THE RICHMOND GATE

HOTEL

2009

GUIDE

42nd edition September 2008.
First published by the Automobile Association as the Hotel and Restaurant Guide, 1967
© Automobile Association Developments Limited 2008. Automobile Association Developments
Limited retains the copyright in the current edition © 2008 and in all subsequent editions, reprints
and amendments to editions. The information contained in this directory is sourced entirely from
the AA's information resources.
The contents of this publication are believed correct at the time
of printing. Nevertheless, the publishers cannot be held responsible for any errors or omissions or
for any changes in the details given in this guide or for the consequences of any reliance on the
information provided by the same. This does not affect your statutory rights. Assessments of AA
inspected establishments are based on the experience of the Hotel and Restaurant Inspectors on
the occasion(s) of their visit(s) and therefore descriptions given in this guide necessarily contain
an element of subjective opinion which may not reflect or dictate a reader's own opinion on
another occasion. See 'AA Star Classification' at the end of the guide for a clear explanation of
how, based on our Inspectors' inspection experiences, establishments are graded. If the meal or
meals experienced by an Inspector or Inspectors during an inspection fall between award levels
the restaurant concerned may be awarded the lower of any award levels considered applicable.
The AA strives to ensure accuracy of the information in this guide at the time of printing. Due to the
constantly evolving nature of the subject matter the information is subject to change. The AA will
gratefully receive any advice from our readers of any necessary updated information. Please contact:
Advertising Sales Department: advertisingsales@theAA.com
Editorial Department: lifestyleguides@theAA.com
AA Hotel Scheme Enquiries: 01256 844455

Cover Credits: Front Cover: Main Gary Houlder/Getty Images; bl Mike Caldwell/London Marriott Hotel
West India Quay; br Headland Hotel, Newquay
Back Cover: bl Sheffield Park Hotel, Sheffield; bc Stockbyte; br Crown Hotel, Exford

Typeset/Repro: Servis Filmsetting Ltd, Stockport, Greater Manchester
Printed and bound in Spain by Printer Industria Grafica S.A., Barcelona
This directory is compiled by the AA Hotel Services Department; managed in the Librios Information
Management System and generated by the AA establishment database system.

Published by AA Publishing, a trading name of Automobile Association Developments Limited,
whose registered office is Fanum House, Basing View, Basingstoke, Hampshire RG21 4EA.
Registered number 1878835
A CIP catalogue record for this book is available from the British Library
ISBN-13: 978-0-7495-5790-4
A03682

Maps prepared by the
Mapping Services Department of
The Automobile Association.

Maps © Automobile Association Developments
Limited 2008.

 This product includes
mapping data licensed
from Ordnance Survey® with the permission of
the Controller of Her Majesty's Stationery Office.
© Crown copyright 2008.
All rights reserved.
Licence number 100021153.

 This material is Crown Copyright
and is reproduced with the
permission of Land and Property
Services under delegated authority from the
Controller of Her Majesty's Stationery Office,
© Crown copyright and database rights LA59
© Crown copyright 2008.
Permit number 80036.

© Ordnance Survey Ireland/Government of
Ireland.
Copyright permit No. MP000108

Information on National Parks in England
provided by the Countryside Agency
(Natural England).
Information on National Parks in Scotland
provided by Scottish Natural Heritage.
Information on National Parks in Wales
provided by The Countryside Council for Wales.

Contents

How to use the guide

1 LOCATION
Town listed alphabetically within county

2 MAP REFERENCE
Map page number followed by a 2-figure National Grid reference (see also page 7)

3 HOTEL NAME
Where the name appears in *italic* type the information that follows has not been confirmed by the establishment for 2009

4 GRADING
Hotels are listed in star rating and merit score order within each location (for full explanation of ratings and awards see page 786)
★ Star rating
% Merit score
◉ Rosette award

5 TYPE OF HOTEL
(see opposite)

6 HOTEL LOGO
If a symbol appears here it represents a hotel group or consortium (See pages 33-41)

7 PICTURE
Optional photograph supplied by establishment

8 ADDRESS AND CONTACT DETAILS

9 DIRECTIONS
Brief details of how to find the hotel

10 DESCRIPTION
Written by the AA inspector at the time of the last visit

11 ROOMS
Number of rooms and prices (see page 6)

12 FACILITIES
Additional facilities including those for children and for leisure activities

13 CONFERENCE
Conference facilities as available (see page 6)

14 NOTES
Additional information (see pages 6-7)

1 GULWORTHY — Map 3 SX47 — **2**

3 Horn of Plenty — LOGO — **6**

4 ★★★ 85% ◉◉◉ HOTEL — **5**

7

8 ☎ 01822 832528 📄 01822 834390
PL19 8JD
e-mail: enquiries@thehornofplenty.co.uk
web: www.thehornofplenty.co.uk

9 dir: from Tavistock take A390 W for 3m. Right at Gulworthy Cross. In 400yds turn left, hotel in 400yds on right

10 With stunning views over the Tamar Valley, The Horn of Plenty maintains its reputation as one of Britain's best country-house hotels. The bedrooms are well equipped and have many thoughtful extras with the garden rooms offering impressive levels of comfort and quality. Cuisine here is also impressive and local produce provides interesting and memorable dining.

11 Rooms 10 (6 annexe) (3 fmly) (4 GF)
S £150-£240; D £160-£250 (incl. bkfst)*
12 Facilities New Year
13 Conf Class 20 Board 16 Thtr 28 Parking 25
14 Notes Closed 24-26 Dec Civ Wed 80

KEY TO SYMBOLS AND ABBREVIATIONS

★	Black stars
★	Red stars – indicate AA Inspectors' Choice
@	AA Rosettes – indicate an AA award for food
	For full explanation of AA ratings and awards see page 786
%	Inspector's Merit score (see page 6)
▲	Associate Hotels (see this page)
O	Hotel due to open during the currency of the guide
ⓤ	Star rating not confirmed (see this page)
Fmly	Number of family rooms available
GF	Ground floors rooms available
Smoking	Number of bedrooms allocated for smokers
pri facs	Bedroom with separate private facilities (Restaurant-with-rooms only)
S	Single room
D	Double room
*	2008 prices
fr	From
incl. bkfst	Breakfast included in the price
FTV	Freeview
STV	Satellite television
Wi-fi	Wireless network connection
Air con	Air conditioning
ⓢ	Heated indoor swimming pool
⌁	Outdoor swimming pool
⌁	Heated outdoor swimming pool
♫	Entertainment
Child facilities	Children's facilities (see page 6)
Xmas/New Year	Special programme for Christmas/New Year
♞	Tennis court
♘	Croquet lawn
⚑	Golf course
CONF	Conference facilities
Thtr	Number of theatre style seats
Class	Number of classroom style seats
Board	Number of boardroom style seats
⊗	No dogs allowed (guide dogs for the blind and assist dogs should be allowed)
No children	Children cannot be accommodated
RS	Restricted opening time
Civ Wed	Establishment licensed for civil weddings (+ maximum number of guests at ceremony)
LB	Special leisure breaks available
Spa	Hotel has its own spa

TYPES OF HOTEL

The majority of establishments in this guide come under the category of Hotel; other categories are listed below.

TOWN HOUSE HOTEL A small, individual city or town centre property, which provides a high degree of personal service and privacy

COUNTRY HOUSE HOTEL These are quietly located in a rural area

SMALL HOTEL Has fewer than 20 bedrooms and is owner-managed

METRO HOTEL A hotel in an urban location that does not offer an evening meal

BUDGET HOTEL These are usually purpose built modern properties offering inexpensive accommodation. Often located near motorways and in town or city centres

RESTAURANT WITH ROOMS This category of accommodation is now assessed under the AA's Guest Accommodation scheme, therefore, although they continue to have an entry in this guide, we do not include their star rating. Most Restaurants with Rooms have been awarded AA Rosettes for their food and the rooms will meet the required AA standard. For more detailed information about any Restaurant with Rooms please consult The AA Bed and Breakfast Guide or see www.theAA.com

▲ These are establishments that have not been inspected by the AA but which have been inspected by other national tourist boards in Britain and Northern Ireland. An establishment marked as "Associate" has paid to belong to the AA Associate Hotel Scheme and therefore receives a limited entry in the guide. Descriptions of these hotels can be found on the AA website.*

ⓤ A small number of hotels in the guide have this symbol because their star classification was not confirmed at the time of going to press. This may be due to a change of ownership or because the hotel has only recently joined the AA rating scheme.

O These hotels were not open at the time of going to press, but will open in late 2008, or in 2009.

* Check the AA website **www.theAA.com** for current information and ratings

How to use the guide *continued*

Merit Score (%)

AA inspectors supplement their reports with an additional quality assessment of everything the hotel provides, including hospitality, based on their findings as a 'mystery guest'. This wider ranging quality assessment results in an overall Merit Score which is shown as a percentage beside the hotel name. When making your selection of hotel accommodation this enables you to see at a glance that a three star hotel with a percentage score of 79% offers a higher standard overall than one in the same star classification but with a percentage score of 69%. To gain AA recognition, a hotel must achieve a minimum quality score of 50%.

AA Awards

Every year the AA presents a range of awards to the finest AA-inspected and rated hotels from England, Scotland, Wales and the Republic of Ireland. The Hotel of the Year is our ultimate accolade and is awarded to those hotels that are recognised as outstanding examples in their field. Often innovative, the winning hotels always set high standards in hotel keeping. The winners for 2008-9 are listed on pages 8-11.

Rooms

Each entry shows the total number of en suite rooms available, (this total will include any annexe rooms). The total number may be followed by a breakdown of the type of rooms available, i.e. the number of annexe rooms; number of family rooms (fmly); number of ground-floor rooms (GF); number of rooms available for smokers.

Bedrooms in an annexe or extension are only noted if they are at least equivalent in quality to those in the main building, but facilities and prices may differ. In some hotels all bedrooms are in an annexe or extension.

Prices

Prices are per room per night and are provided by the hoteliers in good faith. These prices are indications and not firm quotations. ✳ indicates 2008 prices.

Payment

As most hotels now accept credit or debit cards we only indicate if an establishment does not accept any cards for payment. Credit cards may be subject to a surcharge – check when booking if this is how you intend to pay. Not all hotels accept travellers' cheques.

Children

Child facilities may include baby intercom, baby sitting service, playroom, playground, laundry, drying/ironing facilities, cots, high chairs or special meals. In some hotels children can sleep in parents' rooms at no extra cost – check when booking.

If 'No children' is indicated a minimum age may be also given e.g. No children 4yrs would mean no children under 4 years of age would be accepted.

Some hotels, although accepting children, may not have any special facilities for them so it is well worth checking before booking.

Leisure breaks

Some hotels offer special leisure breaks, and these prices may differ from those quoted in this guide and the availability may vary through the year.

Parking

We indicate the number of parking spaces available for guests. These may include under cover parking and/or charged spaces.

Civil Weddings (Civ Wed)

Indicates that the establishment holds a civil wedding licence, and we indicate the number of guests that can be accommodated at the ceremony.

Conference Facilities

We include three types of meeting layouts – Theatre, Classroom and Boardroom style and include the maximum number of delegates for each. The price shown is the maximum 24-hour rate per delegate. Please note that as arrangements vary between a hotel and a business client, VAT may or may not be included in the price quoted in the guide. We also show if Wi-fi connectivity is available, but please check with the hotel if this is suitable for your requirements.

Dogs

Although many hotels allow dogs, they may be excluded from some areas of the hotel and some breeds, particularly those requiring an exceptional license, may not be acceptable at all. Under the Disability Discrimination Act 1995 access should be allowed for guide dogs and assistance dogs. Please check the hotel's policy when making your booking.

Entertainment (♫)

This indicates that live entertainment should be available at least once a week all year. Some hotels provide live entertainment only in summer or on special occasions – check when booking.

Hotel logos

If an establishment belongs to a hotel group or consortium their logo is included in their entry and these are listed on pages 33-41.

Map references

Each town is given a map reference – the map page number and a two-figure map reference based on the National Grid. For example: **Map 05 SU 48**:

05 refers to the page number of the map section at back of the guide

SU is the National Grid lettered square (representing 100,000sq metres) in which the location will be found

4 is the figure reading across the top or bottom of the map page

8 is the figure reading down at each side of the map page.

Restricted Service

Some hotels have restricted service (RS) during quieter months, usually during the winter months, and at this time some of the listed facilities will not be available. If your booking is out-of-season, check with the hotel and enquire specifically.

Smoking regulations

If a bedroom has been allocated for smokers, the hotel is obliged to clearly indicate that this is the case. If either the freedom to smoke, or to be in a non-smoking environment is important to you, please check with the hotel when you book.

Spa

For the purposes of this guide the word **Spa** in an entry indicates that the hotel has its own spa which is either managed by themselves or outsourced to an external management company. Facilities will vary but will include a minimum of two treatment rooms. Any specific details are also given, and these are as provided to us by the establishment. (i.e. steam room, beauty therapy etc).

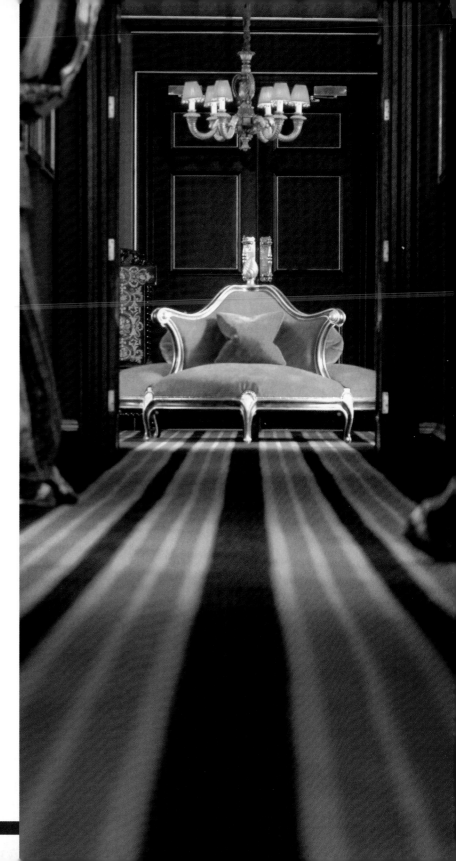

Hotels of the Year

ENGLAND

JESMOND DENE HOUSE HOTEL & RESTAURANT
NEWCASTLE UPON TYNE, TYNE & WEAR

★★★★ ◉◉

Just a short drive from Newcastle's city centre, this grand house was built by the Victorian industrialist, Lord Armstrong and later donated to the city. The house overlooks a wooded valley, and peace and tranquillity are guaranteed. A mix of retro and classical design make for really interesting interiors – fresh, light colours contrasting with the polished floors, huge windows and inglenook fireplaces. There are handsome rooms for dining, meeting and celebrating – from the wood-panelled Great Hall to the light-filled Garden Room.

Of the 40 individually designed bedrooms, eight are in the New House, a modern interpretation of the Arts & Crafts style; the remainder are in the main house and boast big beds, crisp Egyptian cotton linen, organic bespoke toiletries, oversized bathtubs, large walk-in showers, and have ample space to work and to chill out.

The atmosphere throughout is relaxed, and the friendly staff provide warm and attentive service, so from the minute you drive up to the front door you are made to feel like a special guest. The award-winning food, under the guiding hand of Terry Laybourn, leading chef and restaurateur and also a co-director of the hotel, is prepared by talented chef Pierre Rigothier. Local, seasonal, organic produce is used to produce innovative cuisine.

SCOTLAND

NORTON HOUSE HOTEL & RESTAURANT
EDINBURGH

★★★★ 86% ◉◉◉

Dating back to 1840 and situated in 55 acres of wooded grounds, Norton House has always provided opulent surroundings for the families that have resided under its roof. Today the extended mansion house continues to offer understated luxury; the marble columns, period furnishings and the grand oak staircase contrast with contemporary design. Just outside Edinburgh and convenient for the airport, this hotel proves a popular destination for leisure and business guests and also makes a delightful wedding venue.

The bedroom styles vary from modern to traditional and recent investment has resulted in additional bedrooms and a stunning new spa. Here you will find a swimming and hydrotherapy pool, experience shower, crystal steam room, sauna and state-of-the-art fitness studios with the latest technically advanced equipment, along with a range of treatment rooms offering a comprehensive list of rejuvenate techniques and experiences. There is a choice of restaurants with the intimate, fine dining Ushers, with three AA rosettes, serving modern cuisine, underpinned by a classical theme. Skilled, precise cooking allows fine-quality Scottish ingredients to shine through, resulting in clean, clear, balanced flavours in deceptively simple dishes. Together with existing meeting facilities there is a stable block in the grounds that has now been converted into a self-contained conference and business centre.

WALES

LAKE COUNTRY HOUSE HOTEL & SPA
LLANGAMMARCH WELLS, POWYS

★★★ ◉◉

A Victorian country house hotel peacefully set in 50 acres of parkland with lawns, rhododendrons, riverside walks and a 9-hole par 3 golf course. The building dates back to 1840 but was refashioned in 1900 to reveal an architectural mix of styles including mock-Tudor timbering and French windows that lead out onto colonial verandas.

There are spacious lounges, furnished with antiques and beautiful paintings, that have roaring fires to relax by on colder days. Every afternoon guests can enjoy traditional Welsh teas that are served in the drawing room or on the patio in the summer. Each of the superbly comfortable bedrooms in the main house has its own character and charm, and in addition there are twelve lodge bedroom suites that have their own open-plan sitting rooms.

The kitchen brigade uses the best local produce to create an award-winning menu; there is an outstanding choice of some 300 wines to accompany.

Guests can banish the stresses of modern life in the lakeside Kingfisher Spa by choosing from the wide range of health and beauty treatments on offer. There's also a coffee shop that makes an ideal place for golfers and non-golfers to meet up.

REPUBLIC OF IRELAND

THE BROOKLODGE HOTEL & WELLS SPA
MACREDDIN, COUNTY WICKLOW

★★★★ 86%, ◉◉

Less than an hour's drive from Dublin in a lovely valley, this is a privately owned luxurious country house hotel where the owners are very involved in the day to day running of the establishment and committed to ongoing improvements.

In addition to the comfortable accommodation in the original house, there are also mezzanine-style suites in the landscaped grounds, and in Brook Hall, the new addition, there are ground-floor rooms with their own small patios, and upstairs rooms with floor-to-ceiling French doors overlooking the 18th hole of Macreddin Golf Course. The award-winning Strawberry Tree Restaurant, specialising in organic and wild foods, is a really romantic setting for an enjoyable meal. The hotel's Acton Country Pub serves home brewed beer and stout, and The Orchard Café offers modern home cooking.

For complete relaxation a visit to the spa is a must. Here you will find many beauty and health treatments, including aroma baths, Finnish baths, a Hammam massage room, a floatation room, jacuzzis and an outdoor hot tub. Guests will find that there are lots of other things to see and do – off-road driving, equestrian activities, field and clay pigeon shooting, angling, canoeing, walking, trekking … the list is almost endless!

Hotel Group of the Year

Q HOTELS

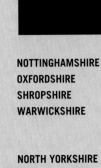

This group has 20 hotels throughout England and one in Scotland. 2007 saw Q Hotels increase its number of hotels after the multi-million pound acquisition of another group and the conclusion of a number of high profile property refurbishments. Investment throughout the portfolio has been impressive and their hotels appeal to a wide range of markets, catering equally well for corporate and leisure guests. The majority of their hotels have Reflections Spa and Leisure Clubs offering a wide variety of treatments together with swimming pools, saunas, steam rooms and state-of-the-art fitness equipment for aerobic workouts. Aldwark Manor, Forest Pines Hotel, Hellidon Lakes, The Westerwood Hotel and Telford Golf & Spa Hotel are at the heart of their own golf courses, and nine hotels have indoor and outdoor tennis courts.

CAMBRIDGESHIRE	The Cambridge Belfry, Cambourne
CHESHIRE	Crewe Hall, Crewe;
	The Park Royal Hotel, Warrington
GLOUCESTERSHIRE	The Chase Hotel, Cheltenham
GREATER MANCHESTER	The Midland, Manchester
HAMPSHIRE	The Hampshire Court, Basingstoke;
	Norton Park, Sutton Scotney
KENT	Ashford International, Ashford;
	Bridgewood Manor, Chatham
LINCOLNSHIRE	Forest Pines Hotel, Scunthorpe
NORTH LANARKSHIRE	The Westerwood Hotel, Cumbernauld
NORTHAMPTONSHIRE	Hellidon Lakes, Hellidon

NOTTINGHAMSHIRE	The Nottingham Belfry, Nottingham
OXFORDSHIRE	The Oxford Belfry, Milton Common
SHROPSHIRE	Telford Golf & Spa Hotel, Telford
WARWICKSHIRE	Chesford Grange Hotel, Kenilworth;
	Stratford Manor & Stratford Victoria,
	Stratford-upon-Avon
NORTH YORKSHIRE	Aldwark Manor, Aldwark
SOUTH YORKSHIRE	Tankersley Manor, Tankersley
WEST YORKSHIRE	Queens Hotel, Leeds

Small Hotel Group of the Year

HOTEL DU VIN

Contemporary style combined with friendly and enthusiastic staff, plus a focus on wine, captures what this group is all about. Hotel du Vin has never been shy of taking on a challenge when it comes to finding new and exciting locations for its establishments. Amongst the eleven hotels in the group they have converted an eye hospital, a sugar warehouse and a brewery. Just a few of the trademarks to look out for are their bistros that serve imaginative yet simply cooked dishes, the wine cellars, and monsoon showers and Egyptian cotton linen in the bedrooms. The people who work for Hotel du Vin are passionate about what they do.

BRISTOL	Hotel du Vin Bristol
CAMBRIDGESHIRE	Hotel du Vin Cambridge
GLOUCESTERSHIRE	Hotel du Vin Cheltenham
HAMPSHIRE	Hotel du Vin Winchester
KENT	Hotel du Vin Tunbridge Wells
OXFORDSHIRE	Hotel du Vin Henley-on-Thames
SUSSEX, EAST	Hotel du Vin Brighton
WEST MIDLANDS	Hotel du Vin Birmingham
YORKSHIRE, NORTH	Hotel du Vin Harrogate & Hotel du Vin York
GLASGOW	Hotel du Vin at One Devonshire Gardens

OPENING IN 2008

DORSET	Hotel du Vin Poole *(Summer 2008)*
TYNE & WEAR	Hotel du Vin Newcastle upon Tyne *(Winter 2008)*
EDINBURGH	Hotel du Vin Edinburgh *(Autumn 2008)*

For current details of these new hotels please see the AA website **www.theAA.com**

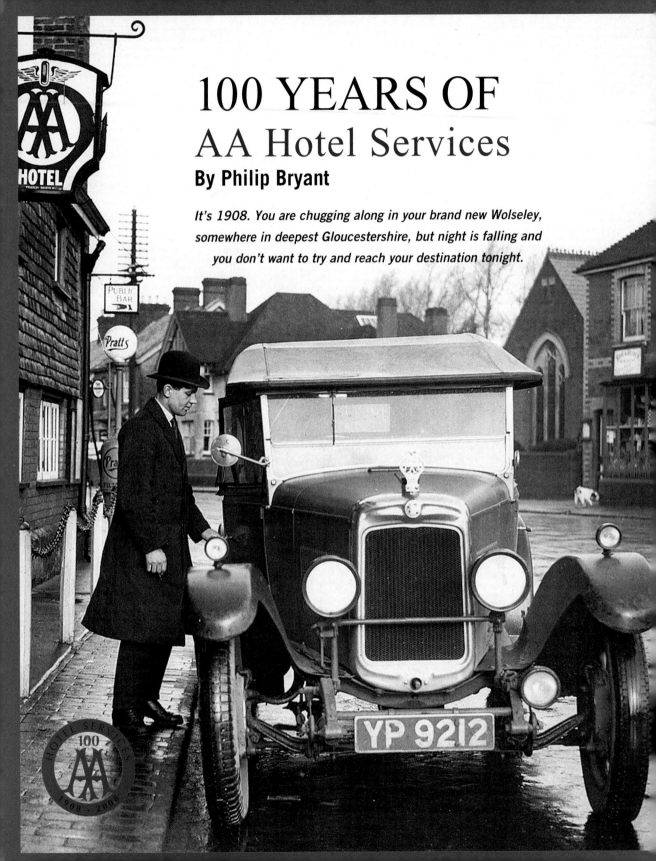

100 YEARS OF
AA Hotel Services
By Philip Bryant

It's 1908. You are chugging along in your brand new Wolseley, somewhere in deepest Gloucestershire, but night is falling and you don't want to try and reach your destination tonight.

A hotel appears, so you pull in and book a room. Next morning you can't wait to leave. Dinner never materialised, the bedbugs were in playful mood, and the concept of pairing 'service' with 'smile' was clearly unknown to your miserable host. What a pity you reflect, as you slam down your payment, that your newly published AA Handbook doesn't list hotels, as it already does garages.

A year later you make the same trip, this time armed with the new second edition of the Handbook, listing AA-appointed hotels alphabetically by town. There, under Chipping Campden, is an entry for the Three Ways House and you gratefully pull on to its forecourt, confident of a decent dinner and a fleabite-free night. (Regrettably, however, you are 76 years too early to enjoy the hotel's world famous Pudding Club, formed in 1985 to promote traditional English desserts).

Signs and Bulletin Boards

The addition of England's leading hotels to the Handbook was part of the AA's aim 'To Make Motoring Pleasant'. Motorists could now look for the AA signs hanging outside a thousand or so hotels – the Headland Hotel in Newquay, for instance, The George at Stamford or the Fairy Glen at Betws-y-Coed, all of which promised an acceptable standard of lunch, dinner and overnight accommodation.

The AA provided these appointed hotels with bulletin boards, which only members, using a special key, could unlock to pick up messages or important travel information, such as tip-offs about speed traps and road repairs. This was how guests at a Devon hotel in 1913 learnt, for example, that the road from North Tawton to Okehampton was in a 'very bad condition'.

By the time this ancient handwritten notice surfaced during hotel renovations in the 1950s, the road had improved sufficiently to become the B3217.

The Inspector Arrives

It wasn't long though before members began to clamour for something more meaningful. What they really wanted, they said, was a guide that told them more about the type of meal or bedroom they would encounter in wherever they fancied stopping - in other words, a classification system.

The Association's secretary, Stenson Cooke, came up with the answer. A former wine and spirit salesman, Cooke was familiar with the star grading system distillers used to classify brandy, three stars, for example, signifying a middling quality that would please most people. Something similar would work well for the AA, he proposed: "We can take a really decent, average middle-class hotel, with good food, English meat, beds and other comforts, which no reasonable motorist will cavil at, and make that our standard three-star".

Promising that recommended hotels would be "classified without fear or favour", the Association's chairman reported at its annual meeting in 1913 that almost all AA-appointed hotels had been inspected and classified and that the revised information would appear in the next Handbook.

Thus was born the AA hotel inspector, for whom the ground rules were uncompromising. They had, for example, to refuse all bribes from hoteliers: "Never, never accept a receipted bill except in return for your money, which is our money," inspectors were warned, on pain of being sacked. And, of course, they had to remain completely anonymous until after they had paid for their meal or overnight stay.

Continued

Under the Eagle Eye

Inspectors were also given copious advice about how to spot tricks of the trade, such as double sets of creases in sheets, apparently a complete giveaway that they hadn't been washed, but simply pressed. A dirty hairbrush was a "horrible thing", and in those pre-Fairy Liquid days cutlery showing traces of cleaning powder was "evidence of slovenly attention". Quite right too!

Naturally enough, bathrooms and lavatories required particular scrutiny. In fact, the AA provided many hotels with members' cabinets containing a supply of brushes and small linen towels.

Hoteliers, not surprisingly, weren't always happy to be interrogated by "some young man, however bright, who might arrive in a two-seater… and proceed to throw his weight about". It was impertinent, they thought, to be asked about their lovely hotel's sanitary arrangements, or whether their garages could be locked. No wonder inspectors were advised to tread lightly, to use their discretion.

Straight-talking was the order of the day for the Association: "Classification must be according to the house as it is built and furnished – or laid out. No house, however large and well decorated, may hope for the AA appointment, or prevent its being withdrawn, if it is badly directed. No landlord or manager of an hotel which is not large enough to merit more than two stars, can be expected to be graded higher on the score of good management or the charm of the landlady's smile".

Setting the Standards

But inspections were having an effect and by 1927 the AA's hotel classification scheme included over 2,300 establishments in England, Scotland and Wales. Standards were definitely rising.

In the run-up to the outbreak of war in September 1939, hotel bookings were heading for bumper levels, perhaps as much as anything because Britons believed that Neville Chamberlain's Munich agreement with Hitler would prevent conflict with Germany. The French government, taking perhaps a more realistic view, went so far as to promise that British motorists touring in France would not have their cars commandeered even if war did break out.

Break out it did, and as a contribution to the general war effort, the AA discontinued its hotel inspections, only reinstating them in 1948 under a Hotel Appointment Committee operated jointly with the RAC and the Royal Scottish Automobile Club (RSAC). In most respects it was similar to the original 1912 scheme in terms of classifications, standards and procedures, and it survived for another 25 years.

It was during the 1950s, however, that new kinds of hotels, such as motels and airport transit accommodation, began to emerge to meet the needs of business travellers. Most could get by quite well without a guidebook, prompting Bob Ryan, the AA's Road Manager, to admit in 1961: "It is probably true to say that about five per cent of members are knowledgeable about hotels and are prepared to pay for good value, whatever the cost.

"At the other end is the large majority who cannot afford to pay Handbook prices and demand information about accommodation at the lower price levels; while in between are those who stay at one- or two-star hotels who seem to be content with the standards provided. The AA Handbook does little to meet these demands, and one of the problems is to decide how best to do so."

Hotels, guesthouses, inns and farmhouses listed in that year's Handbook – all 5,282 of them - paid a two-guinea (£2.10p) fee for the privilege of having an AA inspector rate twenty five features, including fire escape arrangements, facilities for children, reception porterage and atmosphere, indoor games facilities and value for money. On their application form hoteliers had already had to tick a list of amenities - dancing, golf, riding, bathing, fishing, tennis, squash, shooting and boating – that their establishment offered .

Not surprisingly, with so many places to visit, inspectors were always on the move, and it was not unusual for them within a 24-hour period to dine at an AA-recommended restaurant, sleep and breakfast at a hotel, assess a local picnic area, visit another hotel for lunch, then take afternoon tea at a campsite. Waistlines were – and no doubt still are – somewhat vulnerable to expansion.

Progress, Partnerships and Harmonisation

In 1974, after its joint scheme with the RAC and RSAC had ended, the AA revised its classification criteria in co-operation with the British Hotel, Restaurant and Catering Association. Every hotel that applied for reappointment under their independent Appointment Scheme was inspected afresh.

In 1990, the AA devised and introduced a percentage scheme that recognised and reflected the quality of hotels within each star rating. The same year the now well-known one-to-five Rosette grading system arrived, by which hotels, restaurants and pubs are classified according to the quality of their food. The following year separate AA Hotel and Restaurant Guides were published for the first time.

Over the years the inspection and quality standards developed by the AA, the RAC and the English Tourist Board became

quite different and so, in 1997, they agreed to harmonise their schemes in order to end public confusion. Since then there has been even more harmonisation, with inspection and classification of hotels and accommodation under common Quality Standards agreed by the AA, VisitBritain, VisitScotland and VisitWales.

100 Years Strong

Many of the establishments that AA Hotel Services now inspects and recommends featured in that first guide 100 years ago. Some are well into their second, third or even fourth century. Although motoring may not be quite the adventure it was in 1908, at least we can be certain that we are never far from somewhere worth stopping.

Indeed, should you be passing through Chipping Campden, for example, there are now three AA-listed hotels; and if not, you still have many thousand establishments throughout the country to choose from, most with plenty of space to park the Wolseley.

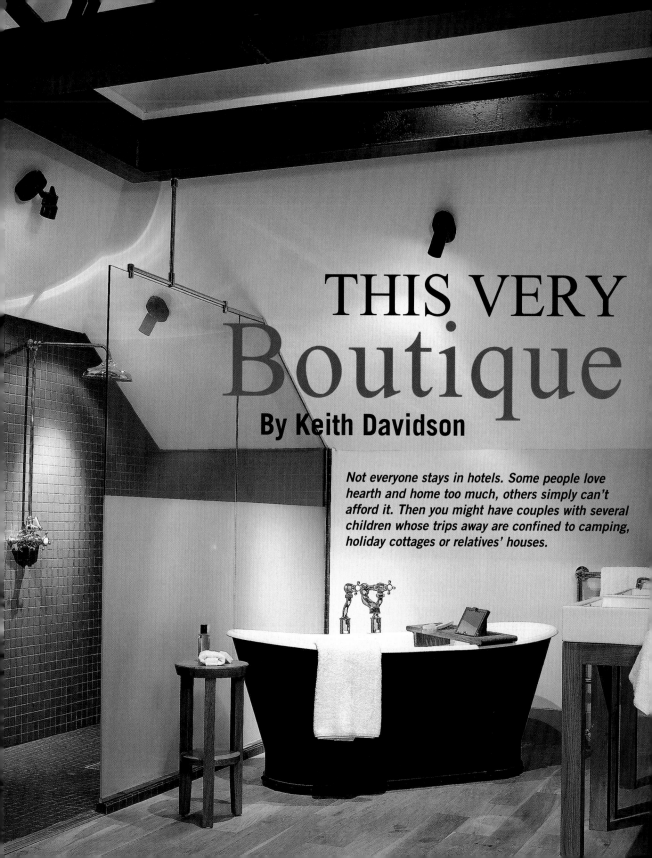

THIS VERY
Boutique
By Keith Davidson

Not everyone stays in hotels. Some people love hearth and home too much, others simply can't afford it. Then you might have couples with several children whose trips away are confined to camping, holiday cottages or relatives' houses.

When hotels are off someone's radar, explaining their attractions is quite a challenge. Outlining the different varieties – budget chains, chintzy guest houses, town houses, those that cater to the business crowd – will certainly take some time. Letting slip that you stayed in a boutique hotel lately is a shortcut to semantic havoc.

What's in a name?

"What's a boutique hotel?" they ask, reasonably. Thereby hangs a tale. Pose that question to a civilian from outside the hospitality industry and they might use words like 'trendy', 'designer', 'expensive' or 'posh'. Even 'overpriced'. Ask an industry insider and they will bang on about 'style', 'aspiration', 'vision' and 'individuality' but since these are marketing buzzwords used to sell anything from sunglasses to sports cars, they don't really provide an answer on their own.

Since recent years have also given us boutique bakers, cheese shops, investment houses and law firms, it's clear that the meaning of 'boutique' is a little fuzzy these days. Back to basics then – what was a boutique in the first place? A clothes shop, obviously. But actually, a little bit more than a clothes shop.

More Quaint than Quant

Boutiques were one facet of the pop culture revolution that hit London in the Swinging Sixties. Around 40 years ago, Barbara Hulanicki's legendary fashion store, Biba, was doing great business in Kensington while the Kings Road and Carnaby Street boasted a legion of other similar shops that were copied untold times across the provinces. Mary Quant was a major name, Mod style was in and the young Diana Rigg was rampaging across television screens in a leather catsuit. This catch-all cultural melting pot also included the Beatles and the Rolling Stones, Twiggy as arguably the first supermodel and Antonioni's Blowup at the movies.

The drabness of the immediate postwar era had been blown away by an affordable pop aesthetic and you could participate for the price of a cinema ticket, by owning the latest Kinks single or buying a miniskirt. It would be easy to overstate the case and slide straight to Pseuds Corner but, in their heyday, boutiques were often a personal expression of style – small businesses showcasing new designers – and a democratisation of fashion. Such retail success was hardly going to stay in tyro hands forever of course; department stores and high street chains soon got in

on the act. By the late 1970s, boutiques were more quaint than Quant, a concept as tired as cider-guzzling punks ten years later.

There the matter would have rested – boutiques having been as much of their time as The Golden Hits of Sandie Shaw – except somewhere, for someone, the word stuck in mind with its echoes of individual flair and accessibility. Meanwhile, in another branch of the post-industrial economy, something was stirring…

In the late 1970s and early 1980s, striking new hotels began to appear in London, New York and elsewhere. These were not run by major international companies, they did make a huge effort to resemble something from an interior design magazine and they provided levels of service that aimed far beyond Stepford Wives blandness, so no rote repetition of "Have a nice day, sir." It was almost as if someone had looked

Continued

Above and below:
Malmaison, Birmingham
Opposite page:
Hotel du Vin, Cambridge

at the hotel business with its stiff and forbidding formality at the top end, Basil Fawlty at the other, and decided to create a third way. These places had furniture you might want to buy, artworks that you actually liked and food you were happy to eat. If you think that sounds rather radical, remember that Basil was based on a real hotelier.

Setting the trend

But what to call these new hotels? Across the years, you can almost hear the consternation of owners, copywriters and reviewers as they rummaged around their lexicon for a suitable epithet to distinguish this new wave from what had gone before. The word eventually pulled off the shelf was 'boutique' and at the time it was accurate. Just like the first tranche of fashion stores in Swinging London, these places were individual, they were stylish, urban and the look often did come from a single designer. In social terms they were accessible too, as long as you had the necessary slack on your credit card.

More than 20 years later, such hotels are everywhere. The Morgans Hotel Group, which runs the estimable Morgans on Madison Avenue in New York City, claims to have introduced the boutique concept back in 1984, although there were certainly very stylish hotels around before then. Après lui, la déluge however. Now you can find boutique hotels in the heart of most major cities across the planet with Britain and Ireland no exception.

The Clarence Hotel in Dublin's Temple Bar area may have started life in the 1850s but it was bought by rock band U2 and relaunched with chunky wooden fittings, ecclesiastical colours and a classy service ethos in 1996. The multiple award-winning One Aldwych opened in a former Edwardian-era newspaper office, in the heart of London, in 1998. Its Lobby Bar has a dual layer of elegance: modern metropolitan chic superimposed on a century-old space. The rooms meanwhile don't announce themselves with a look-at-me design, opting for something more quiet and discreet instead – and it has a decent swimming pool.

Into this decade and Laurence and Helen Beere bought the Queensberry Hotel in Bath in 2003, refurbishing the old place to produce the best-looking accommodation in the city. With just 29 rooms, each individually designed, it operates on a truly human scale. In Scotland, Glasgow had already boasted the Arthouse Hotel since 1999 but it was taken over by hotelier Andrew Brownsword and chef Michael Caines to create Abode Glasgow in 2005. Housed in another Edwardian space – education department offices – the hotel manages to look good without compromising its old institutional history. The list goes on.
Continued

The word is out

Indeed, boutique hotels have been such a success that the big boys long ago appropriated the idea. Lush bolsters, large wooden headboards, artful lighting and funky bathroom fittings can now be found everywhere, from bedzillas out on the bypass to 150-plus room properties in the middle of the Scottish Highlands. Such places may aim for visual splendour but they're hardly bijou little crashpads near Holland Park.

The other factor that bedevils boutique hoteldom is its own limitations. When going great guns, a small bespoke venture may think of expansion. If it opts for small chain status, as was always the strategy for the Abode brand for instance, then it's no longer individual

Top left: The Lobby Bar, One Aldwych
Left: Poolside, One Aldwych
Above: The Screening Room,
One Aldwych

because – by definition – there is more than one. If it decides to get physically bigger, as the Clarence plans to do for sound economic reasons, then it's at risk of losing the small-hotel touch even if service standards are maintained. Back to the original conundrum then: in the here and now, what exactly is a boutique hotel? Sticking to the idea that that it needs to be small, sui generis and in a city, even the likes of One Aldwych, with its 105 bedrooms and suites, may be a little on the large side. The Queensberry in Bath, with just 29 rooms, manages to live with a more strict definition of the term but not many establishments can. As soon as you get prescriptive, the word just stops being useful but phrase like 'attractive, well-run and privately-owned urban accommodation of a manageable size' is neither pithy nor sexy as a more meaningful replacement.

Time to put it to bed

Just as fashion boutiques gave clothes retailing a boost in the 1960s, boutique hotels have certainly given the hospitality industry a kick up the backside since the 1980s. Rubbish aesthetics, poor food and naff service are now far easier to avoid – even if they have not been totally eradicated. Beds are actually more likely to be comfortable, breakfasts better and design values elevated. The ubiquity of the adjective, used for various hotels, endeavours and industries, has long reached the status of cliché however – so perhaps it really is time to put it to bed.

Back in December 1969, when the original boutique phenomenon still had some legs, the BBC transmitted an episode of a comedy show that used the word to throw an already laughing audience even further off balance. In the first ever broadcast of a legendary sketch, John Cleese walked into a shabby pet shop, noting it as "this very boutique" where he had made a recent purchase, then went on complain about a parrot with some grave health issues. Even before those Swinging Sixties drew to a formal close, boutique was a funny word when used so far out of context. If that was the case all those decades ago then it's all the more true now. The term has strayed yet further, applied to classes of hotel with nothing in common except for a woolly notion of 'design', so it really should go and join the choir invisible. Its meaning has ceased to be.

Below: Queensberry Hotel, Bath
Below left: Guest bathroom, Hotel du Vin, Glasgow
Below right: Champagne Bar, Malmaison, London

GOLDEN
Slumbers

What do we want from a good hotel room? Above all, a decent night's sleep, but that isn't always easy. Simon Wright offers some tips for a good night's kip

"I really like hotel rooms, Dad, they're more comfy than home." My youngest son told me this at the age of four and naturally I was a little wounded by his honesty. I could see his point though, hotel bedrooms do have something going for them. I guess it's the convenience, not having to clear up your own mess, a decent sized telly positioned so it can be comfortably watched from a prone position. Even a half-decent hotel room can be a little cocoon of comfort: you don't have to travel far for anything. The bathroom's not down the hall it's just over there by the door. You don't have to go to the kitchen to make tea and coffee, and there are biscuits too. When the newspaper is delivered in the morning it comes straight to your bedroom door, there might be magazines in the room and of course a fridge stocked with the essentials of alcohol, chocolate and potato snacks. You can have movies too, some of them aimed at the business market.

But how do you sleep? That's the real point isn't it? All the other bells and whistles are just add-ons, decoration. It's a little bit like in-flight entertainment, nice to have, but you wouldn't pay a couple of hundred quid to watch the latest blockbuster on a screen the size of a postcard - the point of the exercise is to get from here to there, as fast as possible - just as the point of a hotel room is to provide you with somewhere to sleep. Sleep is the essential part of the deal, it's what you're really paying for but perversely it's the one thing the hotel can't guarantee to provide. Some people can sleep in the kitchen with their feet in the hall, but for many of us it's a thin line between golden slumbers and a troubled night of dark restlessness. In the unfamiliarity of a hotel room the odds on the latter are distinctly shorter. The answer, my insomniac friend, as with so many other things, lies in the preparation. To some extent, you get the night's sleep you deserve. So, instead of cursing your bad luck and spending the following day

heavy-eyed, foggy-headed and irritable, take time to give yourself a fighting chance of a peaceful night. Here's how…

Ask before you buy

The aim is to get a good night's sleep, correct? As with anything else you purchase it makes sense to ensure that what you are buying is fit for purpose. If noise is a problem for you check that they're giving you a quiet room. If light is the issue ask them if the curtains are properly lined. None of these things can be assumed; I've stayed in Five Star hotels with rooms that might as well have been located on the central reservation of the M25 or that leak so much light that you're slapped in the face by a penetrating beam of early morning sun at 5am. A couple of questions at the time of booking will avoid all that. Makes sure you get what you're paying for - sleep.

Don't get alarmed

Maybe you don't have to worry about oversleeping and can get up at your leisure. That's fine, you simply don't set the alarm, but what about the previous occupant who was getting a flight at 6.30am? If you've ever been woken by an alarm set for 4am by yesterday's guest you'll know how horrible it is and you'll also know that as far as getting back to sleep is concerned the situation may be unrecoverable. The answer is simple, if there's an alarm present check it before you nod off.

Build an iron curtain

Often it's dark when you get back to the room and close the curtains. That's why you don't notice that slender gap that in the morning will allow a laser like beam of light to burn its way through your eyelids just after dawn. Early morning light is like water - if there's a way in it will find it. Don't give it an inch.

Get intimate with the air conditioning

On a hot night the air conditioning can be a boon, it's true. Often though it's the most vicious of double-edged swords. On the one hand, it keeps you cool on the other it makes a noise that will drill into your skull like few others. On top of that, to actually get the room at the temperature you want it you may have to stay up all night trying to figure out what all those symbols on the LCD control panel actually mean and how in heaven's name you get the thing to do your bidding. You either turn the whole thing off, throw off the duvet and risk opening the window or you do the obvious and call reception for assistance - that's what they are there for.

Be a devil, use the DND notice

"Do not disturb" notices. They're one of those things all the hotel grading organisations insist upon, like beds and windows. How often do you see one

hanging on a door though? Rarely, and yet when the housekeeper knocks at 8am and you didn't get to bed until 4am you're surprised, dismayed and a little annoyed. You had your chance and the tools were available to you. Hook the notice on the handle and sleep uninterrupted, that's the whole point of the thing.

Familiarity (breeds content)

Sometimes it's the mere fact of being away from home that means you just can't get settled. The solution is to bring a little of home with you, maybe a teddy, maybe a hot water bottle, may be your partner. A friend of mine takes his own pillows wherever he goes so at least his head feels at home. Weird it may be, but who cares? At least he gets his shuteye.

Can't kip? Be a drip

How many of us suffer in a weary silence, tossing and turning, eventually dozing off, only to be reawakened by some clowns in the corridor from the corporate bash in the ballroom, slamming doors and generally having fun at the expense of your sleep. Or maybe it's the heating pipes coughing and spluttering into action or the fact that next doors plumbing seems to be routed through your headboard. Don't despair, there is an answer - complain! You are paying for the room, the use of the bed and the opportunity these things give you to sleep. That's the bargain, you pay the cash, the hotel provides you with rest. If they're not holding up their end of the deal then it's your obligation to let them know that. Ring reception, asked to be moved, speak to the manager, have a really good moan. In fact, make a nuisance of yourself.

But don't lose any sleep over it.

TOP TIPS FOR GETTING A GOOD NIGHT'S SLEEP

- Make sure the bedroom isn't too hot

- Open the windows to let fresh air in unless it's noisy outside

- Take a warm bath

- Avoid a big meal and spicy foods, but a light snack is a good idea

- Wear an eye mask and/or ear plugs

- Read before turning the light out

- Have the radio on quietly in the background

- Take exercise, but not too near bedtime

- Try chamomile tea before sleep (avoid caffeine, alcohol and nicotine)

- Add a dab of lavender or geranium oil to the pillow

You could be forgiven for being confused. In an age when terms such as 'organic' and 'carbon neutral' have become controversial, the fact that there are more awards and schemes for eco-friendly accommodation than there are rooms at the Ritz, is hardly going to help eco-conscious travellers decide where to stay.

GREEN
Hotels

By Robin Barton

Over the last five years, the number of hotels claiming 'green' credentials has increased exponentially. As bandwagons go, the green movement is a juggernaut. And a very fashionable one at that. But what is a 'green' hotel? How do you find one and how do you see through the 'greenwash'? And does it all even matter? First, here's some encouraging news. A survey in 2007 by a popular travel magazine found that 75 percent of respondents evaluated a hotel's environmental policies before making their bookings. Increasing awareness of energy conservation, wasted water and even the source of building materials means that guests are at least asking questions of their hotels. Ten years ago, this would not have been the case. But ten years ago, an eco-friendly hotel would have been a Mongolian yurt not an urban

boutique hotel with a spa and restaurant using seasonal and local produce.

In terms of impact on the environment, the typical hotel doesn't have much to sing about: countless little plastic bottles of lotions, which are discarded if used only once, white towels and bed linen laundered daily in 60c washes, corridor lights left on day and night, televisions and fridges on stand-by in every room and air-conditioning units puffing away in unoccupied rooms. And going back one stage, there's the immense environmental cost of building a hotel, in some cases shipping stone and wood from around the world.

The Right Credentials

So, it's not surprising that hotels large and small are keen to be seen doing their bit for the environment. Of the hotels in

this edition of the Hotel Guide, more than 150 cited some sort of environmental award, from the Marriott Hotel in Huntingdon (a winner of the Huntingdon Post's Sustainable Development prize) to the Best Western Premier Yew Lodge, recipient of an Energy Saving Award from the Considerate Hoteliers' Association. However, among the myriad awards and accreditations, one scheme stands out: the Green Tourism Business Scheme. Conceived in Scotland, the GTBS has been rolled out to other corners of the country. With 1,400 members, it's the largest scheme measuring eco-friendliness in the UK. The criteria for inclusion covers 150 factors evaluated over ten areas, amongst which are energy efficiency, waste disposal, transport and social involvement. Hotels (and other tourism businesses) are then awarded gold, silver and bronze status according to how well they perform. Among the hotels in this edition of the Hotel Guide, gold award winners include national hotel chains and single, independent hotels such as the Pool House Hotel on the west coast of Scotland.

Leading the Way

"We like being monitored," says Elizabeth Harrison of Pool House, "it gives us a chance to show off." For Pool House Hotel, being green is nothing new: "We were environmentally aware long before it was fashionable, partly because we're in an Area of Outstanding Natural Beauty. When you have otters and seals coming right up to the shore you're always aware of what you put down the drains. We've always taken care of the wildlife because our brand of tourism is dependent on it." Perhaps one of Britain's greenest hotels, the Pool House project began as a restoration of the 300-year old building. "All the materials we used were reclaimed – from the stones to the tiles," says Elizabeth Harrison. "Our green hotel has developed over years and mainly off our own bat. It has to be thought through properly. There's no point installing woodchip-fired heating if you have to ship the woodchips in."

There seems to be no limit to the eco-friendly measures taken at Pool House. "Discarded newspapers go into the logmaker for the fires, empty plastic bottles become cloches in the

Continued

**Below: Guest bedroom,
Pool House Hotel**

Above: Pool House Hotel

garden. We've introduced plants, such as poached egg plants and borage, to bring back bees, which pollinate our fruit trees. We've reinstated a Victorian pottager to grow our own veg and herbs – we have potatoes, cabbages, broccoli and heirloom plants - so that when chef is cooking he just has to go outside. We have wind-up radios and torches for the guests and we employ only local people."

Interestingly, however, Elizabeth Harrison doesn't believe that the hotel's green policies, which are not widely publicised, have made a difference to the bookings they get. "In terms of bookings it might take a couple of years. People book us because we have a romantic location not because of our recycling bins. But guests are becoming more environmentally aware once they get here. On the first night of their stay they might leave their lights or TV on but by the second night you can guarantee that the TV and lights will be turned off."

Group contributions

And this is perhaps the most important quality of a 'green' hotel: the capacity to change guests' attitudes without preaching. After all, not every hotel shouts about its 'greenness'; who knew that the Zetter Hotel, deep in London's Clerkenwell, has its own borehole?

But if an individual hotel such as Pool House can encourage eco-friendly behaviour, what about hotel groups with several establishments to manage? Two gold-winning groups in the GTBS stand out: Macdonald Hotels and Apex Hotels. Macdonald's Scottish hotels have been kitted out with sophisticated, energy-efficient lighting systems, such as movement sensors and long-life bulbs. Some of the group's hotels have reduced energy consumption by 20 percent, which also means lower bills. But a concerted 'green' approach to the hotel business doesn't stop at light bulb. Macdonald is working with its suppliers to cut waste and introducing new staff training programmes. And Apex is building a green hotel chain from the ground up, literally. As well as eco-friendly measures in each hotel, such as using ultraviolet light rather than chemicals to clean hot tubs, the group has a policy of developing only existing city-centre buildings rather than building on greenfield sites and offering cycle racks rather than car parks. Arguably, it is the construction of new hotels, even those like the new 1 Hotel and Residences brand from Starwood, which has an explicitly eco-friendly blueprint and will use recycled and local materials, which has the greatest impact on the environment, particularly in sensitive parts of the world: how many 'eco-resorts' still have marble-clad bathrooms? Is it really possible to have, as Starwood claim, 'luxury with a conscience'? The jury's still out on that.

But, arguably, an international hotel group, such as Starwood or Fairmont adopting a series of 'light green' policies does more to raise awareness about environmental impact than a yurt. And, certainly, current trends suggest that the urban 'green' hotel will be an ever more common fixture in city centres in the coming years. They might be a work in progress, but everybody will benefit.

Ongoing expectations

True, debates will continue to rage about whether organically-produced food does more harm than good to the environment and whether carbon neutrality is a sham. But once you're inside the hotel, it should be clear whether the hotel is living up to its promises: are the bathroom products in a refillable dispenser or in single plastic bottles. Is the television on stand-by? Are the brochures printed on recycled paper? Are there newspapers lying unwanted outside all the rooms?

Of course, such scrutiny can take away some of the magic of staying in a hotel. This is why accreditation provided by the Green Tourism Business Scheme is so valuable; leave the job of measuring energy usage to the experts and just enjoy your stay. You can take comfort from the fact that as more hotels adopt eco-friendly policies and the green movement steamrollers into the mainstream, it won't be profitable for any hotel to ignore its impact on the environment.

HOTELS ON LOCATION

Spotting AA Hotels in the Movies and on TV

By Julia Hynard

If films are about losing yourself in a different reality and leaving your everyday life behind, then it could be argued that hotels serve a very similar function. If hotels are the repository of our romanticised lives, then it is no surprise that they often feature in the fictionalised world of film. Whatever the case, it is good fun identifying the hotels that appear in some of our best loved movies.

Fireworks over Luton Hoo Hotel, Golf and Spa

Hotel Groups Information *continued*

Jurys Doyle	**Jury's Doyle** This Irish company has a range of three, four and five star hotels in the UK and the Republic of Ireland.	*00 353 1 607 0070* *www.jurysdoyle.com*
JURYS Inns	**Jury's Inn** A group of 17 three star city centre hotels situated throughout the UK and Ireland.	*08704 100 800* *www.jurysinn.com*
Legacy Hotels	**Legacy Hotels** A small group of three star hotels growing its coverage across the UK.	*0808 329923* *www.legacy-hotels.co.uk*
Leisureplex	**Leisureplex** A group of 17 two star hotels located in many popular seaside resorts.	*08451 305 666 (Head Office)* *www.alfatravel.co.uk*
MACDONALD	**Macdonald** A large group of predominantly four star hotels, both traditional and modern in style and located across the UK.	*0870 830 4812* *www.macdonald-hotels.co.uk*
Malmaison	**Malmaison** A growing brand of modern, three star city centre hotels including new hotels in Reading and Liverpool.	*0845 365 4247* *www.malmaison.com*
MANOR HOUSE	**Manor House** Located throughout Ireland, this group offers a selection of independent, high quality country and manor house hotels.	*00 353 1 295 8900 (local)* *0818 281 281* *www.manorhousehotels.com*
Marriott HOTELS & RESORTS	**Marriott** This international brand has four and five star hotels in primary locations. Most are modern and have leisure facilities with a focus on activities such as golf.	*00800 1927 1927* *www.marriott.co.uk*
MAYBOURNE	**Maybourne Hotels** A newly formed hotel group representing the prestigious London five star hotels - The Berkeley, Claridge's and The Connaught.	*020 7107 8830 (Head Office)* *www.maybourne.com*
Mercure	**Mercure Hotels** A fast growing group with the original hotels in London and Bristol joined by a further 24 throughout the country.	*0870 609 0965* *www.mercure.com*
MenziesHotels	**Menzies Hotels** A group of predominately four star hotels in key locations across the UK.	*0870 600 3013* *www.menzies-hotels.co.uk*
MILLENNIUM	**Millennium** Part of the Millennium and Copthorne group with 6 high-quality four star hotels, mainly in central London.	*0800 41 47 41* *www.millenniumhotels.com*
MORAN HOTELS	**Moran Hotels** A privately owned group with 4 four star Moran Hotels, and 6 three star Bewley's Hotels. All have strategic locations in the UK and Ireland.	*00 353 1 4593650* *www.moranhotels.com*
NOVOTEL	**Novotel** Part of French group Accor, Novotel provides mainly modern three star hotels and a new generation of four star hotels in key locations throughout the UK.	*0870 609 0962* *www.novotel.com*

3 nights for the price of 2

enjoy a short break,
stay friday and saturday night
and get sunday night free!*

breaks available from

£39.95*

per room, per night

more than just a good night's sleep

experience the difference

Whether you're looking for a conveniently located, well equipped business stopover, somewhere local to hold your meeting, or a relaxed getaway visiting friends, family or a special destination, Innkeeper's Lodge provides a warm and relaxing environment when you are away from home.

unlimited free breakfast

▷ Family rooms available at most locations
▷ Fresh food available 12-10pm every day †
▷ Free unlimited continental style buffet breakfast
▷ Free sky sports 1-3, sky one and 24 hour news †
▷ Refreshing en suite shower and hair dryer
▷ Tea and coffee making facilities - free newspaper
▷ Telephone and modem connection
▷ High speed wireless internet access^

www.innkeeperslodge.com | 08451 551 551

request a brochure online or by texting the word **lodge**, your **surname**, **house number** and **postcode** to 63333~

Hotel Groups Information *continued*

	Old English Inns A large collection of former coaching inns that are mainly graded at two and three stars.	0800 917 3085 www.oldenglishinns.co.uk
OXFORD HOTELS & INNS	**Oxford Hotels and Inns** A large group of 45 hotels with good coverage across the UK, and particularly in Scotland. Each hotel has its own individual style and character.	0871 376 9900 www.oxfordhotelsandinns.com
Park Plaza Hotels & Resorts	**Park Plaza Hotels** A European based group increasing its presence in the UK with quality four star hotels in primary locations.	0800 169 6128 www.parkplaza.com
PEEL HOTELS PLC	**Peel Hotels** A group of mainly three star hotels located across the UK.	0845 601 7335 www.peelhotels.co.uk
PRIDE OF BRITAIN HOTELS	**Pride of Britain** A consortium of privately owned British hotels, often in the country house style, many of which have been awarded red stars.	0800 089 3929 www.prideofbritainhotels.com
PH PRINCIPAL HAYLEY	**Principal** A small group of four star hotels currently represented by 5 hotels situated in prime city centre locations.	0870 242 7474 www.principal-hotels.com
QHOTELS	**QHotels** An expanding hotel group currently with 21 individually styled four star hotels across the UK.	0845 074 0060 www.qhotels.co.uk
Radisson EDWARDIAN	**Radisson Edwardian** This high-quality London-based group offers mainly four star hotels in key locations throughout the capital.	020 8757 7900 www.radissonedwardian.com
Radisson SAS HOTELS & RESORTS	**Radisson SAS** A recognised international brand increasing its hotels in the UK and Ireland, and offering high-quality four star hotels in key locations.	0800 374 411 www.radisson.com
RAMADA	**Ramada** A large hotel group with many properties throughout the UK in three brands - Ramada Plaza, Ramada and Ramada Hotel & Resort.	0845 2070 100 www.ramadajarvis.co.uk
Red Carnation HOTELS	**Red Carnation** A unique collection of prestigious four and five star central London hotels, providing luxurious surroundings and attentive service.	0845 634 2665 www.redcarnationhotels.com
RELAIS & CHATEAUX	**Relais et Chateaux** An international consortium of rural, privately owned hotels, mainly in the country house style.	00800 2000 0002 www.relaischateaux.com
RENAISSANCE HOTELS	**Renaissance** One of the Marriott brands, Renaissance is a collection of individual hotels offering comfortable guest rooms, quality cuisine and good levels of service.	00800 1927 1927 www.marriott.co.uk
RICHARDSON	**Richardson Hotels** A group of 6 three and four star hotels located predominantly in Cornwall and Devon, with one hotel in the Lake District.	www.richardsonhotels.co.uk

Hotel Groups Information *continued*

ℛℱ ROCCO FORTE HOTELS	**Rocco Forte Hotels** A small group of luxury hotels spread across Europe. Owned by Sir Rocco Forte, 3 are three hotels in the UK, all situated in major city locations.	*0870 458 4040* *www.roccofortehotels.com*
(logo)	**Scotland's Hotels of Distinction** A consortium of independent Scottish hotels in the three and four star range.	*01333 360 888* *www.hotels-of-distinction.com*
ⓢ Sheraton HOTELS & RESORTS	**Sheraton** Represented in the UK by a small number of four and five star hotels in London and Scotland.	*0800 35 35 35* *www.starwoodhotels.com*
(logo) SHIRE HOTELS	**Shire** A small group of mostly four star hotels many of which feature spa facilities.	*01254 267 444 (Head Office)* *www.shirehotels.com*
(logo)	**Small Luxury Hotels of the World** Part of an international consortium of mainly privately owned hotels, often in the country house style.	*00800 5254 8000* *www.slh.com*
StopInn	**Stop Inn** A brand from Choice Hotels with a small group of hotels in the Midlands and Northern England.	*0800 44 44 44* *www.choicehotelseurope.com*
(logo) THE CIRCLE	**The Circle** A consortium of independently owned, mainly two and three star hotels, across Britain.	*0845 345 1965* *www.circle-hotels.co.uk*
thistle	**Thistle** A large group of approximately 50 hotels across the UK with a significant number in London.	*0870 414 1516* *www.thistlehotels.com*
(logo) TOWER HOTEL GROUP	**Tower Hotel Group** This Irish owned and operated group has quality hotels offering accommodation in convenient locations throughout Ireland.	*00353 1 428 2400* *www.towerhotelgroup.com*
Travelodge	**Travelodge** Good quality, modern, budget accommodation with over 300 properties across the UK and Ireland. Almost every lodge has an adjacent family restaurant, often a Little Chef, Harry Ramsden's or Burger King.	*08700 850 950* *www.travelodge.co.uk*
ⱽℋ VENTURE HOTELS	**Venture Hotels** Small group of business and leisure hotels located in the north of England.	*www.venturehotels.co.uk*
(logo) von Essen hotels	**Von Essen** A privately owned collection of country house hotels, all individual in style and offered in 3 main catagories: classic, luxury family and country.	*01761 240 121* *www.vonessenhotels.co.uk*
WELCOMEBREAK	**Welcome Break** Good quality, modern, budget accommodation at motorway services.	*01908 299 705* *www.welcomebreak.co.uk*

Online booking with **www.theAA.com/travel**

Book online...

Check in...

and Relax...

Take the hassle out of booking accommodation online

Visit

www.theAA.com/travel

to search and book hundreds of AA inspected and
rated hotels and B&Bs in real time.

Tulloch Castle - Highlands

Best Western St Mellons - Cardiff

Carnoustie - Angus

Best Western Gleddoch House - Glasgow

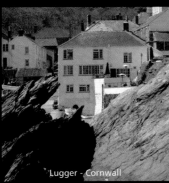

Lugger - Cornwall

Cornwallis - Suffolk

OXFORD
HOTELS & INNS

www.oxfordhotelsandinns.com

Central Reservations **0871 376 9900**

44 stylish and unique properties spread throughout the UK, from the Scottish Isles to the Cornish coast.

20 TO CARRY 3

BINFIELD
Map 5 SU87

Travelodge Bracknell
BUDGET HOTEL

☎ 08719 846 015 📠 01344 485940
London Rd RG12 4AA
web: www.travelodge.co.uk
dir: M4 junct 10 take 1st exit towards Binfield B3408

Travelodge offers good quality, good value, modern accommodation. Ideal for families, the spacious en suite bedrooms include remote-control TV, tea and coffee-making facilities and comfortable beds. Meals can be taken at the nearby family restaurant. See also the Hotel Groups pages.

Rooms 35 S fr £29; D fr £29

BRACKNELL
Map 5 SU86

See also **Crowthorne**

Coppid Beech
★★★★ 77% ⑩⑩ HOTEL

☎ 01344 303333 📠 01344 301200
John Nike Way RG12 8TF
e-mail: sales@coppidbeech.com
web: www.coppidbeech.com
dir: M4 junct 10 take Wokingham/Bracknell onto A329. In 2m take B3408 to Binfield at rdbt. Hotel 200yds on right

This chalet designed hotel offers extensive facilities and includes a ski-slope, ice rink, nightclub, health club and Bier Keller. Bedrooms range from suites to standard rooms - all are impressively equipped. A choice of dining is offered; there's a full bistro menu available in the Keller and for more formal dining, Rowan's restaurant provides award-winning cuisine.

Rooms 205 (6 fmly) **S** £75-£205; **D** £95-£225 (incl. bkfst)* **Facilities** Spa ③ Gym Ice rink Dry ski slope Snow boarding Freestyle park Xmas Wi-fi **Conf** Class 161 Board 24 Thtr 350 Del from £150 to £230* **Services** Lift **Parking** 350 **Notes** LB Civ Wed 200

Stirrups Country House
★★★ 79% HOTEL

☎ 01344 882284 📠 01344 882300
Maidens Green RG42 6LD
e-mail: reception@stirrupshotel.co.uk
web: www.stirrupshotel.co.uk
dir: 3m N on B3022 towards Windsor

Situated in a peaceful location between Maidenhead, Bracknell and Windsor, this hotel has high standards of comfort in the bedrooms, with some rooms boasting a small sitting room area. There is a popular bar, a restaurant, function rooms and delightful grounds.

Rooms 30 (4 fmly) (2 GF) **D** £100-£165 (incl. bkfst) **Facilities** STV Wi-fi **Conf** Class 50 Board 40 Thtr 100 Del from £170 to £190 **Services** Lift **Parking** 100 **Notes** LB Civ Wed 100

BRAY
Map 6 SU97

Monkey Island
★★★ 73% HOTEL

☎ 01628 623400 & 500713 📠 01628 784732
Old Mill Ln SL6 2EE
e-mail: info@monkeyisland.co.uk
dir: M4 junct 8/9/A308 signed Windsor. 1st left into Bray, 1st right

This hotel is in a charming setting on an island in the Thames, yet is within easy reach to major routes. Access is by footbridge or boat, but there is a large car park nearby. The hotel comprises two buildings, one for accommodation and the other for dining and drinking. The ample grounds are beautifully maintained and provide a peaceful haven for wildlife.

Rooms 26 (1 fmly) (12 GF) **Facilities** STV Putt green 🛶 Xmas New Year Wi-fi **Conf** Class 60 Board 70 Thtr 150 Del from £190 to £260* **Parking** 100 **Notes** ⊗ Civ Wed 150

COOKHAM DEAN
Map 5 SU88

The Inn on the Green
⑩⑩ RESTAURANT WITH ROOMS

☎ 01628 482638 📠 01628 487474
The Old Cricket Common SL6 9NZ
e-mail: reception@theinnonthegreen.com
dir: In village centre

A traditional English country inn set in rural Berkshire. Bedrooms are spacious and comfortable, with antique furnishings adding to the character. The building retains many traditional features including a wood panelled dining room and Old English bar with log fire. Food is imaginative and noteworthy and can be enjoyed outside in the garden or terrace in warmer months.

Rooms 9 (9 en suite) (4 GF)

CROWTHORNE
Map 5 SU86

The Waterloo Hotel
★★★ 71% HOTEL

folio Hotels

☎ 0870 609 6111 & 01344 777711 📠 01344 778913
Duke's Ride RG45 6DW
e-mail: waterloo@foliohotels.com
web: www.foliohotels.com/waterloo
dir: A331 to Camberley, follow signs to Sandhurst/ Crowthorne A3095, left B3348, hotel past 2nd rdbt

Situated in a quiet location but convenient for both the M3 and M4, this hotel attracts a high proportion of business guests. The modern bedrooms, which include inter-connecting pairs of rooms, are attractively appointed and well maintained. Public areas include the pleasant Grove Brasserie and Bar.

Rooms 79 (1 fmly) (23 GF) (8 smoking) **S** £65-£175; **D** £75-£195* **Facilities** STV Wi-fi **Conf** Class 16 Board 20 Thtr 50 Del from £120 to £165* **Parking** 96 **Notes** LB ⊗ Civ Wed 50

HUNGERFORD
Map 5 SU36

Bear
★★★ 81% ⑩⑩ HOTEL

☎ 01488 682512 📠 01488 684357
41 Charnham St RG17 0EL
e-mail: info@thebearhotelhungerford.co.uk
web: www.thebearhotelhungerford.co.uk
dir: M4 junct 14, A338 to Hungerford for 3m, left at T-junct onto A4, hotel on left

Situated five miles south of the M4 this hotel dates back as far as early 13th century and was once owned by King Henry VIII. It now has a contemporary feel throughout. Bedrooms are split between the main house, the courtyard and Bear Island. The award-winning restaurant is open for lunch and dinner, and lighter snacks are available in the bar and lounge. Guests can enjoy a sun terrace in the summer and log fires in the winter.

Rooms 39 (26 annexe) (2 fmly) (24 GF) **S** £85-£150; **D** £95-£190* **Facilities** FTV Xmas New Year Wi-fi **Conf** Class 35 Board 34 Thtr 80 **Parking** 68 **Notes** LB Civ Wed 80

Three Swans
★★★ 70% HOTEL

☎ 01488 682721 📠 01488 681708
117 High St RG17 0LZ
e-mail: info@threeswans.net
web: www.threeswans.net
dir: M4 junct 14 follow signs to Hungerford. Hotel half way along High St on left.

Centrally located in the bustling market town of Hungerford this charming former inn, dating back some 700 years, has been renovated in a fresh and airy style. Visitors will still see the original arch under which the

Continued

HUNGERFORD continued

horse-drawn carriages once passed. There is a wood panelled bar, a spacious lounge and attractive rear garden to relax in. The informal restaurant is decorated with a range of artwork by local artists. Bedrooms are well appointed and comfortable.

Rooms 25 (10 annexe) (1 fmly) (5 GF) **S** £85-£115; **D** £115-£155 (incl. bkfst)* **Facilities** STV Access to local private gym Xmas New Year Wi-fi **Conf** Class 40 Board 30 Thtr 55 **Parking** 30 **Notes** LB ⊗

HURLEY   Map 5 SU88

Black Boys Inn

⊛⊛ RESTAURANT WITH ROOMS

☎ 01628 824212
Henley Rd SL6 5NQ
e-mail: info@blackboysinn.co.uk
dir: 1m W of Hurley on A4130

Just a short drive from Henley, the traditional exterior of this friendly establishment is a contrast to the smart modernity within. Popular with locals, the restaurant is the stage for Simon Bonwick's imaginative cuisine, and offers a buzzing atmosphere. The well-appointed bedrooms are situated in converted barns close by.

Rooms 8 (3 en suite) (8 annexe) (5 GF)

KNOWL HILL   Map 5 SU87

Bird In Hand Country Inn

★★★ Ⓐ HOTEL

☎ 01628 826622 & 822781   🖹 01628 826748
Bath Rd RG10 9UP
e-mail: sthebirdinhand@aol.com
web: www.birdinhand.co.uk
dir: on A4 between Maidenhead & Reading

Rooms 15 (1 fmly) (6 GF) **S** £70-£100; **D** £80-£120 (incl. bkfst)* **Facilities** New Year Wi-fi **Conf** Class 30 Board 25 Thtr 50 Del from £130 to £150* **Parking** 80 **Notes** LB

MAIDENHEAD   Map 6 SU88

See also **Bray**

INSPECTORS' CHOICE

Fredrick's Hotel Restaurant Spa

"bespoke" HOTELS

★★★★ ⊛⊛⊛ HOTEL

☎ 01628 581000   🖹 01628 771054
Shoppenhangers Rd SL6 2PZ
e-mail: reservations@fredricks-hotel.co.uk
web: www.fredricks-hotel.co.uk
dir: M4 junct 8/9 onto A404(M) to Maidenhead West & Henley. 1st exit 9a to White Waltham. Left into Shoppenhangers Road to Maidenhead, hotel on right

Just 30 minutes from London, this delightful hotel enjoys a peaceful location yet is within easy reach of the M4 and only 20 minutes' drive from Wentworth and Sunningdale golf courses. The spacious bedrooms are comfortably furnished and very well equipped. An enthusiastic team of staff ensure friendly and efficient service. The imaginative cuisine is a highlight, as is the luxurious spa that offers the ultimate in relaxation and wellbeing.

Rooms 34 (11 GF) **Facilities** Spa ⊛ supervised ⊛ supervised Gym Rasul suite Oriental steam Dead Sea flotation room Wi-fi **Conf** Class 80 Board 60 Thtr 120 **Services** Air con **Parking** 90 **Notes** LB ⊗ Closed 24 Dec-3 Jan Civ Wed 120

Elva Lodge

★★ 72% HOTEL

☎ 01628 622948   🖹 01628 778954
Castle Hill SL6 4AD
e-mail: reservations@elvalodgehotel.co.uk
web: www.elvalodgehotel.co.uk
dir: A4 from Maidenhead towards Reading. Hotel at top of hill on left

Within easy reach of the town centre, this family-run hotel offers a warm welcome and friendly service. Bedrooms are pleasantly decorated, continually maintained, and equipped with thoughtful extras. Spacious public areas include a smart, stylish lounge, a bar, and Lion's Brasserie which offers a wide range of popular dishes.

Rooms 26 (1 fmly) (5 GF) **S** £55-£94.50; **D** £70-£113.50 (incl. bkfst)* **Facilities** Reduced rates at local leisure centre Wi-fi **Conf** Class 30 Board 30 Thtr 50 **Parking** 32 **Notes** Closed 24-30 Dec Civ Wed 60

Holiday Inn Maidenhead/ Windsor

Ⓤ

☎ 0870 400 9053 & 01628 506000   🖹 01628 506001
Manor Ln SL6 2RA
e-mail: reservations-maidenhead@ihg.com
web: www.holidayinn.co.uk
dir: A404 towards High Wycombe. Leave at junct 9A. Left at mini rdbt. Hotel on left

Currently the rating for this establishment is not confirmed. This may be due to a change of ownership or because it has only recently joined the AA rating scheme. For further details please see the AA website: www.theAA.com

Rooms 197 **S** £49-£285; **D** £49-£285* **Facilities** STV ⊛ supervised Gym Steam room Sauna New Year Wi-fi **Conf** Class 200 Board 100 Thtr 400 Del from £99 to £249* **Services** Lift Air con **Parking** 250 **Notes** LB ⊗ Civ Wed 400

Thames Riviera

[U]

☎ 01628 674057 📠 01628 776586
At the Bridge SL6 8DW
e-mail: reservations.thamesriviera@foliohotels.com
web: www.foliohotels.com/thamesriviera
dir: off A4 by Maidenhead Historic Bridge, hotel by bridge

Currently the rating for this establishment is not confirmed. This may be due to a change of ownership or because it has only recently joined the AA rating scheme. For further details please see the AA website: www.theAA.com

Rooms 52 (18 annexe) (5 fmly) (2 GF) **S** £60-£150; **D** £80-£190* **Facilities** FTV New Year Wi-fi **Parking** 45 **Notes** LB ⊗

MEMBURY MOTORWAY SERVICE AREA (M4) Map 5 SU37

Days Inn Membury

BUDGET HOTEL

☎ 01488 72336 📠 01488 72336
Membury Service Area RG17 7TZ
e-mail: membury.hotel@welcomebreak.co.uk
web: www.welcomebreak.co.uk
dir: M4 between junct 14 & 15

This modern building offers accommodation in smart, spacious and well-equipped bedrooms, suitable for families and business travellers, and all with en suite bathrooms. Continental breakfast is available and other refreshments may be taken at the nearby family restaurant. See also the Hotel Groups pages.

Rooms 38 (32 fmly) (17 GF) **S** £39-£59; **D** £49-£69* **Conf** Board 10 Del from £69 to £89*

NEWBURY Map 5 SU46
See also **Andover (Hampshire)**

INSPECTORS' CHOICE

The Vineyard at Stockcross
★★★★★ ◉◉◉◉◉ HOTEL

☎ 01635 528770 📠 01635 528398
Stockcross RG20 8JU
e-mail: general@the-vineyard.co.uk
web: www.the-vineyard.co.uk
dir: from M4 take A34 towards Newbury, exit at 3rd junct for Speen. Right at rdbt then right again at 2nd rdbt.

A haven of style in the Berkshire countryside, this hotel prides itself on a superb art collection, which can be seen throughout the building. Bedrooms come in a variety of styles - many split-level suites that are exceptionally well equipped. Comfortable lounges lead into the stylish restaurant, which serves award-winning, imaginative and precise cooking, complemented by an equally impressive selection of wines from California and around the world. The welcome is warm and sincere, the service professional yet relaxed.

Rooms 49 (15 GF) **Facilities** Spa ⊗ Gym Treatment rooms ♫ Xmas Wi-fi **Conf** Class 50 Board 30 Thtr 100 **Services** Lift Air con **Parking** 100 **Notes** ⊗ Civ Wed 100

Donnington Valley Hotel & Spa
★★★★ 85% ◉◉ HOTEL

CLASSIC BRITISH HOTELS

☎ 01635 551199 📠 01635 551123
Old Oxford Rd, Donnington RG14 3AG
e-mail: general@donningtonvalley.co.uk
web: www.donningtonvalley.co.uk
dir: M4 junct 13, take A34 signed Newbury. Take exit signed Donnington/Services, at rdbt take 2nd exit signed Donnington. Left at next rdbt. Hotel 2m on right

In its own grounds complete with an 18-hole golf course, this stylish hotel boasts excellent facilities for both corporate and leisure guests; from the state-of-the-art spa offering an excellent range of treatments, to an extensive range of meeting and function rooms. Air-conditioned bedrooms are stylish, spacious and particularly well equipped with fridges, lap-top safes and internet access. The Wine Press restaurant offers imaginative food complemented by a superb wine list.

Rooms 111 (3 fmly) (36 GF) **Facilities** Spa ⊗ ♪ 18 Putt green Fishing Gym Sauna Aromatherapy Studio Xmas New Year Wi-fi **Conf** Class 60 Board 40 Thtr 140 **Services** Lift Air con **Parking** 150 **Notes** ⊗ Civ Wed 85

Regency Park Hotel
★★★★ 81% ◉ HOTEL

☎ 01635 871555 📠 01635 871571
Bowling Green Rd, Thatcham RG18 3RP
e-mail: info.newbury@pedersenhotels.com
web: www.pedersenhotels.com
dir: from Newbury take A4 signed Thatcham & Reading. 2nd rdbt exit signed Cold Ash. Hotel 1m on left

This smart, stylish hotel has benefited from major investment over the last few years and is ideal for both business and leisure guests. Spacious, well-equipped bedrooms include a number of contemporary, tasteful

Continued

NEWBURY continued

executive rooms. Smart airy public areas include a state-of-the-art spa and leisure club and the Watermark Restaurant offers imaginative, award-winning cuisine.

Rooms 109 (7 fmly) (9 GF) **Facilities** Spa ☯ Gym Xmas New Year Wi-fi **Conf** Class 80 Board 70 Thtr 200 Del from £165 to £215* **Services** Lift **Parking** 160 **Notes** ⊗ Civ Wed 100

See advert on page 51

Ramada Hotel & Resort Elcot Park

★★★★ 73% HOTEL

☎ 01488 658100 & 0844 815 9060 🖹 01488 658288
RG20 8NJ
e-mail: sales.elcotpark@ramadajarvis.co.uk
web: www.ramadajarvis.co.uk/newbury
dir: M4 junct 13, A338 to Hungerford, A4 to Newbury. Hotel 4m from Hungerford

Enjoying a peaceful location yet within easy access to both the A4 and M4, this country-house hotel is set in 16 acres of gardens and woodland. Bedrooms are comfortably appointed and include some located in an adjacent mews. Public areas include the Orangery Restaurant, which enjoys views over the Kennet Valley, a leisure club and a range of conference rooms.

Rooms 73 (17 annexe) (1 fmly) (25 GF) (5 smoking) **S** £92-£196; **D** £92-£212 **Facilities** FTV ☯ supervised ♨ ♨ Gym Sauna Solarium Steam room Xmas New Year Wi-fi **Conf** Class 45 Board 35 Thtr 110 Del from £169 to £190 **Parking** 130 **Notes** LB ⊗ Civ Wed 120

Newbury Manor Hotel

★★★ 78% ◉ HOTEL

☎ 01635 528838 🖹 01635 523406
London Rd RG14 2BY
e-mail: enquiries@newbury-manor-hotel.co.uk
dir: On A4 between Newbury & Thatcham

A former Georgian watermill, which still features the original millrace, situated beside the River Kennet which flows through the well tended grounds. The character bedrooms that vary in style and size offer many accessories. Guests can dine in the River Bar Restaurant.

Rooms 33 (4 fmly) (11 GF) **D** £120-£135 (incl. bkfst)* **Facilities** Fishing Xmas New Year Wi-fi **Conf** Class 140 Board 90 Thtr 190 **Parking** 100 **Notes** LB ⊗ Civ Wed 100

Best Western West Grange

★★★ 72% HOTEL

☎ 01635 273074 🖹 01635 862351
Cox's Ln, Bath Rd, Midgham RG7 5UP
e-mail: reservations@westgrangehotel.co.uk
dir: A4 Theale, follow signs to Newbury. Hotel on right approx 2m from Woolhampton

This former farmhouse has been turned into a smart and modern hotel that is set in well-managed grounds only a short drive away from Thatcham. Bedrooms offer a quiet and comfortable stay, and guests can relax in the large bar lounge and attractive restaurant. There is also a patio for warmer months.

Rooms 45 (3 fmly) (12 GF) **S** £50-£100; **D** £70-£120* **Facilities** STV New Year Wi-fi **Conf** Class 25 Board 30 Thtr 50 **Services** Lift **Parking** 70 **Notes** ⊗

Hare & Hounds

★★ 78% HOTEL

☎ 01635 521152 🖹 01635 47708
Bath Rd, Speen RG14 1QY
e-mail: reservations@hareandhoundsnewbury.co.uk
web: www.hareandhoundshotel.net
dir: Turn off A34 onto A4 signed for Speen. Hotel 300yds on right

A privately owned, historic hotel just a few minutes from the centre of Newbury. The hotel offers bedrooms in the coach house and in the mews, and all are modern and tastefully decorated. There is a relaxed, informal restaurant offering regularly changing menus, and the bar is popular with locals and guests alike.

Rooms 30 (23 annexe) (3 fmly) (11 GF) **S** £48-£78; **D** £65-£108 (incl. bkfst)* **Facilities** New Year **Parking** 64 **Notes** LB

Chequers

[U]

☎ 01635 38000 🖹 01635 37170
6-8 Oxford St RG14 1JB
e-mail: reservations.chequers@foliohotels.com
web: www.foliohotels.com
dir: M4 junct 13/A34 S onto A339 to Newbury. At 2nd rdbt turn right to town centre. At clock tower rdbt turn right, hotel on right

Currently the rating for this establishment is not confirmed. This may be due to a change of ownership or because it has only recently joined the AA rating scheme. For further details please see the AA website: www.theAA.com

Rooms 56 (11 annexe) (3 fmly) (7 GF) **S** £45-£125; **D** £55-£125* **Facilities** Xmas New Year Wi-fi **Conf** Class 80 Board 40 Thtr 70 Del from £100 to £145* **Parking** 65 **Notes** ⊗ Civ Wed 140

Travelodge Newbury Chieveley (M4)

BUDGET HOTEL

☎ 08719 846 203 🖹 01635 247886
Chieveley, Oxford Rd RG18 9XX
web: www.travelodge.co.uk
dir: on A34, off M4 junct 13

Travelodge offers good quality, good value, modern accommodation. Ideal for families, the spacious en suite bedrooms include remote-control TV, tea and coffee-making facilities and comfortable beds. Meals can be taken at the nearby family restaurant. See also the Hotel Groups pages.

Rooms 127 **S** fr £29; **D** fr £29

Travelodge Newbury Tot Hill

BUDGET HOTEL

☎ 08719 846 204 🖹 01635 278169
Tot Hill Services (A34), Newbury by-pass RG20 9ED
web: www.travelodge.co.uk
dir: Tot Hill Services on A34

Rooms 52 **S** fr £29; **D** fr £29

Holiday Inn Reading West

[U]

☎ 0118 971 4411 🖹 0118 971 4442
Bath Rd RG7 5HT
web: www.holidayinn.co.uk

Currently the rating for this establishment is not confirmed. This may be due to a change of ownership or because it has only recently joined the AA rating scheme. For further details please see the AA website: www.theAA.com

Rooms 50

Elephant at Pangbourne

★★★ 78% ◉ HOTEL

☎ 0118 984 2244 & 07770 268359 🖹 0118 976 7346
Church Rd RG8 7AR
e-mail: paul@hillbrooke.co.uk
web: www.elephanthotel.co.uk
dir: A4 Theale/Newbury, right at 2nd rdbt signed Pangbourne. Hotel on left

Centrally located in this bustling village, just a short drive from Reading town centre. Bedrooms are individual in style but identical in the attention to detail, with handcrafted Indian furniture and rich oriental rugs. Guests can enjoy award-winning cuisine in the restaurant or bistro-style dining in the bar area.

Rooms 22 (8 annexe) (2 fmly) (4 GF) **S** £100; **D** £140 (incl. bkfst)* **Facilities** FTV ♨ Xmas New Year Wi-fi

Conf Class 40 Board 30 Thtr 60 Del from £155*
Parking 10 Notes LB ⊗ Civ Wed 60

READING Map 5 SU77

See also **Swallowfield**

Forbury

★★★★★ 81% ⊛ HOTEL

☎ 08000 789789 & 0118 958 1234 📄 0118 959 0806
26 The Forbury RG1 3EJ
e-mail: reservations@theforburyhotel.co.uk

The imposing exterior of this hotel belies the caring approach of the staff who provide helpful service with a smile. The up-to-the-minute bedrooms have very appealing designs and sensory appeal. For film buffs, a 30-seater cinema is also available, complete with refreshments! Cerise is the convivial and stylish venue for trying the award-winning cuisine.

Rooms 24 (1 fmly) (1 GF) Facilities Xmas New Year Wi-fi
Conf Class 24 Board 24 Thtr 35 Services Lift Parking 20
(charged) Notes ⊗ Civ Wed 50

Millennium Madejski Hotel Reading

★★★★ 81% ⊛⊛ HOTEL

☎ 0118 925 3500 📄 0118 925 3501
Madejski Stadium RG2 0FL
e-mail: sales.reading@millenniumhotels.co.uk
web: www.millenniumhotels.co.uk
dir: M4 junct 11 onto A33, follow signs for Madejski Stadium Complex

A stylish hotel, that features an atrium lobby with specially commissioned water sculpture, is part of the Madejski stadium complex, home to both Reading Football and London Irish Rugby teams. Bedrooms are appointed with spacious workstations and plenty of amenities; there is also a choice of suites and a club floor with its own lounge. The hotel also has an award-winning, fine dining restaurant.

Rooms 201 (39 fmly) (19 smoking) D £69-£230*
Facilities Spa STV ⓢ supervised Gym Wi-fi Conf Class 36
Board 30 Thtr 60 Del from £165 to £220 Services Lift
Air con Parking 250 Notes LB RS Xmas & New Year

Novotel Reading Centre

★★★★ 77% ⊛ HOTEL

☎ 0118 952 2600 📄 0118 952 2610
25b Friar St RG1 1DP
e-mail: h5432@accor.com
web: www.novotel.com
dir: M4 junct 11 or A33 towards Reading, exit on left for Garrard St car park, at rdbt take 3rd exit on Friar St

This attractive and stylish city centre hotel is convenient for Reading's business and shopping centre; it is adjacent to a town centre car park, and has a range of conference facilities and excellent leisure options. The restaurant offers a contemporary style menu and a good wine list too. Bedrooms are comfortable and stylishly designed.

Rooms 178 (15 fmly) S £59-£195; D £59-£195*
Facilities STV FTV ⓢ Gym Steam room Wi-fi
Conf Class 50 Board 36 Thtr 90 Del from £159 to £249*
Services Lift Air con Parking 15 (charged)

Crowne Plaza Reading

★★★★ 77% HOTEL

☎ 0118 925 9988
Caversham Bridge, Richfield Av RG1 8BD
e-mail: info@cp-reading.co.uk
web: www.crowneplaza.co.uk
dir: A33 to Reading. Follow signs for Caversham & Henley. Take 1st exit at rdbt onto Caversham Rd. Left at rdbt & entrance on right.

Located on the banks of the River Thames, this hotel is well positioned for both business and leisure travellers. The air-conditioned bedrooms are smartly appointed and well equipped. Public areas include the stylish Acqua Restaurant, a lounge bar, extensive conference and business facilities and the new Revive health club and spa. Secure parking is a real bonus.

Rooms 122 (9 fmly) S £64-£165; D £64-£165*
Facilities Spa STV ⓢ Gym Xmas New Year Wi-fi
Conf Class 60 Thtr 110 Services Lift Air con Parking 200
Notes LB ⊗ Civ Wed 180

Copthorne Hotel Reading

★★★★ 74% HOTEL

☎ 0118 950 0885 📄 0118 939 1996
Pingewood RG30 3UN
dir: A33 towards Basingstoke. At Three Mile Cross rdbt right signed Burghfield. After 300mtrs 2nd right, over M4, through lights, hotel on left

Enjoying a secluded and rural setting and yet just a few minutes south of Reading, this modern hotel was built around a man-made lake which is occasionally used for water sport. Bedrooms are generally spacious with good facilities, and most have balconies overlooking the lake and wildlife.

Rooms 81 (23 fmly) S £49-£180; D £49-£180*
Facilities STV ⓢ Gym Squash Watersports Wi-fi
Conf Class 60 Board 60 Thtr 110 Del from £125 to £205*
Services Lift Parking 250 Notes LB ⊗ Civ Wed 80

Malmaison Reading

★★★ 78% ⊛ HOTEL

☎ 0118 956 2300 📄 0118 956 2301
Great Western House, 18-20 Station Rd RG1 1JX
e-mail: reading@malmaison.com
web: www.malmaison.com
dir: Opposite Reading train station

This historic hotel has been transformed to a funky, Malmaison style which reflects its proximity and long-standing relationship with the railway. Public areas feature rail memorabilia and excellent pictures, and include a Café Mal and a meeting room. Bedrooms here have all the amenities a modern executive would expect, plus comfort and quality in abundance. Dining is exciting too, with a menu that features home-grown and local produce accompanied by an impressive wine list.

Rooms 75 (6 fmly) S £79-£160; D £79-£160*
Facilities Gym Xmas New Year Wi-fi Conf Board 16
Del from £225* Services Lift Air con

Best Western Calcot Hotel

★★★ 72% HOTEL

☎ 0118 941 6423 📄 0118 945 1223
98 Bath Rd, Calcot RG31 7QN
e-mail: enquiries@calcothotel.co.uk
web: www.calcothotel.co.uk
dir: M4 junct 12 onto A4 towards Reading, hotel in 0.5m on N side of A4

This hotel is conveniently located in a residential area just off the motorway. Bedrooms are well equipped with good business facilities, such as data ports and good workspace. There are attractive public rooms and function suites, and the informal restaurant offers enjoyable food in welcoming surroundings.

Rooms 78 (2 fmly) (6 GF) Facilities FTV ♫ New Year Wi-fi
Conf Class 35 Board 35 Thtr 120 Del from £135 to £165*
Parking 130 Notes ⊗ Closed 25-27 Dec Civ Wed 60

READING continued

The Mill House

THE INDEPENDENTS
HOTEL ASSOCIATION

★★ 78% HOTEL

☎ 0118 988 3124 📄 0118 988 5550
Old Basingstoke Rd, Swallowfield RG7 1PY
e-mail: info@themillhousehotel.co.uk

(For full entry see Swallowfield)

Royal County

★★ 69% HOTEL

☎ 0118 958 3455 & 959 1115 📄 0118 950 4450
4-8 Duke St RG1 4RY
e-mail: meet@royalcountyhotel.com
dir: In town centre adjacent to the Oracle Shopping Centre

Conviniently located in Reading Town Centre for business and shopping, this traditional hotel has had investment in bedrooms and some public areas. Bedrooms are well equipped and bathrooms cosy. The restaurant features Indian Tandoori cooking as well as a choice of European foods on some evenings. Limited on site car parking, but ample in vicinity. Staff are friendly and welcoming.

Rooms 52 (2 fmly) (6 smoking) **S** £49-£105; **D** £75-£125 (incl. bkfst)* **Facilities** FTV Wi-fi **Conf** Class 35 Board 35 Thtr 90 Del from £120 to £154* **Parking** 18 **Notes** ⊗

Comfort Hotel Reading West

Ⓤ
Comfort
INN

☎ 0118 971 3282 📄 0118 971 4238
Bath Rd, Padworth RG7 5HT
e-mail: info@comfortreading.co.uk
web: www.comfortreading.co.uk
dir: M4 junct 12, A4 (Bath Road) signed Newbury. Hotel approx 2m on left

Currently the rating for this establishment is not confirmed. This may be due to a change of ownership or because it has only recently joined the AA rating scheme. For further details please see the AA website: www.theAA.com

Rooms 33 (1 fmly) (20 GF) **S** £60-£90; **D** £99 (incl. bkfst) **Facilities** FTV Wi-fi **Conf** Class 50 Board 50 Thtr 120 Del from £90 to £140 **Parking** 40 **Notes** LB ⊗ Civ Wed 100

See advert on opposite page

Holiday Inn Reading South

Ⓤ

Holiday Inn
HOTELS · RESORTS

☎ 0870 400 9067 📄 0118 931 1958
Basingstoke Rd RG2 0SL
e-mail: reading@ihg.com
web: www.holidayinn.co.uk

Currently the rating for this establishment is not confirmed. This may be due to a change of ownership or because it has only recently joined the AA rating scheme. For further details please see the AA website: www.theAA.com

Rooms 202 **S** £58-£160; **D** £58-£160* **Facilities** Health & fitness centre Xmas Child facilities

Express by Holiday Inn Reading

Express
by Holiday Inn

BUDGET HOTEL

☎ 0118 958 2558 📄 0118 958 2858
Richfield Av RG1 8EQ
e-mail: ebhi-reading@btconnect.com
web: www.hiexpress.com/expressreading
dir: Follow city centre & Caversham signs

A modern hotel ideal for families and business travellers. Fresh and uncomplicated, the spacious rooms include Sky TV, power shower and tea and coffee-making facilities. Continental buffet breakfast is included in the room rate; other meals may be taken at the nearby family pub or restaurant. See also the Hotel Groups pages.

Rooms 74 (28 fmly) **Conf** Class 20 Board 16 Thtr 30

Ibis Reading Centre

ibis
HOTEL

BUDGET HOTEL

☎ 0118 953 3500 📄 0118 953 3501
25A Friar St RG1 1DP
e-mail: H5431@accor.com
web: www.ibishotel.com
dir: Turn off A329 Friar Street. Hotel 2 min from central train station

Budget Hotel in the main shopping area of Reading with handy NCP parking behind. All rooms are well equipped and comfortable and both dinner and breakfast are available in La Table restaurant. See also the Hotel Groups pages.

Rooms 182 (36 fmly) **S** £39-£90; **D** £39-£90*

Travelodge Reading Central

Travelodge

BUDGET HOTEL

☎ 08719 846 211 📄 0118 950 3257
Oxford Rd RG1 7LT
web: www.travelodge.co.uk
dir: M4 junct 11, A33 towards Reading, follow signs for A329 (Oxford road)

Travelodge offers good quality, good value, modern accommodation. Ideal for families, the spacious en suite bedrooms include remote-control TV, tea and coffee-making facilities and comfortable beds. Meals can be taken at the nearby family restaurant. See also the Hotel Groups pages.

Rooms 80 **S** fr £29; **D** fr £29

Travelodge Reading (M4 Eastbound)

BUDGET HOTEL

☎ 08719 846 267 📄 0118 959 2045
Burghfield RG30 3UQ
web: www.travelodge.co.uk
dir: M4 between juncts 11 & 12 eastbound

Rooms 86 **S** fr £29; **D** fr £29 **Conf** Class 20 Board 20 Thtr 20

Travelodge Reading (M4 Westbound)

BUDGET HOTEL

☎ 08719 846 268 📄 0118 958 2350
Burghfield RG30 3UQ
web: www.travelodge.co.uk
dir: M4 between junct 11 & 12 westbound

Rooms 102 **S** fr £29; **D** fr £29

Travelodge Reading Oxford Road

BUDGET HOTEL

☎ 0871 984 6357 📄 0118 956 7220
648-654 Oxford Rd RG30 1EH
web: www.travelodge.co.uk
dir: M4 junct 11, A33 bypass towards town centre, then A329 towards Pangbourne, follow Oxford Road signs

Rooms 96 (15 fmly) **S** fr £29; **D** fr £29 **Conf** Class 50 Board 40 Thtr 100

Travelodge Reading Whitley

BUDGET HOTEL

☎ 08719 846 242 📄 0118 975 1303
387 Basingstoke Rd RG2 0JE
web: www.travelodge.co.uk
dir: M4 junct 11, A33 to Reading, right onto B3031, 1m on right

Rooms 36 **S** fr £29; **D** fr £29

SLOUGH	Map 6 SU97

Copthorne Hotel Slough-Windsor

MILLENNIUM
HOTELS AND RESORTS
MILLENNIUM HOTELS
COPTHORNE HOTELS

★★★★ 76% HOTEL

☎ 01753 516222 📄 01753 516237
400 Cippenham Ln SL1 2YE
e-mail: sales.slough@millenniumhotels.co.uk
web: www.millenniumhotels.co.uk
dir: M4 junct 6 & follow A355 to Slough at next rdbt turn left & left again for hotel entrance

Conveniently located for the motorway and for Heathrow Airport, this modern hotel offers visitors a wide range of indoor leisure facilities, and Turner's Grill offers a British menu. Bedrooms provide a useful range of extras including climate control, satellite TV and a trouser press.

The hotel offers a discounted entrance fee to some of the attractions in the area.

Rooms 219 (47 fmly) **Facilities** STV FTV ☺ Gym Wi-fi **Conf** Class 160 Board 60 Thtr 250 **Services** Lift **Parking** 3 (charged) **Notes** ⊗ Civ Wed 100

The Pinewood Hotel

★★★★ 74% ⊛ HOTEL

☎ 01753 896400 📠 01753 896500
Wexham Park Ln, George Green SL3 6AP
e-mail: info@pinewoodhotel.co.uk
web: www.bespokehotels.com
dir: A4 N from Slough, A412 towards Uxbridge. Hotel 3m on left

This is a small luxury hotel on the outskirts of Slough. Excellent design is at the forefront throughout, together with good levels of comfort. The Eden brasserie specialises in quality produce, carefully prepared, including dishes cooked on the wood-burning stove. Service is friendly and attentive.

Rooms 49 (16 annexe) (4 fmly) (12 GF) **S** £60-£100; **D** £80-£140 (incl. bkfst) **Facilities** Xmas Wi-fi

Conf Class 46 Board 40 Thtr 120 **Del** from £175 to £205 **Services** Lift Air con **Parking** 40 **Notes** LB ⊗ Civ Wed 30

Quality Hotel Heathrow

★★★ 73% HOTEL

☎ 01753 684001 📠 01753 685767
London Rd, Brands Hill SL3 8QB
e-mail: info@qualityheathrow.com
web: www.qualityheathrow.com
dir: M4 junct 5, follow signs for Colnbrook. Hotel approx 250mtrs on right

This stylish, modern hotel is ideally located for Heathrow Airport travellers, and for commercial visitors to Slough. Bedrooms have good facilities, benefit from all-day room service and are smartly furnished. There is a bright and airy open-plan restaurant, bar and lounge. A regular shuttle service, at a small charge, operates for Terminals 1, 2 and 3.

Rooms 128 (23 fmly) (5 GF) **S** £49-£155; **D** £59-£155* **Facilities** Gym Wi-fi **Conf** Class 50 Board 40 Thtr 120 **Del** from £99 to £146* **Services** Lift **Parking** 100 (charged) **Notes** LB ⊗

Holiday Inn Slough-Windsor

Ⓤ

☎ 01753 551551 ☎ 0870 400 7215 📠 01753 553333
1 Church St, Chalvey SL1 2ND
e-mail: reservations@slough.kewgreen.co.uk
web: www.holidayinn.co.uk
dir: M4 junct 6, take 3rd exit on rdbt onto A355 Tuns Lane. 3rd exit at next rdbt, hotel on right

Currently the rating for this establishment is not confirmed. This may be due to a change of ownership or because it has only recently joined the AA rating scheme. For further details please see the AA website: www.theAA.com

Rooms 150 (64 fmly) (6 GF) (18 smoking) **S** £59-£189; **D** £59-£189* **Facilities** STV Xmas Wi-fi **Conf** Class 12 Board 20 Thtr 40 **Del** from £99 to £169 **Services** Lift **Parking** 150 (charged) **Notes** LB ⊗

Express by Holiday Inn Slough

Express by Holiday Inn

BUDGET HOTEL

☎ 0844 499 2890 📠 0844 499 2910
Mill St SL2 5DD
web: www.hiexpress.co.uk

A modern hotel ideal for families and business travellers. Fresh and uncomplicated, the spacious rooms include Sky TV, power shower and tea and coffee-making facilities. Continental buffet breakfast is included in the room rate; other meals may be taken at the nearby family pub or restaurant. See also the Hotel Groups pages.

Rooms 142

Innkeeper's Lodge Slough/ Windsor

Innkeeper's Lodge

BUDGET HOTEL

☎ 0845 112 6108 📠 0845 112 6195
399 London Rd, Langley SL3 8PS
web: www.innkeeperslodge.com/sloughwindsor
dir: M4 junct 5, A4 towards Slough. Lodge on right

Innkeeper's Lodge represents an exciting, high value concept within the budget hotel market. Comfortable bedrooms provide excellent facilities that include satellite TV and modem points. Options include family rooms, and for the corporate guest, cutting edge IT which includes Wi-fi access. A popular Carvery provides all-day food, including an extensive, complimentary continental breakfast.

Rooms 57 (15 fmly) **S** £59.95-£74.95; **D** £59.95-£74.95 (incl. bkfst)

SLOUGH continued

Travelodge Slough

BUDGET HOTEL

☎ 08719 846 253 🖹 0121 521 6026
Landmark Place SL1 1BZ
web: www.travelodge.co.uk

Travelodge offers good quality, good value, modern accommodation. Ideal for families, the spacious en suite bedrooms include remote-control TV, tea and coffee-making facilities and comfortable beds. Meals can be taken at the nearby family restaurant. See also the Hotel Groups pages.

Rooms 157 **S** fr £29; **D** fr £29

SONNING   Map 5 SU77

French Horn

★★★ 81% ◉◉ HOTEL   *Pride of Britain*

☎ 0118 969 2204 🖹 0118 944 2210
RG4 6TN
e-mail: info@thefrenchhorn.co.uk
dir: From A4 into Sonning, follow B478 through village over bridge, hotel on right, car park on left

This long established Thames-side establishment has a lovely village setting and retains the traditions of classic hotel keeping. The restaurant is a particular attraction and provides attentive service. Bedrooms, including four cottage suites, are spacious and comfortable; many offering stunning views over the river. A private boardroom is available for corporate guests.

Rooms 21 (8 annexe) (4 GF) **Facilities** Fishing Wi-fi **Conf** Board 16 **Services** Air con **Parking** 40 **Notes** ⊗ Closed 26-29 Dec

---

STREATLEY   Map 5 SU58

The Swan at Streatley

★★★★ 75% ◉◉ HOTEL

☎ 01491 878800 🖹 01491 872554
High St RG8 9HR
e-mail: sales@swan-at-streatley.co.uk
web: www.swanatstreatley.co.uk
dir: from S right at lights in Streatley, hotel on left before bridge

A stunning location set beside the Thames, ideal for an English summer's day. The bedrooms are well appointed

and many enjoy the lovely views. The hotel offers a range of facilities including meeting rooms, and the Magdalen Barge is moored beside the hotel making an unusual, yet perfect meeting venue. A motor launch is available for hire from April to October. The spa includes an indoor heated mineral pool and offers a range of treatments. Cuisine is accomplished and dining here should not be missed.

Rooms 45 (12 GF) **S** £115-£130; **D** fr £150 (incl. bkfst)*
Facilities Spa STV ③ supervised Fishing ⅃ Gym Electric motor launches for hire Apr-Oct Xmas New Year Wi-fi **Conf** Class 80 Board 60 Thtr 140 **Parking** 170 **Notes** LB Civ Wed 130

SWALLOWFIELD   Map 5 SU76

The Mill House   THE INDEPENDENTS
                      HOTEL ASSOCIATION

★★ 78% HOTEL

☎ 0118 988 3124 🖹 0118 988 5550
Old Basingstoke Rd, Swallowfield RG7 1PY
e-mail: info@themillhousehotel.co.uk
dir: M4 junct 11, S on A33, left at 1st rdbt onto B3349. Approx 1m after sign for Three Mile Cross & Spencer's Wood, hotel on right

This smart Georgian house hotel enjoys a tranquil setting in its own delightful gardens, making it a popular wedding venue. Guests can enjoy fine dining in the conservatory-style restaurant or lighter meals in the cosy bar. Well-equipped bedrooms vary in size and style and include a number of spacious, well-appointed executive rooms.

Rooms 12 (2 fmly) **S** £65-£85; **D** £90-£120 (incl. bkfst)*
Facilities FTV Wi-fi **Conf** Class 100 Board 60 Thtr 250 **Parking** 60 **Notes** Closed 25-30 Dec RS Sun evenings Civ Wed 125

WINDSOR   Map 6 SU97

Oakley Court

★★★★ 79% ◉ HOTEL

☎ 01753 609988 & 609900 🖹 01628 637011
Windsor Rd, Water Oakley SL4 5UR
e-mail: reservations@oakleycourt.com
web: www.oakleycourt.com
dir: M4 junct 6, towards Windsor, then right onto A308 Maidenhead. Pass racecourse & hotel is 2.5m on right.

Built in 1859 this splendid Victorian Gothic mansion is enviably situated in extensive grounds that lead down to the Thames. All rooms are spacious, beautifully furnished and many enjoy river views. Extensive public areas include a range of comfortable lounges, the Oakleaf Restaurant and comprehensive facilities, which also features a 9-hole golf course.

Rooms 118 (109 annexe) (5 fmly) (28 GF) **Facilities** Spa ③ ⅃ 9 ♀ ⅃ Gym Boating Sauna Snooker Xmas New Year Wi-fi **Conf** Class 90 Board 50 Thtr 170 **Services** Air con **Parking** 120 **Notes** LB ⊗ Civ Wed 120

Mercure Castle

★★★★ 77% ◉◉ HOTEL

☎ 01753 851577 🖹 01753 856930
18 High St SL4 1LJ
e-mail: h6618@accor.com
web: www.mercure-uk.com
dir: M4 junct 6/M25 junct 15 - follow signs to Windsor town centre & castle. Hotel at top of hill by castle opposite Guildhall

This is one of the oldest hotels in Windsor, beginning life as a coaching inn in the 16th century. Located opposite Windsor Castle, it is an ideal base from which to explore the town. Stylish bedrooms are thoughtfully equipped and include four-poster and executive rooms. Public areas are spacious and tastefully decorated.

Rooms 108 (70 annexe) (18 fmly) **S** £120-£280;
D £120-£280* **Facilities** STV Xmas New Year Wi-fi **Conf** Class 130 Board 80 Thtr 400 Del from £195 to £310* **Services** Lift Air con **Parking** 110 (charged) **Notes** LB ⊗ Civ Wed 80

Harte & Garter   *folio Hotels*

★★★★ 74% HOTEL

☎ 01753 863426 & 848560 🖹 01753 830527
High St SL4 1PH
e-mail: harteandgarter@foliohotels.com
web: www.foliohotels.com/harteandgarter
dir: M4 junct 6/ A332 follow town centre signs, hotel opposite front entrance to Windsor Castle

Enjoying an enviable location in the centre of Windsor, this hotel overlooks the magnificent Windsor Castle. Bedrooms are comfortably appointed and interiors blend modern and classic styles well. Public areas include the Tower Brasserie and tea room which also enjoys views of the castle, a new spa facility where guests can unwind, and a range of conference and meeting rooms.

Rooms 79 (40 annexe) (3 GF) **S** £70-£175; **D** £110-£350*
Facilities Spa FTV Thermal suite & Hydro pool ♫ Xmas New Year Wi-fi **Conf** Class 80 Board 80 Thtr 260 Del from £210 to £280* **Services** Lift **Notes** LB ⊗ Civ Wed 180

WINDSOR continued

Sir Christopher Wren's House Hotel & Spa

★★★★ 73% ⊚⊚ HOTEL

☎ 01753 861354 📄 01753 860172
Thames St SL4 1PX
e-mail: reservations@wrensgroup.com
web: www.sirchristopherwren.co.uk
dir: M4 junct 6, 1st exit from relief road, follow signs to Windsor, 1st major exit on left, turn left at lights

This hotel has an enviable location right on the edge of the River Thames overlooking Eton Bridge. Diners in Strok's, the award-winning restaurant, enjoy the best views. A variety of well-appointed bedrooms are available, including several in the adjacent courtyard rooms. There is also a health and leisure spa, and secure parking is available.

Rooms 95 (38 annexe) (11 fmly) (3 GF) **S** £85-£170; **D** £97-£320* **Facilities** Spa FTV Gym Health & beauty club Sauna Xmas New Year Wi-fi **Conf** Class 50 Board 50 Thtr 90 Del from £195 to £265* **Parking** 10 (charged) **Notes** LB ⊗ Civ Wed 90

See advert on page 57

Royal Adelaide

★★★★ 71% HOTEL

☎ 01753 863916 & 07710 473130 📄 01753 830682
46 Kings Rd SL4 2AG
e-mail: www.theroyaladelaide.com
web: info@theroyaladeliade.com
dir: M4 junct 6, A322 to Windsor. 1st left off rdbt into Clarence Rd. At 4th lights right into Sheet St and into Kings Rd. Hotel on right

This attractive Georgian-style hotel enjoys a quiet location yet is only a short walk from the town centre and benefiting from off-road parking. Bedrooms vary in size. Public areas are tastefully appointed and include a range of meeting rooms, a bar and an elegant restaurant.

Rooms 42 (4 annexe) (8 GF) **S** £79-£130; **D** £89-£175 (incl. bkfst)* **Facilities** Xmas New Year Wi-fi

Conf Class 80 Board 50 Thtr 100 **Services** Air con **Notes** LB ⊗ Civ Wed

See advert on page 57

Christopher Hotel

★★★ 75% HOTEL

☎ 01753 852359 📄 01753 830914
110 High St, Eton SL4 6AN
e-mail: janet@thechristopher.co.uk
web: www.thechristopher.co.uk
dir: M4 junct 5 (Slough E), Colnbrook Datchet Eton (B470). At rdbt 2nd exit for Datchet. Right at mini rdbt (Eton), left into Eton Rd (3rd rdbt). Left, hotel on right

This hotel benefits from an ideal location in Eton, being only a short stroll across the pedestrian bridge from historic Windsor Castle and the many other attractions the town has to offer. The hotel has comfortable and smartly decorated accommodation, and a wide range of dishes is available in the informal bar and grill. A stylish room is available for private dining or for meetings.

Rooms 33 (22 annexe) (6 fmly) (22 GF) **S** £98.60-£116; **D** £131.80-£185* **Facilities** Xmas New Year Wi-fi **Conf** Board 10 Del from £165 to £185* **Parking** 19 **Notes** LB

See advert on page 57

Innkeeper's Lodge Old Windsor

BUDGET HOTEL

☎ 0845 112 6104 📄 0845 112 6199
14 Straight Rd, Old Windsor SL4 2RR
web: www.innkeeperslodge.com/oldwindsor
dir: M4 or M25 junct 13 towards Windsor Castle/Old Windsor on A308 from either direction. Lodge on A308

Innkeeper's Lodge represents an exciting, high value concept within the budget hotel market. Comfortable bedrooms provide excellent facilities that include satellite TV and modem points. Options include family rooms, and for the corporate guest, cutting edge IT which includes Wi-fi access. A popular Carvery provides all-day food, including an extensive, complimentary continental breakfast.

Rooms 15 (2 fmly) **S** £63-£85; **D** £63-£85 (incl. bkfst)

Travelodge Windsor Central

Travelodge

BUDGET HOTEL

☎ 0871 984 6331
34 King Edward Court SL4 1TG
web: www.travelodge.co.uk
dir: Wthin King Edward Court shopping precinct

Travelodge offers good quality, good value, modern accommodation. Ideal for families, the spacious en suite bedrooms include remote-control TV, tea and coffee-making facilities and comfortable beds. Meals can be taken at the nearby family restaurant. See also the Hotel Groups pages.

Rooms 114 **S** fr £29; **D** fr £29

WOKINGHAM   Map 5 SU86

Best Western Reading Moat House

Best Western

★★★★ 75% HOTEL

☎ 0870 225 0601 📄 0118 935 1646
Mill Ln, Sindlesham RG41 5DF
e-mail: ops.reading@qmh-hotels.com
web: www.bestwestern.co.uk/readingmoathouse
dir: Towards Reading on A329(M), take 1st exit to Winnersh. Follow Lower Earley Way North. Hotel on left

Located just off the M4 on the outskirts of Reading, this smart, modern hotel has been sympathetically built

around a 19th-century mill house. Bedrooms are stylish and have a contemporary feel to them. Spacious public areas include good conference rooms, a spacious bar and restaurant, as well as a business centre and a small fitness area.

Rooms 129 (15 fmly) (22 GF) (10 smoking) **S** £49-£196; **D** £59-£196* **Facilities** Fishing Gym ♫ Xmas New Year Wi-fi **Conf** Class 40 Board 40 Thtr 80 **Services** Lift Air con **Parking** 250 **Notes** ⊗ Civ Wed 80

YATTENDON   Map 5 SU57

Royal Oak

☎ 01635 201325 📄 01635 201926
The Square RG18 0UG
e-mail: info@royaloakyattendon.com
dir: M4 junct 12, A4 towards Theale, 2nd rdbt right towards Pangbourne. 150mtrs left to Bradford follow road through to Yattendon

Currently the rating for this establishment is not confirmed. This may be due to a change of ownership or because it has only recently joined the AA rating scheme. For further details please see the AA website: www.theAA.com

Rooms 5 **S** fr £85; **D** fr £110 (incl. bkfst)* **Facilities** Xmas Wi-fi **Conf** Class 40 Board 20 Thtr 40 **Notes** ⊗

BRISTOL

BRISTOL   Map 4 ST57

Aztec Hotel & Spa

SHIRE HOTELS

★★★★ 80% ⊛ HOTEL

☎ 01454 201090 📄 01454 201593
Aztec West Business Park, Almondsbury BS32 4TS
e-mail: aztec@shirehotels.com
web: www.aztechotelbristol.com
dir: access via M5 junct 16 & M4

Situated close to Cribbs Causeway shopping centre and major motorway links, this stylish hotel offers comfortable, very well-equipped bedrooms. Built in a Nordic style, public rooms boast log fires and vaulted ceilings. Leisure facilities include a popular gym and good size pool. The Quarterjacks restaurant offers relaxed informal dining with a focus on simply prepared, quality regional foods.

Rooms 128 (8 fmly) (29 GF) **S** £97.50-£249; **D** £145-£274 (incl. bkfst)* **Facilities** Spa STV ⟲ Gym Steam room Sauna Children's splash pool Activity studio New Year

Wi-fi **Conf** Class 120 Board 36 Thtr 200 Del from £110 to £189* **Services** Lift **Parking** 240 **Notes** LB ⊗ Civ Wed 120

Bristol Marriott Royal Hotel

Marriott HOTELS & RESORTS

★★★★ 80% ⊛ HOTEL

☎ 0117 925 5100 📄 0117 925 1515
College Green BS1 5TA
e-mail: bristol.royal@marriotthotels.co.uk
web: www.bristolmarriottroyal.co.uk
dir: next to cathedral

A truly stunning hotel located in the centre of the city, next to the cathedral. Public areas are particularly impressive with luxurious lounges and a leisure club. Dining options include the more informal Terrace and the really spectacular, more formal restaurant adjacent to the champagne bar. The spacious bedrooms have the benefit of air-conditioning, comfortable armchairs and marbled bathrooms.

Rooms 242 **Facilities** ⟲ Gym Xmas **Conf** Class 80 Board 84 Thtr 300 **Services** Lift Air con **Parking** 200 (charged) **Notes** LB ⊗ Civ Wed 200

Cadbury House Hotel, Health Club & Spa

CLASSIC BRITISH HOTELS

★★★★ 77% ⊛⊛ HOTEL

☎ 01934 834343 📄 01934 834390
Frost Hill, Congresbury BS49 5AD
e-mail: info@cadburyhouse.com
web: www.cadburyhouse.com
dir: on B3133, approx 0.25m from A370 at Congresbury

Externally, this newly developed hotel presents an interesting blend of old and new, but inside there's contemporary, stylish accommodation with a wide range of facilities, suitable for both business and leisure. The bar has a vibrant atmosphere while the restaurant is more relaxed, and the service friendly. Just a stroll away from the main building is the leisure club and spa, featuring a good sized indoor pool, treatment rooms and an air-conditioned gym with state-of-the-art equipment.

Rooms 72 (4 fmly) **S** £85-£160; **D** £85-£350* **Facilities** Spa FTV ⟲ Gym Xmas New Year Wi-fi **Conf** Class 150 Board 60 Thtr 250 Del from £140 to £185 **Services** Lift Air con **Parking** 350 **Notes** LB ⊗ Civ Wed 130

BRISTOL continued

Mercure Holland House Bristol

★★★★ 77% HOTEL

☎ 0117 968 9900 🖷 0117 968 9866
Redcliffe Hill BS1 6SQ
e-mail: h6698@accor.com
web: www.mercure-uk.com
dir: M4 junct 19 towards city centre, follow signs A4 then A370, take A38 Redcliffe Hill. Hotel opposite St Mary Redcliffe Church

This modern hotel, just a ten minute walk from Bristol Temple Meads, has striking, contemporary style throughout, and offers some impressive facilities including a spa, a fitness suite and meeting rooms. The hotel has a green-bicycle service for guests. Bedrooms are stylishly designed with large plasma screen TVs, comfortable beds and free internet access. Dining is offered in the Phoenix Restaurant and bar.

Rooms 275 (44 GF) **Facilities** FTV ⊛ Gym Free bike rental ♫ Xmas New Year Wi-fi **Conf** Class 150 Board 80 Thtr 240 **Services** Lift Air con **Parking** 140 (charged) **Notes** Civ Wed 240

The Grand by Thistle

thistle

★★★★ 75% ⊛⊛ HOTEL

☎ 0871 376 9042 🖷 0871 376 9142
Broad St BS1 2EL
e-mail: bristol@thistle.co.uk
web: www.thistlehotels.com/bristol
dir: in city centre pass The Galleries, hotel 3rd road on right

This large hotel is situated in the heart of the city, and benefits from its own secure parking. Bedrooms are well equipped and comfortably appointed, and include a number of Premium Executive rooms. The public areas include leisure and therapy treatment rooms and there is an impressive range of conference and banquet facilities.

Rooms 182 (10 fmly) **S** £70-£168; **D** £85-£183 (incl. bkfst)* **Facilities** Spa STV ⊛ supervised Gym Steam room Sauna Solarium Xmas Wi-fi **Conf** Class 250 Board 40 Thtr 600 Del from £125 to £195* **Services** Lift Air con **Parking** 150 (charged) **Notes** LB ⊗ Civ Wed 200

Hotel du Vin Bristol

★★★★ 75% ⊛ TOWN HOUSE HOTEL

☎ 0117 925 5577 🖷 0117 925 1199
The Sugar House, Narrow Lewins Mead BS1 2NU
e-mail: info.bristol@hotelduvin.com
web: www.hotelduvin.com
dir: A4 follow city centre signs. After 400yds pass Rupert Street NCP on right. Hotel on opposite carriageway

This hotel is part of one of Britain's most innovative and expanding hotel groups that offer the high standards of hospitality and accommodation. Housed in a Grade II listed, converted 18th-century sugar refinery, it provides great facilities with a modern, minimalist feel. The bedrooms are exceptionally well designed and the bistro offers an excellent menu and wine list. Hotel du Vin - AA Small Hotel Group of the Year 2008-9.

Rooms 40 (10 fmly) **D** £140-£360* **Facilities** STV FTV Xmas New Year Wi-fi **Conf** Class 36 Board 34 Thtr 72 **Services** Lift **Parking** 9 (charged) **Notes** LB Civ Wed 65

Bristol Marriott City Centre

Marriott
HOTELS & RESORTS

★★★★ 75% HOTEL

☎ 0117 929 4281 🖷 0117 927 6377
Lower Castle St BS1 3AD
web: www.bristolmarriottcitycentre.co.uk
dir: M32 follow signs to Broadmead, take slip road to large rdbt, take 3rd exit. Hotel on right

Situated at the foot of the picturesque Castle Park, this mainly business-orientated hotel is well placed for the city centre. Executive and deluxe bedrooms have high speed internet access. In addition to a coffee bar and lounge menu, the Mediterrano Restaurant offers an interesting selection of well-prepared internationally inspired dishes.

Rooms 300 (135 fmly) **S** £120-£155; **D** £120-£155* **Facilities** ⊛ Gym Steam room **Conf** Class 280 Board 40 Thtr 600 **Services** Lift Air con **Notes** ⊗

Mercure Brigstow Bristol

Mercure

★★★★ 74% ⊛ HOTEL

☎ 0117 929 1030 🖷 0117 929 2030
5-7 Welsh Back BS1 4SP
e-mail: H6548@accor.com
web: www.mercure-uk.com
dir: Left at Baldwin St lights. Take first left into Queen Charlotte St

In a prime position on the river this handsome purpose-built hotel is designed and finished with care. The shopping centre and theatres are within easy walking distance. The stylish bedrooms are extremely well equipped, including plasma TV screens in the bathrooms. There is an integrated state-of-the-art conference and meeting centre, and a smart restaurant and bar overlooking the harbour. Guests have complimentary use of a squash and health club, plus free internet access.

Rooms 116 **S** £59-£149; **D** £59-£149* **Facilities** Gym Wi-fi **Conf** Class 25 Board 23 Thtr 60 **Services** Lift Air con **Notes** LB ⊗ Civ Wed 50

Jurys Bristol Hotel

JURYS DOYLE
HOTELS

★★★★ 74% HOTEL

☎ 0117 923 0333 🖷 0117 923 0300
Prince St BS1 4QF
e-mail: bristol@jurysdoyle.com
web: www.jurysdoyle.com
dir: from Temple Meads at 1st rdbt into Victoria St. At Bristol Bridge lights left into Baldwin St, 2nd left into Marsh St, straight ahead

This modern hotel enjoys an excellent location near Bristol's Millennium project. Bedrooms vary in size and are well appointed with a range of facilities. There is a choice of eating options, including a quayside restaurant and adjoining inn. Extensive conference facilities are also available.

Rooms 192 (17 fmly) **Facilities** STV Complimentary use of nearby gym ♫ Xmas New Year Wi-fi **Conf** Class 160 Board 80 Thtr 400 **Services** Lift **Parking** 400 **Notes** ⊗

Ramada Plaza Bristol

★★★★ 74% HOTEL

☎ 0844 845 9100 📠 0117 925 5054
Redcliffe Way BS1 6NJ
e-mail: sales.plazabristol@ramadajarvis.co.uk
web: www.ramadajarvis.co.uk
dir: 400yds from Temple Meads BR station

This large modern hotel is situated in the heart of the city centre and offers spacious public areas and ample parking. Bedrooms are well equipped for both business and leisure guests. Dining options include a relaxed bar and a unique kiln restaurant where a good selection of freshly prepared dishes is available.

Rooms 201 (4 fmly) (24 smoking) **S** £67-£172; **D** £67-£184 (incl. bkfst)* **Facilities** FTV 🕐 supervised Gym Sauna Steam room Xmas New Year Wi-fi **Conf** Class 332 Board 213 Thtr 332 Del from £145 to £175* **Services** Lift Air con **Parking** 150 (charged) **Notes** LB ⊗ Civ Wed 250

Grange

★★★★ 71% COUNTRY HOUSE HOTEL

☎ 01454 777333 📠 01454 777447
Northwoods, Winterbourne BS36 1RP
e-mail: sales.grange@ramadajarvis.co.uk
web: www.ramadajarvis.co.uk
dir: A38 towards Filton/Bristol. At rdbt take 1st exit into Bradley Stoke Way, at lights take 1st left into Woodlands Lane, at 2nd rdbt turn left into Tench Lane. After 1m turn left at T-junct, hotel 200yds on left

Situated in 18 acres of attractive grounds, this pleasant hotel is only a short drive from the city centre. Bedrooms are spacious and well equipped; there is a leisure centre and pool and a range of meeting facilities.

Rooms 68 (6 fmly) (22 GF) (6 smoking) **S** £87-£196; **D** £87-£212 (incl. bkfst)* **Facilities** Spa STV FTV 🕐

supervised 🏊 Gym Xmas New Year Wi-fi **Conf** Class 120 Board 134 Thtr 150 Del from £150 to £180* **Parking** 150 **Notes** LB Civ Wed 150

Novotel Bristol Centre

★★★★ 70% HOTEL

☎ 0117 976 9988 📠 0117 925 5040
Victoria St BS1 6HY
e-mail: H5622@accor.com
web: www.novotel.com
dir: at end of M32 follow signs for Temple Meads station to rdbt. Final exit, hotel immediately on right

This city centre hotel provides smart, contemporary style accommodation. Most of the bedrooms demonstrate the latest Novotel 'Novation' style with unique swivel desk, internet access, air-conditioning and a host of extras. The hotel is convenient for the mainline railway station and also has its own car park.

Rooms 131 (20 fmly) (4 smoking) **S** £59-£149; **D** £59-£149* **Facilities** STV Gym Wi-fi **Conf** Class 70 Board 35 Thtr 210 Del from £150 to £185* **Services** Lift **Parking** 120 (charged) **Notes** LB Civ Wed 100

Berkeley Square

★★★ 77% HOTEL

☎ 0117 925 4000 📠 0117 925 2970
15 Berkeley Square, Clifton BS8 1HB
e-mail: berkeley@cliftonhotels.com
web: www.cliftonhotels.com/chg.html
dir: M32 follow Clifton signs. 1st left at lights by Nills Memorial Tower (University) into Berkeley Sq

Set in a pleasant square close to the university, art gallery and Clifton Village, this smart, elegant Georgian hotel has modern, stylishly decorated bedrooms that feature many welcome extras. There is a cosy lounge and stylish restaurant on the ground floor and a smart,

contemporary bar in the basement. A small garden is also available at the rear of the hotel.

Rooms 43 (4 GF) **Facilities** Use of local gym and swimming pool **Services** Lift **Parking** 20 (charged)

Arno's Manor

★★★ 72% HOTEL

☎ 0117 971 1461 📠 0117 971 5507
470 Bath Rd, Arno's Vale BS4 3HQ
e-mail: arnos.manor@forestdale.com
web: www.arnosmanorhotel.co.uk
dir: From end of M32 follow signs for Bath hotel on right side of A4 after 2m. Next to ITV West television studio

Once the home of a wealthy merchant, this historic 18th-century building is now a comfortable hotel and offers spacious, well-appointed bedrooms, and some have spa baths. The Chapel Lounge has many original features and is a great place to relax, while meals are taken in the decorative and stylish courtyard restaurant.

Rooms 73 (5 fmly) (7 GF) **S** £103-£109; **D** £133-£139 (incl. bkfst)* **Facilities** Xmas New Year Wi-fi **Conf** Class 40 Board 40 Thtr 150 **Services** Lift **Parking** 200 **Notes** LB ⊗ Civ Wed 100

Redwood Hotel & Country Club

★★★ 68% HOTEL

☎ 0870 609 6144 📠 01275 392104
Beggar Bush Ln, Failand BS8 3TG
e-mail: redwood@foliohotels.com
web: www.foliohotels.com/redwood
dir: M5 junct 19, A369, 3m right at lights. Hotel 1m on left

Situated close to the suspension bridge, this popular hotel offers guests a peaceful environment combined

BRISTOL continued

with excellent leisure facilities, including a cinema, gym, squash, badminton and tennis courts, plus indoor and outdoor pools. Bedrooms have plenty of amenities and are well suited to the business guest.

Rooms 112 (1 fmly) **S** £59-£159; **D** £59-£159*
Facilities 🕲 8 ☺ Gym Squash Cinema Aerobics/Dance studios Badminton courts Xmas New Year Wi-fi **Conf** Class 100 Board 40 Thtr 240 Del from £120 to £160* **Parking** 1000 **Notes** ⊗ Civ Wed 200

Henbury Lodge

★★★ 66% HOTEL

☎ 0117 950 2615 📠 0117 950 9532
Station Rd, Henbury BS10 7QQ
e-mail: contactus@henburylodgehotel.com
web: www.henburylodgehotel.com
dir: M5 junct 17/A4018 towards city centre, 3rd rdbt right into Crow Ln. At end turn right & hotel 200mtrs on right

This comfortable 18th-century country house has a delightful home-from-home atmosphere and is conveniently situated with easy access to the M5 and the city centre. Bedrooms are available both within the main house and in the adjacent converted stables; all are attractively decorated and well equipped. The pleasant dining room offers a selection of carefully prepared dishes using fresh ingredients.

Rooms 21 (9 annexe) (4 fmly) (6 GF) **Conf** Class 20 Board 20 Thtr 32 **Parking** 24 **Notes** LB

Best Western Victoria Square

★★ 79% HOTEL

☎ 0117 973 9058 📠 0117 970 6929
Victoria Square, Clifton BS8 4EW
e-mail: victoriasquare@btinternet.com
dir: M5 junct 19, follow Clifton signs. Over suspension/toll bridge, right into Clifton Down Rd. Left into Merchants Rd then into Victoria Square

This welcoming hotel has now been refurbished to provide high quality, individual bedrooms and bathrooms offering a variety of shapes and sizes. Ideally located the hotel is just one mile from the city centre and a two minute stroll to the heart of Clifton village. The ambience is relaxed, and guests have a choice of dining options - from lighter meals in the bar to a range of imaginative dishes in the main restaurant.

Rooms 41 **S** £79-£123; **D** £89-£139 (incl. bkfst)*
Facilities Wi-fi **Conf** Class 15 Board 20 Thtr 25 Del from £150 to £140* **Parking** 14 **Notes** LB ⊗

Rodney Hotel

★★ 74% ⊛ HOTEL

☎ 0117 973 5422 📠 0117 946 7092
4 Rodney Place, Clifton BS8 4HY
e-mail: rodney@cliftonhotels.com
dir: off Clifton Down Rd

With easy access from the M5, this attractive, listed building in Clifton is conveniently close to the city centre. The individually decorated bedrooms provide a useful range of extra facilities for the business traveller; the public areas include a smart bar and small restaurant offering enjoyable and carefully prepared dishes. A pleasant rear garden provides additional seating in the summer months.

Rooms 31 (1 fmly) (2 GF) **S** £44-£95; **D** £62-£108*
Facilities Wi-fi **Conf** Class 20 Board 20 Thtr 30 Del from £109.95 to £131.95* **Parking** 10 (charged) **Notes** Closed 22 Dec-3 Jan RS Sun

Clifton

★★ 74% HOTEL

☎ 0117 973 6882 📠 0117 974 1082
St Pauls Rd, Clifton BS8 1LX
e-mail: clifton@cliftonhotels.com
web: www.cliftonhotels.com/clifton
dir: M32 follow Bristol/Clifton signs, along Park St. Left at lights into St Pauls Rd

This popular hotel offers very well equipped bedrooms and relaxed, friendly service. There is a welcoming lounge by the reception, and in summer months drinks and meals can be enjoyed on the terrace. Racks Bar and Restaurant offers an interesting selection of modern dishes in informal surroundings. There is some street parking, but for a small charge, secure garage parking is available.

Rooms 59 (2 fmly) **Facilities** Wi-fi **Services** Lift **Parking** 12 (charged)

The Bowl Inn

★★ 69% ⊛ HOTEL

☎ 01454 612757 📠 01454 619910
16 Church Rd, Lower Almondsbury BS32 4DT
e-mail: reception@thebowlinn.co.uk
web: www.thebowlinn.co.uk
dir: M5 junct 16 onto Gloucester road, N for 500yds. Left into Over Lane, right by garden centre. Hotel next to church on right

With easy access to the motorway network, this popular 16th-century village inn has all the comforts of modern life. Each bedroom has been individually furnished to complement the many original features. Dining options include an extensive bar menu with cask ales, and the more intimate Lilies restaurant that offers a varied selection of carefully prepared dishes.

Rooms 13 (2 annexe) (1 GF) **S** £51.50-£87.50; **D** £79-£109.50 (incl. bkfst)* **Conf** Class 20 Board 24 Thtr 30 **Parking** 30 **Notes** ⊗ RS 25 Dec

Westbourne

★★ 60% HOTEL

☎ 0117 973 4214 ▧ 0117 974 3552
40-44 St Pauls Rd, Clifton BS8 1LR
e-mail: westbournehotel@bristol8.fsworld.co.uk
web: www.westbournehotel-bristol.co.uk
dir: M32/A4018 along Park St to Triangle, then
Whiteladies Rd. Turn left at 1st lights opp the BBC onto
St Pauls Rd. Hotel 200yds on right

This privately owned hotel is situated in the heart of
Clifton and is popular with business guests during the
week. It offers comfortable, well-equipped bedrooms.
Freddie's Bar and Restaurant provide a choice of eating
options, and in the summer guests can enjoy a drink on
the terrace.

Rooms 29 (7 fmly) (1 GF) **Parking** 9 **Notes** ⊗

Holiday Inn Bristol Airport

Ⓤ

☎ 01934 861123 ▧ 01934 861133
A38 Bridgwater Rd, Cowslip Garden BS40 5RB
web: www.holidayinn.com

Currently the rating for this establishment is not confirmed.
This may be due to a change of ownership or because it has
only recently joined the AA rating scheme. For further
details please see the AA website: www.theAA.com

Rooms 80

Holiday Inn Bristol Filton

Ⓤ

☎ 0870 400 9014 ▧ 0117 956 9735
Filton Rd, Hambrook BS16 1QX
e-mail: bristol@ihg.com
web: www.holidayinn.co.uk
dir: M4 junct 19/M32 junct 1/A4174 towards Filton &
Bristol. Hotel 800yds on left

Currently the rating for this establishment is not confirmed.
This may be due to a change of ownership or because it has
only recently joined the AA rating scheme. For further
details please see the AA website: www.theAA.com

Rooms 211 (40 fmly) (18 GF) (12 smoking) **Facilities** STV
🏊 supervised Gym Xmas New Year Wi-fi **Conf** Class 120
Board 30 Thtr 250 Del from £145 to £178 **Services** Lift
Air con **Parking** 250 **Notes** ⊗ Civ Wed 150

Express by Holiday Inn Bristol - North

BUDGET HOTEL

☎ 0870 443 0036 ▧ 0870 443 0037
New Rd, Bristol Parkway Business Park BS34 8SJ
e-mail: managerbristolnorth@expressholidayinn.co.uk
web: www.hiexpress.com/bristolnorth
dir: M4 junct 19/M32 junct 1. Follow signs for Bristol
Parkway Station, right at main rdbt, hotel on left. For
access, left at next 2 rdbts onto New Road, hotel entrance
100yds past Bristol & West building

A modern hotel ideal for families and business travellers.
Fresh and uncomplicated, the spacious rooms include Sky
TV, power shower and tea and coffee-making facilities.
Continental buffet breakfast is included in the room rate;
other meals may be taken at the nearby family pub or
restaurant. See also the Hotel Groups pages.

Rooms 133 (106 fmly) **Conf** Class 20 Board 24 Thtr 30

Travelodge Bristol Central

BUDGET HOTEL

☎ 08719 846 223 ▧ 0117 925 5149
Anchor Rd, Harbourside BS1 5TT
web: www.travelodge.co.uk
dir: on Anchor Road (A4) on left

Travelodge offers good quality, good value, modern
accommodation. Ideal for families, the spacious en suite
bedrooms include remote-control TV, tea and coffee-
making facilities and comfortable beds. Meals can be
taken at the nearby family restaurant. See also the Hotel
Groups pages.

Rooms 119 **S** fr £29; **D** fr £29

Travelodge Bristol Cribbs Causeway

BUDGET HOTEL

☎ 08719 846 222 ▧ 0117 950 1530
Cribbs Causeway BS10 7TL
web: www.travelodge.co.uk
dir: A4018, off M5 junct 17

Rooms 56 **S** fr £29; **D** fr £29

Innkeeper's Lodge Aylesbury East

BUDGET HOTEL

☎ 0845 112 6094 ▧ 0845 112 6209
London Rd HP22 5HP
web: www.innkeeperslodge.com/aylesburyeast
dir: A41 N for 10m, follow Wendover, Dunstable & Tring
signs. At top of slip road follow Wendover, Halton & Aston
Clinton signs. Into Aston Clinton (London Road). Lodge on
right

Innkeeper's Lodge represents an exciting, high value
concept within the budget hotel market. Comfortable
bedrooms provide excellent facilities that include satellite
TV and modem points. This carefully restored lodge is in a
picturesque setting and has its own unique style and
quirky character. Food is served all day, and an extensive,
complimentary continental breakfast is offered.

Rooms 11 **S** £53-£75; **D** £53-£75 (incl. bkfst)

Continued

INSPECTORS' CHOICE

Hartwell House Hotel, Restaurant & Spa

★★★★ ⍟⍟⍟ HOTEL

☎ 01296 747444 📠 01296 747450
Oxford Rd HP17 8NL
e-mail: info@hartwell-house.com
web: www.hartwell-house.com
dir: from S - M40 junct 7, A329 to Thame, then A418 towards Aylesbury. After 6m, through Stone, hotel on left. From N - M40 junct 9 for Bicester. A41 to Aylesbury, A418 to Oxford for 2m. Hotel on right

This beautiful, historic house is set in 90 acres of unspoilt parkland. The grand public rooms are truly magnificent, and feature many fine works of art. The service standards are very high, being attentive and traditional without stuffiness. There is an elegant, award-winning restaurant where carefully prepared dishes use the best local produce. Bedrooms are spacious, elegant and very comfortable. Most are in the main house, but some, including suites, are in the nearby, renovated coach house, which also houses a fine spa.

Rooms 46 (16 annexe) (10 GF) **S** fr £160; **D** fr £260 (incl. bkfst)* **Facilities** Spa STV ⍟ supervised ⍟ ⍟ Gym Sauna treatment rooms Steam rooms 🎵 Xmas New Year Wi-fi **Conf** Class 40 Board 40 Thtr 100 Del from £225 to £265* **Services** Lift **Parking** 90 **Notes** LB No children 6yrs RS Xmas/New Year Civ Wed 60

Holiday Inn Aylesbury

[U]

☎ 01296 734000 📠 01296 392211
Aston Clinton Rd HP22 5AA
e-mail: aylesbury@ihg.com
web: www.holidayinn.co.uk
dir: M25 junct 20, follow A41. Hotel on left on entering Aylesbury

Currently the rating for this establishment is not confirmed. This may be due to a change of ownership or because it has only recently joined the AA rating scheme. For further details please see the AA website: www.theAA.com

Rooms 139 (45 fmly) (69 GF) (8 smoking) **D** £65-£140 (incl. bkfst)* **Facilities** Spa STV ⍟ supervised Gym

Steam room Sauna Dance studio New Year Wi-fi **Conf** Class 50 Board 50 Thtr 120 Del from £95 to £160* **Services** Air con **Parking** 160 **Notes** LB Civ Wed

Holiday Inn Garden Court Aylesbury

[U]

☎ 01296 398839 📠 01296 394108
Buckingham Rd, Watermead HP19 3FY
web: www.holidayinn.co.uk

Currently the rating for this establishment is not confirmed. This may be due to a change of ownership or because it has only recently joined the AA rating scheme. For further details please see the AA website: www.theAA.com

Rooms 39

Innkeeper's Lodge Aylesbury South

BUDGET HOTEL

☎ 0845 112 6095 📠 0845 112 6208
40 Main St, Weston Turville HP22 5RW
web: www.innkeeperslodge.com/aylesburysouth
dir: M25 junct 20/A41 towards Hemel Hempstead. Onto A41 towards Aylesbury for 12m to Aston Clinton. Left onto B4544 to Weston Turville. Lodge on left

Innkeeper's Lodge represents an exciting, high value concept within the budget hotel market. Comfortable bedrooms provide excellent facilities that include satellite TV and modem points. Options include family rooms, and for the corporate guest, cutting edge IT includes Wi-fi access. Food is served all day in the adjacent Country Pub. The extensive continental breakfast is complimentary.

Rooms 16 **S** £53-£65; **D** £53-£65 (incl. bkfst)

Innkeeper's Lodge Beaconsfield

BUDGET HOTEL

☎ 0845 112 6096 📠 0845 112 6207
Aylesbury End HP9 1LW
web: www.innkeeperslodge.com/beaconsfield
dir: From M25 junct 16 or M40 junct 2, A355. At rdbt turn left onto A40. Lodge at White Hart on Aylesbury End.

Innkeeper's Lodge represents an exciting, high value concept within the budget hotel market. Comfortable bedrooms provide excellent facilities that include satellite TV and modem points. Options include family rooms, and for the corporate guest, cutting edge IT includes Wi-fi access. Food is served all day in the adjacent Country Pub. The extensive continental breakfast is complimentary.

Rooms 31 (1 fmly) **S** £59.95-£85; **D** £59.95-£85 (incl. bkfst) **Conf** Thtr 24

Buckingham Villiers

★★★★ 74% ⍟⍟ HOTEL

☎ 01280 822444 📠 01280 822113
3 Castle St MK18 1BS
e-mail: villiers@oxfordshire-hotels.co.uk
web: www.oxfordshire-hotels.co.uk
dir: M1 junct 13 (N) or junct 15 (S) follow signs to Buckingham. Castle St by Old Town Hall

Guests can enjoy a town centre location with a high degree of comfort at this 400-year-old former coaching inn. Relaxing public areas feature flagstone floors, oak panelling and real fires whilst bedrooms are modern, spacious and equipped to a high level. Diners can unwind in the atmospheric bar before taking dinner in the award-winning restaurant.

Rooms 46 (43 fmly) **S** £85-£130; **D** £120-£190 (incl. bkfst)* **Facilities** STV Xmas New Year Wi-fi **Conf** Class 120 Board 80 Thtr 250 Del from £120 to £160* **Services** Lift **Parking** 40 **Notes** LB ⍟ Civ Wed 180

Rowton Hall Country House Hotel & Spa

★★★★ 81% ◎◎ HOTEL

☎ 01244 335262 📠 01244 335464
Whitchurch Rd, Rowton CH3 6AD
e-mail: reception@rowtonhallhotelandspa.co.uk
web: www.rowtonhallhotel.co.uk
dir: 2m SE of Chester at Rowton off A41 towards Whitchurch

This delightful Georgian manor house, set in mature grounds, retains many original features such as a superb carved staircase and several eye-catching fireplaces. Bedrooms vary in style and all have been stylishly fitted and have impressive en suites. Public areas include a smart leisure centre, extensive function facilities and a striking restaurant that serves imaginative dishes.

Rooms 37 (4 fmly) (8 GF) **S** £145-£375; **D** £145-£500 **Facilities** Spa FTV ⓣ 🎱 🏊 Gym Xmas New Year Wi-fi **Conf** Class 48 Board 50 Thtr 170 **Parking** 90 **Notes** LB Civ Wed 120

Crowne Plaza Chester

★★★★ 78% HOTEL

☎ 0870 442 1081 & 01244 899988 📠 01244 316118
Trinity St CH1 2BD
e-mail: cpchester@qmh-hotels.com
web: www.crowneplaza.co.uk
dir: M53 junct 12 to A56 onto St Martins Way, under foot bridge, left at lights then 1st right, hotel on right.

Conveniently located in the heart of the city, this modern hotel offers spacious public areas that include the Silks restaurant, leisure club and a range of meeting rooms. Smart air-conditioned bedrooms are comfortably appointed and particularly well equipped. The hotel's own car park is a real bonus.

Crowne Plaza Chester

Rooms 160 (4 fmly) (12 smoking) **S** £95-£235; **D** £95-£235 (incl. bkfst)* **Facilities** ⓣ supervised Gym Wi-fi **Conf** Class 250 Board 100 Thtr 600 Del from £125 to £175* **Services** Lift **Parking** 80 (charged) **Notes** LB ⊗ Civ Wed 150

Best Western The Queen Hotel

★★★★ 75% HOTEL

☎ 01244 305000 📠 01244 318483
City Rd CH1 3AH
e-mail: queenhotel@feathers.uk.com
web: www.feathers.uk.com
dir: follow signs for railway station, hotel opposite

This hotel is ideally located opposite the railway station and just a couple minutes' walk from the city. Public areas include a restaurant, small gym, waiting room bar, separate lounge and Roman-themed gardens. Bedrooms are generally spacious and reflect the hotel's Victorian heritage.

Rooms 131 (6 fmly) (12 GF) **S** £125-£150; **D** £140-£180 (incl. bkfst) **Facilities** STV FTV Gym Xmas New Year Wi-fi **Conf** Class 150 Board 60 Thtr 400 Del from £140 to £170 **Services** Lift **Parking** 100 (charged) **Notes** LB ⊗ Civ Wed 250

Ramada Chester

★★★★ 75% HOTEL RAMADA

☎ 01244 332121 & 0844 815 9001 📠 01244 335287
Whitchurch Rd, Christleton CH3 5QL
e-mail: sales.chester@ramadajarvis.co.uk
web: www.ramadajarvis.co.uk/chester
dir: A41 Whitchurch, hotel on right 200mtrs from A41, 1.3m from city centre

This smart, modern hotel is located just a short drive from the city centre; with extensive meeting and function facilities, a well-equipped leisure club and ample parking, it is a popular conference venue. Bedrooms vary in size and style but all are well equipped for both business and leisure guests. Food is served in both the airy restaurant and in the large open-plan bar lounge.

Rooms 126 (6 fmly) (58 GF) (10 smoking) **S** £67-£182; **D** £67-£194 (incl. bkfst)* **Facilities** STV ⓣ Gym Xmas New Year Wi-fi **Conf** Class 80 Board 60 Thtr 230 Del from £135 to £160* **Services** Lift **Parking** 160 **Notes** LB ⊗ Civ Wed 180

Grosvenor Pulford Hotel & Spa

★★★★ 74% HOTEL

☎ 01244 570560 📠 01244 570809
Wrexham Rd, Pulford CH4 9DG
e-mail: reservations@grosvenorpulfordhotel.co.uk
web: www.grosvenorpulfordhotel.co.uk
dir: M53/A55 at junct signed A483 Chester/Wrexham & North Wales. Left onto B5445, hotel 2m on right

Set in rural surroundings, this modern, stylish hotel features a magnificent spa with a large Roman-style swimming pool. Among the bedrooms available are several executive suites and others containing spiral staircases leading to the bedroom sections. A smart brasserie restaurant and bar provide a wide range of imaginative dishes in a relaxed atmosphere.

Rooms 73 (10 fmly) (21 GF) (6 smoking) **S** £95-£130; **D** £130-£160 (incl. bkfst)* **Facilities** Spa STV FTV ⓣ 🏊 Gym Steam room Sauna Xmas New Year Wi-fi **Conf** Class 100 Board 50 Thtr 200 Del from £115 to £145* **Services** Lift **Parking** 200 **Notes** LB Civ Wed 200

Best Western Westminster

★★★ 80% HOTEL Best Western

☎ 01244 317341 📠 01244 325369
City Rd CH1 3AF
e-mail: westminsterhotel@feathers.uk.com
web: www.feathers.uk.com
dir: A56, 3m to city centre, left signed rail station. Hotel opposite station, on right

Situated close to the railway station and city centre, the Westminster is an old, established hotel. It has an attractive Tudor-style exterior, while bedrooms are brightly decorated with a modern theme. Family rooms are available. There is a choice of bars and lounges, and the dining room serves a good range of dishes.

Rooms 75 (5 fmly) (6 GF) **S** £49-£85; **D** £65-£149 (incl. bkfst)* **Facilities** STV Free gym facilities at sister hotel New Year Wi-fi **Conf** Class 60 Board 40 Thtr 150 Del from £110 to £138* **Services** Lift **Notes** LB ⊗ Civ Wed 100

CHESTER continued

Mill Hotel & Spa Destination

★★★ 79% HOTEL

☎ 01244 350035 📠 01244 345635
Milton St CH1 3NF
e-mail: reservations@millhotel.com
web: www.millhotel.com
dir: M53 junct 12, onto A56, left at 2nd rdbt (A5268), then 1st left , 2nd left

This hotel is a stylish conversion of an old corn mill and enjoys an idyllic canalside location next to the inner ring road and close to the city centre. The bedrooms offer varying styles, and public rooms are spacious and comfortable. There are several dining options and dinner is often served on a large boat that cruises Chester's canal system between courses. A well-equipped leisure centre is also provided.

Rooms 128 (49 annexe) (57 fmly) **S** £73-£93; **D** £91-£112 (incl. bkfst)* **Facilities** Spa STV ⓢ supervised Gym Aerobic studio Hairdresser Sauna Steam room Spa bath Kenesis studio ♫ Xmas New Year Wi-fi **Conf** Class 27 Board 28 Thtr 40 Del from £125 to £145* **Services** Lift **Parking** 120 **Notes** ⊗

Holiday Inn Chester South

★★★ 70% HOTEL

☎ 0870 400 9019 📠 01244 674100
Wrexham Rd CH4 9DL
e-mail: reservations-chester@ihg.com
web: www.holidayinn.co.uk
dir: near Wrexham junct on A483, off A55

Located close to the A55 and opposite to the park-and-ride to the city centre, this hotel offers spacious and comfortable accommodation. Meals can be taken in the attractive bar or in the restaurant. There is also a well-equipped leisure club for residents, and extensive conference facilities are available.

Rooms 143 (21 fmly) (71 GF) (12 smoking) **S** £59-£210; **D** £59-£210 **Facilities** STV FTV ⓢ supervised Gym Xmas New Year Wi-fi **Conf** Class 70 Board 70 Thtr 80 Del from £99 to £150 **Services** Air con **Parking** 150 **Notes** ⊗

Curzon

★★ 77% HOTEL

☎ 01244 678581 📠 01244 680866
52/54 Hough Green CH4 8JQ
e-mail: curzon.chester@virgin.net
web: www.curzonhotel.co.uk
dir: at junct of A55/A483 follow sign for Chester, 3rd rdbt, 2nd exit (A5104). Hotel 500yds on right

This smart period property is located in a residential suburb, close to the racecourse and just a short walk from the city centre. Spacious bedrooms are comfortable, well equipped and include family and four-poster rooms. The atmosphere is friendly, and the dinner menu offers a creative choice of freshly prepared dishes.

Curzon

Rooms 16 (2 fmly) (1 GF) **S** £75-£95; **D** £105-£150 (incl. bkfst) **Facilities** Wi-fi **Parking** 12 **Notes** LB ⊗ Closed 20 Dec-6 Jan

See advert on this page

Dene

★★ 75% HOTEL

VENTURE HOTELS

☎ 01244 321165 📠 01244 350277
95 Hoole Rd CH2 3ND
e-mail: info@denehotel.com
web: www.denehotel.com
dir: M53 junct 12 take A56 for 1m towards Chester. Hotel 1m from M53 next to Alexander Park

This friendly hotel is now part of a small privately owned group and is located close to both the city centre and M53. The bedrooms are very well equipped and many are on ground floor level. Family rooms and interconnecting

FALMOUTH continued

Hotel Anacapri

★★ 75% HOTEL

☎ 01326 311454 📠 01326 311474
Gyllyngvase Rd TR11 4DJ
e-mail: anacapri@btconnect.com
web: www.hotelanacapri.co.uk
dir: A39 (Truro to Falmouth), straight on at lights,
straight on at 2 rdbts. 5th right into Gyllyngvase Rd, hotel
on right

In an elevated position overlooking Gyllyngvase Beach
with views of Falmouth Bay beyond, this family run
establishment extends a warm welcome to all. Bedrooms
have similar standards of comfort and quality, and the
majority have sea views. Public areas include a convivial
bar, a lounge and the smart restaurant, where carefully
prepared and very enjoyable cuisine is on offer.

Rooms 16 **Facilities** Wi-fi **Parking** 20 **Notes** ⊗ No
children 8yrs Closed 13 Dec-10 Jan

Park Grove

★★ 71% HOTEL

☎ 01326 313276 📠 01326 211926
Kimberley Park Rd TR11 2DD
e-mail: reception@parkgrovehotel.com
web: www.parkgrovehotel.com
dir: off A39 at lights by Riders Garage towards harbour.
Hotel 400yds on left opposite park

Within walking distance of the town centre, this friendly
family-run hotel is situated in a pleasant residential area
opposite Kimberley Park. Comfortable accommodation is
provided and public areas include a relaxing and stylish
lounge and a spacious dining room and bar. Bedrooms
are also comfortable and well equipped.

Rooms 17 (6 fmly) (2 GF) **S** £47-£57; **D** £74-£84 (incl.
bkfst)* **Parking** 25 **Notes** LB ⊗ Closed Dec-Feb

Broadmead

★★ 69% SMALL HOTEL

THE CIRCLE
Secured Immersed of Hotels

☎ 01326 315704 📠 01326 311048
66/68 Kimberley Park Rd TR11 2DD
e-mail: frontdesk@broadmead-hotel.co.uk
dir: A39 from Truro to Falmouth, at lights left into
Kimberley Park Rd, hotel 200yds on left

Conveniently located, with views across the park and
within easy walking distance of the beaches and town
centre, this pleasant hotel, has smart and comfortable
accommodation. Bedrooms are well equipped and
attractively decorated. A choice of lounges is available
and, in the dining room, menus offer freshly prepared
home-cooked dishes.

Rooms 12 (2 fmly) (2 GF) **S** £35-£40; **D** £70-£80 (incl.
bkfst)* **Parking** 8 **Notes** LB

Rosslyn

★★ 69% HOTEL

☎ 01326 312699 & 315373 📠 01326 312699
110 Kimberley Park Rd TR11 2JJ
e-mail: mail@rosslynhotel.co.uk
web: www.rosslynhotel.co.uk
dir: on A39 towards Falmouth, to Hillend rdbt, turn right
and over next mini rdbt. At 2nd mini rdbt left into
Trescobeas Rd. Hotel on left past hospital

A relaxed and friendly atmosphere is maintained at this
family-run hotel. Situated on the northern edge of
Falmouth, the Rosslyn is easily located and is suitable for
both business and leisure guests. A comfortable lounge
overlooks the well-tended garden, and enjoyable freshly
prepared dinners are offered in the restaurant.

Rooms 25 (3 fmly) (6 GF) **S** £25-£50; **D** £50-£70 (incl.
bkfst) **Facilities** Internet access in lounge New Year
Conf Class 60 Board 20 **Parking** 22 **Notes** LB

Madeira Hotel

★★ 67% HOTEL

☎ 01326 313531 📠 01326 319143
Cliff Rd TR11 4NY
e-mail: madeira.falmouth@alfatravel.co.uk
dir: A39 (Truro to Falmouth), follow tourist signs 'Hotels'
to seafront

This popular hotel offers splendid sea views and a
pleasant, convenient location, which is close to the town.
Extensive sun lounges are popular haunts in which to
enjoy the views, while additional facilities include an oak
panelled cocktail bar. Bedrooms, many with sea views,
are available in a range of sizes.

Rooms 50 (8 fmly) (7 GF) **S** £37-£49; **D** £60-£84 (incl.
bkfst) **Facilities** FTV 🎵 Xmas New Year **Services** Lift
Parking 11 **Notes** LB ⊗ Closed Dec-Feb (except Xmas)
RS Nov & Mar

Membly Hall

★★ 65% HOTEL

☎ 01326 312869 & 311115 📠 01326 211751
Sea Front, Cliff Rd TR11 4NT
e-mail: memblyhallhotel@tiscali.co.uk
dir: A39 to Falmouth. Follow seafront & beaches sign

Located conveniently on the seafront and enjoying
splendid views, this family-run hotel offers friendly
service. Bedrooms are pleasantly spacious and well

equipped. Carefully prepared and enjoyable meals are
served in the spacious dining room. Live entertainment is
provided on some evenings and there is also a sauna and
spa pool.

Rooms 35 (3 fmly) (6 GF) **S** £37-£45; **D** £74-£90 (incl.
bkfst)* **Facilities** STV FTV Putt green 🏌 Gym Indoor short
bowls Table tennis Pool table 🎵 New Year Wi-fi
Conf Class 130 Board 60 Thtr 150 Del from £55 to £76*
Services Lift **Parking** 30 **Notes** LB ⊗ Closed Xmas week
RS Dec-Jan No credit cards

FOWEY	Map 2 SX15

The Fowey Hotel

★★★★ 71% ⊛⊛ HOTEL

RICHARDSON

☎ 01726 832551 📠 01726 832125
The Esplanade PL23 1HX
e-mail: fowey@richardsonhotels.co.uk
web: www.thefoweyhotel.co.uk
dir: A30 to Okehampton, continue to Bodmin. Then B3269
to Fowey for 1m, on right bend left junct then right into
Dagands Rd. Hotel 200mtrs on left

This attractive hotel stands proudly above the estuary,
with marvellous views of the river from the public areas
and the majority of the bedrooms. High standards are
evident throughout, augmented by a relaxed and
welcoming atmosphere. There is a spacious bar, elegant
restaurant and smart drawing room. Imaginative dinners
make good use of quality local ingredients.

Rooms 37 (2 fmly) **D** £110-£218 (incl. bkfst)*
Facilities Fishing 🏊 Xmas New Year Wi-fi **Conf** Class 60
Board 20 Thtr 100 Del from £180 to £220* **Services** Lift
Parking 18 (charged) **Notes** LB

Fowey Hall

★★★ 83% ◉◉ HOTEL

☎ 01726 833866 📄 01726 834100
Hanson Dr PL23 1ET
e-mail: info@foweyhallhotel.co.uk
web: www.foweyhallhotel.com
dir: In Fowey, over mini rdbt into town centre. Pass school on right, 400mtrs right into Hanson Drive

Built in 1899, this listed mansion looks out on to the English Channel. The imaginatively designed bedrooms offer charm, individuality and sumptuous comfort; the Garden Wing rooms adding a further dimension to staying here. The beautifully appointed public rooms include the wood-panelled dining room where accomplished cuisine is served. Enjoying glorious views, the well-kept grounds have a covered pool and sunbathing area.

Rooms 36 (8 annexe) (30 fmly) (8 GF) **Facilities** ⓣ ⤥
Table tennis Basketball Trampoline Xmas New Year Wi-fi
Child facilities **Conf** Class 20 Board 20 Thtr 30
Parking 40 **Notes** LB Civ Wed 50

See advert on this page

INSPECTORS' CHOICE

Old Quay House

★★ ◉◉ HOTEL

☎ 01726 833302 📄 01726 833668
28 Fore St PL23 1AQ
e-mail: info@theoldquayhouse.com
dir: M5 junct 31 onto A30 to Bodmin. Then A389 through town, then B3269 to Fowey

Looking out across Fowey's busy waterway, situated at the end of steep and winding streets so typical of Cornwall, this hotel offers very comfortable, stylish bedrooms; some have harbour views. The old quay itself is where guests can either dine or enjoy a drink; the cuisine is accomplished and breakfast is also noteworthy.

Rooms 11 **S** £130-£300; **D** £160-£300 (incl. bkfst)*
Facilities STV Wi-fi **Notes** ⊗ No children 12yrs
Civ Wed 100

GOLANT Map 2 SX15

Cormorant

★★★ 77% ◉ HOTEL

☎ 01726 833426 📄 01726 833219
PL23 1LL
e-mail: relax@cormoranthotel.co.uk
web: www.cormoranthotel.co.uk
dir: A390 onto B3269 signed Fowey. In 3m left to Golant, through village to end of road, hotel on right

A refurbished hotel with a focus on traditional hospitality, attentive service and good food. All the bedrooms enjoy the river view and guests can expect goose and down duvets, flat-screen, digital TVs and free Wi-fi access. Breakfast and lunch may be taken on the terrace which overlooks the river.

Rooms 14 (4 GF) **S** £70-£170; **D** £100-£170 (incl. bkfst)*
Facilities FTV ⓣ Xmas New Year Wi-fi **Parking** 14
Notes LB ⊗ No children 12yrs

HAYLE Map 2 SW53

Travelodge Hayle

BUDGET HOTEL

☎ 08719 846 314
Carwin Roundabout TR27 5DG
web: www.travelodge.co.uk
dir: M5 junct 30, A312, after 2m turn right onto A244 (Hounslow road)

Travelodge offers good quality, good value, modern accommodation. Ideal for families, the spacious en suite bedrooms include remote-control TV, tea and coffee-making facilities and comfortable beds. Meals can be taken at the nearby family restaurant. See also the Hotel Groups pages.

Rooms 39 **S** fr £29; **D** fr £29

HELSTON — Map 2 SW62

Gwealdues

★★ 75% HOTEL

☎ 01326 572808 📄 01326 561388
Falmouth Rd TR13 8JX
e-mail: thegwealdueshotel@hotmail.co.uk
web: www.gwealdueshotel.co.uk
dir: off rdbt on A394. On town outskirts

A family owned and run hotel that is within easy access of the coast and the cathedral city of Truro. The staff are friendly and attentive. The comfortable bedrooms include family rooms. There is a well stocked bar and a traditionally styled restaurant.

Rooms 18 (2 fmly) (1 GF) **Facilities** FTV Wi-fi
Conf Class 80 Board 40 Thtr 120 Del from £120 to £300*
Parking 50

LAND'S END — Map 2 SW32

See also **Sennen**

The Land's End Hotel

★★★ 64% HOTEL

☎ 01736 871844 📄 01736 871599
TR19 7AA
e-mail: reservations@landsendhotel.wanadoo.co.uk
web: www.landsendhotel.co.uk
dir: from Penzance take A30, follow Land's End signs. After Sennen 1m to Land's End

This famous location provides a very impressive setting for this well-established hotel. Bedrooms, many with stunning views of the Atlantic, are pleasantly decorated and comfortable. A relaxing lounge and attractive bar are provided. The Longships Restaurant, with far reaching sea views, offers fresh local produce, and fish dishes are a speciality.

The Land's End Hotel

Rooms 33 (2 fmly) **S** £45-£75; **D** £90-£170 (incl. bkfst)*
Facilities Free entry Land's End Visitor Centre Xmas New Year **Conf** Class 100 Board 50 Thtr 200 Del from £50 to £100* **Parking** 1000 **Notes** Civ Wed 110

LAUNCESTON — Map 3 SX38

See also **Lifton (Devon)**

Eagle House

★★ 72% SMALL HOTEL

☎ 01566 772036 & 774488 📄 01566 772036
Castle St PL15 8BA
e-mail: eaglehousehotel@aol.com
dir: from Launceston on Holsworthy Rd follow brown hotel signs

Next to the castle, this elegant Georgian house dates back to 1767 and is within walking distance of all the local amienties. Many of the bedrooms have wonderful views over the Cornish countryside. A short carte is served each evening in the restaurant.

Rooms 14 (1 fmly) **S** £40; **D** £68 (incl. bkfst)*
Facilities Wi-fi **Conf** Class 170 Board 170 Thtr 170 **Parking** 80 **Notes** ⊗ Civ Wed 170

LISKEARD — Map 2 SX26

Well House

★★ 85% ⑩⑩⑩ HOTEL

☎ 01579 342001 📄 01579 343891
St Keyne PL14 4RN
e-mail: enquiries@wellhouse.co.uk
dir: From Liskeard on A38 take B3254 to St Keyne (3m). At church fork left, hotel 0.5m down hill on left

Tucked away in an attractive valley and set in impressive grounds, this hotel enjoys a tranquil setting. Friendly staff provide attentive yet relaxed service which complements the elegant atmosphere of the house. The comfortable lounge offers deep cushioned sofas and an open fire, and the intimate bar has an extensive choice of wines and drinks to choose from. The rosette-awarded cooking is very skilled.

Rooms 9 (1 fmly) (2 GF) **S** £130-£220; **D** £145-£245 (incl. bkfst)* **Facilities** FTV ⌇ ⊚ ⥁ Xmas New Year **Conf** Board 20 **Parking** 30 **Notes** LB ⊗ Civ Wed 25

LIZARD — Map 2 SW71

Housel Bay

★★★ 67% HOTEL

☎ 01326 290417 & 290917 📄 01326 290359
Housel Cove TR12 7PG
e-mail: info@houselbay.com
dir: A39 or A394 to Helston, then A3083. At Lizard sign turn left, left at school, down lane to hotel

This long-established hotel has stunning views across the Western Approaches, equally enjoyable from the lounge and many of the bedrooms. Good cuisine is available in the stylish dining room, from where guests might enjoy a stroll to the end of the garden, which leads directly onto the Cornwall coastal path.

Rooms 20 (1 fmly) **S** £50-£60; **D** £70-£140 (incl. bkfst)*
Facilities FTV Xmas New Year **Services** Lift **Parking** 35 **Notes** LB ⊗

LOOE Map 2 SX25
See also **Portwrinkle**

Trelaske Hotel & Restaurant

★★★ 79% HOTEL

☎ 01503 262159 📠 01503 265360
Polperro Rd PL13 2JS
e-mail: info@trelaske.co.uk
dir: B252 signed Looe, over bridge signed Polperro. Follow
road for 1.9m, hotel signed off road on right.

This small hotel offers comfortable accommodation and
professional yet friendly service and award-winning food.
Set in its own very well tended grounds and only minutes
away from Looe and its attractions.

Rooms 7 (4 annexe) (2 fmly) (2 GF) **Facilities** Mountain
bikes for hire Wi-fi **Conf** Class 30 Board 40 Thtr 100
Del from £110 to £120 **Parking** 50

Hannafore Point

THE INDEPENDENTS
HOTEL ASSOCIATION

★★★ 70% HOTEL

☎ 01503 263273 📠 01503 263272
Marine Dr, West Looe PL13 2DG
e-mail: stay@hannaforepointhotel.com
dir: A38, left onto A385 to Looe. Over bridge turn left.
Hotel 0.5m on left

With panoramic coastal views of St George's Island
around to Rame Head, this popular hotel provides a warm
welcome. The wonderful view is certainly a feature of the
spacious restaurant and bar, providing a scenic backdrop
for both dinners and breakfasts. Additional facilities
include a heated indoor pool and gym.

Rooms 37 (5 fmly) **S** £50-£70; **D** £100-£160 (incl. bkfst)*
Facilities STV 🦢 Gym Spa pool Steam room Sauna 🎵
Xmas New Year Wi-fi **Conf** Class 80 Board 40 Thtr 120
Del from £75* **Services** Lift **Parking** 32 **Notes** LB
Civ Wed 150

See advert on opposite page

Fieldhead Hotel & Horizons Restaurant

THE INDEPENDENTS
HOTEL ASSOCIATION

★★ 76% HOTEL

☎ 01503 262689
Portuan Rd, Hannafore PL13 2DR
e-mail: fieldheadhotel@bluebottle.com
web: www.fieldheadhotel.co.uk
dir: In Looe pass Texaco garage, cross bridge, left to
Hannafore. At Tom Sawyer turn right & right again into
Portuan Rd. Hotel on left

Overlooking the bay, this engaging hotel has a relaxing
atmosphere. Bedrooms are furnished with care and many
have sea views. Smartly presented public areas include a
convivial bar and restaurant, and outside there is a
palm-filled garden with a secluded patio and swimming
pool. The fixed-price menu changes daily and features
quality local produce.

Rooms 16 (2 fmly) (2 GF) **S** £40-£65; **D** £80-£160 (incl.
bkfst) **Facilities** FTV 🦢 New Year Wi-fi **Parking** 15
Notes LB Closed 1 day at Xmas

See advert on this page

LOSTWITHIEL Map 2 SX15

Best Western Restormel Lodge

★★★ 73% HOTEL

Best Western

☎ 01208 872223 📠 01208 873568
Castle Hill PL22 0DD
e-mail: restormellodge@yahoo.co.uk
web: www.restormelhotel.co.uk
dir: on A390 in Lostwithiel

A short drive from the Eden Project, this popular hotel
offers a friendly welcome to all visitors and is ideally
situated for exploring the area. The original building
houses the bar, restaurant and lounges, with original
features adding to the character. Bedrooms are
comfortably furnished, with a number overlooking the
secluded outdoor pool.

Rooms 36 (12 annexe) (2 fmly) (9 GF) **S** £50-£75;
D £75-£110 (incl. bkfst)* **Facilities** FTV 🦢 Xmas New
Year Wi-fi **Conf** Class 12 Board 12 Thtr 12 **Parking** 40
Notes LB

LOSTWITHIEL continued

Lostwithiel Hotel Golf & Country Club

★★★ 67% HOTEL

☎ 01208 873550 📠 01208 873479
Lower Polscoe PL22 0HQ
e-mail: reception@golf-hotel.co.uk
web: www.golf-hotel.co.uk
dir: off A38 at Dobwalls onto A390. In Lostwithiel turn
right & hotel signed

This rural hotel is based around its own golf club and
other leisure activities. The main building offers guests a
choice of eating options, including all-day snacks in the
popular Sports Bar. The bedroom accommodation,
designed to incorporate beamed ceilings, has been
developed from old Cornish barns that are set around a
courtyard.

Rooms 27 (2 fmly) (15 GF) **S** £47-£56; **D** £112 (incl.
bkfst)* **Facilities** 🕑 🏖 18 🏌 Putt green Fishing Gym
Undercover floodlit driving range Indoor golf simulator
Xmas New Year **Conf** Class 60 Board 40 Thtr 120
Del from £70 to £90* **Parking** 120 **Notes** Civ Wed 120

MARAZION   Map 2 SW53

Mount Haven Hotel & St Michaels Restaurant

★★ 84% ◉ HOTEL

☎ 01736 710249 📠 01736 711658
Turnpike Rd TR17 0DQ
e-mail: reception@mounthaven.co.uk
web: www.mounthaven.co.uk
dir: From A30 towards Penzance. At rdbt take exit for
Helston onto A394. Next rdbt right into Marazion, hotel on
left

A stylish and delightfully located hotel where exceptional
views can be enjoyed - sunsets and sunrises can be
particularly splendid. Bedrooms, many with balconies,
are comfortably appointed. Fresh seafood and local

produce are simply treated to produce interesting menus
and enjoyable dining. A range of holistic therapies is
available. Service is attentive and friendly creating a
relaxing and enchanting environment throughout.

Rooms 18 (2 fmly) (6 GF) **S** £65-£90; **D** £90-£190 (incl.
bkfst)* **Facilities** FTV Aromatherapy Reflexology Massage
Reiki Hot rocks Osteopathy Wi-fi **Parking** 30 **Notes** LB ⊗
Closed 20 Dec-5 Feb

Godolphin Arms

★★ 76% SMALL HOTEL

☎ 01736 710202 📠 01736 710171
TR17 0EN
e-mail: enquiries@godolphinarms.co.uk
web: www.godolphinarms.co.uk
dir: from A30 follow Marazion signs for 1m to hotel. At
end of causeway to St Michael's Mount

This 170-year-old waterside hotel is in a prime location
where the stunning views of St Michael's Mount provide a
backdrop for the restaurant and lounge bar. Bedrooms
are colourful, comfortable and spacious. A choice of
menu with the emphasis on locally caught seafood is
offered in the main restaurant and the Gig Bar.

Rooms 10 (2 fmly) (2 GF) **Facilities** Direct access to large
beach New Year Wi-fi **Parking** 48 **Notes** LB Civ Wed 75

Marazion

★★ 69% SMALL HOTEL

☎ 01736 710334
The Square TR17 0AP
e-mail: stephanie@marazionhotel.co.uk
dir: A30 to Penzance, at rdbt follow St Michael's Mount
signs. Hotel on left opposite

Within 50 yards of one of Cornwall's safest beaches, this
family run hotel, offers a relaxed atmosphere with friendly
service. The individually furnished and decorated
bedrooms are comfortable, many with the benefit of
stunning views across to St Michael's Mount. The hotel

incorporates the Cutty Sark public bar and restaurant,
where a wide range of meals is offered to suit all palates
and budgets.

Rooms 10 (3 fmly) **S** £50-£80; **D** £65-£100 (incl. bkfst)*
Parking 20 **Notes** ⊗

MAWGAN PORTH   Map 2 SW86

Bedruthan Steps Hotel

★★★★ 75% ◉ HOTEL

☎ 01637 860555 & 860860 📠 01637 860714
TR8 4BU
e-mail: stay@bedruthan.com
dir: From A39/A30 follow signs to Newquay Airport. Past
airport, right at T-junct to Mawgan Porth. Hotel at top of
hill on left

With stunning views over Mawgan Porth Bay from the
public rooms and the majority of the bedrooms, this is a
child-friendly hotel. Children's clubs for various ages are
provided in addition to children's dining areas and
appropriate meals and times. A homage to architecture of
the 1970s, with a modern, comfortable, contemporary
feel, this hotel also has conference facilities. In the
spacious restaurants, an imaginative fixed-price menu is
offered; a short carte is available from Tuesdays to
Saturdays.

Rooms 101 (60 fmly) (1 GF) **S** £67-£142; **D** £134-£284
(incl. bkfst & dinner)* **Facilities** Spa 🕑 🎾 🏊 Gym
Jungle tumble ball pool Sauna Steam room Hydro pool 🎵
Xmas New Year Wi-fi Child facilities **Conf** Class 60
Board 40 Thtr 180 Del from £120* **Services** Lift
Parking 100 **Notes** ⊗ Closed 23-29 Dec Civ Wed 150

MAWNAN SMITH   Map 2 SW72

Budock Vean-The Hotel on the River

★★★★ 79% ◉ COUNTRY HOUSE HOTEL

☎ 01326 252100 & 0800 833927 📠 01326 250892
TR11 5LG
e-mail: relax@budockvean.co.uk
web: www.budockvean.co.uk
dir: from A39 follow tourist signs to Trebah Gardens.
0.5m to hotel

Set in 65 acres of attractive, well-tended grounds, this
peaceful hotel offers an impressive range of facilities.
Convenient for visiting the Helford River Estuary and the
many local gardens, or simply as a tranquil venue for a
leisure break. Bedrooms are spacious and come in a

NEWQUAY continued

Hotel Riviera

★★★ 68% HOTEL

☎ 01637 874251 & 07920 007977 📠 01637 850823
Lusty Glaze Rd TR7 3AA
e-mail: hotelriviera@btconnect.com
dir: approaching Newquay from Porth right at The Barrowfields. Hotel on right

This popular cliff-top hotel enjoys panoramic views across the gardens to the sea beyond. Bedrooms vary in size and style, and many also have sea views. Comfortable lounges are provided for rest and relaxation, although the more energetic may wish to use the squash court or heated outdoor pool. There is also a range of conference and function facilities.

Rooms 48 (6 fmly) **S** £45-£55; **D** £90-£110 (incl. bkfst)* **Facilities** ⚐ Squash Hairdresser Xmas New Year Wi-fi **Conf** Class 240 Board 100 Thtr 240 Del from £65 to £83.95* **Services** Lift **Parking** 40 **Notes** ⊗ Civ Wed 120

Glendorgal Resort

★★★ 🅰 HOTEL

☎ 01637 874937 & 859981 📠 01637 851341
Lusty Glaze Rd, Porth TR7 3AD
e-mail: info@glendorgal.co.uk
dir: From A30 right onto A392, 2nd rdbt turn right (A3058), at mini rdbt straight on, turn right into Lusty Glaze Rd, follow signs for Glendorgal

Rooms 26 (8 fmly) **S** £72-£105; **D** £118-£178 (incl. bkfst)* **Facilities** ⚕ Gym Steam room Cardiovascular room Sauna Xmas New Year Wi-fi **Conf** Class 36 Board 30 Thtr 60 **Parking** 200 **Notes** LB Civ Wed 65

Whipsiderry

★★ 78% HOTEL

☎ 01637 874777 & 876066 📠 01637 874777
Trevelgue Rd, Porth TR7 3LY
e-mail: info@whipsiderry.co.uk
dir: right onto Padstow road (B3276) out of Newquay, in 0.5m right at Trevelgue Rd

Quietly located, overlooking Porth Beach, this friendly hotel offers bedrooms in a variety of sizes and styles, many with superb views. A daily-changing menu offers interesting and well-cooked dishes with the emphasis on fresh, local produce. An outdoor pool is available, and at dusk guests may be lucky enough to watch badgers in the attractive grounds.

Rooms 20 (5 fmly) (3 GF) **S** £58-£70; **D** £116-£140 (incl. bkfst & dinner)* **Facilities** ⚐ Pool room Xmas **Parking** 30 **Notes** LB Closed Nov-Etr (ex Xmas)

Priory Lodge

★★ 69% HOTEL

☎ 01637 874111 📠 01637 851803
30 Mount Wise TR7 2BN
e-mail: fionapocklington@tiscali.co.uk
dir: From lights in town centre onto Berry Rd, right onto B3282 Mount Wise, 0.5m on right

The hotel enjoys a central location close to the town centre, the harbour and the local beaches. Secure parking is available at the hotel along with a range of leisure facilities including a heated pool, sauna, games room and hot tub. Attractively decorated bedrooms vary in size and style with many offering sea views over Towan Beach and Island.

Rooms 28 (6 annexe) (13 fmly) (1 GF) **S** £35-£45; **D** £70-£85 (incl. bkfst) **Facilities** ⚐ Outdoor hydrotherapy spa bath 🎵 Xmas New Year **Parking** 30 **Notes** LB ⊗ Closed 11-22 Dec & 4 Jan-early Mar

Kilbirnie

★★ 68% HOTEL

☎ 01637 875155 📠 01637 850769
Narrowcliff TR7 2RS
e-mail: info@kilbirniehotel.co.uk
dir: on A392

With delightful views over the Barrowfields and the sea, this privately run hotel offers an impressive range of facilities. The reception rooms are spacious and comfortable, and during summer months feature a programme of entertainment. Bedrooms vary in size and style, and some enjoy fine sea views.

Rooms 66 (6 fmly) (8 GF) **S** £35-£50; **D** £70-£100 (incl. bkfst)* **Facilities** ⚕ ⚐ Gym Fitness room Hair salon Xmas New Year Wi-fi **Conf** Class 50 Board 25 Thtr 100 **Services** Lift Air con **Parking** 50 **Notes** ⊗

Sandy Lodge

★★ 67% HOTEL

☎ 01637 872851 📠 01637 872851
6-12 Hilgrove Rd TR7 2QY
e-mail: info@sandylodgehotel.co.uk

This friendly family run hotel is ideally located for easy access to Newquay seafront, surfing beaches and within walking distance of the town centre and shopping facilities. Accommodation is comfortable with a choice of family, twin and double rooms. Dinner and breakfast is served in the spacious dining room and there is a choice of lounge areas to sit and relax in or join in with the nightly entertainment. The leisure facilities include an indoor and outdoor swimming pool, sauna, jacuzzi, gym and snooker table.

Rooms 81 (8 fmly) (12 GF) **Facilities** ⚕ ⚐ Gym 🎵 Xmas New Year Wi-fi **Conf** Class 40 Board 30 Thtr 100 **Services** Lift **Parking** 50 **Notes** LB ⊗ Closed 5-23 Jan RS Jan

Eliot

★★ 65% HOTEL

Leisureplex

☎ 01637 878177 📠 01637 852053
Edgcumbe Av TR7 2NH
e-mail: eliot.newquay@alfatravel.co.uk
dir: A30 onto A392 towards Quintrell Downs. Right at rdbt onto A3058. 4m to Newquay, left at amusements onto Edgcumbe Av. Hotel on left

Located in a quiet residential area just a short walk from the beaches and the varied attractions of the town, this long-established hotel offers comfortable accommodation. Entertainment is provided most nights throughout the season and guests can relax in the spacious public areas.

Rooms 76 (10 fmly) **S** £34-£40; **D** £54-£66 (incl. bkfst) **Facilities** FTV ⚐ Pool table Table tennis 🎵 Xmas New Year **Services** Lift **Parking** 20 **Notes** LB ⊗ Closed Dec-Jan (ex Xmas) RS Nov & Feb-Mar

PADSTOW Map 2 SW97

Treglos

★★★★ 74% ⚅ COUNTRY HOUSE HOTEL

☎ 01841 520727 📠 01841 521163
Constantine Bay PL28 8JH
e-mail: stay@tregloshotel.com
web: www.tregloshotel.com
dir: in Constantine Bay. At St Merryn x-rds take B3276 towards Newquay. In 500mtrs right to Constantine Bay, follow brown signs

Owned by the Barlow family for over 30 years, this hotel has a tradition of high standards. The genuine welcome, choice of comfortable lounges, indoor pool and children's play facilities entice guests back year after year. Bedrooms vary in size; those with sea views are always popular. The restaurant continues to provide imaginative menus incorporating seasonal local produce.

Rooms 42 (12 fmly) (1 GF) **S** £75.50-£106; **D** £151-£212 (incl. bkfst & dinner)* **Facilities** Spa ⚕ ⚘ 18 Putt green ⚓ Converted boat house for table tennis Infra red treatment cabin 🎵 Wi-fi **Services** Lift **Parking** 50 (charged) **Notes** LB Closed 30 Nov-1 Mar

Hotel St Eia

★★ 69% HOTEL

☎ 01736 795531 📠 01736 793591
Trelyon Av TR26 2AA
e-mail: info@hotelsteia.co.uk
dir: off A30 onto A3074, follow signs to St Ives, approaching town, hotel on right

This smart hotel is conveniently located and enjoys spectacular views over St Ives, the harbour and Porthminster Beach. The friendly proprietors provide a relaxing environment. Bedrooms are comfortable and well equipped, and some have sea views. The spacious lounge bar has a well-stocked bar and views can be enjoyed from the rooftop terrace.

Rooms 18 (3 fmly) **S** £33-£50; **D** £66-£100 (incl. bkfst)* **Parking** 16 **Notes** ⊗ Closed Nov-Mar

Cottage Hotel

★★ 68% HOTEL **Leisureplex**

☎ 01736 795252 📠 01736 798636
Boskerris Rd, Carbis Bay TR26 2PE
e-mail: cottage.stives@alfatravel.co.uk
dir: from A30 take A3074 to Carbis Bay. Right into Porthreptor Rd. Just before railway bridge, left through railway car park and into hotel car park

Set in quiet, lush gardens, this pleasant hotel offers friendly and attentive service. Smart bedrooms are pleasantly spacious and many rooms enjoy splendid views. Public areas are varied and include a snooker room, a comfortable lounge and a spacious dining room with sea views over the beach and Carbis Bay.

Rooms 80 (7 fmly) (2 GF) **S** £34-£44; **D** £54-£74 (incl. bkfst) **Facilities** FTV ↻ Snooker ♫ Xmas New Year **Services** Lift **Parking** 20 **Notes** LB ⊗ Closed Dec-Feb (ex Xmas) RS Nov & Mar

---

ST MAWES   Map 2 SW83

Idle Rocks

★★★ 83% ◉◉ HOTEL

☎ 01326 270771 📠 01326 270062
Harbour Side TR2 5AN
e-mail: reception@idlerocks.co.uk
web: www.idlerocks.co.uk
dir: off A390 onto A3078, 14m to St Mawes. Hotel on left

This hotel has splendid sea views overlooking the attractive fishing port. The lounge and bar also benefit from the views and in warmer months service is available on the terrace. Bedrooms are individually styled and

Continued

ST MAWES continued

tastefully furnished to a high standard. The daily-changing menu served in the restaurant features fresh, local produce in imaginative cuisine.

Idle Rocks

Rooms 27 (4 annexe) (6 fmly) (2 GF) **Facilities** Xmas New Year Wi-fi **Parking** 4 (charged)

SALTASH Map 3 SX45

China Fleet Country Club

★★★ 72% HOTEL

☎ 01752 848668 📠 01752 848456
PL12 6LJ
e-mail: sales@china-fleet.co.uk
web: www.china-fleet.co.uk
dir: A38 towards Plymouth/Saltash. Cross Tamar Bridge, take slip road before tunnel. Right at lights, 1st left follow signs, 0.5m

Set in 180 acres of stunning Cornish countryside overlooking the beautiful Tamar estuary, ideal for access to Plymouth and the countryside, this hotel offers an extensive range of leisure facilities including an impressive golf course. Bedrooms are all located in annexe buildings; each is equipped with its own kitchen. There is a range of dining options, and the restaurant offers interesting and imaginative choices.

Rooms 40 (21 GF) **Facilities** 🏊 supervised ⛳ 18 🏌 Putt green Gym Squash 28-bay floodlit driving range Health & beauty suite Hairdresser Wi-fi **Conf** Class 80 Board 60 Thtr 300 Del from £111* **Services** Lift **Parking** 400 **Notes** ⊗ Civ Wed 300

Travelodge Saltash

BUDGET HOTEL

☎ 08719 846 051 📠 01752 841079
Callington Rd, Carkeel PL12 6LF
web: www.travelodge.co.uk
dir: on A38 Saltash bypass - 1m from Tamar Bridge

Travelodge offers good quality, good value, modern accommodation. Ideal for families, the spacious en suite bedrooms include remote-control TV, tea and coffee-making facilities and comfortable beds. Meals can be taken at the nearby family restaurant. See also the Hotel Groups pages.

Rooms 53 **S** fr £29; **D** fr £29 **Conf** Class 15 Board 12 Thtr 25

SCILLY, ISLES OF

BRYHER Map 2 SV81

INSPECTORS' CHOICE

Hell Bay

★★★ ⍟⍟ HOTEL

☎ 01720 422947 📠 01720 423004
TR23 0PR
e-mail: contactus@hellbay.co.uk
web: www.hellbay.co.uk
dir: access by helicopter or boat from Penzance, plane from Bristol, Exeter, Newquay, Southampton, Land's End

Located on the smallest of the inhabited islands of the Scilly Isles on the edge of the Atlantic, this hotel makes a really special destination. The owners have filled the hotel with original works of art by artists who have connections with the islands, and the interior is decorated in cool blues and greens creating an extremely restful environment. The contemporary bedrooms are equally stylish and many have garden access and stunning sea views. Eating here is a delight, and naturally seafood features strongly on the award-winning, daily-changing menus.

Rooms 25 (25 annexe) (3 fmly) (15 GF)
S £162.50-£600; **D** £260-£600 (incl. bkfst & dinner)*
Facilities STV 🏊 ⛳ 7 Gym Boules Wi-fi **Conf** Class 36 Board 36 Thtr 36 Del from £210* **Notes** LB Closed Nov-Feb

---

ST MARTIN'S Map 2 SV91

INSPECTORS' CHOICE

St Martin's on the Isle

★★★ ⍟⍟⍟ HOTEL

☎ 01720 422090 & 422092 📠 01720 422298
Lower Town TR25 0QW
e-mail: stay@stmartinshotel.co.uk
web: www.stmartinshotel.co.uk
dir: 20-minute helicopter flight to St Mary's, then 10-minute launch to St Martin's

This attractive hotel, complete with its own sandy beach, enjoys an idyllic position on the waterfront overlooking Tresco and Tean. Bedrooms are brightly appointed, comfortably furnished and overlook the sea or the well-tended gardens. There is an elegant, award-winning restaurant and a split-level lounge bar where guests can relax and enjoy the memorable view. Locally caught fish features significantly on the daily-changing menus.

Rooms 30 (10 fmly) (14 GF) **S** £105-£190;
D £210-£420 (incl. bkfst & dinner)* **Facilities** 🏊 🚣 Clay pigeon shooting Boating Bikes Diving Snorkelling Wi-fi Child facilities **Conf** Class 50 Board 50 Thtr 50 **Notes** LB Closed Nov-Feb Civ Wed 100

ST MARY'S Map 2 SV91

St Mary's Hall Hotel

★★★ 82% ⍟ HOTEL

☎ 01720 422316 📠 01720 422252
Church St, Hugh Town TR21 0JR
e-mail: recep@stmaryshallhotel.co.uk

Hospitality, service and the cuisine are all strengths at this elegant hotel which was originally built by a Count Leon de Ferrari. The metropolitan-style brasserie and bar, with its bold paintings and red sofas, has a very stylish and modern feel, whilst the elegant wood-panelled foyer reception and two separate comfortable lounges are more traditional. There are two styles of bedrooms - Godolphin, and the Count Leon rooms which offer more facilities.

Rooms 20 (3 fmly) (4 GF) **Facilities** Xmas New Year Wi-fi **Notes** ⊗

Tregarthens

★★★ 75% HOTEL

☎ 01720 422540 🖹 01720 422089
Hugh Town TR21 0PP
e-mail: reception@tregarthens-hotel.co.uk
dir: 100yds from quay

Opened in 1848 by Captain Tregarthen this is now a well-established hotel. The impressive public areas provide wonderful views overlooking St Mary's harbour and some of the many islands, including Tresco and Bryher. Bedrooms are well equipped and neatly furnished. Traditional cuisine is served in the restaurant.

Rooms 32 (1 annexe) (5 fmly) **S** £100-£135; **D** £200-£290 (incl. bkfst & dinner)* **Notes** ⊗ Closed late Oct-mid Mar

TRESCO Map 2 SV81

INSPECTORS' CHOICE

The Island

★★★ ⊛⊛ HOTEL

☎ 01720 422883 🖹 01720 423008
TR24 0PU
e-mail: islandhotel@tresco.co.uk
web: www.tresco.co.uk/holidays/island_hotel.asp
dir: helicopter service Penzance to Tresco, hotel on NE of island

This delightful colonial-style hotel enjoys a waterside location in its own attractive gardens. The spacious, comfortable lounges, airy restaurant and many of the bedrooms enjoy stunning sea views. All of the rooms are brightly furnished and many benefit from lounge areas, balconies or terraces. Carefully prepared, imaginative cuisine makes good use of locally caught fish.

Rooms 48 (27 fmly) (2 GF) **S** £130-£185; **D** £260-£720 (incl. bkfst & dinner)* **Facilities** ➘ ⍨ Fishing ⚓ Boating Table tennis Bowls Boutique Wi-fi **Conf** Class 80 Board 80 Thtr 80 Del from £150 to £170* **Notes** ⊗ Closed Nov-Mar

New Inn

★★ 78% ⊛ HOTEL

☎ 01720 422844 & 423006 🖹 01720 423200
TR24 0QQ
e-mail: newinn@tresco.co.uk
web: www.tresco.co.uk/holidays/new_inn.asp
dir: by New Grimsby Quay

This friendly, popular inn is located at the island's centre point and offers bright, attractive and well-equipped bedrooms, many with splendid sea views. Guests have an extensive choice from the menu at both lunch and dinner and can also choose where they take their meals - either in the airy bistro-style Pavilion, the popular bar which serves real ales, or the elegant restaurant.

Rooms 16 (2 GF) **Facilities** ➘ ⍨ Sea fishing Bird watching Walking Xmas New Year **Notes** LB ⊗

SENNEN Map 2 SW32

Old Success Inn

★★ 69% HOTEL

☎ 01736 871232 🖹 01736 871457
Sennen Cove TR19 7DG
e-mail: oldsuccess@sennencove.fsbusiness.co.uk
dir: turn right off A30 approx 1m before Land's End, signed Sennen Cove. Hotel on left at bottom of hill

This inn is romantically located at the water's edge, with spectacular views of the cove and the Atlantic Ocean. Popular with locals and visitors alike, the inn offers friendly service and a choice of dining in either the restaurant and bar; there is always a selection of fresh fish dishes.

Rooms 12 (1 fmly) **Facilities** ♫ Xmas **Parking** 12

TINTAGEL Map 2 SX08

Atlantic View

★★ 75% SMALL HOTEL

☎ 01840 770221 🖹 01840 770995
Treknow PL34 0EJ
e-mail: atlantic-view@eclipse.co.uk
web: www.holidayscornwall.com
dir: B3263 to Tregatta, turn left into Treknow, hotel on road to Trebarwith Strand Beach

Conveniently located for all the attractions of Tintagel, this family-run hotel has a wonderfully relaxed and welcoming atmosphere. Public areas include a bar, comfortable lounge, TV/games room and heated swimming pool. Bedrooms are generally spacious and some have the added advantage of distant sea views.

Rooms 9 (1 fmly) **S** £47-£52; **D** £74-£84 (incl. bkfst)* **Facilities** ⊙ **Parking** 10 **Notes** LB ⊗ Closed Nov-Feb RS Mar

TRURO Map 2 SW84

Alverton Manor

★★★ 81% ⊛⊛ HOTEL

☎ 01872 276633 🖹 01872 222989
Tregolls Rd TR1 1ZQ
e-mail: reception@alvertonmanor.co.uk
web: www.connexions.co.uk/alvertonmanor/index.htm
dir: From Carland Cross, take A39 to Truro

Formerly a convent, this impressive sandstone property stands in six acres of grounds, within walking distance of the city centre. It has a wide range of smart bedrooms, combining comfort with character. Stylish public areas include the library and the former chapel, now a striking function room. An interesting range of dishes, using the very best of local produce (organic whenever possible) is offered in the elegant restaurant.

Rooms 32 (3 GF) **Facilities** ♿ 18 Xmas Wi-fi **Conf** Class 60 Board 40 Thtr 80 **Services** Lift **Parking** 120 **Notes** Closed 28 Dec RS 4 Jan Civ Wed 80

Mannings

★★★ 80% HOTEL

☎ 01872 270345 🖹 01872 242453
Lemon St TR1 2QB
e-mail: reception@manningshotels.co.uk
web: www.manningshotels.co.uk
dir: A30 to Carland Cross then Truro. Follow brown signs to hotel in city centre

This popular hotel is located in the heart of Truro and has an engaging blend of traditional and contemporary. Public areas offer a stylish atmosphere with the bar and restaurant proving popular with locals and residents alike. Bedrooms are pleasantly appointed. A wide choice of appetising dishes is available, which feature ethnic, classical and vegetarian as well as daily specials.

Rooms 43 (9 annexe) (4 fmly) (3 GF) **S** £75-£85; **D** £90-£135 (incl. bkfst)* **Facilities** STV Wi-fi **Parking** 43 (charged) **Notes** LB ⊗ Closed 25-26 Dec

See advert on page 116

TRURO continued

Brookdale

★★★ 66% HOTEL

☎ 01872 273513 ▤ 01872 272400
Tregolls Rd TR1 1JZ
e-mail: brookdale@hotelstruro.com
web: www.hotelstruro.com
dir: from A30 onto A39, at A390 junct turn right into city centre. Hotel 600mtrs down hill

Pleasantly situated in an elevated position close to the city centre, the Brookdale provides a range of accommodation options; all rooms are pleasantly spacious and well equipped, and some are located in an adjacent annexe. Meals can be served in guests' rooms, or in the restaurant where an interesting selection of dishes is available.

Rooms 30 (2 fmly) **Facilities** Xmas **Conf** Class 65 Board 30 Thtr 100 **Parking** 30

See advert on opposite page

Carlton

★★ 72% HOTEL

☎ 01872 272450 ▤ 01872 223938
Falmouth Rd TR1 2HL
e-mail: reception@carltonhotel.co.uk
dir: on A39 straight across 1st & 2nd rdbts onto bypass (Morlaix Ave). At top of sweeping bend/hill turn right at mini rdbt into Falmouth Rd. Hotel 100mtrs on right

This family-run hotel is pleasantly located a short stroll from the city centre. A friendly welcome is assured and both business and leisure guests choose the Carlton on a regular basis. A smart, comfortable lounge is available, along with leisure facilities. A wide selection of home-cooked dishes is offered in the dining room.

Carlton

Rooms 29 (4 fmly) (4 GF) **S** £47-£57; **D** £67-£77 (incl. bkfst)* **Facilities** STV **Conf** Class 24 Board 36 Thtr 60 Del from £65 to £85* **Parking** 31 **Notes** Closed 20 Dec-5 Jan

Trenython Manor

★★★ 80% ◉ COUNTRY HOUSE HOTEL

☎ 01726 814797 ▤ 01726 817030
Castle Dore Rd PL24 2TS
e-mail: trenython@clublacosta.com
web: www.trenython.co.uk
dir: A390/B3269 towards Fowey, after 2m right into Castledore. Hotel 100mtrs on left

Dating from the 1800s, there is something distinctly different about Trenython, an English manor house designed by an Italian architect. Peacefully situated in extensive grounds, public areas have grace and elegance with original features, and many of the bedrooms have wonderful views. The splendour of the panelled restaurant is the venue for contemporary cuisine.

Rooms 23 (3 fmly) **D** £125-£225 (incl. bkfst)*
Facilities Spa STV FTV ⊗ supervised ⚽ Gym Woodland walks Health & beauty centre Pool table Xmas New Year Wi-fi Child facilities **Parking** 50 **Notes** ⊗

Nare

★★★★ 85% ◉
COUNTRY HOUSE HOTEL

☎ 01872 501111 ▤ 01872 501856
Carne Beach TR2 5PF
e-mail: office@narehotel.co.uk
web: www.narehotel.co.uk
dir: from Tregony follow A3078 for approx 1.5m. Left at Veryan sign, through village towards sea & hotel

This delightful hotel offers a relaxed, country-house atmosphere in a spectacular coastal setting. The bedrooms, many with balconies, have fresh flowers, carefully chosen artwork and antiques that contribute to the engaging individuality. A choice of dining options is available, from light snacks to superb local seafood.

Rooms 39 (4 fmly) (6 GF) **S** £109-£223; **D** £206-£210 (incl. bkfst)* **Facilities** Spa ⊗ ⚑ ⚽ Gym Health & beauty clinic Hotel sailing boat Shooting Steam room Sauna Xmas New Year **Services** Lift **Parking** 80 **Notes** LB ⊗

See advert on opposite page

The Hotel & Extreme Academy Watergate Bay

★★★ 79% ◉ HOTEL

☎ 01637 860543 ▤ 01637 860333
TR8 4AA
e-mail: hotel@watergatebay.co.uk
web: www.watergatebay.co.uk
dir: A30 onto A3059. Follow airport/Watergate Bay signs

With its own private beach, which is home to the 'Extreme Academy' of beach and watersports activities, this hotel

boasts a truly a spectacular location. The style here is relaxed with a genuine welcome for all the family. Public areas are stylish and contemporary. Many bedrooms share the breathtaking outlook and a number have balconies. Several dining options are on offer, including the Beach Hut, Brasserie and Jamie Oliver's restaurant, Fifteen Cornwall.

Rooms 67 (17 annexe) (36 fmly) **S** £71.25-£221.25; **D** £95-£400 (incl. bkfst)* **Facilities** STV 🎱 🏄 🚣 Surfing Table tennis Billiards Mountain boarding Wave ski-ing Kite surfing Xmas New Year Wi-fi Child facilities **Conf** Class 40 Board 20 Thtr 150 Del from £130 to £450* **Services** Lift **Parking** 72 **Notes** LB Civ Wed 40

CUMBRIA

ALSTON	Map 18 NY74

Lovelady Shield Country House

★★★ 78% ◉◉ COUNTRY HOUSE HOTEL

☎ 01434 381203 & 381305 📠 01434 381515
CA9 3LF
e-mail: enquiries@lovelady.co.uk
dir: 2m E, signed off A689 at junct with B6294

Located in the heart of the Pennines close to England's highest market town, this delightful country house is set in three acres of landscaped gardens. Accommodation is provided in stylish, thoughtfully equipped bedrooms. Carefully prepared meals are served in the elegant dining room and there is a choice of appealing lounges with log fires in the cooler months.

Lovelady Shield Country House

Rooms 10 (1 fmly) **S** £100-£170; **D** £200-£340 (incl. bkfst & dinner) **Facilities** Xmas New Year Wi-fi **Conf** Class 12 Board 12 **Parking** 20 **Notes** LB Civ Wed 100

AMBLESIDE Map 18 NY30

See also **Elterwater**

Waterhead

★★★★ 75% TOWN HOUSE HOTEL

☎ 015394 32566 📄 015394 31255
Lake Rd LA22 0ER
e-mail: waterhead@elhmail.co.uk
web: www.elh.co.uk/hotels/waterhead.htm
dir: A591 into Ambleside, hotel opposite Waterhead Pier

With an enviable location opposite the bay, this well-established hotel offers contemporary and comfortable accommodation with CD/DVD players, plasma screens and internet access. There is a bar with a garden terrace overlooking the lake and a stylish restaurant serving classical cuisine with a modern twist. Staff are very attentive and friendly. Guests can enjoy full use of the Low Wood Hotel leisure facilities nearby.

Rooms 41 (3 fmly) (7 GF) **Facilities** FTV Xmas New Year Wi-fi **Conf** Class 30 Board 26 Thtr 40 **Parking** 43

Rothay Manor

★★★ 82% ⊚ HOTEL

☎ 015394 33605 📄 015394 33607
Rothay Bridge LA22 0EH
e-mail: hotel@rothaymanor.co.uk
web: www.rothaymanor.co.uk/aa
dir: In Ambleside follow signs for Coniston (A593). Hotel 0.25m SW of Ambleside opposite rugby pitch

A long-established hotel, this attractive listed building built in Regency style, is a short walk from both the town centre and Lake Windermere. Spacious bedrooms, including suites, family rooms and rooms with balconies, are comfortably equipped and furnished to a very high standard. Public areas include a choice of lounges, a spacious restaurant and conference facilities.

Rooms 19 (2 annexe) (7 fmly) (3 GF) **S** £90-£140; **D** £140-£215 (incl. bkfst)* **Facilities** Nearby leisure centre free to guests Free fishing permit available Xmas New Year Wi-fi **Conf** Board 18 Thtr 22 Del from £165 to £180* **Parking** 45 **Notes** LB ⊗ Closed 3-23 Jan

See advert on this page

Regent

★★★ 80% ⊚ HOTEL

☎ 015394 32254 📄 015394 31474
Waterhead Bay LA22 0ES
e-mail: info@regentlakes.co.uk
dir: 1m S on A591

This attractive holiday hotel, situated close to Waterhead Bay, offers a warm welcome. Bedrooms come in a variety of styles, including three suites and five bedrooms in the garden wing. There is a modern swimming pool and the restaurant offers a fine dining experience in a contemporary setting.

Rooms 30 (7 fmly) **Facilities** ⊗ New Year Wi-fi **Parking** 38 (charged) **Notes** Closed 19-27 Dec

Best Western Ambleside Salutation Hotel

★★★ 80% HOTEL

☎ 015394 32244 📄 015394 34157
Lake Rd LA22 9BX
e-mail: ambleside@hotelslakedistrict.com
web: www.hotelslakedistrict.com
dir: A591 to Ambleside, onto one-way system down Wansfell Rd into Compston Rd. Right at lights back into village

A former coaching inn, this hotel lies in the centre of the town. Bedrooms are tastefully appointed and thoughtfully equipped; many boast balconies and fine views. Inviting public areas include an attractive restaurant and a choice of comfortable lounges for relaxing, and for the more energetic there is a swimming pool and small gym.

GRASMERE continued

Oak Bank

★★ 76% HOTEL

☎ 015394 35217   📄 015394 35685
Broadgate LA22 9TA
e-mail: info@lakedistricthotel.co.uk
web: www.lakedistricthotel.co.uk
dir: N'bound: M6 junct 36 onto A591 to Windermere, Ambleside, then Grasmere. S'bound: M6 junct 40 onto A66 to Keswick, A591 to Grasmere

This privately owned and personally run hotel provides well-equipped accommodation, including a bedroom on the ground-floor and a four-poster room. Public areas include a choice of comfortable lounges with welcoming log fires when the weather is cold. There is a pleasant bar and an attractive restaurant with a conservatory extension overlooking the garden.

Oak Bank

Rooms 15 (2 fmly) (1 GF) **Facilities** Xmas New Year Wi-fi **Parking** 15 **Notes** LB Closed 2-22 Jan

Queen's Head

★★ 72% ⊕ HOTEL

☎ 015394 36271   📄 015394 36722
Main St LA22 0NS
e-mail: enquiries@queensheadhotel.co.uk
web: www.queensheadhotel.co.uk
dir: M6 junct 36, then A590 to Newby Bridge. Over rdbt, 1st right for 8m into Hawkshead

This 16th-century inn features a wood-panelled bar with low, oak-beamed ceilings and an open log fire. Substantial, carefully prepared meals are served in the bar and in the pretty dining room. The bedrooms, three of which are in an adjacent cottage, are attractively furnished and include some four-poster rooms.

Rooms 14 (3 annexe) (3 fmly) (2 GF) **Facilities** Xmas **Notes** ⊗

See advert on this page

PENRITH

Map 18 NY53

See also **Glenridding and Shap**

North Lakes Hotel & Spa

★★★★ 80% ⊛ HOTEL

SHIRE HOTELS

☎ 01768 868111 📠 01768 868291
Ullswater Rd CA11 8QT
e-mail: nlakes@shirehotels.com
web: www.northlakeshotel.com
dir: M6 junct 40 at junct with A66

With a great location, it's no wonder that this modern hotel is perpetually busy. Amenities include a good range of meeting and function rooms and excellent health and leisure facilities including a full spa. Themed public areas have a contemporary, Scandinavian country style and offer plenty of space and comfort. High standards of service are provided by a friendly team of staff.

Rooms 84 (6 fmly) (22 GF) **S** £95-£162; **D** £140-£229 (incl. bkfst)* **Facilities** Spa STV ⊗ Gym Children's splash pool Steam room Activity & wellness studios Sauna Xmas New Year Wi-fi **Conf** Class 140 Board 30 Thtr 200 Del from £160 to £165* **Services** Lift **Parking** 150 **Notes** LB ⊗ Civ Wed 200

Temple Sowerby House Hotel & Restaurant

★★★ 85% ⊛⊛ HOTEL

☎ 017683 61578 📠 017683 61958
CA10 1RZ
e-mail: stay@templesowerby.com
web: www.templesowerby.com

(For full entry see Temple Sowerby)

Westmorland Hotel

★★★ 81% ⊛ HOTEL

☎ 015396 24351 📠 015396 24354
Westmorland Place, Orton CA10 3SB
e-mail: reservations@westmorlandhotel.com
web: www.westmorlandhotel.com

(For full entry see Tebay)

George

★★★ 75% HOTEL

☎ 01768 862696 📠 01768 868223
Devonshire St CA11 7SU
e-mail: georgehotel@lakedistricthotels.net
dir: M6 junct 40, 1m to town centre. From A6/A66 to Penrith

This inviting and popular hotel dates back to a time when Bonnie Prince Charlie made a visit. Extended over the

Continued

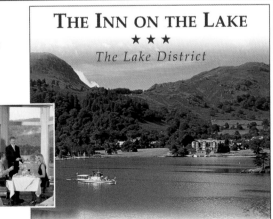

PENRITH continued

years this town centre hotel has been upgraded throughout. The bedrooms are well equipped. The spacious public areas retain a timeless charm and include a choice of lounge areas, popular venues for morning coffees and afternoon teas.

George

Rooms 35 (4 fmly) **Facilities** Xmas New Year Wi-fi **Conf** Class 80 Board 50 Thtr 120 **Parking** 40 **Notes** Civ Wed 120

See advert on page 137

Edenhall Country Hotel

U

☎ 01768 881454 🖹 01768 881266
Edenhall CA11 8SX
e-mail: info@edenhallhotel.co.uk
dir: take A686 from Penrith to Alston. Hotel signed on right in 3m

Currently the rating for this establishment is not confirmed. This may be due to a change of ownership or because it has only recently joined the AA rating scheme. For further details please see the AA website: www.theAA.com

Rooms 25 (8 annexe) (3 fmly) (7 GF) **S** fr £45; **D** £70-£92.50 (incl. bkfst)* **Facilities** STV 🏊 Xmas New Year Wi-fi **Conf** Class 30 Board 30 Thtr 50 **Parking** 60 **Notes** LB ⊗ Civ Wed 60

Travelodge Penrith

BUDGET HOTEL

☎ 08719 846 168 🖹 01768 866958
Redhills CA11 0DT
web: www.travelodge.co.uk
dir: on A66, 0.25m from M6 junct 40

Travelodge offers good quality, good value, modern accommodation. Ideal for families, the spacious en suite bedrooms include remote-control TV, tea and coffee-making facilities and comfortable beds. Meals can be taken at the nearby family restaurant. See also the Hotel Groups pages.

Rooms 54 **S** fr £29; **D** fr £29

RAVENGLASS Map 18 SD09

Pennington

★★★ 79% ◉ HOTEL

☎ 01229 717222 & 717626
CA18 1SD

This hotel has a very relaxed atmosphere throughout and the public areas are open plan with high quality fabrics and artwork. The bedrooms are modern in design and have high spec fixtures and fittings in the bathrooms. Honest cooking, based on local and fine quality ingredients, is offered on the seasonal menus. Staff show exceptional customer awareness by providing very attentive and friendly service.

Rooms 29 (12 annexe) (6 fmly) **Parking** 50

RAVENSTONEDALE Map 18 NY70

The Fat Lamb

★★ 69% HOTEL

☎ 015396 23242 🖹 015396 23285
Crossbank CA17 4LL
e-mail: fatlamb@cumbria.com
dir: on A683, between Kirkby Stephen & Sedbergh

Open fires and solid stone walls feature at this 17th-century inn, set on its own nature reserve. There is a choice of dining options with an extensive menu available in the traditional bar and a more formal dining experience in the restaurant. Bedrooms are bright and cheerful, and include family rooms and easily accessible rooms for guests with limited mobility.

Rooms 12 (4 fmly) (5 GF) **S** £48-£54; **D** £80-£88 (incl. bkfst)* **Facilities** Private 5-acre nature reserve Xmas Wi-fi **Parking** 60 **Notes** LB

ROSTHWAITE Map 18 NY21

See also **Borrowdale**

Scafell

★★★ 63% HOTEL

☎ 017687 77208 🖹 017687 77280
CA12 5XB
e-mail: info@scafell.co.uk
web: www.scafell.co.uk
dir: M6 junct 40 to Keswick on A66. Take B5289 to Rosthwaite

This friendly hotel has long been popular with walkers and enjoys a peaceful location. Bedrooms vary in style from traditional to modern, but are all well equipped and neatly decorated. Public areas include a residents' cocktail bar, lounge and spacious restaurant as well as the popular Riverside Inn pub, offering all-day dining in summer months.

Rooms 24 (2 fmly) (8 GF) **S** £87.50; **D** £175 (incl. bkfst & dinner) **Facilities** FTV Guided walks Xmas New Year **Parking** 50 **Notes** LB Civ Wed 75

Royal Oak

★ 72% HOTEL

☎ 017687 77214 🖹 017687 77214
CA12 5XB
e-mail: info@royaloakhotel.co.uk
web: www.royaloakhotel.co.uk
dir: 6m S of Keswick on B5289 in centre of Rosthwaite

Set in a village in one of Lakeland's most picturesque valleys, this family-run hotel offers friendly and obliging service. There is a variety of accommodation styles, with particularly impressive rooms being located in a converted barn across the courtyard and backed by a stream. Family rooms are available. The cosy bar is for residents and diners only. A set home-cooked dinner is served at 7pm.

Rooms 12 (4 annexe) (5 fmly) (4 GF) **S** £42-£53; **D** £82-£116 (incl. bkfst & dinner)* **Parking** 15 **Notes** LB Closed 6-24 Jan & 7-27 Dec

SEASCALE — Map 18 NY00

Cumbrian Lodge

RESTAURANT WITH ROOMS

☎ 019467 27309 📠 019467 27158
Gosforth Rd CA20 1JG
e-mail: cumbrianlodge@btconnect.com
dir: Off A595 at Gosforth onto B5344 signed Seascale, 2m on left

A relaxed and friendly atmosphere prevails at this well-run restaurant with rooms, where well-prepared tasty dinners are a popular local attraction. Décor and fixtures are modern throughout, and the bedrooms are well-equipped for business and leisure guests. The new thatched garden buildings provide a delightful location for dining al fresco, an elegant setting for groups of up to eight.

Rooms 6 (1 fmly)

SHAP — Map 18 NY51

Best Western Shap Wells

★★★ 74% HOTEL

☎ 01931 716628 📠 01931 716377
CA10 3QU
e-mail: manager@shapwells.com
dir: between A6 and B6261, 4m S of Shap

This hotel occupies a wonderful secluded position amid trees and waterfalls. Extensive public areas include function and meeting rooms, a well-stocked bar, a choice of lounges and a spacious restaurant. Bedrooms vary in size and style but all are equipped with the expected facilities.

Rooms 98 (7 annexe) (10 fmly) (10 GF) **Facilities** Games room Xmas **Conf** Class 80 Board 40 Thtr 170 **Services** Lift **Parking** 200 **Notes** Civ Wed 150

SILLOTH — Map 18 NY15

Golf Hotel

★★ 68% HOTEL

☎ 016973 31438 📠 016973 32582
Criffel St CA7 4AB
e-mail: golf.hotel@virgin.net

A friendly welcome waits at this hotel which occupies a prime position in the centre of the historic market town; it is a popular meeting place for the local community. Bedrooms are mostly well proportioned and are comfortably equipped. The lounge bar is a popular venue for dining with a wide range of dishes on offer. Refurbishment at the hotel is ongoing.

Rooms 22 (4 fmly) (22 smoking) **S** £49-£67.50; **D** £82-£105 (incl. bkfst)* **Facilities** Snooker & Games room **Conf** Class 50 Board 30 Thtr 100 **Notes** LB Closed 24-26 Dec

SOUTHWAITE MOTORWAY SERVICE AREA (M6) — Map 18 NY44

Travelodge Carlisle (M6)

BUDGET HOTEL

☎ 08719 846 128 📠 016974 75354
Broadfield Site CA4 0NT
web: www.travelodge.co.uk
dir: M6 junct 41/42

Travelodge offers good quality, good value, modern accommodation. Ideal for families, the spacious en suite bedrooms include remote-control TV, tea and coffee-making facilities and comfortable beds. Meals can be taken at the nearby family restaurant. See also the Hotel Groups pages.

Rooms 38 **S** fr £29; **D** fr £29

TEBAY — Map 18 NY60

Westmorland Hotel

★★★ 81% HOTEL

☎ 015396 24351 📠 015396 24354
Westmorland Place, Orton CA10 3SB
e-mail: reservations@westmorlandhotel.com
web: www.westmorlandhotel.com
dir: Signed from Westmorland Services between M6 junct 38 & 39

With fine views over rugged moorland, this modern and friendly hotel is ideal for conferences and meetings. Bedrooms are spacious and comfortable, with the executive rooms particularly well equipped. Open-plan public areas provide a Tyrolean touch and include a split-level restaurant.

Rooms 51 (5 fmly) (12 GF) **S** £80-£100; **D** £94-£115 (incl. bkfst)* **Facilities** FTV Xmas New Year Wi-fi **Conf** Class 24 Board 30 Thtr 120 **Services** Lift **Parking** 60 **Notes** LB RS 1 Jan Civ Wed 120

TEMPLE SOWERBY — Map 18 NY62

Temple Sowerby House Hotel & Restaurant

★★★ 85% ⊕⊕ HOTEL

☎ 017683 61578 📠 017683 61958
CA10 1RZ
e-mail: stay@templesowerby.com
web: www.templesowerby.com
dir: in village centre, midway between Penrith & Appleby, 7m from M6 junct 40

The hotel is set in the heart of the Eden Valley, ideal for exploring the northern Lake District and Pennine Fells. Bedrooms are comfortable and stylish, most featuring ultra-modern bathrooms, and there is a choice of pleasant lounges. The new restaurant, with picture windows overlooking the beautiful walled garden, is a splendid addition. Staff throughout are friendly and keen to please.

Rooms 12 (4 annexe) (2 GF) **S** £90-£130; **D** £120-£180 (incl. bkfst) **Facilities** ⅙ New Year Wi-fi **Conf** Class 20 Board 20 Thtr 30 Del from £145 to £165 **Parking** 15 **Notes** LB ⊗ No children 12yrs Closed 20-29 Dec Civ Wed 40

ULLSWATER

See Glenridding & Patterdale

WATERMILLOCK — Map 18 NY42

Macdonald Leeming House

★★★★ 76% ⊕⊕⊕ HOTEL

☎ 0844 879 9142 📠 015394 43432
CA11 0JJ
e-mail: sales/oldengland@macdonald-hotels.co.uk
web: www.macdonald-hotels.co.uk
dir: M6 junct 40, A66 to Keswick. At rdbt A592 (Ullswater). 5m to T-junct, right (A592). Hotel on left in 3m

This hotel enjoys a superb location, being set in 20 acres of mature wooded gardens in the Lake District National Park, and overlooking Ullswater and the towering fells. Many rooms offer views of the lake and the rugged fells beyond, with more than half having their own balcony. Public rooms include three sumptuous lounges, a cosy bar and library.

Rooms 41 (1 fmly) (10 GF) **S** £120-£185; **D** £135-£200 (incl. bkfst)* **Facilities** Fishing ⅙ Xmas New Year **Conf** Class 40 Board 30 Thtr 80 Del from £140 to £155* **Parking** 50 **Notes** Civ Wed 80

WATERMILLOCK continued

INSPECTORS' CHOICE

Rampsbeck Country House
★★★ ⚛⚛⚛ HOTEL

☎ 017684 86442 🖺 017684 86688
CA11 0LP
e-mail: enquiries@rampsbeck.co.uk
web: www.rampsbeck.co.uk
dir: M6 junct 40, A592 to Ullswater, at T-junct (with lake in front) turn right, hotel 1.5m

This fine country house lies in 18 acres of parkland on the shores of Lake Ullswater, and is furnished with many period and antique pieces. There are three delightful lounges, an elegant restaurant and a traditional bar. Bedrooms come in three grades; the most spacious rooms are spectacular and overlook the lake. Service is attentive and the cuisine a real highlight.

Rooms 19 (1 GF) **S** £85-£150; **D** £140-£280 (incl. bkfst)* **Facilities** STV FTV Fishing 🏊 Xmas New Year Wi-fi **Conf** Class 10 Board 15 Thtr 15 Del from £155 to £250* **Parking** 30 **Notes** LB Civ Wed 65

WINDERMERE Map 18 SD49

INSPECTORS' CHOICE

Gilpin Lodge Country House Hotel & Restaurant
★★★★ ⚛⚛⚛ HOTEL

☎ 015394 88818 🖺 015394 88058
Crook Rd LA23 3NE
e-mail: hotel@gilpinlodge.co.uk
web: www.gilpinlodge.co.uk
dir: M6 junct 36, take A590/A591 to rdbt north of Kendal, take B5284, hotel 5m on right

This smart Victorian residence is set amidst delightful gardens leading to the fells, and is just a short drive from the lake. The individually styled bedrooms are stylish and a number benefit from private terraces; all are spacious and thoughtfully equipped, and each has a private sitting room. In addition there are luxury Garden Suites that lead out onto private gardens with cedar wood hot tubs. The welcoming atmosphere is notable and the attractive day rooms are perfect for relaxing, perhaps beside a real fire. Guests can expect vibrant and exciting cuisine.

Rooms 20 (6 annexe) (11 GF) **S** £175; **D** £270-£390 (incl. bkfst & dinner)* **Facilities** 🏊 Free membership at local Leisure Club In-room spa treatment Xmas New Year Wi-fi **Parking** 40 **Notes** LB ⊗ No children 7yrs

---

INSPECTORS' CHOICE

Holbeck Ghyll Country House
★★★★ ⚛⚛⚛ COUNTRY HOUSE HOTEL

☎ 015394 32375 🖺 015394 34743
Holbeck Ln LA23 1LU
e-mail: stay@holbeckghyll.com
dir: 3m N of Windermere on A591, right into Holbeck Lane (signed Troutbeck), hotel 0.5m on left

With a peaceful setting in extensive grounds, this beautifully maintained hotel enjoys breathtaking views over Lake Windermere and the Langdale Fells. Public rooms include luxurious, comfortable lounges and two elegant dining rooms, where memorable meals are served. Bedrooms are individually styled, beautifully furnished and many have balconies or patios. Some in an adjacent, more private lodge are less traditional in design and have superb views. The professionalism and attentiveness of the staff is exemplary.

Rooms 28 (14 annexe) (4 fmly) (6 GF) **S** £155-£300; **D** £250-£550 (incl. bkfst & dinner)* **Facilities** Spa STV 🏌 Putt green 🏋 Gym Steam room Treatment rooms Beauty massage Xmas New Year Wi-fi **Conf** Class 25 Board 25 Thtr 45 Del from £200 to £350* **Parking** 34 **Notes** LB Civ Wed 65

Macdonald Old England
★★★★ 84% ⚛⚛ HOTEL

☎ 0844 879 9144 🖺 015394 43432
Church St, Bowness LA23 3DF
e-mail: sales/oldengland@macdonald-hotels.co.uk
web: www.macdonaldhotels.co.uk
dir: Through Windermere to Bowness, straight across at mini-rdbt . Hotel behind church on right

This hotel stands right on the shore of England's largest lake and boasts superb views. It is currently undergoing a significant refurbishment to upgrade all its accommodation and public areas.

Macdonald Old England

Rooms 106 (3 fmly) (14 GF) **S** £120-£185; **D** £135-£200 (incl. bkfst)* **Facilities** Spa STV ☜ supervised Gym Private jetties Xmas New Year Wi-fi **Conf** Class 60 Board 25 Thtr 100 Del from £140 to £165* **Services** Lift **Parking** 82 **Notes** ⊗ Civ Wed 100

Storrs Hall

★★★★ 75% ⑩⑩ HOTEL

☎ 015394 47111 ▤ 015394 47555
Storrs Park LA23 3LG
e-mail: storrshall@elhmail.co.uk
web: www.elh.co.uk/hotels/storrshall
dir: on A592 2m S of Bowness, on Newby Bridge road

Set in 17 acres of landscaped grounds by the lakeside, this imposing Georgian mansion is delightful. There are numerous lounges to relax in, furnished with fine art and antiques. Individually styled bedrooms are generally spacious and boast impressive bathrooms. Imaginative cuisine is served in the elegant restaurant, which offers fine views across the lawn to the lake and fells beyond.

Rooms 30 **S** £113-£177; **D** £176-£304 (incl. bkfst)
Facilities FTV Fishing 🚣 Use of nearby sports/beauty facilities Xmas New Year Wi-fi **Conf** Class 35 Board 24 Thtr 50 **Parking** 50 **Notes** LB No children 12yrs Civ Wed 94

Low Wood

★★★★ 75% HOTEL

☎ 015394 33338 & 0845 850 3502 ▤ 015394 34275
LA23 1LP
e-mail: lowwood@elhmail.co.uk
dir: M6 junct 36, follow A590 then A591 to Windermere, then 3m towards Ambleside, hotel on right

Benefiting from a lakeside location, this hotel offers an excellent range of leisure and conference facilities. Bedrooms, many with panoramic lake views, are attractively furnished, and include a number of larger executive rooms and suites. There is a choice of bars, a spacious restaurant and the more informal Café del Lago. The poolside bar offers internet and e-mail access.

Rooms 111 (13 fmly) **D** £92-£220 (incl. bkfst)
Facilities ☜ supervised Fishing Gym Squash Water skiing Canoeing Beauty salon Bungy trampoline Wall climbing Marina Xmas New Year Wi-fi **Conf** Class 180 Board 150 Thtr 340 **Services** Lift **Parking** 200 **Notes** LB Civ Wed 200

See advert on this page

WINDERMERE continued

INSPECTORS' CHOICE

Linthwaite House Hotel & Restaurant
★★★ ◉◉ COUNTRY HOUSE HOTEL

☎ 015394 88600 ▤ 015394 88601
Crook Rd LA23 3JA
e-mail: stay@linthwaite.com
web: www.linthwaite.com
dir: A591 towards The Lakes for 8m to large rdbt, take 1st exit (B5284), 6m, hotel on left. 1m past Windermere golf club

Linthwaite House is set in 14 acres of hilltop grounds and enjoys stunning views over Lake Windermere. Inviting public rooms include an attractive conservatory and adjoining lounge and an elegant restaurant. Bedrooms, which are individually decorated, combine contemporary furnishings with classical styles; all are thoughtfully equipped and include CD players. Service and hospitality are attentive and friendly.

Rooms 27 (1 fmly) (7 GF) **S** £120-£165; **D** £160-£380 (incl. bkfst & dinner)* **Facilities** STV Putt green Fishing 🎣 Beauty treatments Massage Xmas New Year Wi-fi **Conf** Class 19 Board 25 Thtr 40 Del from £125 to £299* **Parking** 40 **Notes** LB ⊗ Civ Wed 64

Lindeth Howe Country House Hotel & Restaurant
CLASSIC BRITISH HOTELS

★★★ 87% ◉◉ COUNTRY HOUSE HOTEL

☎ 015394 45759 ▤ 015394 46368
Lindeth Dr, Longtail Hill LA23 3JF
e-mail: hotel@lindeth-howe.co.uk
web: www.lindeth-howe.co.uk
dir: turn off A592, 1m S of Bowness onto B5284 (Longtail Hill) signed Kendal & Lancaster, hotel last driveway on right

Historic photographs commemorate the fact that this delightful house was once the family home of Beatrix Potter. Secluded in landscaped grounds, it enjoys views across the valley and Lake Windermere. Public rooms are plentiful and inviting, with the restaurant being the perfect setting for modern country-house cooking. Deluxe and superior bedrooms are spacious and smartly appointed.

Rooms 36 (3 fmly) (2 GF) **S** £65-£140; **D** £130-£250 (incl. bkfst)* **Facilities** STV ⊗ Gym Sauna Fitness room Xmas New Year Wi-fi **Conf** Class 20 Board 18 Thtr 30 **Parking** 50 **Notes** LB ⊗

Miller Howe
★★★ 86% ◉◉ COUNTRY HOUSE HOTEL

☎ 015394 42536 ▤ 015394 45664
Rayrigg Rd LA23 1EY
e-mail: lakeview@millerhowe.com
dir: M6 junct 36 follow A591 past Windermere village, left at rdbt towards Bowness

This long established hotel of much character enjoys a lakeside setting amidst delightful landscaped gardens. The bright and welcoming day rooms include sumptuous lounges, a conservatory and an opulently decorated restaurant. Imaginative dinners make use of fresh, local produce where possible and there is an extensive, well-balanced wine list. Stylish bedrooms, many with fabulous lake views, include well-equipped cottage rooms and a number with whirlpool baths.

Rooms 15 (3 annexe) (1 GF) **S** £70-£150; **D** £140-£200 (incl. bkfst)* **Facilities** Xmas New Year **Parking** 35 **Notes** LB No children 8yrs Civ Wed 65

Fayrer Garden Hotel
★★★ 83% ◉◉ HOTEL

☎ 015394 88195 ▤ 015394 45986
Lyth Valley Rd, Bowness-on-Windermere LA23 3JP
e-mail: lakescene@fayrergarden.com
web: www.fayrergarden.com
dir: on A5074 1m from Bowness Bay

Sitting in lovely landscaped gardens, this elegant hotel enjoys spectacular views over the lake. The comfortably appointed bedrooms come in a variety of styles and sizes, some with bathrooms of a high specification. There is a choice of lounges and a stylish, conservatory restaurant. The attentive, hospitable staff ensure a relaxing stay.

Rooms 29 (5 annexe) (10 GF) **S** £68-£142; **D** £114-£290 (incl. bkfst & dinner) **Facilities** FTV Free membership of leisure club Xmas New Year Wi-fi **Parking** 40 **Notes** LB No children 5yrs Civ Wed 60

Lindeth Fell Country House Hotel
★★★ 83% ◉ COUNTRY HOUSE HOTEL

☎ 015394 43286 & 44287 ▤ 015394 47455
Lyth Valley Rd, Bowness-on-Windermere LA23 3JP
e-mail: kennedy@lindethfell.co.uk
web: www.lindethfell.co.uk
dir: 1m S of Bowness on A5074

Enjoying delightful views, this smart Edwardian residence stands in seven acres of glorious, landscaped gardens. Bedrooms, which vary in size and style, are comfortably equipped. Skilfully prepared dinners are served in the spacious dining room that commands fine views. The resident owners and their attentive, friendly staff provide high levels of hospitality and service.

Rooms 14 (2 fmly) (1 GF) **S** £50-£85; **D** £100-£170 (incl. bkfst)* **Facilities** Putt green Fishing 🎣 Bowling Xmas New Year Wi-fi **Conf** Class 12 Board 12 Thtr 12 Del from £120 to £150* **Parking** 20 **Notes** LB ⊗ Closed Jan

Beech Hill

RICHARDSON

★★★ 81% ◉◉ HOTEL

☎ 015394 42137 ▤ 015394 43745
Newby Bridge Rd LA23 3LR
e-mail: reservations@beechhillhotel.co.uk
web: www.beechhillhotel.co.uk
dir: A592 from Bowness to Newby Bridge, hotel 4m on right

This stylish, terraced hotel is set on high ground leading to the shore of Lake Windermere and has a spacious, open-plan lounge which, like the restaurant, affords splendid views across the lake. Bedrooms come in a range of styles; some have four-poster beds, and all are well equipped. Leisure facilities and a choice of conference rooms complete the package.

Rooms 57 (4 fmly) (4 GF) **S** £55-£109; **D** £78-£310 (incl. bkfst)* **Facilities** FTV ⊗ Fishing 🎵 Xmas New Year Wi-fi **Parking** 70 **Notes** LB Civ Wed 130

See advert on opposite page

Riber Hall

[U]

☎ 01629 582795 📠 01629 580475
DE4 5JU
e-mail: info@riber-hall.co.uk
web: www.riber-hall.co.uk
dir: 1m off A615 at Tansley

Currently the rating for this establishment is not confirmed. This may be due to a change of ownership or because it has only recently joined the AA rating scheme. For further details please see the AA website: www.theAA.com

Rooms 14 (11 annexe) (6 GF) **Facilities** ☕ Xmas New Year **Conf** Class 25 Board 25 Thtr 45 **Parking** 40 **Notes** Civ Wed 45

MORLEY Map 11 SK34

The Morley Hayes Hotel

★★★★ 73% ⊛ HOTEL

☎ 01332 780480 📠 01332 781094
Main Rd DE7 6DG
e-mail: hotel@morleyhayes.com
web: www.morleyhayes.com
dir: 4m N of Derby on A608

Located in rolling countryside this modern golfing destination provides extremely comfortable, stylish bedrooms with wide-ranging facilities, plasma TVs, and state-of-the-art bathrooms; the plush suites are particularly eye-catching. Creative cuisine is offered in the Dovecote Restaurant, and both Roosters and the Spikes sports bar provide informal eating options.

Rooms 32 (4 fmly) (15 GF) **S** £120-£245; **D** £140-£261 (incl. bkfst) **Facilities** ⚲ 27 Putt green Golf driving range Wi-fi **Conf** Class 130 Board 122 Thtr 165 Del from £169.95 to £189.95* **Services** Lift Air con **Parking** 245 **Notes** LB ⊗ Civ Wed 90

RENISHAW Map 16 SK47

Sitwell Arms

★★★ 70% HOTEL

☎ 01246 435226 & 437327 📠 01246 433915
Station Rd S21 3WF
e-mail: info@sitwellarms.com
web: www.thesitwellarms.co.uk
dir: on A6135 to Sheffield, W of M1 junct 30

This stone-built hotel, parts of which date back to the 18th century, is conveniently situated close to the M1 and offers good value accommodation. The hotel has an extensive gym plus a hair and beauty salon. Bedrooms are of a comfortable size and include modern facilities. There are extensive bars and a restaurant serving a wide range of meals and snacks.

Rooms 31 (8 fmly) (9 GF) (26 smoking) **S** £35.95-£37.95; **D** £70-£82 (incl. bkfst)* **Facilities** STV Gym Fitness studio Hair & beauty salon Xmas New Year Wi-fi **Conf** Class 60 Board 60 Thtr 160 Del from £87* **Services** Lift **Parking** 150 **Notes** ⊗ Civ Wed 150

RISLEY Map 11 SK43

Risley Hall Hotel & Spa

★★★ 78% ⊛ HOTEL

OXFORD
HOTELS & INNS

☎ 0115 939 9000 & 921 8523 📠 0115 939 7766
Derby Rd DE72 3SS
e-mail: reservations.risleyhall@ohiml.com
web: www.oxfordhotelsandinns.com
dir: M1 junct 25, Sandiacre exit into Bostock Lane. left at lights, hotel is on left in 0.25m

Set in 17 acres of private landscaped grounds and attractive mature gardens, this 11th-century manor

house offers a good range of comfortable accommodation and relaxing day rooms. The friendly and attentive service complements the imaginative cuisine in the fine dining restaurant. The spa and beauty treatment rooms prove particularly popular with members and leisure guests alike.

Rooms 35 (8 GF) **Facilities** Spa ⊛ Xmas **Conf** Class 22 Board 20 Thtr 100 **Services** Lift **Notes** LB ⊗ Civ Wed 100

ROWSLEY Map 16 SK26

INSPECTORS' CHOICE

East Lodge Country House

★★★ ⊛⊛ HOTEL

☎ 01629 734474 📠 01629 733949
DE4 2EF
e-mail: info@eastlodge.com
web: www.eastlodge.com
dir: A6, 3m from Bakewell, 5m from Matlock

This hotel enjoys a romantic setting in ten acres of landscaped grounds and gardens. The stylish bedrooms are equipped with many extras such as TVs with DVD players, and most have lovely garden views. The popular restaurant serves much produce sourced from the area, and the conservatory lounge, overlooking the gardens, offers afternoon teas and light meals.

Rooms 12 (2 fmly) (1 GF) **Facilities** ⚲ Xmas New Year Wi-fi **Conf** Class 20 Board 22 Thtr 75 **Parking** 40 **Notes** LB ⊗ No children 7yrs Civ Wed 100

ROWSLEY continued

The Peacock at Rowsley

★★★ 87% ⊛ HOTEL

☎ 01629 733518 📠 01629 732671
Bakewell Rd DE4 2EB
e-mail: reception@thepeacockatrowsley.com
web: www.thepeacockatrowsley.com
dir: A6, 3m before Bakewell, 6m from Matlock towards Bakewell

Owned by Haddon Hall this hotel is a smart, contemporary destination although many of the property's original features can still be seen. The menus are well balanced and use local produce. Dry fly fishing is a great attraction here as the hotel owns fishing rights in the area. The staff are delightful and deliver high standards of service.

Rooms 16 (5 fmly) **Facilities** Fishing ⤸ Free use of Woodlands Fitness Centre Free membership to Bakewell Golf Club ♫ New Year Wi-fi **Conf** Class 8 Board 16 Thtr 16 **Parking** 25 (charged) **Notes** No children 10yrs Civ Wed 20

SANDIACRE | Map 11 SK43

Holiday Inn Derby/ Nottingham

U

☎ 0870 400 9062 📠 0115 949 0469
Bostocks Ln NG10 5NJ
e-mail: rachel.shipley@ihg.com
web: www.holidayinn.co.uk
dir: M1 junct 25 follow exit to Sandiacre, hotel on right

Currently the rating for this establishment is not confirmed. This may be due to a change of ownership or because it has only recently joined the AA rating scheme. For further details please see the AA website: www.theAA.com

Rooms 92 (31 fmly) (53 GF) (7 smoking) **S** £39-£150; **D** £39-£150 (incl. bkfst) **Facilities** STV Xmas New Year Wi-fi **Conf** Class 32 Board 30 Thtr 75 Del from £110 to £155 **Services** Air con **Parking** 200 **Notes** Civ Wed 50

SOUTH NORMANTON | Map 16 SK45

The Derbyshire Hotel

U

☎ 01773 812000 📠 01773 813413
Carter Lane East DE55 2EH
e-mail: reservations.derbyshire@principal-hayley.com
dir: M1 junct 28, E on A38 to Mansfield

Currently the rating for this establishment is not confirmed. This may be due to a change of ownership or because it has only recently joined the AA rating scheme. For further details please see the AA website: www.theAA.com

Rooms 157 (10 fmly) (61 GF) (10 smoking) **Facilities** Spa STV 🗘 Gym Steam room Sauna New Year Wi-fi **Conf** Class 120 Board 25 Thtr 250 Del from £120 to £160 **Parking** 220 **Notes** Civ Wed 150

SUDBURY | Map 10 SK13

The Boars Head

★★★ 74% HOTEL

☎ 01283 820344 📠 01283 820075
Lichfield Rd DE6 5GX
e-mail: enquiries@boars-head-hotel.co.uk
web: www.boars-head-hotel.co.uk
dir: off A50 onto A515 towards Lichfield, hotel 1m on right

This popular hotel offers comfortable accommodation in well-equipped bedrooms. There is a relaxed atmosphere in the public rooms, which consists of a several bars and dining options. The beamed lounge bar provides informal dining thanks to a popular carvery, while the restaurant and cocktail bar offer a more formal environment.

Rooms 23 (1 annexe) (1 fmly) **Facilities** Xmas **Parking** 85 **Notes** LB

See advert on page 446

THORPE (DOVEDALE) | Map 16 SK15

Izaak Walton

★★★ 79% ⊛⊛ HOTEL

☎ 01335 350555 📠 01335 350539
Dovedale DE6 2AY
e-mail: reception@izaakwaltonhotel.com
web: www.izaakwaltonhotel.com
dir: A515 onto B5054, to Thorpe village, continue straight over cattle grid & 2 small bridges, 1st right & sharp left

This hotel is peacefully situated, with magnificent views over the valley of Dovedale to Thorpe Cloud. Many of the bedrooms have lovely views, and the executive rooms are particularly spacious. Meals are served in the bar area, with more formal dining in the Haddon Restaurant. Staff are friendly and efficient. Fishing on the River Dove can be arranged.

Rooms 35 (6 fmly) (8 GF) **S** fr £110; **D** fr £145 (incl. bkfst)* **Facilities** Fishing ⤸ Xmas New Year Wi-fi **Conf** Class 40 Board 50 Thtr 50 Del from £155* **Parking** 80 **Notes** Civ Wed 80

See advert on page 145

DEVON

ASHBURTON | Map 3 SX77

Dartmoor Lodge

★★ Ⓐ HOTEL

☎ 01364 652232 📠 01364 653990
Peartree Cross TQ13 7JW
e-mail: dartmoor.ashburton@newbridgeinns.co.uk
web: www.oldenglish.co.uk
dir: Exit A38 at 2nd exit for Ashburton, turn right across bridge, turn left at garage, hotel on right.

Rooms 29 (7 fmly) (9 GF) **Facilities** Xmas **Conf** Class 36 Board 36 Thtr 90 **Services** Lift **Parking** 100 **Notes** LB

OKEHAMPTON Map 3 SX59

Ashbury

★★ 72% HOTEL

☎ 01837 55453 🖹 01837 55468
Higher Maddaford, Southcott EX20 4NL
dir: off A30 at Sourton Cross onto A386. Left onto A3079 to Bude at Fowley Cross. After 1m right to Ashbury. Hotel 0.5m on right

With no less than five courses and a clubhouse with lounge, bar and dining facilities, The Ashbury is a golfer's paradise. The majority of the well-equipped bedrooms are located in the farmhouse and courtyard-style development around the putting green. Guests can enjoy the many on-site leisure facilities or join the activities available at the adjacent sister hotel.

Rooms 143 (30 annexe) (52 fmly) (75 GF) **S** £39-£185; **D** £74-£185 (incl. bkfst & dinner)* **Facilities** 🕲 🏊 99 🏌 Putt green Fishing Driving range Indoor bowls Ten-pin bowling Outdoor chess Golf simulator Xmas New Year **Parking** 150 **Notes** LB ⊗

Manor House Hotel

★★ 71% HOTEL

☎ 01837 53053 🖹 01837 55027
Fowley Cross EX20 4NA
e-mail: ali@manorhousehotel.co.uk
web: www.manorhousehotel.co.uk
dir: off A30 at Sourton Cross flyover, right onto A386. Hotel 1.5m on right

Enjoying views to Dartmoor in the distance, this hotel is set within 17 acres of grounds and is located close to the A30. An impressive range of facilities, including golf at the adjacent sister hotel, is available at this friendly establishment, which specialises in short breaks. Bedrooms, many located on the ground floor, are comfortable and well equipped.

Rooms 196 (91 fmly) (90 GF) **S** £62-£96; **D** £112-£183 (incl. bkfst & dinner)* **Facilities** Spa 🕲 🏊 Fishing 🎣 Gym Squash Craft centre Indoor bowls Shooting range Laser clay pigeon shooting Aerobics Xmas New Year **Parking** 200 **Notes** LB ⊗

See advert on this page

White Hart

★★ 71% HOTEL

☎ 01837 52730 & 54514 🖹 01837 53979
Fore St EX20 1HD
e-mail: enquiry@thewhitehart-hotel.com
dir: in town centre, adjacent to lights, car park at rear of hotel

Dating back to the 17th century, the White Hart offers modern facilities. Bedrooms are well equipped and spacious and some have four-poster beds. A range of bar meals is offered, or more relaxed dining may be taken in the Courtney Restaurant or Vines pizzeria. Guests can relax in the lounge or choice of bars, as well as a traditional skittles and games room.

Rooms 19 (2 fmly) **Facilities** Xmas **Conf** Class 30 Board 40 Thtr 100 **Parking** 20

OKEHAMPTON continued

Travelodge Okehampton Whiddon Down

BUDGET HOTEL

☎ 08719 846 047 📄 01647 231626
Whiddon Down EX20 2QT
web: www.travelodge.co.uk
dir: at Merrymeet rdbt on A30/A382

Travelodge offers good quality, good value, modern accommodation. Ideal for families, the spacious en suite bedrooms include remote-control TV, tea and coffee-making facilities and comfortable beds. Meals can be taken at the nearby family restaurant. See also the Hotel Groups pages.

Rooms 40 **S** fr £29; **D** fr £29

OTTERY ST MARY   **Map 3 SY19**

Tumbling Weir Hotel

★★ 76% SMALL HOTEL

☎ 01404 812752 📄 01404 812752
Canaan Way EX11 1AQ
e-mail: reception@tumblingweirhotel.com
web: www.tumblingweir-hotel.co.uk
dir: off A30 take B3177 into Ottery St Mary, hotel signed off Mill St, access through old mill

Quietly located between the River Otter and its millstream and set in well-tended gardens, this family-run hotel offers friendly and attentive service. Bedrooms are attractively presented and equipped with modern comforts. In the dining room, where a selection of carefully prepared dishes makes up the carte menu, beams and subtle lighting help to create an intimate atmosphere.

Rooms 10 (1 fmly) **S** £50-£63; **D** £80-£100 (incl. bkfst) **Facilities** ❧ Wi-fi **Conf** Class 60 Board 50 Thtr 90 Del from £95 to £100 **Parking** 10 **Notes** LB ⊗ Closed 26 Dec-10 Jan Civ Wed 80

PAIGNTON   **Map 3 SX86**

Redcliffe

★★★ 75% HOTEL

☎ 01803 526397 📄 01803 528030
Marine Dr TQ3 2NL
e-mail: redclfe@aol.com
dir: on seafront at Torquay end of Paignton Green

Set at the water's edge in three acres of well-tended grounds, this popular hotel enjoys uninterrupted views across Tor Bay. Offering a diverse range of facilities including a leisure complex, beauty treatments and lots of outdoor family activities in the summer. Bedrooms are pleasantly appointed and comfortably furnished, while public areas offer ample space for rest and relaxation.

Rooms 68 (8 fmly) (3 GF) **S** £55-£62; **D** £110-£124 (incl. bkfst)* **Facilities** Spa ❀ supervised ⚘ Putt green

---

Fishing Gym Table tennis Carpet bowls Xmas New Year Wi-fi **Conf** Class 50 Board 50 Thtr 150 Del from £95 to £102* **Services** Lift **Parking** 80 **Notes** LB ⊗ Civ Wed 150

Summerhill

★★ 🅰 HOTEL

☎ 01803 558101 📄 01803 226106
Braeside Rd TQ4 6BX
e-mail: info@summerhillhotel.co.uk
web: www.summerhillhotel.co.uk
dir: with harbour on left, follow for 600yds

Rooms 25 (8 fmly) (4 GF) **Facilities** ❧ Free membership to nearby leisure centre Wi-fi **Services** Lift **Parking** 40 **Notes** LB ⊗

PLYMOUTH   **Map 3 SX45**

See also **St Mellion (Cornwall & Isles of Scilly)**

Holiday Inn Plymouth

★★★★ 73% HOTEL

☎ 0870 225 0301 & 01752 63998 📄 01752 673816
Armada Way PL1 2HJ
e-mail: hiplymouth@qmh-hotels.com
web: www.holidayinn.co.uk
dir: Exit A38 at Plymouth city centre & follow signs for Barbican/Hoe. Into Notte St, left into Hoe Approach, right into Citadel Rd. Hotel on right

Overlooking The Hoe and out towards Plymouth Sound, this modern, high-rise hotel offers extensive facilities, including a leisure club and impressive conference and function rooms. Most bedrooms are very spacious; sea-facing rooms are the most popular. Spectacular, panoramic views of the city can be enjoyed from the restaurant and bar on the top floor.

Rooms 211 (10 fmly) (12 GF) **Facilities** ⊙ Gym Beauty salon Dance studio Sauna Steam room Xmas New Year Wi-fi **Conf** Class 260 Board 60 Thtr 425 **Services** Lift Air con **Parking** 30 (charged) **Notes** LB ⊗ Civ Wed 250

Best Western Duke of Cornwall

★★★ 77% ◉ HOTEL

☎ 01752 275850 & 275855 📄 01752 275854
Millbay Rd PL1 3LG
e-mail: dukereservations@hotmail.com
web: www.thedukeofcornwallhotel.com
dir: follow city centre, then Plymouth Pavilions Conference & Leisure Centre signs

A historic landmark, this city centre hotel is conveniently located. The spacious public areas include a popular bar, comfortable lounge and multi functional ballroom. Bedrooms, many with far reaching views, are individually styled and comfortably appointed. The range of dining options includes meals in the bar, or guests might choose the elegant dining room for a more formal atmosphere.

Rooms 71 (6 fmly) (20 smoking) **S** £105-£230; **D** £120-£230 (incl. bkfst) **Facilities** STV Xmas New Year Wi-fi **Conf** Class 125 Board 84 Thtr 300 Del from £140 to £220 **Services** Lift **Parking** 50 **Notes** LB Civ Wed 300

Langdon Court Hotel & Restaurant

★★★ 77% ◉ HOTEL

☎ 01752 862358 & 07944 483162 📄 01752 863428
Langdon, Wendbury PL9 0DY
e-mail: enquiries@langdoncourt.com
web: www.langdoncourt.co.uk/
dir: from Elburton follow HMS Cambridge signs & tourist signs on A379

This magnificent Grade II listed Tudor manor, set in seven acres of lush countryside, has a direct path leading to the beach at Wembury and coastal footpaths. Bedrooms enjoy countryside views while public areas include a stylish bar and brasserie restaurant where the contemporary menu incorporates local produce with excellent seafood.

Rooms 18 (3 fmly) **S** £79-£129; **D** £99-£169 (incl. bkfst)* **Facilities** FTV ♫ Xmas New Year Wi-fi **Conf** Class 20 Board 15 Thtr 30 Del from £139 to £149* **Parking** 60 **Notes** LB ⊗ Civ Wed 90

Elfordleigh Hotel Golf Leisure

★★★ 74% HOTEL

☎ 01752 336428 ▤ 01752 344581
Colebrook, Plympton PL7 5EB
e-mail: reception@elfordleigh.co.uk
dir: Leave A38 at city centre exit, at Marsh Mills/
Sainsbury's rdbt take Plympton road. At 4th lights left
into Larkham Ln, at end right then left into Crossway. At
end left into The Moors, hotel 1m

Located in the beautiful Plym Valley, this well-established
hotel is set in attractive wooded countryside. Bedrooms,
many with lovely views, are spacious and comfortable.
There is an excellent range of leisure facilities including
an 18-hole golf course. A choice of dining options is
available - a friendly brasserie and the more formal
restaurant.

Rooms 34 (2 fmly) (7 GF) **Facilities** ☜ ⚓ 18 ⛳ Putt
green Fishing ⚓ Gym Squash Hairdresser Beautician
Dance/Aerobics studio 5 aside football pitch (hard) Xmas
Conf Class 120 Board 50 Thtr 200 **Services** Lift
Parking 200 **Notes** LB Civ Wed 200

Invicta

★★★ 74% HOTEL

☎ 01752 664997 ▤ 01752 664994
11-12 Osborne Place, Lockyer St, The Hoe PL1 2PU
e-mail: info@invictahotel.co.uk
web: www.invictahotel.co.uk
dir: A38 to Plymouth, follow city centre signs, then Hoe
Park signs. Hotel opposite park entrance

Just a short stroll from the city centre, this elegant
Victorian establishment stands opposite the famous
bowling green. The atmosphere is relaxed and friendly
and bedrooms are neatly presented, well-equipped and
attractively decorated. Dining options include bar meals
or the more formal setting of the dining room.

Rooms 23 (6 fmly) (1 GF) **Facilities** Xmas Wi-fi
Conf Board 45 **Parking** 14 **Notes** LB ⊗

New Continental

★★★ 73% HOTEL

☎ 01752 220782 ▤ 01752 227013
Millbay Rd PL1 3LD
e-mail: newconti@tiscali.co.uk
web: www.newcontinental.co.uk
dir: A38, follow city centre signs for Continental Ferryport.
Hotel is before ferryport & next to Plymouth Pavilions
Conference Centre

Within easy reach of the city centre and The Hoe, this
privately owned hotel continues to offer high standards of
service and hospitality. A variety of bedroom sizes and
styles is available, all with the same levels of equipment
and comfort. The hotel is a popular choice for conferences
and functions.

Rooms 99 (20 fmly) **S** £70-£93; **D** £85-£108 (incl. bkfst)*
Facilities ☜ supervised Gym Beautician Pool table
Sauna Steam room Wi-fi **Conf** Class 100 Board 70
Thtr 350 **Services** Lift **Parking** 100 (charged) **Notes** LB
⊗ Closed 24 Dec-2 Jan Civ Wed 110

Jurys Inn Plymouth

★★★ 71% HOTEL

☎ 01752 631000
50 Exeter St PL4 0AZ
e-mail: elaine-mellotte@jurysinn.com

Modern, prupose built hotel in a very convenient location
with nearby public parking. Bedrooms provide good guest
comfort and in-room facilities are ideal for both the
business and leisure traveller. Public areas include a
number of meeting rooms, restaurant and a popular bar.

Rooms 247

Novotel Plymouth

★★★ 71% HOTEL

☎ 01752 221422 ▤ 01752 223922
Marsh Mills PL6 8NH
e-mail: h0508@accor.com
web: www.novotel.com
dir: Exit A38 at Marsh Mills, follow Plympton signs, hotel
on left

Conveniently located on the outskirts of the city, close to
Marsh Mills roundabout, this modern hotel offers good
value accommodation. All rooms are spacious and
designed with flexibility for family use. Public areas are
open-plan with meals available throughout the day in
either the Garden Brasserie, the bar, or from room service.

Rooms 100 (17 fmly) (18 GF) **Facilities** ⚑ Xmas New
Year **Conf** Class 120 Board 100 Thtr 300 **Services** Lift
Parking 140 **Notes** LB

Copthorne Hotel Plymouth

Ⓤ

MILLENNIUM

☎ 01752 224161 ▤ 01752 670688
Armada Way PL1 1AR
e-mail: sales.plymouth@millenniumhotels.co.uk
web: www.millenniumhotels.co.uk
dir: from M5 follow A38 to Plymouth city centre. Follow
ferryport signs over 2 rdbts. Hotel on 1st exit left before
4th rdbt

Currently the rating for this establishment was not
confirmed. This may be due to a change of ownership or
because it has only recently joined the AA rating scheme.
For further details please see the AA website:
www.theAA.com

Rooms 135 (29 fmly) **S** £62-£129; **D** £62-£129*
Facilities Gym Xmas New Year Wi-fi **Conf** Class 60
Board 60 Thtr 140 **Del** from £110 to £160* **Services** Lift
Parking 10 (charged) **Notes** ⊗ Civ Wed 65

Ibis Hotel Plymouth

BUDGET HOTEL

☎ 01752 601087 ▤ 01752 223213
Marsh Mills, Longbridge Rd, Forder Valley PL6 8LD
e-mail: H2093@accor-hotels.com
web: www.ibishotel.com
dir: A38 to Plymouth, 1st exit after flyover towards
Estover, Leigham and Parkway Industrial Est. At rdbt,
hotel on 4th exit

Modern, budget hotel offering comfortable
accommodation in bright and practical bedrooms.
Breakfast is self-service and dinner is available in the
restaurant. See also the Hotel Groups pages.

Rooms 52 (26 GF)

Innkeeper's Lodge Plymouth

BUDGET HOTEL

☎ 0845 112 6087 ▤ 0845 112 6216
399 Tavistock Rd PL6 7HB
web: www.innkeeperslodge.com/plymouthroborough
dir: From A38 towards Plymouth onto A386 follow airport
signs. Lodge on left by airport, opposite B3432
(Plymbridge Rd)

Innkeeper's Lodge represents an exciting, high value
concept within the budget hotel market. Comfortable
bedrooms provide excellent facilities that include satellite
TV and modem points. Options include family rooms, and
for the corporate guest, cutting edge IT includes Wi-fi
access. Food is served all day in the adjacent Country
Pub. The extensive continental breakfast is
complimentary.

Rooms 40 **S** £55-£57.50; **D** £55-£57.50 (incl. bkfst)

PLYMOUTH continued

Innkeeper's Lodge Plymouth (Derriford)

BUDGET HOTEL

☎ 0845 112 6088 📠 0845 112 6215
8-9 Howeson Ln PL6 8BB
web: www.innkeeperslodge.com/plymouth
dir: From A38 towards Plymouth. At junct with A386 north towards airport. At Derriford rdbt (hospital & airport), take 3rd exit into Derriford Rd. Lodge on left

Innkeeper's Lodge represents an exciting, high value concept within the budget hotel market. Comfortable bedrooms provide excellent facilities that include satellite TV and modem points. Options include family rooms, and for the corporate guest, cutting edge IT includes Wi-fi access. Food is served all day in the adjacent Country Pub. The extensive continental breakfast is complimentary.

Rooms 75 **S** £55-£57.50; **D** £55-£57.50 (incl. bkfst)
Conf Thtr 30

Travelodge Plymouth

BUDGET HOTEL

☎ 08719 846 251
Derry's Cross PL1 2SW
web: www.travelodge.co.uk

Travelodge offers good quality, good value, modern accommodation. Ideal for families, the spacious en suite bedrooms include remote-control TV, tea and coffee-making facilities and comfortable beds. Meals can be taken at the nearby family restaurant. See also the Hotel Groups pages.

Rooms 96 **S** fr £29; **D** fr £29

ST MARY CHURCH

See Torquay

SALCOMBE   Map 3 SX73

See also **Hope Cove**

Thurlestone

★★★★ 79% ⊛ HOTEL

☎ 01548 560382 📠 01548 561069
TQ7 3NN
e-mail: enquiries@thurlestone.co.uk
web: www.thurlestone.co.uk

(For full entry see Thurlestone)

Soar Mill Cove

★★★★ 78% ⊛⊛ HOTEL

☎ 01548 561566 📠 01548 561223
Soar Mill Cove, Malborough TQ7 3DS
e-mail: info@soarmillcove.co.uk
web: www.soarmillcove.co.uk
dir: 3m W of town off A381 at Malborough. Follow Soar signs

Situated amid spectacular scenery with dramatic sea views, this hotel is ideal for a relaxing stay. Family-run, with a committed team, keen standards of hospitality and service are upheld. Bedrooms are well equipped and many rooms have private terraces. There are different seating areas where impressive cream teas are served, and for the more active, there's a choice of swimming pools. Local produce and seafood are used to good effect in the restaurant.

Rooms 22 (5 fmly) (21 GF) **S** £70-£100; **D** £140-£199 (incl. bkfst) **Facilities** FTV ⌕ 8 ⛳ Putt green Table tennis Games room ♪♪ Xmas New Year Wi-fi **Conf** Class 50 Board 50 Thtr 100 **Parking** 30 **Notes** LB Closed 2 Jan-8 Feb

See advert on this page

Buckland-Tout-Saints

★★★ 85% ⊛⊛
COUNTRY HOUSE HOTEL

☎ 01548 853055 📠 01548 856261
Goveton TQ7 2DS
e-mail: buckland@tout-saints.co.uk
web: www.tout-saints.co.uk

(For full entry see Kingsbridge)

Tides Reach

★★★ 81% ⊛ HOTEL

☎ 01548 843466 📠 01548 843954
South Sands TQ8 8LJ
e-mail: enquire@tidesreach.com
web: www.tidesreach.com
dir: Off A38 at Buckfastleigh to Totnes. Then A381 to Salcombe, follow signs to South Sands

Superbly situated at the water's edge, this personally run, friendly hotel has splendid views of the estuary and beach. Bedrooms, many with balconies, are spacious and comfortable. In the bar and lounge, attentive service can be enjoyed along with the view, and the Garden Room restaurant serves appetising and accomplished cuisine.

Rooms 35 (7 fmly) **S** £75-£143; **D** £124-£320 (incl. bkfst & dinner)* **Facilities** FTV ⌕ supervised Gym Squash Windsurfing Sailing Kayaking Scuba diving Hair & beauty treatment ♪♪ Wi-fi **Services** Lift **Parking** 100 **Notes** LB No children 8yrs Closed Dec-early Feb

---

Soar Mill Cove Hotel

Soar Mill Cove, Malborough,

Salcombe TQ7 3DS

Tel: 01548 561566

Fax: 01548 561223

Email: info@soarmillcove.co.uk

www.soarmillcove.co.uk

SAMPFORD PEVERELL
Map 3 ST01

Travelodge Tiverton

BUDGET HOTEL

☎ 0871 984 6057 📠 01884 821087
Sampford Peverell Service Area EX16 7HD
web: www.travelodge.co.uk
dir: M5 junct 27

Travelodge offers good quality, good value, modern accommodation. Ideal for families, the spacious en suite bedrooms include remote-control TV, tea and coffee-making facilities and comfortable beds. Meals can be taken at the nearby family restaurant. See also the Hotel Groups pages.

Rooms 40 **S** fr £29; **D** fr £29

SAUNTON
Map 3 SS43

Saunton Sands

Brend Hotels

★★★★ 78% HOTEL

☎ 01271 890212 & 892001 📠 01271 890145
EX33 1LQ
e-mail: reservations@sauntonsands.com
web: www.sauntonsands.com
dir: off A361 at Braunton, signed Croyde B3231, hotel 2m on left

Stunning sea views and direct access to five miles of sandy beach are just two of the highlights at this popular hotel. The majority of sea-facing rooms have balconies, and splendid views can be enjoyed from all of the public areas, which include comfortable lounges. The Sands café/bar is a successful innovation and provides an informal eating option.

Rooms 92 (39 fmly) **S** £86-£124; **D** £164-£354*
Facilities STV ⊗ ⬩ ⬩ Putt green Gym Squash OFSTED registered nursery ♫ Xmas New Year Wi-fi Child facilities **Conf** Class 180 Board 50 Thtr 200 **Services** Lift **Parking** 140 **Notes** LB ⊗ Civ Wed 200

See advert on this page

SIDMOUTH
Map 3 SY18

Victoria

Brend Hotels

★★★★ 83% ⊛ HOTEL

☎ 01395 512651 📠 01395 579154
The Esplanade EX10 8RY
e-mail: info@victoriahotel.co.uk
web: www.victoriahotel.co.uk
dir: on seafront

This imposing building, with manicured gardens, is situated overlooking the town. Wonderful sea views can be enjoyed from many of the comfortable bedrooms and elegant lounges. With indoor and outdoor leisure, the hotel caters to a year-round clientele. Carefully prepared meals are served in the refined atmosphere of the restaurant, with staff providing a professional and friendly service.

Rooms 61 (18 fmly) **S** £115-£145; **D** £155-£305*
Facilities STV ⊗ ⬩ ⬩ Putt green ♫ Xmas New Year Wi-fi Child facilities **Conf** Thtr 60 **Services** Lift **Parking** 100 (charged) **Notes** LB ⊗

See advert on page 176

Riviera

★★★★ 80% ⊛⊛ HOTEL

☎ 01395 515201 📠 01395 577775
The Esplanade EX10 8AY
e-mail: enquiries@hotelriviera.co.uk
web: www.hotelriviera.co.uk
dir: M5 junct 30 & follow A3052

Overlooking the sea and close to the town centre, the Riviera is a fine example of Regency architecture. The large number of guests that become regular visitors here pay testament to the high standards of service and hospitality offered. The front-facing bedrooms benefit from wonderful sea views. The daily-changing menu places an emphasis on fresh, local produce.

Rooms 26 (6 fmly) **S** £114-£170; **D** £228-£368 (incl. bkfst & dinner)* **Facilities** Putt green ♫ Xmas New Year **Conf** Class 60 Board 30 Thtr 85 **Services** Lift Air con **Parking** 6 (charged) **Notes** LB

See advert on page 177

The most luxurious choice in East Devon

The Victoria
★ ★ ★ ★ Hotel

Perfectly positioned on Sidmouth's famous esplanade, the Victoria is one of the resort's finest and most picturesque hotels. It's extensive leisure facilities include indoor and outdoor pools, sauna, solarium, spa bath, putting green, tennis court and snooker room. The hotel's resturant has been awarded an AA Rosette for fine cuisine.

Telephone: 01395 512651

www.victoriahotel.co.uk Email: info@victoriahotel.co.uk

The Belmont Hotel
★ ★ ★ ★

The Belmont too commands spectacular views from the famous esplanade. As inviting in January as July, the hotel offers fine cusine and superb service that brings guests back year after year. With the indoor and outdoor leisure facilities of the adjacent Victoria Hotel at your disposal, the Belmont provides the perfect location for your holiday.

Telephone: 01395 512555

www.belmont-hotel.co.uk Email: info@belmont-hotel.co.uk

SIDMOUTH continued

Belmont

★★★★ 75% HOTEL

☎ 01395 512555 📠 01395 579101
The Esplanade EX10 8RX
e-mail: reservations@belmont-hotel.co.uk
web: www.belmont-hotel.co.uk
dir: on seafront

Prominently positioned on the seafront just a few minutes' walk from the town centre, this traditional hotel has a regular following. A choice of comfortable lounges provide ample space for relaxation, and the air-conditioned restaurant has a pianist most evenings. Bedrooms are attractively furnished and many have fine views over the esplanade. Leisure facilities are available at the adjacent sister hotel, the Victoria.

Rooms 50 (4 fmly) (2 GF) **S** £100–£140; **D** £130–£210* **Facilities** STV Putt green ♫ Xmas New Year Wi-fi Child facilities **Conf** Thtr 50 **Services** Lift **Parking** 45 **Notes** LB ⊗ Civ Wed 110

See advert on opposite page

Westcliff

★★★ 80% HOTEL

☎ 01395 513252 📠 01395 578203
Manor Rd EX10 8RU
e-mail: stay@westcliffhotel.co.uk
web: www.westcliffhotel.co.uk
dir: Exit A3052 to Sidmouth then to seafront & esplanade, turn right, hotel directly ahead

This charming hotel is ideally located within walking distance of Sidmouth's elegant promenade and beaches. The spacious lounges and the cocktail bar open onto a terrace which leads to the pool and croquet lawn. Bedrooms, several with balconies and glorious sea views, are spacious and comfortable, whilst the restaurant offers a choice of well-prepared dishes.

Rooms 40 (4 fmly) (5 GF) **S** £60–£120; **D** £80–£220 (incl. bkfst)* **Facilities** ⌁ Putt green ⌁ Pool table Table tennis Xmas New Year Wi-fi **Conf** Class 20 Board 15 Thtr 30 Del from £120 to £180* **Services** Lift **Parking** 40 **Notes** LB Civ Wed 80

Royal Glen

★★★ 73% HOTEL

☎ 01395 513221 & 513456 📠 01395 514922
Glen Rd EX10 8RW
e-mail: info@royalglenhotel.co.uk
dir: A303 to Honiton, A375 to Sidford, follow seafront signs, right onto esplanade, right at end into Glen Rd

This historic 17th-century, Grade I listed hotel has been owned by the same family for several generations. The comfortable bedrooms are furnished in period style. Guests may use the well-maintained gardens and a heated indoor pool, and can enjoy well-prepared food in the dining room.

Rooms 32 (4 fmly) (3 GF) **S** £40–£62; **D** £80–£124 (incl. bkfst)* **Facilities** STV ⌁ **Parking** 14 (charged) **Notes** LB Closed 2 Jan-1 Feb RS Dec

SIDMOUTH continued

Bedford

★★★ 70% HOTEL

☎ 01395 513047 & 0797 394 0671 📠 01395 578563
Esplanade EX10 8NR
e-mail: info@bedfordhotelsidmouth.co.uk
web: www.bedfordhotelsidmouth.co.uk
dir: M5 junct 30/A3052 & to Sidmouth. Hotel at centre of Esplanade

Situated on the seafront, this long established, family-run hotel provides a warm welcome and relaxing atmosphere. Bedrooms are well appointed and many have the added bonus of wonderful sea views. Public areas combine character and comfort with a choice of lounges in which to relax. In addition to the hotel dining room, Pyne's bar and restaurant is also available, offering an interesting range of dishes in a convivial environment.

Rooms 37 (1 GF) **S** £48-£82; **D** £96-£164 (incl. bkfst & dinner)* **Facilities** Xmas **Services** Lift **Parking** 6

Kingswood

★★ 79% HOTEL

☎ 01395 516367 📠 01395 513185
The Esplanade EX10 8AX
e-mail: kingswood@hotels-sidmouth.co.uk
web: www.hotels-sidmouth.co.uk
dir: take A375 off A3052 towards seafront. Hotel in centre of Esplanade

Super standards of hospitality are only surpassed by this hotel's prominent position on the esplanade. All bedrooms have modern facilities and some enjoy the stunning sea views. The two lounges offer comfort and space and the attractive dining room serves good traditional cooking.

Rooms 26 (7 fmly) (2 GF) **S** £54-£76; **D** £54-£76 (incl. bkfst & dinner)* **Facilities** Guests receive vouchers for local swimming pool Discounts for local golf course Xmas **Services** Lift **Parking** 17 **Notes** Closed 28 Dec-9 Feb

Royal York & Faulkner

★★ 79% HOTEL

☎ 01395 513043 & 0800 220714 📠 01395 577472
The Esplanade EX10 8AZ
e-mail: stay@royalyorkhotel.co.uk
web: www.royalyorkhotel.co.uk
dir: M5 junct 30 take A3052, 10m to Sidmouth, hotel in centre of Esplanade

This seafront hotel, owned and run by the same family for generations, maintains its Regency charm and grandeur. The attractive bedrooms vary in size; many have balconies and sea views. Public rooms are spacious and traditional dining is offered plus Blinis Café-Bar, which is more contemporary in style and offers coffees, lunch and afternoon teas. The spa facilities include a hydrotherapy pool, steam room, sauna and a variety of treatments.

Rooms 70 (2 annexe) (8 fmly) (5 GF) **S** £52-£92; **D** £104-£184 (incl. bkfst & dinner)* **Facilities** Spa ⊛ Steam cabin Snooker table Sauna ♬ Xmas New Year Wi-fi **Services** Lift **Parking** 20 **Notes** LB Closed Jan

Hotel Elizabeth

★★ 78% HOTEL

☎ 01395 513503 📠 01395 578000
The Esplanade EX10 8AT
e-mail: elizabeth@hotels-sidmouth.co.uk
web: www.hotels-sidmouth.co.uk
dir: M5 junct 30, then A3052 to Sidmouth. 1st exit on right to Sidmouth, then left onto esplanade

Occupying a prime location on Sidmouth's dignified Esplanade, this elegant hotel attracts many loyal guests who return to enjoy the relaxed atmosphere and attentive service. Bedrooms are both comfortable and smartly appointed; all have sea views and some have balconies. The spacious lounge and sunny patio, with wonderful views across the bay, are perfect places to sit and watch the world go by.

Rooms 28 (3 fmly) (1 GF) **S** £54-£76; **D** £108-£112 (incl. bkfst & dinner)* **Facilities** FTV Xmas **Services** Lift **Parking** 16 **Notes** ⊛ Closed 28 Dec-10 Feb

Mount Pleasant

★★ 78% HOTEL

☎ 01395 514694
Salcombe Rd EX10 8JA
dir: exit A3052 at Sidford x-rds, in 1.25m turn left into Salcombe Rd, opposite Radway Cinema. Hotel on right after bridge

Quietly located within almost an acre of gardens, this modernised Georgian hotel is minutes from the town centre and seafront. Bedrooms and public areas provide good levels of comfort and high quality furnishings. Guests return on a regular basis especially for the friendly, relaxed atmosphere. The light and airy restaurant that overlooks the pleasant garden, offers a

daily-changing menu of imaginative, yet traditional home-cooked dishes.

Rooms 17 (1 fmly) (3 GF) **S** £54-£68; **D** £108-£136 (incl. bkfst & dinner)* **Facilities** Putt green **Parking** 20 **Notes** ⊛ No children 8yrs Closed Dec-Feb

Devoran

★★ 76% HOTEL

☎ 01395 513151 📠 01395 579929
Esplanade EX10 8AU
e-mail: devoran@hotels-sidmouth.co.uk
web: www.hotels-sidmouth.co.uk
dir: turn off B3052 at Bowd Inn, follow Sidmouth sign for approx 2m, turn left onto seafront, hotel 50yds at centre of Esplanade

This long established hotel is located in the heart of Sidmouth's elegant esplanade, and refurbishment has resulted in high standards throughout. The elegant public rooms have wonderful sea views. Bedrooms are neatly presented, and some have sea facing balconies. Dinner is an enjoyable and civilised occasion with caring staff ensuring a relaxing and pleasant experience.

Rooms 24 (5 fmly) **S** £48-£72; **D** £76-£144 (incl. bkfst & dinner)* **Facilities** FTV Wi-fi **Services** Lift **Parking** 3 (charged) **Notes** ⊛ Closed 30 Oct-10 Mar

Hunters Moon

★★ 76% HOTEL

☎ 01395 513380 📠 01395 514270
Sid Rd EX10 9AA
e-mail: huntersmoon.hotel@virgin.net
dir: from Exeter on A3052 to Sidford, right at lights into Sidmouth, 1.5m, at cinema turn left. Hotel in 0.25m

Set amid three acres of attractive and well-tended grounds, this friendly, family-run hotel is peacefully located in a quiet area within walking distance of the town and esplanade. The light and airy bedrooms, some located at ground floor level, are comfortable and well equipped. There is a lounge and a cosy bar. Dining provides a choice of imaginative dishes and tea may be taken on the lawn.

Rooms 33 (4 fmly) (11 GF) **S** £71-£75; **D** £124-£142 (incl. bkfst & dinner)* **Facilities** Putt green Xmas Wi-fi **Parking** 33 **Notes** LB No children 3yrs Closed Jan-9 Feb RS Dec & Feb

The Woodlands Hotel

★★ 72% HOTEL

☎ 01395 513120 📠 01395 513348
Cotmaton Cross EX10 8HG
e-mail: info@woodlands-hotel.com
web: www.woodlands-hotel.com
dir: follow signs for Sidmouth

Located in the heart of the town and ideally situated for exploring Devon and Dorset, this listed property has numerous character features. There is a spacious bar and

modern comforts. The restaurant is a relaxed location for enjoying innovative food, and the hotel offers the benefit of a smart conservatory ideal for functions and limited courtyard parking.

Rooms 27 (2 annexe) (2 fmly) **Facilities** Wi-fi **Conf** Class 40 Board 40 Thtr 80 **Parking** 12 **Notes** ⊗ Closed 23-30 Dec

EVERSHOT — Map 4 ST50

INSPECTORS' CHOICE

Summer Lodge Country House Hotel, Restaurant & Spa

★★★★ ◉◉◉ COUNTRY HOUSE HOTEL

☎ 01935 482000 ≣ 01935 482040
DT2 0JR
e-mail: summer@relaischateaux.com
dir: 1m W of A37 halfway between Dorchester & Yeovil

This picturesque hotel is situated in the heart of Dorset and is the ideal retreat for getting away from it all. It's worth arriving in time for afternoon tea. Bedrooms are appointed to a very high standard; they are individually designed with upholstered walls and come with a wealth of luxurious facilities. Delightful public areas include a sumptuous lounge complete with an open fire and the elegant restaurant where the cuisine continues to be the high point of any stay.

Rooms 24 (14 annexe) (6 fmly) (2 GF) (1 smoking) **S** £195-£515; **D** £225-£515 (incl. bkfst)* **Facilities** Spa STV FTV ◉ ♨ ♨ Gym Xmas New Year Wi-fi **Conf** Class 16 Board 16 Thtr 24 **Services** Air con **Parking** 40 **Notes** LB Civ Wed 30

FERNDOWN — Map 5 SU00

Bridge House

★★ 🅰 HOTEL

☎ 01202 578828 ≣ 01202 572620
2 Ringwood Rd, Longham BH22 9AN
e-mail: 6416@greeneking.co.uk
web: www.oldenglish.co.uk
dir: on A348 towards Poole

Rooms 33 (4 fmly) (1 GF) **Facilities** Fishing ♫ Xmas **Conf** Class 60 Board 50 Thtr 120 **Parking** 300 **Notes** LB ⊗ Civ Wed 120

GILLINGHAM — Map 4 ST82

INSPECTORS' CHOICE

Stock Hill Country House Hotel & Restaurant

★★★ ◉◉ COUNTRY HOUSE HOTEL

☎ 01747 823626 & 822741 ≣ 01747 825628
Stock Hill SP8 5NR
e-mail: reception@stockhillhouse.co.uk
web: www.stockhillhouse.co.uk
dir: 3m E on B3081, off A303

Set in eleven acres, this lovely hotel has an impressive beech-lined driveway and beautiful gardens. The luxurious bedrooms, tastefully furnished with antiques, combine high standards of comfort with modern facilities. Public rooms are delightful in every way with sumptuous fabrics and furnishings. The complete tranquillity makes taking tea in front of fires a very enjoyable experience. Accomplished cooking based on top-quality local ingredients shows strong Austrian influences. Nita and Peter Hauser and their team are clearly dedicated to their guests' enjoyment of this small hotel.

Rooms 9 (3 annexe) (3 GF) **S** £135-£165; **D** £250-£320 (incl. bkfst & dinner)* **Facilities** ♨ ♨ Croquet Bird watching Xmas New Year **Conf** Thtr 12 Del from £165 to £220* **Parking** 20 **Notes** LB ⊗ No children 7yrs

LYME REGIS — Map 4 SY39

Hotel Alexandra and Restaurant

★★★ 76% ◉ HOTEL

☎ 01297 442010 ≣ 01297 443229
Pound St DT7 3HZ
e-mail: enquiries@hotelalexandra.co.uk
dir: from A30 , A35, then onto A358, A3052 to Lyme Regis

This welcoming, family-run hotel is Grade II listed and dates back to 1735. Public areas are spacious and comfortable, with ample seating areas to relax, unwind and enjoy the magnificent views. The elegant restaurant offers imaginative, innovative dishes. Bedrooms vary in size and shape, and are decorated with pretty chintz fabrics and attractive furniture.

Rooms 25 (1 annexe) (3 fmly) (3 GF) **S** £65; **D** £105-£165 (incl. bkfst)* **Facilities** Child facilities **Conf** Class 30 Board 25 Thtr 60 **Parking** 17 **Notes** ⊗ Closed Xmas & Jan Civ Wed 75

Royal Lion

★★ 69% HOTEL

☎ 01297 445622 ≣ 01297 445859
Broad St DT7 3QF
e-mail: enquiries@royallionhotel.com
web: www.royallionhotel.com
dir: From W on A35, take A3052 or from E take B3165 to Lyme Regis. Hotel in centre of town, opp The Fossil Shop

This 17th-century, former coaching inn is full of character and charm, and is situated a short walk from the seafront. Bedrooms vary in size; those in the newer wing are more spacious and some have balconies, sea views or a private terrace. In addition to the elegant dining room and guest lounges, a heated pool, jacuzzi, sauna and small gym are available. There is a car park at the rear.

Rooms 29 (11 fmly) **Facilities** ◉ Gym Games room Pool table Table tennis New Year Wi-fi **Conf** Class 20 Board 20 Thtr 50 **Parking** 30 **Notes** LB Closed 24-26 Dec

Swallows Eaves

☎ 01297 553184 ≣ 01297 553574
Swan Hill Rd EX24 6QJ
e-mail: swallows_eaves@hotmail.com
web: www.lymeregis.com/swallowseaveshotel

(For full entry see Colyford (Devon))

MUDEFORD

See Christchurch

POOLE — Map 4 SZ09

Harbour Heights

★★★★ 80% ⚛⚛ HOTEL

☎ 01202 707272 & 0845 337 1550 ▤ 01202 708594
73 Haven Rd, Sandbanks BH13 7LW
e-mail: enquiries@harbourheights.net
web: www.fjbhotels.co.uk
dir: Follow signs for Sandbanks, hotel on left after
Canford Cliffs

The unassuming appearance of this hotel belies a wealth of innovation, quality and style. The very stylish, contemporary bedrooms, many with sea views, combine state-of-the-art facilities with traditional comforts; all have spa baths. The smart public areas include the Harbar brasserie, popular bars and sitting areas where picture windows accentuate panoramic views of Poole Harbour. The sun deck is the perfect setting for watching the cross-channel ferries come and go.

Rooms 38 (2 fmly) **S** £165-£215; **D** £260-£360 (incl. bkfst)* **Facilities** STV Spa bath in all rooms Xmas New Year Wi-fi **Conf** Class 36 Board 22 Thtr 70 Del from £175 to £195* **Services** Lift Air con **Parking** 50 **Notes** LB ⊗ Civ Wed 120

See advert on page 189

Sandbanks

★★★★ 74% ⚛ HOTEL

☎ 01202 707377 & 0845 337 1550 ▤ 01202 708885
15 Banks Rd, Sandbanks BH13 7PS
e-mail: reservations@sandbankshotel.co.uk
web: www.fjbhotels.co.uk
dir: A338 from Bournemouth onto Wessex Way, to Liverpool Victoria rdbt. Left, then 2nd exit onto B3965. Hotel on left

Set on the delightful Sandbanks Peninsula, this well loved hotel has direct access to the blue flag beach and stunning views across Poole Harbour. Most of the

spacious bedrooms have sea view; some are air-conditioned. There is an extensive range of leisure facilities, including a state-of-the-art crèche.

Rooms 110 (31 fmly) (4 GF) **S** £75-£155; **D** £150-£310 (incl. bkfst)* **Facilities** Spa STV FTV ⊗ supervised Gym Sailing Mountain bikes Children's play area Massage room Xmas New Year Wi-fi Child facilities **Conf** Class 40 Board 25 Thtr 150 Del from £120 to £150* **Services** Lift **Parking** 120 **Notes** LB ⊗ Civ Wed 70

See advert on page 189

Haven

★★★★ 73% ⚛⚛ HOTEL

☎ 01202 707333 & 0845 337 1550 ▤ 01202 708796
Banks Rd, Sandbanks BH13 7QL
e-mail: reservations@havenhotel.co.uk
web: www.fjbhotels.co.uk
dir: B3965 towards Poole Bay, left onto the Peninsula. Hotel 1.5m on left next to Swanage Toll Ferry point

Enjoying an enviable location at the water's edge with views of Poole Bay, this well established hotel was once the home of radio pioneer, Guglielmo Marconi. A friendly team of staff provide good levels of customer care. Bedrooms vary in size and style; many have balconies and wonderful sea views. Leisure facilities are noteworthy.

Rooms 78 (4 fmly) **S** £100-£145; **D** £200-£440 (incl. bkfst)* **Facilities** Spa STV ⊗ supervised ⊗ supervised ⊗ Dance studio Health & Beauty suite Sauna Steam room Xmas New Year Wi-fi **Conf** Class 70 Board 50 Thtr 160 **Services** Lift **Parking** 160 **Notes** LB ⊗ Civ Wed 100

See advert on page 189

Thistle Poole

★★★ 79% ⚛ HOTEL — **thistle**

☎ 0871 376 9032 ▤ 0871 376 9132
The Quay BH15 1HD
e-mail: poole@thistle.co.uk
web: www.thistlehotels.com/poole
dir: on quay next to Dolphin Marina

Situated on the quayside overlooking the harbour, this modern hotel is situated close to the ferry terminal and is also a good base for exploring the beautiful Dorset countryside. Many of the bedrooms have views of Poole harbour. There is a restaurant and two bars, plus two meeting rooms are available.

Rooms 70 (24 GF) **Facilities** Xmas New Year Wi-fi **Conf** Class 50 Board 50 Thtr 180 **Services** Lift **Parking** 120 (charged) **Notes** Civ Wed 80

Arndale Court

★★★ 68% HOTEL

☎ 01202 683746 ▤ 01202 668838
62/66 Wimborne Rd BH15 2BY
e-mail: info@arndalecourthotel.com
web: www.arndalecourthotel.com
dir: on A349, opp Poole Stadium

Ideally situated for the town centre and ferry terminal, this is a small, privately owned hotel. Bedrooms are well equipped, spacious and comfortable. Particularly well suited to business guests, this hotel has a pleasant range of stylish public areas and good parking.

Rooms 39 (7 fmly) (14 GF) **Facilities** Wi-fi **Conf** Class 35 Board 35 Thtr 50 **Parking** 40

Salterns Harbourside

★★★ 68% HOTEL

☎ 01202 707321 ▤ 01202 707488
38 Salterns Way, Lilliput BH14 8JR
e-mail: reception@salterns-hotel.co.uk
web: www.salterns-hotel.co.uk
dir: in Poole follow B3369 Sandbanks road. 1m at Lilliput shops turn into Salterns Way by Barclays Bank

Located next to the marina with superb views across to Brownsea Island, this modernised hotel used to be the headquarters for the flying boats in WWII and was later a yacht club. Bedrooms are spacious and some have private balconies, whilst the busy bar and restaurant both share harbour views.

Rooms 20 (4 fmly) **S** £70-£100; **D** £80-£130 (incl. bkfst)
Facilities Xmas Wi-fi **Conf** Class 50 Board 30 Thtr 100
Parking 40 **Notes** LB Civ Wed 120

Quarterdeck

★★ 71% HOTEL

☎ 01202 740066 ▤ 01202 736780
2 Sandbanks Rd BH14 8AQ
e-mail: reception@quarterdeckhotel.co.uk
dir: A35 to Civic Centre, hotel next to Poole Park, opposite
police station

A family run hotel adjacent to Poole Park and close to
Poole Harbour and Dorset beaches. Bedrooms are
comfortable and well equipped. Enjoy afternoon tea in the
cosy lounge, a drink in the bar and dinner in the colourful
restaurant. There's a sun terrace perfect for the summer
months.

Rooms 15 (5 GF) **S** £68-£88; **D** £78-£98 (incl. bkfst)*
Facilities Wi-fi **Parking** 30 **Notes** ⊗

Antelope Inn

★★ Ⓐ

☎ 01202 672029 ▤ 01202 678286
8 High St BH15 1BP
e-mail: 6603@greeneking.co.uk
web: www.oldenglish.co.uk

Rooms 21 (2 fmly) **Facilities** Xmas **Parking** 17 **Notes** LB

Hotel du Vin Poole

Ⓤ HOTEL

☎ 01202 685666 ▤ 01202 665709
Thames St BH15 1JN
web: www.hotelduvin.com
dir: A31 to Poole, follow channel ferry signs. Left at Poole
bridge onto Poole Quay, 1st left into Thames St. Hotel
opposite St James Church

Currently the rating for this establishment is not
confirmed. This may be due to a change of ownership or
because it has only recently joined the AA rating scheme.
For further details please see the AA website:
www.theAA.com

Hotel du Vin - AA Small Hotel Group of the Year 2008-9.

Rooms 38

Express by Holiday Inn Poole

BUDGET HOTEL

☎ 01202 649222 ▤ 01202 649666
Walking Field Ln, Seldown Bridge Site BH15 1TJ
e-mail: sales@exhipoole.co.uk
web: www.hiexpress.com/pooleuk
dir: A350 to town centre, pass bus station. Right at next
rdbt, take slip road to left. Hotel next to Dolphin
Swimming Pool

A modern hotel ideal for families and business travellers.
Fresh and uncomplicated, the spacious rooms include Sky
TV, power shower and tea and coffee-making facilities.
Continental buffet breakfast is included in the room rate;
evening meals are available in the spacious café/bar. See
also the Hotel Groups pages.

Rooms 85 (42 fmly) **Conf** Class 16 Board 18 Thtr 30

ST LEONARDS — Map 5 SU10

St Leonards

★★ Ⓐ HOTEL

☎ 01425 471220 ▤ 01425 480274
Ringwood Rd BH24 2NP
e-mail: 9230@greeneking.co.uk
web: www.oldenglish.co.uk
dir: At end of M27 continue to 1st rdbt. Take slip road on
left

Rooms 35 (5 fmly) (15 GF) **Facilities** Xmas **Conf** Class 40
Board 40 Thtr 100 **Services** Lift **Parking** 50 **Notes** LB
Civ Wed 60

SANDBANKS

See Poole

SHAFTESBURY — Map 4 ST82

Best Western Royal Chase

★★★ 71% ⊛ HOTEL

☎ 01747 853355 ▤ 01747 851969
Royal Chase Roundabout SP7 8DB
e-mail: royalchasehotel@btinternet.com
web: www.theroyalchasehotel.co.uk
dir: A303 to A350 signed Blandford Forum. Avoid town
centre, follow road to 3rd rdbt

Equally suitable for both leisure and business guests,
this well-known local landmark is situated close to the
famous Gold Hill. Both Standard and Crown bedrooms
offer good levels of comfort and quality. In addition to the
fixed-price menu in the Byzant Restaurant, guests have
the option of eating more informally in the convivial bar.

Rooms 33 (13 fmly) (6 GF) **S** £54-£160; **D** £54-£160*
Facilities ⓣ Turkish steam room Xmas New Year Wi-fi
Conf Class 90 Board 50 Thtr 180 Del from £112.50 to
£121.50* **Parking** 100 **Notes** LB Civ Wed 76

La Fleur de Lys Restaurant with Rooms

⊛⊛ RESTAURANT WITH ROOMS

☎ 01747 853717 ▤ 01747 853130
Bleke St SP7 8AW
e-mail: info@lafleurdelys.co.uk
dir: 0.25m off the junct of A30 with A350 at Shaftesbury
towards town centre

Located just a few minutes walk from the famous Gold
Hill, this light and airy restaurant with rooms combines
efficient service in a relaxed and friendly atmosphere.
Bedrooms, which are suitable for both business and
leisure guests, vary in size but all are well equipped,
comfortable and tastefully furnished. A relaxing guest
lounge and courtyard are available for afternoon tea or
pre-dinner drinks.

Rooms 7 (4 en suite) (2 fmly) (1 GF)

SHERBORNE — Map 4 ST61

The Grange at Oborne

★★★ 79% HOTEL

☎ 01935 813463 ▤ 01935 817464
Oborne DT9 4LA
e-mail: reception@thegrange.co.uk
web: www.thegrangeatoborne.co.uk
dir: Turn off A30 & follow signs through village

Set in beautiful gardens in a quiet hamlet, this 200-year-
old, family run, country-house hotel has a wealth of
charm and character. It offers friendly hospitality
together with attentive service. Bedrooms are comfortable
and tastefully appointed. Public areas are elegantly
furnished and the popular restaurant offers a good
selection of dishes.

Rooms 18 (3 fmly) (5 GF) **S** £90-£100; **D** £109-£150 (incl.
bkfst) **Facilities** Guest laundry Xmas New Year Wi-fi
Conf Class 40 Board 30 Thtr 80 Del from £115 to £125*
Parking 45 **Notes** LB ⊗ Civ Wed 80

SHERBORNE continued

Eastbury

★★★ 75% ◎◎ HOTEL

☎ 01935 813131 📄 01935 817296
Long St DT9 3BY
e-mail: enquiries@theeastburyhotel.co.uk
web: www.theeastburyhotel.co.uk
dir: From A30 westbound, left into North Rd, then St Swithin's, left at bottom, hotel 800yds on right

Much of the original Georgian charm and elegance is maintained at this smart, comfortable hotel. Just five minutes' stroll from the abbey and close to the town centre, the Eastbury's friendly and attentive staff ensure a relaxed and enjoyable stay. Award-winning cuisine is served in the attractive dining room that overlooks the walled garden.

Rooms 23 (1 fmly) (3 GF) **S** £68; **D** £125-£165 (incl. bkfst)* **Facilities** STV FTV ⚓ New Year **Conf** Class 40 Board 28 Thtr 80 Del from £121 to £166* **Parking** 30 **Notes** LB ⊗ Civ Wed 80

The Sherborne Hotel

★★ 62% HOTEL

☎ 01935 813191 📄 01935 816493
Horsecastles Ln DT9 6BB
e-mail: info@sherbornehotel.co.uk
dir: at junction of A30 & A352

This hotel has an attractive setting, within its own grounds, and provides a quiet location. Bedrooms are spacious and well equipped. The open-plan lounge and bar area are comfortable and satellite TV is available in this area. Cuisine offers a good range of choice and the dining room looks out to the garden.

Rooms 60 (24 GF) **Facilities** ⚓ Xmas New Year Wi-fi **Conf** Class 35 Board 30 Thtr 80 Del from £70 to £90* **Parking** 90 **Notes** ⊗

SWANAGE Map 5 SZ07

Purbeck House

★★★ 72% HOTEL

☎ 01929 422872 📄 01929 421194
91 High St BH19 2LZ
e-mail: reservations@purbeckhousehotel.co.uk
web: www.purbeckhousehotel.co.uk
dir: A351 to Swanage via Wareham, right into Shore Road, on into Institute Road, right into High Street

Located close to the town centre, this former convent is set in well-tended grounds. The attractive bedrooms are located in the original building and also in an annexe. In addition to a very pleasant and spacious conservatory, the smartly presented public areas have some stunning features, such as painted ceilings, wood panelling and fine tiled floors.

Rooms 38 (20 annexe) (5 fmly) (10 GF) **Facilities** ⚓ New Year Wi-fi **Conf** Class 36 Board 25 Thtr 100 **Parking** 50 **Notes** LB ⊗ Civ Wed 100

The Pines

★★★ 71% HOTEL

☎ 01929 425211 📠 01929 422075
Burlington Rd BH19 1LT
e-mail: reservations@pineshotel.co.uk
web: www.pineshotel.co.uk
dir: A351 to seafront, left then 2nd right. Hotel at end of road

Enjoying a peaceful location with spectacular views over the cliffs and sea, The Pines is a pleasant place to stay. Many of the comfortable bedrooms have sea views. Guests can take tea in the lounge, enjoy appetising bar snacks in the attractive bar, and interesting and accomplished cuisine in the restaurant.

Rooms 41 (26 fmly) (6 GF) **S** £63; **D** £126-£152 (incl. bkfst)* **Facilities** ♫ Xmas New Year **Conf** Class 80 Board 80 Thtr 80 Del from £92.40* **Services** Lift **Parking** 60 **Notes** LB

See advert on opposite page

Grand

★★★ 70% HOTEL

☎ 01929 423353 📠 01929 427068
Burlington Rd BH19 1LU
e-mail: reservations@grandhotelswanage.co.uk
web: www.grandhotelswanage.co.uk

Dating back to 1898, this hotel is located on the Isle of Purbeck and has spectacular views across Swanage Bay and Peveril Point. Bedrooms are individually decorated and well equipped; public rooms offer a number of choices from relaxing lounges to extensive leisure facilities. The hotel also has its own private beach.

Rooms 30 (2 fmly) **Facilities** ⚲ supervised Fishing Gym Table tennis Xmas **Conf** Class 40 Board 40 Thtr 120 **Services** Lift **Parking** 15 **Notes** ⊗ Closed 10 days in Jan (dates on application) Civ Wed

---

WAREHAM Map 4 SY98

Worgret Manor

★★★ 73% HOTEL

☎ 01929 552957 📠 01929 554804
Worgret Rd BH20 6AB
e-mail: admin@worgretmanorhotel.co.uk
web: www.worgretmanorhotel.co.uk
dir: on A352 (Wareham to Wool), 500mtrs from Wareham rdbt

On the edge of Wareham, with easy access to major routes, this privately owned Georgian manor house has a friendly, cheerful atmosphere. The bedrooms come in a variety of sizes. Public rooms are well presented and comprise a popular bar, a quiet lounge and an airy restaurant.

Rooms 12 (1 fmly) (3 GF) **S** £65-£80; **D** £110-£120 (incl. bkfst)* **Facilities** Wi-fi **Conf** Class 20 Board 20 Thtr 40 Del from £125 to £140* **Parking** 30 **Notes** LB

WEST BAY
See Bridport

WEST BEXINGTON Map 4 SY58

The Manor

★★ 74% HOTEL

☎ 01308 897616 📠 01308 897704
Beach Rd DT2 9DF
e-mail: themanorhotel@btconnect.com
dir: B3157 to Burton Bradstock, continue to The Bull public house in Swire. Immediately right to West Bexington.

Surrounded by scenic splendour and just a short stroll from the magnificent sweep of Chesil Beach, the atmosphere is relaxed and welcoming with snug lounges and crackling wood fires. Bedrooms are individual in style, many with wonderful sea views and the sound of

---

waves in the background. With an abundance of excellent local produce, dining here, in either the convivial Cellar Bar, or the elegant dining room is recommended.

Rooms 13 (2 fmly) **Facilities** Xmas New Year **Conf** Class 40 Board 40 Thtr 40 **Parking** 80 **Notes** Civ Wed 65

WEST LULWORTH Map 4 SY88

Cromwell House

★★ 75% HOTEL

☎ 01929 400253 & 400332 📠 01929 400566
Lulworth Cove BH20 5RJ
e-mail: catriona@lulworthcove.co.uk
web: www.lulworthcove.co.uk
dir: 200yds beyond end of West Lulworth, left onto high slip road, hotel 100yds on left opposite beach car park

Built in 1881 by the Mayor of Weymouth, specifically as a guest house, this family-run hotel now provides visitors with an ideal base for touring the area and for exploring the beaches and coast. Cromwell House enjoys spectacular views across the sea and countryside. Bedrooms, many with sea views, are comfortable and some have been specifically designed for family use.

Rooms 18 (1 annexe) (3 fmly) (2 GF) **S** £40-£65; **D** £80-£105 (incl. bkfst) **Facilities** ⚲ Access to Dorset coastal footpath & Jurassic Coast **Parking** 17 **Notes** LB Closed 22 Dec-3 Jan

Moonfleet Manor

★★★ 75% ⚙⚙
COUNTRY HOUSE HOTEL

☎ 01305 786948 📄 01305 774395
Fleet DT3 4ED
e-mail: info@moonfleetmanorhotel.co.uk
web: www.moonfleetmanor.com
dir: A354 to Weymouth, right on B3157 to Bridport. At Chickerell left at mini rdbt to Fleet

This enchanting hideaway, peacefully located at the end of the village of Fleet, enjoys a wonderful sea-facing position. Children are especially welcomed throughout the hotel. Many of the well-equipped bedrooms overlook Chesil Beach and the hotel is furnished with style and panache, particularly in the sumptuous lounges.. Accomplished cuisine is served in the beautiful restaurant.

Rooms 39 (6 annexe) (26 fmly) **Facilities** 🏊 supervised 🎱 🏌 Squash Children's nursery Xmas **Conf** Class 18 Board 26 Thtr 50 **Services** Lift **Parking** 50 **Notes** LB

Hotel Rembrandt

★★★ 73% HOTEL

☎ 01305 764000 📄 01305 764022
12-18 Dorchester Rd DT4 7JU
e-mail: reception@hotelrembrandt.co.uk
web: www.hotelrembrandt.co.uk
dir: 0.75m on left after Manor Rdbt on A354 from Dorchester

Only a short distance from the seafront and town centre, this hotel is ideal for visiting local attractions. Facilities include indoor leisure, a bar and extensive meeting rooms. The restaurant offers impressive carvery and carte menu choices and is popular with locals and residents alike.

Rooms 78 (4 fmly) (7 GF) **S** £45.50-£99; **D** £91-£125 (incl. bkfst) **Facilities** STV 🏊 Gym Steam room Sauna Wi-fi **Conf** Class 100 Board 60 Thtr 200 Del from £109 to £115 **Services** Lift **Parking** 80 **Notes** LB ⊗ Civ Wed 100

Best Western Hotel Prince Regent

★★★ 71% HOTEL

☎ 01305 771313 📄 01305 778100
139 The Esplanade DT4 7NR
e-mail: info@princeregentweymouth.co.uk
web: www.princeregentweymouth.co.uk
dir: from A354 follow seafront signs. Left at Jubilee Clock, 25mtrs on seafront

Dating back to 1855, this welcoming resort hotel boasts splendid views over Weymouth Bay from the majority of public rooms and front-facing bedrooms. It is conveniently close to the town centre and harbour, and is opposite the beach. The restaurant offers a choice of menus, and entertainment is regularly provided in the ballroom during the season.

Rooms 70 (14 fmly) (5 GF) **S** £52-£95; **D** £75-£115 (incl. bkfst)* **Facilities** STV Xmas New Year Wi-fi **Conf** Class 150 Board 150 Thtr 180 Del from £89 to £99* **Services** Lift **Parking** 13 **Notes** LB ⊗ Civ Wed 200

See advert on this page

Hotel Rex

★★★ 67% HOTEL

☎ 01305 760400 📄 01305 760500
29 The Esplanade DT4 8DN
e-mail: rex@kingshotels.co.uk
web: www.kingshotels.co.uk
dir: on seafront opp Alexandra Gardens

Originally built as the summer residence for the Duke of Clarence, this hotel benefits from its seafront location with stunning views across Weymouth Bay. Bedrooms include several sea-facing rooms and all are well equipped. A wide range of imaginative dishes is served in the popular vaulted restaurant.

Rooms 31 (5 fmly) S £57-£72; D £94-£124 (incl. bkfst)*
Facilities New Year Wi-fi Conf Class 30 Board 25 Thtr 40
Services Lift Parking 6 (charged) Notes LB ⊗ Closed
Xmas

Crown

★★ 71% HOTEL

☎ 01305 760800 📄 01305 760300
51-53 St Thomas St DT4 8EQ
e-mail: crown@kingshotels.co.uk
web: www.kingshotels.co.uk
dir: From Dorchester, A354 to Weymouth. Follow Back
Water on left & cross 2nd bridge

This popular hotel is conveniently located adjacent to the
old harbour and is ideal for shopping, local attractions
and transportation links, including the ferry. Public areas
include an extensive bar, ballroom and comfortable
residents' lounge on the first floor. Themed events, such
as mock cruises, are a speciality.

Rooms 86 (15 fmly) S £48-£53; D £90-£100 (incl. bkfst)*
Facilities ♫ New Year Services Lift Parking 6 (charged)
Notes LB ⊗ Closed 25-26 Dec

Central

★★ 69% HOTEL

☎ 01305 760700 📄 01305 760300
17-19 Maiden St DT4 8BB
e-mail: central@kingshotels.co.uk

Centrally located for both the town and the beach with
some off road parking, this hotel offers comfortable
bedrooms and friendly staff. It is privately owned and has
sister properties nearby.

Rooms 28 (5 fmly) (4 GF) S £40-£49; D £60-£86 (incl.
bkfst)* Facilities ♫ Services Lift Parking 16 (charged)
Notes LB ⊗ Closed mid Dec-1 Mar

Fairhaven

★★ 68% HOTEL

☎ 01305 760200 📄 01305 760300
37 The Esplanade DT4 8DH
e-mail: fairhaven@kingshotels.co.uk
dir: on right just before Alexandra Gardens

A popular sea facing, family-run hotel which has a
friendly young team of staff. Bedrooms are comfortable
and well maintained, and the hotel boasts two bars, one
with panoramic views of the bay. Entertainment is
provided most nights during the season.

Rooms 82 (23 fmly) (1 GF) S £40-£49; D £60-£86 (incl.
bkfst)* Facilities ♫ Services Lift Parking 16 (charged)
Notes LB ⊗ Closed Nov-1 Mar

Russell

★★ 68% HOTEL

☎ 01305 786059 📄 01305 775723
135-13 The Esplanade DT4 7NG
e-mail: russell@hollybushhotels.co.uk
dir: 500yds from Clock Tower on Esplanade

This hotel offers comfortable and spacious
accommodation. It is situated on the seafront so many
rooms benefit from magnificent views. With a sister hotel
next door, banqueting facilities in a superb ballroom can
be offered. Live music and entertainment are also
provided.

Rooms 93 (23 GF) Facilities ♫ Xmas Services Lift
Parking 20 Notes LB ⊗ No children 18yrs

WIMBORNE MINSTER   Map 5 SZ06

Kings Head

★★ Ⓐ HOTEL

☎ 01202 880101 📄 01202 881667
The Square BH21 1JG
e-mail: 6474@greeneking.co.uk
web: www.oldenglish.co.uk
dir: From A31 Dorchester take B3073 into Wimborne.
Follow signs to town centre, hotel in square on left

Rooms 27 (1 fmly) Facilities Xmas Conf Board 20 Thtr 25
Services Lift Parking 20 Notes LB

Les Bouviers Restaurant with Rooms

◉◉ RESTAURANT WITH ROOMS

☎ 01202 889555 📄 01202 639428
Arrowsmith Rd, Canford Magna BH21 3BD
e-mail: info@lesbouviers.co.uk
dir: A31 on to A349. In 0.6m turn left. In approx 1m turn
right into Arrowsmith Rd. Establishment approx 100yds
on right.

A very well patronised restaurant with rooms in a great
location, set in six acres of grounds. Food is a highlight of
any stay here as is the friendly, attentive service.
Bedrooms are extremely well equipped and beds are
supremely comfortable.

Rooms 6 (4 en suite) (4 fmly)

CO DURHAM

BARNARD CASTLE   Map 19 NZ01

The Morritt

★★★ 79% HOTEL

☎ 01833 627232 📄 01833 627392
Greta Bridge DL12 9SE
e-mail: relax@themorritt.co.uk
web: www.themorritt.co.uk
dir: turn off A1 (A1(M)) at Scotch Corner onto A66
westbound towards Penrith. Greta Bridge 9m on left

Set off the main road at Greta Bridge, this 17th-century
former coaching house provides comfortable public rooms
full of character. The bar, with its interesting Dickensian
mural, is very much focused on food, but in addition a
fine dining is offered in the oak-panelled restaurant.
Bedrooms come in individual styles and of varying sizes.
The attentive service is noteworthy.

Rooms 27 (7 annexe) (3 fmly) (4 GF) S £85-£170;
D £110-£170 (incl. bkfst) Facilities Xmas New Year
Conf Class 60 Board 50 Thtr 200 Parking 40 Notes LB
Civ Wed 200

Jersey Farm Country Hotel

★★★ Ⓐ HOTEL

☎ 01833 638223 📄 01833 631988
Darlington Rd DL12 8TA
e-mail: enquiries@jerseyfarm.co.uk
web: www.jerseyfarm.co.uk
dir: On A67 1m E of Barnard Castle

Rooms 22 (11 annexe) (3 fmly) (8 GF) S £68-£85;
D £99-£150 (incl. bkfst)* Facilities FTV Pool table Xmas
New Year Wi-fi Conf Class 80 Board 60 Thtr 200
Parking 150 Notes LB Civ Wed

BEAMISH   Map 19 NZ25

Beamish Park

★★★ 78% ◉◉ HOTEL

☎ 01207 230666 📄 01207 281260
Beamish Burn Rd, Marley Hill NE16 5EG
e-mail: reception@beamish-park-hotel.co.uk
web: www.beamish-park-hotel.co.uk
dir: A1 junct 63 onto A693 Stanley. Exit rdbt onto A6076,
hotel 2m on right

The Metro Centre, Beamish Museum and south Tyneside
are all within striking distance of this modern hotel, set
in open countryside alongside its own golf course and
floodlit range. Bedrooms, some with their own patios,
provide a diverse mix of styles and sizes. The conservatory
bistro offers an interesting modern menu.

Rooms 42 (4 fmly) (27 GF) S £62.50-£79; D £72.50-£95*
Facilities FTV ⚘ 9 Putt green New Year Wi-fi
Conf Class 50 Board 50 Thtr 100 Del from £130*
Parking 100 Notes Closed 24 Dec-1 Jan

CHESTER-LE-STREET Map 19 NZ25

Lumley Castle

★★★★ 75% HOTEL

☎ 0191 389 1111 & 0191 389 5854 📄 0191 387 1437
Lumley Castle DH3 4NX
e-mail: reservations@lumleycastle.com
dir: A1(M) junct 63, follow Chester-le-Street signs. Follow signs for Riverside then Lumley Castle

The castle describes itself as 'no ordinary hotel' and has every justification for doing so. In terms of quality standards and entertainment, it really is something else. Deep tones, carefully selected fine silks, fabrics and atmospheric lighting have been combined to give an overwhelming feeling of restfulness and relaxation. The hotel offers large castle rooms and suites plus courtyard rooms in the converted stable block.

Rooms 74 (48 annexe) (3 fmly) (8 GF) **S** £89-£399; **D** £219-£399 (incl. bkfst)* **Facilities** STV FTV 🎵 New Year Wi-fi **Conf** Class 65 Board 50 Thtr 150 Del from £145 to £150* **Services** Lift **Parking** 200 **Notes** LB ⊗ Closed 24-26 Dec & 1 Jan Civ Wed 80

See advert on this page

Innkeeper's Lodge Durham North

BUDGET HOTEL

☎ 0845 112 6014 📄 0845 112 6287
Church Mouse, Great North Rd, Chester Moor DH2 3RJ
web: www.innkeeperslodge.com/durhamnorth
dir: A1(M) junct 63, take A167 S Durham/Chester-Le-Street. Straight on at 3 rdbts. Lodge on left

Innkeeper's Lodge represents an exciting, high value concept within the budget hotel market. Comfortable bedrooms provide excellent facilities that include satellite TV and modem points. Options include family rooms, and

for the corporate guest, cutting edge IT includes Wi-fi access. Food is served all day in the adjacent Country Pub. The extensive continental breakfast is complimentary.

Rooms 21 (4 fmly) **S** £59.95-£65; **D** £59.95-£65 (incl. bkfst)

CONSETT Map 19 NZ15

Best Western Derwent Manor

★★★ 73% HOTEL

☎ 01207 592000 📄 01207 502472
Allensford DH8 9BB
e-mail: gm@derwent-manor-hotel.com
web: www.oxfordhotelsandinns.com
dir: on A68

This hotel, built in the style of a manor house, is set in open grounds overlooking the River Derwent. Spacious bedrooms, including a number of suites, are comfortably equipped. A popular wedding venue, there are also extensive conference facilities and an impressive leisure suite. The Grouse & Claret bar serves a wide range of drinks and light meals, and Guinevere's restaurant offers the fine dining option.

Rooms 48 (3 fmly) (26 GF) **S** £92; **D** £122 (incl. bkfst)* **Facilities** FTV 🅦 supervised Gym Xmas New Year **Conf** Class 200 Board 60 Thtr 300 **Services** Lift **Parking** 100 **Notes** Civ Wed 300

DARLINGTON Map 19 NZ21

Headlam Hall

★★★ 80% ⊛ HOTEL

☎ 01325 730238 📄 01325 730790
Headlam, Gainford DL2 3HA
e-mail: admin@headlamhall.co.uk
web: www.headlamhall.co.uk
dir: 2m N of A67 between Piercebridge & Gainford

This impressive Jacobean hall lies in farmland north-east of Piercebridge and has its own 9-hole golf course. The main house retains many historical features, including flagstone floors and a pillared hall. Bedrooms are well proportioned and traditionally styled. A converted coach house contains the more modern rooms, as well as a conference and leisure centre.

Rooms 40 (22 annexe) (4 fmly) (10 GF) **S** £85-£155; **D** £110-£180 (incl. bkfst)* **Facilities** Spa STV 🅦 ⚓ 9 ⚑ Putt green Fishing ⚓ Gym New Year Wi-fi **Conf** Class 40 Board 40 Thtr 150 Del from £125* **Services** Lift **Parking** 80 **Notes** LB Closed 24-26 Dec Civ Wed 150

The Blackwell Grange Hotel

★★★ 78% HOTEL

☎ 0870 609 6121 & 01325 509955 🖹 01325 380899
Blackwell Grange DL3 8QH
e-mail: blackwell.grange@forestdale.com
web: www.blackwellgrangehotel.com
dir: on A167, 1.5m from central ring road

This beautiful 17th-century mansion is peacefully situated in nine acres of its own grounds yet is convenient for the motorway network. The pick of the bedrooms are in a courtyard building or the impressive feature rooms in the original house. The Havelock restaurant offers a range of traditional and continental menus.

Rooms 110 (11 annexe) (3 fmly) (36 GF) **D** £95-£99 (incl. bkfst)* **Facilities** 🕓 Gym Beauty room Xmas **Conf** Class 110 Board 50 Thtr 300 **Services** Lift **Parking** 250 **Notes** LB Civ Wed 200

Best Western Walworth Castle Hotel

★★★ 75% HOTEL

☎ 01325 485470 🖹 01325 462257
Walworth DL2 2LY
e-mail: enquiries@walworthcastle.co.uk
web: www.walworthcastle.co.uk
dir: A1(M) junct 58 follow signs to Corbridge. Left at The Dog pub. Hotel on left after 2m

This 12th-century castle is privately owned and has been tastefully converted. Accommodation is offered in a range of styles, including an impressive suite and more compact rooms in an adjoining wing. Dinner can be taken in the fine dining Hansards Restaurant or the more relaxed Farmer's Bar. A popular venue for conferences and weddings.

Rooms 34 (14 annexe) (4 fmly) (8 GF) **S** £85-£105; **D** £120-£245 (incl. bkfst) **Facilities** 🏊 Xmas New Year Wi-fi **Conf** Board 40 Thtr 120 Del from £115 to £135 **Parking** 100 **Notes** 🚫 Civ Wed

Best Western Croft

★★★ 74% HOTEL

☎ 01325 720319 🖹 01325 721252
Croft-on-Tees DL2 2ST
e-mail: enquiries@croft-hotel.co.uk
web: www.croft-hotel.co.uk
dir: from Darlington take A167 (Northallerton road). Hotel 3m S

Set in the village of Croft-on-Tees, this hotel offers smart well-equipped accommodation that includes a series of themed bedrooms that reflect different eras and countries around the world. The impressive Raffles Restaurant sports a colonial style and offers an interesting contemporary brasserie menu.

Rooms 20 (2 fmly) **S** £72.50-£170; **D** £77.50-£170 (incl. bkfst)* **Facilities** STV Gym Sauna Steam room Xmas New Year Wi-fi **Conf** Class 120 Board 50 Thtr 200 Del from £140 to £180* **Parking** 60 **Notes** 🚫 Closed 24-25 Dec Civ Wed 150

Hall Garth Hotel, Golf and Country Club

★★★ 73% HOTEL

☎ 0870 609 6131 🖹 01325 310083
Coatham Mundeville DL1 3LU
e-mail: hallgarth@foliohotels.com
web: www.foliohotels.com/hallgarth
dir: A1(M) junct 59, A167 towards Darlington. After 600yds left at top of hill, hotel on right

Peacefully situated in grounds that feature a golf course, this hotel is just a few minutes from the motorway

network. The well-equipped bedrooms come in various styles - it's worth asking for one of the trendy, modern rooms. Public rooms include relaxing lounges, a fine-dining restaurant and a separate pub. The extensive leisure and conference facilities are an important focus here.

Rooms 52 (12 annexe) (2 fmly) (1 GF) **S** £65-£140; **D** £110-£260* **Facilities** Spa STV FTV 🕓 supervised ♨ 9 Putt green Gym Steam room Beauty Salon Xmas New Year Wi-fi **Conf** Class 160 Board 80 Thtr 250 Del from £100 to £148* **Parking** 150 **Notes** LB Civ Wed 170

Durham Marriott Hotel, Royal County

★★★★ 76% HOTEL

☎ 0191 386 6821 🖹 0191 386 0704
Old Elvet DH1 3JN
e-mail: mhrs.xvudm.frontdesk@marriotthotels.com
web: www.durhammarriottroyalcounty.co.uk
dir: from A1(M) junct 62, then A690 to Durham, over 1st rdbt, left at 2nd rdbt left at lights, hotel on left

In a wonderful position on the banks of the River Wear, the hotel's central location makes it ideal for visiting the attractions of this historic city. The building was developed from a series of Jacobean town houses. The bedrooms are tastefully styled and the County Restaurant and lounge bar have been refurbished.

Continued

DURHAM continued

Rooms 150 (8 annexe) (10 fmly) (15 GF) (8 smoking)
Facilities STV 🄬 supervised Gym Turkish steam room
Plunge pool Sanarium Tropical fun shower Wi-fi
Conf Class 50 Board 50 Thtr 120 Del from £130 to £160
Services Lift **Parking** 76 **Notes** Civ Wed 70

Ramside Hall

★★★★ 73% HOTEL

☎ 0191 386 5282 🖷 0191 386 0399
Carrville DH1 1TD
e-mail: mail@ramsidehallhotel.co.uk
web: www.ramsidehall.co.uk
dir: from A1(M) junct 62 take A690 to Sunderland.
Straight on at lights. 200mtrs after railway bridge turn
right

With its proximity to the motorway and delightful
parkland setting, this establishment combines the best
of both worlds - convenience and tranquillity. The hotel
boasts 27 holes of golf, a choice of lounges, two eating
options and two bars. Bedrooms are furnished and
decorated to a very high standard and include two very
impressive presidential suites.

Rooms 80 (10 fmly) (28 GF) **Facilities** ♿ 27 Putt green
Steam room Sauna Golf academy Driving range 🎵 Wi-fi
Conf Class 160 Board 40 Thtr 400 **Services** Lift
Parking 500 **Notes** LB Civ Wed 400

See advert on page 207

Best Western Whitworth Hall Hotel

★★★ 77% COUNTRY HOUSE HOTEL

☎ 01388 811772 🖷 01388 818669
Whitworth Hall Country Park DL16 7QX
e-mail: enquiries@whitworthhall.co.uk
web: www.whitworthhall.co.uk

(For full entry see Spennymoor)

Hallgarth Manor Country Hotel & Restaurant

★★★ 70% HOTEL

☎ 0191 372 1188 🖷 0191 372 1249
Pittington DH6 1AB
e-mail: sales@hallgarthmanorhotel.com
dir: A1 junct 62/A690 signed Sunderland for 0.5m turn
right across dual carriageway, follow brown tourist signs
to hotel.

This traditional 16th-century country house is set in quiet
and beautifully maintained grounds just a few miles from
Durham. The public areas and the restaurant have been
tastefully modernised yet retain many original features.
The individually styled bedrooms are all situated on the
top two floors of the building. A large function room is
available.

Rooms 23 (2 fmly) **Facilities** Xmas New Year
Conf Class 75 Board 60 Thtr 250 **Parking** 200 **Notes** LB
🄬 Civ Wed 200

Bowburn Hall

★★★ 66% HOTEL

☎ 0191 377 0311 🖷 0191 377 3459
Bowburn DH6 5NH
e-mail: info@bowburnhallhotel.co.uk
dir: towards Bowburn. Right at Cooperage Pub, then 0.5m
to junct signed Durham. Hotel on left

A former country mansion, this hotel lies in five acres of
grounds in a residential area, but within easy reach of
the A1. The comfortable and spacious lounge bar and
conservatory overlook the gardens, and offer both bar and
restaurant meals. Bedrooms are not large but are very
smartly presented and well equipped.

Rooms 19 (1 fmly) **S** £75; **D** £85 (incl. bkfst)*
Facilities STV Wi-fi **Conf** Class 80 Board 30 Thtr 150
Parking 100 **Notes** RS 24-26 Dec & 1 Jan Civ Wed 120

Travelodge Durham

BUDGET HOTEL

☎ 08719 846 136 🖷 0191 386 5461
Station Rd, Gilesgate DH1 1LJ
web: www.travelodge.co.uk
dir: A1(M) junct 62 onto A690 towards Durham, 1st rdbt,
1st left into Station Rd

Travelodge offers good quality, good value, modern
accommodation. Ideal for families, the spacious en suite
bedrooms include remote-control TV, tea and coffee-
making facilities and comfortable beds. Meals can be
taken at the nearby family restaurant. See also the Hotel
Groups pages.

Rooms 57 **S** fr £29; **D** fr £29

Grand

★★★ 75% HOTEL

☎ 01429 266345 🖷 01429 265217
Swainson St TS24 8AA
e-mail: grandhotel@tavistockleisure.com
dir: A689 into town centre. Left onto Victoria Rd, hotel on
right.

This hotel has undergone a complete refurbishment yet
retains many original features; the public areas include
the grand ballroom, an open-plan lounge bar and the
basement restaurant, Italia. The bedrooms are modern in
design and have high spec fixtures and fittings. The staff
provide attentive and friendly service.

Rooms 47 (1 fmly) (17 smoking) **S** £55-£65; **D** £65-£75
(incl. bkfst & dinner)* **Facilities** STV FTV Affiliation with
local gym 🎵 New Year **Conf** Class 200 Board 60 Thtr 250
Del from £85 to £99* **Services** Lift **Parking** 50 **Notes** LB
🄬 Civ Wed 200

The Teesdale Hotel

★★ 65% HOTEL

☎ 01833 640264 🖷 01833 640651
Market Place DL12 0QG
e-mail: enquiries@teesdalehotel.co.uk
web: www.teesdalehotel.co.uk
dir: from Barnard Castle take B6278, follow signs for
Middleton-in-Teesdale & Highforce. Hotel in town centre

Located in the heart of the popular village, this family-
run hotel offers a relaxed and friendly atmosphere.
Bedrooms and bathrooms are well equipped and offer a
good standard of quality and comfort. Public areas
include a residents' lounge on the first floor, a spacious
restaurant and a lounge bar which is popular with locals.

Rooms 14 (1 fmly) **S** £30-£42.50; **D** £75 (incl. bkfst)*
Facilities Xmas **Conf** Class 20 Board 20 Thtr 40
Parking 20 **Notes** LB

Barceló Redworth Hall Hotel

★★★★ 76% HOTEL

☎ 01388 770600 🖷 01388 770654
DL5 6NL
e-mail: redworthhall@barcelo-hotels.co.uk
web: www.barcelo-hotels.co.uk
dir: from A1(M) junct 58/A68 signed Corbridge. Follow
hotel signs

This imposing Georgian building includes a health club
with state-of-the-art equipment and impressive
conference facilities making this a popular destination
for business travellers. There are several spacious
lounges to relax in along with the Conservatory
Restaurant. Bedrooms are very comfortable and well
equipped.

Rooms 143 (12 fmly) **S** £69-£150; **Facilities**
Gym Bodysense Health & Leisure Club ♫ Xmas New Year
Wi-fi **Conf** Class 144 Board 90 Thtr 300 **Services** Lift
Parking 300 **Notes** Civ Wed

ROMALDKIRK   Map 19 NY92

INSPECTORS' CHOICE

Rose & Crown
★★ ◉◉ HOTEL

☎ 01833 650213   📄 01833 650828
DL12 9EB
e-mail: hotel@rose-and-crown.co.uk
web: www.rose-and-crown.co.uk
dir: 6m NW from Barnard Castle on B6277

This charming country inn is located in the heart of
the village, overlooking fine fell scenery. Attractively
furnished bedrooms, including suites, are split
between the main house and the rear courtyard. There
is a cosy bar, warmed by log fires, and a welcoming
restaurant. Good local produce features extensively on
the menu. Service is both friendly and attentive.

Rooms 12 (5 annexe) (1 fmly) (5 GF) **S** £85-£115;
D £135-£165 (incl. bkfst)* **Facilities** STV New Year
Parking 20 **Notes** LB Closed 24-26 Dec

SEAHAM   Map 19 NZ44

INSPECTORS' CHOICE

Seaham Hall Hotel
★★★★★ HOTEL

☎ 0191 516 1400   📄 0191 516 1410
Lord Byron's Walk SR7 7AG
e-mail: reservations@seaham-hall.com
web: www.seaham-hall.com
dir: from A19 take B1404 to Seaham. At lights straight
over level crossing. Hotel approx 0.25m on right

This imposing house was the setting for Lord
Byron's marriage to Annabella Milbanke in 1815.
Now restored to their opulant glory, the bedrooms,
including some stunning suites, offer cutting edge
technology, contemporary artwork and a real sense
of style. Bathrooms are particularly lavish, with
two-person baths a feature. Public rooms are equally
impressive. The stunning Oriental Spa, accessed via
an underground walkway, offers guests a wide range
of treatments plus a Thai brasserie. At the time of
going to press the rosette award for the cuisine was
suspended as there had been a change of chef. For
up-to-date details visit the AA website www.theAA.com

Rooms 19 (4 GF) **Facilities** Spa ⊗ Gym Xmas
New Year Wi-fi **Conf** Class 48 Board 40 Thtr 120
Services Lift Air con **Parking** 120 **Notes** LB ⊗
Civ Wed 100

SEDGEFIELD   Map 19 NZ32

Best Western Hardwick Hall
★★★ 80% HOTEL

☎ 01740 620253   📄 01740 622771
TS21 2EH
e-mail: info@hardwickhallhotel.co.uk
dir: off A1(M) junct 60 towards Sedgefield, left at 1st
rdbt, hotel 400mtrs on left

Set in extensive parkland, this 18th-century house suits
leisure and corporate guests very well. It is a top
conference and function venue that offers an impressive
meeting and banqueting complex. The bedrooms include
a wing of stunning bedrooms to augment those in the
original house; all are appointed to the same high

standard and many have feature bathrooms and some
have stunning views over the lake. The modern lounge
bar and Cellar Bistro both offer a relaxed atmosphere.

Rooms 51 (6 fmly) **Facilities** STV FTV **Conf** Board 80
Thtr 700 Del from £145 to £165 **Services** Lift
Parking 200 **Notes** ⊗ Civ Wed 450

Travelodge Sedgefield
BUDGET HOTEL

☎ 08719 846 174   📄 01740 623399
TS21 2JX
web: www.travelodge.co.uk
dir: on A689, 3m E of A1(M) junct 60

Travelodge offers good quality, good value, modern
accommodation. Ideal for families, the spacious en suite
bedrooms include remote-control TV, tea and coffee-
making facilities and comfortable beds. Meals can be
taken at the nearby family restaurant. See also the Hotel
Groups pages.

Rooms 40 **S** fr £29; **D** fr £29

SPENNYMOOR   Map 19 NZ23

Best Western Whitworth Hall Hotel
★★★ 77% COUNTRY HOUSE HOTEL

☎ 01388 811772   📄 01388 818669
Whitworth Hall Country Park DL16 7QX
e-mail: enquiries@whitworthhall.co.uk
web: www.whitworthhall.co.uk
dir: A688 to Spennymoor, then Bishop Auckland. At rdbt
right to Middlestone Moor. Left at lights, hotel on right

This hotel, peacefully situated in its own grounds in the
centre of the deer park, offers comfortable
accommodation. Spacious bedrooms, some with excellent
views, offer stylish and elegant decor. Public areas
include a choice of restaurants and bars, a bright
conservatory and well-equipped function and conference
rooms.

Rooms 29 (4 fmly) (17 GF) **S** £74-£118; **D** £74-£118*
Facilities Fishing Wi-fi Child facilities **Conf** Class 40
Board 30 Thtr 100 Del from £135 to £150 **Parking** 100
Notes LB ⊗ Civ Wed 120

Best Western Parkmore Hotel & Leisure Park

★★★ 79% HOTEL

☎ 01642 786815 🖷 01642 790485
636 Yarm Rd, Eaglescliffe TS16 0DH
e-mail: enquiries@parkmorehotel.co.uk
dir: off A19 at Crathorne, follow A67 to Yarm. Through Yarm bear right onto A135 to Stockton. Hotel 1m on left

Set in its own gardens, this smart hotel has grown from its Victorian house origins to provide stylish public areas, as well as extensive leisure and beauty facilities including a hydrotherapy pool and conference facilities. The well-equipped bedrooms include junior suites. The restaurant known as J's@636 boasts a reputation for creativity meals. Service is friendly and obliging.

Rooms 55 (8 fmly) (9 GF) **S** £76-£83; **D** £94-£122* **Facilities** Spa STV 🟦 supervised Gym Beauty salon Badminton Aerobics studio Hydrotherapy Xmas New Year Wi-fi **Conf** Class 40 Board 40 Thtr 130 **Parking** 90 **Notes** LB Civ Wed 130

Express by Holiday Inn Stockton-on-Tees

BUDGET HOTEL

☎ 01740 644000 🖷 01740 644111
Junction A19 & A689, Coal Ln, Wynyard Park Services, Wolviston TS22 5PZ
e-mail: ebhi-stockton@btconnect.com
web: www.hiexpress.com/stocktonuk
dir: A1(M) junct 60, follow signs for Hartlepool & Teeside. On A689 straight across at small rdbts. Hotel on left on entering Wynyard Park Services.

A modern hotel ideal for families and business travellers. Fresh and uncomplicated, the spacious rooms include Sky TV, power shower and tea and coffee-making facilities. Continental buffet breakfast is included in the room rate; other meals may be taken at the nearby family pub or restaurant. See also the Hotel Groups pages.

Rooms 49 (20 fmly) **Conf** Class 12 Board 16 Thtr 30

The Manor House Hotel & Country Club

★★★ 79% HOTEL

☎ 01388 834834 🖷 01388 833566
The Green DL14 9HW
e-mail: enquiries@manorhousehotelcountydurham.co.uk
web: www.manorhousehotelcountydurham.co.uk
dir: A1(M) junct 58, then A68 to West Auckland. At T-junct turn left, hotel 150yds on right

This historic manor house, dating back to the 14th century, is full of character. Welcoming log fires await guests on cooler evenings. Comfortable bedrooms are individual in style, tastefully furnished and well equipped. The brasserie and Juniper's restaurant both offer an interesting selection of freshly prepared dishes. Well-equipped leisure facilities are available.

Rooms 35 (11 annexe) (6 fmly) (2 GF) **S** £55-£95; **D** £90-£140 (incl. bkfst)* **Facilities** FTV 🟦 Gym Xmas New Year **Conf** Class 80 Board 50 Thtr 100 Del from £95 to £120* **Parking** 150 **Notes** ⊗ Civ Wed 120

Chichester

★★★ 78% HOTEL

☎ 01268 560555 🖷 01268 560580
Old London Rd, Wickford SS11 8UE
e-mail: reception@chichester-hotel.com
web: www.chichester-hotel.com
dir: off A129

Set in landscaped gardens and surrounded by farmland, this friendly hotel has been owned and run by the same family for over 25 years. Spacious bedrooms are located around an attractive courtyard, and each is pleasantly decorated and thoughtfully equipped. Public rooms include a cosy lounge bar and a smart restaurant.

Rooms 34 (32 annexe) (4 fmly) (16 GF) **S** £54.95-£69.95; **D** £54.95-£69.95* **Facilities** FTV Wi-fi **Parking** 150 **Notes** ⊗

Holiday Inn Basildon

🝋

☎ 0870 400 9003 & 01268 824000 🖷 01268 530119
Waterfront Walk, Festival Leisure Park SS14 3DG
e-mail: reservations-basildon@ihg.com
web: www.holidayinn.co.uk
dir: A127 then A176 Basildon Billericay exit. Follow brown signs to Festival Leisure Park

Currently the rating for this establishment is not confirmed. This may be due to a change of ownership or because it has only recently joined the AA rating scheme. For further details please see the AA website: www.theAA.com

Rooms 148 (10 fmly) (8 GF) (16 smoking) **S** £99-£123; **D** £99-£123* **Facilities** STV Use of nearby leisure club New Year Wi-fi **Conf** Class 80 Board 80 Thtr 300 Del from £110 to £170* **Services** Lift Air con **Parking** 200 **Notes** LB Civ Wed

Campanile Basildon

BUDGET HOTEL

☎ 01268 530810 🖷 01268 286710
Pipps Hill, Southend Arterial Rd SS14 3AE
e-mail: basildon@campanile.com
dir: M25 junct 29 Basildon exit, back under A127, then left at rdbt

This modern building offers accommodation in smart, well-equipped bedrooms, all with en suite bathrooms. Refreshments may be taken at the informal bistro. See also the Hotel Groups pages.

Rooms 97 (97 annexe) (8 fmly) **Conf** Class 18 Board 24 Thtr 35

Travelodge Basildon

BUDGET HOTEL

☎ 08719 846 008 🖷 01268 186559
Festival Leisure Park, Festival Way SS14 3WB
web: www.travelodge.co.uk
dir: M25 junct 29, A127 follow signs Basildon town centre, onto A176 signed Festival Leisure Park

Travelodge offers good quality, good value, modern accommodation. Ideal for families, the spacious en suite bedrooms include remote-control TV, tea and coffee-making facilities and comfortable beds. Meals can be taken at the nearby family restaurant. See also the Hotel Groups pages.

Rooms 60 (27 fmly) **S** fr £29; **D** fr £29

BIRCHANGER GREEN MOTORWAY SERVICE AREA (M11) — Map 6 TL52

Days Inn London Stansted

BUDGET HOTEL

☎ 01279 656477 📠 01279 656590
CM23 5QZ
e-mail: birchanger.hotel@welcomebreak.co.uk
web: www.welcomebreak.co.uk
dir: M11 junct 8

This modern building offers accommodation in smart, spacious and well-equipped bedrooms, suitable for families and business travellers, and all with en suite bathrooms. Continental breakfast is available and other refreshments may be taken at the nearby family restaurant. See also the Hotel Groups pages.

Rooms 60 (57 fmly) **S** £49-£69; **D** £69-£89*

BRAINTREE — Map 7 TL72

White Hart

★★★ Ⓐ HOTEL

☎ 01376 321401 📠 01376 552628
Bocking End CM7 9AB
web: www.oldenglish.co.uk
dir: off A120 towards town centre. Hotel at junct B1256 & Bocking Causeway

Rooms 31 (8 fmly) **Conf** Class 16 Board 24 Thtr 40
Parking 40 **Notes** ⊗

Express by Holiday Inn Braintree - Essex

BUDGET HOTEL

☎ 01376 551141 📠 01376 551142
Galley's Corner, Cressing Rd CM77 8DH
e-mail: ebhi-braintree@btconnect.com
web: www.hiexpress.com/braintree
dir: off A120 onto B1018 at Galley's Corner. Hotel next to Wyevale Garden Centre

A modern hotel ideal for families and business travellers. Fresh and uncomplicated, the spacious rooms include Sky TV, power shower and tea and coffee-making facilities. Continental buffet breakfast is included in the room rate; other meals may be taken at the nearby family pub or restaurant. See also the Hotel Groups pages.

Rooms 47 (19 GF) **Conf** Class 15 Board 20 Thtr 30

BRENTWOOD — Map 6 TQ59

Marygreen Manor

★★★★ 80% ◉◉ HOTEL

☎ 01277 225252 📠 01277 262809
London Rd CM14 4NR
e-mail: info@marygreenmanor.co.uk
web: www.marygreenmanor.co.uk
dir: M25 junct 28, onto A1023 over 2 sets of lights, hotel on left

A 16th-century house which was built by Robert Wright, who named the house 'Manor of Mary Green' after his young bride. Public rooms exude character and have a wealth of original features that include exposed beams, carved panelling and the impressive Tudors restaurant. Bedrooms are tastefully decorated and thoughtfully equipped.

Rooms 44 (40 annexe) (35 GF) (9 smoking) **S** fr £135;
D fr £150 **Facilities** STV FTV **Conf** Class 20 Board 25
Thtr 50 Del from £215 **Parking** 100 **Notes** ⊗ Civ Wed 60

See advert on this page

De Rougemont Manor

★★★★ 78% HOTEL

☎ 01277 226418 & 220483 📠 01277 239020
Great Warley St CM13 3JP
e-mail: enquiries@derougemontmanor.com
web: www.derougemontmanor.com
dir: M25 junct 29, A127 to Southend then B186 towards Great Warley

Expect a warm welcome at this family owned and managed hotel, situated on the outskirts of Brentwood just off the M25. The stylish bedrooms are divided between the main hotel and a bedroom wing; each one is tastefully appointed and well equipped. Public rooms include a smart lounge bar, restaurant and a choice of seating areas.

Rooms 81 (11 fmly) (16 GF) **S** £89-£109; **D** £99-£139*
Facilities STV ⚊ ⚑ Gym Xmas New Year Wi-fi
Conf Class 120 Board 16 Thtr 200 **Services** Lift Air con
Parking 133 **Notes** ⊗ Civ Wed 90

Weald Park Hotel, Golf & Country Club

★★★ 77% HOTEL

☎ 01277 375101 📠 01277 374888
Coxtie Green Rd, South Weald CM14 5RJ
e-mail: info@wealdpark.net
dir: M25 junct 28 Brentwood, left at 1st lights. Left at T-junct, follow winding road for 1.5m. 2nd right, hotel 1m on right

Expect a warm welcome at this family-run hotel situated in a peaceful rural location yet just a short drive from the M25 and M11. The spacious, tastefully appointed and well-equipped bedrooms are situated in attractive courtyard-style blocks adjacent to the main building. Public rooms include a first-floor function room, a lounge bar, a stylish restaurant and a conservatory.

Rooms 32 (32 annexe) (2 fmly) (25 GF) **S** £65-£125;
D £65-£125* **Facilities** ⚸ 18 Putt green Wi-fi
Conf Class 40 Board 20 Thtr 80 Del from £145 to £165*
Parking 180 **Notes** LB ⊗ No children 12yrs

BRENTWOOD continued

Holiday Inn Brentwood

☎ 0870 400 9012 📠 01277 264264
Brook St CM14 5NF
e-mail: reservations-brentwoodm25@ihg.com
web: www.holidayinn.co.uk
dir: close to M25/A12 interchange

Currently the rating for this establishment is not confirmed. This may be due to a change of ownership or because it has only recently joined the AA rating scheme. For further details please see the AA website: www.theAA.com

Rooms 149 (28 fmly) (47 smoking) **D** £49-£149 (incl. bkfst)* **Facilities** STV 🌀 Gym New Year Wi-fi **Conf** Class 60 Board 50 Thtr 140 Del from £99 to £180* **Services** Lift Air con **Parking** 276 **Notes** LB Civ Wed

---

BUCKHURST HILL   **Map 6 TQ49**

Express by Holiday Inn London-Buckhurst Hill

BUDGET HOTEL

☎ 020 8504 4450 📠 020 8498 0011
High Rd IG9 5HT
e-mail: ebhi-buckhurst@btinternet.com
web: www.hiexpress.com/buckhursthill

A modern hotel ideal for families and business travellers. Fresh and uncomplicated, the spacious rooms include Sky TV, power shower and tea and coffee-making facilities. Continental buffet breakfast is included in the room rate; other meals may be taken at the nearby family pub or restaurant. See also the Hotel Groups pages.

Rooms 49 (20 fmly) **Conf** Class 20 Board 16 Thtr 30

CHELMSFORD   **Map 6 TL70**

County Hotel

★★★ 85% HOTEL   CLASSIC BRITISH HOTELS

☎ 01245 455700 📠 01245 492762
29 Rainsford Rd CM1 2PZ
e-mail: kloftus@countyhotelgroup.co.uk
web: www.countyhotelgroup.co.uk
dir: from town centre, past rail and bus station. Hotel 300yds left beyond lights

This popular hotel is ideally situated within easy walking distance of the railway station, bus depot and town centre. Stylish bedrooms offer spacious comfort and plentiful extras including free Wi-fi. There is a smart restaurant, bar and lounge as well as sunny outdoor terraces for making the most of warm weather. The hotel also has a range of meeting rooms and banqueting facilities.

Rooms 54 (2 fmly) (1 GF) **S** £70-£120; **D** £90-£190 (incl. bkfst)* **Facilities** FTV Xmas Wi-fi **Conf** Class 84 Board 64 Thtr 160 **Services** Lift **Parking** 80 **Notes** ⊗ Closed 27-30 Dec Civ Wed 80

Pontlands Park Country Hotel

★★★ 79% HOTEL

☎ 01245 476444 📠 01245 478393
West Hanningfield Rd, Great Baddow CM2 8HR
e-mail: sales@pontlandsparkhotel.co.uk
web: www.pontlandsparkhotel.co.uk
dir: A12/A130/A1114 to Chelmsford. 1st exit at rdbt, 1st slip road on left. Left towards Gt Baddow, 1st left into West Hanningfield Rd. Hotel 400yds on left

A Victorian country-house hotel situated in a peaceful rural location amidst attractive landscaped grounds. The stylishly furnished bedrooms are generally quite spacious; each is individually decorated and equipped with modern facilities. The elegant public rooms include a tastefully furnished sitting room, a cosy lounge bar, smart conservatory restaurant and an intimate dining room.

Rooms 35 (10 fmly) (11 GF) **Facilities** 🌀 ⚒ Gym Beauty Room Wi-fi **Conf** Class 30 Board 30 Thtr 100 **Parking** 100 **Notes** LB ⊗ Closed 24 Dec-3 Jan (ex 31 Dec) Civ Wed 100

Best Western Atlantic

★★★ 77% ⚜ HOTEL

☎ 01245 268168 📠 01245 268169
New St CM1 1PP
e-mail: info@atlantichotel.co.uk
dir: From Chelmsford rail station, left onto Victoria Rd, left at lights into New St, hotel on right

Ideally situated just a short walk from the railway station with its quick links to London, this modern, purpose-built hotel has contemporary-style bedrooms equipped with modern facilities. The open-plan public areas include the popular New Street Brasserie, a lounge bar and a conservatory.

Rooms 59 (3 fmly) (27 GF) **Facilities** Gym Complimentary use of facilities at Fitness First 🎵 Wi-fi **Conf** Board 10 Thtr 15 **Services** Air con **Parking** 60 **Notes** LB ⊗ Closed 23 Dec-3 Jan

---

Best Western Ivy Hill

★★★ 75% HOTEL

☎ 01277 353040 📠 01277 355038
Writtle Rd, Margaretting CM4 0EH
e-mail: sales@ivyhillhotel.co.uk
web: www.heritageleisure.co.uk
dir: A12 junct 14 from London. Hotel on left at top of slip road

A smartly appointed hotel conveniently situated just off the A12. The spacious bedrooms are tastefully decorated, have co-ordinated fabrics and all the usual facilities. Public rooms include a choice of lounges, a cosy bar, a smart conservatory and restaurant, as well as a range of conference and banqueting facilities.

Rooms 33 (5 fmly) (11 GF) **D** £110-£170* **Facilities** FTV Wi-fi **Conf** Class 80 Board 40 Thtr 180 Del from £135 to £150* **Parking** 60 **Notes** LB ⊗ Closed 23-30 Dec Civ Wed 100

Boswell House

★★ 🄰 SMALL HOTEL

☎ 01245 287587 📠 01245 287587
118/120 Springfield Rd CM2 6LF
e-mail: boswell118@aol.com
dir: 500yds E of town centre. Signs to Riverside Ice & Leisure Centre, over river at junct Victoria Rd

Rooms 13 (2 fmly) (4 GF) **S** £55-£60; **D** £70-£75 (incl. bkfst)* **Facilities** FTV Wi-fi Child facilities **Parking** 15 **Notes** ⊗ Closed 24 Dec-4 Jan

---

CLACTON-ON-SEA   **Map 7 TM11**

Esplanade Hotel

★★ 68% HOTEL

☎ 01255 220450 📠 01255 221800
27-29 Marine Parade East CO15 1UU
e-mail: mjs@esplanadehoteluk.com
web: www.esplanadehoteluk.com
dir: from A133 to Clacton-on-Sea, follow seafront signs. At seafront turn right. Hotel on right in 50yds

Ideally situated on the seafront overlooking the pier and just a short walk from the town centre. Bedrooms vary in size and style: each one is pleasantly decorated and well equipped; some rooms have lovely sea views. Public rooms include a comfortable lounge bar and Coasters Restaurant.

Rooms 29 (2 fmly) (3 GF) **Facilities** Xmas **Conf** Class 50 Board 50 Thtr 80 **Parking** 13 **Notes** LB ⊗ Civ Wed 85

COGGESHALL   **Map 7 TL82**

White Hart

★★★ 77% ⚜ HOTEL

☎ 01376 561654 📠 01376 561789
Market End CO6 1NH
e-mail: 6529@greeneking.co.uk
web: www.oldenglish.co.uk
dir: from A12 through Kelvedon & onto B1024 to Coggeshall

A delightful inn situated in the centre of this bustling market town. Bedrooms vary in size and style; each one offers good quality and comfort with extras such as CD players, fruit and mineral water. The heavily beamed public areas include a popular bar serving a varied menu, a large restaurant offering Italian cuisine and a cosy residents' lounge.

Rooms 18 (1 fmly) **Facilities** 🎵 Xmas Child facilities **Conf** Class 10 Board 22 Thtr 30 **Parking** 40

RANGEWORTHY — Map 4 ST68

Rangeworthy Court

★★ 71% HOTEL

☎ 01454 228347 📄 01454 228945
Church Ln, Wotton Rd BS37 7ND
e-mail: reception@rangeworthycourt.com
dir: Signed from B4058. Hotel at end of Church Lane

This welcoming manor house hotel is peacefully located in its own grounds, and is within easy reach of the motorway network. The character bedrooms come in a variety of sizes and there is a choice of comfortable lounges in which to enjoy a drink before dinner. The relaxing restaurant offers a selection of carefully prepared, enjoyable dishes.

Rooms 13 (4 fmly) **S** fr £82.25; **D** fr £99.87 (incl. bkfst) **Facilities** FTV 🗲 Wi-fi **Conf** Class 14 Board 16 Thtr 22 Del from £150 to £190 **Parking** 30 **Notes** Closed 24-30 Dec Civ Wed 50

SEVERN VIEW MOTORWAY SERVICE AREA (M48) — Map 4 ST58

Travelodge Bristol Severn View (M48)

BUDGET HOTEL

☎ 08719 846 052 📄 01454 632482
M48 Motorway, Severn Bridge BS35 4BH
web: www.travelodge.co.uk
dir: M48 junct 1

Travelodge offers good quality, good value, modern accommodation. Ideal for families, the spacious en suite bedrooms include remote-control TV, tea and coffee-making facilities and comfortable beds. Meals can be taken at the nearby family restaurant. See also the Hotel Groups pages.

Rooms 50 **S** fr £29; **D** fr £29

SOUTH CERNEY — Map 5 SU09

Cotswold Water Park Four Pillars Hotel

★★★★ 76% HOTEL

☎ 01285 864000 📄 01285 864000
Lake 6 Spine Road East GL7 5FP
e-mail: waterpark@four-pillars.co.uk
web: www.four-pillars.co.uk/cotswoldwaterpark
dir: off A419, 3m from Cirencester

A purpose-built hotel, overlooking the water park, that offers accommodation that includes executive rooms. There is a popular brasserie, cocktail bar, atrium lounges, indoor heated pool, gym, sauna and steam room. A wide range of conference facilities is available and parking is extensive.

Rooms 219 (35 fmly) (71 GF) **Facilities** Spa STV 🏊 Fishing Gym Treatment rooms & therapies Xmas New Year Wi-fi **Conf** Class 144 Board 34 Thtr 360 Del from £135 to £185* **Services** Lift **Parking** 200 **Notes** LB ⊗ Civ Wed 320

STONEHOUSE — Map 4 SO80

Stonehouse Court

★★★ 79% ⚜⚜ HOTEL

☎ 0871 871 3240 & 01453 794 950 📄 0871 871 3241
GL10 3RA
e-mail: info@stonehousecourt.co.uk
dir: M5 junct 13, off A419. Follow signs for Stonehouse, hotel on right 0.25m after 2nd rdbt

Set in six acres of secluded gardens, this Grade II listed manor house dates back to 1601. Bedrooms vary greatly in size and style and include some stylish feature rooms. Elegant public areas include a lounge, bar and small gym. In warmer weather, guests can enjoy afternoon tea on the terrace. Dinner, featuring local and seasonal items, is available in Henry's restaurant or alternatively,

guests might choose to eat in the lounge. Extensive conference facilities are available.

Rooms 36 (27 annexe) (2 fmly) (6 GF) **Facilities** 🗲 Gym 🎵 Xmas New Year Wi-fi **Conf** Class 75 Board 70 Thtr 150 **Parking** 200 **Notes** LB Civ Wed 150

Travelodge Stonehouse

BUDGET HOTEL

☎ 0871 9846054 📄 01453 828590
A419, Easington GL10 3SQ
web: www.travelodge.co.uk
dir: M5 junct 13, onto A419

Travelodge offers good quality, good value, modern accommodation. Ideal for families, the spacious en suite bedrooms include remote-control TV, tea and coffee-making facilities and comfortable beds. Meals can be taken at the nearby family restaurant. See also the Hotel Groups pages.

Rooms 40 **S** fr £29; **D** fr £29

STOW-ON-THE-WOLD — Map 10 SP12

Fosse Manor

CLASSIC BRITISH HOTELS

★★★ 81% ⚜⚜ HOTEL

☎ 01451 830354 📄 01451 832486
GL54 1JX
e-mail: enquiries@fossemanor.co.uk
web: www.fossemanor.co.uk
dir: 1m S on A429, 300yds past junct with A424

Deriving its name from the historic Roman Fosse Way, this popular hotel is ideally situated for exploring the many delights of this picturesque area. Bedrooms, located both in the main building and the adjacent coach house, offer high standards of comfort and quality. Public areas include a small lounge, spacious bar and light and airy restaurant. Classy cuisine is on offer with quality produce used to create imaginative dishes.

Rooms 19 (8 annexe) (3 fmly) (5 GF) **S** £95; **D** £130-£230 (incl. bkfst)* **Facilities** 🗲 Xmas New Year Wi-fi **Conf** Class 20 Board 26 Thtr 60 Del from £132.50 to £155* **Parking** 30 **Notes** LB ⊗

STOW-ON-THE-WOLD continued

The Unicorn

★★★ 75% ◉ SMALL HOTEL

☎ 01451 830257 📄 01451 831090
Sheep St GL54 1HQ
e-mail: reception@birchhotels.co.uk
dir: at junct of A429 & A436

This attractive limestone hotel dates back to the 17th century. Individually designed bedrooms include some delightful four-poster rooms. Spacious public areas retain much character and include a choice of inviting lounges and a traditional bar offering a good selection of bar meals and ales. The restaurant provides a stylish venue for impressive cuisine.

Rooms 20 **S** £95-£100; **D** £125-£190 (incl. bkfst & dinner)* **Facilities** Xmas New Year Wi-fi **Conf** Class 20 Board 28 Thtr 50 **Parking** 40 **Notes** LB Civ Wed 45

Stow Lodge

★★★ 75% SMALL HOTEL

☎ 01451 830485 📄 01451 831671
The Square GL54 1AB
e-mail: enquiries@stowlodge.com
web: www.stowlodge.com
dir: in town centre

Situated in smart grounds, this family-run hotel has direct access to the market square and provides high standards of customer care. Bedrooms, located in the main building and in the converted coach house, provide similar standards of homely comfort. Extensive menus and an interesting wine list make for an enjoyable dining experience.

Rooms 21 (10 annexe) (1 fmly) **S** £60-£150; **D** £80-£170 (incl. bkfst)* **Parking** 30 **Notes** LB ⊗ No children 5yrs Closed Xmas-end Jan

The Royalist

★★★ 74% ◉◉ HOTEL

☎ 01451 830670 📄 01451 870048
Digbeth St GL54 1BN
e-mail: stay@theroyalisthotel.com
web: www.theroyalisthotel.com
dir: Off A436

Verified as the oldest inn in England, this charming hotel has a wealth of history and character. Bedrooms and public areas have been stylishly and sympathetically decorated to ensure high levels of comfort at every turn. Some rooms are in an adjoining annexe. There are two eating options: the restaurant offers high-quality cooking and the Eagle and Child provides a more informal alternative.

Rooms 14 (4 annexe) (1 fmly) (2 GF) **S** £65-£110; **D** £100-£160 (incl. bkfst)* **Facilities** Xmas New Year Wi-fi **Parking** 8 **Notes** LB Civ Wed

Grapevine

★★★ 73% ◉◉ HOTEL

☎ 01451 830344 📄 01451 832278
Sheep St GL54 1AU
e-mail: enquiries@vines.co.uk
web: www.vines.co.uk
dir: on A436 towards Chipping Norton. 150yds on right, facing green

Situated in the heart of this unique market town, the Grapevine is a delightful 17th-century hotel with lots of charm and character. Original features abound, such as stone-flagged floors and aged beams. Individually styled bedrooms combine comfort and quality, and each is equipped with thoughtful extras. Canopied by an ancient vine, the Conservatory Restaurant is a lovely setting for accomplished cuisine. Alternatively, lighter meals can be enjoyed either in the popular bar or in La Vigna, a Mediterranean-style bistro.

Rooms 22 (10 annexe) (2 fmly) (5 GF) **S** £85-£95; **D** £140-£160 (incl. bkfst)* **Facilities** Xmas New Year Wi-fi **Conf** Class 18 Board 20 Thtr 30 **Parking** 25 **Notes** LB ⊗ Civ Wed 85

See advert on this page

Old Stocks

★★ 71% SMALL HOTEL

☎ 01451 830666 📠 01451 870014
The Square GL54 1AF
e-mail: aa@theoldstockshotel.co.uk
web: www.oldstockshotel.co.uk
dir: Exit A429 to town centre. Hotel facing village green

Overlooking the old market square, this Grade II listed, mellow Cotswold-stone building is a comfortable and friendly base from which to explore this picturesque area. There's lots of character throughout, and the bedrooms offer individuality and charm. Facilities include a guest lounge, restaurant and bar, whilst outside, the patio is a popular summer venue for refreshing drinks and good food.

Rooms 18 (3 annexe) (5 fmly) (4 GF) **Facilities** Xmas New Year **Parking** 12 **Notes** LB

Wyck Hill House

☎ 01451 831936 📠 01451 832243
Burford Rd GL54 1HY
e-mail: enquiries@wyckhillhouse.com
dir: turn off A429. Hotel 1m on right

Currently the rating for this establishment is not confirmed. This may be due to a change of ownership or because it has only recently joined the AA rating scheme. For further details please see the AA website: www.theAA.com

Rooms 32 (16 annexe)

Burleigh Court

★★★ 78% ◉◉ HOTEL

☎ 01453 883804 📠 01453 886870
Burleigh, Minchinhampton GL5 2PF
e-mail: info@burleighcourthotel.co.uk
dir: From Stroud A419 towards Cirencester. Right after 2.5m signed Burleigh & Minchinhampton. Left after 500yds signed Burleigh Court. Hotel 300yds on right

Dating back to the 18th century, this former gentleman's manor house is in a secluded yet accessible elevated position with some wonderful countryside views. Public rooms are elegantly styled and include an oak-panelled bar for pre-dinner drinks beside a crackling fire. Combining comfort and quality, each bedroom is different, and some are in an adjoining coach house.

Rooms 18 (2 fmly) (3 GF) **S** £85-£105; **D** £130-£190 (incl. bkfst)* **Facilities** ↖ ⛴ New Year Wi-fi **Conf** Class 30 Board 30 Thtr 50 **Parking** 40 **Notes** LB Civ Wed 50

The Bear of Rodborough

★★★ 77% HOTEL

☎ 01453 878522 📠 01453 872523
Rodborough Common GL5 5DE
e-mail: info@bearofrodborough.info
web: www.cotswold-inns-hotels.co.uk
dir: M5 junct 13, A419 to Stroud. Follow signs to Rodborough. Up hill, left at top at T-junct. Hotel on right.

This popular 17th-century coaching inn is situated high above Stroud within acres of National Trust parkland. Character abounds in the lounges and cocktail bar, and in the Box Tree Restaurant where the cuisine utilises fresh local produce. Bedrooms offer equal measures of comfort and style with plenty of extra touches. There is also a traditional and well-patronised public bar.

Rooms 46 (2 fmly) **S** £75-£105; **D** £120-£240 (incl. bkfst)* **Facilities** STV Putt green ⛴ Xmas New Year Wi-fi **Conf** Class 35 Board 30 Thtr 60 Del from £125 to £155* **Parking** 70 **Notes** LB Civ Wed 70

INSPECTORS' CHOICE

Calcot Manor

★★★★ ◉◉ HOTEL

☎ 01666 890391 📠 01666 890394
Calcot GL8 8YJ
e-mail: reception@calcotmanor.co.uk
web: www.calcotmanor.co.uk
dir: 3m West of Tetbury at junct A4135/A46

Cistercian monks built the ancient barns and stables around which this lovely English farmhouse is set. No two rooms are identical, and each is beautifully decorated in a variety of styles and equipped with the contemporary comforts. Sumptuous sitting rooms, with crackling log fires in the winter, look out over immaculate gardens. There are two dining options: the elegant conservatory restaurant and the informal Gumstool Inn. There are also ample function rooms. A superb health and leisure spa includes an indoor pool, high-tech gym, massage tables, complementary therapies and much more. For children, a supervised crèche and 'playzone' are a great attraction.

Rooms 35 (23 annexe) (13 fmly) (17 GF) **S** £198-£223; **D** £220-£420 (incl. bkfst)* **Facilities** Spa ⊕ ↖ ⛴ ⛴ Gym Clay pigeon shooting Archery Xmas New Year Wi-fi Child facilities **Conf** Class 40 Board 35 Thtr 120 Del from £280 to £305* **Parking** 150 **Notes** LB ⊗ Civ Wed 100

TETBURY continued

Best Western Hare & Hounds

★★★ 77% HOTEL

☎ 01666 880233 & 881000 📠 01666 880241
Westonbirt GL8 8QL
e-mail: enquiries@hareandhoundshotel.com
web: www.hareandhoundshotel.com
dir: 2.5m SW of Tetbury on A433

This popular hotel, set in extensive grounds, is situated close to Westonbirt Arboretum and has remained under the same ownership for over 50 years. Bedrooms are individual in style; those in the main house are more traditional and the stylish cottage rooms are contemporary in design. Public rooms include the informal bar and light, airy lounges - one with a log fire in colder months. Guests can eat either in the bar or the attractive restaurant.

Rooms 45 (21 annexe) (8 fmly) (13 GF) **S** £88-£93;
D £110-£125 (incl. bkfst)* **Facilities** FTV 🏌 Putt green ⛲ Xmas New Year Wi-fi **Conf** Class 80 Board 40 Thtr 120 **Parking** 85 (charged) **Notes** LB Civ Wed 200

Snooty Fox

★★★ 74% SMALL HOTEL

☎ 01666 502436 📠 01666 503479
Market Place GL8 8DD
e-mail: res@snooty-fox.co.uk
web: www.snooty-fox.co.uk
dir: in town centre

Centrally situated, the Snooty Fox is a popular venue for weekend breaks, and retains many of the historic features associated with a 16th-century coaching inn. The relaxed and friendly atmosphere, the high standard of accommodation, and the food offered in the bar and restaurant, make good reasons why many guests return here.

Rooms 12 **S** £60-£185; **D** £70-£210 (incl. bkfst)*
Facilities Xmas New Year **Conf** Class 12 Board 16 Thtr 24 **Notes** LB

The Priory Inn

★★★ 72% SMALL HOTEL

☎ 01666 502251 📠 01666 503534
London Rd GL8 8JJ
e-mail: info@theprioryinn.co.uk
web: www.theprioryinn.co.uk
dir: on A433 (Cirencester to Tetbury road). Hotel 200yds from Market Square

A warm welcome is guaranteed at this attractive inn where friendly service is of a high priority to the team. Public areas and bedrooms have a contemporary style that mixes well with more traditional features, such as an open fireplace in the cosy bar dining room. Cuisine is a highlight of any stay, with locally sourced produce skilfully prepared. For those in need of a little pampering, the hotel also has a partnership with a beauty and well-being centre on site.

Rooms 14 (1 fmly) (4 GF) (4 smoking) **S** £69-£79;
D £109-£119 (incl. bkfst)* **Facilities** STV Health & beauty centre 🎵 Xmas New Year Wi-fi Child facilities
Conf Class 28 Board 28 Thtr 30 Del from £109 to £125* **Parking** 35 **Notes** LB ⊗

Ormond at Tetbury

★★★ 64% HOTEL

☎ 01666 505690 📠 01666 505956
23 Long St GL8 8AA
e-mail: info@theormond.co.uk
dir: Turn off A433 from Cirencester into Long St. Hotel approx 100yds on left

Located on the main street of this charming town, The Ormond provides a selection of individually styled and comfortably furnished bedrooms in a variety of shapes and sizes. The ambience here is relaxed and friendly, and guests may chose to dine in either the popular bar area or in the adjoining restaurant. In warmer weather, a range of outdoor seating is available in the courtyard.

Rooms 15 (3 fmly) **S** fr £55; **D** £69-£140* **Facilities** FTV Xmas New Year Wi-fi Child facilities **Conf** Class 20 Board 20 Thtr 40 Del from £99 to £125* **Notes** ⊗

Close

★★★ 🅰 SMALL HOTEL

☎ 01666 502272 📠 01666 504401
8 Long St GL8 8AQ
e-mail: reception@theclosehotel.co.uk
web: www.oldenglish.co.uk
dir: M4 junct 17 onto A429 or M5 junct 14 onto B4509, follow Tetbury signs

Rooms 15 **Facilities** ⛲ Xmas **Conf** Board 22 Thtr 50 **Parking** 22 **Notes** Civ Wed 50

Corse Lawn House Hotel

⊛⊛   Corse Lawn, Gloucestershire GL19 4LZ   ★★★
Tel: 01452 780771 Fax: 01452 780840
Email: enquiries@corselawn.com
www.corselawn.com

Family owned and run luxury country house hotel situated in a tranquil backwater of Gloucestershire yet within easy access of M5, M50, Gloucester, Cheltenham, the Cotswolds, Malverns and Forest of Dean.
The highly acclaimed restaurant and bistro are open daily and the 12 acre grounds include an indoor swimming pool, all-weather tennis court, croquet lawn and table tennis.
Pets most welcome. Short break rates always available.

Thornbury Castle Hotel

Castle Street, Thornbury, Bristol BS35 1HH
Tel: 01454 281182 Fax: 01454 416188
www.thornburycastle.co.uk

von Essen hotels
A PRIVATE COLLECTION
www.vonessenhotels.com

Kings and queens have stayed here. Courtiers have flirted with ladies-in-waiting in the ancient yew-hedged gardens. Serving girls have chattered in the stone-flagged courtyard. Today, Thornbury Castle still resonates with history and is the only Tudor castle in England to be open as a hotel…and it's only 15 minutes from the M5.

However, step behind the heavy oak doors and you'll find a magnificent hotel with roaring fires, delicious modern cuisine and sumptuous bedchambers - a truly special setting for an overnight stay, a weekend away or for more formal occasions.

Henry VIII and Anne Boleyn once walked these rooms and grounds. Today, the 500 year-old castle-palace with its beautiful oriel windows, Tudor hall and historic parkland is yours for the duration of your stay. There has even been a vineyard within the castle walls for over 500 years, from which Thornbury Castle wine is still produced.

Enjoy a regal night's sleep in the Duke's Bedchamber where King Henry VIII and Anne Boleyn slept or favour the Mary 1st Bedchamber and wake up to a view of the oldest Tudor gardens in England - the Privy Garden and Goodly Garden.

TETBURY continued

Hunters Hall

★★ 🅰 SMALL HOTEL

☎ 01453 860393 📠 01453 860707
Kingscote GL8 8XZ
e-mail: huntershall.kingscote@greeneking.co.uk
web: www.oldenglish.co.uk
dir: M4 junct 18, take A46 towards Stroud. 10m turn left
signed Kingscote, follow road to T-junct, turn left, hotel
0.5m on left.

Rooms 12 (12 annexe) (1 fmly) (8 GF) **Facilities** Pool
table Xmas Child facilities **Conf** Class 12 Board 20
Thtr 30 **Parking** 100 **Notes** LB

TEWKESBURY   **Map 10 S083**

Tewkesbury Park Hotel Golf & Country Club

★★★★ 72% HOTEL

☎ 0870 609 6101 📠 01684 292386
Lincoln Green Ln GL20 7DN
e-mail: tewkesburypark@foliohotels.com
web: www.foliohotels.com/tewkesburypark
dir: M5 junct 9/A438 through Tewkesbury, A38 (pass
Abbey on left), right into Lincoln Green Lane

Only two miles from the M5, this extended 18th-century
manor house boasts wonderful views across the Malvern
Hills from its hilltop position. Bedrooms have
contemporary comforts and many enjoy countryside
views. In addition to the well-established golf course, an
indoor pool, gym, sauna, squash and tennis courts are
also available.

Rooms 82 (8 fmly) (27 GF) **D** £78-£148 (incl. bkfst)*
Facilities Spa STV ⌾ supervised ♨ 18 ⛳ Putt green Gym
Squash Xmas New Year Wi-fi **Conf** Class 100 Board 50
Thtr 300 Del from £135 to £154* **Parking** 250 **Notes** LB
Civ Wed 150

Bell

★★ 🅰 HOTEL

☎ 01684 293293 📠 01684 295938
52 Church St GL20 5SA
e-mail: 6408@greeneking.co.uk
web: www.oldenglish.co.uk
dir: M5 junct 9, follow brown tourist signs for Tewkesbury
Abbey, hotel directly opposite Abbey.

Rooms 24 (1 fmly) (4 GF) **Facilities** Xmas **Conf** Class 16
Board 24 Thtr 60 **Parking** 20 **Notes** LB

THORNBURY   **Map 4 ST69**

Thornbury Castle

★★★ ⊛⊛ HOTEL

☎ 01454 281182 📠 01454 416188
Castle St BS35 1HH
e-mail: info@thornburycastle.co.uk
web: www.thornburycastle.co.uk
dir: on A38 N'bound from Bristol take 1st turn to
Thornbury. At end of High St left into Castle St, follow
brown sign, entrance to Castle on left behind St Mary's
Church

Henry VIII ordered the first owner of this castle to
be beheaded! Guests today have the opportunity of
sleeping in historical surroundings fitted out with all
the modern amenities. Most rooms have four-poster
or coronet beds and real fires. Tranquil lounges enjoy
views over the gardens, while elegant, wood-panelled
dining rooms make memorable settings for a leisurely
award-winning meal.

Rooms 27 (3 fmly) (4 GF) **S** £140-£215; **D** £155-£435
(incl. bkfst)* **Facilities** STV FTV ⛵ Archery Helicopter
ride Clay pigeon shooting Massage treatment Xmas
New Year Wi-fi **Conf** Class 40 Board 30 Thtr 70
Del from £220 to £280* **Parking** 50 **Notes** LB
Civ Wed 70

See advert on page 233

Thornbury Golf Lodge

★★ 67% HOTEL

☎ 01454 281144 📠 01454 281177
Bristol Rd BS35 3XL
e-mail: info@thornburygc.co.uk
web: www.thornburygc.co.uk
dir: M5 junct 16, A38 towards Thornbury. At lights
(Berkeley Vale Motors) turn left. Hotel entrance 1m on left

The old farmhouse exterior of Thornbury Golf Lodge
disguises an interior with spacious, well equipped and
comfortable bedrooms. Many have pleasant views over
the centre's two golf courses or towards the Severn
Estuary. Meals are taken in the adjacent clubhouse which
has a full bar and serves a range of hot and cold food all
through the day.

Rooms 11 (7 GF) **S** fr £58.95; **D** fr £68.95* **Facilities** STV
♨ 36 Putt green **Conf** Class 40 Board 40 Thtr 100
Parking 150 **Notes** LB ⊗ No children 5yrs Closed 25 Dec

TORMARTON   **Map 4 ST77**

Best Western Compass Inn

★★ 78% HOTEL

☎ 01454 218242 & 218577 📠 01454 218741
GL9 1JB
e-mail: info@compass-inn.co.uk
web: www.compass-inn.co.uk
dir: 0.5m from M4 junct 18

Originally a coaching inn dating from the 18th century,
this hostelry has grown considerably over the years.
Bedrooms are spacious and well equipped, whilst public
areas include a choice of bars and varied dining options.
A range of conference rooms is also available, providing
facilities for varied functions.

Rooms 26 (6 fmly) (12 GF) (4 smoking) **S** £67.50-£98;
D £76.50-£130* **Facilities** FTV French boules Golf driving
nets New Year Wi-fi **Conf** Class 30 Board 34 Thtr 80
Del from £135* **Parking** 160 **Notes** LB Closed 24-26 Dec
Civ Wed 100

Campanile Manchester

BUDGET HOTEL

☎ 0161 833 1845 📠 0161 833 1847
55 Ordsall Ln, Regent Rd, Salford M5 4RS
e-mail: manchester@campanile.com
dir: M602 to Manchester, then A57. After large rdbt with Sainsbury's on left, left at next lights. Hotel on right

This modern building offers accommodation in smart, well-equipped bedrooms, all with en suite bathrooms. Refreshments may be taken at the informal bistro. See also the Hotel Groups pages.

Rooms 104 (25 GF) **Conf** Class 40 Board 30 Thtr 50

Express by Holiday Inn - Manchester Salford Quays

BUDGET HOTEL

☎ 0161 868 1000 📠 0161 868 10 68
Waterfront Quay, Salford Quays M50 3XW
e-mail: dutymanagersalfordquays@expressholidayinn.co.uk
web: www.hiexpress.com/salfordquays

A modern hotel ideal for families and business travellers. Fresh and uncomplicated, the spacious rooms include Sky TV, power shower and tea and coffee-making facilities. Continental buffet breakfast is included in the room rate; other meals may be taken at the nearby family pub or restaurant. See also the Hotel Groups pages.

Rooms 120 **Conf** Class 10 Board 12 Thtr 25

Ibis Hotel Manchester

BUDGET HOTEL

☎ 0161 272 5000 📠 0161 272 5010
Charles St, Princess St M1 7DL
e-mail: H3143@accor-hotels.com
web: www.ibishotel.com
dir: M62, M602 towards Manchester Centre, follow signs to UMIST(A34)

Modern, budget hotel offering comfortable accommodation in bright and practical bedrooms. Breakfast is self-service and dinner is available in the restaurant. See also the Hotel Groups pages.

Rooms 126 (9 smoking) **D** £59-£95*

Ibis Manchester City Centre

BUDGET HOTEL

☎ 0161 234 0600 📠 0161 234 0610
96 Portland St M1 4GY
e-mail: H3142@accor.com
web: www.ibishotel.com
dir: In city centre, between Princess St & Oxford St. 10min walk from Piccadilly

Rooms 127 (16 fmly) (7 smoking) **S** £61-£75; **D** £61-£75*

Travelodge Ashton Under Lyne

BUDGET HOTEL

☎ 08719 846 284
Lord Sheldon Way OL7 0DN
web: www.travelodge.co.uk
dir: W of M60 junct 23, A635 follow signs for Snipe Retail Park into Lord Sheldon Way. Lodge on left

Travelodge offers good quality, good value, modern accommodation. Ideal for families, the spacious en suite bedrooms include remote-control TV, tea and coffee-making facilities and comfortable beds. Meals can be taken at the nearby family restaurant. See also the Hotel Groups pages.

Rooms 62 **S** fr £29; **D** fr £29

Travelodge Manchester Ancoats

BUDGET HOTEL

☎ 08719 846 282 📠 0161 235 8631
22 Great Ancoats St, Ancoats M4 5AZ
web: www.travelodge.co.uk
dir: M60 junct 11 to A57, take 5th exit off rdbt. Follow M60/M602 junct 3. Follow signs for A62 to Lodge.

Rooms 117 **S** fr £29; **D** fr £29

Travelodge Manchester Central

BUDGET HOTEL

☎ 08719 846 159 📠 0161 839 5181
Townbury House, 11 Blackfriars St M3 5AL
web: www.travelodge.co.uk
dir: N on Deansgate, junct of Blackfriars St & St Mary Gate, turn left over bridge

Rooms 181 **S** fr £29; **D** fr £29

Travelodge Manchester Sportcity

BUDGET HOTEL

☎ 08719 846 293
Hyde Rd, Birch St, West Gorton M12 5NT
web: www.travelodge.co.uk
dir: M60 junct 24, follow A57 towards city centre for 2m, hotel on right

Rooms 90 (6 fmly) (28 GF) **S** fr £29; **D** fr £29
Conf Class 50 Board 50 Thtr 100

Travelodge Manchester Trafford Park

BUDGET HOTEL

☎ 08719 846 338 📠 0161 747 7419
17 Trafford Way, Urmston M17 8DD
web: www.travelodge.co.uk
dir: B5214 Trafford Boulevard towards Trafford Centre. At rdbt take 1st left

Rooms 54 **S** fr £29; **D** fr £29

MANCHESTER AIRPORT Map 15 SJ88

See also **Altrincham**

Manchester Airport Marriott

Marriott HOTELS & RESORTS

★★★★ 81% HOTEL

☎ 0161 904 0301 📠 0161 980 1787
Hale Rd, Hale Barns WA15 8XW
e-mail: london.regional.reservations@marriott.com
web: www.manchesterairportmarriott.co.uk
dir: M56 junct 6, in left lane (Hale, Altrincham). Left at lights, on approach to bridge into right lane. At rdbt 3rd exit into hotel car park

With good airport links and convenient access to the city, this sprawling modern hotel is a popular destination. The hotel offers extensive leisure and business facilities, a choice of eating and drinking options and ample parking. Bedrooms are situated around courtyards and have a comprehensive range of facilities.

Rooms 215 (22 fmly) **Facilities** ☃ supervised Gym
Conf Class 70 Board 50 Thtr 160 **Services** Lift
Parking 400 (charged) **Notes** LB ⊗ Civ Wed 110

MANCHESTER continued

Stanneylands

★★★★ 80% ◉◉ HOTEL

☎ 01625 525225 📠 01625 537282
Stanneylands Rd SK9 4EY
e-mail: reservations@stanneylandshotel.co.uk
web: www.stanneylandshotel.co.uk
dir: from M56 at airport turn off, follow signs to
Wilmslow. Left into Station Rd, onto Stanneylands Rd.
Hotel on right

This traditional hotel offers well-equipped bedrooms and
delightful, comfortable day rooms. The cuisine in the
restaurant is of a high standard and ranges from
traditional favourites to more imaginative contemporary
dishes. Staff throughout are friendly and obliging.

Rooms 54 (2 fmly) (10 GF) **S** £50–£125; **D** £60–£145*
Facilities STV FTV 𝄞 Wi-fi **Conf** Class 50 Board 40
Thtr 120 Del from £125 to £145* **Services** Lift
Parking 108 **Notes** LB ⊗ Civ Wed 100

Radisson SAS Hotel Manchester Airport

Radisson

★★★★ 78% HOTEL

☎ 0161 490 5000 📠 0161 490 5100
Chicago Av M90 3RA
e-mail: sales.manchester@radissonsas.com
web: www.manchester.radissonsas.co.uk
dir: M56 junct 5, follow signs for Terminal 2. At rdbt 2nd
left and follow signs for railway station. Hotel next to
station

All the airport terminals are quickly accessed by covered,
moving walkways from this modern hotel. There is an
excellent and well-equipped leisure club complete with
indoor pool, and extensive conference and banqueting
facilities are available. Air-conditioned bedrooms are
thoughtfully equipped and come in a variety of decorative
themes. Super views of the runway can be enjoyed in the

Phileas Fogg Restaurant that offers creative international
cuisine; there's also an all-day brasserie.

Rooms 360 (27 fmly) (23 smoking) **Facilities** ⊗ Gym
Health & beauty treatments Wi-fi **Conf** Class 160
Board 60 Thtr 350 **Services** Lift Air con **Parking** 222
(charged) **Notes** ⊗ Civ Wed 230

Crowne Plaza Manchester Airport

CROWNE PLAZA
HOTELS & RESORTS

★★★★ 74% HOTEL

☎ 0870 400 9055 📠 0161 436 2340
Ringway Rd M90 3NS
e-mail: reservations-manchesterairport@ihg.com
web: www.crowneplaza.co.uk
dir: M56 junct 5 signed to Manchester Airport. At airport,
follow signs to Terminal 1 & 3. Hotel next to Terminal 3.
Long stay car park on left

Located close to Terminal 3 this smart, modern hotel
offers well equipped, comfortable bedrooms, all with
fitted with air conditioning and effective double glazing.
A choice of dining styles and bars is available, and the
hotel has spacious leisure facilities and ample on-site
parking. Hospitality is friendly with several long-serving
staff members who greet regular customers as friends.

Rooms 294 (100 fmly) (51 GF) **Facilities** ⊗ supervised
Gym Wi-fi **Conf** Class 25 Board 20 Thtr 30 **Services** Lift
Air con **Parking** 300 (charged)

Etrop Grange Hotel

folio Hotels

★★★ 78% ◉ HOTEL

☎ 0870 609 6123 & 0161 499 0500 📠 0161 499 0790
Thorley Ln M90 4EG
e-mail: etrop@foliohotels.com
web: www.foliohotels.com/etropgrange
dir: M56 junct 5 follow signs for Terminal 2, on slip road
to rdbt take 1st exit. Immediately left, hotel 400yds

This Georgian country-house style hotel is close to
Terminal 2 but one would never know once inside. Stylish,
comfortable bedrooms provide modern comforts and good
business facilities. Elegant day rooms include the Coach
House Restaurant that serves creative dishes.
Complimentary chauffeured transport to the airport is
available for guests using the airport.

Rooms 64 **S** £75–£149; **D** £75–£149* **Facilities** STV New
Year Wi-fi **Conf** Class 35 Board 35 Thtr 80 Del from £130
to £175* **Parking** 80 **Notes** LB ⊗ Civ Wed 90

Holiday Inn Manchester Airport

Holiday Inn
HOTELS · RESORTS

★★★ 74% HOTEL

☎ 0870 443 6961 📠 01625 531876
Altrincham Rd SK9 4LR
e-mail: himanchester@qmh-hotels.com
web: www.holidayinn.co.uk
dir: take A538 for approx 1m, hotel on left

Just a short distance from Manchester Airport and the
M56 motorway, this pleasant hotel offers comfortable
public areas, modern leisure and meeting facilities. The
restaurant provides a wide choice of formal and informal
dining. Bedrooms are fully equipped with air-conditioning
and have 24-hour room service.

Rooms 126 (6 fmly) (19 GF) **Facilities** ⊗ Gym Squash
Floatation room Sauna Steam room Beauty salon Squash
court Xmas New Year Wi-fi **Conf** Class 150 Board 90
Thtr 300 **Services** Lift Air con **Parking** 529 (charged)
Notes ⊗ RS 23-31 Dec Civ Wed 300

Bewleys Hotel Manchester Airport

☎ 0161 498 0333 & 498 1390 📠 0161 498 0222
Outwood Ln M90 4HL
e-mail: man@bewleyshotels.com
web: www.bewleyshotels.com
dir: at Manchester Airport. Follow signs to Manchester Airport Terminal 3. Hotel on left on Terminal 3 rdbt.

Currently the rating for this establishment is not confirmed. This may be due to a change of ownership or because it has only recently joined the AA rating scheme. For further details please see the AA website: www.theAA.com

Rooms 365 (111 fmly) (30 GF) **S** £79-£99; **D** £79-£99
Facilities Wi-fi **Conf** Class 35 Board 18 Thtr 60
Del from £139 to £169* **Services** Lift **Parking** 300
(charged) **Notes** LB ⊗

Menzies Pinewood

MenziesHotels

☎ 01625 529211 📠 01625 536812
180 Wilmslow Rd, Handforth SK9 3LG
e-mail: pinewood@menzieshotels.co.uk
web: www.menzieshotels.co.uk
dir: M60 junct 3 follow A34 towards Wilmslow at 3rd rdbt turn right following tourist signs. At end of dual carriageway turn left, hotel on left.

Currently the rating for this establishment is not confirmed. This may be due to a change of ownership or because it has only recently joined the AA rating scheme. For further details please see the AA website: www.theAA.com

Rooms 58 (4 fmly) (6 smoking) **S** £75-£125; **D** £75-£125
Facilities STV Xmas New Year Wi-fi **Conf** Class 100
Board 60 Thtr 200 Del from £120 to £160 **Services** Lift
Parking 160 (charged) **Notes** ⊗ Civ Wed 130

Travelodge Manchester Airport

Travelodge

BUDGET HOTEL

☎ 08719 846 6181
Runger Ln WA15 8XW
web: www.travelodge.co.uk

Travelodge offers good quality, good value, modern accommodation. Ideal for families, the spacious en suite bedrooms include remote-control TV, tea and coffee-

making facilities and comfortable beds. Meals can be taken at the nearby family restaurant. See also the Hotel Groups pages.

S fr £29; **D** fr £29

Best Western Hotel Smokies Park

★★★ 80% HOTEL

☎ 0161 785 5000 📠 0161 785 5010
Ashton Rd, Bardsley OL8 3HX
e-mail: sales@smokies.co.uk
web: www.smokies.co.uk
dir: on A627 between Oldham and Ashton-under-Lyne

This modern, stylish hotel offers smart, comfortable bedrooms and suites. A wide range of Italian and English dishes is offered in the Mediterranean-style restaurant and there is a welcoming lounge bar with live entertainment at weekends. There is a small yet well equipped, residents' only fitness centre and extensive function facilities are also available.

Rooms 73 (2 fmly) (22 GF) **S** £75-£95; **D** £85-£105 (incl. bkfst)* **Facilities** Gym Xmas New Year Wi-fi
Conf Class 100 Board 40 Thtr 400 Del from £105 to
£145* **Services** Lift **Parking** 120 **Notes** LB ⊗ RS 25
Dec-3 Jan Civ Wed 120

Clough Manor

★★★ 73% ⊛ HOTEL

☎ 01457 871040 📠 01457 873804
Rochdale Rd, Denshaw OL3 5UE
e-mail: reception@cloughmanor.com
dir: M62 junct 21, right at rdbt onto A640, under motorway, left at Wagon & Horses public house. Hotel 500yds on left

Situated in open moorland and convenient for the M62 this friendly hotel has been refurbished and offers comfortable, well equipped bedrooms. The hub of the hotel is the attractive restaurant which serves interesting meals using seasonal and fresh local produce. There is also a large well equipped function room.

Rooms 25 **S** £65-£75; **D** £80-£100 (incl. bkfst)*
Facilities FTV New Year Wi-fi **Conf** Class 120 Board 100
Thtr 250 **Parking** 80 **Notes** LB ⊗ Civ Wed 120

Innkeeper's Lodge Oldham

BUDGET HOTEL

☎ 0845 112 6025 📠 0845 112 6276
Burnley Ln, Chadderton OL1 2QS
web: www.innkeeperslodge.com/oldham
dir: M62 junct 20, A627(M) S towards Oldham. At junct with A663 into Burnley Lane. Lodge on left

Innkeeper's Lodge represents an exciting, high value concept within the budget hotel market. Comfortable bedrooms provide excellent facilities that include satellite

---

TV and modem points. Options include family rooms, and for the corporate guest, cutting edge IT which includes Wi-fi access. A popular Carvery provides all-day food, including an extensive, complimentary continental breakfast.

Rooms 30 **S** £53-£55; **D** £53-£55 (incl. bkfst)
Conf Thtr 30

Travelodge Oldham

Travelodge

BUDGET HOTEL

☎ 08719 846 236 📠 0161 681 9021
432 Broadway, Chadderton OL9 8AU
web: www.travelodge.co.uk

Travelodge offers good quality, good value, modern accommodation. Ideal for families, the spacious en suite bedrooms include remote-control TV, tea and coffee-making facilities and comfortable beds. Meals can be taken at the nearby family restaurant. See also the Hotel Groups pages.

Rooms 50 **S** fr £29; **D** fr £29

Fairways Lodge & Leisure Club

☎ 0161 798 8905 📠 0161 773 5562
George St, (Off Bury New Road) M25 9WS
e-mail: info@fairwayslodge.co.uk
dir: M60 junct 17, A56 for 1.5m, right into George St

Currently the rating for this establishment is not confirmed. This may be due to a change of ownership or because it has only recently joined the AA rating scheme. For further details please see the AA website: www.theAA.com

Rooms 40 (2 fmly) (19 GF) **Facilities** Gym Squash ♫
Xmas Child facilities **Conf** Class 120 Thtr 100 **Parking** 80
Notes LB ⊗ Civ Wed 50

Old Mill

★★★ 70% HOTEL

☎ 01706 822991 📠 01706 822291
Springwood BL0 9DS
e-mail: reservations@oldmill-uk.com
dir: M66 junct 4, A56 towards Rawtenstall. 1st left into Bridge St. Over rail crossing, on at lights into Carr St. 2nd left into Springwood, to end of road, right to hotel

Extended from an original water mill, this friendly hotel enjoys fine views over the town and Rossendale Valley. The bedrooms have attractive floral furnishings, and inter-connecting family rooms are available. In addition to a comfortable bar and beamed restaurant, a well-equipped leisure centre is available to guests during their stay.

Rooms 29 (6 fmly) **S** £60-£99; **D** £65-£110 (incl. bkfst)*
Facilities STV ⊙ supervised Gym Steam room Sauna
Wi-fi **Conf** Class 30 Board 20 Thtr 70 Del from £130 to
£149* **Parking** 50 **Notes** LB Civ Wed 100

ROCHDALE — Map 16 SD81

Mercure Norton Grange Hotel & Spa

★★★★ 77% HOTEL

☎ 0870 1942119 📠 01706 649313
Manchester Rd, Castleton OL11 2XZ
web: www.mercure-uk.com
dir: M62 junct 20, follow signs for A664 Castleton. Right at next 2 rdbts for hotel 0.5m on left

Standing in nine acres of grounds and mature gardens, this Victorian house provides comfort in elegant surroundings. The well-equipped bedrooms provide a host of extras for both the business and leisure guest. Public areas include the Pickwick bistro and bar and a smart restaurant, both offering a good choice of dishes. There is also an impressive leisure centre.

Rooms 81 (17 fmly) (10 GF) **Facilities** Spa ✪ Gym Leisure centre Indoor/Outdoor hydrotherapy pool Thermal suite Rock sauna Xmas New Year Wi-fi **Conf** Class 120 Board 70 Thtr 220 **Services** Lift **Parking** 150 **Notes** LB Civ Wed 150

SALE — Map 15 SJ79

Amblehurst Hotel

★★★ 68% HOTEL

☎ 0161 973 8800 📠 0161 905 1697
44 Washway Rd M33 7QZ
e-mail: reception@theamblehurst.com
web: www.theamblehurst.com
dir: M60 junct 7 onto A56 (Washway Rd)

This hotel is located in the centre of Sale which is only a short distance from the centre of Manchester. It offers spacious accommodation and a small function room. Meals are available in the formal dining room or in the popular lounge bar.

Rooms 66 (4 fmly) (21 GF) (14 smoking) **S** £55-£60; **D** £65-£70 (incl. bkfst)* **Facilities** ♫ Xmas New Year Wi-fi **Conf** Class 65 Board 30 Thtr 80 **Services** Lift **Parking** 50 **Notes** ⊗

STOCKPORT — Map 16 SJ89

See also **Manchester Airport**

Bredbury Hall Hotel & Country Club

THE INDEPENDENTS
HOTEL ASSOCIATION

★★★ 77% HOTEL

☎ 0161 430 7421 📠 0161 430 5079
Goyt Valley SK6 2DH
e-mail: reservations@bredburyhallhotel.com
dir: M60 junct 25 signed Bredbury, right at lights, left onto Osbourne St, hotel 500mtrs on right

With views over open countryside, this large modern hotel is conveniently located for the M60. The well-equipped bedrooms offer space and comfort and the restaurant serves a very wide range of freshly prepared dishes.

Rooms 150 (2 fmly) (50 GF) **Facilities** STV Fishing Night club (Thu, Fri & Sat eve) Casino 36 Stockport ♫ Xmas New Year Wi-fi **Conf** Class 120 Board 60 Thtr 200 **Services** Lift **Parking** 450 **Notes** ⊗ Civ Wed 80

Alma Lodge Hotel

★★★ 75% HOTEL

☎ 0161 483 4431 📠 0161 483 1983
149 Buxton Rd SK2 6EL
e-mail: reception@almalodgehotel.com
web: www.almalodgehotel.com
dir: M60 junct 1 at rdbt take 2nd exit under rail viaduct at lights opposite. At Debenhams turn right onto A6. Hotel approx 1.5m on left

A large hotel, located on the main road close to the town, offering modern and well-equipped bedrooms. It is family owned and run and serves a good range of quality Italian cooking in Luigi's restaurant. Good function rooms are also available. Free internet access is also available.

Rooms 52 (32 annexe) (2 fmly) **S** £45-£67; **D** £80-£94 (incl. bkfst)* **Facilities** FTV Wi-fi **Conf** Class 100 Board 60 Thtr 250 **Parking** 120 **Notes** ⊗ RS Bank Hols Civ Wed 200

Wycliffe

★★★ 72% HOTEL

☎ 0161 477 5395 📠 0161 476 3219
74 Edgeley Rd, Edgeley SK3 9NQ
e-mail: reception@wycliffe-hotel.com
web: www.wycliffe-hotel.com
dir: M60 junct 2 follow A560 for Stockport, at 1st lights turn right, hotel 0.5m on left

This family-run, welcoming hotel provides immaculately maintained and well-equipped bedrooms within main building, and more simply appointed rooms in two houses opposite. There is a well stocked bar and a popular restaurant where the menu has an Italian bias. There is ample, convenient parking.

Rooms 20 (6 annexe) (3 fmly) (2 GF) **S** £50-£73.50; **D** £75-£88 (incl. bkfst)* **Facilities** FTV Wi-fi **Conf** Class 20 Board 20 Thtr 30 **Parking** 46 **Notes** ⊗ Closed 25-27 Dec RS BH

Innkeeper's Lodge Stockport

BUDGET HOTEL

☎ 0845 112 6027 📠 0845 112 6274
271 Wellington Rd, North Heaton Chapel SK4 5BP
web: www.innkeeperslodge.com/stockport
dir: M60 junct 1. Follow A5145/Town Centre signs. Left at lights (signed Manchester) into George's Rd. Over rdbt, left at lights, left onto A6/Wellington Road North. Lodge on right

Innkeeper's Lodge represents an exciting, high value concept within the budget hotel market. Comfortable bedrooms provide excellent facilities that include satellite TV and modem points. Options include family rooms, and for the corporate guest, cutting edge IT which includes Wi-fi access. A popular Carvery provides all-day food, including an extensive, complimentary continental breakfast.

Rooms 22 **S** £53-£55; **D** £53-£55 (incl. bkfst)* **Conf** Thtr 80

WIGAN Map 15 SD50

Macdonald Kilhey Court

★★★★ 73% ⊛ HOTEL

☎ 0870 1942122 📄 01257 422401
Chorley Rd, Standish WN1 2XN
e-mail: general.kilheycourt@macdonald-hotels.co.uk
web: www.macdonald-hotels.co.uk/kilheycourt
dir: M6 junct 27, A5209 Standish, over at lights, past church on right, left at T-junct, hotel on right 350yds. M61 junct 6, signed Wigan & Haigh Hall. 3m & right at T-junct. Hotel 0.5 m on right

This hotel is peacefully situated in its own grounds yet conveniently located for the motorway network. The accommodation is comfortable and the rooms are split between the Victorian house and a modern extension. Public areas display many original features and the split-level restaurant has views over the Worthington Lakes. This hotel is a very popular venue for weddings.

Rooms 62 (8 GF) **Facilities** STV ☞ Gym Aerobics & yoga classes Private fishing arranged Beauty treatments Xmas New Year Wi-fi **Conf** Class 180 Board 60 Thtr 400 **Services** Lift **Parking** 200 **Notes** ⊗ Civ Wed 300

Best Western Wrightington Hotel & Country Club

★★★ 80% HOTEL

☎ 01257 425803 📄 01257 425830
Moss Ln, Wrightington WN6 9PB
e-mail: info@wrightingtonhotel.co.uk
dir: M6 junct 27, 0.25m W, hotel on right after church

Situated in open countryside close to the M6, this privately owned hotel offers friendly hospitality. Accommodation is well equipped and spacious, and public areas include an extensive leisure complex complete with hair salon, boutique and sports injury lab. Blazers Restaurant, two bars and air-conditioned banqueting facilities appeal to a broad market.

Rooms 74 (6 fmly) (36 GF) **Facilities** ☞ Gym Squash Hairdressing salon Beauty spa Sports injury clinic Wi-fi **Conf** Class 120 Board 40 Thtr 200 **Services** Lift **Parking** 240 **Notes** RS 24 Dec-3 Jan Civ Wed 100

The Beeches

RESTAURANT WITH ROOMS

☎ 01257 426432 & 421316 📄 01257 427503
School Ln, Standish WN6 0TD
e-mail: mail@beecheshotel.co.uk
dir: M6 junct 27, A5209 into Standish on School Ln

Located a short drive from M6, this elegant Victorian house has been renovated to provide high standards of comfort. Bedrooms are equipped with practical and homely extras, and public areas include spacious lounges, a popular brasserie, and a self-contained function suite.

Rooms 10 (6 en suite) (4 fmly)

WORSLEY Map 15 SD70

Novotel Manchester West

★★★ 68% HOTEL

☎ 0161 799 3535 📄 0161 703 8207
Worsley Brow M28 2YA
e-mail: H0907@accor.com
web: www.novotel.com
dir: adjacent to M60 junct 13

Well placed for access to the Peak and the Lake District, as well as the City of Manchester, this modern hotel successfully caters for both families and business guests. The spacious bedrooms have sofa beds and a large work area; the hotel boasts an outdoor swimming pool, children's play area, and secure parking.

Rooms 119 (10 fmly) (41 GF) **Facilities** ⚊ Wi-fi **Conf** Class 140 Board 25 Thtr 200 **Services** Lift **Parking** 95 **Notes** LB Civ Wed 140

HAMPSHIRE

ALDERSHOT Map 5 SU85

Potters International

★★★ 68% HOTEL

☎ 01252 344000 📄 01252 311611
1 Fleet Rd GU11 2ET
e-mail: reservations@pottersinthotel.com
dir: access via A325 & A321 towards Fleet

This modern hotel is located within easy reach of Aldershot. Extensive air-conditioned public areas include ample lounge areas, a pub and a more formal restaurant; there are also conference rooms and a very good leisure club. Bedrooms, mostly spacious, are well equipped and have been attractively decorated and furnished.

Rooms 100 (5 fmly) (7 GF) **S** £55-£120; **D** £77-£140 (incl. bkfst)* **Facilities** STV ☞ Gym Wi-fi **Conf** Class 250 Board 100 Thtr 400 **Services** Lift **Parking** 120 **Notes** ⊗

ALTON Map 5 SU73

Alton Grange

★★★ 74% ⊛⊛ HOTEL

☎ 01420 86565 📄 01420 541346
London Rd GU34 4EG
e-mail: info@altongrange.co.uk
web: www.altongrange.co.uk
dir: from A31 right at rdbt signed Alton/Holybourne/Bordon B3004. Hotel 300yds on left

A friendly family owned hotel, conveniently located on the outskirts of this market town and set in two acres of lovingly tended gardens. The individually styled bedrooms, including three suites, are all thoughtfully equipped. Diners can choose between the more formal Truffles Restaurant or relaxed Muffins Brasserie. The attractive public areas include a function suite.

Rooms 30 (4 annexe) (4 fmly) (7 GF) **Facilities** Hot air ballooning Wi-fi **Conf** Class 30 Board 40 Thtr 80 **Parking** 48 **Notes** LB No children 3yrs Closed 24 Dec-2 Jan Civ Wed 100

ANDOVER Map 5 SU34

Esseborne Manor

★★★ 78% ⊛ HOTEL

☎ 01264 736444 📄 01264 736725
Hurstbourne Tarrant SP11 0ER
e-mail: info@esseborne-manor.co.uk
web: www.esseborne-manor.co.uk
dir: halfway between Andover & Newbury on A343, just 1m N of Hurstbourne Tarrant

Set in two acres of well-tended gardens, this attractive manor house is surrounded by the open countryside of the North Wessex Downs. Bedrooms are delightfully individual and are split between the main house, an adjoining courtyard and separate garden cottage. There's a wonderfully relaxed atmosphere throughout, and public rooms combine elegance with comfort. *Continued*

ANDOVER continued

Rooms 19 (8 annexe) (2 fmly) (6 GF) **S** £110-£130;
D £125-£180 (incl. bkfst)* **Facilities** STV 🏊 🐕 Wi-fi
Conf Class 40 Board 30 Thtr 60 **Parking** 50 **Notes** LB
Civ Wed 100

Quality Hotel Andover

★★★ 63% HOTEL

☎ 01264 369111 📠 01264 369000
Micheldever Rd SP11 6LA
e-mail: andover@quality-hotels.co.uk
dir: off A303 at A3093. 1st rdbt take 1st exit, 2nd rdbt
take 1st exit. Turn left immediately before Total petrol
station, then left again

Located on the outskirts of the town, this hotel is popular
with business guests. Bedrooms provide useful
accessories; public areas consist of a cosy lounge, a hotel
bar and a traditional style restaurant serving a range of

meals. There is also a large conference suite available
and a pleasant garden with patio seating.

Rooms 49 (36 annexe) (13 GF) **S** £55-£65; **D** £59-£85
(incl. bkfst)* **Facilities** Wi-fi **Conf** Class 60 Board 60
Thtr 180 Del from £65 to £95* **Parking** 100 **Notes** LB ⊗
Civ Wed 85

BARTON STACEY Map 5 SU44

Travelodge Barton Stacey

BUDGET HOTEL

☎ 08719 846 007 📠 01264 720260
SO21 3NP
web: www.travelodge.co.uk
dir: on A303 westbound

Travelodge offers good quality, good value, modern
accommodation. Ideal for families, the spacious en suite
bedrooms include remote-control TV, tea and coffee-
making facilities and comfortable beds. Meals can be

taken at the nearby family restaurant. See also the Hotel
Groups pages.

Rooms 20 **S** fr £29; **D** fr £29

BASINGSTOKE Map 5 SU65

See also **Odiham & Stratfield Turgis**

INSPECTORS' CHOICE

Tylney Hall

★★★★ 🏵🏵 HOTEL

☎ 01256 764881 📠 01256 768141
RG27 9AZ
e-mail: sales@tylneyhall.com
web: www.tylneyhall.com

(For full entry see Rotherwick)

The Hampshire Court

QHOTELS

★★★★ 78% ◉ HOTEL

☎ 01256 319700 🖷 01256 319730
Centre Dr, Chineham RG24 8FY
e-mail: hampshirecourt@qhotels.co.uk
web: www.qhotels.co.uk
dir: off A33 (Reading road) behind Chineham Shopping
Centre via Great Binfields Rd

Having completed a multi-million pound transformation,
this hotel now boasts a range of smart, comfortable and
stylish bedrooms, and leisure facilities that are unrivalled
locally. Facilities include indoor and outdoor tennis
courts, two swimming pools, a gym and a number of
treatment rooms. Q Hotels - AA Hotel Group of the Year
2008-9.

Rooms 90 (6 fmly) **S** £60-£160; **D** £70-£170 (incl. bkfst)*
Facilities Spa STV ℞ 🏊 Gym Steam room Beauty salon
Sauna Exercise studios Xmas New Year Wi-fi
Conf Class 130 Board 60 Thtr 220 Del from £145 to
£189* **Services** Lift **Parking** 200 **Notes** LB Civ Wed 220

See advert on opposite page

Audleys Wood

HANDPICKED HOTELS

★★★★ 76% ◉◉ COUNTRY HOUSE HOTEL

☎ 01256 817555 🖷 01256 817500
Alton Rd RG25 2JT
e-mail: info@audleyswood.com
web: www.audleyswood.com
dir: M3 junct 6. From Basingstoke take A339 towards
Alton, hotel on right

A long sweeping drive leads to this old Victorian hunting
lodge, now a traditional country-house hotel that has
some modern twists. Smart and traditional public areas
have log fires, and good food is served in the
contemporary conservatory with a small minstrels'
gallery. All the bedrooms and bathrooms are well
equipped and spacious.

Rooms 72 (23 fmly) (34 GF) **S** £105-£195; **D** £125-£295
(incl. bkfst)* **Facilities** STV ⛳ Xmas New Year Wi-fi
Conf Class 80 Board 60 Thtr 200 Del from £165 to £205*
Parking 60 **Notes** LB ⊗ Civ Wed 100

See advert on opposite page

Apollo

CLASSIC
BRITISH HOTELS

★★★★ 76% ◉ HOTEL

☎ 01256 796700 🖷 01256 796701
Aldermaston Roundabout RG24 9NU
e-mail: admin@apollohotels.com
web: www.apollohotels.com
dir: M3 junct 6. Follow ringroad N, exit A340
(Aldermaston). Hotel on rdbt, 5th exit into Popley Way for
access

This modern hotel provides well-equipped
accommodation and spacious public areas, appealing to
both the leisure and business guest. Facilities include a
smartly appointed leisure club, a business centre, along
with a good choice of formal and informal eating in two
restaurants; Vespers is the fine dining option.

Rooms 125 (32 GF) **Facilities** Spa FTV ℞ supervised Gym
Sauna Steam room Xmas New Year Wi-fi **Conf** Class 196
Board 30 Thtr 255 **Services** Lift Air con **Parking** 200
Notes ⊗ Civ Wed 100

BASINGSTOKE continued

Barceló Basingstoke Country Hotel

★★★★ 74% HOTEL

☎ 01256 764161 ▤ 01256 768341
Scures Hill, Nately Scures, Hook RG27 9JS
e-mail: basingstokecountry@barcelo-hotels.co.uk
web: www.barcelo-hotels.co.uk
dir: M3 junct 5, A287 towards Newnham. Left at lights.
Hotel 200mtrs on right

This popular hotel is close to Basingstoke and its country location ensures a quiet stay. Bedrooms are available in a number of styles, and guests have a choice of dining in the formal restaurant, or for lighter meals and snacks there is a relaxed café and a smart bar. Extensive conference and leisure facilities complete the picture.

Rooms 100 (26 GF) **S** £65-£160; **Facilities** ♨ Gym Sauna Solarium Steam room Dance studio Beauty treatments New Year Wi-fi **Conf** Class 85 Board 80 Thtr 240 **Services** Lift Air con **Parking** 200 **Notes** RS 24 Dec-2 Jan Civ Wed 90

Romans

★★★ 70% HOTEL

☎ 0118 970 0421 ▤ 0118 970 0691
Little London Rd RG7 2PN
e-mail: romanhotel@hotmail.com

(For full entry see SILCHESTER)

See advert on page 249

Holiday Inn Basingstoke

Ⓤ

☎ 0870 400 9004 ▤ 01256 840081
Grove Rd RG21 3EE
e-mail: reservations-basingstoke@ihg.com
web: www.holidayinn.co.uk
dir: on A339 (Alton road) S of Basingstoke

Currently the rating for this establishment is not confirmed. This may be due to a change of ownership or because it has only recently joined the AA rating scheme. For further details please see the AA website: www.theAA.com

Rooms 86 (5 fmly) (43 GF) (4 smoking) **S** £39-£149; **D** £39-£149 **Facilities** FTV Xmas New Year Wi-fi **Conf** Class 70 Board 70 Thtr 140 Del from £110 to £180 **Services** Air con **Parking** 150 **Notes** LB ⊗

Travelodge Basingstoke

BUDGET HOTEL

☎ 08719 846 009 ▤ 01256 843566
Stag and Hounds, Winchester Rd RG22 6HN
web: www.travelodge.co.uk
dir: off A30, S of town centre

Travelodge offers good quality, good value, modern accommodation. Ideal for families, the spacious en suite bedrooms include remote-control TV, tea and coffee-making facilities and comfortable beds. Meals can be

taken at the nearby family restaurant. See also the Hotel Groups pages.

Rooms 44 **S** fr £29; **D** fr £29

BEAULIEU   Map 5 SU30

INSPECTORS' CHOICE

Montagu Arms

★★★ ◉◉ HOTEL

☎ 01590 612324 & 0845 123 5613
▤ 01590 612188
Palace Ln SO42 7ZL
e-mail: reservations@montaguarmshotel.co.uk
web: www.montaguarmshotel.co.uk
dir: M27 junct 2, turn left at rdbt, follow signs for Beaulieu. Continue to Dibden Purlieu, then right at rdbt. Hotel on left

Surrounded by the glorious scenery of the New Forest, this lovely hotel manages to achieve the impression of almost total seclusion, though it is within easy reach of the major towns and cities in the area. Bedrooms, each named after a species of tree, are individually decorated and come with a range of thoughtful extras.

Public rooms include a cosy lounge, an adjoining conservatory and a choice of two dining options, the informal Monty's, or the stylish Terrace Restaurant.

Rooms 22 (3 fmly) **Facilities** ⚓ Complimentary use of spa in Brockenhurst Xmas New Year Wi-fi **Conf** Class 16 Board 26 Thtr 50 **Parking** 80 **Notes** ⊗ Civ Wed 50

See advert on opposite page

Master Builders House Hotel

★★★ 78% ⍟⍟ HOTEL

☎ 01590 616253 📄 01590 616297
Buckler's Hard SO42 7XB
e-mail: res@themasterbuilders.co.uk
web: www.themasterbuilders.co.uk
dir: M27 junct 2, follow Beaulieu signs. At T-junct left onto B3056, 1st left to Buckler's Hard. Hotel 2m on left before village

The name of the hotel is a testament to the master shipbuilder Henry Adams who once owned the property. A full list of the famous ships built in the village may be found in the Yachtsman's Bar. The Riverside Restaurant and many of the individually styled bedrooms enjoy views over the Beaulieu River. For guests wishing to travel to the Isle of Wight, the hotel has its own boat.

Rooms 25 (17 annexe) (2 fmly) (8 GF) **S** £140-£170; **D** £190-£242 (incl. bkfst)* **Facilities** Sailing on Beaulieu

River Mountain biking Xmas New Year Wi-fi **Conf** Class 18 Board 25 Thtr 50 **Parking** 70 **Notes** LB ⊗ Civ Wed 70

Beaulieu

★★★ 73% ⍟ HOTEL

☎ 023 8029 3344 📄 023 8029 2729
Beaulieu Rd SO42 7YQ
e-mail: beaulieu@newforesthotels.co.uk
web: www.newforesthotels.co.uk
dir: M27 junct 1/A337 towards Lyndhurst. Left at lights, through Lyndhurst, right onto B3056, continue for 3m

Conveniently located in the heart of the New Forest and close to Beaulieu Road railway station, this popular, small hotel provides an ideal base for exploring this lovely area. Facilities include an indoor swimming pool, an outdoor children's play area and an adjoining pub. A daily changing menu is offered in the restaurant.

Rooms 23 (3 annexe) (2 fmly) (3 GF) **Facilities** ⍟ Steam room Xmas **Conf** Class 100 Board 160 Thtr 290 **Services** Lift **Parking** 60 **Notes** Civ Wed 205

Macdonald Botley Park, Golf & Country Club

★★★★ 76% ⍟ COUNTRY HOUSE HOTEL

☎ 01489 780 888 & 0870 194 2132 📄 01489 789 242
Winchester Rd, Boorley Green SO32 2UA
e-mail: botleypark@macdonald-hotels.co.uk
web: www.macdonald-hotels.co.uk/botleypark
dir: A334 towards Botley, left at 1st rdbt past M&S, continue over next 4 mini-rdbts, at 3rd rdbt follow hotel signs

This modern and spacious hotel sits peacefully in the midst of its own 176-acre parkland golf course. Bedrooms are comfortably appointed with a good range of extras and an extensive range of leisure facilities is on offer. Attractive public areas include a relaxing restaurant and the more informal Swing and Divot Bar.

Rooms 130 (30 fmly) (44 GF) **Facilities** Spa ⍟ ⚓ 18 ⛳ Putt green Gym Squash Dance studio Xmas New Year Wi-fi **Conf** Class 180 Board 100 Thtr 450 **Services** Air con **Parking** 250 **Notes** ⊗ Civ Wed 400

See advert on this page

BROCKENHURST — Map 5 SU30

INSPECTORS' CHOICE

Rhinefield House

HandPICKED

★★★★ ◉◉ HOTEL

☎ 01590 622922 📠 01590 622800
Rhinefield Rd SO42 7QB
e-mail: rhinefieldhouse@handpicked.co.uk
web: www.handpicked.co.uk
dir: A35 towards Christchurch. 3m from Lyndhurst turn left to Rhinefield, 1.5m to hotel

This stunning 19th-century, mock-Elizabethan mansion is set in 40 acres of beautifully landscaped gardens and forest. Bedrooms are spacious and great consideration is given to guest comfort. The elegant and award-winning Armada Restaurant is richly furnished, and features a fireplace carving (nine years in the making) that is worth taking time to admire. If the weather permits, the delightful terrace is just the place for enjoying alfresco eating.

Rooms 50 (10 fmly) (2 GF) **S** £175-£240; **D** £185-£250 (incl. bkfst)* **Facilities** STV ◌ supervised ⌇ ⌣ ⌣ Gym Hydro-therapy pool Plunge pool Steam room Sauna Xmas New Year Wi-fi **Conf** Class 72 Board 56 Thtr 160 Del from £250* **Services** Lift **Parking** 100 **Notes** LB ⊗ Civ Wed 110

Careys Manor

★★★★ 78% ◉◉ HOTEL

☎ 01590 623551 & 08707 512305 📠 01590 622799
SO42 7RH
e-mail: stay@careysmanor.com
web: www.careysmanor.com
dir: M27 junct 3, M271, A35 to Lyndhurst. A337 towards Brockenhurst. Hotel on left after 30mph sign

This smart property offers a host of facilities that include an Oriental-style spa and leisure suite with an excellent range of unusual treatments, and three very contrasting restaurants that offer a choice of Thai, French or modern British cuisine. Many of the spacious and well appointed bedrooms have balconies overlooking the gardens. Extensive function and conference facilities are also available.

Rooms 80 (62 annexe) (32 GF) **Facilities** ◌ supervised ⌣ Gym Steam room Beauty therapists Treatment rooms Hydrotherapy pool Xmas **Conf** Class 70 Board 40 Thtr 120 **Services** Lift **Parking** 180 **Notes** ⊗ No children 16yrs Civ Wed 100

INSPECTORS' CHOICE

Whitley Ridge Hotel

★★★ ◉◉◉ COUNTRY HOUSE HOTEL

☎ 01590 622354 📠 01590 622856
Beaulieu Rd SO42 7QL
e-mail: info@whitleyridge.co.uk
web: www.whitleyridge.com
dir: At Brockenhurst onto B3055 Beaulieu Road. 1m on left up private road.

This charming hotel enjoys a secluded picturesque setting in the heart of the New Forest. The newly extended and relaxing public areas, delightful grounds, smart and comfortable bedrooms and a team of helpful and attentive staff all contribute to a memorable stay. The cuisine of the well-established Le Poussin restaurant is a highlight at this venue.

Rooms 18 (2 GF) **S** £85-£160; **D** £135-£320 (incl. bkfst & dinner)* **Facilities** ⌣ Xmas New Year Wi-fi **Conf** Class 20 Board 20 Thtr 35 **Parking** 35 **Notes** LB Civ Wed 60

Balmer Lawn

★★★ 85% ◉ HOTEL

☎ 01590 623116 📠 01590 623864
Lyndhurst Rd SO42 7ZB
e-mail: info@balmerlawnhotel.com
dir: just off A337 from Brockenhurst towards Lymington

Situated in the heart of the New Forest, this peacefully located hotel provides comfortable public rooms and a wide range of bedrooms. A selection of carefully prepared and enjoyable dishes is offered in the spacious restaurant. The extensive function and leisure facilities make this popular with both families and conference delegates.

Rooms 55 (10 fmly) **S** £99-£110; **D** £150-£180 (incl. bkfst) **Facilities** FTV ◌ ⌇ ⌣ Gym Squash Indoor leisure suite ♫ Xmas New Year Wi-fi **Conf** Class 76 Board 48 Thtr 150 Del from £125 to £170* **Services** Lift **Parking** 100 **Notes** LB Civ Wed 120

See advert on opposite page

New Park Manor

von Essen hotels
A PRIVATE COLLECTION

★★★ 82% ◉◉
COUNTRY HOUSE HOTEL

☎ 01590 623467 📠 01590 622268
Lyndhurst Rd SO42 7QH
e-mail: info@newparkmanorhotel.co.uk
web: www.newparkmanorhotel.co.uk
dir: M27 junct 1, A337 to Lyndhurst & Brockenhurst. Hotel 1.5m on right

Once the favoured hunting lodge of King Charles II, this well presented hotel enjoys a peaceful setting in the New Forest and comes complete with an equestrian centre. The bedrooms are divided between the old house and a purpose-built wing. An impressive spa offers a range of treatments.

Rooms 24 (6 fmly) **S** £118-£208; **D** £135-£315 (incl. bkfst)* **Facilities** Spa STV FTV ◌ 8 ⌣ Gym Mountain biking Xmas New Year Wi-fi **Conf** Class 52 Board 60 Thtr 120 Del from £160 to £175* **Parking** 70 **Notes** LB Civ Wed 120

Forest Park
★★★ 73% HOTEL

☎ 01590 622844 🖷 01590 623948
Rhinefield Rd SO42 7ZG
e-mail: forest.park@forestdale.com
web: www.forestparkhotel.co.uk
dir: A337 to Brockenhurst turn into Meerut Rd, follow road through Waters Green. Right at T-junct into Rhinefield Rd

Situated in the heart of the New Forest, this former vicarage and war field hospital is now a hotel which offers a warm and friendly welcome to all its guests. The hotel offers a heated pool, riding, a log cabin sauna and tennis courts. The bedrooms and public areas are comfortable and stylish.

Rooms 38 (2 fmly) (7 GF) **S** £85-£90; **D** £123-£129 (incl. bkfst)* **Facilities** ⚒ ♨ Xmas New Year Wi-fi **Conf** Class 20 Board 24 Thtr 50 **Parking** 80 **Notes** LB Civ Wed 50

Cloud
★★ 82% SMALL HOTEL

☎ 01590 622165 & 622354 🖷 01590 622818
Meerut Rd SO42 7TD
e-mail: enquiries@cloudhotel.co.uk
web: www.cloudhotel.co.uk
dir: 1st right off A337, follow tourist signs

This charming hotel enjoys a peaceful location on the edge of the village. The bedrooms are bright and comfortable with pine furnishings and smart en suite facilities. Public rooms include a selection of cosy lounges, a delightful rear garden with outdoor seating and a restaurant specialising in home-cooked, wholesome English food.

Rooms 17 (1 fmly) (2 GF) **S** £98-£110; **D** £110 (incl. bkfst & dinner)* **Facilities** Xmas **Conf** Class 12 Board 12 Thtr 40 **Parking** 20 **Notes** LB ⊗ No children 8yrs Closed 28 Dec-10 Jan

Watersplash
★★ 64% HOTEL

☎ 01590 622344
The Rise SO42 7ZP
e-mail: bookings@watersplash.co.uk
web: www.watersplash.co.uk
dir: M3 junct 13/M27 junct 1/A337 S through Lyndhurst & Brockenhurst. The Rise on left, hotel on left

This popular, welcoming hotel that dates from Victorian times, has been in the same family for over 40 years. Bedrooms have co-ordinated decor and good facilities. The restaurant overlooks the neatly tended garden and there is also a comfortably furnished lounge, separate bar and an outdoor pool.

Rooms 23 (6 fmly) (3 GF) **Facilities** ⚒ Xmas New Year **Conf** Class 20 Board 20 Thtr 80 **Parking** 25 (charged)

Bell Inn
★★★ 81% ◉◉ HOTEL

☎ 023 8081 2214 🖷 023 8081 3958
SO43 7HE
e-mail: bell@bramshaw.co.uk
web: www.bellinnbramshaw.co.uk
dir: M27 junct 1 onto B3079, hotel 1.5m on right

The inn is part of the Bramshaw Golf Club and has tailored its style to suit this market, but it is also an ideal base for visiting the New Forest. Bedrooms are comfortable and attractively furnished, and the public areas, particularly the welcoming bar, have a cosy and friendly atmosphere.

Rooms 27 (2 annexe) (1 fmly) (8 GF) **S** £50-£80; **D** £90-£120 (incl. bkfst) **Facilities** FTV ♨ 54 Putt green Xmas New Year Wi-fi **Conf** Class 20 Board 30 Thtr 50 Del from £85 to £100 **Parking** 150 **Notes** ⊗

BURLEY
Map 5 SU20

Burley Manor
★★★ 75% HOTEL

☎ 01425 403522 📠 01425 403227
Ringwood Rd BH24 4BS
e-mail: burley.manor@forestdale.com
web: www.theburleymanorhotel.co.uk
dir: exit A31at Burley sign, hotel 3m on left

Set in extensive grounds, this 18th-century mansion house enjoys a relaxed ambience and a peaceful setting. Half of the well-equipped, comfortable bedrooms, including several with four-posters, are located in the main house. The remainder, many with balconies, are in the adjacent converted stable block overlooking the outdoor pool. Cosy public rooms benefit from log fires in winter.

Rooms 38 (17 annexe) (2 fmly) (17 GF) **D** £129-£139 (incl. bkfst)* **Facilities** ⚲ Xmas New Year Wi-fi **Conf** Class 40 Board 40 Thtr 60 **Parking** 60 **Notes** LB Civ Wed 70

Moorhill House
★★★ 70% ⚜ COUNTRY HOUSE HOTEL

☎ 01425 403285 📠 01425 403715
BH24 4AH
e-mail: moorhill@newforesthotels.co.uk
web: www.newforesthotels.co.uk
dir: M27, A31, follow signs to Burley village, through village, up hill, turn right opposite school and cricket grounds

Situated deep in the heart of the New Forest and formerly a grand gentleman's residence, this charming hotel offers a relaxed and friendly environment. Bedrooms, of varying sizes, are smartly decorated. A range of facilities is provided and guests can relax by walking around the extensive grounds. Both dinner and breakfast offer a choice of interesting and freshly prepared dishes.

Rooms 31 (13 fmly) (3 GF) **S** £60-£75; **D** £120-£156 (incl. bkfst)* **Facilities** ⚲ Putt green ⚲ Gym Badminton (Apr-Sep) Xmas New Year Wi-fi **Conf** Class 60 Board 65 Thtr 120 Del from £100 to £110* **Parking** 50 **Notes** LB Civ Wed 80

CADNAM
Map 5 SU31

Bartley Lodge
★★★ 75% ⚜ HOTEL

☎ 023 8081 2248 📠 023 8081 2075
Lyndhurst Rd SO40 2NR
e-mail: bartley@newforesthotels.co.uk
web: www.newforesthotels.co.uk
dir: M27 junct 1 at 1st rdbt 1st exit, at 2nd rdbt 3rd exit onto A337. Hotel sign on left

This 18th-century former hunting lodge is very quietly situated, yet is just minutes from the M27. Bedrooms vary in size but all are well equipped. There is a selection of small lounge areas, a cosy bar and an indoor pool, together with a small fitness suite. The Crystal dining room offers a tempting choice of well prepared dishes.

Rooms 31 (12 fmly) (2 GF) **S** £60-£78; **D** £120-£156 (incl. bkfst)* **Facilities** ⚲ Gym Xmas New Year Wi-fi **Conf** Class 60 Board 60 Thtr 120 Del from £100 to £110* **Parking** 60 **Notes** LB Civ Wed 80

See advert on opposite page

DOGMERSFIELD
Map 5 SU75

INSPECTORS' CHOICE

Four Seasons Hotel Hampshire
★★★★★ ⚜

☎ 01252 853000 📠 01252 853010
Dogmersfield Park, Chalky Ln RG27 8TD
e-mail: reservations.ham@fourseasons.com
dir: M3 junct 5 onto A287 Farnham. After 1.5m take left Dogmersfield, hotel 0.6m on left

This Georgian manor house, set in 500 acres of rolling grounds and English Heritage listed gardens, offers the upmost in luxury and relaxation, just an hour from London. The spacious and stylish bedrooms are particularly well appointed and offer up-to-date technology. Fitness and spa facilities include nearly every conceivable indoor and outdoor activity, in addition to luxurious pampering. An elegant restaurant, a healthy eating spa café and a trendy bar are popular venues.

Rooms 133 (23 GF) **S** £240.88-£334.88; **D** £240.88-£334.88* **Facilities** Spa STV ⚲ ⚲ Fishing ⚲ Gym Clay pigeon shooting Bikes Canal boat Falconry ⚲ Xmas New Year Wi-fi **Conf** Class 110 Board 60 Thtr 260 Del from £411.13 to £540.50* **Services** Lift Air con **Parking** 165 **Notes** Civ Wed 200

EASTLEIGH
Map 5 SU41

Concorde Club & Hotel
★★★ 🅰 HOTEL

☎ 023 8065 1478 & 8061 3989 📠 023 8065 1479
Stoneham Ln SO50 9HQ
e-mail: hotel@theconcordeclub.com
web: www.theconcordeclub.com
dir: M27 junct 5, at rdbt follow Chandlers Ford signs, hotel 500yds on right

Rooms 35 (18 GF) **S** £60-£120; **D** £70-£140 (incl. bkfst) **Facilities** Fishing ⚲ Wi-fi **Conf** Class 50 Board 40 Thtr 200 Del from £120 to £150 **Services** Lift Air con **Parking** 250 **Notes** LB No children 18yrs Closed 24-26 Dec

Holiday Inn Southampton-Eastleigh M3, Jct 13

🆄

☎ 0870 400 9075 📠 023 8064 3945
Leigh Rd SO50 9PG
e-mail: reservations-eastleigh@ihg.com
web: www.holidayinn.co.uk
dir: follow A335 to Eastleigh, hotel on right

Currently the rating for this establishment is not confirmed. This may be due to a change of ownership or because it has only recently joined the AA rating scheme. For further details please see the AA website: www.theAA.com

Rooms 129 **S** £49-£175; **D** £49-£175*

Travelodge Southampton Eastleigh

BUDGET HOTEL

☎ 08719 846 213 📠 023 8061 6813
Twyford Rd SO50 4LF
web: www.travelodge.co.uk
dir: M3 junct 12 on A335 Eastleigh & Boyatt Wood to next rdbt, take 2nd exit signed Eastleigh town centre

Travelodge offers good quality, good value, modern accommodation. Ideal for families, the spacious en suite bedrooms include remote-control TV, tea and coffee-making facilities and comfortable beds. Meals can be taken at the nearby family restaurant. See also the Hotel Groups pages.

Rooms 32 **S** fr £29; **D** fr £29

EMSWORTH   Map 5 SU70

Brookfield

★★★ 77% HOTEL

☎ 01243 373363   📄 01243 376342
Havant Rd PO10 7LF
e-mail: bookings@brookfieldhotel.co.uk
dir: From A27 onto A259 towards Emsworth. Hotel 0.5m
on left

This well-established family-run hotel has spacious
public areas with popular conference and banqueting
facilities. Bedrooms are in a modern style, and
comfortably furnished. The popular Hermitage Restaurant
offers a seasonally changing menu and an interesting
wine list.

Rooms 40 (6 fmly) (16 GF) **Facilities** New Year Wi-fi
Conf Class 50 Board 50 Thtr 100 **Parking** 80 **Notes** ⊗
Closed 24-27 Dec Civ Wed 100

Travelodge Chichester Emsworth

BUDGET HOTEL

☎ 08719 846 024   📄 01243 370877
PO10 7RB
web: www.travelodge.co.uk
dir: E'bound carriageway of A27

Travelodge offers good quality, good value, modern
accommodation. Ideal for families, the spacious en suite
bedrooms include remote-control TV, tea and coffee-
making facilities and comfortable beds. Meals can be
taken at the nearby family restaurant. See also the Hotel
Groups pages.

Rooms 36 **S** fr £29; **D** fr £29

---

36 on the Quay

🏵🏵🏵 RESTAURANT WITH ROOMS

☎ 01243 375592   & 372257
47 South St PO10 7EG

Occupying a prime position with far reaching views over
the estuary, this 16th-century house is the scene for
some accomplished and exciting cuisine. The elegant
restaurant occupies centre stage with peaceful pastel
shades, local art and crisp napery together with glimpses
of the bustling harbour outside. The contemporary
bedrooms offer style, comfort and thoughtful extras.

Rooms 5 (5 en suite)

FAREHAM   Map 5 SU50

Solent Hotel & Spa

★★★★ 81% 🏵 HOTEL

☎ 01489 880000   📄 01489 880007
Rookery Av, Whiteley PO15 7AJ
e-mail: solent@shirehotels.com
web: www.solenthotel.com
dir: M27 junct 9, hotel on Solent Business Park

Close to the M27 with easy access to Portsmouth, the
New Forest and other attractions, this smart, purpose-
built hotel enjoys a peaceful location. Bedrooms are
spacious and very well appointed and there is a well-
equipped spa with new health and beauty facilities.

Rooms 111 (9 fmly) (39 GF) **S** £95-£260; **D** £140-£295
(incl. bkfst)* **Facilities** Spa STV 🕙 ♨ Gym Steam room
Sauna Children's splash pool Activity studio Xmas New
Year Wi-fi **Conf** Class 100 Board 80 Thtr 200
Del from £145 to £184* **Services** Lift **Parking** 200
Notes LB ⊗ Civ Wed 160

Lysses House

★★★ 71% 🏵 HOTEL

☎ 01329 822622   📄 01329 822762
51 High St PO16 7BQ
e-mail: lysses@lysses.co.uk
web: www.lysses.co.uk
dir: M27 junct 11 stay in left lane. At rdbt 3rd exit into
East St & follow into High St. Hotel at top on right

This attractive Georgian hotel is situated on the edge of
the town in a quiet location and provides spacious and
well-equipped accommodation. There are conference
facilities, and a lounge bar serving a range of snacks
together with the Richmond Restaurant that offers
accomplished and imaginative cuisine.

Rooms 21 (7 GF) **S** £59.50-£85; **D** £87.50-£107.50 (incl.
bkfst)* **Facilities** FTV Wi-fi **Conf** Class 42 Board 28
Thtr 95 Del from £130 to £135* **Services** Lift **Parking** 30
Notes ⊗ Closed 25 Dec-1 Jan RS 24 Dec & BHs
Civ Wed 100

Holiday Inn Fareham-Solent

Ⓤ

☎ 0870 400 9028   📄 01329 844666
Cartwright Dr, Titchfield PO15 5RJ
e-mail: fareham@ihg.com
web: www.holidayinn.co.uk
dir: M27 junct 9, follow signs for A27. Over Segensworth
rdbt 1.5m, left at next rdbt

Currently the rating for this establishment is not confirmed.
This may be due to a change of ownership or because it has
only recently joined the AA rating scheme. For further
details please see the AA website: www.theAA.com

Rooms 124 **S** £49-£210; **D** £59-£220 (incl. bkfst)*

FARNBOROUGH — Map 5 SU85

Falcon

★★★ 64% HOTEL

☎ 01252 545378 📠 01252 522539
68 Farnborough Rd GU14 6TH
e-mail: hotel@falconfarnborough.com
web: www.falconfarnborough.com
dir: A325 off M3, pass Farnborough Gate Retail Park. Left
at next rdbt & straight at next 2 rdbts. Hotel on left at
junct of aircraft esplanade & A325

This well-presented hotel is conveniently located for
business guests. Modern bedrooms are practically
furnished and equipped with a useful range of extras.
Public areas include the conservatory restaurant offering
a range of contemporary and traditional fare. Aircraft
enthusiasts will be interested to know that there is an
aeronautical centre adjacent.

Rooms 30 (1 fmly) (3 GF) **S** £68-£112; **D** £78-£114 (incl.
bkfst)* **Facilities** STV Wi-fi **Conf** Class 20 Board 16
Thtr 25 **Parking** 25 **Notes** ⊗ RS 23 Dec-4 Jan Civ Wed 50

Holiday Inn Farnborough

[U]

☎ 0870 400 9029 & 01252 894300 📠 01252 523166
Lynchford Rd GU14 6AZ
e-mail: reservations-farnborough@ihg.com
web: www.holidayinn.co.uk
dir: M3 junct 4, follow A325 through Farnborough towards
Aldershot. Hotel on left at The Queen's rdbt

Currently the rating for this establishment is not confirmed.
This may be due to a change of ownership or because it has
only recently joined the AA rating scheme. For further
details please see the AA website: www.theAA.com

Rooms 142 (31 fmly) (35 GF) (7 smoking) **S** £60-£199;
D £60-£199* **Facilities** STV ⟳ supervised Sauna Steam
room Beauty room ♫ Xmas Wi-fi **Conf** Class 80 Board 60
Thtr 180 Del from £125 to £185* **Services** Air con
Parking 170 **Notes** LB Civ Wed 180

FLEET — Map 5 SU85

Lismoyne

★★★ 72% HOTEL

☎ 01252 628555 📠 01252 811761
Church Rd GU51 4NE
e-mail: info@lismoynehotel.com
web: www.lismoynehotel.com
dir: M3 junct 4a. B3013, over railway bridge to town
centre. Through lights, take 4th right. Hotel 0.25m on left

Set in extensive grounds, this attractive hotel is located
close to the town centre. Public rooms include a
comfortable lounge and pleasant bar with a conservatory
overlooking the garden, and a traditional restaurant.
Accommodation is divided between the bedrooms in the
original building and those in the modern extension;
styles vary but all rooms are well equipped.

Rooms 62 (3 fmly) (19 GF) **S** £50-£130; **D** £75-£160 (incl.
bkfst) **Facilities** STV Gym Xmas New Year Wi-fi
Conf Class 92 Board 80 Thtr 170 Del from £110 to £175
Parking 150 **Notes** LB ⊗ Civ Wed 170

Innkeeper's Lodge Fleet

BUDGET HOTEL

☎ 0845 112 6101 📠 0845 112 6197
Cove Rd GU51 2SH
web: www.innkeeperslodge.com/fleet
dir: M3 junct 4a, south on A327 towards Fleet. Right at
1st rdbt (continue on A327). Lodge at next rdbt at A3013
& B3014 junct.

Innkeeper's Lodge represent an exciting, high value
concept within the budget hotel market. Comfortable
bedrooms provide excellent facilities that include satellite
TV and modem points. Options include spacious family
rooms, and for the corporate guest, cutting edge IT is
provided with Wi-fi access. All-day food is provided in the
adjacent pub restaurant. The extensive continental
breakfast is complimentary.

Rooms 40 **S** £52.95-£75; **D** £52.95-£75 (incl. bkfst)

FLEET MOTORWAY SERVICE AREA (M3) — Map 5 SU75

Days Inn Fleet

BUDGET HOTEL

☎ 01252 815587 📠 01252 815587
Fleet Services GU51 1AA
e-mail: fleet.hotel@welcomebreak.co.uk
web: www.welcomebreak.co.uk
dir: between junct 4a & 5 southbound on M3

This modern building offers accommodation in smart,
spacious and well-equipped bedrooms, suitable for
families and business travellers, and all with en suite
bathrooms. Continental breakfast is available and other
refreshments may be taken at the nearby family
restaurant. See also the Hotel Groups pages.

Rooms 58 (46 fmly) **S** £49-£69; **D** £59-£79*
Conf Board 10 Del from £69 to £89*

FOUR MARKS — Map 5 SU63

Travelodge Alton Four Marks

BUDGET HOTEL
Travelodge

☎ 08719 846 002 📠 01420 562659
156 Winchester Rd GU34 5HZ
web: www.travelodge.co.uk
dir: 5m S of Alton on A31 N'bound

Travelodge offers good quality, good value, modern
accommodation. Ideal for families, the spacious en suite
bedrooms include remote-control TV, tea and coffee-
making facilities and comfortable beds. Meals can be
taken at the nearby family restaurant. See also the Hotel
Groups pages.

Rooms 31 **S** fr £29; **D** fr £29

HARTLEY WINTNEY — Map 5 SU75

Elvetham

★★★ 79% HOTEL

☎ 01252 844871 📠 01252 844161
RG27 8AR
e-mail: enq@theelvetham.co.uk
web: www.theelvetham.co.uk
dir: M3 junct 4A W, junct 5 E (or M4 junct 11, A33,
B3011). Hotel signed from A323 between Hartley Wintney
& Fleet

A spectacular 19th-century mansion set in 35 acres of
grounds with an arboretum. All bedrooms are individually
styled and many have views of the manicured gardens. A
popular venue for weddings and conferences, the hotel
lends itself to team building events and outdoor pursuits.

Rooms 70 (29 annexe) (7 GF) **S** £110; **D** £135-£200 (incl.
bkfst)* **Facilities** STV ⚲ Putt green ⚒ Gym Badminton
Boules Volleyball Wi-fi **Conf** Class 80 Board 48 Thtr 110
Parking 200 **Notes** Closed 24 Dec-1 Jan Civ Wed 200

ISLE OF WIGHT

See Wight, Isle of

LIPHOOK — Map 5 SU83

Old Thorns Hotel Golf & Country Estate

★★★ 82% HOTEL

☎ 01428 724555 📠 01428 725036
Griggs Green GU30 7PE
e-mail: sales@oldthorns.com
dir: Griggs Green exit off A3 hotel 0.5m off exit

This hotel is peacefully located in 400 acres of rolling
countryside with a championship golf course, and has
easy access to the A3. Bedrooms and bathrooms are
stylish in design and offer high levels of comfort and
space. Leisure facilities are extensive, and the Greenview
Restaurant, overlooking the 9th and 18th greens, offers
all day dining.

Rooms 33 (2 fmly) (14 GF) **S** £75-£170; **D** £99-£195 (incl.
bkfst) **Facilities** Spa STV FTV ⟳ supervised ⚑ 18 ⚲ Putt
green Gym Xmas New Year Wi-fi **Conf** Class 100 Board 30
Thtr 250 Del from £130 to £185 **Parking** 100 **Notes** LB
Civ Wed 250

Travelodge Liphook

BUDGET HOTEL

☎ 08719 846 044 ▤ 01428 727619
GU30 7TT
web: www.travelodge.co.uk
dir: on N'bound carriageway of A3, 1m from Griggs Green
exit at Shell services

Travelodge offers good quality, good value, modern
accommodation. Ideal for families, the spacious en suite
bedrooms include remote-control TV, tea and coffee-
making facilities and comfortable beds. Meals can be
taken at the nearby family restaurant. See also the Hotel
Groups pages.

Rooms 40 **S** fr £29; **D** fr £29

LYMINGTON	Map 5 SZ39

Passford House

★★★ 82% HOTEL

☎ 01590 682398 ▤ 01590 683494
Mount Pleasant Ln SO41 8LS
e-mail: sales@passfordhousehotel.co.uk
web: www.passfordhousehotel.co.uk
dir: from A337 at Lymington over 2 mini rdbts. 1st right
at Tollhouse pub, then after 1m right into Mount Pleasant
Lane

A peaceful hotel set in attractive grounds on the edge of
town. Bedrooms vary in size but all are comfortably
furnished and well equipped. Extensive public areas
include lounges, a smartly appointed restaurant and bar
plus leisure facilities. The friendly and well-motivated
staff provide attentive service.

Rooms 51 (2 annexe) (10 GF) **Facilities** ⊗ ⅄ ⅊ Putt
green ⅊ Gym Petanque Table tennis Pool table Xmas
New Year **Conf** Class 30 Board 30 Thtr 80 **Parking** 100
Notes LB No children 8yrs Civ Wed 40

Stanwell House

★★★ 80% ⊛ HOTEL

☎ 01590 677123 ▤ 01590 677756
14-15 High St SO41 9AA
e-mail: enquiries@stanwellhouse.com
dir: M27 junct 1, follow signs to Lyndhurst into Lymington
centre & High Street

Stanwell House Hotel is a privately owned Georgian House
situated on the wide High Street of Lymington, only a few
minutes from the town's marina and a short drive from
the stunning New Forest. Accommodation is comfortable
and public areas have been redecorated to a high
standard. Dining options include the informal Bistro or
the intimate atmosphere of the new Seafood Restaurant.
Service is friendly and attentive. A meeting room is
available for hire which benefits from doors leading out
onto the attractive garden and patio area.

Rooms 27 (3 fmly) (4 GF) **S** fr £99; **D** fr £135 (incl. bkfst)*
Facilities FTV Xmas New Year Wi-fi **Conf** Class 25
Board 20 Thtr 70 Del from £125* **Notes** LB Civ Wed 70

Macdonald Elmers Court Hotel & Resort

★★★ 79% HOTEL

☎ 0844 879 9060 ▤ 01590 679780
South Baddesley Rd SO41 5ZB
e-mail: elmerscourt@macdonald-hotels.co.uk
web: www.macdonaldhotels.co.uk
dir: M27 junct 1, through Lyndhurst, Brockenhurst &
Lymington, hotel 200yds right after Lymington ferry
terminal

Originally known as The Elms, this Tudor manor house
dates back to the 1820s. Ideally located at the edge of
the New Forest and overlooking The Solent with views
towards the Isle of Wight, the hotel offers suites and
self-catering accommodation in the grounds, along with
a host of leisure facilities.

Rooms 42 (42 annexe) (8 fmly) (22 GF) **S** £75-£140;
D £85-£180 (incl. bkfst)* **Facilities** Spa ⊗ ⅄
supervised ⅊ Putt green ⅊ Gym Squash Steam room
Aerobics classes Sauna ♫ Xmas New Year Wi-fi
Conf Class 40 Board 40 Thtr 100 Del from £145 to £180*
Parking 100 **Notes** LB ⊗ Civ Wed 100

Bell Inn

★★★ 81% HOTEL

☎ 023 8081 2214 📄 023 8081 3958
SO43 7HE
e-mail: bell@bramshaw.co.uk
web: www.bellinnbramshaw.co.uk

(For full entry see Brook (Near Cadnam)

Best Western Forest Lodge

★★★ 79%  HOTEL

☎ 023 8028 3677 📄 023 8028 2940
Pikes Hill, Romsey Rd SO43 7AS
e-mail: forest@newforesthotels.co.uk
web: www.newforesthotels.co.uk
dir: M27 junct 1, A337 towards Lyndhurst. In village, with
police station & courts on right, take 1st right into Pikes
Hill

Situated on the edge of Lyndhurst, this hotel is set well
back from the main road. The smart, contemporary
bedrooms include four-poster rooms and family rooms;
children are very welcome here and parents will find that
the hotel offers many child-friendly facilities. The eating
options are the Forest Restaurant and the fine-dining
Glasshouse Restaurant. There is an indoor swimming
pool and Nordic sauna.

Rooms 28 (7 fmly) (6 GF) **Facilities** ⚱ Xmas New Year
Wi-fi **Conf** Class 70 Board 60 Thtr 120 **Parking** 50
Notes LB Civ Wed 60

Best Western Crown

★★★ 75% HOTEL

☎ 023 8028 2922 📄 023 8028 2751
High St SO43 7NF
e-mail: reception@crownhotel-lyndhurst.co.uk
web: www.crownhotel-lyndhurst.co.uk
dir: in centre of village, opposite church

The Crown, with its stone mullioned windows, panelled
rooms and elegant period decor evokes the style of an
Edwardian country house. Bedrooms are generally a good
size and offer a useful range of facilities. Public areas
have style and comfort and include a choice of function
and meeting rooms. The pleasant garden and terrace are
havens of peace and tranquillity.

Rooms 39 (8 fmly) **S** £73-£98; **D** £95-£185 (incl. bkfst)*
Facilities FTV Xmas New Year Wi-fi **Conf** Class 30
Board 45 Thtr 70 Del from £132 to £145* **Services** Lift
Parking 60 **Notes** LB Civ Wed 70

Lyndhurst Park

★★★ 72% HOTEL

☎ 023 8028 3923 📄 023 8028 3019
High St SO43 7NL
e-mail: lyndhurst.park@forestdale.com
web: www.lyndhurstparkhotel.co.uk
dir: M27 junct 1-3 to A35 to Lyndhurst. Hotel at bottom of
High St

Although it is just by the High Street, this hotel is
afforded seclusion and tranquillity from the town due to
its five acres of mature grounds. The comfortable
bedrooms include home-from-home touches such as
ducks in the bath! The bar offers a stylish setting for a
snack whilst the oak-panelled Tudor restaurant provides
a more formal dining venue.

Rooms 59 (3 fmly) **S** £90-£95; **D** £113-£129 (incl. bkfst)*
Facilities ⚲ 🏊 Sauna Xmas New Year Wi-fi
Conf Class 120 Board 40 Thtr 300 **Services** Lift
Parking 100 **Notes** LB Civ Wed 120

Penny Farthing Hotel

★★ 78% METRO HOTEL

☎ 023 8028 4422 📄 023 8028 4488
Romsey Rd SO43 7AA
e-mail: stay@pennyfarthinghotel.co.uk
dir: in Lyndhurst, hotel on left opposite old thatched
cottage

This friendly, well-appointed establishment on the edge
of town is suitable for business or for exploring the New
Forest area. The attractive bedrooms are well-equipped,
with some located in an adjacent cottage. There is a
spacious breakfast room, a comfortable lounge bar and a
bicycle store.

Rooms 20 (4 annexe) (1 fmly) (1 GF) **S** £59; **D** £78-£118
(incl. bkfst)* **Facilities** FTV Wi-fi **Parking** 25 **Notes** ⊗
Closed Xmas week & New Year

Ormonde House

★★ 75% HOTEL

☎ 023 8028 2806 📄 023 8028 2004
Southampton Rd SO43 7BT
e-mail: enquiries@ormondehouse.co.uk
web: www.ormondehouse.co.uk
dir: 800yds E of Lyndhurst on A35 to Southampton

Set back from the main road on the edge of Lyndhurst,
this welcoming hotel combines an efficient mix of relaxed
hospitality and attentive service. Bedrooms, including
some on the ground floor, are well furnished and
equipped. Larger suites with kitchen facilities are also
available. Home-cooked dinners feature a range of
carefully presented fresh ingredients.

Rooms 25 (6 annexe) (1 fmly) (8 GF) **S** £40-£60;
D £70-£120 (incl. bkfst)* **Facilities** New Year **Parking** 26
Notes LB Closed Xmas week

Knightwood Lodge

THE INDEPENDENTS
HOTEL ASSOCIATION

★★ 68% HOTEL

☎ 023 8028 2502 📄 023 8028 3730
Southampton Rd SO43 7BU
e-mail: jackie4r@aol.com
web: www.knightwoodlodge.co.uk
dir: M27 junct 1 follow A337 to Lyndhurst. Left at traffic
lights in village onto A35 towards Southampton. Hotel
0.25m on left

This friendly, family-run hotel is situated on the outskirts
of Lyndhurst. Comfortable bedrooms are modern in style
and well equipped with many useful extras. The hotel
offers an excellent range of facilities including a
swimming pool, a jacuzzi and a small gym area. Two
separate cottages are available for families or larger
groups, and dogs are also welcome to accompany their
owners in these units.

Rooms 18 (4 annexe) (2 fmly) (3 GF) **S** £35-£55;
D £70-£110 (incl. bkfst)* **Facilities** FTV ⛹ Gym Steam
room Sauna Spa bath **Parking** 15 **Notes** LB

Travelodge Stoney Cross Lyndhurst

Travelodge

BUDGET HOTEL

☎ 0871 9846200 📄 02380 811544
A31 Westbound SO43 7GN
web: www.travelodge.co.uk
dir: M27 w'bound becomes A31, on left after Rufus Stone
sign

Travelodge offers good quality, good value, modern
accommodation. Ideal for families, the spacious en suite
bedrooms include remote-control TV, tea and coffee-
making facilities and comfortable beds. Meals can be
taken at the nearby family restaurant. See also the Hotel
Groups pages.

Rooms 32 **S** fr £29; **D** fr £29

Westover Hall

★★★ 88% COUNTRY HOUSE HOTEL

☎ 01590 643044 📄 01590 644490
Park Ln SO41 0PT
e-mail: info@westoverhallhotel.com
dir: M3 & M27 W onto A337 to Lymington, follow signs to
Milford-on-Sea onto B3058, hotel outside village centre
towards cliff

Just a few moments' walk from the beach and boasting
uninterrupted views across Christchurch Bay to the Isle of
Wight in the distance, this late-Victorian mansion offers
a relaxed, informal and friendly atmosphere together with
efficient standards of hospitality and service. Bedrooms

do vary in size and aspect, but all have been decorated with flair and style. Architectural delights include dramatic stained-glass windows, extensive oak panelling and a galleried entrance hall. The cuisine is prepared with much care and attention to detail.

Rooms 12 (2 fmly) **S** £130-£200; **D** £190-£340 (incl. bkfst & dinner) **Facilities** Xmas New Year Wi-fi **Conf** Class 14 Board 18 Thtr 35 Del from £155 to £175* **Parking** 50 **Notes** LB Civ Wed 50

See advert on page 257

South Lawn
★★★ 62% HOTEL

☎ 01590 643911 📄 01590 644820
Lymington Rd SO41 0RF
e-mail: enquiries@southdown.co.uk
web: www.oxfordhotelsandinns.com
dir: M27 junct 1, take A337 to Lymington, follow signs for Christchurch, after 3m turn left on B3058 signed Milford-on-Sea, hotel 1m on right

Close to the coast and enjoying a quiet location, this pleasant hotel is set in well tended and spacious grounds

this hotel is a comfortable place to stay. Bedrooms are spacious and well appointed. Guests can relax or take afternoon tea in the lounge; the restaurant menu offers a good range of choice. Staff are friendly and attentive.

Rooms 24 (3 fmly) (3 GF) **D** £90-£150 (incl. bkfst & dinner)* **Facilities** Xmas New Year **Conf** Class 40 Board 30 Thtr 100 Del from £115 to £135* **Parking** 60 **Notes** ⊗ Civ Wed 120

NEW ALRESFORD   Map 5 SU53

Swan
★★ 67% HOTEL

☎ 01962 732302 & 734427 📄 01962 735274
11 West St SO24 9AD
e-mail: swanhotel@btinternet.com
web: www.swanhotelalresford.com
dir: off A31 onto B3047

This former coaching inn dates back to the 18th century and remains a busy and popular destination for travellers and locals alike. Bedrooms are in the main building and the more modern wing. The lounge bar and adjacent restaurant are open all day; for more traditional dining there is another restaurant which overlooks the busy village street.

Rooms 23 (12 annexe) (3 fmly) (5 GF) **S** £45-£55; **D** £75-£85 (incl. bkfst)* **Conf** Class 60 Board 40 Thtr 90 Del from £75 to £100* **Parking** 25 **Notes** RS 25 Dec

See advert on this page

NEW MILTON   Map 5 SZ29

INSPECTORS' CHOICE

Chewton Glen Hotel & Spa
★★★★★ ⊛⊛⊛ HOTEL

☎ 01425 275341 📄 01425 272310
Christchurch Rd BH25 5QS
e-mail: reservations@chewtonglen.com
web: www.chewtonglen.com
dir: A35 from Lyndhurst for 10m, left at staggered junct. Follow tourist sign for hotel through Walkford, take 2nd left

This outstanding hotel has been at the forefront of British hotel-keeping for many years. Once past the wrought iron entrance gates, guests are transported into a world of luxury. Log fires and afternoon tea are part of the tradition here, and lounges enjoy fine views over sweeping croquet lawns. Most bedrooms are very spacious, with private patios or balconies. Dining is a treat, and the extensive wine lists are essential reading for the enthusiast. The spa and leisure facilities are among the best in the country.

Rooms 58 (9 GF) **S** £295-£1280; **D** £295-£1280* **Facilities** Spa FTV ⓢ ⌇ ⅃ 9 ⌂ Putt green ⅃ Gym Hydrotherapy spa Hot tub Dance studio Cycling & jogging trail ♪ Xmas New Year Wi-fi **Conf** Class 70 Board 40 Thtr 150 Del from £250 to £400* **Services** Air con **Parking** 100 **Notes** LB ⊗ Civ Wed 140

ODIHAM — Map 5 SU75

George

★★★ 72% HOTEL

☎ 01256 702081   📠 01256 704213
High St RG29 1LP
e-mail: reception@georgehotelodiham.com
web: www.georgehotelodiham.com
dir: M3 junct 5 follow Alton & Odiham signs. Through
North Warnborough into Odiham left at top of hill, hotel
on left

The George is over 450 years old and is a fine example of
an old English inn. Bedrooms come in a number of styles;
the older part of the property has beams and period
features, whilst newer rooms have a contemporary feel.
Guests can dine in the all-day bistro or the popular
restaurant.

Rooms 28 (9 annexe) (1 fmly) (6 GF) (4 smoking)
S £65-£95; **D** £85-£135 (incl. bkfst)* **Facilities** STV Wi-fi
Conf Class 10 Board 26 Thtr 30 Del from £135 to £150*
Parking 20 **Notes** LB Closed 24-26 Dec

PETERSFIELD — Map 5 SU72

Langrish House

★★★ 74% ◉◉ HOTEL

☎ 01730 266941   📠 01730 260543
Langrish GU32 1RN
e-mail: frontdesk@langrishhouse.co.uk
web: www.langrishhouse.co.uk
dir: A3 onto A272 towards Winchester. Hotel signed, 2.5m
on left

Located in an idyllic country location just outside
Petersfield, this family home dates back to the 17th
century. Rooms offer good levels of comfort with beautiful
views over the countryside. The public areas consist of a
small cosy restaurant, a bar in the vaults, and conference
and banqueting rooms that are popular for weddings.
Staff throughout are friendly and nothing is too much
trouble.

Rooms 13 (1 fmly) (3 GF) **S** £72-£90; **D** £104-£155 (incl.
bkfst)* **Facilities** Fishing ↷ Xmas New Year Wi-fi
Conf Class 18 Board 25 Thtr 60 **Parking** 80 **Notes** LB
Closed 2 weeks in Jan Civ Wed 60

PORTSMOUTH & SOUTHSEA — Map 5 SU60

Portsmouth Marriott Hotel   Marriott HOTELS & RESORTS

★★★★ 74% HOTEL

☎ 0870 400 7285   📠 0870 400 7385
Southampton Rd PO6 4SH
web: www.portsmouthmarriott.co.uk
dir: M27 junct 12 keep left and hotel on left

Close to the motorway and ferry port, this hotel is well
suited to the business trade. The comfortable and well
laid-out bedrooms provide a comprehensive range of
facilities including up-to-date workstations. The leisure
club offers a pool, a gym, and a health and beauty salon.

Rooms 174 (77 fmly) **Facilities** 🏊 supervised Gym
Exercise studio, Beauty salon Xmas **Conf** Class 180
Board 30 Thtr 350 **Services** Lift Air con **Parking** 250
Notes Civ Wed 100

Best Western Royal Beach   Best Western

★★★ 74% HOTEL

☎ 023 9273 1281   📠 023 9281 7572
South Pde, Southsea PO4 0RN
e-mail: enquiries@royalbeachhotel.co.uk
web: www.royalbeachhotel.co.uk
dir: M27 to M275, follow signs to seafront. Hotel on
seafront

This former Victorian seafront hotel is a smart and
comfortable venue suitable for leisure and business
guests alike. Bedrooms and public areas are well
presented and generally spacious, and the smart Coast
Bar is an ideal venue for a relaxing drink.

Rooms 124 (18 fmly) (47 smoking) **S** £60-£95;
D £80-£125 (incl. bkfst) **Facilities** 🎵 Xmas New Year
Wi-fi **Conf** Class 180 Board 40 Thtr 280 Del from £119.95
Services Lift **Parking** 50 **Notes** LB

Westfield Hall

★★★ 74% HOTEL

☎ 023 9282 6971   📠 023 9287 0200
65 Festing Rd, Southsea PO4 0NQ
e-mail: enquiries@whhotel.info
web: www.whhotel.info
dir: From M275 follow Southsea seafront signs. Left onto
Clarence Esplanade on South Parade Pier, left onto St
Helens Parade, hotel 150yds

This hotel is situated in a quiet side road close to the
seafront and town centre. The accommodation is split
between two identical houses and all rooms are smartly
appointed and well equipped. Public rooms are
attractively decorated and include three lounges, a bar
and a restaurant.

Rooms 26 (11 annexe) (12 fmly) (6 GF) **S** £50-£62;
D £72-£120 (incl. bkfst) **Facilities** STV FTV Wi-fi
Parking 16 **Notes** ⊗

Queen's

★★★ 73% HOTEL

☎ 023 9282 2466   📠 023 9282 1901
Clarence Pde, Southsea PO5 3LJ
e-mail: queenshotelports@aol.com
web: www.queenshotelportsmouth.com
dir: M27 junct 12 onto M275. Follow Southsea seafront
signs, hotel on seafront. From A3, follow south to
Portsmouth, take A27, follow signs to seafront

This hotel occupies a prominent position, only a couple of
minutes from the seafront and Southsea centre; the
restaurant and many of the bedrooms offer stunning sea
views. Accommodation offers comfort and thoughtful
accessories throughout. Enjoyable dinners and
substantial breakfasts are available in the grand
restaurant overlooking the well maintained gardens.

Rooms 72 (6 fmly) **S** £60-£79.50; **D** £99-£149*
Facilities STV Xmas New Year Wi-fi **Conf** Class 80
Board 60 Thtr 150 Del from £120 to £130* **Services** Lift
Parking 60 (charged) **Notes** ⊗ Civ Wed 150

SWAY — Map 5 SZ29

Sway Manor Restaurant & Hotel

★★★ 75% HOTEL

☎ 01590 682754 📠 01590 682955
Station Rd SO41 6BA
e-mail: info@swaymanor.com
web: www.swaymanor.com
dir: exit B3055 (Brockenhurst/New Milton road) into village centre

Built at the turn of the 20th century, this attractive mansion is set in its own grounds, and conveniently located in the village centre. Bedrooms are well appointed and generously equipped; most have views over the gardens and pool. The bar and conservatory restaurant, both with views over the gardens, are popular with locals.

Rooms 15 (3 fmly) **S** £63.50-£69.50; **D** £109-£139 (incl. bkfst)* **Facilities** 🎿 🎵 Xmas **Services** Lift **Parking** 40 **Notes** LB Civ Wed 80

WICKHAM — Map 5 SU51

Old House Hotel & Restaurant

★★★ 77% ⚜⚜ HOTEL

☎ 01329 833049 📠 01329 833672
The Square PO17 5JG
e-mail: enquiries@oldhousehotel.co.uk
web: www.oldhousehotel.co.uk
dir: M27 junct 10, N on A32 for 2m towards Alton.

This hotel, a grade II listed building, occupies a convenient location in the heart of historic Wickham, not far from Portsmouth and Southampton. Bedrooms and bathrooms are smartly co-ordinated, and include stylish Garden Suites that look out on the delightful garden. The public areas have much character and charm. The service is attentive and friendly, and the award-winning cuisine utilises seasonal, local produce.

Rooms 12 (4 annexe) (2 fmly) (4 GF) **D** £90-£165 (incl. bkfst)* **Facilities** FTV Xmas New Year Wi-fi **Parking** 8 **Notes** ⊗ Civ Wed 80

WINCHESTER — Map 5 SU42

INSPECTORS' CHOICE

Lainston House

★★★★ ⚜⚜⚜ HOTEL

☎ 01962 776088 📠 01962 776672
Sparsholt SO21 2LT
e-mail: enquiries@lainstonhouse.com
web: www.exclusivehotels.co.uk
dir: 2m NW off B3049 towards Stockbridge

This graceful example of a William and Mary House enjoys a countryside location amidst mature grounds and gardens. Staff provide good levels of courtesy and care with a polished, professional service. Bedrooms are tastefully appointed and include some spectacular spacious rooms with stylish handmade beds and stunning bathrooms. Public rooms include a cocktail bar built entirely from a single cedar and stocked with an impressive range of rare drinks and cigars.

Rooms 50 (6 fmly) (18 GF) **Facilities** 🎣 Putt green Fishing 🏋 Gym Archery Clay pigeon shooting Cycling Hot air ballooning Walking 🎵 Xmas New Year Wi-fi **Conf** Class 80 Board 40 Thtr 166 **Parking** 150 **Notes** LB Civ Wed 200

WINCHESTER continued

The Winchester Hotel

★★★★ 78% ⊛ HOTEL

☎ 01962 709988 📄 01962 840862
Worthy Ln SO23 7AB
e-mail: gillianrobinson@pedersenhotels.com
web: www.pedersenhotels.com/winchester
dir: A33 then A3047, hotel 1m on right

This hotel is just a few minutes' walk from the city centre; it is very smartly appointed throughout and now includes a great leisure centre. The staff are extremely friendly and helpful; award-winning food is served in the contemporary Hutton's Brasserie.

Rooms 71 (2 fmly) (8 GF) **Facilities** ⓧ supervised Gym Xmas Wi-fi **Conf** Class 100 Board 40 Thtr 200 **Services** Lift Air con **Parking** 70 **Notes** LB ⊗ Civ Wed 180

Hotel du Vin Winchester

★★★★ 75% ⊛⊛ TOWN HOUSE HOTEL

☎ 01962 841414 📄 01962 842458
Southgate St SO23 9EF
e-mail: info@winchester.hotelduvin.com
web: www.hotelduvin.com
dir: M3 junct 11 towards Winchester, follow signs. Hotel in approx 2m on left just past cinema

Continuing to set high standards, this inviting hotel is best known for its high profile bistro. The individually decorated bedrooms, each sponsored by a different wine house, show considerable originality of style, and are very well equipped. The bistro serves imaginative yet simply cooked dishes from a seasonal, daily-changing menu, by a very willing young team. Hotel du Vin - AA Small Hotel Group of the Year 2008-9.

Rooms 24 (4 annexe) (4 GF) **Facilities** Xmas New Year Wi-fi **Conf** Class 30 Board 20 Thtr 40 **Parking** 35 **Notes** Civ Wed 60

Mercure Wessex

★★★★ 71% HOTEL

☎ 01962 861611 📄 01962 841503
Paternoster Row SO23 9LQ
web: www.mercure-uk.com
dir: M3, follow signs for town centre, at rdbt by King Alfred's statue past Guildhall, next left, hotel on right

Occupying an enviable location in the centre of this historic city and adjacent to the spectacular cathedral, this hotel is quietly situated on a side street. Inside, the atmosphere is restful and welcoming, with public areas and some bedrooms enjoying unrivalled views of the hotel's centuries-old neighbour.

Rooms 94 (6 fmly) **Facilities** STV Gym Xmas New Year Wi-fi **Conf** Class 60 Board 60 Thtr 100 Del from £125 to £160* **Services** Lift **Parking** 60 (charged) **Notes** Civ Wed 100

The Winchester Royal

★★★ 79% ⊛ HOTEL

☎ 01962 840840 📄 01962 841582
Saint Peter St SO23 8BS
e-mail: winchester.royal@forestdale.com
web: www.thewinchesterroyalhotel.co.uk
dir: M3 junct 9 to Winnall Trading Estate. Follow to city centre, cross river, left, 1st right. Onto one-way system, take 2nd right. Hotel immediately on right

Situated in the heart of the former capital of England, a warm welcome awaits at this friendly hotel, which in parts, dates back to the 16th century. The bedrooms may vary in style but they are all comfortable and well equipped; the modern annexe rooms overlook the attractive well-tended gardens. The conservatory restaurant makes a very pleasant setting for enjoyable meals.

Rooms 75 (56 annexe) (1 fmly) (27 GF) **D** £139-£149 (incl. bkfst)* **Facilities** Xmas New Year Wi-fi **Conf** Class 40 Board 40 Thtr 120 **Parking** 50 **Notes** LB Civ Wed 100

Marwell

★★★ 71% HOTEL

"bespoke"

☎ 01962 777681 📄 01962 777625
Thompsons Ln, Colden Common, Marwell SO21 1JY
e-mail: info@marwellhotel.co.uk
web: www.marwellhotel.co.uk
dir: B3354 through Twyford. 1st exit at rdbt continue on B3354, then left onto B2177 signed Bishop Waltham. Turn left into Thomsons Ln after 1m, hotel on left

Taking its theme from the adjacent zoo, this unusual hotel is based on the famous TreeTops safari lodge in Kenya. Bedrooms are well appointed and equipped, while the smart public areas include an airy lobby bar and an 'Out of Africa' style restaurant. There is also a selection of meeting and leisure facilities.

Rooms 66 (10 fmly) (36 GF) **S** £65-£105; **D** £85-£125 (incl. bkfst)* **Facilities** STV ⓧ supervised ⬚ 18 Gym New Year Wi-fi **Conf** Class 60 Board 60 Thtr 175 **Parking** 120 **Notes** LB Civ Wed 150

WOODLANDS   Map 5 SU31

The Woodlands Lodge

★★★ 73% HOTEL

☎ 023 8029 2257 📄 023 8029 3090
Bartley Rd, Woodlands SO40 7GN
e-mail: reception@woodlands-lodge.co.uk
web: www.woodlands-lodge.co.uk
dir: M27 junct 2, A326 towards Fawley. 2nd rdbt turn right, left after 0.25m by White Horse PH. In 1.5m cross cattle grid, hotel 70yds on left

An 18th-century former hunting lodge, this hotel is set in four acres of impressive and well-tended grounds on the edge of the New Forest. Well-equipped bedrooms come in varying sizes and styles and all bathrooms have a jacuzzi bath. Public areas provide a pleasant lounge and intimate cocktail bar.

Rooms 16 (1 fmly) (3 GF) **S** £60-£85; **D** £109-£169 (incl. bkfst)* **Facilities** FTV ⬚ Xmas New Year Wi-fi **Conf** Class 14 Board 20 Thtr 55 Del from £140 to £160* **Parking** 30 **Notes** LB Civ Wed 90

Casa dei Cesari Restaurant & Hotel

★★★ 71% HOTEL

☎ 01252 873275 📄 01252 870614
Handford Ln GU46 6BT
e-mail: reservations@casadeicesari.co.uk
dir: M3 junct 4a, follow signs for town centre. Hotel signed

This delightful hotel where a warm welcome is guaranteed is ideally located for transportation networks. It boasts rooms with quality and comfort, and the Italian-themed restaurant, which is very popular locally, serves an extensive traditional menu.

Rooms 63 (2 fmly) (15 GF) (33 smoking) **S** £75-£145; **D** £75-£165 (incl. bkfst)* **Facilities** FTV Xmas New Year Wi-fi **Conf** Class 60 Board 60 Thtr 150 Del from £129.95 to £159.95* **Services** Lift **Parking** 80 **Notes** LB ⊗ Civ Wed 150

HEREFORDSHIRE

HEREFORD Map 10 SO54

See also **Leominster**

Castle House

★★★ 87% ◉◉◉ HOTEL

☎ 01432 356321 📄 01432 365909
Castle St HR1 2NW
e-mail: info@castlehse.co.uk
web: www.castlehse.co.uk
dir: Follow signs to City Centre East. At junct of Commercial Rd & Union St follow hotel signs

Enjoying a prime city centre location and overlooking the castle moat, this delightful Victorian mansion is the epitome of elegance and sophistication. The character bedrooms are equipped with every luxury to ensure a memorable stay and are complemented perfectly by the well-proportioned and restful lounge and bar, together with the topiary-style restaurant.

Rooms 15 (1 GF) **S** £120; **D** £175-£220 (incl. bkfst)* **Facilities** FTV Free membership at local spa Xmas New Year Wi-fi **Services** Lift **Parking** 12 **Notes** LB ⊗

See advert on page 268

Belmont Lodge & Golf

★★★ 74% HOTEL

☎ 01432 352666 📄 01432 358090
Belmont HR2 9SA
e-mail: info@belmont-hereford.co.uk
web: www.belmont-hereford.co.uk
dir: from Hereford towards Abergavenny on A465. Pass Tesco on right, straight on at rdbt. 0.25m turn right into Ruckhall Ln (signed Belmont Golf Course). Hotel on right in 0.5m

This impressive complex, surrounded by its own golf course, commands delightful views over the River Wye and the surrounding countryside, and is less than a 10-minute drive from the city centre. Bedrooms, in a modern lodge, are comfortable and well equipped while the smart restaurant and the bar, in the main house, offer an excellent choice of food.

Belmont Lodge & Golf

Rooms 30 (4 fmly) (15 GF) **S** £61-£65; **D** £65-£75 **Facilities** ⅃ 18 ♣ Putt green Fishing ⤳ Games room with pool table Xmas **Conf** Class 25 Board 25 Thtr 50 **Parking** 150 **Notes** LB ⊗

Three Counties Hotel

★★★ 73% HOTEL

☎ 01432 299955 📄 01432 275114
Belmont Rd HR2 7BP
e-mail: enquiries@threecountieshotel.co.uk
web: www.threecountieshotel.co.uk
dir: on A465 Abergavenny Rd

A mile west of the city centre, this large, privately owned, modern complex has well-equipped, spacious bedrooms, many of which are located in separate single-storey buildings around the extensive car park. There is a spacious, comfortable lounge, a traditional bar and an attractive restaurant.

Rooms 60 (32 annexe) (4 fmly) (46 GF) **S** £63.50-£80; **D** £75.50-£103 (incl. bkfst)* **Facilities** STV Wi-fi **Conf** Class 154 Board 80 Thtr 350 Del from £88 to £98* **Parking** 250 **Notes** LB Civ Wed 250

See advert on this page

HEREFORD continued

Travelodge Hereford

BUDGET HOTEL

☎ 08719 846 343 📠 01432 351819
Pomana Place HR4 0EF
web: www.travelodge.co.uk
dir: A438, left onto Grimmer Rd, then left onto Pomana Place

Travelodge offers good quality, good value, modern accommodation. Ideal for families, the spacious en suite bedrooms include remote-control TV, tea and coffee-making facilities and comfortable beds. Meals can be taken at nearby convenient restaurants. See also the Hotel Groups pages.

Rooms 52 **S** fr £29; **D** fr £29

KINGTON   Map 9 SO25

Burton

★★★ 74% HOTEL

☎ 01544 230323 📠 01544 239023
Mill St HR5 3BQ
e-mail: info@burtonhotel.co.uk
web: www.burtonhotel.co.uk
dir: rdbt at A44/A411 junct take road signed Town Centre

Situated in the town centre, this friendly, privately-owned hotel offers spacious, pleasantly proportioned and well-equipped bedrooms. Smartly presented public areas include a lounge bar, leisure facilities including a swimming pool, and an attractive restaurant where carefully prepared cuisine can be enjoyed. There are function and meeting facilities available in a purpose-built, modern wing.

Burton

Rooms 16 (5 fmly) **S** £50-£79; **D** £89-£120 (incl. bkfst)*
Facilities Spa FTV 🏊 supervised Gym Steam room Therapy rooms Xmas New Year Wi-fi **Conf** Class 100 Board 20 Thtr 150 Del from £80 to £95* **Services** Lift **Parking** 50 **Notes** LB Civ Wed 120

LEDBURY   Map 10 SO73

Verzon House

★★★ 82% ◎◎ HOTEL

☎ 01531 670381 📠 01531 670830
Hereford Rd, Trumpet HR8 2PZ
e-mail: info@verzonhouse.com
web: www.verzonhouse.com
dir: M5 junct 8/M50 junct 2, follow signs for Hereford A438. Hotel on right

Dating back to 1790 this elegant establishment stands in extensive gardens with far-reaching views over the Malvern Hills. Bedrooms are very well appointed and spacious; one has a four-poster bed. Stylish public areas include the popular bar and brasserie restaurant where a range of well-executed dishes can be enjoyed.

Rooms 8 **S** £105-£135; **D** £155-£175 (incl. bkfst)*
Facilities Wi-fi **Conf** Class 15 Board 24 Thtr 50 Del from £125 to £175* **Parking** 70 **Notes** LB ⊗ No children 8yrs Closed 3-14 Jan

---

Feathers

★★★ 80% @ HOTEL

☎ 01531 635266 🖹 01531 638955
High St HR8 1DS
e-mail: mary@feathers-ledbury.co.uk
web: www.feathers-ledbury.co.uk
dir: S from Worcester on A449, E from Hereford on A438, N from Gloucester on A417. Hotel in High St

A wealth of authentic features can be found at this historic timber-framed hotel, set in the middle of town. The comfortably equipped bedrooms are tastefully decorated; there are now three additional bedrooms - one a cottage room and two contemporary apartments which have two bedrooms and bathrooms each, and prove ideal for families. Well-prepared meals can be taken in Fuggles Brasserie with its adjoining bar, and breakfast is served in Quills Restaurant.

Rooms 22 (3 annexe) (2 fmly) S £82.50-£125; D £120-£195 (incl. bkfst)* Facilities STV ⓣ Gym Steam room New Year Wi-fi Conf Class 80 Board 40 Thtr 140 Del from £130* Parking 30 Notes Civ Wed 100

LEOMINSTER Map 10 SO45

Best Western Talbot

★★★ 75% HOTEL

☎ 01568 616347 🖹 01568 614880
West St HR6 8EP
e-mail: talbot@bestwestern.co.uk
dir: from A49, A44 or A4112, hotel in centre of town

This charming former coaching inn is located in the town centre and offers an ideal base from which to explore this delightful area. Public areas feature original beams and antique furniture, and include an atmospheric bar and elegant restaurant. Bedrooms vary in size but all are comfortably furnished and equipped. Facilities are available for private functions and conferences.

Rooms 28 (3 fmly) Conf Class 25 Board 30 Thtr 130 Parking 26 Notes LB

ROSS-ON-WYE Map 10 SO52

Wilton Court Hotel

★★★ 80% @@ HOTEL

☎ 01989 562569 🖹 01989 768460
Wilton Ln HR9 6AQ
e-mail: info@wiltoncourthotel.com
web: www.wiltoncourthotel.com
dir: M50 junct 4 onto A40 towards Monmouth at 3rd rdbt turn left signed Ross-on-Wye then take 1st right, hotel on right

Dating back to the 16th century, this hotel has great charm and a wealth of character. Standing on the banks of the River Wye and just a short walk from the town centre, there is a genuinely relaxed, friendly and unhurried atmosphere here. Bedrooms are tastefully furnished and well equipped, while public areas include a comfortable lounge, traditional bar and pleasant restaurant with a conservatory extension overlooking the garden. High standards of food using fresh locally-sourced ingredients is offered.

Rooms 10 (1 fmly) S £80-£125; D £105-£145 (incl. bkfst)* Facilities FTV Fishing ⚓ Boule Xmas New Year Wi-fi Conf Class 25 Board 25 Thtr 40 Del from £130 to £150* Parking 24 Notes LB Civ Wed 50

Chase

★★★ 80% @ HOTEL

CLASSIC BRITISH HOTELS

☎ 01989 763161 & 760644 🖹 01989 768330
Gloucester Rd HR9 5LH
e-mail: res@chasehotel.co.uk
web: www.chasehotel.co.uk
dir: M50 junct 4, 1st left exit towards rdbt, left at rdbt towards A40. Right at 2nd rdbt towards town centre, hotel 0.5m on left

This attractive Georgian mansion sits in its own landscaped grounds and is only a short walk from the town centre. Bedrooms, including two four-poster rooms,

---

vary in size and character; all rooms are appointed to impressive standards. There is also a light and spacious bar, and also Harry's restaurant that offers an excellent selection of enjoyable dishes.

Rooms 36 (1 fmly) S £85-£155; D £99-£179 (incl. bkfst)* Facilities STV New Year Wi-fi Conf Class 100 Board 80 Thtr 300 Parking 150 Notes LB ⊗ Closed 24-27 Dec Civ Wed 300

Best Western Pengethley Manor

Best Western

★★★ 75% HOTEL

☎ 01989 730211 🖹 01989 730238
Pengethley Park HR9 6LL
e-mail: reservations@pengethleymanor.co.uk
web: www.pengethleymanor.co.uk
dir: 4m N on A49 (Hereford road), from Ross-on-Wye

This fine Georgian mansion is set in extensive grounds with glorious views and two successful vineyards that produce over 1,000 bottles a year. The bedrooms are tastefully appointed and come in a wide variety of styles; all are well equipped. The elegant public rooms are furnished in a style that is in keeping with the house's character. Dinner provides a range of enjoyable options and is served in the spacious restaurant.

Rooms 25 (14 annexe) (3 fmly) (4 GF) S £79-£115; D £120-£160 (incl. bkfst)* Facilities ⚓ ⚘ 9 ⛳ Golf improvement course Xmas New Year Wi-fi Conf Class 25 Board 28 Thtr 70 Parking 70 Notes LB Civ Wed 90

ROSS-ON-WYE continued

Glewstone Court

★★★ 73% ® COUNTRY HOUSE HOTEL

☎ 01989 770367 🖷 01989 770282
Glewstone HR9 6AW
e-mail: glewstone@aol.com
web: www.glewstonecourt.com
dir: from Ross-on-Wye Market Place take A40/A49
Monmouth/Hereford, over Wilton Bridge to rdbt, turn left
onto A40 to Monmouth, after 1m turn right for Glewstone

This charming hotel enjoys an elevated position with
views over Ross-on-Wye, and is set in well-tended
gardens. Informal service is delivered with great
enthusiasm by Bill Reeve-Tucker, whilst the kitchen is the
domain of Christine Reeve-Tucker who offers an extensive
menu of well executed dishes. Bedrooms come in a
variety of sizes and are tastefully furnished and well
equipped.

Rooms 8 (2 fmly) **S** £80-£95; **D** £118-£135 (incl. bkfst)*
Facilities ⛳ New Year Wi-fi **Conf** Board 12 Thtr 18
Parking 25 **Notes** LB Closed 25-27 Dec

Pencraig Court Country House Hotel

★★★ 70% COUNTRY HOUSE HOTEL

☎ 01989 770306 🖷 01989 770040
Pencraig HR9 6HR
e-mail: info@pencraig-court.co.uk
web: www.pencraig-court.co.uk
dir: off A40, into Pencraig 4m S of Ross-on-Wye

This Georgian mansion commands impressive views of
the River Wye to Ross-on-Wye beyond. Guests can be
assured of a relaxing stay and the proprietors are on
hand to ensure personal attention and service. The
bedrooms have a traditional feel and include one room
with a four-poster bed. The country-house atmosphere is
carried through in the lounges and the elegant
restaurant.

Rooms 11 (1 fmly) **S** £49-£65; **D** £89-£99 (incl. bkfst)*
Facilities ⛳ Wi-fi **Conf** Class 10 Board 10 Thtr 20
Del from £100 to £125* **Parking** 20 **Notes** LB RS 24-27
Dec

The Royal

★★★ 🅰 HOTEL

☎ 01989 565105 🖷 01989 768058
Palace Pound HR9 5HZ
e-mail: 6504@greeneking.co.uk
web: www.oldenglish.co.uk
dir: at end of M50 take A40 signed 'Monmouth'. At 3rd
rdbt, left to Ross-on-Wye, over bridge, take road signed
'The Royal Hotel' after left bend

Rooms 42 (1 fmly) **Facilities** Xmas **Conf** Class 20
Board 28 Thtr 85 **Parking** 44 **Notes** LB Civ Wed 75

Castle Lodge Hotel

★★ 75% HOTEL

☎ 01989 562234 🖷 01989 768322
Wilton HR9 6AD
e-mail: info@castlelodge.co.uk
web: www.castlelodge.co.uk
dir: on rdbt at junct of A40/A49, 0.5m from centre of
Ross-on-Wye

This friendly hotel dates back to the 16th century and
offers a convenient base on the outskirts of the town.
Bedrooms are well equipped and comfortably furnished,
and those choosing to eat in will find there is a good
selection of bar meals plus a varied restaurant menu
which features a wide range of fresh seafood.

Rooms 10 **Facilities** ⛱ **Conf** Class 80 Board 60 Thtr 100
Parking 40

Chasedale

★★ 69% SMALL HOTEL

☎ 01989 562423 & 565801 🖷 01989 567900
Walford Rd HR9 5PQ
e-mail: chasedale@supanet.com
web: www.chasedale.co.uk
dir: from town centre, S on B4234, hotel 0.5m on left

This large, mid-Victorian property is situated on the
south-west outskirts of the town. Privately owned and
personally run, it provides spacious, well-proportioned
public areas and extensive grounds. The accommodation
is well equipped and includes ground floor and family
rooms, whilst the restaurant offers a wide selection of
wholesome food.

Rooms 10 (2 fmly) (1 GF) **S** £41-£42.50; **D** £82-£85 (incl.
bkfst) **Facilities** Xmas Wi-fi **Conf** Class 30 Board 25
Thtr 40 **Parking** 14 **Notes** LB

King's Head

★★ 68% HOTEL

☎ 01989 763174 🖷 01989 769578
8 High St HR9 5HL
e-mail: enquiries@kingshead.co.uk
web: www.kingshead.co.uk
dir: in town centre, turn right past Royal Hotel

This establishment dates back to the 14th century and
has a wealth of charm and character. Bedrooms are well
equipped and include both four-poster and family rooms.
The restaurant doubles as a coffee shop during the day
and is a popular venue with locals. There is also a very
pleasant bar and comfortable lounge.

Rooms 15 (1 fmly) **S** £53.50; **D** £90 (incl. bkfst)
Facilities Wi-fi **Parking** 13 **Notes** LB

Bridge House

®® RESTAURANT WITH ROOMS

☎ 01989 562655 🖷 01989 567652
Wilton HR9 6AA
e-mail: info@bridge-house-hotel.com
dir: Off junct A40 & A49 into Ross-on-Wye, 300yds on left

Built about 1740, this elegant house is just a stroll
across the bridge from delightful Ross-on-Wye. Standards
here are impressive and bedrooms offer ample space,
comfort and genuine quality. Period features in the public
areas add to the stylish ambience, and the gardens run
down to the river. The restaurant serves accomplished
cuisine.

Rooms 9 (2 en suite)

HERTFORDSHIRE

BALDOCK   Map 12 TL23

Travelodge Baldock Hinxworth

BUDGET HOTEL

☎ 08719 846 005   📄 01462 835329
Great North Rd, Hinxworth SG7 5EX
web: www.travelodge.co.uk
dir: on A1, southbound

Travelodge offers good quality, good value, modern accommodation. Ideal for families, the spacious en suite bedrooms include remote-control TV, tea and coffee-making facilities and comfortable beds. Meals can be taken at the nearby family restaurant. See also the Hotel Groups pages.

Rooms 40 **S** fr £29; **D** fr £29

BISHOP'S STORTFORD   Map 6 TL42

Down Hall Country House

★★★★ 76% ◉◉ HOTEL

☎ 01279 731441   📄 01279 730416
Hatfield Heath CM22 7AS
e-mail: reservations@downhall.co.uk
web: www.downhall.co.uk
dir: A1060, at Hatfield Heath keep left. Turn right into lane opposite Hunters Meet restaurant & left at end, follow sign

Imposing Victorian country-house hotel set amidst 100 acres of mature grounds in a peaceful location just a short drive from Stansted Airport. Bedrooms are generally quite spacious; each one is pleasantly decorated, tastefully furnished and equipped with modern facilities. Public rooms include a choice of restaurants, a cocktail bar, two lounges and leisure facilities.

Rooms 99 (20 GF) (10 smoking) **S** £99-£104; **D** £104-£140 (incl. bkfst)* **Facilities** ◉ ◉ ◉ Giant chess Whirlpool Sauna Snooker room Gym equipment Xmas New Year Wi-fi **Conf** Class 140 Board 68 Thtr 200 Del from £189 to £214* **Services** Lift **Parking** 150 **Notes** LB Civ Wed 120

BOREHAMWOOD   Map 6 TQ19

Holiday Inn London - Elstree

★★★★ 71% HOTEL

☎ 0870 443 1271   & 020 8214 9988   📄 020 8207 6817
Barnet Bypass WD6 5PU
e-mail: hielstree@qmh-hotels.com
web: www.holidayinn.co.uk
dir: M25 junct 23 take A1 S towards London. After 2m take B5135 towards Borehamwood. Hotel next to 1st rdbt

Ideally located for motorway links and easy travel into the city, this hotel boasts excellent conference and event facilities, secure parking and leisure and beauty treatment options. A range of bedroom sizes is available; all are well equipped and have air conditioning. Dining is available in either the restaurant, which offers both carvery and carte choices, or in the bar serving a range of dishes.

Rooms 135 (5 fmly) (25 GF) **Facilities** ◉ Gym Steam room Beauty salon Xmas Wi-fi **Conf** Class 150 Board 60 Thtr 400 **Services** Lift Air con **Parking** 350 **Notes** LB ◉ Civ Wed 250

Innkeeper's Lodge London Borehamwood

BUDGET HOTEL

☎ 0845 112 6120   📄 0845 112 6183
Studio Way WD6 5JY
web: www.innkeeperslodge.com/borehamwood
dir: M25 junct 23/A1(M) signed to London. Follow signs to Borehamwood after double rdbt turn into Studio Way

Innkeeper's Lodge represents an exciting, high value concept within the budget hotel market. Comfortable bedrooms provide excellent facilities that include satellite TV and modem points. Options include family rooms, and for the corporate guest, cutting edge IT which includes

Wi-fi access. A popular Carvery provides all-day food, including an extensive, complimentary continental breakfast.

Rooms 55 (8 fmly) **S** £55-£59.95; **D** £55-£59.95 (incl. bkfst) **Conf** Thtr 36

CHESHUNT   Map 6 TL30

Cheshunt Marriott

★★★★ 76% HOTEL

☎ 01992 451245   📄 01992 440120
Halfhide Ln, Turnford EN10 6NG
web: www.cheshuntmarriott.co.uk
dir: Exit A10 at Broxbourne, right and right again at rdbt, hotel on right at next rdbt.

This popular suburban hotel has an attractive courtyard garden, overlooked by many of the guest bedrooms. All rooms are spacious and air conditioned. Public areas include a small, unsupervised leisure facility, along with the busy Washington Bar and Restaurant.

Rooms 143 (37 fmly) (39 GF) **Facilities** STV ◉ Gym ♫ Xmas New Year Wi-fi **Conf** Class 72 Board 56 Thtr 150 **Services** Lift Air con **Parking** 200 **Notes** ◉ Civ Wed 120

De Vere Theobalds Park

[U]

☎ 01992 633375   📄 01992 634212
Lieutenant Ellis Way EN7 5HW
e-mail: thereception@deverevenues.co.uk
web: www.devere.co.uk
dir: M25 junct 25, N on A10 to 1st rdbt, take take 1st left, left into driveway

Currently the rating for this establishment is not confirmed. This may be due to a change of ownership or because it has only recently joined the AA rating scheme. For further details please see the AA website: www.theAA.com

Rooms 110 (3 fmly) (25 GF) **Facilities** ◉ Gym Xmas New Year Wi-fi **Conf** Class 70 Board 54 Thtr 180 **Services** Lift **Parking** 230 **Notes** LB ◉ Civ Wed 120

Travelodge Cheshunt

BUDGET HOTEL

☎ 0871 9846 349
Park Plaza EN8 8DY
web: www.travelodge.co.uk
dir: M25 junct 25, A10 N'bound towards Cheshunt/Waltham Cross. Hotel 500mtrs from junct on east side

Travelodge offers good quality, good value, modern accommodation. Ideal for families, the spacious en suite bedrooms include remote-control TV, tea and coffee-making facilities and comfortable beds. A breakfast buffet is available in the large dining room. See also the Hotel Groups pages.

Rooms 100 **S** fr £29; **D** fr £29

ELSTREE — Map 6 TQ19

Corus hotel Elstree

★★★ 74% HOTEL

☎ 020 8953 8227 & 0844 736 8602 📠 020 8207 3668
Barnet Ln WD6 3RE
e-mail: elstree@corushotels.com
web: www.corushotels.com
dir: M1 junct 5, A41 to Harrow, left onto A411 into Elstree. Through x-rds into Barnet Ln, hotel on right

Sitting in ten acres of landscaped gardens this hotel is full of charm and character, with a Tudor-style façade and interiors of a traditional design. The oak-panelled bar, with two large fireplaces, and the stately Cavendish restaurant enjoy wonderful views over the gardens and the city beyond.

Rooms 49 (36 annexe) (4 fmly) (13 GF) **S** £129-£260;
D £129-£260* **Facilities** STV FTV Wi-fi **Conf** Class 35 Board 35 Thtr 80 Del from £160 to £200* **Parking** 100
Notes LB ⊗ Civ Wed 90

HARPENDEN — Map 6 TL11

Harpenden House Hotel

folio Hotels

★★★ 77% HOTEL

☎ 0870 609 6170 📠 01582 769858
18 Southdown Rd AL5 1PE
e-mail: harpendenhouse@foliohotels.com
web: www.foliohotels.com/harpendenhouse
dir: M1 junct 10 left at rdbt. Next rdbt right onto A1081 to Harpenden. Over 2 mini rdbts, through town centre. Next rdbt left, hotel 200yds on left

This attractive Grade II listed Georgian building overlooks East Common. The hotel gardens are particularly attractive and the public areas are stylishly decorated, including the restaurant that has an impressively decorated ceiling. Some of the bedrooms and a large suite are located in the original house but most of the accommodation is in the annexe.

Rooms 76 (59 annexe) (13 fmly) (2 GF)
Facilities Complimentary use of local leisure centre Wi-fi
Conf Class 60 Board 60 Thtr 150 Del from £105 to £179*
Parking 80 **Notes** ⊗ RS wknds & BHs Civ Wed 120

HATFIELD — Map 6 TL20

Beales

★★★★ 80% ⑩⑩ HOTEL

☎ 01707 288500 📠 01707 256282
Comet Way AL10 9NG
e-mail: hatfield@bealeshotels.co.uk
web: www.bealeshotels.co.uk
dir: On A1001 opposite Galleria Shopping Mall - follow signs for Galleria

This hotel is a stunning contemporary property. Within easy access of the M25, its striking exterior incorporates giant glass panels and cedar wood slats. Bedrooms have luxurious baths, flat-screen TVs and smart bathrooms. Public areas include a small bar and attractive restaurant, which opens throughout the day.

Rooms 53 (3 fmly) (21 GF) **S** £100-£130; **Facilities** STV FTV Use of nearby leisure club Xmas New Year Wi-fi
Conf Class 124 Board 64 Thtr 300 Del from £175 to £195* **Services** Lift **Parking** 126 **Notes** LB ⊗ RS 27-30 Dec Civ Wed 300

Bush Hall

★★★ 77% ⑩⑩ HOTEL

☎ 01707 271251 📠 01707 272289
Mill Green AL9 5NT
e-mail: enquiries@bush-hall.com
dir: A1(M) junct 4, 2nd left at rdbt onto A414 signed Hertford & Welwyn Garden City. Left at rdbt, take A1000. Hotel on left

Standing in delightful grounds with a river running through it, this hotel boasts extensive facilities. Outdoor enthusiasts can enjoy a range of activities including go-karting and clay pigeon shooting. Bedrooms and public areas are comfortable and tastefully decorated. Kipling's restaurant continues to offer a wide range freshly prepared dishes using quality produce; service is both professional and friendly.

Rooms 25 (2 fmly) (8 GF) **S** £50-£90; **D** £80-£110*
Facilities Clay pigeon shooting Archery Wi-fi
Conf Class 70 Board 50 Thtr 150 **Parking** 100 **Notes** ⊗ Closed 24 Dec-3 Jan Civ Wed 160

Ramada Hatfield

⊕ RAMADA

★★★ 75% HOTEL

☎ 01707 265411 📠 01707 264019
301 St Albans Road West AL10 9RH
e-mail: sales.hatfield@ramadajarvis.co.uk
web: www.ramadajarvis.co.uk
dir: A1(M) junct 3, take 2nd exit at rdbt signed Hatfield. Hotel on left

Conveniently located close to the A1(M) with good links to London, this large hotel is a themed, Grade II listed art deco building and retains many of its original 1930s features. Spacious bedrooms are comfortably appointed in a modern style and very well equipped. Public areas include a substantial range of conference rooms, a small gym and the popular Arts Bar & Grill.

Rooms 128 (4 fmly) (53 GF) (12 smoking) **S** £67-£211;
D £67-£223 (incl. bkfst)* **Facilities** Wi-fi **Conf** Class 100 Board 60 Thtr 120 Del from £145 to £175* **Parking** 150
Notes LB RS between Xmas & New Year Civ Wed 140

Travelodge Hatfield Central

BUDGET HOTEL

☎ 08719 846 316 📠 01707 266331
Comet Way AL10 0XR
web: www.travelodge.co.uk
dir: A1001 to 1st rdbt, right signed Hatfield Business Park, left at Porsche dealership, hotel signed

Travelodge offers good quality, good value, modern accommodation. Ideal for families, the spacious en suite bedrooms include remote-control TV, tea and coffee-making facilities and comfortable beds. Meals can be taken at the nearby family restaurant. See also the Hotel Groups pages.

Rooms 120 **S** fr £29; **D** fr £29

HEMEL HEMPSTEAD — Map 6 TL00

The Bobsleigh Inn

MACDONALD HOTELS & RESORTS

★★★ 78% HOTEL

☎ 0844 879 9033 📠 01442 832471
Hempstead Rd, Bovingdon HP3 0DS
e-mail: bobsleigh@macdonald-hotels.co.uk
web: www.macdonald-hotels.co.uk
dir: turn left after Hemel Hempstead station onto B4505 towards Chesham and follow into Bovingdon, hotel on left

Located just outside the town, the hotel enjoys a pleasant rural setting, yet is within easy reach of local transport links and the motorway network. Bedrooms vary in size; all are modern in style. There is an open-plan lobby, a bar area and an attractive dining room with views over the garden.

Rooms 47 (15 annexe) (8 fmly) (29 GF) S £59-£120;
D £59-£120* Facilities STV Xmas New Year Wi-fi
Conf Class 50 Board 40 Thtr 150 Del from £110 to £160*
Parking 60 Notes LB Civ Wed 100

Ramada Hemel Hempstead

★★★ 75% HOTEL

☎ 01582 792105 📠 01582 792001
Hemel Hempstead Rd, Redbourn AL3 7AF
e-mail: sales.hemel@ramadajarvis.co.uk
web: www.ramadajarvis.co.uk
dir: M1 junct 9 follow Hemel Hempstead & St Albans
signs for 3m, straight across 2 rdbts onto B487 signed
Hemel Hempstead. Hotel on right

With easy access to both the M1 and M25 motorways, this
well presented hotel is set in six acres of landscaped
gardens. Bedrooms are comfortably appointed for both
business and leisure guests.

Rooms 137 (4 fmly) (67 GF) S £67-£211; D £67-£223
(incl. bkfst)* Facilities Xmas Wi-fi Conf Class 50
Board 40 Thtr 100 Del from £145 to £175* Services Lift
Parking 150 Notes LB Civ Wed 100

Best Western The Watermill

★★★ 74% HOTEL

☎ 01442 349955 📠 01442 866130
London Rd, Bourne End HP1 2RJ
e-mail: info@hotelwatermill.co.uk
web: www.hotelwatermill.co.uk
dir: from M25 & M1 follow signs to Aylesbury on A41, then
A4251 to Bourne End. Hotel 0.25m on right

In the heart of the county this modern hotel has been
built around an old flour mill on the banks of the River
Bulbourne with water meadows adjacent. The
thoughtfully equipped, contemporary bedrooms are
located in three annexes situated around the complex. A
good range of air-conditioned conference and meeting
rooms complement the lounge bar and restaurant.

Rooms 75 (67 annexe) (9 fmly) (35 GF) S £65-£120;
D £75-£135* Facilities Fishing Xmas Conf Class 60
Board 50 Thtr 100 Parking 100 Notes LB ⊗ Civ Wed 90

Holiday Inn Hemel Hempstead

Ⓤ

☎ 0870 400 9041 📠 01442 211283
Breakspear Way HP2 4UA
web: www.holidayinn.co.uk
dir: M1 junct 8, over rdbt and 1st left after BP garage

Currently the rating for this establishment is not confirmed.
This may be due to a change of ownership or because it has
only recently joined the AA rating scheme. For further
details please see the AA website: www.theAA.com

Rooms 144 S £155-£180; D £155-£180*

Express by Holiday Inn Hemel Hempstead

BUDGET HOTEL

☎ 0870 4585485 📠 0870 4585488
Stationers Place, Apsley Lock HP3 9RH
e-mail: hemel@expressholidayinn.co.uk
web: www.hiexpress.com/hemelhempstead

A modern hotel ideal for families and business travellers.
Fresh and uncomplicated, the spacious rooms include Sky
TV, power shower and tea and coffee-making facilities.
Continental buffet breakfast is included in the room rate;
other meals may be taken at the nearby family pub or
restaurant. See also the Hotel Groups pages.

Rooms 116 Conf Class 18 Board 18 Thtr 40

Travelodge Hemel Hempstead

BUDGET HOTEL

☎ 08719 846 036 📠 01442 266887
Wolsey House, Wolsey Rd HP2 4SS
web: www.travelodge.co.uk
dir: M1 junct 8 into city centre, 5th rdbt turn back
towards M1, take 1st left

Travelodge offers good quality, good value, modern
accommodation. Ideal for families, the spacious en suite
bedrooms include remote-control TV, tea and coffee-
making facilities and comfortable beds. Meals can be
taken at the nearby family restaurant. See also the Hotel
Groups pages.

Rooms 53 S fr £29; D fr £29

HITCHIN Map 12 TL12

Redcoats Farmhouse Hotel

★★★ 71% ◉ SMALL HOTEL

☎ 01438 729500 📠 01438 723322
Redcoats Green SG4 7JR
e-mail: sales@redcoats.co.uk
web: www.redcoats.co.uk
dir: A602 to Wymondley. Turn left to Redcoats Green. At
top of hill straight over at junct

This delightful 15th-century property is situated in four
acres of landscaped grounds only a short drive from the
A1(M). Bedrooms in the main house and courtyard
annexe are well appointed and spacious. Breakfast and
dinner are served in the conservatory which overlooks the
garden, and a series of intimate dining rooms is also
available.

Rooms 13 (9 annexe) (1 fmly) (9 GF) S £62-£115;
D £70-£145 (incl. bkfst)* Facilities FTV ⚑ New Year
Wi-fi Conf Board 15 Thtr 30 Del from £160 to £180*
Parking 50 Notes LB Closed BH & Xmas-7Jan Civ Wed 75

Firs

THE INDEPENDENTS
HOTEL ASSOCIATION

★★ 🅰 HOTEL

☎ 01462 422322 📠 01462 432051
83 Bedford Rd SG5 2TY
e-mail: info@firshotel.co.uk
web: www.firshotel.co.uk
dir: on A600/A602 for Hitchin, next to Shell petrol station

Rooms 29 (4 fmly) (9 GF) S £55-£60; D £60-£68 (incl.
bkfst)* Facilities FTV Wi-fi Conf Class 24 Board 20
Thtr 30 Parking 30 Notes ⊗

Lord Lister

★★ 🅰 METRO HOTEL

☎ 01462 432712 📠 01462 438506
1 Park St SG4 9AH
e-mail: info@lordlisterhotel.co.uk
web: www.lordlisterhotel.co.uk
dir: 200yds S of town centre at mini rdbt on B656 (off
A602)

Rooms 20 (4 annexe) (2 fmly) (2 GF) S £60-£80;
D £70-£90 (incl. bkfst)* Facilities Wi-fi Parking 16
Notes ⊗ Closed 24 Dec-3 Jan

HITCHIN continued

Sun

★★ **A** HOTEL

☎ 01462 432092 & 436411 📄 01462 431488
Sun St SG5 1AF
e-mail: sun.hitchin@greeneking.co.uk
web: www.oldenglish.co.uk

Rooms 32 (6 GF) **Conf** Thtr 100 **Parking** 24 **Notes** LB ⊗
Civ Wed 100

Innkeeper's Lodge St Albans

BUDGET HOTEL

☎ 0845 112 6058 📄 0845 112 6245
1 Barnet Rd AL2 1BL
web: www.innkeeperslodge.com/stalbans
dir: M25 junct 22 (keep in left lane), A1081at rdbt 1st left
& straight over to next rdbt. Lodge 500yds on right

Innkeeper's Lodge represents an exciting, high value
concept within the budget hotel market. Comfortable
bedrooms provide excellent facilities that include satellite
TV and modem points. This carefully restored lodge is in a
picturesque setting and has its own unique style and
quirky character. Food is served all day, and an extensive,
complimentary continental breakfast is offered.

Rooms 13 **S** £52.95-£65; **D** £52.95-£65 (incl. bkfst)

Ponsbourne Park Hotel

★★★★ 76% ◎◎ HOTEL

☎ 01707 876191 & 879277 📄 01707 875190
Newgate Street Village SG13 8QT
e-mail: reservations@ponsbournepark.co.uk
web: www.ponsbournepark.com

Set within 200 acres of quiet parkland, this 17th-century
country house offers contemporary accommodation and
public rooms, along with a flexible range of leisure and
conference facilities. Smart modern bedrooms are located
in the main house and adjacent annexe; each room is
well equipped, but typically main house rooms are more
spacious. The fine dining restaurant is supplemented by
a bistro.

Rooms 51 (28 annexe) (8 fmly) (10 GF) **Facilities** STV ⌁
⌁ 9 ♨ Gym New Year Wi-fi **Conf** Class 40 Board 40
Thtr 100 Del from £150 to £160* **Parking** 125 **Notes** ⊗
Civ Wed 92

See also **Chenies, Buckinghamshire**

The Grove

★★★★★ 89% ◎◎◎ HOTEL

☎ 01923 807807 📄 01923 221008
Chandler's Cross WD3 4TG
e-mail: info@thegrove.co.uk
web: www.thegrove.co.uk
dir: From M25 follow A411 signs towards Watford. Hotel
entrance on right. From M1 follow brown hotel signs

Set amid 300 acres of rolling countryside, much of which
is a golf course, the hotel combines its historic
characteristics with cutting-edge, modern design. The
spacious bedrooms feature the latest in temperature
control, flat-screen TVs and lighting technology; many
have balconies. Suites in the original mansion are

particularly stunning. Championship golf, a world-class
spa and three dining options are just a few of the
treasures to sample here. The award-winning cuisine in
Colette's restaurant takes its inspiration from the
seasons and uses produce from specialist suppliers; the
restaurant has a private terrace for enjoying an aperitif in
the summer months.

Rooms 227 (32 fmly) (35 GF) **S** £295-£1050;
D £295-£1050 (incl. bkfst)* **Facilities** Spa STV FTV ⌁ ⌁
supervised ⌁ 18 ♨ Putt green Fishing ⌁ Gym Kids' club
Artificial beach Walking & cycling trails Xmas New Year
Wi-fi Child facilities **Conf** Class 300 Board 78 Thtr 450
Del from £360 to £475* **Services** Lift Air con **Parking** 400
Notes ⊗ Civ Wed 450

Long Island

★★ **A** HOTEL

☎ 01923 779466 📄 01923 896248
2 Victoria Close WD3 4EQ
e-mail: office@longisland.fsbusiness.co.uk
web: www.oldenglish.co.uk
dir: M25 junct 18 onto A404, 1.5m. Turn left at rdbt onto
Nightingale Rd, 1st left

Rooms 50 (3 fmly) (12 GF) **Facilities** ♫ **Parking** 120
Notes ⊗

The Noke by Thistle
thistle

★★★★ 77% ◎ HOTEL

☎ 0870 333 9144 📄 0870 333 9244
Watford Rd AL2 3DS
e-mail: reservations.stalbans@thistle.co.uk
web: www.thistlehotels.com/stalbans
dir: M1 junct 6/M25 junct 21a, follow St. Albans signs,
A405. Hotel 0.5m

Conveniently located for access to both the M1 and M25,
this Victorian hotel lies within its own grounds and has
secure parking. Bedrooms are neatly appointed in a
traditional style. Public areas include a choice of
restaurants, The Noke or the more informal Oak and
Avocado, and there is also a small modern leisure club.

Rooms 111 (4 fmly) (58 GF) (16 smoking) **S** £89-£160;
D £99-£160 (incl. bkfst)* **Facilities** Spa ⌁ supervised
Gym Xmas New Year Wi-fi **Conf** Class 22 Board 24 Thtr 60
Del from £135 to £165* **Parking** 150 **Notes** LB ⊗
Civ Wed 150

Sopwell House

★★★★ 77% ⊛ HOTEL

☎ 01727 864477 📄 01727 844741
Cottonmill Ln, Sopwell AL1 2HQ
e-mail: enquiries@sopwellhouse.co.uk
web: www.sopwellhouse.co.uk
dir: M25 junct 22, A1081 St Albans. At lights left into Mile House Ln, over mini-rdbt into Cottonmill Ln

This imposing Georgian house retains an exclusive ambience. Bedrooms vary in style and include a number of self-contained cottages within the Sopwell Mews. Meeting and function rooms are housed in a separate section, and leisure and spa facilities are particularly impressive. Dining options include the brasserie and the fine-dining Magnolia restaurant.

Rooms 129 (16 annexe) (12 fmly) (11 GF) **Facilities** Spa ⓣ Gym Hairdressing salon ♫ Xmas New Year **Conf** Class 220 Board 120 Thtr 400 **Services** Lift **Parking** 350 **Notes** LB ⊗ Civ Wed 250

St Michael's Manor

★★★★ 74% ⊛⊛ HOTEL

☎ 01727 864444 📄 01727 848909
Fishpool St AL3 4RY
e-mail: reservations@stmichaelsmanor.com
dir: from St Albans Abbey follow Fishpool Street towards St Michael's village. Hotel 0.5m on left

Hidden from the street, adjacent to listed buildings, mills and ancient inns, this hotel, with a history dating back 500 years, is set in six acres of beautiful landscaped grounds. Inside there is a real sense of luxury, the high standard of decor and attentive service is complemented by award-winning food; the elegant restaurant overlooks the gardens and lake. The bedrooms are individually styled and have satellite TVs, DVDs and free internet access.

Rooms 30 (1 fmly) (4 GF) (6 smoking) **S** £125-£345; **D** £125-£345 (incl. bkfst)* **Facilities** ⥥ Xmas New Year Wi-fi **Conf** Class 20 Board 24 Thtr 30 Del from £230 to £310 **Parking** 70 **Notes** ⊗ Civ Wed 90

Holiday Inn Luton South

★★★ 75% HOTEL

☎ 0870 4431 781 & 01582 449988 📄 01582 449041
London Rd, Markyate AL3 8HH
e-mail: hiluton@qmh-hotels.com
web: www.holidayinn.co.uk
dir: M1 junct 9 N towards Dunstable/Whipsnade, hotel 1m on right

Situated a short drive from the M1 and Luton Airport, this hotel has a pleasant setting with country views. There is a health and fitness club and a good range of air-conditioned conference and meeting facilities. The contemporary bedrooms are well appointed and have a good range of facilities.

Rooms 140 (12 fmly) (44 GF) **Facilities** ⓣ Gym Sauna Beauty salon Wi-fi **Conf** Class 90 Board 50 Thtr 200 **Services** Lift **Parking** 260 **Notes** LB ⊗ Civ Wed 80

Ardmore House

★★★ 73% HOTEL

☎ 01727 859313 📄 01727 859313
54 Lemsford Rd AL1 3PR
e-mail: info@ardmorehousehotel.co.uk
web: www.ardmorehousehotel.co.uk
dir: A1081 signed St Albans, over 3 sets of lights & 2 mini rdbts. Right at 3rd mini rdbt, across 2 sets of lights. Hotel on right after 800yds

Located in immaculate surroundings close to the town centre and cathedral, this extended Edwardian house and annexe has been carefully renovated, providing a range of facilities much appreciated by a loyal commercial clientele. The practically furnished bedrooms offer a good range of facilities and the extensive public areas include a spacious conservatory dining room.

Rooms 40 (4 annexe) (5 fmly) (5 GF) **S** £63-£95; **D** £73-£135 (incl. bkfst)* **Facilities** STV Wi-fi **Conf** Class 17 Board 18 Thtr 130 Del from £130 to £150 **Parking** 40 **Notes** ⊗ Civ Wed 150

Quality Hotel St Albans

★★★ 71% HOTEL

☎ 01727 857858 📄 01727 855666
232-236 London Rd AL1 1JQ
e-mail: st.albans@quality-hotels.net
dir: M25 junct 22 follow A1081 to St Albans, after 2.5m hotel on left, before overhead bridge

This smartly presented property is conveniently situated close to the major road networks and the railway station. The contemporary style bedrooms have co-ordinated fabrics and a good range of useful facilities. Public rooms include an open-plan lounge bar and brasserie restaurant. A leisure complex has been created, along with air-conditioned meeting rooms.

Rooms 81 (7 fmly) (14 GF) (6 smoking) **S** £50-£95; **D** £70-£130 (incl. bkfst)* **Facilities** STV ⓣ supervised Gym Saunarium Sunbed Beauty treatments Wi-fi **Conf** Class 40 Board 50 Thtr 220 Del from £110 to £145* **Services** Lift **Parking** 80 **Notes** ⊗

ST ALBANS continued

Express by Holiday Inn Luton-Hemel

BUDGET HOTEL

☎ 0845 1126132 📄 01582 842486
London Rd, Flamstead AL3 8HT
e-mail: ebhi-flamstead@btconnect.com
web: www.hiexpress.com/luton-hemel
dir: Turn off M1 junct 9/A5 to Dunstable. Next to
Harvester Restaurant

A modern hotel ideal for families and business travellers.
Fresh and uncomplicated, the spacious rooms include Sky
TV, power shower and tea and coffee-making facilities.
Continental buffet breakfast is included in the room rate;
other meals may be taken at the nearby family pub or
restaurant. See also the Hotel Groups pages.

Rooms 75 (37 fmly) **Conf** Class 12 Board 15 Thtr 20

SAWBRIDGEWORTH   Map 6 TL41

Manor of Groves Hotel, Golf & Country Club

★★★ 78% HOTEL

☎ 01279 600777 & 0870 410 8833 📄 01279 600374
High Wych CM21 0JU
e-mail: info@manorofgroves.co.uk
web: www.manorofgroves.com
dir: A1184 to Sawbridgeworth, left to High Wych, right at
village green & hotel 200yds left

Delightful Georgian manor house set in 150 acres of
secluded grounds and gardens, with its own 18-hole
championship golf course and superb leisure facilities.
Public rooms include an imposing open-plan glass atrium
that features a bar, lounge area and modern restaurant.
The spacious bedrooms are smartly decorated and
equipped with modern facilities.

Manor of Groves Hotel, Golf & Country Club

Rooms 80 (2 fmly) (17 GF) **S** £80-£120; **D** £120-£150
(incl. bkfst)* **Facilities** Spa STV 🕃 supervised ᠘ 18 Putt
green Gym Dance studio Beauty salon Sauna Steam
rooms Xmas New Year Wi-fi **Conf** Class 250 Board 50
Thtr 500 Del from £145 to £169* **Services** Lift
Parking 350 **Notes** ⊗ RS 24 Dec-2 Jan Civ Wed 300

See advert on this page

SOUTH MIMMS SERVICE AREA (M25) Map 6 TL20

Days Inn South Mimms

BUDGET HOTEL

☎ 01707 665440 📄 01707 660189
Bignells Corner EN6 3QQ
e-mail: south.mimms@welcomebreak.co.uk
web: www.welcomebreak.co.uk
dir: M25 junct 23, at rdbt follow signs

This modern building offers accommodation in smart,
spacious and well-equipped bedrooms, suitable for
families and business travellers, and all with en suite
bathrooms. Continental breakfast is available and other
refreshments may be taken at the nearby family
restaurant. See also the Hotel Groups pages.

Rooms 74 (55 fmly) **S** £49-£69; **D** £59-£79*
Conf Board 10 Del from £95 to £109*

STEVENAGE   Map 12 TL22

Novotel Stevenage

★★★ 77% HOTEL

☎ 01438 346100 📄 01438 723872
Knebworth Park SG1 2AX
e-mail: H0992@accor.com
web: www.novotel.com
dir: A1(M) junct 7, at entrance to Knebworth Park

Ideally situated just off the A1(M) is this purpose built
hotel, which is a popular business and conference venue.
Bedrooms are pleasantly decorated and equipped with a
good range of useful extras. Public rooms include a large
open plan lounge bar serving a range of snacks, and a
smartly appointed restaurant.

Rooms 101 (20 fmly) (30 GF) **Facilities** 🏋 Free use of
local health club New Year Wi-fi **Conf** Class 80 Board 70
Thtr 150 **Services** Lift **Parking** 120 **Notes** Civ Wed 120

Best Western Roebuck Inn

★★★ 71% HOTEL

☎ 01438 365445 📄 01438 741308
London Rd, Broadwater SG2 8DS
e-mail: hotel@roebuckinn.com
dir: A1(M) junct 7, right towards Stevenage. At 2nd rdbt
take 2nd exit signed Roebuck-London/Knebworth/B197.
Hotel in 1.5m

Suitable for both the business and leisure traveller, this
hotel provides spacious contemporary accommodation in
well-equipped bedrooms. The older part of the building,
where there is a restaurant and a cosy public bar with log
fire and real ales, dates back to the 15th century.

Rooms 26 (8 fmly) (13 GF) **S** £39.50-£85; **D** £45-£95
Facilities STV Xmas New Year Wi-fi **Conf** Class 20
Board 30 Thtr 50 Del from £105 to £130 **Parking** 50
Notes ⊗

Express by Holiday Inn Stevenage

BUDGET HOTEL

☎ 01438 344300 ▤ 01438 344301
Danestreet SG1 1XB
e-mail: admin@exhistevenage.com
web: www.hiexpress.com/stevenage

A modern hotel ideal for families and business travellers. Fresh and uncomplicated, the spacious rooms include Sky TV, power shower and tea and coffee-making facilities. Continental buffet breakfast is included in the room rate; other meals may be taken at the nearby family pub or restaurant. See also the Hotel Groups pages.

Rooms 129 **Conf** Class 20 Board 20 Thtr 40

Ibis Stevenage Centre

BUDGET HOTEL

☎ 01438 779955 ▤ 01438 741880
Danestrete SG1 1EJ
e-mail: H2794@accor.com
web: www.ibishotel.com
dir: in town centre adjacent to Tesco & Westgate Multi-Store

Modern, budget hotel offering comfortable accommodation in bright and practical bedrooms. Breakfast is self-service and dinner is available in the restaurant. See also the Hotel Groups pages.

Rooms 98 (10 smoking) **S** £37-£47; **D** £37-£47*

TRING   Map 6 SP91

Pendley Manor

★★★★ 76% ◉ HOTEL

☎ 01442 891891 ▤ 01442 890687
Cow Ln HP23 5QY
e-mail: info@pendley-manor.co.uk
web: www.pendley-manor.co.uk
dir: M25 junct 20, A41 (Tring exit). At rdbt follow Berkhamsted/London signs. 1st left signed Tring Station & Pendley Manor

This impressive Victorian mansion is set in extensive and mature landscaped grounds where peacocks roam. The spacious bedrooms are situated in both the manor house and the wing, and offer a useful range of facilities. Public areas include a cosy bar, a conservatory lounge and an intimate restaurant as well as a leisure centre.

Rooms 73 (6 fmly) (17 GF) **Facilities** Spa ◐ ♨ ♨ Gym Steam room Dance Studio Beauty spa Sauna Snooker room New Year Wi-fi **Conf** Class 80 Board 80 Thtr 250 **Services** Lift **Parking** 150 **Notes** ⊗ Civ Wed 200

The Rose & Crown Hotel

★★★ 70% HOTEL

☎ 01442 824071 ▤ 01442 890735
High St HP23 5AH
e-mail: salesrose-crown@pendley-manor.co.uk
dir: off A41 between Aylesbury & Hempstead, hotel in town centre

This Tudor-style manor house in the centre of town, offers a great deal of charm. Bedrooms vary in size and style but all are generally well equipped. The restaurant and bar form the centre of the hotel and are popular with locals and residents alike.

Rooms 27 (3 fmly) **Facilities** Full indoor leisure facilities available at sister hotel **Conf** Class 30 Board 30 Thtr 80 **Parking** 60 **Notes** ⊗ Civ Wed 100

WARE   Map 6 TL31

Marriott Hanbury Manor Hotel & Country Club

★★★★★ 81% ◉◉ COUNTRY HOUSE HOTEL

☎ 01920 487722 & 0870 400 7222 ▤ 01920 487692
SG12 0SD
e-mail: mhrs.stngs.guestrelations@marriotthotels.com
web: www.marriotthanburymanor.co.uk
dir: M25 junct 25, take A10 north for 12m, then A1170 exit, right at rdbt, hotel on left

Set in 200 acres of landscaped grounds, this impressive Jacobean-style mansion boasts an enviable range of leisure facilities, including an excellent health club and championship golf course. Bedrooms are traditionally and comfortably furnished in the country-house style and have lovely marbled bathrooms. There are a number of food and drink options, including the renowned Zodiac and Oakes restaurants.

Rooms 161 (27 annexe) (3 GF) **Facilities** Spa ◐ supervised ♨ 18 ♨ Putt green ♨ Gym Health & beauty treatments Aerobics Yoga Dance class Xmas Wi-fi **Conf** Class 76 Board 36 Thtr 120 **Services** Lift **Parking** 200 **Notes** LB Civ Wed 120

Roebuck

★★★ 74% HOTEL

☎ 01920 409955 ▤ 01920 468016
Baldock St SG12 9DR
e-mail: roebuck@forestdale.com
web: www.theroebuckhotel.co.uk
dir: A10 onto B1001, left at rdbt, 1st left behind fire station

The Roebuck is a comfortable and friendly hotel situated close to the old market town of Ware, it is also within easy reach of Stansted Airport, Cambridge and Hertford. The hotel has spacious bedrooms, a comfortable lounge, bar and conservatory restaurant. There is also a range of air-conditioned meeting rooms.

Rooms 50 (1 fmly) (16 GF) **S** £84-£89; **D** £114-£125 (incl. bkfst)* **Facilities** Wi-fi **Conf** Class 75 Board 60 Thtr 200 **Services** Lift **Parking** 64 **Notes** LB Civ Wed 80

WATFORD   Map 6 TQ19

Ramada Watford

★★★ 77% HOTEL

☎ 020 8901 0000 ▤ 020 8950 7809
A41, Watford Bypass WD25 8JH
e-mail: sales.watford@ramadajarvis.co.uk
web: www.ramadajarvis.co.uk
dir: M1 junct 5, A41 S to London. Straight on at island, hotel 1m on left

This large, modern hotel is conveniently located close to both the M1 and M25 and is a popular venue for conferences. Bedroom options include stylish studio rooms with leather easy chairs; all bedrooms are well equipped and comfortably appointed for both business and leisure guests. A good choice of meals is served in the contemporary Arts Restaurant and Bar.

Rooms 218 (6 fmly) (80 GF) **S** £67-£211; **D** £67-£223 (incl. bkfst)* **Facilities** Spa FTV ◐ Gym ♨ Xmas New Year Wi-fi **Conf** Class 434 Board 310 Thtr 728 Del from £140 to £165* **Services** Lift **Parking** 250 **Notes** LB Civ Wed 180

WATFORD continued

Best Western White House

★★★ 73% HOTEL

☎ 01923 237316 📠 01923 233109
Upton Rd WD18 0JF
e-mail: info@whitehousehotel.co.uk
web: www.whitehousehotel.co.uk
dir: from main Watford centre ring road into Exchange Rd, Upton Rd left turn off, hotel on left

This popular commercial hotel is situated within easy walking distance to the town centre. Bedrooms are pleasantly decorated and offer a good range of facilities that include interactive TV with internet. The public areas are open plan in style; they include a comfortable lounge/bar, cosy snug and an attractive conservatory restaurant with a sunny open terrace for summer dining. Functions suites are also available.

Rooms 57 (8 GF) **S** £59-£139; **D** £79-£139 (incl. bkfst)*
Facilities STV Wi-fi **Conf** Class 80 Board 50 Thtr 200
Del from £135 to £145* **Services** Lift **Parking** 50
Notes ⊗ RS 25 Dec-2 Jan Civ Wed 120

Travelodge Watford Central

BUDGET HOTEL

☎ 0871 984 6320 📠 01923 213502
23-25 Market Steet WD18 0PA
web: www.travelodge.co.uk
dir: A4008 towards town centre. In 1m take left slip lane to bypass 1st rdbt. At next rdbt take 2nd exit towards town centre. Bear left onto ring road. Hotel on right in 0.5m

Travelodge offers good quality, good value, modern accommodation. Ideal for families, the spacious en suite bedrooms include remote-control TV, tea and coffee-making facilities and comfortable beds. A tasty breakfast buffet is available in the spacious dining room See also the Hotel Groups pages.

Rooms 93 **S** fr £29; **D** fr £29

WELWYN GARDEN CITY   Map 6 TL21

Tewin Bury Farm Hotel

★★★★ 74% ❀ HOTEL

☎ 01438 717793 📠 01438 840440
Hertford Road (B1000) AL6 0JB
e-mail: reservations@tewinbury.co.uk
dir: From A1(M) junct 6, 1st exit onto A1000, at rdbt 1st exit onto Hertford Rd, 0.5m, Tewinbury Rd on left

Situated not far from the A1(M) and within easy reach of Stevenage and Knebworth House, this delightful country-house hotel is part of a thriving farm. Stylish, well-equipped bedrooms of varying sizes are perfectly suited for both leisure and business guests. An award-winning restaurant and meeting rooms are all part of this family-run establishment.

Rooms 39 (30 annexe) (6 fmly) (26 GF) **S** £114-£134;
D £122-£142 (incl. bkfst)* **Facilities** STV FTV Fishing
New Year Wi-fi **Conf** Board 40 Thtr 500 Del from £157 to £165* **Services** Lift **Parking** 400 **Notes** LB ⊗
Civ Wed 150

Best Western Homestead Court Hotel

★★★ 73% HOTEL

☎ 01707 324336 📠 01707 326447
Homestead Ln AL7 4LX
e-mail: enquiries@homesteadcourt.co.uk
web: www.bw-homesteadcourt.co.uk
dir: off A1000, left at lights at Bushall Hotel. Right at rdbt into Howlands, 2nd left at Hollybush public house into Hollybush Lane. 2nd right at War Memorial into Homestead Lane

A friendly hotel ideally situated less than two miles from the city centre in a tranquil location adjacent to parkland. The property boasts stylish, brightly decorated public areas that include a smart lounge bar and a large restaurant. Bedrooms are pleasantly appointed and

equipped with modern facilities. Conference rooms are also available.

Rooms 75 (8 annexe) (9 fmly) (2 GF) **S** £70-£90;
D £75-£95 **Facilities** STV Wi-fi **Conf** Class 60 Board 60
Thtr 200 Del from £125 to £140 **Services** Lift **Parking** 70
Notes ⊗ Civ Wed 110

KENT

ASHFORD   Map 7 TR04

INSPECTORS' CHOICE

Eastwell Manor

★★★★ ❀❀ HOTEL

☎ 01233 213000 📠 01233 635530
Eastwell Park, Boughton Lees TN25 4HR
e-mail: enquiries@eastwellmanor.co.uk
dir: on A251, 200yds on left when entering Boughton Aluph

Set in 62 acres of landscaped grounds, this lovely hotel dates back to the Norman Conquest and boasts a number of interesting features, including carved wood-panelled rooms and huge baronial stone fireplaces. Accommodation is divided between the manor house and the courtyard mews cottages. The luxury Pavilion Spa in the grounds has an all-day brasserie, whilst fine dining in the main restaurant is a highlight of any stay.

Rooms 62 (39 annexe) (2 fmly) **D** £140-£440 (incl. bkfst)* **Facilities** Spa STV ⊛ ⊰ ₰ 9 ⌣ Putt green ⚒ Gym Boules Xmas New Year Wi-fi **Conf** Class 60
Board 48 Thtr 200 Del from £240* **Services** Lift
Parking 200 **Notes** LB ⊗ Civ Wed 250

Ashford International

★★★★ 81% HOTEL

☎ 01233 219988 📠 01233 647743
Simone Weil Av TN24 8UX
e-mail: ashford@qhotels.co.uk
web: www.qhotels.co.uk
dir: M20 junct 9, 3rd exit for Ashford/Canterbury. Left at 1st rdbt, hotel 200mtrs on left

Situated just off the M20 and with easy links to the Eurotunnel, Eurostar and ferry terminals, this hotel has been stunningly appointed. The slick, stylishly presented bedrooms are equipped with the latest amenities. Public areas include the spacious Horizons Wine Bar and

Restaurant serving a competitively priced menu, and Quench Sports Bar for relaxing drinks. The Reflections leisure club boasts a pool, fully-equipped gym, spa facilities and treatment rooms. Q Hotels - AA Hotel Group of the Year 2008-9.

Rooms 179 (25 fmly) **S** £120; **D** £130* **Facilities** Spa ⓣ supervised Gym Aroma steam room Xmas New Year Wi-fi **Conf** Class 160 Board 26 Thtr 400 Del from £140 to £179* **Services** Lift Air con **Parking** 400 (charged) **Notes** LB Civ Wed 150

See advert on this page

Holiday Inn Ashford-Central

★★★ 77% HOTEL

☎ 0870 400 9001 🖷 01233 643176
Canterbury Rd TN24 8QQ
e-mail: reservations-ashford@ihg.com
web: www.holidayinn.co.uk
dir: A28, at 2nd lights turn left. Hotel approx 90mtrs on right

Ideally situated within easy reach of Eurostar and Eurotunnel terminals and a short drive to historic Canterbury, this popular hotel offers stylish facilities for both business and leisure travellers. Comfortable, well-equipped bedrooms vary in size and include spacious family rooms with modern sofa beds. Public areas include a casual restaurant, lounges, bar and attractive garden area.

Rooms 103 (40 fmly) (50 GF) (12 smoking) **D** £59-£129 (incl. bkfst)* **Facilities** STV Xmas Wi-fi **Conf** Class 64 Board 40 Thtr 120 Del from £105 to £120* **Parking** 120 **Notes** LB Civ Wed

---

Holiday Inn Ashford-North A20

Ⓤ

☎ 01233 713333 🖷 01233 712082
Maidstone Rd, Hothfield TN26 1AR
web: www.holidayinn.co.uk

Currently the rating for this establishment is not confirmed. This may be due to a change of ownership or because it has only recently joined the AA rating scheme. For further details please see the AA website: www.theAA.com

Rooms 92

Travelodge Ashford

BUDGET HOTEL

☎ 08719 846 004 🖷 01233 622676
Eureka Leisure Park TN25 4BN
web: www.travelodge.co.uk
dir: M20 junct 9, take 1st exit on left

Travelodge offers good quality, good value, modern accommodation. Ideal for families, the spacious en suite bedrooms include remote-control TV, tea and coffee-making facilities and comfortable beds. Meals can be taken at the nearby family restaurant. See also the Hotel Groups pages.

Rooms 67 **S** fr £29; **D** fr £29

BRANDS HATCH   Map 6 TQ56

Thistle Brands Hatch   thistle

★★★★ 83% ⓢⓢ HOTEL

☎ 0870 333 9128 🖷 0870 333 9228
DA3 8PE
e-mail: brandshatch@thistle.co.uk
web: www.thistlehotels.com/brandshatch
dir: Follow Brands Hatch signs, hotel on left of racing circuit entrance

Ideally situated overlooking Brands Hatch race track and close to the major road networks (M20/M25). The open-plan public areas include a choice of bars, large lounge and an award-winning restaurant. Bedrooms are stylishly appointed and well equipped for both leisure and business guests. Extensive meeting rooms and Otium leisure facilities are also available.

Rooms 121 (4 fmly) (43 GF) **Facilities** ⓣ Gym Health & beauty treatments Solarium **Conf** Class 120 Board 66 Thtr 270 **Parking** 180 **Notes** Civ Wed 65

BRANDSHATCH continued

Brandshatch Place Hotel and Spa

HandPICKED HOTELS

★★★★ 75% @ HOTEL

☎ 01474 875000 📄 01474 879652
Brands Hatch Rd, Fawkham DA3 8NQ
e-mail: brandshatchplace@handpicked.co.uk
web: www.handpicked.co.uk
dir: M25 junct 3/A20 West Kingsdown. Left at paddock entrance/Fawkham Green sign. 3rd left signed Fawkham Rd. Hotel 500mtrs on right

This charming 18th-century Georgian country house close to the famous racing circuit offers stylish and elegant rooms. Bedrooms are appointed to a very high standard, offering impressive facilities and excellent levels of comfort and quality. The hotel also features an excellent and comprehensive leisure club with substantial crèche facilities.

Rooms 38 (12 annexe) (1 fmly) (6 GF) **S** £95-£235; **D** £105-£245 (incl. bkfst)* **Facilities** Spa STV ⊙ ⊝ Gym Squash Xmas New Year Wi-fi **Conf** Class 60 Board 50 Thtr 160 Del from £160 to £220* **Services** Lift **Parking** 100 **Notes** LB ⊗ Civ Wed 110

BROADSTAIRS
Map 7 TR36

See advert on this page

CANTERBURY
Map 7 TR15

Abode Canterbury

aBode

★★★★ 80% @@ HOTEL

☎ 01227 766266 📄 01227 451512
High St CT1 2RX
e-mail: reservationscanterbury@abodehotels.co.uk
web: www.abodehotels.co.uk
dir: M2 junct 7. Follow Canterbury signs onto ringroad. At Wincheap rdbt turn into city. Left into Rosemary Ln, into Stour St. Hotel at end

Dating back to the 12th century this hotel reflects the Abode Hotels' lifestyle concept. Fine dining is offered in the Michael Caines Restaurant, and there is also a Champagne bar, as well as more informal dining in the Tavern. Bedrooms are individually decorated, and have comfortable beds and an impressive range of facilities.

Rooms 72 (3 fmly) **Facilities** Gym & treatment room Xmas **Conf** Class 60 Board 45 Thtr 130 **Services** Lift Air con **Parking** 16 (charged) **Notes** ⊗ Civ Wed 80

Best Western Abbots Barton

Best Western

★★★ 88% HOTEL

☎ 01227 760341 📄 01227 785442
New Dover Rd CT1 3DU
e-mail: sales@abbotsbartonhotel.com
dir: A2 onto A2050 at bridge, S of Canterbury. Hotel 0.75m past Old Gate Inn on left

Delightful property with a country-house hotel feel set amid two acres of pretty landscaped gardens close to the city centre and major road networks. The spacious accommodation includes a range of stylish lounges, a smart bar and the Fountain Restaurant, which serves imaginative food. Conference and banqueting facilities are also available.

Rooms 50 (2 fmly) (6 GF) **Facilities** Xmas New Year Wi-fi **Conf** Class 80 Board 60 Thtr 150 **Services** Lift Air con **Parking** 80 **Notes** LB Civ Wed 100

Chaucer

★★★ 71% HOTEL

☎ 01227 464427 & 453779 📄 01227 450397
Ivy Ln CT1 1TU
e-mail: res.chaucer@crerarmgmt.com
dir: Towards city on A2, exit at Harbledown. Right at 5th rdbt, then 1st left

This historic hotel is located just a short walk from Canterbury Cathedral and the city centre. Retaining much of its original character it offers well-appointed, comfortable bedrooms and modern amenities including Wi-fi. Public areas include the popular Pilgrims lounge/bar and more formal Restaurant 63.

Rooms 42 **S** £74-£105; **D** £89-£130 (incl. bkfst)* **Facilities** STV Xmas New Year Wi-fi **Conf** Class 50 Board 50 Thtr 100 Del from £100 to £120* **Parking** 42 **Notes** LB ⊗ Civ Wed 100

Victoria

★★★ 68% HOTEL

☎ 01227 459333 📄 01227 781552
59 London Rd CT2 8JY
e-mail: info@thevictoriahotel.co.uk
dir: M2/A2 onto A2052, on entering city hotel on left off 1st rdbt

Well situated on the outskirts of the city centre yet just a short walk from the shops and within sight of the cathedral. Bedrooms vary in size; each one is pleasantly decorated and has a good range of useful facilities such as free Wi-fi. Public areas include a stylish bar/lounge, sunny conservatory and a carvery restaurant. Spacious parking is available.

Rooms 33 (3 fmly) (10 GF) **Facilities** Xmas Wi-fi **Conf** Class 20 Board 20 Thtr 20 **Parking** 70 **Notes** LB ⊗

Canterbury Cathedral Lodge

★★★ **A** METRO HOTEL

☎ 01227 865350 ▤ 01227 865388
The Precincts CT1 2EH
e-mail: stay@canterbury-cathedral.org
web: www.canterburycathedrallodge.org/
dir: Within grounds of cathedral

Rooms 35 (6 annexe) (1 fmly) (13 GF) **S** £69-£99;
D £99-£119 (incl. bkfst)* **Facilities** Wi-fi **Conf** Class 95
Board 40 Thtr 250 Del from £139 to £149* **Services** Lift
Parking 15 **Notes** LB ⊗ RS Xmas

Falstaff

★★ 67% HOTEL

☎ 01227 462138 ▤ 01227 463525
8-10 St Dunstan's St CT2 8AF
web: www.foliohotels.com/falstaff
dir: M2 junct 7/A2 (Canterbury & Dover). After 5m follow
1st sign for Canterbury. At 1st rdbt turn left (St Dunstan's
Hotels). At 2nd mini-rdbt, hotel on left

Situated next to the historic Westgate, parts of this old
coaching inn date back to the early 15th century and the
building is mentioned in many ancient documents.
Conveniently located just a few minutes from shops, bars
and tourist sites this hotel has a varied selection of
comfortably appointed rooms with modern amenities
such as Wi-fi. Public areas retain much original character
and include a bar, cosy lounges and a stylish restaurant.
Limited parking is available.

Rooms 46 (22 annexe) (1 fmly) (16 GF) **S** £60-£95;
D £70-£110* **Facilities** New Year **Conf** Board 12 Thtr 20
Del from £127 to £167* **Parking** 30 **Notes** LB ⊗

Express by Holiday Inn Canterbury

BUDGET HOTEL

☎ 01227 865000 ▤ 01227 865100
A2 Dover Rd, Upper Harbledown CT2 9HX
e-mail: canterbury@exbhi.co.uk
web: www.hiexpress.com/canterburyuk
dir: On A2, 4m from city centre. Hotel accessed via Texaco
petrol station at Upper Harbledown

A modern hotel ideal for families and business travellers.
Fresh and uncomplicated, the spacious rooms include Sky
TV, power shower and tea and coffee-making facilities.
Continental buffet breakfast is included in the room rate;
other meals may be taken at the nearby family pub or
restaurant. See also the Hotel Groups pages.

Rooms 89 (55 fmly) **Conf** Class 20 Board 20 Thtr 36

Innkeeper's Lodge Canterbury

BUDGET HOTEL

☎ 0845 112 6099
162 New Dover Rd CT1 3EL
web: www.innkeeperslodge.com/canterbury
dir: M2 junct 7, A2 towards Canterbury/Dover. Take exit
for OBridge, right at end of sliproad, then right again.
Right at road end & follow A2050/Canterbury signs.
Lodge 1m on left

Innkeeper's Lodge represents an exciting, high value
concept within the budget hotel market. Comfortable
bedrooms provide excellent facilities that include satellite
TV and modem points. This carefully restored lodge is in a
picturesque setting and has its own unique style and
quirky character. Food is served all day, and an extensive,
complimentary continental breakfast is offered.

Innkeeper's Lodge Canterbury

Rooms 9 (1 fmly) **S** £65; **D** £65 (incl. bkfst)

Travelodge Canterbury Dunkirk

BUDGET HOTEL

☎ 08719 846 023 ▤ 01227 752781
A2 Gate Services, Dunkirk ME13 9LN
web: www.travelodge.co.uk
dir: 5m W on A2 northbound

Travelodge offers good quality, good value, modern
accommodation. Ideal for families, the spacious en suite
bedrooms include remote-control TV, tea and coffee-
making facilities and comfortable beds. Meals can be
taken at the nearby family restaurant. See also the Hotel
Groups pages.

Rooms 40 **S** fr £29; **D** fr £29

CHATHAM
Map 7 TQ76

Bridgewood Manor Hotel

★★★★ 76% ◉◉ HOTEL

☎ 01634 201333 📠 01634 201330
Bridgewood Roundabout, Walderslade Woods ME5 9AX
e-mail: bridgewoodmanor@qhotels.co.uk
web: www.qhotels.co.uk
dir: adjacent to Bridgewood rdbt on A229. Take 3rd exit signed Walderslade & Lordswood. Hotel 50mtrs on left

A modern, purpose-built hotel situated on the outskirts of Rochester. Bedrooms are pleasantly decorated, comfortably furnished and equipped with many thoughtful touches. The hotel has an excellent range of leisure and conference facilities. Guests can dine in the informal Terrace Bistro or experience fine dining in the more formal Squires restaurant, where the service is both attentive and friendly. Q Hotels - AA Hotel Group of the Year 2008-9.

Rooms 100 (12 fmly) (26 GF) **S** £75-£109; **D** £75-£120 (incl. bkfst)* **Facilities** Spa STV ◉ supervised ♨ Putt green Gym Beauty treatments Xmas New Year Wi-fi **Conf** Class 110 Board 80 Thtr 200 **Services** Lift **Parking** 170 **Notes** LB ⊗ Civ Wed 130

See advert on page 281

Holiday Inn Rochester-Chatham
Holiday Inn
HOTELS · RESORTS

U

☎ 0870 400 9069 & 01634 673500 📠 01634 673673
Maidstone Rd ME5 9SF
e-mail: maggie.kennerley@ihg.com
web: www.holidayinn.co.uk
dir: M2 junct 3 or M20 junct 6, then A229 for Chatham

Currently the rating for this establishment is not confirmed. This may be due to a change of ownership or because it has only recently joined the AA rating scheme. For further details please see the AA website: www.theAA.com

Rooms 149 (29 fmly) (53 GF) (16 smoking) **S** £60-£134; **D** £60-£134* **Facilities** ◉ supervised Gym Steam room Sauna Pilates & beauty evenings Xmas New Year Wi-fi **Conf** Class 45 Board 45 Thtr 100 Del from £110 to £145* **Services** Lift Air con **Parking** 200 **Notes** LB Civ Wed 100

DARTFORD
Map 6 TQ57

Rowhill Grange Hotel & Utopia Spa
★★★★ 82% ◉◉◉ HOTEL

☎ 01322 615136 📠 01322 615137
DA2 7QH
e-mail: admin@rowhillgrange.co.uk
web: www.rowhillgrange.co.uk
dir: M25 junct 3 take B2173 to Swanley, then B258 to Hextable

Set within nine acres of mature woodland this hotel enjoys a tranquil setting, yet is accessible to road networks. Bedrooms are stylishly and individually decorated; many have four-poster or sleigh beds. There is a smart, conservatory restaurant offering memorable, seasonal dishes, and also a more informal brasserie. The elegant lounge is popular for afternoon teas. The leisure and conference facilities are impressive.

Rooms 38 (8 annexe) (4 fmly) (3 GF) **S** £175-£260; **D** £200-£370 (incl. bkfst)* **Facilities** Spa STV FTV ◉ ♨ Gym Beauty treatment Hair salon Aerobic studio Japanese Therapy pool Xmas New Year Wi-fi **Conf** Class 64 Board 34 Thtr 160 Del from £185 to £225* **Services** Lift **Parking** 150 **Notes** LB ⊗ Civ Wed 150

Campanile Dartford
Campanile
BUDGET HOTEL

☎ 01322 278925 📠 01322 278948
1 Clipper Boulevard West, Crossways Business Park DA2 6QN
e-mail: dartford@campanile.com
dir: follow signs for Ferry Terminal from Dartford Bridge

This modern building offers accommodation in smart, well-equipped bedrooms, all with en suite bathrooms. Refreshments may be taken at the informal bistro. See also the Hotel Groups pages.

Rooms 125 (14 fmly) **Conf** Class 30 Board 30 Thtr 40

Express by Holiday Inn Dartford Bridge
Express
by Holiday Inn
BUDGET HOTEL

☎ 01322 290333 📠 01322 290444
Dartford Bridge, University Way DA1 5PA
e-mail: gm.dartford@expressholidayinn.co.uk
web: www.hiexpress.com/dartfordbridge
dir: A206 to Erith. Hotel off University Way via signed sliproad

A modern hotel ideal for families and business travellers. Fresh and uncomplicated, the spacious rooms include Sky TV, power shower and tea and coffee-making facilities. Continental buffet breakfast is included in the room rate; other meals may be taken at the nearby family pub or restaurant. See also the Hotel Groups pages.

Rooms 126 (34 fmly) **Conf** Board 25 Thtr 35

Travelodge Dartford
Travelodge
BUDGET HOTEL

☎ 08719 846 025 📠 01322 387854
Charles St, Greenhithe DA9 9AP
web: www.travelodge.co.uk
dir: M25 junct 1a, take A206 towards Gravesend

Travelodge offers good quality, good value, modern accommodation. Ideal for families, the spacious en suite bedrooms include remote-control TV, tea and coffee-making facilities, Wi-fi and comfortable beds. Breakfast and light meals are available in the ground floor café. See also the Hotel Groups pages.

Rooms 65 **S** fr £29; **D** fr £29

DEAL
Map 7 TR35

Dunkerleys Hotel & Restaurant
★★★ 80% ◉◉ HOTEL

☎ 01304 375016 📠 01304 380187
19 Beach St CT14 7AH
e-mail: ddunkerley@btconnect.com
web: www.dunkerleys.co.uk
dir: from M20 or M2 follow signs for A258 Deal. Hotel close to Pier

This hotel is centrally located and on the seafront. Bedrooms are furnished to a high standard with a good range of amenities. The restaurant and bar offer a comfortable and attractive environment in which to relax and to enjoy the cuisine that makes the best use of local ingredients. Service throughout is friendly and attentive.

Rooms 16 (2 fmly) **S** £70-£90; **D** £100-£130 (incl. bkfst)* **Facilities** STV FTV Xmas Wi-fi **Notes** ⊗ RS Mon morning

DOVER Map 7 TR34

Ramada Hotel Dover
RAMADA

★★★★ 74% HOTEL

☎ 01304 821230 📠 01304 825576
Singledge Ln, Whitfield CT16 3EL
e-mail: reservations@ramadadover.co.uk
web: www.ramadadover.co.uk
dir: from M20 follow signs to A2 towards Canterbury. Turn right after Whitfield rdbt. From A2 towards Dover, turn left before Whitfield rdbt

A modern purpose-built hotel situated in a quiet location between Dover and Canterbury, close to the ferry port and seaside. The open-plan public areas are contemporary in style and include a lounge, a bar and Bleriot's Restaurant. The stylish bedrooms are simply decorated with co-ordinated soft furnishings and many thoughtful extras.

Rooms 68 (19 fmly) (68 GF) **S** £62-£141; **D** £62-£141
Facilities Gym Xmas New Year Wi-fi **Conf** Class 200 Board 30 Thtr 300 Del from £99 to £129 **Parking** 80 **Notes** LB ⊗ Civ Wed 300

Wallett's Court Country House Hotel & Spa

★★★ 82% ⑩⑩ HOTEL

☎ 01304 852424 & 0800 035 1628 📠 01304 853430
West Cliffe, St Margarets-at-Cliffe CT15 6EW
e-mail: wc@wallettscourt.com
web: www.wallettscourt.com
dir: from Dover take A258 towards Deal. 1st right to St Margarets-at-Cliffe & West Cliffe, 1m on right opposite West Cliffe church

A lovely Jacobean manor situated in a peaceful location on the outskirts of town. Bedrooms in the original house are traditionally furnished whereas the rooms in the courtyard buildings are more modern; all are equipped to a high standard. Public rooms include a smart bar, a

lounge and a restaurant that utilises local organic produce. An impressive spa facility is housed in converted barn buildings in the grounds.

Rooms 16 (13 annexe) (2 fmly) (7 GF) **S** £109-£139; **D** £129-£169 (incl. bkfst)* **Facilities** Spa FTV ⓢ ⥉ Putt green ⤳ Gym Treatment suite Aromatherapy massage Golf pitching range Beauty therapy New Year Wi-fi Child facilities **Conf** Class 25 Board 16 Thtr 25 Del from £193 to £233* **Parking** 30 **Notes** LB ⊗ Closed 24-26 Dec

Best Western Churchill Hotel and Health Club
 Best Western

★★★ 72% HOTEL

☎ 01304 203633 📠 01304 216320
Dover Waterfront CT17 9BP
e-mail: enquiries@churchill-hotel.com
web: www.bw-churchillhotel.co.uk
dir: A20 follow Hoverport signs, left onto seafront, hotel in 800yds

Attractive terraced waterfront hotel overlooking the harbour that offers a wide range of facilities including meeting rooms, health club, hairdresser and beauty treatments. Some of the tastefully decorated bedrooms have balconies, some have broadband access and many of the rooms have superb sea views. Public rooms include a large, open-plan lounge bar and a smart bistro restaurant.

Rooms 81 (5 fmly) **S** £60-£78; **D** £65-£95* **Facilities** STV Gym Health club Hair & beauty salons Xmas New Year Wi-fi **Conf** Class 60 Board 50 Thtr 110 Del from £90 to £120 **Services** Lift **Parking** 32 **Notes** LB ⊗ Civ Wed 100

White Cliffs
Ⓤ

☎ 01304 852229 & 852400 📠 01304 851880
High St, St Margaret's-at-Cliffe CT15 6AT
e-mail: mail@thewhitecliffs.com
dir: Opposite church in village centre

Currently the rating for this establishment is not confirmed. This may be due to a change of ownership or because it has only recently joined the AA rating scheme. For further details please see the AA website: www.theAA.com

Rooms 15 (9 annexe) (2 fmly) (4 GF) **S** £49-£89; **D** £79-£129 (incl. bkfst)* **Facilities** FTV Xmas New Year Wi-fi Child facilities **Conf** Class 20 Board 14 Thtr 20 Del from £108 to £148* **Parking** 20 **Notes** LB

FAVERSHAM Map 7 TR06

Travelodge Canterbury Whitstable
 Travelodge

BUDGET HOTEL

☎ 08719 846 022 📠 01227 281135
Thanet Way ME13 9EL
web: www.travelodge.co.uk
dir: M2 from junct 7, A299 to Ramsgate. Lodge 4m on left

Travelodge offers good quality, good value, modern accommodation. Ideal for families, the spacious en suite bedrooms include remote-control TV, tea and coffee-making facilities and comfortable beds. Meals can be taken at the nearby family restaurant. See also the Hotel Groups pages.

Rooms 40 **S** fr £29; **D** fr £29

FOLKESTONE Map 7 TR23

Best Western Clifton
 Best Western

★★★ 75% HOTEL

☎ 01303 851231 📠 01303 223949
The Leas CT20 2EB
e-mail: reservations@thecliftonhotel.com
dir: M20 junct 13, 0.25m W of town centre on A259

This privately-owned Victorian-style hotel occupies a prime location, looking out across the English Channel. The bedrooms are comfortably appointed and most have views of the sea. Public areas include a traditionally furnished lounge, a popular bar serving a good range of beers and several well-appointed conference rooms.

Continued

FOLKESTONE continued

Rooms 80 (5 fmly) **Facilities** Games room Xmas New Year Wi-fi **Conf** Class 36 Board 32 Thtr 80 **Services** Lift **Notes** LB ⊗

The Burlington

★★★ 73% HOTEL

☎ 01303 255301 🖹 01303 251301
Earls Av CT20 2HR
e-mail: info@theburlingtonhotel.com
dir: M20 junct 13. At rdbt 3rd exit signed A20/Folkstone. At next rdbt 2nd exit into Cherry Garden Lane. To lights, take middle lane into Beachborough Rd, under bridge, left into Shorncliffe Rd. 5th right signed Hythe & Hastings. Hotel at end on right

Situated close to the beach in a peaceful side road just a short walk from the town centre. The public rooms include a choice of lounges, the Bay Tree restaurant and a large cocktail bar. Bedrooms are pleasantly decorated and equipped with modern facilities; some rooms have superb sea views.

Rooms 50 (6 fmly) (5 GF) (27 smoking) **S** £42–£98;
D £54–£123* **Facilities** FTV Putt green Xmas New Year Wi-fi **Conf** Class 100 Board 80 Thtr 240 Del from £125* **Services** Lift **Parking** 20 **Notes** LB Civ Wed 100

The Southcliff

★★ 69% HOTEL

☎ 01303 850075 🖹 01303 850070
22-26 The Leas CT20 2DY
e-mail: sales@thesouthcliff.co.uk
web: www.thesouthcliff.co.uk
dir: M20 junct 13, follow signs for The Leas. Left at rdbt onto Sandgate Rd, right at Blockbusters, right at end of road, hotel on right

Perched atop the south cliff with a bird's eye view of the sea this historical Victorian hotel is perfectly located for the Folkestone channel crossings and is only minutes from the town centre. The bedrooms are spacious and airy with some boasting balconies and sea views. Enjoy dinner in the spacious restaurant or contemporary on-site bistro. Parking is available by arrangement.

Rooms 68 (2 fmly) (12 smoking) **S** £35–£69.50;
D £49.50–£79.50 (incl. bkfst) **Facilities** STV ♫ Xmas New Year Wi-fi **Conf** Class 120 Board 50 Thtr 200 Del from £45 to £65 **Services** Lift **Parking** 10 (charged) **Notes** ⊗

GILLINGHAM Map 7 TQ76

Travelodge Medway (M2)

BUDGET HOTEL

☎ 08719 846 198 🖹 01634 263187
Medway Motorway Service Area, Rainham ME8 8PQ
web: www.travelodge.co.uk
dir: between junct 4 & 5 of M2 westbound

Travelodge offers good quality, good value, modern accommodation. Ideal for families, the spacious en suite bedrooms include remote-control TV, tea and coffee-making facilities and comfortable beds. Meals can be taken at the nearby family restaurant. See also the Hotel Groups pages.

Rooms 58 **S** fr £29; **D** fr £29

GRAVESEND Map 6 TQ67

Best Western Manor Hotel

★★★ 77% HOTEL

☎ 01474 353100 🖹 01474 354978
Hever Court Rd DA12 5UQ
e-mail: manor@bestwestern.co.uk
web: www.bw-manorhotel.co.uk
dir: at junct of A2 Gravesend East exit

Situated close to the major road networks with links to Dover, Channel Tunnel and Bluewater shopping village. The attractively decorated bedrooms are generally quite spacious and each one is equipped with many useful facilities. Public rooms include a bar and a smart restaurant as well as an impressive health club.

Rooms 59 (3 fmly) (20 GF) **S** £80–£120; **D** £85–£140 (incl. bkfst)* **Facilities** 🏊 supervised Gym Fitness centre Steam room New Year Wi-fi **Conf** Class 100 Board 25 Thtr 200 Del from £120 to £140* **Parking** 100 **Notes** LB ⊗ Closed 24-26 & 31 Dec

HADLOW Map 6 TQ65

Hadlow Manor

★★★ 77% HOTEL

☎ 01732 851442 🖹 01732 851875
Goose Green TN11 0JH
e-mail: hotel@hadlowmanor.co.uk
dir: On A26 (Maidstone to Tonbridge road). 1m E of Hadlow

This is a friendly, independently owned country-house hotel, ideally situated between Maidstone and Tonbridge. Traditionally styled bedrooms are spacious and attractively furnished with many amenities. Public areas include a sunny restaurant, bar and lounge. The gardens are delightful and there's a seated area ideal for relaxation in warmer weather. Meeting and banqueting facilities are available.

Rooms 29 (2 fmly) (8 GF) **S** £60–£85; **D** £60–£85* **Facilities** STV New Year Wi-fi **Conf** Class 90 Board 103 Thtr 200 Del from £120 to £140* **Parking** 120 **Notes** ⊗ Civ Wed 200

HOLLINGBOURNE Map 7 TQ85

Ramada Hotel & Resort Maidstone

★★★ 75% HOTEL

☎ 01622 631163 🖹 01622 735290
Ashford Rd ME17 1RE
e-mail: sales.maidstone@ramadajarvis.co.uk
web: www.ramadajarvis.co.uk
dir: M20 junct 8, follow Leeds Castle signs, at 3rd rdbt turn right

A large, purpose-built hotel that is conveniently close to the M20, Channel Tunnel and Leeds Castle. Public areas include an attractive contemporary bar, restaurant and comfortable lounge. Bedrooms are stylishly decorated and furnished, with modern amenities such as flat-screen TVs, internet and movie channels.

Rooms 126 (4 fmly) **Facilities** 🏊 supervised ♨ Fishing ♨ Gym Running track Clay pigeon and air rifle shooting Archery ♫ Xmas Wi-fi **Conf** Class 220 Board 60 Thtr 650 **Services** Lift **Parking** 500 **Notes** LB ⊗ Civ Wed 150

HYTHE — Map 7 TR13

Mercure Hythe Imperial
★★★★ 74% HOTEL

☎ 01303 267441 📠 01303 264610
Princes Pde CT21 6AE
web: www.mercure-uk.com
dir: M20, junct 11 onto A261. In Hythe follow Folkestone signs. Right into Twiss Rd to hotel

This impressive seafront hotel is enhanced by impressive grounds including a 13-hole golf course, tennis court and extensive gardens. Bedrooms are varied in style but all offer modern facilities, and many enjoy stunning sea views. The elegant restaurant, bar and lounges are traditional in style and retain many original features. The leisure club includes a gym, a squash court, an indoor pool, and the spa offers a range of luxury treatments.

Rooms 100 (5 fmly) (6 GF) **Facilities** Spa ⟨ᘔ⟩ ⛵ 13 ⚑ Putt green 🏌 Gym Squash Beauty salon Fitness assessments Xmas New Year Wi-fi **Conf** Class 100 Board 50 Thtr 220 **Services** Lift **Parking** 200 **Notes** ⊗ Civ Wed 220

Best Western Stade Court
★★★ 74% HOTEL

☎ 01303 268263 📠 01303 261803
West Pde CT21 6DT
e-mail: stadecourt@bestwestern.co.uk
dir: M20 junct 11 follow signs for Hythe town centre. Follow brown tourist sign for hotel

This privately owned hotel is built on the site of a landing place or 'stade', and is located on the seafront in this historic Cinque Port. Many of its well-maintained bedrooms enjoy splendid sea views and some of these have additional seating areas. Guests can also enjoy the well-tended garden in warmer months and just watch the world go by.

Rooms 42 (5 fmly) **Facilities** Fishing Xmas New Year Wi-fi **Conf** Class 20 Board 30 Thtr 40 **Services** Lift **Parking** 11 **Notes** LB Civ Wed 60

KINGSGATE — Map 7 TR37

The Fayreness
★★★ 77% HOTEL

☎ 01843 868641 📠 01843 608750
Marine Dr CT10 3LG
e-mail: info@fayreness.co.uk
web: www.fayreness.co.uk
dir: A28 onto B2051 which becomes B2052. Pass Holy Trinity Church on right and '19th Hole' public house. Next left, down Kingsgate Ave, hotel at end on left

Situated on the cliff top overlooking the English Channel, just a few steps from a sandy beach and adjacent to the North Foreland Golf Club. The spacious bedrooms are tastefully furnished with many thoughtful touches including free Wi-fi; some rooms have stunning sea views. Public rooms include a large open-plan lounge/bar, a function room, dining room and conservatory restaurant.

Rooms 29 (3 fmly) (5 GF) (4 smoking) **S** £55.50–£143; **D** £71–£153 (incl. bkfst)* **Facilities** STV New Year Wi-fi **Conf** Class 28 Board 36 Thtr 50 Del from £100 to £150* **Parking** 70 **Notes** LB Civ Wed 80

See advert on page 280

LENHAM — Map 7 TQ85

INSPECTORS' CHOICE

Chilston Park
★★★★ ◉◉ HOTEL

☎ 01622 859803 📠 01622 858588
Sandway ME17 2BE
e-mail: chilstonpark@handpicked.co.uk
web: www.handpicked.co.uk
dir: from A20 turn off to Lenham, turn right onto High St, pass station on right, 1st left, over x-roads, hotel 0.25m on left

This elegant Grade I listed country house is set in 23 acres of immaculately landscaped gardens and parkland. An impressive collection of original paintings and antiques creates a unique environment. The sunken Venetian-style restaurant serves modern British food with French influences. Bedrooms are individual in design, some have four-poster beds and many have garden views.

Rooms 53 (23 annexe) (2 fmly) (3 GF) **S** £95–£180; **D** £105–£190 (incl. bkfst)* **Facilities** STV FTV ⚑ Fishing 🏌 Xmas New Year Wi-fi **Conf** Class 60 Board 50 Thtr 100 **Services** Lift **Parking** 100 **Notes** LB ⊗ Civ Wed 90

MAIDSTONE — Map 7 TQ75

Marriott Tudor Park Hotel & Country Club
★★★★ 77% HOTEL

☎ 01622 734334 & 632004 📠 01622 735360
Ashford Rd, Bearsted ME14 4NQ
e-mail: mhrs.tdmgs.salesadmin@marriotthotels.com
web: www.marriotttudorpark.co.uk
dir: M20 junct 8 to Lenham. Right at rdbt towards Bearsted and Maidstone on A20. Hotel 1m on left

Located on the outskirts of Maidstone in a wooded valley below Leeds Castle, this fine country hotel is set amidst 220 acres of parkland. Spacious bedrooms provide good levels of comfort and a comprehensive range of extras. Facilities include a championship golf course, a fully equipped gym and two dining options.

Rooms 120 (48 fmly) (60 GF) **Facilities** ⟨ᘔ⟩ ⛵ 18 ⚑ Putt green Gym Driving range Beauty salon Steam room Xmas New Year Wi-fi **Conf** Class 100 Board 60 Thtr 250 **Services** Lift **Parking** 250 **Notes** ⊗

Grange Moor
★★★ 77% HOTEL

☎ 01622 677623 📠 01622 678246
St Michael's Rd ME16 8BS
e-mail: reservations@grangemoor.co.uk
dir: from town centre towards A26 (Tonbridge road). Hotel 0.25m on left, just after church

Expect a warm welcome at this friendly, privately owned hotel, which is ideally situated, within easy walking distance of the town centre. The smartly decorated bedrooms have co-ordinated soft fabrics and many thoughtful touches. Public areas include a popular bar, a cosy restaurant and a small residents' lounge.

Rooms 50 (12 annexe) (6 fmly) (12 GF) (11 smoking) **S** £48–£58; **D** £58–£70 (incl. bkfst)* **Facilities** FTV Wi-fi **Conf** Class 60 Board 40 Thtr 120 **Parking** 60 **Notes** ⊗ Closed 24-30 Dec Civ Wed 80

Best Western Russell
★★★ 75% HOTEL

☎ 01622 692221 📠 01622 762084
136 Boxley Rd ME14 2AE
e-mail: res@therussellhotel.com
dir: M20 junct 7, A249 Maidstone. At 2nd rdbt take 2nd exit to Boxley. Left at 3rd rdbt, hotel on left at top of hill

Since its days as a Carmelite convent, this Victorian building has been extended and modernised. Set in attractive grounds and offering a range of function rooms, the hotel is a popular venue for weddings and conferences. The well-maintained bedrooms are contemporary in style and equipped with modern facilities.

Continued

MAIDSTONE continued

Rooms 42 (4 fmly) **S** £85-£105; **D** £95-£115 (incl. bkfst)* **Facilities** STV Free use of facilities at David Lloyd Health & Fitness Centre Xmas New Year Wi-fi **Conf** Class 100 Board 70 Thtr 300 Del from £105 to £125* **Parking** 100 **Notes** ⊗ Civ Wed 250

Larkfield Priory

★★★ 67% HOTEL

☎ 01732 846858
London Rd, Larkfield ME20 6HJ
e-mail: reservations@larkfieldpriory.com
web: www.larkfieldpriory.com
dir: A228 West Malling, Larkfield. At 1st lights take A20 towards Maidstone. Hotel 0.5m on left at 2nd lights

This hotel was built in 1890 and is full of character. Situated just four miles from the centre of Maidstone, and with easy access to the M20, it makes a good stop-off if travelling to or from the Channel ports. The conservatory restaurant offers an extensive menu.

Rooms 52 (6 fmly) (10 GF) **S** £55-£85; **D** £65-£95 (incl. bkfst)* **Facilities** STV FTV Xmas New Year Wi-fi **Conf** Class 35 Board 35 Thtr 70 Del from £99.99 to £155* **Parking** 46 **Notes** LB Civ Wed 80

Innkeeper's Lodge Maidstone

BUDGET HOTEL

☎ 0845 112 6103 ▤ 0845 112 6200
Sandling Rd ME14 2RF
web: www.innkeeperslodge.com/maidstone
dir: M20 junct 6, A229 towards Maidstone. Left at 3rd rdbt into Station Road, left into Sandling Road. Lodge on left

Innkeeper's Lodge represents an exciting, high value concept within the budget hotel market. Comfortable bedrooms provide excellent facilities that include satellite TV and modem points. This carefully restored lodge is in a picturesque setting and has its own unique style and quirky character. Food is served all day, and an extensive, complimentary continental breakfast is offered.

Rooms 12 (1 fmly) **S** £59.95-£69.95; **D** £59.95-£69.95 (incl. bkfst)

MARGATE Map 7 TR37

Smiths Court

★★★ 🅰 HOTEL

☎ 01843 222310 ▤ 01843 222312
Eastern Esplanade, Cliftonville CT9 2HL
e-mail: info@smithscourt.co.uk
dir: from clocktower on seafront take left fork on A28 for approx 1m. Hotel on right Eastern Esplanade at junct with Godwin Rd.

Rooms 43 (10 fmly) (4 GF) **S** £50-£60; **D** £75-£85 (incl. bkfst) **Facilities** FTV Gym ♫ New Year Wi-fi **Conf** Class 50 Board 80 Thtr 80 Del from £60 to £80 **Services** Lift **Parking** 15 **Notes** Civ Wed 80

RAMSGATE Map 7 TR36

Pegwell Bay

★★★ 77% HOTEL

☎ 01843 599590 ▤ 01843 599591
81 Pegwell Rd, Pegwell Village CT11 0NJ
e-mail: reception@pegwellbayhotel.co.uk
dir: A28 to Ramsgate. Follow directions to Pegwell. Continue on Chiltern Lane, hotel on left

Boasting stunning views over The Channel, this historic cliff-top hotel makes an ideal location for guests either on business or for leisure. Spacious, comfortable bedrooms are well equipped and include Wi-fi. A modern lounge, majestic dining room and traditional pub offer a variety of options for eating and for relaxation.

Rooms 42 (1 fmly) (6 GF) **Facilities** FTV Xmas New Year Wi-fi **Conf** Class 65 Board 65 Thtr 100 **Services** Lift **Notes** ⊗

Comfort Inn Ramsgate

★★★ 74% HOTEL

☎ 01843 592345 ▤ 01843 580157
Victoria Pde, East Cliff CT11 8DT
e-mail: reservations@comfortinnramsgate.co.uk
web: www.comfortinnramsgate.co.uk
dir: From M2 take A299 signed Ramsgate, B2054 to Victoria Parade, follow sign to harbour

This Victorian hotel stands on the seafront, close to the ferry and the town. Bedrooms, some with balconies, are generously sized and well equipped. Meals are served both in the bar lounge and in the restaurant, which serves a particularly wide choice of dishes ranging from traditional British cuisine to Indian favourites.

Rooms 44 (5 fmly) **Facilities** Xmas New Year Wi-fi **Conf** Class 30 Board 60 Thtr 130 **Services** Lift **Parking** 10 **Notes** ⊗

The Oak Hotel

★★ 84% HOTEL

☎ 01843 583686 & 581582 ▤ 01843 581606
66 Harbour Pde CT11 8LN
e-mail: reception@oakhotel.co.uk
dir: Follow road around harbour & turn right into Harbour Pde

Located within easy reach of the railway station, ferry terminal and the town centre's shops, this stylish hotel enjoys spectacular views of the marina and harbour. The comfortable bedrooms are attractively presented and very well equipped. The Atlantis fish restaurant, Caffe Roma and the contemporary bar offer a variety of dining options.

Rooms 34 (9 fmly) **S** £49.50-£98; **D** £65.50-£110 (incl. bkfst)* **Facilities** Wi-fi **Conf** Class 60 Board 50 Thtr 100 **Notes** ⊗

Express by Holiday Inn Kent International Airport-Minster

BUDGET HOTEL

☎ 0208 554 9933 ▤ 0208 554 1898
Tothill St, Ramsgate in Thaner CT12 4AU
e-mail: reservations@express-kia.co.uk
web: www.hiexpress.co.uk

A modern hotel ideal for families and business travellers. Fresh and uncomplicated, the spacious rooms include Sky TV, power shower and tea and coffee-making facilities. Continental buffet breakfast is included in the room rate; other meals may be taken at the nearby family pub or restaurant. See also the Hotel Groups pages.

Rooms 105

SANDWICH Map 7 TR35

Blazing Donkey Country Hotel & Restaurant

★★★ 72% HOTEL

☎ 01304 617362 ▤ 01304 615264
Hay Hill, Ham CT14 0ED
e-mail: info@blazingdonkey.co.uk
web: www.blazingdonkey.co.uk
dir: off A256 at Eastry into village, right at Five Bells public house, hotel 0.75m on left

This distinctive inn with its beautiful landscaped grounds is set in the heart of peaceful Kentish farmland. Delightful outdoor terraced dining is available and convivial interior public rooms include a bar, a lounge and a more formal dining area. Comfortably appointed bedrooms are in the main house and also arranged around a rustic courtyard. This is an ideal venue for wedding celebrations.

Rooms 22 (3 annexe) (2 fmly) (19 GF) **Facilities** Putt green ♨ Xmas **Conf** Class 200 Board 200 Thtr 200 **Services** Air con **Parking** 108 **Notes** LB Civ Wed 250

SEVENOAKS — Map 6 TQ55

Best Western Donnington Manor

★★★ 73% HOTEL

☎ 01732 462681 📠 01732 458116
London Rd, Dunton Green TN13 2TD
e-mail: fdesk@donningtonmanorhotel.co.uk
web: www.bw-donningtonmanor.co.uk
dir: M25 junct 4, follow signs for Bromley/Orpington to rdbt. Left onto A224 (Dunton Green), left at 2nd rdbt. Left at Rose & Crown, hotel 300yds on right

An extended 15th-century manor house situated on the outskirts of Sevenoaks. Public rooms in the original part of the building have a wealth of character; they include an attractive oak-beamed restaurant, a comfortable lounge and a cosy bar. The purpose-built bedrooms are smartly decorated and well equipped. The hotel also has leisure facilities.

Rooms 60 (2 fmly) (16 GF) **S** £75-£95; **D** £80-£110 (incl. bkfst) **Facilities** STV ⊗ Gym Xmas New Year Wi-fi **Conf** Class 70 Board 50 Thtr 180 Del from £140 to £145 **Services** Lift Air con **Parking** 120 **Notes** ⊗ Civ Wed 130

SITTINGBOURNE — Map 7 TQ96

Hempstead House Country Hotel

★★★ 83% ⍟ HOTEL

☎ 01795 428020 📠 01795 436362
London Rd, Bapchild ME9 9PP
e-mail: info@hempsteadhouse.co.uk
web: www.hempsteadhouse.co.uk
dir: 1.5m from town centre on A2 towards Canterbury

Expect a warm welcome at this charming detached Victorian property, situated amidst four acres of mature landscaped gardens. Bedrooms are attractively decorated with lovely co-ordinated fabrics, tastefully furnished and equipped with many thoughtful touches. Public rooms feature a choice of elegant lounges as well as a superb

conservatory dining room. In summer guests can eat on the terraces. The new spa and fitness suite opens in the Autumn of 2008.

Rooms 34 (7 fmly) (1 GF) **S** £80-£110; **D** £100-£150 (incl. bkfst) **Facilities** Spa STV FTV ⊗ ♨ Gym Fitness studio Steam room Sauna Hydrotherapy pool Xmas New Year Wi-fi **Conf** Class 150 Board 100 Thtr 150 **Services** Lift **Parking** 100 **Notes** LB Civ Wed 150

TENTERDEN — Map 7 TQ83

Best Western London Beach Country Hotel & Golf Club

★★★ 78% HOTEL

☎ 01580 766279 📠 01580 763884
Ashford Rd TN30 6HX
e-mail: enquiries@londonbeach.com
web: www.londonbeach.com
dir: M20 junct 9, A28 follow signs to Tenterden (10m). Hotel on right 1m before Tenterden.

A modern purpose-built hotel situated in mature grounds on the outskirts of Tenterden. The spacious bedrooms are smartly decorated, have co-ordinated soft furnishings and most rooms have balconies with superb views over the golf course. The open-plan public rooms feature a brasserie-style restaurant, where an interesting choice of dishes is served.

Rooms 26 (2 fmly) **S** £75-£95; **D** £130-£190 (incl. bkfst)* **Facilities** ⊗ ↓ 9 Putt green Fishing Driving range Xmas New Year Wi-fi **Conf** Class 75 Board 40 Thtr 100 **Services** Lift **Parking** 100 **Notes** LB ⊗ Civ Wed 100

Little Silver Country Hotel

Ⓤ

☎ 01233 850321 📠 01233 850647
Ashford Rd, St Michael's TN30 6SP
e-mail: enquiries@little-silver.co.uk
web: www.little-silver.co.uk
dir: M20 junct 8, A274 signed Tenterden

Currently the rating for this establishment is not confirmed. This may be due to a change of ownership or because it has only recently joined the AA rating scheme. For further details please see the AA website: www.theAA.com

Rooms 16 (2 fmly) (6 GF) **S** £60-£95; **D** £95-£185 (incl. bkfst)* **Facilities** STV FTV Xmas Wi-fi **Conf** Class 50 Board 25 Thtr 75 **Parking** 70 **Notes** LB ⊗ Civ Wed 120

TONBRIDGE — Map 6 TQ54

Best Western Rose & Crown

★★★ 74% HOTEL

☎ 01732 357966 📠 01732 357194
125 High St TN9 1DD
e-mail: rose.crown@bestwestern.co.uk
dir: M25 junct 5, A21 to Hastings. At 2nd junct take B245 through Hildenborough. Continue to Tonbridge. At 1st lights right, straight on at next set. Hotel on left

A 15th-century coaching inn situated in the heart of this bustling town centre, the hotel still retains much of its original character such as oak beams and Jacobean panelling. Bedrooms are stylishly decorated, spacious and well presented; amenities include Wi-fi access. A choice of traditional restaurant or comfortable bar is available for dining. The attractive coffee lounge provides a cosy option for impromptu meetings.

Rooms 56 (2 fmly) (10 GF) **Facilities** STV Xmas New Year Wi-fi **Conf** Class 60 Board 60 Thtr 125 **Parking** 47 **Notes** ⊗ Civ Wed 40

The Langley

★★★ 67% HOTEL

☎ 01732 353311 📠 01732 771471
18-20 London Rd TN10 3DA
e-mail: thelangley@btconnect.com
dir: from Tonbridge towards Hildenborough N, hotel on Tonbridge/Hildenborough border

Privately owned hotel located just a short drive from the centre of Tonbridge and ideally situated for business and leisure guests alike. Bedrooms are generally quite spacious; each one is pleasantly decorated and equipped with modern facilities. The restaurant offers a varied menu of carefully prepared fresh produce.

Rooms 39 (3 fmly) (8 GF) **Facilities** Xmas New Year **Conf** Class 50 Board 40 Thtr 150 **Services** Lift **Parking** 60 **Notes** ⊗ Civ Wed 150

TUNBRIDGE WELLS (ROYAL)   Map 6 TQ53

The Spa

★★★★ 77% ⑳ HOTEL

☎ 01892 520331 🖷 01892 510575
Mount Ephraim TN4 8XJ
e-mail: reservations@spahotel.co.uk
web: www.spahotel.co.uk
dir: off A21 to A26, follow signs to A264 East Grinstead, hotel on right

Set in 14 acres of beautifully tended grounds, this imposing 18th-century country house has undergone an impressive refurbishment programme. Spacious, modern bedrooms are stylishly decorated and thoughtfully equipped. The public rooms include an elegant lounge, the Chandelier Restaurant and excellent leisure facilities. State-of-the-art conference rooms are also available.

Rooms 69 (5 fmly) (2 GF) **S** fr £105; **D** fr £150*
Facilities Spa STV ⑳ ⊇ ⬥ Gym ♫ Xmas New Year Wi-fi
Conf Class 90 Board 45 Thtr 250 **Services** Lift
Parking 150 **Notes** LB ⊗ Civ Wed 150

Hotel du Vin Tunbridge Wells

★★★★ 74% ⑳ TOWN HOUSE HOTEL

☎ 01892 526455 🖷 01892 512044
Crescent Rd TN1 2LY
e-mail: reception.tunbridgewells@hotelduvin.com
web: www.hotelduvin.com
dir: follow town centre to main junct of Mount Pleasant Road & Crescent Road/Church Road. Hotel 150yds on right just past Phillips House

This impressive Grade II listed building dates from 1762, and as a princess, Queen Victoria often stayed here. The spacious bedrooms are available in a range of sizes, beautifully and individually appointed, and equipped with a host of thoughtful extras. Public rooms include a bistro-style restaurant, two elegant lounges and a small bar. Hotel du Vin - AA Small Hotel Group of the Year 2008-9.

Rooms 34 **D** £115-£325* **Facilities** STV Boules court in garden Wi-fi **Conf** Class 30 Board 25 Thtr 40
Del from £199* **Services** Lift **Parking** 30 **Notes** LB
Civ Wed 84

Ramada Tunbridge Wells   ⑳RAMADA.

★★★★ 72% HOTEL

☎ 01892 823567 🖷 01892 823931
8 Tonbridge Rd, Pembury TN2 4QL
e-mail: sales.tunwells@ramadajarvis.co.uk
web: www.ramadatunbridgewells.co.uk
dir: From M25 junct 5 follow A21 S. Turn left at 1st rdbt signed Pembury Hospital. Hotel on left, 400yds past hospital

Built in the style of a traditional Kentish oast house, this well presented hotel is conveniently located just off the A21 with easy access to the M25. Bedrooms are comfortably appointed for both business and leisure guests. Public areas include a leisure club and a range of meeting rooms.

Rooms 84 (8 fmly) (40 GF) **S** £72-£162; **D** £72-£174 (incl. bkfst)* **Facilities** ⑳ Steam room Sauna Xmas New Year Wi-fi **Conf** Class 150 Board 107 Thtr 390 Del from £145 to £170* **Parking** 200 **Notes** LB Civ Wed 70

Russell

★★ 61% METRO HOTEL

☎ 01892 544833 🖷 01892 515846
80 London Rd TN1 1DZ
e-mail: sales@russell-hotel.com
web: www.russell-hotel.com
dir: at junct A26/A264 uphill onto A26, hotel on right

This detached Victorian property is situated just a short walk from the centre of town. The generously proportioned bedrooms in the main house are pleasantly decorated and well equipped. In addition, there are several smartly appointed self-contained suites in an adjacent building. The public rooms include a lounge and cosy bar.

Rooms 25 (5 annexe) (5 fmly) (1 GF) **Facilities** Wi-fi
Conf Class 10 Board 10 Thtr 10 **Parking** 15 **Notes** ⊗

Brew House

⑤

☎ 01892 520587 & 552591 🖷 01892 534979
1 Warwick Park TN2 5TA
e-mail: frontoffice@brewhousehotel.com
web: www.brewhousehotel.com
dir: A267, 1st left onto Warwick Park, hotel immediately on left

Currently the rating for this establishment is not confirmed. This may be due to a change of ownership or because it has only recently joined the AA rating scheme. For further details please see the AA website: www.theAA.com

Rooms 10 **S** £105-£150; **D** £150-£195 (incl. bkfst)*
Facilities STV Xmas New Year Wi-fi **Services** Lift Air con
Parking 8 **Notes** ⊗

See advert on this page

Innkeeper's Lodge Tunbridge Wells

BUDGET HOTEL

☎ 0845 112 6109 📠 0845 112 6194
21 London Rd, Southborough TN4 0RL
web: www.innkeeperslodge.com/tunbridgewells
dir: M25, A21, A26 (Tonbridge/Southborough). Lodge in Southborough on A26, opposite cricket green

Innkeeper's Lodge Select represents an exciting, stylish concept within the hotel market. Contemporary style bedrooms provide excellent facilities that include LCD TVs with satellite channels, and modem points. Options include spacious family rooms, and for the corporate guest there is Wi-fi access. All-day food is served in a modern country pub and eating house. The extensive continental breakfast is complimentary.

Rooms 14 (3 fmly) **S** £75; **D** £75 (incl. bkfst)

WROTHAM Map 6 TQ65

Holiday Inn Maidstone Sevenoaks

★★★ 73% HOTEL

☎ 0870 400 9054 📠 01732 885850
London Rd, Wrotham Heath TN15 7RS
e-mail: reservations-maidstone@ihg.com
web: www.holidayinn.co.uk
dir: M26 junct 2A onto A20. Hotel on left

This purpose-built hotel is located within easy reach of the world famous Brands Hatch racing circuit as well as historic Leeds and Hever castles. Rooms are very spacious, comfortably furnished with many accessories. A fully equipped leisure centre, bar, restaurant and lounges are also available as well as a selection of modern meeting rooms.

Rooms 105 (16 fmly) (6 GF) (10 smoking) **D** £55-£159 (incl. bkfst)* **Facilities** STV ⊗ supervised Gym Steam room Sauna New Year Wi-fi **Conf** Class 35 Board 30 Thtr 70 Del from £125 to £150* **Services** Air con **Parking** 120 **Notes** LB Civ Wed 60

LANCASHIRE

ACCRINGTON Map 18 SD72

Mercure Dunkenhalgh Hotel & Spa

★★★★ 72% ◉ HOTEL

☎ 01254 398021 📠 01254 872230
Blackburn Rd, Clayton-le-Moors BB5 5JP
e-mail: H6617@accor.com
web: www.mercure-uk.com
dir: M65 junct 7, left at rdbt, left at lights, hotel 100yds on left

Set in delightfully tended grounds yet a stones' throw from the M65, this fine mansion has conference and banqueting facilities that attract the wedding and corporate markets. The state-of-the-art thermal suite allows guests to relax and take life easy. Bedrooms come in a variety of styles, sizes and standards; some outside the main hotel building.

Rooms 175 (119 annexe) (36 fmly) (43 GF) (9 smoking) **Facilities** Spa STV ⊗ Gym Thermal suite Aerobics studio Xmas New Year Wi-fi **Conf** Class 200 Board 100 Thtr 400 **Services** Lift **Parking** 400 **Notes** ⊗ Civ Wed 300

Sparth House Hotel

★★★ 77% SMALL HOTEL

☎ 01254 872263 📠 01254 872263
Whalley Rd, Clayton Le Moors BB5 5RP
e-mail: mail.sparth@btinternet.com
web: www.sparthhousehotel.co.uk
dir: A6185 to Clitheroe along Dunkenhalgh Way, right at lights onto A678, left at next lights, A680 to Whalley. Hotel on left after 2 sets of lights

This 18th-century listed building sits in three acres of well-tended gardens. Bedrooms offer a choice of styles from the cosy modern rooms ideal for business guests, to the spacious classical rooms - including one with furnishings from one of the great cruise liners. Public rooms feature a panelled restaurant and plush lounge bar.

Rooms 16 (3 fmly) **S** £68-£95; **D** £89-£110 (incl. bkfst)* **Facilities** FTV **Conf** Class 50 Board 40 Thtr 160 **Parking** 50 **Notes** ⊗ Civ Wed

---

BARTON Map 18 SD53

Barton Grange

CLASSIC BRITISH HOTELS

★★★★ 76% ◉ HOTEL

☎ 01772 862551 📠 01772 861267
Garstang Rd PR3 5AA
e-mail: stay@bartongrangehotel.com
web: www.bartongrangehotel.co.uk
dir: M6 junct 32, follow Garstang (A6) signs for 2.5m. Hotel on right

Situated close to the M6, this modern, stylish hotel benefits from extensive public areas that include an award-winning garden centre and leisure facilities. Comfortable, well-appointed bedrooms include four-poster and family rooms, as well as attractive rooms in an adjacent cottage. The unique Walled Garden restaurant offers all-day eating, whilst Healy's restaurant offers dishes prepared with flair and creativity.

Rooms 51 (8 annexe) (4 fmly) (4 GF) **S** £65-£90; **D** £75-£115* **Facilities** STV ⊗ Gym Xmas New Year Wi-fi **Conf** Class 100 Board 80 Thtr 300 Del from £115 to £150* **Services** Lift **Parking** 250 **Notes** ⊗ Civ Wed 120

BLACKBURN Map 18 SD62

See also **Langho**

Millstone at Mellor

★★ 85% ◉◉ HOTEL SHIRE HOTELS

☎ 01254 813333 📠 01254 812628
Church Ln, Mellor BB2 7JR
e-mail: info@millstonehotel.co.uk
web: www.millstonehotel.co.uk
dir: 3m NW off A59

Once a coaching inn, the Millstone is situated in a village just outside the town. The hotel provides a very high standard of accommodation, professional and friendly service and good food. Bedrooms, some in an adjacent house, are comfortable and generally spacious, and all are very well equipped. A room for less able guests is also available.

Rooms 23 (6 annexe) (5 fmly) (8 GF) **S** £74.50-£124; **D** £99-£155 (incl. bkfst)* **Facilities** STV New Year Wi-fi **Parking** 40 **Notes** LB ⊗ Civ Wed 60

BLACKBURN continued

Stanley House

"bespoke" HOTELS

☎ 01254 769200 ▤ 01254 769206
Off Further Ln, Mellor BB2 7NP
e-mail: info@stanleyhouse.co.uk
web: www.stanleyhouse.co.uk
dir: A677 pass The Windmill pub in 2.3m on left, through pedestrian lights. Right, hotel entrance on left.

Currently the rating for this establishment is not confirmed. This may be due to a change of ownership or because it has only recently joined the AA rating scheme. For further details please see the AA website: www.theAA.com

Rooms 12 (4 GF) **Facilities** Wi-fi **Conf** Class 60 Board 32 Thtr 200 **Services** Lift **Parking** 150 **Notes** LB ⊗ No children 3yrs Civ Wed 100

BLACKPOOL Map 18 SD33

De Vere Herons' Reach

DE VERE heritage

★★★★ 75% HOTEL

☎ 01253 838866 ▤ 01253 798800
East Park Dr FY3 8LL
e-mail: reservations.herons@devere-hotels.com
web: www.devere.co.uk
dir: A583. At 4th lights turn right into South Park Dr for 0.25m, right at mini-rdbt onto East Park Dr, hotel 0.25m on right

Set in over 200 acres of grounds, this hotel is popular with both business and leisure guests. The pleasure beach is a few minutes' walk from the hotel, and the Lake District and the Trough of Bowland are just an hour away. Extensive indoor and outdoor leisure facilities include an 18-hole championship golf course. Bedrooms include a number of suites and smart, well-appointed clubrooms.

Rooms 172 (20 GF) **Facilities** Spa ⊗ ⌦ 18 ⛳ Putt green Gym Squash Aerobic studio Beauty room Spinning studio Xmas New Year Wi-fi **Conf** Class 250 Board 70 Thtr 650 **Services** Lift **Parking** 500 **Notes** LB ⊗ Civ Wed 650

Barceló Blackpool Imperial Hotel

 Barceló HOTELS & RESORTS

★★★★ 74% HOTEL

☎ 01253 623971 ▤ 01253 751784
North Promenade FY1 2HB
e-mail: imperialblackpool@barcelo-hotels.co.uk
web: www.barcelo-hotels.co.uk
dir: M55 junct 2, take A583 North Shore, follow signs to North Promenade. Hotel on seafront, north of tower.

Enjoying a prime seafront location, this grand Victorian hotel offers smartly appointed, well-equipped bedrooms and spacious, elegant public areas. Facilities include a smart leisure club; a comfortable lounge, the No.10 bar and an attractive split-level restaurant that overlooks the seafront. Conferences and functions are extremely well catered for.

Rooms 180 (16 fmly) **S** £64-£158; **Facilities** Spa ⊗ supervised supervised Gym Xmas New Year Wi-fi **Conf** Class 280 Board 70 Thtr 600 **Services** Lift **Parking** 150 (charged) **Notes** Civ Wed 200

Big Blue Hotel

 CLASSIC BRITISH HOTELS

★★★★ 71% HOTEL

☎ 0845 367 3333 & 01253 400045 ▤ 01253 400046
Ocean Boulevard FY4 1ND
e-mail: reservations@bigbluehotel.com
dir: M6 junct 32 onto M55. Follow tourist signs for Pleasure Beach. Hotel on Pleasure Beach near south train station

This stylish hotel is ideally located adjacent to the Pleasure Beach, boasting excellent family facilities. A large proportion of family suites offer separate children's rooms furnished with bunk beds, each with their own individual TV screens. Spacious executive rooms boast seating areas with flat screen TVs and DVD players. Public areas include a smart bar and brasserie, a range of meeting facilities and a residents' gym.

Rooms 157 (84 fmly) (37 GF) (4 smoking) **S** £75-£290; **D** £85-£300 (incl. bkfst)* **Facilities** Gym Xmas New Year Wi-fi **Conf** Class 25 Board 30 Thtr 55 Del from £115 to £150* **Services** Lift Air con **Parking** 250 **Notes** ⊗ Civ Wed 100

Briar Dene

★★★ 77% HOTEL

☎ 01253 852312 & 338300 ▤ 01253 338301
56 Kelso Av, Thornton, Cleveleys FY5 3JG
dir: M55 junct 3 signed Fleetwood A585. Towards Cleveleys centre on A585. Left at Morrisons rdbt. Left at lights. Hotel on left

This friendly, long-established family-run establishment is near the centre of Cleveleys, one block from the promenade and a short tram ride from Blackpool. The superb bedrooms have homely extras, and imaginative food is served in the attractive dining room.

Rooms 16 (4 fmly) **Facilities** Xmas New Year **Conf** Class 40 Board 40 Thtr 50 **Parking** 8

Best Western Carlton

Best Western

★★★ 76% HOTEL

☎ 01253 628966 ▤ 01253 752587
282-286 North Promenade FY1 2EZ
e-mail: mail@carltonhotelblackpool.co.uk
web: www.carltonhotelblackpool.co.uk
dir: M6 junct 32/M55 follow signs for North Shore. Between Blackpool Tower & Gynn Sq

Enjoying a prime seafront location, this hotel offers bedrooms that are brightly appointed and modern in style. Public areas include an open-plan dining room and lounge bar, and a spacious additional bar where lunches are served. Functions are well catered for and ample parking is available.

Rooms 58 **Facilities** Xmas New Year Wi-fi **Conf** Class 40 Board 40 Thtr 90 **Services** Lift **Parking** 43 **Notes** LB ⊗ Civ Wed 80

Carousel

★★★ 75% HOTEL

☎ 01253 402642 ▤ 01253 341100
663-671 New South Prom FY4 1RN
e-mail: carousel.reservations@sleepwellhotels.com
web: www.sleepwellhotels.com
dir: from M55 follow signs to airport, pass airport to lights. Turn right, hotel 100yds on right

This friendly seafront hotel, close to the Pleasure Beach, offers smart, contemporary accommodation. Bedrooms are comfortably appointed and have a modern, stylish feel to them. An airy restaurant and a spacious bar/lounge both overlook the Promenade. The hotel has good conference/meeting facilities and its own car park.

Rooms 92 (7 fmly) **S** £55-£90; **D** £90-£140 (incl. bkfst) **Facilities** STV ♫ Xmas New Year Wi-fi **Conf** Class 30 Board 40 Thtr 100 **Services** Lift **Parking** 28 **Notes** LB ⊗ Civ Wed 150

Viking

★★ 75% HOTEL

☎ 0845 458 4222 📠 01253 754222
479 South Promenade FY4 1AY
e-mail: reservations@choice-hotels.co.uk
dir: M55 junct 3, follow Pleasure Beach signs

Located close to the centre of the South Promenade, the Viking Hotel offers well equipped accommodation and a warm welcome. Meals are served in the attractive sea view restaurant and entertainment is available in the renowned "Talk of the Coast" night club. Leisure facilities at sister hotels are also available free of charge.

Rooms 101 (10 GF) **Facilities** 🎵 Xmas **Services** Lift **Parking** 50 **Notes** LB ⊗ No children

Claremont

★★ 74% HOTEL

☎ 0845 458 4222 📠 01253 754222
270 North Promenade FY1 1SA
e-mail: reservations@choice-hotels.co.uk
dir: M55 junct 3 follow sign for promenade. Hotel beyond North Pier

Conveniently situated this is a popular family holiday hotel. The bedrooms are bright and attractively decorated. The extensive public areas include a spacious air-conditioned restaurant which offers a good choice of dishes. There is a well equipped, supervised children's play room, and entertainment is provided during the season.

Rooms 143 (50 fmly) **D** £64-£94 (incl. bkfst & dinner)* **Facilities** 🏊 Gym 🎵 Xmas New Year **Conf** Class 300 Board 75 Thtr 530 Del from £73 to £94.50* **Services** Lift **Parking** 40 **Notes** LB ⊗

Cliffs

★★ 74% HOTEL

☎ 0845 458 4222 & 01253 595559 📠 01253 754222
Queens Promenade FY2 9SG
e-mail: reservations@choice-hotels.co.uk
dir: M55 junct 3, follow Promenade signs. Hotel just after rdbt

This large, privately owned and extremely popular hotel is within easy reach of the town centre. The bedrooms, including spacious family rooms, vary in size. Public areas offer an all-day coffee shop, a smart restaurant and a family room where children are entertained.

Rooms 163 (53 fmly) **D** £68-£106* **Facilities** 🏊 supervised Gym 🎵 Xmas New Year **Conf** Class 210 Board 50 Thtr 475 **Services** Lift **Parking** 30 **Notes** ⊗

Hotel Sheraton

★★ 69% HOTEL

☎ 01253 352723 📠 01253 595499
54-62 Queens Promenade FY2 9RP
e-mail: email@hotelsheraton.co.uk
web: www.hotelsheraton.co.uk
dir: 1m N from Blackpool Tower towards Fleetwood

This family-owned and run hotel is situated at the quieter, northern end of the promenade. Public areas include a choice of spacious lounges with sea views, a large function suite where popular dancing and cabaret evenings are held, and a heated indoor swimming pool. The smartly appointed bedrooms come in a range of sizes and styles.

Rooms 104 (45 fmly) (15 smoking) **S** £20-£75; **D** £40-£150 (incl. bkfst)* **Facilities** 🏊 Table tennis Darts 🎵 Xmas New Year **Conf** Class 100 Board 150 Thtr 200 **Services** Lift **Parking** 20 **Notes** ⊗

Belgrave Madison

★★ 67% HOTEL

☎ 01253 351570 📠 01253 500698
270-274 Queens Promenade FY2 9HD
e-mail: info@belgravemadison.co.uk
dir: From M55 follow signs for Tower/Promenade, turn right onto Promenade. Hotel 2.5m N of tower

This family-run hotel enjoys a seafront location at the quieter end of town. Thoughtfully equipped bedrooms vary in size and include family and four-poster rooms. Spacious public areas include a choice of lounges with views over the promenade, a bar lounge where guests can enjoy live entertainment and a bright restaurant.

Rooms 43 (10 fmly) (2 GF) **Facilities** 🎵 Xmas **Services** Lift **Parking** 28 **Notes** LB ⊗

Headlands

★★ 67% HOTEL

☎ 01253 341179 📠 01253 342657
611-613 South Promenade FY4 1NJ
e-mail: headlands@blackpool.net
dir: M55 & filter left, right at rdbt to Promenade, turn right & hotel 0.5m on right

This friendly, family owned hotel stands on the South Promenade, close to the Pleasure Beach and many of the town's major attractions. Bedrooms are traditionally furnished, many enjoying sea views. There is a choice of lounges and live entertainment is provided regularly. Home cooked food is served in the panelled dining room.

Rooms 41 (10 fmly) **S** £39.95-£49.50; **D** £79.90 (incl. bkfst)* **Facilities** Darts Games room Pool Snooker 🎵 Xmas New Year **Services** Lift **Parking** 38 **Notes** LB Closed 2-15 Jan

BURNLEY Map 18 SD83

Oaks

★★★ 80% HOTEL

☎ 01282 414141 📠 01282 433401
Colne Rd, Reedley BB10 2LF
e-mail: oaks@lavenderhotels.co.uk
dir: 2m N, off A682

Once a Victorian coffee merchant's house this hotel, set in its own peaceful grounds, offers traditional public areas and modern well-equipped bedrooms that come in a variety of styles and sizes. There is a good leisure club, extensive function facilities, and it is a popular venue for weddings.

Rooms 51 (22 fmly) (14 GF) **S** £59-£105; **D** £67-£113 (incl. bkfst)* **Facilities** STV 🏊 supervised Gym Xmas New Year Wi-fi **Conf** Class 50 Board 30 Thtr 120 Del from £99 to £140* **Parking** 100 **Notes** LB Civ Wed 100

Best Western Higher Trapp Country House

★★★ 78% HOTEL

☎ 01282 772781 📠 01282 772782
Trapp Ln, Simonstone BB12 7QW
e-mail: reception@highertrapphotel.co.uk

Set in beautifully maintained gardens with rolling countryside beyond, this hotel offers spacious, comfortable bedrooms, some of which are located in the Lodge, a smart annexe building. Public areas include a pleasant lounge, bar and conservatory restaurant where guests will find service friendly and attentive.

Rooms 29 (10 annexe) (3 fmly) (4 GF) **S** £50-£90; **D** £58-£98 (incl. bkfst & dinner) **Facilities** Xmas **Conf** Class 30 Board 30 Thtr 100 **Parking** 100 **Notes** LB Civ Wed 100

Rosehill House

★★★ 78% HOTEL

☎ 01282 453931 📠 01282 455628
Rosehill Av BB11 2PW
e-mail: rhhotel@provider.co.uk
dir: 0.5m S of town centre, off A682

This fine Grade II listed building stands its own leafy grounds in a quiet area of town. There are two

Continued

BURNLEY continued

restaurants (one a tapas bar) and stylish lounge bar. The hotel features original and beautifully ornate ceilings and mosaic flooring. The boutique-style bedrooms are tastefully finished and comfortably equipped; the two loft conversions and the former coach house offer spacious yet more traditional-style accommodation.

Rooms 34 (3 fmly) (4 GF) **Conf** Class 30 Board 30 Thtr 50 **Parking** 50 **Notes** LB ⊗ Civ Wed 90

Travelodge Burnley

BUDGET HOTEL

☎ 08719 846 125 🖹 01282 416039
Cavalry Barracks, Barracks Rd BB11 4AS
web: www.travelodge.co.uk
dir: at junct of A671/A679

Travelodge offers good quality, good value, modern accommodation. Ideal for families, the spacious en suite bedrooms include remote-control TV, tea and coffee-making facilities and comfortable beds. Meals can be taken at the nearby family restaurant. See also the Hotel Groups pages.

Rooms 32 **S** fr £29; **D** fr £29

**CHARNOCK RICHARD
MOTORWAY SERVICE AREA (M6)** Map 15 SD51

Welcome Lodge Charnock Richard

BUDGET HOTEL

☎ 01257 791746 🖹 01257 793596
Welcome Break Service Area PR7 5LR
e-mail: charnockhotel@welcomebreak.co.uk
web: www.welcomebreak.co.uk
dir: between junct 27 & 28 of M6 N'bound. 500yds from Camelot Theme Park via Mill Lane

This modern building offers accommodation in smart, spacious and well-equipped bedrooms, suitable for families and business travellers, and all with en suite bathrooms. Continental breakfast is available and other refreshments may be taken at the nearby family restaurant. See also the Hotel Groups pages.

Rooms 100 (68 fmly) (32 GF) **S** £39-£59; **D** £49-£69*
Conf Class 16 Board 24 Thtr 40 Del from £55 to £95*

CHORLEY Map 15 SD51

Best Western Park Hall

★★★ 74% HOTEL

☎ 01257 455000 🖹 01257 451838
Park Hall Rd, Charnock Richard PR7 5LP
e-mail: conference@parkhall-hotel.co.uk
web: www.parkhall-hotel.co.uk
dir: between Preston & Wigan, signed from M6 junct 27 N'bound & junct 28 S'bound, or from M61 junct 8

The popular Camelot Theme Park is just a short stroll across the grounds from this hotel, which focuses on the leisure and corporate/conference markets. Conveniently located for the motorway network, this idyllic country retreat is shared between the main hotel and The Village, a series of chalet bungalows. The Cadbury and Bassett rooms with special themed furnishings prove a real hit with children.

Rooms 140 (84 annexe) (52 fmly) (84 GF) **S** £70-£95; **D** £70-£95 (incl. bkfst)* **Facilities** Spa ⊛ supervised Gym Steam room Sauna Solarium Dance studio Xmas New Year Wi-fi **Conf** Class 240 Board 70 Thtr 700 Del from £99 to £145* **Services** Lift **Parking** 2600 **Notes** LB ⊗ Civ Wed 200

Travelodge Preston Chorley

BUDGET HOTEL

☎ 08719 846 172 🖹 01772 311963
Preston Rd, Clayton-le-Woods PR6 7JB
web: www.travelodge.co.uk
dir: M6 junct 28, B5256 for 2m. Lodge adjacent to Halfway House pub

Travelodge offers good quality, good value, modern accommodation. Ideal for families, the spacious en suite bedrooms include remote-control TV, tea and coffee-making facilities and comfortable beds. Meals can be taken at the nearby family restaurant. See also the Hotel Groups pages.

Rooms 40 **S** fr £29; **D** fr £29

CLITHEROE Map 18 SD74

Eaves Hall Country Hotel

★★★ 74% HOTEL

☎ 01200 425271 🖹 01200 425131
Eaves Hall Ln, West Bradford BB7 3JG
e-mail: reservations@eaveshall.co.uk
web: www.eaveshall.co.uk
dir: A59 onto Pimlico link. Take 3rd left towards Waddington. At T-junct turn left, hotel 1st on right

A country-house hotel set in 13 acres of landscaped gardens with its own crown bowling green, tennis courts and pitch & putt among other activities. Eaves Hall offers the perfect place to relax and 'get away from it all'. Bedrooms are spacious and well equipped; at the time of inspection they were in the process of being upgraded. Jonathan's Restaurant, with lovely views over the grounds, is the setting for meals, and the hotel is a popular venue for weddings.

Rooms 34 (7 fmly) **S** £59-£79; **D** £158-£210 (incl. bkfst)* **Facilities** ⚓ 9 🏌 Putt green Fishing 🏊 Xmas New Year Wi-fi **Conf** Class 90 Board 50 Thtr 130 Del from £106 to £206* **Services** Lift **Parking** 70 **Notes** LB Civ Wed 195

Shireburn Arms

★★★ 73% HOTEL

☎ 01254 826518 🖹 01254 826208
Whalley Rd, Hurst Green BB7 9QJ
e-mail: sales@shireburnarmshotel.com
web: www.shireburnarmshotel.com
dir: A59 to Clitheroe, left at lights to Ribchester, follow Hurst Green signs. Hotel on B6243 at entrance to Hurst Green village

This long established, family-owned hotel dates back to the 17th century and enjoys panoramic views over the Ribble Valley. Rooms are individually designed and thoughtfully equipped. The lounge bar offers a selection of real ales, and the spacious restaurant, opening onto an attractive patio and garden, offers home-cooked food.

Rooms 22 (3 fmly) **S** £50-£60; **D** £80-£120 (incl. bkfst)* **Facilities** STV FTV Xmas Wi-fi **Conf** Class 50 Board 50 Thtr 100 **Parking** 71 **Notes** Civ Wed 100

DARWEN | Map 15 SD62

Travelodge Blackburn

BUDGET HOTEL

☎ 08719 846 122 📠 01254 776058
Darwen Motorway Services BB3 0AT
web: www.travelodge.co.uk

Travelodge offers good quality, good value, modern accommodation. Ideal for families, the spacious en suite bedrooms include remote-control TV, tea and coffee-making facilities and comfortable beds. Meals can be taken at the nearby family restaurant. See also the Hotel Groups pages.

Rooms 48 (45 fmly) **S** fr £29; **D** fr £29

FORTON MOTORWAY SERVICE AREA (M6) | Map 18 SD55

Travelodge Lancaster (M6)

BUDGET HOTEL

☎ 08719 846 154 📠 01524 791703
White Carr Ln, Bay Horse LA2 9DU
web: www.travelodge.co.uk
dir: between junct 32 & 33 of M6

Travelodge offers good quality, good value, modern accommodation. Ideal for families, the spacious en suite bedrooms include remote-control TV, tea and coffee-making facilities and comfortable beds. Meals can be taken at the nearby family restaurant. See also the Hotel Groups pages.

Rooms 53 **S** fr £29; **D** fr £29

GARSTANG | Map 18 SD44

Crofters Hotel & Tavern

★★★ 75% ⊛ HOTEL

☎ 01995 604128 📠 01772 289347
New Rd, A6 Cabus PR3 1PH
e-mail: bookings@croftershotel.co.uk
dir: on A6, midway between junct 32 & 33 of M6

This is an attractive hotel close to the charming market town of Garstang. Bedrooms are spacious and well equipped and meals are available either in the Crofter's Brasserie or the Tavern bar. There are also extensive function facilities.

Rooms 22 (2 fmly) **S** £45-£59; **D** £75-£95 (incl. bkfst)*
Facilities FTV Xmas New Year Wi-fi **Conf** Class 150 Board 80 Thtr 250 Del from £95* **Parking** 200 **Notes** LB ⊗ Civ Wed 200

Best Western Garstang Country Hotel & Golf Club

★★★ 75% HOTEL

☎ 01995 600100 📠 01995 600950
Garstang Rd, Bowgreave PR3 1YE
e-mail: reception@ghgc.co.uk
web: www.garstanghotelandgolf.com
dir: M6 junct 32 take 1st right after Rogers Esso garage on A6 onto B6430. 1m, hotel on left

This smart, purpose-built hotel enjoys a peaceful location alongside its own 18-hole golf course. Comfortable and spacious bedrooms are well equipped for both business and leisure guests, whilst inviting public areas include a restaurant and a choice of bars - one serving food.

Rooms 32 (16 GF) **S** £55-£75; **D** £65-£85 (incl. bkfst)*
Facilities STV FTV ♨ 18 Golf driving range Xmas New Year Wi-fi **Conf** Class 100 Board 80 Thtr 200 Del from £77.50 to £85* **Services** Lift **Parking** 172 **Notes** LB ⊗ Civ Wed 200

LANCASTER | Map 18 SD46

Lancaster House

★★★★ 76% ⊛ HOTEL

☎ 01524 844822 📠 01524 844766
Green Ln, Ellel LA1 4GJ
e-mail: lancaster@elhmail.co.uk
web: www.elh.co.uk/hotels/lancaster
dir: M6 junct 33 N towards Lancaster. Through Galgate and into Green Ln. Hotel before university on right

This modern hotel enjoys a rural setting south of the city and close to the university. The attractive open-plan reception and lounge boast a roaring log fire in colder

---

months. Bedrooms are spacious, and include 19 rooms that are particularly well equipped for business guests. There are leisure facilities with a hot tub and a function suite.

Rooms 99 (29 fmly) (44 GF) **S** £74-£120; **D** £84-£120 (incl. bkfst)* **Facilities** Spa STV ♨ supervised Gym Beauty salon Outside hot tub Xmas New Year Wi-fi **Conf** Class 60 Board 48 Thtr 200 Del from £110* **Parking** 120 **Notes** LB Civ Wed 100

Best Western Royal Kings Arms

★★★ 72% HOTEL

☎ 01524 32451 📠 01524 841698
Market St LA1 1HP
e-mail: reservations.lancaster@ohiml.com
web: www.oxfordhotelsandinns.com
dir: M6 junct 33, follow A6 to city centre, turn 1st left, after Market Hotel. Hotel at lights before Lancaster Castle

A distinctive period building located in the town centre, close to the castle. Bedrooms and bathrooms are comfortable and suitable for both business and leisure guests. Public areas include a small lounge on the ground floor and The Castle Bar and Brasserie Restaurant on the first floor. The hotel also has a private car park.

Rooms 55 (14 fmly) **Facilities** Xmas **Conf** Class 60 Board 40 Thtr 100 **Services** Lift **Parking** 26 **Notes** Civ Wed 100

The Greaves Hotel

★★ 65% HOTEL

☎ 01524 63943 📠 01524 382679
Greaves Rd LA1 4UW
e-mail: greaves@mitchellshotels.co.uk
dir: M6 junct 34 signed Lancaster, through town centre, signed M6 S, hotel on right after hospital.

Located to the south of the city centre, this popular hotel enjoys a good local following. There are comfortable open-plan public areas where guests can enjoy a range of real ales and bar meals. Bedrooms are well equipped with both practical and homely extras.

Rooms 16 (4 fmly) **S** £45; **D** £65 (incl. bkfst)*
Facilities STV **Conf** Class 40 Board 30 Thtr 60 **Parking** 35 **Notes** LB ⊗

Holiday Inn Lancaster

[U]

☎ 01524 541313 & 0870 400 9047 📠 01524 841265
Waterside Park, Caton Rd LA1 3RA
e-mail: reservations-lancaster@ihg.com
web: www.holidayinn.co.uk
dir: M6 junct 34 towards Lancaster. Hotel 1st on right

Currently the rating for this establishment is not confirmed. This may be due to a change of ownership or because it has

Continued

LANCASTER continued

only recently joined the AA rating scheme. For further details please see the AA website: www.theAA.com

Rooms 156 (72 fmly) (25 GF) (8 smoking) **S** £55-£105; **D** £55-£105* **Facilities** ♨ supervised Gym Fitness classes Xmas New Year Wi-fi **Conf** Class 60 Board 60 Thtr 120 Del from £99 to £145* **Services** Lift Air con **Parking** 200 **Notes** LB

LANGHO	Map 18 SD73

Northcote Manor

★★★★ 80% ⊚⊚⊚
SMALL HOTEL

☎ 01254 240555 📠 01254 246568
Northcote Rd BB6 8BE
e-mail: sales@northcotemanor.com
web: www.northcotemanor.com
dir: M6 junct 31, 9m to Northcote. Follow Clitheroe (A59) signs, Hotel on left before rdbt

This is a gastronomic haven where guests return to sample the delights of its famous kitchen. Excellent cooking includes Lancashire's finest fare, and fruit and herbs from the hotel's own beautifully laid out organic gardens. Drinks can be enjoyed in the comfortable, elegantly furnished lounges and bar. The stylish bedrooms have been individually furnished and thoughtfully equipped.

Rooms 14 (2 fmly) (4 GF) **S** £150-£195; **D** £180-£225 (incl. bkfst)* **Facilities** STV FTV ♨ Wi-fi **Conf** Class 10 Board 20 Thtr 36 **Parking** 50 **Notes** LB ⊗ Closed 25 Dec Civ Wed 40

Mytton Fold Hotel and Golf Complex

★★★ 🅰 HOTEL

☎ 01254 240662 & 245392 📠 01254 248119
Whalley Rd BB6 8AB
e-mail: reception@myttonfold.co.uk
web: www.myttonfold.co.uk
dir: At large rdbt on A59, follow signs for Whalley, exit onto Whalley New Road. Hotel on right

Rooms 28 (2 fmly) (3 GF) **S** £57-£71; **D** £91-£102 (incl. bkfst)* **Facilities** STV ♨ 18 Putt green Wi-fi **Conf** Class 60 Board 40 Thtr 290 Del from £80.50 to £90.50* **Parking** 300 **Notes** LB ⊗ RS 24-26 Dec & 1 Jan Civ Wed 150

The Avenue Hotel & Restaurant

★★ 79% HOTEL

☎ 01254 244811 📠 01254 244812
Brockhall Village BB6 8AY
e-mail: info@theavenuehotel.co.uk
dir: exit A59 by Northcote Manor, follow for 1m. Right then 1st left into Brockhall Village

The Avenue offers a modern and relaxed atmosphere throughout. The bedrooms are especially stylish being very well equipped and delightfully furnished. A wide range of dishes are available in the café bar/restaurant, and good conference facilities are on offer.

Rooms 21 (9 fmly) (11 GF) **Facilities** STV Xmas New Year **Conf** Class 30 Board 40 Thtr 50 **Parking** 30 **Notes** ⊗ Closed 24-25 Dec

LEYLAND	Map 15 SD52

Best Western Premier Leyland

★★★★ 77% HOTEL

☎ 01772 422922 📠 01772 622282
Leyland Way PR25 4JX
e-mail: leylandhotel@feathers.uk.com
web: www.feathers.uk.com
dir: M6 junct 28 turn left at end of slip road, hotel 100mtrs on left

This purpose-built hotel enjoys a convenient location, just off the M6, within easy reach of Preston and Blackpool. Spacious public areas include extensive conference and banqueting facilities as well as a smart leisure club.

Rooms 93 (4 fmly) (31 GF) **S** £94-£104; **D** £99-£109 (incl. bkfst)* **Facilities** STV FTV ♨ supervised Gym Xmas New Year Wi-fi **Conf** Class 250 Board 250 Thtr 500 **Parking** 150 **Notes** Civ Wed 200

Farington Lodge

Ⓤ

☎ 01772 421321 📠 01772 455388
Stanifield Ln, Farington PR25 4QR
e-mail: info.farington@classiclodges.co.uk
web: www.classiclodges.co.uk
dir: Left at rdbt at end of M6 & left at next rdbt. Entrance 1m on right after lights.

Currently the rating for this establishment is not confirmed. This may be due to a change of ownership or because it has only recently joined the AA rating scheme. For further details please see the AA website: www.theAA.com

Rooms 27 (3 fmly) (6 GF) **Facilities** Xmas **Conf** Class 80 Board 60 Thtr 180 **Parking** 90 **Notes** LB ⊗ Civ Wed 150

LOWER BARTLE	Map 18 SD43

Bartle Hall

★★★ 75% HOTEL

☎ 01772 690506 📠 01772 690841
Lea Lane PR4 0HA
e-mail: chris@bartlehall.co.uk
dir: M6 junct 32 onto Tom Benson Way, follow signs for Woodplumpton

Ideally situated between Preston and Blackpool, Bartle Hall is within easy access of the M6 and the Lake District. Set in its own extensive grounds the hotel offers comfortable, well-equipped and renovated accommodation. The restaurant cuisine uses local produce and there is a large comfortable bar and lounge. There are also extensive conference facilities and this is a popular wedding venue.

Rooms 13 (1 annexe) (3 fmly) (1 GF) **S** £65-£75; **D** £75-£140 (incl. bkfst)* **Facilities** Xmas New Year Wi-fi Child facilities **Conf** Class 50 Board 40 Thtr 200 Del from £115 to £135* **Parking** 250 **Notes** LB ⊗ Closed 25-26 Dec Civ Wed 110

Clifton Arms Hotel

★★★★ 79% ® HOTEL

☎ 01253 739898 📠 01253 730657
West Beach, Lytham FY8 5QJ
e-mail: welcome@cliftonarms-lytham.com
web: www.cliftonarms-lytham.com
dir: on A584 along seafront

This well established hotel occupies a prime position overlooking Lytham Green and the Ribble estuary beyond. Bedrooms vary in size and are appointed to a high standard; front-facing rooms are particularly spacious and enjoy splendid views. There is an elegant restaurant, a stylish open-plan lounge and cocktail bar as well as function and conference facilities.

Rooms 48 (2 fmly) **S** £70-£130; **D** £100-£185 (incl. bkfst)* **Facilities** STV FTV Xmas New Year Wi-fi **Conf** Class 100 Board 60 Thtr 200 Del from £139 to £155* **Services** Lift **Parking** 50 **Notes** LB ® Civ Wed 100

See advert on this page

Grand

★★★★ 76% HOTEL

☎ 01253 721288 & 643424 📠 01253 714459
South Promenade FY8 1NB
e-mail: book@the-grand.co.uk
web: www.the-grand.co.uk
dir: M6 junct 32 take M55 to Blackpool then A5230 to South Shore. Follow signs for St Annes

This beautiful Victorian property stands in its own grounds with wonderful views of the coastline; Royal Lytham and other major golf courses are within easy reach. Elegant public areas include a contemporary restaurant and bar, an inviting lounge, extensive function facilities and an impressive leisure club. Stylish, well-equipped bedrooms include a number of stunning, spacious executive rooms and suites.

Rooms 55 (4 GF) **S** £80-£135; **D** £100-£160 (incl. bkfst)* **Facilities** STV FTV ® supervised ® Gym Saunarium New Year Wi-fi **Conf** Class 80 Board 30 Thtr 160 **Services** Lift **Parking** 75 **Notes** LB ® Closed 24-26 Dec Civ Wed 150

Bedford

★★★ 79% HOTEL

☎ 01253 724636 📠 01253 729244
307-311 Clifton Drive South FY8 1HN
e-mail: reservations@bedford-hotel.com
web: www.bedford-hotel.com
dir: from M55 follow signs for airport to last lights. Left through 2 sets of lights. Hotel 300yds on left

This popular family-run hotel is close to the town centre and the seafront. Bedrooms vary in size and style and include superior and club class rooms. The newer bedrooms are particularly elegant and tastefully appointed. Spacious public areas include a choice of lounges, a coffee shop, fitness facilities and an impressive function suite.

Rooms 45 (6 GF) **S** fr £59; **D** £90-£120 (incl. bkfst)* **Facilities** STV Gym Hydro-therapy spa bath Xmas New Year Wi-fi **Conf** Class 140 Board 60 Thtr 200 Del from £95* **Services** Lift **Parking** 25 **Notes** LB ® Civ Wed 200

Chadwick

THE INDEPENDENTS
HOTEL ASSOCIATION

★★★ 77% HOTEL

☎ 01253 720061 📠 01253 714455
South Promenade FY8 1NP
e-mail: info@thechadwickhotel.com
web: www.thechadwickhotel.com
dir: M6 junct 32 take M55 to Blackpool then A5230 to South Shore. Follow signs for St Annes, hotel on promenade south end

This popular, comfortable and traditional hotel enjoys a seafront location. Bedrooms vary in size and style, but all are very thoughtfully equipped; those at the front boast panoramic sea views. Public rooms are spacious and comfortably furnished and the smart bar is stocked with some 200 malt whiskies. The hotel has a well-equipped, air-conditioned gym and indoor pool.

Rooms 75 (28 fmly) (13 GF) **S** £52-£80; **D** £75-£110 (incl. bkfst) **Facilities** FTV ® Gym Turkish bath Games room Soft play adventure area Sauna Solarium ♫ Xmas New Year Wi-fi Child facilities **Conf** Class 24 Board 28 Thtr 72 Del from £79.50 to £92.50 **Services** Lift **Parking** 40 **Notes** LB ®

See advert on page 296

LYTHAM ST ANNES continued

Dalmeny Hotel

★★★ 77% HOTEL

☎ 01253 712236 🖹 01253 724447
19-33 South Promenade FY8 1LX
e-mail: reservations@dalmenyhotel.co.uk
web: www.dalmenyhotel.co.uk

With a superb seafront location and extensive facilities including comfortable lounges, leisure centre, beauty and hair salons and conference rooms. There are three restaurants: the Patio Restaurant, The Carvery and the contemporary, split level Atrium Restaurant. Children are well catered for; spacious bedrooms, many with sea views, include family rooms.

Rooms 125 (68 fmly) (11 GF) **S** £75-£113.50; **D** £95-£167 (incl. bkfst)* **Facilities** FTV ⓘ Gym Squash Beauty salon Aerobics centre 🎵 New Year Wi-fi **Conf** Class 80 Board 50 Thtr 150 Del from £85 to £120* **Services** Lift **Parking** 120 **Notes** LB ⊗ Closed 24-26 Dec

Best Western Glendower Hotel

★★★ 74% HOTEL

☎ 01253 723241 🖹 01253 640069
North Promenade FY8 2NQ
e-mail: recp@theglendowerhotel.co.uk
web: www.theglendowerhotel.co.uk
dir: M55 follow airport signs. Left at Promenade to St Annes. Hotel 500yds from pier

Located on the seafront and with easy access to the town centre, this popular, friendly hotel offers comfortably furnished, well-equipped accommodation. Bedrooms vary in size and style, and include four-poster rooms and very popular family suites. Public areas feature a choice of smart, comfortable lounges, a bright, modern leisure club and function facilities.

Rooms 60 (17 fmly) **Facilities** FTV ⓘ supervised Gym Children's playroom Snooker Xmas New Year Wi-fi **Conf** Class 120 Board 50 Thtr 150 Del from £110 to £160* **Services** Lift **Parking** 45 **Notes** ⊗

See advert on this page

Elms

★★★ 71% HOTEL

☎ 01524 411501 🖹 01524 831979
Bare Village LA4 6DD
e-mail: elms@mitchellshotels.co.uk
dir: M6 junct 34, follow Morecambe signs to large rdbt. Take 4th exit into Hall Drive which becomes Bare Lane. Over rail crossing. Hotel 200yds on right

This long-established hotel lies just off the North Promenade and is popular with both business and leisure guests. Public rooms include a spacious lounge bar, a classical style restaurant and function facilities, plus a pub in the grounds.

Rooms 39 (3 fmly) **S** £65; **D** £90 (incl. bkfst)* **Facilities** STV Xmas New Year Wi-fi **Conf** Class 72 Board 60 Thtr 200 **Services** Lift **Parking** 80 **Notes** LB Civ Wed 100

Clarendon

★★★ 68% HOTEL

☎ 01524 410180 📠 01524 421616
76 Marine Road West, West End Promenade LA4 4EP
e-mail: clarendon@mitchellshotels.co.uk
dir: M6 junct 34 follow Morecambe signs. At rdbt (with
'The Shrimp' on corner) 1st exit to Westgate, follow to
seafront. Right at lights, hotel 3rd block

This traditional seafront hotel offers modern facilities,
and several long serving key staff ensure guests
experience a home-from-home atmosphere. Well
maintained throughout, it offers bright, cheerful public
areas and ample convenient parking.

Rooms 29 (4 fmly) **S** fr £60; **D** fr £90 (incl. bkfst)*
Facilities Xmas New Year Wi-fi **Conf** Class 40 Board 40
Thtr 90 **Services** Lift **Parking** 22 **Notes** LB Civ Wed 60

Hotel Prospect

★ 75% HOTEL

☎ 01524 417819 📠 01524 417819
363 Marine Road East LA4 5AQ
e-mail: peter@hotel-prospect.fsnet.co.uk

Situated on the promenade, this friendly, family-run
establishment has panoramic views over the bay to the
Lakeland mountains. Bedrooms are comfortably
proportioned and thoughtfully furnished, and the bright
dining room extends into a small lounge area which has a
well-stocked bar and overlooks the sea.

Rooms 13 (4 fmly) (2 GF) **S** fr £20; **D** £40 (incl. bkfst)*
Facilities Xmas **Parking** 14

ORMSKIRK Map 15 SD40

West Tower Country House

Ⓤ

☎ 01695 423328 📠 01695 420704
Mill Ln, Aughton L39 7HJ
e-mail: info@westtower.com
web: www.westtower.co.uk

Currently the rating for this establishment is not confirmed.
This may be due to a change of ownership or because it has
only recently joined the AA rating scheme. For further
details please see the AA website: www.theAA.com

Rooms 12 (12 annexe) (7 GF) **Facilities** FTV Xmas Wi-fi
Conf Class 100 Board 50 Thtr 150 **Parking** 100 **Notes** ⊗
Civ Wed 110

PRESTON Map 18 SD52

See also **Garstang**

Barton Grange

★★★★ 76% ⑳ HOTEL

☎ 01772 862551 📠 01772 861267
Garstang Rd PR3 5AA
e-mail: stay@bartongrangehotel.com
web: www.bartongrangehotel.co.uk

(For full entry see Barton)

Preston Marriott Hotel

Marriott HOTELS & RESORTS

★★★★ 76% HOTEL

☎ 01772 864087 📠 01772 861728
Garstang Rd, Broughton PR3 5JB
e-mail: reservations.preston@marriotthotels.co.uk
web: www.prestonmarriott.co.uk
dir: M6 junct 32 onto M55 junct 1, follow A6 towards
Garstang. Hotel 0.5m on right

Exuding a country-club atmosphere this stylish hotel
enjoys good links to both the city centre and motorway
network. There are two dining options and the extensive
leisure facilities ensure that there is plenty to do. The
bedrooms are smartly decorated and equipped with a
comprehensive range of extras.

Rooms 149 (40 fmly) (63 GF) **S** £105-£155; **D** £115-£165
(incl. bkfst)* **Facilities** STV Ⓢ supervised Gym Steam
room Beauty salon Hairdressing New Year Wi-fi
Conf Class 100 Board 70 Thtr 220 Del from £125 to
£165* **Services** Lift Air con **Parking** 250 **Notes** ⊗
Civ Wed 180

Pines

★★★ 80% ⑳ HOTEL

☎ 01772 338551 📠 01772 629002
570 Preston Rd, Clayton-Le-Woods PR6 7ED
e-mail: mail@thepineshotel.co.uk
dir: From A6 towards Preston/Whittle-le-Woods. Approx
2.5m, hotel on right

This unique and stylish hotel sits in four acres of mature
grounds just a short drive from the motorway network.
Elegant bedrooms are individually designed and offer
high levels of comfort and facilities. Day rooms include a
smart bar and Haworth's restaurant, while extensive
function rooms make this hotel a popular venue for
weddings.

Continued

PRESTON continued

Pines

Rooms 35 (2 fmly) (14 GF) **Facilities** STV FTV ♫ Xmas New Year Wi-fi **Conf** Class 250 Board 100 Thtr 400 **Parking** 120 **Notes** ⊗ Civ Wed 25

Macdonald Tickled Trout

★★★ 75% HOTEL

☎ 0870 1942120 🖷 01772 877463
Preston New Rd, Samlesbury PR5 0UJ
e-mail: tickledtrout@macdonald-hotels.co.uk
web: www.macdonald-hotels.co.uk
dir: close to M6 junct 31

On the banks of the River Ribble, this hotel is conveniently located for the motorway, making it a popular venue for both business and leisure guests. Smartly appointed bedrooms are all tastefully decorated and equipped with a thoughtful range of extras. The hotel boasts a stylish wing of meeting rooms.

Rooms 102 (6 fmly) **Facilities** Fishing ♫ Xmas **Conf** Class 60 Board 50 Thtr 120 **Services** Lift **Parking** 240 **Notes** LB Civ Wed 100

See advert on page 297

Haighton Manor Country House

★★ 71% HOTEL

☎ 01772 663170 🖷 01772 663171
Haighton Green Ln, Haighton PR2 5SQ
e-mail: info@haightonmanor.com
web: www.haightonmanor.com
dir: Off A6 onto Durton Rd, or from M6 junct 32 right at rdbt & right onto Durton Rd. Right at end into Haighton Lane. Hotel 2m on left

Located in sleepy, rolling countryside just ten minutes east of the city, this impressive hotel is ideally situated for both the business and leisure guest. External appearances are deceptive, for once inside, this 17th-century manor house has ultra-modern bedrooms and stylishly fashioned day rooms providing a wonderful fusion of traditional and modern. Wide-ranging creative menus can be sampled in the candlelit restaurant. This hotel is a popular wedding venue.

Rooms 8 (2 fmly) **S** £70-£90; **D** £90-£140 (incl. bkfst)* **Facilities** STV ♫ Xmas New Year **Conf** Class 80 Board 80 Thtr 100 Del from £90 to £110* **Parking** 70 **Notes** LB ⊗ Civ Wed 200

Holiday Inn Preston

Ⓤ

☎ 0870 400 9066 🖷 01772 201923
Ringway PR1 3AU
e-mail: prestonhi@ichotelsgroup.com
web: www.holidayinn.co.uk
dir: M6 junct 31, A59 signs for town centre. Right at T-junct, hotel on left

Currently the rating for this establishment is not confirmed. This may be due to a change of ownership or because it has only recently joined the AA rating scheme. For further details please see the AA website: www.theAA.com

Rooms 133

Express by Hoilday Inn Preston - South

BUDGET HOTEL

☎ 01772 689711 🖷 01772 330063
Lostock Ln, Bamber Bridge PR5 6BZ
e-mail: ebhi-preston@btconnect.com
web: www.hiexpress.com/prestonsouth

A modern hotel ideal for families and business travellers. Fresh and uncomplicated, the spacious rooms include Sky TV, power shower and tea and coffee-making facilities. Continental buffet breakfast is included in the room rate; other meals may be taken at the nearby family pub or restaurant. See also the Hotel Groups pages.

Rooms 74 **Conf** Class 12 Board 16 Thtr 20

Ibis Preston North

BUDGET HOTEL

☎ 01772 861800 🖷 01772 861900
Garstang Rd, Broughton PR3 5JE
e-mail: H3162@accor.com
web: www.ibishotel.com
dir: M6 junct 32, then M55 junct 1. Left lane onto A6. Left at slip road, left again at mini-rdbt. 2nd turn, hotel on right past pub

Modern, budget hotel offering comfortable accommodation in bright and practical bedrooms. Breakfast is self-service, food is available all day and a full dinner menu is available in the restaurant. See also the Hotel Groups pages.

Rooms 82 (27 fmly) (16 GF) (12 smoking) **S** £47-£51; **D** £47-£51* **Conf** Class 20 Board 20 Thtr 30

Travelodge Preston Central

BUDGET HOTEL

☎ 08719 846 150
Preston Farmers Office, New Hall Ln PR1 5JX
web: www.travelodge.co.uk
dir: M6 junct 31. Follow signs for Preston. Lodge on right

Travelodge offers good quality, good value, modern accommodation. Ideal for families, the spacious en suite bedrooms include remote-control TV, tea and coffee-making facilities and comfortable beds. Meals can be taken at the nearby family restaurant. See also the Hotel Groups pages.

Rooms 72 **S** fr £29; **D** fr £29

ST ANNES

See Lytham St Annes

WREA GREEN   Map 18 SD33

Villa Country House

★★★ 75% HOTEL

☎ 01772 684347 🖷 01772 687647
Moss Side Ln PR4 2PE
e-mail: info@the-villahotel.co.uk
dir: M55 junct 3 follow signs to Kirkham at Wrea Green follow signs to Lytham

This 19th-century residence stands in a peaceful location close to the village of Wrea Green. There are extensive bars and a good range of quality food is served either in the bar or the many-roomed restaurant. The modern, air-conditioned bedrooms are very well designed. The staff are friendly and helpful.

Rooms 25 (1 fmly) (10 GF) **S** £85-£130; **D** £115-£150 (incl. bkfst)* **Facilities** STV Xmas New Year Wi-fi **Conf** Class 15 Board 14 Thtr 60 Del from £115 **Services** Lift **Parking** 75 **Notes** LB Civ Wed 60

LEICESTERSHIRE

APPLEBY MAGNA — Map 10 SK30

Ramada Tamworth ⓡRAMADA.

★★★ 73% HOTEL

☎ 01530 279500 & 273102 ▤ 01530 279501
DE12 7BQ
e-mail: gm@ramada-tamworth.com
web: www.ramada-tamworth.com
dir: M42 junct 11/A444 to Nuneaton, hotel on left

Having undergone a major refurbishment program in the public areas, the hotel now offers a brand new reception, bar, restaurant and conference rooms and proves a good choice for both business and leisure guests. It is just a short journey away from the NEC and all the Midlands' tourist attractions. The bedrooms have all the expected facilities, and premier rooms are available. Reubens' restaurant serves contemporary bistro food.

Rooms 94 (10 fmly) (47 GF) **S** £49-£90; **D** £49-£90 (incl. bkfst)* **Facilities** Wi-fi **Conf** Class 70 Board 50 Thtr 120 **Services** Lift **Parking** 90 **Notes** Civ Wed 120

ASHBY-DE-LA-ZOUCH — Map 11 SK31

Royal

Ⓤ

☎ 01530 412833 ▤ 01530 564548
Station Raod LE65 2GP
e-mail: theroyalhotel@email.com
web: www.royalhotelashby.co.uk
dir: A42 junct 12, 3m hotel on right

Currently the rating for this establishment is not confirmed. This may be due to a change of ownership or because it has only recently joined the AA rating scheme. For further details please see the AA website: www.theAA.com

Rooms 34 (5 fmly) **Facilities** New Year Wi-fi **Conf** Class 26 Board 26 Thtr 70 **Parking** 95 **Notes** LB Civ Wed 65

BELTON — Map 11 SK42

The Queen's Head

◉◉ RESTAURANT WITH ROOMS

☎ 01530 222359 ▤ 01530 224680
2 Long St LE12 9TP
e-mail: enquiries@thequeenshead.org
dir: From Loughborough turn left onto B5324, 3m into Belton

This well furnished inn is found in the village centre and has public rooms with a modern feel. Bedrooms are also along modern lines while quality cooking is provided in the delightful dining room.

Rooms 6 (2 en suite)

CASTLE DONINGTON
See East Midlands Airport

COALVILLE — Map 11 SK41

Hermitage Park

★★★ 70% HOTEL

☎ 01530 814814 ▤ 01530 814202
Whitwick Rd LE67 3FA
e-mail: hotel@hermitageparkhotel.co.uk

Relaxed and friendly environment throughout this modern building which sits within easy access of major road networks. Bedrooms are contemporary and well equipped; a number of ground floor rooms are available. Open plan public areas include a lounge bar and informal dining area.

Rooms 28 (5 fmly) (14 GF) **S** £62-£77.50; **D** £72-£87.50 (incl. bkfst)* **Facilities** STV ♫ Xmas New Year Wi-fi **Conf** Class 30 Board 30 Thtr 50 **Parking** 40 **Notes** LB ⊗ Civ Wed 100

EAST MIDLANDS AIRPORT — Map 11 SK42

Best Western Premier Yew Lodge Hotel

★★★★ 80% ◉ HOTEL

☎ 01509 672518 ▤ 01509 674730
Packington Hill, Kegworth DE74 2DF
e-mail: info@yewlodgehotel.co.uk
web: www.yewlodgehotel.co.uk
dir: M1 junct 24. Follow signs to Loughborough & Kegworth on A6. On entering village, 1st right, after 400yds hotel on right

This smart, family-owned hotel is close to both the motorway and airport, yet is peacefully located. Modern, stylish bedrooms and public areas are thoughtfully appointed and smartly presented. The restaurant serves interesting dishes, while lounge service and extensive conference facilities are available. A very well equipped spa and leisure centre complete the picture.

Rooms 100 (22 fmly) **D** £75-£160 (incl. bkfst)* **Facilities** Spa STV ⏱ Gym Beauty therapy suite Foot spas Steam room Sauna Xmas New Year Wi-fi **Conf** Class 150 Board 84 Thtr 330 Del from £119 to £180* **Services** Lift **Parking** 180 **Notes** LB Civ Wed 260

The Priest House *Hand*PICKED

★★★★ 78% ◉◉ HOTEL

☎ 01332 810649 ▤ 01332 811141
Kings Mills, Castle Donington DE74 2RR
e-mail: enquiries@priesthouse.co.uk
web: www.handpicked.co.uk
dir: M1 junct 24, onto A50, take 1st slip road signed Castle Donington. Right at lights, hotel in 2m

A historic hotel peacefully situated in a picturesque riverside setting. Public areas include a fine dining restaurant, a modern brasserie and conference rooms. Bedrooms are situated in both the main building and converted cottages, and the executive rooms feature state-of-the-art technology.

Rooms 42 (18 annexe) (5 fmly) (16 GF) **S** £85-£105; **D** £95-£125 (incl. bkfst)* **Facilities** STV FTV Fishing Xmas New Year Wi-fi **Conf** Class 40 Board 40 Thtr 120 Del from £160 to £180* **Parking** 200 **Notes** LB ⊗ Civ Wed 100

EAST MIDLANDS AIRPORT continued

Thistle East Midlands Airport
thistle

★★★★ 75% HOTEL

☎ 01332 815700 📠 0870 333 9232
DE74 2SH
e-mail: eastmidlandsairport@thistle.co.uk
web: www.thistlehotels.com/eastmidlandsairport
dir: on A453, at entrance to East Midlands Airport

This large, well-presented hotel is conveniently located next to East Midlands Airport with easy access to the M1. Accommodation is generally spacious. Substantial public areas include the popular Lord Byron bar, a comprehensive range of meeting rooms and an Otium health and leisure club.

Rooms 164 (10 fmly) (100 GF) **S** £60-£230; **D** £65-£260*
Facilities STV 🄌 supervised Gym Sauna Steam room Treatment room Xmas Wi-fi **Conf** Class 140 Board 55 Thtr 220 Del from £100 to £170* **Services** Air con **Parking** 300 (charged) **Notes** LB Civ Wed 180

Donington Manor

★★★ 80% ⊛ HOTEL

☎ 01332 810253 📠 01332 850330
High St DE74 2PP
e-mail: enquiries@doningtonmanorhotel.co.uk
dir: 1m into village on B5430, left at lights

Near the village centre, this refined Georgian building offers high standards of hospitality and a professional service. Many of the original architectural features have been preserved; the elegant dining room is particularly appealing. Bedrooms are individually designed, and the newer suites are especially comfortable and well equipped.

Rooms 33 (6 annexe) (8 fmly) (4 GF) **S** £50-£75;
D £59-£115 (incl. bkfst)* **Facilities** STV New Year Wi-fi **Conf** Class 60 Board 40 Thtr 120 Del from £120 to £145* **Parking** 40 **Notes** LB RS 24-30 Dec Civ Wed 100

Express by Holiday Inn East Midlands Airport

BUDGET HOTEL

☎ 01509 678000 📠 01509 670954
Hunter Rd, Pegasus Business Park DE74 2TQ
e-mail: ema@expressholidayinn.co.uk
web: www.hiexpress.com/emidlandsapt
dir: signs for East Midlands Airport, right into Pegasus Business Park, hotel on left

A modern hotel ideal for families and business travellers. Fresh and uncomplicated, the spacious rooms include Sky TV, power shower and tea and coffee-making facilities. Continental buffet breakfast is included in the room rate; other meals may be taken at the nearby family pub or restaurant. See also the Hotel Groups pages.

Rooms 90 (55 fmly) **Conf** Class 26 Board 20 Thtr 40

Travelodge East Midlands Airport

BUDGET HOTEL

☎ 08719 846 073 📠 01509 673494
DE74 2TN
web: www.travelodge.co.uk
dir: M1 junct 23a follow signs for A453

Travelodge offers good quality, good value, modern accommodation. Ideal for families, the spacious en suite bedrooms include remote-control TV, tea and coffee-making facilities and comfortable beds. Meals can be taken at the nearby family restaurant. See also the Hotel Groups pages.

Rooms 80 **S** fr £29; **D** fr £29

GRIMSTON

Best Western Leicester North

★★★ 71% HOTEL

☎ 01664 823212 📠 01664 823371
A46 Fosse Way, Station Rd, Upper Broughton LE14 3BH
e-mail: info@lnhotel.co.uk
dir: A46 towards Grantham. Hotel at junct for Upper Broughton & Willoughby

Very conveniently located right next to the Fosse Way (A46), this hotel offers well equipped and smart bedrooms. There is a small restaurant and bar area as well as very large conferencing facilities. Ample parking is a bonus. This makes an ideal base for visits to Nottingham, Leicester, Loughborough and Belvoir Castle.

Rooms 75 **S** £50-£80; **D** £60-£90* **Facilities** Wi-fi **Conf** Class 100 Board 100 Thtr 300 Del from £85 to £105* **Parking** 200 **Notes** ⊗

HINCKLEY
Map 11 SP49

Sketchley Grange

★★★★ 79% ⊛ HOTEL

☎ 01455 251133 📠 01455 631384
Sketchley Ln, Burbage LE10 3HU
e-mail: info@sketchleygrange.co.uk
web: www.sketchleygrange.co.uk
dir: SE of town, off A5/M69 junct 1, take B4109 to Hinckley. Left at 2nd rdbt. 1st right onto Sketchley Lane

Close to motorway connections, this hotel is peacefully set in its own grounds, and enjoys open country views. Extensive leisure facilities include a stylish health and leisure spa with a crèche. Modern meeting facilities, a choice of bars, and two dining options, together with comfortable bedrooms furnished with many extras, make this a special hotel.

Rooms 52 (9 fmly) (1 GF) **S** £65-£130; **D** £65-£140*
Facilities Spa 🄌 supervised Gym Steam room Hairdressing Crèche 🎵 Wi-fi **Conf** Class 150 Board 30 Thtr 300 **Services** Lift **Parking** 200 **Notes** Civ Wed 300

See advert on opposite page

Barceló Hinckley Island Hotel

★★★★ 76% HOTEL

☎ 01455 631122 📠 01455 634536
Watling Street (A5) LE10 3JA
e-mail: hinckleyisland@barcelo-hotels.co.uk
web: www.barcelo-hotels.co.uk
dir: on A5, S of junct 1 on M69

A large, constantly improving hotel offering good facilities for both leisure and business guests. Bedrooms are well equipped, with the Club Floors providing high levels of comfort and workspace. A choice of dining styles is available in the Brasserie or Conservatory restaurants and the Triumph Bar is a must for motor cycle enthusiasts. The modern leisure club also offers a range of spa treatments.

Rooms 362 (14 GF) **S** £55-£130; **Facilities** 🄌 supervised Gym Steam room Wi-fi **Conf** Class 240 Board 40 Thtr 400 **Services** Lift Air con **Parking** 600 (charged) **Notes** ⊗ Civ Wed 350

KEGWORTH

See East Midlands Airport

LEICESTER   Map 11 SK50

See also Rothley

Leicester Marriott

 Marriott
HOTELS & RESORTS

★★★★ 79% HOTEL

☎ 0116 282 0100   📄 0116 282 0101
Smith Way, Grove Park, Enderby LE19 1SW
web: www.leicestermarriott.co.uk
dir: M1 junct 21/A563 signed Leicester. At rdbt take 1st left onto A563. Into right lane, at 2nd slip road turn right. At rdbt take last exit, hotel straight ahead

This purpose-built hotel offers stylish bedrooms, some of which are executive rooms with access to the executive lounge. There is a popular brasserie, cocktail bar, atrium lounge, indoor heated pool, gym, sauna and steam room. 18 meeting rooms provide conference facilities for up to 500 delegates and parking is extensive.

Rooms 227 (91 fmly) **S** £69-£155; **D** £69-£155*
Facilities STV ⓈⓉ supervised Gym Wi-fi **Conf** Class 180 Board 52 Thtr 500 Del from £145 to £190* **Services** Lift Air con **Parking** 280 (charged) **Notes** LB ⊗ Civ Wed 300

Best Western Belmont Hotel

 Best Western

★★★ 85% HOTEL

☎ 0116 254 4773   📄 0116 247 0804
De Montfort St LE1 7GR
e-mail: info@belmonthotel.co.uk
web: www.belmonthotel.co.uk
dir: from A6 take 1st right after rail station. Hotel 200yds on left

This well established hotel, under the same family ownership, has been welcoming guests for over 70 years. It is conveniently situated within easy walking distance of the railway station and city centre though it sits in a quiet leafy residential area. Extensive public rooms are smartly appointed and include the informal Bowie's Bistro, Jamie's Bar with its relaxed atmosphere, and the more formal Cherry Restaurant.

Rooms 77 (7 fmly) (9 GF) (10 smoking) **S** £70-£120; **D** £80-£130* **Facilities** FTV Gym Wi-fi **Conf** Class 75 Board 65 Thtr 175 Del from £130 to £160* **Services** Lift **Parking** 75 **Notes** LB Closed 25-26 Dec Civ Wed 150

Ramada Leicester

 Ⓡ RAMADA.

★★★ 79% HOTEL

☎ 0116 255 5599   📄 0116 254 4736
Granby St LE1 6ES
e-mail: sales.leicester@ramadajarvis.co.uk
web: www.ramadajarvis.co.uk
dir: A5460 into city. Follow Leicester Central Station signs. Granby Street is left off St. Georges Way, A594

This Grade II listed Victorian hotel is set in the heart of the commercial and shopping centre. Although bedrooms vary in size, all offer modern amenities and comfort; there is a popular restaurant and ample private parking.

Rooms 104 (4 fmly) **Facilities** Xmas New Year **Conf** Class 200 Board 35 Thtr 450 **Services** Lift **Parking** 120 **Notes** LB ⊗ Civ Wed 60

Best Western Leicester Stage Hotel

Best Western

★★★ 74% HOTEL

☎ 0116 288 6161   📄 0116 257 3900
Leicester Rd, Wigston LE18 1JW
e-mail: reservations@stagehotel.co.uk
web: www.stagehotel.co.uk
dir: M69/M1 junct 21 take ring road S to Leicester. Follow Oadby & Wigston signs, right onto A5199 towards Northampton. Hotel on left

This striking, purpose-built, glass-fronted building is situated to the south of the city centre. Bedrooms vary in style and include executive rooms and four-poster bridal suites. Open-plan public areas include a lounge bar, restaurant and a further seating area in the entrance hall. Staff are friendly and nothing is too much trouble. Ample parking is an added bonus.

Rooms 77 (10 fmly) (39 GF) **Facilities** ⓈⓉ supervised Gym Steam room Sauna Xmas **Conf** Class 320 Board 120 Thtr 500 **Parking** 200 **Notes** LB ⊗ Civ Wed 200

LEICESTER continued

Westfield House Hotel

★★★ 73% HOTEL

☎ 0870 609 6106 📄 0116 278 1974
Enderby Rd, Blaby LE8 4GD
e-mail: westfield@foliohotels.com
web: www.foliohotels.com/westfieldhouse
dir: M1 junct 21, A5460 to Leicester. 4th exit at 1st rdbt, ahead at 2nd, left at 3rd. Follow signs to Blaby, over 4th rdbt. Hotel on left

This establishment is situated in a quiet location on the outskirts of the city, yet is convenient for the adjacent link road. Public areas include a bar/brasserie, Hunters Restaurant, various meeting rooms and an extensive gym and indoor pool. Bedrooms are comfortably appointed and generally quite spacious; many are decorated to a very high standard.

Rooms 48 (12 annexe) (5 fmly) (11 GF) **S** £49-£125; **D** £49-£125* **Facilities** 🏊 Gym Steam room Sauna Solarium Xmas Wi-fi **Conf** Class 36 Board 36 Thtr 70 Del from £110 to £145* **Parking** 110 **Notes** Civ Wed 60

Regency

★★★ 71% HOTEL

☎ 0116 270 9634 📄 0116 270 1375
360 London Rd LE2 2PL
e-mail: info@the-regency-hotel.com
dir: on A6, 1.5m from city centre

This friendly hotel is located on the edge of town and provides smart accommodation, suitable for both business and leisure guests. Dining options include a cosy conservatory brasserie and a formal restaurant. A relaxing lounge bar is also available, along with good banqueting and conference facilities. Bedrooms come in a variety of styles and sizes and include some spacious and stylish rooms.

Rooms 32 (2 fmly) (5 smoking) **S** £45-£49; **D** £62-£67 (incl. bkfst)* **Facilities** STV 🎵 Xmas New Year Wi-fi **Conf** Class 40 Board 30 Thtr 50 **Parking** 32 **Notes** ⊗ Civ Wed 140

Holiday Inn Leicester

Ⓤ

☎ 0116 253 1161 📄 0116 251 3169
St Nicholas Circle LE1 5LX
web: www.holidayinn.co.uk

Currently the rating for this establishment is not confirmed. This may be due to a change of ownership or because it has only recently joined the AA rating scheme. For further details please see the AA website: www.theAA.com

Rooms 188

Campanile Leicester

BUDGET HOTEL

☎ 0116 261 6600 📄 0116 261 6601
St Matthew's Way, 1 Bedford Street North LE1 3JE
e-mail: leicester@campanile.com
dir: A5460. Right at end of road, left at rdbt on A594. Follow Vaughan Way, Burleys Way then St. Matthews Way. Hotel on left

This modern building offers accommodation in smart, well-equipped bedrooms, all with en suite bathrooms. Refreshments may be taken at the informal bistro. See also the Hotel Groups pages.

Rooms 93 **Conf** Class 30 Board 30 Thtr 40

Days Inn Leicester Central

BUDGET HOTEL

☎ 0116 251 0666 & 0870 033 9633 📄 0870 033 9634
14-17 Abbey St LE1 3TE
e-mail: reception.leicester.central@daysinn.co.uk
web: www.daysinn.com

This modern building offers accommodation in smart, spacious and well-equipped bedrooms, suitable for families and business travellers, and all with en suite bathrooms. Continental breakfast is available and other refreshments may be taken at the nearby family restaurant. See also the Hotel Groups pages.

Rooms 73 **Conf** Class 100 Board 40 Thtr 150

Express by Holiday Inn Leicester - Walkers

BUDGET HOTEL

☎ 0116 249 4590 📄 0116 249 4591
Filbert Way, Raw Dykes Rd LE2 7FQ
e-mail: info@exhileicester.co.uk
web: www.hiexpress.com/leicesterwalke

A modern hotel ideal for families and business travellers. Fresh and uncomplicated, the spacious rooms include Sky TV, power shower and tea and coffee-making facilities. Continental buffet breakfast is included in the room rate; other meals may be taken at the nearby family pub or restaurant. See also the Hotel Groups pages.

Rooms 110 **Conf** Class 40 Board 35 Thtr 70

Ibis Leicester

BUDGET HOTEL

☎ 0116 248 7200 📄 0116 262 0880
St Georges Way, Constitution Hill LE1 1PL
e-mail: H3061@accor.com
web: www.ibishotel.com
dir: From M1/M69 junct 21, follow town centre signs, central ring road (A594)/railway station, hotel opposite Leicester Mercury

Modern, budget hotel offering comfortable accommodation in bright and practical bedrooms. Breakfast is self-service and dinner is available in the restaurant. See also the Hotel Groups pages.

Rooms 94 (15 fmly) **S** fr £53; **D** fr £53*

Innkeeper's Lodge Leicester

BUDGET HOTEL

☎ 0845 112 6048 📄 0845 112 6254
Hinckley Rd LE3 3PG
web: www.innkeeperslodge.com/leicester
dir: M1(M69) junct 21, A5460 towards Leicester. Left towards ring road, right at rdbt onto A563. Left at A47 rdbt towards Hinckley. Through lights (B5380 junct). Lodge on right

Innkeeper's Lodge represents an exciting, high value concept within the budget hotel market. Comfortable bedrooms provide excellent facilities that include satellite TV and modem points. Options include family rooms, and for the corporate guest, cutting edge IT includes Wi-fi access. Food is served all day in the adjacent Country Pub. The extensive continental breakfast is complimentary.

Rooms 31 **S** £53-£55; **D** £53-£55 (incl. bkfst)

Travelodge Leicester Central

BUDGET HOTEL

☎ 08719 846254 📄 0116 251 0560
Vaughan Way LE1 4NN
web: www.travelodge.co.uk

Travelodge offers good quality, good value, modern accommodation. Ideal for families, the spacious en suite bedrooms include remote-control TV, tea and coffee-making facilities and comfortable beds. Meals can be taken at the nearby family restaurant. See also the Hotel Groups pages.

Rooms 95 **S** fr £29; **D** fr £29

Days Inn Leicester Forest East

BUDGET HOTEL

☎ 0116 239 0534 🗎 0116 239 0546
Leicester Forest East, Junction 21 M1 LE3 3GB
e-mail: leicester.hotel@welcomebreak.co.uk
web: www.welcomebreak.co.uk
dir: on M1 northbound between junct 21 & 21A

This modern building offers accommodation in smart, spacious and well-equipped bedrooms, suitable for families and business travellers, and all with en suite bathrooms. Continental breakfast is available, and other refreshments may be taken at the nearby family restaurant. See also the Hotel Groups pages.

Rooms 92 (71 fmly) **S** £39-£59; **D** £39-£59*
Conf Board 10 Del from £69 to £89*

Quorn Country

★★★★ 79% HOTEL

☎ 01509 415050 & 415061 🗎 01509 415557
Charnwood House, 66 Leicester Rd LE12 8BB
e-mail: reservations@quorncountryhotel.co.uk
web: www.quorncountryhotel.co.uk

(For full entry see Quorn)

Travelodge Lutterworth

BUDGET HOTEL

☎ 08719 846 182
Mill Farm LE17 4BP
web: www.travelodge.co.uk

Travelodge offers good quality, good value, modern accommodation. Ideal for families, the spacious en suite bedrooms include remote-control TV, tea and coffee-making facilities and comfortable beds. Meals can be taken at the nearby family restaurant. See also the Hotel Groups pages.

Rooms 40 **S** fr £29; **D** fr £29

Best Western Three Swans

★★★ 74% HOTEL

☎ 01858 466644 🗎 01858 433101
21 High St LE16 7NJ
e-mail: sales@threeswans.co.uk
web: www.threeswans.co.uk
dir: M1 junct 20 take A4304 to Market Harborough. Through town centre on A6 from Leicester, hotel on right

Public areas in this former coaching inn include an elegant fine dining restaurant and cocktail bar, a smart foyer lounge and popular public bar areas. Bedroom styles and sizes vary, but are very well appointed and equipped. Those in the wing are particularly impressive, offering high quality and spacious accommodation.

Rooms 61 (43 annexe) (8 fmly) (12 GF) **Facilities** Xmas Wi-fi **Conf** Class 180 Board 180 Thtr 250 **Services** Lift **Parking** 100 **Notes** LB Civ Wed 140

Field Head

★★★ Ⓐ HOTEL

☎ 01530 245454 🗎 01530 243740
Markfield Ln LE6 9PS
e-mail: 9160@greeneking.co.uk
web: www.oldenglish.co.uk
dir: M1 junct 22, towards Leicester. At rdbt turn left, then right

Rooms 28 (1 fmly) (13 GF) **Facilities** ♫ Xmas
Conf Board 36 Thtr 60 **Parking** 65 **Notes** Civ Wed 50

Travelodge Leicester Markfield

BUDGET HOTEL

☎ 08719 846 083 🗎 01530 244580
Littleshaw Ln LE6 0PP
web: www.travelodge.co.uk
dir: on A50 from M1 junct 22

Travelodge offers good quality, good value, modern accommodation. Ideal for families, the spacious en suite bedrooms include remote-control TV, tea and coffee-making facilities and comfortable beds. Meals can be taken at the nearby family restaurant. See also the Hotel Groups pages.

Rooms 60 **S** fr £29; **D** fr £29

The Horse & Trumpet

⊛⊛ RESTAURANT WITH ROOMS

☎ 01858 565000 🗎 01858 565551
Old Green LE16 8DX
e-mail: info@horseandtrumpet.com
dir: In village centre, opposite church

Tucked away behind the village bowling green, this carefully restored and re-thatched former farmhouse and pub now offers fine dining and quality accommodation. The golden stone three-storey building hosts three dining rooms, in which chef Gary Maganani and his team provides imaginative food from high quality produce; service is both professional and friendly. The smartly appointed bedrooms are located to the rear of the building in a barn conversion; attractively furnished and thoughtfully equipped for modern travellers.

Rooms 4 (2 en suite) (4 annexe) (2 GF)

INSPECTORS' CHOICE

Stapleford Park
★★★★ ◉◉ HOTEL

☎ 01572 787000   📠 01572 787651
Stapleford LE14 2EF
e-mail: reservations@stapleford.co.uk
web: www.staplefordpark.com
dir: 1m SW of B676, 4m E of Melton Mowbray & 9m W of Colsterworth

This stunning mansion, dating back to the 14th century, sits in over 500 acres of beautiful grounds. Spacious, sumptuous public rooms include a choice of lounges and an elegant restaurant; an additional brasserie-style restaurant is located in the golf complex. The hotel also boasts a spa with health and beauty treatments and gym, plus horse-riding and many other country pursuits. Bedrooms are individually styled and furnished to a high standard. Attentive service is delivered with a relaxed yet professional style. Dinner, in the impressive dining room, is a highlight of any stay.

Rooms 55 (7 annexe) (10 fmly) **S** £225-£275; **D** £295-£850 (incl. bkfst)* **Facilities** Spa STV FTV ⓢ ⬥ 18 ♨ Putt green Fishing ⬥ Gym Archery Croquet Falconry Horse riding Petanque Shooting Billiards Xmas New Year Wi-fi **Conf** Class 140 Board 80 Thtr 200 Del from £395 to £410* **Services** Lift **Parking** 120 **Notes** LB Civ Wed 150

Sysonby Knoll
★★★ 75% HOTEL

☎ 01664 563563   📠 01664 410364
Asfordby Rd LE13 0HP
e-mail: reception@sysonby.com
web: www.sysonby.com
dir: 0.5m from town centre beside A6006

This well-established hotel is on the edge of town and set in attractive gardens. A friendly and relaxed atmosphere prevails and the many returning guests have become friends. Bedrooms, including superior rooms in the annexe, are generally spacious and thoughtfully equipped. There is a choice of lounges, a cosy bar, and a smart a restaurant that offers carefully prepared meals.

Rooms 30 (7 annexe) (1 fmly) (7 GF) **S** £68-£89; **D** £82-£115 (incl. bkfst)* **Facilities** FTV Fishing ⬥ Wi-fi

Conf Class 25 Board 34 Thtr 50 Del from £115 to £135* **Parking** 48 **Notes** LB Closed 25 Dec-1 Jan

See advert on opposite page

Quorn Lodge
★★★ 71% HOTEL

☎ 01664 566660   📠 01664 480660
46 Asfordby Rd LE13 0HR
e-mail: quornlodge@aol.com
dir: from town centre take A6006. Hotel 300yds from junct of A606/A607 on right

Centrally located, this smart privately owned and managed hotel offers a comfortable and welcoming atmosphere. Bedrooms are individually decorated and thoughtfully designed. The public rooms consist of a bright restaurant overlooking the garden, a cosy lounge bar and a modern function suite. High standards are maintained throughout and parking is a bonus.

Rooms 19 (2 fmly) (3 GF) **S** fr £60; **D** fr £75 (incl. bkfst)* **Facilities** Wi-fi **Conf** Class 70 Board 80 Thtr 100 Del from £105 to £115* **Parking** 38 **Notes** LB ⊗ Civ Wed 80

Scalford Hall
★★★ Ⓐ HOTEL

☎ 0845 400 1403   📠 01664 444487
Scalford Rd LE14 4UB
e-mail: sales@scalfordhall.co.uk
dir: A6006 towards Melton Mowbray. Left at 2nd lights into Scalford Rd, hotel 3m down on left

Rooms 88 (21 annexe) (6 fmly) (19 GF) **S** £40-£72.50; **D** £50-£92.50 (incl. bkfst)* **Facilities** FTV Putt green ⬥ Gym New Year Wi-fi **Conf** Class 36 Board 40 Thtr 150 Del from £89 to £145* **Parking** 120 **Notes** LB ⊗ Civ Wed 100

Kilworth House
★★★★ 84% ◉◉ HOTEL   *Pride of Britain*

☎ 01858 880058   📠 01858 880349
Lutterworth Rd LE17 6JE
e-mail: info@kilworthhouse.co.uk
web: www.kilworthhouse.co.uk
dir: A4304 towards Market Harborough, after Walcote, hotel 1.5m on right

A restored Victorian country house located in 38 acres of private grounds offering state-of-the-art conference rooms. The gracious public areas feature many period pieces and original art works. The bedrooms are very comfortable and well equipped, and the large Orangery is now used for informal dining, while the opulent Wordsworth Restaurant has a more formal air.

Rooms 44 (2 fmly) (13 GF) **Facilities** FTV Fishing ⬥ Gym Beauty therapy rooms Xmas Wi-fi **Conf** Class 30 Board 30 Thtr 80 Del from £200 to £260* **Services** Lift **Parking** 140 **Notes** ⊗ Civ Wed 130

Quorn Country
★★★★ 79% HOTEL

☎ 01509 415050 & 415061   📠 01509 415557
Charnwood House, 66 Leicester Rd LE12 8BB
e-mail: reservations@quorncountryhotel.co.uk
web: www.quorncountryhotel.co.uk
dir: M1 junct 23 onto A512 into Loughborough. Follow A6 signs. At 1st rdbt towards Quorn, through lights, hotel 500yds from 2nd rdbt

Professional service is one of the key strengths of this pleasing hotel, which sits beside the river in four acres of landscaped gardens and grounds. The smart modern conference centre and function suites are popular for both corporate functions and weddings. Public rooms include a smart comfortable lounge and bar, whilst guests have the choice from two dining options: the formal Shires restaurant and the informal conservatory-style Orangery.

Rooms 30 (2 fmly) (9 GF) **S** £70-£140; **D** £80-£160* **Facilities** STV Fishing New Year Wi-fi **Conf** Class 162 Board 40 Thtr 300 Del from £125 to £155* **Services** Lift **Parking** 100 **Notes** LB ⊗ Civ Wed 200

ROTHLEY   Map 11 SK51

Rothley Court

★★★ Ⓐ HOTEL

☎ 0116 237 4141 📄 0116 237 4483
Westfield Ln LE7 7LG
e-mail: 6501@greeneking.co.uk
web: www.oldenglish.co.uk
dir: on B5328

Rooms 30 (18 annexe) (3 fmly) (6 GF) **Facilities** Xmas **Conf** Class 35 Board 35 Thtr 100 **Parking** 100 **Notes** LB ⊗ Civ Wed 85

SIBSON   Map 11 SK30

Millers

★★ Ⓐ HOTEL

☎ 01827 880223 📄 01827 880990
Twycross Rd CV13 6LB
e-mail: 6483@greeneking.co.uk
web: www.oldenglish.co.uk
dir: A5 onto A444 towards Burton. Hotel 3m on right.

Rooms 35 (3 fmly) (15 GF) **Facilities** 🎵 **Conf** Class 24 Board 35 Thtr 50 **Parking** 90 **Notes** ⊗ Civ Wed 80

SUTTON IN THE ELMS   Map 11 SP59

Mill on the Soar

BUDGET HOTEL

☎ 01455 282419 📄 01455 285937
Coventry Rd LE9 6QA
e-mail: 1968@greeneking.co.uk
web: www.oldenglish.co.uk
dir: M1 junct 21, follow signs for Narborough. After 3m hotel on left.

This is a popular inn, set in grounds with two rivers and a lake, that caters especially well for family dining. The open-plan bar offers meals and snacks throughout the day, and is divided into family and adults-only areas; for the summer months, there is also an attractive patio.

Practical bedrooms are housed in a lodge-style annexe within the grounds. See also the Hotel Groups pages.

Mill on the Soar

Rooms 25 (5 annexe) (19 fmly) (13 GF) **Conf** Class 25 Board 25 Thtr 50

THRUSSINGTON   Map 11 SK61

Travelodge Leicester Thrussington

BUDGET HOTEL

☎ 08719 846 084 📄 0870 1911584
LE7 4TF
web: www.travelodge.co.uk
dir: on A46, southbound

Travelodge offers good quality, good value, modern accommodation. Ideal for families, the spacious en suite

Continued

THRUSSINGTON continued

bedrooms include remote-control TV, tea and coffee-making facilities and comfortable beds. Meals can be taken at the nearby family restaurant. See also the Hotel Groups pages.

Rooms 32 **S** fr £29; **D** fr £29

ULLESTHORPE
Map 11 SP58

Best Western Ullesthorpe Court Hotel & Golf Club

★★★★ 76% HOTEL

☎ 01455 209023 ▤ 01455 202537
Frolesworth Rd LE17 5BZ
e-mail: bookings@ullesthorpecourt.co.uk
web: www.bw-ullesthorpecourt.co.uk
dir: M1 junct 20 towards Lutterworth. Follow brown tourist signs

Complete with its own golf club, this impressively equipped hotel is within easy reach of the motorway network, NEC and Birmingham airport. Public areas include both formal and informal eating options, conference and extensive leisure facilities. Spacious bedrooms are thoughtfully equipped for both the corporate or leisure guests, and a four-poster room is available.

Rooms 72 (3 fmly) (16 GF) **S** £64.80-£138; **D** £69.30-£148 (incl. bkfst)* **Facilities** Spa ⓣ supervised ⌁ 18 ⛳ Putt green Gym Beauty room Steam room Sauna Snooker room Wi-fi **Conf** Class 48 Board 30 Thtr 80 Del from £130 to £140* **Services** Lift **Parking** 280 **Notes** LB ⊗ RS 25 & 26 Dec Civ Wed 120

LINCOLNSHIRE

ALFORD
Map 17 TF47

Half Moon Hotel & Restaurant

★★★ Ⓐ HOTEL

☎ 01507 463477 ▤ 01507 462916
25-28 West St LN13 9DG
e-mail: halfmoonalford25@aol.com
dir: Exit A16 at Ulceby, at rdbt take A1104 into Alford, 3m. Hotel opposite The Manor House

Rooms 16 (2 annexe) (2 fmly) (4 GF) **S** £42.50-£57.50; **D** £72-£80 (incl. bkfst)* **Conf** Class 50 Board 50 Thtr 50 Del from £70 to £90* **Parking** 16 **Notes** LB ⊗

BARTON-UPON-HUMBER
Map 17 TA02

Best Western Reeds
★★★ 77% HOTEL

☎ 01652 632313 ▤ 01652 636361
Westfield Lakes, Far Ings Rd DN18 5RG
e-mail: info@reedshotel.co.uk
dir: A15 rdbt take 2nd exit (Humber Bridge) & exit at Barton-upon-Humber, left at rdbt. In 200yds right at hotel sign, down hill & hotel at junct

This hotel is situated in a quiet wildlife sanctuary, just upstream from the Humber Bridge. A very attractive lakeside restaurant commands tranquil views, and there is a health spa offering various alternative therapies. Bedrooms are comfortable and well equipped, and service is both friendly and helpful.

Rooms 25 (2 fmly) **S** £87-£110; **D** £105-£134 (incl. bkfst)* **Facilities** Spa STV FTV Xmas New Year Wi-fi **Conf** Class 200 Board 70 Thtr 300 Del from £110 to £129* **Services** Lift **Parking** 100 **Notes** ⊗ Civ Wed 300

BELTON
Map 11 SK93

De Vere Belton Woods
DE VERE heritage

★★★★ 74% HOTEL

☎ 01476 593200 ▤ 01476 574547
NG32 2LN
e-mail: belton.woods@devere-hotels.com
web: www.devere.co.uk
dir: A1 to Gonerby Moor Services. B1174 towards Great Gonerby. At top of hill turn left towards Manthorpe/Belton. At T-junct turn left onto A607. Hotel 0.25m on left

Beautifully located amidst 475 acres of picturesque countryside, this is a destination venue for lovers of sport, especially golf, as well as a relaxing executive retreat for seminars. Comfortable and well-equipped accommodation complements the elegant and spacious public areas, which provide a good choice of drinking and dining options.

Rooms 136 (136 fmly) (68 GF) **Facilities** Spa ⓣ supervised ⌁ 45 ⛳ Putt green Fishing ⛟ Gym Squash Outdoor activity centre (quad biking, laser shooting etc) Xmas New Year Wi-fi **Conf** Class 180 Board 80 Thtr 245 **Services** Lift **Parking** 350 **Notes** ⊗ Civ Wed 80

BOSTON
Map 12 TF34

Boston West
★★★ 71% HOTEL

☎ 01205 292969 & 290670 ▤ 01205 290725
Hubberts Bridge PE20 3QX
e-mail: info@bostonwesthotel.co.uk
dir: A1121 signed Boston, hotel on left after speed camera

A modern, purpose-built hotel situated in a rural location on the outskirts of town. The smartly appointed bedrooms are spacious and thoughtfully equipped; some rooms have balconies with stunning countryside views. Public rooms include a restaurant and a large open-plan lounge bar which overlooks the golf course.

Rooms 24 (5 fmly) (12 GF) **S** £54.50-£65.50; **D** £54.50-£71 (incl. bkfst) **Facilities** FTV ⌁ 18 Putt green Driving range Xmas New Year Wi-fi **Conf** Board 40 Thtr 80 **Services** Lift **Parking** 24 **Notes** ⊗ Civ Wed 110

Poacher's Country Hotel
★★ 72% HOTEL

☎ 01205 290310 ▤ 01205 290254
Swineshead Rd, Kirton Holme PE20 1SQ
e-mail: poachers@kirtonholme.wandoo.co.uk
dir: A17 Bicker Bar, turn at rdbt onto A52, hotel 2m

A delightfully furnished and comfortable hotel offering a very wide range of well prepared dishes. The bedrooms are modern and have been delightfully furnished. Expect attentive and friendly service.

Rooms 16 (2 fmly) (7 GF) **S** £37.50-£45; **D** £49.50-£55 (incl. bkfst)* **Facilities** FTV Xmas New Year Wi-fi **Conf** Class 100 Board 40 Thtr 150 Del from £70 to £80* **Parking** 60 **Notes** LB Civ Wed 150

CLEETHORPES
Map 17 TA30

Kingsway
★★★ 77% ⊛ HOTEL

☎ 01472 601122 ▤ 0871 236 0671
Kingsway DN35 0AE
e-mail: reception@kingsway-hotel.com
web: www.kingsway-hotel.com
dir: Exit A180 at Grimsby, to Cleethorpes seafront. Hotel at Kingsway & Queen Parade junct (A1098)

This seafront hotel has been in the same family for four generations and continues to provide traditional comfort and friendly service. The lounges are comfortable and good food is served in the pleasant dining room. The bedrooms are bright and nicely furnished - most are comfortably proportioned.

Rooms 49 **S** £73-£86; **D** £90-£103 (incl. bkfst)* **Facilities** STV Wi-fi **Conf** Board 18 Thtr 22 **Services** Lift **Parking** 30 (charged) **Notes** ⊗ No children 5yrs Closed 25-26 Dec

Dovedale Hotel & Restaurant

★★ 72% HOTEL

☎ 01472 692988 ⓘ 01472 692992
14 Albert Rd DN35 8LX
web: www.dovedalehotel.com
dir: In town centre. Off A1098 (Alexandra Rd)

This hotel stands in a quite side road just off the seafront. The bedrooms offer good all round comforts, and there is a modern bar and lounge. Cooking offers a wide choice of dishes that are served in delightful restaurant. Service is both friendly and attentive.

Rooms 22 (9 fmly) (4 GF) **S** £69-£85; **D** £79-£99 (incl. bkfst)* **Facilities** FTV Wi-fi **Parking** 12 **Notes** LB

COLSTERWORTH	Map 11 SK92

Travelodge Grantham Colsterworth

BUDGET HOTEL

☎ 08719 846 075 ⓘ 01476 860680
NG35 5JR
web: www.travelodge.co.uk
dir: on A1/A151 s'bound at junct with A151/B676

Travelodge offers good quality, good value, modern accommodation. Ideal for families, the spacious en suite bedrooms include remote-control TV, tea and coffee-making facilities and comfortable beds. Meals can be taken at the nearby family restaurant. See also the Hotel Groups pages.

Rooms 31 **S** fr £29; **D** fr £29

GAINSBOROUGH	Map 17 SK88

Hickman Hill

★★ 63% HOTEL

☎ 01427 613639 ⓘ 01427 677591
Cox's Hill DN21 1HH
e-mail: info@hickmanhill.co.uk
web: www.hickmanhill.co.uk
dir: Right off B1433 after railway bridge, hotel up hill 100mtrs on right

Dating back to 1795, and once a school, this establishment became a hotel over 25 years ago; it retains many original features. The stylish and spacious bedrooms are named after the school's head teachers. The two-acre gardens are ideal for relaxing in after the stressful day. The restaurant is in the old school hall and

offers tasty home-made dishes; themed Thai nights are a speciality.

Rooms 9 (1 fmly) (1 GF) **S** £72-£85; **D** £85-£120 (incl. bkfst)* **Facilities** FTV Wi-fi **Conf** Class 40 Board 30 Thtr 60 **Parking** 25 **Notes** ⊗

GRANTHAM	Map 11 SK93

Angel & Royal

★★★ 75% ◉ HOTEL

☎ 01476 565816 ⓘ 01476 567149
High St NG31 6PN
e-mail: enquiries@angelandroyal.co.uk
web: www.angelandroyal.co.uk
dir: Take Grantham exit off A1 & follow signs to town centre

This former coaching inn in the centre of town claims to be one of the oldest in the country and retains many original features. The accommodation is varied in size, but all rooms are stylish and comfortable. The bar offers over 200 whiskies and the brasserie provides a modern selection of dishes. Additionally, the historic King's Room restaurant is open at weekends.

Rooms 29 (3 annexe) (4 fmly) (1 GF) **Facilities** Xmas Wi-fi **Conf** Class 30 Board 34 Thtr 65 **Parking** 70 **Notes** LB ⊗ Civ Wed 65

Best Western Kings

★★★ 73% HOTEL

☎ 01476 590800 ⓘ 01476 577072
North Pde NG31 8AU
e-mail: kings@bestwestern.co.uk
web: www.bw-kingshotel.co.uk
dir: S on A1, 1st exit to Grantham. Through Great Gonerby, 2m on left

A friendly atmosphere exists at this extended Georgian house. Modern bedrooms are attractively decorated and furnished, suitably equipped to meet the needs of corporate and leisure guests. Dining options include the formal Victorian restaurant and the popular Orangery, which also operates as an informal coffee shop and breakfast room; a lounge bar and a comfortable open-plan foyer lounge are also available.

Rooms 21 (3 fmly) (3 GF) **S** £58.50-£84; **D** £68.50-£94 (incl. bkfst)* **Facilities** STV New Year Wi-fi **Conf** Class 50 Board 40 Thtr 90 Del from £91.50 to £107.50* **Parking** 40 **Notes** Closed 25-26 Dec RS 24 Dec

Ramada Grantham

®RAMADA.

Ⓤ

☎ 01476 593000 ⓘ 01476 592592
Swingbridge Rd NG31 7XT
e-mail: amanda.burton@ramadagrantham.co.uk
dir: exit A1 at Grantham/Melton Mowbray junct onto A607. From N: 1st exit at mini rdbt, hotel on right. From S: at rdbt 2nd exit. Next left at T-junct. At mini rdbt 2nd exit. Hotel on right

Currently the rating for this establishment is not confirmed. This may be due to a change of ownership or because it has only recently joined the AA rating scheme. For further details please see the AA website: www.theAA.com

Rooms 89 (44 GF) (10 smoking) **S** £64-£99; **D** £69-£105* **Facilities** STV ⓢ Gym Steam room Sunbed Xmas New Year Wi-fi **Conf** Class 90 Board 60 Thtr 200 Del from £132 to £145* **Parking** 102 **Notes** LB ⊗ Civ Wed 200

Travelodge Grantham (A1)

Travelodge

BUDGET HOTEL

☎ 08719 846 077 ⓘ 01476 577500
Grantham Service Area, Grantham North, Gonerby Moor NG32 2AB
web: www.travelodge.co.uk
dir: 4m N on A1

Travelodge offers good quality, good value, modern accommodation. Ideal for families, the spacious en suite bedrooms include remote-control TV, tea and coffee-making facilities and comfortable beds. Meals can be taken at the nearby family restaurant. See also the Hotel Groups pages.

Rooms 39 **S** fr £29; **D** fr £29

GRIMSBY	Map 17 TA21

Millfields

★★★ Ⓐ HOTEL

☎ 01472 356068 ⓘ 01472 250286
53 Bargate DN34 5AD
e-mail: info@millfieldshotel.co.uk
web: www.millfieldshotel.co.uk
dir: A180, right at KFC rdbt then left at next rdbt. Right at 2nd lights & right onto Bargate, hotel 0.5m on left after Wheatsheaf pub

Rooms 26 (4 annexe) (7 fmly) (13 GF) **Facilities** Gym Squash Sauna Steam room Hairdresser Beauty salon Wi-fi **Conf** Class 25 Board 25 Thtr 50 **Parking** 75 **Notes** LB Civ Wed 50

HORNCASTLE

Map 17 TF26

Best Western Admiral Rodney

★★★ 72% HOTEL

☎ 01507 523131 📠 01507 523104
North St LN9 5DX
e-mail: reception@admiralrodney.com
web: www.admiralrodney.com
dir: off A153 (Louth to Horncastle)

Once a coaching inn and enjoying a prime location in the town centre, this smart hotel offers a high standard of accommodation. Bedrooms are well appointed and thoughtfully equipped for both business and leisure guests. Public areas include the Rodney Bar ideal for enjoying a drink, a selection of meeting and conference rooms and a conservatory-style restaurant and adjoining lounge.

Rooms 31 (3 fmly) (7 GF) (7 smoking) **S** £70-£75;
D £90-£100 (incl. bkfst)* **Facilities** Xmas New Year Wi-fi
Conf Class 60 Board 50 Thtr 140 **Services** Lift
Parking 60 **Notes** LB ⊗

LACEBY

Map 17 TA20

Legacy Oaklands

Ⓤ

☎ 0870 832 9909 📠 0870 832 9910
Barton St DN37 7LF
e-mail: res-oaklands@legacy-hotel.co.uk
web: www.legacy-hotels.co.uk
dir: A18 to rdbt, straight over, hotel 75yds on right

Currently the rating for this establishment is not confirmed. This may be due to a change of ownership or because it has only recently joined the AA rating scheme. For further details please see the AA website: www.theAA.com

Rooms 45 (3 fmly) (10 GF) **S** £47.50-£90; **D** £47.50-£95
(incl. bkfst)* **Facilities** STV Xmas New Year Wi-fi
Conf Class 60 Board 40 Thtr 200 **Parking** 110 **Notes** LB
Civ Wed

LINCOLN

Map 17 SK97

Best Western Bentley Hotel & Leisure Club

★★★ 85% HOTEL

☎ 01522 878000 📠 01522 878001
Newark Rd, South Hykeham LN6 9NH
e-mail: infothebentleyhotel@btconnect.com
web: www.thebentleyhotel.uk.com
dir: from A1 take A46 E towards Lincoln for 10m. Over 1st rdbt on Lincoln Bypass to hotel 50yds on left

This modern hotel is on a ring road, so it is conveniently located for all local attractions. Attractive bedrooms, most with air conditioning are well equipped and spacious. The hotel has a leisure suite with gym and large pool (with a hoist for the less able). Extensive conference facilities are available.

Rooms 80 (5 fmly) (26 GF) **S** £90-£105; **D** £105-£140
(incl. bkfst) **Facilities** STV ⓢ Gym Beauty salon Steam room Xmas Wi-fi **Conf** Class 150 Board 30 Thtr 300
Del from £115 to £120* **Services** Lift **Parking** 170
Notes LB ⊗ Civ Wed 120

Branston Hall

★★★ 74% ⊛⊛ COUNTRY HOUSE HOTEL

☎ 01522 793305 📠 01522 790734
Branston Park, Branston LN4 1PD
e-mail: info@branstonhall.com
web: www.branstonhall.com
dir: on B1188

Many original features have been retained in this country house, which sits in beautiful grounds complete with a lake. There is an elegant restaurant, a spacious bar and a beautiful lounge in addition to impressive conference and leisure facilities. Individually styled bedrooms vary in size and include several with four-poster beds.

Rooms 50 (7 annexe) (3 fmly) (4 GF) **S** £79.50-£89.50;
D £109.50-£179.50 (incl. bkfst)* **Facilities** Spa ⓢ Gym Jogging circuit Xmas New Year Wi-fi **Conf** Class 54
Board 40 Thtr 200 **Services** Lift **Parking** 100 **Notes** LB ⊗
Civ Wed 160

The Lincoln

"bespoke"

★★★ 72% HOTEL

☎ 01522 520348 📠 01522 510780
Eastgate LN2 1PN
e-mail: reservations@thelincolnhotel.com
web: www.thelincolnhotel.com
dir: adjacent to cathedral

This privately owned modern hotel enjoys superb uninterrupted views of Lincoln Cathedral. There are ruins of the Roman wall and Eastgate in the grounds. Bedrooms are contemporary with up-to-the-minute facilities. An airy restaurant and bar, plus a comfortable lounge are provided, in addition to substantial conference and meeting facilities.

Rooms 72 (4 fmly) **Facilities** Wi-fi **Conf** Class 50
Board 40 Thtr 120 **Services** Lift **Parking** 120 **Notes** ⊗
Civ Wed 150

Washingborough Hall

★★★ 72% ◉ HOTEL

☎ 01522 790340 📄 01522 792936
Church Hill, Washingborough LN4 1BE
e-mail: enquiries@washingboroughhall.com
web: www.washingboroughhall.com
dir: B1190 into Washingborough. Right at rdbt, hotel
500yds on left

This Georgian manor stands on the edge of the quiet
village of Washingborough among attractive gardens.
Public rooms are pleasantly furnished and comfortable,
whilst the restaurant offers interesting menus. Bedrooms
are individually designed, and most have views out over
the grounds and countryside.

Rooms 12 (3 fmly) **S** £60–£120; **D** £85–£140 (incl. bkfst)*
Facilities 🚲 Bicycles for hire Xmas New Year Wi-fi
Conf Class 25 Board 25 Thtr 50 Del from £120 to £140*
Parking 50 **Notes** LB ⊗ Civ Wed 48

The White Hart

★★★ 68% HOTEL

☎ 01522 526222 & 563293 📄 01522 531798
Bailgate LN1 3AR
e-mail: info@whitehart-lincoln.co.uk
web: www.whitehart-lincoln.co.uk
dir: turn off A46 onto B1226, through Newport Arch. Hotel
0.5m on left as road bends left

Lying in the shadow of Lincoln's magnificent cathedral,
this hotel is perfectly positioned for exploring the shops
and sights of this medieval city. The attractive bedrooms
are furnished and decorated in a traditional style and
many have views of the cathedral. Given the hotel's
central location, parking is a real benefit.

Rooms 50 **S** £88–£110; **D** £113–£140 (incl. bkfst)*
Facilities FTV Xmas New Year Wi-fi **Conf** Class 80
Board 103 Thtr 160 **Services** Lift **Parking** 20
Notes Civ Wed 120

Castle

★★ 79% ◉ HOTEL

☎ 01522 538801 📄 01522 575457
Westgate LN1 3AS
e-mail: aa@castlehotel.net
web: www.castlehotel.net
dir: follow signs for Historic Lincoln. Hotel at NE corner of
castle

Located in the heart of historic Lincoln, this privately
owned and run hotel has been carefully restored to offer
comfortable, attractive, well-appointed accommodation.
Bedrooms are thoughtfully equipped, particularly the
deluxe rooms and the spacious Lincoln Suite. Specialising
in traditional fayre, Knights Restaurant has an
interesting medieval theme.

Rooms 19 (3 annexe) (5 GF) **S** £70–£115; **D** £89–£150
(incl. bkfst)* **Facilities** Wi-fi **Conf** Class 40 Board 30
Thtr 20 Del from £117.50 to £138.50* **Parking** 20
Notes LB No children 8yrs RS 25-26 Dec evening

Tower Hotel

★★ 69% HOTEL

☎ 01522 529999 📄 01522 560596
38 Westgate LN1 3BD
e-mail: tower.hotel@btclick.com
dir: from A46 follow signs to Lincoln N then to Bailgate
area. Through arch and 2nd left

This hotel faces the Norman castle wall and is in a very
convenient location for the city. The relaxed and friendly
atmosphere is very noticeable here. There's a modern
conservatory bar and a stylish restaurant where
contemporary dishes are available throughout the day.

Rooms 15 (1 fmly) **Facilities** Wi-fi **Conf** Class 24
Board 16 Thtr 24 **Parking** 4 **Notes** LB Closed 24-27 Dec &
1 Jan

Holiday Inn Lincoln

Ⓤ

☎ 01522 544244 📄 01522 560805
Brayford Wharf North LN1 1YW
e-mail: reservations@lincoln.kewgreen.co.uk
web: www.holidayinn.co.uk
dir: From A46 onto A57 to Lincoln Central. Left at lights,
right, take next right onto Lucy Tower St then right onto
Brayford Wharf North for hotel on right

Currently the rating for this establishment is not confirmed.
This may be due to a change of ownership or because it has
only recently joined the AA rating scheme. For further
details please see the AA website: www.theAA.com

Rooms 97 (32 fmly) (9 GF) **S** £82–£121; **D** £82–£121 (incl.
bkfst)* **Facilities** Gym Wi-fi **Conf** Class 15 Board 18
Thtr 30 Del from £125 to £155* **Services** Lift Air con
Parking 100 (charged) **Notes** LB

Ibis Lincoln

BUDGET HOTEL

☎ 01522 698333 📄 01522 698444
Runcorn Rd (A46), off Whisby Rd LN6 3QZ
e-mail: H3161@accor-hotels.com
web: www.ibishotel.com
dir: off A46 ring road onto Whisby Rd. 1st turning on left

Enjoying a convenient location, adjacent to the A46 on
the edge of the city, this modern purpose-built hotel
offers well-equipped en suite bedrooms, suitable for both
leisure and business guests. The open-plan public rooms
are light and contemporary in style. See also the Hotel
Groups pages.

Rooms 86 (19 fmly) (8 GF) **Conf** Class 12 Board 20
Thtr 35

Travelodge Lincoln Thorpe
on the Hill

BUDGET HOTEL

☎ 08719 846 085 📄 01522 697213
Thorpe on the Hill LN6 9AJ
web: www.travelodge.co.uk
dir: on A46 Newark/Lincoln rdbt

Travelodge offers good quality, good value, modern
accommodation. Ideal for families, the spacious en suite
bedrooms include remote-control TV, tea and coffee-
making facilities and comfortable beds. Meals can be
taken at the nearby family restaurant. See also the Hotel
Groups pages.

Rooms 32 **S** fr £29; **D** fr £29

LINCOLN continued

The Old Bakery

@@ RESTAURANT WITH ROOMS

☎ 01522 576057
26/28 Burton Rd LN1 3LB
e-mail: enquiries@theold-bakery.co.uk
dir: Exit A46 at Lincoln North follow signs for cathedral.
3rd exit at 1st rdbt, 1st exit at next rdbt

Situated close to the castle at the top of the town, this
converted bakery offers well-equipped bedrooms and a
delightful dining operation. The cooking is international
with a leaning towards the use of local produce. Expect
good friendly service from a dedicated staff.

Rooms 4 (2 pri facs) (1 en suite) (1 fmly)

| LONG SUTTON | Map 12 TF42 |

Travelodge King's Lynn Long Sutton

BUDGET HOTEL

☎ 08719 846 082 📠 01406 362230
Wisbech Rd PE12 9AG
web: www.travelodge.co.uk
dir: on junct A17/A1101 rdbt

Travelodge offers good quality, good value, modern
accommodation. Ideal for families, the spacious en suite
bedrooms include remote-control TV, tea and coffee-
making facilities and comfortable beds. Meals can be
taken at the nearby family restaurant. See also the Hotel
Groups pages.

Rooms 40 **S** fr £29; **D** fr £29

| LOUTH | Map 17 TF38 |

Brackenborough Hotel

★★★ 86% @ HOTEL

☎ 01507 609169 📠 01507 609413
Cordeaux Corner, Brackenborough LN11 0SZ
e-mail: arlidgard@oakridgehotels.co.uk
web: www.oakridgehotels.co.uk
dir: off A16 2m N of Louth

Set amid well-tended gardens and patios, this hotel
offers attractive bedrooms, each individually decorated
with co-ordinated furnishings and many extras. Tippler's
Retreat lounge bar offers informal dining; the more
formal Signature Restaurant provides dishes using the

best of local produce including fish from Grimsby. Wi-fi is
also available.

Rooms 24 (2 fmly) (6 GF) **S** £79-£119; **D** £95-£149 (incl.
bkfst)* **Facilities** FTV ♫ Xmas New Year Wi-fi
Conf Class 40 Board 30 Thtr 70 Del from £94.95 to
£114.95* **Services** Air con **Parking** 90 **Notes** LB ⊗
Civ Wed 80

Best Western Kenwick Park

★★★ 79% HOTEL

☎ 01507 608806 📠 01507 608027
Kenwick Park Estate LN11 8NR
e-mail: enquiries@kenwick-park.co.uk
web: www.kenwick-park.co.uk
dir: A16 from Grimsby, then A157 Mablethorpe/Manby Rd.
Hotel 400mtrs down hill on right

This elegant Georgian house is situated on the 320-acre
Kenwick Park estate, overlooking its own golf course.
Bedrooms are spacious, comfortable and provide modern
facilities. Public areas include a restaurant and a
conservatory bar that overlook the grounds. There is also
an extensive leisure centre and state-of-the-art
conference and banqueting facilities.

Rooms 34 (5 annexe) (10 fmly) **Facilities** Spa ⊕
supervised ♨ 18 ⛳ Putt green Gym Squash Health &
beauty centre Xmas New Year Wi-fi **Conf** Class 40
Board 90 Thtr 250 **Parking** 100 **Notes** LB Civ Wed 200

Beaumont

★★★ 72% HOTEL

☎ 01507 605005 📠 01507 607768
66 Victoria Rd LN11 0BX
e-mail: beaumonthotel@aol.com

This smart, family-run hotel enjoys a quiet location,
within easy reach of the town centre. Bedrooms are
spacious and individually designed. Public areas include
a smart restaurant serving Mediterranean-influenced
cuisine, and an inviting lounge bar with comfortable deep
sofas and open fires.

Rooms 16 (2 fmly) (6 GF) **S** £62-£75; **D** £88-£98 (incl.
bkfst)* **Conf** Class 50 Board 46 Thtr 70 **Services** Lift
Parking 70 **Notes** RS Sun

| MARSTON | Map 11 SK84 |

The Olde Barn

★★★ 72% HOTEL

☎ 01400 250909 📠 01400 250130
Toll Bar Rd NG32 2HT
e-mail: reservations@theoldebarnhotel.com
dir: From A1 N: left to Marston next to petrol station. From
A1 S: 1st right after Gonerby rdbt signed Marston

Located in the countryside one mile from the A1, this
sympathetically renovated and extended former period
barn provides a range of thoughtfully furnished
bedrooms, ideal for both business and leisure customers.

Imaginative food is offered in an attractive beamed
restaurant and extensive leisure facilities include a
swimming pool, sauna, steam room and a well-equipped
gym.

Rooms 103 (11 fmly) (51 GF) (6 smoking) **S** £69-£134;
D £79-£144 (incl. bkfst) **Facilities** STV ⊕ Gym Xmas New
Year Wi-fi **Conf** Class 180 Board 100 Thtr 300
Del from £115 to £145* **Services** Lift **Parking** 280
Notes LB Civ Wed 250

| SCUNTHORPE | Map 17 SE81 |

Forest Pines Hotel

★★★★ 77% HOTEL

☎ 01652 650770 📠 01652 650495
Ermine St, Broughton DN20 0AQ
e-mail: forestpines@qhotels.co.uk
web: www.qhotels.co.uk
dir: 200yds from M180 junct 4, on Brigg-Scunthorpe rdbt

This smart hotel provides a comprehensive range of
leisure facilities. Extensive conference rooms, a modern
health and beauty spa, and a championship golf course
ensure that it is a popular choice with both corporate and
leisure guests. Extensive public areas include a choice of
dining options, with fine dining available in The Beech
Tree Restaurant or more informal eating in the Garden
Room or Mulligan's Bar. Bedrooms are modern, spacious
and very well equipped. Q Hotels - AA Hotel Group of the
Year 2008-9.

Rooms 188 (66 fmly) (67 GF) **S** £89-£149; **D** £99-£159
(incl. bkfst)* **Facilities** Spa STV FTV ⊕ supervised ♨ 27
Putt green Gym Mountain bikes Jogging track Xmas New
Year Wi-fi **Conf** Class 170 Board 96 Thtr 370
Del from £129 to £189* **Services** Lift **Parking** 300
Notes LB Civ Wed 250

See advert on opposite page

Wortley House

★★★ 74% HOTEL

☎ 01724 842223 📠 01724 280646
Rowland Rd DN16 1SU
e-mail: reception@wortleyhousehotel.co.uk
web: www.wortleyhousehotel.co.uk
dir: M180 junct 3 take A18. Follow signs for Grimsby/
Humberside airport, 2nd left into Brumby Wood Ln, over
rdbt into Rowland Rd. Hotel 200yds on right

A friendly hotel with good facilities for conferences,
meetings, banquets and other functions. Bedrooms offer
modern comfort and facilities. An extensive range of
dishes is available in both the formal restaurant and the
more relaxed bar.

Rooms 42 (4 annexe) (5 fmly) (4 GF) **S** £55-£75;
D £75-£150 (incl. bkfst) **Facilities** FTV Xmas New Year
Wi-fi **Conf** Class 250 Board 50 Thtr 300 Del from £70 to
£150 **Parking** 100 **Notes** Civ Wed 250

Travelodge Scunthorpe

BUDGET HOTEL

☎ 08719 846 286 ᠍ 01724 289 391
Doncaster Rd, Gunness DN15 8TE
web: www.travelodge.co.uk
dir: M18 junct 5, take M180 towards Scunthorpe. 1st exit signed Scunthorpe. In 1.5 m take 3rd exit at traffic island. Lodge on right

Travelodge offers good quality, good value, modern accommodation. Ideal for families, the spacious en suite bedrooms include remote-control TV, tea and coffee-making facilities and comfortable beds. Meals can be taken at the nearby family restaurant. See also the Hotel Groups pages.

Rooms 40 **S** fr £29; **D** fr £29

SKEGNESS   Map 17 TF56

Crown

★★★ 70% HOTEL

☎ 01754 610760 ᠍ 01754 610847
Drummond Rd PE25 3AB
e-mail: enquiries@crownhotel.biz
dir: On entering town follow Gibraltar Point Nature Reserve signs

The Crown is ideally situated just a short walk from the seafront and town centre, close to Seacroft Golf Course and the bird sanctuary. Homely bedrooms are attractively decorated and thoughtfully equipped. Public areas include a spacious bar offering a wide selection of dishes, a formal restaurant, residents' TV lounge and indoor pool; ample parking is provided.

Rooms 29 (4 fmly) **Facilities** ⓧ Wi-fi **Conf** Class 60 Board 60 Thtr 100 **Services** Lift **Parking** 52 **Notes** LB ⊗ Civ Wed 120

See advert on page 312

Best Western Vine

★★★ 67% HOTEL

☎ 01754 763018 & 610611 ᠍ 01754 769845
Vine Rd, Seacroft PE25 3DB
e-mail: info@thevinehotel.com
dir: A52 to Skegness, S towards Gibraltar Point, turn right on to Drummond Rd, after 0.5m turn right into Vine Rd

Reputedly the second oldest building in Skegness, this traditional style hotel offers two character bars that serve excellent local beers. Freshly prepared dishes are served in both the bar and the restaurant; service is both friendly and helpful. The smartly decorated bedrooms are well equipped and comfortably appointed.

Rooms 25 (3 fmly) **S** £41-£50; **D** £58-£71* **Facilities** FTV Xmas New Year Wi-fi **Conf** Class 25 Board 30 Thtr 100 Del from £85 to £120* **Parking** 50 **Notes** LB Civ Wed 100

North Shore Hotel & Golf Course

★★ 72% HOTEL

☎ 01754 763298 ᠍ 01754 761902
North Shore Rd PE25 1DN
e-mail: golf@northshorehotel.co.uk
dir: 1m N of town centre on A52, turn right into North Shore Rd (opposite Fenland laundry)

This hotel enjoys an enviable position on the beachfront, adjacent to its own championship golf course and only ten minutes from the town centre. Spacious public areas include a terrace bar serving informal meals and real ales, a formal restaurant and impressive function rooms. Bedrooms are smartly decorated and thoughtfully equipped.

Rooms 36 (3 annexe) (4 fmly) **S** £38-£61; **D** £59-£83 (incl. bkfst)* **Facilities** ⌡ 18 Putt green Xmas New Year Wi-fi **Conf** Class 60 Board 60 Thtr 220 Del from £80 to £120* **Parking** 200 **Notes** ⊗ Civ Wed 180

SLEAFORD
Map 12 TF04

Carre Arms Hotel & Conference Centre

★★★ 68% SMALL HOTEL

☎ 01529 303156 ▤ 01529 303139
1 Mareham Ln NG34 7JP
e-mail: enquiries@carrearmshotel.co.uk
web: www.carrearmshotel.co.uk
dir: take A153 to Sleaford, hotel on right at level crossing

This friendly, family run hotel is located close to the station and offers suitably appointed accommodation. Public areas include a smart brasserie and two spacious bars where a good selection of meals is offered. There is also a conservatory and a former stable that houses the spacious function room.

Rooms 13 (2 fmly) **Facilities** Wi-fi **Conf** Class 70 Board 40 Thtr 120 **Parking** 100 **Notes** ⊗

The Lincolnshire Oak

THE INDEPENDENTS
HOTEL ASSOCIATION

★★★ 68% HOTEL

☎ 01529 413807 ▤ 01529 413710
East Rd NG34 7EH
e-mail: reception@lincolnshire-oak.co.uk
web: www.lincolnshire-oak.co.uk
dir: From A17 (by-pass) exit on A153 into Sleaford. Hotel 0.75m on left

Located on the edge of the town in well-tended grounds, this hotel has a relaxed and friendly atmosphere. A comfortable open-plan lounge bar is complemented by a cosy restaurant that looks out onto the rear garden. There are also several meeting rooms. Bedroom styles differ, but all rooms are well furnished and suitably equipped; the superior rooms, as expected, are more comfortably appointed.

Rooms 17 **S** £67-£87.75; **D** £78-£103.50 (incl. bkfst)*
Facilities FTV Wi-fi **Conf** Class 70 Board 50 Thtr 140
Parking 80 **Notes** LB ⊗ Civ Wed 90

Travelodge Sleaford

BUDGET HOTEL

☎ 08719 846 104 ▤ 01529 414752
Holdingham NG34 8PN
web: www.travelodge.co.uk
dir: 1m N, at rdbt A17/A15

Travelodge offers good quality, good value, modern accommodation. Ideal for families, the spacious en suite bedrooms include remote-control TV, tea and coffee-making facilities and comfortable beds. Meals can be taken at the nearby family restaurant. See also the Hotel Groups pages.

Rooms 40 **S** fr £29; **D** fr £29

SOUTH WITHAM — Map 11 SK91

Travelodge Grantham South Witham

BUDGET HOTEL

☎ 08719 846 076 📠 01572 767 586
New Fox NG33 5LN
web: www.travelodge.co.uk
dir: on A1, northbound

Travelodge offers good quality, good value, modern accommodation. Ideal for families, the spacious en suite bedrooms include remote-control TV, tea and coffee-making facilities and comfortable beds. Meals can be taken at the nearby family restaurant. See also the Hotel Groups pages.

Rooms 32 **S** fr £29; **D** fr £29

SPALDING — Map 12 TF22

Woodlands

★★★ 79% HOTEL

☎ 01775 769933 📠 01775 711365
80 Pinchbeck Rd PE11 1QF
e-mail: woodlands@kingscountryhotels.co.uk
dir: A16 turn left at rdbt, cross double bridges onto Elloe Rd. Left at lights, hotel 20yds on left

A delightful 19th-century Victorian house ideally situated just a short walk from the town centre. The public areas have many original features; they include the Oakleaf dining room, the Silver Birch meeting room and the Willows bar. The smartly decorated bedrooms have lovely co-ordinated soft furnishings and many thoughtful touches.

Rooms 17 (5 GF) **S** £70; **D** £90-£115 (incl. bkfst)
Facilities STV **Conf** Class 30 Board 30 Thtr 60 **Notes** ⊗ Civ Wed 60

Cley Hall

★★ 74% ⊛ SMALL HOTEL

☎ 01775 725157 📠 01775 710785
22 High St PE11 1TX
e-mail: cleyhall@kingscountryhotels.co.uk
dir: A16/A151 rdbt towards Spalding, keep river on right, hotel 1.5m on left

This Georgian house overlooks the River Welland, with landscaped gardens to the rear. Most bedrooms are in an adjacent building; all are smart and include modern amenities. Public rooms include a choice of dining options that feature a brasserie restaurant and guests also have the use of a smart lounge bar.

Rooms 15 (11 annexe) (2 GF) **S** fr £70; **D** £90-£105 (incl. bkfst)* **Facilities** Xmas New Year **Conf** Class 20 Board 18 Thtr 35 **Parking** 13 **Notes** ⊗ Civ Wed 40

STALLINGBOROUGH — Map 17 TA11

Stallingborough Grange Hotel

★★★ 72% HOTEL

☎ 01469 561302 📠 01469 561338
Riby Rd DN41 8BU
e-mail: grange.hot@virgin.net
web: www.stallingborough-grange.com
dir: from A180 follow Stallingborough Interchange signs. Through village. From rdbt take A1173/Caistor. Hotel 1m on left just past windmill

This 18th-century country house has been tastefully extended to provide spacious and well-equipped bedrooms, particularly in the executive wing. A family-run hotel that is popular with locals who enjoy the wide range of food offered in either the bar or the restaurant.

Rooms 41 (6 fmly) (9 GF) **S** £90-£110; **D** £105-£125 (incl. bkfst)* **Facilities** STV FTV Wi-fi **Conf** Class 40 Board 28 Thtr 60 **Parking** 100 **Notes** ⊗ Civ Wed 65

STAMFORD — Map 11 TF00

The George of Stamford

★★★ 85% ⊛ HOTEL

☎ 01780 750750 & 750700 (res) 📠 01780 750701
71 St Martins PE9 2LB
e-mail: reservations@georgehotelofstamford.com
web: www.georgehotelofstamford.com
dir: A1, 15m N of Peterborough onto B1081, hotel 1m on left

Steeped in hundreds of years of history, this delightful coaching inn provides spacious public areas that include a choice of dining options, inviting, lounges, a business centre and a range of quality shops. A highlight is afternoon tea, taken in the colourful courtyard when weather permits. Bedrooms are stylishly appointed and range from traditional to contemporary in design.

Rooms 47 (18 fmly) **S** £90-£130; **D** £130-£245 (incl. bkfst)* **Facilities** STV ⏬ Complimentary membership to local gym Xmas New Year Wi-fi **Conf** Class 25 Board 25 Thtr 50 Del from £145 to £170* **Parking** 80 **Notes** LB Civ Wed 50

Crown

★★★ 75% HOTEL

☎ 01780 763136 📠 01780 756111
All Saints Place PE9 2AG
e-mail: reservations@thecrownhotelstamford.co.uk
web: www.thecrownhotelstamford.co.uk
dir: off A1 onto A43, through town to Red Lion Sq, hotel behind All Saints Church

This small, privately owned hotel where hospitality is spontaneous and sincere, is ideally situated in the town centre. Unpretentious British food is served in the modern dining areas and the spacious bar is popular with locals. Bedrooms are appointed to a very high standard being quite contemporary in style and very well equipped; some have four-poster beds. Additional 'superior' rooms are located in a renovated Georgian town house just a short walk up the street.

Rooms 24 (7 annexe) (2 fmly) (1 GF) **S** fr £85; **D** £110-£160 (incl. bkfst)* **Facilities** STV Use of local health/gym club Wi-fi **Conf** Class 12 Board 12 Thtr 20 **Parking** 21 **Notes** LB ⊗

Garden House

★★★ 70% HOTEL

☎ 01780 763359 📠 01780 763339
High St, St Martins PE9 2LP
e-mail: enquiries@gardenhousehotel.com
web: www.gardenhousehotel.com
dir: A1 to South Stamford, B1081, signed Stamford & Burghley House. Hotel on left on entering town

Situated within a few minutes' walk of the town centre, this transformed 18th-century town house provides pleasant accommodation. Bedroom styles vary; all are well equipped and comfortably furnished. Public rooms include a charming lounge bar, conservatory restaurant

Continued

STAMFORD continued

and a smart breakfast room. Service is attentive and friendly throughout.

Rooms 20 (2 fmly) (4 GF) **Facilities** Xmas **Conf** Class 20 Board 20 Thtr 40 **Parking** 20 **Notes** LB Closed 26-30 Dec RS 1-12 Jan Civ Wed 60

Candlesticks

RESTAURANT WITH ROOMS

☎ 01780 764033 🖹 01780 756071
1 Church Ln PE9 2JU
e-mail: info@candlestickshotel.co.uk
dir: On B1081 High Street St Martins. Church Ln opposite St Martin Church

This stone-built, family-run property sits within the oldest part of Stamford, the building dating back to 1730 and retaining many original features. Converted to a restaurant and run by the same family since 1975, Candlesticks offers a lounge bar and intimate restaurant in the ground floor and cellar rooms. Continental breakfasts are served in the well-equipped bedrooms.

Rooms 8 (3 en suite)

The Grange & Links

★★★ 73% ⚫ HOTEL

☎ 01507 441334 🖹 01507 443033
Sea Ln, Sandilands LN12 2RA
e-mail: grangeandlinkshotel@btconnect.com
web: www.grangeandlinkshotel.co.uk
dir: A1111 to Sutton-on-Sea, follow signs to Sandilands

This friendly, family-run hotel sits in five acres of grounds, close to both the beach and its own 18-hole links golf course. Bedrooms are pleasantly appointed and are well equipped for both business and leisure guests. Public rooms include ample lounge areas, a formal restaurant and a traditional bar, serving a wide range of meals and snacks.

Rooms 23 (10 fmly) (3 GF) **S** £64.50; **D** £84 (incl. bkfst)*
Facilities STV ⚓ 18 ☉ Putt green ⚲ Gym Bowls Xmas New Year **Conf** Class 200 Board 100 Thtr 200 **Parking** 60 **Notes** LB ⊗ Civ Wed 150

INSPECTORS' CHOICE

Winteringham Fields

◉◉ RESTAURANT WITH ROOMS

☎ 01724 733096 🖹 01724 733898
DN15 9PF
e-mail: wintfields@aol.com
dir: In centre of village at x-rds

This highly regarded restaurant with rooms, located deep in the countryside in Winteringham village, is six miles west of the Humber Bridge. Public rooms and bedrooms, some of which are housed in renovated barns and cottages, are delightfully cosseting. Award-winning food is available in the restaurant.

Rooms 10 (10 en suite) (6 annexe) (3 GF)

Petwood

★★★ 74% HOTEL

☎ 01526 352411 🖹 01526 353473
Stixwould Rd LN10 6QG
e-mail: reception@petwood.co.uk
web: www.petwood.co.uk
dir: from Sleaford take A153 (signed Skegness). At Tattershall turn left on B1192. Hotel is signed from village

This lovely Edwardian house, set in 30 acres of gardens and woodlands, is adjacent to Woodhall Golf Course. Built in 1905, the house was used by 617 Squadron, the famous Dambusters, as an officers' mess during World War II. Bedrooms and public areas are spacious and comfortable, and retain many original features. Weddings and conferences are well catered for in modern facilities.

Rooms 53 (3 GF) **S** £99-£124; **D** £145-£170 (incl. bkfst)*
Facilities Putt green ⚲ Complimentary pass to leisure centre ♫ Xmas New Year **Conf** Class 100 Board 50 Thtr 250 Del from £100 to £110* **Services** Lift **Parking** 140 **Notes** LB Civ Wed 200

Woodhall Spa

★★★ 71% HOTEL

☎ 01526 353231 🖹 01526 352797
The Broadway LN10 6ST
e-mail: reception@woodhallspahotel.co.uk
web: www.woodhallspahotel.co.uk
dir: In village centre, 500tmrs from golf course

This family owned hotel is located in the centre of town, close to local shops and golf courses. Modern bedrooms are equipped for both business and leisure guests. Public areas include a bar and lounge, and a formal restaurant where a good range of dishes to suit all tastes is offered. Conference and meeting facilities are also available.

Rooms 25 (2 fmly) (2 GF) **S** £65; **D** £84.50-£114.50 (incl. bkfst)* **Facilities** FTV Xmas Wi-fi **Conf** Class 40 Board 40 Thtr 100 **Services** Lift **Parking** 30 **Notes** LB ⊗ Civ Wed 86

Golf Hotel

★★★ 67% HOTEL

☎ 01526 353535 🖹 01526 353096
The Broadway LN10 6SG
e-mail: reception@thegolf-hotel.com
web: www.thegolf-hotel.com
dir: from Lincoln take B1189 to Metheringham onto B1191 towards Woodhall Spa. Hotel on left in approx 500yds from rdbt

Located near the centre of the village, this traditional hotel is ideally situated to explore the Lincolnshire countryside and coast. The adjacent golf course makes this a popular venue for golfers, and the hotel's hydrotherapy suite uses the original spa water supplies. Bedrooms vary in size.

Rooms 50 (4 fmly) (8 GF) **S** £25-£60; **D** £50-£120* **Facilities** Spa STV Use of private leisure centre in 1m Xmas New Year Wi-fi **Conf** Class 50 Board 50 Thtr 150 Del from £95 to £105* **Services** Lift **Parking** 100 **Notes** LB Civ Wed 150

London

Index of London Hotels

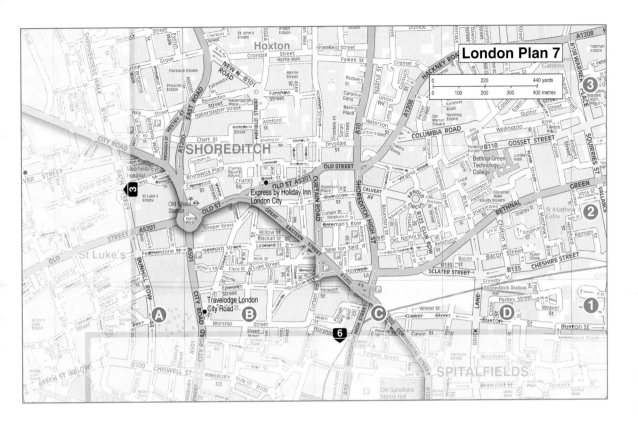

London Plan 7

0 100 200 300 400 metres
0 220 440 yards

London Plan 8

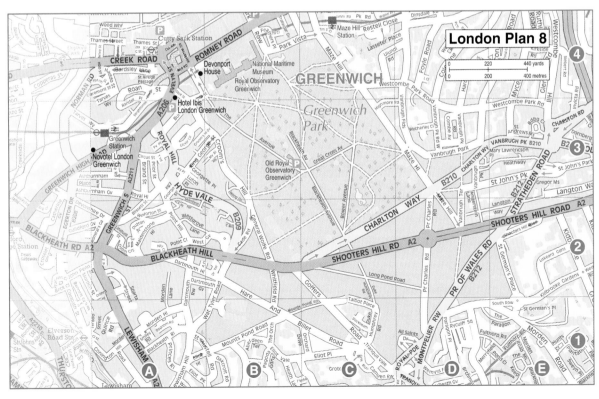

0 200 400 metres
0 220 440 yards

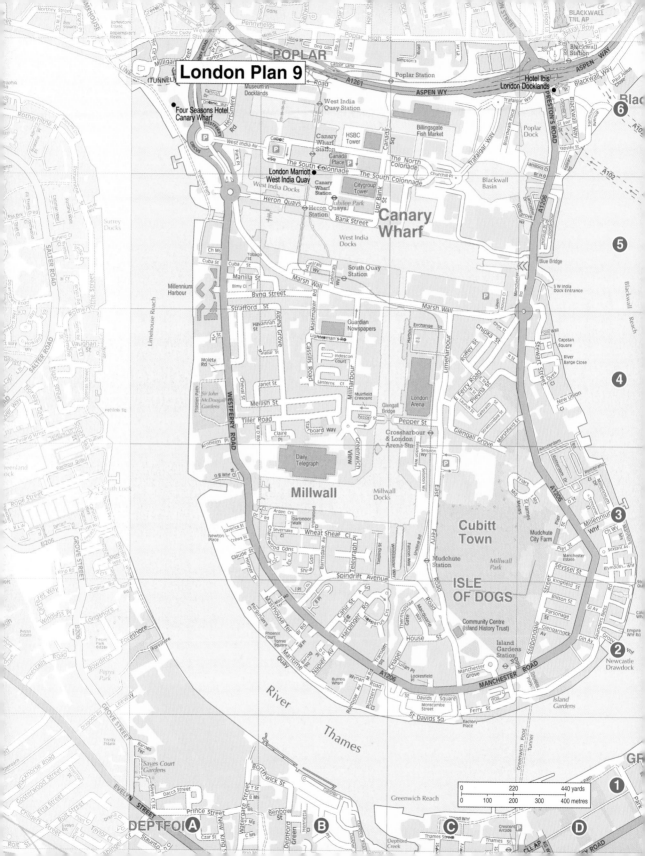

A new Thistle

It's a big statement. But there's much more to it than just words: we're transforming what we do, and how we do it.

We believe experience is everything. A relaxing, comfortable ambience in which you can work or rest at your pace. Personal service delivered in a warm, efficient, straightforward manner – every time. And to bring it to life, we're investing over £100m in the next two years. Stay relaxed. Leave refreshed.

With nationwide coverage, including 9 locations in central London, the name may be same, but we're showing the world a very different face.

To find out more about the new Thistle experience call **0871 376 9000** or visit **www.thistle.com**

Discover the new Thistle in London:

Thistle Bloomsbury

Thistle Bloomsbury Park

Thistle City Barbican

Thistle Euston

Thistle Kensington Gardens

Thistle Piccadilly

Thistle Westminster

The Royal Trafalgar, by Thistle

Whites, by Thistle

thistle

The way it should be

LONDON

LONDON

Greater London Plans 1-9, pages 320-332. (Small scale maps 6 & 7 at back of guide.) Hotels are listed below in postal district order, commencing East, then North, South and West, with a brief indication of the area covered. Detailed plans 2-9 show the locations of AA-appointed hotels within the Central London postal districts. If you do not know the postal district of the hotel you want, please refer to the index preceding the street plans for the entry and map pages. The plan reference for each AA-appointed hotel also appears within its directory entry.

E1 STEPNEY AND EAST OF THE TOWER OF LONDON

See also LONDON plan 1 G4

The Tower

★★★★ 75% HOTEL PLAN 6 D3

☎ 0870 333 9106 🗎 0870 333 9206
St Katherine's Way E1W 1LD
e-mail: tower@guoman.com
dir: Follow signs for Tower Bridge, turn left into St. Katharine's Way. Approach car park by barrier control.

This extensive modern hotel enjoys superb views over the Thames, Tower Bridge and St Katherine's Docks. Public areas include several lounges, a modern, contemporary bar and a choice of restaurants. Bedrooms are traditionally furnished and include a selection of impressive suites.

Rooms 801 (34 fmly) (90 smoking) Facilities Gym Xmas New Year Wi-fi Conf Class 350 Board 65 Thtr 500 Del from £105* Services Lift Air con Parking 80 (charged) Notes ⊗ Civ Wed 500

Crowne Plaza Hotel London - Shoreditch

★★★★ 71% HOTEL

☎ 020 7613 9800 🗎 020 7613 9811
100 Shoreditch High St E1 6JQ
e-mail: info@cplondon.com
web: www.crowneplaza.co.uk

The Crowne Plaza London - Shoreditch is located in London's fashionable east end, close to the financial district and many attractions. The hotel is contemporary in style and rooms are well appointed and tastefully decorated, air conditioning and mini bar are only two of the many amenities available. Dinner and breakfast are served in the rooftop restaurant with fantastic views of London.

Rooms 196

Express by Holiday Inn London-Limehouse

BUDGET HOTEL

☎ 020 7791 3850 🗎 020 7791 3851
469-475 The Highway E1W 3HN
e-mail: jcniclas@exhi-limehouse.co.uk
web: www.hiexpress.com/limehouse

A modern hotel ideal for families and business travellers. Fresh and uncomplicated, the spacious rooms include Sky TV, power shower and tea and coffee-making facilities. Continental buffet breakfast is included in the room rate; other meals may be taken at the nearby family pub or restaurant. See also the Hotel Groups pages.

Rooms 150 Conf Class 26 Board 25 Thtr 60

Travelodge London Liverpool Street

BUDGET HOTEL PLAN 6 C5

☎ 08719 846 190 🗎 020 7626 1105
1 Harrow Place E1 7DB
web: www.travelodge.co.uk

Travelodge offers good quality, good value, modern accommodation. Ideal for families, the spacious en suite bedrooms include remote-control TV, tea and coffee-making facilities and comfortable beds. Meals can be taken at the nearby family restaurant. See also the Hotel Groups pages.

Rooms 142 S fr £29; D fr £29

E4 CHINGFORD   Map 6 TQ39

See LONDON plan 1 G6

Ridgeway

★★ 57% SMALL HOTEL

☎ 020 8529 1964 🗎 020 8524 9130
115/117 The Ridgeway, North Chingford E4 6QU
e-mail: reception@ridgewayhotel.com
dir: M25 junct 26, Sewardstone Rd

The Ridgeway is within easy reach of the North Circular and the M25 and can cater for meetings and functions. Bedrooms vary in size and style, including a four-poster room, and public areas include a smart dining room, lounge bar and an attractive garden.

Rooms 20 (2 fmly) (4 GF) S £54; D £67-£73 (incl. bkfst)*
Facilities Wi-fi Conf Class 40 Board 20 Thtr 30 Parking 9

Express by Holiday Inn London Chingford

BUDGET HOTEL

☎ 0870 444 2789 🗎 0870 444 2790
5 Walthamstow Av, Chingford E4 8ST
e-mail: dgmchingford@expressholidayinn.co.uk
web: www.hiexpress.com/lonchingford
dir: on A406 (North Circular) at Crooked Billet rdbt, adjacent to A112 (Chingford-Walthamstow)

A modern hotel ideal for families and business travellers. Fresh and uncomplicated, the spacious rooms include Sky TV, power shower and tea and coffee-making facilities. Continental buffet breakfast is included in the room rate; other meals may be taken at the nearby family pub or restaurant. See also the Hotel Groups pages.

Rooms 102 (65 fmly) Conf Class 10 Board 16 Thtr 20

E11 SNARESBROOK

See LONDON plan 1 G5

Innkeeper's Lodge London Snaresbrook

BUDGET HOTEL

☎ 0845 112 6122 🗎 0845 112 6181
73 Hollybush Hill, Snaresbrook E11 1PE
web: www.innkeeperslodge.com/snaresbrook
dir: M11 junct 4 onto A406. Left, at rdbt take A12 (The City). Left (Wanstead). Right at lights (High Street). Continue over lights with Hollybush

Innkeeper's Lodge represents an exciting, high value concept within the budget hotel market. Comfortable bedrooms provide excellent facilities that include satellite TV and modem points. Options include family rooms, and for the corporate guest, cutting edge IT which includes Wi-fi access. A popular Carvery provides all-day food, including an extensive, complimentary continental breakfast.

Rooms 24 S £79.95; D £79.95 (incl. bkfst)

E14 CANARY WHARF & LIMEHOUSE
See also LONDON plan 1 G3

INSPECTORS' CHOICE

Four Seasons Hotel Canary Wharf
★★★★★ ◎◎ HOTEL PLAN 9 A6

☎ 020 7510 1999 📄 020 7510 1998
Westferry Circus, Canary Wharf E14 8RS
e-mail: res.canarywharf@fourseasons.com
web: www.fourseasons.com/canarywharf
dir: From A13 follow signs to Canary Wharf, Isle of Dogs and Westferry Circus. Hotel off 3rd exit of Westferry Circus rdbt

With superb views over the London skyline, this stylish modern hotel enjoys a delightful riverside location. Spacious contemporary bedrooms are particularly thoughtfully equipped. Public areas include the Italian Quadrato Bar and Restaurant, an impressive business centre and gym. Guests also have complimentary use of the impressive Holmes Place health club and spa. Welcoming staff provide exemplary levels of service and hospitality.

Rooms 142 (20 smoking) **S** £370-£2200; **D** £370-£2200* **Facilities** Spa STV FTV⌖ supervised ♨ Gym Fitness centre ♫ Xmas New Year Wi-fi **Conf** Class 120 Board 56 Thtr 200 **Services** Lift Air con **Parking** 25 (charged) **Notes** LB Civ Wed 200

London Marriott West India Quay
Marriott HOTELS & RESORTS
★★★★★ 83% ◎ HOTEL PLAN 9 B6

☎ 020 7093 1000 📄 020 7093 1001
22 Hertsmere Rd, Canary Wharf E14 4ED
web: www.londonmarriottwestindiaquay.co.uk
dir: Exit Aspen Way at Hertsmere Road. Hotel opposite, adjacent to Canary Wharf

This spectacular skyscraper with curved glass façade is located at the heart of the docklands, adjacent to Canary Wharf and overlooking the water. The hotel is modern, but not pretentiously trendy; eye-catching floral displays add warmth to the public areas. Bedrooms, many of which overlook the quay, provide every modern convenience, including broadband and air-conditioning. Curve Restaurant offers good quality cooking focusing on fresh fish dishes.

Rooms 301 (22 fmly) **Facilities** Gym Massage & facial treatments Wi-fi **Conf** Class 132 Board 27 Thtr 290 **Services** Lift Air con **Notes** ⊗ Civ Wed 290

Ibis London Docklands
ibis HOTEL
BUDGET HOTEL PLAN 9 D6

☎ 020 7517 1100 📄 020 7987 5916
1 Baffin Way E14 9PE
e-mail: H2177@accor.com
web: www.ibishotel.com
dir: from Tower Bridge follow City Airport and Royal Docks signs,exit for 'Isle of Dogs'. Hotel on 1st left opposite McDonalds

Modern, budget hotel offering comfortable accommodation in bright and practical bedrooms. Breakfast is self-service and dinner is available in the restaurant. See also the Hotel Groups pages.

Rooms 87

Travelodge London Docklands
 Travelodge
BUDGET HOTEL

☎ 08719 846 192 📄 020 7515 9178
Coriander Av, East India Dock Rd E14 2AA
web: www.travelodge.co.uk
dir: on A13 at East India Dock Rd

Travelodge offers good quality, good value, modern accommodation. Ideal for families, the spacious en suite bedrooms include remote-control TV, tea and coffee-making facilities and comfortable beds. Meals can be taken at the nearby family restaurant. See also the Hotel Groups pages.

Rooms 232 **S** fr £29; **D** fr £29

E15 STRATFORD
See LONDON plan 1 G4

Express by Holiday Inn London - Stratford
Express by Holiday Inn
BUDGET HOTEL

☎ 0870 240 5708 📄 020 8536 8036
196 High St, Stratford E15 2PD
e-mail: reservations@express-holidayinn.com
web: www.hiexpress.com/londonstratfrd

A modern hotel ideal for families and business travellers. Fresh and uncomplicated, the spacious rooms include Sky TV, power shower and tea and coffee-making facilities. Continental buffet breakfast is included in the room rate; other meals may be taken at the nearby family pub or restaurant. See also the Hotel Groups pages.

Rooms 114 (62 fmly) **Conf** Class 16 Board 24 Thtr 35

Ibis London Stratford
 ibis HOTEL
BUDGET HOTEL

☎ 020 8536 3700 📄 020 8519 5161
1A Romford Rd, Stratford E15 4LJ
e-mail: h3099@accor.com
web: www.ibishotel.com

Modern, budget hotel offering comfortable accommodation in bright and practical bedrooms. Breakfast is self-service and dinner is available in the restaurant. See also the Hotel Groups pages.

Rooms 108 (15 fmly) **S** £62-£105; **D** £62-£105*

E16 SILVERTOWN

See LONDON plan 1 H3/H4

Novotel London ExCel

★★★★ 74% HOTEL

☎ 020 7540 9700 & 0870 850 4560 🗎 020 7540 9710
7 Western Gateway, Royal Victoria Docks E16 1AA
e-mail: H3656@accor.com
web: www.novotel.com
dir: M25 junct 30. A13 towards 'City', exit at Canning
Town. Follow signs to 'ExCel West'. Hotel adjacent

This hotel is situated adjacent to the ExCel exhibition
centre and overlooks the Royal Victoria Dock. Design
throughout the hotel is contemporary and stylish. Public
rooms include a range of meeting rooms, a modern coffee
station, indoor leisure facilities and a smart bar and
restaurant, both with a terrace overlooking the dock.
Bedrooms feature modern décor, a bath and separate
shower and an extensive range of extras.

Rooms 257 (211 fmly) **Facilities** Gym Steam room
Relaxation room with massage bed Wi-fi **Conf** Class 55
Board 30 Thtr 70 **Services** Lift Air con **Parking** 80
(charged) **Notes** Civ Wed 50

Crowne Plaza-London Docklands

★★★★ 72% HOTEL

☎ 0870 990 9692 🗎 0870 990 9693
Royal Victoria Dock, Western Gateway E16 1AL
e-mail: sales@crowneplazadocklands.co.uk
web: www.crowneplaza.co.uk
dir: A1020 towards Excel. Follow signs for Excel West.
Hotel on left 400mtrs before Excel

Ideally located for the ExCel Exhibition Centre, Canary
Wharf and London City airport, this unique, contemporary
hotel overlooking Royal Victoria Dock, offers
accommodation suitable for both the leisure and
business travellers. Rooms are spacious and equipped
with all modern facilities. The hotel houses a busy bar, a
contemporary restaurant and health and fitness facilities
with an indoor pool, Jacuzzi and sauna.

Rooms 210 (12 fmly) (42 smoking) **S** £89-£285;
D £89-£285* **Facilities** STV FTV 🏊 supervised Gym
Beauty treatments Sauna Steam room Xmas New Year
Wi-fi **Conf** Class 140 Board 62 Thtr 275 Del from £260 to
£360* **Services** Lift Air con **Parking** 75 (charged)
Notes LB ⊗ Civ Wed 275

Express by Holiday Inn London Royal Docks

BUDGET HOTEL

☎ 020 7540 4040 🗎 020 7540 4050
1 Silvertown Way, Silvertown E16 1EA
e-mail: info@exhi-royaldocks.co.uk
web: www.hiexpress.com/londonroyal
dir: From A13 take A1011 towards Silvertown, City Airport
& Excel. Hotel on left

A modern hotel ideal for families and business travellers.
Fresh and uncomplicated, the spacious rooms include Sky
TV, power shower and tea and coffee-making facilities.
Continental buffet breakfast is included in the room rate;
other meals may be taken at the nearby family pub or
restaurant. See also the Hotel Groups pages.

Rooms 136 (48 fmly) **Conf** Class 30 Board 30 Thtr 80

Ibis London ExCel

BUDGET HOTEL

☎ 020 7055 2300 🗎 020 7055 2310
9 Western Gateway, Royal Victoria Docks E16 1AB
e-mail: H3655@accor-hotels.com
web: www.ibishotel.com
dir: M25 then A13 to London, City Airport, ExCel East

Modern, budget hotel offering comfortable
accommodation in bright and practical bedrooms.
Breakfast is self-service and dinner is available in the
restaurant See also the Hotel Groups pages.

Rooms 278 (64 fmly) **S** £65-£105; **D** £65-£120*

Travelodge London City Airport

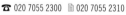

BUDGET HOTEL

☎ 08719 846 290 🗎 020 7474 2671
Hartman Rd, Silvertown E16 2BZ
web: www.travelodge.co.uk
dir: Follow signs for London City Airport. Travelodge at
airport entrance at junct of A1011 & A112

Travelodge offers good quality, good value, modern
accommodation. Ideal for families, the spacious en suite
bedrooms include remote-control TV, tea and coffee-
making facilities and comfortable beds. Meals can be
taken at the nearby family restaurant. See also the Hotel
Groups pages.

Rooms 142 **S** fr £29; **D** fr £29

EC1 CITY OF LONDON

Zetter

★★★★ 🅰 HOTEL PLAN 3 F4

☎ 020 7324 4422 & 7324 4444 🗎 020 7324 4445
St John's Square, 86-88 Clerkenwell Rd EC1M 5RJ
e-mail: info@thezetter.com
dir: From West A401, Clerkenwell Rd A5201. Hotel
200mtrs on left

Rooms 59 (13 smoking) **S** £188-£399.50;
D £188-£399.50* **Facilities** STV Wi-fi **Conf** Class 28
Board 32 Thtr 50 Del from £350 to £550* **Services** Lift
Air con **Parking** 1 (charged) **Notes** LB ⊗

Malmaison Charterhouse Square

★★★ 86% ⊛⊛ HOTEL PLAN 3 G4

☎ 020 7012 3700 🗎 020 7012 3702
18-21 Charterhouse Square, Clerkenwell EC1M 6AH
e-mail: london@malmaison.com
web: www.malmaison.com
dir: Exit Barbican Station turn left, take 1st left. Hotel on
far left corner of Charterhouse Square

Situated in a leafy and peaceful square, Malmaison
Charterhouse maintains the same focus on quality
service and food as the other hotels in the group. The
bedrooms, stylishly decorated in calming tones, have all
the expected facilities including power showers, CD
players and free internet access. The brasserie and bar at
the hotel's centre has a buzzing atmosphere and
traditional French cuisine.

Rooms 97 (5 GF) **S** £125-£250; **D** £125-£475*
Facilities STV Gym Wi-fi **Conf** Board 16 Thtr 30
Services Lift Air con **Notes** LB

Thistle City Barbican

thistle

★★★ 75% HOTEL PLAN 3 G5

☎ 0870 333 9101 🗎 0870 333 9201
Central St, Clerkenwell EC1V 8DS
e-mail: citybarbican@thistle.co.uk
web: www.thistlehotels.com/citybarbican
dir: From Kings Cross E, follow Pentonville Rd, right into
Goswell Rd. At lights left into Lever St. Hotel at junct of
Lever St & Central St

Situated on the edge of the City, this modern hotel offers
a complimentary shuttle bus to Barbican, Liverpool Street
and Moorgate tube stations at peak times. Bedrooms are
well equipped and include some smart executive and
superior rooms; public areas include a bar, a coffee shop
and restaurant along with a smart Otium leisure club.

Rooms 463 (166 annexe) (20 fmly) **Facilities** Spa 🏊
supervised Gym Wi-fi **Conf** Class 80 Board 60 Thtr 200
Services Lift **Parking** 12 (charged) **Notes** LB ⊗

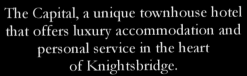

SW3 CHELSEA, BROMPTON continued

INSPECTORS' CHOICE

The Levin

★★★★ TOWN HOUSE HOTEL PLAN 4 F4

☎ 020 7589 6286 📠 020 7823 7826
28 Basil St, Knightsbridge SW3 1AS
e-mail: reservations@thelevin.co.uk
web: www.thelevinhotel.co.uk
dir: 20yds from Harrods

This sophisticated town house is the sister property to the adjacent Capital Hotel and enjoys a prime location on the doorstep of Knightsbridge's stylish department and designer stores. Bedrooms and en suites offer stylish elegance alongside a host of up-to-date modern comforts; extra touches include champagne bars and state-of-the-art audio-visual systems. Guests can enjoy all-day dining in the stylish, popular, lower ground floor Metro Restaurant.

Rooms 12 **Facilities** STV Wi-fi **Conf** Board 24 Thtr 30 **Services** Lift Air con **Parking** 3 (charged) **Notes** ⊗ No children 12yrs

The Beaufort

★★★★ 79% TOWN HOUSE HOTEL PLAN 4 F3

☎ 020 7584 5252 📠 020 7589 2834
33 Beaufort Gardens SW3 1PP
e-mail: reservations@thebeaufort.co.uk
web: www.thebeaufort.co.uk
dir: 100yds past Harrods on left of Brompton Rd

This friendly, attractive town house enjoys a peaceful location in a tree-lined cul-de-sac just a few minutes' walk from Knightsbridge. Air-conditioned bedrooms are thoughtfully equipped with chocolates, fruit, fresh flowers, videos, CD players, free internet and movie channel access. Guests are offered complimentary drinks

and afternoon tea, served in the attractive drawing room. A good continental breakfast is served in guests' rooms.

Rooms 29 (3 GF) **Facilities** STV Wi-fi **Conf** Thtr 10 **Services** Lift Air con **Notes** ⊗

Parkes

★★★★ 78% TOWN HOUSE HOTEL PLAN 4 E4

☎ 020 7581 9944 📠 020 7581 1999
41 Beaufort Gardens, Knightsbridge SW3 1PW
e-mail: reception@parkeshotel.com
web: www.parkeshotel.com
dir: off Brompton Rd, 100yds from Harrods

This sophisticated and friendly hotel is located in a tree-lined square in the heart of fashionable Knightsbridge. Stylish bedrooms and spacious suites with kitchens are beautifully appointed and equipped with every conceivable extra including UK/US modems and sockets, wireless ADSL and mini-bars. Whilst there is no hotel restaurant, a wide range of dishes from local eateries can be delivered to your room.

Rooms 33 (16 fmly) (4 GF) **Facilities** Arrangement with nearby gym **Conf** Board 12 **Services** Lift Air con **Notes** ⊗

SW5 EARL'S COURT

London Marriott Kensington

★★★★ 82% HOTEL PLAN 4 B3

Marriott
HOTELS & RESORTS

☎ 020 7973 1000 📠 020 7370 1685
Cromwell Rd SW5 0TH
e-mail: kensington.marriott@marriotthotels.com
web: www.londonmarriottkensington.co.uk
dir: On A4, opposite Cromwell Rd Hospital

This stylish contemporary hotel features a stunning glass exterior and a seven-storey atrium lobby. Fully air conditioned throughout, the hotel has elegant design

combined with a great range of facilities, including indoor leisure, a range of conference rooms and parking. Smart bedrooms offer a host of extras including the very latest communications technology.

Rooms 216 (39 fmly) **S** £135-£285; **D** £135-£285* **Facilities** STV FTV ⊙ Gym Wi-fi **Conf** Class 100 Board 60 Thtr 200 **Services** Lift Air con **Parking** 20 (charged) **Notes** ⊗ Civ Wed 60

Cranley

★★★★ 80% TOWN HOUSE HOTEL PLAN 4 C2

☎ 020 7373 0123 📠 020 7373 9497
10 Bina Gardens, South Kensington SW5 0LA
e-mail: info@thecranley.com
web: www.steinhotels.com/cranley
dir: Gloucester Rd towards Old Brompton Rd. 3rd right after station into Hereford Sq, then 3rd left into Bina Gardens

This period building, in the heart of South Kensington, is well located for fashionable shops and restaurants, with an NCP nearby. Small elegant public areas are furnished with quality pieces of artwork. Individually styled bedrooms are very well designed; all rooms have modern facilities with safes, internet access and mini bars; many rooms boast feature beds.

Rooms 39 (5 GF) **Facilities** Wi-fi **Services** Lift Air con **Notes** ⊗

The Rockwell

★★★★ 74% HOTEL PLAN 4 B3

☎ 020 7244 2000 📠 020 7244 2001
181-183 Cromwell Rd SW5 0SF
e-mail: enquiries@therockwell.com
dir: From central London W on A4 (Cromwell Rd), hotel on left after Marloes Rd

This property enjoys a convenient location, just a few minutes' walk from both Gloucester Road and Earls Court tube stations. Stylish bedrooms are smartly appointed and benefit from a host of extra facilities such as safes, mini bars and broadband access. A small bar and restaurant open onto a delightful garden terrace offering alfresco dining in warmer months.

Rooms 40 (4 fmly) (2 GF) **S** £120-£130; **D** £160-£200 **Facilities** FTV Wi-fi **Conf** Board 10 Del from £180 to £220 **Services** Lift Air con **Notes** LB ⊗

Twenty Nevern Square

★★★★ 71% TOWN HOUSE HOTEL PLAN 4 A2

☎ 020 7565 9555 & 7370 4934 📠 020 7565 9444
20 Nevern Square, Earls Court SW5 9PD
e-mail: hotel@twentynevernsquare.co.uk
web: www.twentynevernsquare.co.uk
dir: from station take Warwick Rd exit, right, 2nd right
into Nevern Sq. Hotel 30yds on right

This smart boutique style town house hotel is discreetly
located in Nevern Square and is ideally situated for both
Earls Court and Olympia. The stylish bedrooms, which
vary in shape and size, are appointed to a high standard
and are well equipped. Public areas include a delightful
lounge and Café Twenty where breakfast and light meals
are served.

Rooms 20 (3 GF) **Facilities** Wi-fi **Services** Lift **Parking** 4
(charged) **Notes** ⊗

K + K Hotel George

★★★ 75% HOTEL PLAN 4 A2

☎ 020 7598 8700 & 7598 8707 📠 020 7370 2285
1-15 Templeton Place, Earl's Court SW5 9NB
e-mail: hotelgeorge@kkhotels.co.uk
web: www.kkhotels.com/george
dir: A3220 Earls Court Rd, right onto Trebovir Rd, right
onto Templeton Place

This smart hotel enjoys a central location, just a few
minutes' walk from Earls Court and with easy access to
London's central attractions. Smart public areas include
a bar/bistro, an executive lounge and meeting facilities
and a stylish restaurant that overlooks the attractive rear
garden. Bedrooms are particularly well equipped with a
host of useful extras including free, high-speed internet
access.

Rooms 154 (38 fmly) (8 GF) (28 smoking) **S** £205.62;
D £235 (incl. bkfst)* **Facilities** STV FTV Gym Wellness
area with exercise machines Sauna Wi-fi **Conf** Class 14
Board 18 Thtr 35 **Services** Lift Air con **Parking** 20
(charged) **Notes** LB

Best Western Burns Hotel

★★★ 70% METRO HOTEL PLAN 4 B2

☎ 020 7373 3151 📠 020 7370 4090
18-26 Barkston Gardens, Kensington SW5 0EN
e-mail: burnshotel@vienna-group.co.uk
dir: Off A4, right to Earls Court Rd (A3220), 2nd left.
Hotel in Barkston Gardens, 2nd left past Earls Court
underground station.

This friendly Victorian hotel overlooks a leafy garden in a
quiet residential area not far from the Earls Court
exhibition centre and tube station. Bedrooms are
attractively appointed, with modern facilities; beds have
duvets. Public areas, although not extensive, are stylish.

Rooms 105 (10 fmly) **Services** Lift **Notes** ⊗

N H Kensington

🅿 PLAN 4 A3

☎ 020 7244 1441 📠 020 7244 1442
202/222 Cromwell Rd SW5 0SW
e-mail: nhkensington@nh-hotels.com
dir: M4 junct 4b, A4, Earls Court

Currently the rating for this establishment is not confirmed.
This may be due to a change of ownership or because it has
only recently joined the AA rating scheme. For further
details please see the AA website: www.theAA.com

Rooms 121 (12 fmly) (3 GF) **Facilities** Wi-fi
Conf Board 17 Thtr 25 **Services** Lift Air con **Parking** 18
(charged) **Notes** LB ⊗

SW6 FULHAM
See also LONDON plan 1 D2/3 & E3

Millennium & Copthorne Hotels at Chelsea FC

★★★★ 75% HOTEL

☎ 020 7565 1400 📠 020 7565 1450
Stamford Bridge, Fulham Rd SW6 1HS
e-mail: reservations@chelseafc.com
web: www.millenniumhotels.co.uk
dir: 4 mins walk from Fulham Broadway tube station

A unique destination in a fashionable area of the city.
Situated at Chelsea's famous Stamford Bridge football
club, and having undergone a multi-million pound refit,
the accommodation offered here is very up-to-the-minute.
Bedroom facilities include flat-screen LCD TVs, video on
demand, broadband, Wi-fi and good sized desk space;
larger Club rooms have additional features. For eating
there's a brasserie, the Bridge Bar and sports bar, and
for corporate guests a flexible arrangement of meeting
and event rooms is available.

Rooms 275 (64 fmly) **S** £79-£169; **D** £89-£179
Facilities Spa STV FTV ⓣ Gym Health club Treatments ♫
Xmas New Year Wi-fi **Conf** Class 600 Board 30 Thtr 950
Del from £200 to £300 **Services** Lift Air con **Parking** 180
(charged) **Notes** LB ⊗ Civ Wed 50

Jurys Inn Chelsea

★★★ 74% HOTEL

☎ 020 7411 2200 📠 020 7411 2444
Imperial Rd, Imperial Wharf SW6 2GA
e-mail: info@jurysinns.com
web: www.jurysinns.com
dir: From A3 onto A219, after 1.5m turn right onto A308.
Turn right & right again in 1.5m

This modern hotel is located in Chelsea close to the
Wharf. Bedrooms provide good guest comfort and in-room
facilities are ideal for both leisure and business markets.
Public areas include a number of meeting rooms, a
restaurant and a popular bar.

Rooms 172 (172 fmly) **S** £109-£150; **D** £109-£150*
Facilities New Year Wi-fi **Conf** Board 10 Thtr 15
Services Lift Air con **Notes** ⊗ Closed 24-26 Dec

Ibis London Earls Court

★★★ 71% HOTEL PLAN 4 A1

☎ 020 7610 0880 📠 020 7381 0215
47 Lillie Rd SW6 1UD
e-mail: h5623@accor.com
web: www.ibishotel.com
dir: From Hammersmith flyover towards London, keep in
right lane, right at Kings pub on Talgarth Rd to join North
End Rd. At mini-rdbt turn right. Hotel on left

Situated opposite the Earls Court Exhibition Centre, this
large, modern hotel is popular with business and leisure
guests. Bedrooms are comfortable and well equipped.
There is a café bar open all day and a restaurant that
serves evening meals. There are also extensive conference
facilities and an underground car park.

Rooms 504 (20 fmly) **Facilities** Health club & gym nearby
Wi-fi **Conf** Class 750 Board 25 Thtr 1200 **Services** Lift
Parking 130

SW7 SOUTH KENSINGTON

INSPECTORS' CHOICE

Baglioni
★★★★★ ◉◉ HOTEL PLAN 4 C4

☎ 020 7368 5700 🖩 020 7368 5701
60 Hyde Park Gate, Kensington Rd, Kensington SW7 5BB
e-mail: info@baglionihotellondon.com
web: www.baglionihotellondon.com
dir: on corner of Palace Gate Road

Located in the heart of Kensington and overlooking Hyde Park, this small hotel buzzes with Italian style and chic. Bedrooms, predominantly suites, are generously sized, with bold dark colours and feature espresso machines, interactive plasma TV screens and a host of other excellent touches. Service is both professional and friendly, with personal butlers for the bedrooms. Public areas include the main open-plan space with bar, lounge and award-winning Brunello restaurant, all merging together with great elan; there is a small health club and a fashionable private club bar downstairs.

Rooms 67 (16 fmly) **S** £385; **Facilities** Spa STV FTV Gym Xmas New Year Wi-fi **Conf** Class 35 Board 32 Thtr 60 **Services** Lift Air con **Notes** LB Civ Wed 60

The Bentley
★★★★★ 87% ◉◉ HOTEL PLAN 4 C2

☎ 020 7244 5555 🖩 020 7244 5566
27-33 Harrington Gardens SW7 4JX
e-mail: info@thebentley-hotel.com
web: www.thebentley-hotel.com
dir: S of A4 into Knightsbridge at junct with Gloucester Rd, right, 2nd right turn, hotel on left just after mini-rdbt

This hotel, discreetly located in the heart of Kensington, features lavish opulence throughout the public areas.

Spacious air-conditioned bedrooms are equally luxurious, and the marble clad bathrooms have jacuzzi baths and walk-in showers. Public areas include the Peridot where breakfast and lunch are served, and the cocktail bar, Malachite. The fine dining restaurant, 1880, which is open for dinner, provides excellent contemporary cuisine and highly professional service.

Rooms 64 **Facilities** Spa Gym Traditional Turkish Hamam ♬ Xmas New Year Wi-fi **Conf** Class 60 Board 50 Thtr 70 **Services** Lift Air con **Notes** Civ Wed 80

Jurys Kensington Hotel
★★★★ 78% HOTEL PLAN 4 D2

☎ 020 7589 6300 🖩 020 7581 1492
109-113 Queensgate, South Kensington SW7 5LR
e-mail: kensington@jurysdoyle.com
web: www.jurysdoyle.com
dir: From A4 take Cromwell Rd, turn right at V&A Museum onto Queensgate, hotel at end on left

This beautiful building is in an excellent location for visitors to London. Smartly appointed public areas include an open-plan lobby/bar, Copplestones restaurant with adjoining library lounge and the lively Kavanagh's bar. Bedrooms vary in size and are well equipped.

Rooms 174 (174 annexe) (10 fmly) **Facilities** Local health club at discounted rate ♬ Xmas Child facilities **Conf** Class 45 Board 40 Thtr 90 **Services** Lift Air con **Notes** ⊗

Millennium Gloucester Hotel London Kensington
★★★★ 76% HOTEL PLAN 4 C2

☎ 020 7373 6030 🖩 020 7373 0409
4-18 Harrington Gardens SW7 4LH
e-mail: reservations.gloucester@millenniumhotels.co.uk
web: www.millenniumhotels.co.uk
dir: opposite Gloucester Rd underground station

This spacious, stylish hotel is centrally located, close to The Victoria & Albert Museum and Gloucester Road tube station. Air-conditioned bedrooms are furnished in a variety of contemporary styles and Clubrooms benefit from a dedicated club lounge with complimentary breakfast and snacks. A wide range of eating options includes Singaporean and Mediterranean cuisine.

Rooms 610 (6 fmly) (66 smoking) **Facilities** STV Gym Wi-fi **Conf** Class 300 Board 40 Thtr 500 **Services** Lift Air con **Parking** 110 (charged) **Notes** ⊗ Civ Wed 500

Harrington Hall
★★★★ 73% HOTEL PLAN 4 C2

☎ 020 7396 9696 🖩 020 7396 9090
5-25 Harrington Gardens SW7 4JW
e-mail: book.london@nh-hotels.com
web: www.nh-hotels.com
dir: 2 mins walk from Gloucester Road underground station

This splendid period property is centrally located just a stone's throw from Gloucester Road tube station and is convenient for visiting the museums and shopping in Knightsbridge. Spacious bedrooms are smartly appointed and boast a host of extra touches. The public areas include extensive meeting facilities, a lounge bar and a restaurant.

Rooms 200 **Facilities** Gym Xmas New Year Wi-fi **Conf** Class 100 Board 50 Thtr 240 **Services** Lift Air con **Notes** ⊗ Civ Wed 200

Millennium Bailey's Hotel London Kensington
★★★★ 73% HOTEL PLAN 4 C3

☎ 020 7373 6000 🖩 020 7370 3760
140 Gloucester Rd SW7 4QH
e-mail: reservations.baileys@millenniumhotels.co.uk
web: www.millenniumhotels.co.uk
dir: A4, turn right at Cromwell Hospital into Knaresborough Place, follow to Courtfield Rd to corner of Gloucester Rd, hotel opposite underground station

This elegant hotel has a townhouse feel to it and enjoys a prime location opposite Gloucester Road tube station. Air-conditioned bedrooms are smartly appointed and thoughtfully equipped, particularly the club rooms which benefit from DVD players. Public areas include a stylish contemporary restaurant and bar. Guests may also use the facilities at the adjacent, larger sister hotel.

Rooms 211 (20 smoking) **Facilities** STV Gym Wi-fi **Conf** Class 12 Board 12 Thtr 12 **Services** Lift Air con **Parking** 110 (charged) **Notes** ⊗

Holiday Inn London-Kensington Forum

★★★★ 71% HOTEL PLAN 4 C3

☎ 0870 400 9100 🖩 020 7373 1448
97 Cromwell Rd SW7 4DN
e-mail: hikensingtonforum@ihg.com
web: www.holidayinn.co.uk
dir: from S Circular onto N Circular at Chiswick Flyover. Onto A4 Cromwell Rd as far as Gloucester Rd

This large hotel is easily accessed and provides a good location for central London, Knightsbridge and Hyde Park. There are a range of bedroom types, many with panoramic views of the city. The hotel has a pub as well as a restaurant and both offer good dining choices. Covered parking is available.

Rooms 906 (26 fmly) (106 smoking) **S** £115-£305; **D** £115-£305* **Facilities** STV FTV Gym Xmas New Year Wi-fi **Conf** Class 150 Board 35 Thtr 300 Del from £135 to £230* **Services** Lift Air con **Parking** 76 (charged) **Notes** LB ⊗

Radisson Edwardian Vanderbilt

★★★★ 🅰 HOTEL PLAN 4 C3

☎ 020 7761 9000 📄 020 7761 9001
68-86 Cromwell Rd SW7 5BT
e-mail: resvand@radisson.com
dir: A4 into central London on Cromwell Rd. Hotel on left at junct of Gloucester Rd & Cromwell Rd

Rooms 215 (18 fmly) (28 GF) **Facilities** Fitness room Wi-fi **Conf** Class 56 Board 40 Thtr 100 **Services** Lift Air con **Notes** ⊗ No children 16 yrs

Holiday Inn London-Kensington

★★★★ 🅰 HOTEL PLAN 4 C3

☎ 020 7373 2222 📄 020 7373 0559
100 Cromwell Rd SW7 4ER
web: www.holidayinn.co.uk

Rooms 162

Best Western The Cromwell

★★★ 80% METRO HOTEL PLAN 4 C2

☎ 020 7244 1720 📄 020 7373 3706
110-112 Cromwell Rd, Kensington SW7 4ES
e-mail: reception@thecromwell.com
dir: M4/A4 towards London, pass Cromwell Hospital, hotel in 0.5m

Just minutes away from the tube station and within easy access of all main tourist attractions, this refurbished hotel offers comfortable, modern accommodation. Fully air conditioned and with free Wi-fi this is an ideal location for both leisure and business guests. Amenities include an on-site meeting room, and secure parking is available nearby.

Rooms 57 (3 fmly) (7 GF) **Facilities** Wi-fi **Conf** Board 8 **Services** Lift Air con **Notes** ⊗

SW10 WEST BROMPTON
See LONDON plan 1 D/E3

Wyndham Grand London Chelsea Harbour

★★★★★ 86% ⊛ HOTEL

☎ 020 7823 3000 📄 020 7351 6525
Chelsea Harbour SW10 0XG
e-mail: wyndhamlondon@wyndham.com
web: www.wyndham.com
dir: A4 to Earls Court Rd S towards river. Right into Kings Rd, left down Lots Rd. Chelsea Harbour in front

Against the picturesque backdrop of Chelsea Harbour's small marina, this modern hotel offers spacious, comfortable accommodation. All rooms are suites, which are superbly equipped; many enjoy splendid views of the marina. In addition, there are also several luxurious penthouse suites. Public areas include a modern bar and restaurant, excellent leisure facilities and extensive meeting and function rooms.

Rooms 160 (39 fmly) (46 smoking) **Facilities** STV ⊛ Gym ♫ Xmas New Year Wi-fi Child facilities **Conf** Class 120 Board 50 Thtr 280 **Services** Lift Air con **Parking** 7 (charged) **Notes** Civ Wed 200

SW11 BATTERSEA
See LONDON plan 1 E3

Travelodge London Battersea

BUDGET HOTEL

☎ 08719 846189 📄 020 7978 5898
200 York Rd, Battersea SW11 3SA
web: www.travelodge.co.uk
dir: from Wandsworth Bridge southern rdbt, take A3205 (York Rd) towards Battersea. 0.5m on left

Travelodge offers good quality, good value, modern accommodation. Ideal for families, the spacious en suite bedrooms include remote-control TV, tea and coffee-making facilities and comfortable beds. Meals can be taken at the nearby family restaurant. See also the Hotel Groups pages.

Rooms 87 **S** fr £29; **D** fr £29

SW15 PUTNEY
See LONDON plan 1 D2/3

Best Western Lodge

★★★ 77% METRO HOTEL

☎ 020 8874 1598 📄 020 8874 0910
52 -54 Upper Richmond Rd, Putney SW15 2RN
e-mail: res@thelodgehotellondon.com
dir: M25 junct 10/A3 towards central London. A219 to Putney, right to Upper Richmond, left at lights after 0.5m

This friendly hotel is conveniently located for East Putney tube station. Public areas include a bar/lounge with satellite TV and conference and banqueting facilities. A buffet breakfast is served in the garden conservatory. Thoughtfully equipped, comfortable bedrooms include a selection of executive rooms and suites. Parking for residents is an asset.

Rooms 64 (12 fmly) (15 GF) (12 smoking) **S** £79-£160; **D** £79-£180* **Facilities** STV FTV Wi-fi **Conf** Class 40 Board 30 Thtr 90 Del from £150 to £175* **Parking** 35 **Notes** LB Civ Wed 100

SW19 WIMBLEDON
See LONDON plan 1 D2

Cannizaro House

★★★★ 77% ⊛⊛ COUNTRY HOUSE HOTEL

☎ 020 8879 1464 📄 020 8879 7338
West Side, Wimbledon Common SW19 4UE
e-mail: info@cannizarohouse.com
dir: from A3 follow A219 signed Wimbledon into Parkside, right onto Cannizaro Rd, sharp right onto Westside Common

This unique, elegant 18th-century house has a long tradition of hosting the rich and famous of London society. A few miles from the city centre, the landscaped grounds provide a peaceful escape and a country-house ambience; fine art, murals and stunning fireplaces feature throughout. Spacious bedrooms are individually furnished and equipped to a high standard.

Rooms 46 (10 fmly) (5 GF) **D** £155-£595 (incl. bkfst)* **Facilities** STV ⚘ Xmas New Year Wi-fi **Conf** Class 50 Board 40 Thtr 120 Del from £199 to £350* **Services** Lift **Parking** 95 **Notes** LB Civ Wed 100

SW19 WIMBLEDON continued

Express by Holiday Inn London Wimbledon-South

BUDGET HOTEL

☎ 020 8545 7300 📄 020 8545 7301
Miller's Meadhouse, 200 High St, Colliers Wood SW19 2BH
e-mail: info@exhiwimbledon.co.uk
web: www.hiexpress.com/wimbledonso
dir: M25/A3 signed central London, then A238, past Wimbledon for 3.2m. Hotel on left opposite large office block

A modern hotel ideal for families and business travellers. Fresh and uncomplicated, the spacious rooms include Sky TV, power shower and tea and coffee-making facilities. Continental buffet breakfast is included in the room rate; other meals may be taken at the nearby family pub or restaurant. See also the Hotel Groups pages.

Rooms 83 (60 fmly) **Conf** Class 16 Board 22 Thtr 40

W1 WEST END

INSPECTORS' CHOICE

Claridge's
★★★★★ ⑭⑭⑭
HOTEL PLAN 2 H2

MAYBOURNE
HOTEL
GROUP

☎ 020 7629 8860 📄 020 7499 2210
Brook St W1A 2JQ
e-mail: info@claridges.co.uk
dir: 1st turn after Green Park underground station to Berkeley Sq & 4th exit into Davies St. 3rd right into Brook St

Once renowned as the resort of kings and princes, Claridge's today continues to set the standards by which other hotels are judged. The sumptuous, air-conditioned bedrooms are elegantly themed to reflect the Victorian or art deco architecture of the building. Gordon Ramsay at Claridge's has fast become one of London's most popular dining venues, while the stylish cocktail bar is proving to be equally well supported by residents and non-residents alike. Service throughout is punctilious and thoroughly professional.

Rooms 203 (144 fmly) **S** £249-£490; **D** £279-£5700*
Facilities Spa STV Gym Beauty & health treatments Use of sister hotel's swimming pool ♫ Xmas Wi-fi **Conf** Class 130 Board 60 Thtr 250 **Services** Lift Air con **Notes** LB ⊗ Civ Wed 200

INSPECTORS' CHOICE

The Dorchester
★★★★★ ⑭⑭⑭ HOTEL PLAN 4 G6

☎ 020 7629 8888 📄 020 7629 8080
Park Ln W1A 2HJ
e-mail: info@thedorchester.com
dir: halfway along Park Ln between Hyde Park Corner & Marble Arch

One of London's finest, The Dorchester remains one of the best-loved hotels in the country and always delivers. The spacious bedrooms and suites are beautifully appointed and feature fabulous marble bathrooms. Leading off from the foyer, The Promenade is the perfect setting for afternoon tea or drinks. In the evenings guests can relax to the sound of live jazz in the bar, and enjoy a cocktail or a meal in the Grill. Further dining options include the sophisticated Chinese restaurant, China Tang.

Rooms 250 **S** £275-£480; **D** £430-£625*
Facilities Spa STV FTV Gym Steam rooms ♫ Xmas New Year Wi-fi **Conf** Class 300 Board 42 Thtr 500 **Services** Lift Air con **Notes** LB ⊗ Civ Wed 500

INSPECTORS' CHOICE

The Ritz London
★★★★★ ⑭⑭ HOTEL PLAN 5 A6

☎ 020 7493 8181 📄 020 7493 2687
150 Piccadilly W1J 9BR
e-mail: enquire@theritzlondon.com
web: www.theritzlondon.com
dir: from Hyde Park Corner E on Piccadilly. Hotel on right after Green Park

This renowned, stylish hotel offers guests the ultimate in sophistication whilst still managing to retain all of its former historical glory. Bedrooms and suites are exquisitely furnished in Louis XVI style, with fine

---

marble bathrooms and every imaginable comfort. Elegant reception rooms include the Palm Court with its legendary afternoon teas, the beautiful fashionable Rivoli Bar and the sumptuous Ritz Restaurant, complete with gold chandeliers and extraordinary trompe-l'oeil decoration.

Rooms 137 (44 fmly) (27 smoking) **S** £411.25; **D** £528.75-£2115* **Facilities** STV Gym Treatment room Hairdressing Fitness centre The Ritz Club ♫ Xmas New Year **Conf** Class 40 Board 30 Thtr 60 **Services** Lift Air con **Parking** 10 (charged) **Notes** LB ⊗ Civ Wed 60

INSPECTORS' CHOICE

Athenaeum Hotel & Apartments
★★★★★ ⑭ HOTEL PLAN 4 H5

☎ 020 7499 3464 📄 020 7493 1860
116 Piccadilly W1J 7BJ
e-mail: info@athenaeumhotel.com
web: www.athenaeumhotel.com
dir: on Piccadilly, overlooking Green Park

With a discreet address in Mayfair, this well-loved hotel offers bedrooms appointed to the highest standard; several boast views over Green Park. The delightful bar has an excellent stock of whiskies which complements the stunning Garden Lounge and stylish restaurant. A row of Edwardian townhouses adjacent to the hotel offers a range of spacious and well-appointed apartments. There is an extensive range of beauty treatments available along with conference and meeting facilities.

Rooms 157 **D** fr £295 **Facilities** STV FTV Gym Steam rooms Sauna Hairdressing salon Xmas New Year Wi-fi **Conf** Class 35 Board 36 Thtr 55 **Services** Lift Air con **Notes** LB Civ Wed 80

Connaught

MAYBOURNE HOTEL GROUP

★★★★★ HOTEL PLAN 2 G1

☎ 020 7499 7070 🖨 020 7495 3262
Carlos Place W1K 2AL
e-mail: info@the-connaught.co.uk
dir: between Grosvenor Sq and Berkeley Sq in Mayfair

Following a multi-million pound restoration The Connaught has been brought well and truly into the 21st century whilst preserving the authentic elegance so beloved of its guests. Discreetly located in the heart of Mayfair, this hotel offers intuitive and personal service in intimate surroundings where every guest is pampered; butlers and valets respond at the touch of a button and nothing is too much trouble. 2008 sees many changes to the eating options at the hotel and also the arrival of a new head chef, Hèléne Darroze who comes from the Landes region of France. Unfortunately at the time of going to press we had not been able to assess the new cuisine. Please see the AA website for up-to-date information. www.theAA.com

Rooms 123 (17 smoking) **Facilities** STV FTV Gym Fitness studio Health club facilities at sister hotels Wi-fi **Conf** Board 18 **Services** Lift Air con **Notes** ⊗ Civ Wed 20

The Langham, London

★★★★★ 86% ⊛⊛⊛ HOTEL PLAN 2 H4

☎ 020 7636 1000 🖨 020 7323 2340
Portland Place W1B 1JA
e-mail: lon.info@langhamhotels.com
dir: N of Regent St, left opposite All Soul's Church

Originally opened in 1865, this elegant hotel enjoys a central location ideal for both theatreland and principal shopping areas. Bedrooms offer a choice of styles from traditional through to modern; all are comfortably appointed with a full range of amenities. Public areas include the elegant Palm Court ideal for afternoon tea, Memories restaurant and an extensive health club complete with a 16-metre pool.

Rooms 382 (5 fmly) **S** £210-£4876; **D** £210-£4876*
Facilities STV ⊛ Gym Health club and spa facilities ♫ Xmas Wi-fi **Conf** Class 380 Board 260 Thtr 584 **Services** Lift Air con **Notes** ⊗ Civ Wed 280

Brown's

★★★★★ 86% ⊛⊛ HOTEL PLAN 3 A1

☎ 020 7493 6020 🖨 020 7493 9381
Albemarle St, Mayfair W1S 4BP
e-mail: reservations.browns@roccofortecollection.com
web: www.roccofortecollection.com
dir: a short walk from Green Park, Bond St & Piccadilly

Brown's is a London landmark that retains much charm in a successful balance of traditional and contemporary. Bedrooms are luxurious, furnished to a high standard and come with all the modern comforts expected of such a grand Mayfair hotel. The elegant restaurant (the oldest hotel restaurant in London) serves a traditional selection of popular dishes; the lounges prove popular venues for afternoon tea.

Rooms 117 (12 smoking) **S** £240-£3200; **D** £240-£3200*
Facilities Spa STV Gym ♫ Xmas New Year Wi-fi
Conf Class 30 Board 30 Thtr 70 **Services** Lift Air con
Notes LB ⊗ Civ Wed 70

Hyatt Regency London - The Churchill

★★★★★ 84% ⊛⊛⊛⊛ HOTEL PLAN 2 F2

☎ 020 7486 5800 🖨 020 7486 1255
30 Portman Square W1A 4ZX
e-mail: london.churchill@hyattintl.com
dir: from Marble Arch rdbt, follow signs for Oxford Circus onto Oxford St. Left turn after 2nd lights onto Portman St. Hotel on left

This smart hotel enjoys a central location overlooking Portman Square. Excellent conference, hairdressing and beauty facilities plus a fitness room make this the ideal choice for both corporate and leisure guests. The Montagu restaurant offers contemporary dining within the hotel. The restaurant, Locanda Locatelli, which situated in the hotel has been awarded four AA rosettes.

Rooms 444 (87 smoking) **S** £193.87-£446.50;
D £217.38-£470* **Facilities** STV FTV ⊛ Gym Jogging track ♫ Xmas New Year Wi-fi **Conf** Class 160 Board 68 Thtr 250 Del from £418 to £550* **Services** Lift Air con **Parking** 48 (charged) **Notes** ⊗ Civ Wed 250

The Metropolitan

★★★★★ 84% ⊛⊛ HOTEL PLAN 4 G5

☎ 020 7447 1000 🖨 020 7447 1100
Old Park Ln W1K 1LB
e-mail: res.lon@metropolitan.como.bz
dir: on corner of Old Park Ln and Hertford St, within 200mtrs from Hyde Park corner

Overlooking Hyde Park this hotel is located within easy reach of the fashionable stores of Knightsbridge and Mayfair. The hotel's contemporary style allows freedom and space to relax. Understated luxury is the key here with bedrooms enjoying great natural light. There is also a Shambhala Spa, steam room and fully equipped gym. For those seeking a culinary experience, Nobu offers innovative Japanese cuisine with an upbeat atmosphere.

Rooms 150 **S** £375-£2800; **D** £375-£2800* **Facilities** Spa STV FTV Gym Treatments Wi-fi **Conf** Board 30 Thtr 40 **Services** Lift Air con **Parking** 15 (charged) **Notes** Civ Wed 30

InterContinental London Park Lane

INTER-CONTINENTAL HOTELS AND RESORTS

★★★★★ 83% ⊛⊛⊛ HOTEL PLAN 4 G5

☎ 020 7409 3131 🖨 020 7493 3476
1 Hamilton Place, Hyde Park Corner W1J 7QY
e-mail: london@interconti.com
dir: at Hyde Park Corner, on corner of Park Lane and Piccadilly

A well-known and well-loved landmark on Hyde Park Corner, this hotel boasts elegant guest rooms and spectacular suites, including the split level loft style London Suite and a stunning Club InterContinental lounge. A choice of restaurants includes the superb Theo Randall. Public areas also include a chic urban spa run in partnership with Elemis and a contemporary event space with a ballroom and 12 meeting rooms.

Rooms 447 **Facilities** Spa Gym ♫ Xmas New Year Wi-fi **Conf** Class 340 Board 62 Thtr 750 **Services** Lift Air con **Parking** 100 (charged) **Notes** ⊗ Civ Wed 750

See advert on page 356

W1 WEST END continued

Grosvenor House, London

★★★★★ 82% HOTEL PLAN 2 G1

☎ 020 7499 6363 & 7399 8400 ▤ 020 7493 3341
Park Ln W1K 7TN
e-mail: grosvenor.house@marriotthotels.com
web: www.londongrosvenorhouse.co.uk
dir: centrally located on Park Ln, between Hyde Park
Corner & Oxford St

This quintessentially British hotel, overlooking Hyde Park
is undergoing an extensive restoration. Grosvenor House
promises approachable luxury and epitomises the fine
hotel culture and history of London. The property boasts
the largest ballroom in Europe, and now has a French-
style brasserie and Champagne Bar. The Park Room is
the perfect setting for afternoon tea.

Rooms 494 (113 smoking) **Facilities** STV ⓣ Gym Health
& Fitness centre Xmas New Year Wi-fi **Conf** Class 800
Board 140 Thtr 1500 **Services** Lift Air con **Parking** 6
(charged) **Notes** ⊗ Civ Wed 1500

London Marriott Hotel Park Lane

★★★★★ 81% HOTEL PLAN 2 F2

☎ 020 7493 7000 ▤ 020 7493 8333
140 Park Ln W1K 7AA
e-mail: mhrs.parklane@marriotthotels.com
web: www.londonmarriottparklane.co.uk
dir: From Hyde Park Corner left on Park Ln onto A4202,
0.8m. At Marble Arch onto Park Ln. Take 1st left onto
North Row. Hotel on left

This modern and stylish hotel is situated in a prominent
position in the heart of central London. Bedrooms are
superbly appointed and air conditioned. Public rooms
include a popular lounge/bar, and there are excellent
leisure facilities and an executive lounge.

Rooms 157 (31 smoking) **Facilities** STV ⓣ Gym Steam
room Xmas New Year Wi-fi **Conf** Class 33 Board 42
Thtr 72 **Services** Lift Air con **Notes** ⊗

Radisson Edwardian May Fair Hotel

★★★★★ Ⓐ HOTEL PLAN 5 A6

☎ 020 7629 7777 ▤ 020 7629 1459
Stratton St W1J 8LL
e-mail: mayfair@interconti.com
dir: from Hyde Park Corner or Piccadilly left onto Stratton
Street, hotel on left

Rooms 289 (14 fmly) **Facilities** Spa Gym ♫ Xmas Wi-fi
Conf Class 108 Board 60 Thtr 292 **Services** Lift Air con
Notes ⊗ No children 16 yrs Civ Wed 250

London Marriott Hotel Grosvenor Square

★★★★ 86% ⚘⚘ HOTEL PLAN 2 G2

☎ 020 7493 1232 ▤ 020 7514 1528
Grosvenor Square W1K 6JP
e-mail: philip.hyland@marriotthotels.com
web: www.londonmarriottgrosvenorsquare.co.uk
dir: M4 E to Cromwell Rd through Knightsbridge to Hyde
Park Corner. Park Lane right at Brook Gate onto Upper
Brook St to Grosvenor Sq

Situated adjacent to Grosvenor Square in the heart of
Mayfair, this hotel boasts convenient access to the city,
West End and some of London's most exclusive shops.
Bedrooms and public areas are furnished and decorated
to a high standard and retain the traditional elegance for
which the area is known. The hotel's eating options are
Gordon Ramsay's Maze Grill (2 AA rosettes), and Maze (4
AA rosettes) with impressive cooking by Jason Atherton.

Rooms 236 (26 fmly) **Facilities** Gym Exercise & fitness
centre Xmas Wi-fi **Conf** Class 500 Board 120 Thtr 900
Services Lift Air con **Parking** 80 (charged) **Notes** LB ⊗
Civ Wed 600

Chesterfield Mayfair

★★★★ 84% ⚘ HOTEL PLAN 4 H6

☎ 020 7491 2622 ▤ 020 7491 4793
35 Charles St, Mayfair W1J 5EB
e-mail: bookch@rchmail.com
web: www.chesterfieldmayfair.com
dir: Hyde Park Corner along Piccadilly, left into Half Moon
St. At end left & 1st right into Queens St, then right into
Charles St

Quiet elegance and an atmosphere of exclusivity
characterise this stylish Mayfair hotel where attentive,
friendly service is a highlight. Bedrooms have been

Mitre House

★★ 65% METRO HOTEL PLAN 2 D2

☎ 020 7723 8040 📠 020 7402 0990
178-184 Sussex Gardens, Hyde Park W2 1TU
e-mail: reservations@mitrehousehotel.com
web: www.mitrehousehotel.com
dir: parallel to Bayswater Rd & one block from
Paddington Station

This family-run hotel continues to offers a warm welcome
and attentive service. It is ideally located, close to
Paddington station and near the West End and major
attractions. Bedrooms include a number of family suites
and there is a lounge bar. Limited parking is available.

Rooms 69 (7 fmly) (7 GF) **S** £70-£80; **D** £90 (incl. bkfst)*
Facilities STV Wi-fi **Services** Lift **Parking** 20 **Notes** ⊗

Thistle Kensington Gardens   thistle

🅄 PLAN 2 C1

☎ 0870 333 9102 📠 0870 333 9202
104 Bayswater Rd W2 3HL
e-mail: kensingtongardens@thistle.co.uk
web: www.thistlehotels.com/kensingtongardens

Currently the rating for this establishment is not confirmed.
This may be due to a change of ownership or because it has
only recently joined the AA rating scheme. For further
details please see the AA website: www.theAA.com

Rooms 175 (12 fmly) (12 smoking) **Facilities** STV FTV
Wi-fi **Conf** Class 22 Board 30 Thtr 45 **Services** Lift Air con
Parking 72 (charged) **Notes** ⊗

Central Park

🅄 PLAN 2 B2

☎ 020 7229 2424 & 7313 5984 📠 020 7221 9847
49-67 Queensborough Ter W2 3SS
e-mail: cph@centralparklondon.co.uk
dir: 3 mins walk from Queensway and Bayswater
underground stations

Currently the rating for this establishment is not confirmed.
This may be due to a change of ownership or because it has
only recently joined the AA rating scheme. For further
details please see the AA website: www.theAA.com

Rooms 294 (5 fmly) (10 GF) **S** £42-£72; **D** £56-£98 (incl.
bkfst)* **Facilities** STV Xmas New Year Wi-fi
Conf Class 120 Board 80 Thtr 200 Del from £45 to £120*
Services Lift **Parking** 18 (charged) **Notes** ⊗

Days Inn London Hyde Park

BUDGET HOTEL PLAN 2 D2

☎ 020 7723 2939 📠 020 7723 6225
148/152 Sussex Gardens W2 1UD
e-mail: reservations@daysinnhydepark.com
web: www.daysinn.com
dir: on N side of Hyde Park. 2 min walk from Paddington
Station

This modern building offers accommodation in smart,
spacious and well-equipped bedrooms, suitable for
families and business travellers, and all with en suite
bathrooms. Continental breakfast is available and other
refreshments may be taken at the nearby family
restaurant. See also the Hotel Groups pages.

Rooms 57 (5 fmly) (11 GF) **S** £80-£95; **D** £100-£115 (incl.
bkfst)*

W3 ACTON

See LONDON plan 1 C3/4

Ramada Encore London   @ncore
West

★★★ 75% HOTEL

☎ 0870 0667 123 📠 0870 0667 144
**4 Portal Way, Gypsy Corner, A40 Western Avenue
W3 6RT**
e-mail: reservations@encorelondonwest.co.uk
web: www.encorelondonwest.co.uk

Conveniently situated on the A40 this modern, purpose
built, glass fronted hotel is ideal for visitors to London.
Air-conditioned bedrooms offer smartly appointed modern
accommodation with en suite power shower rooms.
Open-plan public areas include a popular Asian and
European restaurant and a 2go café serving Starbucks
coffee. Secure parking and a range of meeting rooms
complete the picture.

Ramada Encore London West

Rooms 150 (35 fmly) (15 smoking) **S** £64.95-£159.95;
D £64.95-£159.95* **Facilities** STV FTV Wi-fi
Conf Class 28 Board 26 Thtr 50 Del from £134 to £199*
Services Lift Air con **Parking** 72 (charged) **Notes** LB ⊗

Express by Holiday Inn   Express
London-Park Royal

BUDGET HOTEL

☎ 020 8896 4460 📠 020 8896 4461
Victoria Rd, Acton W3 6UB
e-mail: info@exhiparkroyal.co.uk
web: www.hiexpress.com/exparkroyal

A modern hotel ideal for families and business travellers.
Fresh and uncomplicated, the spacious rooms include Sky
TV, power shower and tea and coffee-making facilities.
Continental buffet breakfast is included in the room rate;
other meals may be taken at the nearby family pub or
restaurant. See also the Hotel Groups pages.

Rooms 104 **Conf** Class 60 Board 30 Thtr 30

Travelodge London Park
Royal

BUDGET HOTEL

☎ 08719 846 195 📠 020 8752 1134
A40 Western Ave, Acton W3 0TE
web: www.travelodge.co.uk
dir: off A40 Western Ave eastbound

Travelodge offers good quality, good value, modern
accommodation. Ideal for families, the spacious en suite
bedrooms include remote-control TV, tea and coffee-
making facilities and comfortable beds. Meals can be
taken at the nearby family restaurant. See also the Hotel
Groups pages.

Rooms 64 **S** fr £29; **D** fr £29

W4 CHISWICK

See LONDON plan 1 C3

Chiswick Moran

★★★★ 79% HOTEL

☎ 020 8996 5200 📠 020 8996 5201
626 Chiswick High Rd W4 5RY
e-mail: chiswickres@moranhotels.com
dir: 200yds from M4 junct 2

This stylish, modern hotel is conveniently located for Heathrow and central London, with Gunnersby tube station just a few minutes walk away. Airy, spacious public areas include a modern restaurant, a popular bar and excellent meeting facilities. Fully air-conditioned bedrooms are stylish and extremely well appointed with broadband, laptop safes and flat screen TVs. All boast spacious, modern bathrooms, many with walk-in rain showers.

Rooms 122 (6 fmly) **S** £109-£230; **D** £109-£230 (incl. bkfst)* **Facilities** STV Gym Wi-fi **Conf** Class 45 Board 40 Thtr 90 Del from £209 to £250* **Services** Lift Air con **Parking** 20 (charged) **Notes** LB ⊗ Civ Wed 80

W5 EALING

See LONDON SECTION plan 1 C4

Ramada Ealing

ⓇRAMADA

★★★ 79% HOTEL

☎ 0844 815 9035 📠 020 8992 7082
Ealing Common W5 3HN
e-mail: sales.ealing@ramadajarvis.co.uk
web: www.ramadajarvis.co.uk
dir: at junct of North Circular A406 & Uxbridge Road, A4020

This large modern, comfortable hotel is conveniently located a few minutes' walk from Ealing Common underground and easy access to the M40. Bedrooms, which vary in size, are comfortably appointed for both business and leisure guests. There is substantial parking, a spacious Arts restaurant and a range of meeting rooms.

Rooms 189 (3 fmly) **S** £72-£211; **D** £72-£223 (incl. bkfst)* **Facilities** FTV New Year Wi-fi **Conf** Class 110 Board 80 Thtr 200 Del from £170 to £190* **Services** Lift Air con **Parking** 150 (charged) **Notes** LB ⊗ Civ Wed 200

Crowne Plaza London Ealing

Ⓤ

☎ 0870 400 9114 & 020 8233 3216 📠 020 8233 3242
Western Av, Hanger Ln, Ealing W5 1HG
e-mail: info@hi-londonealing.co.uk
web: www.crowneplaza.co.uk
dir: From Central London A40 towards M40. Exit at Ealing & North Circular A406 sign. At rdbt 2nd exit signed A40. Hotel on left

Currently the rating for this establishment is not confirmed. This may be due to a change of ownership or because it has only recently joined the AA rating scheme. For further details please see the AA website: www.theAA.com

Rooms 131 (17 GF) (15 smoking) **S** £90-£235; **D** £90-£235* **Facilities** FTV Gym Steam room Xmas New Year Wi-fi **Conf** Class 48 Board 35 Thtr 80 Del from £190 to £250* **Services** Lift Air con **Parking** 85 (charged) **Notes** ⊗

W6 HAMMERSMITH

See LONDON plan 1 D3

Novotel London West

★★★★ 71% HOTEL

☎ 020 8741 1555 📠 020 8741 2120
1 Shortlands W6 8DR
e-mail: H0737@accor.com
web: www.novotel.com
dir: M4 (A4) & A316 junct at Hogarth rdbt. Along Great West Rd, left for Hammersmith before flyover. On Hammersmith Bridge Rd to rdbt, take 5th exit. 1st left into Shortlands, 1st left to hotel main entrance

A Hammersmith landmark, this substantial hotel is a popular base for both business and leisure travellers. Spacious, air-conditioned bedrooms have a good range of extras and many have additional beds, making them suitable for families. The hotel also has its own car park, business centre and shop and boasts one of the largest convention centres in Europe.

Rooms 630 (148 fmly) **S** £110-£1850; **D** £110-£205* **Facilities** STV Gym Wi-fi **Conf** Class 525 Board 200 Thtr 1000 Del from £199 to £274* **Services** Lift Air con **Parking** 240 (charged) **Notes** LB Civ Wed 1400

Express by Holiday Inn London - Hammersmith

BUDGET HOTEL

☎ 020 8746 5100 📠 020 8746 5199
120 -124 King St W6 0QU
e-mail: gsm.hammersmith@expressholidayinn.co.uk
web: www.hiexpress.com/hammersmith
dir: M4/A4 junct 1 to Hammersmith Broadway. 2nd left to A315 towards Chiswick (King St). Hotel on right

A modern hotel ideal for families and business travellers. Fresh and uncomplicated, the spacious rooms include Sky TV, power shower and tea and coffee-making facilities.

Continental buffet breakfast is included in the room rate; other meals may be taken at the nearby family pub or restaurant. See also the Hotel Groups pages.

Rooms 135 (49 fmly) **Conf** Class 18 Board 20 Thtr 35

W8 KENSINGTON

INSPECTORS' CHOICE

Milestone Hotel & Apartments

★★★★★ ⊛⊛ HOTEL PLAN 4 B4

☎ 020 7917 1000 📠 020 7917 1010
1 Kensington Court W8 5DL
e-mail: bookms@rchmail.com
web: www.milestonehotel.com
dir: From Warwick Rd right into Kensington High St. Hotel 400yds past Kensington underground

This delightful town house enjoys a wonderful location opposite Kensington Palace and is near the elegant shops. Individually themed bedrooms include a selection of stunning suites that are equipped with every conceivable extra. Public areas include the luxurious Park Lounge where afternoon tea is served, a delightful panelled bar, a sumptuous restaurant and a small gym and resistance pool.

Rooms 57 (3 fmly) (2 GF) (5 smoking) **S** £275-£311; **D** £370-£405* **Facilities** STV FTV ⊗ Gym Health club ♫ Xmas New Year Wi-fi **Conf** Class 20 Board 20 Thtr 50 Del from £395 to £445* **Services** Lift Air con **Parking** 1 (charged) **Notes** LB Civ Wed 30

See advert on opposite page

The Milestone Hotel

★★★★★

STYLE AND IMAGINATION

Overlooking Kensington Palace and Hyde Park, this distinguished, AA five Red Star hotel is a landmark of unique character and 21st century elegance. Impeccable service and sumptuous, individually designed rooms provide the utmost in comfort and style. No request is too large, no detail too small.

RANKED NO. 1 HOTEL IN THE WORLD – Travel and Leisure Worlds Best Service Awards 2008
VOTED NO.1 BRITISH HOTEL – Condé Nast Traveler Gold List World's Best Hotels 2008
Awarded Two Rosettes For Dining by The AA

For reservations or a brochure please call
020 7917 1000 or visit www.milestonehotel.com

MEMBERS OF THE
RED CARNATION
HOTEL COLLECTION

A member of
The Leading
Small Hotels
of the World

1 Kensington Court, London W8 5DL | www.milestonehotel.com

W8 KINSINGTON continued

Royal Garden Hotel

★★★★★ ◎◎ HOTEL PLAN 4 B5

☎ 020 7937 8000 ▤ 020 7361 1991
2-24 Kensington High St W8 4PT
e-mail: sales@royalgardenhotel.co.uk
web: www.royalgardenhotel.co.uk
dir: next to Kensington Palace

This well-known landmark hotel is just a short walk from the Royal Albert Hall. Bedrooms are of contemporary design, equipped with many up-to-date facilities; many are spacious and offer super views over Kensington Gardens. The summer of 2008 sees the opening of a new restaurant - Min Jueng. Unfortunately we were unable to make an inspection before the guide deadlines. For up-to-date information please see the AA website, www.theAA.com

Rooms 396 (19 fmly) **S** £175-£317; **D** £245-£452*
Facilities Spa STV Gym Health & fitness centre ♫ Xmas New Year Wi-fi **Conf** Class 260 Board 80 Thtr 550 **Services** Lift Air con **Parking** 160 (charged) **Notes** LB ⊗ Civ Wed 400

Copthorne Tara Hotel London Kensington

★★★★ 75% HOTEL PLAN 4 B4

☎ 020 7937 7211 ▤ 020 7937 7100
Scarsdale Place, Wrights Ln W8 5SR
e-mail: reservations.tara@millenniumhotels.co.uk
web: www.millenniumhotels.com/tara
dir: off Kensington High Street down Wright Ln

This expansive hotel is ideally the stylish shops and also the tube station. Smart public areas include a trendy coffee shop, a gym, a stylish Brasserie and bar and extensive conference facilities. Bedrooms include several well-equipped rooms for less mobile guests in addition to a number of Connoisseur rooms that include use of a club lounge with many complimentary facilities.

Rooms 833 (3 fmly) **S** £94-£260; **D** £94-£260*
Facilities STV Gym Beauty room Xmas New Year Wi-fi **Conf** Class 160 Board 90 Thtr 280 **Services** Lift Air con **Parking** 16 (charged) **Notes** LB ⊗ Civ Wed 280

Kensington House

★★★★ 70% TOWN HOUSE HOTEL PLAN 4 B4

☎ 020 7937 2345 ▤ 020 7368 6700
15-16 Prince of Wales Ter W8 5PQ
e-mail: sales@kenhouse.com
web: www.kenhouse.com
dir: off Kensington High St, opposite Kensington Palace

This beautiful and elegantly restored 19th-century property is located just off Kensington High Street and convenient for the park, The Royal Albert Hall and most of the major attractions. Bedrooms vary in size but all are stylish, comfortable and thoughtfully equipped - many have air conditioning. Tiger Bar provides an airy, informal setting for light snacks, meals and refreshments throughout the day.

Rooms 41 (2 fmly) (3 GF) (3 smoking) **S** £155; **D** £180 (incl. bkfst) **Facilities** Arrangement with local health club Wi-fi **Services** Lift **Notes** LB ⊗

See LONDON plan 1 B3

K West Hotel & Spa

★★★★ 80% HOTEL PLAN 1 D3

☎ 020 8008 6600 ▤ 020 8008 6650
Richmond Way W14 0AX
e-mail: info@k-west.co.uk
web: www.k-west.co.uk
dir: From A40/M take Shepherd's Bush Exit. Holland Park rdbt 3rd exit. Take 1st left & left again. Hotel ahead

This stylish, contemporary hotel is conveniently located for Notting Hill, the exhibition halls and the BBC; Bond Street is only a 10-minute tube journey away. Funky, minimalist public areas include a trendy lobby bar and mezzanine style restaurant, and free internet access is available. Spacious bedrooms are extremely well appointed and offer luxurious bedding, Aveda toiletries and a host of extras such as CD and DVD players.

Rooms 220 (31 GF) (44 smoking) **S** £119-£775; **D** £129-£775 **Facilities** Spa STV Gym ♫ Xmas New Year Wi-fi **Conf** Class 20 Board 25 Thtr 50 Del from £255 to £375 **Services** Lift Air con **Parking** 100 (charged) **Notes** LB ⊗

Express by Holiday Inn London-Earl's Court

BUDGET HOTEL PLAN 4 A1

☎ 020 7384 5151 ▤ 020 7384 5152
295 North End Rd W14 9NS
e-mail: info@exhiearlscourt.co.uk
web: www.hiexpress.com/lonearlscourt

A modern hotel ideal for families and business travellers. Fresh and uncomplicated, the spacious rooms include Sky TV, power shower and tea and coffee-making facilities. Continental buffet breakfast is included in the room rate; other meals may be taken at the nearby family pub or restaurant. See also the Hotel Groups pages.

Rooms 100 **Conf** Class 12 Board 12 Thtr 50

Renaissance Chancery Court

★★★★★ 86% ◎◎◎ HOTEL
PLAN 3 D3

☎ 020 7829 9888 ▤ 020 7829 9889
252 High Holborn WC1V 7EN
e-mail: sales.chancerycourt@renaissancehotels.com
web: www.renaissancechancerycourt.co.uk
dir: A4 along Piccadilly onto Shaftesbury Av. Into High Holborn, hotel on right

This is a grand place with splendid public areas, decorated from top to bottom in rare marble. Craftsmen have meticulously restored the sweeping staircases, archways and stately rooms of the 1914 building. The result is a spacious, relaxed hotel offering everything from stylish, luxuriously appointed bedrooms to a health club and state-of-the-art meeting rooms. The sophisticated Pearl Restaurant & Bar offers an impressive standard of cooking.

Renaissance Chancery Court

Rooms 356 **S** £165-£375; **D** £165-£375* **Facilities** Spa Gym ♫ Xmas New Year Wi-fi **Conf** Class 234 Board 40 Thtr 435 **Services** Lift Air con **Parking** 4 (charged) **Notes** ⊗ Civ Wed 280

The Montague on the Gardens

★★★★ 84% ⊛ HOTEL PLAN 3 C4

☎ 020 7637 1001 ▤ 020 7637 2516
15 Montague St, Bloomsbury WC1B 5BJ
e-mail: bookmt@rchmail.com
web: www.montaguehotel.com
dir: just off Russell Square, adjacent to British Museum

This stylish hotel is situated right next to the British Museum. A special feature is the alfresco terrace overlooking a delightful garden. Other public rooms include the Blue Door Bistro and Chef's Table, a bar, a lounge and a conservatory where traditional afternoon teas are served. The bedrooms are beautifully appointed and range from split-level suites to more compact rooms.

Rooms 100 (19 GF) (10 smoking) **S** £115-£210; **D** £135-£260* **Facilities** STV Gym ♫ Xmas New Year Wi-fi Child facilities **Conf** Class 50 Board 50 Thtr 120 Del from £199 to £295* **Services** Lift Air con **Notes** LB Civ Wed 90

Jurys Great Russell Street

★★★★ 77% ⊛ HOTEL PLAN 3 C3

☎ 020 7347 1000 ▤ 020 7347 1001
16-22 Great Russell St WC1B 3NN
e-mail: restaurant_grs@jurysdoyle.com
web: www.jurysdoyle.com
dir: A40 onto A400, Gower St then south to Bedford Sq. Turn right, then 1st left to end of road

On the doorstep of Covent Garden, Oxford Street and the West End, this impressive building, designed by the renowned Sir Edwin Lutyens in the 1930s, retains many

original features. Bedrooms are attractively appointed and benefit from an excellent range of facilities. Public areas include a grand reception lounge, an elegant bar and restaurant plus extensive conference facilities.

Rooms 170 (5 GF) **S** £99.88-£352.50; **D** £99.88-£352.50* **Facilities** STV Xmas Wi-fi **Conf** Class 180 Board 60 Thtr 300 Del from £300 to £430* **Services** Lift Air con **Notes** ⊗ Civ Wed 200

The Hotel Russell

★★★★ 74% HOTEL PLAN 3 C4

☎ 020 7837 6470 ▤ 020 7837 2857
Russell Square WC1B 5BE
web: www.principal-hotels.com
dir: from A501 into Woburn Place. Hotel 500mtrs on left

This landmark Grade II, Victorian hotel is located on Russell Square, within walking distance of the West End and theatre district. Many bedrooms are stylish and state-of-the-art in design, and others are more traditional. Spacious public areas include the impressive foyer with a restored mosaic floor, a choice of lounges and an elegant restaurant.

Rooms 373 **Facilities** Wi-fi **Conf** Class 200 Board 75 Thtr 450 **Services** Lift Air con **Notes** ⊗ Civ Wed 300

Holiday Inn Kings Cross/ Bloomsbury

★★★★ 71% HOTEL PLAN 3 E5

☎ 020 7833 3900 ▤ 020 7917 6163
1 Kings Cross Rd WC1X 9HX
e-mail: sales@holidayinnlondon.com
web: www.holidayinn.co.uk
dir: 0.5m from Kings Cross Station on corner of King Cross Rd and Calthorpe St

Conveniently located for Kings Cross station and the City, this modern hotel offers smart, spacious air-conditioned accommodation with a wide range of facilities. The hotel offers a choice of restaurants including one serving Indian cuisine, versatile meeting rooms, a bar and a well-equipped fitness centre.

Rooms 405 (163 fmly) (126 smoking) **S** £90-£250; **D** £115-£275* **Facilities** STV FTV ☆ Gym **Conf** Class 120 Board 30 Thtr 220 Del from £190 to £290* **Services** Lift Air con **Parking** 3 (charged) **Notes** LB ⊗

Park Inn, London

★★★★ 70% HOTEL PLAN 3 D4

☎ 020 7242 2828 ▤ 020 7831 9170
92 Southampton Row WC1B 4BH
e-mail: info.russellsquare@rezidorparkinn.com
web: www.london-russell-square.parkinn.co.uk
dir: M40 Euston Rd. Opposite station turn S into Upper Woburn Place past Russell Sq into Southampton Row. Hotel on left

With its beautiful Edwardian façade, the newly-renovated hotel is ideally located in Bloomsbury. It has

contemporary accommodation which is fresh and stylish. Bedrooms are equipped with a good range of amenities suitable for both business and leisure travellers. The restaurant offers a vibrant choice of dishes.

Park Inn, London

Rooms 214 **S** £99-£159; **D** £129-£199* **Facilities** Fitness room ♫ Wi-fi **Conf** Class 80 Board 50 Thtr 200 Del from £220 to £300* **Services** Lift Air con **Notes** ⊗

Radisson Edwardian Kenilworth

★★★★ Ⓐ HOTEL PLAN 3 C3

☎ 020 7637 3477 ▤ 020 636 0532
Great Russell St WC1B 3LB
e-mail: reskeni@radisson.com
dir: from New Oxford St into Bloomsbury St, then Great Russell St

Rooms 186 (15 fmly) **Facilities** Fitness room Xmas Wi-fi **Conf** Class 50 Board 35 Thtr 120 **Services** Lift Air con **Notes** ⊗ No children 16 yrs

Radisson Edwardian Marlborough

★★★★ Ⓐ HOTEL PLAN 3 C3

☎ 020 7636 5601 ▤ 020 7636 0532
Bloomsbury St WC1B 3QD
e-mail: resmarl@radisson.com
dir: past Oxford St, down New Oxford St, into Bloomsbury St

Rooms 173 (3 fmly) **Facilities** Xmas Wi-fi **Conf** Class 150 Board 70 Thtr 300 **Services** Lift **Notes** ⊗ No children 16 yrs

The Kingsley by Thistle

thistle

★★★ 70% HOTEL PLAN 3 C3

☎ 0870 333 9103 ▤ 0870 333 9203
Bloomsbury Way WC1A 2SD
e-mail: bloomsbury@thistle.co.uk
web: www.thistlehotels.com/bloomsbury
dir: A40(M) to A501 (Marylebone Rd), take sliproad before underpass to Holborn. Into Gower St, Bloomsbury St (A400). Left into Oxford St & onto Bloomsbury Way

Well situated for theatregoers, this hotel enjoys a convenient central location. The well-equipped rooms are generally spacious with good quality fabrics and *Continued*

WC1 BLOOMSBURY, HOLBORN continued

furnishings, with both family rooms and executive suites available. The ground-floor bar and lounge areas are well appointed. There is a public car park nearby.

Rooms 138 (7 fmly) **S** fr £99; **D** fr £99* **Facilities** Wi-fi **Conf** Class 55 Board 35 Thtr 100 Del from £230 to £345* **Services** Lift **Notes** LB ⊗

Bedford

★★★ 66% HOTEL PLAN 3 D4

☎ 020 7636 7822 & 7692 3620 📠 020 7837 4653
83-93 Southampton Row WC1B 4HD
e-mail: info@imperialhotels.co.uk

Just off Russell Square, this intimate hotel is ideal for visits to the British Museum and Covent Garden. The bedrooms are well equipped with all the expected facilities including modem points if requested. The ground floor has a lounge, a bar and restaurant plus there's a delightful secret rear garden. An underground car park is a bonus.

Rooms 183 (1 fmly) **S** £72; **D** £97 (incl. bkfst) **Facilities** FTV Xmas New Year Wi-fi **Conf** Board 12 Del from £97 to £120* **Services** Lift **Parking** 50 (charged) **Notes** ⊗

Holiday Inn London Bloomsbury

🅤 PLAN 3 C4

☎ 0870 400 9222 📠 020 7837 5374
Coram St WC1N 1HT
e-mail: bloomsbury@ihg.com
web: www.holidayinn.co.uk
dir: off Upper Woburn Place near Russell Sq

Currently the rating for this establishment is not confirmed. This may be due to a change of ownership or because it has only recently joined the AA rating scheme. For further details please see the AA website: www.theAA.com

Rooms 311 (30 fmly) (16 smoking) **D** £90-£195 (incl. bkfst) **Facilities** Wi-fi **Conf** Class 180 Board 80 Thtr 300 **Services** Lift Air con **Notes** ⊗ Civ Wed 50

Travelodge London Farringdon

BUDGET HOTEL PLAN 3 E6

☎ 08719 846 274 📠 020 7837 3776
10-42 Kings Cross Rd WC1X 9QN
web: www.travelodge.co.uk

Travelodge offers good quality, good value, modern accommodation. Ideal for families, the spacious en suite bedrooms include remote-control TV, tea and coffee-making facilities and comfortable beds. Meals can be taken at the nearby family restaurant. See also the Hotel Groups pages.

Rooms 211 (18 fmly) **S** fr £29; **D** fr £29 **Conf** Class 18 Board 30 Thtr 50

Travelodge London Kings Cross

BUDGET HOTEL PLAN 3 D6

☎ 08719 846 256 📠 020 7278 7396
Willing House, Grays Inn Rd, Kings Cross WC1X 8BH
web: www.travelodge.co.uk

Rooms 140 **S** fr £29; **D** fr £29

Travelodge London Kings Cross Royal Scot

BUDGET HOTEL PLAN 3 E5

☎ 08719 846 272 📠 020 7833 0798
100 Kings Cross Rd WC1X 9DT
web: www.travelodge.co.uk

Rooms 351 (22 fmly) **S** fr £29; **D** fr £29 **Conf** Class 60 Board 50 Thtr 170

WC2 SOHO, STRAND

INSPECTORS' CHOICE

One Aldwych

★★★★★ ⑳⑳ HOTEL PLAN 3 D2

☎ 020 7300 1000 & 7300 0500 📠 020 7300 1001
1 Aldwych WC2B 4RH
e-mail: reservations@onealdwych.com
web: www.onealdwych.com
dir: at Aldwych & The Strand junct, opposite Waterloo Bridge

Although well established for some years now, One Aldwych continues to be highly considered for its blend of chic design and consistent high standards. Bedrooms vary in size, but all are stylish, very well equipped and have excellent beds with giant pillows and high quality bedding. There are a host of facilities - two fine restaurants, Axis with a separate entrance and open-plan Indigo, a health club with underwater music in the therapeutic pool, the Lobby Bar and also a private screening room.

Rooms 105 (18 fmly) (36 smoking) **D** £446.50-£1363* **Facilities** Spa STV ⑤ Gym Sauna Steam & Treatment rooms ♫ Xmas New Year Wi-fi **Conf** Board 40 Thtr 60 **Services** Lift Air con **Notes** LB ⊗ Civ Wed 60

Swissôtel The Howard, London

★★★★★ 85% HOTEL PLAN 3 E2

☎ 020 7836 3555 📠 020 7379 4547
Temple Place WC2R 2PR
e-mail: london@swissotel.com
web: www.london.swissotel.com
dir: From E turn off Aldwych, keep left of church (in centre of road). Turn left into Surrey St. Hotel at end

This smart hotel enjoys wonderful views across London's historic skyline from its riverside location, and the Eurostar terminal, Covent Garden and Theatreland are all within easy reach. The air-conditioned bedrooms offer a host of extra facilities. The bar opens out onto a delightful garden where alfresco dining is possible when the weather permits.

Rooms 189 **Facilities** Complimentary use of nearby health club ♫ Xmas New Year Wi-fi **Conf** Class 60 Board 60 Thtr 120 **Services** Lift Air con **Parking** 30 (charged) **Notes** LB ⊗ Civ Wed 120

Radisson Edwardian Hampshire Hotel

★★★★★ 🅰 HOTEL PLAN 3 C1

☎ 020 7839 9399 📠 020 7930 8122
31 Leicester Square WC2H 7LH
e-mail: reshamp@radisson.com
dir: from Charing Cross Rd turn into Cranbourn St at Leicester Sq. Left at end, hotel at bottom of square

Rooms 124 (5 fmly) **Facilities** Gym Fitness room Wi-fi **Conf** Class 48 Board 35 Thtr 100 **Services** Lift Air con **Notes** ⊗ No children 16 yrs

Charing Cross

★★★★ 76% ⑳ HOTEL PLAN 3 C1

☎ 0871 376 9012 📠 0870 333 9205
The Strand WC2N 5HX
e-mail: charingcross@guoman.co.uk
web: www.guoman.com
dir: E along The Strand towards Trafalgar Square, right into station forecourt

This centrally located and historic landmark hotel provides a friendly welcome. Spacious in design, the original architecture blends nicely with the modern style of interior appointments, particularly in the bedrooms and bathrooms. There is a choice of dining options - for those in a hurry try Co-Motion which offers a range of snacks and speedy service. More leisurely dining can be enjoyed in The Strand Terrace, which has splendid views of London especially at night.

Rooms 239 (83 annexe) (12 fmly) (8 smoking) **S** £109-£370; **D** £129-£370* **Facilities** STV ♫ Xmas New Year Wi-fi **Conf** Class 96 Board 46 Thtr 140 Del from £209 to £495* **Services** Lift Air con **Notes** LB Civ Wed 140

Radisson Edwardian Mountbatten

★★★★ Ⓐ HOTEL PLAN 3 C2

☎ 020 7836 4300 🖺 020 7240 3540
Monmouth St, Seven Dials, Covent Garden WC2H 9HD
e-mail: resmoun@radisson.com
dir: off Shaftesbury Av, on corner of Seven Dials rdbt

Rooms 151 **S** £120–£180; **D** £130–£200* **Facilities** FTV Fitness room Xmas New Year Wi-fi **Conf** Class 45 Board 32 Thtr 90 Del from £300 to £385 **Services** Lift Air con **Notes** ⊗

The Royal Trafalgar by Thistle   **thistle**

★★★ 75% HOTEL PLAN 3 C2

☎ 0870 333 9119 🖺 0870 333 9219
Whitcomb St WC2H 7HG
e-mail: trafalgarsquare@thistle.co.uk
web: www.thistlehotels.com/tralalgarsquare
dir: 100mtrs from Trafalgar Sq adjacent to Sainsbury Wing of National Gallery

Quietly located, this handily placed hotel is just a short walk from Trafalgar Square and Theatreland. Bedrooms offer good levels of comfort with a variety of standards available. Dining options include the Savoria brasserie, or alternatively, light meals can be taken in the traditionally styled bar.

Rooms 116 (20 smoking) **S** £99–£215; **D** £99–£230* **Facilities** STV FTV ♫ Xmas New Year Wi-fi **Services** Lift Air con **Notes** LB ⊗

Strand Palace

★★★ 74% HOTEL PLAN 3 D2

☎ 020 7836 8080 & 0870 400 8702 🖺 020 7836 2077
372 The Strand WC2R 0JJ
e-mail: reservations@strandpalacehotel.co.uk
dir: From Trafalgar Square, on A4 to Charing Cross, 150mtrs, hotel on left.

At the heart of Theatreland, this vast hotel is proud of its friendly and efficient staff. The bedrooms vary in style and include bright Club rooms with enhanced facilities. The extensive public areas include shops, a popular cocktail bar and there is the Strand Carvery and Johnson's Brasserie as eating options.

Rooms 785 **Facilities** Xmas **Conf** Class 90 Board 40 Thtr 200 **Services** Lift **Notes** LB ⊗

Radisson Edwardian Pastoria Hotel

★★★ Ⓐ HOTEL PLAN 3 C1

☎ 020 7930 8641 & 020 7451 0227 🖺 020 7451 0191
3-6 Saint Martins St WC2H 7HL
e-mail: reshamp@radisson.com
dir: from Whitcomb Street left into Panton Street. Saint Martins Street off Leicester Square

Rooms 58 **Facilities** Gym **Services** Lift **Notes** ⊗

Travelodge London Covent Garden

BUDGET HOTEL PLAN 3 D2

☎ 08719 846 845 🖺 01376 572 724
10 Drury Ln, High Holborn WC2B 5RE
web: www.travelodge.co.uk
dir: on High Holborn off Drury Lane

Travelodge offers good quality, good value, modern accommodation. Ideal for families, the spacious en suite bedrooms include remote-control TV, tea and coffee-making facilities and comfortable beds. Meals can be taken at the nearby family restaurant. See also the Hotel Groups pages.

Rooms 163 (4 fmly) **S** fr £29; **D** fr £29 **Conf** Class 40 Board 30 Thtr 100

LONDON GATEWAY MOTORWAY SERVICE AREA (M1)   Map 6 TQ19

Days Hotel London North

★★★ 67% HOTEL

☎ 020 8906 7000 🖺 020 8906 7011
Welcome Break Service Area NW7 3HU
e-mail: lgw.hotel@welcomebreak.co.uk
web: www.welcomebreak.co.uk
dir: on M1 between junct 2/4 northbound & southbound

This modern building offers accommodation in smart, spacious and well-equipped bedrooms, suitable for families and business travellers, and all with en suite bathrooms. Continental breakfast is available and other refreshments may be taken at the nearby family restaurant.

Rooms 200 (190 fmly) (80 GF) **S** £59–£89; **D** £59–£99* **Facilities** STV Wi-fi **Conf** Class 30 Board 50 Thtr 70 Del from £65 to £95* **Services** Lift Air con **Parking** 160

LONDON, GREATER

BARKING
See LONDON SECTION plan 1 H4

Ibis London Barking

BUDGET HOTEL

☎ 020 8477 4100 🖺 020 8477 4101
Highbridge Rd IG11 7BA
e-mail: H2042@accor.com
web: www.ibishotel.com
dir: exit Barking from A406 or A13

Modern, budget hotel offering comfortable accommodation in bright and practical bedrooms. Breakfast is self-service and dinner is available in the restaurant. See also the Hotel Groups pages.

Rooms 86 (26 GF) (9 smoking) **S** £56–£100; **D** £56–£100*

BECKENHAM
See LONDON SECTION plan 1 G1

Innkeeper's Lodge London Beckenham

BUDGET HOTEL

☎ 0845 112 6126 🖺 0845 112 6184
422 Upper Elmers End Rd BR3 3HQ
web: www.innkeeperslodge.com/beckenham
dir: From M25 junct 6 Croydon, A22 towards Croydon, then A232 for Shirley. At West Wickham take A214. Lodge opposite Eden Park Station

Innkeeper's Lodge represents an exciting, high value concept within the budget hotel market. Comfortable bedrooms provide excellent facilities that include satellite TV and modem points. Options include family rooms, and for the corporate guest, cutting edge IT which includes Wi-fi access. A popular Carvery provides all-day food, including an extensive, complimentary continental breakfast.

Rooms 24 (1 fmly) **S** £59.95–£75; **D** £59.95–£75 (incl. bkfst)

BEXLEY   Map 6 TQ47

Bexleyheath Marriott Hotel   *Marriott* HOTELS & RESORTS

★★★★ 75% HOTEL

☎ 020 8298 1000 🖺 020 8298 1234
1 Broadway DA6 7JZ
e-mail: bexleyheath@marriotthotels.co.uk
web: www.bexleyheathmarriott.co.uk
dir: M25 junct 2/A2 towards London. Exit at Black Prince junct onto A220, signed Bexleyheath. Left at 2nd lights into hotel

Well positioned for access to major road networks, this large, modern hotel offers spacious, air-conditioned bedrooms with a comprehensive range of extra facilities. Planters Bar is a popular venue for pre-dinner drinks and offers guests a choice of lighter dining, whilst a more formal restaurant is also available. The hotel boasts a well-equipped leisure centre and undercover parking.

Rooms 142 (16 fmly) (26 GF) **S** £75–£124; **D** £85–£134* **Facilities** STV ⊕ supervised Gym Steam room Health beauty treatment Xmas New Year Wi-fi **Conf** Class 120 Board 34 Thtr 250 Del from £135 to £155* **Services** Lift Air con **Parking** 6 (charged) **Notes** LB ⊗ Civ Wed 40

BEXLEY continued

Holiday Inn London - Bexley

U

☎ 0870 400 9006 & 01322 625513 🖹 01322 526113
Black Prince Interchange, Southwold Rd DA5 1ND
e-mail: bexley@ihg.com
web: www.holidayinn.co.uk
dir: A2 to exit for A220/A223 Black Prince interchange
Bexley/Bexleyheath. Hotel on left

Currently the rating for this establishment is not confirmed.
This may be due to a change of ownership or because it has
only recently joined the AA rating scheme. For further
details please see the AA website: www.theAA.com

Rooms 107 (11 fmly) (33 GF) (16 smoking) **S** £85-£125;
D £85-£125 **Facilities** New Year Wi-fi **Conf** Class 42
Board 50 Thtr 120 Del from £135 to £155* **Services** Lift
Air con **Parking** 200 (charged) **Notes** LB Civ Wed 80

BRENTFORD

See LONDON plan 1 C3

Holiday Inn London Brentford Lock

★★★★ 75% HOTEL

☎ 020 8232 2000 🖹 020 8232 2001
High St TW8 8JZ
e-mail: info@holidayinnbrentford.co.uk
web: www.holidayinn.co.uk
dir: M4 junct 2 onto A4. At rdbt take 4th exit onto A315,
hotel on right.

This smart, modern hotel is located beside the Grand
Union Canal in the heart of Brentford. Central London, the
major motorway networks and Heathrow Airport are all
within easy reach. Stylish bedrooms are thoughtfully
equipped and contemporary public areas include a bar/
lounge, restaurant, conference and function facilities and
a spacious underground car park.

Rooms 134 (30 fmly) (30 smoking) **S** £69-£249;
D £69-£249* **Facilities** Wi-fi **Conf** Class 200 Board 120
Thtr 700 Del from £175 to £225* **Services** Lift Air con
Parking 60 (charged) **Notes** ⊗ Civ Wed 180

Travelodge London Kew Bridge

BUDGET HOTEL

☎ 08719 846 040 🖹 020 8758 1190
North Rd, High St TW8 0BD
web: www.travelodge.co.uk

Travelodge offers good quality, good value, modern
accommodation. Ideal for families, the spacious en suite
bedrooms include remote-control TV, tea and coffee-
making facilities and comfortable beds. Meals can be

taken at the nearby family restaurant. See also the Hotel
Groups pages.

Rooms 111 **S** fr £29; **D** fr £29

BROMLEY

See LONDON SECTION plan 1 G1

Best Western Bromley Court

★★★ 77% HOTEL

☎ 020 8461 8600 🖹 020 8460 0899
Bromley Hill BR1 4JD
e-mail: info@bromleycourthotel.co.uk
web: www.bw-bromleycourthotel.co.uk
dir: N of town centre, off A21. Private drive opposite
Volkswagen garage on Bromley Hill

Set amid three acres of grounds, this smart hotel enjoys a
peaceful location, in a residential area on the outskirts of
town. Well maintained bedrooms are smartly appointed
and thoughtfully equipped. The contemporary-style
restaurant offers a good choice of meals in comfortable
surroundings. Extensive facilities include a leisure club
and a good range of meeting rooms.

Rooms 114 (4 fmly) **S** £85-£105; **D** £95-£120 (incl.
bkfst)* **Facilities** STV Gym Steam room Spa pool Wi-fi
Conf Class 80 Board 45 Thtr 150 Del from £140 to £160*
Services Lift **Parking** 100 **Notes** LB ⊗ Civ Wed 55

CHESSINGTON   Map 6 TQ16

Holiday Inn London- Chessington

★★★★ 71% HOTEL

☎ 01372 734600 🖹 01372 734600
Leatherhead Rd KT9 2NE
e-mail: enquiries@holidayinnchessington.co.uk
web: www.holidayinn.co.uk
dir: Follow signs for Chessington World of Adventures.
Hotel at North car park entrance of CWOA

Ideally located just off the M25 at Junction 9, the Hotel is
only 2 miles from the A3 in the heart of Surrey and 12
miles from London. The great location also makes it ideal
for visiting Chessington World of Adventures and
Chessington Zoo, both are on-site, and Epsom
Racecourse near-by. An African animal/safari theme
predominates public areas and bedrooms. Good leisure
facilities. Ample dedicated car parking.

Rooms 150 (56 fmly) (10 smoking) **S** £59-£229;
D £59-£229* **Facilities** Spa STV FTV 🏊 Gym Sauna
Steam room Aqua aerobics Xmas New Year Wi-fi Child
facilities **Conf** Class 150 Board 70 Thtr 300
Del from £125 to £245* **Services** Lift Air con **Parking** 120
Notes LB Civ Wed 100

CROYDON   Map 6 TQ36

Coulsdon Manor

★★★★ 73% HOTEL

☎ 020 8668 0414 🖹 020 8668 3118
Coulsdon Court Rd, Coulsdon CR5 2LL
e-mail: reservations.coulsdon@ohiml.com
web: www.oxfordhotelsandinns.com
dir: M23/25 junct 7, A23, 2.5m, B2030 for 1m, left onto
Coulsdon Rd, then 0.5m

This delightful Victorian manor house is peacefully set
amidst 140 acres of landscaped parkland, complete with
its own professional 18-hole golf course. Bedrooms are
spacious and comfortable, whilst public areas include a
choice of lounges and an elegant restaurant serving
carefully prepared, imaginative food.

Rooms 35 (4 fmly) **S** £75-£120; **D** £85-£150 (incl. bkfst)*
Facilities STV FTV ♪ 18 ⛳ Putt green Gym Squash
Aerobic studio Steam room Sauna Xmas New Year Wi-fi
Conf Class 90 Board 70 Thtr 180 Del from £150 to £215*
Services Lift **Parking** 200 **Notes** LB ⊗ Civ Wed 60

Selsdon Park Hotel & Golf Club

★★★★ 73% HOTEL

☎ 020 8657 8811 🖹 020 8651 6171
Addington Rd, Sanderstead CR2 8YA
e-mail: sales.selsdonpark@principal-hotels.com
dir: 3m SE of Croydon, off A2022

Surrounded by 200 acres of mature parkland with its own
18-hole golf course, this imposing Jacobean mansion is
less than 20 minutes from central London. The hotel's
impressive range of conference rooms along with the
spectacular views of the North Downs countryside, make
this a popular venue for both weddings and meetings.
The leisure facilities are impressive.

Rooms 204 (12 fmly) (12 GF) **Facilities** 🏊 🎾 supervised
♪ 18 ⛳ Putt green ♣ Gym Squash Boules Jogging track
♪ Xmas Child facilities **Conf** Class 220 Board 60
Thtr 350 **Services** Lift **Parking** 300 **Notes** LB ⊗
Civ Wed 120

Aerodrome

★★★ 80% HOTEL

☎ 020 8710 9000 & 8680 1999 📄 020 8681 6438
Purley Way CR9 4LT
e-mail: info@aerodrome-hotel.co.uk
web: www.aerodrome-hotel.co.uk
dir: Follow A23/Central London. Hotel on left next to Airport House

The Croydon Aerodrome was the world's first international airport and the starting point for Amy Johnson's record-breaking flight to Darwin. The hotel has benefited from substantial investment in recent years. Bedrooms and suites are smartly designed and include an integrated internet and entertainment facility. Public areas, with Wi-fi, include two restaurants, bars and conference facilities. There's also a terrace garden.

Rooms 110 (1 fmly) (24 smoking) **S** £60-£112.95;
D £80-£142.95 (incl. bkfst) **Facilities** FTV Complimentary pass to nearby health club Xmas New Year Wi-fi
Conf Class 60 Board 40 Thtr 170 Del from £125 to £145
Services Lift **Parking** 200 **Notes** LB ⊗ Civ Wed 140

Jurys Inn Croydon

JURYS Inns

★★★ 78% HOTEL

☎ 020 8448 6000 📄 020 8448 6111
Wellesley Rd CR0 9XY
e-mail: jurysinncroydon@jurysinns.com
web: www.jurysinns.com
dir: Off A212, in town centre adjacent to Whitgift Centre

This modern hotel, located in the town centre, has spacious bedrooms with air conditioning. The contemporary public areas include a choice of eating options and a busy state-of-the-art conference centre. Parking is available in a nearby multi-storey at reduced rates.

Rooms 240 (168 fmly) (50 smoking) **S** £65-£110;
D £65-£110* **Facilities** New Year Wi-fi **Conf** Class 50
Board 40 Thtr 100 Del from £105 to £131* **Services** Lift
Air con **Notes** LB ⊗ Closed 24-26 Dec

South Park Hotel

★★★ 74% HOTEL

☎ 020 8688 5644 📄 020 8760 0861
3-5 South Park Hill Rd, South Croydon CR2 7DY
e-mail: reception@southparkhotel.co.uk
web: www.southparkhotel.co.uk
dir: follow A235 to town centre. At Coombe Rd lights turn right (A212) towards Addington, 0.5m to rdbt take 3rd exit into South Park Hill Rd, hotel on left

This intimate hotel has easy access to rail and road networks with some off-street parking available. Attractively decorated bedrooms vary in size and offer a good range of in-room facilities. Public areas consist of a bar and lounge with large sofas and an informal dining area where meals are served.

Rooms 30 (2 fmly) (9 GF) **Facilities** FTV Wi-fi
Conf Class 50 Board 30 Thtr 60 Del from £115 to £135*
Parking 15 **Notes** ⊗

Express by Holiday Inn London-Croydon

BUDGET HOTEL

☎ 0208 2531200 📄 0208 2531201
1 Priddys Yard, Off Frith Rd CR0 1TS
e-mail: admin@exhicroydon.com
web: www.hiexpress.com/london-croydon

A modern hotel ideal for families and business travellers. Fresh and uncomplicated, the spacious rooms include Sky TV, power shower and tea and coffee-making facilities. Continental buffet breakfast is included in the room rate; other meals may be taken at the nearby family pub or restaurant. See also the Hotel Groups pages.

Rooms 156 **Conf** Class 30 Board 30 Thtr 60

Innkeeper's Lodge Croydon South

BUDGET HOTEL

☎ 0845 112 6118 📄 0845 112 6185
415 Brighton Rd CR2 6EJ
web: www.innkeeperslodge.com/croydon
dir: M23 junct 7/A23 or M25 junct 6/A22. At Purley take A235 Brighton road, N towards South Croydon, for 1m. Lodge on right

Innkeeper's Lodge represents an exciting, high value concept within the budget hotel market. Comfortable bedrooms provide excellent facilities that include satellite TV and modem points. Options include family rooms, and for the corporate guest, cutting edge IT which includes Wi-fi access. A popular Carvery provides all-day food, including an extensive, complimentary continental breakfast.

Rooms 30 (5 fmly) **S** £59.95-£75; **D** £59.95-£75 (incl. bkfst)

Travelodge Croydon Central

BUDGET HOTEL

☎ 08719 846 318 📄 020 8686 7808
Norfolk House, Wellesley Rd CR0 1LH
web: www.travelodge.co.uk
dir: A212 signed Central Croydon. Croydon Underpass, hotel on right.

Travelodge offers good quality, good value, modern accommodation. Ideal for families, the spacious en suite bedrooms include remote-control TV, tea and coffee-making facilities and comfortable beds. A breakfast buffet is available in the large dining room beside a comfortable TV lounge See also the Hotel Groups pages.

Rooms 147 **S** fr £29; **D** fr £29

ENFIELD — Map 6 TQ39

Royal Chace

★★★★ 77% ⊛ HOTEL

☎ 020 8884 8181 📄 020 8884 8150
The Ridgeway EN2 8AR
e-mail: enquiries@royalchacehotel.co.uk
dir: M25 junct 24 take A1005 towards Enfield. Hotel 3m on right

This professionally run, privately owned hotel enjoys a peaceful location with open fields to the rear. Public rooms are smartly appointed; the first-floor Chace Brasserie is particularly appealing with its warm colour schemes and friendly service. Bedrooms are well presented and thoughtfully equipped.

Rooms 92 (5 fmly) (32 GF) **S** £150-£295; **D** £150-£295
(incl. bkfst)* **Facilities** FTV ⚓ Gym New Year Wi-fi
Conf Class 100 Board 40 Thtr 250 Del from £145 to
£155* **Parking** 200 **Notes** LB ⊗ Closed 24-30 Dec
RS Lunchtime/Sun eve Civ Wed 220

ENFIELD continued

Comfort Hotel Enfield

★★★ 72% HOTEL

☎ 020 8366 3511 🖹 020 8366 2432
52 Rowantree Rd EN2 8PW
e-mail: admin@comfortenfield.co.uk
web: www.comfortenfield.co.uk
dir: M25 junct 24 follow signs for A1005 towards Enfield. Hospital on left, across mini-rdbt, 3rd left onto Bycullah Rd, 2nd left into Rowantree Rd.

This hotel is situated in a quiet residential area, close to the centre of Enfield. Comfortable accommodation is provided in the thoughtfully equipped bedrooms, which include ground floor and family rooms. Public areas include a cosy bar and lounge, conference and function rooms and the smart Etruscan Restaurant.

Rooms 34 (34 annexe) (3 fmly) **S** £45-£89; **D** £55-£99 (incl. bkfst)* **Facilities** Wi-fi **Conf** Class 25 Board 25 Thtr 65 **Parking** 17 **Notes** LB ⊗ Civ Wed 65

See advert on this page

FELTHAM

See LONDON plan 1 A2

Travelodge Feltham

BUDGET HOTEL

☎ 08719 846 319 🖹 020 8890 0664
Res Centre, High St TW13 4EX
web: www.travelodge.co.uk
dir: A308 Staines. Right at Shears junct onto A244 Cadbury Rd, A244 onto Feltham High St

Travelodge offers good quality, good value, modern accommodation. Ideal for families, the spacious en suite bedrooms include remote-control TV, tea and coffee-making facilities and comfortable beds. Meals can be taken at the nearby family restaurant. See also the Hotel Groups pages.

Rooms 115 **S** fr £29; **D** fr £29

HADLEY WOOD   Map 6 TQ29

West Lodge Park

★★★★ 80% ❀❀ HOTEL

☎ 020 8216 3900 🖹 020 8216 3937
Cockfosters Rd EN4 0PY
e-mail: westlodgepark@bealeshotels.co.uk
web: www.bealeshotels.co.uk
dir: on A111, 1m S of M25 junct 24

Stylish country house set in stunning parkland and gardens, yet only 12 miles from central London and a few miles from the M25. Bedrooms are individually decorated, in traditional style and offer excellent in-room facilities. Annexe rooms feature air-conditioning and have access to an outdoor patio area. Public rooms include the award-winning Cedar Restaurant, cosy bar area and separate lounge.

Rooms 59 (13 annexe) (1 fmly) (11 GF) **S** £70-£85; **D** £90-£115* **Facilities** STV Putt green ⛳ Massage Manicure Free use of nearby leisure club 🎵 Xmas New Year Wi-fi **Conf** Class 30 Board 30 Thtr 64 Del from £180 to £205* **Services** Lift **Parking** 200 **Notes** LB ⊗ Civ Wed 72

HAMPTON COURT

See LONDON SECTION plan 1 B1

The Carlton Mitre

★★★★ 74% HOTEL

☎ 020 8979 9988 🖹 020 8979 9777
Hampton Court Rd KT8 9BN
e-mail: mitre@carltonhotels.co.uk
dir: M3 junct 1 follow signs to Sunbury & Hampton Court Palace. At Hampton Court Palace rdbt right, hotel on right

This hotel, dating back in parts to 1655, enjoys an enviable setting on the banks of the River Thames opposite Hampton Court Palace. The riverside restaurant and Edge bar/brasserie command wonderful views as well as spacious terraces for alfresco dining. Bedrooms are spacious and elegant with excellent facilities. Parking is limited.

Rooms 36 (2 fmly) **D** £135-£180 (incl. bkfst)* **Facilities** STV Xmas New Year Wi-fi **Conf** Class 60 Board 40 Thtr 120 Del from £200 to £250* **Services** Lift Air con **Parking** 13 **Notes** LB ⊗ Civ Wed 100

Liongate

★★ 69% HOTEL

☎ 020 8977 8121 🖹 020 8943 4029
Hampton Court Rd KT8 9DD
e-mail: lionres@dhillonhotels.co.uk
dir: M25 junct 12/M3 towards London. M3 junct 1, A308 at mini-rdbt turn left. Hotel opposite Hampton Court Palace gates

Dating back to 1721 this hotel enjoys a wonderful location opposite the Lion Gate entrance to Hampton Court and beside the gate into Bushy Park. Despite the hotel's age the bedrooms have a contemporary style. The public bar, restaurant and lounge area are open-plan and

Rooms 115 (39 fmly) (15 smoking) **S** £55-£129;
D £55-£129* **Facilities** Spa STV ⓣ supervised Gym
Xmas New Year Wi-fi **Conf** Class 100 Board 70 Thtr 180
Del from £130 to £175* **Services** Lift Air con **Parking** 100
(charged) **Notes** LB ⊗ Civ Wed 140

TEDDINGTON

See **LONDON** plan 1 B/C2

Park

Ⓤ

☎ 020 8614 9700 ▤ 020 8614 9701
Park Rd TW11 0AB
e-mail: reservations.park@foliohotels.com
web: www.foliohotels.com
dir: A312 Kingston, 1st exit signed Teddington. Straight
onto Broad St to T-junct, hotel in front.

Currently the rating for this establishment is not confirmed.
This may be due to a change of ownership or because it has
only recently joined the AA rating scheme. For further
details please see the AA website: www.theAA.com

Rooms 43 (30 annexe) (8 fmly) (10 GF) **S** £190; **D** £190*
Facilities ♫ Xmas New Year Wi-fi **Services** Lift
Parking 24 **Notes** LB ⊗

TOLWORTH Map 6 TQ16

Travelodge Chessington Tolworth

BUDGET HOTEL

☎ 08719 846 210
Tolworth Tower KT6 7EL
web: www.travelodge.co.uk
dir: Leave A3 at Tolworth junct. At rdbt take 2nd exit
signed London (A3). Immediate left onto Ewell Rd. Lodge
on left

Travelodge offers good quality, good value, modern
accommodation. Ideal for families, the spacious en suite
bedrooms include remote-control TV, tea and coffee-
making facilities and comfortable beds. Meals can be
taken at the nearby family restaurant. See also the Hotel
Groups pages.

Rooms 120 **S** fr £29; **D** fr £29

TWICKENHAM

London Marriott Hotel Twickenham

Marriott
HOTELS & RESORTS

○

Rugby Rd TW1 1DS

Due to open early 2009.

Rooms 156

WEMBLEY

See **LONDON SECTION** plan 1 C5

Quality Hotel, Wembley

★★★ 71% HOTEL

☎ 020 8733 9000 ▤ 020 8733 9001
Empire Way HA9 0NH
e-mail: sales@hotels-wembley.com
dir: M1 junct 6 onto A406, right onto A404. Right onto
Empire Way, after rdbt at lights, Hotel on right.

Conveniently situated within walking distance of both the
Arena and conference centres this modern hotel offers
smart, comfortable, spacious bedrooms; many are air
conditioned. All rooms offer an excellent range of
amenities. Air-conditioned public areas include a large
restaurant serving a wide range of contemporary dishes.

Rooms 165 (70 fmly) (3 GF) (76 smoking) **S** £125-£149;
D £135-£169 (incl. bkfst) **Facilities** STV FTV Wi-fi
Conf Class 90 Board 90 Thtr 120 Del from £145
Services Lift Air con **Parking** 65 **Notes** ⊗

Ibis London Wembley

ibis
HOTEL

BUDGET HOTEL

☎ 0870 220 6581 ▤ 020 8453 5110
Southway HA9 6BA
e-mail: H3141@accor.com
web: www.ibishotel.com
dir: from Hanger Lane on A40, take A406 north, exit at
Wembley. A404 to lights junct with Wembley Hill Road,
turn right then 1st right into Southway. Hotel 75mtrs on
left

Modern, budget hotel offering comfortable
accommodation in bright and practical bedrooms.
Breakfast is self-service and dinner is available in the
restaurant. See also the Hotel Groups pages.

Rooms 210 (44 fmly)

WEST DRAYTON

Hotels are listed under Heathrow Airport

WOODFORD BRIDGE

See **LONDON** plan 1 H6

Menzies Prince Regent   **MenziesHotels**

★★★★ 72% HOTEL

☎ 020 8505 9966 ▤ 020 8506 0807
Manor Rd IG8 8AE
e-mail: princeregent@menzieshotels.co.uk
web: www.menzieshotels.co.uk
dir: M25 junct 26, to Loughton and Chigwell, hotel on
Manor Rd

Situated on the edge of Woodford Bridge and Chigwell,
this hotel with delightful rear gardens, offers easy access

into London as well as the M11 and M25. There is a good
range of spacious, well-equipped bedrooms. Extensive
conference and banqueting facilities are particularly well
appointed, and are well suited to weddings and business
events.

Rooms 61 (4 fmly) (15 GF) (10 smoking) **S** £90-£135;
D £110-£240 **Facilities** STV Xmas New Year Wi-fi
Conf Class 150 Board 80 Thtr 350 Del from £130 to £170
Services Lift **Parking** 200 **Notes** Civ Wed 350

WOODFORD GREEN

See **LONDON SECTION** plan 1 G6

Innkeeper's Lodge Chigwell

BUDGET HOTEL

☎ 0845 112 6117 ▤ 0845 112 6186
735 Chigwell Rd IG8 8AS
web: www.innkeeperslodge.com/chigwell
dir: M25 junct 26, A121 towards Loughton. Left at mini
rdt onto A1168 (signed Chigwell) to junct with A113. Turn
right, lodge 2m on left

Innkeeper's Lodge represents an exciting, high value
concept within the budget hotel market. Comfortable
bedrooms provide excellent facilities that include satellite
TV and modem points. Options include family rooms, and
for the corporate guest, cutting edge IT includes Wi-fi
access. Food is served all day in the adjacent Country
Pub. The extensive continental breakfast is
complimentary.

Rooms 34 **S** £59.95-£75; **D** £59.95-£75 (incl. bkfst)

MERSEYSIDE

BEBINGTON Map 15 SJ38

Travelodge Wirral Eastham

BUDGET HOTEL

☎ 0871 984 6184 ▤ 0151 327 2489
New Chester Rd CH62 9AQ
web: www.travelodge.co.uk
dir: on A41, N'bound off M53 junct 5

Travelodge offers good quality, good value, modern
accommodation. Ideal for families, the spacious en suite
bedrooms include remote-control TV, tea and coffee-
making facilities and comfortable beds. Meals can be
taken at the nearby family restaurant. See also the Hotel
Groups pages.

Rooms 31 **S** fr £29; **D** fr £29

BIRKENHEAD · Map 15 SJ38

Riverhill

★★★ 79% HOTEL

☎ 0151 653 3773 · 0151 653 7162
Talbot Rd, Prenton CH43 2HJ
e-mail: reception@theriverhill.co.uk
dir: M53 junct 3, A552. Left onto B5151 at lights, hotel 0.5m on right

Pretty lawns and gardens provide the setting for this friendly, privately owned hotel, which is conveniently situated about a mile from the M53. Attractively furnished, well-equipped bedrooms include ground floor, family, and four-poster rooms. Business meetings and weddings can be catered for. A wide choice of dishes is available in the restaurant, which overlooks the garden.

Rooms 15 (1 fmly) **S** £69.75; **D** £79.75-£89.75
Facilities STV FTV Free use of local leisure facilities Wi-fi **Conf** Class 30 Board 52 Thtr 50 **Parking** 32 **Notes** ⊗ Civ Wed 40

See advert on this page

FORMBY · Map 15 SD30

Formby Hall Golf Resort & Spa

Ⓤ

☎ 01704 875699 · 01704 832134
Southport Old Rd L37 0AB
e-mail: salesmanager@formbyhallgolfresort.co.uk
web: www.formbyhallgolfresort.co.uk
dir: A565 to 2nd rdbt, follow brown signs

Currently the rating for this establishment is not confirmed. This may be due to a change of ownership or because it has only recently joined the AA rating scheme. For further details please see the AA website: www.theAA.com

Rooms 62 (10 fmly) (29 GF) **S** £135-£195; **D** £135-£195*
Facilities Spa STV FTV ⊗ ♨ 18 Putt green Gym Kinesis studio Driving range Short ball area Xmas New Year Wi-fi **Conf** Class 60 Board 40 Thtr 300 **Services** Lift Air con **Parking** 457 **Notes** LB ⊗ Civ Wed 100

HAYDOCK · Map 15 SJ59

Thistle Haydock

★★★★ 76% ⊛ HOTEL

☎ 0871 376 9044 · & 01942 272000 · 0871 376 9144
Penny Ln WA11 9SG
e-mail: haydock@thistle.co.uk
web: www.thistlehotels.com/haydock
dir: M6 junct 23, follow Racecourse signs (A49) towards Ashton-in-Makerfield, 1st left, after bridge 1st turn

A smart, purpose-built hotel which offers an excellent standard of thoughtfully equipped accommodation. It is conveniently situated between Liverpool and Manchester, just off the M6. The wide range of leisure and meeting facilities prove popular with guests.

Rooms 137 (13 fmly) (78 GF) **S** £56-£170; **D** £66-£170*
Facilities Spa STV ⊗ supervised Gym Children's play area Xmas New Year Wi-fi **Conf** Class 140 Board 80 Thtr 300 Del from £99 to £230* **Parking** 200 **Notes** LB Civ Wed 110

Travelodge Haydock St Helens

BUDGET HOTEL

☎ 08719 846 145 · 01942 272067
Piele Rd WA11 0JZ
web: www.travelodge.co.uk
dir: 1m W of junct 23 on M6, on A580 westbound

Travelodge offers good quality, good value, modern accommodation. Ideal for families, the spacious en suite bedrooms include remote-control TV, tea and coffee-making facilities and comfortable beds. Meals can be taken at the nearby family restaurant. See also the Hotel Groups pages.

Rooms 62 **S** fr £29; **D** fr £29

KNOWSLEY · Map 15 SJ49

Suites Hotel Knowsley

★★★★ 72% HOTEL

☎ 0151 549 2222 · 0151 549 1116
Ribblers Ln L34 9HA
e-mail: enquiries@suiteshotelgroup.com
web: www.suiteshotelgroup.com
dir: M57 junct 4, at x-rds of A580 East Lancashire Rd.

Located a close to the M54, this hotel is just a 10-minute drive from Liverpool's city centre. It offers superior, well-equipped accommodation and there is a choice of lounges plus Handley's Restaurant. Guests have the use of the impressive leisure centre, and there are extensive conference facilities.

Rooms 101 (39 fmly) (20 GF) (20 smoking) **S** £65-£107; **D** £65-£127 (incl. bkfst)* **Facilities** STV ⊗ supervised Gym Xmas New Year Wi-fi **Conf** Class 60 Board 50 Thtr 240 Del from £110 to £142* **Services** Lift Air con **Parking** 200 **Notes** LB ⊗ Civ Wed 140

LIVERPOOL | Map 15 SJ39

Radisson SAS Hotel Liverpool

★★★★ 79% @ HOTEL

☎ 0151 966 1500 📠 0151 966 1501
107 Old Hall St L3 9BD
e-mail: info.liverpool@radissonsas.com
web: www.liverpool.radissonsas.co.uk
dir: Follow Liverpool City Centre & Albert Dock signs. Left onto Old Hall Street from Leeds Street dual carriageway

This smart hotel enjoys an enviable location on the city's waterfront. The stylish, well-equipped bedrooms are designed in two eye-catching schemes - Ocean and Urban; junior suites and business rooms offer additional choices. Public areas include extensive conference and leisure facilities, and the trendy White Bar and Filini Restaurant serve imaginative Italian cuisine.

Rooms 194 (44 smoking) **S** £99-£170; **D** £99-£170*
Facilities Spa STV 🅣 supervised Gym Wi-fi **Conf** Class 60 Board 44 Thtr 180 **Services** Lift Air con **Parking** 25 (charged) **Notes** ✪ Civ Wed 130

Liverpool Marriott Hotel South

★★★★ 79% HOTEL

☎ 0151 494 5000 📠 0151 494 5053
Speke Aerodrome L24 8QD
e-mail: liverpool.south@marriotthotels.co.uk
web: www.liverpoolmarriottsouth.co.uk
dir: M62 junct 6, take Knowsley Expressway towards Speke. At end of Expressway right onto A561 towards Liverpool. Approx 4m, hotel on left just after Estuary Commerce Park

Previously Liverpool Airport's building where fans gathered in the 1960s to see The Beatles, this hotel is now Grade II listed. It has a distinctive look, reflected in its art deco architecture and interior design. The spacious bedrooms are fully air-conditioned and feature a comprehensive range of facilities. Feature rooms include the Presidential Suite in the base of the old control tower.

Rooms 164 (50 fmly) (46 GF) **Facilities** 🅣 ⤳ supervised 🅢 Gym Squash Wi-fi **Conf** Class 120 Board 24 Thtr 280 **Services** Lift Air con **Parking** 200 **Notes** ✪ Civ Wed 200

Thornton Hall Hotel and Spa CLASSIC BRITISH HOTELS

★★★★ 77% @@ HOTEL

☎ 0151 336 3938 📠 0151 336 7864
Neston Rd CH63 1JF
e-mail: reservations@thorntonhallhotel.com
web: www.thorntonhallhotel.com

(For full entry see Thornton Hough)

Liverpool Marriott Hotel City Centre **Marriott** HOTELS & RESORTS

★★★★ 77% HOTEL

☎ 0151 476 8000 📠 0151 474 5000
1 Queen Square L1 1RH
e-mail: liverpool.city@marriotthotels.com
web: www.liverpoolmarriottcitycentre.co.uk
dir: end of M62 follow city centre signs, A5047, Edge Lane. From city centre follow signs for Queens Square parking

An impressive modern hotel located in the heart of the city. The elegant public rooms include a ground-floor café bar, and a cocktail bar and stylish Oliver's Restaurant on the first floor. The hotel also boasts a well-equipped, indoor leisure health club with pool. Bedrooms are stylishly appointed and benefit from a host of extra facilities.

Rooms 146 (29 fmly) **Facilities** 🅣 Gym Boxercise Aqua aerobics Body sculpture Xmas New Year Wi-fi **Conf** Class 90 Board 30 Thtr 300 **Services** Lift Air con **Parking** 8 (charged) **Notes** LB ✪ Civ Wed 150

Crowne Plaza Liverpool   CROWNE PLAZA

★★★★ 74% HOTEL

☎ 0151 243 8000 📠 0151 243 8008
St Nicholas Place, Princes Dock, Pier Head L3 1QW
web: www.crowneplaza.co.uk

Situated right on the waterfront, yet still within striking distance of the city centre this hotel offers comprehensive leisure and meeting facilities, whether taking a snack in the spacious lounge or using the business centre. Contemporary in style with superb quality, this hotel offers a welcome to business or leisure guests alike.

Rooms 159 **D** fr £99* **Facilities** Spa STV FTV 🅣 Gym New Year Wi-fi **Conf** Class 340 Board 30 Thtr 500 **Services** Lift Air con **Parking** 150 (charged) **Notes** ✪ Civ Wed 500

Malmaison Liverpool *Malmaison*

★★★ 82% @ HOTEL

☎ 0151 229 5000 📠 0151 229 5025
7 William Jessop Way, Princes Dock L3 1QZ
e-mail: liverpool@malmaison.com
dir: A5080 follow signs for Pier Head/Southport/Bootle. Into Baln St to rdbt, 1st exit at rdbt, immediately left onto William Jessop Way

Malmaison Liverpool is a purpose built hotel with cutting edge and contemporary style, a strong brand standard of this company. 'Mal' Liverpool has a stunning location, alongside the river and docks, and in the heart of the city's regeneration. Bedrooms are stylish and comfortable and are provided with lots of extra facilities. The public areas are packed with fun and style, and there is a number of meeting rooms as well as private dining available here, including a chef's table.

Rooms 130 **Facilities** Gym Wi-fi **Conf** Class 28 Board 18 Thtr 50 **Services** Lift Air con

The Royal THE INDEPENDENTS HOTEL ASSOCIATION

★★★ 80% HOTEL

☎ 0151 928 2332 📠 0151 949 0320
Marine Ter, Waterloo L22 5PR
e-mail: enquiries@liverpool-royalhotel.co.uk
web: www.liverpool-royalhotel.co.uk
dir: 6.5m NW of city centre, left from A565 (Liverpool to Southport road) at monument. Hotel at bottom of road

Dating back to 1815, this Grade II listed hotel is situated on the outskirts of the city, beside the Marine Gardens. Bedrooms are smartly appointed and some feature four-poster beds and spa baths. Spacious public areas enjoy splendid views and include an elegant restaurant, an attractive bar lounge and a conservatory.

Rooms 25 (5 fmly) **S** £59.50-£120; **D** £69.50-£160 (incl. bkfst) **Facilities** FTV New Year Wi-fi **Conf** Class 70 Board 40 Thtr 100 **Parking** 25 **Notes** ✪

LIVERPOOL continued

Best Western Alicia

★★★ 77% HOTEL

☎ 0151 727 4411 📠 0151 727 6752
3 Aigburth Dr, Sefton Park L17 3AA
e-mail: aliciahotel@feathers.uk.com
web: www.feathers.uk.com
dir: From end of M62 take A5058 to Sefton Park, then left, follow park around

This stylish and friendly hotel overlooks Sefton Park and is just a few minutes' drive from both the city centre and John Lennon Airport. Bedrooms are well equipped and comfortable. Day rooms include a striking modern restaurant and bar. Extensive, stylish function facilities make this a popular wedding venue.

Rooms 41 (8 fmly) **S** £64-£119; **D** £74-£199*
Facilities STV Xmas New Year Wi-fi **Conf** Class 80 Board 40 Thtr 120 Del from £119 to £159* **Services** Lift **Parking** 40 **Notes** LB ✪ Civ Wed 120

Jurys Inn Liverpool

★★★ 73% HOTEL

☎ 0151 244 3777 📠 0151 244 3888
No 31 Keel Wharf L3 4FN

Centrally located adjacent to the railway station, this modern, stylish hotel is easily accessible from major road networks. Bedrooms provide good guest comfort and in-room facilities are suited for both leisure and business markets. Public areas include a number of meeting rooms and a popular bar and restaurant.

Rooms 310

Holiday Inn Liverpool

★★★ Ⓐ HOTEL

☎ 0151 709 7090 📠 0151 709 0137
St John's Precinct, Lime St L1 1NQ
web: www.holidayinn.co.uk

Rooms 139

Atlantic Tower by Thistle

thistle

Ⓤ

☎ 0871 376 9025 📠 0871 376 9125
Chapel St L3 9RE
e-mail: liverpool@thistle.co.uk
web: www.thistlehotels.com/liverpool
dir: M6 onto M62 follow signs for Albert Dock, turn right at Liver Building. Stay in lane marked Chapel St, hotel on left.

Currently the rating for this establishment is not confirmed. This may be due to a change of ownership or because it has only recently joined the AA rating scheme. For further details please see the AA website: www.theAA.com

Rooms 225 (28 fmly) (24 smoking) **S** £79-£170;
D £89-£170 (incl. bkfst)* **Facilities** STV FTV New Year Wi-fi **Conf** Class 40 Board 30 Thtr 120 **Services** Lift Air con **Parking** 56 (charged) **Notes** LB Civ Wed 80

Campanile Liverpool

Campanile

BUDGET HOTEL

☎ 0151 709 8104 📠 0151 709 8725
Chaloner St, Queens Dock L3 4AJ
e-mail: liverpool@campanile.com
dir: follow tourist signs marked Albert Dock. Hotel on waterfront

This modern building offers accommodation in smart, well-equipped bedrooms, all with en suite bathrooms. Refreshments may be taken at the informal bistro. See also the Hotel Groups pages.

Rooms 100 (4 fmly) (33 GF) **Conf** Class 18 Board 24 Thtr 35

Express by Holiday Inn Liverpool - Knowsley

BUDGET HOTEL

☎ 0151 549 2700 📠 0151 549 2800
Ribblers Ln, Knowsley L34 9HA
e-mail: liverpool@exhi.co.uk
web: www.hiexpress.com/lpool-knowsley
dir: M57 junct 4, last exit off rdbt, then 1st left. Hotel on left

A modern hotel ideal for families and business travellers. Fresh and uncomplicated, the spacious rooms include Sky TV, power shower and tea and coffee-making facilities. Continental buffet breakfast is included in the room rate; other meals may be taken at the nearby family pub or restaurant. See also the Hotel Groups pages.

Rooms 86 (62 fmly)

Ibis Liverpool City Centre

BUDGET HOTEL

☎ 0151 706 9800 📠 0151 706 9810
27 Wapping L1 8LY
e-mail: H3140@accor-hotels.com
web: www.ibishotel.com
dir: from M62 follow Albert Dock signs. Opposite Dock entrance

Modern, budget hotel offering comfortable accommodation in bright and practical bedrooms. Breakfast is self-service and dinner is available in the restaurant. See also the Hotel Groups pages.

Rooms 127 (15 fmly) (23 GF)

Innkeeper's Lodge Liverpool North

BUDGET HOTEL

☎ 0845 112 6023 📠 0845 112 6278
502 Queen's Dr, Stoneycroft L13 0AS
web: www.innkeeperslodge.com/liverpoolnorth
dir: From lights at end of M62, right onto A5080. Under flyover, right onto A5080 (ring road) signed Bootle. At lights with A57, straight over into Queen's Drive. Lodge on left.

Innkeeper's Lodge represents an exciting, high value concept within the budget hotel market. Comfortable bedrooms provide excellent facilities that include satellite TV and modem points. Options include family rooms, and for the corporate guest, cutting edge IT which includes Wi-fi access. A popular Carvery provides all-day food, including an extensive, complimentary continental breakfast.

Rooms 21 (6 fmly) **S** £53-£55; **D** £53-£55 (incl. bkfst)

Innkeeper's Lodge Liverpool South (Airport)

BUDGET HOTEL

☎ 0845 112 6024 📠 0845 112 6277
531 Aigburth Rd L19 9DN
web: www.innkeeperslodge.com/liverpoolsouth
dir: M62 junct 6 or M57 junct 1, A5300, follow Liverpool (S)/Airport signs. At rdbt take A562 (signed Airport). Then A561 through Garston. Lodge on right opposite Liverpool Cricket Ground.

Innkeeper's Lodge represents an exciting, high value concept within the budget hotel market. Comfortable bedrooms provide excellent facilities that include satellite TV and modem points. Options include family rooms, and for the corporate guest, cutting edge IT which includes Wi-fi access. A popular Carvery provides all-day food, including an extensive, complimentary continental breakfast.

Rooms 32 (6 fmly) **S** £53-£55; **D** £53-£55 (incl. bkfst) **Conf** Thtr 12

Travelodge Liverpool Central

BUDGET HOTEL

☎ 08719 846 156 ▤ 0151 227 5838
25 Haymarket L1 6ER
web: www.travelodge.co.uk

Travelodge offers good quality, good value, modern accommodation. Ideal for families, the spacious en suite bedrooms include remote-control TV, tea and coffee-making facilities and comfortable beds. Meals can be taken at the nearby family restaurant. See also the Hotel Groups pages.

Rooms 105 **S** fr £29; **D** fr £29

Travelodge Liverpool Docks

BUDGET HOTEL

☎ 08719 846 030 ▤ 0151 707 7769
Brunswick Dock, Sefton St L3 4BH
web: www.travelodge.co.uk

Rooms 31 **S** fr £29; **D** fr £29

MORETON	Map 15 SJ28

Leasowe Castle

★★★ 75% HOTEL

☎ 0151 606 9191 ▤ 0151 678 5551
Leasowe Rd CH46 3RF
e-mail: reservations@leasowecastle.com
web: www.leasowecastle.com
dir: M53 junct 1, 1st exit from rdbt onto A551. Hotel 0.75m on right

Located adjacent to Leasowe Golf Course and within easy reach of Liverpool, Chester and all of the Wirral's attractions, this historic hotel dates back to 1592. Bedrooms are smartly appointed and well equipped, many enjoying ocean views. Public areas retain many original features. Weddings and functions are well catered for.

Rooms 47 (3 fmly) **S** £65-£85; **D** £75-£95 (incl. bkfst)* **Facilities** Gym Water sports Sea Fishing Sailing Health club Xmas New Year Wi-fi **Conf** Class 200 Board 80 Thtr 400 **Services** Lift **Parking** 200 **Notes** LB ⊗ Civ Wed 250

NEWTON-LE-WILLOWS	Map 15 SJ59

Kirkfield Hotel

★★ 63% HOTEL

☎ 01925 228196 ▤ 01925 291540
2/4 Church St WA12 9SU
e-mail: enquiries@kirkfieldhotel.co.uk
dir: on A49, opposite St Peter's Church

A conveniently located, family-run hotel that offers comfortable accommodation. Guests receive a friendly

---

welcome and there is an informal atmosphere throughout. A set menu is available and there are options for lighter dining in the attractive bar area.

Rooms 15 (3 fmly) (1 GF) (6 smoking) **Facilities** Wi-fi **Conf** Class 60 Board 20 Thtr 70

Holiday Inn

Ⓤ

☎ 0870 400 9039 ▤ 01942 718419
Lodge Ln, Newton Le Willows WA12 0JG
e-mail: haydock@ihg.com
web: www.holidayinn.co.uk
dir: M6 junct 23, take A49 to Ashton-in-Makerfield. Hotel 0.25m on right by racecourse

Currently the rating for this establishment is not confirmed. This may be due to a change of ownership or because it has only recently joined the AA rating scheme. For further details please see the AA website: www.theAA.com

Rooms 136 (12 fmly) (23 GF) (38 smoking) **Facilities** STV Ⓣ Gym Xmas New Year **Conf** Class 70 Board 60 Thtr 180 Del from £99 to £145* **Services** Lift Air con **Parking** 204 **Notes** Civ Wed 120

SOUTHPORT	Map 15 SD31

Scarisbrick

★★★ 77% HOTEL

☎ 01704 543000 ▤ 01704 533335
Lord St PR8 1NZ
e-mail: info@scarisbrickhotel.com
web: www.scarisbrickhotel.co.uk
dir: from S: M6 junct 26, M58 to Ormskirk then Southport. From N: A59 from Preston, well signed

Centrally located on Southport's famous Lord Street, this privately owned hotel offers a high standard of attractively furnished, thoughtfully equipped accommodation. A wide range of eating options is available, from the bistro style of Maloney's Kitchen to the more formal Knightsbridge restaurant. Extensive leisure and conference facilities are also available.

Rooms 88 (5 fmly) **S** £50-£85; **D** £60-£160 (incl. bkfst) **Facilities** STV Ⓣ Gym Use of private leisure centre Beauty & aromatherapy studio ♫ Xmas New Year Wi-fi **Conf** Class 100 Board 80 Thtr 200 Del from £90 to £120 **Services** Lift **Parking** 66 **Notes** LB ⊗ Civ Wed 170

Best Western Stutelea Hotel & Leisure Club

★★★ 75% HOTEL

☎ 01704 544220 ▤ 01704 500232
Alexandra Rd PR9 0NB
e-mail: greg@warnerhotels.co.uk
dir: off promenade

This family owned and run hotel enjoys a quiet location in a residential area, a short walk from Lord Street and the promenade. Bedrooms vary in size and style and include

---

family suites and rooms with balconies overlooking the attractive gardens. The elegant restaurant has a cosmopolitan theme; alternatively the Garden Bar, in the leisure centre, offers light snacks throughout the day.

Rooms 22 (4 fmly) (3 GF) **Facilities** Ⓣ Gym Games room Keep fit classes Steam room **Services** Lift **Parking** 15 **Notes** ⊗

Best Western Royal Clifton Hotel & Spa

★★★ 73% HOTEL

☎ 01704 533771 ▤ 01704 500657
Promenade PR8 1RB
e-mail: sales@royalclifton.co.uk
dir: adjacent to Marine Lake

This grand, traditional hotel benefits from a prime location on the promenade. Bedrooms range in size and style, but all are comfortable and thoughtfully equipped. Public areas include the lively Bar C, the elegant Pavilion Restaurant and a modern, well-equipped leisure club. Extensive conference and banqueting facilities make this hotel a popular function venue.

Rooms 120 (23 fmly) (6 GF) **S** £45-£85; **D** £60-£125 (incl. bkfst)* **Facilities** Spa STV Ⓣ supervised Gym Hair & beauty Steam room Aromatherapy ♫ Xmas New Year Wi-fi **Conf** Class 100 Board 65 Thtr 250 Del from £85 to £125* **Services** Lift **Parking** 60 **Notes** LB ⊗ Civ Wed 150

Cambridge House

★★ 81% HOTEL

☎ 01704 538372 ▤ 01704 547183
4 Cambridge Rd PR9 9NG
e-mail: info@cambridgehouse.co.uk
dir: A565 N from town centre, over 2 rdbts

This delightful house is in a peaceful location close to Hesketh Park, a short drive from Lord Street. The

Continued

SOUTHPORT continued

spacious, individually styled bedrooms, including a luxurious honeymoon suite, are furnished to a very high standard. Stylish public areas include a lounge, a cosy bar and a dining room. Attentive service and delicious food complete the picture.

Rooms 16 (2 fmly) **S** £63-£90; **D** £78-£118 (incl. bkfst)* **Facilities** Wi-fi **Conf** Class 30 Thtr 30 Del from £90 to £120* **Parking** 20 **Notes** LB

Bold Hotel

★★ 76% HOTEL

☎ 01704 532578 📠 01704 532528
585 Lord St PR9 0BE
e-mail: info@boldhotel.com
dir: M6 junct 26/M58/A570 towards Southport. In Southport follow signs to Lord St. Hotel on junct with Seabank Rd

Enjoying a central location, this family hotel is just a minute's walk from the promenade and local attractions. Thoughtfully equipped spacious bedrooms are suitable for business or leisure guests. There is a large bar and also a popular brasserie.

Rooms 23 (8 fmly) **S** £50-£60; **D** £65-£90 (incl. bkfst)* **Facilities** Xmas New Year **Conf** Class 120 Board 100 Thtr 200 **Parking** 12 **Notes** LB ⊗

Balmoral Lodge

★★ 71% HOTEL

☎ 01704 544298 & 530751 📠 01704 501224
41 Queens Rd PR9 9EX
e-mail: balmorallg@aol.com
web: www.balmorallodge.co.uk
dir: edge of town on A565 (Preston road). Turn E at rdbt at North Lord St, left at lights, hotel 200yds on left

Situated in a quiet residential area close to Lord Street, this friendly hotel is particularly popular with golfers. Smartly appointed bedrooms are well equipped for both business and leisure guests; some benefit from private patios overlooking the attractive gardens. Stylish public areas include the restaurant and an attractive bar lounge.

Rooms 15 (4 annexe) (1 fmly) (4 GF) **Facilities** Wi-fi **Parking** 12 **Notes** LB ⊗

Thornton Hall Hotel and Spa

★★★★ 77% ⊛⊛ HOTEL   CLASSIC BRITISH HOTELS

☎ 0151 336 3938 📠 0151 336 7864
Neston Rd CH63 1JF
e-mail: reservations@thorntonhallhotel.com
web: www.thorntonhallhotel.com
dir: M53 junct 4, B5151/Neston onto B5136 to Thornton Hough (signed)

Dating back to the mid 1800s, this country-house hotel has been carefully extended and restored. Public areas include an impressive leisure spa boasting excellent facilities, a choice of restaurants and a spacious bar. Bedrooms vary in style and include feature rooms in the main house and more contemporary rooms in the garden wing. Delightful grounds and gardens, and impressive function facilities make this a popular wedding venue.

Rooms 63 (6 fmly) (28 GF) **S** £65-£125; **D** £65-£125* **Facilities** Spa 🏊 ⛳ Gym Hot tub Beauty spa Hairdressing salon Wi-fi **Conf** Class 225 Board 80 Thtr 450 Del from £120 to £155* **Parking** 250 **Notes** LB ⊗ Closed 1 Jan Civ Wed 400

Grove House

★★★ 78% HOTEL

☎ 0151 639 3947 & 0151 630 4558 📠 0151 639 0028
Grove Rd CH45 3HF
e-mail: reception@thegrovehouse.co.uk
dir: M53 junct 1, A554 (Wallasey New Brighton), right after church onto Harrison Drive, left after Windsors Garage onto Grove Rd

Pretty lawns and gardens provide the setting for this friendly hotel, conveniently situated about a mile from the M53. Attractively furnished, well-equipped bedrooms include family and four-poster rooms. Business meetings and weddings can be catered for. A wide choice of dishes is available in the restaurant that overlooks the garden.

Rooms 14 (7 fmly) **S** fr £69.50; **D** £85-£115* **Facilities** FTV Wi-fi **Conf** Class 30 Board 50 Thtr 50 Del from £108.90 to £126.90* **Parking** 28 **Notes** LB ⊗ RS Bank holidays Civ Wed 50

See advert on this page

NORFOLK

ACLE
Map 13 TG41

Travelodge Great Yarmouth Acle

BUDGET HOTEL

☎ 08719 846 032 📄 01493 751970
NR13 3BE
web: www.travelodge.co.uk
dir: junct of A47 & Acle bypass

Travelodge offers good quality, good value, modern accommodation. Ideal for families, the spacious en suite bedrooms include remote-control TV, tea and coffee-making facilities and comfortable beds. Meals can be taken at the nearby family restaurant. See also the Hotel Groups pages.

Rooms 40 **S** fr £29; **D** fr £29

ALBURGH
Map 13 TM28

The Dove Restaurant with Rooms

◉◉ RESTAURANT WITH ROOMS

☎ 01986 788315 📄 01986 788315
Holbrook Hill IP20 0EP
e-mail: thedovenorfolk@freeula.com
dir: Between Harleston & Bungay at junct A143 & B1062

Expect a warm welcome from the hosts at this restaurant with rooms, situated just off the A143 between Harleston and Bungay. Bedrooms are pleasantly decorated, furnished with pine pieces and have modern facilities. Public rooms include a lounge area with a small bar, and a smart restaurant with well-spaced tables.

Rooms 2 (1 pri facs) (1 fmly)

BARNHAM BROOM
Map 13 TG00

Barnham Broom Hotel, Golf & Restaurant

★★★ 83% ◉◉ HOTEL

☎ 01603 759393 📄 01603 758224
NR9 4DD
e-mail: amortimer@barnham-broom.co.uk
web: www.barnham-broom.co.uk
dir: A11/A47 towards Swaffham, follow brown tourist signs

Situated in a peaceful rural location just a short drive from Norwich, this hotel offers contemporary style bedrooms, tastefully furnished and thoughtfully equipped. The Sports Bar serves a range of snacks and meals throughout the day, or guests may choose from the carte menu in Flints Restaurant. There also are extensive leisure, conference and banqueting facilities.

Rooms 52 (7 fmly) (22 GF) **S** £49-£120; **D** £59-£140 (incl. bkfst)* **Facilities** STV ⊕ supervised ♨ 36 ⚘ Putt green Gym Squash Sauna Steam room Personal trainers Xmas New Year Wi-fi **Conf** Class 100 Board 80 Thtr 250 Del from £95 to £140* **Parking** 150 **Notes** LB Civ Wed 200

BLAKENEY   Map 13 TG04

INSPECTORS' CHOICE

Morston Hall
★★★ ◉◉◉ HOTEL

☎ 01263 741041   🖷 01263 740419
Morston, Holt NR25 7AA
e-mail: reception@morstonhall.com
web: www.morstonhall.com
dir: 1m W of Blakeney on A149 (King's Lynn Cromer road)

This delightful 17th-century country-house hotel enjoys a tranquil setting amid well-tended gardens. The comfortable public rooms offer a choice of attractive lounges and a sunny conservatory, while the elegant dining room is the perfect setting to enjoy Galton Blackiston's award-winning cuisine. The spacious bedrooms are individually decorated and stylishly furnished with modern opulence.

Rooms 13 (6 annexe) (7 GF) **D** £260-£300 (incl. bkfst & dinner)* **Facilities** STV New Year Wi-fi **Parking** 40 **Notes** LB Closed 1 Jan-2 Feb & 2 days Xmas

The Blakeney
★★★ 82% ◉ HOTEL

☎ 01263 740797   🖷 01263 740795
The Quay NR25 7NE
e-mail: reception@blakeney-hotel.co.uk
web: www.blakeney-hotel.co.uk
dir: off A149 coast road, 8m W of Sheringham

A traditional, privately owned hotel situated on the quayside with superb views across the estuary and the salt marshes to Blakeney Point. Public rooms feature an elegant restaurant, ground-floor lounge, a bar and a first-floor sun lounge overlooking the harbour. Bedrooms are smartly decorated and equipped with modern facilities, some enjoy the lovely sea views.

Rooms 64 (16 annexe) (20 fmly) (18 GF) **S** £84-£140; **D** £168-£304 (incl. bkfst & dinner)* **Facilities** 🟢 Gym Billiards Snooker Table tennis Sauna Steam room Spa bath Xmas New Year Wi-fi **Conf** Class 100 Board 100 Thtr 150 Del from £120* **Services** Lift **Parking** 60 **Notes** LB

Blakeney Manor
★★ 76% HOTEL

☎ 01263 740376   🖷 01263 741116
The Quay NR25 7ND
e-mail: reception@blakeneymanor.co.uk
dir: exit A149 at Blakeney towards Blakeney Quay. Hotel at end of quay between Mariner's Hill & Friary Hills

An attractive Norfolk flint building overlooking Blakeney Marshes close to the town centre and quayside. The bedrooms are located in flint-faced barns in a courtyard adjacent to the main building. The spacious public rooms include a choice of lounges, a conservatory, a popular bar and a large restaurant offering an interesting choice of dishes.

Rooms 35 (28 annexe) (26 GF) **Facilities** Xmas **Parking** 40 **Notes** LB No children 14yrs

The Pheasant
★★ 76% HOTEL

☎ 01263 588382   🖷 01263 588101
Coast Rd, Kelling NR25 7EG
e-mail: enquiries@pheasanthotelnorfolk.co.uk
dir: on A149 coast road, mid-way between Sheringham & Blakeney

Popular hotel ideally situated on the main coast road just a short drive from the bustling town of Holt. Bedrooms are split between the main house and a modern wing of spacious rooms to the rear of the property. Public rooms include a busy lounge bar, a residents' lounge and a large restaurant.

Rooms 30 (1 fmly) (24 GF) **S** £52-£62; **D** £104-£114 (incl. bkfst)* **Facilities** Xmas New Year **Conf** Class 50 Board 50 Thtr 80 **Parking** 80 **Notes** LB

BRANCASTER STAITHE   Map 13 TF74

White Horse
★★★ 79% ◉◉ HOTEL

☎ 01485 210262   🖷 01485 210930
PE31 8BY
e-mail: reception@whitehorsebrancaster.co.uk
web: www.whitehorsebrancaster.co.uk
dir: on A149 coast road midway between Hunstanton & Wells-next-the-Sea

A charming hotel situated on the north Norfolk coast with contemporary bedrooms in two wings, some featuring an interesting cobbled fascia. Each room is attractively decorated and thoughtfully equipped. There is a large bar and a lounge area leading through to the conservatory restaurant, with stunning tidal marshland views across to Scolt Head Island.

Rooms 15 (8 annexe) (4 fmly) (8 GF) **S** £75-£114; **D** £100-£178 (incl. bkfst)* **Facilities** Xmas New Year Wi-fi **Parking** 60 **Notes** LB

BURNHAM MARKET — Map 13 TF84

Hoste Arms

★★★ 86% ◉◉ HOTEL

☎ 01328 738777 📠 01328 730103
The Green PE31 8HD
e-mail: reception@hostearms.co.uk
web: www.hostearms.co.uk
dir: signed on B1155, 5m W of Wells-next-the-Sea

A stylish, privately-owned inn situated in the heart of a bustling village close to the north Norfolk coast. The extensive public rooms feature a range of dining areas that include a conservatory with plush furniture, a sunny patio and a traditional pub. The tastefully furnished and thoughtfully equipped bedrooms are generally very spacious and offer a high degree of comfort.

Rooms 35 (7 GF) **S** £114-£119; **D** £145-£160 (incl. bkfst & dinner)* **Facilities** STV Xmas New Year Wi-fi **Conf** Board 16 Thtr 25 **Services** Air con **Parking** 45

See advert on this page

CROMER — Map 13 TG24

Elderton Lodge Hotel & Langtry Restaurant

★★★ 87% ◉◉ HOTEL

☎ 01263 833547 📠 01263 834673
Gunton Park NR11 8TZ
e-mail: enquiries@eldertonlodge.co.uk
web: www.eldertonlodge.co.uk
dir: at North Walsham take A149 towards Cromer, hotel 3m on left, just before Thorpe Market

Ideally placed for touring the north Norfolk coastline, this delightful former shooting lodge is set amidst six acres of mature gardens adjacent to Gunton Hall estate. The individually decorated bedrooms are tastefully furnished and thoughtfully equipped. Public rooms include a smart lounge bar, an elegant restaurant and a sunny conservatory breakfast room.

Elderton Lodge Hotel & Langtry Restaurant

Rooms 11 (2 fmly) (2 GF) **S** £65; **D** £100-£120 (incl. bkfst)* **Facilities** Xmas New Year Wi-fi **Parking** 50 **Notes** LB Civ Wed 55

Sea Marge

★★★ 86% ◉ HOTEL

☎ 01263 579579 📠 01263 579524
16 High St NR27 0AB
e-mail: info@mackenziehotels.com
dir: A140 from Norwich then A149 to Cromer, B1159 to Overstrand. Hotel in village centre

An elegant Grade II listed Edwardian mansion perched on the clifftop amidst pretty landscaped gardens which lead down to the beach. Bedrooms are tastefully decorated and thoughtfully equipped; many have superb sea views. Public rooms offer a wide choice of areas in which to relax, including Frazer's restaurant and a smart lounge bar.

Rooms 25 (6 annexe) (6 fmly) (2 GF) **S** £83-£198; **D** £124-£198 (incl. bkfst & dinner)* **Facilities** ⌣ Xmas New Year Wi-fi **Conf** Class 55 Board 30 Thtr 70 **Del** from £106.50 to £126.50* **Services** Lift **Parking** 50 **Notes** LB

Virginia Court Hotel

★★★ 75% HOTEL

☎ 01263 512398 📠 01263 515529
Cliff Av NR27 0AN
e-mail: info@virginiacourt.co.uk
web: www.virginiacourt.co.uk
dir: A148 into town centre, pass church, left at lights, 1st right. A140 into Cromer over mini-rdbt then 1st right

Originally built in 1899 as a clubhouse for King Edward VII, this property is situated in a peaceful side road just a short walk from the town centre and seafront. The spacious bedrooms are smartly decorated and thoughtfully equipped. Public rooms include a smart restaurant, a cosy lounge bar and a further residents' lounge.

Rooms 25 (2 fmly) (3 GF) **S** £50-£65; **D** £100-£130 (incl. bkfst)* **Facilities** Xmas **Conf** Class 30 Board 20 Thtr 30 **Del** from £100 to £140* **Parking** 25 **Notes** LB ⊗

CROMER continued

The Cliftonville

★★★ 72% HOTEL

☎ 01263 512543 📄 01263 515700
NR27 9AS
e-mail: reservations@cliftonvillehotel.co.uk
web: www.cliftonvillehotel.co.uk
dir: From A149 (coastal road), 500yds from town centre, northbound on clifftop by sunken gardens

An imposing Edwardian hotel situated on the main coast road with stunning views of the sea. Public rooms feature a magnificent staircase, minstrels' gallery, coffee shop, lounge bar, a further residents' lounge, Boltons Bistro and an additional restaurant. The pleasantly decorated bedrooms are generally quite spacious and have lovely sea views.

Rooms 30 (5 fmly) **S** £50-£77; **D** £100-£154 (incl. bkfst)*
Facilities Xmas New Year Wi-fi **Conf** Class 100 Board 60
Thtr 150 Del from £74.50 to £106.50* **Services** Lift
Parking 20 **Notes** LB

Red Lion

★★ 78% HOTEL

☎ 01263 514964 📄 01263 512834
Brook St NR27 9HD
e-mail: enquiries@yeolderedlionhotel.co.uk
web: www.yeolderedlionhotel.co.uk
dir: from town centre 1st left after church

A Victorian property situated in an elevated position overlooking the beach and the sea. The smartly appointed public areas include a billiard room, lounge bar, a popular restaurant, a sunny conservatory and a first-floor residents' lounge with superb sea views. The spacious bedrooms are tastefully decorated, with co-ordinated soft furnishings and many thoughtful touches.

Rooms 12 (1 fmly) **Facilities** Discount for local leisure centre **Conf** Class 50 Board 60 Thtr 100 **Parking** 12
Notes LB ⊗ Closed 25 Dec

Hotel de Paris

★★ 69% HOTEL

Leisureplex

☎ 01263 513141 📄 01263 515217
High St NR27 9HG
e-mail: deparis.cromer@alfatravel.co.uk
dir: enter Cromer on A140 (Norwich road). Left at lights onto Mount St. At 2nd lights right into Prince of Wales Rd. 2nd right into New St leading into High St

An imposing, traditional-style resort hotel, situated in a prominent position overlooking the pier and beach. The bedrooms are pleasantly decorated and equipped with a good range of useful extras; many rooms have lovely sea views. The spacious public areas include a large lounge bar, restaurant, games room and a further lounge.

Rooms 56 (5 fmly) **S** £37-£49; **D** £60-£84 (incl. bkfst)
Facilities FTV Games room 🎵 Xmas New Year
Services Lift **Parking** 14 **Notes** LB ⊗ Closed Dec-Feb
(except Xmas) RS Mar & Nov

Hill House

★★★ 85% HOTEL

☎ 01362 699857
26 Market Place NR19 2AP
e-mail: hillhouse@mjbhotels.com
dir: Follow town centre signs into main street through town. Right at mini-rdbt, take right fork. Hotel car park 1st left

A delightful 16th-century Queen Anne property situated in the heart of this bustling town centre. The extensive public rooms include a smart lounge, an open-plan bar/carvery, a wine bar and a stylish restaurant. The tastefully furnished bedrooms offer a high degree of comfort and have many thoughtful touches.

Rooms 22 (1 fmly) (6 GF) **Parking** 12 **Notes** ⊗

George

★★ 78% HOTEL

☎ 01362 696801 📄 01362 695711
Swaffham Rd NR19 2AZ
web: www.lottiesrestaurant.co.uk
dir: From A47 follow Dereham signs. In High St to memorial, hotel on left

Delightful old inn situated in the heart of this bustling market town and ideally placed for touring Norfolk. The spacious bedrooms are pleasantly decorated, furnished with pine pieces and have many thoughtful touches. Public rooms include a smart restaurant, a stylish lounge with leather sofas, a conservatory dining room and a large lounge bar.

Rooms 8 (2 fmly) **Facilities** New Year **Parking** 50
Notes ⊗ Closed 26 Dec Civ Wed 50

Scole Inn

★★★ 64% HOTEL

OXFORD
HOTELS & INNS

☎ 01379 740481 📄 01379 740762
Ipswich Rd, Scole IP21 4DR
e-mail: manager.scoleinn@ohiml.com
web: www.oxfordhotelsandinns.com
dir: A140, Diss rdbt signed Scole, left at T-junct, hotel on left

A charming 17th-century inn situated in the heart of the village where King Charles II and highwayman John Belcher are said to have stayed. Bedrooms come in a variety of styles; each one is pleasantly decorated and well equipped. The hotel retains a wealth of original features such as exposed brickwork, huge open fires and a superb carved wooden staircase. The public areas include a bar, restaurant and lounge bar.

Rooms 23 (12 annexe) (1 fmly) (7 GF) **S** £50-£90;
D £60-£120 (incl. bkfst)* **Facilities** 🎵 Xmas Wi-fi
Conf Class 26 Board 35 Thtr 45 **Parking** 60 **Notes** LB
Civ Wed 50

Castle

★★ 78% HOTEL

☎ 01366 384311 📄 01366 384311
High St PE38 9HF
e-mail: howards@castle-hotel.com
dir: M11 take A10 for Ely into Downham Market. Hotel opp lights on corner of High St

This popular coaching inn is situated close to the centre of town and has been welcoming guests for over 300 years. Well maintained public areas include a cosy lounge bar and two smartly appointed restaurants. Inviting bedrooms, some with four-poster beds, are attractively decorated, thoughtfully equipped, and have bright, modern decor.

Rooms 12 **S** £69-£79; **D** £89-£120 (incl. bkfst)
Facilities Xmas **Conf** Class 30 Board 40 Thtr 60
Parking 26 **Notes** LB

Wensum Lodge

★★ 🅰 HOTEL

☎ 01328 862100 📄 01328 863365
Bridge St NR21 9AY
e-mail: enquiries@wensumlodge.fsnet.co.uk
web: www.wensumlodge.com

Rooms 17 (2 fmly) **Facilities** Putt green Fishing Xmas
Conf Class 85 Board 90 Thtr 120 **Parking** 19 **Notes** LB
Civ Wed 100

FRITTON
Map 13 TG40

Caldecott Hall Golf & Leisure
★★★ 78% HOTEL

☎ 01493 488488 📠 01493 488561
Caldecott Hall, Beccles Rd NR31 9EY
e-mail: hotel@caldecotthall.co.uk
web: www.caldecotthall.co.uk
dir: On A143 (Beccles to Great Yarmouth road), 4m from Great Yarmouth

Ideally situated in its own attractive, landscaped grounds that has an 18-hole golf course, fishing lakes and the Redwings horse sanctuary. The individually decorated bedrooms are spacious, and equipped with many thoughtful touches. Public rooms include a smart sitting room, a lounge bar, restaurant, clubhouse and smart leisure complex.

Rooms 8 (3 fmly) **S** £75-£95; **D** £85-£110* **Facilities** FTV
🕐 supervised ⚓ 36 Putt green Gym Driving range
Conf Class 80 Board 20 Thtr 100 **Parking** 100 **Notes** LB
⊗ Civ Wed 150

Fritton House
★★ 85% ⊛ HOTEL

☎ 01493 484008 📠 01493 488355
Church Ln NR31 9HA
e-mail: frittonhouse@somerleyton.co.uk
web: www.frittonhouse.co.uk
dir: within grounds of Somereley Estate, off A143, between Great Yarmouth & Fritton

This charming 15th-century property is set amidst parkland on the banks of Fritton Lake on the Somerleyton Estate. The contemporary-style public rooms include a large open-plan lounge bar, a dining room, a further lounge and a terraced area for alfresco dining. The individually decorated bedrooms are tastefully appointed and thoughtfully equipped.

Rooms 9 (2 fmly) **Facilities** Putt green Fishing ⚓ Xmas New Year **Conf** Thtr 20 **Notes** Civ Wed 100

GORLESTON ON SEA
Map 13 TG50

See also **Great Yarmouth**

The Pier
★★★ 72% HOTEL

☎ 01493 662631 📠 01493 440263
Harbourmouth, South Pier NR31 6PL
e-mail: info@pierhotelgorleston.co.uk
dir: from A143 left into Shrublands, into Church Ln, to Baker St, right into Pier Plain, left into Pier Walk, right into Quay Rd

This small, family-run hotel sits adjacent to the harbour wall, with splendid views along the sandy beach. The smartly appointed public rooms include a popular bar and a pleasant restaurant where an interesting choice of home cooked food is available. Bedrooms are pleasantly decorated and equipped with modern facilities.

Rooms 19 (2 smoking) **S** £40-£45; **D** £65-£125 (incl. bkfst) **Facilities** STV Xmas New Year Wi-fi **Conf** Class 80 Board 80 Thtr 140 **Parking** 30 **Notes** LB ⊗ No children Civ Wed 140

GREAT BIRCHAM
Map 13 TF73

Kings Head
★★★ 86% ⊛ HOTEL

☎ 01485 578265 📠 01485 578635
PE31 6RJ
e-mail: welcome@the-kings-head-bircham.co.uk
web: www.the-kings-head-bircham.co.uk
dir: From King's Lynn take A149 towards Fakenham. After Hillington, turn left onto B1153, to Great Bircham

This inn is situated in a peaceful village location close to the north Norfolk coastline. The spacious, individually decorated bedrooms are tastefully appointed with superb co-ordinated furnishings and many thoughtful touches. The contemporary, public rooms include a brasserie restaurant, a relaxing lounge, a smart bar and a private dining room.

Rooms 12 (8 fmly) **Facilities** Xmas **Conf** Class 14 Board 20 Thtr 40 **Parking** 25 **Notes** LB Civ Wed 130

GREAT YARMOUTH
Map 13 TG50

See also **Gorleston on Sea**

Imperial
★★★ 80% ⊛ HOTEL

☎ 01493 842000 📠 01493 852229
North Dr NR30 1EQ
e-mail: reservations@imperialhotel.co.uk
web: www.imperialhotel.co.uk
dir: follow signs to seafront, turn left. Hotel opposite tennis courts

This friendly, family-run hotel is situated at the quieter end of the seafront within easy walking distance of the town centre. Bedrooms are attractively decorated with co-ordinated soft furnishings and many thoughtful touches; most rooms have superb sea views. Public areas include the smart Savoie Lounge Bar and the Rambouillet Restaurant.

Rooms 39 (4 fmly) **S** £60-£90; **D** £78-£110 (incl. bkfst) **Facilities** STV Xmas New Year Wi-fi **Conf** Class 40 Board 30 Thtr 140 Del from £95 to £150 **Services** Lift **Parking** 50 **Notes** LB Civ Wed 140

Comfort Hotel Great Yarmouth
★★★ 75% HOTEL

☎ 01493 855070 & 850044 📠 01493 853798
Albert Square NR30 3JH
e-mail: sales@comfortgreatyarmouth.co.uk
web: www.comfortgreatyarmouth.co.uk
dir: from seafront left at Wellington Pier into Kimberley Terrace. Left into Albert Square, hotel on left

A large hotel situated in the quieter end of town, just off the seafront and within easy walking distance of the town centre. The pleasantly decorated, well-equipped bedrooms are generally quite spacious and include Wi-fi. Public rooms include a comfortable lounge, a bar and smart brasserie-style restaurant. The hotel has an outdoor swimming pool.

Rooms 50 (6 fmly) (3 GF) (12 smoking) **S** £54-£74; **D** £79-£99 (incl. bkfst) **Facilities** STV ⚓ Xmas New Year Wi-fi **Conf** Class 50 Board 30 Thtr 120 **Parking** 7 **Notes** LB ⊗ Civ Wed 120

See advert on page 388

GREAT YARMOUTH continued

Furzedown

★★★ 70% HOTEL

☎ 01493 844138 📄 01493 844138
19-20 North Dr NR30 4EW
e-mail: paul@furzedownhotel.co.uk
web: www.furzedownhotel.co.uk
dir: at end of A47 or A12, towards seafront, left, hotel opposite Waterways

Expect a warm welcome at this family-run hotel situated at the northern end of the seafront overlooking the town's Venetian Waterways. Bedrooms are pleasantly decorated and thoughtfully equipped; many rooms have superb sea views. The stylish public areas include a comfortable lounge bar, a smartly appointed restaurant and a cosy TV room.

Rooms 20 (11 fmly) **S** £53-£59; **D** £72-£84 (incl. bkfst)* **Facilities** FTV New Year Wi-fi **Conf** Class 80 Board 40 Thtr 75 Del from £82 to £92* **Parking** 30

Burlington Palm Hotel

★★★ 67% HOTEL

☎ 01493 844568 & 842095 📄 01493 331848
11 North Dr NR30 1EG
e-mail: enquiries@burlington-hotel.co.uk
web: www.burlington-hotel.co.uk
dir: A12 to seafront, left at Britannia Pier. Hotel near tennis courts

This privately owned hotel is situated at the quiet end of the resort, overlooking the sea. Bedrooms come in a variety of sizes and styles; they are pleasantly decorated and well equipped, and many have lovely sea views. The spacious public rooms include a range of seating areas, a choice of dining rooms and two bars.

Rooms 70 (9 fmly) (1 GF) **Facilities** ⓢ Turkish steam room Xmas Wi-fi **Conf** Class 60 Board 30 Thtr 120 **Services** Lift **Parking** 70 **Notes** LB ⊗ Closed Jan-Feb RS Dec-Feb

See advert on page 384

The Arden Court Hotel

★★ 76% HOTEL

☎ 01493 855310 📄 01493 843413
93-94 North Denes Rd NR30 4LW
e-mail: info@ardencourt-hotel.co.uk
web: www.ardencourt-hotel.co.uk
dir: At seafront left along North Drive. At boating lake left along Beaconsfield Rd. At mini rdbt right into North Denes Rd

Friendly, family-run hotel situated in a residential area just a short walk from the seafront. The individually decorated bedrooms are smartly furnished and equipped with a good range of useful extras. Public rooms are attractively presented; they include a smart lounge bar and a restaurant serving an interesting choice of dishes.

Rooms 14 (5 fmly) (2 GF) **S** £35-£50; **D** £64-£84 (incl. bkfst)* **Facilities** Xmas **Parking** 10 **Notes** LB ⊗

New Beach Hotel

★★ 69% HOTEL Leisureplex

☎ 01493 332300 📄 01493 331880
67 Marine Pde NR30 2EJ
e-mail: newbeach.gtyarmouth@alfatravel.co.uk
dir: Follow signs to seafront. Hotel facing Britannia Pier

This Victorian building is centrally located on the seafront, overlooking Britannia Pier and the sandy beach. Bedrooms are pleasantly decorated and equipped with modern facilities; many have lovely sea views. Dinner is taken in the restaurant which doubles as the ballroom, and guests can also relax in the bar or sunny lounge.

Rooms 75 (3 fmly) **S** £34-£44; **D** £54-£74 (incl. bkfst) **Facilities** FTV ♫ Xmas New Year **Services** Lift **Notes** LB ⊗ Closed Dec-Feb (except Xmas) RS Nov & Mar

GRIMSTON
Map 12 TF72

INSPECTORS' CHOICE

Congham Hall Country House Hotel

★★★ ◉◉ HOTEL

☎ 01485 600250 ≣ 01485 601191
Lynn Rd PE32 1AH
e-mail: info@conghamhallhotel.co.uk
web: www.conghamhallhotel.co.uk
dir: at A149/A148 junct, NE of King's Lynn, take A148 towards Fakenham for 100yds. Right to Grimston, hotel 2.5m on left

Elegant 18th-century Georgian manor set amid 30 acres of mature landscaped grounds and surrounded by parkland. The inviting public rooms provide a range of tastefully furnished areas in which to sit and relax. Imaginative cuisine is served in the Orangery Restaurant which has an intimate atmosphere and panoramic views of the gardens. The bedrooms, tastefully furnished with period pieces, have modern facilities and many thoughtful touches.

Rooms 14 (1 GF) **S** £90-£110; **D** £155-£385 (incl. bkfst)* **Facilities** ☋ Putt green ☋ Xmas New Year Wi-fi **Conf** Class 12 Board 20 Thtr 50 Del from £175* **Parking** 50 **Notes** LB ⊗ Civ Wed 100

HETHERSETT
Map 13 TG10

Park Farm

★★★ 82% ◉ HOTEL

☎ 01603 810264 ≣ 01603 812104
NR9 3DL
e-mail: enq@parkfarm-hotel.co.uk
web: www.parkfarm-hotel.co.uk
dir: 5m S of Norwich, off A11 on B1172

Elegant Georgian farmhouse set in landscaped grounds surrounded by open countryside. The property has been

owned and run by the Gowing family since 1958. Bedrooms are pleasantly decorated and tastefully furnished; some rooms have patio doors with a sun terrace. Public rooms include a stylish conservatory, a lounge bar, a smart restaurant and superb leisure facilities.

Rooms 53 (50 annexe) (15 fmly) (26 GF) **S** £99-£140; **D** £130-£195 (incl. bkfst)* **Facilities** ⊛ supervised Gym Beauty salon Hairdressing Xmas New Year Wi-fi **Conf** Class 50 Board 50 Thtr 120 **Parking** 150 **Notes** LB ⊗ Civ Wed 100

See advert on page 391

HOLKHAM
Map 13 T84

The Victoria at Holkham

★★ 83% ◉◉ SMALL HOTEL

☎ 01328 711008 ≣ 01328 711009
Park Rd NR23 1RG
e-mail: victoria@holkham.co.uk
web: www.victoriaatholkham.co.uk
dir: A149, 2m W of Wells-next-the-Sea

A Grade II listed property, built from local flint, is ideally situated on the north Norfolk coast road and forms part of the Holkham Estate. Decor is very much influenced by the local landscape: the stylish bedrooms are individually decorated and tastefully furnished with pieces specially made for the hotel in India. The brasserie-style restaurant serves an interesting choice of dishes.

Rooms 10 (1 annexe) (2 fmly) (1 GF) **Facilities** Fishing Shooting on Holkham Estate, Bird watching reserve nearby Xmas Child facilities **Conf** Class 40 Board 30 Thtr 12 **Parking** 30 **Notes** LB ⊗ Civ Wed 70

HOLT
Map 13 TG03

The Lawns

◉ RESTAURANT WITH ROOMS

☎ 01263 713390
26 Station Rd NR25 6BS
e-mail: mail@lawnsatholt.co.uk
dir: A148 (Cromer Rd). 0.25m from Holt rdbt, turn left, 400yds along Station Rd

Superb Georgian house situated in the centre of this delightful North Norfolk market town. The open-plan public areas include a large wine bar with plush sofas, a conservatory and a smart restaurant. The spacious bedrooms are tastefully appointed with co-ordinated soft furnishings and have many thoughtful touches.

Rooms 8 (8 en suite)

HORNING
Map 13 TG31

Innkeeper's Lodge Norfolk Broads - Horning

BUDGET HOTEL

☎ 0845 112 6060
The Swan Inn, Lower St NR12 8AA

Innkeeper's Lodge represents an exciting, high value concept within the budget hotel market. Comfortable bedrooms provide excellent facilities that include satellite TV and modem points. This carefully restored lodge is in a picturesque setting and has its own unique style and quirky character. Food is served all day, and an extensive, complimentary continental breakfast is offered.

Rooms 8

HUNSTANTON
Map 12 TF64

Best Western Le Strange Arms

★★★ 81% HOTEL

☎ 01485 534411 ≣ 01485 534724
Golf Course Rd, Old Hunstanton PE36 6JJ
e-mail: reception@lestrangearms.co.uk
dir: off A149 1m N of Hunstanton. Left at sharp right bend by pitch & putt course

Impressive hotel with superb views from the wide lawns down to the sandy beach and across The Wash. Bedrooms in the main house have period furnishings whereas the rooms in the wing are more contemporary in style. Public rooms include a comfortable lounge bar and an attractive restaurant, where an interesting choice of dishes is served.

Rooms 36 (2 fmly) (8 smoking) **S** £75-£85; **D** £120-£145 (incl. bkfst)* **Facilities** STV Xmas New Year Wi-fi **Conf** Class 150 Board 50 Thtr 180 **Services** Lift **Parking** 80 **Notes** LB Civ Wed 70

HUNSTANTON continued

Caley Hall

★★★ 80% HOTEL

☎ 01485 533486 ▤ 01485 533348
Old Hunstanton Rd PE36 6HH
e-mail: mail@caleyhallhotel.co.uk
web: www.caleyhallhotel.co.uk
dir: 1m from Hunstanton, on A149

Situated within easy walking distance of the seafront.
The tastefully decorated bedrooms are in a series of
converted outbuildings; each is smartly furnished and
thoughtfully equipped. Public rooms feature a large
open-plan lounge/bar with plush leather seating, and a
restaurant offering an interesting choice of dishes.

Rooms 40 (20 fmly) (30 GF) **S** £55-£150; **D** £78-£199
(incl. bkfst)* **Facilities** STV Wi-fi Child facilities
Parking 50 **Notes** LB Closed 18 Dec-20 Jan

Sutton House

★★ 79% ⊛ HOTEL

☎ 01485 532552 ▤ 01485 532552
24 Northgate PE36 6AP
e-mail: benelli@freeuk.com
web: www.suttonhousehotel.co.uk
dir: Off A149 (Cromer road) onto Greevegate, 2nd right

Expect a warm welcome at this delightful, small, family
run hotel situated in a peaceful residential area close to
the seafront. Bedrooms are thoughtfully equipped, and
some rooms have superb sea views. The public rooms
include a cosy residents' lounge, a small bar and 'Luigi's
Trattoria' which is well known locally for its authentic
Italian cuisine.

Rooms 8 (1 fmly) **S** £30-£50; **D** £50-£70 (incl. bkfst)
Facilities New Year Wi-fi **Conf** Board 20 Del from £80 to
£100* **Parking** 4 **Notes** LB ⊗

The Neptune Inn & Restaurant

⊛⊛⊛ RESTAURANT WITH ROOMS

☎ 01485 532122
85 Old Hunstanton Rd, Old Hunstanton PE36 6HZ
e-mail: reservations@theneptune.co.uk
dir: On A149, past Hunstanton, 200mtrs on left after post
office

This charming 18th-century coaching, now a restaurant
with rooms, is ideally situated for touring the Norfolk
coastline. The smartly appointed bedrooms are brightly

finished with co-ordinated fabrics and handmade New
England furniture. Public rooms feature white clapboard
walls, polished dark wood floors, fresh flowers and Lloyd
Loom furniture. The food is very much a draw here with
the carefully prepared, award-winning cuisine utilising
excellent local produce, from oysters and mussels from
Thornham to quinces grown on a neighbouring farm.

Rooms 7

KING'S LYNN Map 12 TF62

Congham Hall Country House Hotel

★★★ ⊛⊛ HOTEL

von Essen hotels A PRIVATE COLLECTION

☎ 01485 600250 ▤ 01485 601191
Lynn Rd PE32 1AH
e-mail: info@conghamhallhotel.co.uk
web: www.conghamhallhotel.co.uk

(For full entry see Grimston)

Best Western Knights Hill

★★★ 78% HOTEL

Best Western

☎ 01553 675566 ▤ 01553 675568
Knights Hill Village, South Wootton PE30 3HQ
e-mail: reception@knightshill.co.uk
dir: junct A148/A149

This hotel village complex is set on a 16th-century site on
the outskirts of town. The smartly decorated, well-
equipped bedrooms are situated in extensions of the
original hunting lodge. Public areas have a wealth of
historic charm; they include the Garden Restaurant and
the Farmers Arms pub. The hotel also has conference and
leisure facilities.

Rooms 79 (12 annexe) (1 fmly) (38 GF) **S** £60-£120;
D £65-£150* **Facilities** Spa STV ⊙ ॐ ≊ Gym Xmas New
Year Wi-fi **Conf** Class 150 Board 30 Thtr 200 **Parking** 350
Notes LB ⊗ Civ Wed 90

Stuart House

★★ 72% HOTEL

☎ 01553 772169 ▤ 01553 774788
35 Goodwins Rd PE30 5QX
e-mail: reception@stuarthousehotel.co.uk
web: www.stuarthousehotel.co.uk
dir: at A47/A10/A149 rdbt take signs to King's Lynn town
centre. Under Southgate Arch, right into Guanock Terrace
and right into Goodwins Rd

Small privately-owned hotel situated in a peaceful
residential area just a short walk from the town centre.
Bedrooms come in a variety of styles and sizes; all are
pleasantly decorated and thoughtfully equipped. There is
a choice of dining options with informal dining in the bar
and a daily-changing menu in the elegant restaurant.

Rooms 18 (2 fmly) **S** £72; **D** £89-£150 (incl. bkfst)*
Facilities ♫ Wi-fi **Conf** Class 30 Board 20 Thtr 50
Del from £75 to £105* **Parking** 30 **Notes** LB ⊗ RS 25-26
Dec & 1 Jan Civ Wed 60

Grange

★★ 68% HOTEL

☎ 01553 673777 & 671222 ▤ 01553 673777
Willow Park, South Wootton Ln PE30 3BP
e-mail: info@thegrangehotelkingslynn.co.uk
dir: A148 towards King's Lynn for 1.5m. At lights left into
Wootton Rd, 400yds on right into South Wootton Ln. Hotel
1st on left

Expect a warm welcome at this Edwardian house which is
situated in a quiet residential area in its own grounds.
Public rooms include a smart lounge bar and a cosy
restaurant. The spacious bedrooms are pleasantly
decorated and equipped with many thoughtful touches;
some are located in an adjacent wing.

Rooms 9 (4 annexe) (2 fmly) (4 GF) **Facilities** Xmas
Conf Class 15 Board 12 Thtr 20 **Parking** 15

NORTH WALSHAM
Map 13 TG23

INSPECTORS' CHOICE

Beechwood
★ ★ ★ ◉◉ HOTEL

☎ 01692 403231 🖷 01692 407284
Cromer Rd NR28 0HD
e-mail: enquiries@beechwood-hotel.co.uk
web: www.beechwood-hotel.co.uk
dir: B1150 from Norwich. At North Walsham left at 1st lights, then right at next

Expect a warm welcome at this elegant 18th-century house, situated just a short walk from the town centre. The individually styled bedrooms are tastefully furnished with well-chosen antique pieces, attractive co-ordinated soft fabrics and many thoughtful touches. The spacious public areas include a lounge bar with plush furnishings, a further lounge and a smartly appointed restaurant.

Rooms 17 (4 GF) **S** £72; **D** £90-£160 (incl. bkfst) **Facilities** ➳ New Year Wi-fi **Conf** Class 20 Board 20 Thtr 20 Del from £130 **Parking** 20 **Notes** LB No children 10yrs

The Scarborough Hill Country Inn
★ ★ ★ 71% HOTEL

☎ 01692 402151 🖷 01692 406686
Old Yarmouth Rd NR28 9NA
e-mail: scarboroughhill@nascr.net
web: www.arlingtonhotelgroup.co.uk
dir: From Norwich B1150, straight through lights, across mini rdbt, right at next rdbt, hotel 1m on right

A delightful country-house hotel situated on the outskirts of town, in a peaceful location amidst landscaped grounds. Public rooms include a smart lounge bar with plush sofas, an intimate dining room and a large conservatory. Bedrooms are generally quite spacious; each one is pleasantly furnished and thoughtfully equipped.

Rooms 9 (1 fmly) (1 GF) **S** £45-£52.50; **D** £50-£70 (incl. bkfst)* **Facilities** FTV Wi-fi **Conf** Class 80 Board 60 Thtr 120 **Parking** 80 **Notes** ⊗ Civ Wed

NORWICH
Map 13 TG20

Marriott Sprowston Manor Hotel & Country Club
★ ★ ★ ★ 80% ◉◉ HOTEL

Marriott HOTELS & RESORTS

☎ 01603 410871 🖷 01603 423911
Sprowston Park, Wroxham Rd, Sprowston NR7 8RP
e-mail: mhrs.nwigs.frontdesk@marriotthotels.com
web: www.marriottsprowstonmanor.co.uk
dir: From A11/A47, 2m NE on A115 (Wroxham road). Follow signs to Sprowston Park

Surrounded by open parkland, this imposing property is set in attractively landscaped grounds and is just a short drive from the city centre. Bedrooms are spacious and feature a variety of decorative styles. The hotel also has extensive conference, banqueting and leisure facilities. Other public rooms include an array of seating areas and the elegant Manor Restaurant.

Rooms 94 (3 fmly) (5 GF) **Facilities** ☉ supervised ↥ 18 Putt green Gym Xmas **Conf** Class 50 Board 50 Thtr 500 **Services** Lift **Parking** 150 **Notes** ⊗ Civ Wed 300

NORWICH continued

St Giles House

★★★★ 80% ◎ HOTEL

☎ 01603 275180 📠 0845 299 1905
41-45 St Giles St NR2 1JR
e-mail: info@stgileshousehotel.com
web: www.stgileshousehotel.com
dir: A11 into central Norwich. Left at rdbt (Chapelfield Shopping Center). 3rd exit at next rdbt. Left onto St Giles St. Hotel on left

A stylish 19th-century, Grade II listed building situated in the heart of the city. The property has a wealth of magnificent original features such as wood-panelling, ornamental plasterwork and marble floors. Public areas include an open-plan lounge bar/restaurant, a smart lounge with plush sofas and a Parisian style terrace. The spacious, contemporary bedrooms are individually designed and have many thoughtful touches.

Rooms 24 **S** £120-£210; **D** £130-£220 (incl. bkfst)* **Facilities** Spa Xmas New Year Wi-fi **Conf** Class 20 Board 24 Thtr 45 **Services** Lift **Parking** 23 **Notes** LB ⊗

De Vere Dunston Hall

DE VERE heritage

★★★★ 78% ◎ HOTEL

☎ 01508 470444 📠 01508 471499
Ipswich Rd NR14 8PQ
e-mail: dhreception@devere-hotels.com
web: www.devere.co.uk
dir: from A47 take A140 (Ipswich road). 0.25m, hotel on left

Imposing Grade II listed building set amidst 170 acres of landscaped grounds just a short drive from the city centre. The spacious bedrooms are smartly decorated, tastefully furnished and equipped to a high standard. The attractively appointed public rooms offer a wide choice of areas in which to relax, and the hotel also boasts a superb range of leisure facilities including an 18-hole PGA golf course, floodlit tennis courts and a football pitch.

Rooms 169 (16 fmly) (16 GF) **Facilities** Spa ⓢ ⛳ 18 Putt green Gym Floodlit driving range Xmas New Year Wi-fi **Conf** Class 140 Board 80 Thtr 300 **Services** Lift **Parking** 500 **Notes** ⊗ Civ Wed 90

Holiday Inn Norwich-North

★★★★ 71% HOTEL

☎ 01603 410544 📠 01603 487701
Cromer Rd NR6 6JA
e-mail: frontoffice@hinorwich.com
web: www.holidayinn.co.uk
dir: A140 signed for Cromer, turn right at lights signed 'Airport Passengers'. Hotel on right

Modern purpose built hotel situated to the north of Norwich at the airport. Bedrooms are smartly decorated, equipped with modern facilities and have a good range of useful extras. Public areas include a large open-plan lounge bar and restaurant, as well as meeting rooms, a banqueting suite and leisure facilities.

Rooms 121 (8 fmly) (34 GF) (4 smoking) **S** £95-£125; **D** £95-£125* **Facilities** ⓢ Gym ♫ Wi-fi **Conf** Class 200 Board 50 Thtr 500 Del from £110 to £150* **Services** Lift Air con **Parking** 300 (charged) **Notes** ⊗ Civ Wed 500

Best Western Annesley House

★★★ 85% ◎◎ HOTEL

☎ 01603 624553 📠 01603 621577
6 Newmarket Rd NR2 2LA
e-mail: annesleyhouse@bestwestern.co.uk
dir: on A11, 0.5m before city centre

Delightful Georgian property set in three acres of landscaped gardens close to the city centre. Bedrooms are split between three separate houses, two of which are linked by a glass walkway. Each one is attractively decorated, tastefully furnished and thoughtfully equipped. Public rooms include a comfortable lounge/bar and a smart conservatory restaurant which overlooks the gardens.

Rooms 26 (8 annexe) (1 fmly) (7 GF) **S** £70-£80; **D** £80-£90* **Facilities** Wi-fi **Conf** Board 16 Thtr 16 **Parking** 25 **Notes** LB ⊗ Closed 24 Dec-2 Jan

Barnham Broom Hotel, Golf & Restaurant

★★★ 83% ◎◎ HOTEL

☎ 01603 759393 📠 01603 758224
NR9 4DD
e-mail: amortimer@barnham-broom.co.uk
web: www.barnham-broom.co.uk

(For full entry see Barnham Broom)

Beeches Hotel & Victorian Gardens

THE INDEPENDENTS HOTEL ASSOCIATION

★★★ 81% HOTEL

☎ 01603 621167 📠 01603 620151
2-6 Earlham Rd NR2 3DB
e-mail: reception@beeches.co.uk
web: www.mjbhotels.com
dir: W of city centre on B1108, next to St Johns Cathedral, off inner ring road

Ideally situated just a short walk from the city centre, and set amidst landscaped grounds that include a lovely sunken Victorian garden. The bedrooms are in five separate buildings; each one is tastefully decorated and equipped with many thoughtful touches. Public rooms include a smart lounge bar, a bistro-style restaurant and a residents' lounge.

Rooms 41 (30 GF) **Facilities** Xmas **Parking** 50 **Notes** ⊗ No children 12yrs

Ramada Norwich

RAMADA

★★★ 78% HOTEL

☎ 01603 787260 📠 01603 400466
121-131 Boundary Rd NR3 2BA
e-mail: gm.norwich@ramadajarvis.co.uk
web: www.ramadajarvis.co.uk
dir: approx 2m from airport on A140 (Norwich ring road)

Purpose-built hotel conveniently situated on the outer ring road close to the city centre. Bedrooms are pleasantly decorated and equipped with a good range of useful facilities. Public rooms include a large open-plan lounge bar and a smart restaurant. Meeting rooms as well as banqueting suites and leisure facilities are available.

Rooms 107 (8 fmly) (22 GF) (5 smoking) **S** £72-£152; **D** £72-£164 (incl. bkfst)* **Facilities** ⓢ Gym Xmas **Conf** Class 150 Board 80 Thtr 300 Del from £135 to £155* **Parking** 230 **Notes** LB ⊗ Civ Wed 400

Wensum Valley Hotel Golf & Country Club

★★★ 73% HOTEL

☎ 01603 261012 📠 01603 261664
Beech Av, Taverham NR8 6HP
e-mail: enqs@wensumvalley.co.uk
web: www.wensumvalleyhotel.co.uk
dir: off A1067 (Norwich to Fakenham road) at Taverham into Beech Ave. Hotel on right next to High School

A family-run hotel set amid 350 acres of lovely countryside just a short distance from the city centre and Norwich Airport. The modern, purpose-built bedrooms are generally spacious and thoughtfully equipped. Public rooms include a choice of bars, a lounge and a large restaurant overlooking the green. The hotel has superb golf and leisure facilities.

Rooms 90 (12 fmly) (32 GF) **S** fr £54; **D** fr £90 (incl. bkfst)* **Facilities** Spa ⓢ supervised ⛳ 36 Putt green Fishing Gym Beauty therapy Golf driving range Hairdressing salon Sauna Steam room ♫ Xmas New Year Wi-fi **Conf** Board 40 Thtr 200 Del from £90 to £100* **Parking** 250 **Notes** LB ⊗ Civ Wed 100

Best Western George Hotel

★★★ 72% ⊛ HOTEL

☎ 01603 617841 🖷 01603 663708
10 Arlington Ln, Newmarket Rd NR2 2DA
e-mail: reservations@georgehotel.co.uk
web: www.arlingtonhotelgroup.co.uk
dir: from A11 follow city centre signs. Newmarket Rd towards centre. Hotel on left

Within just 10 minutes' walk of the town centre, this friendly, family-run hotel is well placed for guests wishing to explore the many sights of this historic city. The hotel occupies three adjacent buildings; the restaurant, bar and most bedrooms are located in the main building, while the adjacent cottages have been converted into comfortable and modern guest bedrooms.

Rooms 43 (5 annexe) (4 fmly) (19 GF) **Facilities** Beauty therapist Holistic treatments Xmas New Year
Conf Class 30 Board 30 Thtr 70 Del from £95 to £125*
Parking 40 **Notes** ⊗

The Maids Head Hotel

folio Hotels

★★★ 72% HOTEL

☎ 0870 609 6110 🖷 01603 613688
Tombland NR3 1LB
e-mail: maidshead@foliohotels.com
web: www.foliohotels.com/maidshead
dir: follow city centre signs past Norwich Castle. 3rd turn after castle into Upper King St. Hotel opposite cathedral

Imposing 13th-century building situated close to the impressive Norman cathedral, the Anglian TV studios and within easy walking distance of the city centre. The bedrooms are pleasantly decorated and thoughtfully equipped; some rooms have original oak beams. The spacious public rooms include a Jacobean bar, a range of seating areas and the Courtyard restaurant.

Rooms 84 (10 fmly) **Facilities** Treatment room Xmas New Year Wi-fi **Conf** Class 30 Board 50 Thtr 180 Del from £120 to £150* **Services** Lift **Parking** 70 **Notes** ⊗ Civ Wed 100

INSPECTORS' CHOICE

The Old Rectory

★★ ⊛⊛⊛ SMALL HOTEL

☎ 01603 700772 🖷 01603 300772
103 Yarmouth Rd, Thorpe St Andrew NR7 0HF
e-mail: enquiries@oldrectorynorwich.com
web: www.oldrectorynorwich.com
dir: from A47 southern bypass onto A1042 towards Norwich N & E. Left at mini rdbt onto A1242. After 0.3m through lights. Hotel 100mtrs on right

This delightful Grade II listed Georgian property is ideally located in a peaceful area overlooking the River Yare, just a few minutes' drive from the city centre. Spacious bedrooms are individually designed with carefully chosen soft fabrics, plush furniture and many thoughtful touches; many of the rooms overlook the swimming pool and landscaped gardens. Accomplished cooking is offered via an interesting daily-changing menu, which features skilfully prepared local produce.

Rooms 8 (3 annexe) **S** £85-£115; **D** £115-£145 (incl. bkfst)* **Facilities** FTV ⚲ Wi-fi **Conf** Class 18 Board 16 Thtr 25 **Parking** 15 **Notes** LB ⊗ Closed 23 Dec-1 Jan RS 2-6 Jan

Stower Grange

★★ 85% ⊛ HOTEL

☎ 01603 860210 🖷 01603 860464
School Rd, Drayton NR8 6EF
e-mail: enquiries@stowergrange.co.uk
web: www.stowergrange.co.uk
dir: Norwich ring road N to Asda supermarket. Take A1067 (Fakenham road) at Drayton, right at lights into School Rd. Hotel 150yds on right

Expect a warm welcome at this 17th-century, ivy-clad property situated in a peaceful residential area close to the city centre and airport. The individually decorated

bedrooms are generally quite spacious; each one is tastefully furnished and equipped with many thoughtful touches. Public rooms include a smart open-plan lounge bar and an elegant restaurant.

Rooms 11 (1 fmly) **Facilities** ⚲ New Year Wi-fi **Conf** Class 45 Board 30 Thtr 100 **Parking** 40 **Notes** LB Civ Wed 100

Holiday Inn Norwich City

U

☎ 0870 890 1000 🖷 0870 890 1111
Carrow Rd NR1 1HU
e-mail: info.norwich@kewgreen.co.uk
web: www.holidayinn.co.uk
dir: A11 turn right to A47 signed football ground. Hotel at Norwich City Football Club

Currently the rating for this establishment is not confirmed. This may be due to a change of ownership or because it has only recently joined the AA rating scheme. For further details please see the AA website: www.theAA.com

Rooms 150 **S** £85-£120; **D** £95-£140 **Facilities** STV Gym Xmas Wi-fi **Conf** Class 25 Board 16 Thtr 30 Del from £120 to £140 **Services** Lift Air con **Parking** 57 **Notes** LB ⊗

Holiday Inn Norwich

U

☎ 0870 400 9060 & 0800 405060 🖷 01603 506400
Ipswich Rd NR4 6EP
e-mail: reservations-norwich@ihg.com
web: www.holidayinn.co.uk
dir: A47 Great Yarmouth then A140 Norwich. 1m, hotel on right

Currently the rating for this establishment is not confirmed. This may be due to a change of ownership or because it has only recently joined the AA rating scheme. For further details please see the AA website: www.theAA.com

Rooms 119 (41 fmly) (39 GF) (10 smoking) **S** £65-£155; **D** £65-£155 (incl. bkfst)* **Facilities** FTV ⚲ supervised Gym Sauna Steam room Xmas New Year Wi-fi **Conf** Class 48 Board 40 Thtr 150 Del from £105 to £145* **Services** Air con **Parking** 250 **Notes** LB ⊗ Civ Wed 120

Express by Holiday Inn Norwich

Express by Holiday Inn

BUDGET HOTEL

☎ 01603 780010 🖷 01603 780011
Drayton High Rd, Hellesdon NR6 5DU
e-mail: gm@exhinorwich.co.uk
web: www.hiexpress.com/norwich
dir: at junct of A140 (ring road) & A1067 to Fakenham, follow brown tourist signs

A modern hotel ideal for families and business travellers. Fresh and uncomplicated, the spacious rooms include Sky TV, power shower and tea and coffee-making facilities. Continental buffet breakfast is included in the room rate;

Continued

NORWICH continued

other meals may be taken at the nearby family pub or restaurant. See also the Hotel Groups pages.

Rooms 78 (2 fmly)

Travelodge Norwich Central

BUDGET HOTEL

☎ 0871 984 6297 ≣ 01603 768262
Queens road NR1 2AA
web: www.travelodge.co.uk

Travelodge offers good quality, good value, modern accommodation. Ideal for families, the spacious en suite bedrooms include remote-control TV, tea and coffee-making facilities and comfortable beds. Meals can be taken at the nearby family restaurant. See also the Hotel Groups pages.

Rooms 104 **S** fr £29; **D** fr £29

Travelodge Norwich Cringleford

BUDGET HOTEL

☎ 08719 846 205 ≣ 0870 191 1704
Thickthorn Service Area, Norwich Southern Bypass NR9 3AU
web: www.travelodge.co.uk
dir: at A11/A47 junct

Rooms 62 **S** fr £29; **D** fr £29

REEPHAM   Map 13 TG12

Old Brewery House

Ⓤ   OXFORD
                           HOTELS & INNS

☎ 01603 870881 ≣ 01603 870969
Market Place NR10 4JJ
e-mail: reservations.oldbreweryhouse@ohiml.com
web: www.oxfordhotelsandinns.com
dir: A1067, right at Bawdeswell onto B1145 into Reepham, hotel on left in Market Place

Currently the rating for this establishment is not confirmed. This may be due to a change of ownership or because it has only recently joined the AA rating scheme. For further details please see the AA website: www.theAA.com

Rooms 23 (2 fmly) (7 GF) **S** £45-£55; **D** £65-£85 (incl. bkfst)* **Facilities** Ⓢ Gym Squash Xmas **Conf** Class 80 Board 30 Thtr 200 Del from £55 to £65* **Parking** 40 **Notes** LB Civ Wed 45

SHERINGHAM   Map 13 TG14

Dales Country House Hotel

★★★★ 76% ◉ HOTEL

☎ 01263 824555 ≣ 01263 822647
Lodge Hill, Upper Sheringham NR26 8TJ
e-mail: dales@mackenziehotels.com
dir: on B1157 1m S of Sheringham, from A148 take turn at entrance to Sheringham Park, 0.5m, hotel on left

Superb Grade II listed building situated in extensive landscaped grounds on the edge of Sheringham Park. The attractive public rooms are full of original character; they include a choice of lounges as well as an intimate restaurant, a cosy lounge bar. The spacious bedrooms are individually decorated, with co-ordinated soft furnishings and many thoughtful touches.

Rooms 21 (5 GF) **S** £88-£194; **D** £136-£204 (incl. bkfst & dinner)* **Facilities** ⚘ ⚘ Giant garden games - chess & Jenga Xmas New Year Wi-fi **Conf** Class 20 Board 27 Thtr 40 Del from £106.50 to £134.50* **Services** Lift **Parking** 50 **Notes** LB ⊗ No children 14yrs

Roman Camp Inn

★★★ 78% SMALL HOTEL

☎ 01263 838291 ≣ 01263 837071
Holt Rd, Aylmerton NR11 8QD
e-mail: enquiries@romancampinn.co.uk
web: www.romancampinn.co.uk
dir: on A148 between Sheringham and Cromer, approx 1.5m from Cromer

A smartly presented hotel ideally placed for touring the north Norfolk coastline. The property provides spacious, pleasantly decorated bedrooms with a good range of useful facilities. Public rooms include a smart conservatory-style restaurant, a comfortable open-plan lounge/bar and a dining area.

Rooms 15 (1 fmly) (10 GF) **S** £54-£70; **D** £88-£120 (incl. bkfst)* **Facilities** STV **Conf** Class 12 Board 16 Thtr 25 **Parking** 50 **Notes** LB ⊗ Closed 25 Dec

See advert on page 383

Beaumaris

★★ 78% HOTEL

☎ 01263 822370 ≣ 01263 821421
South St NR26 8LL
e-mail: beauhotel@aol.com
web: www.thebeaumarishotel.co.uk
dir: turn off A148, turn left at rdbt, 1st right over railway bridge, 1st left by church, 1st left into South St

Situated in a peaceful side road just a short walk from the beach, town centre and golf course. This friendly hotel has been owned and run by the same family for over 60 years and continues to provide comfortable, thoughtfully equipped accommodation throughout. Public rooms feature a smart dining room, a cosy bar and two quiet lounges.

Rooms 21 (5 fmly) (2 GF) **S** £55-£60; **D** £110-£120 (incl. bkfst)* **Parking** 25 **Notes** LB ⊗ Closed mid Dec-1 Mar

---

SNETTISHAM   Map 12 TF63

Rose & Crown

★★ 78% ◉ HOTEL

☎ 01485 541382 ≣ 01485 543172
Old Church Rd PE31 7LX
e-mail: info@roseandcrownsnettisham.co.uk
web: www.roseandcrownsnettisham.co.uk
dir: A149 towards Hunstanton. In village centre turn into Old Church Rd, hotel 100yds on left

This lovely village inn provides comfortable, well-equipped bedrooms. A range of quality meals is served in the many dining areas, complemented by a good variety of real ales and wines. Service is friendly and a delightful atmosphere prevails. A walled garden is available on sunny days, as is a children's play area.

Rooms 16 (3 fmly) (2 GF) **S** £70-£90; **D** £90-£110 (incl. bkfst)* **Facilities** FTV ⚘ ⚘ Xmas New Year Wi-fi **Parking** 70 **Notes** LB

SWAFFHAM
Map 13 TF80

Best Western George Hotel

★★★ 73% ⊛ HOTEL

☎ 01760 721238 📠 01760 725333
Station Rd PE37 7LJ
e-mail: georgehotel@bestwestern.co.uk
web: www.arlingtonhotelgroup.co.uk
dir: exit A47 signed Swaffham. Hotel opposite St Peter & St Paul church

A Georgian hotel situated in the heart of this bustling market town, which is ideally placed for touring north Norfolk. Bedrooms vary in size and style; each one is pleasantly decorated and well equipped. Public rooms include a cosy restaurant, a lounge and a busy bar where a range of drinks and snacks is available.

Rooms 29 (1 fmly) **S** £55-£80; **D** £70-£95 (incl. bkfst)
Facilities New Year Wi-fi **Conf** Class 70 Board 70 Thtr 150 Del from £80 to £95 **Parking** 100 **Notes** LB

THETFORD
Map 13 TL88

Bell
★★★ Ⓐ HOTEL

☎ 01842 754455 📠 01842 755552
King St IP24 2AZ
e-mail: bell.thetford@oldenglishinns.co.uk
web: www.oldenglish.co.uk
dir: From S exit A11, 2m to 1st set of lights, turn right onto A134. 100yds turn left into Bridge St, 150yds & over bridge

Rooms 46 (1 fmly) **Facilities** Xmas **Conf** Class 45 Board 40 Thtr 70 **Parking** 55 **Notes** LB

The Thomas Paine Hotel
THE INDEPENDENTS
HOTEL ASSOCIATION
★★ 68% HOTEL

☎ 01842 755631 📠 01842 766505
White Hart St IP24 1AA
e-mail: bookings@thomaspainehotel.com
dir: N'bound on A11, at rdbt immediately before Thetford take A1075, hotel on right on approach to town

This Grade II listed building is situated close to the town centre and Thetford Forest Park is just a short drive away. Public rooms include a large lounge bar, a pleasantly appointed restaurant and a meeting room. Bedrooms vary in size and style; each one is attractively decorated and thoughtfully equipped.

Rooms 13 (2 fmly) **S** fr £55; **D** fr £66 (incl. bkfst)
Facilities Xmas Wi-fi **Conf** Class 35 Board 30 Thtr 70 **Parking** 30 **Notes** LB

THORNHAM
Map 12 TF74

Lifeboat Inn
★★ 78% ⊛ HOTEL

☎ 01485 512236 📠 01485 512323
Ship Ln PE36 6LT
e-mail: reception@lifeboatinn.co.uk
web: www.lifeboatinn.co.uk
dir: follow A149 from Hunstanton for approx 6m. 1st left after Thornham sign

This popular 16th-century smugglers' alehouse enjoys superb views across open meadows to Thornham Harbour. The tastefully decorated bedrooms are furnished with pine pieces and have many thoughtful touches. The public rooms have a wealth of character and feature open fireplaces, exposed brickwork and oak beams.

Rooms 13 (3 fmly) (1 GF) **S** £72-£82; **D** £104-£124 (incl. bkfst)* **Facilities** Xmas New Year Wi-fi **Conf** Class 30 Board 30 Thtr 50 **Parking** 120

The Orange Tree
⊛⊛ RESTAURANT WITH ROOMS

☎ 01485 512213 📠 01485 512424
High St PE36 6LY
e-mail: email@theorangetreethornham.co.uk
dir: On A149 in centre of village.

The Orange Tree is a smart inn on the north Norfolk coast. Bedrooms are located in an annexe adjacent to the main building; each one is pleasantly decorated and thoughtfully equipped. Public areas feature a contemporary open-plan bar/restaurant where an interesting choice of freshly prepared dishes is on offer.

Rooms 6 (1 fmly) (6 GF)

THURSFORD

The Old Forge Seafood Restaurant
⊛ RESTAURANT WITH ROOMS

☎ 01328 878345
Seafood Restaurant, Fakenham Rd NR21 0BD
e-mail: sarah.goldspink@btconnect.com
dir: On A148 (Fakenham to Holt road), next to garage at Thursford

Expect a warm welcome at this delightful relaxed restaurant with rooms. The open-plan public areas include a lounge bar area with comfy sofas, and a intimate restaurant with pine tables. Bedrooms are pleasantly decorated and equipped with a good range of useful facilities.

Rooms 2 (1 pri facs)

TITCHWELL
Map 13 TF74

Titchwell Manor
★★★ 82% ⊛⊛ HOTEL

☎ 01485 210221 📠 01485 210104
PE31 8BB
e-mail: margaret@titchwellmanor.com
web: www.titchwellmanor.com
dir: on A149 coast road between Brancaster and Thornham

Friendly family-run hotel ideally placed for touring the north Norfolk coastline. The tastefully appointed bedrooms are very comfortable; some in the adjacent annexe offer ground floor access. Smart public rooms include a lounge area, relaxed informal bar and a delightful conservatory restaurant, overlooking the walled garden. Imaginative menus feature quality local produce and fresh fish.

Rooms 26 (18 annexe) (4 fmly) (16 GF) **D** £100-£200 (incl. bkfst) **Facilities** Xmas New Year Child facilities **Conf** Class 25 Board 25 Thtr 25 **Parking** 50 **Notes** LB

WATTON
Map 13 TF90

Broom Hall Country Hotel
★★★ Ⓐ HOTEL

☎ 01953 882125 📠 01953 885325
Richmond Rd, Saham Toney IP25 7EX
e-mail: enquiries@broomhallhotel.co.uk
web: www.broomhallhotel.co.uk
dir: Leave A11 at Thetford onto A1075 to Watton (12m), B1108 towards Swaffham, in 0.5m at rdbt turn right to Saham Toney, hotel 0.5m on left

Rooms 15 (5 annexe) (3 fmly) (5 GF) **S** £75-£95; **D** £95-£175 (incl. bkfst) **Facilities** ⓢ Massage Wi-fi **Conf** Class 30 Board 22 Thtr 80 Del from £100 to £115 **Parking** 30 **Notes** LB Closed 24 Dec-4 Jan Civ Wed 70

WROXHAM
Map 13 TG31

Broad House Country Estate
★★★ Ⓐ COUNTRY HOUSE HOTEL

☎ 01603 783567 📠 01494 400333
The Avenue NR12 8TS
e-mail: info@broadhousehotel.co.uk

Rooms 9 (1 fmly) **S** £130-£210; **D** £130-£210 (incl. bkfst)* **Facilities** FTV ⓢ Fishing ⓢ Gym Xmas New Year Wi-fi **Conf** Class 30 Board 30 Thtr 60 Del from £130 to £200* **Parking** 60 **Notes** LB No children 12yrs Civ Wed 50

WROXHAM continued

Hotel Wroxham

★★ 71% HOTEL

☎ 01603 782061 📠 01603 784279
The Bridge NR12 8AJ
e-mail: reservations@hotelwroxham.co.uk
web: www.arlingtonhotelgroup.co.uk
dir: From Norwich, A1151 signed Wroxham & The Broads
for approx 7m. Over bridge at Wroxham take 1st right, &
sharp right again. Hotel car park on right

Perfectly placed for touring the Norfolk Broads in the
heart of this bustling town centre. The bedrooms are
pleasantly decorated and well equipped; some rooms
have balconies with lovely views of the busy waterways.
The open-plan public rooms include the lively riverside
bar, a lounge, a large sun terrace and a smart restaurant.

Rooms 18 **Facilities** Fishing Boating facilities (by
arrangement) Xmas New Year Wi-fi **Conf** Class 50
Board 20 Thtr 200 **Parking** 45 **Notes** LB ⊗ Civ Wed 40

WYMONDHAM   Map 13 TG10

Hill House

★★★ 74% HOTEL

☎ 01953 602148 📠 01953 606247
10 Church St NR18 0PH
e-mail: abbey@mjbhotels.com
web: www.mjbhotels.com
dir: from A11 follow Wymondham sign. At lights left, then
1st left into one-way system. Left into Church St

Charming 16th-century hotel situated close to the abbey
just off the main high street of this delightful market
town. The spacious bedrooms are pleasantly decorated,
tastefully furnished and thoughtfully equipped; five
superior rooms are available. Public rooms include a cosy
lounge bar, the Benims restaurant and a further sitting
room.

Rooms 28 (1 annexe) (3 fmly) (6 GF) **Facilities** Xmas
Services Lift **Parking** 3 **Notes** LB ⊗

Wymondham Consort

★★ 78% METRO HOTEL

☎ 01953 606721 📠 01953 601361
28 Market St NR18 0BB
e-mail: wymondham@bestwestern.co.uk
dir: off A11 (M11) left at lights and left again

A privately-owned hotel situated in the centre of this
bustling market town. The individually styled bedrooms
come in a variety of sizes; each one is pleasantly
decorated and thoughtfully equipped. Public rooms
include a cosy bar, a separate lounge, the Rendezvous
wine bar and an intimate restaurant that overlooks the
busy high street.

Rooms 20 (1 fmly) (3 GF) **Facilities** Wi-fi **Conf** Board 20
Thtr 20 **Parking** 16 **Notes** LB

NORTHAMPTONSHIRE

CASTLE ASHBY   Map 11 SP85

Falcon

★★ Ⓐ HOTEL

☎ 01604 696200 📠 01604 696673
NN7 1LF
e-mail: falcon.castleashby@oldenglishinns.co.uk
web: www.oldenglish.co.uk
dir: off A428

Rooms 16 (11 annexe) (1 fmly) **Facilities** Xmas
Conf Class 30 Board 25 Thtr 50 **Parking** 75
Notes Civ Wed 60

CORBY   Map 11 SP88

Holiday Inn Corby-Kettering A43

Ⓤ

☎ 01536 401020 📠 01536 400767
Geddington Rd NN18 8ET
e-mail: gm@hicorby.com
web: www.holidayinn.co.uk
dir: M1 junct 19, A14 towards Kettering. Exit at junct 7
towards Corby. Follow Stamford & Corby East, A43. At end
of road left through Geddington. After Eurohub rdbt turn
left at next lights

Currently the rating for this establishment is not confirmed.
This may be due to a change of ownership or because it has
only recently joined the AA rating scheme. For further
details please see the AA website: www.theAA.com

Rooms 105 (9 GF) (16 smoking) **Facilities** STV FTV Ⓧ
Gym Sauna Steam room Xmas New Year Wi-fi
Conf Thtr 250 Del from £99 to £135* **Services** Lift Air con
Parking 250 **Notes** Civ Wed 70

CRICK   Map 11 SP57

Holiday Inn Rugby/Northampton

Ⓤ

☎ 0870 400 9059 & 0800 405060 📠 01788 823 8955
NN6 7XR
e-mail: rugbyhi@ihg.com
web: www.holidayinn.co.uk
dir: 0.5m from M1 junct 18

Currently the rating for this establishment is not confirmed.
This may be due to a change of ownership or because it has
only recently joined the AA rating scheme. For further
details please see the AA website: www.theAA.com

Rooms 90 (19 fmly) (42 GF) (12 smoking) **S** £65-£150;
D £65-£150* **Facilities** STV Ⓧ Gym New Year Wi-fi
Conf Class 90 Board 64 Thtr 170 Del from £99 to £150*
Services Lift Air con **Parking** 250 **Notes** LB Civ Wed

Ibis Rugby East

BUDGET HOTEL

☎ 01788 824331 📠 01788 824332
Parklands NN6 7EX
e-mail: H3588@accor-hotels.com
web: www.ibishotel.com
dir: M1 junct 18, follow Daventry/Rugby A5 signs. At rdbt
3rd exit signed DIRFT East. Hotel on right

Modern, budget hotel offering comfortable
accommodation in bright and practical bedrooms.
Breakfast is self-service and dinner is available in the
café restaurant. See also the Hotel Groups pages.

Rooms 111 (47 fmly) (12 GF) **Conf** Class 25 Board 25
Thtr 40

DAVENTRY   Map 11 SP56

INSPECTORS' CHOICE

Fawsley Hall

★★★★ ✿✿✿ HOTEL

☎ 01327 892000   📠 01327 892001
Fawsley NN11 3BA
e-mail: reservations@fawsleyhall.com
web: www.fawsleyhall.com
dir: A361 (Daventry), follow for 12m. Turn right, signed
Fawsley Hall.

Dating back to the 15th century, this delightful hotel
is peacefully located in beautiful gardens designed
by 'Capability' Brown. Spacious, individually designed
bedrooms and stylish public areas are beautifully
furnished with antique and period pieces. Afternoon
tea is served in the impressive Great Hall with its
sumptuous deep cushioned sofas and real fires. Dinner
in Knightly Restaurant offers imaginative cuisine with
Mediterranean influences.

Rooms 52 (8 annexe) (2 GF) **S** fr £159; **D** £159-£459
(incl. bkfst)* **Facilities** STV ☁ ⌣ Gym Health &
beauty treatment rooms Fitness studio Xmas New Year
Wi-fi **Conf** Class 64 Board 40 Thtr 120 Del from £199*
Parking 140 **Notes** LB Civ Wed 120

Barceló Daventry Hotel

★★★★ 71% HOTEL

☎ 01327 307000   📠 01327 706313
Sedgemoor Way NN11 0SG
e-mail: daventry@barcelo-hotels.co.uk
web: www.barcelo-hotels.co.uk
dir: M1 junct 16/A45 to Daventry, at 1st rdbt turn right to
Kilsby/M1(N). Hotel on right in 1m

This modern, striking hotel overlooking Drayton Water
boasts spacious public areas that include a good range
of banqueting, meeting and leisure facilities. It is a
popular venue for conferences. Bedrooms are suitable for
both business and leisure guests.

Rooms 155 (14 fmly) **S** £55-£135; **Facilities** ⌕
supervised Gym Steam room Health & beauty salon Wi-fi
Conf Class 200 Board 100 Thtr 600 **Services** Lift
Parking 350 **Notes** Civ Wed 250

HELLIDON   Map 11 SP55

Hellidon Lakes   QHOTELS

★★★★ 71% HOTEL

☎ 01327 262550   📠 01327 262559
NN11 6GG
e-mail: hellidonlakes@qhotels.co.uk
web: www.qhotels.co.uk
dir: off A361 between Daventry and Banbury, signed

Some 220 acres of beautiful countryside, which include
27 holes of golf and 12 lakes, combine to form a rather
spectacular backdrop to this impressive hotel. Bedroom
styles vary, from ultra smart, modern rooms through to
those in the original wing that offer superb views. There
is an extensive range of facilities available from meeting
rooms to swimming pool, gym and ten-pin bowling.
Golfers of all levels can try some of the world's most
challenging courses on the indoor golf simulator. Q Hotels
- AA Hotel Group of the Year 2008-9.

Rooms 110 **Facilities** Spa STV ⌕ ⌣ 27 ⛳ Putt green ⌣
Gym Beauty therapist Indoor smart golf 10-pin bowling
Steam room Xmas New Year Wi-fi **Conf** Class 150
Board 80 Thtr 300 **Services** Lift **Parking** 150
Notes Civ Wed 220

See advert on this page

HORTON   Map 11 SP85

The New French Partridge
★★ 85% ◎◎ HOTEL

☎ 01604 870033 📠 01604 870032
Newport Pagnell Rd NN7 2AP
e-mail: info@newfrenchpartridge.co.uk
web: www.newfrenchpartridge.co.uk
dir: On B526 (Newport Pagnell road), 0.5m from
Northampton & Milton Keynes

Set in private grounds within the rural village of Horton, a
short drive from Northampton, this unique and historic
manor house offers superb accommodation and good
food. Individually appointed bedrooms are attractively
presented and extremely well equipped, well suited to
both corporate and leisure guests. Accomplished cooking
is served in the restaurant, whilst the friendly team
provide attentive service. The day rooms include small
lounge areas and a character cellar bar.

Rooms 10 (2 fmly) **Facilities** Xmas New Year
Conf Class 40 Board 25 Thtr 50 **Parking** 30 **Notes** LB
Civ Wed 70

KETTERING   Map 11 SP87

Rushton Hall Hotel and Spa
★★★★ 83% ◎◎ COUNTRY HOUSE HOTEL

☎ 01536 713001 📠 01536 713010
NN14 1RR
e-mail: enquiries@rushtonhall.com
web: www.rushtonhall.com
dir: A14 junct 7. A43 to Corby then A6003 to Rushton turn
after bridge

Elegant country house hotel set amidst 30 acres of
parkland and surrounded by open countryside. The stylish
public rooms include a library, a superb open-plan lounge
bar with a magnificent vaulted ceiling and plush sofas,
and an oak-panelled dining hall. The tastefully appointed
bedrooms have co-ordinated fabrics and many thoughtful
touches.

Rooms 42 (6 fmly) (3 GF) **S** £140-£300; **D** £150-£350
(incl. bkfst)* **Facilities** Spa FTV ⊗ ⌇ Fishing ⚓ Gym
Billiard table Sauna Wi-fi **Conf** Class 250 Board 40
Thtr 250 Del from £215* **Services** Lift **Parking** 140
Notes LB ⊗ Civ Wed 160

See advert on this page

Kettering Park Hotel & Spa
★★★★ 80% ◎ HOTEL

☎ 01536 416666 📠 01536 416171
Kettering Parkway NN15 6XT
e-mail: kpark@shirehotels.com
web: www.ketteringparkhotel.com
dir: off A14 junct 9 (M1 to A1 link road), hotel in Kettering
Venture Park

Expect a warm welcome at this stylish hotel situated just
off the A14. The spacious, smartly decorated bedrooms
are well equipped and meticulously maintained. Guests
can choose from classical or contemporary dishes in the
restaurant and lighter meals are served in the bar. The
extensive leisure facilities are impressive.

Rooms 119 (29 fmly) (35 GF) **S** £97.50-£204;
D £145-£229 (incl. bkfst)* **Facilities** STV ⊗ Gym Steam
room Sauna Children's splash pool Activity studio New
Year Wi-fi **Conf** Class 120 Board 40 Thtr 260
Del from £135 to £189* **Services** Lift Air con **Parking** 200
Notes LB ⊗ Civ Wed 120

Travelodge Kettering
BUDGET HOTEL

☎ 08719 846 081
A14 (Westbound) NN14 1RW
web: www.travelodge.co.uk
dir: M6 junct 1 or M1 junct 19, take A14, 0.5m past A43
junct

Travelodge offers good quality, good value, modern
accommodation. Ideal for families, the spacious en suite
bedrooms include remote-control TV, tea and coffee-
making facilities and comfortable beds. Meals can be
taken at the nearby family restaurant. See also the Hotel
Groups pages.

Rooms 40 **S** fr £29; **D** fr £29

NORTHAMPTON — Map 11 SP76

Northampton Marriott Hotel

 Marriott HOTELS & RESORTS

★★★★ 73% HOTEL

☎ 01604 768700 🖷 01604 769011
Eagle Dr NN4 7HW
e-mail: mhrs.ormnh.salesadmin@marriotthotels.com
web: www.northamptonmarriott.co.uk
dir: M1 junct 15, follow signs to Delapre Golf Course, hotel on right

Located on the outskirts of town, close to major road networks, this modern hotel caters to a cross section of guests. A self-contained management centre makes this a popular conference venue, and its spacious and well designed bedrooms will suit business travellers particularly well. This makes a good base for exploring the attractions the area has to offer.

Rooms 120 (10 fmly) (52 GF) (10 smoking) **S** £78-£199; **D** £78-£199 (incl. bkfst)* **Facilities** STV ✨ supervised Gym Steam room Beauty treatment room Solarium Sauna Xmas New Year Wi-fi **Conf** Class 72 Board 30 Thtr 250 Del from £110 to £165* **Services** Air con **Parking** 200 **Notes** LB ⊗ Civ Wed 180

Best Western Lime Trees

Best Western

★★★ 71% HOTEL

☎ 01604 632188 🖷 01604 233012
8 Langham Place, Barrack Rd NN2 6AA
e-mail: info@limetreeshotel.co.uk
web: www.limetreeshotel.co.uk
dir: from city centre 0.5m N on A508 towards Market Harborough, near racecourse & cathedral

This well presented hotel is popular with business travellers during the week and leisure guests at the weekend. Service is both efficient and friendly. Bedrooms are comfortable and in addition to all the usual facilities, many offer air conditioning. Notable features include an internal courtyard and a row of charming mews houses that have been converted into bedrooms.

Rooms 28 (8 annexe) (4 fmly) (5 GF) **Facilities** FTV Xmas New Year Wi-fi **Conf** Class 50 Board 45 Thtr 140 **Services** Air con **Parking** 25 **Notes** Civ Wed 140

Holiday Inn

 Holiday Inn HOTELS · RESORTS

☎ 01327 349022 🖷 01327 349017
High St, Flore NN7 4LP
e-mail: sarah.potter@kewgreen.co.uk
web: www.holidayinn.co.uk

Currently the rating for this establishment is not confirmed. This may be due to a change of ownership or because it has only recently joined the AA rating scheme. For further details please see the AA website: www.theAA.com

Rooms 53 (9 fmly) (42 GF) (5 smoking) **D** £50-£200 (incl. bkfst)* **Facilities** STV FTV Gym Xmas New Year Wi-fi **Conf** Class 50 Board 40 Thtr 150 Del from £125 to £155* **Services** Air con **Parking** 150 **Notes** LB Civ Wed 120

Holiday Inn Northampton

 Holiday Inn HOTELS · RESORTS

☎ 01604 622777 & 0870 400 7214 🖷 0870 400 7314
Bedford Rd NN4 7YF
e-mail: reservations@northampton.kewgreen.co.uk
web: www.holidayinn.co.uk
dir: M1 junct 15 onto A508 towards Northampton. Follow A45 towards Wellingborough for 2m then A428 towards Bedford, hotel on left

Currently the rating for this establishment is not confirmed. This may be due to a change of ownership or because it has only recently joined the AA rating scheme. For further details please see the AA website: www.theAA.com

Rooms 104 (3 fmly) (26 GF) **D** £65-£139 (incl. bkfst)* **Facilities** STV Gym Xmas New Year Wi-fi **Conf** Class 30 Board 35 Thtr 70 Del from £125 to £185* **Services** Lift Air con **Parking** 125 **Notes** ⊗

Campanile Northampton

 Campanile HOTEL RESTAURANT

BUDGET HOTEL

Cheaney Dr, Grange Park NN4 5FB
dir: M1 junction 15 onto A508 towards Northampton. 2nd exit at first roundabout and 2nd exit at second roundabout into Grange Park.

This modern building offers accommodation in smart, well-equipped bedrooms, all with en suite bathrooms. Refreshments may be taken at the informal bistro. See also the Hotel Groups pages.

Rooms 87

Express by Holiday Inn Northampton M1 Jct 15

 Express by Holiday Inn

BUDGET HOTEL

☎ 01604 432800 🖷 01604 432832
Loake Close, Grange Park NN4 5EZ
e-mail: northampton@expressholidayinn.co.uk
web: www.hiexpress.com/exnorthampton

A modern hotel ideal for families and business travellers. Fresh and uncomplicated, the spacious rooms include Sky TV, power shower and tea and coffee-making facilities. Continental buffet breakfast is included in the room rate; other meals may be taken at the nearby family pub or restaurant. See also the Hotel Groups pages.

Rooms 126 **Conf** Class 28 Board 28 Thtr 70

Ibis Northampton Centre

 ibis HOTEL

BUDGET HOTEL

☎ 01604 608900 🖷 01604 608910
Sol Central, Marefair NN1 1SR
e-mail: H3657@accor-hotels.com
web: www.ibishotel.com
dir: M1 junct 15/15a & city centre towards railway station

Modern, budget hotel offering comfortable accommodation in bright and practical bedrooms. Breakfast is self-service and dinner is available in the restaurant. See also the Hotel Groups pages.

Rooms 151 (14 fmly)

Innkeeper's Lodge Northampton East

Innkeeper's Lodge

BUDGET HOTEL

☎ 0845 112 6049 🖷 0845 112 6253
Talavera Way, Round Spinney NN3 8RN
web: www.innkeeperslodge.com/northamptoneast
dir: M1 junct 15, A508 towards Northampton. Under flyover, immediately left, right at rdbt into London Rd. Lodge on right

Innkeeper's Lodge represents an exciting, high value concept within the budget hotel market. Comfortable bedrooms provide excellent facilities that include satellite TV and modem points. Options include family rooms, and for the corporate guest, cutting edge IT which includes Wi-fi access. A popular Carvery provides all-day food, including an extensive, complimentary continental breakfast.

Rooms 31 **S** £53-£55; **D** £53-£55 (incl. bkfst)
Conf Thtr 40

Innkeeper's Lodge Northampton M1 Jct 15

BUDGET HOTEL

☎ 0845 112 6050 🖷 0845 112 6252
London Rd, Wootton NN4 0TG
web: www.innkeeperslodge.com/northamptonsouth
dir: M1 junct 15 take A508, towards Northampton. Pass under flyover, exit left immediately & turn right at rdbt into London Rd. Lodge on right.

Innkeeper's Lodge represents an exciting, high value concept within the budget hotel market. Comfortable bedrooms provide excellent facilities that include satellite TV and modem points. Options include family rooms, and for the corporate guest, cutting edge IT which includes Wi-fi access. A popular Carvery provides all-day food, including an extensive, complimentary continental breakfast.

Rooms 51 (21 fmly) **S** £53-£55; **D** £53-£55 (incl. bkfst)
Conf Thtr 100

NORTHAMPTON continued

Travelodge Northampton Upton Way

BUDGET HOTEL

☎ 0871 984 6089 ▤ 01604 758395
Upton Way NN5 6EG
web: www.travelodge.co.uk
dir: A45, towards M1 junct 16

Travelodge offers good quality, good value, modern accommodation. Ideal for families, the spacious en suite bedrooms include remote-control TV, tea and coffee-making facilities and comfortable beds. Meals can be taken at the nearby family restaurant. See also the Hotel Groups pages.

Rooms 62 **S** fr £29; **D** fr £29

OUNDLE   Map 11 TL08

Talbot

★★ Ⓐ HOTEL

☎ 01832 273621 ▤ 01832 274545
New St PE8 4EA
e-mail: talbot.oundle@oldenglishinns.co.uk
web: www.oldenglish.co.uk
dir: A1(M) junct 17 take A605. At 3rd rdbt turn right signed Oundle A427. Hotel in town centre.

Rooms 35 (3 fmly) (11 GF) **Facilities** Xmas **Conf** Class 70 Board 100 Thtr 200 **Parking** 25 **Notes** LB ⊗ Civ Wed 60

RUSHDEN   Map 11 SP96

Travelodge Wellingborough Rushden

BUDGET HOTEL

☎ 0871 984 6115 ▤ 01933 57008
Saunders Lodge NN10 6AP
web: www.travelodge.co.uk
dir: on A45, eastbound

Travelodge offers good quality, good value, modern accommodation. Ideal for families, the spacious en suite bedrooms include remote-control TV, tea and coffee-making facilities and comfortable beds. Meals can be taken at the nearby family restaurant See also the Hotel Groups pages.

Rooms 40 **S** fr £29; **D** fr £29

THRAPSTON   Map 11 SP97

Travelodge Kettering Thrapston

BUDGET HOTEL

☎ 08719 846 111 ▤ 01832 735199
Thrapston Bypass NN14 4UR
web: www.travelodge.co.uk
dir: on A14 link road A1/M1

Travelodge offers good quality, good value, modern accommodation. Ideal for families, the spacious en suite bedrooms include remote-control TV, tea and coffee-making facilities and comfortable beds. Meals can be taken at the nearby family restaurant. See also the Hotel Groups pages.

Rooms 40 **S** fr £29; **D** fr £29

TOWCESTER   Map 11 SP64

Saracens Head

★★ Ⓐ HOTEL

☎ 01327 350414 ▤ 01327 359879
219 Watling St NN12 7BX
e-mail: saracenshead.towcester@greeneking.co.uk
web: www.oldenglish.co.uk
dir: A5 to Towcester. Follow signs into town centre

Rooms 21 (3 fmly) **Facilities** ♫ Xmas **Conf** Class 50 Board 50 Thtr 80 **Parking** 20 **Notes** LB ⊗ RS 25 Dec Civ Wed 90

Travelodge Towcester Silverstone

BUDGET HOTEL

☎ 0871 984 6112 ▤ 01327 359105
NN12 6TQ
web: www.travelodge.co.uk
dir: A43 East Towcester by-pass

Travelodge offers good quality, good value, modern accommodation. Ideal for families, the spacious en suite bedrooms include remote-control TV, tea and coffee-making facilities and comfortable beds. Meals can be taken at the nearby family restaurant. See also the Hotel Groups pages.

Rooms 55 **S** fr £29; **D** fr £29

WELLINGBOROUGH   Map 11 SP86

The Hind

★★ 64% HOTEL

☎ 01933 222827 ▤ 01933 441921
Sheep St NN8 1BY
e-mail: enquiries@thehind.co.uk
dir: on A509 in town centre

Dating back to Jacobean times, this centrally located hotel provides a good base for business and leisure guests visiting the town. A good choice of dishes is available in the restaurant; alternatively the all-day coffee shop offers light snacks. Bedrooms come in a variety of styles, mostly of spacious dimensions.

Rooms 34 (2 fmly) (5 GF) **Facilities** Pool table **Conf** Class 40 Board 40 Thtr 70 **Parking** 15 **Notes** RS 24 Dec-2 Jan Civ Wed 70

Ibis Wellingborough

BUDGET HOTEL

☎ 01933 228333 ▤ 01933 228444
Enstone Court NN8 2DR
e-mail: H3164@accor-hotels.com
web: www.ibishotel.com
dir: at junct of A45 & A509 towards Kettering, SW outskirts of Wellingborough

Modern, budget hotel offering comfortable accommodation in bright and practical bedrooms. Breakfast is self-service and dinner is available in the restaurant. See also the Hotel Groups pages.

Rooms 78 (20 fmly) (2 GF)

WHITTLEBURY   Map 11 SP64

Whittlebury Hall

★★★★ 80% ⊛⊛ HOTEL

☎ 01327 857857 ▤ 01327 857867
NN12 8QH
e-mail: sales@whittleburyhall.co.uk
web: www.whittleburyhall.co.uk
dir: A43/A413 towards Buckingham, through Whittlebury, turn for hotel on right (signed)

A purpose-built, Georgian-style country house hotel with excellent spa and leisure facilities and pedestrian access to the Silverstone circuit. Grand public areas include F1 car racing memorabilia and the accommodation includes some lavishly appointed suites. Food is a strength, with a choice of various dining options. Particularly noteworthy are the afternoon teas in the spacious, comfortable lounge and the fine dining in Murray's Restaurant.

Rooms 211 (3 fmly) **Facilities** Spa ⓣ Gym Beauty treatments Relaxation room Hair studio Heat & Ice experience Leisure club Xmas New Year Wi-fi Child facilities **Conf** Class 175 Board 40 Thtr 500 **Services** Lift **Parking** 450 **Notes** ⊗

NORTHUMBERLAND

ALNWICK
Map 21 NU11

See also **Embleton**

White Swan

★★★ 80% HOTEL

☎ 01665 602109 ◫ 01665 510400
Bondgate Within NE66 1TD
e-mail: info.whiteswan@classiclodges.co.uk
web: www.classiclodges.co.uk
dir: from A1 follow town centre signs. Hotel in town centre
near Bondgate Tower

Situated in the heart of the historic town, this charming
300-year-old coaching inn has now undergone a full
refurbishment but still retains many authentic period
features. The Olympic restaurant with its original oak
panelling and stained glass windows, salvaged from the
SS Olympic (sister ship of the ill fated Titanic) blends
well with the modern Hardy's bistro. All the bedrooms
have also been stylishly refurbished and are well
equipped.

Rooms 56 (5 fmly) (11 GF) **S** £80-£85; **D** £120-£170 (incl.
bkfst)* **Facilities** Xmas New Year Wi-fi **Conf** Class 50
Board 40 Thtr 150 Del from £95 to £150* **Parking** 25
Notes LB ⊗ Civ Wed 150

Oaks

★★ 🅰 SMALL HOTEL

☎ 01665 510014 ◫ 01665 603219
South Rd NE66 2PN
e-mail: kentheoakshotel@alncom.net
dir: From S, leave A1 at 1st exit for Alnwick and at rdbt
take 2nd exit. At 2nd rdbt take last exit, car park 1st right

Rooms 12 (3 annexe) (3 fmly) (5 GF) **S** £50; **D** £80 (incl.
bkfst)* **Facilities** FTV Wi-fi **Conf** Class 16 Board 20
Thtr 22 **Parking** 27 **Notes** Closed 25 Dec RS 26 Dec &
1 Jan

BAMBURGH
Map 21 NU13

Waren House

★★★ 78% COUNTRY HOUSE HOTEL

☎ 01668 214581 ◫ 01668 214484
Waren Mill NE70 7EE
e-mail: enquiries@warenhousehotel.co.uk
web: www.warenhousehotel.co.uk
dir: 2m E of A1 turn onto B1342 to Waren Mill, at T-junct
turn right, hotel 100yds on right

This delightful Georgian mansion is set in six acres of
woodland and offers a welcoming atmosphere and views
of the coast. The individually themed bedrooms and
suites include many with large bathrooms. Good, home-
cooked food is served in the elegant dining room. A
comfortable lounge and library are also available.

Rooms 13 (1 GF) **S** £85-£143; **D** £113-£223 (incl. bkfst)*
Facilities FTV Xmas New Year Wi-fi **Conf** Class 16
Board 16 Del from £140 to £200* **Parking** 20 **Notes** No
children 14yrs

Victoria

★★ 80% HOTEL

☎ 01668 214431 ◫ 01668 214404
Front St NE69 7BP
e-mail: enquiries@victoriahotel.net
web: www.victoriahotel.net
dir: off A1, N of Alnwick onto B1342, near Belford & follow
signs to Bamburgh. Hotel in town centre

Overlooking the village green, this hotel offers an
interesting blend of traditional and modern. Public areas
including the residents'/diners' bar lounge are relaxing
venues throughout the day and evening, while the
brasserie, with its conservatory roof, provides a more
contemporary dinner menu. Bedrooms come in a variety
of styles and sizes.

Rooms 29 (2 fmly) (2 GF) **Facilities** Xmas **Conf** Class 30
Board 20 Thtr 50 **Notes** LB Closed 8-23 Jan Civ Wed 50

The Lord Crewe

★★ 78% HOTEL

☎ 01668 214243 & 214613 ◫ 01668 214273
Front St NE69 7BL
e-mail: enquiries@lordcrewe.co.uk
dir: just below the castle

Located in the heart of the village in the shadow of
impressive Bamburgh Castle, this hotel has been
developed from an old inn. Public areas include a choice
of lounges, a cosy bar and a smart modern restaurant.
Bedrooms vary in size, all offer good levels of comfort and
are well equipped.

Rooms 17 **Facilities** FTV **Parking** 20 **Notes** ⊗ No
children 5yrs Closed Dec & Jan

BELFORD
Map 21 NU13

Blue Bell

★★★ 64% HOTEL

☎ 01668 213543 ◫ 01668 213787
Market Place NE70 7NE
e-mail: bluebel@globalnet.co.uk
web: www.bluebellhotel.com
dir: centre of village on left of St Mary's Church

Formerly a coaching inn, this popular and long
established hotel is located in the village square. It offers
a choice of superior and standard bedrooms all in
classical style. Well-prepared meals can be enjoyed in the
restaurant and in addition to the bar there is a
comfortable lounge in which to relax.

Rooms 28 (11 annexe) (2 fmly) (13 GF) **S** £45-£70;
D £90-£140 (incl. bkfst & dinner) **Facilities** FTV Xmas
New Year **Conf** Class 40 Board 30 Thtr 80 **Parking** 16
Notes ⊗ Civ Wed 100

Purdy Lodge

★★ 74% HOTEL

☎ 01668 213000 ◫ 01668 213131
Adderstone Services NE70 7JU
e-mail: stay@purdylodge.co.uk
web: www.purdylodge.co.uk
dir: turn off A1 onto B1341 then immediately left

Situated on the A1, this family-owned lodge provides
quiet bedrooms that look out over fields towards
Bamburgh Castle. Food is readily available in the
attractive restaurant, the smart 24-hour café, and the
cosy lounge bar.

Rooms 20 (4 fmly) (10 GF) **Facilities** Xmas **Parking** 60

BERWICK-UPON-TWEED — Map 21 NT95

Marshall Meadows Country House

★★★ 70% COUNTRY HOUSE HOTEL

☎ 01289 331133 📠 01289 331438
TD15 1UT
e-mail: gm.marshallmeadows@classiclodges.co.uk
web: www.classiclodges.co.uk
dir: signed directly off A1, 300yds from Scottish border

This stylish Georgian mansion is set in wooded grounds flanked by farmland and has convenient access from the A1. A popular venue for weddings and conferences, it offers comfortable and well-equipped bedrooms. Public rooms include a cosy bar, a relaxing lounge and a two-tier restaurant, which serves imaginative dishes.

Rooms 19 (1 fmly) **Facilities** ⚒ Xmas New Year **Conf** Class 120 Board 40 Thtr 200 **Parking** 85 **Notes** LB Civ Wed 200

Queens Head

★★ 74% HOTEL

☎ 01289 307852 📠 01289 307858
Sandgate TD15 1EP
e-mail: info@queensheadberwick.co.uk
dir: A1 towards centre & town hall, along High St. Turn right at bottom to Hide Hill. Hotel next to cinema

This small hotel is situated in the town centre, close to the old walls of this former garrison town. The bright stylish bedrooms are furnished in pine and are well equipped. For eating the focus is on a daily-changing blackboard menu that offers an impressive choice of tasty, freshly prepared dishes served in the reception lounge or dining room.

Rooms 11 (2 fmly) **S** £60; **D** £45-£60 (incl. bkfst)* **Facilities** FTV Wi-fi **Notes** ⊗

Travelodge Berwick-upon-Tweed

BUDGET HOTEL

☎ 08719 846 279 📠 01289 306555
Loaning Meadow, North Rd TD15 1UQ
web: www.travelodge.co.uk
dir: From A1 to rdbt with A1167

Travelodge offers good quality, good value, modern accommodation. Ideal for families, the spacious en suite bedrooms include remote-control TV, tea and coffee-making facilities and comfortable beds. Meals can be taken at the nearby family restaurant. See also the Hotel Groups pages.

Rooms 40 **S** fr £29; **D** fr £29

CORNHILL-ON-TWEED — Map 21 NT83

Tillmouth Park Country House

★★★ 85% ⊛⊛ HOTEL

☎ 01890 882255 📠 01890 882540
TD12 4UU
e-mail: reception@tillmouthpark.force9.co.uk
web: www.tillmouthpark.co.uk
dir: off A1(M) at East Ord rdbt at Berwick-upon-Tweed. Take A698 to Cornhill and Coldstream. Hotel 9m on left

An imposing mansion set in landscaped grounds by the River Till. Gracious public rooms include a stunning galleried lounge with a drawing room adjacent. The quiet, elegant dining room overlooks the gardens, whilst lunches and early dinners are available in the bistro. Bedrooms retain much traditional character and include several magnificent master rooms.

Rooms 14 (2 annexe) (1 fmly) **S** £68; **D** £90-£195 (incl. bkfst)* **Facilities** FTV ⚒ Game shooting Fishing New Year Wi-fi **Conf** Class 20 Board 20 Thtr 50 Del from £125* **Parking** 50 **Notes** LB Closed 2 Jan-6 Apr 09 Civ Wed 50

CRAMLINGTON — Map 21 NZ27

Innkeeper's Lodge Cramlington

BUDGET HOTEL

☎ 0845 112 6013 📠 0845 112 6288
Blagdon Ln NE23 8AU
web: www.innkeeperslodge.com/cramlington
dir: from A1 onto A19. At rdbt, left onto A1068. Lodge at junct of Blagdon Lane & Fisher Lane

Innkeeper's Lodge represents an exciting, high value concept within the budget hotel market. Comfortable bedrooms provide excellent facilities that include satellite TV and modem points. Options include family rooms, and for the corporate guest, cutting edge IT includes Wi-fi access. Food is served all day in the adjacent Country Pub. The extensive continental breakfast is complimentary.

Rooms 18 **S** £65; **D** £65 (incl. bkfst)

EMBLETON — Map 21 NU22

Dunstanburgh Castle Hotel

★★ 76% HOTEL

☎ 01665 576111 📠 01665 576203
NE66 3UN
e-mail: stay@dunstanburghcastlehotel.co.uk
web: www.dunstanburghcastlehotel.co.uk
dir: from A1, take B1340 to Denwick past Rennington & Masons Arms. Take next right signed Embleton

The focal point of the village, this friendly, family-run hotel has a dining room and grill room that offer different menus, plus a cosy bar and two lounges. In addition to the main bedrooms, a barn conversion houses three stunning suites, each with a lounge and gallery bedroom above.

Rooms 20 (4 fmly) **S** £37.50-£52.50; **D** £75-£105 (incl. bkfst)* **Parking** 15 **Notes** LB Closed Dec-Jan

HEDDON-ON-THE-WALL — Map 21 NZ16

Close House

★★★★ 75% HOTEL

☎ 01661 852255 & 856002 📠 01661 853322
NE15 0HT
e-mail: gary.pierce@closehouse.co.uk
dir: A1 N, A69 W. Follow B6528 at junct turn left, hotel signed

Dating back to 1779, this is a magnificent country house set in 300 acres of woodland and parkland in the beautiful Tyne Valley. It is just 20 minutes from Newcastle city centre that has good national and international transport links. The hotel provides accommodation designed to make a stay relaxing and special. All the bedrooms are equipped with high-tech mod cons. There is a magnificent restaurant and bar, and 24-hour room service is also available.

Rooms 19 **S** £96-£172.50; **D** £132-£285 (incl. bkfst) **Facilities** STV ⚑ 18 Putt green Fishing Xmas New Year Wi-fi Child facilities **Conf** Class 30 Board 30 Thtr 140 **Parking** 87 **Notes** LB Civ Wed 200

KINGHAM — Map 10 SP22

Mill House Hotel & Restaurant

★★★ 81% ◉◉ HOTEL

☎ 01608 658188 🖹 01608 658492
OX7 6UH
e-mail: stay@millhousehotel.co.uk
web: www.millhousehotel.co.uk
dir: off A44 onto B4450. Hotel indicated by tourist sign

This Cotswold-stone, former mill house has been carefully converted into a comfortable and attractive hotel. It is set in well-kept grounds bordered by its own trout stream. Bedrooms are comfortable and provide thoughtfully equipped accommodation. There is a peaceful lounge and bar, plus an atmospheric restaurant where the imaginative, skilfully cooked dishes are a highlight of any stay.

Rooms 23 (2 annexe) (1 fmly) (7 GF) **S** £85-£95; **D** £120-£140 (incl. bkfst) **Facilities** STV FTV Fishing ➴ Xmas New Year Wi-fi **Conf** Class 24 Board 24 Thtr 70 Del from £120 to £145 **Parking** 60 **Notes** Civ Wed 100

KIRTLINGTON — Map 11 SP41

Dashwood Hotel and Restaurant

★★★ 81% HOTEL

☎ 01869 352707 🖹 01869 351432
South Green, Heyford Rd OX5 3HJ
e-mail: info@thedashwood.co.uk
web: www.thedashwood.co.uk
dir: M40 junct 10, S on B430 signed Middleton Stoney. After lights in Middleton Stoney, right onto A4095 signed Kirtlington. In village, hotel approx 800mtrs on right just before sharp bend.

This former inn in the centre of the village provides striking, modern bedrooms with LCD flat-screen TVs, broadband and tailor-made oak furniture. The sophisticated bar and restaurant have a wealth of period features and look onto the open-plan kitchen where well-sourced seasonal produce is used to prepare modern cuisine.

Rooms 12 (7 annexe) (1 fmly) (3 GF) **S** £85-£150; **D** £110-£150 (incl. bkfst)* **Facilities** Xmas **Parking** 27 **Notes** LB ⊗ Closed New Year

MIDDLETON STONEY — Map 11 SP52

Best Western Jersey Arms

★★ 72% HOTEL

☎ 01869 343234 🖹 01869 343565
OX25 4AD
e-mail: jerseyarms@bestwestern.co.uk
web: www.jerseyarms.co.uk
dir: 3m from A34, on B430, 10m N of Oxford, between junct 9 & 10 of M40

With a history dating back to the 13th century, the Jersey Arms combines old-fashioned charm with contemporary style and elegance. The individually designed bedrooms are well equipped and comfortable. The lounge has an open fire, and the smart and spacious restaurant provides a calm atmosphere in which to enjoy the hotel's popular cuisine.

Rooms 20 (14 annexe) (3 fmly) (9 GF) **S** fr £85; **D** fr £99 (incl. bkfst)* **Facilities** FTV Xmas New Year Wi-fi **Conf** Board 20 Del from £130 to £150* **Parking** 55 **Notes** LB ⊗

MILTON COMMON — Map 5 SP60

The Oxford Belfry

QHOTELS

★★★★ 78% HOTEL

☎ 01844 279381 🖹 01844 279624
OX9 2JW
e-mail: oxfordbelfry@qhotels.co.uk
web: www.qhotels.co.uk
dir: M40 junct 7 onto A329 to Thame. Left onto A40, hotel 300yds on right

This modern hotel has a relatively rural location and enjoys lovely views of the countryside to the rear. The hotel is built around two very attractive courtyards and has a number of lounges and conference rooms, as well as indoor leisure facilities and outdoor tennis courts. Bedrooms are large and feature a range of extras. Q Hotels - AA Hotel Group of the Year 2008-9.

Rooms 154 (20 fmly) (66 GF) **S** £79-£165; **D** £89-£175 (incl. bkfst)* **Facilities** Spa STV ⊗ ♨ ➴ Gym Steam room Sauna Xmas New Year Wi-fi **Conf** Class 150 Board 100 Thtr 350 Del from £135 to £199* **Services** Lift **Parking** 250 **Notes** LB ⊗ Civ Wed 300

See advert on this page

OXFORD Map 5 SP50

INSPECTORS' CHOICE

Le Manoir Aux Quat' Saisons
★★★★★ ◉◉◉◉◉ HOTEL
RELAIS & CHATEAUX

☎ 01844 278881 📠 01844 278847
Church Rd OX44 7PD
e-mail: lemanoir@blanc.co.uk
web: www.manoir.com

(For full entry see Great Milton)

Macdonald Randolph
★★★★★ 81% ◉◉ HOTEL

 MACDONALD HOTELS & RESORTS

☎ 01865 256400 📠 01865 791678
Beaumont St OX1 2LN
e-mail: randolph@macdonald-hotels.co.uk
web: www.macdonaldhotels.co.uk
dir: M40 junct 8, A40 towards Oxford. Follow city centre signs, leading to St Giles, hotel on right

Superbly located near the city centre, The Randolph boasts impressive neo-Gothic architecture and tasteful decor. The spacious and traditional restaurant, complete with picture windows, is an ideal place to watch the world go by while enjoying freshly prepared, modern dishes. Bedrooms include a mix of classical and contemporary wing rooms, which have been appointed to a high standard. Parking is a real bonus.

Rooms 151 **S** £119-£265; **D** £129-£275* **Facilities** Spa STV Gym Treatment rooms Thermal suite Mini gym ♬ Xmas New Year Wi-fi **Conf** Class 130 Board 60 Thtr 300 Del from £145 to £270* **Services** Lift **Parking** 60 (charged) **Notes** LB Civ Wed 120

The Old Bank Hotel
★★★★ 78% ◉ TOWN HOUSE HOTEL

☎ 01865 799599 📠 01865 799598
92-94 High St OX1 4BN
e-mail: info@oldbank-hotel.co.uk
web: www.oldbank-hotel.co.uk
dir: from Magdalen Bridge into High St, hotel 50yds on left

Located close to the city centre and the colleges this former bank benefits from an excellent location. An eclectic collection of modern pictures and photographs, many by well-known artists, are on display. Bedrooms are smart with excellent business facilities plus the benefit of air conditioning. Public areas include the vibrant all-day Quod Bar and Restaurant. The hotel also has the benefit of its own car park - a definite advantage in this busy city.

Rooms 42 (10 fmly) (1 GF) **S** £170-£200; **D** £185-£200* **Facilities** STV Discounts with various leisure facilities ♬ Wi-fi **Conf** Class 30 Board 40 Thtr 50 **Services** Lift Air con **Parking** 60 **Notes** LB ⊗

See advert on opposite page

Barceló Oxford Hotel
★★★★ 76% HOTEL

 Barceló HOTELS & RESORTS

☎ 01865 489988 📠 01865 489952
Godstow Rd, Wolvercote Roundabout OX2 8AL
e-mail: oxford@barcelo-hotels.co.uk
web: www.barcelo-hotels.co.uk
dir: adjacent to A34/A40, 2m from city centre

Conveniently located on the northern edge of the city centre, this purpose-built hotel offers bedrooms that are bright, modern and well equipped. Guests can eat in the 'Medio' restaurant or try the Cappuccino bar menu. The hotel offers impressive conference, business and leisure facilities.

Rooms 168 (11 fmly) (89 GF) **S** £69-£145; **Facilities** ⊙ supervised Gym Squash Steam room New Year Wi-fi **Conf** Class 130 Board 110 Thtr 320 **Parking** 250 (charged) **Notes** Civ Wed 250

See advert on opposite page

Cotswold Lodge
★★★★ 75% ◉ HOTEL

 CLASSIC BRITISH HOTELS

☎ 01865 512121 📠 01865 512490
66a Banbury Rd OX2 6JP
e-mail: info@cotswoldlodgehotel.co.uk
web: www.cotswoldlodgehotel.co.uk
dir: off A40 Oxford ring road onto A4165 (Banbury road) Signed city centre & Summertown. Hotel 2m on left

This Victorian property is located close to the centre of Oxford and offers smart, comfortable accommodation. Stylish bedrooms and suites are attractively presented and some have balconies. The public areas have an elegant country-house feel. The hotel is popular with business guests and caters for conferences and banquets.

Rooms 49 (14 GF) **S** £50-£140; **D** £50-£160* **Facilities** STV New Year Wi-fi **Conf** Class 60 Board 60 Thtr 100 **Parking** 40 **Notes** LB ⊗

Old Parsonage
★★★★ 73% ◉ TOWN HOUSE HOTEL

☎ 01865 310210 📠 01865 311262
1 Banbury Rd OX2 6NN
e-mail: info@oldparsonage-hotel.co.uk
web: www.oldparsonage-hotel.co.uk
dir: from Oxford ring road to city centre via Summertown. Hotel last building on right next to St Giles Church before city centre

Dating back in parts to the 16th century, this stylish hotel offers great character and charm and is conveniently located at the northern edge of the city centre. Bedrooms are attractively styled and particularly well appointed. The focal point of the operation is the busy all-day bar and restaurant; the small garden areas and terraces prove popular in summer months.

Rooms 30 (4 fmly) (10 GF) **S** £150-£185; **D** £170-£185* **Facilities** FTV Beauty treatments Free use of nearby leisure facilities, punt & house bikes ♬ Xmas Wi-fi **Conf** Board 12 Del from £250* **Services** Air con **Parking** 14 **Notes** Civ Wed 20

See advert on opposite page

Oxford Thames Four Pillars Hotel
★★★★ 73% HOTEL

 PILLARS HOTELS

☎ 0800 374 692 & 01865 334444 📠 01865 334400
Henley Rd, Sandford-on-Thames OX4 4GX
e-mail: thames@four-pillars.co.uk
web: www.four-pillars.co.uk
dir: M40 junct 8 towards Oxford, follow ring road. Left at rdbt towards Cowley. At rdbt with lights turn left to Littlemore, hotel approx 1m on right

The main house of this hotel is built from local, yellow stone. The spacious and traditional River Restaurant has superb views of the hotel's own boat, moored on the river. The gardens can be enjoyed from the patios or balconies in the newer bedroom wings. Public rooms include a beamed bar and lounge area with minstrels' gallery.

Rooms 62 (4 fmly) (24 GF) **S** £79-£139; **D** £89-£159 (incl. bkfst) **Facilities** ⊙ ♨ Gym Steam room Sauna Weights room Xmas New Year Wi-fi **Conf** Class 80 Board 60 Thtr 160 Del from £160 to £210 **Parking** 120 **Notes** LB ⊗ Civ Wed 120

OXFORD continued

Oxford Spires Four Pillars Hotel

★★★★ 71% HOTEL

☎ 0800 374 692 & 01865 324324 📠 01865 324325
Abingdon Rd OX1 4PS
e-mail: spires@four-pillars.co.uk
web: www.four-pillars.co.uk
dir: M40 junct 8 towards Oxford. Left towards Cowley. At 3rd rdbt follow city centre signs. Hotel 1m

This purpose-built hotel is surrounded by extensive parkland, yet is only a short walk from the city centre. Bedrooms are attractively furnished, well equipped and include several apartments. Public areas include a spacious restaurant, open plan bar/lounge, leisure club and extensive conference facilities.

Rooms 160 (18 fmly) (53 GF) **S** £99-£160; **D** £105-£210 (incl. bkfst)* **Facilities** FTV 🏊 Gym Beauty Steam room Sauna Xmas New Year Wi-fi **Conf** Class 96 Board 76 Thtr 266 Del from £140 to £195* **Services** Lift **Parking** 95 **Notes** LB ⊗ Civ Wed 140

Malmaison Oxford

Malmaison

★★★ 85% ⊛ HOTEL

☎ 01865 268400 📠 01865 268402
3 Oxford Castle, New Rd OX1 1AY
web: www.malmaison.com
dir: M40 junct 9, A34 N to Botley interchange. Follow city centre & rail station signs. At rail station continue straight ahead to 2nd lights. Turn right, at next lights turn left into Park End St. Straight on at next lights, hotel 2nd turn on left

Once the city's prison, this is definitely a hotel with a difference. Many of the rooms are actually converted from the old cells. Not to worry there have been many improvements since the previous occupants left; exceedingly comfortable beds and luxury bathrooms are just two of the changes! The hotel has a popular brasserie with quality and value much in evidence. A small amount of parking space is available.

Rooms 94 (5 GF) **S** £145-£230; **D** £145-£230* **Facilities** STV Gym Xmas New Year Wi-fi **Conf** Del from £270 to £310* **Services** Lift **Parking** 20 (charged) **Notes** Civ Wed 80

Weston Manor

★★★ 78% ⊛⊛ HOTEL

☎ 01869 350621 📠 01869 350901
OX25 3QL
e-mail: reception@westonmanor.co.uk
web: www.westonmanor.co.uk

(For full entry see Weston-on-the-Green)

Mercure Eastgate

 Mercure

★★★ 78% METRO HOTEL

☎ 0870 400 8201 & 01865 248332 📠 01865 791681
73 High St OX1 4BE
e-mail: h6668-sb@accor.com
web: www.mercure-uk.com
dir: A40 follow signs to Headington & Oxford city centre, over Magdalen Bridge, stay in left lane, through lights, left into Merton St, entrance to car park on left

Just a short stroll from the city centre, this hotel, as its name suggests, occupies the site of the city's medieval East Gate and boasts its own car park. Bedrooms are appointed and equipped to a high standard. Stylish public areas include the all-day Town House Brasserie and Bar.

Rooms 63 (3 fmly) **Conf** Board 16 **Services** Lift Air con **Parking** 40 (charged) **Notes** LB ⊗

Hawkwell House

 "bespoke"

★★★ 74% ⊛ HOTEL

☎ 01865 749988 📠 01865 748525
Church Way, Iffley Village OX4 4DZ
e-mail: reservations@hawkwellhouse.co.uk
web: www.bespokehotels.com
dir: A34 follow signs to Cowley. At Littlemore rdbt take A4158 exit onto Iffley Rd. After lights turn left to Iffley

Set in a peaceful residential location, Hawkwell House is just a few minutes' drive from the Oxford ring road. The spacious rooms are modern, attractively decorated and well equipped. Public areas are tastefully appointed and the conservatory-style restaurant offers an interesting choice of dishes. The hotel also has a range of conference and function facilities.

Rooms 66 (10 fmly) (4 GF) **S** £65-£95; **D** £75-£125 (incl. bkfst)* **Facilities** FTV Xmas New Year Wi-fi **Conf** Class 100 Board 80 Thtr 200 **Services** Lift **Parking** 120 **Notes** ⊗ Civ Wed 150

Best Western Linton Lodge

Best Western

★★★ 73% HOTEL

☎ 01865 553461 📠 01865 553691
11-13 Linton Rd OX2 6UJ
e-mail: sales@lintonlodge.com
web: www.lintonlodge.com
dir: to Oxford city centre, along Banbury Rd. After 0.5m right into Linton Rd. Hotel opposite St Andrews Church

Located in a residential area, this hotel is within walking distance of the city centre. Bedrooms are modern, well equipped and comfortable. The oak-panelled Linton's Restaurant serves both set and carte menus, and the Dragon Bar, overlooking the extensive lawned gardens, is the ideal place to relax and have a drink.

Rooms 71 (2 fmly) (14 GF) **S** £60-£100; **D** £70-£150* **Facilities** FTV Putt green 🎣 Wi-fi **Conf** Class 50 Board 40 Thtr 120 Del from £99 to £155* **Services** Lift **Parking** 40 **Notes** LB ⊗ Civ Wed 120

Westwood Country Hotel

★★★ 73% HOTEL

☎ 01865 735408 📠 01865 736536
Hinksey Hill, Boars Hill OX1 5BG
e-mail: reservations@westwoodhotel.co.uk
web: www.westwoodhotel.co.uk
dir: off Oxford ring road at Hinksey Hill junct towards Boars Hill & Wootton. At top of hill road bends to left. Hotel on right

This Edwardian country-house hotel is prominently set in terraced landscaped grounds and is within easy reach of the city centre by car. The hotel is modern in style with very comfortable, well-equipped and tastefully decorated bedrooms. Public areas include a contemporary bar, a cosy lounge and a restaurant overlooking the pretty garden.

Rooms 20 (6 fmly) (6 GF) **S** £65-£85; **D** £95-£135 (incl. bkfst)* **Facilities** Arrangement with local health club Xmas New Year Wi-fi **Conf** Class 36 Board 35 Thtr 60

Del from £135 to £155* **Parking** 50 **Notes** LB ⊗
Civ Wed 200

Manor House

★★ 68% METRO HOTEL

☎ 01865 727627 ▤ 01865 200478
250 Iffley Rd OX4 1SE
dir: on A4158, 1m from city centre

This family run establishment is easily accessible from
the city centre and all major road links. The hotel provides
informal but friendly and attentive service. The
comfortably furnished bedrooms are well equipped. The
hotel has a bar but there is a selection of restaurants and
popular pubs within easy walking distance. Private
parking is also available.

Rooms 7 (2 fmly) **S** £69-£99; **D** £69-£99 (incl. bkfst)*
Parking 6 **Notes** ⊗ Closed 20 Dec-20 Jan

Victoria

★★ 65% METRO HOTEL

☎ 01865 724536 ▤ 01865 794909
180 Abingdon Rd OX1 4RA
e-mail: info@victoriahotelox.com
web: www.victoriahotelox.com
dir: from M40/A40 take Eastern bypass and A4144 into
city

Located within easy reach of Oxford city centre and the
motorway networks, this metro hotel offers comfortable
bedrooms, well maintained and furnished to a high
standard. A conservatory bar with large flat screen TV is
an ideal place to relax.

Rooms 20 (5 annexe) (2 fmly) (6 GF) **Facilities** Xmas
Wi-fi **Parking** 20 **Notes** ⊗

The Balkan Lodge Hotel

★★ 60% METRO HOTEL

☎ 01865 244524 ▤ 01865 251090
315 Iffley Rd OX4 4AG
e-mail: balkanlodge@aol.co.uk
web: www.hometown.aol.com/balkanlodge
dir: from M40/A40 take eastern bypass, into city on
A4158

Conveniently located for the city centre and the ring road,
this family operated metro hotel offers a comfortable
stay. Bedrooms are attractive and well equipped. Public
areas include a lounge and bar. A large, secure private
car park is located to the rear of the building.

Rooms 13 **Facilities** Wi-fi **Notes** LB ⊗

Bath Place

★★ 57% METRO HOTEL

☎ 01865 791812 ▤ 01865 791834
4-5 Bath Place, Holywell St OX1 3SU
e-mail: info@bathplace.co.uk
dir: on S side of Holywell St running parallel to High St

The hotel has been created from a group of 17th-century
cottages originally built by Flemish weavers who were
permitted to settle outside the city walls. This lovely hotel
is very much at the heart of the city today and offers
individually designed bedrooms, including some with
four-posters.

Rooms 14 (2 fmly) (3 GF) **S** £75-£125; **D** £105-£150 (incl.
bkfst)* **Facilities** FTV Wi-fi **Parking** 14 (charged)
Notes LB

River Hotel

★ 70% METRO HOTEL

☎ 01865 243475 ▤ 01865 724306
17 Botley Rd OX2 0AA
e-mail: reception@riverhotel.co.uk
dir: A34 southern by-pass to A420 Botley/ Seacourt West
exit. From slip road left onto Botley Rd, hotel 1m on right

This hotel situated on the banks of the River Thames
occupies a convenient location only a few minutes walk
from the historic sights of Oxford; the train station and
various restaurants are all within walking distance too.
Most bedrooms are spacious, and comfortable seating is
available in the bar/lounge area. Free parking with CCTV
is definitely a bonus.

Rooms 20 (7 annexe) (5 fmly) **S** £70-£75; **D** £80-£90
(incl. bkfst)* **Conf** Class 20 Board 20 Thtr 30 **Parking** 25
Notes ⊗ Closed Xmas/New Year

Holiday Inn Oxford

Ⓤ

☎ 0870 400 9086 ▤ 01865 888321
Peartree Roundabout, Woodstock Rd OX2 8JD
e-mail: reservations-oxford@ihg.com
web: www.holidayinn.co.uk
dir: A34 Peartree Interchange signed Oxford & Services.
Hotel within service area

Currently the rating for this establishment is not confirmed.
This may be due to a change of ownership or because it has
only recently joined the AA rating scheme. For further
details please see the AA website: www.theAA.com

Rooms 154 (25 fmly) (23 GF) (14 smoking) **Facilities** Spa
STV ⓒ supervised Gym Wi-fi **Conf** Class 65 Board 65
Thtr 150 **Services** Lift Air con **Notes** ⊗ Civ Wed 120

Express by Holiday Inn Oxford-Kassam Stadium

BUDGET HOTEL

☎ 01865 780888 ▤ 01865 780999
Grenoble Rd OX4 4XP
e-mail: reservations@expressoxford.com
web: www.hiexpress.com/oxfrdkassam
dir: M40 junct 8 onto A40 for 4m. Left at McDonald's onto
A4142. After 3.5m left onto A4074, take 1st exit signed
Science Park & Kassam Stadium

A modern hotel ideal for families and business travellers.
Fresh and uncomplicated, the spacious rooms include Sky
TVs, power showers and tea and coffee-making facilities.
A continental buffet breakfast is included in the room
rate; other meals may be taken at the nearby family pub
or restaurant. See also the Hotel Groups pages.

Rooms 162 (131 fmly) **Conf** Class 18 Board 28 Thtr 30

Travelodge Oxford Peartree

BUDGET HOTEL

☎ 08719 846 206 ▤ 01865 513474
Peartree Roundabout, Woodstock Rd OX2 8JZ
web: www.travelodge.co.uk
dir: at junct of A34/A44

Travelodge offers good quality, good value, modern
accommodation. Ideal for families, the spacious en suite
bedrooms include remote-control TV, tea and coffee-
making facilities and comfortable beds. Meals can be
taken at the nearby family restaurant. See also the Hotel
Groups pages.

Rooms 150 **S** fr £29; **D** fr £29 **Conf** Class 150 Board 60
Thtr 300

Travelodge Oxford Wheatley

BUDGET HOTEL

☎ 0871 984 6207 ▤ 01865 875905
London Rd, Wheatley OX33 1JH
web: www.travelodge.co.uk
dir: off A40 next to The Harvester on outskirts of Wheatley

Rooms 36 **S** fr £29; **D** fr £29

OXFORD MOTORWAY SERVICE AREA (M40) — Map 5 SP60

Days Inn Oxford

BUDGET HOTEL

☎ 01865 877000 🖨 01865 877016
M40 junction 8A, Waterstock OX33 1LJ
e-mail: oxford.hotel@welcomebreak.co.uk
web: www.welcomebreak.co.uk
dir: M40 junct 8a, at Welcome Break service area

This modern building offers accommodation in smart, spacious and well-equipped bedrooms, suitable for families and business travellers, and all with en suite bathrooms. Continental breakfast is available and other refreshments may be taken at the nearby family restaurant. See also the Hotel Groups pages.

Rooms 59 (56 fmly) **S** £39-£59; **D** £49-£69*

STEEPLE ASTON — Map 11 SP42

The Holt Hotel

★★★ 70% HOTEL

☎ 01869 340259 🖨 01869 340865
Oxford Rd OX25 5QQ
e-mail: info@holthotel.co.uk
web: www.holthotel.co.uk
dir: junct of B4030/A4260

This attractive former coaching inn has given hospitality to many over the centuries, not least to Claude Duval, a notorious 17th-century highwayman. Today guests are offered well-equipped, modern bedrooms and attractive public areas, which include a relaxing bar, restaurant and a well-appointed lounge. A selection of meeting rooms is available.

Rooms 86 (19 fmly) **Facilities** Xmas New Year Wi-fi **Conf** Class 70 Board 44 Thtr 140 **Parking** 200 **Notes** Civ Wed 100

THAME — Map 5 SP70

Travelodge Thame

BUDGET HOTEL

☎ 0871 9846215 🖨 01844 218740
OX9 3AX
web: www.travelodge.co.uk
dir: A418/B4011

Travelodge offers good quality, good value, modern accommodation. Ideal for families, the spacious en suite bedrooms include remote-control TV, tea and coffee-making facilities and comfortable beds. Meals can be taken at the nearby family restaurant. See also the Hotel Groups pages.

Rooms 31 **S** fr £29; **D** fr £29

WALLINGFORD — Map 5 SU68

The Springs Hotel & Golf Club

★★★ 80% 🏵 HOTEL

☎ 01491 836687 🖨 01491 836877
Wallingford Rd, North Stoke OX10 6BE
e-mail: info@thespringshotel.com
web: www.thespringshotel.com
dir: off A4074 (Oxford-Reading road) onto B4009 (Goring). Hotel approx 1m on right

Set on its own golf course, this Victorian mansion has a timeless and peaceful atmosphere. The generously equipped bedrooms vary in size but many are spacious. The elegant restaurant enjoys splendid views over the spring-fed lake where a variety of wildfowl enjoy the natural surroundings. There is also a comfortable lounge with original features, and a cosy bar to relax in.

Rooms 32 (4 fmly) (8 GF) **S** £95-£120; **D** £115-£135 (incl. bkfst)* **Facilities** STV FTV ᴿ↖ ♨ 18 Putt green Fishing ⤴ Clay pigeon shooting nearby Horse riding ♫ Xmas New Year Wi-fi **Conf** Class 16 Board 26 Thtr 60 Del from £140 to £155* **Parking** 150 **Notes** LB Civ Wed 150

Shillingford Bridge

★★★ 74% HOTEL

☎ 01865 858567 🖨 01865 858636
Shillingford OX10 8LZ
e-mail: shillingford.bridge@forestdale.com
web: www.shillingfordbridgehotel.com
dir: M4 junct 10, A329 through Wallingford towards Thame, then B4009 through Watlington. Right on A4074 at Benson, then left at Shillingford rdbt (unclass road) Wallingford Road

This hotel enjoys a superb position right on the banks of the River Thames, and benefits from private moorings and has a waterside open-air swimming pool. Public areas are stylish with a contemporary feel and have large picture windows making the best use of the view. Bedrooms are well equipped and furnished with guest comfort in mind.

Rooms 40 (8 annexe) (6 fmly) (9 GF) **S** £89-£95; **D** £119-£130 (incl. bkfst)* **Facilities** ᴿ↖ supervised Fishing Table tennis ♫ Xmas New Year Wi-fi **Conf** Class 36 Board 36 Thtr 80 **Parking** 100 **Notes** LB Civ Wed 150

The George

★★★ 73% HOTEL

PEEL HOTELS PLC

☎ 01491 836665 🖨 01491 825359
High St OX10 0BS
e-mail: info@george-hotel-wallingford.com
web: www.peelhotel.com
dir: E side of A329 on N entry to town

Old world charm and modern facilities merge seamlessly in this former coaching inn. Bedrooms in the main house have character in abundance. Those in the wing have a more contemporary style, but all are well equipped and attractively decorated. Diners can choose between the restaurant and bistro, or relax in the cosy bar.

Rooms 39 (1 fmly) (9 GF) **S** £120-£140; **D** £135-£150* **Facilities** STV Xmas New Year Wi-fi **Conf** Class 60 Board 50 Thtr 150 Del from £125 to £145* **Parking** 60 **Notes** LB ⊗ Civ Wed 100

WESTON-ON-THE-GREEN — Map 11 SP51

Weston Manor

★★★ 78% 🏵🏵 HOTEL

☎ 01869 350621 🖨 01869 350901
OX25 3QL
e-mail: reception@westonmanor.co.uk
web: www.westonmanor.co.uk
dir: M40 junct 9, A34 towards Oxford. Turn right at rdbt (B4030), hotel 100yds on left

Character, charm and sophistication blend effortlessly in this friendly hotel set in well-tended grounds. Bedrooms are well equipped and are located in the main house, coach house or a cottage annexe. Award-winning food can be enjoyed in the impressive vaulted restaurant, complete with original oak panelling and minstrels' gallery; other public areas include an atmospheric foyer lounge, a bar and meeting facilities.

Rooms 35 (20 annexe) (5 fmly) (6 GF) **Facilities** ᴿ↖ ⤴ New Year Wi-fi **Conf** Class 20 Board 32 Thtr 60 **Parking** 100 **Notes** LB ⊗ Civ Wed 100

WITNEY — Map 5 SP31

Witney Four Pillars Hotel

★★★ 75% HOTEL

☎ 0845 850 8855 & 01993 779777 📄 01993 703467
Ducklington Ln OX28 4TJ
e-mail: witney@four-pillars.co.uk
web: www.four-pillars.co.uk
dir: M40 junct 9, A34 to A40, exit A415 Witney/Abingdon.
Hotel on left, 2nd exit for Witney

This attractive modern hotel is close to Oxford and
Burford and offers spacious, well-equipped bedrooms.
The cosy Spinners Bar has comfortable seating areas and
the popular Weavers Restaurant offers a good range of
dishes. Other amenities include extensive function and
leisure facilities, complete with indoor swimming pool.

Rooms 86 (16 fmly) (20 GF) **S** £100-£120; **D** £125-£144
(incl. bkfst)* **Facilities** 🏊 Gym Steam room Sauna Xmas
New Year Wi-fi **Conf** Class 80 Board 46 Thtr 160
Del from £125 to £169* **Parking** 170 **Notes** LB ⊗
Civ Wed 120

WOODSTOCK — Map 11 SP41

Macdonald Bear

MACDONALD HOTELS & RESORTS

★★★★ 76% @@ HOTEL

☎ 0844 879 9143 📄 01993 813380
Park St OX20 1SZ
e-mail: gm.bear@macdonaldhotels.co.uk
web: www.macdonaldhotels.co.uk
dir: M40 junct 9 follow signs for Oxford & Blenheim
Palace. A44 to town centre hotel on left

With its ivy-clad façade, oak beams and open fireplaces,
this 13th-century coaching inn exudes charm and
cosiness. The bedrooms are decorated in a modern style
that remains in keeping with the historic character of the
building. Public rooms include a variety of function
rooms, an intimate bar area and an attractive restaurant
where attentive service and good food are offered.

Rooms 54 (18 annexe) (1 fmly) (8 GF) **S** £86-£250;
D £86-£250 **Facilities** STV Xmas New Year Wi-fi
Conf Class 12 Board 24 Thtr 40 Del from £140 to £240
Parking 40 **Notes** LB

Feathers

★★★ 83% @@ HOTEL

☎ 01993 812291 📄 01993 813158
Market St OX20 1SX
e-mail: enquiries@feathers.co.uk
dir: from A44 (Oxford to Woodstock), 1st left after lights.
Hotel on left

This intimate and unique hotel enjoys a town centre
location with easy access to nearby Blenheim Palace.
Public areas are elegant and full of traditional character
from the cosy drawing room to the atmospheric
restaurant. Individually styled bedrooms are appointed to
a high standard and are furnished with attractive period
and reproduction furniture.

Rooms 20 (5 annexe) (4 fmly) (2 GF) **S** £99-£169;
D £169-£279 (incl. bkfst) **Facilities** FTV 1 suite has
steam room Xmas New Year Wi-fi **Conf** Class 20 Board 30
Thtr 20 Del from £150* **Notes** LB

Kings Arms

★★★ 77% HOTEL

☎ 01993 813636 📄 01993 813737
19 Market St OX20 1SU
e-mail: stay@kingshotelwoodstock.co.uk
web: www.kings-hotel-woodstock.co.uk
dir: in town centre, on corner of Market St & A44

This appealing and contemporary hotel is situated in the
centre of town just a short walk from Blenheim Palace.
Public areas include an attractive bistro-style restaurant
and a smart bar. Bedrooms and bathrooms are
comfortably furnished and equipped, and appointed to a
high standard.

Rooms 15 **S** £75-£100; **D** £140-£150 (incl. bkfst)
Facilities FTV Wi-fi **Notes** LB ⊗ No children 12yrs

RUTLAND

GREETHAM — Map 11 SK91

Greetham Valley

★★★ 74% HOTEL

☎ 01780 460444 📄 01780 460623
Wood Ln LE15 7NP
e-mail: info@gvgc.co.uk
web: www.greethamvalley.co.uk

Spacious bedrooms with storage facilities designed for
golfers, offer high levels of comfort and many have
superb views over the two 18-hole golf courses. Meals are
taken in the clubhouse restaurants with a choice of
informal or more formal styles. A beauty suite and
extensive conference facilities are ideal for both large
and small groups.

Rooms 35 (17 GF) **Facilities** ⅃ 36 Putt green Fishing 4x4
course Off road training course Archery centre Xmas Child
facilities **Conf** Class 150 Board 80 Thtr 200 **Services** Lift
Parking 300 **Notes** LB ⊗ Civ Wed 200

MORCOTT — Map 11 SK90

Travelodge Uppingham Morcott

BUDGET HOTEL

☎ 0871 984 6113 📄 01572 747719
Uppingham LE15 8SA
web: www.travelodge.co.uk
dir: on A47, eastbound

Travelodge offers good quality, good value, modern
accommodation. Ideal for families, the spacious en suite
bedrooms include remote-control TV, tea and coffee-
making facilities and comfortable beds. Meals can be
taken at the nearby family restaurant. See also the Hotel
Groups pages.

Rooms 40 **S** fr £29; **D** fr £29

NORMANTON   Map 11 SK90

Best Western Normanton Park

★★★ 72% HOTEL

☎ 01780 720315 ▤ 01780 721086
Oakham LE15 8RP
e-mail: info@normantonpark.co.uk
web: www.normantonpark.com
dir: From A1 follow A606 towards Oakham, 1m. Turn left, 1.5m. Hotel on right

This delightful hotel, on Rutland Water's south shore, is appointed to a high standard and there are two dining styles available including an extensive Chinese menu. Bedrooms are well furnished and there are ample public rooms for guest to relax in.

Rooms 30 (7 annexe) (6 fmly) (11 GF) **S** £80–£90; **D** £80–£140 (incl. bkfst)* **Facilities** FTV ⤳ Xmas New Year Wi-fi **Conf** Class 60 Board 80 Thtr 200 Del from £135 to £145* **Parking** 100 **Notes** LB Civ Wed 100

OAKHAM   Map 11 SK80

INSPECTORS' CHOICE

Hambleton Hall
★★★★ ⚜⚜⚜⚜
COUNTRY HOUSE HOTEL

☎ 01572 756991 ▤ 01572 724721
Hambleton LE15 8TH
e-mail: hotel@hambletonhall.com
web: www.hambletonhall.com
dir: 3m E off A606

Established over 25 years ago by Tim and Stefa Hart this delightful country house enjoys tranquil and spectacular views over Rutland Water. The beautifully manicured grounds are a delight to walk in. The bedrooms in the main house are stylish, individually decorated and equipped with a range of thoughtful extras. A two-bedroom folly, with its own sitting and breakfast room, is only a short walk away. Day rooms include a cosy bar and a sumptuous drawing room, both featuring open fires. The elegant restaurant serves skilfully prepared, award-winning cuisine with menus highlighting locally sourced, seasonal produce - some grown in the hotel's own grounds.

Rooms 17 (2 annexe) **S** £170–£200; **D** £200–£600 (incl. bkfst)* **Facilities** STV ⤳ ⚘ ⤳ Private access to lake Xmas New Year Wi-fi **Conf** Board 24 Thtr 40 Del from £260 to £290* **Services** Lift **Parking** 40 **Notes** LB Civ Wed 64

Barnsdale Lodge

★★★ 77% ⚘ HOTEL

☎ 01572 724678 ▤ 01572 724961
The Avenue, Rutland Water, North Shore LE15 8AH
e-mail: enquiries@barnsdalelodge.co.uk
web: www.barnsdalelodge.co.uk
dir: off A1 onto A606. Hotel 5m on right, 2m E of Oakham

A popular and interesting hotel converted from a farmstead overlooking Rutland Water. The public areas are dominated by a very successful food operation with a good range of appealing meals on offer for either formal or informal dining. Bedrooms are comfortably appointed with excellent beds enhanced by contemporary soft furnishings and thoughtful extras.

Rooms 44 (2 fmly) (15 GF) **S** £68.25–£89.25; **D** £84–£120.75 (incl. bkfst) **Facilities** STV Fishing ⤳ Archery Beauty treatments Golf Shooting Xmas New Year **Conf** Class 120 Board 76 Thtr 330 **Parking** 200 **Notes** LB Civ Wed 160

Old Wisteria

★★★ 🅰 HOTEL

☎ 01572 722844 ▤ 01572 724473
4 Catmose St LE15 6HW
e-mail: enquiries@wisteriahotel.co.uk
web: www.wisteriahotel.co.uk
dir: At A606/A6003 junct. Opposite council offices. Private driveway entrance from South St

Rooms 25 (8 GF) **S** £60–£80; **D** £80–£100 (incl. bkfst)* **Facilities** Xmas New Year Wi-fi **Conf** Class 30 Board 30 Thtr 60 **Parking** 16 **Notes** LB

Nick's Restaurant at Lord Nelson's House

⚘⚘ RESTAURANT WITH ROOMS

☎ 01572 723199
11 Market Place LE15 6HR
e-mail: simon@nicksrestaurant.co.uk
dir: A1(M) onto A606, after 2nd rdbt, Market Place on right

Tucked away in the corner of Oakham's market square, this restaurant with rooms offers fine dining and four individually appointed bedrooms with a range of antiques and knick-knacks. Service is attentive and helpful, and the food a delight, offering a selection of carefully crafted dishes using the best of quality seasonal produce.

Rooms 4

UPPINGHAM   Map 11 SP89

The Lake Isle

⚘⚘ RESTAURANT WITH ROOMS

☎ 01572 822951 ▤ 01572 824400
16 High Street East LE15 9PZ
e-mail: info@lakeisle.co.uk

This attractive, townhouse hotel centres round a delightful restaurant and small elegant bar. There is also an inviting first-floor guest lounge. Bedrooms are extremely well appointed and thoughtfully equipped and include spacious split-level cottage suites situated in a quiet courtyard. Imaginative cooking and an extremely impressive wine list are highlights.

Rooms 12 (9 en suite) (3 annexe) (1 fmly) (1 GF)

SHROPSHIRE

ALVELEY   Map 10 SO78

Mill Hotel & Restaurant

★★★★ 78% HOTEL

☎ 01746 780437 ▤ 01746 780850
WV15 6HL
e-mail: info@themill-hotel.co.uk
web: www.themill-hotel.co.uk
dir: midway between Kidderminster & Bridgnorth, turn off A442 signed Enville & Turley Green

Built around a 17th-century water mill, with the original water wheel still on display, this extended and renovated hotel is set in eight acres of landscaped grounds. Bedrooms are pleasant, well equipped and include some superior rooms, which have sitting areas. There are also some rooms with four-poster beds. The restaurant provides carefully prepared dishes and there are extensive wedding and function facilities.

Rooms 41 (5 fmly) **S** £60–£88; **D** £80–£150 (incl. bkfst)* **Facilities** STV Gym Xmas New Year Wi-fi **Conf** Class 180 Board 80 Thtr 250 Del from £125 to £135* **Services** Lift **Parking** 212 **Notes** LB ⊗ Civ Wed 140

BRIDGNORTH · Map 10 SO79

INSPECTORS' CHOICE

Old Vicarage Hotel
★★★ ◉◉◉ HOTEL

☎ 01746 716497 🖹 01746 716552
Worfield WV15 5JZ
e-mail: admin@the-old-vicarage.demon.co.uk
web: www.oldvicarageworfield.com
dir: off A454, approx 3.5m NE of Bridgnorth, 5m S of
Telford's southern business area. Follow brown signs

This delightful property is set in acres of wooded
farmland in a quiet and peaceful area of Shropshire.
Service is friendly and helpful, and customer care
is one the many strengths of this charming small
hotel. The well-equipped bedrooms are individually
appointed, and thoughtfully and luxuriously furnished.
The lounge and conservatory are the perfect places
to enjoy a pre-dinner drink or the complimentary
afternoon tea. The restaurant is a joy, serving
award-winning modern British cuisine in elegant
surroundings.

Rooms 14 (4 annexe) (1 fmly) (2 GF) **S** £65–£110;
D £99.50–£175 (incl. bkfst) **Facilities** FTV 🏊 New
Year Wi-fi **Conf** Class 40 Board 30 Thtr 60 **Parking** 30
Notes LB

Parlors Hall
★ 75% HOTEL

☎ 01746 761931 🖹 01746 767058
Mill St WV15 5AL
e-mail: info@parlorshallhotel.co.uk
dir: from A454, right & right again in 200yds

Parlors Hall has been a hotel since 1929 and retains
many original features, such as oak panelling and
magnificent fireplaces. Named after the family who lived
here between 1419 and 1539, the property now features
well-equipped bedrooms, some with four-poster beds, a
restaurant and a cosy comfortable bar.

Rooms 13 (2 fmly) **S** £46–£50; **D** £66–£70 (incl. bkfst)*
Facilities Xmas New Year Wi-fi **Conf** Class 20 Board 20
Thtr 40 **Parking** 23 **Notes** ⊗

CHURCH STRETTON · Map 15 SO49

Longmynd Hotel
★★ 75% HOTEL

☎ 01694 722244 🖹 01694 722718
Cunnery Rd SY6 6AG
e-mail: info@longmynd.co.uk
web: www.longmynd.co.uk
dir: A49 into town centre on Sandford Ave, left at Lloyds
TSB, over mini-rdbt, 1st right into Cunnery Rd, hotel at
top of hill on left

This family-run hotel overlooks this country town and the
views from many of the rooms are breathtaking.
Bedrooms are generally spacious, comfortable and well
equipped. Facilities include a range of comfortable
lounges and the hotel is set in attractive grounds and
gardens.

Rooms 50 (6 fmly) **S** £50–£65; **D** £100–£130 (incl. bkfst)
Facilities 🏌 Putt green Pitch and putt Sauna Xmas New
Year Wi-fi **Conf** Class 50 Board 40 Thtr 100 **Services** Lift
Parking 100 **Notes** LB Civ Wed 100

HADNALL · Map 15 SJ52

Saracens at Hadnall
◉ RESTAURANT WITH ROOMS

☎ 01939 210877 🖹 01939 210877
Shrewsbury Rd SY4 4AG
e-mail: reception@saracensathadnall.co.uk
dir: M54 onto A5, at junct of A5/A49 take A49 towards
Whitchurch. Follow A49 until Hadnall, diagonal from
church

This Georgian Grade II listed former farmhouse and
village pub has been tastefully converted into a very
smart restaurant-with-rooms, without any loss of its
original charm and character. The bedrooms are
thoughtfully equipped and include a family room. Skilfully
prepared meals are served in either the elegant dining
room or the adjacent conservatory where the glass-topped
well is a feature.

Rooms 5 (1 fmly)

LLANFAIR WATERDINE · Map 9 SO27

The Waterdine
◉◉ RESTAURANT WITH ROOMS

☎ 01547 528214
LD7 1TU
e-mail: info@waterdine.com
dir: Off B4355 into village, last property on left before
church

Standing in pretty, mature gardens within an Area of
Outstanding Natural Beauty, which includes part of
Offa's Dyke, this former 16th-century drovers' inn retains
much of its original character. Bedrooms are filled with a
wealth of thoughtful extras and have modern bathrooms.

Public areas include a cosy lounge bar and an elegant
restaurant, the setting for imaginative dinners that use
quality, seasonal local produce.

Rooms 3

LUDLOW · Map 10 SO57

Overton Grange Hotel and Restaurant
★★★ 85% ◉◉ HOTEL

☎ 01584 873500 & 0845 476 1000 🖹 01584 873524
Old Hereford Rd SY8 4AD
e-mail: info@overtongrangehotel.com
web: www.overtongrangehotel.com
dir: off A49 at B4361 to Ludlow. Hotel 200yds on left

This is a traditional country-house hotel with stylish,
comfortable bedrooms, and high standards of guest care.
Food is an important part of what the hotel has to offer
and the restaurant serves classically based, French-style
cuisine using locally sourced produce where possible.
Meeting and conference rooms are available.

Rooms 14 **S** £75–£140; **D** £105–£240 (incl. bkfst)
Facilities 🕙 Xmas New Year Wi-fi **Conf** Class 50
Board 30 Thtr 100 **Del** from £135 to £150 **Parking** 45
Notes LB ⊗ No children 7yrs Civ Wed 70

Fishmore Hall
★★★ 80% ◉◉ SMALL HOTEL

☎ 01584 875148 & 07919 174595 🖹 01584 877907
Fishmore Rd SY8 3DP
e-mail: laura@fishmorehall.co.uk
web: www.fishmorehall.co.uk
dir: A49 onto Henley Rd. Follow until mini rdbt, right onto
Fishmore Rd, hotel on right.

Located in a rural area within easy reach of town centre,
this Palladian styled Georgian house has been
sympathetically renovated and extended to provide high
standards of comfort and facilities. A contemporary
styled interior highlights the many retained period
features and public areas include a comfortable lounge
and restaurant, the setting for imaginative cooking.

Rooms 15 (1 GF) **S** £70–£210; **D** £100–£250 (incl. bkfst)
Facilities FTV 🏊 Xmas New Year Wi-fi **Conf** Class 20
Board 30 Thtr 40 **Del** from £140.25 to £165* **Services** Lift
Parking 48 **Notes** LB Civ Wed 60

LUDLOW continued

Feathers

★★★ 79% ◉ HOTEL

☎ 01584 875261 🖹 01584 876030
The Bull Ring SY8 1AA
e-mail: feathers.ludlow@btconnect.com
web: www.feathersatludlow.co.uk
dir: from A49 follow town centre signs to centre. Hotel on left

Famous for the carved woodwork outside and in, this picturesque 17th-century hotel is one of the town's best-known landmarks and is in an excellent location. Bedrooms are traditional in style and décor. Public areas have retained much of the traditional charm; the first-floor lounge is particularly stunning.

Rooms 40 (3 fmly) **S** £87.50; **D** £130-£195 (incl. bkfst)*
Facilities FTV Xmas New Year Wi-fi **Conf** Class 40 Board 40 Thtr 80 **Services** Lift **Parking** 33 **Notes** LB Civ Wed 50

Cliffe

★★ 75% SMALL HOTEL

☎ 01584 872063 🖹 01584 873991
Dinham SY8 2JE
e-mail: thecliffehotel@hotmail.com
dir: in town centre turn left at castle gates to Dinham, follow over bridge. Take right fork, hotel 200yds on left

Built in the 19th century and standing in extensive grounds and gardens, this privately owned and personally run hotel is quietly located close to the castle and the river. It provides well-equipped accommodation, and facilities include a lounge bar, a pleasant restaurant and a patio overlooking the garden.

Rooms 9 (2 fmly) **S** £50-£60; **D** £80-£100 (incl. bkfst)
Parking 22 **Notes** LB

Travelodge Ludlow

BUDGET HOTEL

☎ 08719 846 347 🖹 01584 879098
Foldgate Ln SY8 1LS
web: www.travelodge.co.uk
dir: A49. At rdbt 1st exit Sheet Rd, left onto Foldgate Ln, hotel on right

Travelodge offers good quality, good value, modern accommodation. Ideal for families, the spacious en suite bedrooms include remote-control TV, tea and coffee-making facilities and comfortable beds. Meals can be taken at the nearby family restaurant. See also the Hotel Groups pages.

Rooms 41 **S** fr £29; **D** fr £29

Travelodge Ludlow Woofferton

BUDGET HOTEL

☎ 08719 846 086 🖹 01584 711695
Woofferton SY8 4AL
web: www.travelodge.co.uk
dir: on A49 at junct A456/B4362

Rooms 32 **S** fr £29; **D** fr £29

The Clive Bar & Restaurant with Rooms

◉◉ RESTAURANT WITH ROOMS

☎ 01584 856565 & 856665 🖹 01584 856661
Bromfield SY8 2JR
e-mail: info@theclive.co.uk
dir: 2m N of Ludlow on A49 in village of Bromfield

The Clive is just two miles from the busy town of Ludlow and is a convenient base for visiting the local attractions or for business. The bedrooms are spacious and very well equipped, and some are suitable for families. Meals are available in the well-known Clive Restaurant or the Cookhouse café bar. A small meeting room is also available.

Rooms 15 (14 en suite) (15 annexe) (9 fmly) (11 GF)

Goldstone Hall

★★★ 82% ◉◉ HOTEL

☎ 01630 661202 🖹 01630 661585
Goldstone TF9 2NA
e-mail: enquiries@goldstonehall.com
dir: 4m S of Market Drayton off A529 signed Goldstone Hall Hotel. 4m N of Newport signed from A41

Situated in extensive grounds, this charming period property is a family-run hotel. It provides traditionally furnished, well-equipped accommodation, with some contemporary artistic touches. Public rooms are extensive and include a choice of lounges, a snooker room and a conservatory. The hotel has a well deserved reputation for good food.

Rooms 12 (2 GF) **S** £88-£108; **D** £132-£165 (incl. bkfst)
Facilities STV FTV Snooker table New Year Wi-fi
Conf Class 30 Board 30 Thtr 50 **Parking** 60 **Notes** ⊗
Civ Wed 96

Rosehill Manor

★★ 78% ◉ HOTEL

☎ 01630 638532 🖹 01630 637008
Rosehill, Ternhill TF9 2JF
dir: from rdbt at Ternhill A53 S towards Newport. Hotel 2m on right

Parts of this charming old house, which stands in mature gardens, date back to the 16th century. Privately owned and personally run, it provides well-equipped accommodation including family rooms. Public areas comprise a pleasant restaurant serving award-winning cuisine, a bar and a comfortable lounge. There is also a conservatory which is available for functions.

Rooms 8 (2 fmly) **S** £57.50; **D** £85 (incl. bkfst)*
Facilities ॐ Wi-fi **Conf** Class 60 Board 40 Thtr 100
Parking 80 **Notes** Civ Wed 100

Ternhill Farm House & The Cottage Restaurant

◉ RESTAURANT WITH ROOMS

☎ 01630 638984 🖹 01630 638752
Ternhill TF9 3PX
e-mail: info@ternhillfarm.co.uk
dir: On junct A53 & A41, archway off A53 to back of property

The elegant Grade II listed Georgian farmhouse stands in a large pleasant garden and has been modernised to provide quality accommodation. There is a choice of comfortable lounges, and the Cottage Restaurant features imaginative dishes using local produce. Secure parking is an additional benefit.

Rooms 5 (2 fmly)

Raven

★★★ 75% ◉ HOTEL

☎ 01952 727251 🖹 01952 728416
Barrow St TF13 6EN
e-mail: enquiry@ravenhotel.com
web: www.ravenhotel.com
dir: M54 junct 4 or 5, take A442 S, then A4169 to Much Wenlock

This town centre hotel is spread across several historic buildings with a 17th-century coaching inn at its centre. Accommodation is well furnished and equipped to offer modern comfort, with some ground floor rooms. Public areas feature an interesting collection of prints and memorabilia connected with the modern-day Olympic Games - an idea which was, interestingly, born in Much Wenlock.

Rooms 15 (7 annexe) **Facilities** Beauty salon
Conf Board 16 Thtr 16 **Parking** 30 **Notes** ⊗

Gaskell Arms

★★ 79% HOTEL

☎ 01952 727212 🖷 01952 728505
Bourton Rd TF13 6AQ
e-mail: maxine@gaskellarms.co.uk
web: www.gaskellarms.co.uk
dir: M6 junct 10A onto M54, exit at junct 4, follow signs for Ironbridge/Much Wenlock & A4169

This 17th-century former coaching inn has exposed beams and log fires in the public areas. In addition to the lounge bar and restaurant, offering a wide range of meals and snacks, there is a small bar which is popular with locals. Well-maintained bedrooms, some located within stylishly renovated stables, have good standards of comfort and facilities.

Rooms 16 (3 fmly) (5 GF) **S** £65-£80; **D** £85-£110 (incl. bkfst)* **Parking** 40 **Notes** LB ⊗

NORTON   Map 10 SJ70

Hundred House Hotel

★★ 82% ◉◉ HOTEL

☎ 01952 730353 🖷 01952 730355
Bridgnorth Rd TF11 9EE
e-mail: reservations@hundredhouse.co.uk
web: www.hundredhouse.co.uk
dir: between Telford & Bridgnorth on A442. In town centre

Primarily Georgian, but with parts dating back to the 14th century, this friendly family owned and run hotel offers individually styled, well-equipped bedrooms which have period furniture and attractive soft furnishings. Public areas include cosy bars and intimate dining areas where memorable meals are served. There is an attractive conference centre in the old barn.

Rooms 10 (4 fmly) **Facilities** Xmas New Year Wi-fi **Conf** Class 30 Board 32 Thtr 80 **Parking** 45 **Notes** LB Closed 25 & 26 Dec nights RS Sun evenings Civ Wed

OSWESTRY   Map 15 SJ22

Wynnstay

★★★ 87% ◉◉ HOTEL   Best Western

☎ 01691 655261 🖷 01691 670606
Church St SY11 2SZ
e-mail: info@wynnstayhotel.com
web: www.wynnstayhotel.com
dir: B4083 to town, fork left at Honda Garage, right at lights. Hotel opposite church

This Georgian property was once a coaching inn and posting house and surrounds a unique 200-year-old Crown Bowling Green. Elegant public areas include a health, leisure and beauty centre, which is housed in a former coach house. Well-equipped bedrooms are individually styled and decorated and include several suites, four-poster rooms and a self-catering apartment. The Four Seasons Restaurant has a well deserved reputation for its food, and the adjacent Wilsons café/bar is a stylish informal alternative.

Rooms 34 (5 fmly) **S** £65-£85; **D** £85-£110*
Facilities Spa FTV ☜ Gym Crown Green Bowling Beauty suite New Year Wi-fi **Conf** Class 150 Board 50 Thtr 290 **Parking** 80 **Notes** LB ⊗ Civ Wed 90

See advert on this page

Pen-y-Dyffryn Country Hotel

WELSH RAREBITS

★★★ 82% ◉◉ HOTEL

☎ 01691 653700 🖷 01978 211004
Rhydycroesau SY10 7JD
e-mail: stay@peny.co.uk
web: www.peny.co.uk
dir: from A5 into Oswestry town centre. Follow signs to Llansilin on B4580, hotel 3m W of Oswestry before Rhydycroesau village

Peacefully situated in five acres of grounds, this charming old house dates back to around 1840, when it was built as a rectory. The tastefully appointed public rooms have real fires during cold weather, and the accommodation includes several mini-cottages, each with its own patio. This hotel attracts many guests for its food and attentive, friendly service.

Rooms 12 (4 annexe) (1 fmly) (1 GF) **S** £86; **D** £114-£186 (incl. bkfst)* **Facilities** STV Guided walks Xmas New Year Wi-fi **Parking** 18 **Notes** LB No children 3yrs Closed 18 Dec-19 Jan

OSWESTRY continued

Sebastian's Hotel & Restaurant

★★ 85% ◎◎ SMALL HOTEL

☎ 01691 655444 📠 01691 653452
45 Willow St SY11 1AQ
e-mail: sebastians.rest@virgin.net
web: www.sebastians-hotel.co.uk
dir: Follow town centre signs. Take road towards Selattyn & Llansilin for 300yds into Willow St, hotel on left

Parts of this privately owned and personally run small hotel and restaurant date back to 1640. It has a wealth of charm and character, enhanced by original features such as exposed beams and oak panelling in the cosy lounge, bar and popular bistro-style restaurant, where skilfully prepared dishes are served. The well equipped bedrooms including four in a separate building at the rear, are tastefully appointed in a style befitting the age and character of the property.

Rooms 6 (4 annexe) (6 fmly) (2 GF) **S** £65; **D** £85*
Facilities Wi-fi **Parking** 7 **Notes** ⊗

Travelodge Oswestry

BUDGET HOTEL

☎ 08719 846 096 📠 0870 191 1596
Mile End Service Area SY11 4JA
web: www.travelodge.co.uk
dir: at junct of A5/A483

Travelodge offers good quality, good value, modern accommodation. Ideal for families, the spacious en suite bedrooms include remote-control TV, tea and coffee-making facilities and comfortable beds. Meals can be taken at the nearby family restaurant. See also the Hotel Groups pages.

Rooms 40 **S** fr £29; **D** fr £29

SHIFNAL Map 10 SJ70

Park House

★★★★ 75% HOTEL

☎ 01952 460128 📠 01952 461658
Park St TF11 9BA
e-mail: reception@parkhousehotel.net
dir: M54 junct 4 follow A464 (Wolverhampton road) for approx 2m, under railway bridge, hotel 100yds on left

This hotel was created from what were originally two country houses of very different architectural styles. Located on the edge of the historic market town, it offers guests easy access to motorway networks, a choice of banqueting and meeting rooms, and leisure facilities.

Rooms 54 (16 annexe) (4 fmly) (8 GF) **S** £75-£90;
D £90-£200 (incl. bkfst)* **Facilities** STV FTV 🏊 Gym Steam room Sauna Beauty room Xmas New Year Wi-fi **Conf** Class 80 Board 40 Thtr 160 Del from £132.50 to £137.50* **Services** Lift **Parking** 90 **Notes** LB Civ Wed 200

Haughton Hall

★★★ 71% HOTEL

☎ 01952 468300 📠 01952 468313
Haughton Ln TF11 8HG
e-mail: reservations@haughtonhall.com
dir: M54 junct 4 take A464 into Shifnal. Turn left into Haughton Lane, hotel 600yds on left

This listed building dates back to 1718 and stands in open parkland close to the town. It is well geared for the conference trade and also has a 9-hole par 4 golf course, fishing lake and fine leisure club. Comfortable public rooms are available and the dinner menu is extensive. Bedrooms are comfortable and well equipped.

Rooms 36 (6 annexe) (5 fmly) (3 GF) **S** £65-£110;
D £65-£145 (incl. bkfst) **Facilities** FTV 🏊 supervised ⚓ 9 🎯 Fishing Gym Steam room Therapy room Solarium Xmas New Year Wi-fi **Conf** Class 60 Board 25 Thtr 120 Del from £125 to £165 **Parking** 60 **Notes** LB ⊗ Civ Wed 120

SHREWSBURY Map 15 SJ41

See also **Church Stretton**

Mercure Albrighton Hall Hotel & Spa

★★★★ 78% ◎◎ HOTEL

☎ 01939 291000 📠 01939 291123
Albrighton SY4 3AG
e-mail: H6629@accor.com
web: www.mercure-uk.com
dir: from S: M6 junct 10a to M54 to end. From N: M6 junct 12 to M5 then M54. Follow signs Harlescott & Ellesmere to A528

Dating back to 1630, this former ancestral home is set within 15 acres of attractive gardens. Rooms are generally spacious and the stable rooms are particularly popular. Elegant public rooms have rich oak panelling and there is a modern, well-equipped health and fitness centre.

Rooms 87 (16 annexe) (6 fmly) (21 GF) **Facilities** Spa 🏊 ♨ Gym Squash Beauty treatment rooms Thermal suite Relax room Spray tan Aerobics Xmas New Year Wi-fi **Conf** Class 150 Board 80 Thtr 300 **Services** Lift **Parking** 200 **Notes** LB Civ Wed 250

Albright Hussey Manor Hotel & Restaurant

★★★★ 73% ◎ HOTEL

☎ 01939 290571 & 290523 📠 01939 291143
Ellesmere Rd SY4 3AF
e-mail: info@albrighthussey.co.uk
web: www.albrighthussey.co.uk
dir: 2.5m N of Shrewsbury on A528, follow signs for Ellesmere

First mentioned in the Domesday Book, this enchanting medieval manor house is complete with a moat. Bedrooms are situated in either the sumptuously appointed main house or in the more modern wing. The intimate restaurant displays an abundance of original features and there is also a comfortable cocktail bar and lounge.

Rooms 26 (4 fmly) (8 GF) **Facilities** ⮑ Xmas New Year Wi-fi **Conf** Class 180 Board 80 Thtr 250 Del from £125 to £155* **Parking** 100 (charged) **Notes** Civ Wed 180

Rowton Castle Hotel
★★★ 88% ⚙ HOTEL

☎ 01743 884044 📄 01743 884949
Halfway House SY5 9EP
e-mail: post@rowtoncastle.com
web: www.rowtoncastle.com
dir: from A5 near Shrewsbury take A458 to Welshpool. Hotel 4m on right

Standing in 17 acres of grounds where a castle has stood for nearly 800 years, this Grade II listed building dates in

parts back to 1696. Many original features remain, including the oak panelling in the restaurant and a magnificent carved oak fireplace. Most bedrooms are spacious and all have modern facilities; some have four-poster beds. The hotel has a well deserved reputation for its food and is understandably a popular venue for weddings.

Rooms 19 (3 fmly) **Facilities** ⮑ Wi-fi **Conf** Class 30 Board 30 Thtr 80 **Parking** 100 **Notes** ⊗ Civ Wed 110

Prince Rupert
★★★ 82% HOTEL

CLASSIC BRITISH HOTELS

☎ 01743 499955 📄 01743 357306
Butcher Row SY1 1UQ
e-mail: post@prince-rupert-hotel.co.uk
web: www.prince-rupert-hotel.co.uk
dir: follow town centre signs, over English Bridge & Wyle Cop Hill. Right into Fish St, 200yds

Parts of this popular town centre hotel date back to medieval times and many bedrooms have exposed beams and other original features. Luxury suites, family rooms and rooms with four-poster beds are all available. As an alternative to the main Royalist Restaurant, diners have two less formal options including an Italian restaurant and a popular bar-bistro. The hotel's car parking service comes recommended.

Prince Rupert

Rooms 70 (4 fmly) **S** £79-£85; **D** £105-£175 (incl. bkfst) **Facilities** FTV Gym Weight training room Steam shower Sauna Snooker room Xmas New Year Wi-fi **Conf** Class 80 Board 40 Thtr 120 Del from £125 to £140 **Services** Lift **Parking** 70 **Notes** LB ⊗

See advert on this page

SHREWSBURY continued

Mytton & Mermaid

★★★ 77% ◉◉ HOTEL

☎ 01743 761220 🗎 01743 761292
Atcham SY5 6QG
e-mail: admin@myttonandmermaid.co.uk
web: www.myttonandmermaid.co.uk
dir: from Shrewsbury over old bridge in Atcham. Hotel
opposite main entrance to Attingham Park

Convenient for Shrewsbury, this ivy-clad former coaching
inn enjoys a pleasant location beside the River Severn.
Some bedrooms, including family suites, are in a
converted stable block adjacent to the hotel. There is a
large lounge bar, a comfortable lounge, and a brasserie
that has gained a well-deserved local reputation for the
quality of its food.

Rooms 18 (7 annexe) (1 fmly) **S** £80-£85; **D** £105-£165
(incl. bkfst)* **Facilities** Fishing 🎵 New Year Wi-fi
Conf Class 24 Board 28 Thtr 70 **Parking** 50 **Notes** ⊗
Closed 25 Dec Civ Wed 80

Lord Hill

★★★ 74% HOTEL

☎ 01743 232601 🗎 01743 369734
Abbey Foregate SY2 6AX
e-mail: reservations@lordhill.u-net.com
web: www.lordhill.u-net.com
dir: from M54 take A5, at 1st rdbt left then 2nd rdbt take
4th exit into London Rd. At next rdbt (Lord Hill Column)
take 3rd exit, hotel 300yds on left

This pleasant, attractively appointed hotel is located
close to the town centre. Most of the modern bedrooms
are set in a separate purpose-built property, but those in
the main building include one with a four-poster, as well
as full suites. There is also a conservatory restaurant and
a large function suite.

Rooms 36 (24 annexe) (2 fmly) (8 GF) **Facilities** Wi-fi
Conf Class 180 Board 180 Thtr 250 **Parking** 110
Notes Civ Wed 70

The Lion

★★★ 68% HOTEL

☎ 01743 353107 🗎 01743 352744
Wyle Cop SY1 1UY
e-mail: info@thelionhotelshrewsbury.com
dir: from S cross English Bridge, fork right, hotel at hill
top on left. From N follow Castle St into Dogpole, hotel
ahead

A 14th-century coaching inn, located in the town centre,
boasts Charles Dickens as one of its previous guests.
Bedrooms come in a variety of sizes, those at the rear
being quieter. Public areas include the magnificent
ballroom plus a bar and restaurant with oak beams and
original fireplace.

Rooms 59 (3 fmly) **S** £80; **D** £98 (incl. bkfst)
Facilities Xmas New Year Wi-fi **Conf** Class 80 Board 60
Thtr 200 **Services** Lift **Parking** 59 **Notes** LB ⊗
Civ Wed 200

Lion & Pheasant

★★ 65% HOTEL

☎ 01743 236288 🗎 01743 244475
49-50 Wyle Cop SY1 1XJ
e-mail: lionandpheasant@aol.com
dir: In town centre

Located close to The English Bridge and within easy
walking distance of the historic centre, this traditional
coaching hotel provides a range of bedrooms, some of
which are situated in an extension. Public areas include a
cottage style restaurant, a café bar and a cosy foyer
lounge.

Rooms 27 (2 fmly) (12 smoking) **Conf** Class 30 Board 30
Thtr 30 **Parking** 22 **Notes** Closed Xmas

Travelodge Shrewsbury Battlefield

BUDGET HOTEL

☎ 0871 984 6120 🗎 01743 465754
A49/A53 Roundabout, Battlefield SY4 3EQ
web: www.travelodge.co.uk

Travelodge offers good quality, good value, modern
accommodation. Ideal for families, the spacious en suite
bedrooms include remote-control TV, tea and coffee-
making facilities and comfortable beds. Meals can be

taken at the nearby family restaurant. See also the Hotel
Groups pages.

Rooms 41 **S** fr £29; **D** fr £29

Travelodge Shrewsbury Bayston Hill

BUDGET HOTEL

☎ 08719 846 103 🗎 01743 874256
Bayston Hill Services SY3 0DA
web: www.travelodge.co.uk
dir: A5/A49 junct

Rooms 40 **S** fr £29; **D** fr £29

TELFORD   Map 10 SJ60

Telford Golf & Spa

★★★★ 75% HOTEL

☎ 01952 429977 🗎 01952 586602
Great Hay Dr, Sutton Heights TF7 4DT
e-mail: dparrett@qhotels.co.uk
web: www.qhotels.co.uk
dir: M54 junct 4, A442. Follow signs for Telford Golf Club

Set on the edge of Telford with panoramic views of the
famous Ironbridge Gorge, this hotel has now completed a
£7m refurbishment and offers excellent standards. Smart
bedrooms are complemented by spacious public areas,
large conference facilities, a spa with treatment rooms, a
golf course and a driving range. Ample parking is
available. Q Hotels - AA Hotel Group of the Year 2008-9.

Rooms 114 (8 fmly) (50 GF) **Facilities** Spa STV ⊛ ⚓ 18
Putt green Gym Xmas New Year Wi-fi **Conf** Class 220
Board 100 Thtr 350 **Services** Lift **Parking** 200
Notes Civ Wed

See advert on opposite page

Best Western Valley

★★★ 80% ◉◉ HOTEL

☎ 01952 432247 🗎 01952 432308
TF8 7DW
e-mail: info@thevalleyhotel.co.uk
dir: M6, M54 junct 6 onto A5223 to Ironbridge

This privately owned hotel is situated in attractive
gardens, close to the famous Iron Bridge. It was once the
home of the Maws family who manufactured ceramic
tiles, and fine examples of their craft are found
throughout the house. Bedrooms vary in size and are split
between the main house and a mews development;
imaginative meals are served in the attractive Chez
Maws restaurant.

Rooms 44 (3 fmly) (8 GF) **S** £55-£90; **D** £80-£130 (incl.
bkfst)* **Facilities** FTV Wi-fi **Conf** Class 80 Board 60
Thtr 150 Del from £128 to £160* **Services** Lift
Parking 100 **Notes** LB ⊗ Closed 24 Dec-2 Jan RS 25 Dec
Civ Wed 150

Hadley Park House

★★★ 77% ® HOTEL

☎ 01952 677269 📠 01952 676938
Hadley Park TF1 6QJ
e-mail: info@hadleypark.co.uk
dir: off Hadley Park Island off A442 to Whitchurch

Located in Telford, but close to Ironbridge this elegant Georgian mansion is situated within three acres of its own grounds. Bedrooms are spacious and well equipped. There is a comfortable bar and lounge and meals are served in the attractive conservatory-style restaurant.

Rooms 12 (3 fmly) **S** £75-£95; **D** £85-£105 (incl. bkfst)* **Facilities** FTV New Year Wi-fi **Conf** Class 40 Board 30 Thtr 80 Del from £105 to £145* **Parking** 40 **Notes** LB ⊗ Closed 26 Dec & 1 Jan Civ Wed 80

Buckatree Hall

★★★ 70% HOTEL

☎ 01952 641821 📠 01952 247540
The Wrekin, Wellington TF6 5AL
dir: M54 junct 7, left & left, hotel 0.25m

The name Buckatree means 'the well where deer drink'. Little wonder then that the hotel started life as a hunting lodge. The extensive wooded estates on the slopes of the Wrekin make for a peaceful retreat for guests as well as providing a scenic wedding venue. Bedrooms are furnished and decorated in a traditional style and some have balconies.

Rooms 62 (5 fmly) (15 GF) **S** £75-£95; **D** £85-£105 (incl. bkfst)* **Facilities** STV Xmas New Year Wi-fi **Conf** Class 110 Board 48 Thtr 180 Del from £122* **Services** Lift **Parking** 85 **Notes** LB Civ Wed 180

Holiday Inn Telford/ Ironbridge

U

☎ 01952 527000 📠 01952 291949
St Quentin Gate TF3 4EH
e-mail: holidayinn.telford@virgin.net
web: www.holidayinn.co.uk

Currently the rating for this establishment is not confirmed. This may be due to a change of ownership or because it has only recently joined the AA rating scheme. For further details please see the AA website: www.theAA.com

Rooms 151

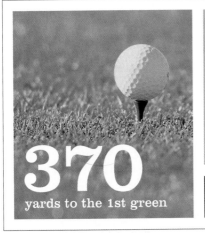

TELFORD continued

Travelodge Telford Shawbirch

BUDGET HOTEL

☎ 0871 984 6110 📄 01952 246534
Whitchurch Dr, Shawbirch TF1 3QA
web: www.travelodge.co.uk
dir: 1m NW, on A5223 at junct of A442 & B5063

Travelodge offers good quality, good value, modern accommodation. Ideal for families, the spacious en suite bedrooms include remote-control TV, tea and coffee-making facilities and comfortable beds. Meals can be taken at the nearby family restaurant. See also the Hotel Groups pages.

Rooms 40 **S** fr £29; **D** fr £29

TELFORD SERVICE AREA (M54) **Map 10 SJ70**

Days Inn Telford

BUDGET HOTEL

☎ 01952 238400 📄 01952 238410
Telford Services, Priorslee Rd TF11 8TG
e-mail: telford.hotel@welcomebreak.co.uk
web: www.welcomebreak.co.uk
dir: M54 junct 4

This modern building offers accommodation in smart, spacious and well-equipped bedrooms, suitable for families and business travellers, and all with en suite bathrooms. Continental breakfast is available, and other refreshments may be taken at the nearby family restaurant. See also the Hotel Groups pages.

Rooms 48 (45 fmly) (21 GF) **S** £39-£59; **D** £49-£69*

WHITCHURCH **Map 15 SJ54**

Macdonald Hill Valley

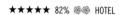

★★★★ 75% HOTEL

☎ 0870 194 2133 📄 01948 667373
Tarporley Rd SY13 4JH
e-mail: gm.hillvalley@macdonald-hotels.co.uk
web: www.macdonald-hotels.co.uk/hillvalley
dir: 2nd exit off A41 towards Whitchurch

This new hotel offers spacious and well-equipped bedrooms. Public areas include popular bar and restaurant, and in addition there are two 18-hole golf courses.

Rooms 81 (27 GF) **S** £69-£149; **D** £83-£163 (incl. bkfst)*
Facilities STV 🕐 ⚑ 18 Putt green Gym Xmas New Year Wi-fi **Conf** Class 150 Board 150 Thtr 300 **Services** Lift **Parking** 300 **Notes** Civ Wed 300

Dodington Lodge

★★★ 71% SMALL HOTEL

☎ 01948 662539 📄 01948 667992
Dodington SY13 1EN
e-mail: info@dodingtonlodge.co.uk
web: www.dodingtonlodge.co.uk
dir: from S on A41/A49 towards Whitchurch, hotel on left

This privately owned hotel is conveniently situated close to the centre of the town, within easy reach of Chester and North Wales. Bedrooms are tastefully decorated and well equipped, and guests will find a welcoming atmosphere in the lounge bar. A choice of eating options is offered - from a light snack to a full meal. The function suite is a popular choice for weddings and meetings.

Rooms 10 (2 fmly) **Conf** Class 40 Board 25 Thtr 60 **Parking** 45 **Notes** LB ⊗

SOMERSET

BATH **Map 4 ST76**

See also **Colerne (Wiltshire) & Hinton Charterhouse**

Macdonald Bath Spa

★★★★★ 84% ⊛⊛ HOTEL

☎ 0844 879 9106 ☏ 01225 444424 📄 01225 444006
Sydney Rd BA2 6JF
e-mail: sales.bathspa@macdonald-hotels.co.uk
web: www.bathspahotel.com
dir: A4, left onto A36 at 1st lights. Right at lights after pedestrian crossing left into Sydney Place. Hotel 200yds on right

A delightful Georgian mansion set amidst seven acres of pretty landscaped grounds, just a short walk from the many and varied delights of the city centre. A timeless elegance pervades the gracious public areas and bedrooms. Facilities include a popular leisure club, a choice of dining options and a number of meeting rooms.

Rooms 129 (3 fmly) (17 GF) **S** £138-£778; **D** £149-£778 (incl. bkfst) **Facilities** Spa STV 🕐 supervised 🏊 Gym

---

Macdonald Bath Spa

Beauty treatment Thermal suite Outdoor hydro pool 🎵 Xmas New Year Wi-fi **Conf** Class 100 Board 50 Thtr 130 Del from £229 to £299 **Services** Lift **Parking** 160 **Notes** LB Civ Wed 130

The Royal Crescent

★★★★★ 82% ⊛ ⊛ HOTEL

☎ 01225 823333 📄 01225 339401
16 Royal Crescent BA1 2LS
e-mail: info@royalcrescent.co.uk
web: www.vonessenhotels.co.uk
dir: from A4, right at lights. 2nd left onto Bennett St. Continue into The Circus, 2nd exit onto Brock St

John Wood's masterpiece of fine Georgian architecture provides the setting for this elegant hotel in the centre of the world famous Royal Crescent. Spacious, air-conditioned bedrooms are individually designed and furnished with antiques. Delightful central grounds lead to a second house, which is home to further rooms, the award-winning Dower House restaurant and the Bath House which offers therapies and treatments.

Rooms 45 (8 fmly) (7 GF) **D** £225-£320 (incl. bkfst)*
Facilities Spa STV FTV 🕐 🏊 Gym 1920s river launch Xmas New Year Wi-fi **Conf** Class 25 Board 24 Thtr 50 Del from £270 to £305* **Services** Lift Air con **Parking** 10 **Notes** LB Civ Wed 50

INSPECTORS' CHOICE

The Bath Priory Hotel Restaurant & Spa
★★★★ ◉◉◉ HOTEL

☎ 01225 331922 📠 01225 448276
Weston Rd BA1 2XT
e-mail: mail@thebathpriory.co.uk
web: www.thebathpriory.co.uk
dir: adjacent to Victoria Park

Set in delightful walled gardens, this attractive Georgian house provides peace and tranquillity and yet is near to this historic city centre. An extensive display of paintings and fine art creates an impression of opulence, and the sumptuously furnished public rooms offer great comfort. The cuisine, using excellently sourced ingredients, is accomplished and complemented by an impressive wine list. Bedrooms are well proportioned and provide the many thoughtful touches expected in an establishment of this quality.

Rooms 27 (6 fmly) (3 GF) **D** £245-£360 (incl. bkfst)*
Facilities Spa STV ◉ ↖ ⚘ Gym Holistic beauty therapy & treatments Steam room Xmas New Year Wi-fi **Conf** Board 25 Thtr 32 **Parking** 40 **Notes** ⊗ Civ Wed 64

Barceló Combe Grove Manor
★★★★ 74% ◉ HOTEL

Barceló HOTELS & RESORTS

☎ 01225 834644 📠 01225 834961
Brassknocker Hill, Monkton Combe BA2 7HS
e-mail: combegrovemanor@barcelo-hotels.co.uk
web: www.barcelo-hotels.co.uk
dir: Exit A36 at Limpley Stoke onto Brassknocker Hill. Hotel 0.5m up hill on left

Set in over 80 acres of gardens, this Georgian mansion commands stunning views over Limpley Stoke Valley. Most bedrooms are in the Garden Lodge, a short walk from the main house. The superb range of indoor and outdoor leisure facilities includes a beauty clinic with holistic therapies, golf, tennis and two pools.

Rooms 42 (33 annexe) (5 fmly) (8 GF) **S** £65-£145;
Facilities ◉ supervised ↖ ⅃ 5 ॐ Putt green ⚘ Gym Squash Driving range Xmas New Year **Conf** Class 60 Board 30 Thtr 90 **Parking** 400 **Notes** ⊗ Civ Wed 50

INSPECTORS' CHOICE

Queensberry
★★★ ◉◉ HOTEL

☎ 01225 447928 📠 01225 446065
Russel St BA1 2QF
e-mail: reservations@thequeensberry.co.uk
web: www.thequeensberry.co.uk
dir: 100mtrs from the Assembly Rooms

This charming family-run hotel, situated in a quiet residential street near the city centre, consists of four delightful townhouses. The spacious bedrooms offer deep armchairs, marble bathrooms and a range of modern comforts. Sumptuously furnished sitting rooms add to The Queensberry's appeal and allow access to the very attractive and peaceful walled gardens. The Olive Tree is a stylish restaurant that combines Georgian opulence with contemporary simplicity. Innovative menus are based on best quality ingredients and competent cooking. Valet parking proves a useful service.

Rooms 29 (2 fmly) (2 GF) **S** £110-£165; **D** £115-£230*
Facilities FTV Wi-fi **Conf** Board 25 Thtr 35
Del from £210 to £275* **Services** Lift **Parking** 6
Notes ⊗

BATH continued

Best Western Cliffe

★★★ 84% ☺ HOTEL

☎ 01225 723226 🖷 01225 723871
Cliffe Dr, Crowe Hill, Limpley Stoke BA2 7FY
e-mail: cliffe@bestwestern.co.uk
dir: A36 S from Bath onto B3108 at lights left towards
Bradford-on-Avon, 0.5m. Right before bridge through
village, hotel on right

With stunning countryside views, this attractive country
house is just a short drive from the City of Bath.
Bedrooms vary in size and style but are well equipped;
several are particularly spacious and a number of rooms
are on the ground floor. The restaurant overlooks the
well-tended garden and offers a tempting selection of
carefully prepared dishes. Wi-fi is available throughout.

Rooms 11 (3 annexe) (2 fmly) (4 GF) **S** £102-£130;
D £124-£160 (incl. bkfst)* **Facilities** ⌇ Xmas New Year
Wi-fi **Conf** Class 15 Board 10 Thtr 20 Del from £145 to
£160* **Parking** 20 **Notes** LB

See advert on page 431

Dukes

★★★ 82% ☺☺ SMALL HOTEL

☎ 01225 787960 🖷 01225 787961
Great Pulteney St BA2 4DN
e-mail: info@dukesbath.co.uk
web: www.dukesbath.co.uk
dir: A46 to Bath, at rdbt right on A4. 4th set of lights turn
left (A36), then right onto Great Pulteney St. Hotel on left.

A fine elegant, Grade I listed Georgian building, just a few
minutes' walk from Pulteney Bridge. The well-equipped
bedrooms, which differ in size and style, have
comfortable beds and flat-screen TVs; some suites and
some ground-floor rooms are available. Staff are
particularly friendly and attentive; the atmosphere is
relaxed. There is a courtyard terrace, leading from the

lounge/bar, where guests can enjoy an aperitif or lunch
during the summer months. The Cavendish restaurant
offers a very creative and interesting menu.

Rooms 17 (5 fmly) (2 GF) **S** £99-£140; **D** £131-£232 (incl.
bkfst)* **Facilities** FTV Xmas New Year **Conf** Board 20
Thtr 35 Del from £145 to £165* **Notes** LB

Mercure Francis

★★★ 73% HOTEL

☎ 01225 424105 & 338970 🖷 01225 319715
Queen Square BA1 2HH
e-mail: h6636@accor.com
web: www.mercure.com
dir: M4 junct 18/A46 to Bath junct. 3rd exit onto A4, right
into George St, left into Gay St into Queen Sq. Hotel on left

Overlooking Queen Square in the centre of the city, this
elegant Georgian hotel is situated within walking
distance of Bath's many attractions. Public rooms provide
a variety of environments where guests can eat, drink
and relax - from the informal café-bar to the traditional
lounge and more formal restaurant. Bedrooms have air
conditioning.

Rooms 95 (17 fmly) (5 smoking) **S** £68-£140;
D £73-£150* **Facilities** Xmas New Year Wi-fi
Conf Class 40 Board 30 Thtr 80 Del from £135 to £175*
Services Lift **Parking** 40 (charged) **Notes** LB Civ Wed 100

Best Western Abbey Hotel

★★★ 72% HOTEL

☎ 0845 130 2556 & 01225 461603 🖷 0870 950 2443
North Pde BA1 1LF
e-mail: ahres@compasshotels.co.uk
dir: close to the Abbey in city centre

Originally built for a wealthy merchant in the 1740s and
forming part of a handsome Georgian terrace, this
welcoming hotel is situated in the heart of the city. The
thoughtfully equipped bedrooms vary in size and style.
Public areas include a smart lounge bar and although the

restaurant is available, many guests take dinner in the
lounge or choose from extensive room service menu.

Rooms 60 (4 fmly) (2 GF) **Facilities** Xmas Wi-fi
Services Lift **Notes** LB ⊗

Pratt's

★★★ 72% HOTEL

☎ 01225 460441 🖷 01225 448807
South Pde BA2 4AB
e-mail: pratts@forestdale.com
web: www.prattshotel.co.uk
dir: A46 into city centre. Left at 1st lights (Curfew Pub),
right at next lights. 2nd exit at next rdbt, right at lights,
left at next lights, 1st left into South Pde

Built in 1743 this popular Georgian hotel still has many
original features and is centrally placed to explore Bath.
The hotels bedrooms each with their own individual
character and style offer great comfort. The lounge has
original open fire places and offers a relaxing venue for
afternoon tea.

Rooms 46 (2 fmly) **S** £90-£95; **D** £129-£139 (incl. bkfst)*
Facilities Xmas New Year Wi-fi **Conf** Class 12 Board 20
Thtr 50 **Services** Lift **Notes** LB

Haringtons

★★ 83% SMALL HOTEL

☎ 01225 461728 & 445883 🖷 01225 444804
8-10 Queen St BA1 1HE
e-mail: post@haringtonshotel.co.uk
web: www.haringtonshotel.co.uk
dir: A4 to George St & turn into Milsom St. 1st right into
Quiet St & 1st left into Queen St

Dating back to the 18th century, this hotel is situated in
the heart of the city and provides all the expected modern
facilities and comforts. The café-bistro is light and airy
and is open throughout the day for light meals and
refreshments. A warm welcome is assured from the
proprietors and staff, making this a delightful place to
stay.

Rooms 13 (3 fmly) **S** £79-£148; **D** £88-£148 (incl. bkfst)*
Facilities STV FTV Xmas Wi-fi **Conf** Class 10 Board 12
Thtr 18 Del from £120 to £220* **Parking** 11 (charged)
Notes ⊗

Old Malt House

★★ 72% HOTEL

☎ 01761 470106 🖷 01761 472726
Radford, Timsbury BA2 0QF
e-mail: hotel@oldmalthouse.co.uk
dir: A367 towards Radstock for 1m pass Park & Ride,
right onto B3115 towards Tunley/Timsbury. At sharp bend
straight ahead & hotel 2nd left

Dating back to 1835, this building was originally the malt
house for the Radford Brewery. Just a few miles from
Bath, this small and welcoming family-run hotel is an
ideal base for exploring the many places of interest in the

area. Bedrooms are individual in style and all have lovely views over surrounding countryside. In addition to the convivial bar/lounge, the patio is also a popular venue for pre-dinner drinks before enjoying some good honest home cooking in the restaurant.

Rooms 11 (1 fmly) (2 GF) **Parking** 25 **Notes** LB ⊗ Closed Xmas & New Year

Wentworth House Hotel

★★ 67% HOTEL

☎ 01225 339193 🖹 01225 310460
106 Bloomfield Rd BA2 2AP
e-mail: stay@wentworthhouse.co.uk
web: www.wentworthhouse.co.uk
dir: A36 towards Bristol at railway arches, hotel on right

This hotel is located on the outskirts of Bath yet is within walking distance of the city. Bedrooms vary in size and style; ground-floor rooms have their own conservatory seating area, some have four-posters and one has superb city views. The dinner menu features authentic home-cooked Indian dishes. There is a garden, which has a pool to enjoy in fine weather.

Rooms 19 (2 fmly) **S** £70-£85; **D** £70-£125 (incl. bkfst)*
Facilities STV FTV ⚡ Xmas Wi-fi **Parking** 19 **Notes** LB ⊗ No children 7yrs

Bailbrook House

U

☎ 01225 855100 🖹 01225 855200
Eveleigh Av, London Road West BA1 7JD
e-mail: bailbrook@hilwoodresorts.com
web: www.bailbrookhouse.co.uk
dir: M4 junct 18/A46, at bottom of long hill take slip road to city centre. At rdbt take 1st exit, London Rd. Hotel 200mtrs on left

Currently the rating for this establishment is not confirmed. This may be due to a change of ownership or because it has only recently joined the AA rating scheme. For further details please see the AA website: www.theAA.com

Rooms 78 (78 annexe) (2 fmly) (26 GF) **S** £75-£120; **D** £79-£158 (incl. bkfst)* **Facilities** FTV ⚡ Gym Sauna Wi-fi **Conf** Class 72 Board 40 Thtr 160 Del from £140 to £209* **Parking** 120 **Notes** ⊗ Civ Wed 120

Express by Holiday Inn Bath

BUDGET HOTEL

☎ 0870 444 2792 🖹 0870 444 2793
Lower Bristol Rd, Brougham Hayes BA2 3QU
e-mail: bath@ebhi.fsnet.co.uk
web: www.hiexpress.co.uk/bath
dir: from A4, right into Bathwick St, over rdbt onto Pulteney Rd. Into Claverton St, straight over at next rdbt (Lower Bristol Rd). Hotel opposite Sainsburys

A modern hotel ideal for families and business travellers. Fresh and uncomplicated, the spacious rooms include Sky TV, power shower and tea and coffee-making facilities. Continental buffet breakfast is included in the room rate; other meals may be taken at the nearby family pub or restaurant. See also the Hotel Groups pages.

Rooms 126 (75 fmly) (31 GF) **Conf** Class 10 Board 20 Thtr 30

Travelodge Bath Central

BUDGET HOTEL

☎ 08719 846 219 🖹 01225 442061
York Buildings, George St BA1 2EB
web: www.travelodge.co.uk
dir: at corner of George St (A4) & Broad St

Travelodge offers good quality, good value, modern accommodation. Ideal for families, the spacious en suite bedrooms include remote-control TV, tea and coffee-making facilities and comfortable beds. Meals can be taken at the nearby family restaurant. See also the Hotel Groups pages.

Rooms 66 **S** fr £29; **D** fr £29

BECKINGTON   Map 4 ST85

Woolpack Inn

★★ Ⓐ SMALL HOTEL

☎ 01373 831244 🖹 01373 831223
BA12 6SP
web: www.oldenglish.co.uk
dir: on A36

Rooms 12 **Facilities** Xmas **Conf** Class 20 Board 20 Thtr 30 **Parking** 16 **Notes** No children 5yrs

BECKINGTON continued

Travelodge Beckington

BUDGET HOTEL

☎ 08719 846 220 📠 01373 830251
BA11 6SF
web: www.travelodge.co.uk
dir: at junct of A36/A361

Travelodge offers good quality, good value, modern accommodation. Ideal for families, the spacious en suite bedrooms include remote-control TV, tea and coffee-making facilities and comfortable beds. Meals can be taken at the nearby family restaurant. See also the Hotel Groups pages.

Rooms 40 **S** fr £29; **D** fr £29

BRENT KNOLL   Map 4 ST35

Woodlands Country House

★★ 78% HOTEL

☎ 01278 760232 📠 01278 769090
Hill Ln TA9 4DF
e-mail: info@woodlands-hotel.co.uk
web: www.woodlands-hotel.co.uk
dir: A38 take 1st left into village, then 5th right & 1st left, follow brown tourist signs

Located at the foot of Brent Knoll in four-acre grounds, this is an ideal base for both business and leisure travellers as it is within easy reach of the M5. The atmosphere is relaxed and welcoming with attentive service at all times. Bedrooms are all individually styled and reflect much charm. The elegant dining room has lovely views across the countryside and offers a well balanced menu featuring excellent local produce.

Rooms 9 (1 fmly) (1 GF) **Facilities** 8 Xmas New Year **Conf** Class 20 Board 30 Thtr 30 **Parking** 16 **Notes** ⊗ RS Sun Civ Wed 65

Brent Knoll Lodge & Fox & Goose Inn

★★ 75% HOTEL

☎ 01278 760008 📠 01278 769236
Bristol Rd TA9 4HH
e-mail: reception@brentknolllodge.com
web: www.brentknolllodge.com
dir: On A38 approx 500mtrs N of M5 junct 22

This accommodation is conveniently located just a few minutes drive from the M5 and is next door to the Fox and Goose Inn which offers a wide range of beverages and freshly prepared dishes. Bedrooms, some located at ground-floor level, are well equipped and quite spacious.

Rooms 14 (3 fmly) (7 GF) **S** £55-£75; **D** £65-£95* **Facilities** FTV Pool table Skittles Xmas Wi-fi **Conf** Class 32 Board 20 Thtr 32 Del from £85 to £110* **Services** Lift Air con **Parking** 60

Battleborough Grange Country Hotel & Restaurant

★★ 71% HOTEL

☎ 01278 760208 📠 01278 761950
Bristol Rd TA9 4HJ
e-mail: info@battleboroughgrangehotel.co.uk
dir: M5 junct 22, right at rdbt onto A38 past garden centre on right, hotel 500yds on left

Conveniently located, this popular hotel is surrounded by mellow Somerset countryside. Bedrooms, including four-poster rooms, are well equipped; some have superb views of the Iron Age fort of Brent Knoll. In the Conservatory Restaurant, both fixed-price and carte menus, using locally sourced ingredients, are offered. Guests can relax in the convivial bar after a busy day exploring the area's many attractions. Extensive function facilities are also provided.

Rooms 23 (2 fmly) (2 GF) **S** £62-£82; **D** £72-£139 (incl. bkfst)* **Facilities** FTV Wi-fi **Conf** Class 40 Board 40 Thtr 85 **Parking** 60 **Notes** LB ⊗ Closed 26 Dec-2 Jan Civ Wed 100

BRIDGWATER   Map 4 ST23

See also **Holford**

Best Western Walnut Tree

★★★ 73% ◉ HOTEL

☎ 01278 662255 & 0845 370 6000 📠 01278 663946
North Petherton TA6 6QA
e-mail: reservations@walnuttreehotel.com
web: www.walnuttreehotel.com
dir: M5 junct 24 centre of North Petherton.

Popular with both business and leisure guests, this 18th-century former coaching inn is conveniently located within easy reach of the M5. The spacious and smartly decorated bedrooms are well furnished to ensure a comfortable and relaxing stay. An extensive selection of dishes is offered in either the restaurant, or the more informal setting of the bistro.

Rooms 30 (3 fmly) (3 GF) **S** £80-£140; **D** £100-£200 (incl. bkfst)* **Facilities** FTV Xmas New Year Wi-fi **Conf** Class 60 Board 50 Thtr 100 **Parking** 70 **Notes** LB ⊗ Civ Wed 100

Apple Tree

★★ 72% HOTEL

☎ 01278 733238 📠 01278 732693
Keenthorne TA5 1HZ
e-mail: reservations@appletreehotel.com
web: www.appletreehotel.com

(For full entry see Nether Stowey)

Travelodge Bridgwater (M5)

BUDGET HOTEL

☎ 0871 984 6243 📠 01278 450 432
Huntsworth Business Park TA6 6TS
web: www.travelodge.co.uk
dir: M5 junct 24 A38 towards Bridgwater. Follow signs for Services. Lodge in Service Area

Travelodge offers good quality, good value, modern accommodation. Ideal for families, the spacious en suite bedrooms include remote-control TV, tea and coffee-making facilities and comfortable beds. Meals can be taken at the nearby family restaurant. See also the Hotel Groups pages.

Rooms 29 **S** fr £29; **D** fr £29

CASTLE CARY   Map 4 ST63

The George

★★ 64% HOTEL

☎ 01963 350761 📠 01963 350035
Market Place BA7 7AH
e-mail: castlecarygeorge@aol.co.uk
dir: A303 onto A371. Signed Castle Cary, 2m on left

This 15th-century coaching inn provides well-equipped bedrooms that are generally spacious. Most rooms are at the back of the house, enjoying a quiet aspect, and some are on the ground floor; one is suitable for less able guests. Diners can choose to eat in the more formal dining room, or in one of the two cosy bars.

Rooms 17 (5 annexe) (1 fmly) (5 GF) **S** £59.50; **D** £79.50 (incl. bkfst) **Facilities** Xmas New Year Wi-fi **Conf** Class 40 Board 20 Thtr 50 **Parking** 7

LICHFIELD
Map 10 SK10

INSPECTORS' CHOICE

Swinfen Hall
★★★★ ◉◉ HOTEL

☎ 01543 481494 📠 01543 480341
Swinfen WS14 9RE
e-mail: info@swinfenhallhotel.co.uk
web: www.swinfenhallhotel.co.uk
dir: set back from A38, 2.5m outside Lichfield, towards Birmingham

Dating from 1757, this lavishly decorated mansion has been painstakingly restored by the present owners. Set in 100 acres of parkland which includes a deer park. Public rooms are particularly stylish, with intricately carved ceilings and impressive oil portraits. Bedrooms on the first floor boast period features and tall sash windows; those on the second floor (the former servants' quarters) are smaller and more contemporary by comparison. Service within the award-winning restaurant is both professional and attentive.

Rooms 17 **S** £135-£265; **D** £160-£295 (incl. bkfst)* **Facilities** STV ⌘ Fishing ⌘ New Year Wi-fi **Conf** Class 50 Board 120 Thtr 96 Del from £180* **Parking** 80 **Notes** LB ⊗ Civ Wed 120

Best Western George
★★★ 77% HOTEL

☎ 01543 414822 📠 01543 415817
12-14 Bird St WS13 6PR
e-mail: mail@thegeorgelichfield.co.uk
web: www.thegeorgelichfield.co.uk
dir: from Bowling Green Island on A461 take Lichfield exit. Left at next island into Swan Road, as road bears left, turn right into Bird St for hotel car park

Situated in the city centre, this privately owned hotel provides good quality, well-equipped accommodation

which includes a room with a four-poster bed. Facilities here include a large ballroom, plus several other rooms for meetings and functions.

Rooms 45 (5 fmly) **S** £50-£99; **D** £68-£150 (incl. bkfst)* **Facilities** FTV Wi-fi **Conf** Class 60 Board 40 Thtr 110 Del from £135 to £165* **Services** Lift **Parking** 45 **Notes** LB ⊗ Civ Wed 110

Angel Croft
★ 72% HOTEL

☎ 01543 258737 📠 01543 415605
Beacon St WS13 7AA
dir: opposite west gate entrance to Lichfield Cathedral

This traditional, family-run, Georgian hotel is close to the cathedral and city centre. A comfortable lounge leads into a pleasantly appointed dining room; there is also a cosy bar on the lower ground floor. Bedrooms vary and most are spacious, particularly those in the adjacent Westgate House.

Rooms 18 (8 annexe) (1 fmly) **Conf** Board 20 Thtr 30 **Parking** 60 **Notes** ⊗ Closed 25 & 26 Dec RS Sun evenings

Innkeeper's Lodge Lichfield
BUDGET HOTEL

☎ 0845 112 6074 📠 0845 112 6232
Stafford Rd WS13 8JB
web: www.innkeeperslodge.com/lichfield
dir: M6 junct 15, A50 towards Burton. A38 south for Lichfield, exit at Streethay onto A5192 to A51(Stafford Rd). From M42 junct 10, A5 towards Tamworth. A51 north through Lichfield

Innkeeper's Lodge represents an exciting, high value concept within the budget hotel market. Comfortable bedrooms provide excellent facilities that include satellite TV and modem points. This carefully restored lodge is in a picturesque setting and has its own unique style and quirky character. Food is served all day, and an extensive, complimentary continental breakfast is offered.

Rooms 10 (2 fmly) **S** £55-£65; **D** £55-£65 (incl. bkfst)

LONGNOR
Map 16 SK06

The Black Grouse
◉ RESTAURANT WITH ROOMS

☎ 01298 83205 & 83194 📠 01298 83689
SK17 0NS
e-mail: food@theblackgrouse.co.uk
dir: In village centre on B5053

Located in the heart of the Peak District National Park this 18th-century coaching inn offers stylish, fully equipped bedrooms each with a modern en suite. Public areas include the oak-panelled bar (featuring real ales) and separate dining room - both offering a tempting range of bar meals and a frequently changing carte menu, using fresh, local ingredients.

Rooms 11 (2 en suite) (3 annexe) (3 fmly) (1 GF)

NEWCASTLE-UNDER-LYME
Map 10 SJ84

Holiday Inn Stoke-on-Trent

Ⓤ

☎ 01782 557000 & 557018 📠 01782 557022
Clayton Rd, Clayton ST5 4DL
e-mail: stoke@ihg.com
web: www.holidayinn.co.uk
dir: Just off M6 junct 15. Follow Clayton Rd signs towards Newcastle-under-Lyme. Hotel 200yds on left

Currently the rating for this establishment is not confirmed. This may be due to a change of ownership or because it has only recently joined the AA rating scheme. For further details please see the AA website: www.theAA.com

Rooms 118 (12 fmly) (8 smoking) **S** £40-£149; **D** £40-£149* **Facilities** STV ⓣ supervised Gym Xmas New Year Wi-fi **Conf** Class 30 Board 22 Thtr 70 Del from £95 to £160* **Services** Air con **Parking** 150 **Notes** ⊗

PATTINGHAM Map 10 SO89

Patshull Park Hotel Golf & Country Club

★★★ 77% HOTEL

☎ 01902 700100 📠 01902 700874
Patshull Park WV6 7HR
e-mail: sales@patshull-park.co.uk
web: www.patshull-park.co.uk
dir: 1.5m W of Pattingham, at church take Patshull Rd, hotel 1.5m on right

There has been a manor house here since before the Norman Conquest - the present house dates back to the 1730s. Sitting within 280 acres of parkland (with good golf and fishing) this comfortably appointed hotel has a range of modern leisure and conference facilities. Public rooms include a lounge bar, coffee shop and restaurant with delightful views over the lake. Bedrooms are well appointed and thoughtfully equipped; most have good views.

Rooms 49 (15 fmly) (16 GF) **S** £99-£124; **D** £119-£169 (incl. bkfst) **Facilities** STV ⓢ ♨ 18 Putt green Fishing Gym Beauty therapist Pool table Cardio suite ♫ New Year Wi-fi **Conf** Class 75 Board 44 Thtr 160 Del from £110 to £165* **Parking** 200 **Notes** LB RS 24-26 Dec Civ Wed 100

See advert on page 429

RUGELEY Map 10 SK01

Travelodge Rugeley

BUDGET HOTEL

☎ 08719 846 102 📠 01889 570096
Western Springs Rd WS15 2AS
web: www.travelodge.co.uk
dir: on A51/B5013

Travelodge offers good quality, good value, modern accommodation. Ideal for families, the spacious en suite bedrooms include remote-control TV, tea and coffee-making facilities and comfortable beds. Meals can be taken at the nearby family restaurant. See also the Hotel Groups pages.

Rooms 32 **S** fr £29; **D** fr £29

STAFFORD Map 10 SJ92

The Moat House

★★★★ 85% ⑧⑧ HOTEL

CLASSIC BRITISH HOTELS

☎ 01785 712217 📠 01785 715344
Lower Penkridge Rd, Acton Trussell ST17 0RJ
e-mail: info@moathouse.co.uk
web: www.moathouse.co.uk
dir: M6 junct 13 onto A449 through Acton Trussell. Hotel on right on exiting village

This 17th-century timbered building, with an idyllic canal-side setting, has been skilfully extended. Bedrooms are stylishly furnished, well equipped and comfortable. The bar offers a range of snacks and the restaurant boasts a popular fine dining option where the head chef displays his skills using top quality produce.

Rooms 41 (4 fmly) (12 GF) **S** £130; **D** £150 (incl. bkfst)* **Facilities** New Year Wi-fi **Conf** Class 60 Board 50 Thtr 200 **Services** Lift **Parking** 200 **Notes** ⊗ Closed 25 Dec & 1 Jan Civ Wed 150

The Swan

★★★ 78% HOTEL

☎ 01785 258142 📠 01785 223372
46 Greengate St ST16 2JA
e-mail: info@theswanstafford.co.uk
dir: from north on A34, access via Mill Street in town centre. From south on A449

This former coaching inn located in the town centre offers spacious, modern public areas that include a popular brasserie, a choice of elegant bars, a coffee shop and conference facilities. Individually styled bedrooms, many with original period features, are tastefully appointed and include two four-poster suites. Executive rooms are air conditioned.

Rooms 31 (2 fmly) **Facilities** Wi-fi **Services** Lift **Parking** 40 **Notes** ⊗ Closed 25 Dec

Abbey

THE INDEPENDENTS

★★ 72% HOTEL

☎ 01785 258531 📠 01785 246875
65-68 Lichfield Rd ST17 4LW
web: www.abbeyhotelstafford.co.uk
dir: M6 junct 13 towards Stafford. Right at Esso garage, to mini-rdbt, follow Silkmore Lane to 2nd rdbt. Hotel 0.25m on right

This friendly privately owned and personally run hotel provides well-equipped accommodation and is particularly popular with commercial visitors. Family and ground floor rooms are both available. Facilities here include a choice of lounges and the spacious car park proves a real benefit to guests in this area of the city.

Rooms 17 (3 fmly) **S** £50-£58; **D** £65-£80 (incl. bkfst) **Facilities** FTV Wi-fi **Parking** 21 **Notes** ⊗ Closed 22 Dec-7 Jan

STAFFORD MOTORWAY SERVICE AREA (M6) Map 10 SJ82

Travelodge Stafford (M6)

BUDGET HOTEL

Travelodge

☎ 08719 846 105 📠 01785 816107
Moto Service Area, Eccleshall Road ST15 0EU
web: www.travelodge.co.uk
dir: between M6 juncts 14 & 15 northbound only

Travelodge offers good quality, good value, modern accommodation. Ideal for families, the spacious en suite bedrooms include remote-control TV, tea and coffee-making facilities and comfortable beds. Meals can be taken at the nearby family restaurant. See also the Hotel Groups pages.

Rooms 49 **S** fr £29; **D** fr £29

STOKE-ON-TRENT Map 10 SJ84

STOKE-ON-TRENT   Map 10 SJ84

Best Western Stoke-on-Trent Moat House

★★★★ 74% HOTEL

☎ 0870 225 4601 & 01782 206101 ⓐ 01782 206101
Etruria Hall, Festival Way, Etruria ST1 5BQ
e-mail: reservations.stoke@qmh-hotels.com
web: www.bestwestern.co.uk/content/hotel-details-leisure.aspx/hotel/83862
dir: M6/A500. A53 Festival Park. Keep in left lane exit, take first slip road on left. Left at island, hotel opposite at next island

A large, modern hotel located in Stoke's Festival Park, that adjoins Etruria Hall, the former home of Josiah Wedgwood. The bedrooms are spacious and well equipped and include family rooms, suites and executive rooms. Public areas include a spacious lounge bar and restaurant as well as a business centre, extensive conference facilities and a leisure club.

Rooms 147 (63 fmly) (22 smoking) **S** £59-£139;
D £59-£139* **Facilities** ⓣ supervised Gym Beauty salon Sauna Steam room Solarium Dance studio Xmas New Year Wi-fi **Conf** Class 400 Board 40 Thtr 550 **Services** Lift Air con **Parking** 350 **Notes** ⊗ Civ Wed 80

Best Western Manor House

★★★ 82% HOTEL

☎ 01270 884000 ⓐ 01270 882483
Audley Rd ST7 2QQ
e-mail: mhres@compasshotels.co.uk
web: www.compasshotels.co.uk

(For full entry see Alsager (Cheshire))

Haydon House

★★★ 67% HOTEL

☎ 01782 711311 & 753690 ⓐ 01782 717470
Haydon St, Basford ST4 6JD
e-mail: enquiries@haydon-house-hotel.co.uk
dir: A500/A53 (Hanley/Newcastle), turn left at rdbt, 2nd left at brow of hill, into Haydon St. Hotel on left

A Victorian property, within easy reach of Newcastle-under-Lyme. The public rooms are furnished in a style befitting the age and character of the house; several rooms are located in a separate house across the road. The hotel has a good reputation for its food and is popular with locals.

Rooms 17 (1 fmly) **S** £47.50-£75; **D** £57.50-£85 (incl. bkfst)* **Conf** Class 30 Board 30 Thtr 80 **Parking** 52
Notes Civ Wed 80

Manor at Hanchurch

Ⓤ

☎ 01782 643030 & 07703 744479 ⓐ 01782 643714
Newcastle Rd, Hanchurch ST4 8SD
e-mail: info@hanchurchmanor.co.uk
dir: A519, follow through lights & under M6 bridge. Hotel immediately on right

Currently the rating for this establishment is not confirmed. This may be due to a change of ownership or because it has only recently joined the AA rating scheme. For further details please see the AA website: www.theAA.com

Rooms 7 (1 fmly) **S** £100-£150; **D** £125-£350 (incl. bkfst)* **Facilities** FTV Fishing ♫ Xmas New Year Wi-fi
Conf Class 24 Board 12 Thtr 30 Del from £224 to £444*
Parking 36 **Notes** LB ⊗ No children 12yrs RS Sun & Mon night Civ Wed 40

George

Ⓤ

☎ 01782 577544 ⓐ 01782 837496
Swan Square, Burslem ST6 2AE
e-mail: reception@georgehotelstoke.com
dir: A527 towards Tunstall/Burslem, follow sign at rdbt for Burslem. After Ceramica in town centre, at main lights turn right 200mtrs. Hotel on right

Currently the rating for this establishment is not confirmed. This may be due to a change of ownership or because it has only recently joined the AA rating scheme. For further details please see the AA website: www.theAA.com

Rooms 39 (3 fmly) **Facilities** ♫ Xmas New Year Wi-fi
Conf Class 100 Board 75 Thtr 170 Del from £85 to £115*
Services Lift **Parking** 15 **Notes** Civ Wed 150

Express by Holiday Inn Stoke-on-Trent

BUDGET HOTEL

☎ 01782 377000 ⓐ 01782 377037
Sir Stanley Matthews Way, Trentham Lakes ST4 4EG
e-mail: stokeontrent@expressholidayinn.co.uk
web: www.hiexpress.com/stoke-on-trent
dir: M6 junct 15, follow signs for Uttoxeter/Derby which leads to A50. Hotel adjacent to Britannia Stadium

A modern hotel ideal for families and business travellers. Fresh and uncomplicated, the spacious rooms include Sky TV, power shower and tea and coffee-making facilities. Continental buffet breakfast is included in the room rate; other meals may be taken at the nearby family pub or restaurant. See also the Hotel Groups pages.

Rooms 123 (73 fmly) **Conf** Class 16 Board 18 Thtr 35

Innkeeper's Lodge Stoke-on-Trent

BUDGET HOTEL

☎ 0845 112 6074 ⓐ 0845 112 6229
Longton Rd ST4 8BU
web: www.innkeeperslodge.com/stokeontrent
dir: M6 junct 15, A500 to slip road for A34 towards Stone. At rdbt take left onto A5035. Lodge 0.5m on right

Innkeeper's Lodge represents an exciting, high value concept within the budget hotel market. Comfortable bedrooms provide excellent facilities that include satellite TV and modem points. Options include family rooms, and for the corporate guest, cutting edge IT which includes Wi-fi access. A popular Carvery provides all-day food, including an extensive, complimentary continental breakfast.

Rooms 30 (8 fmly) **S** £58; **D** £58 (incl. bkfst)

Weathervane

BUDGET HOTEL

☎ 01782 388799 ⓐ 01782 388804
Lysander Rd ST3 7WA
e-mail: 5305@greenking.co.uk
web: www.oldenglish.co.uk

A few minutes from A50 and convenient for both the city and industrial areas, this popular, modern pub and restaurant, under the 'Hungry Horse' brand, provides hearty, well-cooked food at reasonable prices. Adjacent bedrooms are furnished for both commercial and leisure customers. See also the Hotel Groups pages.

Rooms 39 (8 fmly) (18 GF) **Conf** Class 20 Board 20 Thtr 20

STONE — Map 10 SJ93

Crown

★★★ 74% HOTEL

☎ 01785 813535 🖷 01785 815942
38 High St ST15 8AS
e-mail: info@stonehotels.co.uk
dir: M6 junct 14, A34 N to Stone. M6 junct 15, A34 S to Stone

A former coaching inn within the town centre where staff are helpful and friendly. The hotel has a glass domed restaurant that offers a choice of menus, and the front lounge is delightfully furnished. Bedrooms, some of which are located in a separate building, are well equipped and comfortable.

Rooms 29 (16 annexe) (2 fmly) (8 GF) **S** £59-£110; **D** £59-£120* **Conf** Class 80 Board 60 Thtr 150 **Parking** 40 **Notes** ⊗ Civ Wed 100

Stone House

★★★ 71% HOTEL

OXFORD
HOTELS & INNS

☎ 01785 815531 🖷 01785 814764
Stafford Rd ST15 0BQ
e-mail: reservations.stone@ohiml.com
web: www.oxfordhotelsandinns.com
dir: M6 junct 14 (N) or junct 15 (S). Hotel on A34

This former country house, set in attractive grounds, is located within easy reach of the M6. Attractive comfortable bedrooms and tastefully appointed public areas together with leisure and conference facilities make the hotel popular with both corporate and leisure guests. A light menu is offered in the bar and lounge areas, or guests can choose to dine in the stylish restaurant.

Rooms 50 (1 fmly) (15 GF) **S** £65-£86; **D** £70-£93 (incl. bkfst)* **Facilities** ⓢ supervised Gym New Year **Conf** Class 80 Board 60 Thtr 150 Del from £97.50 to £125* **Parking** 100 **Notes** LB ⊗ Civ Wed 60

TALKE — Map 15 SJ85

Travelodge Stoke Talke

BUDGET HOTEL

☎ 0871 9846106 🖷 01782 777000
Newcastle Rd ST7 1UP
web: www.travelodge.co.uk
dir: at junct of A34/A500

Travelodge offers good quality, good value, modern accommodation. Ideal for families, the spacious en suite bedrooms include remote-control TV, tea and coffee-making facilities and comfortable beds. Meals can be taken at the nearby family restaurant. See also the Hotel Groups pages.

Rooms 62 **S** fr £29; **D** fr £29 **Conf** Class 25 Board 32 Thtr 50

TAMWORTH — Map 10 SK20

Drayton Court Hotel

★★ 80% HOTEL

☎ 01827 285805 🖷 01827 284842
65 Coleshill St, Fazeley B78 3RG
e-mail: draytoncthotel@yahoo.co.uk
web: www.draytoncourthotel.co.uk
dir: M42 junct 9, A446 to Lichfield, at next rdbt right onto A4091. 2m, Drayton Manor Theme Park on left. Hotel on right

Conveniently located close to the M42, this lovingly restored hotel offers bedrooms that are elegant and have been thoughtfully equipped to suit both business and leisure guests. Beds are particularly comfortable, and one room has a four-poster. Public areas include a panelled bar, a relaxing lounge and an attractive restaurant.

Rooms 19 (3 fmly) **S** £60-£75; **D** £75-£105 (incl. bkfst) **Facilities** Wi-fi **Conf** Board 12 **Parking** 22 **Notes** ⊗ Closed 22 Dec-1 Jan

Travelodge Tamworth (M42)

BUDGET HOTEL

☎ 0871 984 6109 & 0800 850950 🖷 01827 260145
Green Ln B77 5PS
web: www.travelodge.co.uk
dir: A5/M42 junct 10

Travelodge offers good quality, good value, modern accommodation. Ideal for families, the spacious en suite bedrooms include remote-control TV, tea and coffee-making facilities and comfortable beds. Meals can be taken at the nearby family restaurant. See also the Hotel Groups pages.

Rooms 62 **S** fr £29; **D** fr £29

UTTOXETER — Map 10 SK03

Travelodge Uttoxeter

BUDGET HOTEL

☎ 0871 984 6114 🖷 01889 562043
Ashbourne Rd ST14 5AA
web: www.travelodge.co.uk
dir: on A50/B5030

Travelodge offers good quality, good value, modern accommodation. Ideal for families, the spacious en suite bedrooms include remote-control TV, tea and coffee-making facilities and comfortable beds. Meals can be taken at the nearby family restaurant. See also the Hotel Groups pages.

Rooms 32 **S** fr £29; **D** fr £29

SUFFOLK

ALDEBURGH — Map 13 TM45

Wentworth

★★★ 88% ⊛⊛ HOTEL

☎ 01728 452312 🖷 01728 454343
Wentworth Rd IP15 5BD
e-mail: stay@wentworth-aldeburgh.co.uk
web: www.wentworth-aldeburgh.com
dir: off A12 onto A1094, 6m to Aldeburgh, with church on left, left at bottom of hill

A delightful privately owned hotel overlooking the beach. The attractive, well-maintained public rooms include three stylish lounges as well as a cocktail bar and elegant restaurant. Bedrooms are smartly decorated with co-ordinated fabrics and have many thoughtful touches; some rooms have superb sea views. Several very spacious Mediterranean-style rooms are located across the road.

Rooms 35 (7 annexe) (5 GF) **S** £56-£100; **D** £96-£224 (incl. bkfst)* **Facilities** FTV Xmas New Year Wi-fi **Conf** Class 12 Board 12 Thtr 15 **Parking** 30 **Notes** LB

See advert on opposite page

The Brudenell

★★★ 86% ⊛⊛ HOTEL

☎ 01728 452071 🖷 01728 454082
The Parade IP15 5BU
e-mail: info@brudenellhotel.co.uk
dir: A12/A1094, on reaching town, turn right at junct into High St. Hotel on seafront adjoining Fort Green car park

Situated at the far end of the town centre just a step away from the beach, this hotel has a contemporary appearance, enhanced by subtle lighting and quality soft furnishings. Many of the bedrooms have superb sea views; they include deluxe rooms with king-sized beds and superior rooms suitable for families.

Holiday Inn

U

☎ 01473 272244   📠 01473 272484
3 The Havens, Ransomes Europark IP3 9SJ
e-mail: malcolm.allen@kewgreencourt.co.uk
web: www.holidayinn.co.uk
dir: off A14 Ipswich Bypass at 1st junct after Orwell
Bridge signed Ransomes Europark. Hotel faces slip road

Currently the rating for this establishment is not confirmed.
This may be due to a change of ownership or because it has
only recently joined the AA rating scheme. For further
details please see the AA website: www.theAA.com

Rooms 60 (2 fmly) (30 GF) (16 smoking) **S** £45-£145;
D £45-£145 **Facilities** STV Gym Xmas New Year Wi-fi
Conf Class 70 Board 55 Thtr 160 Del from £99 to £145
Services Lift **Parking** 100 **Notes** LB ⊗ Civ Wed 110

Holiday Inn Ipswich

U

☎ 0870 400 9045   📠 01473 680412
London Rd IP2 0UA
e-mail: reservations-ipswich@ichotelsgroup.com
web: www.holidayinn.co.uk

Currently the rating for this establishment is not confirmed.
This may be due to a change of ownership or because it has
only recently joined the AA rating scheme. For further
details please see the AA website: www.theAA.com

Rooms 108 **Notes** ⊗

Express by Holiday Inn Ipswich

BUDGET HOTEL

☎ 01473 222279   📠 01473 222297
Adj to the Beagle Vintage Inn, Old Hadleigh Rd,
Sproughton IP8 3AR
e-mail: ebhi-ipswich@btconnect.com
web: www.hiexpress.com/ipswich
dir: from A12/A14 junct follow town centre signs on
A1214. At lights at hotel, left onto A1071. At mini rdbt
right onto B113. Hotel on right

A modern hotel ideal for families and business travellers.
Fresh and uncomplicated, the spacious rooms include Sky
TV, power shower and tea and coffee-making facilities.
Continental buffet breakfast is included in the room rate;
other meals may be taken at the nearby family pub or
restaurant. See also the Hotel Groups pages.

Rooms 49 (20 fmly) **Conf** Class 12 Board 16 Thtr 30

Travelodge Ipswich Capel St Mary

BUDGET HOTEL

☎ 08719 846 042   📠 0870 1911542
Capel St Mary IP9 2JP
web: www.travelodge.co.uk
dir: 5m S on A12

Travelodge offers good quality, good value, modern
accommodation. Ideal for families, the spacious en suite
bedrooms include remote-control TV, tea and coffee-
making facilities and comfortable beds. Meals can be
taken at the nearby family restaurant. See also the Hotel
Groups pages.

Rooms 32 **S** fr £29; **D** fr £29

KESGRAVE

Milsoms Kesgrave Hall

U

Hall Rd IP5 2PU
e-mail: enquiries@kesgravehall.com
web: www.kesgravehall.com
dir: A12 N of Ipswich, left at Ipswich/Woodbridge rdbt
onto B1214. Right after 0.5m into Hall Rd. Hotel 200yds
on left

Currently the rating for this establishment is not confirmed.
This may be due to a change of ownership or because it has
only recently joined the AA rating scheme. For further
details please see the AA website: www.theAA.com

Rooms 15 (4 fmly) (2 GF) **S** £90-£135; **D** £110-£185*
Facilities STV Xmas Wi-fi **Conf** Board 24 **Parking** 100

LAVENHAM   Map 13 TL94

The Swan

★★★★ 81% ◎◎ HOTEL

☎ 01787 247477   📠 01787 248286
High St CO10 9QA
e-mail: info@theswanatlavenham.co.uk
web: www.theswanatlavenham.co.uk
dir: from A12 or A14 onto A134, then B1071 to Lavenham

A delightful collection of listed buildings dating back to
the 14th century, lovingly restored to retain their original
charm. Public rooms include comfortable lounge areas, a
charming rustic bar, an informal brasserie and a fine-
dining restaurant. Bedrooms are tastefully furnished and
equipped with many thoughtful touches. The friendly
staff are helpful, attentive and offer professional service.

Rooms 46 (4 fmly) (11 GF) **S** £85-£105; **D** £95-£115 (incl.
bkfst & dinner)* **Facilities** STV FTV Xmas Wi-fi
Conf Class 36 Board 30 Thtr 50 **Parking** 62
Notes Civ Wed 100

Lavenham Great House 'Restaurant With Rooms'

◎◎ RESTAURANT WITH ROOMS

☎ 01787 247431   📠 01787 248007
Market Place CO10 9QZ
e-mail: info@greathouse.co.uk
dir: Off A1141 onto Market Ln, behind cross on Market
Place

The 18th-century front on Market Place conceals a 15th-
century timber-framed building that houses a restaurant
with rooms. The Great House has recently undergone
major refurbishment, and remains a pocket of France
offering high-quality rural cuisine served by French staff.
The spacious bedrooms are individually decorated and
thoughtfully equipped with many useful extras; some
rooms have a separate lounge area.

Rooms 5 (4 en suite) (1 fmly)

LONG MELFORD — Map 13 TL84

The Black Lion

★★★ 81% ⊛ HOTEL

☎ 01787 312356 📠 01787 374557
Church Walk, The Green CO10 9DN
e-mail: enquiries@blacklionhotel.net
web: www.blacklionhotel.net
dir: at junct of A134 & A1092

This charming 15th-century hotel is situated on the edge
of this bustling town overlooking the green. Bedrooms are
generally spacious and each is attractively decorated,
tastefully furnished and equipped with useful extras. An
interesting range of dishes is served in the lounge bar or
guests may choose to dine from the same innovative
menu in the more formal restaurant.

Rooms 10 (1 fmly) **D** £120-£195 (incl. bkfst)*
Facilities Xmas New Year Wi-fi Child facilities
Conf Class 28 Board 28 Thtr 50 **Parking** 10 **Notes** LB
Civ Wed 50

The Bull

★★★ Ⓐ HOTEL

☎ 01787 378494 📠 01787 880307
Hall St CO10 9JG
e-mail: bull.longmelford@greeneking.co.uk
web: www.oldenglish.co.uk
dir: 3m N of Sudbury on A134

Rooms 25 (4 fmly) **Facilities** Xmas **Conf** Class 40
Board 30 Thtr 100 **Parking** 35 **Notes** LB ⊗ Civ Wed 100

LOWESTOFT — Map 13 TM59

Ivy House Country Hotel

★★★ 82% ⊛⊛ HOTEL

☎ 01502 501353 & 588144 📠 01502 501539
Ivy Ln, Beccles Rd, Oulton Broad NR33 8HY
e-mail: aa@ivyhousecountryhotel.co.uk
web: www.ivyhousecountryhotel.co.uk
dir: on A146 SW of Oulton Broad turn into Ivy Ln beside
Esso petrol station. Over railway bridge, follow private
drive

Peacefully located, family-run hotel set in three acres of
mature landscaped grounds just a short walk from Oulton
Broad. Public rooms include an 18th-century thatched
barn restaurant where an interesting choice of dishes is
served. The attractively decorated bedrooms are housed
in garden wings, and many have lovely views of the
grounds to the countryside beyond.

Rooms 20 (20 annexe) (1 fmly) (17 GF) **S** £99-£115;
D £135-£170 (incl. bkfst)* **Facilities** FTV Reduced rates
at nearby leisure club Wi-fi **Conf** Board 22 Thtr 55
Del from £135 to £155* **Parking** 50 **Notes** LB Closed 23
Dec-6 Jan Civ Wed 80

Hotel Victoria

★★★ 80% HOTEL

☎ 01502 574433 📠 01502 501529
Kirkley Cliff NR33 0BZ
e-mail: info@thehotelvictoria.co.uk
dir: A12 to seafront on one-way system signed A12
Ipswich. Hotel on seafront just beyond thatched cottage

Attractive Victorian building situated on the esplanade
overlooking the sea and has direct access to the beach.
Bedrooms are pleasantly decorated and thoughtfully
equipped; many rooms have sea views. Public rooms
include modern conference and banqueting facilities, a
choice of lounges, a comfortable bar and a restaurant,
which overlooks the pretty garden.

Rooms 24 (4 fmly) **Facilities** Xmas New Year Wi-fi
Conf Class 150 Board 50 Thtr 200 **Services** Lift
Parking 45 **Notes** ⊗ Civ Wed 200

Carlton Manor

★★★ 77% ⊛ HOTEL

☎ 01502 566511 📠 01502 581847
Chapel Rd, Carlton Colville NR33 8BL
e-mail: reservations@thecarltonmanor.com
web: www.thecarltonmanor.com
dir: off A146 Beccles/Lowestoft follow signs to Carlton
Manor & Transport Museum

Expect a warm welcome at this delightful hotel which is
situated on the outskirts of town. The spacious public
areas include a smart lounge bar, an intimate restaurant
and a further seating area with plush sofas. Bedrooms
are tastefully decorated and equipped with a good range
of useful extras.

Rooms 14 (2 fmly) (8 GF) **Facilities** Xmas New Year Wi-fi **Conf** Class 150 Board 70 Thtr 150 **Parking** 200 **Notes** ⊗ Civ Wed 70

MILDENHALL Map 12 TL77

Riverside Hotel, Bar and Restaurant

★★★ 73% HOTEL

☎ 01638 717274 📄 01638 715997
Mill St IP28 7DP
e-mail: reservations.riverside@ohiml.com
web: www.oxfordhotelsandinns.com
dir: M11 junct 9 onto A11, at Fiveways rdbt take A1101 signed Milenhall, straight over rdbt, left onto High St for 0.5m onto Mill St, hotel on left before bridge

An 18th-century, red brick building situated in the heart of this charming town on the banks of the River Lark. Public rooms include a smart restaurant, which overlooks the river and the attractive gardens at the rear. The smartly decorated bedrooms have co-ordinated soft furnishings and many thoughtful touches.

Rooms 22 (6 annexe) (3 fmly) (4 GF) **Facilities** Xmas New Year Wi-fi **Conf** Class 50 Board 30 Thtr 120 **Services** Lift **Parking** 35 **Notes** Civ Wed 100

NEEDHAM MARKET Map 13 TM05

Travelodge Ipswich Beacon Hill

BUDGET HOTEL

☎ 08719 846 041 📄 01449 721640
Beacon Hill IP6 8LP
web: www.travelodge.co.uk
dir: A14/A140

Travelodge offers good quality, good value, modern accommodation. Ideal for families, the spacious en suite bedrooms include remote-control TV, tea and coffee-making facilities and comfortable beds. Meals can be taken at the nearby family restaurant. See also the Hotel Groups pages.

Rooms 40 **S** fr £29; **D** fr £29

NEWMARKET Map 12 TL66

Bedford Lodge Hotel

★★★★ 81% ◉◉ HOTEL

☎ 01638 663175 📄 01638 667391
Bury Rd CB8 7BX
e-mail: info@bedfordlodgehotel.co.uk
web: www.bedfordlodgehotel.co.uk
dir: from town centre take A1304 towards Bury St Edmunds, hotel 0.5m on left

Imposing 18th-century Georgian hunting lodge set in three acres of secluded landscaped gardens. Public rooms feature the elegant Orangery restaurant, a smart lounge bar and a small lounge. The hotel also features superb leisure facilities and self-contained conference and banqueting suites. Contemporary bedrooms have a light, airy feel, and each is tastefully furnished and well equipped.

Rooms 55 (3 fmly) (16 GF) (3 smoking) **S** £110-£220; **D** £130-£325 (incl. bkfst)* **Facilities** FTV ⟲ Gym Steam room Sauna Xmas New Year Wi-fi **Conf** Class 80 Board 60 Thtr 200 Del from £150 to £195* **Services** Lift **Parking** 120 **Notes** LB ⊗ RS Sat lunch Civ Wed 150

Swynford Paddocks

★★★ 82% ◉ HOTEL

☎ 01638 570234 📄 01638 570283
CB8 0UE
e-mail: info@swynfordpaddocks.com
web: www.swynfordpaddocks.com

(For full entry see Six Mile Bottom, Cambridgeshire)

Rutland Arms

★★★ 79% ◉ HOTEL

☎ 01638 664251 📄 01638 666298
High St CB8 8NB
e-mail: reservations.rutlandarms@ohiml.com
web: www.oxfordhotelsandinns.com
dir: A14 junct 37 onto A142, or M11 junct 9 onto A11 then A1304 - follow signs for town centre

Expect a warm welcome at this former 16th century coaching inn situated in the heart of town. The property is built around a cobbled courtyard and still retains many of its original features. Public rooms include a large lounge bar and Carriages, a contemporary restaurant and wine bar. Bedrooms are smartly appointed and well equipped.

Rooms 46 (1 fmly) **S** £50-£115; **D** £70-£175 (incl. bkfst)* **Facilities** Wi-fi **Conf** Class 40 Board 30 Thtr 70 Del from £105 to £125* **Parking** 40 **Notes** LB ⊗

Best Western Heath Court

★★★ 78% HOTEL

☎ 01638 667171 📄 01638 666533
Moulton Rd CB8 8DY
e-mail: quality@heathcourthotel.com
dir: leave A14 at Newmarket & Ely exit onto A142. Follow town centre signs over mini rdbt. At clocktower left into Moulton Rd

Modern red-brick hotel situated close to Newmarket Heath and perfectly placed for the town centre. Public rooms include a choice of dining options - informal meals can be taken in the lounge bar or a modern carte menu is offered in the restaurant. The smartly presented bedrooms are mostly spacious and some have air conditioning.

Rooms 41 (2 fmly) **S** £55-£105; **D** £60-£120* **Facilities** STV Health & beauty salon New Year Wi-fi **Conf** Class 50 Board 40 Thtr 130 Del from £95 to £145* **Services** Lift **Parking** 60 **Notes** LB Civ Wed 80

ORFORD   Map 13 TM45

The Crown & Castle

★★ 85% ◉◉ HOTEL

☎ 01394 450205
IP12 2LJ
e-mail: info@crownandcastle.co.uk
web: www.crownandcastle.co.uk
dir: turn right from B1084 on entering village, towards
castle

Delightful inn situated adjacent to the Norman castle
keep. Contemporary style bedrooms are spilt between the
main house and the garden wing; the latter are more
spacious and have patios with access to the garden. The
restaurant has an informal atmosphere with polished
tables and local artwork; the menu features quality,
locally sourced produce.

Rooms 19 (12 annexe) (1 fmly) (11 GF) **S** £92-£124;
D £115-£155 (incl. bkfst)* **Facilities** Xmas New Year
Wi-fi **Conf** Board 10 **Parking** 20 **Notes** LB No children
9yrs Closed 5-8 Jan

SOUTHWOLD   Map 13 TM57

Swan

★★★ 81% ◉◉ HOTEL

☎ 01502 722186 📠 01502 724800
Market Place IP18 6EG
e-mail: swan.hotel@adnams.co.uk
dir: A1095 to Southwold. Hotel in town centre. Parking via
archway to left of building

A charming 17th-century coaching inn situated in the
heart of this bustling town centre overlooking the market
place. Public rooms feature an elegant restaurant, a
comfortable drawing room, a cosy bar and a lounge where
guests can enjoy afternoon tea. The spacious bedrooms are
attractively decorated, tastefully furnished and
thoughtfully equipped.

Rooms 42 (17 annexe) (17 GF) **S** £50-£98; **D** £80-£220
(incl. bkfst) **Facilities** Xmas New Year **Conf** Class 24
Board 12 Thtr 40 Del from £150 to £180 **Services** Lift
Parking 35 **Notes** LB Civ Wed 40

The Crown

★★ 85% ◉ HOTEL

☎ 01502 722275 📠 01502 727263
90 High St IP18 6DP
e-mail: crown.hotel@adnams.co.uk
dir: A12 onto A1095 to Southwold. Hotel on left in High
Street

Delightful old posting inn situated in the heart of this
bustling town. The property combines a pub, wine bar
and restaurant with superb accommodation. The
tastefully decorated bedrooms have attractive co-
ordinated soft furnishings and many thoughtful touches.
Public rooms feature an elegant lounge and a back room
bar serving traditional Adnams ales.

Rooms 14 (2 fmly) **S** £86-£96; **D** £132-£212 (incl. bkfst)*
Facilities Xmas New Year **Conf** Board 8 **Parking** 15
Notes LB ⊗

Blyth

★★ 85% SMALL HOTEL

☎ 01502 722632 & 0845 348 6867 📠 01502 724123
Station Rd IP18 6AY
e-mail: reception@blythhotel.com

Expect a warm welcome at this delightful family run hotel
which is situated just a short walk from the town centre.
The spacious public rooms include a smart residents'
lounge, an open-plan bar and a large restaurant.
Bedrooms are tastefully appointed with co-ordinated
fabrics and have many thoughtful touches.

Rooms 13 **S** £65-£75; **D** £100-£140 (incl. bkfst)*
Facilities FTV Xmas New Year Wi-fi **Parking** 8 **Notes** LB

Sutherland House

◉◉ RESTAURANT WITH ROOMS

☎ 01502 724544
56 High St IP18 6DN
e-mail: enquiries@sutherlandhouse.co.uk
dir: A1095 into Southwold, on High St on left after
Victoria St

Expect a warm welcome at this delightful 16th-century
house situated in the heart of the bustling town centre.
The property has a wealth of original character that
includes oak beams, exposed brickwork, open fireplaces
and two superb ornate plasterwork ceilings. The stylish
bedrooms are tastefully decorated, have co-ordinated
fabrics and many thoughtful touches. Public rooms
feature a large open-plan contemporary style restaurant
with plush furniture.

Rooms 4 (4 en suite) (1 fmly)

STOWMARKET   Map 13 TM05

Cedars

★★★ 71% HOTEL

THE INDEPENDENTS
HOTEL ASSOCIATION

☎ 01449 612668 📠 01449 674704
Needham Rd IP14 2AJ
e-mail: info@cedarshotel.co.uk
dir: A14 junct 15, A1120 towards Stowmarket. At
junct with A1113 turn right. Hotel on right

Expect a friendly welcome at this privately owned hotel,
which is situated just off the A14 within easy reach of the
town centre. Public rooms are full of charm and character
with features such as exposed beams and open
fireplaces. Bedrooms are pleasantly decorated and
thoughtfully equipped with modern facilities.

Rooms 25 (3 fmly) (9 GF) **S** fr £65; **D** fr £72 (incl. bkfst)*
Facilities Wi-fi **Conf** Class 60 Board 40 Thtr 150
Del from £85* **Parking** 75 **Notes** LB Closed 25 Dec-1 Jan

Travelodge Ipswich Stowmarket

BUDGET HOTEL

Travelodge

☎ 08719 846 043 📠 01449 615347
IP14 3PY
web: www.travelodge.co.uk
dir: on A14 westbound

Travelodge offers good quality, good value, modern
accommodation. Ideal for families, the spacious en suite
bedrooms include remote-control TV, tea and coffee-
making facilities and comfortable beds. Meals can be
taken at the nearby family restaurant. See also the Hotel
Groups pages.

Rooms 40 **S** fr £29; **D** fr £29

THORPENESS
Map 13 TM45

Thorpeness Hotel

★★★ 77% HOTEL

☎ 01728 452176 ▤ 01728 453868
Lakeside Av IP16 4NH
e-mail: info@thorpeness.co.uk
web: www.thorpeness.co.uk
dir: A1094 towards Aldeburgh, then coast road north for 2m

Ideally situated in an unspoilt, tranquil setting close to Aldeburgh and Snape Maltings. The extensive public rooms include a choice of lounges, a restaurant, a smart bar, a snooker room and clubhouse. The spacious bedrooms are pleasantly decorated, tastefully furnished and equipped with modern facilities. An 18-hole golf course and tennis courts are also available.

Rooms 30 (30 annexe) (10 fmly) (10 GF) **S** £81–£113; **D** £92–£156 (incl. bkfst)* **Facilities** ⅃ 18 ⚲ Putt green Fishing Cycle hire Rowing boat hire Birdwatching Xmas New Year Wi-fi **Conf** Class 30 Board 24 Thtr 130 **Parking** 60 **Notes** LB Civ Wed 130

WESTLETON
Map 13 TM46

Westleton Crown

★★★ 77% ◉◉ HOTEL

☎ 01728 648777 ▤ 01728 648239
The Street IP17 3AD
e-mail: reception@westletoncrown.co.uk
web: www.westletoncrown.co.uk
dir: A12 N, turn right for Westleton just after Yoxford. Hotel opposite on entering Westleton

Charming coaching inn situated in a peaceful village location just a few minutes from the A12. Public rooms include a smart, award-winning restaurant, comfortable lounge, and busy bar with exposed beams and open fireplaces. The stylish bedrooms are tastefully decorated and equipped with many thoughtful little extras.

Rooms 25 (3 annexe) (3 fmly) (8 GF) **S** £85–£95; **D** £95–£160 (incl. bkfst) **Facilities** Xmas New Year Wi-fi **Conf** Class 40 Board 30 Thtr 60 **Parking** 26 **Notes** Closed 25 Dec

WOODBRIDGE
Map 13 TM24

Seckford Hall

★★★ 81% ◉◉ HOTEL

☎ 01394 385678 ▤ 01394 380610
IP13 6NU
e-mail: reception@seckford.co.uk
web: www.seckford.co.uk
dir: signed on A12. (Do not follow signs for town centre)

An elegant Tudor manor house set amid landscaped grounds just off the A12. It is reputed that Queen Elizabeth I visited this property, and it retains much of its original character. Public rooms include a superb panelled lounge, a cosy bar and an intimate restaurant. The spacious bedrooms are attractively decorated, tastefully furnished and thoughtfully equipped.

Rooms 32 (10 annexe) (4 fmly) (7 GF) **S** £85–£145; **D** £140–£215 (incl. bkfst)* **Facilities** ⚲ ⅃ 18 Putt green Fishing Gym Beauty salon New Year Wi-fi **Conf** Class 46 Board 40 Thtr 100 Del from £160 to £180* **Parking** 100 **Notes** LB Closed 25 Dec Civ Wed 120

Best Western Ufford Park Hotel Golf & Leisure

★★★ 78% HOTEL

☎ 01394 383555 ▤ 0844 4773727
Yarmouth Rd, Ufford IP12 1QW
e-mail: mail@uffordpark.co.uk
web: www.uffordpark.co.uk
dir: A12 N to A1152, in Melton left at lights, follow B1438, hotel 1m on right

A modern hotel set in open countryside boasting superb leisure facilities including a challenging golf course. The spacious public rooms provide a wide choice of areas in which to relax and include a busy lounge bar, a carvery restaurant and the Vista Restaurant. Bedrooms are smartly appointed and pleasantly decorated, each thoughtfully equipped; many rooms overlook the golf course.

Rooms 87 (20 fmly) (32 GF) **S** £90–£120; **D** £110–£170 (incl. bkfst)* **Facilities** Spa FTV ⚲ supervised ⅃ 18 ⚲ Putt green Fishing Gym Golf Academy with PGA tuition 32 bay floodlit driving range Dance Studio Xmas New Year Wi-fi **Conf** Class 80 Board 80 Thtr 200 Del from £116* **Services** Lift **Parking** 250 **Notes** LB ✖ Civ Wed 120

YAXLEY
Map 13 TM17

The Auberge

◉◉ RESTAURANT WITH ROOMS

☎ 01379 783604 ▤ 01379 788486
Ipswich Rd IP23 8BZ
e-mail: deestenhouse@fsmail.net
dir: On A140 between Norwich & Ipswich at B1117 x-rds Eye/Stadbloke

A warm welcome awaits at this charming 15th-century property, which has been lovingly converted by the present owners into a smart restaurant with rooms. The public areas have a wealth of character, such as exposed brickwork and beams. The spacious bedrooms are tastefully appointed and have many thoughtful touches.

Rooms 4 (2 GF)

YOXFORD
Map 13 TM36

Satis House

★★★ 86% ◉◉ COUNTRY HOUSE HOTEL

☎ 01728 668418 ▤ 01728 668640
IP17 3EX
e-mail: enquiries@satishouse.co.uk
web: www.satishouse.co.uk
dir: off A12 between Ipswich & Lowestoft. 9m E Aldeburgh & Snape

Expect a warm welcome from the caring hosts at this delightful 18th-century, Grade II listed property set in three acres of parkland. The stylish public areas have a really relaxed atmosphere; they include a choice of dining rooms, a smart bar and a cosy lounge. The individually decorated bedrooms are tastefully appointed and thoughtfully equipped.

Rooms 8 (1 annexe) (1 fmly) (1 GF) **S** £60–£125; **D** £90–£155 (incl. bkfst)* **Facilities** STV FTV Xmas New Year **Conf** Class 40 Board 40 Thtr 40 **Parking** 30 **Notes** LB Civ Wed 30

SURREY

BAGSHOT
Map 6 SU96

INSPECTORS' CHOICE

Pennyhill Park Hotel & The Spa

★★★★★ ⚜⚜⚜ COUNTRY HOUSE HOTEL

☎ 01276 471774 🖷 01276 473217
London Rd GU19 5EU
e-mail: enquiries@pennyhillpark.co.uk
web: www.exclusivehotels.co.uk
dir: on A30 between Bagshot & Camberley

This delightful country-house hotel set in 120-acre grounds provides every modern comfort. The stylish bedrooms are individually designed and have impressive bathrooms. The award-winning Latymer Restaurant is among the range of dining options and there is a choice of lounges and bars. Leisure facilities include a jogging trail, a golf course and a state-of-the-art spa with a thermal sequencing experience, ozone treated swimming and hydrotherapy pools along with a comprehensive range of therapies and treatments.

Rooms 123 (97 annexe) (6 fmly) (26 GF)
D £250-£925* **Facilities** Spa STV ⓣ ⤵ ⚶ 9 ⚬ Fishing ⚲ Gym Archery Clay shooting Plunge pool Turkish steam room Rugby/football pitch ♫ Xmas New Year Wi-fi **Conf** Class 80 Board 60 Thtr 160 Del from £265 to £375* **Services** Lift **Parking** 500 **Notes** LB Civ Wed 140

CAMBERLEY
Map 6 SU86

See also **Yateley (Hampshire)**

Macdonald Frimley Hall Hotel & Spa

★★★★ 78% ⚜⚜ HOTEL

☎ 0844 879 9110 🖷 01276 670362
Lime Av GU15 2BG
e-mail: sales.frimleyhall@macdonald-hotels.co.uk
web: www.macdonaldhotels.co.uk/frimleyhall
dir: M3 junct 3, A321 follow Bagshot signs. Through lights, left onto A30 signed Camberley & Basingstoke. To rdbt, 2nd exit onto A325, take 5th right

The epitome of classic English elegance this ivy-clad Victorian manor house is set in two acres of immaculate grounds in the heart of Surrey. The bedrooms and public areas are smart and feature a modern decorative theme. The hotel boasts an impressive health club and spa with treatment rooms, a fully equipped gym and heated indoor swimming pool.

Rooms 98 (15 fmly) **S** £80-£239; **D** £80-£239 (incl. bkfst) **Facilities** Spa STV ⓣ Gym Beauty treatment rooms Technogym Sauna Steam room Relaxation Xmas New Year Wi-fi **Conf** Class 100 Board 60 Thtr 250 Del from £210 to £300 **Parking** 150 **Notes** LB Civ Wed 220

Lakeside International

★★★ 70% HOTEL

☎ 01252 838000 🖷 01252 837857
Wharf Rd, Frimley Green GU16 6JR
e-mail: info@lakesideinthotel.com
dir: off A321 at mini-rdbt turn into Wharf Rd. Lakeside complex on right

This hotel, geared towards the business market, enjoys a lakeside location with noteworthy views. Bedrooms are modern, comfortable and with a range of facilities. Public areas are spacious and include a residents' lounge, bar and games room, a smart restaurant and an established health and leisure club.

Rooms 98 (1 fmly) (31 GF) **Facilities** ⓣ Gym Squash Wi-fi **Conf** Class 100 Board 40 Thtr 120 **Services** Lift **Parking** 250 **Notes** ⊗ Civ Wed 100

Travelodge Camberley

BUDGET HOTEL

☎ 08719 846 315 🖷 01276 82839
507-537 London Rd GU15 3UR
web: www.travelodge.co.uk
dir: A30 for 3m

Travelodge offers good quality, good value, modern accommodation. Ideal for families, the spacious en suite bedrooms include remote-control TV, tea and coffee-making facilities and comfortable beds. Meals can be taken at the nearby family restaurant. See also the Hotel Groups pages.

Rooms 66 **S** fr £29; **D** £29

CATERHAM
Map 6 TQ35

Travelodge Caterham Whyteleafe

BUDGET HOTEL

☎ 08719 846 317 🖷 01883 627581
431 Godstone Rd, Whyteleaf CR3 0BF
web: www.travelodge.co.uk
dir: A22 towards London. Straight over at rdbt to Whyteleafe, 1m. Right across carriageway to car park

Travelodge offers good quality, good value, modern accommodation. Ideal for families, the spacious en suite bedrooms include remote-control TV, tea and coffee-making facilities and comfortable beds. Meals can be taken at the nearby family restaurant. See also the Hotel Groups pages.

Rooms 60 **S** fr £29; **D** fr £29

CHERTSEY
Map 6 TQ06

Bridge

Ⓤ

folio Hotels

☎ 01932 565644 🖷 01932 565692
Bridge Rd KT16 8JZ
e-mail: reservations.bridge@foliohotels.com
web: www.foliohotels.com/bridgehotel
dir: M25 junct 11, follow Chertsey/A317 signs. At 1st rdbt follow Chertsey/A387 signs. To dual carriageway, straight over at lights to T-junct. Right onto B375 signed Shepperton. Hotel 300mtrs on left immediately before bridge

Currently the rating for this establishment is not confirmed. This may be due to a change of ownership or because it has only recently joined the AA rating scheme. For further details please see the AA website: www.theAA.com

Rooms 37 (14 fmly) (5 GF) (37 smoking) **S** £60-£120; **D** £60-£120* **Facilities** FTV ♫ Xmas New Year Wi-fi **Services** Lift **Notes** LB ⊗

CHURT
Map 5 SU83

Best Western Frensham Pond Hotel

★★★ 76% HOTEL

☎ 01252 795161 📠 01252 792631
Bacon Ln GU10 2QB
e-mail: info@frenshampondhotel.co.uk
web: www.frenshampondhotel.co.uk
dir: A3 onto A287. 4m left at 'Beware Horses' sign. Hotel 0.25m

This 15th-century house occupies a superb location on the edge of Frensham Pond. Many bedrooms are a more recent addition; mainly they are spacious, and the superior executive garden annexe rooms have their own patio, air conditioning and flat screen TVs. The contemporary bar and lounge offers a range of snacks, and the leisure club has good facilities.

Rooms 51 (12 annexe) **Facilities** ⊙ supervised Gym Squash Steam room Sauna Xmas New Year **Conf** Class 45 Board 40 Thtr 120 **Parking** 120 **Notes** LB ⊗ Civ Wed 130

DORKING
Map 6 TQ14

Mercure Burford Bridge

Mercure

★★★★ 81% ◉◉ HOTEL

☎ 01306 884561 📠 01306 880386
Burford Bridge, Box Hill RH5 6BX
e-mail: h6635@accor.com
web: www.mercure-uk.com
dir: M25 junct 9/A245 towards Dorking. Hotel within 5m on A24

Steeped in history, this hotel was reputedly where Lord Nelson and Lady Hamilton met for the last time, and it is said that the landscape around the hotel has inspired many poets. The hotel has a contemporary feel throughout. The grounds, running down to the River Mole, are extensive, and there are good transport links to major centres, including London.

Rooms 57 (22 fmly) (3 GF) **Facilities** ⚲ ♫ Xmas New Year Wi-fi **Conf** Class 80 Board 60 Thtr 120 **Parking** 130 **Notes** LB ⊗ Civ Wed 200

Gatton Manor Hotel & Golf Club

★★★ 79% HOTEL

☎ 01306 627555 📠 01306 627713
Standon Ln RH5 5PQ
e-mail: info@gattonmanor.co.uk
web: www.gattonmanor.co.uk

(For full entry see Ockley)

Mercure White Horse

Mercure

★★★ 63% HOTEL

☎ 0870 400 8282 📠 01306 887241
High St RH4 1BE
web: www.mercure-uk.com
dir: M25 junct 9, A24 S towards Dorking. Hotel in town centre

The hotel was first established as an inn in 1750, although parts of the building date back as far as the 15th century. Its town centre location and Dickensian charm have long made this a popular destination for travellers. There's beamed ceilings, open fires and four-poster beds; more contemporary rooms can be found in the garden wing.

Rooms 78 (41 annexe) (2 fmly) (5 GF) **Facilities** Xmas **Conf** Class 30 Board 30 Thtr 50 Del from £140 to £180* **Parking** 73

Travelodge Dorking

BUDGET HOTEL

☎ 08719 846 026 📠 01306 741673
Reigate Rd RH4 1QB
web: www.travelodge.co.uk
dir: 0.5m E of Dorking, on A25

Travelodge offers good quality, good value, modern accommodation. Ideal for families, the spacious en suite bedrooms include remote-control TV, tea and coffee-making facilities and comfortable beds. Meals can be taken at the nearby family restaurant. See also the Hotel Groups pages.

Rooms 55 **S** fr £29; **D** fr £29

EAST HORSLEY
Map 6 TQ05

Ramada Guildford/Leatherhead

Ⓡ RAMADA

★★★ 80% HOTEL

☎ 01483 280500 📠 01483 284222
Guildford Rd KT24 6TB
e-mail: sales.guildford@ramadajarvis.co.uk
web: www.ramadajarvis.co.uk
dir: A25 towards Leatherhead & Dorking. Pass West Horsley, hotel 0.5m on left

With easy access to the M25 the hotel's 19th-century oak beamed exterior conceals a wide range of modern facilities. Bedrooms are comfortably appointed for both business and leisure guests.

Rooms 87 (11 fmly) (20 GF) **S** £75-£191; **D** £75-£207 (incl. bkfst)* **Facilities** FTV Xmas New Year Wi-fi **Conf** Class 70 Board 66 Thtr 170 Del from £145 to £175* **Services** Lift **Parking** 110 **Notes** LB Civ Wed 120

EGHAM
Map 6 TQ07

Runnymede Hotel & Spa

★★★★ 78% HOTEL

☎ 01784 436171 📠 01784 436340
Windsor Rd TW20 0AG
e-mail: info@runnymedehotel.com
web: www.runnymedehotel.com
dir: M25 junct 13, onto A308 towards Windsor

Enjoying a peaceful location beside the River Thames, this large modern hotel, with its excellent range of facilities, balances both leisure and corporate business well. The extensive function suites, together with spacious lounges and stylish, well laid out bedrooms are impressive. Superb spa facilities are available, and the good food and beverage venues offer wonderful river views.

Rooms 180 (19 fmly) **S** £98-£258; **D** £155-£345* **Facilities** Spa STV ⓘ ♨ ♒ Gym Dance studio Children's play area River boat hire Treatment suite ♫ New Year Wi-fi **Conf** Class 250 Board 76 Thtr 300 **Services** Lift Air con **Parking** 280 **Notes** LB ⊗ RS Sat lunch/Sun dinner Civ Wed 140

See advert on page 58

EPSOM
Map 6 TQ26

Chalk Lane Hotel

★★★ 77% ◉◉ HOTEL

☎ 01372 721179 📠 01372 727878
Chalk Ln, Woodcote End KT18 7BB
e-mail: smcgregor@chalklanehotel.com
web: www.chalklanehotel.com
dir: M25 junct 9 onto A24 to Epsom. Right at lights by BP garage. Left into Avenue Rd, right into Worple Rd. Left at T-junct & hotel on right

This delightful, privately owned hotel enjoys a peaceful location just a ten minute walk from Epsom Racecourse. Stylish bedrooms are generally spacious and all are appointed to a high standard. Public areas are attractively furnished and include a choice of lounges, an excellent range of function and meeting facilities. A smartly appointed restaurant offers imaginative, accomplished cuisine.

Rooms 22 (1 fmly) **S** £95; **D** £130-£180 (incl. bkfst)* **Facilities** STV Complimentary membership at local health club Wi-fi **Conf** Class 40 Board 30 Thtr 140 **Parking** 60

EWELL
Map 6 TQ26

Nonsuch Park Hotel

★★ 64% SMALL HOTEL

☎ 020 8393 0771 📠 020 8393 1415
355-357 London Rd KT17 2DE
e-mail: reservations@nonsuchparkhotel.com
web: www.nonsuchparkhotel.com
dir: A240 onto A24 (London Rd) for 0.75m

This comfortable accommodation stands opposite Nonsuch Park. The attractive bedrooms have good facilities, and the public areas include a small bar area and a lounge-dining room overlooking the rear patio.

Rooms 11 (2 fmly) (4 GF) **Parking** 11 **Notes** ⊗ Closed 2-3 wks Xmas

FARNHAM
Map 5 SU84

Best Western Frensham Pond Hotel

★★★ 76% HOTEL

☎ 01252 795161 📠 01252 792631
Bacon Ln GU10 2QB
e-mail: info@frenshampondhotel.co.uk
web: www.frenshampondhotel.co.uk

(For full entry see Churt)

Mercure Bush

★★★ 73% HOTEL

☎ 0870 400 8225 & 01252 715237 📠 01252 733530
The Borough GU9 7NN
e-mail: H6621@accor.com
web: www.mercure-uk.com
dir: M3 junct 4, A31, follow town centre signs. At East Street lights turn left, hotel on right

Dating back to the 17th century, this extended coaching inn is attractively presented and has a courtyard and a lawned garden. The bedrooms are well appointed, with quality fabrics and good facilities. The public areas include the panelled Oak Lounge, a smart cocktail bar and a conference facility, developed in an adjoining building.

Rooms 83 (3 fmly) (22 GF) (5 smoking) **Facilities** STV New Year Wi-fi **Conf** Class 80 Board 30 Thtr 140 Del from £145 to £205* **Parking** 70 **Notes** Civ Wed 90

FRIMLEY
Map 5 SU85

Innkeeper's Lodge Camberley Frimley

BUDGET HOTEL

☎ 0845 112 6098 📠 0845 112 6205
114 Portsmouth Rd GU15 1HS
web: www.innkeeperslodge.com/frimley
dir: M3 junct 4, A331 then left onto A325 (Portsmouth road). Straight on at 2 rdbts. Lodge approx 1m on left

Innkeeper's Lodge represents an exciting, high value concept within the budget hotel market. Comfortable bedrooms provide excellent facilities that include satellite TV and modem points. Options include family rooms, and for the corporate guest, cutting edge IT which includes Wi-fi access. A popular Carvery provides all-day food, including an extensive, complimentary continental breakfast.

Rooms 43 (2 fmly) **S** £55-£75; **D** £55-£75 (incl. bkfst) **Conf** Thtr 30

GODALMING
Map 6 SU94

Innkeeper's Lodge Godalming

BUDGET HOTEL

☎ 0845 112 6102 📠 0845 112 6201
Ockford Rd GU7 1RH
web: www.innkeeperslodge.com/Godalming
dir: M25 junct 10 south towards Guildford on A3. Left at Milford junct, at rdbt take A283. Left towards Godalming on A3100, into Ockford Road. Lodge on right just after rail bridge

Innkeeper's Lodge Select represents an exciting, stylish concept within the hotel market. Contemporary style bedrooms provide excellent facilities that include LCD TVs with satellite channels, and modem points. Options include spacious family rooms, and for the corporate guest there is Wi-fi access. All-day food is served in a modern country pub and eating house. The extensive continental breakfast is complimentary.

Rooms 14 **S** £75-£99; **D** £75-£99 (incl. bkfst)

GUILDFORD
Map 6 SU94

Holiday Inn Guildford

Ⓤ

☎ 0870 400 9036 📠 01483 457256
Egerton Rd GU2 7XZ
e-mail: reservations-guildford@ihg.com
web: www.holidayinn.co.uk
dir: A3 to Guildford. Exit at sign for Research Park/Onslow Village. 3rd exit at 1st rdbt, 2nd exit at 2nd rdbt

Currently the rating for this establishment is not confirmed. This may be due to a change of ownership or because it has only recently joined the AA rating scheme. For further details please see the AA website: www.theAA.com

Rooms 168 (52 fmly) (66 GF) (9 smoking) **D** £199* **Facilities** Spa STV ⓣ Gym Fitness studio Beauty treatments Wi-fi **Conf** Class 100 Board 60 Thtr 180 **Services** Air con **Parking** 230 **Notes** LB ⊗ Civ Wed

Travelodge Guildford

BUDGET HOTEL

☎ 08700 850 890 📠 01483 450174
Woodbridge Rd, Woodbridge Meadows GU1 1BD
web: www.travelodge.co.uk
dir: Follow A322 onto A25 Middleton Rd. Right onto A25 to Woodbridge Meadows, then turn right.

Travelodge offers good quality, good value, modern accommodation. Ideal for families, the spacious en suite bedrooms include remote-control TV, tea and coffee-making facilities and comfortable beds. Meals can be taken at the nearby family restaurant. See also the Hotel Groups pages.

Rooms 152 **S** fr £29; **D** fr £29

HASLEMERE
Map 6 SU93

Lythe Hill Hotel and Spa

★★★★ 77% ⊛⊛ HOTEL

☎ 01428 651251 📠 01428 644131
Petworth Rd GU27 3BQ
e-mail: lythe@lythehill.co.uk
web: www.lythehill.co.uk
dir: left from High St onto B2131. Hotel 1.25m on right

This privately owned hotel sits in 30 acres of attractive parkland with lakes, complete with roaming geese. The hotel has been described as a hamlet of character buildings, each furnished in a style that complements the

Boship Farm

★★★ 73% HOTEL

☎ 01323 844826 & 442600 🖻 01323 843945
Lower Dicker BN27 4AT
e-mail: info@boshipfarmhotel.co.uk
dir: On A22. At A267 & 271 junct (Boship rdbt

Dating back to 1652, a lovely old farmhouse forms the hub of this hotel, which is set in 17 acres of well-tended grounds. Guests have the use of an all-weather tennis court, an outdoor pool and a croquet lawn. Bedrooms are smartly appointed and well equipped; most have views across open fields and countryside.

Rooms 47 (3 fmly) (21 GF) **S** £60-£85; **D** £90-£135 (incl. bkfst)* **Facilities** ⚓ 🏊 💆 Gym Badminton Sauna Steam room Xmas New Year **Conf** Class 40 Board 46 Thtr 175 **Parking** 110 **Notes** LB Civ Wed 140

The Olde Forge Hotel & Restaurant

★★ 75% HOTEL

☎ 01323 842893 🖻 01323 842893
Magham Down BN27 1PN
e-mail: theoldeforgehotel@tesco.net
web: www.theoldeforgehotel.co.uk
dir: off Boship rdbt on A271 to Bexhill & Herstmonceux. Hotel 3m on left

In the heart of the countryside, this family-run hotel offers a friendly welcome and an informal atmosphere. The bedrooms are attractively decorated with thoughtful extras. The restaurant, with its timbered beams and log fires, was a forge in the 16th century; today it has a good local reputation for both its cuisine and service.

Rooms 7 **S** £48; **D** £80 (incl. bkfst)* **Facilities** Wi-fi **Parking** 11 **Notes** LB

Travelodge Hellingly Eastbourne

BUDGET HOTEL

☎ 08719 846 035 🖻 01323 844556
Boship Roundabout, Hellingly BN27 4DT
web: www.travelodge.co.uk
dir: on A22 at Boship rdbt

Travelodge offers good quality, good value, modern accommodation. Ideal for families, the spacious en suite bedrooms include remote-control TV, tea and coffee-

making facilities and comfortable beds. Meals can be taken at the nearby family restaurant See also the Hotel Groups pages.

Rooms 58 **S** fr £29; **D** fr £29

Halland Forge

★★ 64% HOTEL

☎ 01825 840456 🖻 01825 840773
BN8 6PW
e-mail: info@hallandforgehotel.co.uk
dir: on A22 at junct with B2192, 4.5m S of Uckfield

Conveniently located, this hotel offers comfortable annexed accommodation with parking spaces directly outside the bedrooms. Public areas include a spacious lounge bar, attractive outdoor seating (weather permitting) and an informal restaurant serving generous portions at dinner. An attractively presented room is available for private dining, special occasions or for meetings by prior arrangement.

Rooms 20 (20 annexe) (2 fmly) (8 GF) **Conf** Class 20 Board 26 Thtr 45 **Parking** 70 **Notes** ⊗

The Chatsworth Hotel

★★★ 72% ⚙ HOTEL

☎ 01424 720188 🖻 01424 445865
Carlisle Pde TN34 1JG
e-mail: info@chatsworthhotel.com
dir: A21 to town centre. At seafront turn right before next lights

Enjoying a central position on the seafront, close to the pier, this much-improved hotel is a short walk from the old town and within easy reach of the county's many attractions. Bedrooms are smartly decorated, equipped with a range of extras and many rooms enjoy splendid sea views. Guests can also enjoy an exciting Indian meal in the contemporary restaurant.

Rooms 52 (5 fmly) **Facilities** Xmas New Year Wi-fi **Conf** Class 20 Board 20 Thtr 40 **Services** Lift **Parking** 8 **Notes** LB ⊗

Best Western Royal Victoria

★★★ 72% HOTEL

☎ 01424 445544 🖻 01424 721995
Marina, St Leonards-on-Sea TN38 0BD
e-mail: reception@royalvichotel.co.uk
web: www.royalvichotel.co.uk
dir: on A259 (seafront road) 1m W of Hastings pier

This imposing 18th-century property is situated in a prominent position overlooking the sea. A superb marble staircase leads up from the lobby to the main public areas on the first floor which has panoramic views of the sea. The spacious bedrooms are pleasantly decorated and well equipped, and include duplex and family suites.

Rooms 50 (15 fmly) **Facilities** Xmas **Conf** Class 40 Board 40 Thtr 100 **Services** Lift **Parking** 6 **Notes** LB Civ Wed 50

High Beech

★★★ 68% HOTEL

☎ 01424 851383 🖻 01424 854265
Eisenhower Dr, Battle Rd, St Leonards on Sea TN37 7BS
e-mail: highbeech@barbox.net
dir: Off A2100 into Washington Ave from Battle Rd.

A privately owned hotel situated between the historic towns of Hastings and Battle in a woodland setting. The generously proportioned bedrooms are pleasantly decorated and thoughtfully equipped. Public rooms include the Mountbatten Bar, which also doubles as the lounge area, and the elegant Wedgwood Restaurant where an interesting and varied menu is served.

Rooms 17 (4 fmly) **Facilities** New Year Wi-fi **Conf** Class 100 Board 50 Thtr 200 **Parking** 70 **Notes** LB ⊗ Civ Wed 55

See advert on page 475

HASTINGS & ST LEONARDS continued

Travelodge Hastings

BUDGET HOTEL

☎ 08719 846 310 ▤ 01424 437277
Bohemia Rd TN34 1ET
web: www.travelodge.co.uk
dir: A21 into Hastings. Police HQ and courts on left, hotel
next left before ambulance HQ

Travelodge offers good quality, good value, modern
accommodation. Ideal for families, the spacious en suite
bedrooms include remote-control TV, tea and coffee-
making facilities and comfortable beds. Meals can be
taken at the nearby family restaurant. See also the Hotel
Groups pages.

Rooms 40 (8 fmly) **S** fr £29; **D** fr £29 **Conf** Class 150
Board 120 Thtr 250

HOVE

See Brighton & Hove

LEWES   Map 6 TQ41

Shelleys

★★★ 86% ◉◉ HOTEL

☎ 01273 472361 & 483403 ▤ 01273 483152
136 High St BN7 1XS
e-mail: reservations@shelleys-hotel-lewes.com
dir: A23 to Brighton onto A27 to Lewes. At 1st rdbt left for
town centre, after x-rds hotel on left

Originally a coaching inn dating from the 16th Century,
this charming establishment is the perfect base for
exploring the South Downs and a relaxing venue when
shopping in nearby Brighton. All rooms are comfortably
furnished in a traditional style and equipped with modern
amenities such as Wi-fi. As well as a cosy bar and lounge,
a fine dining restaurant is available, and homemade
cream teas in the stunning garden are a speciality.

Rooms 19 (1 fmly) **Facilities** ⤴ Xmas New Year Wi-fi
Conf Class 20 Board 25 Thtr 60 **Parking** 20 **Notes** LB
Civ Wed 60

NEWICK   Map 6 TQ42

INSPECTORS' CHOICE

Newick Park Hotel & Country Estate
★★★ ◉◉◉ HOTEL

☎ 01825 723633 ▤ 01825 723969
BN8 4SB
e-mail: bookings@newickpark.co.uk
web: www.newickpark.co.uk
dir: Exit A272 at Newick Green, 1m, pass church &
pub. Turn left, hotel 0.25m on right

Delightful Grade II listed Georgian country house set
amid 250 acres of Sussex parkland and landscaped
gardens. The spacious, individually decorated
bedrooms are tastefully furnished, thoughtfully
equipped and have superb views of the grounds;
many rooms have huge American king-size beds. The
comfortable public rooms include a study, a sitting
room, lounge bar and an elegant restaurant.

Rooms 16 (3 annexe) (5 fmly) (1 GF) **S** £125-£245;
D £165-£285 (incl. bkfst) **Facilities** FTV ↖ ⤜ Fishing
⤴ Badminton Clay pigeon shooting Helicopter rides
Quad biking Tank driving Xmas Wi-fi **Conf** Class 40
Board 40 Thtr 80 **Parking** 50 **Notes** Civ Wed 100

See advert on opposite page

PEASMARSH   Map 7 TQ82

Best Western Flackley Ash

★★★ 79% HOTEL

☎ 01797 230651 ▤ 01797 230510
TN31 6YH
e-mail: enquiries@flackleyashhotel.co.uk
web: www.flackleyashhotel.co.uk
dir: exit A21 onto A268 to Newenden, next left A268 to
Rye. Hotel on left on entering Peasmarsh

Five acres of beautifully kept grounds make a lovely
backdrop to this elegant Georgian country house. The
hotel is superbly situated for exploring the many local
attractions, including the ancient Cinque Port of Rye.
Stylishly decorated bedrooms are comfortable and boast
many thoughtful touches. A sunny conservatory dining
room, luxurious beauty spa and a swimming pool are
available.

Rooms 45 (5 fmly) (19 GF) **D** £144-£190 (incl. bkfst &
dinner)* **Facilities** Spa STV ⊛ supervised Putt green ⤴
Gym Beauty salon Steam room Saunas Xmas New Year

Wi-fi Child facilities **Conf** Class 60 Board 40 Thtr 100
Del from £125* **Parking** 80 **Notes** LB Civ Wed 100

RYE   Map 7 TQ92

George in Rye

★★★★ 79% HOTEL

☎ 01797 222114 ▤ 01797 224065
98 High St TN31 7JT
e-mail: stay@thegeorgeinrye.com
dir: M20 junct 10, then A2070 to Brenzett then A259 to
Rye

This attractive 16th-century property, situated in the
heart of historic Rye, has been sympathetically styled to
retain many original features including a stunning
Georgian ballroom complete with a minstrels' gallery. The
bedrooms are stylishly appointed and filled with an
abundance of thoughtful touches. Contemporary public
areas include a bar, lounge and dining room and an
excellent alfresco area for summer dining.

Rooms 24 (3 GF) **S** £95-£125; **D** £125-£225 (incl. bkfst)*
Facilities FTV Xmas New Year Wi-fi **Conf** Class 65
Board 40 Thtr 100 Del from £155 to £185* **Notes** LB ⊗
Civ Wed 100

Mermaid Inn

★★★ 79% ◉ HOTEL

☎ 01797 223065 & 223788 ▤ 01797 225069
Mermaid St TN31 7EY
e-mail: info@mermaidinn.com
web: www.mermaidinn.com
dir: A259, follow signs to town centre, then into Mermaid
Street

Situated near the top of a cobbled side street, this
famous smugglers' inn is steeped in history. The
charming interior has many architectural features such
as attractive stone work. The bedrooms vary in size and
style but all are tastefully furnished. Delightful public
rooms include a choice of lounges, cosy bar and smart
restaurant.

Rooms 31 (5 fmly) **S** £80-£90; **D** £160-£220 (incl. bkfst)*
Facilities Xmas New Year Wi-fi **Conf** Class 40 Board 30
Thtr 50 **Parking** 25 **Notes** ⊗

RYE continued

The Hope Anchor

★★★ 75% SMALL HOTEL

☎ 01797 222216 📠 01797 223796
Watchbell St TN31 7HA
e-mail: info@thehopeanchor.co.uk
web: www.thehopeanchor.co.uk
dir: from A268, Quayside, turn right into Wish Ward, up
Mermaid St, right into West St, right into Watchbell
Street, hotel at end

This historic inn sits high above the town with enviable
views out over the harbour and Romney Marsh, and is
accessible via delightful cobbled streets. A relaxed and
friendly atmosphere prevails within the cosy public
rooms, while the attractively furnished bedrooms are well
equipped and many enjoy good views over the marshes.

Rooms 15 (1 fmly) **S** £65-£95; **D** £75-£120 (incl. bkfst)
Facilities FTV Xmas New Year Wi-fi **Conf** Class 30
Board 20 Thtr 40 Del from £120 to £160 **Parking** 12
Notes LB

Rye Lodge

★★★ 75% HOTEL

☎ 01797 223838 📠 01797 223585
Hilders Cliff TN31 7LD
e-mail: info@ryelodge.co.uk
web: www.ryelodge.co.uk
dir: one-way system in Rye, follow signs for town centre,
through Landgate arch, hotel 100yds on right

Standing in an elevated position, Rye Lodge has
panoramic views across Romney Marshes and the Rother
Estuary. Traditionally styled bedrooms come in a variety
of sizes; they are attractively decorated and thoughtfully
equipped. Public rooms feature indoor leisure facilities
and the Terrace Room Restaurant where home-made
dishes are offered. Lunch and afternoon tea are served on
the flower-filled outdoor terrace in warmer months.

Rooms 18 (5 GF) **S** £70-£160; **D** £120-£220 (incl. bkfst)*
Facilities STV ⊗ Aromatherapy Steam cabinet Sauna
Exercise machines Xmas **Parking** 20 **Notes** LB

See advert on page 475

White Vine House

RESTAURANT WITH ROOMS

☎ 01797 224748
24 High St TN31 7JF
e-mail: info@whitevinehouse.co.uk
dir: In the middle of Rye high street

Situated in the heart of the ancient Cinque Port town of
Rye, White Vine House's origins go back to the 13th
century. The cellar is the oldest part, but the current
building dates from 1560, and boasts an impressive
Georgian frontage. The original timber framework is
visible in many areas, and certainly adds to the house's
feeling of history. The bedrooms have period furniture
along with luxury bath or shower rooms. One bedroom has
an antique four-poster which tops off the atmosphere for
a special stay.

Rooms 7 (3 en suite) (1 fmly)

ST LEONARDS-ON-SEA

See Hastings & St Leonards

TICEHURST — Map 6 TQ63

Dale Hill Hotel & Golf Club

★★★★ 82% ⊛ HOTEL

☎ 01580 200112 📠 01580 201249
TN5 7DQ
e-mail: info@dalehill.co.uk
web: www.dalehill.co.uk
dir: M25 junct 5/A21. 5m after Lamberhurst turn right at
lights onto B2087 to Flimwell. Hotel 1m on left

This modern hotel is situated just a short drive from the
village. Extensive public rooms include a lounge bar, a
conservatory brasserie, a formal restaurant and the Spike
Bar, which is mainly frequented by golf club members
and has a lively atmosphere. The hotel also has two
superb 18-hole golf courses, a swimming pool and gym.

Rooms 35 (8 fmly) (23 GF) **S** £120-£140; **D** £130-£250
(incl. bkfst)* **Facilities** STV ⊗ ↥ 36 Putt green Gym
Covered driving range Pool table Xmas New Year Wi-fi
Conf Class 50 Board 50 Thtr 120 **Services** Lift
Parking 220 **Notes** LB ⊗ Civ Wed 150

UCKFIELD — Map 6 TQ42

Buxted Park Country House Hotel

★★★★ 84% ⊛⊛ HOTEL

Hand PICKED HOTELS

☎ 01825 733333 📠 01825 732 990
Buxted TN22 4AY
e-mail: buxtedpark@handpicked.co.uk
web: www.handpicked.co.uk
dir: From A26 (Uckfield bypass) take A272 signed Buxted.
Through lights, hotel 1m on right

An attractive Grade II listed Georgian mansion dating
back to the 17th century. The property is set amidst 300
acres of beautiful countryside and landscaped gardens.
The stylish, thoughtfully equipped bedrooms are split
between the main house and the modern Garden Wing. An
interesting choice of dishes is served in the restaurant.

Rooms 44 (6 fmly) (16 GF) **S** £175-£365; **D** £175-£365*
Facilities FTV Putt green Fishing ⊰ Gym Fishing
Mountain biking Orienteering Xmas New Year Wi-fi
Conf Class 80 Board 60 Thtr 180 Del from £180 to £280*
Services Lift **Parking** 150 **Notes** LB ⊗ Civ Wed 130

INSPECTORS' CHOICE

Horsted Place

★★★ ⊛⊛ HOTEL

☎ 01825 750581 📠 01825 750459
Little Horsted TN22 5TS
e-mail: hotel@horstedplace.co.uk
dir: 2m S on A26 towards Lewes

This 17th-century property is one of Britain's finest
examples of Gothic revivalist architecture. It is
situated in extensive landscaped grounds, with a
tennis court and croquet lawn, and is adjacent to
the East Sussex National Golf Club. The spacious
bedrooms are attractively decorated, tastefully
furnished and equipped with many thoughtful touches
such as flowers and books. Most rooms also have a
separate sitting area.

Rooms 20 (3 annexe) (5 fmly) (2 GF) **S** £130-£350;
D £130-£350 (incl. bkfst)* **Facilities** STV ↥ 36 ⊗
⊰ ♫ Xmas Wi-fi **Conf** Class 50 Board 40 Thtr 80
Del from £160* **Services** Lift **Parking** 30 **Notes** LB ⊗
No children 7yrs Civ Wed 100

WILMINGTON

Map 6 TQ50

Crossways

◎◎ RESTAURANT WITH ROOMS

☎ 01323 482455 📠 01323 487811
Lewes Rd BN26 5SG
e-mail: stay@crosswayshotel.co.uk
dir: On A27 between Lewes & Polegate, 2m E of Alfriston rdbt

A well-established restaurant with a good local reputation is the focus of this attractive property. Bedrooms are also provided, and all are individually decorated with taste and style and superior rooms are available. Guest comfort is paramount so there are excellent facilities and the kind of hospitality that ensures guests return often.

Rooms 7 (3 en suite)

SUSSEX, WEST

AMBERLEY

Map 6 TQ01

INSPECTORS' CHOICE

Amberley Castle

★★★★ ◎◎◎
COUNTRY HOUSE HOTEL

☎ 01798 831992 📠 01798 831998
BN18 9LT
e-mail: info@amberleycastle.co.uk
web: www.amberleycastle.co.uk
dir: on B2139, off A29 between Bury & Storrington

This delightful castle, set in idyllic and well manicured grounds in the Sussex countryside, boasts 900 years of history. The old battlements, complete with a mighty oak portcullis (one of the few remaining working ones in Europe), enclose the main hotel; beyond the walls are 12 acres of stunning parkland that features gardens,

ponds, and a thatched-roof furnished tree-house with a rope bridge. Tennis, an 18-hole putting green and croquet are available too. Dining is available in the magnificent Queens Room - pre-booking is essential.

Rooms 19 (5 annexe) (6 GF) **Facilities** 🛎 Putt green
⬆ 🎵 Xmas New Year **Conf** Class 25 Board 30 Thtr 50
Parking 40 **Notes** ⊗ No children 12yrs Civ Wed 110

ARUNDEL

Map 6 TQ00

Norfolk Arms

★★★ 75% HOTEL

☎ 01903 882101 📠 01903 884275
High St BN18 9AB
e-mail: norfolk.arms@forestdale.com
web: www.norfolkarmshotel.com
dir: On High St in city centre

Built by the 10th Duke of Norfolk, this Georgian coaching inn enjoys a superb setting beneath the battlements of Arundel Castle. Bedrooms vary in sizes and character - all are comfortable and well equipped. Public areas include two bars serving 'real ale', comfortable lounges with roaring log fires, a traditional English restaurant and a range of meeting and function rooms.

Rooms 34 (13 annexe) (4 fmly) (8 GF) **S** £72-£79;
D £117-£129 (incl. bkfst)* **Facilities** Xmas New Year
Wi-fi **Conf** Class 40 Board 40 Thtr 100 **Parking** 19
Notes LB Civ Wed 60

ARUNDEL continued

Comfort Inn

★★ 67% HOTEL

☎ 01903 840840 📄 01903 849849
Crossbush BN17 7QQ
e-mail: reservations@comfortinnarundel.co.uk
dir: A27/A284, 1st right into services

This modern, purpose-built hotel provides a good base for exploring the nearby historic town. Good access to local road networks and a range of meeting rooms, all air-conditioned, also make this an ideal venue for business guests. Bedrooms are spacious, smartly decorated and well equipped.

Rooms 53 (4 fmly) (25 GF) (12 smoking) **S** £50-£120; **D** £55-£120 (incl. bkfst) **Facilities** STV FTV Xmas New Year Wi-fi **Conf** Class 30 Board 30 Thtr 30 Del from £75 to £95 **Parking** 53 **Notes** LB

Innkeeper's Lodge Arundel Chichester (Fontwell Park)

BUDGET HOTEL

☎ 0845 112 6093 📄 0845 112 6210
Fontwell Park Racecourse, Fontwell BN18 0SY
web: www.innkeeperslodge.com/arundelchichester
dir: Lodge at Fontwell Park Racecourse on A27/A29 rdbt between Chichester & Arundel

Innkeeper's Lodge represents an exciting, high value concept within the budget hotel market. Comfortable bedrooms provide excellent facilities that include satellite TV and modem points. Options include family rooms, and for the corporate guest, cutting edge IT includes Wi-fi access. Food is served all day in the adjacent Country Pub. The extensive continental breakfast is complimentary.

Rooms 40 **S** £59.95; **D** £59.95 (incl. bkfst)

The Townhouse

◉ RESTAURANT WITH ROOMS

☎ 01903 883847
65 High St BN18 9AJ
dir: Follow A27 to Arundel, onto High Street, establishment on left at top of hill

This an elegant, Grade II-listed Regency building overlooking Arundel Castle, just a short walk from the shops and sights of Arundel. Bedrooms and public areas retain the unspoilt style of the building. The ceiling in the dining room is particularly spectacular, and comes all the way from 16th-century Florence. The owners can be justifiably proud of the enterprise they took on just a short years ago.

Rooms 4

BOGNOR REGIS Map 6 SZ99

Beachcroft

★★★ 72% HOTEL

☎ 01243 827142 📄 01243 863500
Clyde Rd, Felpham Village PO22 7AH
e-mail: reservations@beachcroft-hotel.co.uk
web: www.beachcroft-hotel.co.uk
dir: From A259 between Chichester & Littlehampton at Felpham, follow village signs, hotel signed

This popular hotel overlooks a secluded part of the seafront. Bedrooms are bright and spacious, and leisure facilities include a heated indoor swimming pool and treatment rooms. Diners may choose from the varied choice of the traditional restaurant menus or the more informal cosy bar.

Rooms 35 (4 fmly) (6 GF) **S** £54.50-£74; **D** £64.50-£94 (incl. bkfst) **Facilities** ◊ Xmas New Year Wi-fi **Conf** Class 30 Board 30 Thtr 60 **Parking** 27 **Notes** ⊗

Royal Norfolk

★★★ 72% HOTEL

☎ 01243 826222 📄 01243 826325
The Esplanade PO21 2LH
e-mail: accommodation@royalnorfolkhotel.com
web: www.royalnorfolkhotel.com
dir: from A259 follow Longford Rd through lights to Canada Grove to T-junct. Right, take 2nd exit at rdbt. Hotel on right

On the Esplanade, but set back behind lawns and gardens, this fine-looking hotel has been welcoming guests since Regency times. Today the traditionally furnished bedrooms, four with four-poster beds, are well provided with all the modern comforts. Public areas offer sea views from the elegant restaurant and comfortable lobby lounge.

Rooms 43 (4 fmly) **S** £55-£70; **D** £100-£130 (incl. bkfst)* **Facilities** ♫ Xmas New Year Wi-fi **Conf** Class 140

Board 140 Thtr 140 Del from £90* **Services** Lift **Parking** 60 **Notes** LB

The Inglenook

★★★ 68% HOTEL

☎ 01243 262495 & 265411 📄 01243 262668
255 Pagham Rd, Nyetimber PO21 3QB
e-mail: reception@the-inglenook.com
dir: A27 to Vinnetrow Road left at Walnut Tree, 2.5m on right

This 16th-century inn retains much of its original character, including exposed beams throughout. Bedrooms are individually decorated and vary in size. There is a cosy lounge, a well-kept garden and a bar that offers a popular evening menu and convivial atmosphere. The restaurant, overlooking the garden, also serves enjoyable cuisine.

Rooms 18 (1 fmly) (2 GF) **S** £50-£70; **D** £80-£200 (incl. bkfst)* **Facilities** FTV Xmas New Year Wi-fi **Conf** Class 50 Board 50 Thtr 100 **Parking** 35 **Notes** LB Civ Wed 80

The Royal

★★ Ⓐ HOTEL

☎ 01243 864665 📄 01243 863175
The Esplanade PO21 1SZ
e-mail: david@royalhotelbognor.co.uk
dir: opposite Bognor Pier, 300yds from town centre

Rooms 22 (3 fmly) **Facilities** Xmas **Conf** Class 30 Board 30 Thtr 60 **Services** Lift **Notes** LB

BOSHAM Map 5 SU80

The Millstream

★★★ 83% ◉◉ HOTEL

☎ 01243 573234 📄 01243 573459
Bosham Ln PO18 8HL
e-mail: info@millstream-hotel.co.uk
web: www.millstream-hotel.co.uk
dir: 4m W of Chichester on A259, left at Bosham rdbt. After 0.5m right at T-junct signed to church & quay. Hotel 0.5m on right

Lying in the idyllic village of Bosham, this attractive hotel provides comfortable, well-equipped and tastefully decorated bedrooms. Many guests regularly return here for the relaxed atmosphere created by the notably efficient and friendly staff. Public rooms include a cocktail bar that opens onto the garden, and a pleasant restaurant where varied and freshly prepared cuisine can be enjoyed.

Rooms 35 (2 annexe) (2 fmly) (9 GF) **S** £85-£95; **D** £145-£165 (incl. bkfst)* **Facilities** FTV Painting & Bridge breaks ♫ Xmas New Year Wi-fi **Conf** Class 20 Board 20 Thtr 45 **Parking** 44 **Notes** LB ⊗ Civ Wed 92

CHICHESTER   Map 5 SU80

The Goodwood Park Hotel

★★★★ 77% ◉◉ HOTEL

☎ 01243 775537 ▤ 01243 520120
PO18 0QB
e-mail: reservations@thegoodwoodparkhotel.co.uk
web: www.thegoodwoodparkhotel.co.uk

(For full entry see Goodwood)

Crouchers Country Hotel & Restaurant

★★★ 79% ◉ HOTEL

☎ 01243 784995 ▤ 01243 539797
Birdham Rd PO20 7EH
e-mail: crouchers@btconnect.com
dir: off A27 to A286, 1.5m from Chichester centre opposite Black Horse pub

This friendly, family-run hotel, situated in open countryside, is just a short drive from the harbour. The comfortable and well-equipped bedrooms include some in a separate barn and coach house, and the open-plan public areas have pleasant views.

Rooms 20 (17 annexe) (2 fmly) (12 GF) **S** £75-£110; **D** £110-£140 (incl. bkfst) **Facilities** FTV Xmas New Year Wi-fi **Conf** Class 80 Board 50 Thtr 80 Del from £120 to £140 **Parking** 80 **Notes** LB

See advert on page 477

INSPECTORS' CHOICE

West Stoke House

◉◉◉ RESTAURANT WITH ROOMS

☎ 01243 575226 ▤ 01243 574655
Downs Rd, West Stoke PO18 9BN
e-mail: info@weststokehouse.co.uk
dir: 3m NW of Chichester. Off B286 to West Stoke, next to St Andrew's Church

This fine country house, part Georgian and part medieval, with over five acres of lawns and gardens, lies on the edge of the South Downs. The large uncluttered bedrooms have smart modern bathrooms and great country views. The restaurant provides very good cooking in a relaxed atmosphere. Public rooms have a light-filled elegance and are adorned with an eclectic mix of period furniture and contemporary art.

Rooms 8 (1 pri facs) (2 en suite) (1 fmly)

CLIMPING   Map 6 SU90

Bailiffscourt Hotel & Spa

★★★ 83% ◉◉ HOTEL   *Pride of Britain*

☎ 01903 723511 ▤ 01903 718987
Climping St BN17 5RW
e-mail: bailiffscourt@hshotels.co.uk
web: www.hshotels.co.uk
dir: A259, follow Climping Beach signs. Hotel 0.5m on right

This delightful 'medieval manor' dating back only to the 1920s has the appearance of having been in existence for centuries. Bedrooms vary from atmospheric feature rooms with log fires, oak beams and four-poster beds to spacious, stylish and contemporary rooms located in the grounds. Classic European cooking is a highlight, and a stylish spa plus a choice of cosy lounges complete the package.

Rooms 39 (30 annexe) (25 fmly) (16 GF) **S** £185-£455; **D** £205-£510 (incl. bkfst)* **Facilities** Spa STV ⊙ supervised ⌇ supervised ☺ ⌇ Gym Xmas New Year Wi-fi **Conf** Class 20 Board 26 Thtr 40 Del from £175* **Parking** 100 **Notes** LB Civ Wed 60

COPTHORNE

See Gatwick Airport

CRAWLEY

See Gatwick Airport

CUCKFIELD   Map 6 TQ32

INSPECTORS' CHOICE

Ockenden Manor

★★★ ◉◉ HOTEL   *Pride of Britain*

☎ 01444 416111 ▤ 01444 415549
Ockenden Ln RH17 5LD
e-mail: reservations@ockenden-manor.com
web: www.hshotels.co.uk
dir: A23 towards Brighton. 4.5m left onto B2115 towards Haywards Heath. Cuckfield 3m. Ockenden Lane off High St. Hotel at end

This charming 16th-century hotel enjoys fine views of the South Downs. Bedrooms offer high standards of accommodation, some with historic features. Public rooms, retaining much original character, include an elegant sitting room with all the elements for a

relaxing afternoon in front of the fire. Imaginative, noteworthy cuisine is a highlight to any stay.

Ockenden Manor

Rooms 22 (4 fmly) (4 GF) **S** £105-£195; **D** £170-£360 (incl. bkfst)* **Facilities** STV FTV ⌇ Xmas New Year Wi-fi **Conf** Class 20 Board 26 Thtr 50 Del from £252.63 to £290* **Parking** 43 **Notes** LB Civ Wed 75

EAST GRINSTEAD   Map 6 TQ33

Felbridge Hotel & Spa

★★★★ 86% ◉◉ HOTEL

☎ 01342 337700 ▤ 01342 410778
London Rd RH19 2BH
e-mail: info@felbridgehotel.co.uk
dir: From W exit M23 junct 10, follow signs to A22. From N, exit M25 junct 6. Hotel on A22 at Felbridge

This luxurious hotel is within easy of the M25 and Gatwick as well as Eastbourne and the glorious south coast. All bedrooms are beautifully styled and offer a wealth of amenities. Diners can choose from the Bay Tree Brasserie, Anise Fine Dining Restaurant or contemporary QUBE Bar. Facilities include a selection of modern meeting rooms, the luxurious Chakra Spa and swimming pool.

Rooms 120 (16 fmly) (53 GF) (9 smoking) **S** £79-£290; **D** £79-£290* **Facilities** Spa STV FTV ⊙ supervised Gym Sauna Steam room Hairdresser Xmas New Year Wi-fi **Conf** Class 120 Board 100 Thtr 500 Del from £160 to £290* **Services** Air con **Parking** 300 **Notes** LB ⊗ Civ Wed 150

EAST GRINSTEAD continued

INSPECTORS' CHOICE

Gravetye Manor
★★★ ⛁⛁⛁ HOTEL

☎ 01342 810567 🖷 01342 810080
RH19 4LJ
e-mail: info@gravetyemanor.co.uk
web: www.gravetyemanor.co.uk
dir: B2028 to Haywards Heath. 1m after Turners Hill
fork left towards Sharpthorne, immediate 1st left into
Vowels Lane

This beautiful Elizabethan mansion was built in 1598
and enjoys a tranquil setting. It was one of the first
country-house hotels and remains a shining example
in its class. There are several day rooms, each with
oak panelling, fresh flowers and open fires that offer
guests a relaxing atmosphere. Bedrooms are decorated
in traditional English style, furnished with antiques
and with many thoughtful extras. The cuisine is
excellent and makes full use of home grown fruit and
vegetables. Guests should make a point of exploring
the outstanding gardens.

Rooms 18 **S** £115-£175; **D** £170-£340* **Facilities** STV
Fishing ⅃ Wi-fi **Conf** Board 12 Del from £260 to
£350* **Parking** 35 **Notes** ⊗ No children 7yrs RS 25
Dec Civ Wed 45

FIVE OAKS
Map 6 TQ02

Travelodge Billingshurst
Five Oaks

BUDGET HOTEL

☎ 08719 846 013 🖷 01403 782711
Staines St RH14 9AE
web: www.travelodge.co.uk
dir: on A29, northbound, 1m N of Billingshurst

Travelodge offers good quality, good value, modern
accommodation. Ideal for families, the spacious en suite
bedrooms include remote-control TV, tea and coffee-
making facilities and comfortable beds. Meals can be
taken at the nearby family restaurant. See also the Hotel
Groups pages.

Rooms 26 **S** fr £29; **D** fr £29

FONTWELL
Map 6 SU90

Travelodge Arundel
Fontwell

BUDGET HOTEL

☎ 08719 846 014 🖷 01243 543973
BN18 0SB
web: www.travelodge.co.uk
dir: on A27/A29 rdbt

Travelodge offers good quality, good value, modern
accommodation. Ideal for families, the spacious en suite
bedrooms include remote-control TV, tea and coffee-
making facilities and comfortable beds. Meals can be
taken at the nearby family restaurant. See also the Hotel
Groups pages.

Rooms 62 **S** fr £29; **D** fr £29

GATWICK AIRPORT (LONDON)
Map 6 TQ24

See also **Dorking & Reigate (Surrey), East Grinstead
(Sussex, West)**

INSPECTORS' CHOICE

Langshott Manor
★★★★ ⛁⛁ COUNTRY HOUSE HOTEL

☎ 01293 786680 🖷 01293 783905
Langshott Ln RH6 9LN
e-mail: admin@langshottmanor.com
dir: from A23 take Ladbroke Rd, off Chequers rdbt to
Langshott, after 0.75m hotel on right

Charming timber-framed Tudor house set amidst
beautifully landscaped grounds on the outskirts of
town. The stylish public areas feature a choice of
inviting lounges with polished oak panelling, exposed
beams and log fires. The individually decorated
bedrooms combine the most up-to-date comforts
with flair, individuality and traditional elegance. The
Mulberry restaurant overlooks a picturesque pond and
offers an imaginative menu.

Rooms 22 (8 annexe) (2 fmly) (8 GF) **S** £110-£130;
D £150-£320 (incl. bkfst)* **Facilities** STV FTV ⅃
Xmas New Year Wi-fi **Conf** Class 20 Board 22 Thtr 40
Del from £195 to £250* **Parking** 25 **Notes** LB ⊗
Civ Wed 60

Sofitel London Gatwick
★★★★ 78% HOTEL SOFITEL
ACCOR HOTELS & RESORTS

☎ 01293 567070 & 555000 🖷 01293 567739
North Terminal RH6 0PH
e-mail: h6204-re@accor.com
dir: M23 junct 9, follow to 2nd rdbt. Hotel large white
building straight ahead

One of the closest hotels to the airport, this modern,
purpose-built hotel is located only minutes from the
terminals. Bedrooms are contemporary and all are air-
conditioned. Guests have a choice of eating options
including a French-style café, brasserie and oriental
restaurant.

Rooms 518 (19 fmly) (68 smoking) **S** £116.33-£229.12;
D £116.33-£229.12 **Facilities** Gym Wi-fi **Conf** Class 150
Board 90 Thtr 300 Del from £155 to £180 **Services** Lift
Air con **Parking** 200 (charged) **Notes** ⊗

Ramada Plaza Gatwick
★★★★ 75% HOTEL ⓡRAMADA PLAZA

☎ 01293 561186 🖷 01293 561169
Tinsley Lane South, Three Bridges RH10 8XH
e-mail: sales.plazagatwick@ramadajarvis.co.uk
web: www.ramadajarvis.co.uk
dir: M23 junct 10, A2011 to Crawley. Hotel at 1st rdbt on
left

This modern, purpose built hotel is just four miles from
the airport with easy access to the M23. Spacious
bedrooms are comfortably appointed and well equipped;
some family rooms are available. Air-conditioned public
areas include a brightly appointed Arts restaurant, first
floor conference centre and Sebastian Coe health club.

Rooms 151 (31 fmly) **S** £75-£162; **D** £75-£174 (incl.
bkfst)* **Facilities** STV ⊙ supervised Gym Beauty salon
Hairdresser New Year Wi-fi **Conf** Class 80 Board 40
Thtr 210 Del from £155 to £170* **Services** Lift Air con
Parking 150 (charged) **Notes** LB ⊗ Closed 24-25 Dec
Civ Wed 100

Menzies Chequers

 MenziesHotels

★★★★ 74% HOTEL

☎ 01293 766750 📠 01293 820625
Brighton Rd RH6 8PH
e-mail: chequers@menzieshotels.co.uk
web: www.menzieshotels.co.uk
dir: M23 junct 9, A23 towards Redhill. At 'Longbridge' rdbt take 3rd exit signed Horley/A23. 1m to Sainsburys/ Shell rdbt. Take 1st exit, hotel on right

A popular hotel located close to the town centre and also convenient for Gatwick Airport; original parts of the building date back to the 1750s. Bedrooms are comfortable and well equipped with good facilities. Dining areas include the contemporary restaurant and the traditional Chequers pub. Secure parking is available.

Rooms 104 (10 fmly) (46 GF) (6 smoking) **S** £75-£125; **D** £75-£125 **Facilities** STV ♬ Xmas New Year Wi-fi **Conf** Class 25 Board 32 Thtr 70 Del from £120 to £160 **Services** Lift **Parking** 140 (charged) **Notes** ⊗

Copthorne Hotel and Resort Effingham Park London Gatwick

 MILLENNIUM

★★★★ 73% HOTEL

☎ 01342 714994 📠 01342 716039
West Park Rd RH10 3EU
e-mail: sales.effingham@millenniumhotels.co.uk
web: www.millenniumhotels.co.uk
dir: M23 junct 10, A264 towards East Grinstead. Over rdbt, at 2nd rdbt left onto B2028. Effingham Park on right

A former stately home, set in 40 acres of grounds, this hotel is popular for conference and weekend functions. The main restaurant is an open-plan brasserie serving modern continental cuisine, and snacks are also available in the bar. Bedrooms are spacious and well

equipped. Facilities include a golf course and a leisure club.

Rooms 122 (7 fmly) (20 GF) **Facilities** STV ⊞ ♨ 9 ♨ Putt green Gym Aerobic & Dance studios Xmas New Year Wi-fi **Conf** Class 450 Board 250 Thtr 900 Del from £130 to £250* **Services** Lift **Parking** 500 (charged) **Notes** ⊗ Civ Wed 600

Crowne Plaza Hotel Gatwick-Crawley

 CROWNE PLAZA

★★★★ 71% HOTEL

☎ 01293 608608 📠 01293 515913
Langley Dr RH11 7SX
e-mail: info@cpgatwick.com
web: www.crowneplaza.co.uk
dir: M23 junct 10, 3rd exit at rdbt & 3rd exit at next rdbt. At lights take 3rd exit at rdbt

Ideally located for Gatwick Airport, this contemporary hotel offers comfortable and well-furnished rooms suitable for both the leisure and business travellers. Elite Health and Fitness Centre is a relaxing leisure centre, which house a stunning indoor swimming pool. Cube Restaurant & bar offers a relaxed dining experience and the Gallery Sports Bar an informal alternative. The hotel also offers extensive conference facilities.

Rooms 286 **S** £62-£159; **D** £62-£159* **Facilities** STV FTV ⊞ supervised Gym Sauna Pool spa Steam room Wi-fi **Conf** Class 110 Board 40 Thtr 230 Del from £89 to £170* **Services** Lift Air con **Parking** 170 (charged) **Notes** LB ⊗ Civ Wed

Copthorne Hotel London Gatwick

 MILLENNIUM

★★★★ 70% HOTEL

☎ 01342 348800 & 348888 📠 01342 348833
Copthorne Way RH10 3PG
e-mail: sales.gatwick@millenniumhotels.co.uk
web: www.millenniumhotels.co.uk
dir: on A264, 2m E of A264/B2036 rdbt

Situated in a tranquil position, the Copthorne is set in 100 acres of wooded, landscaped gardens containing jogging tracks, a putting green and a petanque pit. The sprawling building is built around a 16th-century farmhouse and has comfortable bedrooms; many are air conditioned. There are three dining options, ranging from the informal bar or carvery to the more formal Lion d'Or.

Rooms 227 (10 fmly) **S** £59-£188; **D** £59-£188* **Facilities** STV ⊞ ♨ Gym Squash Aerobic studio Wi-fi **Conf** Class 60 Board 40 Thtr 135 **Services** Lift **Parking** 300 (charged) **Notes** LB ⊗ Civ Wed 100

Stanhill Court

★★★ 87% ◉◉ HOTEL

☎ 01293 862166 📠 01293 862773
Stanhill Rd, Charlwood RH6 0EP
e-mail: enquiries@stanhillcourthotel.co.uk
web: www.stanhillcourthotel.co.uk
dir: N of Charlwood towards Newdigate

This hotel dates back to 1881 and enjoys a secluded location in 35 acres of well-tended grounds with views over the Downs. Bedrooms are individually furnished and decorated, and many have four-poster beds. Public areas include a library, a bright Spanish-style bar and a traditional wood-panelled restaurant. Extensive and varied function facilities make this a popular wedding venue.

Rooms 34 (3 fmly) (1 GF) **Facilities** Putt green Fishing **Conf** Class 120 Board 66 Thtr 300 **Parking** 110 **Notes** LB Civ Wed 220

GATWICK AIRPORT (LONDON) continued

Best Western Gatwick Moat House

★★★ 80% HOTEL

☎ 0870 443 1671 & 01293 899988 📄 01293 899904
Longbridge Roundabout RH6 0AB
e-mail: gatwick@qmh-hotels.com
web: www.bestwestern.co.uk/content/hotel-details-leisure.aspx/hotel/83860
dir: M23 junct 9, follow signs for North Terminal, take 4th exit at rdbt signed A23/Redhill. At 1st rdbt take 1st exit then 1st left

Ideally situated for both terminals, this hotel provides a shuttle service to the airport and boasts secure undercover parking. Modern conference facilities and a spacious break-out area are provided. The smart bedrooms have air conditioning and a contemporary feel; some family suites can sleep up to seven guests.

Rooms 125 (20 fmly) **S** £59-£139; **D** £59-£139*
Facilities Xmas New Year Wi-fi **Conf** Class 20 Board 18 Thtr 40 **Services** Lift Air con **Parking** 8 (charged)
Notes ⊗

Gatwick Worth Hotel

★★★ 73% HOTEL

☎ 01293 884806 📄 01293 882444
Crabbet Park, Turners Hill Rd, Worth RH10 4ST
e-mail: reception@gatwickworthhotel.co.uk
web: www.gatwickworthhotel.co.uk
dir: M23 junct 10, left to A264. At 1st rdbt take last exit. Take 1st left and 1st right at T-junct, hotel next right.

This purpose-built hotel is ideally placed for access to Gatwick Airport. The bedrooms are spacious and suitably appointed with good facilities. Public areas consist of a light and airy bar area and a brasserie-style restaurant offering good value meals. Guests have use of the superb leisure club next door.

Rooms 118 (24 fmly) (56 GF) **Facilities** Wi-fi
Conf Class 110 Board 100 Thtr 360 **Parking** 150
Notes ⊗ Civ Wed 70

Holiday Inn Gatwick Airport

🔟

☎ 0870 400 9030 & 01293 787648 📄 01293 771054
Povey Cross Rd RH6 0BA
web: www.holidayinn.co.uk
dir: M23 junct 9, follow Gatwick, then Reigate signs. Hotel on left after 3rd rdbt

Currently the rating for this establishment is not confirmed. This may be due to a change of ownership or because it has only recently joined the AA rating scheme. For further details please see the AA website: www.theAA.com

Rooms 216 **Facilities** STV 🎵 Xmas Wi-fi **Conf** Class 70 Board 50 Thtr 150 **Services** Lift Air con **Parking** 600 (charged)

Express by Holiday Inn Gatwick - Crawley

BUDGET HOTEL

☎ 01293 529991 📄 01293 525529
Haslett Av, The Squareabout RH10 1UA
e-mail: ebhi-crawley@btconnect.com
web: www.hiexpress.com/crawleyuk

A modern hotel ideal for families and business travellers. Fresh and uncomplicated, the spacious rooms include Sky TV, power shower and tea and coffee-making facilities. Continental buffet breakfast is included in the room rate; other meals may be taken at the nearby family pub or restaurant. See also the Hotel Groups pages.

Rooms 74 (55 fmly) **Conf** Class 12 Board 16 Thtr 35

Ibis London Gatwick Airport

BUDGET HOTEL

☎ 01293 590300 📄 01293 590310
London Rd, County Oak RH10 9GY
e-mail: H1889@accor.com
web: www.ibishotel.com
dir: M23 junct 10, A2011 towards Crawley. Onto A23 left towards Crawley/Brighton. Hotel on left

Modern, budget hotel offering comfortable accommodation in bright and practical bedrooms. Breakfast is self-service and dinner is available in the restaurant. See also the Hotel Groups pages.

Rooms 141

Travelodge Gatwick Airport

BUDGET HOTEL

☎ 08719 846 031 📄 01293 535369
Church Rd, Lowfield Heath RH11 0PQ
web: www.travelodge.co.uk
dir: M23 junct 10, follow signs for Crawley, take A23 to Gatwick

Travelodge offers good quality, good value, modern accommodation. Ideal for families, the spacious en suite bedrooms include remote-control TV, tea and coffee-making facilities and comfortable beds. Meals can be taken at the nearby family restaurant. See also the Hotel Groups pages.

Rooms 186 **S** fr £29; **D** fr £29 **Conf** Class 25 Board 25 Thtr 60

The Goodwood Park Hotel

★★★★ 77% ®® HOTEL

☎ 01243 775537 📄 01243 520120
PO18 0QB
e-mail: reservations@thegoodwoodparkhotel.co.uk
web: www.thegoodwoodparkhotel.co.uk
dir: off A285, 3m NE of Chichester

Set in the middle of the 12,000-acre Goodwood Estate, this attractive hotel boasts extensive indoor and outdoor leisure facilities, along with a range of meeting rooms plus conference and banqueting facilities. Bedrooms are furnished to a consistently high standard. Public rooms include the Richmond Restaurant and a smart cocktail bar which reflects the motor-racing heritage at Goodwood.

Rooms 94 **S** £75-£175; **D** £90-£175 (incl. bkfst)*
Facilities Spa ⓒ ♨ Putt green Gym Golf driving range Sauna Steam room Fitness studio Xmas New Year Wi-fi **Conf** Class 60 Board 50 Thtr 150 Del from £150 to £185* **Parking** 350 **Notes** LB ⊗ Civ Wed 120

Best Western The Birch Hotel

★★★ 74% HOTEL

☎ 01444 451565 📄 01444 440109
Lewes Rd RH17 7SF
e-mail: info@birchhotel.co.uk
dir: on A272 opposite Princess Royal Hospital and behind Shell Garage

Originally the home of an eminent Harley Street surgeon, this attractive Victorian property has been extended to combine modern facilities with the charm of its original period. Public rooms include the conservatory-style Pavilion Restaurant, along with an open-plan lounge and brasserie-style bar serving a range of light meals.

Rooms 51 (3 fmly) (12 GF) **S** £82-£87; **D** £87-£92 (incl. bkfst)* **Facilities** STV Wi-fi **Conf** Class 30 Board 26 Thtr 60 Del from £120 to £135* **Parking** 60 **Notes** LB Civ Wed 60

Holiday Inn Stratford-upon-Avon

Rooms 259 (8 fmly) **Facilities** ⊗ supervised Gym Sauna, Beauty Salon Xmas New Year Wi-fi **Conf** Class 340 Board 42 Thtr 550 **Services** Lift Air con **Parking** 350 (charged) **Notes** ⊗

Thistle Stratford-upon-Avon   thistle

★★★ 81% HOTEL

☎ 0871 376 9035 ▤ 0871 376 9135
Waterside CV37 6BA
e-mail: stratforduponavon@thistle.co.uk
web: www.thistlehotels.com/stratforduponavon
dir: M40 junct 15, A46 to Stratford-upon-Avon, take 1st exit at rdbt towards town centre, A439.

The hotel is located just a very short walk from the town centre, sitting directly opposite the world famous Shakespeare and Swan theatres and is fronted by award-winning gardens. Service throughout the day rooms is both friendly and professional, offering separate bar and lounge areas, with the dining room providing interesting menu selections. Bedrooms are well equipped and comfortably appointed.

Rooms 63 (4 fmly) **S** £70–£175; **D** £90–£205 (incl. bkfst)* **Facilities** STV Xmas New Year Wi-fi **Conf** Class 20 Board 20 Thtr 50 Del from £95 to £165* **Parking** 55 (charged) **Notes** LB Civ Wed 50

Best Western Salford Hall

★★★ 80% ⊛ HOTEL

☎ 01386 871300 & 0800 212671 ▤ 01386 871301
WR11 5UT
e-mail: reception@salfordhall.co.uk
web: www.salfordhall.co.uk

(For full entry see Abbot's Salford)

Best Western Grosvenor House

★★★ 78% HOTEL

☎ 01789 269213 ▤ 01789 266087
Warwick Rd CV37 6YT
e-mail: info@bwgh.co.uk
web: www.bwgh.co.uk
dir: M40 junct 15, follow Stratford signs to A439 Warwick Rd. Hotel 7m, on one-way system

This hotel is a short distance from the town centre and many of the historic attractions. Bedroom styles and sizes vary and the friendly staff offer an efficient service.

Refreshments are served in the lounge all day, plus room service is available. The Garden Room restaurant offers a choice of dishes from set priced and carte menus.

Rooms 73 (16 fmly) (25 GF) **S** £50–£130; **D** £50–£140* **Facilities** Xmas New Year Wi-fi **Conf** Class 45 Board 50 Thtr 100 Del from £99 to £160* **Parking** 46 **Notes** ⊗ Civ Wed 70

Macdonald Swan's Nest

★★★ 74% METRO HOTEL

☎ 0844 879 9140 ▤ 01789 414547
Bridgefoot CV37 7LT
e-mail: sales.swansnest@macdonald-hotels.co.uk
web: www.macdonald-hotels.co.uk/swansnest
dir: A439 towards Stratford, follow one-way system, turn left (A3400) over bridge, hotel on right.

Dating back to the 17th century, this hotel is said to be one of the earliest brick-built houses in the town. The hotel occupies a prime position on the banks of the River Avon and is ideally situated for exploring the town and the Warwickshire countryside. Bedrooms, all named after birds, are appointed to a high standard.

Rooms 67 (2 fmly) (25 GF) **S** £139; **D** £163 (incl. bkfst)* **Facilities** Use of facilities at Alveston Manor New Year Wi-fi **Conf** Class 100 Board 60 Thtr 140 Del from £120 to £165* **Parking** 80 **Notes** Civ Wed

Charlecote Pheasant Hotel   *folio Hotels*

★★★ 64% HOTEL

☎ 0870 609 6159 ▤ 01789 470222
Charlecote CV35 9EW
e-mail: charlecote@foliohotels.com
web: www.foliohotels.com/charlcotepheasant
dir: M40 junct 15, A429 towards Cirencester through Barford. In 2m right into Charlecote, hotel opposite Charlecote Park

Located just outside Stratford, this hotel is set in extensive grounds and is a popular conference venue. Various bedroom styles are available within the annexe wings, ranging from standard rooms to executive suites. The main building houses the restaurant and a lounge bar area.

Rooms 70 (39 fmly) **S** £70–£120; **D** £90–£140* **Facilities** FTV ⊰ ⊗ Children's play area Xmas New Year Wi-fi **Conf** Class 70 Board 40 Thtr 160 **Parking** 100 **Notes** LB Civ Wed 176

The New Inn Hotel & Restaurant

★★ 72% HOTEL

☎ 01789 293402 ▤ 01789 292716
Clifford Chambers CV37 8HR
e-mail: thenewinn65@aol.com
web: www.thenewinnhotel.co.uk
dir: A3400 onto B4632, 500yds on left

This welcoming, family-run hotel is located in the pretty village of Clifford Chambers. The bar has an open log fire

and, together with the restaurant, offers a choice of dining options. Bedrooms are appealing; some rooms have four-poster beds and there are rooms suitable for disabled guests.

Rooms 13 (2 fmly) (3 GF) **S** £65–£125; **D** £75–£125 (incl. bkfst) **Facilities** ♫ New Year Wi-fi Child facilities **Parking** 40 **Notes** LB ⊗ Closed 23-28 Dec

White Swan

★★ 68% HOTEL

☎ 01789 297022 & 269283 ▤ 01789 268773
Rother St CV37 6NH
e-mail: thewhiteswan.stratford@pebblehotels.com
dir: M40 junct 15 signed Stratford-on-Avon. Hotel opposite Market Square

This quintessential English inn is in the heart of historic Stratford. Much of the original charm and atmosphere remain; with unique wood panelling, low beams and antique furniture. Bedrooms are comfortable and remain in keeping with the style of the property.

Rooms 41 (3 fmly) **Facilities** ♫ Xmas New Year Wi-fi **Conf** Class 60 Board 60 Thtr 100 **Notes** LB ⊗ Civ Wed 100

Legacy Falcon   LEGACY HOTELS

Ⓤ

☎ 0870 832 9905 ▤ 0870 832 9906
Chapel St CV37 6HA
e-mail: res-falcon@legacy-hotels.co.uk
web: www.legacy-hotels.co.uk
dir: M40 junct 15, follow signs to town centre, turn into Chapel St, 2nd right into Scholars Lane, right again into hotel car park

Currently the rating for this establishment is not confirmed. This may be due to a change of ownership or because it has only recently joined the AA rating scheme. For further details please see the AA website: www.theAA.com

Rooms 84 (11 annexe) (6 fmly) (3 GF) **S** £56–£140; **D** £66–£165 (incl. bkfst)* **Facilities** STV Xmas New Year Wi-fi **Conf** Del from £125 to £155* **Services** Lift **Parking** 122 **Notes** Civ Wed

STUDLEY   Map 10 SP06

Best Western Studley Castle

★★★ 72% HOTEL

☎ 01527 853111 & 855200 ▤ 01527 855000
Castle Rd B80 7AJ
e-mail: bookings@studleycastle.com
dir: A435 S into Studley, left at castle sign, hotel 1m on right

This hotel has a delightful parkland location close to Stratford. Specialising in providing meeting room venues, the hotel has an impressive range of public areas. The restaurant also offers a relaxing environment and lovely

Continued

STUDLEY continued

views across the countryside. Bedrooms are available in a range of sizes and all are well equipped.

Rooms 57 (2 fmly) **S** £60-£85; **D** £70-£125 (incl. bkfst)*
Facilities STV Gym Sauna Xmas New Year Wi-fi
Conf Class 66 Board 20 Thtr 150 Del from £117.50 to £170.37* **Services** Lift **Parking** 150 **Notes** LB ⊗ Civ Wed 150

WARWICK   Map 10 SP26

See also **Honiley & Leamington Spa (Royal)**

Chesford Grange

★★★★ 80% HOTEL

☎ 01926 859331 📄 01926 859272
Chesford Bridge CV8 2LD
e-mail: chesfordgrangereservations@qhotels.co.uk
web: www.qhotels.co.uk

(For full entry see Kenilworth)

Ardencote Manor Hotel, Country Club & Spa

★★★★ 77% ⊛⊛ HOTEL

☎ 01926 843111 📄 01926 842646
The Cumsey, Lye Green Rd, Claverdon CV35 8LT
e-mail: hotel@ardencote.com
web: www.ardencote.com

(For full entry see Claverdon)

Express by Holiday Inn Warwick

BUDGET HOTEL

☎ 01926 483000 📄 01926 483033
Stratford Rd CV34 6TW
e-mail: warwick@expressbyholidayinn.co.uk
web: www.hiexpress.com/warwickuk
dir: M40 junct 15, follow signs A429 to Warwick. Take 1st right

A modern hotel ideal for families and business travellers. Fresh and uncomplicated, the spacious rooms include Sky TV, power shower and tea and coffee-making facilities. Continental buffet breakfast is included in the room rate; other meals may be taken at the nearby family pub or restaurant. See also the Hotel Groups pages.

Rooms 138 (59 fmly) **Conf** Class 18 Board 20 Thtr 40

WARWICK MOTORWAY SERVICE AREA (M40)   Map 10 SP35

Days Inn Warwick North

BUDGET HOTEL

☎ 01926 651681 📄 01926 651634
Warwick Services, M40 Northbound Junction 12-13, Banbury Road CV35 0AA
e-mail: warwick.north.hotel@welcomebreak.co.uk
web: www.welcomebreak.co.uk
dir: M40 northbound between junct 12 & 13

This modern building offers accommodation in smart, spacious and well-equipped bedrooms, suitable for families and business travellers, and all with en suite bathrooms. Continental breakfast is available and other refreshments may be taken at the nearby family restaurant. See also the Hotel Groups pages.

Days Inn Warwick North

Rooms 54 (45 fmly) **S** £39-£59; **D** £49-£69*
Conf Board 30 Del from £79 to £99*

Days Inn Warwick South

BUDGET HOTEL

☎ 01926 650168 📄 01926 651601
Warwick Services, M40 Southbound, Banbury Road CV35 0AA
e-mail: warwick.south.hotel@welcomebreak.co.uk
web: www.welcomebreak.co.uk
dir: M40 southbound between junct 14 & 12

Rooms 40 (38 fmly) **S** £39-£59; **D** £49-£69*

WELLESBOURNE   Map 10 SP25

Barceló Walton Hall

★★★★ 77% HOTEL

☎ 01789 842424 📄 01789 470418
Walton CV35 9HU
e-mail: waltonhall.mande@barcelo-hotels.co.uk

Once occupied by the Churchill family, this delightful Queen Anne house is set in 14 acres of attractive gardens on the edge of Ascot. Public areas include a comfortable lounge bar, an attractive restaurant that overlooks the rear gardens and extensive conference facilities. The main house has been skilfully extended to offer smart, well-equipped bedrooms.

Rooms 56 (19 annexe) (11 GF) **Facilities** Spa STV FTV ⊗ supervised ⚑ Gym Dance studio Beauty salon Xmas New Year Wi-fi **Conf** Class 60 Board 36 Thtr 240 Del from £189* **Services** Air con **Parking** 240 **Notes** ⊗ Civ Wed 240

Innkeeper's Lodge Stratford-upon-Avon East

BUDGET HOTEL

☎ 0845 112 6075 📠 0845 112 6228
Warwick Rd CV35 9LX
web: www.innkeeperslodge.com/stratford
dir: M40 junct 15 S onto A429 towards Wellesbourne. Turn left at rdbt onto B4086. Lodge 300yds on right

Innkeeper's Lodge represents an exciting, high value concept within the budget hotel market. Comfortable bedrooms provide excellent facilities that include satellite TV and modem points. This carefully restored lodge is in a picturesque setting and has its own unique style and quirky character. Food is served all day, and an extensive, complimentary continental breakfast is offered.

Rooms 9 **S** £59.95-£65; **D** £59.95-£65 (incl. bkfst)

WROXALL Map 10 SP27

Wroxall Abbey Estate

★★★ 78% HOTEL

☎ 01926 484470 📠 01926 485206
Birmingham Rd CV35 7NB
e-mail: info@wroxall.com
dir: Between Solihull & Warwick on A4141

Situated in 27 acres of open parkland, yet only 10 miles from the NEC and Birmingham International Airport, this hotel is a magnificent Victorian mansion. Some of the individually designed bedrooms have traditional décor but there are some modern loft rooms as well; some rooms have four-posters. Sonnets Restaurant, with its

impressive fireplace and oak panelling, makes the ideal setting for fine dining.

Rooms 70 (22 annexe) (10 GF) **S** £99-£299; **D** £109-£399* **Facilities** Spa STV ⊗ ⚬ Fishing Gym Ten pin bowling Walks/jogging trail ♫ Xmas New Year Wi-fi **Conf** Class 80 Board 60 Thtr 160 Del from £199 to £259* **Services** Lift **Parking** 200 **Notes** LB ⊗ No children 12yrs Civ Wed 200

WEST MIDLANDS

BALSALL COMMON Map 10 SP27

Nailcote Hall

★★★★ 78% HOTEL

☎ 024 7646 6174 📠 024 7647 0720
Nailcote Ln, Berkswell CV7 7DE
e-mail: info@nailcotehall.co.uk
web: www.nailcotehall.co.uk
dir: on B4101

This 17th-century house, set in 15 acres of grounds, boasts a 9-hole championship golf course and Roman bath-style swimming pool amongst its many facilities. Rooms are spacious and elegantly furnished. The eating options are the fine dining restaurant where smart casual dress is required, or in The Piano Bar for informal meals.

Rooms 40 (19 annexe) (2 fmly) (15 GF) **S** £100-£175; **D** £110-£185 (incl. bkfst)* **Facilities** STV ⊗ supervised ⚬ 9 ⚬ Putt green ⚑ Gym Beauty room ♫ Xmas New Year Wi-fi **Conf** Class 80 Board 44 Thtr 140 Del from £145 to £165* **Services** Lift **Parking** 200 **Notes** ⊗ Civ Wed 120

Haigs

★★★ 71% HOTEL

☎ 01676 533004 📠 01676 535132
Kenilworth Rd CV7 7EL
e-mail: info@haigshotel.co.uk
dir: A45 towards Coventry, at Stonebridge Island turn right, 4m S of M42 junct 6

Conveniently located just five miles from Birmingham Airport and twelve miles from Stratford-upon-Avon. This hotel offers a comfortable stay at a small family run operation. Enjoyable meals can be taken in Mckees Brasserie.

Rooms 23 (2 fmly) (5 GF) **S** £65-£80; **D** £75-£112.50 (incl. bkfst)* **Facilities** Xmas New Year Wi-fi **Conf** Board 20 Thtr 25 **Parking** 23 **Notes** LB ⊗ Civ Wed 60

BIRMINGHAM Map 10 SP08

See also **Bromsgrove (Worcestershire), Lea Marston (Warwickshire), Oldbury & Sutton Coldfield**

Birmingham Marriott Hotel Marriott HOTELS & RESORTS

★★★★ 80% HOTEL

☎ 0121 452 1144 📠 0121 456 3442
12 Hagley Rd, Five Ways B16 8SJ
e-mail: pascal.demarchi@marriotthotels.com
web: www.birminghammarriott.co.uk
dir: Leebank Middleway to Five Ways rdbt, 1st left then right. Follow signs for hotel

Situated in the suburb of Edgbaston, this Edwardian hotel is a prominent landmark on the outskirts of the city centre. Air-conditioned bedrooms are decorated in a comfortable, modern style and provide a comprehensive range of extra facilities. Public rooms include the contemporary, brasserie-style West 12 Bar and Restaurant.

Rooms 104 **S** £84-£165; **D** £84-£165* **Facilities** Spa STV ⊗ Gym Steam room Wi-fi **Conf** Board 35 Thtr 80 Del from £150 to £210* **Services** Lift Air con **Parking** 50 (charged) **Notes** LB ⊗ Civ Wed 60

Hotel du Vin Birmingham

★★★★ 79% ⊗ TOWN HOUSE HOTEL

☎ 0121 200 0600 📠 0121 236 0889
25 Church St B3 2NR
e-mail: info@birmingham.hotelduvin.com
web: www.hotelduvin.com
dir: M6 junct 6/A38(M) to city centre, over flyover. Keep left & exit at St Chads Circus signed Jewellery Quarter. At lights & rdbt take 1st exit, follow signs for Colmore Row, opposite cathedral. Right into Church St, across Barwick St. Hotel on right

The former Birmingham Eye Hospital has become a chic and sophisticated hotel. The stylish, high-ceilinged rooms, all with a wine theme, are luxuriously appointed and feature stunning bathrooms, sumptuous duvets and Egyptian cotton sheets. The Bistro offers relaxed dining and a top-notch wine list, while other attractions include a champagne bar, a wine boutique and a health club.

Hotel du Vin - AA Small Hotel Group of the Year 2008-9.

Rooms 66 **D** £150-£425* **Facilities** Spa STV Gym Treatment rooms Steam room Sauna Xmas New Year Wi-fi **Conf** Class 40 Board 40 Thtr 84 **Services** Lift Air con **Notes** LB Civ Wed 84

Macdonald Burlington   MACDONALD HOTELS & RESORTS

★★★★ 77% HOTEL

☎ 0844 879 9019 & 0121 643 9191 📠 0121 628 5005
Burlington Arcade, 126 New St B2 4JQ
e-mail: events.burlington@macdonald-hotels.co.uk
web: www.macdonaldhotels.co.uk/burlington
dir: M6 junct 6, follow signs for city centre, then take A38

The Burlington's original Victorian grandeur - the marble and iron staircases and the high ceilings - blend

Continued

BIRMINGHAM continued

seamlessly with modern facilities. Bedrooms are equipped to a good standard and public areas include a stylish bar and coffee lounge. The Berlioz Restaurant specialises in innovative dishes using fresh produce.

Rooms 112 (6 fmly) **Facilities** STV New Year Wi-fi **Conf** Class 175 Board 60 Thtr 400 Del from £175 to £225 **Services** Lift **Notes** ⊗ Closed 24-26 Dec Civ Wed 400

Copthorne Hotel Birmingham

★★★★ 71% HOTEL

☎ 0121 200 2727 📠 0121 200 1197
Paradise Circus B3 3HJ
e-mail: reservations.birmingham@millenniumhotels. co.uk
web: www.copthornebirmingham.co.uk
dir: M6 junct 6, city centre A38(M). After Queensway Tunnel emerge left, follow International Convention Centre signs. At Paradise Circus island follow right lane. Hotel in centre

This hotel is one of the few establishments in the city that benefits from its own car park. Bedrooms are spacious and come in a choice of styles, all with excellent facilities. Guests can enjoy a variety of dining options, including the contemporary menu in Goldies Brasserie.

Rooms 212 **S** £60-£170; **D** £60-£170* **Facilities** STV Xmas New Year Wi-fi **Conf** Class 120 Board 30 Thtr 200 Del from £130 to £195* **Services** Lift **Parking** 30 (charged) **Notes** ⊗

Novotel Birmingham Centre

★★★★ 70% HOTEL

☎ 0121 643 2000 📠 0121 643 9796
70 Broad St B1 2HT
e-mail: h1077@accor.com
web: www.novotel.com
dir: A38/A456, hotel on right beyond International Convention Centre

This large, modern, purpose-built hotel benefits from an excellent city centre location, with the bonus of secure parking. Bedrooms are spacious, modern and well equipped especially for business users; four rooms have facilities for less able guests. Public areas include the Garden Brasserie, function rooms and a fitness room.

Rooms 148 (148 fmly) (11 smoking) **S** £155-£175; **D** £155-£185* **Facilities** Gym Fitness room Cardio-vascular equipment Spa bath Wi-fi **Conf** Class 120 Board 90 Thtr 300 Del from £140 to £250* **Services** Lift Air con **Parking** 53 (charged) **Notes** LB

Best Western Westley

★★★ 80% HOTEL

☎ 0121 706 4312 📠 0121 706 2824
80-90 Westley Rd, Acocks Green B27 7UJ
e-mail: reservations@westley-hotel.co.uk
dir: A41 signed Birmingham on Solihull by-pass, continue to Acocks Green. At rdbt, 2nd exit B4146 Westley Rd. Hotel 200yds on left

Situated in the city suburbs and conveniently located for the N.E.C. and the airport, this friendly hotel provides well-equipped, smartly presented bedrooms. In addition to the main restaurant, there is also a lively bar and brasserie together with a large function room.

Rooms 37 (11 annexe) (1 fmly) **S** £90-£140; **D** £130-£160 (incl. bkfst) **Facilities** STV ♫ New Year Wi-fi **Conf** Class 80 Board 50 Thtr 200 Del from £140 to £160 **Parking** 150 **Notes** ⊗ Civ Wed 200

Malmaison Birmingham

★★★ 80% HOTEL

☎ 0121 246 5000 📠 0121 246 5002
1 Wharfside St, The Mailbox B1 1RD
e-mail: birmingham@malmaison.com
web: www.malmaison.com
dir: M6 junct 6, follow A38 towards Birmingham. Hotel within The Mailbox, signed from A38

The 'Mailbox' development, of which this stylish and contemporary hotel is a part, incorporates the very best in fashionable shopping, an array of restaurants and ample parking. Air-conditioned bedrooms are stylishly decorated and feature comprehensive facilities. Public rooms include a contemporary bar and brasserie which prove a hit with guests and locals alike. Gymtonic and a Petit Spa are also available, offering rejuvenating treatments.

Rooms 189 **S** £99-£160; **D** £99-£160* **Facilities** Gym Wi-fi **Conf** Class 40 Board 24 Thtr 50 **Services** Lift Air con **Notes** LB

The Royal Angus by Thistle

thistle

★★★ 80% HOTEL

☎ 0870 333 9126 📠 0870 333 9226
St Chads, Queensway B4 6HY
e-mail: reservations.birmingham@thistle.co.uk
web: www.thistlehotels.com/birminghamcity
dir: From M6 junct 6 onto Aston Expressway towards city centre, after 1m exit A38 signed Jewellery Quarter. Hotel on left

This hotel benefits from a central location and is convenient for both the motorway network and extensive parking facilities. Bedrooms range in size and style with executive rooms providing air conditioning and a host of thoughtful extras. A modern comfortable lounge bar links to a terrace.

Rooms 133 (3 fmly) **Facilities** Xmas New Year Wi-fi **Conf** Class 80 Board 30 Thtr 180 **Services** Lift **Notes** LB ⊗ Civ Wed 140

Menzies Strathallan

MenziesHotels

★★★ 77% HOTEL

☎ 0121 455 9777 📠 0121 454 9432
225 Hagley Rd, Edgbaston B16 9RY
e-mail: strathallan@menzieshotels.co.uk
web: www.menzies-hotels.co.uk
dir: From A38 follow signs for ICC onto Broad St, towards Five Ways island, take underpass to Hagley Rd. Hotel 1m

Located just a few minutes from the city's central attractions and with the benefit of excellent parking, this hotel provides a range of newly refurbished, comfortable and well-equipped bedrooms. A modern lounge bar and contemporary restaurant offer a good range of dining options.

Rooms 135 **S** £39-£135; **D** £49-£145 **Facilities** STV FTV Xmas New Year Wi-fi **Conf** Class 90 Board 50 Thtr 170 **Services** Lift **Parking** 50 (charged) **Notes** LB ⊗ Civ Wed 40

The Westmead Hotel

folio
Hotels

★★★ 70% HOTEL

☎ 0870 609 6119 📠 0121 445 6163
Redditch Rd, Hopwood B48 7AL
e-mail: westmead@foliohotels.com
web: www.foliohotels.com/westmead
dir: M42 junct 2, A441 towards Birmingham. 1m. Hotel on right

In a quiet location on the outskirts of the city, yet close to the M42, this hotel offers a number of meeting and conference rooms. The bedrooms are generally spacious, well equipped and comfortable. A spacious bar offers carvery lunches, and dinner is served in the adjacent restaurant.

Rooms 56 (2 fmly) (4 GF) **Facilities** STV Free access to LA Fitness Complex New Year Wi-fi **Conf** Class 120 Board 80 Thtr 220 Del from £110 to £140* **Parking** 200 **Notes** ⊗ Civ Wed 120

Jurys Inn Birmingham

★★★ 68% HOTEL

☎ 0121 626 0626 & 606 9000 📠 0121 626 0627
245 Broad St B1 2HQ
e-mail: jurysinn_birmingham@jurysinns.com
web: www.jurysinns.com
dir: on A456 in city centre

This large hotel is ideally located in the centre of the city
and offers extensive conference facilities. The modern
bedrooms are spacious and the restaurant is designed for
efficiency, offering a buffet-style operation.

Rooms 445 (336 fmly) **Conf** Class 144 Board 44 Thtr 280
Services Lift Air con **Parking** 230 (charged) **Notes** ⊛
Closed 24-26 Dec

Great Barr Hotel & Conference Centre

★★★ 66% HOTEL

☎ 0121 357 1141 📠 0121 357 7557
Pear Tree Dr, Newton Rd, Great Barr B43 6HS
e-mail: sales@thegreatbarrhotel.com
web: www.thegreatbarrhotel.com
dir: M6 junct 7, at Scott Arms x-rds right towards West
Bromwich (A4010) Newton Rd. Hotel 1m on right

This busy hotel, situated in a leafy residential area, is
particularly popular with business clients; after a major
refurbishment the hotel has excellent, state-of-the-art
training and seminar facilities. There is a traditional
oak-panelled bar and formal restaurant. The refit has
extended to many of the bedrooms too; all are appointed
to a good standard and have the expected amenities.

Rooms 105 (6 fmly) **S** £45-£69; **D** £650-£85 (incl. bkfst)*
Facilities STV Xmas Wi-fi **Conf** Class 90 Board 60
Thtr 200 Del from £95 to £145* **Parking** 200 **Notes** LB ⊛
RS BH (Restaurant may close) Civ Wed 200

Copperfield House

★★ 75% HOTEL

☎ 0121 472 8344 📠 0121 415 5655
60 Upland Rd, Selly Park B29 7JS
e-mail: info@copperfieldhousehotel.fsnet.co.uk
dir: M6 junct 6/A38 through city centre. After tunnels,
right at lights into Belgrave Middleway. Right at rdbt onto
A441. At Selly Park Tavern, right into Upland Rd

A delightful Victorian hotel, situated in a leafy suburb,
close to the BBC's Pebble Mill Studios and within easy
reach of the centre. Accommodation is smartly presented
and well equipped, and the executive rooms are
particularly spacious. There is a lounge with an honesty
bar and the restaurant offers carefully prepared,
seasonally-inspired food accompanied by a well-chosen
wine list.

Rooms 17 (1 fmly) (2 GF) (5 smoking) **S** £50-£82.50;
D £70-£100 (incl. bkfst)* **Facilities** FTV Wi-fi **Parking** 11
Notes LB Closed 24 Dec - 2 Jan

Woodlands

★★ 60% METRO HOTEL

☎ 0121 420 2341 📠 0121 429 3935
379-381 Hagley Rd, Edgbaston B17 8DL
e-mail: hotel@woodlands2000.freeserve.co.uk
web: www.thewoodlandshotel.co.uk
dir: Follow sign to city centre along A456 (Hagley Rd) for
3.5m. Hotel on left where Sandon Rd meets Hagley Rd

Ideally located for major links to the west of city, this
modern hotel provides a range of thoughtfully furnished
bedrooms; some are suitable for families. Public areas
are both comfortable and spacious, and the large car
park is a real benefit.

Rooms 20 (4 fmly) **S** £45-£50; **D** £56-£64 (incl. bkfst)*
Facilities FTV Wi-fi **Parking** 20 **Notes** ⊛ Civ Wed 100

Grove

U

☎ 0121 429 2502 📠 0121 4201207
409/411 Hagley Rd, Edgbaston B17 8BL
e-mail: info@thegrovehotelbirmingham.com

Currently the rating for this establishment is not confirmed.
This may be due to a change of ownership or because it has
only recently joined the AA rating scheme. For further
details please see the AA website: www.theAA.com

Rooms 36 **S** £30-£40; **D** £40-£50 (incl. bkfst)*

Crowne Plaza Birmingham City

U

☎ 0870 400 9150 📠 0121 643 9018
Central Square B1 1HH
web: www.crowneplaza.co.uk
dir: A38, follow city centre signs. After 2nd tunnel (Suffolk
Queensway) join left slip road, follow signs for New St
Station & The Mailbox. Hotel next to The Mailbox

At the time of going to press the rating for this
establishment was not confirmed. This may be due to a
change of ownership or because it has only recently
joined the AA rating scheme. For further details please
see the AA website. www.theAA.com

Rooms 284

Holiday Inn Birmingham M6 Jct 7

U

☎ 0870 400 9009 & 0121 357 7303 📠 0121 357 7503
Chapel Ln, Great Barr B43 7BG
web: www.holidayinn.co.uk
dir: M6 junct 7/A34 signed Walsall. Hotel 200yds on right
across carriageway in Chapel Lane

Currently the rating for this establishment is not confirmed.
This may be due to a change of ownership or because it has
only recently joined the AA rating scheme. For further
details please see the AA website: www.theAA.com

Rooms 190 (45 fmly) (67 GF) (12 smoking) **S** £55-£129;
D £55-£129* **Facilities** STV ⊕ supervised Gym Xmas
New Year Wi-fi **Conf** Class 75 Board 50 Thtr 160
Services Air con **Parking** 250 **Notes** LB Civ Wed 100

Holiday Inn Birmingham City

U

☎ 0870 400 9008 📠 0121 631 2528
Smallbrook Queensway B5 4EW
e-mail: birminghamcity@ichotelsgroup.com
web: www.holidayinn.co.uk

Currently the rating for this establishment is not confirmed.
This may be due to a change of ownership or because it has
only recently joined the AA rating scheme. For further
details please see the AA website: www.theAA.com

Rooms 280

BIRMINGHAM continued

Campanile Birmingham

BUDGET HOTEL

☎ 0121 359 3330 📠 0121 359 1223
Chester St, Aston B6 4BE
e-mail: birmingham@campanile.com
dir: next to rdbt at junct of A4540/A38

This modern building offers accommodation in smart,
well-equipped bedrooms, all with en suite bathrooms.
Refreshments may be taken at the informal bistro. See
also the Hotel Groups pages.

Rooms 109 (3 fmly)

Express by Holiday Inn Birmingham

BUDGET HOTEL

☎ 0121 747 6633 📠 0121 747 6644
1200 Chester Rd, Castle Bromwich B35 7AF
e-mail: castlebromwich@holidayinnexpress.co.uk
web: www.hiexpress.com/birminghamex
dir: M6 junct 5/6/A38 for Tyburn, right into Chester Rd,
follow Park signs

A modern hotel ideal for families and business travellers.
Fresh and uncomplicated, the spacious rooms include Sky
TV, power shower and tea and coffee-making facilities.
Continental buffet breakfast is included in the room rate;
other meals may be taken at the nearby family pub or
restaurant. See also the Hotel Groups pages.

Rooms 110 (21 fmly) (12 GF) **Conf** Class 16 Board 16
Thtr 20

Express by Holiday Inn Birmingham City Centre

BUDGET HOTEL

☎ 0845 1126151 📠 0121 200 1910
65 Lionel St B3 1JE
e-mail: ebhi.birminghamcc@mbplc.com
web: www.hiexpress.com/exb'minghamc

Rooms 120 **Conf** Class 16 Board 16 Thtr 30

Express by Holiday Inn Birmingham - North

BUDGET HOTEL

☎ 0121 358 4044 📠 0121 358 4644
Beacon Birmingham Rd, Great Barr B43 7AG
e-mail: ebhi-walsall@btconnect.com
web: www.hiexpress.com/bhx-walsall
dir: M6 junct 7, onto A34 towards Walsall

Rooms 32 (12 GF) **Conf** Class 16 Board 16 Thtr 25

Express by Holiday Inn Birmingham - South

BUDGET HOTEL

☎ 0121 744 4414 📠 0121 744 4700
Stratford Rd, Hall Green B28 9ES
e-mail: ebhi-hallgreen@btconnect.com
web: www.hiexpress.com/birminghamso
dir: M42 junct 4, follow city centre signs (A34) for 7km,
hotel on rdbt at junct with A4040

Rooms 51 (16 fmly) **Conf** Class 12 Board 12 Thtr 20

Ibis Birmingham Bordesley Circus

BUDGET HOTEL

☎ 0121 506 2600 📠 0121 506 2610
1 Bordesley Park Rd, Bordesley B10 0PD
e-mail: H2178@accor-hotels.com
web: www.ibishotel.com

Modern, budget hotel offering comfortable
accommodation in bright and practical bedrooms.
Breakfast is self-service and dinner is available in the
restaurant. See also the Hotel Groups pages.

Rooms 87

Ibis Birmingham City Centre

BUDGET HOTEL

☎ 0121 622 6010 📠 0121 622 6020
Arcadian Centre, Ladywell Walk B5 4ST
e-mail: h1459@accor-hotels.com
web: www.ibishotel.com
dir: From motorways follow city centre signs. Then follow
Bullring or Indoor Market signs. Hotel next to market

Rooms 159 (5 fmly) **Conf** Class 60 Board 40 Thtr 100

Ibis Birmingham Holloway Circus

BUDGET HOTEL

☎ 0121 622 4925 📠 0121 622 4195
55 Irving St B1 1DH
e-mail: H2092@accor.com
web: www.ibishotel.com
dir: from M6 take A38/City Centre, left after 2nd tunnel.
Right at rdbt, 4th left (Sutton St) into Irving St. Hotel on
left

Rooms 51 (26 GF) (7 smoking) **D** £42-£67*

Innkeeper's Lodge Birmingham West (Quinton)

BUDGET HOTEL

☎ 0845 112 6066 📠 0845 112 6237
563 Hagley Road West, Quinton B32 1HP
web: www.innkeeperslodge.com/birminghamwest
dir: M5 junct 3, A456 east towards Birmingham. Lodge on
opposite side of dual carriageway, cross short distance
from rdbt.

Innkeeper's Lodge represents an exciting, high value
concept within the budget hotel market. Comfortable
bedrooms provide excellent facilities that include satellite
TV and modem points. Options include family rooms, and
for the corporate guest, cutting edge IT which includes
Wi-fi access. A popular Carvery provides all-day food,
including an extensive, complimentary continental
breakfast.

Rooms 24 (9 fmly) **S** £53-£55; **D** £53-£55 (incl. bkfst)
Conf Thtr 40

Travelodge Birmingham Central

BUDGET HOTEL

☎ 08719 846 325 📠 0121 644 5251
230 Broad St B15 1AY
web: www.travelodge.co.uk
dir: lodge on left corner of Broad St/Granville St

Travelodge offers good quality, good value, modern
accommodation. Ideal for families, the spacious en suite
bedrooms include remote-control TV, tea and coffee-
making facilities and comfortable beds. Meals can be
taken at the nearby family restaurant. See also the Hotel
Groups pages.

Rooms 136 **S** fr £29; **D** fr £29

Travelodge Birmingham Central Broadway Plaza

BUDGET HOTEL

☎ 0870 191 1825 📄 0121 455 8733
Broadway Plaza, 220 Ladywood, Middleway B16 8LP
web: www.travelodge.co.uk
dir: A38(M) Birmingham Central. Stay in second lane for
approx 2m & follow signs for city centre

Rooms 74 S fr £29; D fr £29

Travelodge Birmingham Fort Dunlop

BUDGET HOTEL

☎ 08719 846 312 📄 0121 747 9958
Fort Parkway, Erdington B24 9FD
web: www.travelodge.co.uk

Rooms 100 S fr £29; D fr £29

Travelodge Birmingham Maypole

BUDGET HOTEL

☎ 08719 846 304 📄 0121 430 7565
Maypole Ln B14 5JF
web: www.travelodge.co.uk
dir: A435 (Alcester Road) towards city centre. Hotel at 3rd
rdbt on corner of Alcester Rd & Maypole Lane

Rooms 60 S fr £29; D fr £29

Travelodge Birmingham Yardley

BUDGET HOTEL

☎ 08719 846 065 📄 0121 764 5882
A45 Coventry Rd, Acocks Green, Yardley B26 1DS
web: www.travelodge.co.uk
dir: on A45 approx 5m from M42 junct 6

Rooms 40 S fr £29; D fr £29

BIRMINGHAM AIRPORT   Map 10 SP08

Novotel Birmingham Airport

★★★ 74% HOTEL

☎ 0121 782 7000 & 782 4111 📄 0121 782 0445
B26 3QL
e-mail: H1158@accor.com
web: www.novotel.com
dir: M42 junct 6/A45 to Birmingham, signed to airport.
Hotel opposite main terminal.

This large, purpose-built hotel is located opposite the
main passenger terminal. Bedrooms are spacious,
modern in style and well equipped, including Playstations
to keep the children busy. Several rooms have facilities
for less able guests. The Garden Brasserie is open from
noon until midnight, the bar is open 24 hours and a full
room service is available.

Rooms 195 (36 fmly) (20 smoking) S £75-£159;
D £75-£159* Facilities STV Wi-fi Conf Class 20 Board 22
Thtr 35 Del from £149 to £179* Services Lift Notes LB

Holiday Inn Birmingham Airport

[I]

☎ 0870 400 9007 📄 0121 782 2476
Coventry Rd B26 3QW
web: www.holidayinn.co.uk

Currently the rating for this establishment is not confirmed.
This may be due to a change of ownership or because it has
only recently joined the AA rating scheme. For further
details please see the AA website: www.theAA.com

Rooms 141

BIRMINGHAM (NATIONAL EXHIBITION CENTRE)   Map 10 SP18

Nailcote Hall

★★★★ 78% ⊛ HOTEL

☎ 024 7646 6174 📄 024 7647 0720
Nailcote Ln, Berkswell CV7 7DE
e-mail: info@nailcotehall.co.uk
web: www.nailcotehall.co.uk

(For full entry see Balsall Common)

Crowne Plaza Birmingham NEC

★★★★ 75% HOTEL

☎ 0870 400 9160 📄 0121 781 4321
National Exhibition Centre, Pendigo Way B40 1PS
e-mail: necroomsales@ihg.com
web: www.crowneplaza.co.uk
dir: M42 junct 6, follow signs for NEC, take 2nd exit on
left, South Way for hotel entrance 50mtrs on right

On the doorstep of the NEC and overlooking Pendigo Lake,
this hotel has contemporary design and offers well-
equipped bedrooms with air-conditioning. Rooms have
ample working space and high-speed internet access (for
an additional charge). Eating options include the modern
Pendigo Restaurant overlooking the lake, the bar and
24-hour room service.

Rooms 242 (12 fmly) (15 smoking) S £139-£250;
D £149-£260 (incl. bkfst)* Facilities STV Gym Sauna
Wi-fi Conf Class 140 Board 56 Thtr 200 Services Lift
Air con Parking 348 Notes LB ⊗ Civ Wed 160

BIRMINGHAM (NATIONAL EXHIBITION CENTRE) continued

Best Western Premier Moor Hall Hotel & Spa

★★★★ 74% HOTEL

☎ 0121 308 3751 📠 0121 308 8974
Moor Hall Dr, Four Oaks B75 6LN
e-mail: mail@moorhallhotel.co.uk
web: www.moorhallhotel.co.uk

(For full entry see Sutton Coldfield)

Arden Hotel & Leisure Club

★★★ 71% HOTEL

☎ 01675 443221 📠 01675 445604
Coventry Rd, Bickenhill B92 0EH
e-mail: enquiries@ardenhotel.co.uk
dir: M42 junct 6/A45 towards Birmingham. Hotel 0.25m on right, just off Birmingham International railway island

This smart hotel neighbouring the NEC offers modern rooms and well-equipped leisure facilities. After dinner in the formal restaurant, the place to relax is the spacious lounge area. A buffet breakfast is served in the bright and airy Meeting Place.

Rooms 216 (6 fmly) (6 GF) **Facilities** Spa 🏊 supervised Gym Sports therapy Beautician 🎵 Xmas New Year Wi-fi **Conf** Class 40 Board 60 Thtr 200 **Services** Lift **Parking** 300 **Notes** LB RS 25-28 Dec Civ Wed 100

See advert on page 505

Haigs

★★★ 71% HOTEL

☎ 01676 533004 📠 01676 535132
Kenilworth Rd CV7 7EL
e-mail: info@haigshotel.co.uk

(For full entry see Balsall Common)

Heath Lodge

★★ 63% HOTEL

☎ 0121 779 2218 📠 0121 770 5648
117 Coleshill Rd, Marston Green B37 7HT
e-mail: reception@heathlodgehotel.freeserve.co.uk
dir: 1m N of NEC or Birmingham International Airport & station. From M6 take A446, then A452 junct 4

This privately owned and personally run hotel is ideally located for visitors to the NEC and Birmingham Airport. Hospitality and service standards are high and while some bedrooms are compact, all are well equipped and comfortable. Public areas include a bar and a lounge, and a dining room that overlooks the pretty garden.

Rooms 17 (1 fmly) (1 GF) **Facilities** Child facilities **Conf** Class 16 Board 14 Thtr 20 **Parking** 24 **Notes** LB Closed 25-26 Dec & 1 Jan

---

| CASTLE BROMWICH | Map 10 SP18 |

Innkeeper's Lodge Birmingham Castle Bromwich

BUDGET HOTEL

☎ 0845 112 6076
Chester Rd B36 0AG
web: www.innkeeperslodge.com
dir: A452 signed Leamington. Right into Parkfield Drive then right into Beechcroft Rd. Left at rdbt into Chester Road, B4118. Lodge on right

Innkeeper's Lodge represents an exciting, high value concept within the budget hotel market. Comfortable bedrooms provide excellent facilities that include satellite TV and modem points. Options include family rooms, and for the corporate guest, cutting edge IT which includes Wi-fi access. A popular Carvery provides all-day food, including an extensive, complimentary continental breakfast.

Rooms 30 **S** £45-£50; **D** £45-£50

| COVENTRY | Map 10 SP37 |

See also **Brandon, Meriden & Nuneaton (Warwickshire)**

Novotel Coventry

★★★ 71% HOTEL

☎ 024 7636 5000 📠 024 7636 2422
Wilsons Ln CV6 6HL
e-mail: h0506@accor-hotels.com
web: www.novotel.com
dir: M6 junct 3. Follow signs for B4113 towards Longford and Bedworth. 3rd exit on large rdbt

A modern hotel convenient for Birmingham, Coventry and the motorway network, offering spacious, well-equipped accommodation. The bright brasserie has extended dining hours, and alternatively there is an extensive room-service menu. Family rooms and a play area make this a child-friendly hotel, and there is also a selection of meeting rooms.

Rooms 98 (33 fmly) (25 GF) (16 smoking) **S** £55-£150; **D** £55-£150* **Facilities** STV 🏊 Wi-fi **Conf** Class 100 Board 40 Thtr 200 Del from £125 to £145* **Services** Lift **Parking** 120 **Notes** LB Civ Wed 50

Brooklands Grange Hotel & Restaurant

★★★ 70% HOTEL

☎ 024 7660 1601 📠 024 7660 1277
Holyhead Rd CV5 8HX
e-mail: info@brooklands-grange.co.uk
web: www.brooklands-grange.co.uk
dir: exit A45 at city centre rdbt. At next rdbt take A4114. Hotel 100yds on left

Behind the Jacobean façade of Brooklands Grange is a well run modern and comfortable business hotel. Well-appointed bedrooms are thoughtfully equipped and a

---

smartly appointed four-poster bedroom is available. Contemporary, well-flavoured dishes are on offer

Rooms 31 (3 fmly) (11 GF) **Conf** Class 10 Board 14 Thtr 20 **Parking** 52 **Notes** LB Closed 26-28 Dec & 1-2 Jan RS 24 Dec-2 Jan

The Chace

★★★ 70% HOTEL

☎ 0844 736 8607 📠 024 7630 1816
London Rd, Toll Bar End CV3 4EQ
e-mail: chacehotel@corushotels.com
web: www.corushotels.com
dir: A45 or A46 follow to Toll Bar Roundabout/Coventry Airport, take B4116 to Willenhall, over mini-rdbt, hotel on left

A former doctor's mansion, the main building retains many of its original Victorian features, including public rooms with high ceilings, stained glass windows, oak panelling and an impressive staircase; there is also a patio and well-kept gardens. Bedroom styles and sizes vary; most are attractively appointed, bright and modern.

Rooms 66 (23 fmly) (24 GF) (8 smoking) **S** £93; **D** £93* **Facilities** ☄ Nearby leisure centre New Year Wi-fi **Conf** Class 60 Board 45 Thtr 100 Del from £100 to £135* **Parking** 120 **Notes** LB ⊗ RS Xmas period Civ Wed 150

Holiday Inn Coventry South

Ⓤ

☎ 024 7630 1585 & 0870 400 7216 📠 0870 400 7216
London Rd, Ryton on Dunsmore CV8 3DY
e-mail: reservations@coventrykewgreen.co.uk
web: www.holidayinn.co.uk
dir: M6 junct 2, take A46 towards Warwick, then A45 London at Coventry Airport

Currently the rating for this establishment is not confirmed. This may be due to a change of ownership or because it has only recently joined the AA rating scheme. For further details please see the AA website: www.theAA.com

Rooms 51 (15 fmly) (27 GF) (6 smoking) **Facilities** STV Gym New Year Wi-fi **Conf** Class 100 Board 60 Thtr 300 Del from £120 to £165 **Parking** 150 **Notes** ⊗ Civ Wed 280

Best Western Ventnor Towers

★★★ 73% HOTEL

☎ 01983 852277 🖷 01983 855536
54 Madeira Rd PO38 1QT
e-mail: reservations@ventnortowers.com
web: www.ventnortowers.com
dir: From E, 1st left off A3055 just before pelican crossing

This mid-Victorian hotel, set in spacious grounds from where a path leads down to the shore, is high above the bay and enjoys splendid sea views. Many potted plants and fresh flowers grace the day rooms, which include two lounges and a spacious bar. Bedrooms include two four-poster rooms and some that have their own balconies.

Rooms 25 (4 fmly) (6 GF) **Facilities** ↸ 🏌 Putt green **Conf** Class 60 Board 44 Thtr 100 **Parking** 20 **Notes** LB Closed 24-26 Dec

---

Eversley

★★★ 68% HOTEL

☎ 01983 852244 & 852462 🖷 01983 856534
Park Av PO38 1LB
e-mail: eversleyhotel@yahoo.co.uk
web: www.eversleyhotel.com
dir: on A3055 W of Ventnor, next to Ventnor Park

Located west of Ventnor, this hotel enjoys a quiet location and has some rooms with garden and pool views. The spacious restaurant is sometimes used for local functions, and there is a bar, television room, lounge area, a card room as well as a jacuzzi and gym. Bedrooms are generally a good size.

Rooms 30 (8 fmly) (2 GF) **Facilities** ↸ Gym Pool table Xmas **Conf** Class 40 Board 20 **Parking** 23 **Notes** Closed 30 Nov-22 Dec & 2 Jan-8 Feb

---

Wellington

★★★ Ⓐ HOTEL

☎ 01983 856600 🖷 01983 856611
Belgrave Rd PO38 1JH
e-mail: enquiries@thewellingtonhotel.net
web: www.thewellingtonhotel.net

Rooms 28 (5 fmly) (7 GF) (14 smoking) **S** £60-£100; **D** £90-£135 (incl. bkfst)* **Facilities** STV Xmas New Year Wi-fi **Conf** Class 28 Board 28 Thtr 28 Del from £85 to £150* **Parking** 10 **Notes** LB ⊗ Civ Wed 60

Burlington

★★ 69% HOTEL

☎ 01983 852113 🖷 01983 857462
Bellevue Rd PO38 1DB
e-mail: info@burlingtonhotel.uk.com
dir: In one way system turn left at lights. Up hill, take 2nd right & immediate right into Bellevue Rd. Hotel 100mtrs on left.

Eight of the attractively decorated bedrooms at this establishment benefit from balconies, and the three ground floor rooms have French doors that lead onto the garden. There is a cosy bar, a comfortable lounge and a dining room where home-made bread rolls accompany the five-course dinners. Service is friendly and attentive.

Rooms 24 (12 fmly) (3 GF) **Facilities** ↸ Wi-fi **Parking** 20 **Notes** ⊗ No children 3yrs Closed Etr-Nov

---

Hambrough

◉◉ RESTAURANT WITH ROOMS

☎ 01983 856333 🖷 01983 857260
Hambrough Rd PO38 1SQ
e-mail: info@thehambrough.com

A former Victorian villa set on the hillside above Ventnor and with memorable views out to sea. It has a modern, stylish interior with well-equipped and comfortable bedrooms. The team's passion for food is clearly evident in the superb cuisine served in the minimalist themed restaurant.

Rooms 7 (6 en suite)

YARMOUTH Map 5 SZ38

INSPECTORS' CHOICE

George Hotel

★★★ ◉◉ HOTEL

☎ 01983 760331 🖷 01983 760425
Quay St PO41 0PE
e-mail: res@thegeorge.co.uk
dir: between castle and pier

This delightful 17th-century hotel enjoys a wonderful location at the water's edge, adjacent to the castle and the quay. Public areas include a bright brasserie where organic and local produce are utilised, a cosy bar and an inviting lounge. Individually styled bedrooms, with many thoughtful extras, are beautifully appointed; some benefit from spacious balconies. The hotel's motor yacht is available for hire by guests.

Rooms 17 (1 GF) **S** £100-£162.50; **D** £190-£267.50 (incl. bkfst)* **Facilities** STV Sailing from Yarmouth Mountain biking Xmas New Year Wi-fi **Conf** Class 10 Board 18 Thtr 30 **Notes** No children 10yrs

---

WILTSHIRE

AMESBURY Map 5 SU14

Travelodge Amesbury Stonehenge

BUDGET HOTEL

☎ 08719 846 218 🖷 01980 625273
Countess Services SP4 7AS
web: www.travelodge.co.uk
dir: at junct A345 & A303 eastbound

Travelodge offers good quality, good value, modern accommodation. Ideal for families, the spacious en suite bedrooms include remote-control TV, tea and coffee-making facilities and comfortable beds. Meals can be taken at the nearby family restaurant. See also the Hotel Groups pages.

Rooms 48 **S** fr £29; **D** fr £29

BRADFORD-ON-AVON — Map 4 ST86

Woolley Grange
★★★ 82% ◉◉ HOTEL

☎ 01225 864705 ▤ 01225 864059
Woolley Green BA15 1TX
e-mail: info@woolleygrangehotel.co.uk
web: www.woolleygrangehotel.co.uk
dir: A4 onto B3109. Bradford Leigh, left at x-roads, hotel 0.5m on right at Woolley Green

This splendid Cotswold manor house is set in beautiful countryside. Children are made especially welcome; there is a trained nanny on duty in the nursery. Bedrooms and public areas are charmingly furnished and decorated in true country-house style, with many thoughtful touches and luxurious extras. The hotel offers a varied and well-balanced menu selection, including ingredients from the hotel's own garden.

Rooms 26 (14 annexe) (8 fmly) **Facilities** ⚑ Putt green ⛱ Badminton Beauty treatments Football games room Table tennis Xmas New Year Wi-fi Child facilities **Conf** Class 12 Board 22 Thtr 35 **Parking** 40 **Notes** Civ Wed 30

Best Western Leigh Park Hotel
★★★ 78% COUNTRY HOUSE HOTEL

☎ 01225 864885 ▤ 01225 862315
Leigh Park West BA15 2RA
e-mail: inof@leighparkhotel.eclipse.co.uk
dir: A363 between Bath signed Holt/Woolley Green. Hotel 0.25m on right on x-roads of B3105/B3109. N side of Bradford-on-Avon

Enjoying splendid countryside views, this relaxing Georgian hotel is set in five acres of well-tended grounds, complete with a vineyard. Combining charm and character with modern facilities, the hotel is equally well suited to business and leisure travellers. The restaurant serves dishes cooked to order, using home-grown fruit and vegetables, and wine from the vineyard.

Rooms 22 (4 fmly) (7 GF) **Facilities** Vineyard Xmas New Year Wi-fi **Conf** Class 60 Board 60 Thtr 120 **Parking** 80 **Notes** LB Civ Wed 120

Widbrook Grange
★★★ 74% ◉ COUNTRY HOUSE HOTEL

☎ 01225 864750 & 863173 ▤ 01225 862890
Trowbridge Rd, Widbrook BA15 1UH
e-mail: stay@widbrookgrange.com
dir: 1m SE from Bradford on A363, hotel diagonally opposite Bradford Marina & Arabian Stud

This former farmhouse, built as a model farm in the 18th century, has been carefully renovated to provide modern comforts, suitable for both business and leisure guests. Some bedrooms are in the main house, but most are in adjacent converted buildings, and these rooms have their own courtyard entrance and many are located on the ground floor. The lounges offer a good level of comfort. The friendly staff provide a personal and relaxed service.

Rooms 20 (15 annexe) (6 fmly) (13 GF) **S** £95-£120; **D** £120-£140 (incl. bkfst)* **Facilities** ⛾ Gym Children's weekend play room New Year Wi-fi Child facilities **Conf** Class 35 Board 25 Thtr 50 Del from £150 to £200* **Parking** 50 **Notes** ⊗ Closed 24-30 Dec Civ Wed 50

Old Manor
★★ 69% HOTEL

☎ 01225 777393 ▤ 01225 765443
Trowle Common BA14 9BL
e-mail: romanticbeds@oldmanorhotel.com
dir: on A363 between Bradford on Avon & Trowbridge

This hotel stands in its own grounds and has been developed from farm buildings and retains much character and charm. The establishment is filled with antiques. Bedrooms are mostly located in annexes and are individually styled; some having four-poster beds. The lounge and restaurant are open-plan and the atmosphere is relaxed.

Rooms 19 (15 annexe) (4 fmly) (15 GF) **Facilities** Wi-fi **Conf** Class 40 Board 30 Thtr 70 **Parking** 60 **Notes** LB

CALNE — Map 4 ST97

Lansdowne
★★★ 66% HOTEL

☎ 01249 812488 ▤ 01249 815323
The Strand SN11 0EH
e-mail: reservations@lansdownestrand.co.uk
dir: From Chippenham A4 signed Calne. Straight over at both rdbts, hotel in town centre

Situated in this picturesque market town, The Lansdowne was originally built in the 16th century as a coaching inn, and it still retains much of the charm and character of that era. Bedrooms are spacious and furnished in a traditional style. Guests may enjoy dinner in the pleasant bistro, in either of the bar areas or choose from a varied room-service menu. An outdoor courtyard seating area is also available.

Rooms 26 (4 fmly) **S** £40-£60; **D** £50-£90 (incl. bkfst)* **Facilities** STV FTV Wi-fi **Conf** Class 60 Board 50 Thtr 60 Del from £60 to £85* **Parking** 15 **Notes** LB ⊗

CASTLE COMBE — Map 4 ST87

INSPECTORS' CHOICE

Manor House Hotel and Golf Club
★★★★ ◉◉◉ COUNTRY HOUSE HOTEL

☎ 01249 782206 ▤ 01249 782159
SN14 7HR
e-mail: enquiries@manor-housecc.co.uk
web: www.exclusivehotels.co.uk
dir: M4 junct 17 follow Chippenham signs onto A420 Bristol, then right onto B4039. Through village, right after bridge

This delightful hotel is situated in a secluded valley adjacent to a picturesque village, where there have been no new buildings for 300 years. There are 365 acres of grounds to enjoy, complete with an Italian garden and an 18-hole golf course. Bedrooms, some in the main house and some in a row of stone cottages, have been superbly furnished, and public rooms include a number of cosy lounges with roaring fires. Service is a pleasing blend of professionalism and friendliness. The food offered utilises top quality local produce.

Rooms 48 (26 annexe) (8 fmly) (12 GF) **S** £150-£800; **D** £180-£800* **Facilities** STV ⚴ 18 ⛳ Putt green Fishing ⛱ Jogging track Hot air ballooning Xmas New Year Wi-fi **Conf** Class 70 Board 30 Thtr 100 Del from £280 to £320* **Parking** 100 **Notes** LB Civ Wed 110

include purpose-designed disabled access rooms. The air-conditioned restaurant and bar open onto a large patio which overlooks the 18th green, and there are splendid leisure facilities including a techno gym and 18-metre swimming pool; beauty treatments are also on offer.

Rooms 58 (3 fmly) (29 GF) **S** £75-£90; **D** £85-£120 (incl. bkfst & dinner)* **Facilities** Spa STV ⓒ ♨ 27 Putt green Gym Beauty salon Sauna Spa Steam room Wi-fi **Conf** Class 120 Board 30 Thtr 250 **Services** Lift **Parking** 200 **Notes** LB ⊗ Closed 24-25 Dec Civ Wed 80

WORCESTERSHIRE

ABBERLEY
Map 10 SO76

The Elms Hotel & Restaurant

★★★ 88% ◉◉ HOTEL

☎ 01299 896666 ▤ 01299 896804
Stockton Rd WR6 6AT
e-mail: info@theelmshotel.co.uk
web: www.theelmshotel.co.uk
dir: on A443 2m beyond Great Witley

This imposing Queen Anne mansion set in delightful grounds dates back to 1710 and offers a sophisticated yet relaxed atmosphere throughout. The spacious public rooms and generously proportioned bedrooms offer elegance and charm. The hotel is particularly well geared for families with a host of child friendly facilities and features that include a crèche, children's play area and wonderful high teas. Imaginative cooking is served in the elegant restaurant.

Rooms 23 (6 annexe) (1 fmly) (3 GF) **Facilities** Spa FTV ⓒ ♨ ♨ Gym Xmas New Year Wi-fi Child facilities **Conf** Class 30 Board 30 Thtr 70 Del from £175 to £205* **Parking** 100 **Notes** ⊗ Civ Wed 70

BEWDLEY
Map 10 SO77

Ramada Hotel & Resort Kidderminster

RAMADA
HOTEL & RESORT
★★★ 79% HOTEL

☎ 01299 406400 ▤ 01299 400921
Habberley Rd DY12 1LA
e-mail: sales.kidderminster@ramadajarvis.co.uk
web: www.ramadajarvis.co.uk
dir: A456 towards Kidderminster to ring road, follow signs to Bewdley. Pass Safari Park then exit A456/Town Centre, take sharp right after 200yds onto B4190, hotel 400yds on right

Located within 16 acres of landscaped grounds, this Victorian house has been sympathetically renovated and extended to provide good standards of comfort and facilities. A wide range of well equipped bedrooms include both family and executive rooms and the hotel benefits from an on site Sebastian Coe Health Club, available to guests.

Rooms 44 (3 fmly) (18 GF) (3 smoking) **S** £63-£162; **D** £63-£174 (incl. bkfst)* **Facilities** STV ⓒ supervised ♨ Gym Beauty & hair salon Dance studio Steam room Sauna Sun bed New Year **Conf** Class 120 Board 60 Thtr 350 Del from £142 to £155* **Parking** 150 **Notes** LB ⊗ Civ Wed 250

BROADWAY
Map 10 SP03

See also **Buckland (Gloucestershire)**

Barceló The Lygon Arms

Barceló
HOTELS & RESORTS
★★★★ 78% ◉◉ HOTEL

☎ 01386 852255 ▤ 01386 854470
High St WR12 7DU
e-mail: thelygonarms@barcelo-hotels.co.uk
web: www.barcelo-hotels.co.uk
dir: From Evesham take A44 signed Oxford, 5m. Follow Broadway signs. Hotel on left

A hotel with a wealth of historic charm and character, the Lygon Arms dates back to the 16th century. There is a choice of restaurants, a stylish cosy bar, an array of lounges and a smart spa and leisure club. Bedrooms vary in size and style, but all are thoughtfully equipped and include a number of stylish contemporary rooms as well as a cottage in the grounds.

Barceló The Lygon Arms

Rooms 77 (9 GF) **S** £109-£229; **Facilities** Spa ⓒ ♨ ♨ Gym Xmas New Year **Conf** Class 46 Board 30 Thtr 80 **Parking** 200 **Notes** Civ Wed 80

Dormy House

Pride of Britain
★★★ 85% ◉◉ HOTEL

☎ 01386 852711 ▤ 01386 858636
Willersey Hill WR12 7LF
e-mail: reservations@dormyhouse.co.uk
web: www.dormyhouse.co.uk
dir: 2m E off A44, top of Fish Hill, turn for Saintbury/Picnic area. After 0.5m left, hotel on left

A converted 17th-century farmhouse set in extensive grounds and with stunning views over Broadway. Some rooms are in an annexe at ground-floor level, some have contemporary style. The best traditions are retained - customer care, real fires, comfortable sofas and afternoon teas. Dinner features an interesting choice of dishes, created by a skilled kitchen brigade.

Rooms 45 (20 annexe) (8 fmly) (21 GF) **S** £128; **D** £170-£255 (incl. bkfst)* **Facilities** STV Putt green ♨ Gym Games room Nature & jogging trail Sauna Steam room Xmas New Year Wi-fi **Conf** Class 100 Board 25 Thtr 170 **Parking** 80 **Notes** Closed 25-26 Dec Civ Wed 170

BROADWAY continued

Broadway

★★★ 77% HOTEL

CLASSIC BRITISH HOTELS

☎ 01386 852401 🖷 01386 853879
The Green, High St WR12 7AA
e-mail: info@broadwayhotel.info
web: www.cotswold-inns-hotels.co.uk
dir: Follow signs to Evesham, then Broadway

A half-timbered Cotswold stone property, built in the 15th century as a retreat for the Abbots of Pershore. The hotel combines modern, attractive decor with original charm and character. Bedrooms are tastefully furnished and well equipped while public rooms include a relaxing lounge, cosy bar and charming restaurant; alfresco all-day dining in summer months proves popular.

Rooms 19 (1 fmly) (3 GF) **S** £95-£140; **D** £140-£200 (incl. bkfst)* **Facilities** Xmas New Year Wi-fi **Conf** Board 12 Thtr 20 **Parking** 20 **Notes** LB Civ Wed 50

Russell's

◉◉ RESTAURANT WITH ROOMS

☎ 01386 853555 🖷 01386 853555
20 High St WR12 7DT
e-mail: info@russellsofbroadway.com
dir: Opposite village green

Situated in the centre of a picturesque Cotswold village this restaurant with rooms is a great base for exploring local attractions. Bedrooms, each with their own character, boast superb quality, air conditioning and a wide range of extras for guests. Cuisine is a real draw with freshly-prepared local produce used with skill.

Rooms 7 (7 en suite) (3 annexe) (4 fmly)

The Bromsgrove Hotel

★★★★ 71% HOTEL

☎ 01527 576600 🖷 01527 878981
Kidderminster Rd B61 9AB
e-mail: info.bromsgrove@pedersenhotels.com

Public areas in this striking building have a Mediterranean theme with white-washed walls, a courtyard garden and plenty of natural light. Bedrooms are in a variety of styles; some are more compact than others but all offer an excellent working environment for

the business guest. Leisure facilities include a steam room, sauna, pool and gym.

Rooms 111 (10 fmly) (34 GF) **Facilities** Spa STV ⊗ supervised Gym Beauty salon 2 treatment rooms Wi-fi **Conf** Class 120 Board 50 Thtr 250 **Services** Lift Air con **Parking** 250 **Notes** ⊗ Civ Wed 180

Ladybird Lodge

★★★ 78% HOTEL

☎ 01527 889900 🖷 01527 889949
2 Finstall Rd, Aston Fields B60 2DZ
e-mail: info@ladybirdlodge.co.uk
web: www.ladybirdlodge.co.uk
dir: Enter Bromsgrove on A38, follow signs for Aston Fields (B4184)

Located on the town's outskirts, this attractive modern hotel is an extension of the popular Ladybird Inn, popular for its range of quality pub food. Bedrooms are very well equipped for both business and leisure guests and Rosado's Italian Restaurant is the perfect setting for an intimate dinner.

Rooms 43 (9 fmly) (14 GF) **S** £46-£100; **D** £60-£110 (incl. bkfst)* **Facilities** STV Wi-fi **Conf** Class 25 Board 30 Thtr 40 **Services** Lift **Parking** 60 **Notes** LB ⊗

Innkeeper's Lodge Bromsgrove

BUDGET HOTEL

☎ 0845 112 6067 🖷 0845 112 6236
462 Birmingham Rd, Marlbrook B61 0HR
web: www.innkeeperslodge.com/bromsgrove
dir: M5 junct 4 or M42 junct 1 w'bound only (restricted junction). Lodge on A38 (Birmingham road).

Innkeeper's Lodge represents an exciting, high value concept within the budget hotel market. Comfortable bedrooms provide excellent facilities that include satellite TV and modem points. Options include family rooms, and for the corporate guest, cutting edge IT which includes Wi-fi access. A popular Carvery provides all-day food, including an extensive, complimentary continental breakfast.

Rooms 29 (3 fmly) **S** £53-£55; **D** £53-£55 (incl. bkfst) **Conf** Thtr 25

INSPECTORS' CHOICE

Brockencote Hall Country House

★★★ ◉◉ HOTEL

☎ 01562 777876 🖷 01562 777872
DY10 4PY
e-mail: info@brockencotehall.com
web: www.brockencotehall.com
dir: 0.5m W, off A448, opposite St Cassians Church

Glorious countryside extends all around this magnificent mansion, and grazing sheep can be seen from the conservatory. Not surprisingly, relaxation comes high on the list of priorities here. Despite its very English location the hotel's owner actually hails from Alsace and the atmosphere is very much that of a provincial French château. The chef too is French (from Paris) and the chandeliered dining room is a popular venue for the accomplished modern French cuisine.

Rooms 17 (2 fmly) (5 GF) **S** £96-£116; **D** £120-£190 (incl. bkfst) **Facilities** FTV ⊗ Fishing ⊗ Reflexology Aromatherapy Massage Facials Xmas New Year Wi-fi **Conf** Class 20 Board 20 Thtr 30 Del from £175 to £190 **Services** Lift **Parking** 45 **Notes** LB ⊗ Closed 1-18 Jan Civ Wed 70

Express by Holiday Inn Droitwich M5 Jct 5

BUDGET HOTEL

☎ 0870 442 5658 🖷 0870 442 5659
Worcester Rd, Wychbold WR9 7PA
e-mail: dgmdroitwich@expressholidayinn.co.uk
web: www.hiexpress.com/droitwichm5j
dir: M5 junct 5, at rdbt take A38 towards Bromsgrove. Hotel 300yds on left next to MacDonalds

A modern hotel ideal for families and business travellers. Fresh and uncomplicated, the spacious rooms include Sky TV, power shower and tea and coffee-making facilities. Continental buffet breakfast is included in the room rate; other meals may be taken at the nearby family pub or restaurant. See also the Hotel Groups pages.

Rooms 94 (44 fmly) **Conf** Class 18 Board 20 Thtr 40

Travelodge Droitwich

BUDGET HOTEL

☎ 08719 846 074 📠 01527 861807
Rashwood Hill WR9 0BJ
web: www.travelodge.co.uk
dir: 0.5m W of M5 junct 5

Travelodge offers good quality, good value, modern accommodation. Ideal for families, the spacious en suite bedrooms include remote-control TV, tea and coffee-making facilities and comfortable beds. Meals can be taken at the nearby family restaurant. See also the Hotel Groups pages.

Rooms 32 **S** fr £29; **D** fr £29

Northwick Hotel

★★★ 82% ⊚ HOTEL

☎ 01386 40322 📠 01386 41070
Waterside WR11 1BT
e-mail: enquiries@northwickhotel.co.uk
dir: off A46 onto A44 over lights and right at next set onto B4035. Past hospital, hotel on right opposite river

Located close to the centre of the town, the hotel benefits from its position overlooking the River Avon and its adjacent park. Bedrooms are traditional in style and feature broadband access; one room has been adapted for disabled access. Public areas offer a choice of drinking options, meeting rooms and a restaurant.

Rooms 29 (4 fmly) (1 GF) **S** £87; **D** £118 (incl. bkfst)* **Facilities** STV FTV New Year Wi-fi **Conf** Class 150 Board 80 Thtr 240 **Parking** 110 **Notes** LB ⊗ Closed 25-29 Dec Civ Wed 70

See advert on this page

The Evesham

★★★ 79% ⊚ HOTEL

☎ 01386 765566 & 0800 716969 (Res)
📠 01386 765443
Coopers Ln, Off Waterside WR11 1DA
e-mail: reception@eveshamhotel.com
web: www.eveshamhotel.com
dir: Coopers Lane is off road by River Avon

Dating from 1540 and set in extensive grounds, this delightful hotel has well-equipped accommodation that includes a selection of quirkily themed rooms - Alice in Wonderland, Egyptian, and Aquarium (which has a tropical fish tank in the bathroom). A reputation for food is well deserved, with a particularly strong choice for vegetarians. Children are welcome and toys are always available.

Rooms 40 (1 annexe) (3 fmly) (11 GF) **S** £73-£83; **D** £117 (incl. bkfst)* **Facilities** ⊗ Putt green ⛳ New Year **Conf** Class 12 Board 12 Thtr 12 **Parking** 50 **Notes** LB Closed 25-26 Dec

Dumbleton Hall

★★★ 75% HOTEL

☎ 01386 881240 📠 01386 882142
WR11 7TS
e-mail: dh@pofr.co.uk

(For full entry see Dumbleton)

Travelodge Hartlebury

BUDGET HOTEL

☎ 08719 846 079 📠 01299 251774
Shorthill Nurseries DY13 9SH
web: www.travelodge.co.uk
dir: A449 southbound

Travelodge offers good quality, good value, modern accommodation. Ideal for families, the spacious en suite bedrooms include remote-control TV, tea and coffee-making facilities and comfortable beds. Meals can be taken at the nearby family restaurant. See also the Hotel Groups pages.

Rooms 32 **S** fr £29; **D** fr £29

Stone Manor

★★★★ 78% HOTEL

☎ 01562 777555 📠 01562 777834
Stone DY10 4PJ
e-mail: enquiries@stonemanorhotel.co.uk
web: www.stonemanorhotel.co.uk
dir: 2.5m from Kidderminster on A448, on right

This converted, much extended former manor house stands in 25 acres of impressive grounds and gardens. The well-equipped accommodation includes rooms with four-poster beds and luxuriously appointed annexe bedrooms. Quality furnishing and decor styles throughout the public areas highlight the intrinsic charm of the interior; the hotel is a popular venue for wedding receptions.

Rooms 57 (5 annexe) (7 GF) **S** £75-£120; **D** £75-£120 **Facilities** 8 ⌧ ⛳ Pool table Complimentary use of local leisure centre **Conf** Class 48 Board 60 Thtr 150 **Parking** 400 **Notes** LB ⊗ Civ Wed 150

KIDDERMINSTER continued

Gainsborough House

★★★ 80% HOTEL

☎ 01562 820041 📠 01562 66179
Bewdley Hill DY11 6BS
e-mail: reservations@gainsboroughhousehotel.com
web: www.gainsboroughhousehotel.com
dir: Follow A456 to Kidderminster (West Midlands Safari
Park), pass hospital, hotel 500yds on left

Now totally refurbished, this listed Georgian hotel
provides a wide range of thoughtfully furnished bedrooms
with smart modern bathrooms. The contemporary décor
and furnishing style throughout the public areas
highlights the many retained period features. A large
function suite and several meeting rooms are also
available.

Rooms 42 (16 fmly) (12 GF) **S** £50-£75; **D** £75-£95 (incl.
bkfst)* **Facilities** STV FTV Xmas New Year Wi-fi
Conf Board 60 Thtr 250 Del from £95 to £120*
Parking 90 **Notes** ⊗ Civ Wed 250

The Granary Hotel & Restaurant

★★★ 78% ◎◎ HOTEL

☎ 01562 777535 📠 01562 777722
Heath Ln, Shenstone DY10 4BS
e-mail: info@granary-hotel.co.uk
web: www.granary-hotel.co.uk
dir: On A450 between Stourbridge & Worcester, 1m from
Kidderminster

This modern hotel offers spacious, well-equipped
accommodation with many rooms enjoying views towards
Great Witley and the Amberley Hills. Public areas include
a cocktail lounge and an attractive modern restaurant
featuring locally sourced produce, cooked with flair and
imagination. There are also extensive conference facilities
and the hotel is popular as a wedding venue.

Rooms 18 (1 fmly) (18 GF) **S** £75-£95; **D** £90-£140 (incl.
bkfst)* **Facilities** FTV Wi-fi **Conf** Class 80 Board 70
Thtr 200 **Parking** 96 **Notes** LB Closed 24-26 Dec
Civ Wed 120

MALVERN Map 10 SO74

The Cottage in the Wood Hotel

★★★ 83% ◎◎ HOTEL

☎ 01684 575859 📠 01684 560662
Holywell Rd, Malvern Wells WR14 4LG
e-mail: reception@cottageinthewood.co.uk
web: www.cottageinthewood.co.uk
dir: 3m S of Great Malvern off A449, 500yds N of B4209,
on opposite side of road

Sitting high up on a wooded hillside, this delightful,
family-run hotel boasts lovely views over the Severn
Valley. The bedrooms are divided between the main
house, Beech Cottage and the Pinnacles. The public areas
are very stylishly decorated, and imaginative food is
served in an elegant dining room, overlooking the
immaculate grounds.

Rooms 30 (23 annexe) (9 GF) **S** £79-£109; **D** £99-£179
(incl. bkfst)* **Facilities** Direct access to Malvern Hills
Xmas New Year Wi-fi **Conf** Board 14 Thtr 20
Del from £145 to £155* **Parking** 40 **Notes** LB

Colwall Park Hotel, Bar & Restaurant

★★★ 81% ◎◎ HOTEL

☎ 01684 540000 📠 01684 540847
Walwyn Rd, Colwall WR13 6QG
e-mail: hotel@colwall.com
web: www.colwall.co.uk
dir: Between Malvern & Ledbury in centre of Colwall on
B4218

Standing in extensive gardens, this hotel was purpose
built in the early 20th century to serve the local racetrack.
Today the proprietors and loyal staff provide high levels
of hospitality and service. The Seasons Restaurant has a
well-deserved reputation for its cuisine. Bedrooms are
tastefully appointed and public areas help to create a
fine country-house atmosphere.

Rooms 22 (1 fmly) **S** £80-£95; **D** £120-£150 (incl. bkfst)*
Facilities FTV 🏊 Boules Xmas New Year Wi-fi
Conf Class 80 Board 50 Thtr 150 **Parking** 40 **Notes** LB

Cotford Hotel & L'Amuse Bouche Restaurant

★★★ 79% ◎ HOTEL

☎ 01684 572427 📠 01684 572952
51 Graham Rd WR14 2HU
e-mail: reservations@cotfordhotel.co.uk
web: www.cotfordhotel.co.uk
dir: from Worcester follow signs to Malvern on A449. Left
into Graham Rd signed town centre, hotel on right

This delightful house, built in 1851, reputedly for the
Bishop of Worcester, stands in attractive garden with
stunning views of The Malverns. Rooms have been
authentically renovated, retaining many of the original
features. Food, service and hospitality are all major
strengths.

Rooms 15 (4 fmly) (1 GF) **S** £65-£79; **D** £99-£115 (incl.
bkfst) **Facilities** STV 🏊 Complimentary use of local
leisure centre Wi-fi **Conf** Class 26 Board 12 Thtr 26
Del from £125 to £139 **Parking** 15 **Notes** LB

Best Western Foley Arms

★★★ 72% HOTEL

☎ 01684 573397 📠 01684 569665
14 Worcester Rd WR14 4QS
e-mail: reservations@foleyarmshotel.com
web: www.foleyarmshotel.co.uk
dir: M5 junct 8 N (or junct 7 S) or M50 junct 1 to Great
Malvern on A449

Situated in the centre of town and with spectacular views
of the Severn Valley, this hotel is reputed to be the oldest
hotel in Malvern. The bedrooms are comfortable and
tastefully decorated with period furnishings and modern
facilities. Public areas include the Terrace Restaurant, a
popular bar and a choice of comfortable lounges.

Rooms 28 (2 fmly) **Facilities** Free use of nearby leisure
centre Xmas New Year Wi-fi **Conf** Class 40 Board 45
Thtr 150 **Parking** 60 **Notes** LB Civ Wed 100

HARROGATE continued

Hotel du Vin Harrogate

★★★★ 81% ⑱⑱ TOWN HOUSE HOTEL

☎ 01423 856800 🖹 01423 856801
Prospect Place HG1 1LB
e-mail: info@harrogate.hotelduvin.com
web: www.hotelduvin.com
dir: Enter town centre & stay in right lane, pass West Park Church on right. Hotel on right

This town house was created from eight Georgian-style properties and overlooks The Stray. The spacious, open-plan lobby has seating, a bar and the reception desk. Hidden downstairs is a cosy snug cellar. The French-influenced bistro offers high quality cooking and a great choice of wines. Bedrooms face front and back, and are smart and modern, with excellent 'deluge' showers. Hotel du Vin - AA Small Hotel Group of the Year 2008-9.

Rooms 51 (4 GF) **S** £105-£155; **D** £105-£395*
Facilities STV FTV Xmas New Year Wi-fi **Conf** Board 20 Thtr 50 Del from £155 to £185* **Services** Lift **Parking** 30 **Notes** LB Civ Wed 90

Barceló Harrogate Majestic Hotel

★★★★ 75% HOTEL

☎ 01423 700300 🖹 01423 502283
Ripon Rd HG1 2HU
e-mail: majestic@barcelo-hotels.co.uk
web: www.barcelo-hotels.co.uk
dir: from M1 onto A1(M) at Wetherby. Take A661 to Harrogate. Hotel in town centre adjacent to Royal Hall

Popular for conferences and functions, this grand Victorian hotel is set in 12 acres of landscaped grounds that is within walking distance of the town centre. It benefits from spacious public areas, and the comfortable bedrooms, including some spacious suites, come in a variety of sizes.

Rooms 174 (8 fmly) **S** £69-£140; **Facilities** Spa ⑲ supervised ⑲ Gym Golf practice net Xmas New Year Wi-fi **Conf** Class 260 Board 70 Thtr 500 **Services** Lift **Parking** 250 (charged) **Notes** Civ Wed 200

Holiday Inn Harrogate

★★★★ 72% HOTEL

☎ 0870 4431 761 🖹 01423 524435
Kings Rd HG1 1XX
e-mail: gm.hiharrogate@qmh-hotels.com
web: www.holidayinn.co.uk
dir: A1 to A59. Hotel adjoins International Conference Centre

Situated just a short walk from the town centre, this impressive hotel lies adjacent to the Harrogate International Conference Centre. Bedrooms are stylishly furnished. Extensive conference facilities and a business centre are provided. Public areas include the first-floor restaurant and ground floor lounge bar. Nearby private parking is a bonus.

Rooms 214 (7 fmly) **Facilities** Gym Wi-fi **Conf** Class 150 Board 100 Thtr 300 **Services** Lift **Parking** 160 (charged) **Notes** LB

Best Western Cedar Court

★★★★ 70% HOTEL

☎ 01423 858585 & 858595 (res) 🖹 01423 504950
Queens Buildings, Park Pde HG1 5AH
e-mail: cedarcourt@bestwestern.co.uk
web: www.cedarcourthotels.co.uk
dir: from A1(M) follow signs to Harrogate on A661 past Sainsburys. At rdbt left onto A6040. Hotel right after church

This Grade II listed building was Harrogate's first hotel and enjoys a peaceful location in landscaped grounds, close to the town centre. It provides spacious, well-equipped accommodation. Public areas include a brasserie-style restaurant, a small gym and an open-plan lounge and bar. Functions and conferences are particularly well catered for.

Rooms 100 (8 fmly) (7 GF) **S** £85-£145; **D** £95-£165 (incl. bkfst)* **Facilities** FTV Gym Xmas New Year Wi-fi **Conf** Class 300 Board 240 Thtr 650 Del from £120 to £155* **Services** Lift **Parking** 150 **Notes** LB ⑧ Civ Wed 150

The Boar's Head Hotel

★★★ 83% ⑱⑱ HOTEL

☎ 01423 771888 🖹 01423 771509
Ripley Castle Estate HG3 3AY
e-mail: reservations@boarsheadripley.co.uk
dir: on A61 (Harrogate to Ripon road). Hotel in town centre

Part of the Ripley Castle estate, this delightful and popular hotel is renowned for its warm hospitality and as a dining destination. Bedrooms offer many comforts, and the luxurious day rooms feature works of art from the nearby castle. The banqueting suites in the castle are very impressive.

Rooms 25 (6 annexe) (2 fmly) **Facilities** ⑲ Fishing Clay pigeon shooting Tennis Fishing ♫ Xmas **Conf** Class 80 Board 150 Thtr 150 **Parking** 50 **Notes** LB Civ Wed 120

HARROGATE continued

Grants

★★★ 79% HOTEL

☎ 01423 560666 📠 01423 502550
3-13 Swan Rd HG1 2SS
e-mail: enquiries@grantshotel-harrogate.com
web: www.grantshotel-harrogate.com
dir: off A61

A long established, family-run hotel with an attractive flower bedecked patio. The smartly presented, well-equipped bedrooms include some with four-poster beds. A comfortable lounge bar with plenty of interesting old photographs, and imaginative food in the colourful Chimney Pots Bistro, are just some of the features of this friendly hotel.

Rooms 42 (2 fmly) **Facilities** Use of local Health & Leisure Club Xmas **Conf** Class 20 Board 30 Thtr 70 **Services** Lift **Parking** 26

Old Swan

★★★ 78% HOTEL

☎ 01423 500055 📠 01423 501154
Swan Rd HG1 2SR
e-mail: gm.oldswan@macdonald-hotels.co.uk
dir: from A1, A59 Ripon, left Empress rdbt, stay on left, right Prince of Wales rdbt. Straight across lights & turn left into Swan Rd

In the heart of Harrogate and within walking distance of the Harrogate International Centre and Valley Gardens, this hotel is famed as being Agatha Christie's hiding place during her disappearance in 1926. The fully refurbished bedrooms are stylishly furnished, and the public areas include the Library Restaurant, the Wedgwood Room and the lounge bar. Extensive conference and banqueting facilities are available.

Rooms 136 **S** £62-£162; **D** £76-£176 (incl. bkfst)*
Facilities ♨ Xmas New Year Wi-fi **Conf** Class 130 Board 100 Thtr 450 **Services** Lift **Parking** 200 **Notes** LB ⊗ Civ Wed 300

Studley

★★★ 77% ◉ HOTEL

☎ 01423 560425 📠 01423 530967
Swan Rd HG1 2SE
e-mail: info@studleyhotel.co.uk
web: www.studleyhotel.co.uk
dir: adjacent to Valley Gardens, opposite Mercer Gallery

This friendly, well-established hotel, close to the town centre and Valley Gardens, is well known for its Orchid Restaurant, which provides a dynamic and authentic approach to Pacific Rim and Asian cuisine. Bedrooms are modern and come in a variety of styles and sizes, whilst the stylish bar lounge provides guests with an excellent place for relaxing.

Rooms 31 (1 fmly) **S** £60-£130; **D** £94-£190 (incl. bkfst)*
Facilities Free use of local Health & Spa Club Wi-fi **Conf** Class 15 Board 12 Thtr 15 **Services** Lift **Parking** 15 **Notes** LB

Ascot House

★★★ 75% HOTEL

☎ 01423 531005 📠 01423 503523
53 Kings Rd HG1 5HJ
e-mail: admin@ascothouse.com
web: www.ascothouse.com
dir: follow Town Centre/Conference/Exhibition Centre signs into Kings Rd, hotel on left after park

This late-Victorian house is situated a short distance from the International Conference Centre and provides comfortable, well-equipped bedrooms with smartly presented bathrooms. The attractive public areas include an inviting lounge, bar, elegant dining room and a beautiful stained-glass window on the main staircase.

Rooms 18 (2 fmly) (4 GF) **S** £67-£78; **D** £98-£128 (incl. bkfst) **Facilities** Xmas Wi-fi **Conf** Class 36 Board 36 Thtr 80 Del from £120 to £130 **Parking** 14 **Notes** LB Closed New Year, 25 Jan-8 Feb Civ Wed 86

Yorkshire

★★★ 75% HOTEL

☎ 01423 565071 📠 01423 500082
Prospect Place HG1 1LA
e-mail: gm.yorkshire@foliohotels.com
web: www.foliohotels.com
dir: A1 junct 24/A59 to town centre, right at Betty's Tea Rooms

Ideally situated in the heart of this beautiful spa town of Harrogate. After a refurbishment the hotel was transformed from a typical Victorian property to one that is fresh and contemporary, yet retaining all the elegance of the original features. This transformation also included the stylish Hg1 Brasserie & Bar, a very popular venue for guests and local residents, with meals and light bites available throughout the day.

Rooms 80 (1 fmly) **Facilities** FTV Xmas New Year Wi-fi **Conf** Class 60 Board 45 Thtr 120 **Services** Lift **Parking** 33 **Notes** ✖ Civ Wed 100

Cairn

★★★ 🅰 HOTEL

☎ 01423 504005 📠 01423 500056
Ripon Road HG1 2JD
e-mail: salescairn@strathmorehotels.com

Rooms 135 (6 fmly) **S** £60-£130; **D** £80-£180 (incl. bkfst) **Facilities** STV Gym 🎵 Xmas New Year Wi-fi **Conf** Class 200 Board 100 Thtr 400 Del from £95 to £135* **Services** Lift **Parking** 200 **Notes** LB ✖ Civ Wed 300

See advert on page 657

Innkeeper's Lodge Harrogate West

BUDGET HOTEL

☎ 0845 112 6034 📠 0845 112 6268
Otley Rd, Beckwith Knowle HG3 1PR
web: www.innkeeperslodge.com/harrogatewest
dir: A1(M) junct 47, A59 for Harrogate. Over 2 rdbts, at 3rd take B6162 (Otley Road). Lodge on left opposite church

Innkeeper's Lodge Select represents an exciting, stylish concept within the hotel market. Contemporary style bedrooms provide excellent facilities that include LCD TVs with satellite channels, and modem points. Options include spacious family rooms, and for the corporate guest there is Wi-fi access. All-day food is served in a modern country pub and eating house. The extensive continental breakfast is complimentary.

Rooms 13 (2 fmly) **S** £75-£85; **D** £75-£85 (incl. bkfst)

Travelodge Harrogate

BUDGET HOTEL

☎ 08719 846 238 📠 01423 562734
The Gubbel HG1 2RR
web: www.travelodge.co.uk

Travelodge offers good quality, good value, modern accommodation. Ideal for families, the spacious en suite bedrooms include remote-control TV, tea and coffee-making facilities and comfortable beds. Meals can be taken at the nearby family restaurant. See also the Hotel Groups pages.

Rooms 46 **S** fr £29; **D** fr £29

HAWES   **Map 18 SD88**

Simonstone Hall

★★ 78% HOTEL

☎ 01969 667255 📠 01969 667741
Simonstone DL8 3LY
e-mail: hotel@simonstonehall.demon.co.uk
web: www.simonstonehall.co.uk
dir: 1.5m N on road signed to Muker and Buttertubs

This former hunting lodge provides professional, friendly service and a relaxed atmosphere. There is an inviting drawing room, stylish fine dining restaurant, a bar and conservatory. The generally spacious bedrooms are elegantly finished to reflect the style of the house, and many offer spectacular views of the countryside.

Rooms 18 (10 fmly) (2 GF) **Facilities** Xmas New Year Wi-fi **Conf** Class 20 Board 20 Thtr 50 **Parking** 40 **Notes** LB Civ Wed 72

HELMSLEY   **Map 19 SE68**

Black Swan Hotel

★★★★ 78% ◉◉◉ HOTEL

☎ 01439 770466 📠 01439 770174
Market Place YO62 5BJ
e-mail: enquiries@blackswan-helmsley.co.uk
web: www.blackswan-helmsley.co.uk
dir: A1 junct 49, A168, A170 east, hotel 14m from Thirsk

People have been visiting this establishment for over 200 years and it has become a landmark that dominates the market square. The hotel is renowned for its hospitality and friendliness; many of the staff are long-serving and dedicated. The bedrooms are stylish and include a junior suite and feature rooms. The award-winning cuisine uses the freshest local produce. The hotel also has a Tearoom & Patisserie that is open daily. At the time of our inspection there was a planned refurbishment.

Rooms 45 (4 fmly) **D** £170-£240 (incl. bkfst)* **Facilities** STV 🛁 Use of leisure facilities at nearby sister hotel Xmas New Year Wi-fi **Conf** Class 30 Board 26 Thtr 50 Del from £165* **Parking** 50 **Notes** LB Civ Wed 130

HELMSLEY continued

Feversham Arms Hotel & Spa

★★★ 83% ◉◉ HOTEL

☎ 01439 770766 🖷 01439 770346
1 High St YO62 5AG
e-mail: info@fevershamarmshotel.com
web: www.fevershamarmshotel.com
dir: A168 (signed Thirsk) from A1 then A170 or A64
(signed York) from A1 to York North, then B1363 to
Helmsley. Hotel 125mtrs from Market Place

This long established hotel lies just round the corner from
the main square, and under its caring ownership proves
to be a refined operation, yet without airs and graces.
There are several lounge areas and a restaurant where
good local ingredients are prepared with skill and
minimal fuss. The bedrooms, including four poolside
suites, have their own individual character and decor.
Verbana Spa opens in October 2008.

Rooms 23 (5 annexe) (9 fmly) (8 GF) **S** £125-£285;
D £135-£295 (incl. bkfst)* **Facilities** Spa STV FTV ⚲
Sauna Saunarium Xmas New Year Wi-fi **Conf** Class 20
Board 24 Thtr 35 Del from £185* **Services** Lift
Parking 50 **Notes** LB Civ Wed 50

Pheasant

★★★ 79% HOTEL

☎ 01439 771241 🖷 01439 771744
Harome YO62 5JG
e-mail: reservations@thepheasanthotel.com
web: www.thepheasanthotel.com
dir: 2.5m SE, leave A170 after 0.25m. Right signed
Harome for further 2m. Hotel opposite church

Guests can expect a family welcome at this popular hotel
which has spacious, comfortable bedrooms and enjoys a
delightful setting next to the village pond. The beamed,
flagstone bar leads into the charming lounge and

conservatory dining room, where very enjoyable English
food is served. A separate building contains the
swimming pool. Dinner-inclusive tariffs are available.

Rooms 14 (2 annexe) (1 GF) **S** £85-£95; **D** £170-£190
(incl. bkfst & dinner) **Facilities** FTV 🕭 **Parking** 20
Notes No children 12yrs Closed Xmas & Jan-Feb

HOVINGHAM   Map 19 SE67

Worsley Arms

★★★ 71% HOTEL

☎ 01653 628234 🖷 01653 628130
High St YO62 4LA
e-mail: worsleyarms@aol.com
dir: A64, signed York, towards Malton. At dual
carriageway left to Hovingham. At Slingsby left, then 2m

Overlooking the village green, this hotel has relaxing and
attractive lounges with welcoming open fires. Bedrooms
are also comfortable and several are contained in
cottages across the green. The restaurant provides
interesting quality cooking, with less formal dining in the
Cricketers' Bar and Bistro to the rear.

Rooms 20 (8 annexe) (2 fmly) (4 GF) **Facilities** 🕭
Shooting Xmas New Year **Conf** Class 40 Board 20 Thtr 40
Parking 25 **Notes** Civ Wed 100

See advert on page 558

KNARESBOROUGH   Map 19 SE35

Best Western Dower House

★★★ 77% HOTEL

☎ 01423 863302 🖷 01423 867665
Bond End HG5 9AL
e-mail: enquiries@dowerhouse-hotel.co.uk
dir: A1(M) onto A59 Harrogate Rd. Through
Knaresborough, hotel on right after lights at end of high
street

This attractive 15th-century house stands in pleasant
gardens on the edge of the town. Welcoming real fires
enhance its charm and character. Restaurant 48 has a
relaxed and comfortable atmosphere and overlooks the
garden, plus there is a cosy bar and comfortable lounge.
Other facilities include two function rooms and a popular
health and leisure club.

Rooms 31 (3 annexe) (2 fmly) (3 GF) **S** £65-£85;
D £80-£130 (incl. bkfst)* **Facilities** FTV 🕭 supervised
Gym Sauna Steam room Spa pool Aerobics studio Xmas
New Year Wi-fi **Conf** Class 35 Board 36 Thtr 65
Del from £120 to £135* **Parking** 100 **Notes** LB
Civ Wed 100

Innkeeper's Lodge Harrogate East

BUDGET HOTEL

☎ 0845 112 6033 🖷 0845 112 6269
Wetherby Rd, Plompton HG5 8LY
web: www.innkeeperslodge.com/harrogateeast
dir: A1(M) junct 47, A59 for Harrogate.Then A658 over 2
rdbts. At 3rd rdbt turn right onto A661 (Wetherby Road).
Lodge on left.

Innkeeper's Lodge represents an exciting, high value
concept within the budget hotel market. Comfortable
bedrooms provide excellent facilities that include satellite
TV and modem points. This carefully restored lodge is in a
picturesque setting and has its own unique style and
quirky character. Food is served all day, and an extensive,
complimentary continental breakfast is offered.

Rooms 10 **S** £59.95-£65; **D** £59.95-£65 (incl. bkfst)
Conf Thtr 25

General Tarleton Inn

◉◉ RESTAURANT WITH ROOMS

☎ 01423 340284 🖷 01423 340288
Boroughbridge Rd, Ferrensby HG5 0PZ
e-mail: gfi@generaltarleton.co.uk
dir: A1(M) junct 48 at Boroughbridge, take A6055 to
Knaresborough. 4m on right

Food is a real feature here with skilfully prepared meals
served in the restaurant, traditional bar and modern
conservatory. Accommodation is provided in brightly
decorated and airy rooms, and the bathrooms are
thoughtfully equipped. Enjoying a country location, yet
close to the A1(M), the inn remains popular with both
business and leisure guests.

Rooms 14 (14 en suite) (7 GF)

LASTINGHAM   Map 19 SE79

Lastingham Grange

★★★ 80% HOTEL

☎ 01751 417345 & 417402   🖷 01751 417358
YO62 6TH
e-mail: reservations@lastinghamgrange.com
dir: From A170 follow signs for Appleton-le-Moors,
continue into Lastingham, pass church on left & turn
right then left up hill. Hotel on right

A warm welcome and sincere hospitality have been the
hallmarks of this hotel for over 50 years. Antique furniture
is plentiful, and the lounge and the dining room both look
out onto the terrace and sunken rose garden below. There
is a large play area for older children and the moorland
views are breathtaking.

Rooms 12 (2 fmly) **S** £100-£120; **D** £150-£199 (incl.
bkfst)* **Facilities** 🏊 Large adventure playground Wi-fi
Child facilities **Parking** 30 **Notes** LB Closed Dec-Feb

LEEMING BAR   Map 19 SE28

The White Rose

★★ 64% HOTEL

☎ 01677 422707   🖷 01677 425123
Bedale Rd DL7 9AY
e-mail: john@whiterosehotel.co.uk
dir: A1 onto A684, left towards Northallerton. Hotel 0.25m
on left

Conveniently located just minutes from the A1, this
commercial hotel offers pleasant, well-equipped
bedrooms situated in a modern block to the rear. Good-
value meals are offered in either the traditional bar or
attractive dining room.

Rooms 18 (2 fmly) (1 GF) **Facilities** 🎵 **Parking** 50
Notes LB

LEYBURN   Map 19 SE19

Golden Lion

★ 68% HOTEL

☎ 01969 622161   🖷 01969 623836
Market Place DL8 5AS
e-mail: info@goldenlionleyburn.co.uk
web: www.thegoldenlion.co.uk
dir: on A684 in market square

Dating back to 1765, this traditional inn overlooks the
cobbled market square where weekly markets still take
place. Bedrooms, including some family rooms, have
appropriate levels of comfort. The restaurant, with murals
depicting scenes of the Dales, offers a good range of
meals. Food can also be enjoyed in the cosy bar which is
a popular meeting place for local people.

Rooms 14 (5 fmly) **S** £30-£38; **D** £60-£76 (incl. bkfst)*
Facilities New Year Wi-fi **Services** Lift **Notes** Closed
25-26 Dec

LUMBY

Quality Hotel Leeds Selby

Ⓤ

☎ 01977 682761   🖷 01977 685462
A1/A63 Junction LS25 5LF
e-mail: enquiries@hotels-leeds-selby.com
dir: A1(M) junct 42/A63 signed Selby, hotel on A63 on left

Currently the rating for this establishment is not confirmed.
This may be due to a change of ownership or because it has
only recently joined the AA rating scheme. For further
details please see the AA website: www.theAA.com

Rooms 97 (18 fmly) (40 GF) **S** £35-£90; **D** £50-£105*
Facilities STV 🏊 🏋 🟢 Putt green Gym Xmas New Year Wi-fi
Conf Class 100 Board 80 Thtr 160 Del from £90 to £140*
Parking 250 **Notes** LB Civ Wed 120

MALTON   Map 19 SE77

Talbot

★★ 64% HOTEL

☎ 01653 693355 & 01723 374374   🖷 01653 698165
Yorkersgate YO17 7AJ
e-mail: sales@englishrosehotels.co.uk
dir: off A64 towards Malton. Hotel on right

Situated close to the centre of town this long-established,
creeper-covered hotel looks out towards the River Derwent

and open countryside. Bedroom sizes vary, but all are
comfortable. The public rooms are traditional and
elegantly furnished, and include a bar plus a separate
lounge.

Rooms 31 (3 fmly) **S** £39.50-£60; **D** £75-£100 (incl.
bkfst) **Facilities** Xmas New Year **Conf** Board 20 Thtr 50
Del from £70 to £100 **Parking** 30 **Notes** LB ⊗

Green Man

★★ 63% HOTEL

☎ 01653 600370   🖷 01653 696006
15 Market St YO17 7LY
e-mail: greenman@englishrosehotels.co.uk
dir: from A64 follow signs to Malton. Left into Market St,
hotel on left

This friendly hotel, set in the centre of town, has an
inviting reception lounge where a log fire burns in winter.
There is also a cosy bar, and dining takes place in the
traditional restaurant at the rear. Bedrooms vary in size
and are thoughtfully equipped.

Rooms 24 (4 fmly) **S** £39.50-£49.50; **D** £80-£100 (incl.
bkfst) **Conf** Class 20 Board 40 Thtr 100 Del from £75 to
£105 **Parking** 40 **Notes** LB ⊗

MARKINGTON   Map 19 SE26

Hob Green

★★★ 82% COUNTRY HOUSE HOTEL

☎ 01423 770031   🖷 01423 771589
HG3 3PJ
e-mail: info@hobgreen.com
web: www.hobgreen.com
dir: from A61, 4m N of Harrogate, left at Wormald Green,
follow hotel signs

This hospitable country house is set in delightful gardens
amidst rolling countryside midway between Harrogate
and Ripon. The inviting lounges boast open fires in
season and there is an elegant restaurant with a small
private dining room. The individual bedrooms are very
comfortable and come with a host of thoughtful extras.

Rooms 12 (1 fmly) **S** £100-£115; **D** £120-£135 (incl.
bkfst) **Facilities** 🏊 Xmas New Year **Conf** Class 10
Board 10 Thtr 15 Del from £155 to £185 **Parking** 40
Notes LB Civ Wed 35

See advert on page 542

MASHAM
Map 19 SE28

INSPECTORS' CHOICE

Swinton Park
★★★★ ◉◉◉ HOTEL

☎ 01765 680900 🖷 01765 680901
HG4 4JH
e-mail: enquiries@swintonpark.com
web: www.swintonpark.com
dir: A1 onto B6267/8 to Masham. Follow signs through town centre & turn right into Swinton Terrace. 1m past golf course, over bridge, up hill. Hotel on right

Although extended during the Victorian and Edwardian eras, the original part of this welcoming castle dates from the 17th century. Bedrooms are luxuriously furnished and come with a host of thoughtful extras. Samuel's restaurant (built by the current owner's great-great-great grandfather) is very elegant and serves imaginative dishes using local produce, much being sourced from the Swinton estate itself.

Rooms 30 (4 fmly) **S** £160-£350; **D** £160-£350 (incl. bkfst)* **Facilities** Spa FTV 🏊 9 Putt green Fishing 🦌 Gym Shooting Falconry Pony trekking Cookery school Off-road driving Xmas New Year Wi-fi **Conf** Class 60 Board 40 Thtr 120 Del from £195 to £330* **Services** Lift **Parking** 50 **Notes** LB Civ Wed 120

The Kings Head
★★ 69% HOTEL

☎ 01765 689295 🖷 01765 689070
Market Place HG4 4EF
e-mail: kings.head.6395@thespiritgroup.com
dir: from A1 take B6267/8 to Masham, follow Market Place signs

This historic hotel, with its uneven floors, beamed bars and attractive window boxes, looks out over the large market square. Guests have the option of choosing either the elegant bedrooms in the main building or the more contemporary ones at the rear of the property; all rooms are thoughtfully equipped. Public areas are traditional in style and include a popular bar and smartly appointed restaurant.

Rooms 27 (15 annexe) (4 fmly) (10 GF) **S** £60; **D** £75-£90* **Facilities** FTV Wi-fi **Conf** Class 24 Board 30 Thtr 54 **Parking** 3 **Notes** LB ⊗

MIDDLESBROUGH
Map 19 NZ41

Thistle Middlesbrough
thistle
★★★★ 73% ◉ HOTEL

☎ 01642 232000 & 0871 376 9028 🖷 01642 232655
Fry St TS1 1JH
e-mail: middlesbrough@thistle.co.uk
web: www.thistlehotels.com/middlesbrough
dir: A19 onto A66 signed Middlesbrough. A66 after Zetland car park. 3rd exit at 1st rdbt, 2nd exit at 2nd rdbt

The staff here are committed to guest care and nothing is too much trouble. Located close to the town centre and football ground this establishment offers bedrooms of varying sizes, that are well furnished and comfortably equipped. The contemporary first-floor CoMotion café bar leads into the open plan Gengis restaurant featuring an interesting range of globally inspired dishes. Guests have full use of the hotel's Otium health club.

Rooms 132 (8 fmly) **S** £70-£175; **D** £70-£175 (incl. bkfst)* **Facilities** STV 🏊 Gym Beautician Steam room Sauna Solarium Xmas New Year Wi-fi **Conf** Class 250 Board 50 Thtr 400 Del from £110 to £170* **Services** Lift **Parking** 67 **Notes** LB Civ Wed 200

Best Western The Highfield Hotel

★★★ 72% HOTEL

☎ 01642 817638 🖷 01642 821219
335 Marton Rd TS4 2PA
e-mail: info@thehighfieldhotel.co.uk
dir: From A66 onto A172 to Stokesley, right at rdbt, straight on at mini rdbt. Left at next mini rdbt, hotel 150yds on right

A modernised, small hotel in the residential suburbs offering comfortable and practical bedrooms. Informal dining is very popular in the Tavistock Italia restaurant where guests will find that service is very friendly.

Rooms 23 (2 fmly) **S** £59-£83; **D** £69-£95 (incl. bkfst)* **Facilities** Xmas New Year Wi-fi **Conf** Class 15 Board 15 Thtr 45 **Notes** ⊗ Civ Wed 45

MONK FRYSTON
Map 16 SE52

Monk Fryston Hall
★★★ 81% COUNTRY HOUSE HOTEL

☎ 01977 682369 🖷 01977 683544
LS25 5DU
e-mail: reception@monkfrystonhallhotel.co.uk
web: www.monkfrystonhallhotel.co.uk
dir: A1(M) junct 42/A63 towards Selby. Monk Fryston village in 2m, hotel on left

This delightful 16th-century mansion house enjoys a peaceful location in 30 acres of grounds, yet is only minutes' drive from the A1. Many original features have been retained and the public rooms are furnished with antique and period pieces. Bedrooms are individually styled and thoughtfully equipped for both business and leisure guests.

Rooms 29 (2 fmly) (5 GF) **S** £75-£105; **D** £110-£175 (incl. bkfst)* **Facilities** STV 🦌 Xmas New Year Wi-fi **Conf** Class 30 Board 25 Thtr 70 **Parking** 80 **Notes** LB Civ Wed 72

NORTHALLERTON
Map 19 SE39

Solberge Hall
★★★ 70% HOTEL

☎ 01609 779191 🖷 01609 780472
Newby Wiske DL7 9ER
e-mail: reservations@solbergehall.co.uk
web: www.solbergehall.co.uk
dir: Exit A1 at Leeming Bar, follow A684, turn right at x-rds, hotel in 2m on right

This Grade II listed Georgian country house is set in 16 acres of parkland and commands panoramic views over open countryside. Spacious bedrooms, some with four-poster beds, vary in style. Public areas include a comfortable lounge bar and an elegant drawing room. The restaurant offers an interesting range of carefully prepared dishes.

Rooms 24 (2 fmly) (5 GF) **S** £80-£110; **D** £130-£150 (incl. bkfst)* **Facilities** STV FTV 🦌 Xmas Wi-fi **Conf** Class 20 Board 40 Thtr 100 Del from £129.50 to £139.50* **Parking** 100 **Notes** LB Civ Wed 100

SCARBOROUGH continued

furnished, and many at the front have picturesque views of the coast. There are two large lounges and a spacious dining room in which good-value, traditional food is served.

Rooms 67 (7 fmly) (2 GF) **Facilities** ⟳ Gym Xmas New Year **Conf** Class 25 Board 25 Thtr 40 **Services** Lift **Notes** LB ⊗

Park Manor

★★ 71% HOTEL

☎ 01723 372090 🖥 01723 500480
Northstead Manor Dr YO12 6BB
e-mail: info@parkmanor.co.uk
web: www.parkmanor.co.uk
dir: off A165, next to Peasholm Park

Enjoying a peaceful residential setting with sea views, this smartly presented, friendly hotel provides the seaside tourist with a wide range of facilities. Bedrooms vary in size and style but all are smartly furnished and well equipped. There is a spacious lounge, smart restaurant, games room and indoor pool and steam room for relaxation.

Rooms 42 (6 fmly) **S** £38-£46; **D** £76-£102 (incl. bkfst)* **Facilities** ⟳ Pool table Spa bath Steam room Table tennis Xmas New Year Wi-fi **Conf** Class 20 Board 20 Thtr 30 Del from £60 to £70* **Services** Lift **Parking** 20 **Notes** LB ⊗ No children 3yrs

The Cumberland

★★ 67% HOTEL   Leisureplex

☎ 01723 361826 🖥 01723 500081
Belmont Rd YO11 2AB
e-mail: cumberland.scarborough@alfatravel.co.uk
dir: From A64, turn right onto B1437, left at A165 towards town centre. Right into Ramshill Rd, right into Belmont Rd

On the South Cliff, convenient for the Spa Complex, beach and town centre shops, bedrooms are comfortably appointed and accessed by lift. Entertainment is provided most evenings and attractive meals are carefully cooked and served in the restaurant.

Rooms 86 (6 fmly) **S** £37-£43; **D** £60-£72 (incl. bkfst) **Facilities** FTV ♫ Xmas New Year **Services** Lift **Notes** LB ⊗ Closed Jan RS Nov-Dec & Feb

Delmont

★★ 63% HOTEL

☎ 01723 364500 🖥 01723 363554
18/19 Blenheim Ter YO12 7HE
e-mail: enquiries@delmonthotel.co.uk
dir: Follow signs to North Bay. At seafront to top of cliff. Hotel near castle

Popular with groups, a friendly welcome is found at this hotel on the North Bay. Bedrooms are comfortable, and many have sea views. There are two lounges, a bar and a spacious dining room in which good-value, traditional food is served along with entertainment on most evenings.

Rooms 51 (18 fmly) (5 GF) **S** £25-£27; **D** £50-£70 (incl. bkfst & dinner) **Facilities** Games Room with table tennis etc ♫ Xmas New Year **Services** Lift **Parking** 2

Brooklands

★★ 60% HOTEL

☎ 01723 376576 🖥 01723 341093
Esplanade Gardens, South Cliff YO11 2AW
e-mail: thebrooklands@mccollshotels.co.uk
dir: from A64 York, left at B&Q rdbt, right at next mini-rdbt, 1st left onto Victoria Ave, at end turn left then 2nd left

This is a traditional seaside hotel that offers good value for money and also caters for coach tours. It stands on the South Cliff overlooking Esplanade Gardens, and has easy access of the sea. There are ample lounges to relax in and entertainment is provided every night.

Rooms 59 (9 fmly) **S** £29-£48; **D** £58-£72 (incl. bkfst & dinner)* **Facilities** ♫ Xmas New Year Wi-fi **Conf** Class 40 Board 40 Thtr 100 **Services** Lift

Hotel St Nicholas by Swallow

Ⓤ

☎ 01723 364101 🖥 01723 500538
St Nicholas Cliff YO11 2EU
e-mail: res.stnicholas@crerarmgmt.com
dir: Follow A64/A170 to Scarborough railway station, with station on right, right at lights, left at next lights, across rdbt, first available right turn, hotel on right

Currently the rating for this establishment is not confirmed. This may be due to a change of ownership or because it has only recently joined the AA rating scheme. For further details please see the AA website: www.theAA.com

Rooms 134 (17 fmly) **S** £35-£85; **D** £59-£135 (incl. bkfst) **Facilities** FTV ⟳ Gym ♫ Xmas New Year Wi-fi **Conf** Class 150 Board 50 Thtr 400 Del from £75 to £125 **Services** Lift **Parking** 15 (charged) **Notes** LB ⊗ Civ Wed 350

Rivelyn

Ⓤ

☎ 01723 361248 🖥 01723 361001
1-4 Crown Crescent, South Cliff YO11 2BJ
e-mail: info@rivelynhotel.co.uk
web: www.rivelynhotel.co.uk
dir: A165 into Albion Rd, 50mtrs then left into Crown Crescent, hotel on left

Currently the rating for this establishment is not confirmed. This may be due to a change of ownership or because it has only recently joined the AA rating scheme. For further details please see the AA website: www.theAA.com

Rooms 60 (2 fmly) (5 GF) **S** £20-£40; **D** £40-£80 (incl. bkfst & dinner)* **Facilities** ♫ Xmas New Year Wi-fi **Services** Lift

---

**SCOTCH CORNER
(NEAR RICHMOND)**   Map 19 NZ20

Travelodge Scotch Corner (A1)

BUDGET HOTEL

☎ 08719 846 173 🖥 0870 1911675
Skeeby DL10 5EQ
web: www.travelodge.co.uk
dir: off rdbt at junct of A1/A66, S'bound

Travelodge offers good quality, good value, modern accommodation. Ideal for families, the spacious en suite bedrooms include remote-control TV, tea and coffee-making facilities and comfortable beds. Meals can be taken at the nearby family restaurant. See also the Hotel Groups pages.

Rooms 40 **S** fr £29; **D** fr £29

Travelodge Scotch Corner Skeeby

BUDGET HOTEL

☎ 08719 846 176 📠 01325 377616
Middleton Tyas Ln DL10 6PQ
web: www.travelodge.co.uk
dir: On A1 N'bound, 0.5m S of Scotch Corner

Rooms 50 **S** fr £29; **D** fr £29

SKIPTON Map 18 SD95

The Coniston

★★★ 79% HOTEL

☎ 01756 748080 📠 01756 749487
Coniston Cold BD23 4EB
e-mail: info@theconistonhotel.com
dir: on A65, 6m NW of Skipton

Privately owned and situated on a 1,400 acre estate centred around a beautiful 24-acre lake, this hotel offers guests many exciting outdoor activities. The modern bedrooms are comfortable and most have king-size beds. Macleod's Bar and the main restaurant serve all-day meals, and fine dining is available in the evening from both carte and fixed-price menus. Staff are very friendly and nothing is too much trouble.

Rooms 50 (13 fmly) (25 GF) **Facilities** Fishing Clay pigeon shooting Falconry Off-road Land Rover driving Xmas New Year Wi-fi **Conf** Class 80 Board 50 Thtr 200 **Parking** 120 **Notes** Civ Wed 100

Rendezvous

★★★ 77% HOTEL

CLASSIC BRITISH HOTELS

☎ 01756 700100 📠 01756 700107
Keighley Rd BD23 2TA
e-mail: admin@rendezvous-skipton.com

Located beside the canal just outside the town, the hotel has the advantage of plenty of parking and a leisure club

with pool and gym. Bedrooms are well equipped and spacious, and have delightful views over the rolling countryside. There are extensive conference facilities. This hotel makes an ideal base for touring The Dales.

Rooms 79 (10 fmly) (12 GF) **Facilities** 🏊 supervised Gym Xmas New Year Wi-fi **Conf** Class 200 Board 120 Thtr 500 **Services** Lift **Parking** 120 **Notes** LB ⊗ Civ Wed 400

Herriots Hotel

★★★ 75% HOTEL

☎ 01756 792781 📠 01756 793967
Broughton Rd BD23 1RT
e-mail: info@herriotsforleisure.co.uk
web: www.herriotsforleisure.co.uk
dir: off A59, opposite railway station

Close to the centre of the market town, this friendly hotel offers tastefully decorated bedrooms that are well equipped. The open-plan brasserie is a relaxing place and offers a varied and interesting menu; meals and snacks are also available in the bar. The extension includes modern bedrooms and a stylish conservatory lounge.

Rooms 23 (3 fmly) **S** £50-£75; **D** £65-£100 (incl. bkfst) **Facilities** Xmas New Year Wi-fi **Conf** Class 50 Board 52 Thtr 100 Del from £125 to £145 **Services** Lift **Parking** 26 **Notes** LB ⊗ Civ Wed 80

Travelodge Skipton

BUDGET HOTEL

Travelodge

☎ 08719 846 177 📠 0870 1911676
Gargrave Rd BD23 1UD
web: www.travelodge.co.uk
dir: A65/A59 rdbt

Travelodge offers good quality, good value, modern accommodation. Ideal for families, the spacious en suite bedrooms include remote-control TV, tea and coffee-making facilities and comfortable beds. Meals can be taken at the nearby family restaurant. See also the Hotel Groups pages.

Rooms 32 **S** fr £29; **D** fr £29

TOPCLIFFE Map 19 SE37

The Angel Inn

U

☎ 01845 577237 📠 01845 578000
Long St YO7 3RW
e-mail: info@angelinn.co.uk
dir: Exit A168 (between A1(M) & A19)

Currently the rating for this establishment is not confirmed. This may be due to a change of ownership or because it has only recently joined the AA rating scheme. For further details please see the AA website: www.theAA.com

Rooms 15 (1 fmly) **Facilities** New Year **Conf** Class 60 Board 50 Thtr 150 **Parking** 150 **Notes** ⊗ Civ Wed 130

WEST WITTON Map 19 SE08

Wensleydale Heifer

★★ 82% ⚜ HOTEL

☎ 01969 622322 & 622725 📠 01969 624183
Main St DL8 4LS
e-mail: info@wensleydaleheifer.co.uk
web: www.wensleydaleheifer.co.uk
dir: A1 to Leeming Bar junct, A684 towards Bedale for approx 10m to Leyburn, then towards Hawes 3.5m to West Witton

Describing itself as a boutique hotel, this 17th-century coaching inn has been transformed in recent years. The bedrooms (a four-poster room and junior suite included) are each designed with a unique and interesting theme - for example, Chocolate, Malt Whisky, James Herriott and Shooter. Food is very much the focus here - the informal fish bar and the contemporary style restaurant. The kitchen prides itself on sourcing the freshest fish and locally reared meats.

Rooms 9 (3 fmly) **S** £90; **D** £110-£140 (incl. bkfst)* **Facilities** Xmas New Year **Parking** 40 **Notes** LB

WHITBY | Map 19 NZ81

Dunsley Hall

★★★ 80% ⊛ COUNTRY HOUSE HOTEL

☎ 01947 893437 📠 01947 893505
Dunsley YO21 3TL
e-mail: reception@dunsleyhall.com
web: www.dunsleyhall.com
dir: 3m N of Whitby, signed off A171

Friendly service is found at this fine country mansion set in a quiet hamlet with coastal views north of Whitby. The house has Gothic overtones and boasts fine woodwork and panelling, no more so than in the magnificent lounge. Two lovely dining rooms offer imaginative dishes and there is also a cosy bar.

Rooms 26 (2 fmly) (2 GF) **S** £95-£120; **D** £130-£149 (incl. bkfst)* **Facilities** 🏌 Putt green Xmas New Year
Conf Class 50 Board 40 Thtr 95 Del from £110 to £135*
Parking 30 **Notes** LB ⊗ Civ Wed 100

Saxonville

★★★ 77% HOTEL

☎ 01947 602631 📠 01947 820523
Ladysmith Av, Argyle Rd YO21 3HX
e-mail: newtons@saxonville.co.uk
web: www.saxonville.co.uk
dir: A174 to North Promenade. Turn inland at large four-towered building visible on West Cliff, into Argyle Rd, then 1st right

The friendly service is noteworthy at this long-established holiday hotel. Well maintained throughout it offers comfortable bedrooms and inviting public areas that include a well-proportioned restaurant where quality dinners are served.

Rooms 23 (2 fmly) (1 GF) **S** £65-£90; **D** £130-£160 (incl. bkfst) **Conf** Class 40 Board 40 Thtr 100 **Parking** 20
Notes ⊗ Closed Dec-Jan RS Feb-Mar & Nov

Cliffemount

★★ 79% HOTEL

☎ 01947 840103 📠 01947 841025
Bank Top Ln, Runswick Bay TS13 5HU
e-mail: info@cliffemounthotel.co.uk
dir: exit A174, 8m N of Whitby, 1m to end

Enjoying an elevated position above the cliff-side village and with splendid views across the bay, this hotel offers a warm welcome. The cosy bar leads to the restaurant where locally caught fish features on the extensive menus. The bedrooms, many with sea-view balconies, are well equipped with both practical and homely extras.

Rooms 20 (4 fmly) (5 GF) **S** £50-£65; **D** £90-£135 (incl. bkfst)* **Facilities** Xmas New Year Wi-fi **Parking** 25
Notes LB

Estbek House

⊛ RESTAURANT WITH ROOMS

☎ 01947 893424 📠 01947 893625
East Row, Sandsend YO21 3SU
e-mail: info@estbekhouse.co.uk
dir: On Cleveland Way, within Sandsend, next to East Beck

A speciality seafood restaurant on the first floor is the focus of this listed building in a small coastal village north west of Whitby. Below is a small bar and breakfast room, while up above are four individually presented bedrooms offering luxury and comfort.

Rooms 4 (1 pri facs)

The White Horse & Griffin

⊛ RESTAURANT WITH ROOMS

☎ 01947 825026 & 604857 📠 01947 604857
Church St YO22 4BH
e-mail: info@whitehorseandgriffin.co.uk
dir: From town centre E across Bridge St bridge, 2nd left, 50mtrs on right next to Whitby

This historic inn, now a restaurant with rooms, is as quaint as the cobbled side street in which it lies. Cooking is good with the emphasis on fresh fish. The bedrooms, some reached by steep staircases, retain a rustic charm but are well equipped and include CD players.

Rooms 20 (7 pri facs) (11 en suite) (10 annexe) (1 fmly)

YARM | Map 19 NZ41

INSPECTORS' CHOICE

Judges Country House Hotel

★★★ ⊛⊛⊛ HOTEL

Pride of Britain

☎ 01642 789000 📠 01642 782878
Kirklevington Hall TS15 9LW
e-mail: enquiries@judgeshotel.co.uk
web: www.judgeshotel.co.uk
dir: 1.5m from A19. At A67 junct, follow Yarm road, hotel on left

Formerly a lodging for local circuit judges, this gracious mansion lies in landscaped grounds through which a stream runs. Stylish bedrooms are individually decorated and come with 101 extras, including a pet goldfish! The Conservatory restaurant serves award-winning cuisine, and the genuinely caring and attentive service is equally memorable.

Rooms 21 (3 fmly) (5 GF) **S** £142-£155; **D** £175-£185*
Facilities STV 🏊 Gym Boating 4x4 hire Mountain bikes Nature trails Xmas New Year Wi-fi **Conf** Class 120 Board 80 Thtr 200 **Parking** 102 **Notes** LB ⊗ Civ Wed 200

YORK
Map 16 SE65

See also **Aldwark & Escrick**

INSPECTORS' CHOICE

Middlethorpe Hall & Spa
★★★★ ◉◉ HOTEL

☎ 01904 641241 📠 01904 620176
Bishopthorpe Rd, Middlethorpe YO23 2GB
e-mail: info@middlethorpe.com
dir: A1/A64 follow York West (A1036) signs, then Bishopthorpe, Middlethorpe racecourse signs

This fine house, dating from the reign of William and Mary, sits in acres of beautifully landscaped gardens. The bedrooms vary in size but all are comfortably furnished; some are located in the main house, and others are in a cottage and converted courtyard stables. Public areas include a small spa and a stately drawing room where afternoon tea is quite an event. The delightful panelled restaurant is a perfect setting for enjoying the imaginative cuisine.

Rooms 29 (19 annexe) (2 fmly) (10 GF) **S** £130-£185; **D** £190-£260 (incl. bkfst)* **Facilities** Spa FTV ⏍ ⚑ Gym Health & Beauty spa Xmas New Year Wi-fi **Conf** Class 30 Board 25 Thtr 56 Del from £175 to £190* **Services** Lift **Parking** 70 **Notes** LB ⊗ No children 6yrs RS 25 & 31 Dec Civ Wed 56

Hotel du Vin York
★★★★ 81% ◉ HOTEL

☎ 01904 557350 📠 01904 557351
89 The Mount YO24 1AX
e-mail: info.york@hotelduvin.com
web: www.hotelduvin.com
dir: A1036 towards city centre, 6m. Hotel on right through lights.

This Hotel du Vin makes an unrestrained statement of luxury and quality that will cosset even the most discerning guest. Bedrooms are decadent in design and the bathrooms have huge monsoon showers and 'feature' baths. Dinner in the bistro provides a memorable highlight thanks to exciting menus and a superb wine list. Staff throughout are naturally friendly, nothing is too much trouble. Hotel du Vin - AA Small Hotel Group of the Year 2008-9.

Rooms 44 (3 fmly) (14 GF) **S** £130-£395; **D** £130-£395* **Facilities** STV FTV Wi-fi **Conf** Class 8 Board 22 Thtr 22 **Services** Lift Air con **Parking** 18

Best Western Dean Court
★★★★ 77% ◉◉ HOTEL

☎ 01904 625082 📠 01904 620305
Duncombe Place YO1 7EF
e-mail: info@deancourt-york.co.uk
web: www.deancourt-york.co.uk
dir: city centre opposite York Minster

This smart hotel enjoys a central location overlooking The Minster, and guests will find the service is particularly friendly and efficient. Bedrooms are stylishly appointed and vary in size. Public areas are elegant in a contemporary style and include the popular D.C.H. restaurant which enjoys wonderful views of the cathedral, and The Court café-bistro and bar where a more informal, all-day menu is offered. Valet parking is available.

Rooms 37 (4 fmly) **S** £99-£130; **D** £135-£225 (incl. bkfst)* **Facilities** FTV Xmas New Year Wi-fi **Conf** Class 12 Board 32 Thtr 50 **Services** Lift **Parking** 30 (charged) **Notes** LB ⊗ Civ Wed 80

The Grange
★★★★ 77% ◉◉ HOTEL

☎ 01904 644744 📠 01904 612453
1 Clifton YO30 6AA
e-mail: info@grangehotel.co.uk
web: www.grangehotel.co.uk
dir: on A19 York/Thirsk road, approx 500yds from city centre

This bustling Regency town house is just a few minutes' walk from the centre of York. A professional service is efficiently delivered by caring staff in a very friendly and helpful manner. Public rooms are comfortable and have been stylishly furnished; these include two dining options, the popular and informal Cellar Bar, and main hotel restaurant The Ivy Brasserie, which offers fine dining in a lavishly decorated environment. The individually designed bedrooms are comfortably appointed and have been thoughtfully equipped.

Rooms 36 (6 GF) **S** £117-£188; **D** £130-£225 (incl. bkfst)* **Facilities** Use of nearby health club Xmas New Year Wi-fi **Conf** Class 24 Board 24 Thtr 50 Del from £169.50* **Parking** 26 **Notes** LB Civ Wed 90

York Marriott
★★★★ 76% HOTEL

☎ 01904 701000 📠 01904 702308
Tadcaster Rd YO24 1QQ
e-mail: mhrs.qqyyk.pa@marriotthotels.com
web: www.yorkmarriott.co.uk
dir: from A64 at York 'West' onto A1036, follow signs to city centre. Approx 1.5m, hotel on right after church and lights

Overlooking the racecourse and Knavesmire Parkland, the hotel offers modern accommodation, including family rooms, all with comfort cooling. Within the hotel, guests enjoy the use of extensive leisure facilities including indoor pool, putting green and tennis court. For those wishing to explore the historic and cultural attractions, the city is less than a mile away.

Rooms 151 (14 fmly) (27 GF) (12 smoking) **Facilities** Spa STV ⏍ ⚑ Putt green Gym Beauty treatment New Year Wi-fi **Conf** Class 90 Board 40 Thtr 190 Del from £135 to £170* **Services** Lift Air con **Parking** 160 **Notes** ⊗ Civ Wed 140

See advert on page 558

Holiday Inn Doncaster A1(M) Jct 36

Rooms 102 (6 fmly) (22 GF) **Facilities** ☜ supervised Gym Beautician Steam room Xmas New Year Wi-fi **Conf** Class 250 Board 100 Thtr 250 **Services** Lift **Parking** 250 **Notes** ⊗ Civ Wed 250

Regent

★★★ 74% HOTEL

☎ 01302 364180 & 381960 📠 01302 322331
Regent Square DN1 2DS
e-mail: reservations@theregenthotel.co.uk
web: www.theregenthotel.co.uk
dir: on corner of A630 & A638, 1m from racecourse

This town centre hotel overlooks a delightful small square. Public rooms include the modern bar and delightful restaurant, where an interesting range of dishes is offered. Service is friendly and attentive. Modern bedrooms have been furnished in a contemporary style and offer high levels of comfort.

Rooms 53 (6 fmly) (8 GF) **S** £65-£95; **D** £80-£105 (incl. bkfst)* **Facilities** FTV ♫ Wi-fi **Conf** Class 50 Board 40 Thtr 125 **Del** from £120 to £125* **Services** Lift **Parking** 20 **Notes** Closed 25 Dec & 1 Jan RS BH Civ Wed 120

Grand St Leger

★★★ 66% HOTEL

☎ 01302 364111 📠 01302 329865
Bennetthorpe DN2 6AX
e-mail: sales@grandstleger.com
web: www.grandstleger.com
dir: follow Doncaster Racecourse signs, at Racecourse rdbt hotel on corner

This friendly hotel is located next to the racecourse and is only ten minutes' walk from the town centre. There is a cheerful bar-lounge and a pleasant restaurant offering an extensive choice of dishes. The bedrooms are

comfortable and thoughtfully equipped, including Wi-fi access.

Rooms 20 **S** £65-£85; **D** £75-£105 (incl. bkfst)
Facilities FTV Wi-fi **Conf** Class 50 Board 30 Thtr 80 **Del** from £150 to £180 **Parking** 28 **Notes** ⊗ RS 25 Dec Civ Wed 60

Campanile Doncaster

BUDGET HOTEL

☎ 01302 370770 📠 01302 370813
Doncaster Leisure Park, Bawtry Rd DN4 7PD
e-mail: doncaster@campanile.com
dir: follow signs to Doncaster Leisure Centre, left at rdbt before Dome complex

This modern building offers accommodation in smart, well-equipped bedrooms, all with en suite bathrooms. Refreshments may be taken at the informal bistro. See also the Hotel Groups pages.

Rooms 50 **Conf** Class 15 Board 15 Thtr 25

Express by Holiday Inn Doncaster

BUDGET HOTEL

☎ 0870 890 9988 📠 0870 890 9989
Catesby Business Park, First Point DN4 5JH
e-mail: doncaster@expressbyholidayinn.net
web: www.hiexpress.com/doncaster

A modern hotel ideal for families and business travellers. Fresh and uncomplicated, the spacious rooms include Sky TV, power shower and tea and coffee-making facilities. Continental buffet breakfast is included in the room rate; other meals may be taken at the nearby family pub or restaurant. See also the Hotel Groups pages.

Rooms 94 **Conf** Class 16 Board 20 Thtr 40

Innkeeper's Lodge Doncaster

BUDGET HOTEL

☎ 0845 112 6032 📠 0845 112 6270
Bawtry Rd, Bessacarr DN4 7BS
web: www.innkeeperslodge.com/doncaster
dir: M18 junct 3, A6182 towards Doncaster. At rdbt take A18 (signed Thorne). At next rdbt take A638, pass racecourse. Lodge 1.5m on right

Innkeeper's Lodge represents an exciting, high value concept within the budget hotel market. Comfortable bedrooms provide excellent facilities that include satellite TV and modem points. Options include family rooms, and for the corporate guest, cutting edge IT which includes Wi-fi access. A popular Carvery provides all-day food, including an extensive, complimentary continental breakfast.

Rooms 25 **S** £53; **D** £53 (incl. bkfst) **Conf** Thtr 40

Travelodge Doncaster (M18/M180)

BUDGET HOTEL

☎ 08719 846 132 📠 01302 845469
DN8 5GS
web: www.travelodge.co.uk
dir: M18 junct 5/M180

Travelodge offers good quality, good value, modern accommodation. Ideal for families, the spacious en suite bedrooms include remote-control TV, tea and coffee-making facilities and comfortable beds. Meals can be taken at the nearby family restaurant. See also the Hotel Groups pages.

Rooms 39 **S** fr £29; **D** fr £29

MEXBOROUGH   Map 16 SE40

Pastures

★★ 65% HOTEL

☎ 01709 577707 📠 01709 577795
Pastures Rd S64 0JJ
e-mail: info@pastureshotel.co.uk
web: www.pastureshotel.co.uk
dir: 0.5m from town centre on A6023, left by ATS Tyres, signed Denaby Ings & Cadeby. Hotel on right

This private hotel has a modern, purpose-built block of bedrooms and a separate lodge where food is served. It is in a rural setting beside a working canal and convenient for Doncaster or the Dearne Valley with its nature reserves and leisure centre. Compact bedrooms are quiet, comfortable and equipped with many modern facilities.

Rooms 60 (5 fmly) (28 GF) **S** £60; **D** £65-£120 (incl. bkfst)* **Facilities** STV Xmas New Year Wi-fi **Conf** Class 170 Board 100 Thtr 250 **Services** Lift **Parking** 179 **Notes** LB ⊗ Civ Wed 200

ROSSINGTON
Map 16 SK69

Best Western Mount Pleasant
★★★★ 78% HOTEL

☎ 01302 868696 & 868219 📄 01302 865130
Great North Rd DN11 0HW
e-mail: reception@mountpleasant.co.uk
web: www.mountpleasant.co.uk
dir: on A638 (Great North Road) between Bawtry & Doncaster

This charming 18th-century house stands in 100 acres of wooded parkland. The spacious bedrooms have been thoughtfully equipped and pleasantly furnished; the premier rooms being particularly comfortable. Public rooms include an elegant restaurant and a very comfortable bar lounge. The hotel has extensive conference facilities, and a licence for civil weddings.

Rooms 56 (12 fmly) (28 GF) **S** £85-£150; **D** £99-£175 (incl. bkfst)* **Facilities** STV Beauty salon Wi-fi **Conf** Class 70 Board 70 Thtr 200 **Services** Lift **Parking** 140 **Notes** LB ⊗ Closed 25 Dec RS 24 Dec Civ Wed 180

ROTHERHAM
Map 16 SK49

Hellaby Hall
★★★★ 71% HOTEL

☎ 01709 702701 📄 01709 700979
Old Hellaby Ln, Hellaby S66 8SN
e-mail: reservations@hellabyhallhotel.co.uk
web: www.hellabyhallhotel.co.uk
dir: 0.5m off M18 junct 1, onto A631 towards Maltby. Hotel in Hellaby

This 17th-century house was built to a Flemish design with high, beamed ceilings, staircases which lead off to private meeting rooms and a series of oak-panelled lounges. Bedrooms are elegant and well equipped, and guests can dine in the formal Attic Restaurant. There are extensive leisure facilities and conference areas, and the hotel holds a licence for civil weddings.

Rooms 90 (2 fmly) (17 GF) **S** £55-£115; **D** £65-£126* **Facilities** Spa STV FTV ⊛ Gym Beauty room Exercise studio Xmas New Year Wi-fi **Conf** Class 300 Board 150 Thtr 500 Del from £99 to £145* **Services** Lift **Parking** 250 **Notes** LB ⊗ Civ Wed 200

Best Western Consort Hotel
★★★ 79% HOTEL

☎ 01709 530022 📄 01709 531529
Brampton Rd, Thurcroft S66 9JA
e-mail: info@consorthotel.com
web: www.consorthotel.com
dir: M18 junct 1, right towards Bawtry on A631. 250yds to rdbt, then 200yds turn left then 1.5m to x-rds, hotel opposite

Bedrooms at this modern, friendly hotel are comfortable, attractive and air-conditioned, and include ten superior rooms. A wide range of dishes is served in the open-plan bar and restaurant, and there is a comfortable foyer lounge. There are good conference and function facilities, and entertainment evenings are often hosted here.

Rooms 27 (2 fmly) (9 GF) **S** £57-£98; **D** £79-£110 (incl. bkfst)* **Facilities** FTV 🎵 Wi-fi **Conf** Class 120 Board 50 Thtr 300 Del from £90 to £130* **Services** Air con **Parking** 90 **Notes** LB ⊗ Civ Wed 300

Best Western Elton
★★★ 77% HOTEL

☎ 01709 545681 📄 01709 549100
Main St, Bramley S66 2SF
e-mail: bestwestern.eltonhotel@btinternet.com
web: www.bw-eltonhotel.co.uk
dir: M18 junct 1 follow A631 Rotherham, turn right to Ravenfield, hotel at end of Bramley village, follow brown signs

Within easy reach of the M18, this welcoming, stone-built hotel is set in well-tended gardens. The Elton offers good modern accommodation, with larger rooms in the extension that are particularly comfortable and well equipped. A civil licence is held for wedding ceremonies and conference rooms are available.

Rooms 29 (16 annexe) (4 fmly) (11 GF) **S** £55-£82; **D** £73-£96 (incl. bkfst) **Facilities** FTV Wi-fi **Conf** Class 24 Board 26 Thtr 55 **Parking** 48 **Notes** LB Civ Wed 48

Carlton Park
★★★ 77% HOTEL

☎ 01709 849955 📄 01709 368960
102/104 Moorgate Rd S60 2BG
e-mail: reservations@carltonparkhotel.com
web: www.carltonparkhotel.com
dir: M1 junct 33, onto A631, then A618. Hotel 800yds past hospital

This modern hotel is situated in a pleasant residential area of the town, close to the District General Hospital, yet within minutes of the M1. Bedrooms and bathrooms offer very modern facilities; three have separate sitting rooms. The restaurant and bar provide a lively atmosphere and there is a pool and leisure centre.

Rooms 80 (14 fmly) (16 GF) (7 smoking) **S** £54-£102; **D** £88-£112 (incl. bkfst)* **Facilities** STV ⊛ Gym 🎵 Xmas New Year Wi-fi **Conf** Class 160 Board 60 Thtr 250 Del from £100 to £120* **Services** Lift **Parking** 120 **Notes** ⊗ Civ Wed 150

Restover Lodge
★★ 67% HOTEL

☎ 01709 700255 📄 01709 545169
Hellaby Industrial Estate, Lowton Way, off Denby Way S66 8RY
e-mail: rotherham@envergure.co.uk
dir: M18 junct 1. Follow signs for Maltby. Left at lights, 2nd on left

This modern building offers accommodation in smart, well equipped bedrooms. Refreshments may be taken at the informal restaurant or bar.

Rooms 50 (12 fmly) **Facilities** Xmas **Conf** Class 35 Board 30 Thtr 40 **Parking** 40

Holiday Inn Rotherham-Sheffield M1, Jct 33

🄄

☎ 01709 830630 📄 01709 786005
West Bawtry Rd S60 4NA
web: www.holidayinn.co.uk

Currently the rating for this establishment is not confirmed. This may be due to a change of ownership or because it has only recently joined the AA rating scheme. For further details please see the AA website: www.theAA.com

Rooms 104

Best Western Pennine Manor

★★★ 74% HOTEL

☎ 01484 642368 📠 01484 642866
Nettleton Hill Rd, Scapegoat Hill HD7 4NH
e-mail: penninemanor@bestwestern.co.uk
web: www.bw-penninemanor.co.uk
dir: M62 junct 24, signed Rochdale (A640)/Outlane
Village, left after Commercial pub, hotel signed

Set high in The Pennines, this attractive stone-built hotel
enjoys magnificent panoramic views. Bedrooms are
thoughtfully equipped and stylishly appointed. There is a
popular bar with log burning stove and a cosy
atmosphere, offering a good selection of snacks and
meals. The restaurant and meeting rooms enjoy fine
views over the valley.

Rooms 30 (4 fmly) (15 GF) **Facilities** Wi-fi **Conf** Class 56
Board 40 Thtr 132 **Parking** 115 **Notes** LB ⊗ Civ Wed 100

The Old Golf House Hotel

★★★ 70% HOTEL

☎ 0844 736 8609 & 01422 379311 📠 01422 372694
New Hey Rd, Outlane HD3 3YP
e-mail: oldgolfhouse@corushotels.com
web: www.corushotels.com
dir: M62 junct 23 (eastbound only), or junct 24. Follow
A640 to Rochdale. Hotel on A640

Situated close to the M62, this traditionally styled hotel
offers well-equipped bedrooms. A wide choice of dishes is
offered in the restaurant, and lighter meals are available
in the lounge bar. The hotel, with lovely grounds, is a
popular venue for weddings.

Rooms 52 (4 fmly) (19 GF) (10 smoking) **S** £69-£89;
D £69-£89* **Facilities** STV Putt green Mini golf Xmas New
Year Wi-fi **Conf** Class 35 Board 30 Thtr 70 Del from £85
to £105* **Parking** 100 **Notes** LB RS Xmas Civ Wed 100

Cedar Court

[U]

☎ 01422 375431 📠 01422 314050
Ainley Top HD3 3RH
e-mail: huddersfield@cedarcourthotels.co.uk
web: www.cedarcourthotels.co.uk
dir: 500yds from M62 junct 24

Currently the rating for this establishment is not confirmed.
This may be due to a change of ownership or because it has
only recently joined the AA rating scheme. For further
details please see the AA website: www.theAA.com

Rooms 114 (6 fmly) (10 GF) **Facilities** ⊕ supervised Gym
Steam room **Conf** Class 150 Board 100 Thtr 500
Services Lift **Parking** 250 **Notes** LB Civ Wed 400

Travelodge Huddersfield Mirfield

BUDGET HOTEL

☎ 08719 846 146 📠 01924 489921
Leeds Rd, Mirfield WF14 0BY
web: www.travelodge.co.uk
dir: M62 junct 25, follow A62 across 2 rdbts. Lodge on
right

Travelodge offers good quality, good value, modern
accommodation. Ideal for families, the spacious en suite
bedrooms include remote-control TV, tea and coffee-
making facilities and comfortable beds. Meals can be
taken at the nearby family restaurant. See also the Hotel
Groups pages.

Rooms 27 **S** fr £29; **D** fr £29

Weavers Shed Restaurant with Rooms

⊕⊕ RESTAURANT WITH ROOMS

☎ 01484 654284 📠 01484 650980
86-88 Knowl Rd, Golcar HD7 4AN
e-mail: info@weaversshed.co.uk
dir: 3m W of Huddersfield. A62 onto B6111 to Milnsbridge
& Scar Ln to Golcar, right onto Knowl Rd, signed Colne
Valley Museum

This converted house has spacious bedrooms named
after local textile mills; all are extremely well equipped.
An inviting bar-lounge leads into the well known
restaurant where fresh produce, much from the
establishment's own gardens, forms the basis of
excellent meals.

Rooms 5 (5 en suite) (2 GF)

ILKLEY Map 19 SE14

Best Western Rombalds Hotel & Restaurant

★★★ 83% ⊛ HOTEL

☎ 01943 603201 📠 01943 816586
11 West View, Wells Rd LS29 9JG
e-mail: reception@rombalds.demon.co.uk
web: www.rombalds.co.uk
dir: A65 from Leeds. Left at 3rd main lights, follow Ilkley
Moor signs. Right at HSBC Bank onto Wells Rd. Hotel
600yds on left

This elegantly furnished Georgian townhouse is located in
a peaceful terrace between the town and the moors.
Delightful day rooms include a choice of comfortable
lounges and an attractive restaurant that provides a
relaxed venue in which to sample the skilfully prepared,
imaginative meals. The bedrooms are tastefully
furnished, well equipped and include several spacious
suites.

Rooms 15 (4 fmly) **S** £75-£100; **D** £95-£120 (incl. bkfst)*
Facilities STV Xmas Wi-fi **Conf** Class 40 Board 25 Thtr 70
Del from £115 to £145* **Parking** 28 **Notes** LB Closed 28
Dec-2 Jan Civ Wed 70

ILKLEY continued

The Craiglands

★★★ 68% HOTEL

☎ 01943 430001 & 886450 ▤ 01943 430002
Cowpasture Rd LS29 8RQ
e-mail: reservations@craiglands.co.uk
web: www.craiglands.co.uk
dir: off A65 into Ilkley. Left at T-junct. Past rail station,
fork right into Cowpasture Rd. Hotel opposite school

This grand Victorian hotel is ideally situated close to the
town centre. Spacious public areas and a good range of
services are ideal for business or leisure. Extensive
conference facilities are available along with an elegant
restaurant and traditionally styled bar and lounge.
Bedrooms, varying in size and style, are comfortably
furnished and well equipped.

Rooms 61 (6 fmly) **S** £59-£85; **D** £59-£115 (incl. bkfst)*
Facilities STV Xmas New Year Wi-fi **Conf** Class 200
Board 100 Thtr 500 Del from £120 to £150 **Services** Lift
Parking 200 **Notes** LB ⊗ Civ Wed 500

Innkeeper's Lodge Ilkley

BUDGET HOTEL

☎ 0845 112 6037 ▤ 0845 112 6265
Hangingstone Rd LS29 8BT
web: www.innkeeperslodge.com/ilkley
dir: A65 onto B6382 towards Ilkley. Pass Ilkley Station,
right into Cowpasture Rd, leads into Hangingstone Rd.
Lodge 0.5m on left

Innkeeper's Lodge represents an exciting, high value
concept within the budget hotel market. Comfortable
bedrooms provide excellent facilities that include satellite
TV and modem points. This carefully restored lodge is in a
picturesque setting and has its own unique style and
quirky character. Food is served all day, and an extensive,
complimentary continental breakfast is offered.

Rooms 14 (2 fmly) **S** £59.95; **D** £59.95 (incl. bkfst)
Conf Thtr 24

KEIGHLEY	Map 19 SE04

Dalesgate

★★ 70% HOTEL

☎ 01535 664930 ▤ 01535 611253
406 Skipton Rd, Utley BD20 6HP
e-mail: stephen.e.atha@btinternet.com
dir: In town centre follow A629 over rdbt onto B6265.
Right after 0.75m into St. John's Rd. 1st right into hotel
car park

Originally the residence of a local chapel minister, this
modern, well-established hotel provides well-equipped,
comfortable bedrooms. It also boasts a cosy bar and
pleasant restaurant, serving an imaginative range of
dishes. A large car park is provided to the rear.

Rooms 20 (2 fmly) (3 GF) **S** £40-£45; **D** £60-£65 (incl.
bkfst) **Parking** 25 **Notes** RS 22 Dec-4 Jan

Innkeeper's Lodge Keighley

BUDGET HOTEL

☎ 0845 112 6038 ▤ 0845 112 6264
Bradford Rd BD21 4BB
web: www.innkeeperslodge.com/keighley
dir: M606 onto A6177, at next rdbt A641(city centre).
Follow A650 towards Bingley & Keighley. Lodge on 2nd
rdbt

Innkeeper's Lodge represents an exciting, high value
concept within the budget hotel market. Comfortable
bedrooms provide excellent facilities that include satellite
TV and modem points. Options include family rooms, and
for the corporate guest, cutting edge IT which includes
Wi-fi access. A popular Carvery provides all-day food,
including an extensive, complimentary continental
breakfast.

Rooms 43 **S** £53; **D** £53 (incl. bkfst) **Conf** Thtr 24

KIRKBURTON	Map 16 SE11

Innkeeper's Lodge Huddersfield

BUDGET HOTEL

☎ 0845 112 6035 ▤ 0845 112 6267
36a Penistone Rd HD8 0PQ
web: www.innkeeperslodge.com/huddersfield
dir: M62 junct 24, A629 east towards Huddersfield. Onto
A62 (ring road), left onto A629 towards Wakefield. In
Kirkburton, lodge on right

Innkeeper's Lodge represents an exciting, high value
concept within the budget hotel market. Comfortable
bedrooms provide excellent facilities that include satellite
TV and modem points. Options include family rooms, and
for the corporate guest, cutting edge IT includes Wi-fi
access. Food is served all day in the adjacent Country
Pub. The extensive continental breakfast is
complimentary.

Rooms 23 (3 fmly) **S** £53; **D** £53 (incl. bkfst)
Conf Board 20 Thtr 30

LEEDS	Map 19 SE23

See also **Gomersal & Shipley**

De Vere Oulton Hall

★★★★★ 77% ⑨⑨ HOTEL

DE VERE deluxe

☎ 0113 282 1000 ▤ 0113 282 8066
Rothwell Ln, Oulton LS26 8HN
e-mail: oulton.hall@devere-hotels.com
web: www.devere.co.uk
dir: 2m from M62 junct 30 on left, or 1m from M1
junct 44. Follow Castleford & Pontefract signs on A639

Surrounded by the beautiful Yorkshire Dales, yet within
15 minutes of the city centre, this elegant 19th-century
house really does offer the best of both worlds. Impressive
features of the hotel include the formal gardens, which
have been faithfully restored to their original design, and
the galleried Great Hall. The hotel also offers a choice of
dining options and golfers can book preferential tee times
at the adjacent golf club.

Rooms 152 **Facilities** ⑤ ♨ 27 ⑤ Gym 9 treatment rooms
Beauty therapy Aerobics Xmas New Year **Conf** Class 150
Board 40 Thtr 350 **Services** Lift Air con **Parking** 260
Notes LB ⊗ Civ Wed 200

Thorpe Park Hotel & Spa

★★★★ 83% ⑨ HOTEL

SHIRE HOTELS

☎ 0113 264 1000 ▤ 0113 264 1010
Century Way, Thorpe Park LS15 8ZB
e-mail: thorpepark@shirehotels.com
web: www.thorpeparkhotel.com
dir: M1 junct 46 left at top of slip road, then right at rdbt
into Thorpe Park

Conveniently close to the M1, this hotel offers bedrooms
that are modern in both style and facilities. The terrace
and courtyard offer all-day casual dining and
refreshments, and the restaurant features a
Mediterranean-themed menu. There is also a state-of-
the-art spa and leisure facility.

Rooms 117 (25 GF) **S** £100-£230; **D** £150-£255 (incl.
bkfst)* **Facilities** Spa STV ⑤ Gym Activity studio Steam
room Sauna New Year Wi-fi **Conf** Class 100 Board 50
Thtr 200 Del from £145 to £185* **Services** Lift Air con
Parking 200 **Notes** LB ⊗ Civ Wed 150

Rooms 41 (4 annexe) (4 GF) **S** £90-£170; **D** £120-£200
(incl. bkfst)* **Facilities** FTV Xmas New Year Wi-fi
Conf Class 100 Board 60 Thtr 130 Del from £100 to
£150* **Services** Lift **Parking** 100 **Notes** LB ⊗ Closed 25
Dec-evening only Civ Wed 130

Best Western Rogerthorpe Manor

★★★ 76% HOTEL

☎ 01977 643839 ▤ 01977 641571
Thorpe Ln, Badsworth WF9 1AB
e-mail: ops@rogerthorpemanor.co.uk
dir: A639 from Pontefract to Badsworth. Follow B6474
through Thorpe Audlin, hotel on left at end of village

This Jacobean manor house is situated in extensive
grounds and lovely gardens, within easy access of road
networks. Bedrooms vary between the old house with their
inherent charm, and the more modern rooms in the
extensions. A choice of dining styles, real ales, civil
weddings, modern conference facilities and ample
parking are all offered.

Rooms 22 (4 fmly) **S** £60-£80; **D** £80-£140*
Facilities STV Wi-fi **Conf** Class 80 Board 50 Thtr 250
Del from £90 to £120* **Services** Air con **Parking** 150
Notes LB ⊗ Civ Wed 200

Days Inn Ferrybridge

BUDGET HOTEL

☎ 01977 621129
Barnsdale Bar, A1 Southbound, Wentbridge WF8 3JB
e-mail: manager@daysinnpontefract.co.uk
web: www.daysinn.com

This modern building offers accommodation in smart,
spacious and well-equipped bedrooms, suitable for
families and business travellers, and all with en suite
bathrooms. Continental breakfast is available and other
refreshments may be taken at the nearby family
restaurant. See also the Hotel Groups pages.

Rooms 56

Travelodge Bradford

BUDGET HOTEL

☎ 08719 846 124 ▤ 01274 665436
1 Mid Point, Dick Ln BD3 8QD
web: www.travelodge.co.uk
dir: M62 junct 26 (M606), take A6177 towards Leeds,
A647. Lodge 2m on left

Travelodge offers good quality, good value, modern
accommodation. Ideal for families, the spacious en suite
bedrooms include remote-control TV, tea and coffee-
making facilities and comfortable beds. Meals can be
taken at the nearby family restaurant. See also the Hotel
Groups pages.

Rooms 48 **S** fr £29; **D** fr £29

Marriott Hollins Hall Hotel & Country Club

Marriott HOTELS & RESORTS

★★★★ 78% ◉ HOTEL

☎ 01274 530053 ▤ 01274 534251
Hollins Hill, Baildon BD17 7QW
e-mail: mhrs.lbags.eventorganiser@marriotthotels.com
web: www.marriotthollinshall.co.uk
dir: from A650 follow signs to Salt Mill. At lights in
Shipley take A6038. Hotel 3m on left

The hotel is located close to Leeds and Bradford and is
easily accessible from motorway networks. Built in the
19th-century, this Elizabethan-style building is set within
200 acres of grounds and offers extensive leisure
facilities, including a golf course and gym. Bedrooms are
attractively decorated and have a range of additional
facilities.

Rooms 122 (50 fmly) (25 GF) **Facilities** ⓢ supervised ⌁
18 Putt green ⚑ Gym Crèche Dance studio Swimming
lessons Xmas **Conf** Class 90 Board 80 Thtr 200
Services Lift **Parking** 260 **Notes** ⊗ Civ Wed 70

Ibis Bradford Shipley

BUDGET HOTEL

☎ 01274 589333 ▤ 01274 589444
Quayside, Salts Mill Rd BD18 3ST
e-mail: H3158@accor.com
web: www.ibishotel.com
dir: follow tourist signs for Salts Mill. Follow A650 signs
through & out of Bradford for approx 5m to Shipley

Modern, budget hotel offering comfortable
accommodation in bright and practical bedrooms.
Breakfast is self-service, food is available all day and a
full dinner menu is available in the restaurant. See also
the Hotel Groups pages.

Rooms 78 (20 fmly) (22 GF) **Conf** Class 16 Board 18
Thtr 20

Best Western Waterton Park

★★★★ 72% HOTEL

☎ 01924 257911 & 249800 ▤ 01924 259686
Walton Hall, The Balk, Walton WF2 6PW
e-mail: watertonpark@bestwestern.co.uk
web: www.watertonparkhotel.co.uk
dir: 3m SE off B6378. Exit M1 junct 39 towards Wakefield.
At 3rd rdbt right for Crofton. At 2nd lights right & follow
signs

A stately private house, built on an island in the centre of
a lake in an idyllic setting. The main house contains
many feature bedrooms, and the annexe houses more
spacious rooms, all equally well equipped with modern
facilities. The delightful beamed restaurant, two bars and
leisure centre are located in the old hall, and there is a
licence for civil weddings.

Rooms 65 (43 annexe) (23 GF) **Facilities** STV ⓢ
supervised Fishing Gym Steam room Solarium Sauna New
Year Wi-fi **Conf** Class 80 Board 80 Thtr 150 **Services** Lift
Parking 200 **Notes** ⊗ Civ Wed 130

WAKEFIELD continued

Cedar Court

★★★★ 72% HOTEL

☎ 01924 276310 📠 01924 280221
Denby Dale Rd WF4 3QZ
e-mail: sales@cedarcourthotels.co.uk
web: www.cedarcourthotels.co.uk
dir: adjacent to M1 junct 39

This hotel enjoys a convenient location just off the M1. Traditionally styled bedrooms offer a good range of facilities while open-plan public areas include a busy bar and restaurant operation. Conferences and functions are extremely well catered for and a modern leisure club completes the picture.

Rooms 149 (2 fmly) (74 GF) **Facilities** 🕙 supervised Gym Xmas New Year Wi-fi **Conf** Class 140 Board 80 Thtr 400 **Services** Lift Air con **Parking** 350 **Notes** Civ Wed 250

Hotel St Pierre

★★★ 75% HOTEL

☎ 01924 255596 📠 01924 252746
Barnsley Rd, Newmillerdam WF2 6QG
e-mail: enq@hotelstpierre.co.uk
dir: M1 junct 39 take A636 to Wakefield, turn right at rdbt, on to Asdale Road to lights. Turn right onto A61 towards Barnsley. Hotel just after lake

This well-furnished hotel lies south of Wakefield, close to Newmillerdam. The interior of the modern building has comfortable and thoughtfully equipped bedrooms and smart public rooms. Meals are served in the Pierre's Restaurant, and there is a good selection of conference rooms.

Rooms 54 (3 fmly) (4 GF) **S** £69-£79; **D** £75-£85 (incl. bkfst) **Facilities** STV Xmas New Year Wi-fi **Conf** Class 60 Board 60 Thtr 120 **Services** Lift **Parking** 70 **Notes** ⊗ Civ Wed 120

Holiday Inn Leeds - Wakefield

Ⓤ

☎ 0870 400 9082 📠 01924 230684
Queen's Dr, Ossett WF5 9BE
e-mail: wakefield@ichotelsgroup.com
web: www.holidayinn.co.uk
dir: M1 junct 40 following signs for Wakefield. Hotel is on right after 200yds

Currently the rating for this establishment is not confirmed. This may be due to a change of ownership or because it has only recently joined the AA rating scheme. For further details please see the AA website: www.theAA.com

Rooms 104 (32 fmly) (35 GF) (9 smoking) **S** £49-£109; **D** £49-£109 (incl. bkfst)* **Facilities** STV Xmas New Year Wi-fi **Conf** Class 80 Board 80 Thtr 160 Del from £90 to £145 **Services** Lift Air con **Parking** 105 **Notes** LB Civ Wed 160

Chasley

Ⓤ

☎ 01924 372111 📠 01924 383648
Queen St WF1 1JU
e-mail: admin@chasleywakefield.supanet.com
dir: M1 junct 39, follow town centre signs. Queen Street on left

Currently the rating for this establishment is not confirmed. This may be due to a change of ownership or because it has only recently joined the AA rating scheme. For further details please see the AA website: www.theAA.com

Rooms 64 (8 fmly) **Facilities** New Year Wi-fi **Conf** Class 110 Board 88 Thtr 250 **Services** Lift **Parking** 40 **Notes** ⊗ Civ Wed 250

Campanile Wakefield

BUDGET HOTEL

☎ 01924 201054 📠 01924 290976
Monckton Rd WF2 7AL
e-mail: wakefield@campanile.com
dir: M1 junct 39, A636, 1m towards Wakefield, left into Monckton Rd, hotel on left

This modern building offers accommodation in smart, well-equipped bedrooms, all with en suite bathrooms. Refreshments may be taken at the informal bistro. See also the Hotel Groups pages.

Rooms 76 (76 annexe) (4 fmly) **Conf** Class 15 Board 15 Thtr 25

Days Hotel Leeds / Wakefield

BUDGET HOTEL

☎ 01924 274200 & 0800 0280 400 📠 01924 274246
Fryers Way, Silkwood Park, Ossett WF5 9TJ
e-mail: wakefield@kewgreen.co.uk
web: www.daysinn.com
dir: M1 junct 40, follow signs to Wakefield, hotel is 400yds on left.

This modern building offers accommodation in smart, spacious and well-equipped bedrooms, suitable for families and business travellers, and all with en suite bathrooms. Continental breakfast is available and other refreshments may be taken at the nearby family restaurant. See also the Hotel Groups pages.

Rooms 100 (27 fmly) (20 GF) **Conf** Class 18 Board 22 Thtr 40

Express by Holiday Inn Wakefield, M1 Jct 39

BUDGET HOTEL

☎ 01924 257555 📠 01924 249888
Denby Dale Rd WF4 3BB
e-mail: ebhi_wakefield@btinternet.com
web: www.hiexpress.com/wakefieldm1j39

A modern hotel ideal for families and business travellers. Fresh and uncomplicated, the spacious rooms include Sky TV, power shower and tea and coffee-making facilities. Continental buffet breakfast is included in the room rate; other meals may be taken at the nearby family pub or restaurant. See also the Hotel Groups pages.

Rooms 74 (28 fmly) **Conf** Class 12 Board 12 Thtr 30

WETHERBY **Map 16 SE44**

INSPECTORS' CHOICE

Wood Hall

★★★★ ⧉⧉ COUNTRY HOUSE HOTEL

☎ 01937 587271 📠 01937 584353
Trip Ln, Linton LS22 4JA
e-mail: woodhall@handpicked.co.uk
web: www.handpicked.co.uk
dir: from Wetherby take Harrogate road N (A661) for 0.5m, left to Sicklinghall & Linton. Cross bridge, left to Linton & Wood Hall. Turn right opposite Windmill Inn, 1.25m to hotel

A long sweeping drive leads to this delightful Georgian house situated in 100 acres of parkland. Spacious bedrooms are appointed to an impressive standard and feature comprehensive facilities, including large plasma screen TVs. Public rooms reflect the same elegance and include a smart drawing room and dining room, both with fantastic views. A state-of-the-art Technogym is available.

Rooms 44 (30 annexe) (5 fmly) **Facilities** Spa 🕙 supervised Fishing Gym Beauty spa 2 treatment rooms Xmas New Year Wi-fi **Conf** Class 70 Board 40 Thtr 100 Del from £150 to £175 **Services** Lift **Parking** 200 **Notes** ⊗ Civ Wed 100

See advert on page 540

HERM

HERM   Map 24

White House

★★★ 75% ⚛ HOTEL

☎ 01481 722159 📄 01481 710066
GY1 3HR
e-mail: hotel@herm-island.com
web: www.herm-island.com
dir: close to harbour

Enjoying a unique island setting, this attractive hotel is just 20 minutes from Guernsey by sea. Set in well-tended gardens, the hotel offers neatly decorated bedrooms, located in either the main house or adjacent cottages; the majority of rooms have sea views. Guests can relax in one of several lounges, enjoy a drink in one of two bars and choose from two dining options.

Rooms 40 (23 annexe) (23 fmly) (7 GF) **S** £80-£123; **D** £160-£240 (incl. bkfst & dinner)* **Facilities** ℃ ⚛ ⇟ Fishing trips Yacht & motor boat charters Wi-fi **Conf** Board 10 **Notes** ⊗ Closed Nov-Mar

JERSEY

GOREY   Map 24

Old Court House

★★★ 74% HOTEL

☎ 01534 854444 📄 01534 853587
JE3 9FS
e-mail: ochhotel@itl.net
web: www.ochhoteljersey.com

Situated on the east of the island, a short walk from the beach, this long established hotel continues to have a loyal following for its relaxed atmosphere and friendly staff. Bedrooms are of similar standard throughout and some have balconies overlooking the gardens. Spacious public areas include a comfortable, quiet lounge, a restaurant, and a large bar with a dance floor.

Rooms 58 (4 fmly) (9 GF) **S** £47.50-£71.50; **D** £95-£143 (incl. bkfst)* **Facilities** STV ℃ 🎵 **Services** Lift **Parking** 40 **Notes** LB Closed Nov-Mar

The Moorings Hotel & Restaurant

★★★ 71% HOTEL

☎ 01534 853633 📄 01534 857618
Gorey Pier JE3 6EW
e-mail: reservations@themooringshotel.com
web: www.themooringshotel.com
dir: at foot of Mont Orgueil Castle

Enjoying an enviable position by the harbour, the heart of this hotel is the restaurant where a selection of menus offers an extensive choice of dishes. Other public areas include a bar, coffee shop and a comfortable first-floor residents' lounge. Bedrooms at the front have a fine view of the harbour; three have access to a balcony. A small sun terrace at the back of the hotel is available to guests.

Rooms 15 **S** £50-£65; **D** £100-£130 (incl. bkfst)* **Facilities** STV Xmas New Year Wi-fi **Conf** Class 20 Board 20 Thtr 20 Del from £150 to £180* **Notes** LB ⊗

Dolphin Hotel and Restaurant

★★ 67% HOTEL

☎ 01534 853370 📄 01534 855343
Gorey Pier JE3 6EW
e-mail: dolphinhotel@jerseymail.co.uk
dir: at foot of Mont Orgueil Castle

Located on the main harbour at Gorey, many bedrooms at this popular hotel enjoy views over the sea and beaches. The relaxed and friendly style is apparent from the moment of arrival, and the busy restaurant and bar are popular with locals and tourists alike. Outdoor seating is available in season, and fresh fish and seafood are included on the menu.

Rooms 16 **S** £36-£72; **D** £46.50-£93 (incl. bkfst)* **Facilities** STV Xmas New Year **Conf** Class 20 Board 20 Thtr 20 Del from £150 to £190* **Notes** ⊗

Maison Gorey

★★ 67% HOTEL

☎ 01534 857775 & 07797 736059 📄 01534 857779
Gorey Village Main Rd JE3 9EP
e-mail: maisongorey@jerseymail.co.uk
dir: Next to Jersey Pottery

Located in the middle of Gorey Village this small, relaxing hotel provides well-equipped bedrooms and bathrooms that have now been refurbished. In addition to a spacious bar, a small TV lounge is available for guests. Some off-street car parking is provided in front of the hotel.

Rooms 26 (26 annexe) (2 fmly) **S** £30-£70; **D** £55-£75 (incl. bkfst)* **Facilities** FTV 🎵 Xmas New Year Wi-fi **Parking** 6 **Notes** LB ⊗ No children 5yrs

GROUVILLE   Map 24

Beausite

★★★ 71% HOTEL

☎ 01534 857577 📄 01534 857211
Les Rue des Pres, Grouville Bay JE3 9DJ
e-mail: beausite@jerseymail.co.uk
web: www.southernhotels.com
dir: Opposite Royal Jersey Golf Course

Close to the Royal Jersey Golf Club, this hotel is situated on the south-east side of the island; a short distance from the picturesque harbour at Gorey. With parts dating back to 1636, the public rooms retain original character and charm; bedrooms are generally spacious and modern in design. The indoor swimming pool, fitness room, saunas and spa bath are an added bonus.

Rooms 75 (5 fmly) (18 GF) **Facilities** ⊗ Gym **Parking** 60 **Notes** Closed Nov-Mar

Lavender Villa

★★ 65% HOTEL

☎ 01534 854937 📄 01534 856147
La Rue A Don JE3 9DX
e-mail: lavendervilla@jerseymail.co.uk
dir: Close to Royal Jersey Golf course, 1m from Gorey

A small hotel where guests will receive friendly and personal attention from the resident proprietors and their welcoming team of staff. Bedrooms come in a variety of shapes and sizes but all are comfortable and well equipped. The bar and guest lounge are the ideal places to enjoy a drink before choosing from a range of carefully prepared dishes served in the cosy restaurant.

Rooms 21 (2 fmly) (6 GF) **Facilities** ℃ 🎵 **Parking** 22 **Notes** LB ⊗ Closed Dec-Feb

ROZEL — Map 24

INSPECTORS' CHOICE

Château la Chaire
★★★ ◉◉ HOTEL

☎ 01534 863354 🖷 01534 865137
Rozel Bay JE3 6AJ
e-mail: res@chateau-la-chaire.co.uk
web: www.chateau-la-chaire.co.uk
dir: from St Helier on B38 turn left in village by Rozel
Bay Inn, hotel 100yds on right

Built as a gentleman's residence in 1843, Château la
Chaire is a haven of peace and tranquillity, set within
a secluded wooded valley. Picturesque Rozel Harbour
is within easy walking distance and the house is
surrounded by terraced gardens. There is a wonderful
atmosphere here and the helpful staff deliver high
standards of guest care. Imaginative menus, making
the best use of local produce, are served in the oak-
panelled dining room. Bedrooms styles and sizes are
varied - all are beautifully appointed and include
many nice touches such as flowers and mineral water.

Rooms 14 (2 fmly) (1 GF) **S** £90-£125; **D** £120-£295
(incl. bkfst)* **Facilities** STV Xmas New Year Wi-fi
Conf Class 20 Board 20 Thtr 20 Del from £168 to
£268* **Parking** 30 **Notes** LB ⊗ No children 7yrs
Civ Wed 60

ST AUBIN — Map 24

Somerville
★★★★ 74% ◉◉ HOTEL

☎ 01534 741226 🖷 01534 746621
Mont du Boulevard JE3 8AD
e-mail: somerville@dolanhotels.com
web: www.dolanhotels.com
dir: from village, follow harbour into Mont du Boulevard

Enjoying spectacular views of St Aubin's Bay, this friendly
hotel is very popular. Bedrooms vary in style and a
number of superior rooms offer higher levels of luxury.
Public areas are smartly presented and include a
spacious bar-lounge and elegant dining room; both take
full advantage of the hotel's enviable views. An outdoor
swimming pool is available in summer months.

Rooms 56 (4 GF) **S** £65-£135; **D** £109-£179 (incl. bkfst)*
Facilities STV ⊁ ♫ Xmas New Year Wi-fi **Conf** Class 33
Board 36 Thtr 55 Del from £110 to £125* **Services** Lift
Parking 26 **Notes** ⊗ No children 4yrs Civ Wed 40

See advert on opposite page

Hotel La Tour
★★★ 73% HOTEL

☎ 01534 743770 🖷 01534 747143
La Rue du Crocquet JE3 8BZ
e-mail: enquiries@hotellatour.com
web: www.hotellatour.com
dir: On High St behind church (street parallel to seafront)

This elevated hotel has been furnished in contemporary
style yet retains much historic character. Public rooms
are light and airy, and bedrooms are individually
designed. At dinner guests are offered a choice of dining
at the sister hotel or a local restaurant where all meals
and drinks can be charged direct to the hotel.
Complimentary transport is included to both restaurants,
and can also be arranged for travel to and from the
airport.

Rooms 30 (6 fmly) **S** £49-£63; **D** £98-£126 (incl. bkfst)*
Facilities Indoor/outdoor swimming pool at sister hotel.
Personal trainer on request Xmas New Year Wi-fi
Parking 15 **Notes** LB ⊗

ST BRELADE — Map 24

INSPECTORS' CHOICE

The Atlantic
★★★★ ◉◉◉ HOTEL

☎ 01534 744101 🖷 01534 744102
Le Mont de la Pulente JE3 8HE
e-mail: info@theatlantichotel.com
web: www.theatlantichotel.com
dir: from Petit Port turn right into Rue de la Sergente &
right again, hotel signed

Adjoining the manicured fairways of La Moye
championship golf course, this hotel enjoys a peaceful
setting with breathtaking views over St Ouen's Bay.
Stylish bedrooms look out over the course or the sea
and offer a blend of high quality and reassuring
comfort. An air of understated luxury is apparent
throughout, and the attentive service achieves the
perfect balance of friendliness and professionalism.
The Ocean restaurant offers sophisticated, modern
surroundings in which to enjoy some highly
accomplished cooking.

Rooms 50 (8 GF) **Facilities** ⊛ ⊁ ♨ Gym ♫ Xmas
Conf Class 40 Board 20 Thtr 60 **Services** Lift
Parking 60 **Notes** LB ⊗ Closed 2 Jan-2 Feb

L'Horizon Hotel and Spa

HandPICKED HOTELS

★★★★ 90% ⊛⊛ HOTEL

☎ 01534 743101 📠 01534 746269
St Brelade's Bay JE3 8EF
e-mail: lhorizon@handpicked.co.uk
web: www.handpicked.co.uk/lhorizon
dir: 3m from airport. From airport right at rdbt towards St Brelades & Red Houses. Through Red Houses, hotel 300mtrs on right in centre of bay

The combination of a truly wonderful setting on the golden sands of St Brelade's Bay, a relaxed atmosphere and excellent facilities prove a winning formula here. Bedrooms are stylish and have a real contemporary feel, all with plasma TVs and a host of extras; many have balconies or terraces and superb sea views. Spacious public areas include a spa and leisure club, a choice of dining options and relaxing lounges.

Rooms 106 (1 fmly) (15 GF) **S** £100-£160; **D** £140-£260 (incl. bkfst)* **Facilities** Spa STV 🍽 Gym Treatment rooms Windsurfing Water skiing 🎵 Xmas New Year Wi-fi **Conf** Class 100 Board 50 Thtr 250 Del from £140 to £250* **Services** Lift **Parking** 125 **Notes** LB ⊗ Civ Wed 250

St Brelade's Bay Hotel

★★★★ 79% HOTEL

☎ 01534 746141 📠 01534 747278
JE3 8EF
e-mail: info@stbreladesbayhotel.com
web: www.stbreladesbayhotel.com
dir: SW corner of island

This family hotel overlooking the bay has many loyal guests and members of staff. The attractive tiered grounds, with easy access to the beach, are ablaze with colour in summer. There is an extensive range of indoor and outdoor recreational facilities including a choice of pools. Most bedrooms have king-size beds, many have inter-connecting children's rooms, and there are stunning penthouse suites too. The tariff includes morning and afternoon tea.

Rooms 81 (50 fmly) **S** £83-£132; **D** £130-£324 (incl. bkfst)* **Facilities** STV 🎾 supervised 🏊 Putt green ⛳ Gym Petanque Mini-gym Games room Table tennis 🎵 Wi-fi Child facilities **Conf** Board 12 Thtr 20 **Services** Lift **Parking** 60 **Notes** LB ⊗ Closed 3 Nov-4 Apr

Hotel La Place

★★★★ 77% ⊛ HOTEL

☎ 01534 744261 📠 01534 745164
Route du Coin, La Haule JE3 8BT
e-mail: reservations@hotellaplacejersey.com
dir: Off main St Helier/St Aubin coast road at La Haule Manor (B25). Up hill, 2nd left (to Red Houses), 1st right. Hotel 100mtrs on right

Developed around a 17th-century farmhouse and well placed for exploration of the island. Attentive, friendly service is the ethos here. A range of bedroom types is provided, some have private patios and direct access to the pool area. The cocktail bar is popular for pre-dinner drinks and a traditional lounge has a log fire in colder months. An interesting menu is offered.

Rooms 42 (1 fmly) (10 GF) **Facilities** 🎾 Discount at Les Ormes Country Club, including golf, gym & indoor tennis Xmas Wi-fi **Conf** Class 40 Board 40 Thtr 100 **Parking** 100 **Notes** Civ Wed 100

ST BRELADE continued

Golden Sands

★★★ 78% HOTEL

☎ 01534 741241 📠 01534 499366
St Brelade's Bay JE3 8EF
e-mail: goldensands@dolanhotels.com
web: www.dolanhotels.com
dir: follow St Brelade's Bay signs. Hotel on coastal side of road

With direct access to the beach, this popular hotel overlooks the wonderful sandy expanse of St Brelade's Bay. Many of the comfortable bedrooms are sea facing with balconies where guests can relax and breathe in the fresh air. Public areas include a lounge, bar and restaurant, all of which enjoy bay views.

Rooms 62 (9 fmly) **S** £45-£127; **D** £72-£133 (incl. bkfst)* **Facilities** STV Children's play room ♫ Wi-fi **Services** Lift **Notes** ⊗ Closed Nov-mid Apr

See advert on page 585

Beau Rivage

★★★ HOTEL

☎ 01534 745983 📠 01534 747127
St Brelade's Bay JE3 8EF
e-mail: beau@jerseyweb.demon.co.uk
web: www.jersey.co.uk/hotels/beau
dir: sea side of coast road in centre of St Brelade's Bay, 1.5m S of airport

With direct access to one of Jersey's most popular beaches, residents and non-residents alike are welcome to this hotel's bar and terrace. Most of the well-equipped bedrooms have wonderful sea views, and some have the bonus of balconies. Residents have a choice of lounges, plus a sun deck exclusively for their use. A range of dishes featuring English and Continental cuisine is available on the carte menu.

Rooms 27 (9 fmly) **S** £67.50-£214.50; **D** £75-£222 (incl. bkfst)* **Facilities** STV Games room ♫ Wi-fi **Services** Lift **Parking** 16 **Notes** LB ⊗ Closed Nov-Mar Civ Wed 80

Hotel Miramar

★★ 72% HOTEL

☎ 01534 743831 📠 01534 745009
Mont Gras D'Eau JE3 8ED
e-mail: miramarjsy@localdial.com
dir: From airport take B36 at lights, turn left onto A13, 1st right into Mont Gras D'Eau

A friendly welcome awaits at this family-run hotel set in delightful sheltered gardens, overlooking the beautiful bay. Accommodation is comfortable with well appointed bedrooms; some are on the ground floor, and there are two on the lower ground with their own terrace overlooking the outdoor heated pool. The restaurant offers a varied set menu.

Rooms 38 (2 fmly) (14 GF) **S** £30-£46.75; **D** £60-£93.50 (incl. bkfst)* **Facilities** ⌘ **Parking** 30 **Notes** Closed Oct-mid Apr

Pontac House

★★★ 75% HOTEL

☎ 01534 857771 📠 01534 857031
St Clements Bay JE2 6SE
e-mail: info@pontachouse.com
web: www.pontachouse.com

Overlooking the sandy beach of St Clement's Bay, this hotel is located on the south eastern corner of Jersey. Many guests return on a regular basis to experience the friendly, relaxed style of service. The bedrooms, most with splendid views, are comfortable and well equipped.

Varied menus, featuring local seafood, are served each evening.

Rooms 27 (1 fmly) (5 GF) **S** £31-£59; **D** £62-£118 (incl. bkfst & dinner)* **Facilities** ⌘ **Parking** 35 **Notes** ⊗ Closed 18 Dec-7 Mar

INSPECTORS' CHOICE

The Club Hotel & Spa

★★★★ ❀❀❀❀
TOWN HOUSE HOTEL

☎ 01534 876500 📠 01534 720371
Green St JE2 4UH
e-mail: reservations@theclubjersey.com
web: www.theclubjersey.com
dir: 5 mins walk from main shopping centre

This swish, town-house hotel is conveniently located close to the centre of town and features stylish, contemporary decor throughout. All the guest rooms and suites include power showers and state-of-the-art technology including wide-screen LCD TV, DVD and CD systems. The choice of restaurants includes Bohemia, a sophisticated eating option that continues to offer highly accomplished cooking. For relaxation there is an elegant spa with a luxurious range of treatments.

Rooms 46 (4 fmly) (4 GF) (5 smoking) **S** £195-£425; **D** £195-£425 (incl. bkfst) **Facilities** Spa ⓢ ⌘ Sauna Steam room Salt cabin Hydrothermal bench New Year Wi-fi **Conf** Class 35 Board 32 Thtr 50 Del from £195 to £218 **Services** Lift Air con **Parking** 30 **Notes** LB ⊗

Royal Yacht

★★★★ 81% ◉◉ HOTEL

☎ 01534 720511 📠 01534 767729
The Weighbridge JE2 3NF
e-mail: reception@theroyalyacht.com
dir: in town centre, opposite marina & harbour

Overlooking the marina and steam clock, the Royal Yacht is thought to be the oldest established hotel on the island. Following a refurbishment the hotel offers state-of-the-art technology in all the bedrooms and the two penthouse suites. There is a range of impressive dining options to suit all tastes with Sirocco's Restaurant offering high quality local produce. In addition to a choice of bars and conference facilities guests can enjoy the luxury spa with its indoor pool and gym.

Rooms 110 **D** £115-£750 (incl. bkfst)* **Facilities** Spa STV ◉ Gym ♫ Xmas New Year Wi-fi **Conf** Class 150 Board 40 Thtr 280 **Services** Lift Air con **Notes** LB ⊗ Civ Wed 250

Radisson SAS Waterfront Hotel, Jersey

★★★★ 80% ◉ HOTEL

☎ 01534 671100 & 671173 📠 01534 671101
The Waterfront, La Rue de L'Etau JE2 4HE
e-mail: info.jersey@radissonsas.com
web: www.jersey.radissonsas.com
dir: just before harbour 3rd exit at rdbt

Most of the bedrooms at this new, purpose-built hotel have fabulous views of the coastline. There is a popular brasserie, cocktail bar, lounges, indoor heated pool, gym, sauna and steam room. A wide range of meeting rooms provides conference facilities; parking is extensive.

Rooms 195 **S** £90-£255; **D** £120-£255 (incl. bkfst)* **Facilities** Spa STV ◉ supervised Gym ♫ Xmas New Year Wi-fi **Conf** Class 184 Board 30 Thtr 416 Del from £155 to £305* **Services** Lift Air con **Parking** 95 **Notes** LB ⊗ Civ Wed 280

The Grand, Jersey

★★★★ 79% ◉◉◉ HOTEL

☎ 01534 722301 📠 01534 737815
The Esplanade JE4 8WD
e-mail: kmcalpine@hilwoodresorts.com

A local landmark, the newly refurbished Grand Hotel is set on The Esplanade with pleasant views across St Aubin's Bay to the front and the bustling streets of St Helier to the rear. Bedrooms come in a variety of styles and the majority have been refurbished to a very high standard featuring luxurious beds, stylish ottomans and up-to-date LCD TVs. The public areas, many looking out onto the bay, are elegant and spacious; these include a very popular champagne bar, a modern brasserie and the impressive and intimate Tassili fine dining restaurant. There is a large terrace for alfresco eating and the spa offers an indoor pool, gym and treatment rooms.

Rooms 122 (53 fmly) (6 GF) **Facilities** Spa ◉ supervised Gym ♫ Xmas Wi-fi **Conf** Class 193 Board 112 Thtr 356 **Services** Lift Air con **Parking** 7 **Notes** ⊗ Civ Wed

Pomme d'Or

★★★★ 77% ◉◉ HOTEL

☎ 01534 880110 📠 01534 737781
Liberation Square JE1 3UF
e-mail: enquiries@pommedorhotel.com
dir: opposite harbour

This historic hotel overlooks Liberation Square and the marina and offers comfortably furnished, well-equipped bedrooms. Popular with the business fraternity, a range of conference facilities and meeting rooms are available. Dining options include the traditional fine dining in the Petite Pomme, the smart carvery restaurant and the informal coffee shop.

Rooms 143 (3 fmly) **S** £118-£200; **D** £118-£200 (incl. bkfst)* **Facilities** STV Use of Aquadome at Merton Hotel. Xmas New Year Wi-fi **Conf** Class 100 Board 50 Thtr 220 **Services** Lift Air con **Notes** LB ⊗

Best Western Royal

★★★ 78% ◉ HOTEL

☎ 01534 726521 & 873006 📠 01534 811046
David Place JE2 4TD
e-mail: enquiries@royalhoteljersey.com
web: www.royalhoteljersey.com
dir: follow signs for Ring Rd, pass Queen Victoria rdbt keep left, left at lights, left into Piersons Rd. Follow one-way system to Cheapside, Rouge Bouillon, at A14 turn to Midvale Rd, hotel on left

This long established hotel is located in the centre of town and is within walking distance of the business district and shops. Seasons Restaurant offers a modern approach to dining, and the adjoining bar provides a relaxed venue for residents and locals alike. The bedrooms are individually styled. Extensive conference facilities are available.

Rooms 88 (39 fmly) **S** £49-£63; **D** £98-£125 (incl. bkfst)* **Facilities** Gym Xmas New Year Wi-fi **Conf** Class 120 Board 80 Thtr 300 **Services** Lift **Parking** 15 **Notes** LB ⊗ Civ Wed 30

Apollo

★★★ 72% HOTEL

☎ 01534 725441 📠 01534 722120
St Saviours Rd JE2 4GJ
e-mail: reservations@huggler.com
web: www.huggler.com
dir: on St Saviours Rd at junct with La Motte St

Centrally located, this popular hotel has a relaxed, informal atmosphere. Bedrooms are comfortably furnished and include useful extras. Many guests return regularly to enjoy the variety of leisure facilities including an outdoor pool with water slide and indoor pool with separate jacuzzi. The separate cocktail bar is an ideal place for a pre-dinner drink.

Rooms 85 (5 fmly) **S** £59-£110; **D** £65-£120 (incl. bkfst)* **Facilities** ◉ supervised ◉ supervised Gym Xmas New Year Wi-fi **Conf** Class 100 Board 80 Thtr 150 **Services** Lift **Parking** 50 **Notes** ⊗

Hotel Revere

★★★ 71% HOTEL

☎ 01534 611111 📠 01534 611116
Kensington Place JE2 3PA
e-mail: reservations@revere.co.uk
web: www.revere.co.uk
dir: From Esplanade turn left after De Vere Grand Hotel.

Situated on the west side of the town and convenient for the centre and harbour side, this hotel dates back to the 17th century and retains many period features. The style here is engagingly different, and bedrooms are individually decorated. There are three dining options and a small sun terrace.

Rooms 55 (2 fmly) (3 GF) **S** £45-£75; **D** £90-£150 (incl. bkfst)* **Facilities** STV 8; ♫ Xmas New Year Wi-fi **Notes** ⊗ Civ Wed 50

Millbrook House

★★ 74% HOTEL

☎ 01534 733036 📠 01534 724317
Rue De Trachy, Millbrook JE2 3JN
e-mail: millbrook.house@jerseymail.co.uk
web: www.millbrookhousehotel.com
dir: 1.5m W of town off A1

Peacefully located within its own grounds, this small, personally run hotel offers a friendly welcome and relaxing ambience. Bedrooms and bathrooms vary in size, but many have pleasant, countryside views. In addition to outdoor seating in the warmer months, guests can relax in the library, maybe with a drink before dinner.

Rooms 24 (2 fmly) (5 GF) **S** £39-£44; **D** £78-£88 (incl. bkfst)* **Facilities** ♿ 5 **Services** Lift **Parking** 20 **Notes** ⊗ Closed 1 Oct-13 May

ST HELIER continued

Sarum

★★ 62% METRO HOTEL

☎ 01534 731340 📄 01534 758163
19/21 New St Johns Rd JE2 3LD
e-mail: sarum@jerseyweb.demon.co.uk
dir: On NW edge of St Helier, 0.5m from town centre

This hotel, just 600yds from the beach, offers self-catering bedrooms and a number of suites. The friendly staff provide a warm welcome, and there is a spacious recreational lounge with pool tables, plasma TVs and internet access. A garden and outdoor pool are also available. Local restaurants are just a short walk away and bar snacks are available throughout the day.

Rooms 52 (5 annexe) (6 fmly) (3 GF) **S** £38-£56;
D £60-£92* **Facilities** STV ◔ Wi-fi **Services** Lift
Parking 10 (charged) **Notes** LB ⊗ RS Oct-Mar

ST LAWRENCE   Map 24

Hotel Cristina

★★★ 78% ⊛ HOTEL

☎ 01534 758024 📄 01534 758028
Mont Feland JE3 1JA
e-mail: cristina@dolanhotels.com
web: www.dolanhotels.com
dir: Exit A10 onto Mont Feland Exit, hotel on left

This hotel offers smartly styled and comfortable bedrooms. Public areas reflect a contemporary style that makes this a refreshingly different hotel, with a modern restaurant serving a range of fresh produce in a bistro atmosphere. The terrace is adorned with flowers and is a popular place for soaking up the sun.

Rooms 63 (3 fmly) **S** £43-£109; **D** £68-£125 (incl. bkfst)*
Facilities STV ◔ ♫ Wi-fi **Parking** 60 **Notes** ⊗ Closed
Nov-Mar Civ Wed 30

See advert on page 585

ST MARY   Map 24

West View

★★ 68% HOTEL

☎ 01534 481643 📄 01534 483283
La Grande Rue JE3 3BD
e-mail: westview@jerseymail.co.uk
web: www.westviewhoteljersey.com
dir: at junct of B33 & C103

Located in the quiet parish of St Mary, this welcoming hotel is close to the delightful walks and cycle routes of the north coast. Bedrooms here are well equipped especially the larger, superior rooms. Entertainment is provided in the lounge bar during the summer months, when guests can also enjoy a swim in the heated outdoor pool.

Rooms 42 (3 fmly) (18 GF) **S** £31-£44; **D** £55-£81 (incl.
bkfst)* **Facilities** ◔ Wi-fi **Parking** 38 **Notes** ⊗ Closed
Nov-mid Mar

ST PETER   Map 24

Greenhills Country Hotel

★★★★ 74% ⊛ COUNTRY HOUSE HOTEL

☎ 01534 481042 📄 01534 485322
Mont de L'Ecole JE3 7EL
e-mail: greenhills@messages.co.uk

Centrally located on the island and very close to The Living Legends display, this relaxing country house hotel has a lovely atmosphere and a delightful garden that surrounds it. Bedrooms extend from the main building around the courtyard; all are comfortable and well equipped. A varied menu, based on fresh local produce, is served in the spacious restaurant.

Rooms 31 (2 fmly) (9 GF) **S** £52.50-£76; **D** £115-£162
(incl. bkfst)* **Facilities** STV FTV ◔ Wi-fi **Conf** Class 12
Board 16 Thtr 20 Del from £95 to £115* **Parking** 40
Notes LB ⊗ Closed mid Dec-early Feb Civ Wed 40

ST SAVIOUR   Map 24

INSPECTORS' CHOICE

Longueville Manor

★★★★★ ⊛⊛⊛ HOTEL

☎ 01534 725501 📄 01534 731613
JE2 7WF
e-mail: info@longuevillemanor.com
web: www.longuevillemanor.com
dir: A3 E from St Helier towards Gorey. Hotel 1m on left

Dating back to the 13th century, there is something very special about Longueville Manor, which is why so many guests return. It is set in 17 acres of grounds including woodland walks, a spectacular rose garden and a lake. Bedrooms have great style and individuality boasting fresh flowers, fine embroidered bed linen and a host of extras. The committed team of staff create a welcoming atmosphere and every effort is made to ensure a memorable stay. The accomplished cuisine is also a highlight.

Rooms 30 (1 annexe) (7 GF) **S** £175-£360;
D £200-£570 (incl. bkfst)* **Facilities** STV ◔ ♨ ⛳
Xmas New Year Wi-fi **Conf** Class 30 Board 30 Thtr 45
Services Lift **Parking** 40 **Notes** LB Civ Wed 40

TRINITY   Map 24

Water's Edge

★★★ 78% ⊛⊛ HOTEL

☎ 01534 862777 📄 01534 863645
Bouley Bay JE3 5AS
e-mail: mail@watersedgehotel.co.je
web: www.watersedgehotel.co.je

Set in the tranquil surroundings of Bouley Bay on Jersey's north coast, this hotel is exactly as its name conveys and offers breathtaking views. The bedrooms offer high standards of quality and comfort. Dining options include the relaxed atmosphere of the adjoining Black Dog bar or the more formal award-winning restaurant.

Rooms 50 (3 fmly) **S** £43-£69; **D** £86-£162 (incl. bkfst)* **Facilities** ⚒ ♫ **Conf** Class 25 Board 20 Thtr 30 Del from £95 to £150* **Services** Lift **Parking** 20 **Notes** LB ⊗ Closed mid Oct-mid Apr Civ Wed 80

SARK

SARK	Map 24

Hotel Petit Champ
★★ 80% ◉ SMALL HOTEL

☎ 01481 832046 📠 01481 832469
GY9 0SF
e-mail: info@hotelpetitchamp.co.uk
dir: follow signs from the Methodist Chapel

Guests can expect a very warm welcome from the caring hosts at this delightful small hotel. Most of the bedrooms, the gardens and lounges have wonderful views of the sea and the neighbouring islands. Guest can choose dishes from set or carte menus, and there is a well-stocked wine cellar. A natural sun trap area has a solar heated swimming pool for guests' use.

Rooms 10 (2 fmly) (10 smoking) **S** £66.50-£76.50; **D** £129-£149 (incl. bkfst & dinner) **Facilities** ⚒ Putt green ⚑ Library lounge TV room **Notes** ⊗ No children 6-7yrs Closed early Oct-mid Apr

ISLE OF MAN

DOUGLAS	Map 24 SC37

Sefton
★★★★ 77% ◉ HOTEL

☎ 01624 645500 📠 01624 676004
Harris Promenade IM1 2RW
e-mail: info@seftonhotel.co.im
web: www.seftonhotel.co.im
dir: 500yds from Ferry Dock on promenade

This Victorian hotel has been sympathetically extended over the years. Many of the spacious and comfortably furnished bedrooms have balconies overlooking the atrium water garden, while others enjoy sweeping views across the bay. A choice of comfortable lounges is available and freshly prepared dishes are served in the informal Gallery Restaurant.

Rooms 96 (3 fmly) **Facilities** ⊙ Gym Cycle hire, Steam room, Library ♫ New Year Wi-fi **Conf** Class 30 Board 50 Thtr 150 **Services** Lift **Parking** 36 **Notes** LB ⊗

Mount Murray Hotel and Country Club
★★★★ 74% HOTEL

☎ 01624 661111 📠 01624 611116
Santon IM4 2HT
e-mail: manager@mountmurray.com
web: www.mountmurray.com
dir: 4m from Douglas towards airport. Hotel signed at Santon

This large, modern hotel and country club offers a wide range of sporting and leisure facilities, and a superb health and beauty salon. The attractively appointed public areas give a choice of bars and eating options. The spacious bedrooms are well equipped and many enjoy fine views over the 200-acre grounds and golf course. There is a very large conference suite.

Rooms 100 (4 fmly) (32 GF) (78 smoking) **S** £59-£130; **D** £82-£160 (incl. bkfst)* **Facilities** STV ⊙ ⚑ 18 Putt green Gym Squash Driving range Xmas New Year Wi-fi **Conf** Class 200 Board 100 Thtr 300 Del from £85 to £160* **Services** Lift **Parking** 400 **Notes** LB ⊗

Empress
★★★ 77% HOTEL

☎ 01624 661155 📠 01624 673554
Central Promenade IM2 4RA
e-mail: reservations@theempresshotel.net
web: www.theempresshotel.net

This hotel is a large Victorian building on the central promenade, overlooking Douglas Bay. Well-equipped, modern bedrooms include suites, and rooms with sea views. A pianist entertains in the lounge bar most evenings. Other facilities available include a lounge, a sun lounge and a brasserie-style restaurant.

Rooms 102 (9 fmly) **Facilities** STV FTV ⊙ Gym ♫ Xmas Wi-fi **Conf** Class 150 Board 50 Thtr 200 **Services** Lift **Notes** ⊗

Welbeck Hotel
★★★ 74% HOTEL

☎ 01624 675663 📠 01624 661545
13/15 Mona Dr IM2 4LF
e-mail: mail@welbeckhotel.com
dir: at crossroads of Mona & Empress Drive off Central Promenade

The Welbeck is a privately owned and personally run hotel situated within easy reach of the seafront. It offers guests a friendly welcome and a choice of attractive accommodation, ranging from well-equipped bedrooms to six luxury apartments, each with its own lounge and small kitchen. Other facilities include two rooms for meetings and functions, plus a mini-gym and steam room.

Rooms 27 (7 fmly) **Facilities** STV Gym Steam room Wi-fi **Services** Lift **Notes** ⊗ Closed 19 Dec-5 Jan

PORT ERIN	Map 24 SC16

Port Erin Royal
★★★ Ⓐ HOTEL

☎ 01624 833116 📠 01624 835402
Promenade IM9 6LH
e-mail: aaenq@porterinhotels.com
dir: A5 south to Port Erin. After railway station follow road to right and up promenade, hotel on right

Rooms 79 (23 fmly) **Facilities** Fitness room Table tennis ♫ **Conf** Class 140 Board 100 Thtr 180 **Services** Lift **Parking** 20 **Notes** LB ⊗ Closed Nov-Feb

Falcon's Nest
★★ 69% HOTEL

☎ 01624 834077 📠 01624 835370
The Promenade IM9 6AF
e-mail: falconsnest@enterprise.net
web: www.falconsnesthotel.co.uk
dir: follow coastal road, S from airport or ferry. Hotel on seafront, immediately after steam railway station

Situated overlooking the bay and harbour, this Victorian hotel offers generally spacious bedrooms. There is a choice of bars, one of which attracts many locals. Meals can be taken in the lounge bar, the conservatory or in the attractively decorated main restaurant.

Rooms 35 (9 fmly) (15 smoking) **S** £35-£42.50; **D** £70-£85 (incl. bkfst)* **Facilities** Xmas New Year Wi-fi **Conf** Class 50 Board 50 Thtr 50 Del from £65 to £74.50* **Parking** 40

Achilty

★★★ 73% ◉ SMALL HOTEL

☎ 01997 421355 📄 01997 421923
IV14 9EG
e-mail: info@achiltyhotel.co.uk
web: www.achiltyhotel.co.uk
dir: A9 onto A835, hotel 6m on right

Friendly owners contribute to great hospitality and a relaxed atmosphere at this roadside hotel. Public areas are full of interest; the lounges have books and games and the dining room has a musical theme. The Steading bar features exposed stone walls and offers a good selection of tasty home-cooked meals. Bedrooms are smartly furnished and cheerfully decorated.

Rooms 11 (1 annexe) (3 GF) (1 smoking) **Facilities** New Year **Conf** Class 50 Board 20 Thtr 50 **Parking** 100 **Notes** ⊗ Closed 3-10 Jan

---

Tulloch Castle

★★★★ 74% HOTEL

OXFORD
HOTELS & INNS

☎ 01349 861325 📄 01349 863993
Tulloch Castle Dr IV15 9ND
e-mail: info@tullochcastle.co.uk
web: www.oxfordhotelsandinns.com
dir: A9 N, Tore rdbt 2nd left signed Dingwall, at Dingwall turn left at 4th lights, hotel signed

Overlooking the town of Dingwall this 12th-century castle is still the gathering place of the Clan Davidson and boasts its own ghost in the shape of the Green Lady. The friendly team are very helpful and love to tell you about the history of the castle; the ghost tour after dinner is a must. The hotel has a self contained suite and a number of bedrooms with four-posters.

Rooms 20 (2 fmly) **S** £120; **D** £155 (incl. bkfst)*
Facilities FTV ♫ Xmas New Year Wi-fi **Conf** Class 70 Board 70 Thtr 120 **Parking** 50 **Notes** ⊗ Civ Wed 110

Dornoch Castle Hotel

★★★ 74% ◉ HOTEL

☎ 01862 810216 📄 01862 810981
Castle St IV25 3SD
e-mail: enquiries@dornochcastlehotel.com
web: www.dornochcastlehotel.com
dir: 2m N of Dornoch Bridge on A9, turn right to Dornoch. Hotel in village centre

Set opposite the cathedral, this fully restored ancient castle has become a popular wedding venue. Within the original castle are some splendid themed bedrooms, and elsewhere the more modern bedrooms have all of the expected facilities. There is a character bar and a delightful conservatory restaurant overlooking the garden.

Rooms 21 (3 fmly) (4 GF) **S** £50-£135; **D** £86-£220 (incl. bkfst) **Facilities** FTV New Year Wi-fi **Conf** Class 30 Board 30 Thtr 60 Del from £115 to £145 **Parking** 16 **Notes** LB Civ Wed 95

See advert on this page

2 Quail Restaurant and Rooms

◉◉ RESTAURANT WITH ROOMS

☎ 01862 811811
Castle St IV25 3SN
e-mail: theAA@2quail.com
dir: On main street, 200yds from cathedral

The saying "small is beautiful" aptly applies to this restaurant with rooms. Though set in the main street, the careful reproduction of its Victorian past transports you back in time. Cosy public rooms are ideal for conversation, but there are masses of books for those just wishing to relax. The stylish, individual bedrooms match the character of the house but are thoughtfully equipped to include DVD players. Food is the main feature however, with excellent breakfasts and set four course dinners.

Rooms 3 (1 en suite) (1 fmly)

DRUMNADROCHIT — Map 23 NH53

Loch Ness Lodge

★★★ **A** HOTEL

☎ 01456 450342 🖹 01456 450429
IV63 6TU
e-mail: info@lochness-hotel.com
dir: off A82 onto A831 (Cannich road)

Rooms 50 (4 fmly) (10 GF) **S** £55-£65; **D** £60-£100 (incl. bkfst) **Facilities** FTV Visitors centre Shops Cinema Boat cruises Hairdresser ♫ Wi-fi **Conf** Class 40 Board 40 Thtr 50 **Parking** 80 **Notes** LB ⊗ Closed Nov-Feb Civ Wed 50

FORT AUGUSTUS — Map 23 NH30

Lovat Arms

★★★ 86% ⊛ HOTEL

☎ 0845 450 1100 & 01456 459250 🖹 01320 366677
Loch Ness Side PH32 4DU
e-mail: info@lovatarms-hotel.com
web: www.lovatarms-hotel.com
dir: in town centre on A82

This charming country-house hotel enjoys an elevated position in the pretty town of Fort Augustus. The hotel has impressively styled bedrooms with a host of thoughtful extras. Inviting public areas include a comfortable lounge with a log fire, a stylish bar, and contemporary restaurant were food is cooked with skill and care. The hospitality and commitment to guest care will leave a lasting impression.

Rooms 29 (6 annexe) (4 fmly) (7 GF) **S** £65-£150; **D** £80-£270 (incl. bkfst)* **Facilities** FTV Xmas New Year Wi-fi **Conf** Class 20 Board 20 Thtr 50 Del from £145 to £195* **Services** Lift **Parking** 30

FORT WILLIAM — Map 22 NN17

INSPECTORS' CHOICE

Inverlochy Castle

★★★★★ ⊛⊛⊛
COUNTRY HOUSE HOTEL

☎ 01397 702177 🖹 01397 702953
Torlundy PH33 6SN
e-mail: info@inverlochy.co.uk
web: www.inverlochycastlehotel.com
dir: accessible from either A82 (Glasgow-Fort William) or A9 (Edinburgh-Dalwhinnie). Hotel 3m N of Fort William on A82, in Torlundy

With a backdrop of Ben Nevis, this imposing and gracious castle sits amidst extensive gardens and grounds overlooking the hotel's own loch. Lavishly appointed in classic country-house style, spacious bedrooms are extremely comfortable and boast flat screen TVs and laptops with internet access. The sumptuous main hall and lounge provide the perfect setting for afternoon tea or a pre-dinner cocktail, whilst imaginative cuisine is served in one of three dining rooms. A snooker room and a DVD library are also available.

Rooms 17 (6 fmly) **S** £250-£350; **D** £300-£650 (incl. bkfst)* **Facilities** STV 🎣 Fishing 🎣 Fishing on loch Massage Riding Hunting Stalking Clay pigeon shooting Archery ♫ Xmas New Year Wi-fi **Conf** Class 20 Board 20 Thtr 50 **Parking** 17 **Notes** LB Civ Wed 80

See advert on opposite page

Moorings

★★★ 79% ⊛ HOTEL

☎ 01397 772797 🖹 01397 772441
Banavie PH33 7LY
e-mail: reservations@moorings-fortwilliam.co.uk
web: www.moorings-fortwilliam.co.uk
dir: take A380 (N from Fort William), cross Caledonian Canal, 1st right

Located on the Caledonian Canal next to a series of locks known as Neptune's Staircase and close to Thomas Telford's house, this hotel with its dedicated, young team offers friendly service. Accommodation comes in two distinct styles and the newer rooms are particularly appealing. Meals can be taken in the bars or the spacious dining room.

Rooms 27 (1 fmly) (1 GF) **S** £84-£106; **D** £98-£142 (incl. bkfst)* **Facilities** STV New Year Wi-fi **Conf** Class 60 Board 40 Thtr 140 **Parking** 60 **Notes** LB Civ Wed 120

Lime Tree Hotel & Restaurant

★★★ 78% ⊛ SMALL HOTEL

☎ 01397 701806 🖹 01397 701806
Lime Tree Studio, Achintore Rd PH33 6RQ
e-mail: info@limetreefortwilliam.co.uk
dir: On A82 at entrance to Fort William

The Lime Tree is a charming small hotel with a super art gallery on the ground floor, with lots of original artwork displayed throughout. Evening meals can be enjoyed in the restaurant which has a loyal following. The hotel's comfortable lounges with their real fires are ideal for pre or post dinner drinks or maybe just to relax in. Individually designed bedrooms are spacious with some nice little personal touches courtesy of the artist owner.

Rooms 9 (4 fmly) (4 GF) **S** £60-£75; **D** £80-£100 (incl. bkfst)* **Facilities** New Year Wi-fi **Conf** Class 40 Board 30 Thtr 60 **Parking** 9 **Notes** LB Closed Nov

Alexandra

★★★ 76% HOTEL

☎ 01397 702241 🖹 01397 705554
The Parade PH33 6AZ
e-mail: salesalexandra@strathmorehotels.com
dir: Off A82. Hotel opposite railway station

This charming old hotel enjoys a prominent position in the town centre and is just a short walk from all the major attractions. The bedrooms have now been refurbished and many have views over the town and the spectacular Nevis Range of mountains. There is a choice of restaurants along with several stylish and very comfortable lounges.

Rooms 93 (5 fmly) **S** £45-£100; **D** £79-£160 (incl. bkfst) **Facilities** Free use of nearby leisure club ♫ Xmas Wi-fi **Conf** Class 100 Board 40 Thtr 120 Del from £90 to £140 **Services** Lift **Parking** 50 (charged)

See advert on page 657

Inverlochy Castle Hotel

Torlundy, Fort William PH33 6SN
Tel: 01397 702177 Fax: 01397 702953
www.inverlochycastlehotel.com Email: info@inverlochy.co.uk

Steeped in history Inverlochy was built in 1863 as a private residence and in 1969 was converted into a country house hotel. Nestling in the foothills of the mighty Ben Nevis and sits amidst some of Scotland's finest scenery. Visitors can reflect in the relaxed and tranquil atmosphere of a bygone era, wonderfully crafted and richly decorated, beautiful Venetian crystal chandeliers, frescoed ceiling and a handsome staircase. Each of the 17 bedrooms, all with private bathroom, have their own individual design and character, along with splendid views of the grounds and surrounding mountains. Dinner at Inverlochy is an experience to savour in any of our three dining rooms, each decorated with period and elaborate furniture presented as gifts to Inverlochy Castle from the King of Norway.

Inverlochy Castle is also the perfect location for a Highland wedding. Hotel staff can arrange everything to suit your requirements for your special day.

A wealth of sporting activities can be enjoyed in the surrounding grounds and mountains.

Four miles north of Fort William, on the A82 north towards Inverness.

FORT WILLIAM continued

Best Western Imperial

★★★ 73% HOTEL

☎ 01397 702040 ▤ 01397 706277
Fraser's Square PH33 6DW
e-mail: imperial@bestwestern.co.uk
dir: from town centre, along Middle St, approx 400mtrs
from junct with A82

Benefiting from a town centre location this hotel is
popular with both business and leisure guests, and is
ideally placed for many of the area's attractions. Stylish
public areas include a cosy lounge bar, attractive
restaurant and reception lounge. The smart, modern
bedrooms are comfortable and well equipped.

Rooms 34 (2 fmly) **S** £50-£65; **D** £75-£165 (incl. bkfst)
Facilities FTV Xmas New Year Wi-fi **Conf** Class 12
Board 16 Thtr 60 **Parking** 15 **Notes** LB

Ben Nevis Hotel & Leisure Club

★★ 72% HOTEL

☎ 01397 702331 ▤ 01397 700132
North Rd PH33 6TG
e-mail: bennevismanager@strathmorehotels.com
dir: off A82

This popular hotel is ideally situated on the outskirts of
Fort William. It provides comfortable, well equipped
bedrooms; many with views of the impressive Nevis range
of mountains. The hotel's leisure centre is a firm favourite
with guests at the hotel.

Rooms 119 (3 fmly) (30 GF) **S** £45-£100; **D** £79-£150
(incl. bkfst) **Facilities** ⓢ supervised Gym Beauty salon ♫
Xmas New Year Wi-fi **Conf** Class 60 Board 40 Thtr 150
Parking 100 **Notes** Civ Wed 60

See advert on page 657

Nevis Bank

★★ 69% HOTEL

☎ 01397 705721 ▤ 01397 706275
Belford Rd PH33 6BY
e-mail: info@nevisbankhotel.co.uk
dir: on A82, at junct to Glen Nevis

This long established hotel enjoys a prominent location
on the outskirts of the town and is close to the access
road for the West Highland Way and Glen Nevis. It has a
popular bar and evening meals are served here or in the
more formal restaurant. Bedrooms are of a good standard
and thoughtfully equipped.

Rooms 31 (3 fmly) (2 GF) **Facilities** Xmas New Year
Conf Class 30 Board 25 Thtr 50 **Parking** 50 **Notes** LB ⊗

See advert on opposite page

Croit Anna

★★ 64% HOTEL   **Leisureplex**

☎ 01397 702268 ▤ 01397 704099
Achintore Rd, Drimarben PH33 6RR
e-mail: croitanna.fortwilliam@alfatravel.co.uk
dir: from Glencoe on A82 into Fort William, hotel 1st on
right

Located on the edge of Loch Linnhe, just two miles out of
town, this hotel offers some spacious bedrooms, many
with fine views over the loch. There is a choice of two
comfortable lounges and a large airy restaurant. The
hotel appeals to coach parties and independent travellers
alike.

Rooms 92 (5 fmly) (13 GF) **S** £37-£49; **D** £60-£84 (incl.
bkfst) **Facilities** FTV Pool table ♫ Xmas New Year
Parking 25 **Notes** LB ⊗ Closed Dec-Jan (ex Xmas)
RS Nov, Feb, Mar

Craigdarroch House

Ⓤ

☎ 01456 486400 ▤ 01456 486444
IV2 6XU
e-mail: info@hotel-loch-ness.co.uk
dir: Take B862 form either end of The Loch, then B852
signed to Foyers

Currently the rating for this establishment is not confirmed.
This may be due to a change of ownership or because it has
only recently joined the AA rating scheme. For further
details please see the AA website: www.theAA.com

Rooms 10 (2 fmly) **S** £60-£120; **D** £100-£180 (incl. bkfst)
Facilities FTV Xmas New Year Wi-fi **Conf** Class 25
Board 30 Thtr 25 Del from £150 to £215 **Parking** 24
Notes LB No children 12yrs Civ Wed 25

The Prince's House

★★ 78% ⓖⓖ SMALL HOTEL

☎ 01397 722246 ▤ 01397 722323
PH37 4LT
e-mail: princeshouse@glenfinnan.co.uk
web: www.glenfinnan.co.uk
dir: on A830, 0.5m on right past Glenfinnan Monument.
200mtrs from railway station

This delightful hotel enjoys a well deserved reputation for
fine food and excellent hospitality. The hotel has inspiring
views and sits close to where 'Bonnie' Prince Charlie
raised the Jacobite standard. Comfortably appointed
bedrooms offer pleasing decor. Excellent local game and
seafood can be enjoyed in the restaurant and the bar.

Rooms 9 (1 fmly) **S** £55-£70; **D** £90-£130 (incl. bkfst)*
Facilities Fishing New Year **Conf** Class 20 Thtr 40
Parking 18 **Notes** Closed Xmas & Jan-Feb (ex New Year)
RS Nov-Dec & Mar

GRANTOWN-ON-SPEY — Map 23 NJ03

Culdearn House

★★ 85% @ SMALL HOTEL

☎ 01479 872106 📄 01479 873641
Woodlands Ter PH26 3JU
e-mail: enquiries@culdearn.com
web: www.culdearn.com
dir: from SW into Grantown on A95, left at 30mph sign, hotel opposite

This immaculately maintained small hotel sits in well-tended gardens on the edge of town. The bedrooms have quality and comfort very much to the fore. Hospitality is excellent and every effort is made to make guests feel at home. The hotel has the atmosphere of a relaxed country house.

Rooms 7 (1 GF) **Parking** 12 **Notes** LB ⊗ No children 12yrs Closed Feb

---

Craiglynne

CRERAR

Ⓤ

☎ 01479 872597 📄 01479 873675
Woodlands Ter PH26 3JX
e-mail: admin.craiglynnecrerarhotels.com
dir: A95 from Aviemore to Grantown on Spey, hotel on left as you enter Grantown

Currently the rating for this establishment is not confirmed. This may be due to a change of ownership or because it has only recently joined the AA rating scheme. For further details please see the AA website: www.theAA.com

Rooms 83 (3 fmly) (22 GF) **Facilities** FTV ♫ Xmas New Year Wi-fi **Services** Lift **Parking** 50

INVERGARRY — Map 22 NH30

Glengarry Castle

★★★ 80% @ COUNTRY HOUSE HOTEL

☎ 01809 501254 📄 01809 501207
PH35 4HW
e-mail: castle@glengarry.net
web: www.glengarry.net
dir: on A82 beside Loch Oich, 0.5m from A82/A87 junct

This charming country-house hotel is set in 50 acres of grounds on the shores of Loch Oich. The spacious day rooms include comfortable sitting rooms with lots to read and board games to play. The classical dining room boasts an innovative menu that showcases local Scottish

---

produce. The smart bedrooms vary in size and style but all boast magnificent loch or woodland views.

Rooms 26 (2 fmly) **S** £65-£72; **D** £90-£164 (incl. bkfst) **Facilities** FTV ♨ Fishing Wi-fi **Parking** 30 **Notes** Closed mid Nov-mid Mar

See advert on page 629

INVERGORDON — Map 23 NH76

Kincraig House

★★★★ 77% @ COUNTRY HOUSE HOTEL

☎ 01349 852587 📄 01349 852193
IV18 0LF
e-mail: info@kincraig-house-hotel.co.uk
web: www.kincraig-house-hotel.co.uk
dir: off A9 past Alness towards Tain. Hotel on left 0.25m past Rosskeen Church

This mansion house is set in well-tended grounds in an elevated position with views over the Cromarty Firth. It offers smart well-equipped bedrooms and inviting public areas that retain the original features of the house. However it is the friendly service and commitment to guest care that will leave lasting impression.

Rooms 15 (1 fmly) (1 GF) **S** £65-£150; **D** £80-£300 (incl. bkfst)* **Facilities** STV Xmas Wi-fi **Conf** Class 30 Board 24 Thtr 50 Del from £110 to £200* **Parking** 30 **Notes** LB Civ Wed 70

See advert on page 629

INVERNESS — Map 23 NH64

The New Drumossie

★★★★ 80% @@ HOTEL

☎ 01463 236451 & 0870 194 2110 📄 01463 712858
Old Perth Rd IV2 5BE
e-mail: stay@drumossiehotel.co.uk
dir: from A9 follow signs for Culloden Battlefield, hotel on left after 1m

Set in nine acres of landscaped hillside grounds south of Inverness, this hotel has fine views of the Moray Firth towards Ben Wyvis. Art deco style decoration together with a country-house atmosphere are found throughout. Service is friendly and attentive, the food imaginative and enjoyable and the bedrooms spacious and well presented. The main function room is probably the largest in this area.

Rooms 44 (10 fmly) (6 GF) **Facilities** Fishing Xmas **Conf** Class 200 Board 40 Thtr 500 **Services** Lift **Parking** 200 **Notes** ⊗ Civ Wed 400

Culloden House

★★★★ 78% @@ HOTEL

☎ 01463 790461 📄 01463 792181
Culloden IV2 7BZ
e-mail: reserv@cullodenhouse.co.uk
web: www.cullodenhouse.co.uk
dir: from Inverness take A96, turn right for Culloden. After 1m after 2nd lights left at White Church

Dating from the late 1700s this impressive mansion is set in extensive grounds close to the famous Culloden battlefield. High ceilings and intricate cornices are particular features of the public rooms, including the elegant Adam dining room. Bedrooms come in a range of sizes and styles, with a number situated in a separate house.

Rooms 28 (5 annexe) (1 fmly) **Facilities** ♨ ⛳ Boules Badminton Golf driving net Putting green ♫ **Conf** Class 40 Board 30 Thtr 60 **Parking** 50 **Notes** LB No children 10yrs Closed 24-28 Dec Civ Wed 65

Kingsmills

★★★★ 74% HOTEL

☎ 01463 237166 & 257100 📠 01463 225208
Culcabock Rd IV2 3LP
e-mail: reservations@kingsmillshotel.com
web: www.kingsmillshotel.com
dir: from A9 S, exit Culduthel/Kingsmills 5th exit at rdbt,
0.5m, over mini-rdbt past golf club. Hotel on left after
lights

This manor house hotel is located just a short drive from
the city, and is set in four acres of landscaped grounds.
There is a range of spacious, well-equipped modern
bedrooms; the rooms in newer wing are especially
impressive. There is a choice of restaurants, a
comfortable lounge, a leisure club and conference
facilities.

Rooms 83 (6 annexe) (5 fmly) (34 GF) (6 smoking)
S £90-£161; **D** £90-£171 (incl. bkfst)* **Facilities** Spa STV
🏊 supervised Gym Hairdresser Sauna Steam room Pitch
& putt 🎵 Xmas New Year Wi-fi **Conf** Class 34 Board 40
Thtr 100 **Services** Lift **Parking** 102 **Notes** Civ Wed 80

Bunchrew House

★★★★ 73% ⚫⚫ COUNTRY HOUSE HOTEL

☎ 01463 234917 📠 01463 710620
Bunchrew IV3 8TA
e-mail: welcome@bunchrew-inverness.co.uk
web: www.bunchrew-inverness.co.uk
dir: W on A862. Hotel 2m after canal on right

Overlooking the Beauly Firth this impressive mansion
house dates from the 17th century and retains much
original character. Individually styled bedrooms are
spacious and tastefully furnished. A wood-panelled
restaurant is the setting for artfully constructed cooking
and there is a choice of comfortable lounges complete
with real fires.

Rooms 16 (4 fmly) (1 GF) **S** £105-£180; **D** £150-£260
(incl. bkfst) **Facilities** FTV Fishing New Year
Conf Class 30 Board 30 Thtr 80 Del from £100 to £190
Parking 40 **Notes** ⊗ Closed 24-27 Dec Civ Wed 92

Best Western Lochardil House

★★★★ 73% HOTEL

☎ 01463 235995 📠 01463 713394
Stratherrick Rd IV2 4LF
e-mail: reservations@lochardil.co.uk
dir: From A9 at Police HQ, take Sir Walter Scott Drive
through rdbts, turn right onto Stratherrick Rd

This hotel enjoys a peaceful location in a residential area
just a mile from the town centre. Smart, comfortable
bedrooms ensure a relaxed stay whilst spacious day
rooms include an eye-catching conservatory restaurant, a
stylish lounge bar, and a popular function suite. Staff
throughout are friendly and extend a warm Highland
welcome.

Rooms 28 (16 annexe) (2 fmly) (6 GF) **S** £60-£70;
D £88-£189 (incl. bkfst)* **Facilities** Wi-fi **Conf** Class 100
Board 60 Thtr 200 Del from £120 to £180* **Parking** 120
Notes ⊗ Civ Wed 150

Columba

★★★★ 70% HOTEL

☎ 01463 231391 📠 01463 715526
Ness Walk IV3 5NF
e-mail: reservations.columba@ohiml.com
web: www.oxfordhotelsandinns.com
dir: From A9/A96 follow signs to town centre, past
Eastgate shopping centre onto Academy St, at bottom
take left to Bank St, right over bridge, hotel 1st left

Originally built in 1881, the Columba Hotel lies in the
heart of Inverness overlooking the fast flowing River Ness.
The hotel has undergone major refurbishment, with many
of the original Victorian features retained. The new
bedrooms are very stylish, and public areas include a first
floor restaurant and lounge. A second dining option is the
ever popular McNabs bar bistro, which is ideal for less
formal meals.

Rooms 76 (4 fmly) **S** £75-£110; **D** £89-£215 (incl. bkfst)*
Facilities FTV Complimentary use of leisure facilities
0.5m away 🎵 Xmas New Year Wi-fi **Conf** Class 50
Board 60 Thtr 200 Del from £110 to £160* **Services** Lift
Notes LB ⊗ Civ Wed 80

Glenmoriston Town House Hotel

★★★ 85% ⚫⚫⚫ HOTEL

☎ 01463 223777 📠 01463 712378
20 Ness Bank IV2 4SF
e-mail: reception@glenmoristontownhouse.com
web: www.glenmoristontownhouse.com
dir: on riverside opposite theatre

Bold contemporary designs blend seamlessly with the
classical architecture of this stylish hotel, situated on the
banks of the River Ness. Delightful day rooms include a
cosy cocktail bar and a sophisticated restaurant where
outstanding authentic French cuisine can be sampled.
The smart, modern bedrooms have many facilities,
including CD players, DVD players and flat screen TVs.

Rooms 30 (15 annexe) (1 fmly) (6 GF) **S** £95-£115;
D £130-£170 (incl. bkfst) **Facilities** STV 🎵 Xmas New
Year Wi-fi **Conf** Class 10 Board 10 Thtr 15 Del from £130
to £150 **Parking** 40 **Notes** LB ⊗ Closed 26-28 Dec & 4-6
Jan Civ Wed 70

Royal Highland

★★★ 74% HOTEL

☎ 01463 231926 & 251451 📠 01463 710705
Station Square, Academy St IV1 1LG
e-mail: info@royalhighlandhotel.co.uk
web: www.royalhighlandhotel.co.uk
dir: from A9 into town centre. Hotel next to rail station &
Eastgate Retail Centre

Built in 1858 adjacent to the railway station, this hotel
has the typically grand foyer of the Victorian era with
comfortable seating. The contemporary ASH Brasserie
and bar offers a refreshing style for both eating and
drinking throughout the day. The generally spacious
bedrooms are comfortably equipped for the business
traveller.

Rooms 85 (12 fmly) (2 GF) (25 smoking) **S** £80-£130;
D £99-£180 (incl. bkfst) **Facilities** FTV Gym Xmas New
Year Wi-fi **Conf** Class 80 Board 80 Thtr 200 Del from £80
to £160 **Services** Lift **Parking** 8 **Notes** LB Civ Wed 200

INVERNESS continued

Best Western Palace Hotel & Spa

★★★ 73% HOTEL

☎ 01463 223243 📠 01463 236865
8 Ness Walk IV3 5NG
e-mail: palace@miltonhotels.com
web: www.bw-invernesspalace.co.uk
dir: A82 Glenurquhart Rd onto Ness Walk. Hotel 300yds on right opposite Inverness Castle

Set on the north side of the River Ness close to the Eden Court theatre and a short walk from the town, this hotel now has a contemporary look. Bedrooms offer good levels of comfort and equipment, and a smart leisure centre attracts a mixed market.

Rooms 88 (48 annexe) (4 fmly) **Facilities** Spa FTV ☜ supervised Gym Beautician Steam room Xmas New Year Wi-fi **Conf** Class 40 Board 30 Thtr 80 Del from £119.90 to £189.90 **Services** Lift **Parking** 38

Thistle Inverness

thistle

★★★ 73% HOTEL

☎ 0871 376 9023 📠 0871 376 9123
Millburn Rd IV2 3TR
e-mail: inverness@thistle.co.uk
web: www.thistlehotels.com/inverness
dir: From A9 take Raigmore Interchange exit (towards Aberdeen) then 3rd left towards centre. Hotel opposite

Well located within easy distance of the town centre. This well presented hotel offers modern bedrooms including three suites. There is a well equipped leisure centre along with an informal brasserie and open-plan bar and lounge. Ample parking is an added benefit.

Rooms 118 **S** £85-£125; **D** £95-£155 (incl. bkfst) **Facilities** STV ☜ supervised Gym Xmas New Year Wi-fi **Conf** Class 120 Board 30 Thtr 240 Del from £125 to £155 **Services** Lift **Parking** 150 **Notes** LB ⊗ Civ Wed 240

Glen Mhor

★★★ 68% HOTEL

☎ 01463 234308 📠 01463 218018
8-15 Ness Bank IV2 4SG
e-mail: enquires@glen-mhor.com
web: www.glen-mhor.com
dir: on east bank of River Ness, below Inverness Castle

This hotel is a short walk from the city centre and overlooks the beautiful River Ness. This fine old property has undergone a major refurbishment and new bedrooms, including several suites, feature the latest in design. The public areas include a cosy bar and a comfortable lounge with its log fire.

Rooms 52 (34 annexe) (1 fmly) (12 GF) **S** £57-£115; **D** £75-£195 (incl. bkfst)* **Facilities** FTV ♫ Xmas New Year Wi-fi **Conf** Class 30 Board 35 Thtr 60 Del from £115 to £195 **Parking** 26 **Notes** LB ⊗

Loch Ness House

THE INDEPENDENTS
HOTEL ASSOCIATION

★★★ 66% HOTEL

☎ 01463 231248 📠 01463 239327
Glenurquhart Rd IV3 8JL
e-mail: lnhhchris@aol.com
dir: From A9, left at Longman rdbt, follow signs for A82 for 2.5m

This is a family-run hotel, lying close to the canal, that offers friendly and attentive service. Tasty meals can be chosen from a good range of dishes, available in the restaurant or the bar.

Rooms 21 (3 fmly) (8 GF) **Facilities** STV Xmas New Year Wi-fi **Conf** Class 60 Board 40 Thtr 150 **Parking** 60 **Notes** Civ Wed 75

Ramada Inverness

®RAMADA.

★★★ 🅰 HOTEL

☎ 01463 235181 📠 01463 711206
Church St IV1 1DX
e-mail: sales.inverness@ramadajarvis.co.uk
web: www.ramadajarvis.co.uk
dir: A9 at Kessock Bridge, take 1st exit at rdbt, 2nd exit at next rdbt past Inverness College. 1st exit at 2nd rdbt, right at lights, hotel on left

Rooms 106 (12 fmly) **Facilities** ☜ Gym Xmas New Year Wi-fi **Conf** Class 100 Board 100 Thtr 200 **Services** Lift **Parking** 80 **Notes** LB ⊗ Civ Wed 150

Express by Holiday Inn Inverness

BUDGET HOTEL

☎ 01463 732700 📠 01463 732732
Stoneyfield IV2 7PA
e-mail: inverness@expressholidayinn.co.uk
web: www.hiexpress.com/inverness
dir: from A9 follow A96 & Inverness Airport signs, hotel on right

A modern hotel ideal for families and business travellers. Fresh and uncomplicated, the spacious rooms include Sky TV, power shower and tea and coffee-making facilities. Continental buffet breakfast is included in the room rate; other meals may be taken at the nearby family pub or restaurant. See also the Hotel Groups pages.

Rooms 94 (43 fmly) **Conf** Class 20 Board 15 Thtr 35

Travelodge Inverness

BUDGET HOTEL

☎ 08719 846 148 📠 01463 718152
Stoneyfield, A96 Inverness Rd IV2 7PA
web: www.travelodge.co.uk
dir: at junct of A9/A96

Travelodge offers good quality, good value, modern accommodation. Ideal for families, the spacious en suite bedrooms include remote-control TV, tea and coffee-

making facilities and comfortable beds. Meals can be taken at the nearby family restaurant. See also the Hotel Groups pages.

Rooms 50 **S** fr £29; **D** fr £29

Travelodge Inverness Fairways

BUDGET HOTEL

☎ 08719 846 285 📠 01463 250 703
Castle Heather IV2 6AA
web: www.travelodge.co.uk
dir: From A9 follow Raigmore Hospital signs. At 1st rdbt take 3rd exit, follow B8082 towards Hilton/Culduthel. 1.5m, 2nd exit at rdbt, 3rd exit at next rdbt .At 4th rdbt take 1st exit. Lodge on left

Rooms 80 **S** fr £29; **D** fr £29

KINGUSSIE   Map 23 NH70

INSPECTORS' CHOICE

The Cross at Kingussie

◉◉◉ RESTAURANT WITH ROOMS

☎ 01540 661166 📠 01540 661080
Tweed Mill Brae, Ardbroilach Rd PH21 1LB
e-mail: relax@thecross.co.uk
dir: From lights in Kingussie centre along Ardbroilach Rd, 300yds left onto Tweed Mill Brae

Situated in the valley above the town of Kingussie, this former tweed mill sits next to a river, with wild flower gardens and a sunny terrace. Hospitality and food are clearly highlights of any stay at this special restaurant with rooms. Locally sourced produce is carefully prepared with passion and skill. Bedrooms are spacious and airy, while fluffy towels and hand-made toiletries provide extra luxury.

Rooms 8 (6 en suite) (1 fmly)

KYLE OF LOCHALSH   Map 22 NG72

Kyle

OXFORD
HOTELS & INNS

★★★ 72% HOTEL

☎ 01599 534204 📠 01599 534932
Main St IV40 8AB
e-mail: reservations.kyle@ohiml.com
web: www.oxfordhotelsandinns.com
dir: From Glasgow/Inverness take A87 to Kyle of Lochalsh, right at 1st lights, Main St, hotel 50mtrs on right

Standing on the site of an inn from as far back as the 1700s, the Kyle Hotel is ideally located to explore the charm of the west coast and the beautiful Isle of Skye. Bedrooms are attractively presented, with those at the front somewhat more spacious. There is a popular bar where light snacks and bar food are served; more formal dining can be enjoyed in the restaurant.

Rooms 30 (1 fmly) (8 GF) **Facilities** Xmas New Year **Conf** Class 20 Board 30 Thtr 40

The Smiddy House

◉◉ RESTAURANT WITH ROOMS

☎ 01397 712335 ▤ 01397 712043
Roy Bridge Rd PH34 4EU
e-mail: enquiry@smiddyhouse.co.uk
dir: In village centre, A82 onto A86

Set within the 'Great Glen', which stretches from Fort William to Inverness, this was once the village smithy, and is now a friendly establishment. The attractive bedrooms, which are named after Scottish places and whiskies, are comfortably furnished and well equipped. A relaxing garden room is available for guest use. Delicious evening meals are served in Russell's restaurant.

Rooms 4 (1 fmly)

STRATHPEFFER Map 23 NH45

Ben Wyvis Hotel

CRERAR

★★★ 77% HOTEL

☎ 0870 950 6264 ▤ 01997 421228
IV14 9DN
e-mail: benwyvis@crerarhotels.com
web: www.crerarhotels.com
dir: From S A862 to Dingwall, then A834 to Strathpeffer. Hotel 3rd exit on left

This imposing hotel built in 1877 lies in its own extensive landscaped grounds in the centre of the Victorian spa village of Strathpeffer. It offers spacious lounges with open log fires, sparkling chandeliers and even has its own 32-seat cinema. The hotel is popular for meetings and conferences.

Rooms 92 (5 fmly) (8 GF) **Facilities** Putt green Cinema ♫ Xmas New Year Wi-fi **Conf** Class 180 Board 120 Thtr 200 **Services** Lift **Parking** 40 **Notes** Civ Wed 100

STRONTIAN Map 22 NM86

INSPECTORS' CHOICE

Kilcamb Lodge

★★★ ◉◉ COUNTRY HOUSE HOTEL

☎ 01967 402257 ▤ 01967 402041
PH36 4HY
e-mail: enquiries@kilcamblodge.co.uk
web: www.kilcamblodge.co.uk
dir: off A861, via Corran Ferry

This historic house on the shores of Loch Sunart was one of the first stone buildings in the area and was used as military barracks around the time of the Jacobite uprising. Accommodation is provided in tastefully decorated rooms with high quality fabrics. Accomplished cooking, utilising much local produce, can be enjoyed in the stylish dining room. Warm hospitality is assured.

Rooms 10 (2 fmly) **S** £95-£140; **D** £130-£320 (incl. bkfst)* **Facilities** FTV Fishing Boating Hiking Bird, Whale & Otter watching Island hopping Stalking Xmas New Year Wi-fi **Conf** Class 18 Board 18 Thtr 18 Del from £165 to £195 **Parking** 18 **Notes** LB No children 12yrs Closed 2 Jan-1 Feb RS Nov & Feb Civ Wed 60

TAIN Map 23 NH88

INSPECTORS' CHOICE

Glenmorangie Highland Home at Cadboll

★★★ ◉◉ COUNTRY HOUSE HOTEL

☎ 01862 871671 ▤ 01862 871625
Cadboll, Fearn IV20 1XP
e-mail: relax@glenmorangieplc.co.uk
web: www.theglenmorangiehouse.com
dir: from A9 onto B9175 towards Nigg. Follow tourist signs

This establishment superbly balances top class service with the intimate customer care of an historic highland home. Evenings are dominated by the highly successful 'house party' where guests are introduced in the drawing room, sample whiskies then take dinner (a set six course meal) together around one long table. Conversation can extend well into the evening. Stylish bedrooms are divided between the traditional main house and some cosy cottages in the grounds. This is an ideal base from which to enjoy the world famous whisky tours.

Rooms 9 (3 annexe) (4 fmly) (3 GF) **S** £165; **D** £390 (incl. bkfst & dinner)* **Facilities** Putt green Fishing ⚐ Falconry Clay pigeon shooting Beauty treatments Archery Xmas New Year Wi-fi **Conf** Class 12 Board 12 Thtr 12 Del from £165 to £210* **Parking** 60 **Notes** LB ⊗ No children 14yrs Closed 3-31 Jan Civ Wed 170

THURSO Map 23 ND16

Forss House

★★★★ 76% ◉ SMALL HOTEL

☎ 01847 861201 ▤ 01847 861301
Forss KW14 7XY
e-mail: anne@forsshousehotel.co.uk
web: www.forsshousehotel.co.uk
dir: On A836 between Thurso & Reay

This delightful country house is set in its own 20 acres of woodland and was originally built in 1810. The hotel offers a choice of bedrooms from the traditional styled rooms in main house to the more contemporary annexe rooms in the grounds. All rooms are very well equipped and appointed. The beautiful River Forss runs through the grounds and is a firm favourite with fishermen.

Continued

THURSO continued

Rooms 14 (6 annexe) (1 fmly) (1 GF) **Facilities** FTV Fishing Wi-fi **Conf** Class 12 Board 16 Thtr 20 **Parking** 14 **Notes** Closed 23 Dec–3 Jan Civ Wed 30

See advert on this page

Royal

★★★ 68% HOTEL

☎ 01847 893191 📠 01847 895338
Traill St KW14 8EH
web: www.oxfordhotelsandinns.com
dir: A9 to Thurso, cross Thurso Bridge, at 1st lights turn right. Hotel on right

A fine old town centre hotel which is a perfect base for exploring the beautiful north coast of Scotland. Bedrooms are spacious and well equipped; many have now been refurbished. Tasty evening meals are served in the Orkney Restaurant, and the hotel has a comfortable lounge and a popular public bar.

Rooms 103 (5 fmly) (2 GF) (40 smoking) **S** £25–£80; **D** £40–£100 (incl. bkfst)* **Facilities** FTV Beauty treatments ♫ Xmas New Year Wi-fi **Services** Lift **Parking** 54 **Notes** LB Civ Wed 150

TONGUE — Map 23 NC55

Ben Loyal

★★★ 70% ◉ SMALL HOTEL

☎ 01847 611216 📠 01847 611212
Main St IV27 4XE
e-mail: benloyalhotel@btinternet.com
web: www.benloyal.co.uk
dir: at junct of A838/A836. Hotel by Royal Bank of Scotland

Enjoying a super location close to Ben Loyal and with views of the Kyle of Tongue, this hotel more often that not

marks the welcome completion of a stunning highland and coastal drive. Bedrooms are thoughtfully equipped and brightly decorated whilst day rooms extend to a traditionally styled dining room and a cosy bar. Extensive menus ensure there's something for everyone. Staff are especially friendly and provide useful local information.

Rooms 11 **S** £40; **D** £70–£80 (incl. bkfst)* **Facilities** FTV Fishing Fly fishing tuition and equipment **Parking** 20 **Notes** Closed 30 Nov–1 Mar

Borgie Lodge Hotel

★★ 76% ◉ HOTEL

☎ 01641 521332 📠 01641 521889
Skerray KW14 7TH
e-mail: info@borgielodgehotel.co.uk
dir: A836 between Tongue & Bettyhill. 0.5m from Skerray junct

This small outdoor-sport orientated hotel lies in a glen close to the river of the same name. Whilst fishing parties predominate, those who are not anglers are made equally welcome, and indeed the friendliness and commitment to guest care is paramount. Cosy public rooms offer a choice of lounges and an anglers' bar - they all boast welcoming log fires. The dinner menu is short but well chosen.

Rooms 8 (1 GF) **Facilities** Fishing ⚓ Shooting Stalking Boating **Parking** 20 **Notes** LB No children 12yrs RS 25 Dec

TORRIDON — Map 22 NG95

The Torridon

★★★★ ◉◉ COUNTRY HOUSE HOTEL

☎ 01445 791242 📠 01445 712253
By Achnasheen, Wester Ross IV22 2EY
e-mail: info@thetorridon.com
web: www.thetorridon.com
dir: from A832 at Kinlochewe, take A896 towards Torridon. (Do not turn into village) continue 1m, hotel on right

Delightfully set amidst inspiring loch and mountain scenery, this elegant Victorian shooting lodge has been beautifully restored to make the most of its many original features. The attractive bedrooms are all individually furnished and most enjoy stunning Highland views. Comfortable day rooms feature fine wood panelling and roaring fires in cooler months. The whisky bar is aptly named, boasting over 300 malts and in-depth tasting notes. Outdoor activities include shooting, cycling and walking.

Rooms 19 (2 GF) **S** £135–£170; **D** £220–£475 (incl. bkfst & dinner) **Facilities** STV Fishing ⚓ Mountain biking Archery Clay pigeon shooting Falconry Climbing Kayaking Xmas New Year Wi-fi **Conf** Board 16 **Del** from £205 to £315 **Services** Lift **Parking** 20 **Notes** LB ⊗ Closed 3–27 Jan RS Nov–14 Mar Civ Wed 42

ULLAPOOL
Map 22 NH19

Caledonian

OXFORD
HOTELS & INNS

★★ 74% HOTEL

☎ 01854 612306 📄 01854 612679
Quay St IV26 2UG
e-mail: generalmanager.caledonian@ohiml.com
web: www.oxfordhotelsandinns.com
dir: On A835 (60m from Inverness)

A fine hotel located in the heart of the pretty town of Ullapool. Bedrooms are well equipped and very comfortable and many have wonderful views over the harbour and the dramatic mountains beyond. The bistro restaurant is ideal for less formal dining and has an extensive menu. Public areas include a bright spacious lounge, and the Caley Inn is very popular with guests and locals alike.

Rooms 83 (1 fmly) (17 GF) **Facilities** ♫ Xmas New Year **Parking** 35

Glenfield

OXFORD
HOTELS & INNS

Ⓤ

☎ 01854 612314 📄 01854 612158
North Rd IV26 2TG
e-mail: generalmanager.glenfield@ohiml.com
web: www.oxfordhotelsandinns.com
dir: off A835, on outskirts of Ullapool

Currently the rating for this establishment is not confirmed. This may be due to a change of ownership or because it has only recently joined the AA rating scheme. For further details please see the AA website: www.theAA.com

Rooms 60 (4 fmly) (30 GF) **Facilities** ♫ **Parking** 40 **Notes** LB Closed Oct-Apr

WHITEBRIDGE
Map 23 NH41

Whitebridge

★★ 68% HOTEL

☎ 01456 486226 📄 01456 486413
IV2 6UN
e-mail: info@whitebridgehotel.co.uk
dir: off A9 onto B851, follow signs to Fort Augustus. Off A82 onto B862 at Fort Augustus

Close to Loch Ness and set amid rugged mountain and moorland scenery this hotel is popular with tourists, fishermen and deerstalkers. Guests have a choice of more formal dining in the restaurant or lighter meals in the popular cosy bar. Bedrooms are thoughtfully equipped and brightly furnished.

Rooms 12 (3 fmly) **S** £40-£44; **D** £60-£66 (incl. bkfst) **Facilities** Fishing Wi-fi **Parking** 30 **Notes** Closed 11 Dec-9 Jan

WICK
Map 23 ND35

Mackay's

★★★ 75% HOTEL

☎ 01955 602323 📄 01955 605930
Union St KW1 5ED
e-mail: info@mackayshotel.co.uk
dir: opposite Caithness General Hospital

This well-established hotel is situated just outside the town centre overlooking the River Wick. MacKay's provides well-equipped, attractive accommodation, suited to both the business and leisure traveller. There is a stylish bistro offering food throughout the day and a choice of bars that also offer food.

Rooms 30 (4 fmly) **Facilities** ♫ Wi-fi **Conf** Class 100 Board 60 Thtr 100 **Services** Lift **Notes** ⊗ Closed 25-26 Dec & 1-3 Jan

Norseman

OXFORD
HOTELS & INNS

Ⓤ HOTEL

☎ 01955 603344 📄 01955 605456
Riverside KW1 4NL
e-mail: generalmanager.norseman@ohiml.com
web: www.oxfordhotelsandinns.com
dir: Follow A99 to centre, cross bridge, 1st right, then left

Currently the rating for this establishment is not confirmed. This may be due to a change of ownership or because it has only recently joined the AA rating scheme. For further details please see the AA website: www.theAA.com

Rooms 48 (2 fmly) (16 GF) (24 smoking) **S** £25-£65; **D** £50-£80 (incl. bkfst) **Facilities** ♫ Xmas New Year Wi-fi **Conf** Class 50 Board 40 Thtr 80 Del from £49 to £69 **Parking** 22 **Notes** LB

INVERCLYDE

GREENOCK
Map 20 NS27

Express by Holiday Inn Greenock

Express
by Holiday Inn

BUDGET HOTEL

☎ 01475 786666 📄 01475 786777
Cartsburn PA15 1AE
e-mail: greenock@expressbyholidayinn.net
web: www.hiexpress.com/greenockscot
dir: M8 junct 31, A8 till Greenock, right at 4th rdbt, hotel on the right

A modern hotel ideal for families and business travellers. Fresh and uncomplicated, the spacious rooms include Sky TV, power shower and tea and coffee-making facilities. Continental buffet breakfast is included in the room rate; other meals may be taken at the nearby family pub or restaurant. See also the Hotel Groups pages.

Rooms 71 (11 fmly) **Conf** Class 48 Board 32 Thtr 70

MIDLOTHIAN

BONNYRIGG

Retreat Castle

★★★ Ⓐ SMALL HOTEL

☎ 0131 660 3200 📄 0131 654 1248
1 Cockpen Rd EH19 3HS
e-mail: info@theretreatcastle.com
web: www.theretreatcastle.com
dir: A7 city by pass to Sheriff hall rdbt. A7 S to Galashields, at 4th rdbt take B6392 towards Bonnyrigg, 2nd exit and Hotel on left

Rooms 8 (2 fmly) (5 GF) **S** £55-£65; **D** £70-£120 (incl. bkfst)* **Facilities** ♫ New Year Wi-fi **Parking** 30 **Notes** ⊗ Closed 25-26 Dec Civ Wed 50

MORAY

ARCHIESTOWN
Map 23 NJ24

Archiestown

★★★ 73% ◉ SMALL HOTEL

☎ 01340 810218 📄 01340 810239
AB38 7QL
e-mail: jah@archiestownhotel.co.uk
web: www.archiestownhotel.co.uk
dir: A95 Craigellachie, follow B9102 to Archiestown, 4m

Set in the heart of this Speyside village this small hotel is popular with anglers and locals alike. It is rightly noted for its great hospitality, attentive service and good food. Cosy and comfortable public rooms include a choice of lounges (there is no bar as such) and a bistro offering an inviting choice of dishes at both lunch and dinner.

Rooms 11 (1 fmly) **S** £35-£65; **D** £70-£130 (incl. bkfst)* **Facilities** ⬥ New Year Wi-fi **Conf** Board 12 Thtr 20 Del from £105 to £125* **Parking** 20 **Notes** LB Closed 24-27 Dec & 3 Jan-9 Feb Civ Wed 25

CRAIGELLACHIE   Map 23 NJ24

Craigellachie
★★★ 80% ⊛ HOTEL

OXFORD
HOTELS & INNS

☎ 01340 881204   📠 01340 881253
AB38 9SR
e-mail: info@craigellachie.com
web: www.oxfordhotelsandinns.com
dir: On A95 between Aberdeen & Inverness

This impressive and popular hotel is located in the heart of Speyside, so it is no surprise that malt whisky takes centre stage in the Quaich bar with over 600 featured. Bedrooms come in various sizes, all are tastefully decorated and bathrooms are of a high specification. Creative dinners showcase local ingredients in the traditionally styled dining room.

Rooms 26 (1 fmly) (6 GF) **Facilities** Gym Xmas New Year Wi-fi **Conf** Class 35 Board 30 Thtr 60 Del from £115 to £185* **Parking** 30 **Notes** Civ Wed 60

CULLEN   Map 23 NJ56

Cullen Bay Hotel
★★★ 75% ⊛ SMALL HOTEL

☎ 01542 840432   📠 01542 840900
A98 AB56 4XA
e-mail: stay@cullenbayhotel.com
web: www.cullenbayhotel.com
dir: on A98, 1m west of Cullen

This family-run hotel sits on the hillside west of the town and gives lovely views of the golf course, beach and Moray Firth. The spacious restaurant, which offers a selection of fine dishes, makes the most of the view, as do many of the bedrooms. There is a comfortable modern bar, a quiet lounge and a second dining room where breakfasts are served.

Rooms 14 (3 fmly) **S** £50-£65; **D** £76-£110 (incl. bkfst)* **Facilities** New Year Wi-fi **Conf** Class 80 Board 80 Thtr 200 Del from £90 to £110* **Parking** 100 **Notes** ⊗ Civ Wed 200

The Seafield Arms Hotel
★★★ 68% HOTEL

☎ 01542 840791   📠 01542 840736
Seafield St AB56 4SG
e-mail: info@theseafieldarms.co.uk
dir: in centre of Cullen on A98

Centrally located and benefiting from off-road car parking, this is a small but friendly hotel. Bedrooms differ in size and style but all are comfortable. The popular restaurant serves well cooked meals using the very best of Scottish produce including the famous Cullen Skink.

Rooms 23 (1 fmly) **S** £50-£55; **D** £75-£130 (incl. bkfst)* **Facilities** FTV Xmas New Year Wi-fi **Conf** Class 16 Board 16 Thtr 16 Del from £105 to £185* **Parking** 17 **Notes** LB Civ Wed 200

ELGIN   Map 23 NJ26

Mansion House
★★★ 74% HOTEL

☎ 01343 548811   📠 01343 547916
The Haugh IV30 1AW
e-mail: reception@mhelgin.co.uk
web: www.mansionhousehotel.co.uk
dir: turn off A96 into Haugh Rd, then 1st left

Set in grounds by the River Lossie, this baronial mansion is popular with leisure and business guests as well as being a wedding venue. Bedrooms are spacious, many having views of the river. Extensive public areas include a choice of restaurants, with the bistro contrasting with the classical main restaurant. There is an indoor pool and a beauty and hair salon.

Rooms 23 (5 GF) **Facilities** ⊛ supervised Fishing Gym Xmas Wi-fi **Conf** Thtr 200 **Parking** 50 **Notes** ⊗ Civ Wed 160

See advert on opposite page

Eight Acres
CRERAR
HOTELS
★★★ 72% HOTEL

☎ 01343 543077   📠 01343 540001
Morriston Rd IV30 6UL
e-mail: gm.eightacres@crerarhotels.com
dir: On junct of A96 & Morriston Rd.

This is a purpose built hotel set in its own extensive grounds on the western approach to Elgin. Guests can

dine in the Darroch Restaurant or enjoy a drink in the spacious lounge and bar, whilst the more energetic can utilise the extensive leisure club, complete with heated pool, jacuzzi spa, sauna, gym and squash court. The hotel also has a comprehensive range of meeting and event rooms.

Rooms 53 (1 fmly) **S** £45-£55; **D** £70-£100 (incl. bkfst)* **Facilities** ⊛ Gym Squash Xmas New Year Wi-fi **Conf** Class 100 Board 40 Thtr 250 Del from £95 to £133* **Parking** 150 **Notes** LB Civ Wed 200

FORRES   Map 23 NJ05

Ramnee
★★★ 74% HOTEL

☎ 01309 672410   📠 01309 673392
Victoria Rd IV36 3BN
e-mail: info@ramneehotel.com
dir: off A96 at rdbt on E side of Forres, hotel 200yds on right

Genuinely friendly staff ensure this well-established hotel remains popular with business travellers. Bedrooms, including a family suite, vary in size, although all are well presented. Hearty bar food provides a less formal dining option to the imaginative restaurant menu.

Rooms 19 (4 fmly) **S** £80-£120; **D** £90-£160 (incl. bkfst)* **Facilities** STV Wi-fi **Conf** Class 30 Board 45 Thtr 100 Del from £115 to £135* **Parking** 50 **Notes** LB Closed 25 Dec & 1-3 Jan Civ Wed 100

LOSSIEMOUTH   Map 23 NJ27

Stotfield
★★ 64% HOTEL

OXFORD
HOTELS & INNS

☎ 01343 812011   📠 01343 814820
Stotfield Rd IV31 6QS
e-mail: reservations.stotfield@ohiml.com
web: www.oxfordhotelsandinns.com
dir: A96 to Elgin, A941 to Lossiemouth, follow West Beach/Golf Club sign

This fine old hotel overlooks Lossiemouth Golf Course and out towards the beautiful Morey Firth. The individually designed bedrooms vary in size, with front facing rooms having a spectacular sea view. Spacious public areas include an informal bar and a comfortable lounge. Meals can be taken in the main restaurant or alternatively an extensive menu is available in the bar.

Rooms 47 (5 fmly) **Facilities** Beauty Therapist ♬ Xmas New Year **Conf** Class 140 Board 120 Thtr 250 **Parking** 10 **Notes** LB Civ Wed 100

KENMORE
Map 21 NN74

Kenmore Hotel
★★★ 74% ® HOTEL

☎ 01887 830205 ▤ 01887 830262
The Square PH15 2NU
e-mail: reception@kenmorehotel.co.uk
web: www.kenmorehotel.com
dir: off A9 at Ballinluig onto A827, through Aberfeldy to
Kenmore for hotel in village centre

Dating back to 1572, this riverside hotel is Scotland's
oldest inn and has a rich and interesting history.
Bedrooms have tasteful decor, and meals can be enjoyed
in the restaurant which has panoramic views of the River
Tay. The choice of bars includes one with real fires.

Rooms 40 (13 annexe) (4 fmly) (7 GF) (11 smoking)
D £50-£119 (incl. bkfst)* **Facilities** STV Fishing Salmon
fishing on River Tay Xmas New Year Wi-fi **Conf** Class 60
Board 50 Thtr 80 Del from £99.50* **Services** Lift
Parking 30 **Notes** LB Civ Wed 150

KINCLAVEN
Map 21 NO13

Ballathie House
★★★★ 76% ®® COUNTRY HOUSE HOTEL

☎ 01250 883268 ▤ 01250 883396
PH1 4QN
e-mail: email@ballathiehousehotel.com
web: www.ballathiehousehotel.com
dir: from A9 2m N of Perth, B9099 through Stanley &
signed, or from A93 at Beech Hedge follow signs for
Ballathie, 2.5m

Set in delightful grounds, this splendid Scottish mansion
house combines classical grandeur with modern comfort.
Bedrooms range from well-proportioned master rooms to
modern standard rooms, and many boast antique
furniture and art deco bathrooms. For the ultimate,
request one of the Riverside Rooms, a purpose-built
development right on the banks of the river, complete
with balconies and terraces. The elegant restaurant has
views over the River Tay.

Rooms 41 (16 annexe) (2 fmly) (10 GF) **S** £120-£130;
D £240-£260 (incl. bkfst & dinner)* **Facilities** FTV Putt
green Fishing ⌇ Xmas New Year Wi-fi **Conf** Class 20
Board 30 Thtr 50 Del from £150 to £170* **Services** Lift
Parking 50 **Notes** LB Civ Wed 90

KINLOCH RANNOCH
Map 23 NN65

Dunalastair
★★★ 77% ® HOTEL

☎ 01882 632323 & 632218 ▤ 01882 632371
PH16 5PW
e-mail: robert@dunalastair.co.uk
web: www.dunalastair.co.uk
dir: A9 to Pitlochry, at northern end take B8019 to
Tummel Bridge then A846 to Kinloch Rannoch

A traditional Highland hotel with inviting public rooms
that are full of character - log fires, stags heads, wood
panelling and an extensive selection of malt whiskies.
Standard and superior bedrooms are on offer. However, it
is the friendly attentive service by delightful staff, as well
as first-class dinners that will leave lasting impressions.

Rooms 28 (4 fmly) (9 GF) **S** £50-£75; **D** £110-£170 (incl.
bkfst) **Facilities** Fishing 4x4 safaris Rafting Clay pigeon
shooting Bike hire Archery Xmas New Year Child facilities
Conf Class 40 Board 40 Thtr 60 Del from £95 to £125*
Parking 30 **Notes** LB Civ Wed 70

See advert on this page

KINLOCH RANNOCH continued

Macdonald Loch Rannoch Hotel & Resort

★★★ 73% HOTEL

☎ 0844 879 9059 📠 01882 632201
PH16 5PS
e-mail: loch_rannoch@macdonald-hotels.co.uk
web: www.macdonald-hotels.co.uk
dir: off A9 onto B847 Calvine. Follow signs to Kinloch Rannoch, hotel 1m from village

Set deep in the countryside with elevated views across Loch Rannoch, this hotel is built around a 19th-century hunting lodge and provides a great base for exploring this beautiful area. The superior bedrooms have views over the loch. There is a choice of eating options - The Ptarmigan Restaurant and also the Schiehallan Bar for informal eating. The hotel provides both indoor and outdoor activities.

Rooms 44 (25 fmly) **S** £51-£179; **D** £65-£193 (incl. bkfst)* **Facilities** Fishing Gym Xmas New Year Wi-fi **Conf** Class 80 Board 50 Thtr 160 Del from £125 to £150* **Services** Lift **Parking** 52 **Notes** LB ⊗ Civ Wed 160

KINROSS Map 21 N010

The Green Hotel

★★★★ 75% HOTEL

☎ 01577 863467 📠 01577 863180
2 The Muirs KY13 8AS
e-mail: reservations@green-hotel.com
web: www.green-hotel.com
dir: M90 junct 6 follow Kinross signs, onto A922 for hotel

A long-established hotel offering a wide range of indoor and outdoor activities. Public areas include a classical restaurant, a choice of bars and a well-stocked gift shop. The comfortable, well-equipped bedrooms, most of which are generously proportioned, boast attractive colour schemes and smart modern furnishings.

Rooms 46 (3 fmly) (14 GF) **S** £65-£105; **D** £90-£170 (incl. bkfst)* **Facilities** STV supervised 36 Putt green Fishing Gym Squash Petanque Curling (Sep-Apr) New Year Wi-fi **Conf** Class 75 Board 60 Thtr 130 Del from £120 to £140* **Parking** 60 **Notes** LB Closed 23-24 & 26-28 Dec RS 25 Dec Civ Wed 100

The Windlestrae Hotel & Leisure Centre

U

☎ 0870 609 6153 📠 01577 864733
The Muirs KY13 8AS
e-mail: windlestrae@corushotels.com
web: www.corushotels.com
dir: M90 junct 6 into Kinross, left at 2nd mini rdbt. Hotel 400yds on right

Currently the rating for this establishment is not confirmed. This may be due to a change of ownership or because it has only recently joined the AA rating scheme. For further details please see the AA website: www.theAA.com

Rooms 45 (13 GF) **Facilities** Gym Beautician Steam room Toning tables Xmas **Conf** Class 100 Board 80 Thtr 250 **Parking** 80 **Notes** LB Civ Wed 100

Travelodge Kinross (M90)

BUDGET HOTEL

☎ 08719 846 151 📠 01577 861641
Kincardine Rd, Moto Service Area, Turfhill Tourist Area KY13 0NQ
web: www.travelodge.co.uk
dir: on A977, M90 junct 6, Turthills Tourist Centre

Travelodge offers good quality, good value, modern accommodation. Ideal for families, the spacious en suite bedrooms include remote-control TV, tea and coffee-making facilities and comfortable beds. Meals can be taken at the nearby family restaurant. See also the Hotel Groups pages.

Rooms 35 **S** fr £29; **D** fr £29

PERTH Map 21 N012

Murrayshall Country House Hotel & Golf Course

★★★★ 75% HOTEL

☎ 01738 551171 📠 01738 552595
New Scone PH2 7PH
e-mail: lin.murrayshall@virgin.net
dir: from Perth take A94 (Coupar Angus), 1m from Perth, right to Murrayshall just before New Scone

This imposing country house is set in 350 acres of grounds, including two golf courses, one of which is of championship standard. Bedrooms come in two distinct styles: modern suites in a purpose-built building contrast with more classic rooms in the main building. The Clubhouse bar serves a range of meals all day, whilst more accomplished cooking can be enjoyed in the Old Masters Restaurant.

Rooms 41 (14 annexe) (17 fmly) (4 GF) **Facilities** STV 36 Putt green Driving range New Year Wi-fi **Conf** Class 60 Board 30 Thtr 150 Del from £95 to £135* **Parking** 120 **Notes** Civ Wed 130

Parklands Hotel

★★★ 83% ⑧⑧ HOTEL

☎ 01738 622451 📠 01738 622046
2 St Leonards Bank PH2 8EB
e-mail: info@theparklandshotel.com
web: www.theparklandshotel.com
dir: M90 junct 10, in 1m left at lights at end of park area, hotel on left

Ideally located close to the centre of town, with open views over the South Inch the enthusiastic proprietors continue to invest heavily in the business and the bedrooms have a smart contemporary feel. Public areas include a choice of restaurants with a fine dining experience offered in Acanthus.

Rooms 15 (3 fmly) (4 GF) **S** £89-£139; **D** £109-£189 (incl. bkfst)* **Facilities** STV Wi-fi **Conf** Class 18 Board 20 Thtr 24 **Parking** 30 **Notes** LB Closed 26 Dec-3 Jan Civ Wed 40

Best Western Huntingtower

★★★ 75% ⑧ HOTEL

☎ 01738 583771 📠 01738 583777
Crieff Rd PH1 3JT
e-mail: reservations@huntingtowerhotel.co.uk
web: www.huntingtowerhotel.co.uk
dir: 3m W off A85

Set in landscaped grounds in a rural setting, this Edwardian house has been extended to offer smart, comfortable public areas and a series of high quality bedrooms. It's worth asking for one of the executive bedrooms. Comfortable lounges lead to a conservatory popular at lunchtime, whilst the elegant panelled Oak Room restaurant offers skilfully prepared dinners.

Rooms 34 (3 annexe) (2 fmly) (8 GF) **S** £65-£139; **D** £75-£159 (incl. bkfst)* **Facilities** STV FTV Xmas Wi-fi **Conf** Class 140 Board 30 Thtr 200 Del from £130 to £169* **Services** Lift **Parking** 150 **Notes** LB Civ Wed 200

Lovat

★★★ 74% HOTEL

☎ 01738 636555 📠 01738 643123
90 Glasgow Rd PH2 0LT
e-mail: enquiry@lovat.co.uk
dir: from M90 follow Stirling signs to rdbt. Right into Glasgow Rd, hotel 1.5m on right

This popular and long established hotel on the Glasgow road offers good function facilities and largely attracts a business clientele. There is a bright contemporary brasserie serving a good range of meals through the day until late.

Rooms 30 (1 fmly) (9 GF) **Facilities** Use of facilities at nearby sister hotel Xmas **Conf** Class 60 Board 50 Thtr 200 **Parking** 40 **Notes** LB ⊗ Civ Wed 180

Best Western Queens Hotel

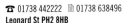

★★★ 71% HOTEL

☎ 01738 442222 📠 01738 638496
Leonard St PH2 8HB
e-mail: enquiry@queensperth.co.uk
dir: from M90 follow to 2nd lights, turn left. Hotel on right, opposite railway station

This popular hotel benefits from a central location close to both the bus and rail stations. Bedrooms vary in size and style with top floor rooms offering extra space and excellent views of the town. Public rooms include a smart leisure centre and versatile conference space. A range of meals is served in both the bar and restaurant.

Rooms 50 (4 fmly) **Facilities** 🕲 Gym Steam room Xmas New Year Wi-fi **Conf** Class 70 Board 50 Thtr 200 **Services** Lift **Parking** 50 **Notes** LB ⊗ Closed 3-7 Jan Civ Wed 220

Salutation

★★★ 70% HOTEL

☎ 01738 630066 📠 01738 633598
South St PH2 8PH
e-mail: salessalutation@strathmorehotels.com
dir: at end of South St on right before River Tay

Situated in heart of Perth, the Salutation is reputed to be one of the oldest hotels in Scotland and has been welcoming guests through its doors since 1699. It offers traditional hospitality with all the modern comforts. Bedrooms vary in size and are thoughtfully equipped. An extensive menu is available in the Adam restaurant with its impressive barrel vaulted ceiling and original features.

Rooms 84 (5 fmly) **S** £40-£100; **D** £60-£150 (incl. bkfst) **Facilities** 🎵 Xmas New Year Wi-fi **Conf** Class 180 Board 60 Thtr 300 **Services** Lift **Notes** Civ Wed 100

See advert on page 657

Ramada Perth

Ⓡ RAMADA.

★★★ Ⓐ HOTEL

☎ 01738 628281 📠 01738 643423
West Mill Street PH1 5QP
e-mail: sales.perth@ramadajarvis.co.uk
web: www.ramadajarvis.co.uk
dir: A93/A989 to city centre, left into Caledonian Rd, right at lights onto Old High St, hotel on left

Rooms 76 (2 fmly) **Facilities** Xmas **Conf** Board 40 Thtr 120 **Parking** 50 **Notes** LB Civ Wed 100

Express by Holiday Inn Perth

BUDGET HOTEL

☎ 01738 636666 📠 01738 633363
200 Dunkeld Rd, Inveralmond PH1 3AQ
e-mail: info@hiexpressperth.co.uk
web: www.hiexpress.com/perthscotland
dir: off A9 (Inverness to Stirling road) at Inveralmond rdbt onto A912 signed Perth. Right at 1st rdbt, follow signs for hotel

A modern hotel ideal for families and business travellers. Fresh and uncomplicated, the spacious rooms include Sky TV, power shower and tea and coffee-making facilities. Continental buffet breakfast is included in the room rate; other meals may be taken at the nearby family pub or restaurant. See also the Hotel Groups pages.

Rooms 81 (43 fmly) **Conf** Class 15 Board 16 Thtr 30

Innkeeper's Lodge Perth A9 (Huntingtower)

BUDGET HOTEL

☎ 0845 112 6007 📠 0845 112 6293
Crieff Road (A85), Huntingtower PH1 3JJ
web: www.innkeeperslodge.com/perthhuntingtower
dir: From M90 junct 1, signed Inverness over Broxden rdbt onto A9. Left signed Perth. At rdbt onto A85. Lodge on left (shared entrance with Dobbies Garden World)

Innkeeper's Lodge represents an exciting, high value concept within the budget hotel market. Comfortable bedrooms provide excellent facilities that include satellite TV and modem points. Options include family rooms, and for the corporate guest, cutting edge IT includes Wi-fi access. Food is served all day in the adjacent Country Pub. The extensive continental breakfast is complimentary.

Rooms 53 **S** £49.95-£52.95; **D** £49.95-£52.95*

Innkeeper's Lodge Perth City Centre

BUDGET HOTEL

☎ 0845 112 6008 📠 0845 112 6292
18 Dundee Rd PH2 7AB
web: www.innkeeperslodge.com/perth
dir: From M90 junct 11, A85 towards Perth. 2m, follow signs for Perth & Scone Palace. After lights at Queens Bridge (A93), turn right into Manse Road. Lodge on left

Innkeeper's Lodge represents an exciting, high value concept within the budget hotel market. Comfortable bedrooms provide excellent facilities that include satellite TV and modem points. Options include family rooms, and for the corporate guest, cutting edge IT which includes Wi-fi access. A popular Carvery provides all-day food, including an extensive, complimentary continental breakfast.

Rooms 41 **S** £49.95-£55; **D** £49.95-£55 (incl. bkfst) **Conf** Class 120 Board 120 Thtr 200

PERTH continued

Travelodge Perth Broxden Junction

BUDGET HOTEL

☎ 0871 984 6250   📠 01738 444783
PH2 0PL
web: www.travelodge.co.uk

Travelodge offers good quality, good value, modern accommodation. Ideal for families, the spacious en suite bedrooms include remote-control TV, tea and coffee-making facilities and comfortable beds. Meals can be taken at the nearby family restaurant. See also the Hotel Groups pages.

S fr £29; **D** fr £29

PITLOCHRY	Map 23 NN95

See also **Kinloch Rannoch**

Pine Trees

★★★★ 73% ⌖ COUNTRY HOUSE HOTEL

☎ 01796 472121   📠 01796 472460
Strathview Ter PH16 5QR
e-mail: info@pinetreeshotel.co.uk
web: www.pinetreeshotel.co.uk
dir: from main street (Atholl Rd), into Larchwood Rd, follow hotel signs

Set in ten acres of tree-studded grounds high above the town, this fine Victorian mansion retains many fine features including wood panelling, ornate ceilings and a wonderful marble staircase. The atmosphere is refined and relaxing, with public rooms looking onto the lawns. Bedrooms come in a variety of sizes and many are well proportioned. Staff are friendly and keen to please.

Pine Trees

Rooms 20 (3 fmly) **S** £40-£62; **D** £80-£134 (incl. bkfst)*
Facilities STV Xmas New Year Wi-fi **Parking** 40 **Notes** LB
No children 12yrs

Green Park

★★★ 85% ⌖ COUNTRY HOUSE HOTEL

☎ 01796 473248   📠 01796 473520
Clunie Bridge Rd PH16 5JY
e-mail: bookings@thegreenpark.co.uk
web: www.thegreenpark.co.uk
dir: turn off A9 at Pitlochry, follow signs 0.25m through town

Guests return year after year to this lovely hotel that is situated in a stunning setting on the shores of Loch Faskally. Most of the thoughtfully designed bedrooms, including a splendid wing, the restaurant and the comfortable lounges enjoy these views. Dinner utilises fresh produce, much of it grown in the kitchen garden.

Rooms 51 (16 GF) **S** £69-£92; **D** £138-£184 (incl. bkfst & dinner) **Facilities** Putt green New Year Wi-fi **Parking** 51

See advert on this page

Scotland's Hotel & Leisure Club

CRERAR HOTELS

★★★ 77% HOTEL

☎ 0870 950 6276   📠 01796 473284
40 Bonnethill Rd PH16 5BT
e-mail: scotlands@crerarhotels.com
web: www.crerarhotels.com
dir: follow A924 (Perth road) into town until War Memorial then take next right for hotel 200mtrs on right

Enjoying a convenient town centre location, this long-established hotel is a popular base for tourists. Bedrooms, including family rooms and some with four-poster beds, come in a variety of styles with several situated in three period properties close by.

Rooms 72 (15 annexe) (21 fmly) (8 GF) **S** £65-£105; **D** £95-£160 (incl. bkfst) **Facilities** ⌖ Gym Beauty & Therapy treatments Aromatherapy Reflexology Sports massage Xmas New Year Wi-fi **Conf** Class 75 Board 30 Thtr 200 Del from £90 to £160 **Services** Lift **Parking** 100 **Notes** LB

Dundarach

★★★ 75% HOTEL

☎ 01796 472862 📠 01796 473024
Perth Rd PH16 5DJ
e-mail: aa@dundarach.co.uk
web: www.dundarach.co.uk
dir: S of town centre on main road

This welcoming, family-run hotel stands in mature grounds at the south end of town. Bedrooms offer a variety of styles, including a block of large purpose-built rooms that will appeal to business guests. Well-proportioned public areas feature inviting lounges and a conservatory restaurant giving fine views of the Tummel Valley.

Rooms 39 (19 annexe) (7 fmly) (12 GF) **S** £49-£68; **D** £98 (incl. bkfst)* **Facilities** Wi-fi **Conf** Class 40 Board 40 Thtr 60 **Parking** 39 **Notes** LB ⊗ Closed Jan RS Dec-early Feb

Moulin Hotel

★★★ 73% SMALL HOTEL

☎ 01796 472196 📠 01796 474098
11-13 Kirkmichael Rd, Moulin PH16 5EW
e-mail: sales@moulinhotel.co.uk
web: www.moulinhotel.co.uk
dir: off A9 take A924 signed Braemar into town centre. Moulin 0.75m from Pitlochry

Steeped in history, original parts of this friendly hotel date back to 1695. The Moulin bar serves an excellent choice of meals as well as real ales from the hotel's own microbrewery. Alternatively, the comfortable restaurant overlooks the Moulin Burn. Bedrooms are well equipped.

Rooms 15 (3 fmly) **S** £45-£70; **D** £60-£85 (incl. bkfst)* **Facilities** New Year Wi-fi **Conf** Class 12 Board 10 Thtr 15 Del from £80 to £100* **Parking** 30 **Notes** LB ⊗

ST FILLANS **Map 20 NN62**

The Four Seasons Hotel

★★★ 83% ⊛⊛ HOTEL

☎ 01764 685333 📠 01764 685444
Loch Earn PH6 2NF
e-mail: info@thefourseasonshotel.co.uk
web: www.thefourseasonshotel.co.uk
dir: on A85, towards W of village

Set on the edge of Loch Earn, this welcoming hotel and many of its bedrooms benefit from fine views. There is a choice of lounges, including a library, warmed by log fires during winter. Local produce is used to good effect in both the Meall Reamhar restaurant and the more informal Tarken Room.

Rooms 18 (6 annexe) (7 fmly) **S** £55-£100; **D** £110-£150 (incl. bkfst)* **Facilities** Xmas New Year Wi-fi **Conf** Class 45 Board 38 Thtr 95 Del from £95 to £132* **Parking** 40 **Notes** LB Closed 2 Jan-Feb RS Nov, Dec, Mar Civ Wed 80

Achray House

★★★ 74% ⊛ SMALL HOTEL

☎ 01764 685231 📠 01764 685320
PH6 2NF
e-mail: info@achray-house.co.uk
dir: follow A85 towards Crainlarich, from Stirling follow A9 then B822 at Braco, B827 to Comrie. Turn left onto A85 to St Fillans

A friendly holiday hotel set in gardens overlooking picturesque Loch Earn, Achray House offers smart, attractive and well-equipped bedrooms. An interesting range of freshly prepared dishes is served both in the conservatory and in the adjoining dining rooms.

Rooms 10 (2 annexe) (2 fmly) (3 GF) **S** £40-£60; **D** £70-£90 (incl. bkfst)* **Facilities** Xmas New Year Wi-fi **Conf** Class 20 Board 20 **Parking** 30 **Notes** Closed 3-24 Jan Civ Wed 40

GLASGOW AIRPORT **Map 20 NS46**

Glynhill Hotel & Leisure Club

★★★ 77% HOTEL

☎ 0141 886 5555 📠 0141 885 2838
Paisley Rd PA4 8XB
e-mail: glynhillleisurehotel@msn.com
dir: M8 junct 27, A741 towards Renfrew. 300yds cross small rdbt, hotel on right

A smart and welcoming hotel with bedrooms ranging from spacious executive rooms to smaller standard rooms. All are tastefully appointed and have a good range of amenities. The hotel boasts a luxurious leisure complex and extensive conference facilities. The choice of contrasting bars and restaurants should suit most tastes and budgets.

Rooms 145 (25 fmly) **Facilities** ⊛ supervised Gym ♬ Xmas **Conf** Class 240 Thtr 450 **Parking** 200 **Notes** ⊗ Civ Wed 450

Ramada Glasgow Airport ⓇRAMADA

★★★ 🅰 HOTEL

☎ 0141 840 2200 📠 0141 889 6830
Marchburn Dr, Glasgow Airport Business Park PA3 2SJ
e-mail: sales.glasgowairport@ramadajarvis.co.uk
web: www.ramadajarvis.co.uk
dir: From Glasgow (& E) exit M8 junct 28. From W exit M8 junct 29

Rooms 108 (108 fmly) (12 GF) **Facilities** Wi-fi **Conf** Class 16 Board 20 Thtr 40 **Services** Lift **Parking** 170 **Notes** ⊗

Holiday Inn Glasgow Airport

🅄

☎ 0870 400 9031 & 0141 887 1266 📠 0141 887 3738
Abbotsinch PA3 2TR
e-mail: operations-glasgow@ihg.com
web: www.holidayinn.co.uk
dir: from E M8 junct 28 follow signs for hotel; from W M8 junct 29, airport slip road to hotel

Currently the rating for this establishment is not confirmed. This may be due to a change of ownership or because it has only recently joined the AA rating scheme. For further details please see the AA website: www.theAA.com

Rooms 300 (6 fmly) (54 smoking) **Facilities** STV Wi-fi **Conf** Class 150 Board 75 Thtr 300 Del from £95 to £165* **Services** Lift Air con **Parking** 56 **Notes** Civ Wed 250

GLASGOW AIRPORT continued

Express by Holiday Inn Glasgow Airport

BUDGET HOTEL

☎ 0141 842 1100 📠 0141 842 1122
St Andrews Dr PA3 2TJ
e-mail: glasgowairport@expressholidayinn.co.uk
web: www.hiexpress.com/ex-glasgow
dir: M8 junct 28, at 1st rdbt turn right, hotel on right

A modern hotel ideal for families and business travellers. Fresh and uncomplicated, the spacious rooms include Sky TV, power shower and tea and coffee-making facilities. Continental buffet breakfast is included in the room rate; other meals may be taken at the nearby family pub or restaurant. See also the Hotel Groups pages.

Rooms 141 (63 fmly) **Conf** Class 20 Board 30 Thtr 70

Travelodge Glasgow Airport

BUDGET HOTEL

☎ 08719 846 335 📠 0141 889 0583
Marchburn Dr, Glasgow Airport Business Park, Paisley PA3 2AR
web: www.travelodge.co.uk
dir: M8 junct 28, 0.5m from Glasgow Airport

Travelodge offers good quality, good value, modern accommodation. Ideal for families, the spacious en suite bedrooms include remote-control TV, tea and coffee-making facilities and comfortable beds. Meals can be taken at the nearby family restaurant. See also the Hotel Groups pages.

Rooms 98 (40 fmly) **S** fr £29; **D** fr £29

HOWWOOD — Map 20 NS36

Bowfield Hotel & Country Club

★★★ 80% ⚙ HOTEL

☎ 01505 705225 📠 01505 705230
PA9 1DZ
e-mail: enquiries@bowfieldhotel.co.uk
web: www.bowfieldhotel.co.uk
dir: M8 junct 28a/29, onto A737 for 6m, left onto B787, right after 2m, follow for 1m to hotel

This former textile mill is now a popular hotel which has become a convenient stopover for travellers using Glasgow Airport. The leisure club has been considerably

expanded and offers very good facilities. Public areas have beamed ceilings, brick and white painted walls, and welcoming open fires. Bedrooms are housed in a separate wing and offer good modern comforts and facilities.

Rooms 23 (3 fmly) (7 GF) **S** £95; **D** £150 (incl. bkfst)*
Facilities Spa FTV 🕭 supervised ⚓ 18 Gym Squash Children's soft play Aerobics studio Health & beauty Xmas New Year Wi-fi **Conf** Class 60 Board 40 Thtr 100 Del from £95 to £120* **Parking** 120 **Notes** LB Civ Wed 80

LANGBANK — Map 20 NS37

Best Western Gleddoch House

★★★ 79% HOTEL

OXFORD
HOTELS & INNS

☎ 01475 540711 📠 01475 540201
PA14 6YE
e-mail: sales.gleddochhouse@ohiml.com
web: www.oxfordhotelsandinns.com
dir: M8 to Greenock, onto A8, left at rdbt onto A789, follow for 0.5m, turn right, 2nd on left

This hotel is set in spacious, landscaped grounds high above the River Clyde with fine views. The period house is appointed to a very high standard. The modern extension remains impressive and offers spacious and very comfortable bedrooms. Warm hospitality and attentive service are noteworthy along with the hotel's parkland golf course and leisure club.

Rooms 70 (20 fmly) (8 GF) **Facilities** 🕭 ⚓ 18 Putt green Xmas New Year **Conf** Class 70 Board 40 Thtr 150 **Parking** 150 **Notes** LB ⊗ Civ Wed 120

RENFREW

For hotels see Glasgow Airport

SCOTTISH BORDERS

EDDLESTON — Map 21 NT24

The Horseshoe Inn

⚙⚙⚙ RESTAURANT WITH ROOMS

☎ 01721 730225 📠 01721 730268
EH45 8QP
e-mail: reservations@horseshoeinn.co.uk
dir: A703, 5m N of Peebles

The Horseshoe Inn is five miles north of Peebles and only 18 miles south of Edinburgh. Originally a blacksmith's shop, it was significantly refurbished by Vivienne Steele

and her partner, Chef Director Patrick Bardoulet. It is now a restaurant with rooms which has a very good reputation for fine dining, and a delightful atmosphere. There are eight bedrooms and ample customer parking to the rear.

Rooms 8 (1 en suite) (1 fmly) (6 GF)

GALASHIELS — Map 21 NT43

Kingsknowes

★★★ 75% SMALL HOTEL

☎ 01896 758375 📠 01896 750377
Selkirk Rd TD1 3HY
e-mail: enq@kingsknowes.co.uk
web: www.kingsknowes.co.uk
dir: off A7 at Galashiels/Selkirk rdbt

An imposing turreted mansion, this hotel lies in attractive gardens on the outskirts of town close to the River Tweed. It boasts elegant public areas and many spacious bedrooms, some with excellent views. There is a choice of bars, one with a popular menu to supplement the restaurant.

Rooms 12 (2 fmly) **Facilities** Wi-fi **Conf** Class 40 Board 30 Thtr 60 **Parking** 65 **Notes** LB Civ Wed 75

KELSO — Map 21 NT73

The Roxburghe Hotel & Golf Course

★★★ 85% ⚙ COUNTRY HOUSE HOTEL

☎ 01573 450331 📠 01573 450611
Heiton TD5 8JZ
e-mail: hotel@roxburghe.net
web: www.roxburghe.net
dir: from A68 Jedburgh take A698 to Heiton, 3m SW of Kelso

Outdoor sporting pursuits are popular at this impressive Jacobean mansion owned by the Duke of Roxburghe, and set in 500 acres of woods and parkland bordering the River Teviot. Gracious public areas are the perfect settings for afternoon teas and carefully prepared meals. The elegant bedrooms are individually designed, some by the Duchess herself, and include superior rooms, some with four posters and log fires.

Rooms 22 (6 annexe) (3 fmly) (3 GF) **S** £147-£170; **D** £185-£390 (incl. bkfst)* **Facilities** Spa STV ⚓ 18 Putt green Fishing 🌢 Clay shooting Health & beauty salon Mountain bike hire Falconry Archery Xmas New Year **Conf** Class 20 Board 20 Thtr 50 **Parking** 150 **Notes** LB ⊗ Civ Wed 60

INSPECTORS' CHOICE

Westin Turnberry Resort
★★★★★ ◉◉ HOTEL

☎ 01655 331000 🖷 01655 331706
KA26 9LT
e-mail: turnberry@westin.com
web: www.westin.com/turnberry
dir: from Glasgow take A77/M77 S towards Stranraer, 2m past Kirkoswald, follow signs for A719/Turnberry. Hotel 500mtrs on right

This famous hotel enjoys magnificent views over to Arran, Ailsa Craig and the Mull of Kintyre. Facilities include a world-renowned golf course, the excellent Colin Montgomerie Golf Academy, a luxurious spa and a host of outdoor and country pursuits. Elegant bedrooms and suites are located in the main hotel, while adjacent lodges provide spacious, well-equipped accommodation. The Ailsa lounge is very welcoming, and in addition to the elegant main restaurant for dining, there is a Mediterranean Terrace Brasserie and the relaxed Clubhouse.

Rooms 219 (89 annexe) (9 fmly) (16 GF) **S** £230–£375; **D** £250–£395 (incl. bkfst)* **Facilities** Spa STV ⓣ supervised ᕽ 36 ⚑ Putt green Fishing Gym Leisure club Outdoor activity centre Colin Montgomerie Golf Academy New Year Wi-fi **Conf** Class 145 Board 80 Thtr 300 Del from £199 to £379* **Services** Lift **Parking** 200 **Notes** LB Closed 25 Dec Civ Wed 220

Malin Court
★★★ 81% ◉ HOTEL

☎ 01655 331457 🖷 01655 331072
KA26 9PB
e-mail: info@malincourt.co.uk
web: www.malincourt.co.uk
dir: on A74 to Ayr then A719 to Turnberry & Maidens

Forming part of the Malin Court Residential and Nursing Home Complex, this friendly and comfortable hotel enjoys delightful views over the Firth of Clyde and Turnberry golf courses. Standard and executive rooms are available; all are well equipped. Public areas are plentiful, with the restaurant serving high teas, dinners and light lunches.

Rooms 18 (9 fmly) **S** £72–£82; **D** £104–£144 (incl. bkfst) **Facilities** STV Putt green Wi-fi **Conf** Class 60 Board 30 Thtr 200 **Services** Lift **Parking** 110 **Notes** ⊗ RS Oct–Mar Civ Wed 80

SOUTH LANARKSHIRE

Days Inn Abington
BUDGET HOTEL

☎ 01864 502782 🖷 01864 502759
ML12 6RG
e-mail: abington.hotel@welcomebreak.co.uk
web: www.welcomebreak.co.uk
dir: M74 junct 13, accessible from N'bound and S'bound carriageways

This modern building offers accommodation in smart, spacious and well-equipped bedrooms, suitable for families and business travellers, and all with en suite bathrooms. Continental breakfast is available and other refreshments may be taken at the nearby family restaurant. See also the Hotel Groups pages.

Rooms 52 (50 fmly) **S** £39–£59; **D** £49–£69* **Conf** Board 10 Del from £69 to £99*

Shieldhill Castle
★★★★ 73% ◉◉ COUNTRY HOUSE HOTEL

☎ 01899 220035 🖷 01899 221092
Quothquan ML12 6NA
e-mail: enquiries@shieldhill.co.uk
web: www.shieldhill.co.uk
dir: A702 onto B7016 (Biggar to Carnwath road), after 2m left into Shieldhill Road. Hotel 1.5m on right

The focus on food and wine are important at this imposing fortified country mansion that dates back almost 800 years. Public room are atmospheric and include the classical Chancellors' Restaurant, oak-panelled lounge and the Gun Room bar that offers its own menu. Bedrooms, many with feature baths, are spacious and comfortable. A friendly welcome is assured, even from the estate's own dogs!

Rooms 26 (10 annexe) (10 GF) **S** £85–£248; **D** £100–£248 (incl. bkfst) **Facilities** FTV ⚑ Cycling Clay shoot Hot air ballooning Falconry Laser & game bird shooting Xmas New Year Wi-fi **Conf** Class 200 Board 250 Thtr 500 Del from £110 to £145 **Parking** 50 **Notes** Civ Wed 200

Tinto

OXFORD
HOTELS & INNS

Ⓤ

☎ 01899 308454 🖷 01899 308520
Symington ML12 6FT
e-mail: generalmanager.tinto@ohiml.com
web: www.oxfordhotelsandinns.com
dir: M74 junct 13 to Edinburgh A702, approx 14m to Symington. On main road before entering village

Currently the rating for this establishment is not confirmed. This may be due to a change of ownership or because it has only recently joined the AA rating scheme. For further details please see the AA website: www.theAA.com

Rooms 37 (8 fmly) (3 GF) **Facilities** New Year Wi-fi **Conf** Thtr 220 **Parking** 150 **Notes** LB Civ Wed 200

BOTHWELL — Map 20 NS75

Bothwell Bridge
★★★ 78% HOTEL

☎ 01698 852246 📠 01698 854686
89 Main St G71 8EU
e-mail: enquiries@bothwellbridge-hotel.com
web: www.bothwellbridge-hotel.com
dir: M74 junct 5 & follow signs to Uddingston, right at mini-rdbt. Hotel just past shops on left

This red-sandstone mansion house is a popular business, function and conference hotel conveniently placed for the motorway. Most bedrooms are spacious and all are well equipped. The conservatory is a bright and comfortable restaurant serving an interesting variety of Italian influenced dishes. The lounge bar offers a comfortable seating area that proves popular as a stop for coffee.

Rooms 90 (14 fmly) (26 GF) (6 smoking) **S** £55-£90; **D** £65-£190 (incl. bkfst)* **Facilities** STV ♪ Xmas New Year Wi-fi **Conf** Class 80 Board 50 Thtr 200 Del from £90 to £103* **Services** Lift **Parking** 125 **Notes** ⊗ Civ Wed 180

EAST KILBRIDE — Map 20 NS65

Macdonald Crutherland House

★★★★ 77% ⑩⑩ HOTEL

☎ 0870 1942109 📠 01355 220855
Strathaven Rd G75 0QZ
e-mail: crutherland@macdonald-hotels.co.uk
web: www.macdonaldhotels.co.uk
dir: Follow A726 signed Strathaven, straight over Torrance rdbt, hotel on left after 250yds

This mansion is set in 37 acres of landscaped grounds two miles from the town centre. Behind its Georgian façade is a very relaxing hotel with elegant public areas plus extensive banqueting and leisure facilities. The bedrooms are spacious and comfortable. Staff provide good levels of attention and enjoyable meals are served in the restaurant.

Rooms 75 (16 fmly) (16 GF) **Facilities** Spa STV ⊗ Gym Sauna Steam room Xmas New Year Wi-fi **Conf** Class 100 Board 50 Thtr 500 **Services** Lift **Parking** 200 **Notes** ⊗ Civ Wed 300

See advert on this page

Holiday Inn Glasgow-East Kilbride

Ⓤ

☎ 01355 236300 📠 01355 233552
Stewartfield Way G74 5LA
e-mail: sales@hieastkilbride.com
web: www.holidayinn.co.uk

Currently the rating for this establishment is not confirmed. This may be due to a change of ownership or because it has only recently joined the AA rating scheme. For further details please see the AA website: www.theAA.com

Rooms 101 (4 fmly) (26 GF) (9 smoking) **S** £60-£145; **D** £60-£145 **Facilities** Spa STV ⊗ Gym Aerobics studio Spin cycle studio Sauna Steam room Wi-fi **Conf** Class 120 Board 40 Thtr 300 Del from £99 to £149* **Services** Lift Air con **Parking** 200 **Notes** LB Civ Wed 200

HAMILTON — Map 20 NS75

Express by Holiday Inn Hamilton

BUDGET HOTEL

☎ 0141 419 3500 📠 0141 419 3500
Keith St ML3 7BL
web: www.hiexpress.com/hamilton

A modern hotel ideal for families and business travellers. Fresh and uncomplicated, the spacious rooms include Sky TV, power shower and tea and coffee-making facilities. Continental buffet breakfast is included in the room rate; other meals may be taken at the nearby family pub or restaurant. See also the Hotel Groups pages.

Rooms 104

LANARK — Map 21 NS84

See also **Biggar**

Best Western Cartland Bridge

★★★ 75% COUNTRY HOUSE HOTEL

☎ 01555 664426 📠 01555 663773
Glasgow Rd ML11 9UF
e-mail: sales@cartlandbridge.co.uk
dir: follow A73 through Lanark towards Carluke. Hotel in 1.25m

Situated in wooded grounds on the edge of the town, this Grade I listed mansion continues to be popular with both business and leisure guests. Public areas feature wood panelling, a gallery staircase and a magnificent dining room. The well-equipped bedrooms vary in size.

Rooms 20 (2 fmly) **S** £45-£65; **D** £75-£112 (incl. bkfst)*
Facilities FTV Xmas New Year Wi-fi **Conf** Class 180
Board 30 Thtr 250 Del from £129 to £135* **Parking** 120
Notes ⊗ Civ Wed 200

NEW LANARK　　　　　　Map 21 NS84

New Lanark Mill Hotel

★★★ 82% HOTEL

☎ 01555 667200 🖷 01555 667222
Mill One, New Lanark Mills ML11 9DB
e-mail: hotel@newlanark.org
web: www.newlanark.org
dir: signed from all major roads, M74 junct 7 & M8

Originally built as a cotton mill in the 18th-century, this
hotel forms part of a fully restored village, now a UNESCO
World Heritage Site. There's a bright modern style
throughout which contrasts nicely with features from the
original mill. There is a comfortable foyer-lounge with a
galleried restaurant above. The hotel enjoys stunning
views over the River Clyde.

Rooms 38 (5 fmly) (10 smoking) **S** £79.50; **D** £119-£144
(incl. bkfst)* **Facilities** STV 🏊 Gym Beauty room Steam
room Sauna Aerobics studios Xmas New Year Wi-fi
Conf Class 60 Board 40 Thtr 200 Del from £120 to £130*
Services Lift **Parking** 75 **Notes** LB Civ Wed 120

ROSEBANK　　　　　　Map 21 NS84

Best Western Popinjay

Ⓤ

☎ 01555 860441 🖷 01555 860204
Lanark Rd ML8 5QB
e-mail: info@popinjay-hotel.co.uk
web: www.popinjayhotel.co.uk
dir: on A72 between Hamilton & Lanark

Currently the rating for this establishment is not confirmed.
This may be due to a change of ownership or because it has
only recently joined the AA rating scheme. For further
details please see the AA website: www.theAA.com

Rooms 34 (4 fmly) (2 GF) **Facilities** Spa 🎣 Fishing Gym
Sunbeds Hairdressing salon Sauna Hydro Spa Whirlpool
Xmas New Year **Conf** Class 120 Board 60 Thtr 250
Parking 300 **Notes** Civ Wed 200

See advert on page 658

STRATHAVEN　　　　　　Map 20 NS74

Best Western Strathaven

★★★ 79% HOTEL

☎ 01357 521778 🖷 01357 520789
Hamilton Rd ML10 6SZ
e-mail: reception@strathavenhotel.com
web: www.strathavenhotel.com

Situated in delightful gardens on the edge of town this
welcoming hotel has been extended with a wing of
modern, stylish bedrooms, which are all well equipped.
Public areas include a comfortable lounge, Lauders
restaurant and a popular bar that serves a range of
freshly prepared meals. Staff are friendly and keen to
please.

Rooms 22 **S** £56-£95; **D** £90-£120 (incl. bkfst)*
Facilities STV FTV Wi-fi **Conf** Class 120 Board 40 Thtr 180
Del from £70 to £115* **Parking** 80 **Notes** ⊗ Closed 1 Jan
Civ Wed 120

STRATHAVEN continued

Rissons at Springvale

◉ RESTAURANT WITH ROOMS

☎ 01357 521131 & 520234 📠 01357 521131
18 Lethame Rd ML10 6AD
e-mail: rissons@msn.com
dir: A71 into Strathaven, W of town centre off Townhead St

You are assured of a warm welcome at this charming establishment close to the town centre. The bedrooms and bathrooms are stylish and well-equipped. Food, though, is the main feature, and a range of interesting, well-prepared dishes is served in Rissons Restaurant.

Rooms 11 (1 en suite) (1 fmly) (2 GF)

STIRLING

ABERFOYLE Map 20 NN50

Macdonald Forest Hills Hotel & Resort

★★★★ 73% HOTEL

☎ 0844 879 9057 & 01877 389500 📠 01877 387307
Kinlochard FK8 3TL
e-mail: forest_hills@macdonald-hotels.co.uk
web: www.macdonald-hotels.co.uk
dir: A84/A873/A81 to Aberfoyle onto B829 along lochside to hotel

Situated in the heart of The Trossachs with wonderful views of Loch Ard, this popular hotel forms part of a resort complex offering a range of indoor and outdoor facilities. The main hotel has relaxing lounges and a restaurant which overlook landscaped gardens. A separate building houses the leisure centre, lounge bar and bistro.

Rooms 50 (16 fmly) (12 GF) **Facilities** Spa STV FTV ⓢ ⌁ Gym Children's playroom Kids' club Snooker ♫ Xmas New Year Wi-fi **Conf** Class 60 Board 45 Thtr 150 Del from £130 to £260* **Services** Lift **Parking** 100 **Notes** ⊗ Civ Wed 100

CALLANDER Map 20 NN60

Roman Camp Country House

★★★ 85% ◉◉◉ COUNTRY HOUSE HOTEL

☎ 01877 330003 📠 01877 331533
FK17 8BG
e-mail: mail@romancamphotel.co.uk
web: www.romancamphotel.co.uk
dir: N on A84, left at east end of High Street. 300yds to hotel

Originally a shooting lodge, this charming country house has a rich history. Twenty acres of gardens and grounds lead down to the River Teith, and the town centre and its attractions are only a short walk away. Food is a highlight of any stay and menus are dominated by high-quality Scottish produce that is sensitively treated by the talented kitchen team. Real fires warm the atmospheric public areas and service is friendly yet professional.

Rooms 14 (3 fmly) (7 GF) **S** £85-£135; **D** £135-£225 (incl. bkfst) **Facilities** STV FTV Fishing Xmas New Year Wi-fi **Conf** Class 40 Board 30 Thtr 100 Del from £155 to £205 **Parking** 80 **Notes** LB Civ Wed 100

Dreadnought

★★ 60% HOTEL

OXFORD
HOTELS & INNS

☎ 01877 330184 📠 01877 330228
Station Rd FK17 8AN
e-mail: generalmanager.dreanought@ohiml.com
web: www.oxfordhotelsandinns.com

Centrally located in the heart of Callander, this once majestic hotel offers good value-for-money accommodation. Public areas are spacious with an array of the original features of this building being retained. Regular entertainment is provided on a number of evenings.

Rooms 61 (4 fmly) (9 GF) **Facilities** ♫ Xmas New Year **Services** Lift **Parking** 20 **Notes** Civ Wed

Callander Meadows

◉ RESTAURANT WITH ROOMS

☎ 01877 330181
24 Main St FK17 8BB
e-mail: mail@callandermeadows.co.uk
dir: M9 junct 10 onto A84 to Callander, on main street just past A81 junct

Located on the high street in Callender, this family-run business offers comfortable accommodation and a restaurant that has quickly become very popular with the locals. Private parking is available to the rear, and out of the three bedrooms, two have been refurbished to a very high standard.

Rooms 3

DRYMEN
Map 20 NS48

Best Western Winnock
★★★ 79% HOTEL

☎ 01360 660245 📠 01360 660267
The Square G63 0BL
e-mail: info@winnockhotel.com
web: www.winnockhotel.com
dir: from S: M74 onto M8 junct 16b through Glasgow.
Follow A809 to Aberfoyle

Occupying a prominent position overlooking the village green, this popular hotel offers well-equipped bedrooms of various sizes and styles. The public rooms include a bar, a lounge and an attractive formal dining room that serves good, locally produced food.

Rooms 73 (18 fmly) (19 GF) (20 smoking) **S** £49-£89;
D £49-£118 (incl. bkfst) **Facilities** Xmas New Year Wi-fi
Conf Class 60 Board 70 Thtr 140 Del from £55 to £99
Parking 60 **Notes** ⊗ Civ Wed 100

Buchanan Arms Hotel and Leisure Club
★★★ 79% HOTEL

☎ 01360 660588 📠 01360 660943
23 Main St G63 0BQ
e-mail: info@buchananarms.co.uk
web: www.buchananarms.co.uk
dir: N from Glasgow on A81 then take A811, hotel at S end of Main Street

This former coaching inn offers comfortable bedrooms in a variety of styles, with spacious public areas that include an intimate bar, a formal dining room, good function and meeting facilities as well as a fully equipped leisure centre. Teas and light meals can be served in the conservatory lounge which looks over the gardens towards Campsie Fells.

Rooms 52 (3 GF) **S** £45-£80; **D** £70-£130 (incl. bkfst)*
Facilities ⊙ supervised Gym Squash Bowling green
Xmas New Year Wi-fi **Conf** Class 140 Board 60 Thtr 250
Del from £90 to £140* **Parking** 100 **Notes** LB ⊗
Civ Wed 180

FINTRY
Map 20 NS68

Culcreuch Castle
★★★ 70% HOTEL

☎ 01360 860555 & 860228 📠 01360 860556
Kippen Rd G63 0LW
e-mail: info@culcreuch.com
web: www.culcreuch.com
dir: on B822, 17m W of Stirling

Peacefully located in 1,600 acres of parkland, this ancient castle dates back to 1296. Tastefully restored accommodation is in a mixture of individually themed castle rooms, some with four-poster beds, and more modern courtyard rooms which are suitable for families. Period style public rooms include a bar, serving light meals, a wood-panelled dining room and an elegant lounge.

Rooms 14 (4 annexe) (3 fmly) (4 GF) **D** £102-£160 (incl. bkfst) **Facilities** FTV Fishing Xmas New Year Wi-fi
Conf Class 70 Board 30 Thtr 140 Del from £118.50 to £128 **Parking** 100 **Notes** LB ⊗ Civ Wed 110

STIRLING
Map 21 NS79

Barceló Stirling Highland Hotel
★★★★ 76% HOTEL

☎ 01786 272727 📠 01786 272829
Spittal St FK8 1DU
e-mail: stirling@barcelo-hotels.co.uk
web: www.barcelo-hotels.co.uk
dir: A84 into Stirling. Follow Stirling Castle signs as far as Albert Hall. Left, left again, follow Castle signs

Enjoying a location close to the castle and historic old town, this atmospheric hotel was previously the High School. Public rooms have been converted from the original classrooms and retain many interesting features. Bedrooms are more modern in style and comfortably equipped. Scholars Restaurant serves traditional and international dishes, and the Headmaster's Study is the ideal venue for enjoying a drink.

Rooms 96 (4 fmly) **S** £60-£140; **Facilities** Spa ⊙ Gym
Squash Steam room Dance studio Beauty therapist Xmas
New Year Wi-fi **Conf** Class 80 Board 60 Thtr 100
Services Lift **Parking** 96 **Notes** Civ Wed 100

Express by Holiday Inn Stirling

BUDGET HOTEL

☎ 01786 449922 📠 01786 449932
Springkerse Business Park FK7 7XH
e-mail: info@hiex-stirling.com
web: www.hiexpress.com/stirling
dir: M9/M80 junct 9/A91, Stirling/St Andrews exit. 2.8m, at 4th rdbt, take 2nd exit to sports stadium, 3rd exit to hotel

A modern hotel ideal for families and business travellers. Fresh and uncomplicated, the spacious rooms include Sky TV, power shower and tea and coffee-making facilities. Continental buffet breakfast is included in the room rate; other meals may be taken at the nearby family pub or restaurant. See also the Hotel Groups pages.

Rooms 78 (36 fmly) **Conf** Class 14 Board 18 Thtr 30

Travelodge Stirling (M80)

BUDGET HOTEL

☎ 0871 9846178 📠 01786 817646
Pirnhall Roundabout, Snabhead FK7 8EU
web: www.travelodge.co.uk
dir: M9/M80 junct 9

Travelodge offers good quality, good value, modern accommodation. Ideal for families, the spacious en suite bedrooms include remote-control TV, tea and coffee-making facilities and comfortable beds. Meals can be taken at the nearby family restaurant. See also the Hotel Groups pages.

Rooms 37 **S** fr £29; **D** fr £29

STRATHYRE
Map 20 NN51

INSPECTORS' CHOICE

Creagan House
◉◉ RESTAURANT WITH ROOMS

☎ 01877 384638 📠 01877 384319
FK18 8ND
e-mail: eatandstay@creaganhouse.co.uk
dir: 0.25m N of Strathyre on A84

Originally a farmhouse dating from the 17th century, Creagan House has operated as a restaurant with rooms for many years. The baronial-style dining room provides a wonderful setting for sympathetic cooking. Warm hospitality and attentive service are the highlights of any stay.

Rooms 5 (4 en suite) (1 fmly) (1 GF)

WEST DUNBARTONSHIRE

BALLOCH — Map 20 NS38

De Vere Deluxe Cameron House

De Vere deluxe

★★★★★ 82% ◉◉◉ HOTEL

☎ 01389 755565 📠 01389 759522
G83 8QZ
e-mail: reservations@cameronhouse.co.uk
web: www.devere.co.uk
dir: M8 (W) junct 30 for Erskine Bridge. A82 for Crainlarich. 14m, at rdbt signed Luss, hotel on right

Enjoying an idyllic location on the banks of Loch Lomond in over 100 acres of wooded parkland, this leisure orientated hotel offers spacious, well-equipped accommodation. Bedrooms vary in size and style and many boast wonderful views of the loch. A choice of restaurants, bars and lounges, a host of indoor and outdoor sporting activities, including two golf courses, the 9-hole 'Wee Demon' and the 18-hole championship 'Carrick', are just some of the facilities available. From Wednesday to Sunday, dinner in the Georgian room is a highlight of any stay.

Rooms 96 (9 fmly) **Facilities** ◉ ♨ 9 ♨ Fishing ♨ Gym Squash Outdoor sports Motor boat on Loch Lomond Hairdresser Xmas **Conf** Class 80 Board 80 Thtr 300 **Services** Lift **Parking** 200 **Notes** LB ⊗ Civ Wed 200

Innkeeper's Lodge Loch Lomond

Innkeeper's Lodge

BUDGET HOTEL

☎ 0845 112 6006 📠 0845 112 6294
Balloch Rd G83 8LQ
web: www.innkeeperslodge.com/lochlomond
dir: M8 junct 30 onto M898. Over Erskine Bridge onto A82 for Crainlarich towards Dumbarton/Loch Lomond. Follow National Park signs, right onto A811, left into Davait Rd, left into Balloch Rd. Lodge opposite.

Innkeeper's Lodge represents an exciting, high value concept within the budget hotel market. Comfortable bedrooms provide excellent facilities that include satellite TV and modem points. This carefully restored lodge is in a picturesque setting and has its own unique style and quirky character. Food is served all day, and an extensive, complimentary continental breakfast is offered.

Rooms 12 (4 fmly) **S** £69.95; **D** £69.95 (incl. bkfst)

CLYDEBANK — Map 20 NS47

Beardmore

★★★★ 74% ◉ HOTEL

☎ 0141 951 6000 📠 0141 951 6018
Beardmore St G81 4SA
e-mail: info@beardmore.scot.nhs.uk
dir: M8 junct 19/A814 towards Clydebank/Dumbarton. At Clydebank follow brown tourist signs. Turn left onto Beardmore St & follow hotel signs

Attracting much business and conference custom, this stylish modern hotel lies beside the River Clyde and shares an impressive site with a hospital (although the latter does not intrude). Spacious and imposing public areas include the stylish Arcoona Restaurant providing innovative contemporary cooking. The café bar offers a more extensive choice of informal lighter dishes.

Rooms 166 **S** £65-£99; **D** £65-£99* **Facilities** STV ◉ supervised Gym Sauna Steam room Whirlpool Xmas New Year Wi-fi **Conf** Class 84 Board 27 Thtr 240 **Services** Lift Air con **Parking** 300 **Notes** LB ⊗ Civ Wed 170

DUMBARTON — Map 20 NS37

Travelodge Dumbarton

BUDGET HOTEL

Travelodge

☎ 08719 846 133 📠 01389 765202
Milton G82 2TZ
web: www.travelodge.co.uk
dir: 2m E of Dumbarton, on A82 westbound

Travelodge offers good quality, good value, modern accommodation. Ideal for families, the spacious en suite bedrooms include remote-control TV, tea and coffee-making facilities and comfortable beds. Meals can be taken at the nearby family restaurant. See also the Hotel Groups pages.

Rooms 32 **S** fr £29; **D** fr £29

WEST LOTHIAN

BATHGATE — Map 21 NS96

Express by Holiday Inn Livingston

Express by Holiday Inn

BUDGET HOTEL

☎ 01506 650650 📠 01506 650651
Bathgate Farm Inn, Starlaw Farm EH48 1LQ
e-mail: ebhi-livingston@btconnect.com
web: www.hiexpress.com/livingstonuk
dir: M8 junct 3A. Follow slip road to 1st rdbt, take 1st exit (Bathgate). Over bridge at 2nd rdbt take 1st exit for hotel 200yds on left

A modern hotel ideal for families and business travellers. Fresh and uncomplicated, the spacious rooms include Sky TV, power shower and tea and coffee-making facilities. Continental buffet breakfast is included in the room rate; other meals may be taken at the nearby family pub or restaurant. See also the Hotel Groups pages.

Rooms 74 (54 fmly)

LIVINGSTON — Map 21 NT06

Ramada Livingston

RAMADA

★★★ 🅰 HOTEL

☎ 01506 431222 & 445708 📠 01506 434666
Almondview EH54 6QB
e-mail: sales.livingston@ramadajarvis.co.uk
web: www.ramadajarvis.co.uk
dir: From M8 junct 3 take A899 towards Livingston, exit at Centre Interchange, left at next rdbt, hotel on left

Rooms 120 (13 fmly) (54 GF) (11 smoking) **D** £170* **Facilities** STV ◉ Gym Steam room Sauna Xmas New Year Wi-fi **Conf** Class 55 Board 60 Thtr 100 **Parking** 130 **Notes** ⊗ Civ Wed 50

Travelodge Livingston

BUDGET HOTEL

Travelodge

☎ 08719 846 288 📠 0121 521 6026
Almondvale Cresent EH54 6QX
web: www.travelodge.co.uk
dir: M8 junct 3 onto A899 towards Livingston. At 2nd rdbt right onto A779. At 2nd rdbt left. Lodge on left

Travelodge offers good quality, good value, modern accommodation. Ideal for families, the spacious en suite bedrooms include remote-control TV, tea and coffee-making facilities and comfortable beds. Meals can be taken at the nearby family restaurant. See also the Hotel Groups pages.

Rooms 60 **S** fr £29; **D** fr £29

UPHALL
Map 21 NT07

Macdonald Houstoun House

★★★★ 78% ⊛ HOTEL

☎ 0844 879 9043 🖷 01506 854220
EH52 6JS
e-mail: houstoun@macdonald-hotels.co.uk
web: www.macdonaldhotels.co.uk
dir: M8 junct 3 follow Broxburn signs, straight over rdbt then at mini-rdbt turn right towards Uphall, hotel 1m on right

This historic 17th-century tower house lies in beautifully landscaped grounds and gardens and features a modern leisure club and spa, a choice of dining options, a vaulted cocktail bar and extensive conference and meeting facilities. Stylish bedrooms, some located around a courtyard, are comfortably furnished and well equipped.

Rooms 71 (47 annexe) (12 fmly) (10 GF) **S** £90-£199; **D** £100-£213 (incl. bkfst) **Facilities** Spa STV ⓣ ☺ Gym Health & beauty salon Xmas New Year Wi-fi **Conf** Class 80 Board 80 Thtr 400 Del from £130 to £170 **Parking** 250 **Notes** LB ⊛ Civ Wed 200

WHITBURN
Map 21 NS96

Best Western Hilcroft

★★★ 78% HOTEL

☎ 01501 740818 & 743372 🖷 01501 744013
East Main St EH47 0JU
e-mail: hilcroft@bestwestern.co.uk
dir: M8 junct 4 follow signs for Whitburn, hotel 0.5m on left

This purpose-built, well-established hotel is popular with business travellers and easily accessible from all major transport routes. Smart contemporary public areas feature a spacious and inviting lounge bar and restaurant. Well-equipped bedrooms come in a variety of sizes.

Rooms 32 (7 fmly) (5 GF) **S** £67.50-£95; **D** £77.50-£110 (incl. bkfst) **Facilities** STV FTV New Year Wi-fi **Conf** Class 50 Board 30 Thtr 200 **Parking** 80 **Notes** ⊛ Civ Wed 180

SCOTTISH ISLANDS
ISLE OF ARRAN

BLACKWATERFOOT
Map 20 NR92

Best Western Kinloch

★★★ 80% HOTEL

☎ 01770 860444 🖷 01770 860447
KA27 8ET
e-mail: reservations@kinlochhotel.eclipse.co.uk
dir: Ferry from Ardrossan to Brodick, follow signs for Blackwaterfoot, hotel in centre of village

Well known for providing an authentic island experience, this long established stylish hotel offers an idyllic venue for exploring the beauty of Arran. Smart public areas include a choice of lounges, popular bars and well-presented leisure facilities. Bedrooms vary in size and style but most enjoy panoramic sea views and several family suites offer excellent value. The spacious restaurant provides a wealth of choice, and although it closes during winter, a creative menu is offered in the comfortable bar.

Rooms 37 (7 fmly) (7 GF) **S** £40-£65; **D** £80-£130 (incl. bkfst) **Facilities** STV ⓣ Gym Squash Beauty therapy ♫ New Year Wi-fi **Conf** Class 20 Board 40 Thtr 120 Del from £95 to £150 **Services** Lift **Parking** 2 **Notes** LB ⊛ Civ Wed 60

BRODICK
Map 20 NS03

Auchrannie House

★★★★ 79% ⊛⊛ HOTEL

☎ 01770 302234 🖷 01770 302812
KA27 8BZ
e-mail: info@auchrannie.co.uk
dir: right from Brodick Ferry terminal, through Brodick, 2nd left after Brodick Golf Course clubhouse, hotel 300yds

Set in beautiful surroundings, with acres of mature, landscaped gardens, this Victorian mansion offers a warm welcome. Bedrooms in the original house have period features, while those in the newer wing are more modern but retain a country house feel; all are well equipped and enjoy panoramic views. A choice of eating options includes the fine-dining Garden Restaurant, and the more informal Brasserie. There is an extensive leisure club with a 20-metre indoor pool, gym, sauna and steam room; an extensive range of treatments and therapies is available in the adjacent spa resort.

Rooms 28 (3 fmly) (4 GF) **Facilities** Spa ⓣ supervised ☺ Gym Hair & Beauty salons Aromatherapy Shiatsu Hockey Badminton Xmas New Year Wi-fi Child facilities **Conf** Class 80 Board 50 Thtr 120 **Parking** 50 **Notes** ⊛ Civ Wed 120

INSPECTORS' CHOICE

Kilmichael Country House
★★★ ⊛⊛ COUNTRY HOUSE HOTEL

☎ 01770 302219 🖷 01770 302068
Glen Cloy KA27 8BY
e-mail: enquiries@kilmichael.com
web: www.kilmichael.com
dir: from Brodick ferry terminal towards Lochranza for 1m. Left at golf course, inland between sports field & church, follow signs

Reputed to be the oldest on the island, this lovely house lies in attractive gardens in a quiet glen less than five minutes' drive from the ferry terminal. It has been lovingly restored to create a stylish, elegant country house, adorned with ornaments from around the world. There are two inviting drawing rooms and a bright dining room, serving award-winning contemporary cuisine. The delightful bedrooms are furnished in classical style; some are contained in a pretty courtyard conversion.

Rooms 8 (3 annexe) (7 GF) **S** £95; **D** £150-£190 (incl. bkfst)* **Facilities** Wi-fi **Parking** 14 **Notes** LB No children 12yrs Closed Nov-Feb (ex for prior bookings)

ISLE OF HARRIS

SCARISTA
Map 22 NG09

Scarista House

⊛⊛ RESTAURANT WITH ROOMS

☎ 01859 550238 🖷 01859 550277
HS3 3HX
e-mail: timandpatricia@scaristahouse.com
dir: On A859, 15m S of Tarbert

A former manse, Scarista House is now a haven for food lovers who seek to explore the magnificent island of Harris. The house enjoys breathtaking views of the Atlantic and is just a short stroll from miles of golden sandy beaches. The house is run in a relaxed country-house manner by the friendly hosts. Expect wellies in the hall and masses of books and CDs in one of two lounges.

Continued

SCARISTA continued

Bedrooms are cosy, and delicious set dinners and memorable breakfasts are provided.

Rooms 5 (5 en suite) (2 annexe) (2 GF)

ISLE OF ISLAY

BOWMORE   Map 20 NR35

The Harbour Inn and Restaurant

☺☺ RESTAURANT WITH ROOMS

☎ 01496 810330   ▤ 01496 810990
PA43 7JR
e-mail: info@harbour.inn.com
dir: Next to harbour

No trip to Islay would be complete without experiencing a night or two at the Harbour Inn. The humble whitewashed exterior conceals a sophisticated, quality environment that draws discerning travellers from all over the world. Spacious bedrooms are appointed to a high standard and the conservatory-lounge has stunning views over Loch Indaal to the peaks of Jura. The cosy bar is popular with locals, while the smart dining room showcases some of the finest seafood in British waters. Welcome peat fires burn in cooler months.

Rooms 7 (5 en suite) (1 GF)

PORT ASKAIG   Map 20 NR46

Port Askaig

★★ 64% SMALL HOTEL

☎ 01496 840245   ▤ 01496 840295
PA46 7RD
e-mail: hotel@portaskaig.co.uk
web: www.portaskaig.co.uk
dir: at ferry terminal

The building of this endearing family-run hotel dates back to the 18th-century. The lounge provides fine views over the Sound of Islay to Jura, and there is a choice of bars that are popular with locals. Traditional dinners are served in the bright restaurant and a full range of bar snacks and meals is also available. The bedrooms are smart and comfortable.

Rooms 8 (1 fmly) (8 GF) **Parking** 15 **Notes** LB

ISLE OF MULL

CRAIGNURE   Map 20 NM73

Isle of Mull Hotel

CRERAR

★★★ 74% HOTEL

☎ 0870 950 6267   ▤ 01680 812462
PA65 6BB
e-mail: isleofmull@crerarhotels.com
web: www.crerarhotels.com
dir: Right from ferry. In 0.5m turn right at hotel sign

With gardens stretching down to the shore, this purpose-built hotel gazes out over beautiful Craignure Bay and is only half a mile from the ferry terminal; a shore path connects the two. A choice of comfortable lounges, two bars and the spacious restaurant, as well as the bedrooms, all enjoy the splendid panoramic views.

Rooms 86 (9 fmly) (18 GF) **S** fr £75; **D** fr £150 (incl. bkfst)* **Facilities** Spa ⓣ supervised Gym Sauna Steam room Hairdresser Children's pool Xmas New Year Wi-fi **Conf** Class 85 Board 60 Thtr 150 Del from £95 to £110* **Parking** 36 **Notes** LB Civ Wed

TOBERMORY   Map 22 NM55

INSPECTORS' CHOICE

Highland Cottage

★★★ ☺☺ SMALL HOTEL

☎ 01688 302030
Breadalbane St PA75 6PD
e-mail: davidandjo@highlandcottage.co.uk
web: www.highlandcottage.co.uk
dir: A848 Craignure/Fishnish ferry terminal, pass Tobermory signs, straight on at mini rdbt across narrow bridge, turn right. Hotel on right opposite fire station

Providing the highest level of natural and unassuming hospitality, this delightful little gem lies high above the island's capital. Don't be fooled by its side street location, a stunning view over the bay is just a few metres away. 'A country house hotel in town' it is an Aladdin's Cave of collectables and treasures, as well as masses of books and magazines. There are two inviting lounges, one with an honesty bar. The cosy dining room offers memorable dinners and splendid breakfasts. Bedrooms are individual; some have four-posters and all are comprehensively equipped to include TVs and music centres.

Rooms 6 (1 GF) **S** £120-£165; **D** £140-£185 (incl. bkfst)* **Facilities** Wi-fi **Parking** 6 **Notes** LB No children 10yrs Closed Nov-Feb

Western Isles

★★★ 72% HOTEL

OXFORD
HOTELS & INNS

☎ 01688 302012   ▤ 01688 302297
PA75 6PR
e-mail: wihotel@aol.com
web: www.oxfordhotelsandinns.com
dir: from ferry follow signs to Tobermory. Over 1st mini-rdbt in Tobermory then over small bridge & immediate right & follow road to T-junct. Right again then keep left & take 1st left for hotel at top of hill on right

Built in 1883 and standing high above the village, this hotel enjoys spectacular views over the harbour and the Sound of Mull. Public rooms range from the classical drawing room and restaurant to the bright modern conservatory bar/bistro. Bedrooms come in a variety of styles; the superior rooms are impressive and include a suite complete with its own piano.

Rooms 28 **Facilities** New Year **Conf** Class 40 Board 30 Thtr 60 **Parking** 15 **Notes** LB

Tobermory

★★ 76% ☺ HOTEL

☎ 01688 302091   ▤ 01688 302254
53 Main St PA75 6NT
e-mail: tobhotel@tinyworld.co.uk
web: www.thetobermoryhotel.com
dir: on waterfront, overlooking Tobermory Bay

This friendly hotel, with its pretty pink frontage, sits on the seafront amid other brightly coloured, picture-postcard buildings. There is a comfortable and relaxing lounge where drinks are served (there is no bar) prior to dining in the stylish restaurant. Bedrooms come in a variety of sizes; all are bright and vibrant.

Rooms 16 (3 fmly) (2 GF) **Facilities** supervised supervised New Year **Notes** LB Closed Xmas

SHETLAND

LERWICK
Map 24 HU44

Lerwick

★★★ 73% HOTEL

☎ 01595 692166 📠 01595 694419
15 South Rd ZE1 0RB
e-mail: reception@lerwickhotel.co.uk
web: www.shetlandhotels.com
dir: near town centre. On main road from airport (25m)

Enjoying fine views across Breiwick Bay from the restaurant and some of the bedrooms, this purpose-built hotel appeals to tourists and business guests alike. Bedrooms, which vary in size and aspect, are attractively furnished and family accommodation is available. The Breiwick restaurant has fine sea views, and there is also a more informal brasserie.

Rooms 34 (3 fmly) **S** fr £85; **D** fr £105 (incl. bkfst)*
Facilities FTV Wi-fi **Conf** Class 40 Board 26 Thtr 100
Parking 50 **Notes** LB ⊗ Civ Wed 100

Shetland

★★★ 71% HOTEL

☎ 01595 695515 📠 01595 695828
Holmsgarth Rd ZE1 0PW
e-mail: reception@shetlandhotel.co.uk
dir: opposite ferry terminal, on main road N from town centre

This purpose-built hotel, situated opposite the main ferry terminal, offers spacious and comfortable bedrooms on three floors. Two dining options are available, including the informal Oasis bistro and Ninians Restaurant. Service is prompt and friendly.

Rooms 64 (4 fmly) **S** £85; **D** £99 (incl. bkfst)
Facilities FTV Wi-fi **Conf** Class 75 Board 50 Thtr 300
Services Lift **Parking** 150 **Notes** LB ⊗ Civ Wed 200

ISLE OF SKYE

ARDVASAR
Map 22 NG60

Ardvasar Hotel

★★ 71% HOTEL

☎ 01471 844223 📠 01471 844495
Sleat IV45 8RS
e-mail: richard@ardvasar-hotel.demon.co.uk
web: www.ardvasarhotel.com
dir: from ferry, 500mtrs & turn left

The Isle of Skye is dotted with cosy, welcoming hotels that make touring the island easy and convenient. This hotel ranks highly amongst its peers thanks to great hospitality and a preservation of community spirit. The hotel sits less than five minutes' drive from the Mallaig ferry and provides comfortable bedrooms and a cosy bar lounge for residents. Seafood is prominent on menus, and meals can be enjoyed in either the popular bar or the attractive dining room.

Rooms 10 (4 fmly) **Facilities** ♫ Xmas New Year
Conf Board 24 Thtr 50 **Parking** 30

See advert on this page

BROADFORD
Map 22 NG62

Dunollie

★★ 72% HOTEL

OXFORD
HOTELS & INNS

☎ 01471 822253 📠 01471 822060
IV49 9AE
e-mail: reservations.dunollie@ohiml.com
web: www.oxfordhotelsandinns.com
dir: A87, after crossing Skye Bridge left at rdbt, 7m to Broadford, hotel on right

This popular hotel, with magnificent views across the sea to Loch Kishorn and the scenic Applecross peninsula, is ideally situated to explore the island. Bedrooms differ in style and size with the front-facing rooms offering magnificent sea views. The restaurant, popular with local and tourists alike, is an ideal venue to watch the sun set of an evening. The cosy bar has a fine collection of malt whiskies.

Rooms 84 (4 fmly) **Facilities** ♫ **Parking** 18 **Notes** LB

COLBOST
Map 22 NG24

INSPECTORS' CHOICE

The Three Chimneys and The House Over-By
◉◉◉ RESTAURANT WITH ROOMS

☎ 01470 511258 📠 01470 511358
IV55 8ZT
e-mail: eatandstay@threechimneys.co.uk
dir: 4m W of Dunvegan village on B884 signed Glendale

A visit to this delightful property and restaurant will make a trip to Skye even more memorable. Shirley Spear's stunning food is the result of a deft approach using quality local ingredients. Breakfast is an impressive array of local fish, meats and cheeses, served with fresh home baking and home-made preserves. The stylish, thoughtfully equipped bedrooms in the House Over-By have spacious en suites and wonderful views across Loch Dunvegan.

Rooms 6 (6 en suite) (1 fmly) (6 GF)

ISLEORNSAY
Map 22 NG71

Duisdale House
★★★★ 74% SMALL HOTEL

☎ 01471 833202 📠 01471 833404
IV43 8QW
e-mail: info@duisdale.com
dir: 5m S of Bradford on A851 towards Armadale.

This grand Victorian house stands in its own landscaped gardens overlooking the Sound of Sleat on the beautiful Isle of Skye. The hotel has a contemporary chic style which compliments the original features of the house. Each bedroom is individually designed and the superior rooms have four-poster beds. The elegant lounge has sumptuous sofas, original artwork and blazing log fires in the colder months.

Rooms 17 (1 fmly) **S** £65-£140; **D** £118-£200 (incl. bkfst)* **Facilities** Sailing on hotel's private yacht Xmas New Year Wi-fi **Conf** Board 28 **Parking** 30 **Notes** LB ⊗ No children 5yrs

Toravaig House Hotel
★★★ 80% ◉ SMALL HOTEL

☎ 0845 055 1117 & 01471 833231 📠 01471 833231
Knock Bay IV44 8RE
e-mail: info@skyehotel.co.uk
web: www.skyehotel.co.uk
dir: cross Skye Bridge, turn left at Broadford onto A851, hotel 11m on left. (Ferry to Armadale, take A851, hotel 4m on right

Set in two acres and enjoying panoramic views to the Knoydart Hills, this hotel is a haven of peace, with stylish, well-equipped and beautifully decorated bedrooms. Here is an inviting lounge complete with deep sofas and an elegant dining room where delicious meals are the order of the day. The hotel provides a sea-going yacht for guests' exclusive use.

Toravaig House Hotel

Rooms 9 **S** £60-£125; **D** £118-£170 (incl. bkfst)* **Facilities** STV Daily excursions for residents on hotel yacht Xmas New Year **Parking** 20 **Notes** ⊗ Civ Wed 18

See advert on this page

Hotel Eilean Iarmain
★★ 80% ◉◉ SMALL HOTEL

THE CIRCLE

☎ 01471 833332 📠 01471 833275
IV43 8QR
e-mail: hotel@eileaniarmain.co.uk
web: www.eileaniarmain.co.uk
dir: A851, A852, right to Isleornsay harbour

A hotel of charm and character, this 19th-century former inn lies by the pier and enjoys fine views across the sea lochs. Bedrooms are individual and retain a traditional style, and a stable block has been converted into four delightful suites. Public rooms are cosy and inviting, and the dining room has an attractive extension.

Rooms 16 (6 fmly) (4 GF) **Facilities** Fishing Shooting Exhibitions Whisky tasting ♪ Xmas **Conf** Class 30 Board 25 Thtr 50 **Parking** 35 **Notes** LB Civ Wed 80

See advert on opposite page

Kinloch Lodge

☎ 01471 833214 & 833333 📄 01471 833277
IV43 8QY
e-mail: reservations@kinloch-lodge.co.uk
web: www.kinloch-lodge.co.uk
dir: 6m S of Broadford on A851, 10m N of Armadale on A851

Currently the rating for this establishment is not confirmed. This may be due to a change of ownership or because it has only recently joined the AA rating scheme. For further details please see the AA website: www.theAA.com

Rooms 14 (1 GF) **D** £150-£345 (incl. bkfst) **Facilities** FTV Fishing New Year Wi-fi **Parking** 40 **Notes** LB

PORTREE   Map 22 NG44

Cuillin Hills

★★★★ 73% ◉◉ HOTEL

☎ 01478 612003 📄 01478 613092
IV51 9QU
e-mail: info@cuillinhills-hotel-skye.co.uk
web: www.cuillinhills-hotel-skye.co.uk
dir: turn right 0.25m N of Portree off A855. Follow hotel signs

This imposing building enjoys a superb location overlooking Portree Bay and the Cuillin Hills. Accommodation is provided in smart, well-equipped rooms that are generally spacious. Some bedrooms are found in an adjacent building. Public areas include a split-level restaurant that takes advantage of the views. Service is particularly attentive.

Rooms 27 (7 annexe) (3 fmly) (8 GF) **S** £65-£80; **D** £110-£280 (incl. bkfst)* **Facilities** STV Xmas New Year Wi-fi **Conf** Class 70 Board 40 Thtr 160 Del from £100 to £180* **Parking** 56 **Notes** LB ❀ Civ Wed 70

See advert on page 666

Bosville

★★★ 80% ◉◉ HOTEL

☎ 01478 612846 📄 01478 613434
Bosville Ter IV51 9DG
e-mail: bosville@macleodhotels.co.uk
web: www.macleodhotels.com
dir: A87 signed Portree, then A855 into town. Cross over zebra crossing, follow road to left.

This stylish, popular hotel enjoys fine views over the harbour. Bedrooms are furnished to a high specification and have a fresh, contemporary feel. Public areas include a smart bar, bistro and the Chandlery restaurant where fantastic local produce is treated with respect and refreshing restraint.

Rooms 19 (2 fmly) **S** £59-£120; **D** £79-£250 (incl. bkfst)* **Facilities** STV Use of nearby leisure club payable Xmas New Year Wi-fi **Conf** Class 20 Board 20 Thtr 20 Del from £140 to £180* **Parking** 10 **Notes** Civ Wed 80

See advert on page 667

PORTREE continued

Rosedale

★★★ 73% ⬡ HOTEL

☎ 01478 613131 📠 01478 612531
Beaumont Crescent IV51 9DB
e-mail: rosedalehotelsky@aol.com
web: www.rosedalehotelskye.co.uk
dir: follow directions to village centre & harbour

The atmosphere is wonderfully warm at this delightful family-run waterfront hotel. A labyrinth of stairs and corridors connects the comfortable lounges, bar and charming restaurant, which are set on different levels. The restaurant offers fine views of the bay. Modern bedrooms offer a good range of amenities.

Rooms 18 (1 fmly) (3 GF) **S** £30-£60; **D** £60-£130 (incl. bkfst)* **Parking** 2 **Notes** LB Closed Nov-mid Mar

---

SKEABOST BRIDGE **Map 22 NG44**

Skeabost Country House

Ⓤ   OXFORD HOTELS & INNS

☎ 01470 532202 📠 01470 532761
IV51 9NP
e-mail: reservations.skeabost@ohiml.com
web: www.oxfordhotelsandinns.com

Currently the rating for this establishment is not confirmed. This may be due to a change of ownership or because it has only recently joined the AA rating scheme. For further details please see the AA website: www.theAA.com

Rooms 14 (5 GF) **Facilities** STV FTV ♿ ฿ 9 Fishing Xmas New Year Wi-fi Child facilities **Conf** Class 20 Board 20 Thtr 40 Del from £149 to £198* **Parking** 40 **Notes** Civ Wed 80

STRUAN **Map 22 NG33**

INSPECTORS' CHOICE

Ullinish Country Lodge

⬡⬡⬡ RESTAURANT WITH ROOMS

☎ 01470 572214 📠 01470 572341
IV56 8FD
e-mail: ullinish@theisleofskye.co.uk
dir: N on A863

Set in some of Scotland's most dramatic landscape, with views of the Black Cuillin and MacLeod's Tables, Ullinish Country Lodge has lochs on three sides. Samual Johnson and James Boswell stayed here in 1773 and were impressed with the hospitality even then! Hosts Brian and Pam hope to extend the same welcome to their guests today. As you would expect, all bedrooms have amazing views, and come with half-tester beds. The restaurant's offerings are very impressive.

Rooms 6

Wales

Nant Gwynant, Snowdonia National Park

AMLWCH
Map 14 SH49

Lastra Farm

★★ 76% SMALL HOTEL

☎ 01407 830906 🖹 01407 832522
Penrhyd LL68 9TF
e-mail: booking@lastra-hotel.com
web: www.lastra-hotel.com
dir: after 'Welcome to Amlwch' sign turn left. Straight across main road, left at T-junct on to Rhosgoch Rd

This 17th-century farmhouse offers pine-furnished, colourfully decorated bedrooms. There is also a comfortable lounge and a cosy bar. A wide range of good-value food is available either in the restaurant or Granary's Bistro. The hotel can cater for functions in a separate purpose-built suite.

Rooms 8 (3 annexe) (1 fmly) (3 GF) **Facilities** Wi-fi
Conf Class 80 Board 30 Thtr 100 **Parking** 40
Notes Civ Wed 100

BEAUMARIS
Map 14 SH67

Best Western Bulkeley Hotel

★★★ 77% HOTEL

☎ 01248 810415 🖹 01248 810146
Castle St LL58 8AW
e-mail: reception@bulkeleyhotel.co.uk
dir: From A55 junct 8a to Beaumaris. Hotel in town centre

A Grade I listed hotel built in 1832, the Bulkeley is just 100 yards from the 13th-century Beaumaris Castle in the centre of the town. The hotel commands fine views from many rooms, and the friendly staff create a relaxed atmosphere. Well-equipped bedrooms are generally spacious, with pretty fabrics and wallpapers. There is a choice of bars and an all-day coffee lounge.

Rooms 43 (5 fmly) **S** £50-£90; **D** £90-£140 (incl. bkfst)
Facilities New Year Wi-fi **Conf** Class 40 Board 25
Thtr 180 Del from £85 to £101 **Services** Lift **Parking** 25
Notes LB Civ Wed 140

Bishopsgate House

★★ 84% ® SMALL HOTEL

☎ 01248 810302 🖹 01248 810166
54 Castle St LL58 8BB
e-mail: hazel@bishopsgatehotel.co.uk
dir: from Menai Bridge onto A545 to Beaumaris. Hotel on left in main street

This immaculately maintained, privately owned and personally run small hotel dates back to 1760. It features fine examples of wood panelling and a Chinese Chippendale staircase. Thoughtfully furnished bedrooms are attractively decorated and two have four-poster beds. Quality cooking is served in the elegant restaurant and guests have a comfortable lounge and cosy bar to relax in.

Rooms 9 **S** £55; **D** £88-£100 (incl. bkfst)* **Parking** 8
Notes LB

HOLYHEAD
Map 14 SH28

Travelodge Holyhead

BUDGET HOTEL

☎ 0871 984 6342
Kingsland Rd LL65 2LB
web: www.travelodge.co.uk
dir: B4545 onto Kingsland Rd, hotel on left

Travelodge offers good quality, good value, modern accommodation. Ideal for families, the spacious en suite bedrooms include remote-control TV, tea and coffee-making facilities and comfortable beds. Meals can be taken at the nearby family restaurant. See also the Hotel Groups pages.

Rooms 54 **S** fr £29; **D** fr £29

TREARDDUR BAY
Map 14 SH27

Trearddur Bay

WELSH RAREBITS

★★★ 80% HOTEL

☎ 01407 860301 🖹 01407 861181
LL65 2UN
e-mail: enquiries@trearddurbayhotel.co.uk
dir: from A5 towards Holyhead left at lights onto B4545 towards Trearddur Bay, (Power garage on right), left opp garage, hotel on right

Facilities at this fine modern hotel include extensive function and conference rooms, an indoor swimming pool and a games room. Bedrooms are well equipped, many

have sea views, and suites are available. An all-day bar serves a wide range of snacks and lighter meals, supplemented by a cocktail bar and the more formal restaurant.

Rooms 40 (6 annexe) (7 fmly) **Facilities** ® Sailing Shooting Horse riding Fishing Diving Golf packages ♫ New Year Wi-fi **Conf** Class 100 Board 78 Thtr 190 **Parking** 200 **Notes** ⊗ Civ Wed 150

BRIDGEND
Map 9 SS97

Coed-Y-Mwstwr

★★★★ 74% COUNTRY HOUSE HOTEL

☎ 01656 860621 🖹 01656 863122
Coychurch CF35 6AF
e-mail: hotel@coed-y-mwstwr.com
web: www.coed-y-mwstwr.com
dir: exit A473 at Coychurch, right at petrol station. Follow signs at top of hill

This former Victorian mansion, set in 17 acres of grounds, is an inviting retreat. Public areas are full of character featuring an impressive contemporary restaurant. Bedrooms have individual styles with a good range of extras, and include two full suites. Facilities include a large and attractive function suite with syndicate rooms, gym and outdoor swimming pool.

Rooms 28 (2 fmly) **S** £98-£122; **D** £125-£165 (incl. bkfst)* **Facilities** STV ᛒ ≋ Gym Xmas New Year Wi-fi **Conf** Class 120 Board 50 Thtr 180 **Services** Lift **Parking** 100 **Notes** LB ⊗ Civ Wed 200

Best Western Heronston

★★★ 73% HOTEL

☎ 01656 668811 & 666085 🖹 01656 767391
Ewenny Rd CF35 5AW
e-mail: reservations@bestwesternheronstonhotel.co.uk
web: www.bw-heronstonhotel.co.uk
dir: M4 junct 35, follow signs for Porthcawl, at 5th rdbt turn left towards Ogmore-by-Sea (B4265), hotel 200yds on left

Situated within easy reach of the town centre and the M4, this large modern hotel offers spacious well-equipped accommodation, including ground floor rooms. Public areas include an open-plan lounge/bar, attractive restaurant and a smart leisure and fitness club. The hotel also has a choice of function/conference rooms and ample parking is available.

Rooms 75 (4 fmly) (37 GF) (8 smoking) **Facilities** STV ⊗ ✗ Gym Steam room Sauna Solarium Xmas New Year Wi-fi **Conf** Class 80 Board 60 Thtr 250 **Services** Lift **Parking** 160 **Notes**

Express by Holiday Inn Bridgend

BUDGET HOTEL

☎ 01656 646200 🖷 01656 663929
The Derwyn CF32 9SH
e-mail: ebhi-bridgend@btconnect.com
web: www.hiexpress.com/exbridgend

A modern hotel ideal for families and business travellers. Fresh and uncomplicated, the spacious rooms include Sky TV, power shower and tea and coffee-making facilities. Continental buffet breakfast is included in the room rate; other meals may be taken at the nearby family pub or restaurant. See also the Hotel Groups pages.

Rooms 68 (35 fmly) **Conf** Class 20 Board 16 Thtr 30

PENCOED — Map 9 SS98

St Mary's Hotel & Country Club

★★★ 71% HOTEL

☎ 01656 861100 🖷 01656 863400
St Marys Golf Club CF35 5EA
e-mail: stmarysgolfhotel@btinternet.com
dir: M4 junct 35, on A473

This charming 16th-century farmhouse has been converted and extended into a modern and restful hotel, surrounded by its own two golf courses. The well equipped bedrooms are generously appointed and most feature whirlpool baths. Guests have a choice of bars which prove popular with club members too, plus there's a good range of dining options.

Rooms 24 (19 fmly) (10 GF) **S** £69.50-£95; **D** £84-£115 (incl. bkfst)* **Facilities** STV ⚒ ⅃ 30 Putt green Floodlit driving range New Year Wi-fi **Conf** Class 60 Board 40 Thtr 120 Del from £105 to £150* **Parking** 140 **Notes** LB ⊗ Civ Wed 120

Travelodge Bridgend Pencoed

BUDGET HOTEL

☎ 08719 846 049 🖷 01656 864404
Old Mill, Felindre Rd CF3 5HU
web: www.travelodge.co.uk
dir: on A473

Travelodge offers good quality, good value, modern accommodation. Ideal for families, the spacious en suite bedrooms include remote-control TV, tea and coffee-making facilities and comfortable beds. Meals can be taken at the nearby family restaurant. See also the Hotel Groups pages.

Rooms 39 **S** fr £29; **D** fr £29

PORTHCAWL — Map 9 SS87

Atlantic

★★★ 72% HOTEL

☎ 01656 785011 🖷 01656 771877
West Dr CF36 3LT
e-mail: enquiries@atlantichotelporthcawl.co.uk
dir: M4 junct 35/37, follow signs to Porthcawl. Then follow Seafront/Promenade signs

This hotel is located on the seafront, a short walk from the town centre. Guests can enjoy sea views from the sun terrace, bright conservatory and some of the bedrooms, which are well equipped and tastefully decorated. A welcoming atmosphere is created here especially in the restaurant where a good selection of tempting dishes is available.

Rooms 18 (2 fmly) **S** £70-£80; **D** £90-£100 (incl. bkfst)* **Facilities** Xmas **Conf** Class 50 Board 25 Thtr 50 **Services** Lift **Parking** 20 **Notes** ⊗

Seabank

★★★ 68% HOTEL

☎ 01656 782261 🖷 01656 785363
The Promenade CF36 3LU
e-mail: info@seabankhotel.co.uk
dir: M4 junct 37, follow A4229 to seafront

This large, privately owned hotel stands on the promenade. The majority of the well-equipped bedrooms enjoy panoramic sea views and several have four-poster beds. There is a spacious restaurant, a lounge bar and a choice of lounges. The hotel is a popular venue for coach-tour parties, as well as weddings and conferences. There is ample parking around the hotel.

Rooms 67 (2 fmly) (5 smoking) **Facilities** Gym ⅃ Xmas New Year **Conf** Class 150 Board 70 Thtr 250 **Services** Lift **Parking** 140 **Notes** ⊗ Civ Wed 100

SARN PARK MOTORWAY SERVICE AREA (M4) — Map 9 SS98

Days Inn Cardiff West

BUDGET HOTEL

☎ 01656 659218 🖷 01656 768665
Sarn Park Services CF32 9RW
e-mail: sarn.hotel@welcomebreak.co.uk
web: www.welcomebreak.co.uk
dir: M4 junct 36

This modern building offers accommodation in smart, spacious and well-equipped bedrooms, suitable for families and business travellers, and all with en suite bathrooms. Continental breakfast is available and other refreshments may be taken at the nearby family restaurant. See also the Hotel Groups pages.

Rooms 40 (39 fmly) (20 GF) **S** £39-£59; **D** £49-£69*

CAERPHILLY

BLACKWOOD — Map 9 ST19

Maes Manor

★★★ 71% COUNTRY HOUSE HOTEL

☎ 01495 220011 🖷 01495 228217
NP12 0AG
e-mail: info@maesmanor.com
dir: A4048 to Tredega. At Pontllanfraith left at rdbt, along Blackwood High St. In 1.25m left at Rock Inn. Hotel 400yds on left

Standing high above the town, this 19th-century manor house is set in nine acres of gardens and woodland. Bedrooms are located either in the main house or an adjacent coach house and are attractively decorated with co-ordinated furnishings. As well as the popular restaurant, public rooms include a choice of bars, a lounge/lobby area and a large function room.

Rooms 28 (14 annexe) (6 fmly) (8 GF) **Facilities** Xmas New Year Wi-fi **Conf** Class 200 Board 50 Thtr 200 **Parking** 175 **Notes** LB ⊗ Closed 24-25 Dec Civ Wed 200

See advert on page 672

MAESYCWMMER · Map 9 SO19

Bryn Meadows Golf, Hotel & Spa

★★★★ 79% HOTEL

☎ 01495 225590 · 🖨 01495 228272
Maesycwmmer, Ystrad Mynach CF82 7SN
e-mail: reception@brynmeadows.co.uk
web: www.brynmeadows.com
dir: A472 signed Ystrad Mynach. 1m before Ystrad
Mynach off Crown rdbt signed for golf course

Surrounded by its own mature parkland and 18-hole golf
course, this impressive hotel, leisure and function
complex provides a range of high quality, well equipped
bedrooms. Several rooms have their own balconies or
patio areas. Public areas are attractively appointed and
include a pleasant restaurant, which like many of the
bedrooms, enjoys impressive views of the golf course and
beyond. The hotel has impressive function facilities and
is a popular venue for weddings.

Rooms 43 (1 annexe) (4 fmly) (21 GF) **S** £95-£130;
D £115-£160 (incl. bkfst)* **Facilities** Spa FTV 🔄
supervised 🏊 18 Putt green Gym Sauna Steam room
Outdoor hot tub Aromatherapy suite New Year Wi-fi
Conf Class 70 Board 60 Thtr 120 **Services** Air con
Parking 120 **Notes** LB ⊗ Closed 25 Dec Civ Wed 250

CARDIFF

CARDIFF · Map 9 ST17

See also **Barry (Vale of Glamorgan)**

St David's Hotel & Spa

★★★★★ 76% HOTEL

☎ 029 2045 4045 · 🖨 029 2031 3075
Havannah St CF10 5SD
e-mail: st.davids.reservations@principal-hotels.com
web: www.thestdavidshotel.com
dir: M4 junct 33/A4232 for 9m, for Techniquest, at top
exit slip road, 1st left at rdbt, 1st right

This imposing contemporary building sits in a prime
position on Cardiff Bay and has a seven-storey atrium
creating a dramatic impression. Leading from the atrium
are the practically designed and comfortable bedrooms.
Tides Restaurant, adjacent to the stylish cocktail bar, has
views across the water to Penarth, and there is a quiet
first-floor lounge for guests seeking peace and quiet. A
well-equipped spa and extensive business areas
complete the package.

Rooms 132 (6 fmly) **S** £105-£260; **D** £105-£260*
Facilities Spa 🔄 supervised Gym Fitness studio
Hydrotherapy pool ♪ Xmas New Year Wi-fi
Conf Class 110 Board 76 Thtr 270 Del from £165 to
£275* **Services** Lift Air con **Parking** 80 (charged)
Notes LB ⊗ Civ Wed 230

Park Plaza Cardiff

★★★★ 80% ⊕ HOTEL

☎ 029 2011 1111 & 2011 1101 · 🖨 029 2011 1112
Greyfriars Rd CF10 3AL
e-mail: ppcres@parkplazahotels.co.uk
web: www.parkplazacardiff.com
dir: From M4 follow city centre (A470) signs. Left into
Boulevard de Nantes then immediately left into Greyfriars
Rd. Hotel on left by New Theatre

A smart hotel located in the city centre that features
eye-catching, contemporary decor, a state-of-the-art
indoor leisure facility, extensive conference and
banqueting facilities and the spacious Laguna kitchen
and bar. Bedrooms are also up-to-the-minute in style and
feature a host of extras including a private bar, a safe
and modem points.

Rooms 129 (20 fmly) **S** £90-£310; **D** £110-£410 (incl.
bkfst) **Facilities** Spa FTV 🔄 Gym Dance studio Steam
room Gym Xmas New Year Wi-fi **Conf** Class 80 Board 60
Thtr 150 Del from £170 to £185* **Services** Lift Air con
Notes LB ⊗ Civ Wed 120

Mercure Holland House Hotel & Spa

★★★★ 77% ◉◉ HOTEL

☎ 029 2043 5000 📠 029 2048 8894
24/26 Newport Rd CF24 0DD
e-mail: h6622@accor.com
web: www.mercure-uk.com
dir: M4 junct 33/A4232 to city centre, turn right at lights facing prison, straight through next lights, hotel car park end of lane facing Magistrates Court.

Conveniently located just a few minutes' walk from the city centre, this exciting hotel combines contemporary styling with a genuinely friendly welcome. Bedrooms, including five luxurious suites, are spacious and include many welcome extras. A state-of-the-art leisure club and spa is available in addition to a large function room. An eclectic menu provides a varied range of freshly prepared, quality dishes.

Rooms 165 (80 fmly) **S** £90-£190; **D** £95-£200 (incl. bkfst)* **Facilities** Spa STV 🏊 supervised Gym Wi-fi **Conf** Class 140 Board 42 Thtr 700 Del from £125 to £215* **Services** Lift Air con **Parking** 90 (charged) **Notes** LB ⊗ Civ Wed 500

Novotel Cardiff Central

★★★★ 76% HOTEL

☎ 029 2047 5000 📠 029 2048 1491
Schooner Way, Atlantic Wharf CF10 4RT
e-mail: h5982@accor.com
web: www.novotel.com
dir: M4 junct 33/A4232 follow Cardiff Bay signs to Atlantic Wharf

Situated in the heart of the city's redevelopment area, this hotel is equally convenient for the centre and Cardiff Bay. Bedrooms vary between standard rooms in the modern extension and executive rooms in the original wing. The hotel offers good seating space in public

rooms, a popular leisure club and the innovative 'Elements' dining concept.

Rooms 138 (100 fmly) **Facilities** 🏊 supervised Gym Wi-fi **Conf** Class 90 Board 65 Thtr 250 **Services** Lift Air con **Parking** 120 **Notes** ⊗ Civ Wed 250

Cardiff Marriott Hotel

★★★★ 75% HOTEL

☎ 029 2039 9944 📠 029 2039 5578
Mill Ln CF10 1EZ
web: www.cardiffmarriott.co.uk
dir: M4 junct 29 follow signs city centre. Turn left into High Street opposite Castle, then 2nd left, at bottom of High St into Mill Lane

A centrally located modern hotel, with spacious public areas and a good range of services, is ideal for business or leisure. Eating options include the informal Chats Café Bar and the contemporary Mediterrano Restaurant. The well-equipped bedrooms are comfortable and air conditioned. The leisure suite includes a gym and a good sized pool.

Rooms 184 (68 fmly) **S** fr £125; **D** fr £125 **Facilities** STV 🏊 Gym Steam room Sauna Xmas New Year Wi-fi **Conf** Class 200 Board 100 Thtr 400 Del from £140 to £165 **Services** Lift Air con **Parking** 146 (charged) **Notes** LB ⊗ Civ Wed 200

Copthorne Hotel Cardiff-Caerdydd

★★★★ 72% ◉◉ HOTEL

☎ 029 2059 9100 📠 029 2059 9080
Copthorne Way, Culverhouse Cross CF5 6DA
e-mail: reservations.cardiff@millenniumhotels.co.uk
web: www.millenniumhotels.co.uk
dir: M4 junct 33, A4232 for 2.5m towards Cardiff West. Then A48 W to Cowbridge

A comfortable, popular and modern hotel, conveniently located for the airport and city. Bedrooms are a good size and some have a private lounge. Public areas are smartly presented and include a gym, pool, meeting rooms and a comfortable restaurant with views of the adjacent lake.

Rooms 135 (7 fmly) (27 GF) **S** £59-£250; **D** £59-£250 **Facilities** STV 🏊 Gym Sauna Steam room 🎵 New Year Wi-fi **Conf** Class 140 Board 80 Thtr 300 Del from £95 to £175 **Services** Lift **Parking** 225 **Notes** LB Civ Wed 200

Barceló Cardiff Angel Hotel

★★★★ 70% HOTEL

☎ 029 2064 9200 📠 029 2039 6212
Castle St CF10 1SZ
e-mail: angel@barcelo-hotels-co.uk
web: www.barcelo-hotels.co.uk
dir: opposite Cardiff Castle

This well-established hotel is in the heart of the city overlooking the castle. All bedrooms offer air conditioning and are decorated and furnished to a high standard. Public areas include an impressive lobby, a modern restaurant and a selection of conference rooms. There is limited parking at the rear of the hotel.

Rooms 102 (3 fmly) **S** £65-£145; **Facilities** Xmas New Year Wi-fi **Conf** Class 120 Board 50 Thtr 300 **Services** Lift Air con **Parking** 60 (charged) **Notes** Civ Wed 200

CARDIFF continued

Manor Parc Country Hotel & Restaurant

★★★ 73% HOTEL

☎ 029 2069 3723   📄 029 2061 4624
Thornhill Rd, Thornhill CF14 9UA
e-mail: enquiry@manorparc.com
dir: M4 junct 32. Turn left at lights, pass Den Inn. Take next left, left at lights on A469

Set in open countryside on the outskirts of Cardiff, this delightful hotel retains traditional values of hospitality and service. Bedrooms, including a suite, are spacious and attractive, whilst public areas comprise a comfortable lounge and a restaurant, with a magnificent lantern ceiling, that overlooks the well-tended grounds.

Rooms 21 (4 fmly) (1 GF) **Facilities** ⚲ **Conf** Class 80 Board 50 Thtr 120 **Parking** 100 **Notes** ✖ Closed 26 Dec-2 Jan Civ Wed 100

Best Western St Mellons Hotel & Country Club

★★★ 72% HOTEL

☎ 01633 680355   📄 01633 680399
Castleton CF3 2XR
e-mail: reservations.stmellons@ohiml.com
web: www.oxfordhotelsandinns.com
dir: M4 junct 28 follow A48 Castleton/St Mellons. Hotel on left past garage

This former Regency mansion has been tastefully converted into an elegant hotel with an adjoining leisure complex that attracts a strong local following. Bedrooms, some in purpose-built wings, are spacious and smart. The public areas retain their pleasing architectural proportions and include relaxing lounges and a restaurant serving a varied choice of carefully prepared and enjoyable dishes.

Rooms 41 (20 annexe) (9 fmly) (5 GF) **Facilities** Spa 🖲 Gym Squash Beauty salon Xmas **Conf** Class 185 Board 179 Thtr 480 **Parking** 100 **Notes** Civ Wed 160

Holiday Inn Cardiff City

★★★ 🅰 HOTEL

☎ 0870 400 8140   📄 029 2023 1482
Castle St CF10 1XB
e-mail: cardiffcity@ihg.com
web: www.holidayinn.co.uk
dir: M4 junct 29E/A48(M) city centre signs, onto A470 follow road, turn left to hotel

Rooms 157 (20 fmly) (10 smoking) **S** £39-£285; **D** £59-£350* **Facilities** 🎵 New Year Wi-fi **Conf** Class 60 Board 50 Thtr 180 Del from £139 to £199* **Services** Lift Air con **Parking** 80 (charged) **Notes** LB ✖

Sandringham

★★ 68% HOTEL

☎ 029 2023 2161   📄 029 2038 3998
21 St Mary St CF10 1PL
e-mail: mm@sandringham-hotel.com
dir: M4 junct 29 follow 'city centre' signs. Opposite castle turn left into High St; leads to St Mary St. Hotel on left

This friendly, privately owned and personally run hotel is near the Millennium Stadium and offers a convenient base for access to the city centre. Bedrooms are well equipped, and diners can relax in Café Jazz, the hotel's adjoining restaurant, where live music is provided most week nights. There is also a separate lounge/bar for residents, and an airy breakfast room.

Rooms 28 (1 fmly) **S** £40-£100; **D** £45-£150 (incl. bkfst) **Facilities** 🎵 **Conf** Class 70 Board 60 Thtr 100 Del from £58 to £100 **Notes** ✖ Closed 24-26 Dec(pm) & 1 Jan(pm)

Mercure The Lodge Cardiff

🅄

☎ 029 2089 4000   📄 029 2049 3695
Wharf Road East, Tyndall St CF10 4BB
e-mail: h6623@accor.com
web: www.mercure-uk.com
dir: M4 junct 29/33 follow city centre signs

Currently the rating for this establishment is not confirmed. This may be due to a change of ownership or because it has only recently joined the AA rating scheme. For further details please see the AA website: www.theAA.com

Rooms 100 (48 fmly) (27 GF) (5 smoking) **S** £60-£150; **D** £60-£150* **Facilities** STV Wi-fi **Services** Lift Air con **Parking** 90

Parc Hotel by Thistle

thistle

🅄

☎ 0871 376 9011   📄 0871 376 9111
Park Place CF10 3UD
e-mail: theparkhotel@thistle.co.uk
web: www.thistlehotels.com/cardiff
dir: M4 junct 29, A48, take 4th exit signed City Centre/A470. At rdbt take 2nd exit signed City Centre/A470

Currently the rating for this establishment is not confirmed. This may be due to a change of ownership or because it has only recently joined the AA rating scheme. For further details please see the AA website: www.theAA.com

Rooms 138 (4 fmly) **S** £85-£350; **D** £85-£350* **Facilities** STV FTV Wi-fi **Conf** Class 170 Board 100 Thtr 300 **Services** Lift Air con **Notes** LB ✖ Civ Wed 250

Campanile Cardiff

Campanile

BUDGET HOTEL

☎ 029 2054 9044   📄 029 2054 9900
Caxton Place, Pentwyn CF23 8HA
e-mail: cardiff@campanile.com
dir: take Pentwyn exit from A489(M), follow signs for hotel

This modern building offers accommodation in smart, well-equipped bedrooms, all with en suite bathrooms. Refreshments may be taken at the informal bistro. See also the Hotel Groups pages.

Rooms 47 (47 annexe) **Conf** Class 18 Board 16 Thtr 35

Days Inn Cardiff

BUDGET HOTEL

☎ 01446 710787   📄 01446 719318
Port Rd, Rhoose, Nr. Barry CF62 3BT
e-mail: daysinncardiff@tiscali.co.uk
web: www.daysinn.com
dir: 0.25m on right before Cardiff Airport

This modern building offers accommodation in smart, spacious and well-equipped bedrooms, suitable for families and business travellers, and with en suite bathrooms. Continental breakfast is available and other refreshments may be taken at the nearby family restaurant. See also the Hotel Groups pages.

Rooms 32 (1 fmly) (12 GF) **Conf** Class 20 Board 20 Thtr 40

Express by Holiday Inn Cardiff Airport

BUDGET HOTEL

☎ 01446 711117 📠 01446 713290
Port Rd, Rhoose CF62 3BT
e-mail: sales@exhicardiffairport.co.uk
web: www.hiexpress.com/cardiffairport

A modern hotel ideal for families and business travellers. Fresh and uncomplicated, the spacious rooms include Sky TV, power shower and tea and coffee-making facilities. Continental buffet breakfast is included in the room rate; other meals may be taken at the nearby family pub or restaurant. See also the Hotel Groups pages.

Rooms 111 **Conf** Board 20 Thtr 40

Express by Holiday Inn Cardiff Bay

BUDGET HOTEL

☎ 029 2044 9000 📠 029 2048 8922
Atlantic Wharf CF10 4EE
e-mail: info@exhicardiff.co.uk
web: www.hiexpress.com/cardiffbay
dir: M4 junct 33, take A4232 & follow road to end. Left at 1st rdbt & left again past the Country Hall on right. Take 1st right, hotel on right

Rooms 87 (48 fmly) **Conf** Board 20 Thtr 30

Ibis Cardiff

BUDGET HOTEL

☎ 029 2064 9250 📠 029 2920 9260
Churchill Way CF10 2HA
e-mail: H2969@accor.com
web: www.ibishotel.com
dir: M4, then A48 2nd exit A4232. Follow signs to City Centre on Newport Rd, left after railway bridge, left after Queen St station.

Modern, budget hotel offering comfortable accommodation in bright and practical bedrooms. Breakfast is self-service and dinner is available in the restaurant. See also the Hotel Groups pages.

Rooms 102 (19 GF) (7 smoking) **S** fr £55; **D** fr £55*

Ibis Cardiff Gate

BUDGET HOTEL

☎ 029 2073 3222 📠 029 2073 4222
Malthouse Av, Cardiff Gate Business Park, Pontprennau CF23 8RA
e-mail: H3159@accor.com
web: www.ibishotel.com
dir: M4 junct 30, follow Cardiff Service Station signs. Hotel on left

Rooms 78 (19 fmly) (22 GF) **S** £39-£120; **D** £120*
Conf Class 24 Thtr 25 Del from £75 to £95*

Innkeeper's Lodge Cardiff

BUDGET HOTEL

☎ 0845 112 6080 📠 0845 112 6223
Tyn-y-Parc Rd, Whitchurch CF14 6BG
web: www.innkeeperslodge.com/cardiff
dir: M4 junct 32 southbound. 0.5m. Lodge on corner of Tyn-y-Parc Rd

Innkeeper's Lodge represents an exciting, high value concept within the budget hotel market. Comfortable bedrooms provide excellent facilities that include satellite TV and modem points. Options include family rooms, and for the corporate guest, cutting edge IT which includes Wi-fi access. A popular Carvery provides all-day food, including an extensive, complimentary continental breakfast.

Rooms 52 (22 fmly) **S** £58; **D** £58 (incl. bkfst)
Conf Thtr 60

Travelodge Cardiff Central

BUDGET HOTEL

☎ 08719 846 224 📠 029 2039 8737
Imperial Gate, Saint Marys St CF10 1FA
web: www.travelodge.co.uk
dir: M4 junct 32, A470 to city centre

Travelodge offers good quality, good value, modern accommodation. Ideal for families, the spacious en suite bedrooms include remote-control TV, tea and coffee-making facilities and comfortable beds. Meals can be taken at the nearby family restaurant. See also the Hotel Groups pages.

Rooms 100 **S** fr £29; **D** fr £29

Travelodge Cardiff Llanedeyrn

BUDGET HOTEL

☎ 08719 846 225 📠 029 2054 9564
Circle Way East, Llanedeyrn CF23 9PD
web: www.travelodge.co.uk
dir: M4 junct 30, A4232 to North Pentwyn junct. A48 & follow Cardiff East & Docks signs. 3rd exit at Llanedeyrn junct, follow Circle Way East signs

Rooms 32 **S** fr £29; **D** fr £29

Travelodge Cardiff (M4)

BUDGET HOTEL

☎ 08719 846 226 📠 029 2089 9412
Granada Service Area M4, Pontyclun CF72 8SA
web: www.travelodge.co.uk
dir: M4, junct 33/A4232

Rooms 50 **S** fr £29; **D** fr £29 **Conf** Board 34 Thtr 45

The Old Post Office

◉ RESTAURANT WITH ROOMS

☎ 029 2056 5400 📠 029 2056 3400
Greenwood Ln, St Fagans CF5 6EL
e-mail: info@theoldpostofficerestaurant.co.uk
dir: 4m W of city centre. M4 junct 33 onto A4232, onto A48 for Cardiff & 1st left for St Fagans

Located just five miles from Cardiff in the historic village of St Fagans, this establishment offers contemporary style based on New England design. Bedrooms, like the dining room, feature striking white walls with spotlights emphasising the fresh, clean design. Delicious meals include a carefully prepared selection of local produce.

Rooms 6 (2 fmly) (6 GF)

CARMARTHENSHIRE

CARMARTHEN   Map 8 SN42

Ivy Bush Royal

★★★ 75% HOTEL

☎ 01267 235111 📠 01267 234914
Spilman St SA31 1LG
e-mail: reception@ivybushroyal.co.uk
web: www.ivybushroyal.co.uk
dir: M4 onto A48 W, over 1st rdbt, 2nd rdbt turn right. Straight over next 2 rdbts. Left at lights. Hotel on right at top of hill

This hotel offers guests spacious, well equipped bedrooms and bathrooms, a relaxing lounge with outdoor patio seating and a comfortable restaurant serving a varied selection of carefully prepared meals. Weddings, meetings and conferences are all well catered for at this friendly, family run establishment.

Rooms 70 (4 fmly) **S** £55-£95; **D** £75-£140 (incl. bkfst)*
Facilities STV FTV Gym Xmas New Year Wi-fi
Conf Class 50 Board 40 Thtr 200 Del from £95 to £150
Services Lift **Parking** 80 (charged) **Notes** LB ⊗
Civ Wed 150

CARMARTHEN continued

Falcon

★★ 72% HOTEL

☎ 01267 234959 & 237152   📄 01267 221277
Lammas St SA31 3AP
e-mail: reception@falconcarmarthen.co.uk
web: www.falconcarmarthen.co.uk
dir: in town centre pass bus station turn left, hotel
200yds on left

This friendly hotel has been owned by the Exton family for
over 45 years. Personally run, it is well placed in the
centre of the town. Bedrooms, some with four-poster
beds, are tastefully decorated with good facilities. There
is a comfortable lounge with adjacent bar, and the
restaurant offers a varied selection of enjoyable dishes at
both lunch and dinner.

Rooms 16 (1 fmly) **Conf** Class 50 Board 40 Thtr 80
Parking 30 **Notes** LB Closed 26 Dec RS Sun

CROSS HANDS   Map 8 SN51

Travelodge Llanelli Cross Hands

BUDGET HOTEL

☎ 08719 846 230   📄 0870 191 1729
SA14 6NW
web: www.travelodge.co.uk
dir: on A48, westbound

Travelodge offers good quality, good value, modern
accommodation. Ideal for families, the spacious en suite
bedrooms include remote-control TV, tea and coffee-
making facilities and comfortable beds. Meals can be
taken at the nearby family restaurant. See also the Hotel
Groups pages.

Rooms 32 **S** fr £29; **D** fr £29

LLANDEILO   Map 8 SN62

The Plough Inn

★★★ 83% ◉ HOTEL

☎ 01558 823431   📄 01558 823969
Rhosmaen SA19 6NP
e-mail: info@ploughrhosmaen.com
web: www.ploughrhosmaen.com
dir: 0.5m N of Llandeilo on A40

This privately owned hotel has memorable views over the
Towy Valley and the Black Mountains. Bedrooms, situated
in a separate wing, are tastefully furnished, spacious and
comfortable. The public lounge bar is popular with locals,
as is the spacious restaurant where freshly prepared food
can be enjoyed. There are also conference facilities, a
gym and a sauna.

Rooms 14 (10 fmly) (5 GF) **S** £70; **D** £90-£120 (incl.
bkfst) **Facilities** STV Gym Xmas New Year Wi-fi
Conf Class 60 Board 30 Thtr 100 **Services** Air con
Parking 70 **Notes** LB ⊗ Civ Wed 100

White Hart Inn

★★ 71% HOTEL

☎ 01558 823419   📄 01558 823089
36 Carmarthen Rd SA19 6RS
e-mail: info@thewhitehartinnwales.co.uk
web: www.whitehartinnwales.co.uk
dir: off A40 onto A483, hotel 200yds on left

This privately owned, 19th-century roadside hostelry is on
the outskirts of town. The modern bedrooms are well
equipped and tastefully furnished, and family rooms are
available. Public areas include a choice of bars where a
wide range of grilled dishes is available. There are
several function rooms, including a large self-contained
suite.

Rooms 11 (3 fmly) **S** £40-£45; **D** £60-£70 (incl. bkfst)*
Facilities STV New Year Wi-fi **Conf** Class 80 Board 40
Thtr 100 **Parking** 50 **Notes** ⊗ Civ Wed 70

LLANELLI   Map 8 SN50

Best Western Diplomat Hotel

★★★ 77% HOTEL

☎ 01554 756156   📄 01554 751649
Felinfoel SA15 3PJ
e-mail: reservations@diplomat-hotel-wales.com
web: www.diplomat-hotel-wales.com
dir: M4 junct 48, A4138, B4303, hotel 0.75m on right

This Victorian mansion, set in mature grounds, has been
extended over the years to provide a comfortable and
relaxing hotel. The well-appointed bedrooms are located
in the main house and there is also a wing of comfortable
modern bedrooms. Public areas include Trubshaw's
Restaurant, a function suite and a modern leisure centre.

Rooms 50 (8 annexe) (2 fmly) (4 GF) **S** £70-£80;
D £95-£100 (incl. bkfst)* **Facilities** ⊗ supervised Gym
Sauna Steam room Sun beds ♫ Xmas New Year Wi-fi
Conf Class 150 Board 100 Thtr 450 Del from £85 to £90*
Services Lift **Parking** 250 **Notes** LB Civ Wed 300

Ashburnham

★★ 74% HOTEL

☎ 01554 834343 & 834455   📄 01554 834483
Ashburnham Rd, Pembrey SA16 0TH
e-mail: info@ashburnham-hotel.co.uk
web: www.ashburnham-hotel.co.uk
dir: M4 junct 48, A4138 to Llanelli, A484 West to
Pembrey. Follow brown information signs

Amelia Earhart stayed at this friendly hotel after finishing
her historic trans-Atlantic flight in 1928. Public areas
include the Brasserie Restaurant, and the Conservatory
Lounge Bar that serves an extensive range of bar meals.
Bedrooms, varying from standard to superior, have
modern furnishings and facilities.

Rooms 13 (2 fmly) **S** £70-£90; **D** £90-£110 (incl. bkfst)*
Facilities Wi-fi **Conf** Class 150 Board 80 Thtr 150
Parking 100 **Notes** ⊗ RS 24-26 Dec Civ Wed 130

ST CLEARS   Map 8 SN21

Travelodge St Clears Carmarthen

BUDGET HOTEL

☎ 08719 846 053   📄 01994 231227
Tenby Rd SA33 4JN
web: www.travelodge.co.uk
dir: A40 westbound, before rdbt junct of A477 & A4066

Travelodge offers good quality, good value, modern
accommodation. Ideal for families, the spacious en suite
bedrooms include remote-control TV, tea and coffee-
making facilities and comfortable beds. Meals can be
taken at the nearby family restaurant. See also the Hotel
Groups pages.

Rooms 32 **S** fr £29; **D** fr £29

CEREDIGION

ABERAERON   Map 8 SN46

Feathers Royal

★★★ 80% SMALL HOTEL

☎ 01545 571750   🖷 01545 571760
Alban Square SA46 0AQ
e-mail: enquiries@feathersroyal.co.uk
dir: A482 Lampeter Rd, hotel opposite recreation grounds

This is a friendly, family run hotel ideally located in the picturesque harbour town of Aberaeron. This charming Grade II listed property was built in 1815 when it was a coaching house, and it was transformed by the present owners to coincide with the town's bicentenary celebrations in 2007. Accommodation is very comfortable with modern fittings and accessories provided. Public areas are also well appointed.

Rooms 13 (2 fmly) **Facilities** Xmas New Year Wi-fi **Conf** Class 120 Board 60 Thtr 200 **Parking** 20 **Notes** LB ⊗

Ty Mawr Mansion

◉◉ RESTAURANT WITH ROOMS

☎ 01570 470033
Cilcennin SA48 8DB
e-mail: info@tymawrmansion.co.uk
dir: on A482 Lampeter to Aberaeron road, 4m from Aberaeron

Surrounded by rolling countryside in its own naturally beautiful gardens, this fine country mansion house is a haven of perfect peace and tranquillity. Careful renovation has recently seen it restored to its former glory and, combined with lush fabrics, top quality beds and sumptuous furnishings, the accommodation is spacious, superbly equipped and very comfortable. Award-winning chefs create mouth-watering dishes from local and seasonal produce, and Martin and Cath McAlpine offer the sort of welcome which makes every visit to Ty Mawr a memorable one.

Rooms 9 (7 en suite) (1 annexe) (1 fmly) (2 GF)

ABERPORTH   Map 8 SN25

The Penrallt

CLASSIC BRITISH HOTELS

★★★ 80% ◉ HOTEL

☎ 01239 810227 & 810927   🖷 01239 811375
SA43 2BS
e-mail: info@thepenrallt.co.uk
dir: take B4333 signed Aberporth. Hotel 1m on right

This magnificent Edwardian mansion is peacefully located in extensive grounds and offers spacious accommodation. The well-maintained public areas feature original carved ceiling beams, an impressive staircase and an eye-catching stained glass window. Guests can enjoy a relaxed atmosphere in the comfortable lounge, the popular bar and elegant restaurant. The leisure and fitness centre features a choice of swimming pools.

Rooms 26 (11 annexe) (1 fmly) (11 GF) **S** £40-£95; **D** £65-£190 (incl. bkfst) **Facilities** FTV ⓣ supervised ⚲ supervised ⚲ 9 ⚘ Putt green Gym Pool table Childrens play area Sauna Xmas New Year Wi-fi **Conf** Class 24 Board 20 **Parking** 100 **Notes** ⊗ Civ Wed 50

ABERYSTWYTH   Map 8 SN58

Conrah

★★★ 83% ◉◉ COUNTRY HOUSE HOTEL

☎ 01970 617941   🖷 01970 624546
Ffosrhydygaled, Chancery SY23 4DF
e-mail: enquiries@conrah.co.uk
dir: on A487, 3.5m S of Aberystwyth

This privately owned and personally run country-house hotel stands in 22 acres of mature grounds. The elegant public rooms include a choice of comfortable lounges with welcoming open fires. Bedrooms are located in the main house, a wing and converted outbuildings. The cuisine, which is modern with international influences, achieves very high standards. Conference facilities are available.

Rooms 17 (6 annexe) (1 fmly) (3 GF) **S** £75-£95; **D** £110-£160 (incl. bkfst)* **Facilities** ⚲ New Year Wi-fi **Conf** Class 40 Board 40 Thtr 60 Del from £140 to £180* **Services** Lift **Parking** 100 **Notes** LB ⊗ No children 5yrs Closed 22-30 Dec Civ Wed 80

Belle Vue Royal

★★★ 75% HOTEL

☎ 01970 617558 & 639240   🖷 01970 612190
Marine Ter SY23 2BA
e-mail: reception@bellevueroyalhotel.co.uk
dir: on promenade, 200yds from pier

This large privately owned seafront hotel dates back more than 170 years and is a short walk from the shops and visitor attractions. All bedrooms are well equipped and include both family and sea-view rooms. Public areas feature extensive function rooms and a choice of bars, and dining options include meals in the bar and a more formal restaurant.

Rooms 34 (6 fmly) (1 GF) **S** £55-£69; **D** £90-£110 (incl. bkfst)* **Facilities** Xmas New Year Wi-fi **Conf** Class 30 Board 30 Thtr 100 Del from £87 to £118* **Parking** 6 **Notes** LB ⊗ Civ Wed 100

Richmond

★★★ 74% SMALL HOTEL

☎ 01970 612201   🖷 01970 626706
44-45 Marine Ter SY23 2BX
e-mail: reservations@richmondhotel.uk.com
web: www.richmondhotel.uk.com
dir: on entering town follow signs for Promenade

This privately owned and personally run, friendly hotel has good sea views from its day rooms and many of the bedrooms. The public areas and bedrooms are comfortably furnished. An attractive dining room and a lounge and bar are provided.

Rooms 15 (2 fmly) **S** £55-£65; **D** £85-£95 (incl. bkfst)* **Facilities** FTV Wi-fi **Conf** Class 22 Board 28 Thtr 60 **Parking** 20 **Notes** LB ⊗ Closed 20 Dec-3 Jan

Marine Hotel & Leisure Suite

★★★ 73% HOTEL

☎ 01970 612444   🖷 01970 617435
The Promenade SY23 2BX
e-mail: marinehotel1@btconnect.com
web: www.marinehotelaberystwyth.co.uk
dir: from W on A44. From N or S Wales on A487. On seafront, west of pier

Located on the central promenade overlooking Cardigan Bay, this long established privately owed hotel has been sympathetically renovated to provide a range of well equipped bedrooms with modern bathrooms. Spacious public areas include a choice of lounges and an elegant dining room. A fitness suite is also available.

Rooms 48 (9 fmly) **S** £35-£75; **D** £65-£110 (incl. bkfst) **Facilities** FTV Gym Steam room Xmas New Year Wi-fi **Conf** Class 150 Board 60 Thtr 220 Del from £70 to £110 **Services** Lift **Parking** 24 (charged) **Notes** LB Civ Wed 200

ABERYSTWYTH continued

Four Seasons Hotel

★★★ 70% HOTEL

☎ 01970 612120 📠 01970 627458
50-54 Portland St SY23 2DX
e-mail: info@fourseasonshotel.demon.co.uk
web: www.fourseasonshotel.uk.com
dir: From rail station left into Terrace Rd by lights, into
North Pde, left into Queens Rd, 2nd left into Portland St.
Hotel on right

This privately owned hotel is soundly maintained and
friendly. Bedrooms are well equipped. A pleasant lounge
bar is provided, plus an attractive restaurant where a
good choice of food is available.

Rooms 16 (1 fmly) **Conf** Class 30 Board 30 Thtr 30
Parking 16 **Notes** ⊗

Queensbridge

★★ 63% METRO HOTEL

☎ 01970 612343 📠 01970 617452
Promenade, Victoria Ter SY23 2DH
dir: 500yds N of town centre near Constitution Hill

The friendly Queensbridge is on the promenade at the
north end of the town. The bedrooms, some suitable for
families, have modern facilities and many have fine sea
views. Public areas include a comfortable lounge with bar
and a spacious lower ground floor dining room, where
buffet breakfast are served. A small passenger lift serves
all floors.

Rooms 15 (2 fmly) (2 smoking) **S** £40-£65; **D** £65-£95
(incl. bkfst)* **Services** Lift **Parking** 4 **Notes** LB

DEVIL'S BRIDGE   Map 9 SN77

The Hafod Hotel

★★★ 72% ⍟ HOTEL

☎ 01970 890232 📠 01970 890394
SY23 3JL
e-mail: hafodhotel@btconnect.com
dir: Exit A44 in Ponterwyd signed Devil's Bridge/
Pontarfynach onto A4120 for 3m, over bridge. Hotel
facing.

This former hunting lodge dates back to the 17th century
and is situated in six acres of grounds. Now a family-
owned and run hotel, it provides accommodation suitable
for both business people and tourists. Family rooms and
a four-poster room are available. In addition to the dining
area and lounge, there are tea rooms.

Rooms 17 (2 fmly) **S** £47.50-£55; **D** £72-£83 (incl.
bkfst)* **Facilities** Xmas New Year Wi-fi **Conf** Class 70
Board 40 Thtr 100 Del from £50 to £80* **Parking** 200
Notes Civ Wed 40

EGLWYSFACH   Map 14 SN69

INSPECTORS' CHOICE

Ynyshir Hall

★★★ ⍟⍟⍟⍟
COUNTRY HOUSE HOTEL

☎ 01654 781209 & 781268 📠 01654 781366
SY20 8TA
e-mail: ynyshir@relaischateaux.com
web: www.ynyshir-hall.co.uk
dir: off A487, 5.5m S of Machynlleth, signed from
main road

Set in beautifully landscaped grounds and surrounded
by a RSBP reserve, Ynyshir Hall is a haven of calm.
Lavishly styled bedrooms, each individually themed
around a great painter, provide high standards of
luxury and comfort. The lounge and bar have different
moods, and both feature abundant fresh flowers. The
dining room offers outstanding cooking using best
ingredients with modern flair.

Rooms 9 (2 annexe) **S** £110-£310; **D** £275-£375 (incl.
bkfst)* **Facilities** ⍦ Xmas New Year **Conf** Class 20
Board 18 Thtr 25 **Parking** 20 **Notes** LB No children
9yrs Civ Wed 40

GWBERT-ON-SEA   Map 14 SN69

The Cliff

★★★ 77% HOTEL

☎ 01239 613241 📠 01239 615391
SA43 1PP
e-mail: reservations@cliffhotel.com
dir: off A487 into Cardigan, follow signs to Gwbert, 3m to
hotel

Set in 30 acres of grounds with a 9-hole golf course, and
enjoying a cliff-top location overlooking Cardigan Bay,
this hotel commands superb sea views. Bedrooms in the

main building offer excellent views and there is also a
wing of 22 modern rooms. Public areas are spacious and
comprise a choice of bars, lounges and the fine dining
restaurant. The spa offers a wide range of up-to-the-
minute leisure facilities.

Rooms 70 (6 fmly) (5 GF) **S** £59-£85; **D** £75-£130 (incl.
bkfst) **Facilities** Spa FTV ⍣ ⍏ ⍦ 9 Fishing Gym Xmas
New Year **Conf** Class 150 Board 140 Thtr 250
Services Lift **Parking** 150 **Notes** LB Civ Wed 200

LAMPETER   Map 8 SN54

Best Western Falcondale
Mansion

★★★ 86% ⍟⍟ COUNTRY HOUSE HOTEL

☎ 01570 422910 📠 01570 423559
SA48 7RX
e-mail: info@falcondalehotel.com
web: www.falcondalehotel.com
dir: 800yds W of High St A475 or 1.5m NW of Lampeter
A482

Built in the Italianate style, this charming Victorian
property is set in extensive grounds and beautiful
parkland. The individually-styled bedrooms are generally
spacious, well equipped and tastefully decorated. Bars
and lounges are similarly well appointed with additional
facilities including a conservatory and function room.
Guests have a choice of either the Valley Restaurant for
fine dining or the less formal Peterwells Brasserie.

Rooms 19 (2 fmly) **S** £99-£178; **D** £139-£200 (incl.
bkfst)* **Facilities** FTV ⍦ Xmas New Year Wi-fi
Conf Class 30 Board 25 Thtr 60 Del from £135 to £205*
Services Lift **Parking** 60 **Notes** LB Civ Wed 60

ABERGELE
Map 14 SH97

Kinmel Manor

★★★ 71% HOTEL

☎ 01745 832014 📠 01745 832014
St George's Rd LL22 9AS
e-mail: reception@kinmelmanorhotel.co.uk
dir: exit A55 at junct 24, hotel entrance on rdbt

Parts of this hotel complex date back to the 16th century and some original features are still in evidence. Set in spacious grounds, it provides well-equipped rooms and extensive leisure facilities.

Rooms 51 (3 fmly) (22 GF) (6 smoking) **S** £65-£100;
D £90-£150 (incl. bkfst)* **Facilities** FTV ⊙ Gym Steam room Sauna Spa bath Xmas New Year Wi-fi
Conf Class 100 Board 100 Thtr 250 Del from £97.50 to £107.50* **Services** Lift **Parking** 120 **Notes** LB Civ Wed 250

The Kinmel Arms

◉ RESTAURANT WITH ROOMS

☎ 01745 832207 📠 01745 822044
The Village, St George LL22 9BP
e-mail: info@thekinmelarms.co.uk
dir: From A55 junct 24a to St George. E on A55, junct 25. 1st left to Rhuddlan, then 1st right into St George. Take 2nd right

This converted 17th-century coaching inn stands close to the church in the village of St George in the beautiful Elwy Valley. The popular, restaurant specialises in produce from Wales and North West England, and the friendly and helpful staff ensures an enjoyable stay. The accommodation consists of four attractive, well-equipped suites, and substantial continental breakfasts are served in the rooms.

Rooms 4 (4 en suite) (2 GF)

BETWS-Y-COED
Map 14 SH75

See also Llanrwst

Royal Oak

★★★ 83% ◉ HOTEL

☎ 01690 710219 📠 01690 710603
Holyhead Rd LL24 0AY
e-mail: royaloakmail@btopenworld.com
web: www.royaloakhotel.net
dir: on A5 in town centre, next to St Mary's church

Centrally situated in the village, this fine, privately owned hotel started life as a coaching inn and now provides smart bedrooms and a wide range of public areas. The choice of eating options includes the Grill Bistro, the Stables Bar which is much frequented by locals, and the more formal Llugwy Restaurant.

Rooms 27 (1 fmly) **S** £70-£100; **D** £90-£150 (incl. bkfst)* **Facilities** STV ♫ New Year Wi-fi **Conf** Class 40 Board 20 Thtr 80 Del from £75 to £115* **Parking** 90 **Notes** LB ⊗ Closed 25-26 Dec Civ Wed 35

See advert on this page

Craig-y-Dderwen Riverside Hotel

★★★ 78% ◉ COUNTRY HOUSE HOTEL

☎ 01690 710293 📠 01690 710362
LL24 0AS
e-mail: info@snowdoniahotel.com
web: www.snowdoniahotel.com
dir: A5 to town, cross Waterloo Bridge, take 1st left

This Victorian country-house hotel is set in well-maintained grounds alongside the River Conwy, at the end of a tree-lined drive. Very pleasant views can be enjoyed from many rooms, and two of the bedrooms have four-poster beds. There are comfortable lounges and the atmosphere throughout is tranquil and relaxing.

Rooms 16 (2 fmly) (1 GF) (3 smoking) **S** £70-£150;
D £80-£160 (incl. bkfst)* **Facilities** STV FTV ⌣ Badminton Volleyball New Year Wi-fi **Conf** Class 25 Board 20 Thtr 50 Del from £110 to £180* **Parking** 50 **Notes** LB Closed 23-26 Dec & 2 Jan-1 Feb Civ Wed 50

BETWS-Y-COED continued

Best Western Waterloo
★★★ 77% HOTEL

☎ 01690 710411 🖷 01690 710986
LL24 0AR
e-mail: reservations@waterloo-hotel.info
web: www.waterloo-hotel.info
dir: A5, near Waterloo Bridge

This long-established hotel, named after the nearby Waterloo Bridge, is ideally located for Snowdonia. Accommodation is split between rooms in the main hotel and modern, cottage-style rooms located in buildings to the rear. The attractive Garden Room Restaurant serves traditional Welsh specialities, and the Wellington Bar offers light meals and snacks.

Rooms 39 (30 annexe) (2 fmly) (30 GF) **S** £70-£85; **D** £110-£130 (incl. bkfst)* **Facilities** 🕙 Gym Steam room Sauna New Year Wi-fi **Conf** Class 18 Board 12 Thtr 40 Del from £106.50 to £136* **Parking** 100 **Notes** LB ⊗ Closed 25-26 Dec

Fairy Glen
★★ 74% SMALL HOTEL

☎ 01690 710269
LL24 0SH
e-mail: fairyglen@youe.fsworld.co.uk
web: www.fairyglenhotel.co.uk
dir: A5 onto A470 S'bound (Dolwyddelan road). Hotel 0.5m on left by Beaver Bridge

This privately owned and personally run former coaching inn is over 300 years old. It is located near the Fairy Glen beauty spot, south of Betws-y-Coed. The modern accommodation is well equipped and service is willing, friendly and attentive. Facilities include a cosy bar and a separate comfortable lounge.

Rooms 8 (1 fmly) **S** £28-£30; **D** £56-£60 (incl. bkfst)* **Parking** 10 **Notes** ⊗ Closed Nov-Jan RS Feb

CAPEL CURIG   Map 14 SH75

Cobdens
★★ 67% SMALL HOTEL

☎ 01690 720243 🖷 01690 720354
LL24 0EE
e-mail: info@cobdens.co.uk
dir: on A5, 4m N of Betws-y-Coed

Situated in the heart of Snowdonia, this hotel has been a centre for mountaineering and other outdoor pursuits for many years. The bedrooms are modern and well equipped, and many enjoy lovely views. A wide range of meals using local produce is served in the restaurant or bar. A sauna room is also available.

Rooms 17 (4 fmly) **Facilities** Fishing Pool table **Conf** Class 25 Board 30 Thtr 50 **Parking** 40 **Notes** Closed Jan RS 24-25 & 31 Dec

COLWYN BAY   Map 14 SH87

Lyndale
★★ 72% HOTEL   THE INDEPENDENTS

☎ 01492 515429 🖷 01492 518805
410 Abergele Rd, Old Colwyn LL29 9AB
e-mail: lyndale@tinyworld.co.uk
dir: A55 junct 22 Old Colwyn, turn left. At rdbt through village, then 1m on A547

A range of accommodation is available at this friendly, family-run hotel, including suites that are suitable for family use and a four-poster bedroom. There is a cosy bar

and a comfortable foyer lounge, and weddings and other functions can be catered for.

Rooms 14 (1 fmly) **S** £39-£49; **D** £59-£69 (incl. bkfst) **Facilities** STV **Conf** Class 20 Board 20 Thtr 30 Del from £55 to £75 **Parking** 20

CONWY   Map 14 SH77

Castle Hotel Conwy   WELSH RAREBITS
★★★ 80% ⊛⊛ HOTEL

☎ 01492 582800 🖷 01492 582300
High St LL32 8DB
e-mail: mail@castlewales.co.uk
web: www.castlewales.co.uk
dir: A55 junct 18, follow town centre signs, cross estuary (castle on left). Right then left at mini-rdbts onto one-way system. Right at Town Wall Gate, right onto Berry St then High St

This family-run, 16th-century hotel is one of Conwy's most distinguished buildings and offers a relaxed and friendly atmosphere. Bedrooms are appointed to an impressive standard and include a stunning suite. Public areas include a popular modern bar and the award-winning Shakespeare's restaurant.

Rooms 28 (2 fmly) **S** £77-£105; **D** £110-£250 (incl. bkfst) **Facilities** New Year Wi-fi **Conf** Class 20 Board 20 Thtr 30 Del from £125 to £175 **Parking** 34 **Notes** LB

Groes Inn   WELSH RAREBITS
★★★ 78% ⊛ HOTEL

☎ 01492 650545 🖷 01492 650855
Tyn-y-Groes LL32 8TN
e-mail: enquiries@thegroes.com
web: www.groesinn.com
dir: A55, over Old Conwy Bridge, 1st left through Castle Walls on B5106 (Trefriw road), hotel 2m on right.

This inn dates back in part to the 16th century and has charming features. It offers a choice of bars and has a beautifully appointed restaurant, with a conservatory extension opening on to the lovely rear garden. The comfortable, well-equipped bedrooms are contained in a separate building; some have balconies or private terraces. The inn has a deservedly good reputation for its food.

Rooms 14 (1 fmly) (6 GF) **S** £85-£157; **D** £103-£189 (incl. bkfst)* **Facilities** New Year Wi-fi **Conf** Class 20 Board 20 Thtr 22 **Parking** 100 **Notes** LB Closed Xmas

---

DEGANWY   Map 14 SH77

Quay Hotel & Spa

★★★★ 85% @@ HOTEL

☎ 01492 564100 🖹 01492 464115
Deganwy Quay LL31 9DJ
e-mail: info@quayhotel.com
dir: M56, A494, A55 junct 18, straight across 2 rdbts. At lights bear left into The Quay. Hotel on right

This boutique hotel occupies a stunning position beside the estuary on Deganwy's Quay. What was once an area for railway storage is now a statement of modern architectural design offering hotel-keeping of the highest standard. Spacious bedrooms, many with balconies and wonderful views, are decorated in neutral colours and boast a host of thoughtful extras, including state-of-the-art communication systems. The friendly staff provide a fluent service in a charmingly informal manner.

Rooms 74 (15 fmly) (30 GF) **S** £120-£275; **D** £175-£275* **Facilities** Spa ③ supervised Gym Steam & sauna room Xmas New Year Wi-fi **Conf** Class 40 Board 40 Thtr 100 Del from £135 to £150 **Services** Lift **Parking** 96 **Notes** LB ⊗ Civ Wed 100

DOLWYDDELAN   Map 14 SH75

Elen's Castle

★★ Ⓐ HOTEL

☎ 01690 750207
LL25 0EJ
e-mail: stay@hotelinsnowdonia.co.uk
web: www.hotelinsnowdonia.co.uk
dir: A470 5m S of Betws-y-Coed in centre of village

Rooms 8 (2 fmly) **S** £40-£90; **D** £60-£95 (incl. bkfst)* **Facilities** Fishing Mountain biking Climbing Xmas New Year Wi-fi **Parking** 20

LLANDUDNO   Map 14 SH78

INSPECTORS' CHOICE

Bodysgallen Hall and Spa

★★★★ @@@ COUNTRY HOUSE HOTEL

☎ 01492 584466 🖹 01492 582519
LL30 1RS
e-mail: info@bodysgallen.com
web: www.bodysgallen.com
dir: A55 junct 19, A470 towards Llandudno. Hotel 2m on right

Situated in idyllic surroundings of its own parkland and formal gardens, this 17th-century house is in an elevated position, with views towards Snowdonia and across to Conwy Castle. The lounges and dining room have fine antiques and great character. Accommodation is provided in the house, but also in delightfully converted cottages, together with a superb spa. Friendly and attentive service is discreetly offered, whilst the restaurant features fine local produce prepared with great skill.

Rooms 31 (16 annexe) (4 fmly) (4 GF) **S** £140-£250; **D** £175-£465 (incl. bkfst) **Facilities** Spa STV ③ ⊌ Gym Beauty treatments Steam room Relaxation room Sauna Xmas New Year Wi-fi **Conf** Class 30 Board 22 Thtr 50 **Parking** 50 **Notes** LB ⊗ No children 6yrs Civ Wed 50

INSPECTORS' CHOICE

Osborne House

★★★★ @ TOWN HOUSE HOTEL

☎ 01492 860330 🖹 01492 860791
17 North House LL30 2LP
e-mail: sales@osbornehouse.com
web: www.osbornehouse.com
dir: exit A55 junct 19. Follow signs for Llandudno then Promenade. Continue to junct, turn right. Hotel on left opposite pier entrance

Built in 1832, this Victorian house was restored and converted into a luxurious townhouse by the Maddocks family. Spacious suites offer unrivalled comfort and luxury, combining antique furnishings with state-of-the-art technology and facilities. Each suite provides super views over the pier and bay. Osborne's café grill is open throughout the day and offers high quality food, whilst the bar blends elegance with plasma screens, dazzling chandeliers and guilt-edged mirrors.

Rooms 6 (6 smoking) **S** £145-£220; **D** £145-£220 (incl. bkfst) **Facilities** STV FTV Use of swimming pool & sauna at Empire Hotel (100 yds) New Year Wi-fi **Services** Air con **Parking** 6 **Notes** ⊗ No children 11yrs Closed 20-30 Dec

See advert on page 682

St George's

★★★★ 77% @ HOTEL

☎ 01492 877544 & 862184 🖹 01492 877788
The Promenade LL30 2LG
e-mail: sales@stgeorgeswales.co.uk
dir: A55-A470, follow to promenade, 0.25m, hotel on corner

This large and impressive seafront property was the first hotel to be built in the town. Restored it to its former glory, the accommodation is of very high quality. Its many Victorian features include the splendid, ornate Wedgwood Room restaurant. The terrace restaurant and main lounges overlook the bay; hot and cold snacks are available all day. Many of the thoughtfully equipped bedrooms enjoy sea views.

Rooms 75 **Facilities** Xmas New Year Wi-fi **Conf** Class 200 Board 45 Thtr 250 Del from £140 to £155* **Services** Lift Air con **Parking** 36 **Notes** ⊗ Civ Wed 200

See advert on page 682

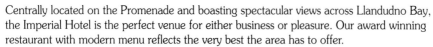

LLANDUDNO continued

Imperial

★★★★ 76% ⊚ HOTEL

☎ 01492 877466 ▤ 01492 878043
The Promenade LL30 1AP
e-mail: reception@theimperial.co.uk
web: www.theimperial.co.uk
dir: A470 to Llandudno

The Imperial is a large and impressive hotel, situated on the promenade, and within easy reach of the town centre and other amenities. Many of the bedrooms have views over the bay and there are also several suites available. The elegant Chantrey Restaurant offers a fixed-price, monthly-changing menu that utilises local produce.

Rooms 98 (10 fmly) **Facilities** FTV ⊕ Gym Beauty therapist Hairdressing ♫ Xmas New Year Wi-fi **Conf** Class 50 Board 50 Thtr 150 **Services** Lift **Parking** 25 **Notes** ⊗ Civ Wed 150

See advert on opposite page

Empire

★★★★ 73% ⊚ HOTEL

☎ 01492 860555 ▤ 01492 860791
Church Walks LL30 2HE
e-mail: reservations@empirehotel.co.uk
web: www.empirehotel.co.uk
dir: from Chester, A55 junct 19 for Llandudno. Follow town centre signs. Hotel at base of Great Orme facing main street of town

Run by the same family for over almost 60 years, the Empire offers luxuriously appointed bedrooms with every modern facility. The 'Number 72' rooms in an adjacent house are particularly sumptuous. The indoor pool is overlooked by a lounge area where snacks are served all day, and in summer an outdoor pool and roof garden are available. The Watkins restaurant offers an interesting fixed-price menu.

Rooms 54 (8 annexe) (1 fmly) (2 GF) (54 smoking) **S** £75-£120; **D** £100-£150 (incl. bkfst) **Facilities** STV FTV ⊕ ⊰ Gym Beauty treatments Sauna Steam room Fitness suite New Year Wi-fi **Conf** Class 20 Board 20 Thtr 24 Del from £97.50 to £107.50 **Services** Lift Air con **Parking** 40 **Notes** LB ⊗ Closed 20-29 Dec

See advert on this page

St Tudno Hotel and Restaurant

★★★ ⊚⊚ HOTEL

WELSH RAREBITS

☎ 01492 874411 ▤ 01492 860407
The Promenade LL30 2LP
e-mail: sttudnohotel@btinternet.com
web: www.st-tudno.co.uk
dir: on Promenade towards pier, hotel opposite pier entrance

A high quality family-owned hotel with friendly, attentive staff, and enjoying fine sea views. The stylish bedrooms are well equipped with mini-bars, robes, satellite TVs and many other thoughtful extras. Public rooms include a lounge, a welcoming bar and a small indoor pool. The Terrace Restaurant, where seasonal and daily-changing menus are offered, has a delightful Mediterranean atmosphere. Afternoon tea is a real highlight.

Rooms 18 (4 fmly) **Facilities** ⊕ supervised ♫ Xmas New Year **Conf** Class 25 Board 20 Thtr 40 **Services** Lift **Parking** 5 **Notes** LB

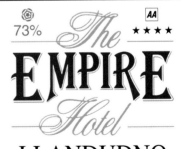

LLANDUDNO continued

Dunoon

★★★ 80% HOTEL

☎ 01492 860787 📠 01492 860031
Gloddaeth St LL30 2DW
e-mail: reservations@dunoonhotel.co.uk
web: www.dunoonhotel.co.uk
dir: exit Promenade at war memorial by pier onto wide
avenue. 200yds on right

This smart, privately owned hotel is centrally located and
offers a variety of styles and sizes of attractive, well-
equipped bedrooms. The elegant public areas include a
tastefully appointed restaurant, where competently
prepared dishes are served along with a good choice of
carefully selected, good-value wines. The caring,
attentive service is noteworthy.

Rooms 49 (7 fmly) **S** £60-£126; **D** £90-£126 (incl. bkfst)*
Facilities Pool table ♫ **Services** Lift **Parking** 24
Notes LB Closed 22 Dec-early Mar Civ Wed 70

Tynedale

★★★ 75% HOTEL

☎ 01492 877426 📠 01492 871213
Central Promenade LL30 2XS
e-mail: enquiries@tynedalehotel.co.uk
web: www.tynedalehotel.co.uk
dir: on promenade opposite bandstand

Tour groups are well catered for at this privately owned
and personally run hotel, and regular live entertainment
is a feature. Public areas include good lounge facilities
and an attractive patio overlooking the bay. The well
maintained bedrooms are fresh and well equipped. Many
have good views over the seafront and the Great Orme.

Rooms 54 (1 fmly) **S** £37-£53; **D** £74-£138 (incl. bkfst)*
Facilities FTV ♫ Xmas New Year Wi-fi **Services** Lift
Parking 20 **Notes** LB ⊗

Merrion

★★★ 68% HOTEL

☎ 01492 860022 📠 01492 860378
Promenade, South Pde LL30 2LN
e-mail: enquiries@merrion-hotel.co.uk
dir: A55 follow Llandudno signs onto Llandudno
Promenade then towards Pier. Hotel close to war
memorial

Located on the sea front close to the centre of town, this
traditional, family run hotel offers comfortable, well
equipped accommodation with many rooms having sea
views. Meals are served in the attractive restaurant and
entertainment is held on a regular basis.

Rooms 65 (6 fmly) (3 GF) **S** £60-£80; **D** £120-£160 (incl.
bkfst & dinner)* **Facilities** STV FTV ♫ Xmas Wi-fi
Conf Class 40 Board 20 Thtr 30 Del from £100 to £125*
Services Lift **Parking** 9 **Notes** LB ⊗ Closed Jan

See advert on this page

Epperstone

★★ 80% SMALL HOTEL

☎ 01492 878746 ▤ 01492 871223
15 Abbey Rd LL30 2EE
e-mail: epperstonehotel@btconnect.com
dir: A55–A470 to Mostyn St. Left at rdbt, 4th right into
York Rd. Hotel on junct of York Rd & Abbey Rd

This delightful hotel is located in wonderful gardens in a
residential part of town, within easy walking distance of
the seafront and shopping area. Bedrooms are
attractively decorated and thoughtfully equipped. Two
lounges and a Victorian-style conservatory are available.
A daily changing menu is offered in the bright dining
room.

Rooms 8 (5 fmly) (1 GF) **Facilities** Xmas Wi-fi **Parking** 8
Notes LB No children 5yrs

Sandringham

★★ 75% HOTEL

☎ 01492 876513 ▤ 01492 877916
West Pde LL30 2BD
e-mail: enquiries@thesandringhamhotel.co.uk
web: www.thesandringhamhotel.co.uk
dir: enter Llandudno on A470 & follow signs for West
Shore

This pleasant and friendly hotel is privately owned and
personally run. It is located at the West Shore area of
Llandudno. The accommodation is well equipped and
there are popular bar and restaurant operations which
provide an extensive choice of wholesome food.

Rooms 18 (3 fmly) (2 GF) **Notes** LB ⊗ RS 1-14 Jan

Hydro Hotel

★★ 71% HOTEL

Leisureplex

☎ 01492 870101 ▤ 01492 870992
Neville Crescent LL30 1AT
e-mail: hydro.llandudno@alfatravel.co.uk
dir: follow signs for theatre to seafront, towards pier.
Hotel near theatre on left

This large hotel is situated on the promenade overlooking
the sea, and offers good, value-for-money, modern
accommodation. Public areas are quite extensive and
include a choice of lounges, a games/snooker room and a
ballroom where entertainment is provided every night.
The hotel is a popular venue for coach tour parties.

Rooms 118 (4 fmly) (8 GF) **S** £34-£44; **D** £54-£74 (incl.
bkfst) **Facilities** FTV Table tennis Snooker ♬ Xmas New
Year **Services** Lift **Parking** 10 **Notes** LB ⊗ Closed Jan-
mid Feb RS Nov-Dec (ex Xmas) & mid Feb-Mar

Esplanade

★★ 68% HOTEL

☎ 0800 318688 & 01492 860300 ▤ 01492 860418
Glan-y-Mor Pde, Promenade LL30 2LL
e-mail: info@esplanadehotel.co.uk
web: www.esplanadehotel.co.uk
dir: A55 at junct 19 onto A470, follow signs to
promenade. Left towards Great Orme. Hotel 500yds left

This family owned and run hotel stands on the
promenade, conveniently close to the town centre and
with views of the bay. Bedrooms vary in size and style,
but all have modern equipment and facilities. Public
areas are bright and attractively appointed, and include
a room for functions and conferences. The hotel is
popular with golfers.

Rooms 59 (17 fmly) **S** £20-£57; **D** £40-£114 (incl. bkfst)*
Facilities ♬ Xmas New Year Wi-fi **Conf** Class 40
Board 40 Thtr 80 Del from £55 to £75* **Services** Lift
Parking 30 **Notes** LB ⊗ Closed 2-29 Jan

LLANRWST Map 14 SH86
See also Betws-y-Coed

Maenan Abbey

★★★ 77% HOTEL

☎ 01492 660247 ▤ 01492 660734
Maenan LL26 0UL
e-mail: reservations@manab.co.uk
dir: 3m N on A470

Set in its own spacious grounds, this privately owned
hotel was built as an abbey in 1850 on the site of a
13th-century monastery. It is now a popular venue for
weddings as the grounds and magnificent galleried
staircase make an ideal backdrop for photographs.
Bedrooms include a large suite and are equipped with
modern facilities. Meals are served in the bar and
restaurant.

Rooms 14 (3 fmly) (4 smoking) **S** £60; **D** £95 (incl.
bkfst)* **Facilities** Fishing Guided mountain walks Xmas
New Year Wi-fi **Conf** Class 30 Board 30 Thtr 50
Parking 60 **Notes** LB Civ Wed 55

DENBIGHSHIRE

LLANDRILLO Map 15 SJ03

Tyddyn Llan

◉◉ RESTAURANT WITH ROOMS

☎ 01490 440264 ▤ 01490 440414
LL21 0ST
e-mail: tyddynllan@compuserve.com
dir: Take B4401 from Corwen to Llandrillo. Tyddyn Llan on
right leaving village

An elegant Georgian house set in its own grounds in a
peaceful and relaxing location. Bedrooms vary in size but
all are comfortably furnished and include some welcome
extras. The restaurant and lounges are quite delightful
and offer pleasant views over the surrounding gardens.
Emphasis is on local produce, carefully prepared by the
chef/proprietor and his team.

Rooms 13 (8 en suite) (1 GF)

RHYL Map 14 SJ08

Barratt's at Ty'N Rhyl

◉◉ RESTAURANT WITH ROOMS

☎ 01745 344138 & 0773 095 4994 ▤ 01745 344138
Ty'n Rhyl, 167 Vale Rd LL18 2PH
e-mail: ebarratt5@aol.com
dir: A55 onto A525 to Rhyl, pass Sainsburys & B&Q,
garden centre on left, Barratt's 400yds on right

This delightful 16th-century house lies in a secluded
location surrounded by attractive gardens. The quality of
food reflects the skill of the owner-chef. Public areas are
smartly furnished and include a panelled lounge and
separate bar with attractive conservatory. Bedrooms are
comfortable and equipped with lots of thoughtful extras.

Rooms 3

RUTHIN   Map 15 SJ15

Ruthin Castle

★★★ 78% ® HOTEL

CLASSIC
BRITISH HOTELS

☎ 01824 702664 ▤ 01824 705978
LL15 2NU
e-mail: reservations@ruthincastle.co.uk
web: www.ruthincastle.co.uk
dir: A550 to Mold, A494 to Ruthin, hotel at end of Castle Street

The main part of this impressive castle was built in the early 19th century, but many ruins in the impressive grounds date back much further. The elegantly panelled public areas include a restaurant and bar along with a medieval banqueting hall. Many of the modern bedrooms are spacious and furnished with fine period pieces.

Rooms 22 (6 fmly) **S** £85-£95; **D** £120-£280 (incl. bkfst)*
Facilities FTV Fishing Gym Beauty suites Snooker ♫
Xmas New Year Wi-fi **Conf** Class 108 Board 48 Thtr 130
Services Lift **Parking** 200 **Notes** LB ⊗ Civ Wed 130

The Wynnstay Arms

®® RESTAURANT WITH ROOMS

☎ 01824 703147
Well St LL15 1AN
e-mail: resevations@wynnstayarms.com
dir: In town centre

This former town centre period inn has been sympathetically renovated to provide good quality accommodation and a smart café-bar. Imaginative food is served in Fusions Brasserie, where a contemporary decor style highlights the many retained period features.

Rooms 7 (5 en suite) (1 fmly)

ST ASAPH   Map 15 SJ07

Oriel House

★★★ 80% ® HOTEL

☎ 01745 582716 ▤ 01745 585208
Upper Denbigh Rd LL17 0LW
e-mail: mail@theorielhotel.com
web: www.theorielhotel.com
dir: A55 onto A525, left at cathedral, 1m on right

Set in several acres of mature grounds south of St Asaph, Oriel House offers generally spacious, well-equipped bedrooms and has a friendly and hospitable staff. The Terrace restaurant serves imaginative food with an emphasis on local produce. Extensive function facilities cater for business meetings and weddings, and the leisure club is available to guests.

Rooms 39 (3 fmly) (13 GF) **S** £59; **D** £69-£120*
Facilities Spa STV ⊛ Gym Steam room Sauna Xmas New Year Wi-fi **Conf** Class 100 Board 50 Thtr 220 **Parking** 200
Notes LB ⊗ Civ Wed 200

Plas Elwy Hotel & Restaurant

★★ 74% SMALL HOTEL

☎ 01745 582263 & 582089 ▤ 01745 583864
The Roe LL17 0LT
e-mail: enquiries@plaselwy.co.uk
dir: off A55 junct 27, A525 signed Rhyl/St Asaph. On left opposite Total petrol station

This hotel, which dates back to 1850, has retained much of its original character. Bedrooms in the purpose-built extension are spacious, and one has a four-poster bed; those in the main building are equally well equipped. Public rooms are smart and comfortably furnished and a range of food options is provided in the attractive restaurant.

Rooms 13 (6 annexe) (3 fmly) (2 GF) **S** £50-£56;
D £65-£75 (incl. bkfst)* **Parking** 25 **Notes** LB ⊗ Closed 25 Dec-1 Jan

EWLOE   Map 15 SJ36

De Vere St David's Park

DE VERE
heritage

★★★★ 74% HOTEL

☎ 01244 520800 ▤ 01244 520930
St Davids Park CH5 3YB
e-mail: reservations.stdavids@devere-hotels.com
web: www.devere.co.uk
dir: M56 onto A494 Queensferry to Mold for 4m, then left slip road B5127 signed Buckley, hotel visible at rdbt

This modern, purpose-built hotel is conveniently situated and offers a range of rooms, including four-poster suites and family rooms. Public areas include leisure and spa facilities, an all-day café, and nearby, the hotel's own golf course. This is a popular venue for conferences and other functions. Younger guests are not forgotten either and can have fun in the Dai the Dove Club.

Rooms 147 (24 fmly) (45 GF) **Facilities** Spa ⊛
supervised Gym Steam bath Sauna Xmas New Year Wi-fi
Conf Class 150 Board 40 Thtr 300 **Services** Lift
Parking 240 **Notes** LB ⊗ Civ Wed 120

HALKYN   Map 15 SJ27

Travelodge Halkyn

Travelodge

BUDGET HOTEL

☎ 08719 846 078 ▤ 01352 781966
CH8 8RF
web: www.travelodge.co.uk
dir: on A55, westbound

Travelodge offers good quality, good value, modern accommodation. Ideal for families, the spacious en suite bedrooms include remote-control TV, tea and coffee-making facilities and comfortable beds. Meals can be taken at the nearby family restaurant. See also the Hotel Groups pages.

Rooms 31 **S** fr £29; **D** fr £29

HOLYWELL   Map 15 SJ17

Stamford Gate

★★ 72% HOTEL

☎ 01352 712942 ▤ 01352 713309
Halkyn Rd CH8 7SJ
dir: take Holywell exit from A55 onto A5026, hotel 1m on right

This popular, friendly hotel enjoys impressive views across the Dee Estuary from its elevated position. It provides well-equipped accommodation, including a number of ground floor bedrooms. Public areas include a smart nautical themed restaurant, a stylish, spacious bar and there are meeting and function facilities.

Rooms 12 (6 GF) **S** £48-£55; **D** £60-£75 (incl. bkfst)*
Facilities New Year **Conf** Class 50 Board 30 Thtr 100
Del from £95 to £120* **Parking** 100 **Notes** ⊗

MOLD   Map 15 SJ26

Beaufort Park Hotel

★★★ 74% HOTEL

☎ 01352 758646 🖷 01352 757132
Alltami Rd, New Brighton CH7 6RQ
e-mail: info@beaufortparkhotel.co.uk
web: www.beaufortparkhotel.co.uk
dir: A55/A494. Through Alltami lights, over mini rdbt by petrol station towards Mold, A5119. Hotel 100yds on right

This large, modern hotel is conveniently located a short drive from the North Wales Expressway and offers various styles of spacious accommodation. There are extensive public areas, and several meeting and function rooms available. There is a wide choice of meals in the formal restaurant and in the popular Arches bar.

Rooms 105 (8 fmly) (32 GF) **Facilities** FTV Squash ♫ Xmas New Year Wi-fi **Conf** Class 120 Board 120 Thtr 250 **Parking** 200 **Notes** Civ Wed 250

NORTHOP HALL   Map 15 SJ26

Northop Hall Country House

THE INDEPENDENTS
HOTEL ASSOCIATION

★★★ 75% HOTEL

☎ 01244 816181 🖷 01244 814661
Chester Rd CH7 6HJ
e-mail: northop@hotel-chester.com
web: www.hotel-chester.com
dir: From Buckley/St David's Park 3rd exit at rdbt, 1st right to Northop Hall 2m. Left at mini-rdbt, 200yds on left

Located within large grounds and woodland, this sympathetically renovated and extended period house retains many original features within public areas and is a popular conference and wedding venue. Bedrooms provide both practical and thoughtful extras and a warm welcome is assured.

Rooms 39 (15 fmly) **S** £55-£65; **D** £85-£125 (incl. bkfst)*
Facilities FTV New Year Wi-fi Child facilities
Conf Class 40 Board 50 Thtr 80 Del from £90 to £120
Parking 70 **Notes** LB Civ Wed 80

Holiday Inn A55 Chester West

🇺

☎ 01244 550011 🖷 01244 550763
Gateway Services, Westbound A55 CH7 6HB
e-mail: bookings@holidayinnchesterwest.co.uk
web: www.holidayinn.co.uk
dir: from M6 junct 20, follow M56 to Queensferry, follow signs for A55 Conwy. Hotel 500yds past A494 slip road

Currently the rating for this establishment is not confirmed. This may be due to a change of ownership or because it has only recently joined the AA rating scheme. For further details please see the AA website: www.theAA.com

Rooms 81 (19 fmly) (31 GF) **S** £42-£86; **D** £42-£86*
Facilities STV Gym New Year Wi-fi **Conf** Class 130 Board 60 Thtr 220 **Services** Lift Air con **Parking** 152 **Notes** LB ⊗ Closed 24-25 Dec Civ Wed 220

Travelodge Chester Northop Hall

Travelodge

BUDGET HOTEL

☎ 08719 846 091 🖷 01244 816473
CH7 6HB
web: www.travelodge.co.uk
dir: on A55, eastbound

Travelodge offers good quality, good value, modern accommodation. Ideal for families, the spacious en suite bedrooms include remote-control TV, tea and coffee-making facilities and comfortable beds. Meals can be taken at the nearby family restaurant. See also the Hotel Groups pages.

Rooms 40 **S** fr £29; **D** fr £29

ABERSOCH   Map 14 SH32

Porth Tocyn

★★★ 80% ⦾⦾ COUNTRY HOUSE HOTEL

☎ 01758 713303 🖷 01758 713538
Bwlch Tocyn LL53 7BU
e-mail: bookings@porthtocyn.fsnet.co.uk
web: www.porth-tocyn-hotel.co.uk
dir: 2.5m S follow Porth Tocyn signs after Sarnbach

Located above Cardigan Bay with fine views over the area, Porth Tocyn is set in attractive gardens. Several elegantly furnished sitting rooms are provided and bedrooms are comfortably furnished. Children are especially welcome and have a playroom. Award-winning food is served in the restaurant.

Rooms 17 (1 fmly) (3 GF) **S** £65-£90; **D** £90-£170 (incl. bkfst)* **Facilities** ↖ ⚲ Table tennis Wi-fi **Parking** 50 **Notes** LB Closed mid Nov-wk before Etr RS some off season nights

See advert on page 688

Neigwl

★★ 81% ⦾ SMALL HOTEL

☎ 01758 712363 🖷 01758 712544
Lon Sarn Bach LL53 7DY
e-mail: relax@neigwl.com
web: www.neigwl.com
dir: on A499, through Abersoch, hotel on left

This delightful, small hotel is privately owned and personally run. It is conveniently located for access to the town, harbour and beach. It has a deservedly high reputation for its food and warm hospitality. Both the attractive restaurant and the pleasant lounge bar overlook the sea, as do several of the tastefully appointed bedrooms.

Rooms 9 (2 fmly) (2 GF) **S** £95; **D** £165 (incl. bkfst & dinner) **Parking** 20 **Notes** LB ⊗ Closed Jan

Riverside

🇺

☎ 01758 712419 🖷 01758 712671
LL53 7HW
e-mail: info@riversideabersoch.co.uk
dir: on A499 from Pwllheli. On entering Abersoch after River Soch, hotel on right

Currently the rating for this establishment is not confirmed. This may be due to a change of ownership or because it has only recently joined the AA rating scheme. For further details please see the AA website: www.theAA.com

Rooms 12 (4 fmly) (3 GF) **S** £50-£72; **D** £70-£116 (incl. bkfst)* **Facilities** FTV Fishing New Year Wi-fi **Parking** 30 **Notes** LB ⊗

BANGOR — Map 14 SH57

Travelodge Bangor
BUDGET HOTEL

📠 0870 1911561
Llys-y-Gwynt LL57 4BG
web: www.travelodge.co.uk
dir: at junct of A5/A55

Travelodge offers good quality, good value, modern accommodation. Ideal for families, the spacious en suite bedrooms include remote-control TV, tea and coffee-making facilities and comfortable beds. Meals can be taken at the nearby family restaurant. See also the Hotel Groups pages.

Rooms 62 **S** fr £29; **D** fr £29

BARMOUTH — Map 14 SH61

Bae Abermaw
★★★ 81% ⊛ HOTEL — WELSH RAREBITS

☎ 01341 280550 📄 01341 280346
Panorama Hill LL42 1DQ
e-mail: enquiries@baeabermaw.com
web: www.baeabermaw.com
dir: off A496 above Barmouth Bridge

Situated on attractive landscaped grounds in an elevated position overlooking the sea, this impressive Victorian house has been sympathetically renovated to provide high standards of comfort and facilities. The interior is furnished and decorated in minimalist style and many bedrooms have stunning views.

Rooms 14 (4 fmly) **S** £70-£107; **D** £90-£158 (incl. bkfst)*
Facilities Xmas New Year **Conf** Class 75 Board 20 Thtr 100 **Parking** 35 **Notes** LB ⊗ Civ Wed 100

BEDDGELERT — Map 14 SH54

The Royal Goat
★★★ 75% HOTEL

THE CIRCLE

☎ 01766 890224 📄 01766 890422
LL55 4YE
e-mail: info@royalgoathotel.co.uk
web: www.royalgoathotel.co.uk
dir: On A498 at Beddgelert

An impressive building steeped in history, the Royal Goat provides well-equipped accommodation. Attractively appointed, comfortable public areas include a choice of bars and restaurants, a residents' lounge and function rooms.

Rooms 32 (4 fmly) **Facilities** Fishing Xmas **Conf** Class 70 Board 30 Thtr 70 **Services** Lift **Parking** 100 **Notes** LB Closed Jan-1 Mar RS Nov-1 Jan

CAERNARFON — Map 14 SH46

INSPECTORS' CHOICE

Seiont Manor
★★★ ⊛⊛ COUNTRY HOUSE HOTEL — HANDPICKED

☎ 01286 673366 📄 01286 672840
Llanrug LL55 2AQ
e-mail: seiontmanor@handpicked.co.uk
web: www.handpicked.co.uk
dir: E on A4086, 2.5m from Caernarfon

A splendid hotel created from authentic rural buildings, set in the tranquil countryside near Snowdonia. Bedrooms are individually decorated and well equipped, with luxurious extra touches. Public rooms are cosy and comfortable and furnished in country-house style. The kitchen team use the best of local produce to provide exciting takes on traditional dishes.

Rooms 28 (2 fmly) (14 GF) **S** £70-£165; **D** £80-£185 (incl. bkfst)* **Facilities** STV ⊗ Fishing Gym Xmas New Year Wi-fi **Conf** Class 40 Board 40 Thtr 100 Del from £125 to £145* **Parking** 60 **Notes** LB ⊗ Civ Wed 90

Celtic Royal Hotel

★★★ 77% HOTEL

☎ 01286 674477 📄 01286 674139
Bangor St LL55 1AY
e-mail: admin@celtic-royal.co.uk
web: www.celtic-royal.co.uk
dir: Exit A55 at Bangor. Follow A487 towards Caernarfon

This large, impressive, privately owned hotel is situated in the town centre. It provides attractively appointed accommodation, which includes bedrooms for less able guests and family rooms. The spacious public areas include a bar, a choice of lounges and a pleasant split-level restaurant. Guests also have the use of the impressive health club.

Rooms 110 (12 fmly) **Facilities** 🏊 Gym Sun shower Steam room Sauna 🎵 Xmas New Year **Conf** Class 120 Board 120 Thtr 300 **Services** Lift **Parking** 180 **Notes** LB ⊗ Civ Wed 200

Stables

★★ 68% HOTEL

☎ 01286 830711 📄 01286 830413
Llanwnda LL54 5SD
dir: 3m S of Caernarfon, on A499

This privately owned and personally run hotel is set in 15 acres of its own land, south of Caernarfon. The bar and restaurant are located in converted stables. The bedrooms are all situated in two purpose-built, motel-style wings.

Rooms 22 (22 annexe) (8 fmly) **Facilities** Xmas **Conf** Class 30 Board 30 Thtr 50 **Parking** 40

CRICCIETH	Map 14 SH43

Bron Eifion Country House

★★★ 86% ⊛ COUNTRY HOUSE HOTEL

☎ 01766 522385 📄 01766 523796
LL52 0SA
e-mail: enquiries@broneifion.co.uk
dir: A497 between Porthmadog & Pwllheli, 0.5m from Criccieth, on right towards Pwheli

This delightful country house built in 1883, is set in extensive grounds to the west of Criccieth. Now a privately owned and personally run hotel, it provides warm and very friendly hospitality as well as attentive service. The interior style highlights the many retained period features; there is a choice of lounges and the very impressive central hall features a minstrels' gallery.

Rooms 19 (1 fmly) (1 GF) **S** £95-£128; **D** £130-£196 (incl. bkfst)* **Facilities** FTV 🎵 Xmas New Year Wi-fi **Conf** Class 40 Board 40 Thtr 50 Del from £140 to £170* **Parking** 50 **Notes** LB ⊗ Civ Wed 50

George IV

★★ 62% HOTEL

Leisureplex

☎ 01766 522168 📄 01766 523340
23-25 High St LL52 0BS
e-mail: georgiv.criccieth@alfatravel.co.uk
dir: on A497 in town centre

Considerable improvements have been completed at this hotel which stands back from the A497 in the town centre. Generally spacious bedrooms are attractively furnished and equipped to meet the needs of both business guests and holidaymakers.

Rooms 47 (11 fmly) **S** £36-£43; **D** £58-£72 (incl. bkfst) **Facilities** FTV 🎵 Xmas New Year **Services** Lift **Parking** 16 **Notes** LB ⊗ Closed Jan RS Nov & Feb-Mar

DOLGELLAU	Map 14 SH71

INSPECTORS' CHOICE

Penmaenuchaf Hall

WELSH RAREBITS

★★★ ⊛⊛ COUNTRY HOUSE HOTEL

☎ 01341 422129 📄 01341 422787
Penmaenpool LL40 1YB
e-mail: relax@penhall.co.uk
web: www.penhall.co.uk
dir: off A470 onto A493 to Tywyn. Hotel approx 1m on left

Built in 1860, this impressive hall stands in 20 acres of formal gardens, grounds and woodland, and enjoys magnificent views across the River Mawddach. Sympathetic restoration has created a comfortable and welcoming hotel with spacious day rooms and thoughtfully furnished bedrooms, some with private balconies. Fresh produce cooked in modern British style is served in an elegant conservatory restaurant, overlooking the surrounding countryside.

Rooms 14 (2 fmly) **S** £95-£145; **D** £150-£240 (incl. bkfst) **Facilities** STV FTV Fishing ⚓ Complimentary salmon & trout fishing Xmas New Year **Conf** Class 30 Board 22 Thtr 50 Del from £149 to £197 **Parking** 30 **Notes** LB No children 6yrs Civ Wed 50

Dolserau Hall

★★★ 81% ⊛ HOTEL

☎ 01341 422522 📄 01341 422400
LL40 2AG
e-mail: welcome@dolserau.co.uk
web: www.dolserau.co.uk
dir: 1.5m outside Dolgellau between A494 to Bala & A470 to Dinas Mawddy

This privately owned, friendly hotel lies in attractive grounds that extend to the river and are surrounded by green fields. Several comfortable lounges are provided and welcoming log fires are lit during cold weather. The smart bedrooms are spacious, well equipped and comfortable. A varied menu offers very competently prepared dishes.

Rooms 20 (5 annexe) (1 fmly) (3 GF) **S** £73-£82; **D** £136-£198 (incl. bkfst & dinner) **Facilities** Fishing Xmas New Year **Services** Lift **Parking** 40 **Notes** No children 10yrs Closed Dec-Jan (ex Xmas & New Year)

Royal Ship

★★ 72% HOTEL

☎ 01341 422209 📄 01341 424693
Queens Square LL40 1AR
dir: in town centre

This establishment dates from 1813 when it was a coaching inn. There are three bars and several lounges, all comfortably furnished and attractively appointed. It is very much the centre of local activities and a wide range of food is available. Bedrooms are tastefully decorated.

Rooms 24 (4 fmly) **Facilities** Fishing arranged Xmas **Conf** Class 60 Board 60 Thtr 80 **Parking** 12 **Notes** LB ⊗

HARLECH — Map 14 SH53

Maes y Neuadd Country House

WELSH RAREBITS

★★★ 80% ◎◎ COUNTRY HOUSE HOTEL

☎ 01766 780200 🖷 01766 780211
LL47 6YA
e-mail: maes@neuadd.com
web: www.neuadd.com
dir: 3m NE of Harlech, signed on unclassified road, off B4573

This 14th-century hotel enjoys fine views over the mountains and across the bay to the Lleyn Peninsula. The team here is committed to restoring some of the hidden features of the house. Bedrooms, some in an adjacent coach house, are individually furnished and many boast fine antique pieces. Public areas display a similar welcoming charm, including the restaurant, which serves many locally-sourced and home-grown ingredients.

Rooms 15 (5 fmly) (3 GF) **S** fr £58; **D** £119-£200 (incl. bkfst)* **Facilities** 🏌 Clay pigeon Cooking tuition Garden breaks Xmas New Year Wi-fi **Conf** Class 10 Board 12 Thtr 15 Del from £185* **Parking** 50 **Notes** LB Civ Wed 65

The Castle

★★ 🅰 HOTEL

☎ 01766 780529 🖷 01766 780499
Castle Square LL46 2YH
dir: directly opposite Harlech Castle entrance

Rooms 7 (1 fmly) **S** £25-£40; **D** £50-£80 (incl. bkfst)* **Parking** 30 **Notes** ⊗

LLANBEDR — Map 14 SH52

Ty Mawr

★★ 69% SMALL HOTEL

☎ 01341 241440 🖷 01341 241440
LL45 2NH
e-mail: tymawrhotel@onetel.com
web: www.tymawrhotel.org.uk
dir: from Barmouth A496 (Harlech road). In Llanbedr turn right after bridge, hotel 50yds on left, brown tourist signs on junct

Located in a picturesque village, this family-run hotel has a relaxed, friendly atmosphere. The pleasant grounds opposite the River Artro makes a popular beer garden during fine weather. The attractive, cane-furnished bar

offers a blackboard selection of food and a good choice of real ales. A more formal menu is available in the restaurant. Bedrooms are smart and brightly decorated.

Rooms 10 (2 fmly) **S** £40-£45; **D** £70-£80 (incl. bkfst)* **Facilities** STV **Conf** Class 25 **Parking** 30 **Notes** LB Closed 24-26 Dec

LLANBERIS — Map 14 SH56

Legacy Royal Victoria

LEGACY HOTELS

★★★ 72% HOTEL

☎ 0870 832 9903 🖷 0870 832 9904
LL55 4TY
e-mail: res-royalvictoria@legacy-hotels.co.uk
web: www.legacy-hotels.co.uk
dir: on A4086 (Caernarfon to Llanberis road), directly opposite Snowdon Mountain Railway

This well-established hotel sits near the foot of Snowdon, between the Peris and Padarn lakes. Pretty gardens and grounds make an attractive backdrop for the many weddings held here. Bedrooms are well equipped. There are spacious lounges and bars, and a large dining room with a conservatory looking out over the lakes.

Rooms 106 (7 fmly) **S** £27.50-£55; **D** £54.50-£109 (incl. bkfst)* **Facilities** STV Mountaineering Cycling Walking 🎵 Xmas New Year **Conf** Class 60 Board 50 Thtr 100 Del from £80 to £105* **Services** Lift **Parking** 100 **Notes** LB Civ Wed 100

PORTHMADOG — Map 14 SH53

Royal Sportsman

★★★ 75% HOTEL

☎ 01766 512015 🖷 01766 512490
131 High St LL49 9HB
e-mail: enquiries@royalsportsman.co.uk
dir: by rdbt, at A497 & A487 junct

Ideally located in the centre of Porthmadog, this former coaching inn dates from the Victorian era and has been restored into a friendly, privately owned and personally run hotel. Rooms are tastefully decorated and well equipped, and some are in an annexe close to the hotel. There is a large comfortable lounge and a wide range of meals is served in the bar or restaurant.

Rooms 28 (9 annexe) (7 fmly) (9 GF) **S** £52-£77; **D** £81-£92 (incl. bkfst)* **Facilities** STV FTV Xmas New Year Wi-fi **Conf** Class 50 Board 30 Thtr 50 **Parking** 6 **Notes** LB

PORTMEIRION — Map 14 SH53

Castell Deudraeth

WELSH RAREBITS

★★★★ 76% ◎ HOTEL

☎ 01766 770000 🖷 01766 771771
LL48 6EN
e-mail: castell@portmeirion-village.com
web: www.portmeirion-village.com
dir: A4212 for Trawsfynydd/Porthmadog. 1.5m beyond Penrhyndeudraeth, hotel on right

A castellated mansion that overlooks Snowdonia and the famous Italianate village featured in the 1960's cult series 'The Prisoner'. An original concept, Castell Deudraeth combines traditional materials, such as oak and slate, with state-of-the-art technology and design. Dynamically styled bedrooms boast underfloor heating, real-flame gas fires, wide-screen TVs with DVDs and cinema surround-sound. The brasserie-themed dining room provides an informal option at dinner.

Rooms 11 (5 fmly) **Facilities** 🎣 🏊 🎵 Xmas New Year **Conf** Class 18 Board 25 Thtr 30 **Services** Lift Air con **Parking** 30 **Notes** ⊗ Civ Wed 30

The Hotel Portmeirion

WELSH RAREBITS

★★★★ 73% ◎ HOTEL

☎ 01766 770000 🖷 01766 771331
LL48 6ET
e-mail: hotel@portmeirion-village.com
web: www.portmeirion-village.com
dir: 2m W, Portmeirion village is S off A487

Saved from dereliction in the 1920s by Clough Williams-Ellis, the elegant Hotel Portmeirion enjoys one of the finest settings in Wales, located beneath the wooded slopes of the village, overlooking the sandy estuary towards Snowdonia. Many rooms have private sitting rooms and balconies with spectacular views. The mostly Welsh-speaking staff provide a good mix of warm hospitality and efficient service.

Rooms 42 (28 annexe) (4 fmly) **S** £135-£265; **D** £170-£300 (incl. bkfst)* **Facilities** STV 🎣 🏊 Xmas New Year Wi-fi **Conf** Class 40 Board 30 Thtr 100 Del from £160 to £190* **Parking** 40 **Notes** LB ⊗ Civ Wed 130

Y FELINHELI — Map 14 SH56

Hotel Plas Dinorwic

★★ 74% HOTEL

☎ 01248 670559 & 0800 328 3910 🖷 01248 670300
Menai Marina LL56 4XA
e-mail: plasdinorwic@btconnect.com
web: www.hotelplasdinrwic.com
dir: A55 junct 10 signed to Caernarfon. At mini rdbt take 1st exit, at next rdbt take 2nd exit. Follow road to village, turn left at Halfway House pub, over bridge and up hill

Plas Dinorwic has an idyllic location alongside the Menai Strait and is an integral part of a marina and village development. Most of the spacious modern bedrooms have spectacular views; many are located in separate cottages and are also available as self-catering accommodation. Facilities include a lounge bar, function room and an indoor swimming pool.

Rooms 30 (18 annexe) (6 fmly) **S** £60-£70; **D** £70-£95* **Facilities** 🕭 Xmas New Year Wi-fi **Conf** Class 40 Board 30 **Notes** ⊗

MERTHYR TYDFIL

MERTHYR TYDFIL   Map 9 SO00

Tregenna

★★★ Ⓐ HOTEL

☎ 01685 723627 & 382055 📄 01685 721951
Park Ter CF47 8RF
e-mail: reception@tregennahotel.co.uk
dir: M4 junct 32, onto A465 follow signs for Merthyr Tydfil signed from town centre

Rooms 21 (6 fmly) (7 GF) **Parking** 12 **Notes** LB

MONMOUTHSHIRE

ABERGAVENNY   Map 9 SO21

Llansantffraed Court

WELSH RAREBITS

★★★ 79% ◉◉ COUNTRY HOUSE HOTEL

☎ 01873 840678 📄 01873 840674
Llanvihangel Gobion, Clytha NP7 9BA
e-mail: reception@llch.co.uk
web: www.llch.co.uk
dir: at A465/A40 Abergavenny junct take B4598 signed Usk (do not join A40). Continue towards Raglan, hotel on left in 4.5m

In a commanding position and in its own extensive grounds, this very impressive property, now a privately owned country-house hotel, has enviable views of the Brecon Beacons. Extensive public areas include a relaxing lounge and a spacious restaurant offering imaginative and enjoyable dishes. Bedrooms are comfortably furnished and have modern facilities.

Rooms 21 (1 fmly) **S** £86-£130; **D** £115-£170 (incl. bkfst) **Facilities** STV FTV ⛳ Putt green Fishing ⛳ Clay pigeon shooting school Wi-fi **Conf** Class 120 Board 100 Thtr 220 Del from £90 to £170 **Services** Lift **Parking** 250 **Notes** LB Civ Wed 150

Angel

★★★ 75% ◉ HOTEL

☎ 01873 857121 📄 01873 858059
15 Cross St NP7 5EN
e-mail: mail@angelhotelabergavenny.com
web: www.angelhotelabergavenny.com
dir: follow town centre signs from rdbt, S of Abergavenny, past rail and bus stations. Turn left by hotel

Once a coaching inn this has long been a popular venue for both local people and visitors; the two traditional function rooms and a ballroom are in regular use. In addition there is a comfortable lounge, a relaxed bar and a smart, award-winning restaurant. In warmer weather there is a central courtyard that is ideal for alfresco eating. The bedrooms include a four-poster room and some that are suitable for families.

Rooms 29 (2 fmly) **S** £65-£90; **D** £85-£130 (incl. bkfst)* **Facilities** ♫ Xmas New Year Wi-fi **Conf** Class 120 Board 60 Thtr 200 Del from £125 to £160* **Parking** 30 **Notes** LB Closed 25 Dec RS 24, 26 & 27 Dec Civ Wed 200

Llanwenarth Hotel & Riverside Restaurant
WELSH RAREBITS

★★ 79% ◉ HOTEL

☎ 01873 810550 📄 01873 811880
Brecon Rd NP8 1EP
e-mail: info@llanwenarthhotel.com
web: www.llanwenarthhotel.com
dir: A40 from Abergavenny towards Brecon. Hotel 3m past hospital on left

Dating from the 16th century and set in magnificent scenery, this delightful hotel offers guests the chance to relax and unwind in style. Bedrooms, in a detached wing, offer plenty of quality and comfort plus pleasant river views; many have a private balcony. The airy conservatory lounge and restaurant offer a varied selection of carefully prepared dishes.

Rooms 17 (3 fmly) (7 GF) **Facilities** Fishing **Parking** 30 **Notes** ⊗

Marriott St Pierre Hotel & Country Club

★★★★ 77% HOTEL

☎ 01291 625261 📄 01291 629975
St Pierre Park NP16 6YA
e-mail: mhrs.cwlgs.frontdesk@marriotthotels.com
web: www.marriottstpierre.co.uk
dir: M48 junct 2. At rdbt on slip road take A466 Chepstow. At next rdbt take 1st exit Caerwent A48. Hotel approx 2m on left

This property dating from the 14th century sits in 400 acres of parkland and offers an extensive range of leisure and conference facilities. Bedrooms are well equipped, comfortable and located either in adjacent wings or in a lakeside cottage complex. The main bar, popular with golfers, overlooks the 18th green, and diners can choose between elegant, oak-panelled Orangery Restaurant and modern brasserie.

Rooms 148 (16 fmly) (75 GF) **S** £98-£129; **D** £98-£143 (incl. bkfst)* **Facilities** Spa STV 🕭 ☀ 36 ⛳ Putt green Fishing ⛳ Gym Health spa Floodlit driving range Chipping green Xmas New Year Wi-fi **Conf** Class 120 Board 90 Thtr 240 Del from £135 to £165* **Parking** 440 **Notes** LB ⊗ Civ Wed 220

Castle View

★★ 69% HOTEL

☎ 01291 620349 📄 01291 627397
16 Bridge St NP16 5EZ
e-mail: castleviewhotel@btconnect.com
dir: M48 junct 2, A466 for Wye Valley, at 1st rdbt right onto A48 towards Gloucester. Follow 2nd sign to town centre, then to Chepstow Castle, hotel directly opposite

This hotel was built around 300 years ago and offers unrivalled views of Chepstow Castle. Accommodation is comfortable - there are family rooms, double bedded rooms, and some bedrooms that are situated in a separate building; a good range of extras for guest comfort are provided. There is a cosy bar area and a small restaurant where home cooked food using fresh, local ingredients is offered.

Rooms 13 (4 annexe) (7 fmly) **Facilities** Xmas New Year Wi-fi **Notes** LB

See advert on page 693

Travelodge Newport Magor

BUDGET HOTEL

☎ 0871 984 6336 📠 01633 881896
Magor Service Area NP26 3YL
web: www.travelodge.co.uk
dir: M4 junct 23a

Travelodge offers good quality, good value, modern accommodation. Ideal for families, the spacious en suite bedrooms include remote-control TV, tea and coffee-making facilities and comfortable beds. Meals can be taken at the nearby family restaurant. See also the Hotel Groups pages.

Rooms 43 **S** fr £29; **D** fr £29

RAGLAN   Map 9 SO40

The Beaufort Arms Coaching Inn & Restaurant

WELSH RAREBITS

★★★ 75% HOTEL

☎ 01291 690412 📠 01291 690935
High St NP15 2DY
e-mail: enquiries@beaufortraglan.co.uk
web: www.beaufortraglan.co.uk
dir: M4 junct 24 (Newport/Abergavenny) A449 then A40 to Raglan. Opposite church in Raglan

This friendly, family-run village inn dating back to the 15th century has historic links with nearby Raglan Castle. The bright, stylish and beautifully appointed bedrooms in the main house are suitably equipped for both tourists and for business guests. Food is served in either the restaurant or traditional lounge, and both offer a relaxed service and an enjoyable selection of carefully prepared dishes.

Rooms 15 (5 annexe) (5 GF) **S** £60; **D** £75-£105 (incl. bkfst)* **Facilities** Wi-fi **Conf** Class 60 Board 30 Thtr 120 Del from £130* **Parking** 30 **Notes** LB ✪ RS 25-26 Dec

Travelodge Monmouth

BUDGET HOTEL

☎ 08719 846 232 📠 01600 740329
Granada Services A40, Nr Monmouth NP5 4BG
web: www.travelodge.co.uk
dir: on A40 near junct with A449

Travelodge offers good quality, good value, modern accommodation. Ideal for families, the spacious en suite bedrooms include remote-control TV, tea and coffee-making facilities and comfortable beds. Meals can be taken at the nearby family restaurant. See also the Hotel Groups pages.

Rooms 43 **S** fr £29; **D** fr £29

ROCKFIELD

The Stonemill & Steppes Farm Cottages

◉◉ RESTAURANT WITH ROOMS

☎ 01600 775424 📠 01600 715257
NP25 5SW
e-mail: michelle@thestonemill.co.uk
dir: A48 to Monmouth, B4233 to Rockfield. 2.6m from Monmouth town centre

Located in Rockfield, a small hamlet just west of Monmouth, close to the Forest of Dean and Wye Valley, this operation offers accommodation comprising of six very well-appointed cottages. The comfortable rooms (for self-catering or on a B&B basis) are architect designed, and lovingly restored with many of the original features remaining. This is also handy for golfers, with a choice of courses within the locality. In a separate, converted 16th-century barn is the Stonemill Restaurant with oak beams, vaulted ceilings and an old cider press. Breakfast is served in the cottages on request.

Rooms 6 (6 fmly) (6 GF)

SKENFRITH   Map 9 SO42

INSPECTORS' CHOICE

The Bell at Skenfrith

◉◉ RESTAURANT WITH ROOMS

☎ 01600 750235 📠 01600 750525
NP7 8UH
e-mail: enquiries@skenfrith.co.uk
dir: On B4521 in Skenfrith, opposite castle

The Bell is a beautifully restored, 17th-century former coaching inn which still retains much of its original charm and character. It is peacefully situated on the banks of the Monnow, a tributary of the River Wye, and is ideally placed for exploring the numerous delights of the area. Natural materials have been used to create a relaxing atmosphere, while the bedrooms, which include full suites and rooms with four-poster beds, are stylish, luxurious and equipped with DVD players.

Rooms 11 (7 en suite)

TINTERN PARVA   Map 4 SO50

Best Western Royal George

★★★ 73% HOTEL

☎ 01291 689205 📠 01291 689448
Wye Valley Rd NP16 6SF
e-mail: royalgeorgetintern@hotmail.com
web: www.royalgeorgetintern.com
dir: off M48/A466, 4m to Tintern, 2nd on left

This privately owned and personally run hotel provides comfortable, spacious accommodation, including bedrooms with balconies overlooking the well-tended garden and there are a number of ground floor bedrooms. The public areas include a lounge bar, and a large function room. A varied and popular menu choice is available in either the bar or restaurant. An ideal place to stay for exploring the counties of Monmouthshire and Herefordshire.

Rooms 16 (14 annexe) (6 fmly) (10 GF) **S** £75-£95; **D** £90-£120 (incl. bkfst)* **Facilities** STV Xmas New Year Wi-fi **Conf** Class 45 Board 30 Thtr 120 Del from £95 to £172.50* **Parking** 50 **Notes** LB Civ Wed 70

USK   Map 9 SO30

Glen-yr-Afon House

★★★ 78% HOTEL

☎ 01291 672302 & 673202 📠 01291 672597
Pontypool Rd NP15 1SY
e-mail: enquiries@glen-yr-afon.co.uk
web: www.glen-yr-afon.co.uk
dir: A472 through High Street, over river bridge, follow to right. Hotel 200yds on left

On the edge of this delightful old market town, Glen-yr-Afon, a unique Victorian villa, offers all the facilities expected of a modern hotel combined with the warm atmosphere of a family home. Bedrooms are furnished to a high standard and several overlook the hotel's well-tended gardens. There is a choice of comfortable sitting areas and a stylish and spacious banqueting suite.

Glen-yr-Afon House

Rooms 27 (2 fmly) **S** £94-£118; **D** £136-£159 (incl. bkfst)* **Facilities** STV FTV 🦢 Complimentary access to Usk Tennis Club New Year Wi-fi **Conf** Class 200 Board 30 Thtr 100 Del from £110 to £130* **Services** Lift **Parking** 100 **Notes** LB Civ Wed 200

INSPECTORS' CHOICE

The Crown at Whitebrook
◎◎ RESTAURANT WITH ROOMS

☎ 01600 860254 📠 01600 860607
NP25 4TX
e-mail: info@crownatwhitebrook.co.uk
dir: 4m from Monmouth on B4293, left at sign to Whitebrook, 2m on unmarked road, Crown on right

In a secluded spot in the wooded valley of the River Wye this former drover's cottage dates back to the 17th century. Refurbished and individually decorated bedrooms boast a contemporary feel with smart modern facilities. The restaurant and lounge combine many original features with a bright fresh look. Memorable cuisine features locally sourced ingredients skilfully prepared.

The Crown at Whitebrook

Rooms 8 (8 en suite)

Castle Hotel
★★★ 70% HOTEL

☎ 01639 641119 📠 01639 641624
The Parade SA11 1RB
e-mail: info@castlehotelneath.co.uk
web: www.castlehotelneath.co.uk
dir: M4 junct 43, follow signs for Neath, 500yds past rail station, hotel on right. Car park on left in 50yds

Situated in the town centre, this Georgian property, once a coaching inn, has a wealth of history and character. Lord Nelson and Lady Hamilton are reputed to have stayed here, and it is where the Welsh Rugby Union was founded in 1881. The hotel provides well-equipped accommodation and pleasant public areas. Bedrooms include family bedded rooms and one with a four-poster bed. Function and meeting rooms are available.

Rooms 29 (3 fmly) (14 smoking) **S** £50-£65; **D** £60-£80 (incl. bkfst) **Facilities** STV New Year **Conf** Class 75 Board 50 Thtr 160 Del from £60 to £95* **Parking** 20 **Notes** LB ⊗ Civ Wed 120

Best Western Aberavon Beach
★★★ 74% HOTEL

☎ 01639 884949 📠 01639 897885
SA12 6QP
e-mail: sales@aberavonbeach.com
web: www.aberavonbeach.com
dir: M4 junct 41/A48 & follow signs for Aberavon Beach & Hollywood Park

This friendly, purpose-built hotel enjoys a prominent position on the seafront overlooking Swansea Bay. Bedrooms, many with sea views, are comfortably appointed and thoughtfully equipped. Public areas include a leisure suite with swimming pool, open-plan bar and restaurant plus a choice of function rooms.

Rooms 52 (6 fmly) **S** £69-£120; **D** £79-£130 (incl. bkfst) **Facilities** FTV 🛝 All weather leisure centre Sauna 🎵 Xmas New Year Wi-fi **Conf** Class 200 Board 100 Thtr 300 Del from £110 to £120 **Services** Lift **Parking** 150 **Notes** LB Civ Wed 300

See advert on page 703

NEWPORT

NEWPORT Map 9 ST38

See also **Cwmbran (Torfaen)**

The Celtic Manor Resort

★★★★★ 84% ◉◉ HOTEL

☎ 01633 413000 📠 01633 412910
Coldra Woods NP18 1HQ
e-mail: postbox@celtic-manor.com
web: www.celtic-manor.com
dir: M4 junct 24, take B4237 towards Newport. Hotel 1st on right

This outstanding resort includes three challenging golf courses, a huge convention centre, superb leisure clubs and two hotels. One hotel is the five star Celtic Manor, and this hotel offers excellent bedrooms, with good space and comfort, several eating options and stylish and extensive public areas set around a spectacular atrium lobby.

Rooms 400 (7 fmly) **S** £66-£256.95; **D** £78-£273.90 (incl. bkfst)* **Facilities** Spa STV ⓣ supervised ♨ 54 ♣ Putt green Gym Golf Academy Clay pigeon shooting Mountain bike trails Art gallery Table tennis ♫ Xmas New Year Wi-fi **Conf** Class 300 Board 50 Thtr 1500 Del from £150 to £260* **Services** Lift Air con **Parking** 1000 **Notes** LB ⊗ Civ Wed 100

Holiday Inn Newport

★★★ 70% HOTEL

☎ 01633 412777 📠 01633 413087
The Coldra NP6 2YG
web: www.holidayinn.co.uk

A purpose-built and modern hotel, in a very convenient location near to the M4, that caters equally well for both leisure and business guests. There is Harpers, the informal restaurant, a small leisure complex and a business centre.

Rooms 119

Newport Lodge

THE INDEPENDENTS HOTEL ASSOCIATION

★★★ 68% HOTEL

☎ 01633 821818 📠 01633 856360
Bryn Bevan, Brynglas Rd NP20 5QN
e-mail: info@newportlodgehotel.co.uk
web: www.newportlodgehotel.co.uk
dir: M4 junct 26 follow signs Newport. Left after 0.5m onto Malpas Rd, up hill, 0.5m to hotel

On the edge of the town centre and convenient for the M4, this purpose-built, friendly hotel provides comfortable and well-maintained bedrooms, with modern facilities. A room with a four-poster bed is available, as are ground floor bedrooms. The bistro-style restaurant offers a wide range of freshly prepared dishes, often using local ingredients.

Rooms 27 (11 GF) **S** £76-£90; **D** £96-£135 (incl. bkfst) **Facilities** FTV Wi-fi **Conf** Class 20 Board 20 Thtr 25 Del from £100 to £150 **Parking** 63 **Notes** LB Civ Wed 55

Manor House

Ⓤ

☎ 01633 413000 📠 01633 410236
The Celtic Manor Resort, Coldra Woods, The Usk Valley NP18 1HQ
e-mail: bookings@celtic-manor.com

Currently the rating for this establishment is not confirmed. This may be due to a change of ownership or because it has only recently joined the AA rating scheme. For further details please see the AA website: www.theAA.com

Rooms 69 **S** £71-£145; **D** £83-£145* **Conf** Class 80 Thtr 200 Del from £150 to £190*

Express by Holiday Inn Newport

Express by Holiday Inn

BUDGET HOTEL

☎ 0870 990 4083 📠 0870 990 4084
Lakeside Dr, Coedkernew NP10 8BB
e-mail: gm.newport@expressholidayinn.co.uk
web: www.hiexpress.com/exnewport

A modern hotel ideal for families and business travellers. Fresh and uncomplicated, the spacious rooms include Sky TV, power shower and tea and coffee-making facilities. Continental buffet breakfast is included in the room rate; other meals may be taken at the nearby family pub or restaurant. See also the Hotel Groups pages.

Rooms 125 **Conf** Class 15 Board 15 Thtr 40

PEMBROKESHIRE

BURTON Map 8 SM90

Beggars Reach

★★★ 80% HOTEL

☎ 01646 600700 📠 01646 600560
SA73 1PD
e-mail: stay@beggars-reach.com
web: www.beggars-reach.com
dir: 8m S of Haverfordwest, 6m N of Pembroke, off A477

This privately owned and personally run hotel was once a Georgian rectory. It stands in four acres of grounds peacefully located close to the village of Burton. It provides modern, well-equipped bedrooms, two of which are located in former stables, which date back to the 14th century. Milford Haven and the ferry terminal at Pembroke Dock are both within easy reach.

Rooms 30 (16 annexe) (4 fmly) (8 GF) (2 smoking) **S** £75-£95; **D** £100-£130 (incl. bkfst)* **Facilities** STV FTV Wi-fi **Conf** Class 60 Board 60 Thtr 100 Del from £110 to £130* **Parking** 80 **Notes** LB ⊗ Civ Wed 130

See advert on opposite page

FISHGUARD Map 8 SM93

Cartref

★★ 63% HOTEL

☎ 01348 872430 & 0781 330 5235 📠 01348 873664
15-19 High St SA65 9AW
e-mail: cartrefhotel@btconnect.com
web: www.cartrefhotel.co.uk
dir: on A40 in town centre

Personally run by the proprietor, this friendly hotel offers convenient access to the town centre and ferry terminal. Bedrooms are well maintained and include some family bedded rooms. There is also a cosy lounge bar and a welcoming restaurant that looks out onto the high street.

Rooms 10 (2 fmly) **S** £35-£41; **D** £60-£65 (incl. bkfst)* **Parking** 2 **Notes** LB

HAVERFORDWEST

Map 8 SM91

Hotel Mariners

★★ 69% HOTEL

☎ 01437 763353 📠 01437 764258
Mariners Square SA61 2DU
e-mail: hotelmariners@aol.com
dir: follow town centre signs, over bridge, up High St, 1st
right, hotel at end

Located a few minutes walk from the town centre, this
privately owned and friendly hotel is said to date back to
1625. The bedrooms are equipped with modern facilities
and are soundly maintained. A good range of food is
offered in the popular bar, which is a focus for the local
community. Facilities include a choice of meeting rooms.

Rooms 28 (5 fmly) **S** £61-£71; **D** £82-£90 (incl. bkfst)*
Facilities STV Wi-fi **Conf** Class 20 Board 20 Thtr 50
Parking 50 **Notes** Closed 25-Dec-2 Jan

MANORBIER

Map 8 SS09

Castle Mead

THE CIRCLE

★★ 71% HOTEL

☎ 01834 871358 📠 01834 871358
SA70 7TA
e-mail: castlemeadhotel@aol.com
web: www.castlemeadhotel.com
dir: A4139 towards Pembroke, turn onto B4585 into
village & follow signs to beach & castle. Hotel on left
above beach

Benefiting from a superb location with spectacular views
of the bay, the Norman church and Manorbier Castle, this
family-run hotel is friendly and welcoming. Bedrooms
which include some in a converted former coach house,
are generally quite spacious and have modern facilities.
Public areas include a sea-view restaurant, bar and
residents' lounge, as well as an extensive garden.

Rooms 8 (3 annexe) (2 fmly) (3 GF) **Parking** 20 **Notes** LB
Closed Dec-Feb RS Nov

PEMBROKE

Map 8 SM90

Best Western Lamphey Court

Best
Western

★★★ 80% HOTEL

☎ 01646 672273 📠 01646 672480
Lamphey SA71 5NT
e-mail: info@lampheycourt.co.uk
web: www.lampheycourt.co.uk
dir: A477 to Pembroke. Turn left at Milton Village for
Lamphey, hotel on right

This former Georgian mansion is set in attractive
countryside and well situated for exploring the stunning
Pembrokeshire coast and beaches. Well-appointed
bedrooms and family suites are situated in a converted
coach house in the grounds. The elegant public areas
include formal and informal dining rooms that both
feature dishes inspired by the local produce. Leisure

Continued

PEMBROKE continued

facilities and grounds are a feature of this elegant building with tennis court, swimming pool, sauna, jaccuzi and multi gym available for guests.

Rooms 38 (12 annexe) (7 fmly) (6 GF) **S** £82-£99; **D** £105-£170 (incl. bkfst)* **Facilities** FTV 🕽 🌊 Gym Yacht charter Xmas New Year Wi-fi **Conf** Class 40 Board 30 Thtr 60 Del from £125 to £155* **Parking** 50 **Notes** LB ⊗ Civ Wed 60

Lamphey Hall

★★★ 77% HOTEL

☎ 01646 672394 📠 01646 672369
Lamphey SA71 5NR
e-mail: andrewjones1990@aol.com
dir: From M4 follow signs for A48 towards Carmarthen, then A40 to St Clears. Follow signs for A477, left at Milton Village

Set in a delightful village, this very friendly, privately owned and efficiently run hotel offers an ideal base from which to explore the surrounding countryside. Bedrooms are well equipped, comfortably furnished and include family rooms and ground floor rooms. Diners have an extensive choice of dishes from the menu and a choice from the three restaurant areas. There is also a small lounge, a bar and attractive gardens.

Rooms 10 (1 fmly) (2 GF) **Parking** 30 **Notes** ⊗

PEMBROKE DOCK   Map 8 SM90

Cleddau Bridge

★★★ 75% HOTEL

☎ 01646 685961 📠 01646 685746
Essex Rd SA72 6EG
e-mail: information@cleddauhotel.co.uk
dir: M4/A40 to St Clears. A477 to Pembroke Dock. At rdbt 2nd exit for Haverfordwest via toll bridge, left before toll bridge

A modern, purpose-built hotel that is situated adjacent to the Cleddau Bridge and with excellent views overlooking the river. The well-equipped bedrooms are all on the ground floor, while the comfortable public areas comprise an attractive bar and restaurant, both taking advantage of the impressive views.

Rooms 40 (2 fmly) (32 GF) **S** £70-£85; **D** £90-£105 (incl. bkfst) **Facilities** Xmas Wi-fi Child facilities **Conf** Class 100 Board 60 Thtr 300 Del from £115 to £140 **Parking** 140 **Notes** LB ⊗ Civ Wed 250

Travelodge Pembroke Dock

BUDGET HOTEL

☎ 08719 846 299 📠 01646 684758
Pier Rd SA72 6DY
web: www.travelodge.co.uk
dir: A4139 right at 1st rdbt, hotel opposite Lidl

Travelodge offers good quality, good value, modern accommodation. Ideal for families, the spacious en suite bedrooms include remote-control TV, tea and coffee-making facilities and comfortable beds. Meals can be taken at nearby convenient restaurants. See also the Hotel Groups pages.

Rooms 51 **S** fr £29; **D** fr £29

ST DAVID'S   Map 8 SM72

Warpool Court   WELSH RAREBITS

★★★ 80% ⚜⚜ COUNTRY HOUSE HOTEL

☎ 01437 720300 📠 01437 720676
SA62 6BN
e-mail: info@warpoolcourthotel.com
web: www.warpoolcourthotel.com
dir: At Cross Square left by Cartref Restaurant (Goat St). Pass Farmers Arms pub, after 400mtrs left, follow hotel signs, entrance on right

Originally the cathedral choir school, this hotel is set in landscaped gardens looking out to sea and is within easy walking distance of the Pembrokeshire Coastal Path. The lounges are spacious and comfortable, and the bedrooms are well furnished and equipped with modern facilities. The restaurant offers delightful cuisine.

Rooms 25 (3 fmly) **S** £105-£120; **D** £180-£290 (incl. bkfst)* **Facilities** 🕽 🌊 ➷ Table tennis Xmas New Year Wi-fi **Conf** Class 25 Board 25 Thtr 40 Del from £115 to £185* **Parking** 100 **Notes** LB Closed Jan Civ Wed 120

SAUNDERSFOOT   Map 8 SN10

Merlewood

★★ 74% HOTEL

☎ 01834 812421 📠 01834 814886
St Brides Hill SA69 9NP
e-mail: merlehotels@aol.com
dir: A477/A4316, hotel through village on St Brides Hill

Offering delightful views over the village and bay, and providing regular live entertainment, this hotel is a popular destination for coach parties. Bedrooms include ground floor and family rooms and there is a comfortable dining room and a large lounge bar. A pleasant outdoor swimming pool is also available for guests.

Rooms 29 (8 fmly) (11 GF) **Facilities** ➷ Putt green Children's swings, Table tennis ♫ Xmas Child facilities **Conf** Class 100 Board 40 Thtr 60 **Parking** 34 **Notes** LB ⊗ Closed Nov-Mar

TENBY   Map 8 SN10

Atlantic

★★★ 78% HOTEL

☎ 01834 842881 📠 01834 840911
The Esplanade SA70 7DU
e-mail: enquiries@atlantic-hotel.uk.com
web: www.atlantic-hotel.uk.com
dir: A478 into Tenby & follow town centre signs, keep town walls on left then turn right at Esplanade, hotel on right

This privately owned and personally run, friendly hotel has an enviable position looking out over South Beach towards Caldy Island. Bedrooms vary in size and style, and are well equipped and tastefully appointed. The comfortable public areas include a choice of restaurants and, in fine weather guests can also enjoy the cliff-top gardens.

Rooms 42 (11 fmly) (4 GF) **S** £76-£87; **D** £100-£182 (incl. bkfst) **Facilities** FTV 🕽 Steam room Spa bath **Conf** Board 6 **Services** Lift **Parking** 25 **Notes** LB Closed mid Dec-mid Jan

Penally Abbey Country House

WELSH RAREBITS

★★★ 77% ⊛ COUNTRY HOUSE HOTEL

☎ 01834 843033 📠 01834 844714
Penally SA70 7PY
e-mail: penally.abbey@btinternet.com
web: www.penally-abbey.com
dir: 1.5m from Tenby, off A4139, near village green

With monastic origins, this delightful country house stands in five acres of grounds with views over Carmarthen Bay. The drawing room, bar and restaurant are tastefully decorated and attractively furnished and set the scene for a relaxing stay. An impressive range of comfortable accommodation is offered. In the main hotel there are country-house style rooms or cottage-style rooms with four posters, and the lodge has rooms that combine classic and contemporary design.

Rooms 12 (4 annexe) (3 fmly) **Facilities** ⊙ Xmas
Conf Board 14 **Parking** 17 **Notes** ⊗ Civ Wed 45

Fourcroft

★★★ 74% HOTEL

☎ 01834 842886 📠 01834 842888
North Beach SA70 8AP
e-mail: staying@fourcroft-hotel.co.uk
web: www.fourcroft-hotel.co.uk
dir: A478, after 'Welcome to Tenby' sign left towards North Beach & Walled Town. At seafront turn sharp left. Hotel on left

This friendly hotel has been owned and run by the same family since 1946. It offers a beach-front location, together with a number of extra facilities that make it particularly suitable for families with children. Guests have direct access to Tenby's North Beach through the hotel's cliff top gardens. Bedrooms are of a good size and have modern facilities.

Rooms 40 (12 fmly) **S** £50-£75; **D** £100-£150 (incl. bkfst)* **Facilities** STV FTV ⊰ Table tennis Giant chess Human gyroscope Snooker Pool New Year Wi-fi
Conf Class 40 Board 50 Thtr 90 Del from £120 to £130*
Services Lift **Parking** 12 (charged) **Notes** LB Civ Wed 90

Clarence House

★★ 62% HOTEL

☎ 01834 844371 📠 01834 844372
Esplanade SA70 7DU
e-mail: clarencehotel@freeuk.com
dir: Off South Parade by town walls onto St Florance Parade & Esplanade

Owned by the same family for over 50 years, this hotel has superb views from its elevated position. Many of the bedrooms have sea views and all are comfortably furnished. The bar leads to a sheltered rose garden or a number of lounges. Entertainment is provided in high season, and this establishment is particularly popular with coach tour parties.

Rooms 68 (6 fmly) **Notes** Closed 18-28 Dec

See advert on this page

WOLF'S CASTLE · Map 8 SM92

Wolfscastle Country Hotel · WELSH RAREBITS

★★★ 78% COUNTRY HOUSE HOTEL

☎ 01437 741688 & 741225 · 🖨 01437 741383
SA62 5LZ
e-mail: enquiries@wolfscastle.com
web: www.wolfscastle.com
dir: on A40 in village at top of hill. 6m N of Haverfordwest

This large stone house, a former vicarage, dates back to the mid-19th century and is now a friendly, privately owned and personally run hotel. It provides stylish, modern, well-maintained and well-equipped bedrooms. There is a pleasant bar and an attractive restaurant, which has a well-deserved reputation for its food.

Rooms 22 (2 annexe) (2 fmly) **S** £70-£90; **D** £100-£135 (incl. bkfst)* **Facilities** FTV New Year Wi-fi **Conf** Class 100 Board 30 Thtr 100 Del from £125 to £160* **Parking** 60 **Notes** LB Closed 24-26 Dec Civ Wed 70

POWYS

BRECON · Map 9 SO02

See also **Llyswen**

Lansdowne Hotel & Restaurant

★★ 65% SMALL HOTEL

☎ 01874 623321 · 🖨 01874 610438
The Watton LD3 7EG
e-mail: reception@lansdownehotel.co.uk
dir: A40/A470 onto B4601

Now a privately owned and personally run hotel, this Georgian house is conveniently located close to the town centre. The accommodation is well equipped and includes family rooms and a bedroom on ground floor level. There is a comfortable lounge and an attractive split-level dining room containing a bar.

Rooms 9 (2 fmly) (1 GF) **S** £40-£50; **D** £60-£70 (incl. bkfst)* **Notes** LB No children 5yrs

Peterstone Court

◉◉ RESTAURANT WITH ROOMS

☎ 01874 665387
Llanhamlach LD3 7YB
e-mail: info@peterstone-court.com
dir: 3m from Brecon on A40 towards Avergavenny

This establishment affords stunning views as it stands on the edge of the Brecon Beacons and overlooks the River Usk. The style is friendly and informal, without any unnecessary fuss. No two bedrooms are alike, but all share comparable levels of comfort, quality and elegance. Public areas reflect similar standards, eclectically styled with a blend of contemporary and traditional. Quality produce is cooked with care in a range of enjoyable dishes.

Rooms 12 (12 en suite) (4 annexe) (2 fmly)

BUILTH WELLS · Map 9 SO05

Caer Beris Manor · THE INDEPENDENTS HOTEL ASSOCIATION

★★★ 75% COUNTRY HOUSE HOTEL

☎ 01982 552601 · 🖨 01982 552586
LD2 3NP
e-mail: caerberis@btconnect.com
web: www.caerberis.com
dir: from town centre follow A483/Llandovery signs. Hotel on left

Guests can expect a relaxing stay at this friendly and privately owned hotel that has extensive landscaped grounds. Bedrooms are individually decorated and furnished to retain an atmosphere of a bygone era. The spacious and comfortable lounge and a lounge bar continue this theme, and there's an elegant restaurant, complete with 16th-century panelling.

Rooms 23 (1 fmly) (3 GF) **S** fr £67.95; **D** fr £115 (incl. bkfst) **Facilities** FTV Fishing 🎣 Gym Clay pigeon shooting Xmas New Year Wi-fi **Conf** Class 75 Board 50 Thtr 100 **Parking** 100 **Notes** LB Civ Wed 200

Pencerrig Gardens

★★ 🅰 COUNTRY HOUSE HOTEL

☎ 01982 553226 · 🖨 01982 552347
Llandrindod Wells Rd LD2 3TF
e-mail: info@pencerrig.co.uk
web: www.pencerrig.co.uk
dir: 2m N on A483 towards Llandrindod Wells

Rooms 20 (10 annexe) (4 fmly) (5 GF) **S** £55-£59.95; **D** £79.95-£89.95 (incl. bkfst)* **Facilities** 🎣 Wi-fi **Conf** Class 90 Board 80 Thtr 135 **Parking** 50 **Notes** LB

INSPECTORS' CHOICE

The Drawing Room

◉◉ RESTAURANT WITH ROOMS

☎ 01982 552493
Cwmbach, Newbridge-on-Wye LD2 3RT
e-mail: post@the-drawing-room.co.uk
dir: 3m NW of Builth on A470

This delightful Georgian country house has been extensively and tastefully renovated by the present owners, to provide three comfortable and very well equipped bedrooms, all with luxurious en suite facilities. Public rooms include two comfortable lounges with welcoming log fires, a room for private dining and a very elegant and intimate dining room, which provides the ideal setting for the cooking skills of Colin Dawson.

Rooms 3

CAERSWS · Map 15 SO09

The Talkhouse

◉◉ RESTAURANT WITH ROOMS

☎ 01686 688919 · 🖨 01686 689134
Pontdolgoch SY17 5JE
e-mail: info@talkhouse.co.uk
dir: 1.5m NW of Caersws on A470

A highlight of this delightful 19th-century inn is the food, home-made dishes making good use of local produce. Bedrooms offer luxury in every area and the cosy lounge, filled with sofas, is the place to while away some time with a glass of wine or a pot of tea. The bar features a large fireplace.

Rooms 3 (1 en suite)

CRICKHOWELL · Map 9 SO21

Gliffaes Country House Hotel

★★★ 80% COUNTRY HOUSE HOTEL

☎ 01874 730371 · 🖨 01874 730463
NP8 1RH
e-mail: calls@gliffaeshotel.com
web: www.gliffaeshotel.com
dir: 1m off A40, 2.5m W of Crickhowell

This impressive Victorian mansion, standing in 33 acres of its own gardens and wooded grounds by the River Usk, is a privately-owned and personally-run hotel. Public rooms retain elegance and generous proportions and include a balcony and conservatory from which to enjoy the views. Bedrooms are very well decorated and furnished and offer high levels of comfort.

Rooms 23 (4 annexe) (1 GF) **S** £84-£105; **D** £92.50-£225 (incl. bkfst)* **Facilities** FTV ⌇ Fishing ⌇ Cycling Xmas New Year Wi-fi **Conf** Class 16 Board 16 Thtr 40 **Parking** 34 **Notes** ⊗ Closed 2-26 Jan Civ Wed 50

Bear

WELSH RAREBITS

★★★ 77% ⊛ HOTEL

☎ 01873 810408 🖹 01873 811696
NP8 1BW
e-mail: bearhotel@aol.com
dir: on A40 between Abergavenny & Brecon

A favourite with locals as well as visitors, the character and friendliness of this 15th-century coaching inn are renowned. The bedrooms come in a variety of sizes and standards including some with four-posters. The bar and restaurant are furnished in keeping with the style of the building and provide comfortable areas in which to enjoy some of the very popular dishes that use the finest locally-sourced ingredients.

Rooms 34 (13 annexe) (6 fmly) (6 GF) **S** £70-£117; **D** £86-£153 (incl. bkfst) **Facilities** STV FTV Xmas New Year Wi-fi **Conf** Class 20 Board 20 Thtr 40 Del from £136 to £180 **Parking** 45 **Notes** RS 25 Dec

Manor

★★★ 74% ⊛ HOTEL

☎ 01873 810212 🖹 01873 811938
Brecon Rd NP8 1SE
e-mail: info@manorhotel.co.uk
web: www.manorhotel.co.uk
dir: on A40, Crickhowell/Brecon, 0.5m from Crickhowell

This impressive manor house, set in a stunning location, was the birthplace of Sir George Everest. The bedrooms

and public areas are elegant, and there are extensive leisure facilities. The restaurant, with panoramic views, is the setting for exciting modern cooking. Guests can also dine informally at the nearby Nantyffin Cider Mill, a sister operation of the hotel.

Rooms 22 (1 fmly) **S** £65-£90; **D** £75-£120 (incl. bkfst)* **Facilities** ⓣ Gym Fitness assessment Sunbed Xmas New Year Wi-fi **Conf** Class 250 Board 150 Thtr 300 Del from £110 to £120* **Parking** 200 **Notes** Civ Wed 150

Ty Croeso

★★★ 72% ⊛ SMALL HOTEL

☎ 01873 810573 🖹 01873 810573
The Dardy, Llangattock NP8 1PU
e-mail: tycroeso@gmail.com
dir: A40 at Shell garage take road opposite, down hill over river bridge. Right, then after 0.5m left, up hill over canal, hotel signed

Ty Croeso, meaning 'House of Welcome' certainly lives up to its name under the careful guidance of the owners. The restaurant offers carefully prepared dishes with a real emphasis on Welsh produce, a theme that continues at breakfast when Glamorgan sausages and laverbread are available. A comfortable lounge features a log fire. Bedrooms are decorated with pretty fabrics and equipped with good facilities.

Rooms 8 (1 fmly) **S** £50; **D** £70-£95 (incl. bkfst)* **Facilities** New Year Wi-fi **Parking** 16 **Notes** LB ⊗

HAY-ON-WYE Map 9 SO24

The Swan-at-Hay

WELSH RAREBITS

★★★ 72% ⊛ HOTEL

☎ 01497 821188 🖹 01497 821424
Church St HR3 5DQ
e-mail: info@theswanathay.co.uk
dir: on B4350 in town centre

This former coaching inn dates back to the 1800s and is only a short walk from the town centre. Bedrooms are well equipped and some are located in either the main hotel or in converted cottages across the courtyard. Spacious, relaxing public areas include a comfortable lounge, a choice of bars and a more formal restaurant. There is also a large function room and a smaller meeting room.

Rooms 18 (4 annexe) (1 fmly) (2 GF) **S** £75; **D** £99-£125 (incl. bkfst)* **Facilities** Fishing New Year Wi-fi **Conf** Class 60 Board 50 Thtr 140 **Parking** 18 **Notes** LB Civ Wed 70

KNIGHTON Map 9 SO27

Milebrook House

WELSH RAREBITS

★★ 85% ⊛⊛ COUNTRY HOUSE HOTEL

☎ 01547 528632 🖹 01547 520509
Milebrook LD7 1LT
e-mail: hotel@milebrook.kc3ltd.co.uk
web: www.milebrookhouse.co.uk
dir: 2m E of Knighton, on A4113

Set in three acres of grounds and gardens in the Teme Valley, this charming house dates back to 1760. Over the years since its conversion into a hotel, it has acquired a well-deserved reputation for its warm hospitality, comfortable accommodation and the quality of its cuisine, that uses local produce and home-grown vegetables.

Rooms 10 (2 fmly) (2 GF) **S** £66-£71; **D** £103-£112.50 (incl. bkfst)* **Facilities** Fishing ⌇ Table tennis Trout fly fishing Xmas New Year Wi-fi **Conf** Class 30 **Parking** 20 **Notes** LB ⊗ No children 8yrs RS Mon lunch

---

LLANDRINDOD WELLS Map 9 SO06

The Metropole

CLASSIC BRITISH HOTELS

★★★ 80% ⊛ HOTEL

☎ 01597 823700 🖹 01597 824828
Temple St LD1 5DY
e-mail: info@metropole.co.uk
web: www.metropole.co.uk
dir: on A483 in town centre

The centre of this famous spa town is dominated by this large Victorian hotel, which has been personally run by the same family for well over 100 years. The lobby leads to Spencers Bar and Brasserie and to the comfortable and elegantly styled lounge. Bedrooms vary in style, but all are quite spacious and well equipped. Facilities include an extensive range of conference and function rooms, as well as a leisure centre.

Continued

LLANDRINDOD WELLS continued

Rooms 120 (11 fmly) **S** £89-£110; **D** £115-£160 (incl. bkfst)* **Facilities** Spa ⓣ Gym Beauty & holistic treatments Sauna Steam room Xmas New Year Wi-fi **Conf** Class 200 Board 80 Thtr 300 **Services** Lift **Parking** 150 **Notes** LB Civ Wed 300

See advert on this page

LLANFYLLIN Map 15 SJ11

Cain Valley

★★ 78% HOTEL

☎ 01691 648366 📠 01691 648307
High St SY22 5AQ
e-mail: info@cainvalleyhotel.co.uk
dir: at end of A490. Hotel in town centre, car park at rear

This Grade II listed coaching inn has a lot of charm and character including features such as exposed beams and a Jacobean staircase. The comfortable accommodation includes family rooms and a wide range of food is available in a choice of bars, or in the restaurant, which has a well-deserved reputation for its locally sourced steaks.

Rooms 13 (2 fmly) (13 smoking) **S** £42-£50; **D** £67-£80 (incl. bkfst)* **Parking** 10 **Notes** LB

LLANGAMMARCH WELLS Map 9 SN94

HOTEL OF THE YEAR
INSPECTORS' CHOICE

The Lake Country House & Spa

★★★ ⓖⓖ COUNTRY HOUSE HOTEL

☎ 01591 620202 & 620474 📠 01591 620457
LD4 4BS
e-mail: info@lakecountryhouse.co.uk
web: www.lakecountryhouse.co.uk
dir: W from Builth Wells on A483 to Garth (approx 6m). Left for Llangammarch Wells, follow hotel signs

Expect good old-fashioned values and hospitality at this Victorian country house hotel. In fact, the service is so traditionally English, guests may believe they have a butler! The establishment offers a 9-hole, par 3 golf course, 50 acres of wooded grounds and a spa where the hot tub overlooks the lake. Bedrooms, some located in an annexe, and some at ground-floor level, are individually styled and have many extra comforts. Traditional afternoon teas are served in the lounge and award-winning cuisine is provided in the spacious and elegant restaurant. AA Hotel of the Year for Wales 2008-9.

Rooms 30 (7 GF) **S** £115-£180; **D** £170-£250 (incl. bkfst)* **Facilities** Spa FTV ⓣ ⓩ 9 ⓢ Putt green Fishing ⓢ Gym Archery Horse riding Mountain biking Quad biking Xmas Wi-fi **Conf** Class 30 Board 25 Thtr 80 **Parking** 70 **Notes** LB Civ Wed 100

LLANWDDYN Map 15 SJ01

Lake Vyrnwy

★★★ 75% ⓖ
COUNTRY HOUSE HOTEL

☎ 01691 870692 📠 01691 870259
Lake Vyrnwy SY10 0LY
e-mail: info@lakevyrnwyhotel.co.uk
web: www.lakevyrnwyhotel.co.uk
dir: on A4393, 200yds past dam turn sharp right into drive

This fine country-house hotel lies in 26,000 acres of woodland above Lake Vyrnwy. It provides a wide range of bedrooms, most with superb views and many with four-poster beds and balconies. The extensive public rooms are elegantly furnished and include a terrace, a choice of bars serving meals and the more formal dining in the restaurant.

Rooms 52 (4 fmly) **S** £95-£185; **D** £120-£210 (incl. bkfst)* **Facilities** Spa STV FTV ⓢ Fishing Gym Archery Birdwatching Canoeing Kayaking Clay shooting Sailing Fly fishing Cycling Xmas New Year Wi-fi **Conf** Class 80 Board 60 Thtr 200 Del from £140 to £160* **Services** Lift **Parking** 70 **Notes** LB Civ Wed 200

LLANWRTYD WELLS   Map 9 SN84

INSPECTORS' CHOICE

Carlton Riverside

RESTAURANT WITH ROOMS

☎ 01591 610248
Irfon Crescent LD5 4SP
e-mail: info@carltonrestaurant.co.uk
dir: In town centre next to bridge

Guests become part of the family at this character property, set beside the river in Wales's smallest town. Carlton Riverside offers award-winning cuisine for which Mary Ann Gilchrist relies on the very best of local ingredients. The set menu is complemented by a well-chosen wine list and dinner is served in the delightfully stylish restaurant which offers a memorable blend of traditional comfort, modern design and river views. Four comfortable bedrooms have tasteful combinations of antique and contemporary furniture, along with welcome personal touches.

Rooms 4 (4 en suite)

Lasswade Country House

RESTAURANT WITH ROOMS

☎ 01591 610515   01591 610611
Station Rd LD5 4RW
e-mail: info@lasswadehotel.co.uk
dir: off A483 into Ifron Terrace, right into Station Rd, hotel 350yds on right

This friendly establishment on the edge of the town has impressive views over the countryside. Bedrooms are comfortably furnished and well equipped, while the public areas consist of a tastefully decorated lounge, an elegant restaurant with a bar, and an airy conservatory which looks out on to the neighbouring hills, for breakfast. The kitchen utilises fresh, local produce to provide an enjoyable dining experience.

Rooms 8 (6 en suite)

LLYSWEN   Map 9 SO13

Llangoed Hall   WELSH RAREBITS

★★★★ 85% ◎◎ COUNTRY HOUSE HOTEL

☎ 01874 754525   01874 754545
LD3 0YP
e-mail: enquiries@llangoedhall.com
web: www.llangoedhall.com
dir: On A470, 2m from Llyswen towards Builth Wells

Set against the stunning backdrop of the Black Mountains and the Wye Valley, this imposing country house is a haven of peace and quiet. The interior is no less impressive, with a noteworthy art collection complementing the many antiques featured in day rooms and bedrooms. Comfortable, spacious bedrooms and suites are matched by equally inviting lounges.

Rooms 23 **S** £175-£350; **D** £210-£400 (incl. bkfst)*
Facilities Fishing ⚓ Maze Clay pigeon shooting ♫ Xmas New Year Wi-fi **Conf** Class 30 Board 30 Thtr 80 Del from £150 to £200* **Parking** 80 **Notes** LB ⊗ No children 8yrs Civ Wed 80

MACHYNLLETH

See Eglwysfach (Ceredigion)

MONTGOMERY   Map 15 SO29

Dragon

★★ 79% ◎ HOTEL

☎ 01686 668359   0870 011 8227
SY15 6PA
e-mail: reception@dragonhotel.com
web: www.dragonhotel.com
dir: behind town hall

This fine 17th-century coaching inn stands in the centre of Montgomery. Beams and timbers from the nearby castle, which was destroyed by Cromwell, are visible in the lounge and bar. A wide choice of soundly prepared, wholesome food is available in both the restaurant and bar. Bedrooms are well equipped and family rooms are available.

Rooms 20 (6 fmly) (2 smoking) **S** £51-£61;
D £87.50-£97.50 (incl. bkfst)* **Facilities** ⊗ ♫ Xmas New Year Wi-fi **Conf** Class 30 Board 25 Thtr 40 **Parking** 21 **Notes** LB

WELSHPOOL   Map 15 SJ20

Royal Oak   WELSH RAREBITS

★★★ 78% ◎ HOTEL

☎ 01938 552217   01938 556652
The Cross SY21 7DG
e-mail: relax@royaloakhotel.info
web: www.royaloakhotel.info
dir: by lights at junct of A483/A458

This traditional market town hotel dates back over 350 years. Sympathetic renovation has provided public areas, furnished in minimalist style to highlight the many retained period features, including exposed beams and open fires. Three different bedroom styles provide good comfort levels and imaginative food is served in the elegant Red Room or adjacent all day café/bar.

Rooms 25 (3 fmly) **S** £60-£90; **D** £80-£110 (incl. bkfst)
Facilities FTV Xmas New Year Wi-fi **Conf** Class 60 Board 60 Thtr 150 **Parking** 30 **Notes** ⊗ Civ Wed

---

RHONDDA CYNON TAFF

MISKIN   Map 9 ST08

Miskin Manor Country Hotel

★★★★ 74% ◎◎ COUNTRY HOUSE HOTEL

☎ 01443 224204   01443 237606
Pendoylan Rd CF72 8ND
e-mail: ben.rosenberg@miskin-manor.co.uk
web: www.miskin-manor.co.uk
dir: M4 junct 34, exit onto A4119, signed Llantrisant, hotel 300yds on left

This historic manor house is peacefully located in 20-acre grounds yet only minutes away from the M4. Bedrooms are furnished to a high standard and include some located in converted stables and cottages. Public areas are spacious and comfortable and include a variety of function rooms. The relaxed atmosphere and the

Continued

MISKIN continued

surroundings ensure this hotel remains popular for wedding functions as well as with business guests.

Rooms 43 (9 annexe) (2 fmly) (7 GF) **Facilities** ⊘ supervised ⚐ Gym Squash Xmas New Year Wi-fi **Conf** Class 80 Board 65 Thtr 160 **Parking** 200 **Notes** Civ Wed 120

PONTYPRIDD Map 9 ST08

Llechwen Hall

★★★ 74% ⊛ COUNTRY HOUSE HOTEL

☎ 01443 742050 & 743020 📠 01443 742189
Llanfabon CF37 4HP
e-mail: steph@llechwen.co.uk
dir: A470 N towards Merthyr Tydfil. At large rdbt take 3rd exit. At mini rdbt take 3rd exit, hotel signed 0.5m on left

Set on top of a hill with a stunning approach, this country house hotel has served many purposes in its 200-year-old history including being a private school and a magistrates' court. Bedrooms are spacious, individually decorated and well equipped, and some are situated in the separate comfortable coach house nearby. There are bedrooms ground-floor, twin, double and family rooms on offer. The Victorian-style public areas are attractively appointed and the hotel is a popular venue for weddings.

Rooms 20 (8 annexe) (6 fmly) (4 GF) **Facilities** FTV New Year Wi-fi **Conf** Class 40 Board 40 Thtr 80 **Parking** 150 **Notes** Closed 24-30 Dec Civ Wed 80

REYNOLDSTON Map 8 SS48

INSPECTORS' CHOICE

Fairyhill
⊛⊛ RESTAURANT WITH ROOMS

☎ 01792 390139 📠 01792 391358
SA3 1BS
e-mail: postbox@fairyhill.net
dir: M4 junct 47 onto A483, at next rdbt turn right onto A484. At Gowerton take B4295 10m

Peace and tranquillity are never far away at this charming Georgian mansion set in the heart of the beautiful Gower peninsula. Bedrooms are furnished with care individuality and are filled with many thoughtful extras. There is also a range of comfortable seating areas with crackling log fires to choose from, and a smart restaurant offering menus based on local produce, complemented by an excellent wine list.

Rooms 8 (8 en suite)

See also **Port Talbot (Neath Port Talbot)**

Swansea Marriott Hotel
Marriott HOTELS & RESORTS

★★★★ 78% HOTEL

☎ 0870 400 7282 📠 0870 400 7382
The Maritime Quarter SA1 3SS
web: www.swanseamarriott.co.uk
dir: M4 junct 42, A483 to city centre past Leisure Centre, then follow signs to Maritime Quarter

Just opposite City Hall, this busy hotel enjoys fantastic views over the bay and marina. Bedrooms are spacious and equipped with a range of extras. Public rooms include a popular leisure club and Abernethy's Restaurant, which overlooks the marina. It is worth noting, however, that lounge seating is limited.

Rooms 122 (50 fmly) (11 GF) **Facilities** ⊘ Gym **Conf** Class 120 Board 30 Thtr 250 **Services** Lift Air con **Parking** 122 **Notes** LB ⊗ Civ Wed 200

Dragon
CLASSIC BRITISH HOTELS

★★★★ 75% ⊛ HOTEL

☎ 01792 657100 & 0870 4299 848 📠 01792 456044
The Kingsway Circle SA1 5LS
e-mail: info@dragon-hotel.co.uk
web: www.dragon-hotel.co.uk
dir: A483 follow signs for city centre. After lights at Sainsbury's right onto Strand then left. Hotel straight ahead

This privately owned hotel is located in the centre of the city and offers spacious modern accommodation. There is a bar and lounge on the first floor along with the dining room for breakfast. On the ground floor the Dragons Brasserie provides award-winning food from a vibrant continental menu for both residents and non-residents. The health and fitness club offers an excellent selection of facilities.

Rooms 106 (5 fmly) (18 smoking) **Facilities** STV ⊘ supervised Gym Beauty therapist Xmas New Year Wi-fi **Conf** Class 120 Board 60 Thtr 230 **Services** Lift Air con **Parking** 40 **Notes** ⊗ Civ Wed 200

Ramada Swansea
⊛RAMADA

★★★ 77% HOTEL

☎ 01792 310330 📠 01792 797535
Phoenix Way, Swansea Enterprise Park SA7 9EG
e-mail: sales.swansea@ramadajarvis.co.uk
web: www.ramadajarvis.co.uk
dir: M4 junct 44, A48 (Llansamlet), left at 3rd lights, right at 1st mini rdbt, left into Phoenix Way at 2nd mini rdbt. Hotel 800mtrs on right

This large, modern hotel is conveniently situated on the outskirts of the city with easy access to the M4. Bedrooms are comfortably appointed for both business and leisure guests. Public areas include the Arts Restaurant, Arts Bar and elegant lounges. 24-hour room service is also available.

Rooms 119 (12 fmly) (50 GF) **S** £63-£162; **D** £63-£174 (incl. bkfst)* **Facilities** STV FTV ⊘ supervised Gym Sauna New Year Wi-fi **Conf** Class 80 Board 60 Thtr 200 Del from £120 to £145* **Parking** 180 **Notes** LB Civ Wed 120

The Grand
Ⓤ

☎ 01792 645898 📠 01792 512159
Ivey Place, High St SA1 1NX
e-mail: info@thegrandhotelswansea.co.uk
dir: M4 junct 42, follow rail station signs

Currently the rating for this establishment is not confirmed. This may be due to a change of ownership or because it has only recently joined the AA rating scheme. For further details please see the AA website: www.theAA.com

Rooms 31 (4 fmly) **S** £70-£120; **D** £75-£120 (incl. bkfst) **Facilities** FTV Gym Sauna Steam room Xmas New Year Wi-fi **Conf** Class 40 Board 40 Thtr 70 Del from £115 to £155 **Services** Lift Air con **Notes** LB ⊗

Express by Holiday Inn Swansea - West

BUDGET HOTEL

☎ 0870 442 5560 📠 0870 442 5561
Neath Rd, Llandarcy SA10 6JQ
e-mail: gm.swansea@expressholidayinn.co.uk
web: www.hiexpress.com/swanseam4j43

A modern hotel ideal for families and business travellers. Fresh and uncomplicated, the spacious rooms include Sky TV, power shower and tea and coffee-making facilities. Continental buffet breakfast is included in the room rate; other meals may be taken at the nearby family pub or restaurant. See also the Hotel Groups pages.

Rooms 91 **Conf** Class 20 Board 16 Thtr 25

Travelodge Swansea Central

BUDGET HOTEL

☎ 0871 9846326
Princess Way SA1 3LW
web: www.travelodge.co.uk
dir: A4067, right onto slip road, then bear right onto Wind St, left after 3m then left onto St Mary St. Hotel on Princess Way

Travelodge offers good quality, good value, modern accommodation. Ideal for families, the spacious, en suite bedroom include remote-control TV, tea and coffee-making facilities, luxury beds and free morning newspaper. Meals can be taken in their own Café Bar or at nearby family restaurants. See also the Hotel Groups pages.

Rooms 70 **S** fr £29; **D** fr £29

Travelodge Swansea (M4)

BUDGET HOTEL

☎ 0871 9846055 📠 01792 898972
Penllergaer SA4 9GT
web: www.travelodge.co.uk
dir: M4 junct 47

Rooms 50 **S** fr £29; **D** fr £29 **Conf** Class 32 Board 20 Thtr 25

TORFAEN

CWMBRAN Map 9 ST29

Best Western Parkway

★★★★ 78% HOTEL

☎ 01633 871199 📠 01633 869160
Cwmbran Dr NP44 3UW
e-mail: enquiries@parkwayhotel.co.uk
web: www.bw-parkwayhotel.co.uk
dir: M4 junct 25A/26/A4051 follow signs Cwmbran-Llantarnam Park. Turn right at rdbt then right for hotel

This hotel is purpose-built and offers comfortable bedrooms and public areas suitable for a wide variety of guests. There is a sports centre and a range of conference and meeting facilities. The coffee shop offers an informal eating option during the day and there is fine dining in Ravello's Restaurant.

Rooms 70 (4 fmly) (34 GF) **S** £70-£150; **D** £80-£160 (incl. bkfst) **Facilities** STV 🏊 Gym Steam room Solaria ♫ Xmas New Year Wi-fi **Conf** Class 240 Board 100 Thtr 500 **Parking** 350 **Notes** LB ⊗ Closed 27-30 Dec Civ Wed 250

PONTYPOOL Map 9 SO20

Express by Holiday Inn Pontypool - Cwmbran

BUDGET HOTEL

☎ 01495 755266 📠 01495 755331
Tyr'felin - Lower Mill Field NP4 0RH
e-mail: exhi-pontypool@btconnect.com
web: www.hiexpress.com/pontypoolgwent
dir: at junct of A4042/A472, adjacent to the Harvester Restaurant

A modern hotel ideal for families and business travellers. Fresh and uncomplicated, the spacious rooms include Sky TV, power shower and tea and coffee-making facilities. Continental buffet breakfast is included in the room rate; other meals may be taken at the nearby family pub or restaurant. See also the Hotel Groups pages.

Rooms 49 (20 fmly)

VALE OF GLAMORGAN

BARRY
Map 9 ST16

Egerton Grey Country House

★★★ 80% ⊛ COUNTRY HOUSE HOTEL WELSH RAREBITS

☎ 01446 711666 🖨 01446 711690
Porthkerry CF62 3BZ
e-mail: info@egertongrey.co.uk
web: www.egertongrey.co.uk
dir: M4 junct 33 follow signs for airport, left at rdbt for Porthkerry, after 500yds turn left down lane between thatched cottages

This former rectory enjoys a peaceful setting and views over delightful countryside with distant glimpses of the sea. The bedrooms are spacious and individually furnished. Public areas offer charm and elegance, and include an airy lounge and restaurant, which has been sympathetically converted from the billiards room.

Rooms 10 (4 fmly) **S** £100-£120; **D** £140-£170 (incl. bkfst)* **Facilities** FTV Putt green ⛳ Xmas New Year Wi-fi **Conf** Class 30 Board 22 Thtr 30 **Parking** 40 **Notes** LB Civ Wed 40

Best Western Mount Sorrel

★★★ 74% HOTEL

☎ 01446 740069 🖨 01446 746600
Porthkerry Rd CF62 7XY
e-mail: reservations@mountsorrel.co.uk
dir: M4 junct 33 onto A4232. Follow signs for A4050 through Barry. At mini-rdbt (with church opposite) turn left, hotel 300mtrs on left

Situated in an elevated position above the town centre, this extended Victorian property is ideally placed for exploring Cardiff and the nearby coast. The public areas include a choice of conference rooms, a restaurant with a bar called Strings, and smart leisure facilities with an indoor swimming pool and multi-gym. There is a comfortable bar and separate, cosy lounge.

Rooms 42 (3 fmly) (5 GF) **Facilities** ⊛ supervised Gym Xmas **Conf** Class 100 Board 50 Thtr 150 **Parking** 17 **Notes** LB ⊗ Civ Wed 150

Innkeeper's Lodge Cardiff Airport

BUDGET HOTEL

☎ 0845 112 6081 🖨 0845 112 6222
Port Road West CF62 3BA
web: www.innkeeperslodge.com/cardiffairport
dir: M4 junct 33, A4232 towards Cardiff. At rdbt with A4050 follow Barry signs. At rdbt with A4226 follow Cardiff Airport signs. Pass rdbt towards Cardiff Airport. Lodge on left

Innkeeper's Lodge represents an exciting, high value concept within the budget hotel market. Comfortable bedrooms provide excellent facilities that include satellite TV and modem points. Options include family rooms, and for the corporate guest, cutting edge IT which includes Wi-fi access. A popular Carvery provides all-day food, including an extensive, complimentary continental breakfast.

Rooms 28 **S** £58; **D** £58 (incl. bkfst)

HENSOL
Map 9 ST07

Vale Hotel Golf & Spa Resort

★★★★ 79% HOTEL

☎ 01443 667800 🖨 01443 665850
Hensol Park CF72 8JY
e-mail: reservations@vale-hotel.com
web: www.vale-hotel.com
dir: M4 junct 34 towards Pendoylan, hotel signed approx 3 mins' drive from junct

A wealth of leisure facilities is offered at this large, modern, purpose-built complex, including two golf courses and a driving range, extensive health spa, gym, swimming pool, squash courts and an orthopaedic clinic. Public areas are spacious and attractive, while bedrooms, many with balconies, are well appointed. Guests can dine either in La Cucina which boasts a wood-fired oven, or the more traditional Lakes restaurant. Meeting and conference facilities are available.

Rooms 143 (114 annexe) (15 fmly) (36 GF) **S** £70-£295; **D** £70-£340 (incl. bkfst)* **Facilities** Spa STV ⊗ ♨ 36 ⛳ Putt green Fishing Gym Squash Children's club Indoor training arena Xmas New Year Wi-fi **Conf** Class 180 Board 60 Thtr 300 Del from £135 to £175* **Services** Lift Air con **Parking** 300 **Notes** ⊗ Civ Wed 200

See advert on page 673

ST GEORGE'S

Greendown Inn

★★ 🅰 HOTEL

☎ 01446 760310 🖨 01446 760937
Drope Rd CF5 6EP
e-mail: enquiries@greendownhotel.co.uk
web: www.greendownhotel.co.uk
dir: A4232, left onto A48 & sharp left onto Michaelstone Rd, left at school onto Drope Rd. Inn 1.5m on left

Rooms 15 (3 fmly) (10 GF) **S** £39.95-£60; **D** £60-£150 (incl. bkfst) **Conf** Class 60 Board 60 Thtr 60 Del from £60 to £100 **Parking** 90 **Notes** Civ Wed 90

WREXHAM

GLYN CEIRIOG
Map 15 SJ23

Golden Pheasant Country Hotel & Inn

★★★ 73% HOTEL

☎ 01691 718281 🖨 01691 718479
Llwynmawr LL20 7BB
e-mail: info@goldenpheasanthotel.co.uk
web: www.goldenpheasanthotel.co.uk
dir: A5/B4500 at Chirk, then 5m to Pontfadog, follow hotel signs, 1st left after Cheshire Home. Take left after bend to Llywnmawr in Dolywern. Hotel at top of small hill

Located in the heart of the unspoilt Ceriog Valley, this period hotel enjoys stunning views of the countryside. Popular with shooting and walking parties, the public areas retain many original features including a fine taxidermy collection of game birds, and a roaring fire burns in the character bars during the cooler months.

Rooms 20 (1 fmly) (1 GF) **S** £50-£60; **D** £90-£110 (incl. bkfst)* **Facilities** Fishing Bike hire Xmas New Year Wi-fi **Conf** Class 24 Board 20 Del from £135 to £150* **Parking** 24 **Notes** LB

LLANARMON DYFFRYN CEIRIOG Map 15 SJ13

West Arms

WELSH RAREBITS

★★★ 87% ◎◎ HOTEL

☎ 01691 600665 & 600612 🖨 01691 600622
LL20 7LD
e-mail: gowestarms@aol.com
dir: Off A483/A5 at Chirk, take B4500 to Ceiriog Valley.
Llanarmon 11m at end of B4500

Set in the beautiful Ceiriog Valley, this delightful hotel
has a wealth of charm and character. There is a
comfortable lounge, a room for private dining and two
bars, as well as a pleasant, award-winning restaurant
offering a set-price menu of freshly cooked dishes. The
attractive bedrooms have a mixture of modern and period
furnishings.

Rooms 15 (2 fmly) (3 GF) **S** £53.50–£118; **D** £87–£225
(incl. bkfst)* **Facilities** Fishing Xmas New Year Wi-fi
Child facilities **Conf** Class 50 Board 50 Thtr 60
Del from £100 to £135* **Parking** 20 **Notes** LB Civ Wed 50

ROSSETT Map 15 SJ35

Rossett Hall

★★★ 83% HOTEL

☎ 01244 571000 🖨 01244 571505
Chester Rd LL12 0DE
e-mail: info@rossetthallhotel.co.uk
web: www.rossetthallhotel.co.uk
dir: M56/M53/A55. Take Wrexham/Chester exit towards
Wrexham. Onto B5445, hotel in village

This privately owned and personally run hotel lies in
several acres of mature gardens in the lovely Welsh
border country. Pretty bedrooms are generally spacious
and well equipped, and include ground-floor rooms and a
full suite. A comfortable foyer lounge is provided and
Oscar's bistro serves a wide range of skilfully prepared
dishes.

Rooms 50 (4 fmly) (20 GF) **S** £65–£100; **D** £75–£130 (incl.
bkfst)* **Facilities** STV Gym Xmas New Year Wi-fi
Conf Class 50 Board 50 Thtr 150 **Parking** 120 **Notes** LB
⊗ Civ Wed 150

Best Western Llyndir Hall

Best Western

★★★ 79% HOTEL

☎ 01244 571648 🖨 01244 571258
Llyndir Ln LL12 0AY
e-mail: llyndirhallhotel@feathers.uk.com
dir: 5m S of Chester on B5445 follow Pulford signs

Located on the English/Welsh border within easy reach of
Chester and Wrexham, this elegant manor house lies in
several acres of mature grounds. The hotel is popular
with both business and leisure guests, and facilities
include conference rooms, The Business Training Centre,
an impressive leisure centre, a choice of comfortable
lounges and a brasserie-style restaurant.

Rooms 48 (3 fmly) (20 GF) **Facilities** Ⓢ supervised Gym
Steam room, Beauty salon. Xmas **Conf** Class 60 Board 40
Thtr 120 **Parking** 80 **Notes** LB ⊗ Civ Wed 120

WREXHAM Map 15 SJ35

Best Western Cross Lanes Hotel & Restaurant

Best Western

★★★ 75% ◎ HOTEL

☎ 01978 780555 🖨 01978 780568
Cross Lanes, Bangor Rd, Marchwiel LL13 0TF
e-mail: guestservices@crosslanes.co.uk
dir: 3m SE of Wrexham, on A525, between Marchwiel &
Bangor-on-Dee

This hotel was built as a private house in 1890 and
stands in over six acres of beautiful grounds. Bedrooms
are well equipped and meet the needs of today's traveller,
and include two with four-poster beds. A fine selection of
well prepared food is available in Kagan's Brasserie.

Rooms 16 (1 fmly) **Facilities** Putt green 🎣 Xmas Wi-fi
Conf Class 60 Board 40 Thtr 120 **Parking** 80 **Notes** ⊗
Closed 25 Dec (night) & 26 Dec Civ Wed 120

Travelodge Wrexham

Travelodge

BUDGET HOTEL

☎ 0871 984 6116 🖨 01978 365705
Wrexham By Pass, Rhostyllen LL14 4EJ
web: www.travelodge.co.uk
dir: 2m S, A483/A5152 rdbt

Travelodge offers good quality, good value, modern
accommodation. Ideal for families, the spacious en suite
bedrooms include remote-control TV, tea and coffee-
making facilities and comfortable beds. Meals can be
taken at the nearby family restaurant. See also the Hotel
Groups pages.

Rooms 32 **S** fr £29; **D** fr £29

Ireland

Blarney Castle, Munster, Co Cork

Additional Information for Northern Ireland & the Republic of Ireland

Licensing Regulations

Northern Ireland: Public houses open Mon-Sat 11.30-23.00. Sun 12.30-22.00. Hotels can serve residents without restriction. Non-residents can be served 12.30-22.00 on Christmas Day. Children under 18 are not allowed in the bar area and may neither buy nor consume liquor in hotels.

Republic of Ireland: General licensing hours are Mon-Thu 10.30-23.30, Fri & Sat 10.30-00.30. Sun 12.30-23.00 (or 00.30 if the following day is a Bank Holiday). There is no service (except for hotel residents) on Christmas Day or Good Friday.

The Fire Services (NI) Order 1984

This covers establishments accommodating more than six people, which must have a certificate from the Northern Ireland Fire Authority. Places accommodating fewer than six people need adequate exits. AA inspectors check emergency notices, fire fighting equipment and fire exits here.

The Republic of Ireland safety regulations are a matter for local authority regulations. For your own and others' safety, read the emergency notices and be sure you understand them.

Telephone numbers

Area codes for numbers in the Republic of Ireland apply only within the Republic. If dialling from outside check the telephone directory (from the UK the international dialling code is 00 353). Area codes for numbers in Britain and Northern Ireland cannot be used directly from the Republic.

For the latest information on the Republic of Ireland visit the AA Ireland's website: www.AAireland.ie

---

NORTHERN IRELAND

CO ANTRIM

ANTRIM

Express by Holiday Inn Antrim M2 Jct 1

BUDGET HOTEL

☎ 0141 419 3500 ▤ 0141 419 3509
Ballymena Rd BT4 1LL
web: www.hiexpress.com/antrim

A modern hotel ideal for families and business travellers. Fresh and uncomplicated, the spacious rooms include Sky TV, power shower and tea and coffee-making facilities. Continental buffet breakfast is included in the room rate; other meals may be taken at the nearby family pub or restaurant. See also the Hotel Groups pages.

Rooms 90

BALLYMENA — Map 1 D5

Galgorm Resort & Spa

★★★★ 80% HOTEL

☎ 028 2588 1001 ▤ 028 2588 0080
BT42 1EA
e-mail: mail@galgorm.com
dir: 1m from Ballymena on A42, between Galgorm & Cullybackey

Standing in 85 acres of private woodland and sweeping lawns beside the River Maine, this 19th-century mansion offers spacious comfortable bedrooms. Public areas include a welcoming cocktail bar and elegant restaurant, as well as Gillies, a lively and atmospheric locals' bar. Also on the estate is an equestrian centre and a conference hall.

Rooms 75 (14 fmly) (25 GF) **Facilities** Spa STV FTV ⊗ Fishing Gym Clay pigeon shooting Archery ♪ Xmas Wi-fi **Conf** Class 200 Board 30 Thtr 500 **Services** Lift **Parking** 300 **Notes** ⊗ Civ Wed 500

CARNLOUGH — Map 1 D6

Londonderry Arms

★★★ 73% ⊛ HOTEL

IRISH COUNTRY HOTELS

☎ 028 2888 5255 ▤ 028 2888 5263
20 Harbour Rd BT44 0EU
e-mail: lda@glensofantrim.com
dir: 14m N from Larne on coast road, A2

This delightful hotel was built in the mid-19th century by Lady Londonderry, whose grandson, Winston Churchill, also owned it at one time. Today the hotel's Georgian architecture and rooms are still evident, and spacious bedrooms can be found in the modern extension. The hotel enjoys a prime location in this pretty fishing village overlooking the Antrim coast.

Rooms 35 (5 fmly) **Facilities** Fishing ♪ Xmas New Year **Conf** Class 60 Board 40 Thtr 120 **Services** Lift **Parking** 50 **Notes** ⊗ Closed Xmas Civ Wed 60

CARRICKFERGUS — Map 1 D5

Dobbins Inn

★★ 65% HOTEL

☎ 028 9335 1905 ▤ 028 9335 1905
6-8 High St BT38 7AP
e-mail: bookingdobbins@btconnect.com
dir: M2 from Belfast, right at rdbt onto A2 to Carrickfergus. Left opposite castle

Colourful window boxes adorn the front of this popular inn near the ancient castle and seafront. Public areas are furnished to a modern standard without compromising the inn's interesting, historical character. Bedrooms vary in size and style, all provide modern comforts. Staff throughout are very friendly and attentive to guests needs.

Rooms 15 (2 fmly) (3 smoking) **S** £50-£52; **D** £72-£76 (incl. bkfst)* **Facilities** STV ♪ New Year **Notes** Closed 25-26 Dec & 1 Jan RS Good Fri

CO ARMAGH

ARMAGH — Map 1 C5

Charlemont Arms Hotel

★★★ 64% HOTEL

☎ 028 3752 2028 ▤ 028 3752 6979
57/65 English St BT61 7LB
e-mail: info@charlemontarmshotel.com
web: www.charlemontarmshotel.com
dir: A3 from Portadown or A28 from Newry, into Armagh. Follow signs to Tourist Information. Hotel 100yds on right

Centrally located for all of this historic city's principal attractions, this hotel has been under the same family ownership for almost 70 years and offers a choice of dining styles and bars. The mostly spacious bedrooms have all been appointed in a contemporary style and provide all the expected facilities.

Rooms 30 (2 fmly) **Facilities** ♫ Xmas **Conf** Class 100 Board 80 Thtr 150 **Services** Lift **Parking** 30 **Notes** LB ⊗ Closed 25-26 Dec

BELFAST

BELFAST	Map 1 D5

Malone Lodge

★★★★ 73% ⊛ HOTEL

☎ 028 9038 8000 📠 028 9038 8088
60 Eglantine Av BT9 6DY
e-mail: info@malonelodgehotel.com
web: www.malonelodgehotel.com
dir: at hospital rdbt exit towards Bouchar Rd, left at 1st rdbt, right at lights at top, then 1st left

Situated in the leafy suburbs of the university area of south Belfast, this stylish hotel forms the centrepiece of an attractive row of Victorian terraced properties. The unassuming exterior belies an attractive and spacious interior with a smart lounge, popular bar and stylish Green Door restaurant. The hotel also has a small, well-equipped fitness room.

Rooms 51 (5 fmly) (1 GF) **Facilities** Gym **Conf** Class 90 Board 40 Thtr 150 **Services** Lift **Parking** 35 **Notes** LB ⊗ Civ Wed 120

Malmaison Belfast

★★★ 81% ⊛ HOTEL

☎ 028 9022 0200 📠 028 9022 0220
34 - 38 Victoria St BT1 3GH
e-mail: hcaters@malmaison.com
web: www.malmaison.com
dir: M1 along Westlink to Grosvenor Rd. Follow city centre signs. Pass City Hall on right, turn left onto Victoria St. Hotel on right

Situated in a former seed warehouse, this smart, contemporary hotel is ideally located for the city centre. Comfortable bedrooms offer a host of modern facilities, whilst the stylish public areas include a popular bar and a brasserie producing carefully prepared meals. The warm hospitality is notable.

Rooms 64 **S** £150-£170; **D** £150-£170* **Facilities** STV Gym Wi-fi **Conf** Board 22 Del from £165 to £230* **Services** Lift **Notes** LB

The Crescent Townhouse

★★★ 75% ⊛ HOTEL

☎ 028 9032 3349 📠 028 9032 0646
13 Lower Crescent BT7 1NR
e-mail: info@crescenttownhouse.com
dir: S towards Queens University, hotel on Botanic Avenue opposite Botanic Train Station

This stylish, smartly presented Regency town house enjoys a central location close to the botanic gardens and railway station. The popular Bar Twelve and Metro Brasserie are found on the ground floor whilst a clubby lounge and well-equipped bedrooms are situated on the upper floors.

Rooms 17 (1 fmly) **Facilities** ♫ Wi-fi **Conf** Class 20 Board 20 Thtr 40 **Notes** LB ⊗ Closed 25-27 Dec, 1 Jan & part of Jul

Jurys Inn Belfast

★★★ 71% HOTEL

☎ 028 9053 3500 📠 028 9053 3511
Fisherwick Place, Great Victoria St BT2 7AP
e-mail: jurysinnbelfast@jurysdoyle.com
web: www.jurysinns.com
dir: at junct of Grosvenor Rd & Great Victoria St, beside Opera House

Enjoying a central location, this modern hotel is well equipped for business guests. Public areas are contemporary in style and include a foyer lounge, a bar and a smart restaurant. Spacious bedrooms provide modern facilities.

Rooms 190 (80 fmly) (38 smoking) **S** £69-£120; **D** £69-£120* **Facilities** ♫ Wi-fi **Conf** Class 16 Board 16 Thtr 30 Del from £140 to £160* **Services** Lift **Notes** LB ⊗ Closed 24-26 Dec

Days Hotel Belfast

★★★ 68% HOTEL

☎ 028 9024 2494 📠 028 9024 2495
40 Hope St BT12 5EE
e-mail: reservations@dayshotelbelfast.co.uk
web: www.daysinn.com
dir: From end of M1 take exit off Grosvenor rdbt, at 1st lights turn right. Over bridge, next left into Hope Street

This large modern hotel is a short walk from the city centre. Bedrooms are comfortable and well equipped, while the smartly appointed public areas include a spacious bistro style restaurant and an open plan bar/

lounge. The hotel is also ideally located for all transport links as it is beside the Great Victoria Street bus and train station. Central Station is just two minutes away, and the City Airport and ferry terminals are within ten minutes drive.

Rooms 250 **Services** Lift **Parking** 300 **Notes** ⊗

Merchant

Ⓤ

☎ 028 9023 4888 📠 028 9024 7775
35-39 Waring St BT1 2DY
e-mail: info@themerchanthotel.com
dir: In city centre, 2nd left at Albert clock onto Waring St. Hotel on left

Currently the rating for this establishment is not confirmed. This may be due to a change of ownership or because it has only recently joined the AA rating scheme. For further details please see the AA website: www.theAA.com

Rooms 26 (5 fmly) **S** £220-£600; **D** £220-£600 (incl. bkfst) **Facilities** FTV ♫ Xmas New Year Wi-fi **Conf** Class 24 Board 20 Thtr 40 Del from £235 to £365 **Services** Lift Air con **Parking** 26 (charged) **Notes** LB ⊗ Civ Wed 50

Holiday Inn Belfast

Ⓤ

☎ 0870 400 9005 📠 028 9062 6546
22 Ormeau Av BT2 8HS
e-mail: belfast@ihg.com
web: www.holidayinn.co.uk
dir: M1/M2 onto West Link at Grosvenor Rd rdbt, follow city centre signs. 1st right then 2nd left into Hope St, at 2nd lights turn left into Bedford St, at next lights turn right into Ormeau Ave, hotel on right

Currently the rating for this establishment is not confirmed. This may be due to a change of ownership or because it has only recently joined the AA rating scheme. For further details please see the AA website: www.theAA.com

Rooms 170 **S** £69-£189; **D** £69-£189*

Travelodge Belfast Central

BUDGET HOTEL

☎ 08719 846188 📠 028 9023 2999
15 Brunswick St BT2 7GE
web: www.travelodge.co.uk
dir: from M2 follow city centre signs to Oxford St. Turn right to May St, take 4th left

Travelodge offers good quality, good value, modern accommodation. Ideal for families, the spacious en suite bedrooms include remote-control TV, tea and coffee-making facilities and comfortable beds. Meals can be taken at the nearby family restaurant. See also the Hotel Groups pages.

Rooms 90 **S** fr £29; **D** fr £29 **Conf** Class 50 Board 34 Thtr 65

CO DOWN

BANGOR
Map 1 D5

The Old Inn
★★★★ 74% ◎◎ HOTEL

☎ 028 9185 3255 🖷 028 9185 2775
15 Main St BT19 1JH
e-mail: info@theoldinn.com
dir: A2, pass Belfast Airport & Holywood, 3m past
Holywood sign for The Old Inn, 100yds left at lights, into
Crawfordsburn, hotel on left

This delightful hotel enjoys a peaceful rural setting just a
short drive from Belfast. Dating from 1614, many of the
day rooms exude charm and character. Individually styled
bedrooms, some with feature beds, offer comfort and
modern facilities. The popular bar and intimate
restaurant both serve dishes from creative menus, and
staff throughout are keen to please.

Rooms 31 (1 annexe) (7 fmly) (6 GF) **Facilities** ♫ Xmas
New Year Wi-fi **Conf** Class 27 Board 40 Thtr 120
Parking 80 **Notes** LB ⊗ Civ Wed 100

Clandeboye Lodge
★★★★ 74% ◎ HOTEL

☎ 028 9185 2500 🖷 028 9185 2772
10 Estate Rd, Clandeboye BT19 1UR
e-mail: info@clandeboyelodge.co.uk
web: www.clandeboyelodge.com
dir: A2 from Belfast turn right at Blackwood Golf Centre &
Hotel sign. 500yds down Ballysallagh Rd turn left into
Crawfordsburn Rd. Hotel 200yds on left

The hotel is located three miles west of Bangor, and sits
in delightful landscaped grounds adjacent to the
Clandeboye Estate. The bedrooms have a contemporary
design and all have Wi-fi, satellite TV and flat-screen
TVs. The hotel has extensive conference, banqueting and
wedding facilities that are separate from the main hotel.
Public areas also include a bright open-plan foyer bar
and attractive lounge area.

Rooms 43 (2 fmly) (13 GF) **S** fr £90; **D** fr £105 (incl. bkfst)
Facilities FTV Xmas New Year Wi-fi **Conf** Class 150
Board 50 Thtr 450 Del from £135 **Services** Lift
Parking 250 **Notes** LB ⊗ Closed 24-26 Dec Civ Wed 400

Marine Court
★★★ 75% HOTEL

☎ 028 9145 1100 🖷 028 9145 1200
The Marina BT20 5ED
e-mail: marinecourt@btconnect.com
web: www.marinecourthotel.net
dir: pass Belfast city airport, follow A2 through Holywood
to Bangor, down main street follow to seafront

Enjoying a delightful location overlooking the marina, this
hotel offers a good range of conference and leisure
facilities suited to both the business and leisure guest.
Extensive public areas include the informal first-floor
Nelson's Restaurant with views over Belfast Lough, the
lively Bar Mocha and the DJ Bar.

Rooms 51 (11 fmly) (22 smoking) **S** £75-£90; **D** £85-£100
(incl. bkfst)* **Facilities** STV FTV ⊛ supervised Gym
Steam room Whirlpool ♫ New Year Wi-fi **Conf** Class 150
Board 60 Thtr 350 Del from £110 to £129.25*
Services Lift **Parking** 30 **Notes** LB ⊗ Closed 25 Dec
Civ Wed 250

Royal
★★★ 61% HOTEL

☎ 028 9127 1866 🖷 028 9146 7810
Seafront BT20 5ED
e-mail: royalhotelbangor@aol.com
web: www.royalhotelbangor.com
dir: A2 from Belfast. Through town centre to seafront.
Turn right, hotel 300yds

This substantial Victorian hotel enjoys a prime seafront
location and overlooks the marina. Bedrooms are
comfortable and practical in style. Public areas are
traditional and include a choice of contrasting bars
whilst traditional Irish cooking can be sampled in a
popular brasserie venue.

Rooms 49 (5 fmly) **S** £58-£68; **D** £70-£90 (incl. bkfst)
Facilities ♫ Wi-fi **Conf** Class 90 Board 80 Thtr 120
Del from £85 to £100 **Services** Lift **Notes** LB ⊗ Closed
25-26 Dec

NEWCASTLE
Map 1 D5

Burrendale Hotel & Country Club
★★★ 77% HOTEL

☎ 028 4372 2599 🖷 028 4372 2328
51 Castlewellan Rd BT33 0JY
e-mail: reservations@burrendale.com
web: www.burrendale.com
dir: on A24 from Belfast. From Newcastle towards
Castlewellan, hotel 0.5m on right

Set in its own grounds this hotel is ideal for both
business and leisure visitors. Bedrooms are comfortable
and many having wonderful views of the Slieve Donard
mountain. Guests can choose to dine in the stylish
restaurant or enjoy lighter meals in the cosy bar. There
are impressive leisure facilities, and the hotel is a firm
favourite with walkers and golfers visiting the nearby
championship course at Royal County Down.

Rooms 69 (13 fmly) (19 GF) **S** £80-£100; **D** £120-£140
(incl. bkfst)* **Facilities** Spa STV ⊛ supervised Putt green
Gym Spin bike room ♫ Xmas New Year **Conf** Class 80
Board 80 Thtr 300 Del from £99 to £125* **Services** Lift
Parking 250 **Notes** LB ⊗ Civ Wed 200

Enniskeen House
★★ 69% HOTEL

☎ 028 4372 2392 🖷 028 4372 4084
98 Bryansford Rd BT33 0LF
e-mail: info@enniskeenhotel.com
dir: from Newcastle town centre follow signs for Tollymore
Forest Park, hotel 1m on left

Set in ten acres of grounds and in the same family
ownership for over 40 years, this hotel is a hospitable
home-from-home. Bedrooms vary but all are well
equipped and many enjoy super mountain and
countryside views. The formal dining room serves
traditional cuisine and the first-floor lounge makes the
most of the coastal views.

Rooms 12 (1 fmly) **S** £60-£75; **D** £100-£120 (incl. bkfst)*
Facilities Wi-fi **Services** Lift **Parking** 45 **Notes** ⊗ Closed
12 Nov-14 Mar

NEWMARKET-ON-FERGUS — Map 1 B3

INSPECTORS' CHOICE

Dromoland Castle

★★★★★ ⑩⑩ HOTEL

☎ 061 368144 📠 061 363355

e-mail: sales@dromoland.ie

dir: N18 to Ennis/Galway from Shannon for 8km to 'Dromoland Interchange' signed Quin. Take slip road left, 4th exit at 1st rdbt, 2nd exit at 2nd rdbt. Hotel 500mtrs on left

Dromoland Castle, dating from the early 18th century, stands on a 375-acre estate and offers extensive indoor leisure activities and outdoor pursuits. The team are wholly committed to caring for guests. The thoughtfully equipped bedrooms and suites vary in style but all provide excellent levels of comfort, and the magnificent public rooms, warmed by log fires, are no less impressive. The hotel has two restaurants, the elegant fine-dining Earl of Thomond, and less formal Fig Tree in the golf clubhouse.

Rooms 99 (20 fmly) **S** €238-€607; **D** €238-€607*
Facilities Spa STV ☷ supervised ⌁ 18 ⛳ Putt green Fishing Gym Beauty clinic Archery Clay shooting Mountain bikes Driven shoots ♫ New Year Wi-fi **Conf** Class 220 Board 80 Thtr 450 Del from €395 to €550* **Services** Lift **Parking** 120 **Notes** ⊗ Closed 25-26 Dec

SPANISH POINT — Map 1 B3

Armada

 IRISH COUNTRY HOTELS

★★★ 73% HOTEL

☎ 065 7084110 📠 065 7084632

e-mail: info@burkesarmadahotel.com

dir: N18 from Ennis take N85 Inagh, then R460 to Miltown Malbay. Follow signs for Spanish Point

Situated on the coastline, overlooking breaking waves and golden sands, this hotel is located in a natural, unspoiled environment. The public areas benefit from views of this stunning location, especially the contemporary restaurant and the Lower Bar. The contemporary bedrooms, many with sea views, include superior spa suites. The Cape Restaurant, overlooking the ocean, serves good food, and the Lower Bar offers a carvery lunch and bar food all day until late.

Rooms 61 (53 fmly) **Facilities** Gym ♫ Xmas **Conf** Class 400 Board 60 Thtr 600 **Services** Lift **Parking** 175 **Notes** LB ⊗

CO CORK

BALLYCOTTON — Map 1 C2

INSPECTORS' CHOICE

Bay View

 MANOR HOUSE HOTELS

★★★ ⑩⑩ HOTEL

☎ 021 4646746 📠 021 4646075

e-mail: res@thebayviewhotel.com

dir: N25 Castlemartyr, turn right through Ladysbridge & Garryvoe, to Ballycotton

Situated in a fishing village overlooking Ballycotton Bay, the Bay View has a very pleasant atmosphere and a stunning outlook. The public rooms and the bedrooms are very comfortable and make the most of the views, but it is the warm and friendly team that impresses most. Dinner in the Capricho Room is a delight.

Rooms 35 (5 GF) (10 smoking) **S** €117-€133; **D** €170-€222 (incl. bkfst)* **Facilities** STV ⛳ Pitch and putt Sea angling **Conf** Class 30 Board 24 Thtr 60 Del from €170 to €190* **Services** Lift Air con **Parking** 40 **Notes** LB ⊗ Closed Nov-Apr Civ Wed 90

BALLYLICKEY — Map 1 B2

INSPECTORS' CHOICE

Sea View House Hotel

 MANOR HOUSE HOTELS

★★★ ⑩⑩ HOTEL

☎ 027 50073 & 50462 📠 027 51555

e-mail: info@seaviewhousehotel.com

web: www.seaviewhousehotel.com

dir: 5km from Bantry, 11km from Glengarriff on N71

Colourful gardens and glimpses of Bantry Bay through the mature trees frame this delightful country house. Owner Kathleen O'Sullivan's team of staff are exceptionally pleasant and there is a relaxed atmosphere in the cosy lounges. Guest comfort and good cuisine are the top priorities. Bedrooms are spacious and individually styled; some on the ground floor are appointed to suit less able guests.

Rooms 25 (3 fmly) (5 GF) **Parking** 32 **Notes** LB Closed mid Nov-mid Mar

BALTIMORE — Map 1 B1

Casey's of Baltimore

 IRISH COUNTRY HOTELS

★★★ 72% ⑩ HOTEL

☎ 028 20197 📠 028 20509

e-mail: info@caseysofbaltimore.com

web: www.caseysofbaltimore.com

dir: from Cork take N71 to Skibbereen, then take R595

This relaxed family run hotel is situated in the sailing and fishing village of Baltimore. Bedrooms are in two areas; both within the hotel and six suites are available in an annexe a few minutes walk away. Traditional music is played in the cosy bar and lounge at weekends. The Casey's ensure that a variety of the freshest seafood, from Michael's fishing trawler and mussel farm is served in the restaurant. They are happy to organise trips to the many nearby islands.

Continued

BALTIMORE continued

Rooms 14 (1 fmly) (4 GF) **S** €99-€150; **D** €154-€182 (incl. bkfst)* **Facilities** STV FTV ♫ New Year **Conf** Class 30 Board 25 Thtr 45 Del from €120 to €175* **Parking** 50 **Notes** LB ⊗ Closed 21-27 Dec

BANTRY — Map 1 B2

Westlodge

★★★ 71% HOTEL

☎ 027 50360 📄 027 50438
e-mail: reservations@westlodgehotel.ie
web: www.westlodgehotel.ie
dir: N71 to West Cork

A superb leisure centre and good children's facilities makes this hotel very popular with families. Its location on the outskirts of the town also makes it an ideal base for touring west Cork and south Kerry. All the staff are friendly and hospitable. There are extensive banqueting facilities and lovely walks in the grounds.

Rooms 90 (20 fmly) (20 GF) **Facilities** ⊛ supervised ♨ Putt green Gym Squash ♫ New Year Wi-fi **Conf** Class 200 Board 24 Thtr 400 Del from €120 to €160 **Services** Lift Air con **Parking** 400 **Notes** ⊗ Closed 23-27 Dec Civ Wed 300

Maritime

Ⓤ

☎ 027 54700 & 54716 📄 027 54701
The Quay
e-mail: info@themaritime.ie
dir: on N71 towards Bantry hotel on right

Currently the rating for this establishment is not confirmed. This may be due to a change of ownership or because it has only recently joined the AA rating scheme. For further details please see the AA website: www.theAA.com

Rooms 114 (30 fmly) **S** €99-€198; **D** €135-€270 (incl. bkfst)* **Facilities** STV ⊛ supervised Gym Sauna Steam room ♫ New Year Wi-fi **Conf** Class 180 Board 120 Thtr 550 **Services** Lift **Parking** 85 **Notes** LB ⊗ Closed 24-28 Dec

BLARNEY — Map 1 B2

Blarney Golf Resort

★★★★ 75% HOTEL

☎ 021 4384477 📄 021 4516453
Tower
e-mail: reservations@blarneygolfresort.com
dir: Exit N20 for Blarney, 4km to Tower, turn right onto Old Kerry Road. Hotel 2km on right.

Set amid a John Daly designed golf course on the outskirts of the village of Tower, this hotel offers a range of well-equipped comfortable bedrooms. Excellent standards of cuisine are on offer in the Inniscarron Restaurant, with more casual eating available throughout the afternoon in Cormac's bar. The hotel also features a Sentosa Spa.

Rooms 117 (56 annexe) (56 fmly) (30 GF) **Facilities** Spa FTV ⊛ supervised ♨ 18 Putt green Gym Steam room Sauna ♫ Xmas New Year Wi-fi **Conf** Class 150 Board 40 Thtr 300 Del from €150 to €195* **Services** Lift Air con **Parking** 250 **Notes** LB ⊗

Blarney Castle

★★★ 70% HOTEL

☎ 021 4385116 📄 021 4385542
The Village Green
e-mail: info@blarneycastlehotel.com
dir: N20 (Cork-Limerick road) onto R617 for Blarney. Hotel on village green

Situated in the centre of the town within walking distance of the renowned Blarney Stone, this friendly hotel has been in the same family since 1873. Many of the bedrooms are spacious, but all are appointed to a very comfortable standard. The popular bar serves good food throughout most of the day.

Rooms 13 (4 fmly) **S** €65-€90; **D** €110-€130 (incl. bkfst)* **Facilities** ♫ **Services** Air con **Parking** 5 **Notes** ⊗ Closed 24-25 Dec

CARRIGALINE — Map 1 B2

Carrigaline Court Hotel

★★★★ 76% HOTEL

☎ 021 4852100 📄 021 4371103
e-mail: reception@carrigcourt.com
web: www.carrigcourt.com
dir: From South Link road (E from airport or W from Dublin/Lee Tunnel) take exit for Carrigaline, stay in right lane

This smart, town centre modern hotel is situated only minutes' drive from Cork City Airport and the Ringaskiddy Port. Bedrooms are spacious and very well appointed. Public areas include Collins, the traditional Irish pub, The Bistro and extensive conference, leisure and beauty facilities. Golf, sailing, angling and horse riding are available locally.

Rooms 91 (3 fmly) **S** €103-€130; **D** €155-€198 (incl. bkfst) **Facilities** Spa STV ⊛ supervised Gym Beauty salon Massage treatment rooms Xmas New Year Wi-fi **Conf** Class 200 Board 35 Thtr 350 Del from €176 to €200 **Services** Lift **Parking** 220 **Notes** LB ⊗ Closed 25 Dec Civ Wed 70

CASTLEMARTYR — Map 1 C2

Capella Hotel at Castlemartyr Resort

Ⓤ

☎ 021 4644050 📄 021 4219002
e-mail: reservations.castlemartyr@capellahotels.com
dir: N25, 3rd exit signed Rosslare. Continue past Carrigtwohill & Midleton exits. At rdbt take 2nd exit into Castlemartyr

Currently the rating for this establishment is not confirmed. This may be due to a change of ownership or because it has only recently joined the AA rating scheme. For further details please see the AA website: www.theAA.com

Rooms 103 (6 fmly) (30 GF) (10 smoking) **S** €225-€2750; **D** €225-€2750 (incl. bkfst)* **Facilities** Spa STV ⊛ ♨ 18 ⛳ Gym Fitness studio Steam room Sauna Xmas New Year Wi-fi **Conf** Class 32 Board 32 Thtr 80 Del from €398 to €650* **Services** Lift Air con **Parking** 200 **Notes** LB Civ Wed 80

CLONAKILTY Map 1 B2

Inchydoney Island Lodge & Spa

★★★★ 81% ◉◉ HOTEL

☎ 023 33143 📠 023 35229
e-mail: reservations@inchydoneyisland.com
dir: follow N71 (West Cork road) to Clonakilty. At rdbt in Clonakilty take 2nd exit, follow signs to hotel

This modern hotel, with a striking interior, has a stunning location on the coast with steps down to two long sandy beaches. Bedrooms are decorated in warm colours and are well appointed. Diners have a choice of the third-floor Gulfstream Restaurant or the more casual Dunes Bar and Bistro. The Island Spa offers many treatments including seawater therapies.

Rooms 67 (24 fmly) (18 GF) **S** €225-€240; **D** €330-€360 (incl. bkfst)* **Facilities** Spa ⊗ supervised Fishing Gym Sauna Steam room ♫ Wi-fi **Conf** Board 50 Thtr 300 **Services** Lift **Parking** 200 **Notes** ⊗ Closed 24-26 Dec

Quality Hotel Clonakilty

★★★ 71% HOTEL

☎ 023 36400 📠 023 35404
Skibbereen Rd
e-mail: info.clonakilty@qualityhotels.ie
web: www.qualityhotelclonakilty.com
dir: In Clonakilty take 2nd exit off small rdbt onto Skibbereen Bypass Rd. Hotel on left after approx 1m

A short distance from the town, in the heart of West Cork, this is good base for exploring the rich history and landscapes of the area. Families are particularly well catered for with a choice of bedroom styles and sizes. Oscars is a lively bar with entertainment at weekends. Use of the facilities of Club Vitae is complimentary to guests.

Rooms 96 (63 fmly) (41 GF) **S** €64-€134; **D** €78-€218 (incl. bkfst)* **Facilities** ⊗ supervised Gym 3-screen cinema Sauna Steam room ♫ New Year Wi-fi Child facilities **Conf** Class 75 Board 40 Thtr 140 Del from €129 to €169* **Services** Lift **Parking** 200 **Notes** LB ⊗ Closed 24-26 Dec

CORK Map 1 B2

INSPECTORS' CHOICE

Hayfield Manor
★★★★ ◉ HOTEL

☎ 021 4845900 📠 021 4316839
Perrott Av, College Rd
e-mail: enquiries@hayfieldmanor.ie
web: www.hayfieldmanor.ie
dir: 1m W of city centre on N22 towards Killarney, turn left at University Gates off Western Rd. Turn right into College Rd, left into Perrott Ave

As part of a landscaped two-acre estate with lovely walled gardens, Hayfield Manor offers luxury and seclusion, just a short distance from UCC. This fine hotel has every modern comfort and maintains an atmosphere of tranquillity, with a choice of two dining options. Bedrooms offer high levels of comfort with many thoughtful extras. Beauty treatments and leisure facilities are available for resident guests.

Rooms 88 (8 fmly) (55 smoking) **S** €190-€380; **D** €220-€380 (incl. bkfst)* **Facilities** Spa STV ⊗ Gym Steam room Hair salon Relaxation room ♫ Xmas New Year Wi-fi **Conf** Class 60 Board 40 Thtr 100 Del from €310 to €340 **Services** Lift Air con **Parking** 100 **Notes** LB ⊗ Civ Wed 50

The Kingsley Hotel

★★★★ 85% HOTEL

☎ 021 4800500 📠 021 4800527
Victoria Cross
e-mail: resv@kingsleyhotel.com
dir: off N22 opposite County Hall

Situated on the banks of the River Lee, this luxurious hotel has excellent facilities. The bedrooms are spacious and feature thoughtful additional touches. The contemporary bar and restaurant have an informal atmosphere, and both the lounge and library are elegant and relaxing.

Rooms 69 (4 fmly) **Facilities** ⊗ supervised Fishing Gym Treatment rooms Xmas **Conf** Class 50 Board 32 Thtr 95 **Services** Lift Air con **Parking** 150 **Notes** LB ⊗

Maryborough Hotel & Spa

★★★★ 79% ◉ HOTEL

☎ 021 4365555 📠 021 4365662
Maryborough Hill
e-mail: info@maryborough.com
dir: from Jack Lynch Tunnel take 2nd exit signed Douglas. Right at 1st rdbt, follow Rochestown road to fingerpost rdbt. Left, hotel on left 0.5m up hill

Dating from 1715, this house was renovated and extended to become a fine hotel set in beautifully landscaped grounds. The suites in the main house and the bedrooms in the wing are well appointed and comfortable. The extensive lounge is very popular for the range of food served throughout the day.

Rooms 93 (6 fmly) **S** €145-€395; **D** €198-€500 (incl. bkfst)* **Facilities** Spa ⊗ supervised Gym Sauna Steam room ♫ New Year Wi-fi **Conf** Class 250 Board 60 Thtr 500 Del from €245 to €260* **Services** Lift **Parking** 300 **Notes** LB ⊗ Closed 24-26 Dec Civ Wed 100

The Clarion Hotel

★★★★ 79% HOTEL

☎ 021 4224900 📠 021 4224901
Lapps Quay
e-mail: info@clarionhotelcorkcity.com

This hotel has commanding views of the River Lee and also City Hall. Rooms are particularly comfortable, with stylish decor and air conditioning. Dining options include Synergie Restaurant, and the popular Kudos bar offering a menu with oriental influences. SanoVitae health club is also a feature. Excellent leisure and meeting facilities are available together with secure underground parking.

Rooms 197 (4 fmly) **S** €260-€350; **D** €260-€355* **Facilities** Spa STV FTV ⊗ supervised Gym Children's pool Aerobics room Steam room Sauna Wi-fi **Conf** Class 175 Board 100 Thtr 350 Del from €210 to €350* **Services** Lift Air con **Notes** ⊗ Closed 24-26 Dec

CORK continued

Rochestown Park Hotel

★★★★ 78% HOTEL

☎ 021 4890800 📠 021 4892178
Rochestown Rd, Douglas
e-mail: info@rochestownpark.com
dir: from Lee Tunnel, 2nd exit left off dual carriageway. 400mtrs then 1st left and right at small rdbt. Hotel 600mtrs on right

This modern hotel is situated in mature gardens on the south side of Cork city. Various bedroom styles, including suites, are available, most rooms are air-conditioned and overlook Mahon Golf Club. Public areas include a traditional bar and Gallery Restaurant. There are extensive leisure, conference and exhibition facilities. Convenient for both the airport and the ferries.

Rooms 150 (17 fmly) (23 GF) **Facilities** Spa ⊕ supervised Gym Thalassotherapy & beauty centre Xmas Wi-fi **Conf** Class 360 Board 100 Thtr 700 **Services** Lift **Parking** 300 **Notes** ⊗ Closed 25-26 Dec

Silver Springs Moran

★★★★ 77% HOTEL

☎ 021 4507533 📠 021 4507641
Tivoli
e-mail: silverspringsres@moranhotels.com
web: www.silverspringshotel.ie
dir: N8 south, Silver Springs exit. Right across overpass then right, hotel on left

The public areas of this hotel create a smart, contemporary atmosphere. Bedrooms are comfortable, many offering good views over the River Lee. Guests have use of a nearby leisure centre. Excellent conference facilities are available in a separate building.

Rooms 109 (29 fmly) **S** €115-€225; **D** €140-€300 (incl. bkfst) **Facilities** ⊕ supervised ⊕ Gym Squash Aerobics classes ♫ Xmas New Year Wi-fi **Conf** Class 400

Board 30 Thtr 800 Del from €146 to €190 **Services** Lift **Parking** 325 **Notes** LB ⊗ Closed 24-26 Dec Civ Wed 800

Imperial Hotel & Escape Salon & Spa

★★★★ 76% HOTEL

☎ 021 4274040 📠 021 4275375
South Mall
e-mail: info@imperialhotelcork.ie
dir: in city centre business area

This long established hotel has a hospitable and welcoming atmosphere. The reception rooms are on a grand scale, especially the foyer and coffee shop. Bedrooms are appointed to a high standard and the bathrooms have power showers. The hotel has comprehensive facilities for conferences and meetings in its business centre. Parking, about five minutes away, is available by prior arrangement.

Rooms 130 (4 fmly) **Facilities** Gym ♫ **Conf** Class 150 Board 80 Thtr 280 **Services** Lift **Notes** LB ⊗ Closed 24-27 Dec

Maldon Hotel Cork

★★★ 70% HOTEL

☎ 021 4529200 📠 021 4529222
John Redmond St
e-mail: res.cork@maldonhotels.com
dir: From N25 at Dunkettle rdbt follow city centre signs. At next rdbt (Glanmire) 1st left (end of dual carriageway) pass Silversprings Moran Hotel. Follow one-way system, 4th lights right into John Redmond St. Hotel 200mtrs on left

Located in the shadows of The Shandon Bells, this hotel offers a choice of bedroom styles that are all comfortably decorated. Within walking distance of the city centre, this hotel is popular with business and leisure guests alike. Lannigan's Steakhouse features a range of food styles, with a good value, fixed price menu available. A leisure centre is available to guests.

Rooms 101 (6 fmly) (33 smoking) **S** €64-€134; **D** €78-€218 (incl. bkfst) **Facilities** STV ⊕ supervised Gym Sauna Steam room Treatments ♫ New Year Wi-fi **Conf** Class 30 Board 30 Thtr 70 **Services** Lift **Parking** 40 **Notes** LB ⊗ RS 24-26 Dec

Travelodge Cork Airport

BUDGET HOTEL

☎ 021 4310722 📠 021 4310723
Blackash
web: www.travelodge.co.uk
dir: at rdbt junct of South Ring Road/Kinsale Rd, R600

Travelodge offers good quality, good value, modern accommodation. Ideal for families, the spacious en suite bedrooms include remote-control TV, tea and coffee-making facilities and comfortable beds. Meals can be taken at the nearby family restaurant. See also the Hotel Groups pages.

Rooms 60 **S** fr €40; **D** fr €40

GARRYVOE — Map 1 C2

Garryvoe

★★★ 74% ⊛ HOTEL

☎ 021 4646718 📠 021 4646824
Ballycotton Bay, Castlemartyr
e-mail: res@garryvoehotel.com
dir: off N25 onto L72 at Castlemartyr (between Midleton & Youghal) then 6km

A comfortable, family-run hotel with caring staff, the Garryvoe offers bedrooms that are appointed to a very high standard. It stands in a delightful position facing a sandy beach and Ballycotton Bay. A popular bar serves light meals throughout the day, with a more formal menu for dinner in the spacious dining room.

Rooms 43 (6 fmly) (10 smoking) **S** €110-€120; **D** €170-€190 (incl. bkfst) **Facilities** STV ⊕ Putt green ♫ Wi-fi **Conf** Class 150 Board 12 Thtr 300 Del from €150 to €170* **Services** Lift **Parking** 100 **Notes** LB ⊗ Closed 24-25 Dec Civ Wed 100

GLANMIRE — Map 1 B2

Fitzgeralds Vienna Woods

★★★ 74% HOTEL

☎ 021 4556800 & 021 4821146 📠 021 4821120
e-mail: reservations@viennawoodshotel.com
dir: 3.5m from Cork city centre

This long established hotel is located in the leafy suburb of Glanmire amid 20 acres of woodland. Bedrooms in the newer wing are comfortably furnished with those in the original house individually decorated. This hotel specialises in family celebrations for which their spacious banqueting room makes an ideal venue.

Rooms 80 (32 annexe) (2 fmly) (20 smoking) **S** €69-€190; **D** €98-€200 (incl. bkfst) **Facilities** STV ♫ New Year Wi-fi Child facilities **Conf** Class 200 Board 70 Thtr 350 **Services** Lift **Parking** 250 **Notes** LB ⊗ Closed 24-26 Dec Civ Wed 300

GOUGANE BARRA — Map 1 B2

Gougane Barra

★★★ 71% ⊛ HOTEL

☎ 026 47069 📠 026 47226
e-mail: gouganebarrahotel@eircom.net
dir: on L4643, off R584 between N22 at Macroom & N71 at Bantry

Picturesquely situated on the shore of Gougane Barra Lake and at the entrance to the National Park this family run hotel offers tranquillity and very good cooking. Bedrooms and public areas are comfortable and enjoy lovely views. In summer guests can experience the unique 'Theatre by the Lake' productions, and bikes and boats are available for exploring the area.

Rooms 26 (12 GF) **S** €85-€100; **D** €130-€150 (incl. bkfst) **Facilities** STV FTV Fishing Boating Cycling ♫ Wi-fi **Parking** 26 **Notes** LB ⊗ Closed 10 Oct-18 Apr

---

KINSALE Map 1 B2

Carlton Hotel Kinsale

★★★★ 76% HOTEL

☎ 021 470 6000 📠 021 470 6001
Rathmore Rd
e-mail: info@carlton.ie
dir: Before Kinsale turn left signed Charles Fort. 2kms, hotel on left

This new hotel is set on an elevated position overlooking Oysterhaven Bay in 90 acres of mature parkland, approximately five kilometres from the town centre. All of the bedrooms are spacious and well appointed; two-bedroom holiday options are available in the grounds. The contemporary public rooms are on the first floor, so making the most of the spectacular views.

Rooms 90 (20 annexe) (20 fmly) (24 GF) (24 smoking) **S** €75-€180; **D** €110-€330 (incl. bkfst)* **Facilities** Spa STV FTV ⏱ supervised Gym Sauna Steam room Wi-fi **Conf** Class 140 Board 60 Thtr 200 Del from €180 to €220* **Services** Lift Air con **Parking** 200 **Notes** LB ⊗ Closed 23-26 Dec

Trident

★★★ 75% ⚜ HOTEL

☎ 021 4779300 📠 021 4774173
Worlds End
e-mail: info@tridenthotel.com
dir: R600 from Cork to Kinsale, along Kinsale waterfront, hotel beyond pier

Located at the harbour's edge, this hotel has its own marina with boats for hire. Many of the bedrooms have superb views and two have balconies. The restaurant and lounge both overlook the harbour, and pleasant staff provide hospitable service.

Rooms 75 (2 fmly) **S** €95-€225; **D** €130-€290 (incl. bkfst)* **Facilities** Gym Steam room Deep sea angling Yacht charter **Conf** Class 130 Board 40 Thtr 200 Del from €150 to €270* **Services** Lift **Parking** 60 **Notes** LB ⊗ Closed 24-26 Dec

Actons

★★★ 74% ⚜ HOTEL

☎ 021 4772135 📠 021 4772231
Pier Rd
e-mail: information@actonshotelkinsale.com
dir: in town centre, 500yds from Yacht Club Marina

Situated overlooking the harbour, Actons is a well established hotel with a good reputation for its friendly and courteous staff. Bedrooms are well appointed and many of them enjoy sea views, as does the restaurant where enjoyable dinners are served. The adjoining leisure centre is well equipped.

Rooms 76 (20 fmly) **Facilities** ⏱ supervised Gym Aerobics studio Outdoor hot tub Steam room ♫ **Conf** Class 200 Board 100 Thtr 300 **Services** Lift **Parking** 70 **Notes** LB ⊗ Closed 24-27 Dec & early-mid Jan

Blue Haven

★★★ 73% HOTEL

☎ 021 4772209 📠 021 4774268
3 Pearse St
e-mail: info@bluehavenkinsale.com
dir: in town centre

At the heart of this historic town, the Blue Haven offers a welcoming lobby lounge, an elegant restaurant with a less formal bistro, and lively, atmospheric bars where music is a feature at weekends and during the summer. Bedrooms vary in size and are furnished to a high standard.

Rooms 17 **S** €85-€140; **D** €99-€230 (incl. bkfst)* **Facilities** ♫ Xmas New Year Wi-fi **Conf** Class 35 Board 25 Thtr 70 Del from €160 to €240* **Notes** LB ⊗ Closed 25 Dec

The White House

⚜ RESTAURANT WITH ROOMS

☎ 021 4772125 📠 021 4772045
Pearse St, The Glen
e-mail: whitehse@indigo.ie
dir: In town centre

Centrally located among the narrow, twisting streets of the charming town of Kinsale, this Restaurant with Rooms dates from 1850. A welcoming hostelry with modern smart and comfortable bedrooms. The bar and bistro is open for lunch and dinner, menu is varied with local fish and beef a speciality. The courtyard is perfect for the summer and there is traditional music in the bar most nights.

Rooms 10 (2 fmly)

MACROOM Map 1 B2

Castle

★★★ 78% ⚜ HOTEL

IRISH COUNTRY HOTELS

☎ 026 41074 📠 026 41505
Main St
e-mail: castlehotel@eircom.net
dir: on N22 midway between Cork & Killarney

This town centre property offers excellent service provided by the Buckley Family and their team. Bedrooms are very comfortable, as are the extensive public areas. Secure parking is available to the rear.

Rooms 58 (6 fmly) (15 smoking) **S** €75-€125; **D** €150-€199 (incl. bkfst) **Facilities** STV ⏱ supervised Gym Steam room ♫ New Year Wi-fi **Conf** Class 80 Board 60 Thtr 200 Del from €155 to €185 **Services** Lift Air con **Parking** 30 **Notes** LB ⊗ Closed 24-28 Dec Civ Wed

MALLOW — Map 1 B2

Longueville House
★★★ ⑨⑨⑨ COUNTRY HOUSE HOTEL

☎ 022 47156 & 47306 🖹 022 47459
e-mail: info@longuevillehouse.ie
dir: 3m W of Mallow via N72 road to Killarney, right turn at Ballyclough junct, hotel entrance 200yds left

This 18th-century Georgian mansion is set in a wooded estate on a 500-acre farm. The beautifully appointed bedrooms overlook the Backwater Valley. Two elegantly furnished sitting rooms feature fine examples of Italian plasterwork. William O'Callaghan's cuisine is served in the Presidents' Restaurant and the Victorian Turner conservatory. Most ingredients are grown or raised on the farm including fish from the river that runs through the estate.

Rooms 20 (3 fmly) **Facilities** Fishing ⚓ Xmas New Year **Conf** Class 30 Board 30 Thtr 50 **Parking** 30 **Notes** LB ⊗ Closed 10 Jan-15 Mar RS mid Nov-early Jan

Springfort Hall Country House Hotel
★★★ 68% HOTEL

☎ 022 21278 🖹 022 21557
e-mail: stay@springfort-hall.com
web: www.springfort-hall.com
dir: on Mallow/Limerick road N20, right at Two Pot House R581, hotel 500mtrs on right

This 18th-century country manor is tucked away amid tranquil woodlands located just 6km from Mallow. There is an attractive oval dining room, drawing room and lounge bar. The comfortable bedrooms are in a wing, and are spacious, well-appointed and command superb country views. There are extensive banqueting and conference facilities.

Rooms 49 (5 fmly) **S** €75-€115; **D** €120-€190 (incl. bkfst)* **Facilities** STV FTV 🎵 **Conf** Class 200 Board 50 Thtr 300 **Parking** 200 **Notes** LB ⊗ Closed 23 Dec-2 Jan

MIDLETON — Map 1 C2

Midleton Park Hotel & Spa
★★★ 79% HOTEL

☎ 021 4631767 🖹 021 4631605
e-mail: info@midletonparkhotel.ie
dir: from Cork exit N25, hotel on right. From Waterford exit N25, over bridge to T-junct, right, hotel on right

This hotel is located just off the N25. The comfortable public areas include a relaxing lobby lounge and bedrooms are spacious and attractively decorated. An interesting menu is available in the popular Park Café Bar while The Park Restaurant offers fine dining. There are extensive banqueting and leisure facilities, and private dining rooms.

Rooms 40 (12 fmly) **Conf** Class 200 Board 40 Thtr 400 **Services** Air con **Parking** 500 **Notes** ⊗ Closed 25 Dec

ROSSCARBERY — Map 1 B2

Celtic Ross
★★★ 73% HOTEL

☎ 023 48722 🖹 023 48723
e-mail: info@celticrosshotel.com
dir: take N71 from Cork, through Bandon towards Clonakilty. Follow signs for Skibbereen

This hotel is situated on the edge of the village overlooking Rosscarbery Bay. Richly textured fabrics add warmth to the polished wood public areas that includes a 5000-year-old Bog Yew Tree sculpture. There is a library plus a bar and a bistro that provides a second dining option. The spacious bedrooms are comfortable and well appointed.

Rooms 66 (30 fmly) **Facilities** ⓢ supervised Gym Steam room Bubble pool 🎵 Xmas **Conf** Class 150 Board 60 Thtr 300 **Services** Lift Air con **Parking** 200 **Notes** ⊗ Closed 24-26 Dec & mid Jan-mid Feb

YOUGHAL — Map 1 C2

Quality Hotel Youghal
★★★ 70% HOTEL

☎ 024 93050 🖹 024 20699
Redbarn
e-mail: info.youghal@qualityhotels.ie
web: www.qualityhotelyoughal.com
dir: From Waterford on N25 towards Cork. Onto R633 towards Ballymacoda, follow hotel signs

Located on the shore of Redbarn Beach, this hotel is ideal for family leisure. Bedrooms are comfortably appointed, some with sea views. Lannigans Restaurant, with a great commanding view of the beach offers good food in the evening, with bar food available in Coast Bar during the day. There are good leisure facilities in the grounds.

Rooms 25 (3 fmly) (5 GF) (3 smoking) **S** €59-€144; **D** €78-€238 (incl. bkfst) **Facilities** Spa STV ⓢ supervised Gym Astro turf sports pitches Games room Crèche Outdoor playground 🎵 New Year **Conf** Class 30 Board 20 Thtr 50 Del from €119 to €159 **Services** Lift **Parking** 200 **Notes** LB ⊗ Closed 23-26 Dec

CO DONEGAL

BALLYSHANNON — Map 1 B5

Heron's Cove
RESTAURANT WITH ROOMS

☎ 071 9822070 🖹 071 9822075
Creevy, Rossnowlagh Rd
e-mail: info@heronscove.ie
dir: From N side of Ballyshannon at rdbt take R231 towards Rossnowlagh 2m. Just after Creevy National School on left

Situated between Ballyshannon and Creevy Pier and close to the sandy beach at Rossnowlagh, the O'Toole family have refurbished Heron's Cove to a high standard. Bedrooms are comfortable, and there is a cosy lounge bar and charming restaurant where menus feature steaks and fresh fish from local suppliers.

Rooms 10 (4 en suite) (1 fmly)

DONEGAL Map 1 B5

Harvey's Point Country Hotel
★★★★ 86% ◉◉ HOTEL

☎ 074 9722208 ◱ 074 9722352
Lough Eske
e-mail: sales@harveyspoint.com
web: www.harveyspoint.com
dir: N56 from Donegal, then 1st right (Loch Eske/Harvey's Point)

Situated by the lakeshore, this hotel is an oasis of relaxation. Comfort and attentive guest care are the norm here. A range of particularly spacious suites are available; they all make the best use of the views. The kitchen brigade maintains consistently high standards in the dining room, with a very popular Sunday buffet lunch served each week.

Rooms 60 (16 GF) **S** €129-€420; **D** €198-€640 (incl. bkfst) **Facilities** ⓣ Treatment rooms Pitch 'n' putt Bicycle hire ♫ Xmas New Year Wi-fi **Conf** Class 200 Board 50 Thtr 200 Del from €179 to €250 **Services** Lift **Parking** 300 **Notes** LB Closed Mon & Tue Nov-Mar Civ Wed 70

Mill Park
★★★ 75% HOTEL

IRISH COUNTRY HOTELS

☎ 074 9722880 ◱ 074 9722640
The Mullins
e-mail: millparkhotel@eircom.net
dir: Take N15 signed Lifford. 2nd exit at rdbt to N56 signed Killybegs. Hotel on right

The gentle flow of the millstream and open fires create a welcoming atmosphere at this hotel that is within walking distance of the town centre. Wood and stone are incorporated with flair in the design of the public areas, as in the first-floor Granary restaurant and the less formal café bar where food is served all day. Bedrooms are spacious and well appointed. There are extensive leisure and banqueting facilities.

Rooms 114 (15 fmly) (44 GF) **S** €75-€125; **D** €110-€250 (incl. bkfst)* **Facilities** ⓣ supervised Gym Wellness centre ♫ New Year Wi-fi **Conf** Class 250 Board 80 Thtr 500 Del from €130 to €180* **Services** Lift **Parking** 250 **Notes** LB Closed 24-26 Dec Civ Wed 200

DUNFANAGHY Map 1 C6

Arnold's
★★★ 73% HOTEL

IRISH COUNTRY HOTELS

☎ 074 9136208 ◱ 074 9136352
e-mail: enquiries@arnoldshotel.com
dir: on N56 from Letterkenny, hotel on left entering the village

This family-run hotel is noted for its warm welcome and good food. It is situated in a coastal village with sandy beaches, links golf courses and beautiful scenery. Public areas and bedrooms are comfortable; there is a traditional bar with food served throughout the day, and a popular bistro-style restaurant. A delightful garden and riding stables are available.

Rooms 30 (10 fmly) **Facilities** Putt green Fishing ♫ **Parking** 60 **Notes** LB Closed Nov-mid Mar

---

DUNGLOW (AN CLOCHÁN LIATH) Map 1 B5

Ostan Na Rosann
★★★ 68% HOTEL

☎ 074 9522444 ◱ 074 9522400
Mill Rd
e-mail: info@ostannarosann.com
dir: N56, at edge of town

Overlooking the spectacular Dungloe Bay within walking distance of the town, this warm family-run hotel is known for its informal and friendly atmosphere. Bedrooms are comfortable. Local ingredients are prepared with care and served in the restaurant, which makes the most of the great views.

Rooms 48 (6 fmly) (24 GF) **Facilities** ⓣ supervised Gym Beautician Steam room ♫ Xmas New Year Wi-fi Child facilities **Conf** Class 200 Board 50 Thtr 300 **Parking** 100 **Notes** LB

DUNKINEELY Map 1 B5

Castle Murray House and Restaurant
◉ RESTAURANT WITH ROOMS

☎ 074 9737022 ◱ 074 9737330
St Johns Point
e-mail: info@castlemurray.com
dir: From Donegal take N56 towards Killybegs. Left to Dunkineely

Situated on the coast road of St. John's Point, this charming family-run house and restaurant overlooks McSwynes Bay and the castle. The bedrooms are individually decorated with guest comfort very much in mind as is the cosy bar and sun lounge. There is a strong French influence in the cooking; locally landed fish, and prime lamb and beef are on the menus.

Rooms 10 (3 en suite) (2 fmly)

LETTERKENNY Map 1 C5

Downings Bay
★★★ 70% HOTEL

☎ 074 9155586 & 9155770 ◱ 074 9154716
Downings
e-mail: info@downingsbayhotel.com
dir: 23m north of Letterkenny. Hotel in village centre

This hotel is situated on Sheephaven Bay in the picturesque village of Downings. There is a cosy lounge, traditional style bar and a restaurant where food is available all day. The bedrooms are comfortable and well appointed. Guests have complimentary use of the local leisure centre, and the night club is open at weekends.

Rooms 40 (8 fmly) (4 smoking) **S** €60-€80; **D** €120-€140 (incl. bkfst) **Facilities** ⓣ supervised Gym ♫ New Year Wi-fi **Conf** Class 175 Board 50 Thtr 350 Del from €120 to €140 **Services** Lift Air con **Parking** 110 **Notes** LB Closed 25 Dec

---

MALIN Map 1 C6

Malin
★★ 67% HOTEL

☎ 074 9370606 ◱ 074 9370770
Malin Town
e-mail: info@malinhotel.ie
dir: From Derry on Molville Rd, turn left at Quigleys Point to Cardonagh, then follow to Malin

Overlooking the village green in the most northerly village in Ireland, the hotel has a friendly, welcoming atmosphere and is an ideal centre for exploring the rugged coastline and sandy beaches. Public areas include an attractive restaurant where dinner is served Wed/Sun and food is available daily in the cosy bar.

Rooms 18 (1 fmly) **S** €45-€100; **D** €80-€150 (incl. bkfst)* **Facilities** STV ⌇ Fishing Gym ♫ Xmas New Year Wi-fi Child facilities **Conf** Class 100 Board 60 Thtr 200 **Services** Lift **Parking** 40 **Notes** LB Civ Wed 200

RATHMULLAN   Map 1 C6

Rathmullan House

★★★★ 79% ◉◉ COUNTRY HOUSE HOTEL

☎ 074 9158188   🖷 074 9158200
e-mail: info@rathmullanhouse.com
dir: From Letterkenny, then Ramelton then Rathmullan
R243. Left at Mace shop, through village, hotel gates on
right

Dating from the 18th-century, this fine property has been
operating as a country-house hotel for the last 40 years
under the stewardship of the Wheeler family. Guests are
welcome to wander around the well-planted grounds and
the walled garden, from where much of the ingredients
for the Weeping Elm Restaurant are grown. The many
lounges are relaxing and comfortable, while many of the
bedrooms benefit from balconies and patio areas.

Rooms 34 (4 fmly) (9 GF) **S** €110-€210; **D** €220-€330
(incl. bkfst)* **Facilities** Spa ⊗ ♨ ♨ New Year Wi-fi
Child facilities **Conf** Class 90 Board 40 Thtr 135
Del from €205* **Parking** 80 **Notes** LB Closed 11 Jan-5
Feb RS 15 Nov-12 Mar Civ Wed 135

Fort Royal Hotel

★★★ 80% ◉ HOTEL

☎ 074 9158100   🖷 074 9158103
Fort Royal
e-mail: fortroyal@eircom.net
dir: R245 from Letterkenny, through Rathmullan, hotel
signed

This family-run period house stands in 18 acres of well-
maintained grounds that include a 9-hole golf and tennis
court. Situated on the shores of Lough Swilly where
private access is available to the secluded sandy beach.
The restful lounges and inviting bar have open log fires,
the fine dining restaurant overlooks the gardens and
comfortable bedrooms enjoy the spectacular views.

Rooms 15 (4 annexe) (1 fmly) **Facilities** ↧ 9 ♨ ♨
Parking 30 **Notes** LB Closed Nov-Mar

ROSSNOWLAGH   Map 1 B5

INSPECTORS' CHOICE

Sandhouse

★★★ ◉ HOTEL

☎ 071 9851777   🖷 071 9852100
e-mail: info@sandhouse-hotel.ie
dir: from Donegal on coast road towards Ballyshannon

The Sandhouse is perched over Rossnowlagh sandy
beach, which is a haven for surfers. It offers very
comfortable lounges with open fires, a restaurant,
a cocktail bar and the Surfers bar. The spacious
bedrooms are well appointed and most enjoy the
splendid sea views. This hotel is well known for
its hospitality, good food and service in a relaxing
environment.

Rooms 55 (6 fmly) (10 smoking) **S** €90-€120;
D €190-€280 (incl. bkfst) **Facilities** Spa STV ♨ Mini-
golf Surfing Canoeing Sailing Whale & bird watching
♫ Wi-fi **Conf** Class 40 Board 30 Thtr 60 **Services** Lift
Parking 40 **Notes** LB Closed Dec & Jan

DUBLIN

DUBLIN   Map 1 D4

INSPECTORS' CHOICE

The Merrion Hotel

★★★★★ ◉◉◉◉ HOTEL

☎ 01 6030600   🖷 01 6030700
Upper Merrion St
e-mail: info@merrionhotel.com
dir: at top of Upper Merrion St on left, beyond
Government buildings on right

This terrace of gracious Georgian buildings, reputed
to have been the birthplace of the Duke of Wellington,
embraces the character of many changes of use
over 200 years. Bedrooms and suites are spacious,
offering comfort and a wide range of extra facilities.
The lounges retain the charm and opulence of days
gone by, while the Cellar bar area is a popular meeting
point. Dining options include The Cellar Restaurant
specialising in prime local ingredients and, for that
very special occasion, award-winning Restaurant
Patrick Guilbaud is Dublin's finest.

Rooms 143 (65 smoking) **S** €455-€2995;
D €475-€2995* **Facilities** Spa STV FTV
⊗ supervised Gym Steam room Sauna Wi-fi
Conf Class 25 Board 25 Thtr 60 Del from €480 to
€510* **Services** Lift Air con **Parking** 60 (charged)
Notes ⊗

Westbury   JURYS DOYLE

★★★★★ 83% HOTEL

☎ 01 6791122   🖷 01 6797078
Grafton St
e-mail: westbury@jurysdoyle.com

Located just off Grafton Street, Dublin's premier shopping
district, this is an oasis of calm; guests are all well cared
for amid smart contemporary surroundings. Public areas
include the relaxing lounge, the Sandbank Bistro and
more formal Russell Room. A range of suites and
bedrooms is available, many overlooking the roofscape of
the city. Valet parking is available.

Rooms 205 **Facilities** Gym ♫ Wi-fi **Conf** Class 100
Board 46 Thtr 220 **Services** Lift Air con **Parking** 100
(charged) **Notes** ⊗

Temple Bar

★★★ 66% HOTEL

☎ 01 6773333 📄 01 6773088
Fleet St, Temple Bar
e-mail: reservations@tbh.ie
web: www.templebarhotel.com
dir: from Trinity College towards O'Connell Bridge. 1st left onto Fleet St. Hotel on right

This hotel is situated in the heart of Dublin's Temple Bar, and in close to the shops, restaurants and cultural life of the city. Bedrooms are comfortable and well equipped. Food is served throughout the day in Buskers theme bar. There is a multi-storey car park nearby.

Rooms 129 (6 fmly) (34 smoking) **S** €65-€220; **D** €80-€300 (incl. bkfst)* **Facilities** Wi-fi **Conf** Class 40 Board 40 Thtr 70 **Services** Lift **Notes** ⊗ Closed 23-25 Dec RS Good Fri

Belverdere Hotel

★★★ 63% HOTEL

☎ 01 8737700 📄 01 8737776
Great Denmark Street
e-mail: info@comfortinndublin.com
dir: From airport follow signs for city centre, up Dorset St, left to Gardiner St, right to Denmark St

Located just off Parnell Square in the city centre, parts of this hotel are set in a Georgian terrace. Bedrooms vary in size, but are all competitively priced and comfortable. The Belvedere is a popular bar where a range of dishes are served throughout the day.

Rooms 92 (6 fmly) **Facilities** ♫ Wi-fi **Conf** Class 20 Board 40 Thtr 60 **Services** Lift **Notes** LB ⊗ Closed 23-26 Dec

West County Hotel

★★ 69% HOTEL

☎ 01 6264011 📄 01 6231378
Chapelizod
e-mail: info@westcountyhotel.ie
dir: From city centre follow signs for N4(W), 4m from city centre between Palmerstown & Ballyfermot on N4

This family run hotel is situated just off the N4 and within walking distance of Chapelizod. Bedrooms are well appointed. Public areas include a comfortable lobby lounge and bar where a carvery lunch is served daily and the Pine restaurant where dinner is served.

Rooms 48 (10 fmly) **S** €55-€110; **D** €89-€180 (incl. bkfst)* **Facilities** ♫ Xmas New Year Wi-fi **Conf** Class 100 Board 60 Thtr 200 Del from €105 to €195* **Services** Lift **Parking** 200 **Notes** LB ⊗ Closed 24-26 Dec

Beacon

[U]

☎ 01 2915000 📄 01 2915005
Sandyford Business Region
e-mail: sales@thebeacon.com
dir: M50 exit 13, 3rd exit at rdbt, right at lights, hotel on right

For further details please see the AA website: www.theAA.com

Rooms 88 (14 smoking) **S** €110-€300; **D** €110-€300* **Facilities** STV FTV ♫ New Year Wi-fi **Conf** Class 20 Board 22 Thtr 40 **Services** Lift **Parking** 54 **Notes** LB ⊗ Closed 24-26 Dec

Radisson SAS St Helen's Hotel

[U]

☎ 01 2186000 📄 01 2186010
Stillorgan Rd
e-mail: info.dublin@radissonsas.com
web: www.sthelens.dublin.radissonsas.com
dir: from centre take N11 south, hotel 4km on left

Currently the rating for this establishment is not confirmed. This may be due to a change of ownership or because it has only recently joined the AA rating scheme. For further details please see the AA website: www.theAA.com

Rooms 151 (102 fmly) (39 GF) (18 smoking) **S** €135-€380; **D** €135-€760 **Facilities** STV Gym Beauty salon ♫ Xmas Wi-fi **Conf** Class 150 Board 70 Thtr 350 Del from €310 to €340 **Services** Lift Air con **Parking** 220 **Notes** ⊗

The Shelbourne

[U]

☎ 01 6634500 📄 01 6616006
27 St Stephen's Green
e-mail: aisling.mcdermott@renaissancehotels.com
web: www.theshelbourne.ie
dir: M1 to city centre, along Parnell St to O'Connell St towards Trinity College, take 3rd right into Kildare St, hotel on right

Currently the rating for this establishment is not confirmed. This may be due to a change of ownership or because it has only recently joined the AA rating scheme. For further details please see the AA website: www.theAA.com

Rooms 265 (20 smoking) **S** €215-€2500; **D** €215-€2500* **Facilities** STV FTV Xmas Wi-fi **Conf** Class 180 Board 60 Thtr 500 **Services** Lift Air con **Notes** Civ Wed 350

Travelodge City Rathmines

BUDGET HOTEL

☎ 01 4911402 📄 01 4967688
Rathmines Rd
web: www.travelodge.co.uk

Travelodge offers good quality, good value, modern accommodation. Ideal for families, the spacious en suite bedrooms include remote-control TV, tea and coffee-making facilities and comfortable beds. Meals can be taken at the nearby family restaurant. See also the Hotel Groups pages.

Rooms 54 **S** fr €40; **D** fr €40

Travelodge Dublin Castleknock

BUDGET HOTEL

☎ 01 8202626
Auburn Avenue Roundabout, Navan Rd, Castleknock
web: www.travelodge.co.uk
dir: just off M50 (Dublin ring road) at junct with Navan Rd, N3 junct 6

Rooms 100 **S** fr €40; **D** fr €40

DUBLIN AIRPORT — Map 1 D4

See also **Portmarnock**

Crowne Plaza Dublin Airport

★★★★ 79% ◉ HOTEL

☎ 01 8628888 🖹 01 8628800
Northwood Park, Santry Demesne, Santry
e-mail: info@crowneplazadublin.ie
web: www.crowneplaza.co.uk

This smart, contemporary hotel is situated in 160 acres of parkland; it is a peaceful, country setting yet very close to Dublin Airport. The air-conditioned bedrooms are furnished to a high standard and the club rooms benefit from having their own lounge. Public areas are stylish with dining options and comfortable lounges. There are extensive conference/banqueting facilities, a multi-storey car park and a courtesy airport coach are available.

Rooms 204 (17 fmly) **Facilities** Gym New Year **Conf** Class 110 Board 45 Thtr 240 **Services** Lift Air con **Parking** 360 (charged) **Notes** LB ⊗ RS 25 Dec

Carlton Hotel Dublin Airport

★★★★ 75% HOTEL

☎ 01 866 7500 🖹 01 862 3114
Old Airport Rd, Cloughran
e-mail: info@carltondublinairport.com
dir: From city centre take M1 to airport rdbt then 1st exit S towards Santry. Hotel 800mtrs on right.

Conveniently located for the airport and the M1, this modern hotel offers courtesy coaches and parking for its guests. Many of the comfortable and smartly appointed bedrooms and suites are air conditioned. Food is served throughout the day in the Kitthawk Bistro, with a more formal dinner served in the atmospheric rooftop Clouds Restaurant.

Rooms 100 (10 fmly) (14 GF) (14 smoking) **S** €350; **D** €350 **Facilities** STV FTV ♫ New Year Wi-fi **Conf** Class 200 Board 100 Thtr 450 **Services** Lift Air con **Parking** 260 **Notes** LB ⊗ Closed 24-26 Dec Civ Wed 100

Bewleys Hotel Dublin Airport

★★★ 73% HOTEL

☎ 01 8711000 🖹 01 8711001
Baskin Ln, Swords
e-mail: dublinairport@bewleyshotels.com
dir: At end of M50 N'bound, 2nd exit at rdbt (N32), left at next rdbt

In a convenient location for Dublin Airport on the M1/M50 interchange, this hotel has the added advantage of secure underground parking and a shuttle bus to the airport. Bedrooms are comfortable, and there is a spacious lounge bar and brasserie with a wide selection of dishes on offer. High quality meeting rooms are available.

Rooms 466 (232 fmly) (36 smoking) **S** €99-€199; **D** €99-€199* **Facilities** Wi-fi **Conf** Class 100 Board 12 Thtr 150 **Services** Lift **Parking** 900 (charged) **Notes** ⊗ Closed 24-25 Dec

Travelodge Dublin Airport

BUDGET HOTEL

☎ 01 8079400 🖹 01 8409235
Swords By Pass
web: www.travelodge.co.uk
dir: on N1 (Dublin/Belfast road) on s'bound carriageway at Swords rdbt

Travelodge offers good quality, good value, modern accommodation. Ideal for families, the spacious en suite bedrooms include remote-control TV, tea and coffee-making facilities and comfortable beds. Meals can be taken at the nearby family restaurant. See also the Hotel Groups pages.

Rooms 100 **S** fr €40; **D** fr €40

CO DUBLIN

DONABATE — Map 1 D4

Waterside House

★★★ 71% HOTEL

☎ 01 8436153 🖹 01 8436111
e-mail: info@watersidehousehotel.ie
web: www.watersidehousehotel.ie
dir: Exit M1 at Swords rdbt, 1st left to Donabate

This family owned hotel is situated in an enviable position overlooking the beach at Donabate and close to Dublin Airport. The public areas and bedrooms are appointed in a contemporary style, with the comfortable lounge bar and restaurant taking advantage of the breathtaking views.

Rooms 35 **S** €65-€155; **D** €120-€260 (incl. bkfst) **Facilities** ♫ Xmas New Year Wi-fi **Conf** Class 150 Board 100 Thtr 350 Del from €110 to €200 **Services** Lift Air con **Parking** 100 **Notes** ⊗ Civ Wed 250

HOWTH — Map 1 D4

Deer Park Hotel, Golf & Spa

IRISH COUNTRY HOTELS

★★★ 72% HOTEL

☎ 01 8322624 🖹 01 8392405
e-mail: sales@deerpark.iol.ie
dir: Follow coast road from Dublin via Clontarf. Through Sutton Cross pass Offington Park. Hotel 0.5m after lights on right

This modern hotel is situated on its own parkland golf courses and overlooking Dublin Bay and Ireland's Eye. The spacious well-equipped bedrooms have spectacular views. Public areas include Four Earls Restaurant, a lively bar and bistro, a spa, gym and swimming pool. Convenient to Dublin Airport, ferry ports and the DART service to the city centre.

Rooms 75 (4 fmly) (36 GF) **Facilities** Spa ⊗ supervised ⌁ 36 ⚐ Putt green Gym Wi-fi **Conf** Class 60 Board 25 Thtr 95 **Parking** 200 **Notes** LB ⊗ Closed 23-26 Dec

Fitzpatrick Castle

★★★★ 80% ⊛ HOTEL

☎ 01 2305400 ▤ 01 2305430
e-mail: reservations@fitzpatricks.com
web: www.fitzpatrickcastle.com
dir: from Dun Laoghaire port turn left, on coast road right at lights, left at next lights. Follow to Dalkey, right at Ivory pub, immediate left, up hill, hotel at top

This family-owned, 18th-century castle is situated in lovely gardens with mature trees and spectacular views over Dublin Bay. The original castle rooms are appointed to a high standard and have four-poster beds, while the rooms in the modern wing are spacious and some have balconies. Lounges are comfortably furnished and PJ's restaurant serves dinner on certain days of the week; more casual fare is available each night in the trendy Dungeon bar and grill. There are extensive leisure and conference facilities.

Rooms 113 (36 fmly) (12 smoking) **S** €140-€275; **D** €150-€340* **Facilities** STV ⊗ supervised Gym Beauty/hairdressing salon Sauna Steam room Fitness centre ♫ New Year Wi-fi **Conf** Class 250 Board 80 Thtr 500 **Services** Lift **Parking** 300 **Notes** LB ⊗ RS 25-Dec

Finnstown Country House Hotel

★★★ 74% ⊛ HOTEL

☎ 01 6010700 ▤ 01 6281088
Newcastle Rd
e-mail: manager@finnstown-hotel.ie
dir: from M1 take 1st exit onto M50 s'bound. 1st exit after Toll Bridge. At rdbt take 3rd left (N4 W). Left at lights

Set in 45 acres of wooded grounds, Finnstown is a calm and peaceful country house. There is a wide choice of bedroom style available, both in the main house and the annexe, with the garden suites being particularly comfortable. Long stay apartments are also available. Lounge areas are numerous, and staff members are very guest focused.

Rooms 78 (51 annexe) (6 fmly) (9 GF) **S** €145-€165; **D** €200-€250 (incl. bkfst)* **Facilities** ⊗ ⚐ ⚐ Gym Turkish bath Table tennis Massage Wi-fi **Conf** Class 150 Board 50 Thtr 300 **Services** Lift Air con **Parking** 300 **Notes** LB Closed 23-26 Dec Civ Wed

Lucan Spa

★★★ 67% HOTEL

☎ 01 6280494 ▤ 01 6280841
e-mail: info@lucanspahotel.ie
dir: on N4, approx 11km from city centre

Set in its own grounds and 20 minutes from Dublin Airport close to the M50, the Lucan Spa is a fine Georgian house with modern extension. Bedrooms vary in size and are well equipped. There are two dining options; dinner is served in Honora D Restaurant and The Earl Bistro for more casual dining. A conference centre is also available.

Rooms 71 (15 fmly) (9 GF) **Facilities** ♫ **Conf** Class 250 Board 80 Thtr 600 **Services** Lift Air con **Parking** 200 **Notes** LB ⊗ Closed 25-Dec

Portmarnock Hotel & Golf Links

★★★★ ⊛⊛ HOTEL

☎ 01 8460611 ▤ 01 8462442
Strand Rd
e-mail: sales@portmarnock.com
web: www.portmarnock.com
dir: From Dublin Airport, N1, rdbt 1st exit, 2nd rdbt 2nd exit, next rdbt 3rd exit, left at T-junct, over x-rds. Hotel on left past Strand

This 19th-century former home of the Jameson whiskey family is now a well run and smartly presented hotel, enjoys a superb location overlooking the sea and the PGA Championship Golf Links. Bedrooms are modern and equipped to high standard, public areas are spacious and very comfortable. The Osborne Restaurant comes highly recommended and a team of friendly staff go out of their way to welcome guests.

Rooms 138 (7 fmly) (44 GF) (30 smoking) **S** €89-€189; **D** €109-€275 (incl. bkfst) **Facilities** Spa STV ⌁ 18 Putt green Gym Beauty therapist Balinotherapy bath & treatments ♫ Xmas Wi-fi **Conf** Class 110 Board 80 Thtr 300 Del from €119 to €395 **Services** Lift **Parking** 200 **Notes** LB ⊗ RS 24 Dec (eve), 25 Dec Civ Wed 200

Redbank House & Restaurant

⊛ RESTAURANT WITH ROOMS

☎ 01 8491005 ▤ 01 8491598
5-7 Church St
e-mail: sales@redbank.ie
dir: N1 north past airport & bypass Swords. 3m N at end of dual carriageway at Esso station right towards Rush, Lusk & Skerries

A comfortable period town house adjacent to the well known restaurant of the same name, this is the latest venture of chef/patron Terry McCoy and his wife Margaret who is responsible for the tasteful refurbishment of the house. Double fronted, with two reception rooms, en suite bedrooms and a secluded garden, there is also secure parking. Convenient for Dublin airport and the ferry port.

Rooms 18 (18 en suite) (2 fmly) (7 GF)

SWORDS — Map 1 D4

The Carnegie Court

★★★ 72% HOTEL

☎ 01 8404384 📠 01 8404505
IFSC, North St, Swords
e-mail: info@carnegiecourt.com
web: www.carnegiecourt.com
dir: From Dublin Airport take N1 towards Belfast. At 5th rdbt take 1st exit for Swords, then sharp left for hotel

This modern hotel has been tastefully built and is conveniently located close to Dublin Airport just off the N1 in Swords. The air-conditioned bedrooms are well appointed, and many are particularly spacious. Public areas include a residents' lounge, contemporary Courtyard Restaurant, a dramatically designed Harp Bar and modern conference and banqueting facilities. Extensive underground parking is available.

Rooms 36 (4 fmly) (1 GF) **S** €135; **D** €240 (incl. bkfst)*
Facilities ♪ **Conf** Class 50 Board 40 Thtr 280
Services Lift Air con **Parking** 150 **Notes** LB ⊗ Closed 25-26 Dec

CO GALWAY

CARNA (CARNA) — Map 1 A4

Carna Bay Hotel

IRISH COUNTRY HOTELS

★★★ 70% HOTEL

☎ 095 32255 📠 095 32530
e-mail: carnabay@iol.ie
dir: from Galway take N59 to Recess, then left onto R340 for approx 10m

This family owned and run hotel is in the little village of Carna on the Connemara coastline and has a very friendly and relaxed atmosphere. Public areas are bright and spacious with casual meals served in the bar at lunch and in the evenings. More formal dinner is available in the restaurant where there is an emphasis on good quality local ingredients.

Rooms 26 (1 fmly) (11 GF) **S** €55-€90; **D** €90-€160 (incl. bkfst) **Facilities** New Year **Parking** 60 **Notes** Closed 23-26 Dec

CASHEL — Map 1 A4

INSPECTORS' CHOICE

Cashel House

★★★ ⊚⊚ COUNTRY HOUSE HOTEL

☎ 095 31001 📠 095 31077
e-mail: info@cashel-house-hotel.com
web: www.cashel-house-hotel.com
dir: S off N59, 1.5km W of Recess, well signed

Cashel House is a mid-19th century property, standing at the head of Cashel Bay, in the heart of Connemara. Quietly secluded in award-winning gardens with woodland walks. Attentive service comes with the perfect balance of friendliness and professionalism from McEvilly family and their staff. The comfortable lounges have turf fires and antique furnishings. The restaurant offers local produce such as the famous Connemara lamb, and fish from the nearby coast.

Rooms 32 (4 fmly) (6 GF) **S** €107-€270;
D €214-€304 (incl. bkfst)* **Facilities** ♨ Xmas New Year **Parking** 40 **Notes** LB Closed 4 Jan-4 Feb

Zetland Country House

MANOR HOUSE HOTELS

★★★ 82% ⊚⊚ HOTEL

☎ 095 31111 📠 095 31117
Cashel Bay
e-mail: zetland@iol.ie
web: www.zetland.com
dir: N59 from Galway towards Clifden, right after Recess onto R340, left after 4m (R341), hotel 1m on right

Standing on the edge of Cashel Bay, this former sporting lodge is a cosy and relaxing family run hotel that exudes charm. Many of the comfortable rooms have sea views, as has the restaurant where very good cuisine is served. Lounge areas feature turf fires.

Rooms 19 (10 fmly) (3 GF) **Facilities** ♨ ♥ Xmas New Year **Conf** Board 20 **Parking** 30 **Notes** LB

CLIFDEN — Map 1 A4

Abbeyglen Castle

MANOR HOUSE HOTELS

★★★★ 78% ⊚ HOTEL

☎ 095 21201 📠 095 21797
Sky Rd
e-mail: info@abbeyglen.ie
dir: N59 from Galway towards Clifden. Hotel 1km from Clifden on Sky Rd

The tranquil setting overlooking Clifden, matched with the dedication of the Hughes's father and son team and their attentive staff, combine to create a magical atmosphere. Well-appointed rooms and very comfortable suites are available, together with a range of relaxing lounge areas.

Rooms 45 (9 GF) **S** €123-€219; **D** €193-€326 (incl. bkfst)* **Facilities** STV ♨ Putt green Beauty treatment & relaxation centre ♪ Xmas New Year Wi-fi **Conf** Class 50 Board 40 Thtr 100 **Services** Lift **Parking** 50 **Notes** LB ⊗ No children Closed 4-29 Jan

Ardagh Hotel & Restaurant

IRISH COUNTRY HOTELS

★★★ 77% ⊚⊚ HOTEL

☎ 095 21384 📠 095 21314
Ballyconneely Rd
e-mail: ardaghhotel@eircom.net
dir: N59 (Galway to Clifden), signed to Ballyconneely

Situated at the head of Ardbear Bay, this family-run hotel takes full advantage of the spectacular scenery. The restaurant is renowned for its cuisine, which is complemented by friendly and knowledgeable service. Many of the spacious and well-appointed bedrooms have large picture windows and plenty of comfort.

Rooms 19 (2 fmly) **S** €120-€140; **D** €180-€210 (incl. bkfst) **Facilities** Pool room ♪ Wi-fi **Parking** 35 **Notes** LB Closed Nov-Mar

Rock Glen Country House Hotel

★★★ 74% HOTEL

☎ 095 21035 📠 095 21737
e-mail: enquiry@rockglenhotel.com
web: www.rockglenhotel.com
dir: N6 from Dublin to Galway. N57 from Galway to
Clifden. Hotel 1.5m from Clifden

The attractive clematis and creeper-framed façade of
this former hunting lodge is an introduction to the
comfort found inside. The hospitality of the staff makes a
visit to this hotel relaxing and very pleasant. Well-
appointed bedrooms and comfortable lounges here have
lovely views of the gardens and the bay.

Rooms 26 (2 fmly) (18 GF) **S** €75-€155; **D** €140-€220
(incl. bkfst & dinner)* **Facilities** ⌁ Putt green ⌁ ♫
Parking 50 **Notes** LB Closed mid Nov-mid Feb (ex New
Year)

Alcock & Brown Hotel

★★★ 70% ⊛ HOTEL

☎ 095 21206 & 21086 📠 095 21842
e-mail: alcockandbrown@eircom.net
dir: take N59 from Galway via Oughterard, hotel in town
centre

This comfortable family owned hotel is situated on the
town square. There is a cosy bar and lounge with open
fire. Brown's restaurant offers a wide ranging menu with
many fresh, local fish specialities. Bedrooms are well
appointed. The friendly and attentive staff provide good
service.

Rooms 19 **Facilities** ♫ New Year **Notes** LB Closed 19-26
Dec

GALWAY   Map 1 B3

INSPECTORS' CHOICE

Glenlo Abbey

★★★★ ⊛ COUNTRY HOUSE HOTEL

☎ 091 526666 📠 091 527800
Bushypark
e-mail: info@glenloabbey.ie
dir: 4km from city centre on N59

This lovingly restored, cut stone abbey was built
in 1740 and features sculpted cornices and fine
antique furniture. There is an elegant drawing room,
a cocktail bar, a library, the delightful River Room
restaurant and a cellar bar. The unique Orient Express
Pullman Restaurant provides a second dining option.
Bedrooms, in the modern wing, are spacious and well
appointed.

Rooms 46 **Facilities** ⌁ 18 Putt green Fishing Boating
Clay pigeon shooting Archery Driving range ♫
New Year Wi-fi **Conf** Class 100 Board 50 Thtr 180
Services Lift **Parking** 150 **Notes** LB ⊛ Closed 24-28
Dec

Ardilaun Hotel & Leisure Club

★★★★ 79% ⊛ HOTEL

☎ 091 521433 📠 091 521546
Taylor's Hill
e-mail: info@theardilaunhotel.ie
web: www.theardilaunhotel.ie
dir: N6 to Galway City West, then follow signs for N59
Clifden, then N6 towards Salthill

The Ardilaun is located on five acres of landscaped
gardens and has undergone a major refurbishment.
Bedrooms have been thoughtfully equipped and furnished
and the new wing of executive rooms and suites are
particularly spacious. Public areas include Camilaun
Restaurant overlooking the garden, comfortable lounges
and Blazers bar, and there extensive banqueting and
leisure facilities.

Rooms 125 (17 fmly) (8 GF) (106 smoking) **S** €95-€165;
D €110-€350 (incl. bkfst)* **Facilities** Spa STV ⌁
supervised Gym Treatment & analysis rooms Beauty salon
Spinning room ♫ New Year Wi-fi **Conf** Class 300
Board 100 Thtr 650 Del from €195 to €315*
Services Lift **Parking** 300 **Notes** LB Closed 24-26 Dec
RS Closed pm 23 Dec Civ Wed 600

Radisson SAS Hotel & Spa

★★★★ 78% HOTEL

☎ 091 538300 📠 091 538380
Lough Atalia Rd
e-mail: sales.galway@radissonsas.com
web: www.radissonhotelgalway.com
dir: take N6 into Galway City. At French rdbt turn 1st left.
At next lights take left fork. 0.5m, hotel at next right
junct at lights

In a prime position on the Lough Atalia's waterfront, it is
the striking interior design and good levels of comfort
that are keynotes at this hotel. Bedrooms are well
equipped and there is an impressive penthouse suite,
plus an executive floor where privacy and personal service
are guaranteed. The corporate and leisure facilities are
also very good.

Rooms 282 (21 annexe) (4 fmly) **S** €130-€450;
D €150-€450* **Facilities** Spa ⌁ supervised Putt green
Gym Outdoor Canadian hot-tub Sauna Steam room ♫
Xmas New Year Wi-fi **Conf** Class 650 Board 70 Thtr 1000
Services Lift Air con **Parking** 260 **Notes** LB ⊛

Galway Bay Hotel Conference & Leisure Centre

★★★★ 77% ⊛ HOTEL

☎ 091 520520 📠 091 520530
The Promenade, Salthill
e-mail: info@galwaybayhotel.com
dir: follow signs to Salthill from all major roads. Hotel on
promenade on coast road to Connemara

This modern hotel enjoys a most spectacular location
overlooking Galway Bay. The spacious bedrooms are well
appointed, public areas include comfortable lounges, sun
patio and bar all enjoying the lovely views. There are two
dining options; fine dining in the Lobster Pot or in the
Bistro featuring a less formal menu. Conference and
banqueting facilities are impressive.

Rooms 153 (10 fmly) (8 GF) **Facilities** ⌁ supervised Gym
Steam room Sauna Treatment rooms ♫ Xmas New Year
Wi-fi Child facilities **Conf** Class 325 Thtr 1100
Services Lift Air con **Parking** 150 **Notes** LB ⊛

GALWAY continued

Park House Hotel & Park Room Restaurant

★★★★ 77% ⚜ HOTEL

☎ 091 564924 📄 091 569219
Forster St, Eyre Square
e-mail: parkhousehotel@eircom.net
web: www.parkhousehotel.ie
dir: city centre

This city centre property offers well decorated and comfortable bedrooms that vary in size. The spacious restaurant has been a popular spot for the people of Galway for many years; a range of bar food is also available in Boss Doyle's bar throughout the day.

Rooms 84 (13 smoking) **Facilities** STV FTV 🎵 Wi-fi
Services Lift Air con **Parking** 26 **Notes** ⊗ Closed 24-26 Dec

See advert on this page

Claregalway

IRISH COUNTRY HOTELS

★★★ 79% HOTEL

☎ 091 738300 & 738302 📄 091 738311
Claregalway Village
e-mail: stay@claregalwayhotel.ie
dir: at junct of N17 (Galway/Sligo) & N18 (Dublin/Limerick)

Within easy reach of Galway city, this hotel offers comfortable bedrooms and spacious public areas. Owner run by the Gill family, food is served throughout the day in the popular bar, with the River Room open in the evenings. Leisure facilities are complimentary to residents.

Rooms 48 (8 fmly) (15 smoking) **S** €49-€320;
D €49-€320* **Facilities** Spa 🕙 supervised Gym Sauna Steam room Sunbeds 🎵 New Year Wi-fi **Conf** Class 250 Board 100 Thtr 400 **Services** Lift Air con **Parking** 160 **Notes** LB ⊗ Closed 23-26 Dec

The Harbour

★★★ 70% HOTEL

☎ 091 569466 📄 091 569455
New Dock Rd
e-mail: stay@harbour.ie
dir: follow signs for Galway City East, at rdbt take 1st exit to city, follow signs to docks, hotel approx 1m

This hotel is situated on the Galway Harbour development in the heart of the city. Contemporary in style, the ground floor includes a large lobby lounge with open fires. Krusoes café bar and restaurant offers modern cuisine. Bedrooms are smartly furnished, comfortable and well equipped. Guests have the benefit of complimentary secure parking at the rear, and there is also a leisure suite with treatment rooms available.

Rooms 96 **Facilities** Gym 🎵 New Year Wi-fi
Conf Class 80 Board 40 Thtr 100 **Services** Lift
Parking 64 (charged) **Notes** ⊗ Closed 23-27 Dec

The House

Ⓤ

☎ 091 538900 📄 091 568262
Lower Merchants Rd
e-mail: info@thehousehotel.ie
web: www.thehousehotel.ie

Currently the rating for this establishment is not confirmed. This may be due to a change of ownership or because it has only recently joined the AA rating scheme. For further details please see the AA website: www.theAA.com

Rooms 40 **Facilities** STV 🎵 New Year Wi-fi **Conf** Board 8 Del from €95 to €150* **Services** Lift Air con **Notes** ⊗

Travelodge Galway City

BUDGET HOTEL

☎ 091 781400
Tuam Rd
web: www.travelodge.co.uk

Travelodge offers good quality, good value, modern accommodation. Ideal for families, the spacious en suite bedrooms include remote-control TV, tea and coffee-making facilities and comfortable beds. Meals can be taken at the nearby family restaurant. See also the Hotel Groups pages.

Rooms 59 **S** fr €40; **D** fr €40

ORANMORE Map 1 B3

Maldon Hotel Galway

★★★ 70% HOTEL

☎ 091 792244 📄 091 792246
e-mail: res.galway@maldonhotels.com
dir: Beside Carrow Moneash rdbt on N6 towards Galway

Located near the village of Oranmore, just a 10 minute drive from the city, this hotel has a friendly and relaxed atmosphere, that proves popular with families. Bedrooms are comfortable, with dining available all day in the Q bar or Lannigans Restaurant. Good leisure facilities are complimentary to guests.

Rooms 113 (39 fmly) **S** €79-€199; **D** €79-€199
Facilities STV 🕙 supervised Gym Health & beauty salon Steam room Sauna Solarium Childrens play ground/room 🎵 New Year Wi-fi **Conf** Class 60 Board 40 Thtr 100 Del from €135 to €155 **Services** Lift Air con
Parking 100 **Notes** ⊗

PORTUMNA — Map 1 B3

Shannon Oaks Hotel & Country Club

★★★ 75% HOTEL

 IRISH COUNTRY HOTELS

☎ 090 9741777 🗎 090 9741357
St Joseph Rd
e-mail: sales@shannonoaks.ie
dir: on N65. From Portumna, on left of St Joseph's Rd

Located in eight acres of parkland by Portumna National Park, this modern hotel offers very comfortable and spacious bedrooms and suites. The popular Idle Hour Bar has food available most of the day, and there is also the Upper Deck Bistro and more formal dining in the Castlegates Restaurant. Extensive conference and leisure facilities are also on site.

Rooms 109 (46 annexe) (21 GF) **S** €110-€125; **D** €170-€190 (incl. bkfst) **Facilities** Spa STV 🐾 supervised Gym Sauna 🎵 Xmas New Year **Conf** Class 320 Board 280 Thtr 600 **Services** Lift Air con **Parking** 400 **Notes** LB 🚫 Civ Wed 360

RECESS (SRAITH SALACH) — Map 1 A4

Ballynahinch Castle

★★★★ 83% 🏵🏵
COUNTRY HOUSE HOTEL

MANOR HOUSE HOTELS

☎ 095 31006 🗎 095 31086
Recess, Connemara
e-mail: bhinch@iol.ie
dir: W from Galway on N59 towards Clifden. After Recess take Roundstone turn on left

Open log fires and friendly professional service are just some of the delights of staying at this castle originating from the 16th century. Set in 350 acres of woodland, rivers and lakes, this hotel has many suites and rooms with stunning views, as does the award-winning

Owenmore restaurant where the linen is crisp and the silver gleams.

Rooms 40 **S** €165-€245; **D** €260-€440 (incl. bkfst) **Facilities** 🎣 Fishing 🚶 River & lakeside walks 🎵 **Conf** Class 20 Board 20 Thtr 30 Del from €240 to €365 **Parking** 55 **Notes** LB 🚫 Closed 1-26 Feb & 20-27 Dec RS Good Fri

---

INSPECTORS' CHOICE

Lough Inagh Lodge

★★★ 🏵 COUNTRY HOUSE HOTEL

 MANOR HOUSE HOTELS

☎ 095 34706 & 34694 🗎 095 34708
Inagh Valley
e-mail: inagh@iol.ie
dir: from Recess take R344 towards Kylemore

This 19th-century, former fishing lodge is akin to a family home where guests are encouraged to relax and enjoy the peace. It is situated between the Connemara Mountains and fronted by a good fishing lake. Bedrooms are smartly decorated and comfortable, there is a choice of lounges with turf fires and a cosy traditional bar. The delightful restaurant specialises in dishes of the local lamb and lake caught fish.

Rooms 13 (1 fmly) (4 GF) **Facilities** Fishing Hill walking Fly fishing Cycling **Conf** Class 20 Board 20 Thtr 20 **Services** Air con **Parking** 16 **Notes** LB Closed mid Dec-mid Mar

---

RENVYLE — Map 1 A4

Renvyle House Hotel

★★★ 74% 🏵 HOTEL

☎ 095 43511 🗎 095 43515
e-mail: info@renvyle.com
web: www.renvyle.com
dir: follow hotel signs from Recess

This comfortable house has been operating as a hotel for over 120 years. Located on the unspoilt coast of Connemara it provides a range of outdoor leisure pursuits. The spacious, comfortable lounges have turf fires and the bedrooms are well equipped. The relaxed, friendly staff will make any visit here memorable.

Rooms 73 (3 annexe) (8 fmly) (15 GF) **Facilities** 🎾 ⚓ 9 🎣 Putt green Fishing 🚶 Clay pigeon shooting 🎵 Xmas New Year Child facilities **Conf** Class 80 Board 80 Thtr 200 **Parking** 60 **Notes** LB Closed 6 Jan-14 Feb

---

ROUNDSTONE — Map 1 A4

Roundstone House Hotel

★★ 70% 🏵 HOTEL

IRISH COUNTRY HOTELS

☎ 095 35864 🗎 095 35944
e-mail: vaughanshotel@eircom.net
dir: From Galway take N59. After Recess take 2nd left. Hotel in 9km

This delightful hotel has been in operation since 1894 and owned by the Vaughan family for many years. The comfortable bedrooms enjoy the magnificent sea views and the rugged Connemara landscape. There is a relaxing residents' lounge, cosy bar and Vaughan's Restaurant that is renowned for its extensive range of seafood.

Rooms 12 (1 fmly) **Notes** 🚫 Closed Oct-Etr Civ Wed

SALTHILL

See Galway

CO KERRY

BALLYHEIGE — Map 1 A2

The White Sands

★★★ 72% HOTEL

IRISH COUNTRY HOTELS

☎ 066 7133102 🗎 066 7133357
e-mail: whitesands@eircom.net
dir: 18km from Tralee on coast road. Hotel in main street

Situated in the seaside town of Ballyheige this family run hotel has friendly staff. Attractively decorated throughout, facilities include a choice of lounges, traditional pub where there is entertainment most nights, good restaurant and comfortable bedrooms. Guests can enjoy the sandy beaches and golf clubs close by.

Rooms 81 (2 fmly) **Facilities** 🎵 Child facilities **Conf** Class 40 Board 40 **Services** Lift Air con **Parking** 40 **Notes** LB 🚫 Closed Nov-Feb RS Mar-Apr & Oct

CAHERDANIEL (CATHAIR DÓNALL) Map 1 A2

Derrynane

★★★ 71% ⊛ HOTEL

☎ 066 9475136 🖷 066 9475160
e-mail: info@derrynane.com
dir: just off main road, (N70)

A super clifftop location overlooking Derrynane Bay with spectacular views add a stunning dimension to this well run hotel where pleasant, efficient staff contribute to the very relaxed atmosphere. Public areas include spacious lounges, a bar and restaurant. Bedrooms are well appointed and most benefit from the views.

Rooms 70 (30 fmly) (32 GF) Facilities ⚑ supervised ⚊ Gym Steam room Seaweed therapy room ♫ Xmas Parking 60 Notes LB ⊗ Closed 4 Oct-15 Apr

CAHERSIVEEN Map 1 A2

Ring of Kerry Hotel

★★★ 71% HOTEL

☎ 066 9472543 🖷 066 9472893
Valentia Rd
e-mail: ringhotel@eircom.net
web: www.ringofkerryhotel.ie
dir: on Ring of Kerry road

This hotel, situated in the town of Cahersiveen, is ideal for touring the Ring of Kerry and the nearby islands. Bedrooms are spacious and attractively decorated. There are two dining options - dinner is served nightly in the cosy restaurant and less formal fare is available in the inviting John D's bar.

Rooms 24 (4 fmly) Facilities ♫ New Year Wi-fi Conf Class 150 Board 80 Thtr 450 Parking 24 Notes LB ⊗

DINGLE (AN DAINGEAN) Map 1 A2

Dingle Skellig Hotel & Peninsula Spa

★★★★ 76% HOTEL

☎ 066 9150200 🖷 066 9151501
e-mail: reservations@dingleskellig.com
dir: Enter Dingle from N86 hotel on harbour

This modern hotel, close to the town, overlooks Dingle Bay and has spectacular views from many of the comfortably furnished bedrooms and suites. Public areas offer a spacious bar and lounge and a bright, airy restaurant. There are extensive health and leisure facilities, and many family activities are organised in the Fungi Kids Club.

Rooms 113 (10 fmly) (31 GF) S €87-€155; D €124-€250 (incl. bkfst)* Facilities Spa STV FTV ⚑ supervised Gym ♫ New Year Wi-fi Child facilities Conf Class 120 Board 100 Thtr 250 Services Lift Parking 110 Notes LB ⊗ Civ Wed 230

Dingle Bay

★★★ 72% HOTEL

☎ 066 9151231 🖷 066 9152740
Strand St
e-mail: info@dinglebayhotel.com

This hotel is in the heart of the town, overlooking the pier and marina. The spacious, individually designed bedrooms have a modern style, and include twin, double, suites and family rooms. Seafood is a speciality of the restaurant, and music features regularly in Paudie's, the popular and stylish bar. Parking is available at the rear.

Rooms 25

Dingle Benners

★★★ 67% HOTEL

☎ 066 9151638 🖷 066 9151412
Main St
e-mail: info@dinglebenners.com

Located in the centre of the town with parking to the rear, this long-established property has a relaxed, traditional character. Bedrooms are well equipped and come in two styles - in the original house and in a newer block. Food is available in the popular bar.

Rooms 52 (2 fmly) (9 GF) Services Lift Parking 32

KENMARE Map 1 B2

From November 2008 the dialling codes for the establishments listed under this location are as shown (ie 064 66). Prior to that date use the 064 prefix only.

Sheen Falls Lodge

★★★★★ 86% ⊛⊛ COUNTRY HOUSE HOTEL

☎ 064 66 41600 🖷 064 66 41386
e-mail: info@sheenfallslodge.ie
dir: from Kenmare take N71 to Glengarriff over suspension bridge, take 1st left

This former fishing lodge has been developed into a beautiful hotel with a friendly team of professional staff. The cascading Sheen Falls are floodlit at night, forming a romantic backdrop to the enjoyment of award-winning cuisine in La Cascade restaurant. Less formal dining is available in Oscar's Restaurant. Bedrooms are very comfortably appointed; many of the suites are particularly spacious. The leisure centre and beauty therapy facilities offer a number of exclusive treatments.

Rooms 66 (14 fmly) (14 GF) Facilities Spa STV ⚑ supervised ⚊ Fishing ⚑ Gym Table tennis Steam room Clay pigeon shooting Cycling Vintage car rides Library ♫ Xmas New Year Wi-fi Conf Class 65 Board 50 Thtr 120 Services Lift Parking 75 Notes LB ⊗ Closed 2 Jan-1 Feb

The Lansdowne Arms Hotel

★★★ 69%

☎ 064 66 41368 🖷 064 66 41114
Main St
e-mail: info@lansdownearms.com
dir: From N22 through Kilgarvan to Kenmare

This was Kenmare's first hotel, dating back to the 1760s, and is now owned by the Quill family. It is appointed to a high standard. Dinner is served in the Quill Room and more casual dining is available in the Poets Bar; traditional music is played in the Bold Thady Quill bar at weekends.

Continued

The Lansdowne Arms Hotel

Rooms 26 (9 GF) **Facilities** 🎵 Child facilities **Parking** 20
Notes LB ⊗ Closed 25 Dec

KILLARNEY   Map 1 B2

From November 2008 the dialling codes for the
establishments listed under this location are as shown
(ie **064 66**). Prior to that date use the **064** prefix only.

INSPECTORS' CHOICE

Aghadoe Heights Hotel & Spa
★★★★★ ◉◉ HOTEL

☎ 064 66 31766 📄 064 66 31345
e-mail: info@aghadoeheights.com
dir: From Killarney via N22. Follow signs for Tralee.
Take 1st left on Tralee Rd, take 1st left at top of hill,
1.5m. Hotel on right

The exterior of this superbly positioned hotel belies
the opulence within. Overlooking Loch Lein with
spectacular views of Killarney's lakes and mountains,
Aghadoe Heights is appointed to the very highest
standard. The friendly team display a genuine
willingness to make everyone's stay special so that
happy memories are assured. Many of the bedrooms
have sun decks making the most of the panoramic
scenery. The Penthouse Suite is truly stunning.

Rooms 74 (12 fmly) (10 GF) **S** €180-€250;
D €250-€370 (incl. bkfst) **Facilities** Spa STV ◓ ⊰
Gym Thermal suite Cycling Guided walks 🎵 Xmas
Wi-fi **Conf** Class 80 Board 60 Thtr 120 **Services** Lift
Parking 82 **Notes** LB ⊗ RS Nov-Feb Civ Wed 150

Killarney Park
★★★★★ 87% ◉◉ HOTEL

☎ 064 66 35555 📄 064 66 35266
e-mail: info@killarneyparkhotel.ie
web: www.killarneyparkhotel.ie
dir: N22 from Cork to Killarney. At 1st rdbt take 1st exit to
town centre. At 2nd rdbt take 2nd exit, 3rd rdbt take 1st
exit. Hotel 2nd left

This charming hotel on the edge of the town combines
elegance with comfort. It has a warm atmosphere with
open fires, restful colours and friendly caring staff who
ensure your stay is an enjoyable one. Bedrooms and
suites are spacious, and many have air conditioning and
open fires. A health spa is included in the leisure
facilities.

Rooms 68 (4 fmly) **S** €275-€400; **D** €275-€400 (incl.
bkfst)* **Facilities** Spa STV ◓ supervised ⊰ Putt green
Gym Outdoor Canadian hot-tub Plunge pool Caldarium
relaxation room Bubble pool Sauna Xmas New Year Wi-fi
Conf Class 70 Board 35 Thtr 150 **Services** Lift Air con
Parking 70 **Notes** LB ⊗ Closed 24-26 Dec Civ Wed 120

Randles Court
★★★★ 81% HOTEL

☎ 064 66 35333 📄 064 66 35206
Muckross Rd
e-mail: info@randlescourt.com
dir: N22 towards Muckross, turn tight at T-junct on right.
From N72 take 3rd exit on 1st rdbt into town & follow
signs for Muckross, hotel on left

Close to all the town's attractions, this is a friendly
family-run hotel with an emphasis on customer care.
Bedrooms are particularly comfortable. Guests can enjoy
a relaxing drink in the cosy bar then dine in the chic
Checkers bistro restaurant where good food is served in
the evenings. A swimming pool and other leisure facilities
are available.

Rooms 52 **Facilities** ◓ Putt green Gym **Conf** Class 60
Board 40 Thtr 80 **Services** Lift **Parking** 39 **Notes** Closed
23-27 Dec

The Brehon
★★★★ 80% ◉ HOTEL

☎ 064 66 30700 📄 064 66 30701
The Brehon Hotel, Muckross Rd
e-mail: info@thebrehon.com
dir: 1m from Killarney on N71

This is a spectacular hotel close to Killarney National
Park and the town. Public areas are particularly spacious
with comfortable lounges, bars and a restaurant.
Bedrooms are well equipped and there is a range of
suites. The hotel offers a Thai spa and extensive
conference facilities. Other leisure facilities are on offer
at their nearby sister hotel.

Rooms 125 (3 fmly) **Facilities** Spa ◓ supervised ⊰ Putt
green Gym 🎵 Xmas New Year Wi-fi **Conf** Class 120
Board 60 Thtr 250 **Services** Lift Air con **Parking** 126
Notes ⊗ Civ Wed 200

Cahernane House
★★★★ 79% ◉◉ HOTEL

☎ 064 66 31895 📄 064 66 34340
Muckross Rd
e-mail: info@cahernane.net
web: www.cahernane.com
dir: On N22 to Killarney, take 1st exit off rdbt then left at
church and 1st exit at next rdbt to Muckross Road

This fine country mansion, former home of the Earls of
Pembroke, has a magnificent mountain backdrop and
panoramic views from its lakeside setting. Elegant period
furniture is complemented by more modern pieces to
create a comfortable hotel offering a warm atmosphere
with a particularly friendly team dedicated to guest care.

Rooms 38 (26 annexe) **S** €145-€195; **D** €190-€290
(incl. bkfst)* **Facilities** ⊰ Fishing ⊰ Wi-fi **Conf** Class 10
Board 10 Thtr 15 **Services** Lift Air con **Parking** 50
Notes LB ⊗ Closed 21 Dec-31 Jan Civ Wed 60

KILLARNEY continued

Lake

★★★ 78% HOTEL

☎ 064 66 31035 📠 064 66 31902
Muckross Rd
e-mail: info@lakehotel.com
dir: N22 to Killarney. Hotel 2km from town on Muckross road

This hotel is located on Killarney's lake shore, it is operated by the Huggard family and a very dedicated and friendly team. There is a relaxed atmosphere with log fires in the lounge and stunning views from the restaurant. Most of the comfortable bedrooms have lake and mountain views, some with balconies and four poster beds. The spa offers good facilities and there are lovely walks and cycle paths.

Rooms 133 (6 fmly) (23 GF) **S** €55-€480; **D** €90-€480 (incl. bkfst)* **Facilities** Spa ⌒ Fishing ⌲ Gym Outdoor hot tub Sauna Steam room ♫ Wi-fi **Conf** Class 60 Board 40 Thtr 80 **Services** Lift **Parking** 140 **Notes** ⊗ Closed 2 Dec-15 Jan Civ Wed 110

Killeen House

★★★ 75% ⊛ HOTEL

☎ 064 66 31711 & 31773 📠 064 66 31811
Aghadoe, Lakes of Killarney
e-mail: charming@indigo.ie
dir: In Aghadoe, just outside Killarney town centre & just off Dingle Road

Dating back to 1838 this charming Victorian country house is situated close to Killarney Park and Lakes. Stylishly decorated public areas include a cosy sitting room and bar where 'golf is spoken'. Excellent cuisine is served in the restaurant which overlooks the beautifully manicured garden. Bedrooms are well appointed and comfortable. The Rosney family and their staff take particular pride in extending a warm welcome to their guests.

Rooms 23 (10 GF) (10 smoking) **S** €120-€160; **D** €180-€240 (incl. bkfst) **Facilities** STV FTV Wi-fi **Parking** 30 **Notes** LB Closed 21 Oct-19 Apr

Castlerosse Hotel & Golf Resort

★★★ 75% HOTEL

☎ 064 66 31144 📠 064 66 31031
e-mail: res@castlerosse.ie
web: www.castlerossehotel.com
dir: from Killarney take R562 for Killorglin & The Ring of Kerry. Hotel 1.5km from town on left

A lovely location on 6,000 acres of land overlooking Lough Leane. Bedrooms are well appointed and comfortable. The restaurant enjoys panoramic views from its elevated position. Golf is available on site, together with a leisure centre and treatment rooms.

Rooms 120 (27 fmly) **Facilities** Spa STV FTV ⌒ supervised ⌲ 9 ⌲ Putt green Gym Golfing & riding arranged ♫ **Conf** Class 100 Board 40 Thtr 200 **Services** Lift **Parking** 100 **Notes** ⊗ Closed Dec-Feb

Scotts Hotel

★★★ 75% HOTEL

☎ 064 66 31060 📠 064 66 36656
College St
e-mail: info@scottshotelkillarney.com
dir: N20, N22 to town, at Friary turn left. 500mtrs on East Avenue Rd to car park entrance

Enjoying a prominent town centre location, this modern hotel has comfortable public areas, a selection of bars and courtyard with nightly live entertainment during the high season and at weekends during the year. Bedrooms are spacious and furnished with guest comfort in mind. The suites have fitted kitchens and splendid views of the mountains. Secure underground parking is available.

Rooms 52 (4 fmly) **Facilities** ♫ Xmas **Services** Lift **Parking** 60 **Notes** ⊗ Closed 24-25 Dec

Gleneagle

★★★ 74% HOTEL

☎ 064 66 36000 📠 064 66 32646
Muckross Rd
e-mail: info@gleneaglehotel.com
web: www.gleneaglehotel.com
dir: 1m outside Killarney on N71 (Kenmare road)

The facilities at this large hotel are excellent and numerous. Family entertainment is a strong element of the Gleneagle experience, popular with the Irish market for over 50 years. Comfortable rooms are matched with a range of lounges, restaurants, a leisure centre and INEC, one of Ireland's largest events' centres.

Rooms 250 (57 fmly) (35 GF) **Facilities** ⌒ supervised ⌲ Gym Squash Pitch & putt Steam room Games room ♫ Xmas New Year Wi-fi **Conf** Class 1000 Board 50 Thtr 2500 **Services** Lift **Parking** 500 **Notes** LB ⊗

Best Western International

★★★ 73% HOTEL

☎ 064 66 31816 📠 064 66 31837
East Avenue Rd
e-mail: inter@iol.ie
dir: N21 from Limerick to Farranfore, then N22 to Killarney, right at 1st rdbt into Killarney, follow bypass to hotel

Quality bedrooms with modern comforts are on offer at this warm and friendly hotel in the heart of the town. Hannigan's bar and brasserie serves food throughout the day, with an inviting mahogany-panelled room open in the evenings. Relaxing lounge areas include a snooker room and a library.

Rooms 90 (6 fmly) **Facilities** Gym Billiards 3-D Golf simulator Infrared sauna ♫ New Year Wi-fi **Conf** Class 100 Board 25 Thtr 150 **Services** Lift **Notes** LB ⊗ Closed 23-27 Dec

Victoria House Hotel

★★★ 72% HOTEL

☎ 064 66 35430 📠 064 66 35439
Muckross Rd
e-mail: info@victoriahousehotel.com
dir: On N71, 1.5km from Killarney overlooking Killarney National Park

This family owned and managed hotel is just one kilometre from the town, and overlooks the National Park and mountains. Friendliness is the key word to the style of service, with good food served in both the restaurant and throughout the day in the bar. Bedrooms are comfortable, well equipped and attractively decorated.

Rooms 35 (2 fmly) (10 GF) **S** €80-€110; **D** €100-€440 (incl. bkfst) **Facilities** STV Bicycle hire ♫ Wi-fi **Parking** 60 **Notes** LB ⊗ Closed 4 Dec-2 Feb

Quality Hotel Killarney

★★★ 70% HOTEL

☎ 064 66 26200 📠 064 66 32438
Cork Rd
e-mail: info@qualityhotelkillarney.com
web: www.qualityhotelkillarney.com
dir: From Cork, approach town on N22. At 1st rdbt straight, hotel immediately on left.

This property is very well suited to the leisure market, with excellent facilities and many activities provided for all ages, particularly families. Bedrooms vary in style, but all are very well appointed and comfortable. Guests have a choice of two bars, where entertainment is a regular feature.

Rooms 269 (87 annexe) (269 fmly) (67 GF) **S** €89-€219; **D** €89-€219 **Facilities** Spa STV ⊙ supervised Gym Sauna Steam room Mini golf Basketball Table tennis ♫ New Year Child facilities **Services** Lift **Parking** 200 **Notes** LB Closed 13-27 Dec & 4 Jan-13 Feb

The Valley Suites

★★★ 70% HOTEL

☎ 064 66 23600 📠 064 66 23601
Fossa
e-mail: killarneyvalley@eircom.net
web: www.killarneyvalley.com
dir: From Killarney N72 (Ring of Kerry). Hotel 3m on right

Located in Fossa Village, not far from Killarney, this hotel offers spacious bedrooms, many of which are interconnecting with kitchenettes and sitting areas. Smart public areas include a popular bar and a first floor restaurant and a penthouse lounge making the most of the views. Close to many golf courses.

Rooms 63 (20 GF) **Facilities** ♫ **Services** Lift **Parking** 74 **Notes** LB ⊗ Closed Nov-Jan

White Gates

★★★ 63% HOTEL

☎ 064 66 31164 📠 064 66 34850
Muckross Rd
e-mail: whitegates@iol.ie
dir: 1km from Killarney on Muckross road on left

The eye is definitely drawn to this hotel with its ochre and blue painted frontage. The same flair for colour is in evidence throughout the interior where bedrooms of mixed sizes are well decorated and very comfortable. There is also a light-filled restaurant, with casual dining in the bar, which has a popular local trade.

Rooms 27 (4 fmly) (4 GF) **Facilities** ♫ **Conf** Class 50 **Parking** 50 **Notes** ⊗ Closed 25-26 Dec

Muckross Park Hotel & Cloisters Spa

[U]

☎ 064 66 23400 📠 064 66 31965
Lakes of Killarney
e-mail: johnkeating@muckrosspark.com
dir: From Killarney take N71 towards Kenmare

Currently the rating for this establishment is not confirmed. This may be due to a change of ownership or because it has only recently joined the AA rating scheme. For further details please see the AA website: www.theAA.com

Rooms 68 (3 fmly) **Facilities** Spa Fishing ⬆ Gym Archery Cycling Yoga ♫ Wi-fi **Conf** Class 280 Board 30 Thtr 350 **Services** Lift Air con **Notes** LB ⊗

PARKNASILLA Map 1 A2
From November 2008 the dialling codes for the establishments listed under this location are as shown (ie 064 66). Prior to that date use the 064 prefix only.

Parknasilla

★★★★ 81% ⊛ HOTEL

☎ 064 66 45122 📠 064 66 45323
e-mail: res@parknasilla-gsh.com
dir: on Kenmare road 3km from Sneem village

This delightful hotel which has been in business for over a hundred years, is a popular haven of relaxation and rejuvenation for generations of Irish families. There are many spacious lounges, that together with the restaurant and many of the bedrooms, have wonderful sea views. Service is warm and friendly, underpinned by smooth professionalism.

Rooms 83 (59 annexe) (6 fmly) **Facilities** ⊙ supervised ♨ 12 ⛳ Putt green Fishing ⬆ Bike hire Windsurfing Clay pigeon shooting Archery ♫ Xmas **Conf** Class 60 Board 20 Thtr 80 **Services** Lift **Parking** 60 **Notes** LB ⊗

STRADBALLY Map 1 A2

Crutch's Hillville House

★★ 65% HOTEL

☎ 066 7138118 📠 066 7138159
Kilcummin, Conor Pass Rd
e-mail: macshome@iol.ie

Located at Kilcummin Junction on the Conor Pass road to Dingle, this hotel is an oasis of calm. Hospitality is very much to the fore, and service is relaxed and informal. Guests will find crackling log fires and cosy lounge areas. Cooking is traditional, with excellent use locally produced ingredients.

Rooms 18

TRALEE Map 1 A2

Manor West

★★★★ 78% ⊛ HOTEL

☎ 066 7194500 📠 066 7194545
Killarney Rd
e-mail: info@manorwesthotel.ie
web: www.manorwesthotel.ie

Just five minutes from the centre of town this hotel is part of a large retail park with many shopping opportunities. Spacious well-equipped bedrooms are matched by smart public areas, including a high spec leisure facility. There is a spa with pools, steam room, sauna and Jacuzzi, and a variety of treatments are offered in the Harmony Wellness suites. The popular Mercantile bar serves food throughout the day, with fine dining available in The Walnut Room in the evening.

Rooms 75 **S** €100-€120; **D** €160-€250 (incl. bkfst)* **Facilities** Spa STV FTV ⊙ supervised Gym Sauna Steam room ♫ New Year Wi-fi **Conf** Class 150 Board 60 Thtr 200 **Services** Lift Air con **Parking** 80 **Notes** ⊗ Closed 24-26 Dec

TRALEE continued

COURTESY & CARE AWARD

Ballygarry House Hotel and Spa

★★★★ 78% HOTEL

☎ 066 7123322 📄 066 7127630
Killarney Rd
e-mail: info@ballygarryhouse.com
web: www.ballygarryhouse.com
dir: 1.5km from Tralee, on N22

Set in six acres of well-tended gardens, this fine hotel has been family run for the last 50 years and is appointed to a very high standard. The elegant and stylishly decorated bedrooms are spacious and relaxing. Good cuisine is served in the split-level restaurant. The staff are friendly and professional. AA Ireland has awarded this hotel their Courtesy & Care Award for the Republic of Ireland 2008-9.

Rooms 64 (10 fmly) (16 GF) **S** €115-€195;
D €155-€195 (incl. bkfst) **Facilities** Spa Outdoor hot tub Steam room Sauna New Year Wi-fi **Services** Lift **Parking** 200 **Notes** ❸ Closed 20-26 Dec Civ Wed 350

Meadowlands Hotel

★★★★ 76% HOTEL

☎ 066 7180444 📄 066 7180964
Oakpark
e-mail: info@meadowlandshotel.com
dir: 1km from Tralee town centre on N69

This smart hotel is within walking distance of the town centre. Bedrooms are tastefully decorated and comfortable. Johnny Frank's is the very popular pub where a wide range of food is offered throughout the day, with more formal dining available in An Pota Stor which specialises in seafood.

Rooms 57 (1 fmly) (4 GF) (4 smoking) **S** €90-€140;
D €160-€195 (incl. bkfst) **Facilities** STV ♫ Wi-fi **Conf** Class 110 Board 30 Thtr 250 **Services** Lift Air con **Parking** 200 **Notes** LB ❸ Closed 24-26 Dec

Fels Point

★★★★ 75% HOTEL

☎ 066 7119986 📄 066 7119987
Fels Point, Dan Spring Rd
e-mail: pmcdermott@felspointhotel.ie

This new, contemporary-style hotel is situated on the ring road and is within walking distance of the town centre. Public areas include a stylish lobby lounge where the grand piano is played at weekends. Bistro food is served in Clarets Bar all day, with finer dining available in Morels Restaurant at night. The smart bedrooms are air conditioned and have LCD TVs and high-speed internet connections. There are extensive conference/banqueting and leisure facilities.

Rooms 166 (29 smoking) **S** €89-€129; **D** €89-€129* **Facilities** STV FTV ➲ Gym ♫ New Year Wi-fi **Conf** Class 250 Board 50 Thtr 350 Del from €125 to €185* **Services** Lift Air con **Parking** 120 **Notes** LB ❸ Closed 24-26 Dec Civ Wed 100

Ballyseede Castle

★★★ 79% HOTEL

☎ 066 7125799 📄 066 7125287
e-mail: info@ballyseedecastle.com
dir: Just outside Tralee on N21

Ballyseede Castle is steeped in history - it has been fought over, lived in and is now lovingly cared for by the Corscadden family. The spacious bedrooms are elegantly and individually furnished. There are gracious reception rooms with ornamental cornice and marble fireplaces, a carved oak library bar, a splendid banqueting hall and 30 acres of mature gardens and woodland.

Rooms 23 (5 fmly) **S** €99-€145; **D** €99-€250 (incl. bkfst) **Facilities** STV FTV **Conf** Class 100 Board 24 Thtr 150 Del from €150 to €200 **Parking** 40 **Notes** LB ❸ Closed 24-26 Dec & 6 Jan-28 Feb Civ Wed 180

WATERVILLE (AN COIREÁN) | Map 1 A2

Butler Arms

★★★ 80% ◉ HOTEL

☎ 066 9474144 📄 066 9474520
e-mail: reservations@butlerarms.com
dir: village centre on seafront. N70 (Ring of Kerry)

This smartly presented hotel on the Ring of Kerry, has been in the Huggard family for four generations. A range of comfortable lounges creates a relaxing atmosphere, and excellent bar food is served in the Fisherman's bar through the day. More formal evening dining is available in the restaurant, which has commanding views of the sea and town.

Rooms 40 (1 fmly) **Facilities** ➲ Fishing Billiards room **Services** Lift **Parking** 50 **Notes** ❸ Closed Nov-Apr

CO KILDARE

ATHY | Map 1 C3

Clanard Court

★★★★ 73% HOTEL

☎ 059 8640666 📄 059 8640888
Dublin Rd
e-mail: sales@clanardcourt.ie
web: www.clanardcourt.ie
dir: Take N7 at Red Cow rdbt, take M7 signed Limerick & Cork. At junct 9 onto M9, exit signed Athy. Right onto N78

Located just one kilometre from Athy on the Dublin road, this family owned hotel enjoys a well earned reputation for hosting weddings and family celebrations. Concerts and events are also a regular feature here. Bedrooms are spaciously sized and attractively decorated. Bailey's is a popular bar serving food throughout the day.

Rooms 38 (2 fmly) (17 GF) **Facilities** Putt green ♫ Xmas New Year Child facilities **Conf** Class 300 Board 20 Thtr 400 **Services** Lift **Parking** 250 **Notes** LB ❸ Closed 25 Dec

CASTLEDERMOT — Map 1 C3

Kilkea Castle Hotel

★★★★ 73% HOTEL

☎ 059 9145156 & 9145100 📠 059 9145187
e-mail: kilkeas@iol.ie
dir: From Dublin take M9 S, take exit for High Cross Inn. Left after pub, hotel 3m on right

Dating from 1180, this is reputed to be Ireland's oldest inhabited castle. Surrounded by an 18-hole golf course, it offers a comfortable bar and lounge, and D'Lacy's, a fine dining restaurant on the first floor. Bedrooms vary in both size and style, but are all well equipped. Popular banqueting and conference facilities are situated in the converted stables.

Rooms 35 (24 annexe) (2 fmly) (5 GF) (25 smoking) S €150-€265; D €200-€230 (incl. bkfst) Facilities STV ℡ supervised ⅃ 18 ⛳ Putt green Fishing Gym Sauna Steam room Wi-fi Conf Class 30 Board 50 Thtr 300 Del from €200 to €250 Services Lift Parking 100 Notes LB ⊗ Closed 23-26 Dec

CLANE — Map 1 C4

Westgrove

Ⓤ

☎ 045 989900 📠 045 989911
Abbeylands
e-mail: info@westgrovehotel.com
dir: From M4 (W of Dublin) follow Naas, Maynooth signs. At rdbt 2nd exit signed Naas, Straffan. At rdbt 3rd exit signed Clane (R403). At next rdbt (before Clane) 1st exit. At next rdbt 2nd exit, hotel on right

Currently the rating for this establishment is not confirmed. This may be due to a change of ownership or because it has only recently joined the AA rating scheme. For further details please see the AA website: www.theAA.com

Rooms 99 (14 fmly) (30 smoking) S €89-€130; D €140-€250 (incl. bkfst)* Facilities Spa STV ℡ supervised Gym New Year Wi-fi Conf Class 220 Board 100 Thtr 500 Del from €162 to €182* Services Lift Parking 300 Notes LB ⊗ Closed 24-25 Dec Civ Wed 300

LEIXLIP — Map 1 D4

Courtyard

★★★★ 74% HOTEL

☎ 01 6295100 📠 01 6295111
Main St
e-mail: info@courtyard.ie
dir: from M4 follow R148 to town centre, then follow Main Street Car Park signs

Situated on the site of the brewery where the Guinness family first started brewing, this hotel has stylish contemporary design that blends seamlessly with the original stonework. The bedrooms have been tastefully appointed with all guest needs catered for. The public areas include a choice of restaurants and bars, and a large open courtyard that often hosts music events during summer months.

Rooms 40 (16 GF) Facilities ♫ Xmas New Year Wi-fi Conf Class 80 Board 80 Thtr 120 Services Lift Air con Parking 100 Notes LB ⊗

Leixlip House

★★★ 79% ◉ HOTEL

☎ 01 6242268 📠 01 6244177
Captains Hill
e-mail: info@leixliphouse.com
dir: from Leixlip motorway junct continue into village. Turn right at lights, up hill

This Georgian house dates back to 1772 and retains many original features. Overlooking Leixlip, the hotel is just eight miles from Dublin city centre. Bedrooms and public areas are furnished and decorated to a high standard. The Bradaun Restaurant offers a wide range of interesting dishes at dinner, with a popular bar menu served throughout the day.

Rooms 19 (2 fmly) S €95-€140; D €115-€200 (incl. bkfst)* Facilities STV Wi-fi Conf Class 60 Board 40 Thtr 130 Del from €165 to €175* Parking 64 Notes LB ⊗ RS 24-27 Dec Civ Wed 60

NAAS — Map 1 D3

Killashee House Hotel and Villa Spa

★★★★ 78% ◉ HOTEL

☎ 045 879277 📠 045 879266
e-mail: reservations@killasheehouse.com
dir: N7, then straight through town on Old Kilcullen Rd (R448), hotel on left, 1.5m from centre of Naas

This Victorian manor house, set among parkland and well-landscaped gardens, has been successfully converted to a large hotel with spacious public areas and very comfortable bedrooms. Two dining options are available - fine dining in Turners Restaurant and more casual fare in the Nuns Kitchen Bar on the lower level. There are extensive banqueting and conference facilities. The Villa Spa and a popular leisure centre are located in the grounds.

Rooms 141 (10 fmly) (48 GF) Facilities Spa ℡ supervised ⅃ Gym Archery Biking Clay pigeon shooting Air Rifle shooting Falconry ♫ Xmas New Year Wi-fi Conf Class 144 Board 84 Thtr 1600 Services Lift Parking 600 Notes ⊗ Closed 25-26 Dec

See advert on this page

NAAS continued

Maudlins House
★★★ 78% ⊛ HOTEL

☎ 045 896999 ▤ 045 906411
Dublin Rd
e-mail: info@maudlinshousehotel.ie
dir: Exit N7 approaching large globe, straight through 2 rdbts. Hotel on right

Located on the outskirts of Naas, this is a modern property incorporating an original country house. Bedrooms are well appointed with some coach rooms making ideal accommodation for long stay guests. The Virginia Restaurant is a series of comfortable rooms to the front of the house where very good food is served at dinner. Less formal dining is available in the bar throughout the day.

Rooms 25 (5 annexe) (5 GF) **S** €99-€350; **D** €150-€350 (incl. bkfst) **Facilities** STV FTV Hair & beauty salon Use of nearby health & fitness club ♫ New Year Wi-fi **Conf** Class 50 Board 50 Thtr 100 Del from €150 to €200 **Services** Lift Air con **Parking** 35 **Notes** LB ⊗ Closed 24-25 Dec

---

NEWBRIDGE   Map 1 C3

Keadeen
★★★★ 81% ⊛⊛ HOTEL

☎ 045 431666 ▤ 045 434402
e-mail: info@keedeenhotel.ie
web: www.keadeenhotel.ie
dir: M7 junct 12, (Newbridge, Curragh) at rdbt follow signs to Newbridge, hotel on left in 1km

This family operated hotel is set in eight acres of award-winning gardens on the outskirts of the town. Comfortable public areas include spacious drawing rooms, an excellent leisure centre, fine dining in the Derby Restaurant and more casual fare in the Club Bar. Ideally located for the nearby Curragh racecourse.

Rooms 75 (4 fmly) (58 GF) **S** €112-€147; **D** €150-€198 (incl. bkfst)* **Facilities** STV ⊗ supervised Gym Aerobics studio Massage Treatment room ♫ Wi-fi **Conf** Class 300 Board 40 Thtr 800 Del from €175 to €189* **Services** Lift **Parking** 200 **Notes** LB ⊗ Closed 24 Dec-2 Jan

---

STRAFFAN   Map 1 D4

The K Club
★★★★★ ⊛⊛⊛ COUNTRY HOUSE HOTEL

☎ 01 6017200 ▤ 01 6017298
e-mail: resortsales@kclub.ie
dir: from Dublin take N4, exit for R406, hotel on right in Straffan

The K Club, which has been host to the Ryder Cup, is set in 700 acres of rolling woodland. There are two magnificent championship golf courses and a spa facility that complements the truly luxurious hotel that is the centrepiece of the resort. Public areas and bedrooms are opulently furnished, and have views of the formal gardens. Fine dining is offered in the elegant Byerly Turk restaurant, with more informal dining offered in Legends and Monza restaurants in the golf pavilions.

Rooms 79 (10 annexe) (10 fmly) **S** €350-€7650; (incl. bkfst)* **Facilities** Spa ⊗ supervised ↓ 36 Putt green Fishing ⊕ Gym Beauty salon Fishing tuition Clay pigeon shooting ♫ Xmas New Year Wi-fi **Conf** Class 300 Board 160 Thtr 300 **Services** Lift **Parking** 200 **Notes** LB ⊗

Barberstown Castle
★★★★ 79% ⊛⊛ HOTEL

☎ 01 6288157 ▤ 01 6277027
e-mail: info@barberstowncastle.ie
web: www.barberstowncastle.ie
dir: R406 signed Naas/Clare, follow signs for Barberstown

With parts dating from the 13th century, the castle is now a hotel providing the very best in standards of comfort. The inviting public areas range from the original keep, which is one of the restaurants, to the warmth of the drawing room. Bedrooms, some in a wing, are elegantly appointed. An airy tea room serves light meals throughout the day.

Rooms 59 (21 GF) **S** €160-€210; **D** €240-€290 (incl. bkfst)* **Facilities** STV ♫ New Year Wi-fi **Conf** Class 120 Board 30 Thtr 150 Del from €209* **Services** Lift **Parking** 200 **Notes** LB ⊗ Closed 24-26 Dec & Jan

---

CO KILKENNY

KILKENNY   Map 1 C3

Kilkenny River Court Hotel
★★★★ 78% ⊛ HOTEL

☎ 056 7723388 ▤ 056 7723389
The Bridge, John St
e-mail: reservations@rivercourthotel.com
dir: at bridge in town centre, opposite castle

Hidden behind archways on John Street, this is a very comfortable and welcoming establishment. The restaurant, bar and many of the well-equipped bedrooms command great views of Kilkenny Castle and the River Nore. Attentive, friendly staff ensure good service in all areas. Excellent corporate and leisure facilities are provided.

Rooms 90 (4 fmly) (45 smoking) **S** €105-€190; **D** €110-€400 (incl. bkfst)* **Facilities** Spa ⊗ supervised Gym Beauty salon Treatment rooms ♫ Wi-fi **Conf** Class 110 Board 45 Thtr 260 Del from €190 to €280* **Services** Lift **Parking** 84 (charged) **Notes** LB ⊗ Closed 23-26 Dec Civ Wed 250

Newpark
★★★★ 76% HOTEL

☎ 056 7760500 ▤ 056 7760555
e-mail: info@newparkhotel.com
dir: On N77 Castlecomer-Durrow road

A short drive from the city centre, set in 40 acres of parkland, this hotel offers a range of well-appointed rooms and suites. There is a range of comfortable lounges, and a leisure club and health spa. Renowned for the friendliness of the staff, a choice of two dining areas is on offer, The Scott Dove Bistro and Gulliver's, a more formal option.

Rooms 129 (20 fmly) (52 GF) **S** €130-€180; **D** €160-€300 (incl. bkfst)* **Facilities** Spa ⊗ supervised Gym Plunge pool ♫ Xmas New Year Wi-fi **Conf** Class 250 Board 50 Thtr 600 **Services** Lift **Parking** 350 **Notes** LB ⊗

Langtons

★★★ 70% HOTEL

☎ 056 7765133 & 5521728 📠 056 7763693
69 John St
e-mail: reservations@langtons.ie
dir: take N9 & N10 from Dublin follow city centre signs at outskirts of Kilkenny, turn left to Langtons. 500mtrs on left after lights

Langtons has a long and well-founded reputation as an entertainment venue, nightclub and bar. There is a range of bedroom accommodation, many in the garden annexe; all are very comfortable, tastefully decorated and well appointed. The busy restaurant is popular with visitors and locals alike.

Rooms 30 (16 annexe) (4 fmly) (8 GF) **Facilities** ♪ Xmas New Year Wi-fi **Conf** Class 250 Board 50 Thtr 600 **Parking** 60 **Notes** LB ⊗ Closed 25 Dec, Good Fri

The Kilkenny Inn Hotel

★★★ 69% HOTEL

☎ 056 7772828 & 7722821 📠 056 7761902
15/16 Vicar St
e-mail: info@kilkennyinn.com
web: www.kilkennyinn.com
dir: N7/N10 from Dublin. N25 from Rosslare to Waterford, N9 to Kilkenny

Within walking distance of the heart of the medieval city this hotel occupies a quite location with the added advantage of complimentary parking. Designed to incorporate traditional features with modern comforts, the public areas include JB's bar and Grill Room Restaurant. Bedrooms are comfortable and stylishly appointed.

Rooms 30 (7 fmly) (10 smoking) **S** €60-€100; **D** €110-€170 (incl. bkfst) **Facilities** Xmas New Year **Conf** Class 18 Board 25 Thtr 45 Del from €90 to €190 **Services** Lift **Parking** 25 **Notes** LB ⊗ Closed 24-26 Dec

---

THOMASTOWN Map 1 C3

INSPECTORS' CHOICE

Mount Juliet Conrad

★★★★ ◉◉ COUNTRY HOUSE HOTEL

☎ 056 7773000 📠 056 7773019
e-mail: info@mountjuliet.ie
dir: M7 from Dublin, N9 towards Waterford then to Mount Juliet via Carlow & Gowran

Mount Juliet Conrad is set in 1,500 acres of parkland with a Jack Nicklaus designed golf course and an equestrian centre. The elegant and spacious public areas retain much of the original architectural features including ornate plasterwork and Adam fireplaces. Bedrooms, in both the main house and the Hunters Yard annexe, are comfortable and well appointed. Fine dining is on offer at Lady Helen, overlooking the river, and more casual dining is available in Kendels in the Hunters Yard, which also has a spa and health club.

Rooms 57 (26 annexe) (14 GF) **S** €145-€365; **D** €155-€375 (incl. bkfst) **Facilities** Spa STV ⓢ supervised ♨ 18 ♣ Putt green Fishing ⛳ Gym Archery Cycling Clay pigeon shooting Xmas Wi-fi **Conf** Class 40 Board 20 Thtr 75 Del from €225 to €400 **Parking** 200 **Notes** LB ⊗

CO LAOIS

PORTLAOISE Map 1 C3

Portlaoise Heritage Hotel

★★★★ 75% HOTEL

☎ 057 8678588 📠 057 8678577
Jessop St
e-mail: info@theheritagehotel.com
dir: off N7 in town centre

The Heritage is situated in the town just off the N7. Public areas include a spacious lobby lounge, two bars and dining options, The Fitzmaurice where breakfast and dinner are served and Spago, an Italian Bistro. Bedrooms are well appointed and there are extensive leisure and conference facilities.

Rooms 110 (6 fmly) **S** €135-€170; **D** €170-€250 (incl. bkfst) **Facilities** Spa ⓢ supervised Gym Health & fitness club Beauty spa ♪ New Year Wi-fi **Conf** Class 300 Board 50 Thtr 500 **Services** Lift **Notes** LB ⊗ Closed 23-27 Dec RS Good Fri

---

Maldon Hotel Portlaoise

★★★ 73% HOTEL

☎ 057 8695900 & 8666702 📠 057 8695901
Tougher Rdbt, Abbeyleix Rd
e-mail: res.portlaoise@maldonhotels.com
dir: From Dublin N7 junct 17, exit S'bound, take 4th exit, 1st right 100mtrs

As part of the Midway development, this purpose built hotel is very successful for business meetings due to its proximity to the motorway. Bedrooms are well equipped and there is a leisure centre available to guests. The on-site restaurant is augmented by a number of more casual options in the food court next door.

Rooms 90 (3 fmly) (8 GF) (27 smoking) **S** €79-€199; **D** €79-€199 **Facilities** Spa STV ⓢ supervised Gym Aerobics room Steam room Sauna Wi-fi **Conf** Class 30 Board 30 Thtr 60 **Services** Lift **Parking** 120 **Notes** LB Closed Xmas

Killeshin

U

☎ 057 8681870 📠 057 8681871
Dublin Rd
e-mail: info@thekilleshin.com
web: www.thekilleshin.com

Currently the rating for this establishment is not confirmed. This may be due to a change of ownership or because it has only recently joined the AA rating scheme. For further details please see the AA website: www.theAA.com

Rooms 91 **Facilities** ⓢ Gym Steam room ♪ New Year Wi-fi **Conf** Class 100 Board 50 Thtr 200 **Services** Lift **Parking** 20 **Notes** ⊗ Closed 23-27 Dec

---

CO LEITRIM

CARRICK-ON-SHANNON Map 1 C4

The Landmark

★★★★ 70% ◉ HOTEL

☎ 071 9622222 📠 071 9622233
e-mail: landmarkhotel@eircom.net
dir: from Dublin on N4 approaching Carrick-on-Shannon, take 1st exit at rdbt, hotel on right

Overlooking the River Shannon, close to the Marina, this hotel offers comfortable public areas and well-equipped bedrooms and suites. Ferrari's Restaurant offers

Continued

CARRICK-ON-SHANNON continued

imaginative cuisine, the Boardwalk café serves food and drinks, and there's the Aroma Café for a variety of coffees, teas and pastries. Pleasant staff will be happy to arrange a cruise, horse riding, golf and angling.

Rooms 50 (4 fmly) **Facilities** ♫ Xmas **Conf** Class 210 Thtr 550 **Services** Lift **Parking** 100 **Notes** LB ⊗ Closed 24-25 Dec RS 26-Dec

Bush Hotel

★★★ 73% HOTEL

☎ 071 9671000 🗏 071 9621180
e-mail: info@bushhotel.com
dir: In town centre (accessed from N4 town bypass, follow signs

With a history dating as far back as the 13th century, this mid-Georgian house has been renovated and expanded into a fine hotel, with a number of bars and dining options. Bedrooms and suites are contemporary in style; there is a choice of lounges including a formal drawing room and an atmospheric bar in the original cellar.

Rooms 49 (3 fmly) (20 smoking) **Facilities** Wi-fi **Conf** Board 60 Thtr 300 **Services** Lift **Parking** 150 **Notes** ⊗ Closed 24 Dec-2 Jan

MOHILL	Map 1 C4

Lough Rynn Castle

★★★★ 77% ⊛ HOTEL

☎ 071 9632700 & 9632714 🗏 071 9632710
e-mail: enquiries@loughrynn.ie

Once to ancestral home of Lord Leitrim, set in 300 acres of parkland, the newly refurbished and extended castle offers a range of luxurious rooms and suites. The many lounges are individually decorated; some feature antique furniture pieces. Additional rooms and a treatment spa facility are currently in development, as is a Nick Faldo designed golf course.

Rooms 43 (16 annexe) (5 fmly) (6 GF) **S** €155-€275; **D** €155-€275 (incl. bkfst)* **Facilities** STV FTV ♫ Xmas New Year Wi-fi **Conf** Class 200 Board 30 Thtr 450 Del from €209 to €285* **Notes** LB ⊗

CO LIMERICK	

ADARE	Map 1 B3

Dunraven Arms

★★★★ 80% ⊛⊛ HOTEL

☎ 061 396633 🗏 061 396541
e-mail: reservations@dunravenhotel.com

This charming hotel was established in 1792 in the heart of one of Ireland's prettiest villages. It is a traditional country inn both in style and atmosphere. Comfortable lounges, spacious bedrooms, attractive gardens, leisure and beauty facilities and good cuisine all add up to an

enjoyable visit at the hotel. Golf, horse racing and equestrian sports are available in the area.

Rooms 86 (2 fmly) (40 GF) **Facilities** ♨ supervised Fishing Gym Beauty salon ♫ Xmas **Conf** Class 60 Board 12 Thtr 180 **Services** Lift **Parking** 90 **Notes** LB

Fitzgeralds Woodlands House Hotel

★★★ 72% HOTEL

☎ 061 605100 🗏 061 396073
Knockanes
e-mail: reception@woodlands-hotel.ie
dir: on N21 S of Limerick at Lantern Lodge rdbt turn left. Hotel 0.5m on right

Located close to the picturesque village of Adare, this family-run hotel is friendly and welcoming. Bedrooms are well appointed. The comfortable public areas include, Woodcock bar, Timmy Mac's traditional bar and bistro and The Brennan Restaurant. There are extensive leisure and beauty facilities. Close to Limerick Racecourse, Adare Manor and many other golf courses.

Rooms 92 (36 fmly) **Facilities** ♨ Gym Health & beauty salon Thermal spa ♫ Xmas **Conf** Class 200 Board 50 Thtr 400 **Services** Air con **Parking** 290 **Notes** LB ⊗ Closed 24-25 Dec

LIMERICK	Map 1 B3

Castletroy Park

★★★★ 81% ⊛ HOTEL

☎ 061 335566 🗏 061 331117
Dublin Rd
e-mail: sales@castletroy-park.ie
web: www.castletroy-park.ie
dir: on Dublin road, 3m from city, opposite University of Limerick

This fine modern hotel is close to the University of Limerick. Public areas combine modern comforts with very attractive decor, and include the Merry Pedler pub and the fine-dining McLaughlins Restaurant, which has a splendid view of the gardens and Clare Hills. Bedrooms are very well equipped to suit both leisure and business guests. There are extensive leisure and banqueting facilities.

Rooms 107 (78 fmly) **S** €180-€205; **D** €195-€230 (incl. bkfst) **Facilities** STV ♨ supervised Gym Steam & Beauty treatment rooms Massage therapy Tanning facility ♫ Xmas New Year Wi-fi **Conf** Class 270 Board 100

Thtr 450 Del from €255 to €390 **Services** Lift **Parking** 160 **Notes** LB ⊗

Clarion Hotel Limerick

★★★★ 76% HOTEL

☎ 061 444100 🗏 061 444101
Steamboat Quay
e-mail: info@clarionhotellimerick.com
dir: From Shannon Airport take N18 W to city, follow Cork/Kerry exit on 1st rdbt. Over Shannon Bridge then 3rd exit onto Dock Rd. Hotel 1st right

The Clarion makes an imposing silhouette on Limerick's skyline, and has a spectacular riverside location on the banks of the River Shannon. The same sleek design is to be found throughout this 17-storey hotel, with contemporary styling combining architectural mastery in the bedrooms and public areas alike. Rooms vary in size and are all well appointed.

Rooms 158 (157 fmly) **S** €120-€240; **D** €140-€280 **Facilities** STV ♨ supervised Gym Steam room Fully equipped leisure centre Sauna Wi-fi **Conf** Class 140 Board 100 Thtr 240 Del from €215* **Services** Lift Air con **Notes** ⊗ Closed 24-25 Dec RS 26 Dec

Hilton Limerick

★★★★ 75% ⊛ HOTEL

☎ 061 421800 🗏 061 421841
Ennis Rd
e-mail: meredith.bevan@hilton.com
dir: From Shannon/Galway follow N18 to Limerick. At Coonagh rdbt follow Ennis road into city centre. Hotel on right on banks of river

This hotel enjoys stunning views over the River Shannon, and all bedrooms are spacious and fitted to a high standard. The public areas make the most of the views, with meeting rooms on the penthouse level. All-day dining is available in the bar, with innovative evening meals served in the River Restaurant. Secure parking is available at a reduced rate for residents.

Rooms 184 (5 fmly) (34 smoking) **S** €79-€229; **D** €89-€239* **Facilities** ♨ supervised Gym Steam room Sauna Spa bath Hydrotherapy bath Monsoon showers ♫ Wi-fi **Conf** Class 250 Board 95 Thtr 420 Del from €180 to €340* **Services** Lift Air con **Parking** 184 (charged) **Notes** LB Closed 24-26 Dec

Maldon Hotel Limerick

★★★ 77% HOTEL

☎ 061 436100 🗏 061 436110
John Carew Link Rd, Roxboro
e-mail: res.limerick@maldonhotels.com

This hotel, five minutes drive south from the city, offers a range of particularly well appointed bedrooms and 16 meeting suites. The rugby themed bar offers food throughout the day, with dinner served in the first-floor

Lannigans Restaurant. The Club Vitae fitness club is complimentary to guests.

Rooms 199 (4 fmly) (25 GF) **Facilities** Spa ⓣ supervised Gym ♫ Wi-fi **Conf** Class 25 Board 25 Thtr 50 **Services** Lift **Parking** 200 **Notes** LB ⊗ Closed 23-26 Dec

Woodfield House

★★★ 66% HOTEL

☎ 061 453022 ▦ 061 326755
Ennis Rd
e-mail: woodfieldhousehotel@eircom.net
dir: on outskirts of city on main Shannon road

This family-run hotel is situated on the N18 a short distance from the city centre and within easy reach of Shannon Airport. There is a relaxing atmosphere in the cosy traditional bar and patio beer garden. Bedrooms are comfortable and well appointed. Food is available in the bar all day and dinner is served in the restaurant.

Rooms 26 (3 fmly) (5 GF) **D** €49-€69* **Facilities** FTV ♨ Wi-fi **Conf** Class 60 Board 60 Thtr 130 **Services** Air con **Parking** 80 **Notes** ⊗ Closed 24-25 Dec Civ Wed 120

Travelodge Limerick

BUDGET HOTEL

☎ 061 457000
Ennis Rd, Clondrinagh
web: www.travelodge.co.uk

Travelodge offers good quality, good value, modern accommodation. Ideal for families, the spacious en suite bedrooms include remote-control TV, tea and coffee-making facilities and comfortable beds. Meals can be taken at the nearby family restaurant. See also the Hotel Groups pages.

Rooms 40 **S** fr €40; **D** fr €40

Boyne Valley Hotel & Country Club

★★★ 70% HOTEL

☎ 041 9837737 ▦ 041 9839188
Stameen, Dublin Rd
e-mail: admin@boyne-valley-hotel.ie
dir: M1 towards Belfast, N of Dublin Airport on right

This historic mansion stands in 16 acres of mature gardens and woodlands on the outskirts of Drogheda. The bedrooms are very smart and provide high standards of comfort. Public areas include relaxing lounges, Terrace Bar, Cellar Bistro, a leisure centre and extensive conference and banqueting facilities.

Rooms 73 (4 fmly) (26 GF) **Facilities** ⓣ supervised ♨ Gym Hot stone therapy ♫ Xmas **Conf** Class 350 Board 25 Thtr 500 **Services** Lift **Parking** 200 **Notes** LB ⊗ Civ Wed 300

D Hotel

Ⓤ

☎ 041 9877700 ▦ 041 9877702
Scotch Hall
e-mail: reservethed@monogramhotels.ie
dir: M1 N from Dublin. Then N1 to Drogheda. Right into Marsh Rd at St Marys Bridge, hotel on left

Currently the rating for this establishment is not confirmed. This may be due to a change of ownership or because it has only recently joined the AA rating scheme. For further details please see the AA website: www.theAA.com

Rooms 104 (30 fmly) **Facilities** Gym ♫ **Conf** Class 60 Board 40 Thtr 100 **Services** Lift **Parking** 200 **Notes** ⊗ Closed 24-29 Dec

Ballymascanlon House

★★★★ 77% HOTEL

☎ 042 9358200 ▦ 042 9371598
e-mail: info@ballymascanlon.com
dir: R173 Carlingford. Take N52 exit off Faughart rdbt. Next rdbt 1st left. Hotel in approx 1km on left

This Victorian mansion is set in 130 acres of woodland at the foot of the Cooley Mountains. The elegantly-designed original house, with its modern extension make this a very comfortable hotel with some really stylish bedrooms. Public areas include a restaurant and spacious lounge and bar, and a well equipped leisure centre. A banqueting facility has been added.

Rooms 90 (11 fmly) (5 GF) (34 smoking) **S** €105-€120; **D** €160-€190 (incl. bkfst)* **Facilities** ⓣ supervised ♨ 18 ♨ Putt green Gym Steam room Plunge pool Outdoor hot tub ♫ Xmas New Year Wi-fi **Conf** Class 220 Board 100 Thtr 400 **Del** from €130 to €200* **Services** Lift **Parking** 250 **Notes** LB Civ Wed 200

Mount Falcon Country House

★★★★ 80% ⑥ HOTEL

☎ 096 74472 ▦ 096 74473
Mount Falcon Estate
e-mail: info@mountfalcon.com
dir: on N26, 6m from Foxford & 3m from Ballina. Hotel on left

Dating from 1876, this house has been lovingly restored to its former glory, and has a bedroom extension that is totally in keeping with the original design. Relaxing lounges look out on the 100-acre estate, which has excellent salmon fishing on The Moy plus well-stocked trout lakes. Dinner is served in the original kitchen with choices from a varied and interesting menu; for lunch there is also the Boathole Bar. A state-of-the-art, air-conditioned gym is available.

Rooms 32 (3 fmly) **S** €215-€575; **D** €240-€600 (incl. bkfst)* **Facilities** Spa STV ⓣ supervised Fishing Gym Sauna Steam room New Year Wi-fi **Conf** Class 120 Board 80 Thtr 200 **Del** from €290 to €440 **Services** Lift **Parking** 260 **Notes** LB ⊗ Closed 6 Jan-5 Feb

Ice House

★★★★ 75% HOTEL

☎ 096 23500 ▦ 096 23598
The Quay
e-mail: chill@theicehouse.ie
dir: On Sligo road through town across river. Turn left at The Quay x-rds. Hotel 2km on left

This new property, situated a mile or so from the town centre, is a stunning mix of old and new. The decor is mainly contemporary, with most rooms enjoying river views. An interesting menu is offered at dinner in the Pier Restaurant, with lighter fare available during the day in the bright and airy riverside bar.

Rooms 32 (7 fmly) (10 GF) **S** €135-€220; **D** €150-€220 (incl. bkfst)* **Facilities** Spa STV New Year Wi-fi Child facilities **Conf** Class 35 Board 30 Thtr 70 **Services** Lift **Parking** 32 **Notes** LB Closed 25 Dec & St Stephens Day

CONG
Map 1 B4

Ashford Castle

★★★★★ 88% ❀❀ HOTEL

☎ 094 9546003 📄 094 9546260
e-mail: ashford@ashford.ie
web: www.ashford.ie
dir: In Cross village left at church onto R345 signed
Cong. Left at Ashford Castle sign, through castle gates

Set in over 300 acres of beautifully grounds, this
magnificent castle, dating from 1228, occupies a
stunning position on the edge of Lough Corrib. Bedrooms
vary in style but all benefit from a pleasing combination
of character, charm and modern comforts. The hotel
offers an extensive range of both indoor and outdoor
leisure pursuits including falconry, golf, shooting, fishing
and an equestrian centre.

Rooms 83 (5 fmly) (22 GF) **Facilities** ♨ 9 ⛳ Putt green
Fishing Gym Archery Clay pigeon shooting Falconry Lake
cruises Treatment rooms ♫ Xmas New Year Wi-fi
Conf Class 65 Thtr 110 **Services** Lift **Parking** 200
Notes ⊗ Civ Wed 150

Lisloughrey Lodge

★★★★ 78% ❀❀ HOTEL

☎ 094 9545400 📄 094 9545424
The Quay
e-mail: lodge@lisloughrey.ie
dir: Take N84 from Galway to Cross. Left at Cong sign.
Left at sign for hotel

Situated in an elevated position overlooking the quay and
Lough Corrib, this new hotel offers contemporary luxury in
a traditional country house setting. Many of the bedrooms
are in a courtyard annexe and all are named after wine
regions of the world. The cuisine is an important focus
here, and dinner in the award-winning Salt Restaurant, is
the highlight of any visit.

Rooms 50 (44 annexe) (5 fmly) (21 GF) **S** €125–€165;
D €150–€350 (incl. bkfst)* **Facilities** Spa STV FTV
Fishing Gym Outdoor hot tub & sauna Beauty salon
Screening room New Year Wi-fi Child facilities
Conf Class 70 Board 40 Thtr 300 Del from €250 to
€300* **Services** Lift **Parking** 100 **Notes** ⊗

KILTIMAGH
Map 1 B4

Park Hotel

★★★ 75% HOTEL

☎ 094 9374922 📄 094 9374924
e-mail: info@parkhotelmayo.com

This smart hotel overlooks a Wetlands Wildlife Park and is
within walking distance of Kiltimagh and ten minutes
from Ireland West Knock Airport. The spacious bedrooms
are furnished with guest comfort in mind. Public areas
include, comfortable lounges, café bar and dinner is
served in the brightly decorated restaurant. There are
treatment rooms and outside hot tubs on the sun
veranda.

Rooms 45

Cill Aodain Court Hotel

IRISH
COUNTRY
HOTELS

★★★ 69% HOTEL

☎ 094 9381761 📄 094 9381838
Main St
e-mail: info@cillaodain.ie
dir: In town centre opposite Market Square

Situated in the heart of historic Kiltimagh and close to
Marian Shrine at Knock and also the airport, this smart,
contemporary hotel offers comfortable well-appointed
bedrooms. Public areas include The Gallery Restaurant,
Court Bar & Bistro. There is off-street parking opposite
the hotel.

Rooms 17 (4 fmly) (7 smoking) **S** €60–€100;
D €100–€140 (incl. bkfst)* **Facilities** STV ♫ New Year
Wi-fi **Conf** Class 30 Board 25 Thtr 50 Del from €80 to
€110* **Notes** ⊗ Closed 24-25 Dec

KNOCK
Map 1 B4

Knock House

★★★ 70% HOTEL

☎ 094 9388088 📄 094 9388044
Ballyhaunis Rd
e-mail: info@knockhousehotel.ie
dir: 0.5km from Knock

Adjacent to the Marian Shrine and Basilica at Knock, this
creatively designed limestone-clad building is surrounded
by landscaped gardens. There is a relaxing lounge bar,
conference rooms and lunch and dinner are served in the
Four Seasons Restaurant daily. Bedrooms are spacious

and well appointed, and some rooms are adapted to
facilitate wheelchair users.

Rooms 68 (12 fmly) (40 GF) **Facilities** Xmas New Year
Wi-fi **Conf** Class 90 Board 45 Thtr 150 **Services** Lift
Parking 150 **Notes** ⊗

Belmont

★★★ 66% HOTEL

☎ 094 9388122 📄 094 9388532
e-mail: reception@belmonthotel.ie
dir: on N17, Galway side of Knock. Turn right at Burke's
supermarket & pub. Hotel 150yds on right

This hotel has an old world charm and offers lounges, a
traditional bar, and the An Bialann Restaurant. Bedroom
standards vary, all are well appointed and comfortable,
and there are specially adapted room for the less able. A
natural health and fitness club offers a range of
therapies. The hotel is close to the Marian Shrine and the
Basilica.

Rooms 62 (5 fmly) (12 GF) **S** €50–€90; **D** €90–€150
(incl. bkfst)* **Facilities** Gym Steam room Natural health
therapies Hydrotherapic bath ♫ Xmas **Conf** Class 100
Board 20 Thtr 500 Del from €65 to €95* **Services** Lift
Parking 110 **Notes** LB ⊗ Closed 25 Dec

MULRANY
Map 1 B4

Park Inn

★★★★ 78% ❀❀ HOTEL

☎ 098 36000 📄 098 36899
e-mail: info@parkinnmulranny.ie
dir: R311 from Castlebar to Newport onto N59. Hotel on
right

Originally a railway hotel dating from the late 1800s, it
has undergone a major renovation. The result is a range
of smart public rooms that have retained many of the
period proportions. Bedrooms vary in size but are
comfortable and decorated in a contemporary style.
Dinner in the Nephin Restaurant is a highlight of any
stay. Set on an elevated site, the property has
commanding views over Clew Bay.

Rooms 61 (22 fmly) (36 GF) **S** €100–€130;
D €150–€210 (incl. bkfst)* **Facilities** ⊛ supervised
Gym Canadian hot tub Steam room Health & Beauty ♫
Xmas New Year Wi-fi **Conf** Class 140 Board 50 Thtr 400
Services Lift **Parking** 200 **Notes** LB ⊗ Closed 4-30 Jan

NEWPORT — Map 1 B4

Hotel Newport
★★★ 68% HOTEL

☎ 098 41155 📠 098 42548
Main St
e-mail: info@hotelnewportmayo.com
dir: On N59 from Westport to Achill Island. Hotel at top of Main St

Situated in the centre of the picturesque town of Newport and close to Achill Island and Westport. This hotel has a modern contemporary style of decor with a traditional exterior appearance. Bedrooms are well appointed and there are comfortable public areas. Food is served all day in the Seven Arches bar and a more formal style is available in the Inish Kee restaurant at night.

Rooms 30 (2 fmly) **Facilities** Fishing 🎵 New Year **Conf** Class 80 Board 40 Thtr 200 **Services** Lift Air con **Parking** 15 **Notes** ⊗ Closed 25 Dec

SWINFORD — Map 1 B4

Kelly's Gateway
★★★ 70% HOTEL

☎ 094 9252156 📠 094 9251328
Main St
e-mail: info@gatewayswinford.com
dir: On main street

This long established town centre hostelry has now been converted to a cosy hotel. The friendly approach at this family run business makes for a very pleasant experience. Bedrooms are warm and inviting, as are the lounge areas. Tasty food is served throughout the day in the bistro and bar, which proves a popular choice with the locals.

Rooms 22 (3 fmly) (5 smoking) **S** €40-€80; **D** €70-€140 (incl. bkfst)* **Facilities** STV FTV 🎵 Wi-fi **Conf** Class 60 Board 40 Thtr 100 **Services** Lift **Parking** 16 **Notes** LB ⊗ Closed 25 Dec

WESTPORT — Map 1 B3

Knockranny House Hotel
★★★★ 80% ⊛ HOTEL

☎ 098 28600 📠 098 28611
e-mail: info@khh.ie
web: www.khh.ie
dir: on N5 (Westport-Castlebar road)

Overlooking Westport with Clew Bay and Croagh Patrick in the distance, the reception rooms of this family-run hotel take full advantage of the lovely views. The luxurious furnishings create an inviting and relaxing atmosphere throughout the lounge, bar and restaurant. The spacious bedrooms are well appointed. There is a helicopter-landing pad in the well-maintained grounds, and also a luxury Spa Salveo.

Rooms 97 (4 fmly) **S** €90-€195; **D** €130-€320 (incl. bkfst)* **Facilities** Spa STV 🖑 supervised Gym 🎵 Xmas New Year Wi-fi **Conf** Class 350 Board 40 Thtr 600 Del from €220 to €350* **Services** Lift **Parking** 150 **Notes** LB ⊗ Closed 24-26 Dec

Carlton Atlantic Coast
★★★★ 74% ⊛ HOTEL

☎ 098 29000 📠 098 29111
The Quay
e-mail: info@carltonatlanticcoasthotel.com
dir: from N5 follow signs into Westport then Louisburgh on R335. 1m from Westport

This distinctive hotel is in a former mill and has been renovated to a good contemporary standard with modern facilities. Many of the rooms have sea views, as has the award-winning restaurant on the fourth floor. The ground floor has comfortable lounge areas and a lively bar. Spa and treatment rooms have been added to the leisure centre.

Rooms 85 (6 fmly) **S** €75-€155; **D** €100-€270 (incl. bkfst) **Facilities** Spa 🖑 supervised Gym Treatment rooms Sauna Steam room Fitness suite 🎵 Xmas New Year Wi-fi Child facilities **Conf** Class 100 Board 70 Thtr 180 Del from €130 to €190 **Services** Lift **Parking** 60 **Notes** LB ⊗ Closed 23-27 Dec

Hotel Westport Leisure, Spa & Conference
★★★ 82% HOTEL

☎ 098 25122 📠 098 26739
Newport Rd
e-mail: reservations@hotelwestport.ie
dir: N5 to Westport. Right at end of Castlebar St, 1st right before bridge, right at lights, left before church. Follow to end of street

Located in private woodlands and just a short river walk to the town, this hotel offers welcoming public areas, a spacious restaurant and comfortable bedrooms. Both leisure and business guests are well catered for by the enthusiastic and friendly team.

Rooms 129 (67 fmly) (42 GF) (18 smoking) **S** €75-€155; **D** €110-€270 (incl. bkfst)* **Facilities** Spa STV 🖑 supervised Gym Children's pool Lounger pool Steam room Sauna 🎵 Xmas New Year Wi-fi Child facilities **Conf** Class 150 Board 60 Thtr 500 Del from €115 to €185* **Services** Lift **Parking** 220 **Notes** LB ⊗

Clew Bay Hotel
★★★ 73% HOTEL

IRISH COUNTRY HOTELS

☎ 098 28088 📠 098 25783
e-mail: info@clewbayhotel.com
dir: at bottom of James St (parallel to main street)

This long established, family-run hotel offers a range of comfortable well-appointed bedrooms together with some very smart public areas. Guest can dine in the Riverside Restaurant or in the very popular Madden's Bistro. Arrangements can be made for residents to use the nearby leisure centre.

Rooms 35 (3 fmly) **Facilities** 🖑 supervised Gym Free use of nearby leisure club 🎵 Child facilities **Conf** Class 12 Board 10 Thtr 20 **Services** Lift **Notes** ⊗ Closed Xmas & New Year

WESTPORT continued

The Wyatt

★★★ 70% HOTEL

☎ 098 25027 📠 098 26316
The Octagon
e-mail: info@wyatthotel.com
dir: Follow one-way system in town. Hotel by tall monument

This stylish, welcoming hotel is situated in the famous town centre Octagon. Bedrooms are attractively decorated and well equipped. Public areas are very comfortable with open fires and include a lively, contemporary bar. There are two dining options, JW for bar food and The Wyatt Restaurant offering more formal eating.

Rooms 51 (2 GF) **S** €65-€115; **D** €95-€220 (incl. bkfst) **Facilities** Complimentary use of nearby leisure park 🎵 New Year **Conf** Class 200 Board 80 Thtr 300 Del from €85 to €120 **Services** Lift Air con **Parking** 20 **Notes** LB ⊗ Closed 25-26 Dec Civ Wed

The Westport Inn

★★ 67% HOTEL

☎ 098 29200 📠 098 29250
Mill St
e-mail: info@westportinn.ie
dir: In town centre

Situated in the centre of Westport close to the shops and many pubs, and ideal for visiting the leisure centre, beaches and many golf courses nearby. Bedrooms are traditional in style and public areas are comfortable. There is a lively bar with entertainment at weekends.

Rooms 34 (3 fmly) **S** €60-€140; **D** €90-€240 (incl. bkfst)* **Facilities** 🎵 New Year Wi-fi **Conf** Class 50 Board 40 Thtr 100 **Services** Lift **Parking** 18 **Notes** LB ⊗ Closed 24-25 Dec

CO MEATH

ASHBOURNE
Map 1 D4

Ashbourne Marriott

Marriott
HOTELS & RESORTS

★★★★ 75% HOTEL

☎ 01 8350800 📠 01 8010301
The Rath
e-mail: info@marriottashbourne.com
dir: on rdbt at end of Ashbourne

Located on the outskirts of Ashbourne and just off the N2 this hotel has been built to a high standard. Contemporary in style the public areas include the upbeat Red Bar and Grill Twenty One. There are extensive leisure, fitness, treatments rooms and banqueting facilities. Bedrooms are spacious and comfortably furnished. The express coach to Dublin Airport is available to guests.

Rooms 148 **Facilities** Spa 🏊 supervised Gym 🎵 New Year Wi-fi **Conf** Class 280 Board 30 Thtr 540 **Services** Lift Air con **Parking** 200 **Notes** ⊗ Closed 25 Dec

DUNBOYNE
Map 1 D4

Dunboyne Castle Hotel & Spa

★★★★ 78% HOTEL

☎ 01 8013500 📠 01 4366801
e-mail: info@dunboynecastlehotel.com
web: www.dunboynecastlehotel.com
dir: In Dunboyne take R157 towards Maynooth. Hotel on left

With a history dating back to the 13th century, this mid-Georgian house has been renovated and expanded into a fine hotel, with a number of bars and dining options. Bedrooms and suites are contemporary in style, with a choice of lounges, a formal drawing room and an atmospheric bar in the original cellar.

Rooms 182 (37 annexe) (36 GF) (36 smoking) **S** €155-€280; **D** €180-€340 (incl. bkfst)* **Facilities** Spa STV Gym 🎵 Xmas New Year Wi-fi **Conf** Class 200 Board 40 Thtr 350 **Services** Lift Air con **Parking** 300 **Notes** LB ⊗

ENFIELD
Map 1 C4

The Hamlet Court Hotel

★★★ 70% HOTEL

☎ 046 9541200 📠 046 9541704
Johnstownbridge
e-mail: info@thehamlet.ie
web: www.thehamlet.ie
dir: After toll bridge take 1st exit at Kilcock on M4. Left then right at rdbt, hotel in 0.5km on left

This hotel has been developed behind the long established Hamlet bar and lounge. It features very comfortable bedrooms, relaxing lounge and the Sabayon Restaurant where food standards are good. This is an ideal location for those with an interest in horseracing and golf. It is also a popular wedding venue.

Rooms 30 (2 fmly) (19 GF) **S** €90-€140; **D** €140-€250 (incl. bkfst)* **Facilities** Fishing 🎵 Xmas New Year Wi-fi **Conf** Class 240 Board 80 Thtr 350 Del from €99* **Services** Lift **Parking** 320 **Notes** LB ⊗ Civ Wed

KELLS
Map 1 C4

Headfort Arms

IRISH COUNTRY HOTELS

★★★ 74% HOTEL

☎ 046 9240063 📠 046 9240587
Headfort Place
e-mail: info@headfortarms.ie
web: www.headfortarms.ie
dir: on N3 between Dublin & Donegal

Situated in the famous heritage town of Kells, the Duff family run a very smart hotel. Appointed to a high standard, there are comfortable lounges with open log fires, a café carvery, Vanilla Pod Brassiere, traditional pub, banqueting facilities and treatment rooms. The bedrooms, in both the newer block and the original building are impressively decorated and furnished.

Rooms 45 (5 fmly) **Facilities** Spa 🎵 Xmas New Year Wi-fi **Conf** Class 200 Board 30 Thtr 400 **Services** Lift **Parking** 45 **Notes** ⊗ Civ Wed 300

KILMESSAN
Map 1 C/D4

The Station House Hotel

★★★ 72% ⊛ HOTEL

☎ 046 9025239 📠 046 9025588
e-mail: info@thestationhousehotel.com
web: www.thestationhousehotel.com
dir: M50, N3 towards Navan. At Dunshaughlin turn left at end of village, follow signs

The Station House saw its last train in 1963, and is now a comfortable, family-run hotel with a popular restaurant. The Carriage House has nicely appointed bedrooms, and the Signal Box houses a suite. There is a sun terrace and conference/banqueting suite.

Rooms 20 (14 annexe) (3 fmly) (5 GF) **S** €75-€130; **D** €150-€220 (incl. bkfst) **Facilities** 🎵 Xmas Wi-fi **Conf** Class 300 Board 100 Thtr 400 Del from €119 to €150 **Parking** 200 **Notes** LB ⊗

TRIM
Map 1 C4

Knightsbrook Hotel Spa & Golf Resort
★★★★ 76% HOTEL

☎ 046 9482100 🖹 046 9482055
Dublin Rd
e-mail: info@knightsbrook.com

Overlooking 180 acres of rolling parkland and a golf
course, a short distance from historical Trim, this hotel
offers excellent facilities. Bedrooms are particularly well
appointed with great attention to detail. The popular bars
have their own styles and their own menus, and more
formal dining is available in Rococo Restaurant.

Rooms 131 (3 fmly) (40 smoking) **S** €95-€150;
D €130-€210 (incl. bkfst)* **Facilities** Spa STV FTV 🕾
supervised ♨ 18 Putt green Gym 🎵 New Year Wi-fi Child
facilities **Conf** Class 300 Board 50 Thtr 1100
Del from €175 to €210* **Services** Lift **Parking** 200
Notes LB ⊗ Closed 24-25 Dec Civ Wed 600

CO MONAGHAN

CARRICKMACROSS
Map 1 C4

Nuremore
★★★★ 79% ⊛⊛⊛ HOTEL

☎ 042 9661438 🖹 042 9661853
e-mail: info@nuremore.com
web: www.nuremore.com
dir: 3km S of Carrickmacross, on N2 (Dublin to Derry
road)

Overlooking its own golf course and lakes, the Nuremore
is a quiet retreat with excellent facilities. Public areas are
spacious and include an indoor pool and gym. Ray
McArdle's award-winning cuisine continues to impress,
with an imaginative range of dishes on offer.

Rooms 72 (6 fmly) (42 smoking) **Facilities** Spa STV FTV
🕾 supervised ♨ 18 ♨ Putt green Fishing Gym Beauty
treatments Aromatherapy Massage 🎵 Xmas New Year
Wi-fi **Conf** Class 300 Board 50 Thtr 600 Del from €195 to
€250 **Services** Lift **Parking** 200 **Notes** ⊗ Civ Wed 200

MONAGHAN
Map 1 C5

Hillgrove Hotel, Leisure & Spa
★★★★ 74% HOTEL

☎ 047 4781288 🖹 047 4784951
Old Armagh Rd
e-mail: info@hillgrovehotel.com
dir: turn off N2 at Cathedral, 400mtrs, hotel on left

This modern hotel on the outskirts of the town offers
spacious bedrooms that are well equipped and
comfortable. The public areas include a split-level dining
room where good food is served, and a popular local bar,
serving snacks throughout the day. Spectacular
banqueting facilities and a well equipped leisure centre
are available.

Rooms 87 (9 fmly) (9 GF) (40 smoking) **S** €150-€180;
D €180-€200 (incl. bkfst)* **Facilities** Spa STV 🕾
supervised Gym New Year Wi-fi **Conf** Class 500 Board 90
Thtr 1500 **Services** Lift Air con **Parking** 300 **Notes** LB ⊗
Closed 25 Dec Civ Wed

CO ROSCOMMON

ROSCOMMON
Map 1 B4

Abbey
★★★ 80% HOTEL

IRISH
COUNTRY
HOTELS

☎ 090 6626240 🖹 090 6626021
Galway Rd
e-mail: info@abbeyhotel.ie
web: www.abbeyhotel.ie
dir: on Galway road

The Grealy family have tastefully restored this fine manor
house. The spacious bedrooms are tastefully furnished
and overlook the magnificent gardens. The smart lounge,
bar and Terrace Restaurant have views of the 12th-
century Dominican Abbey, and the carvery is very popular
at lunchtime. There are extensive leisure and conference
facilities.

Rooms 50 (5 fmly) (10 GF) **Facilities** 🕾 supervised Gym
Sauna Steam room Therapy room Children's pool Wi-fi
Conf Class 140 Board 50 Thtr 250 Del from €145 to
€185 **Services** Lift **Parking** 100 **Notes** ⊗ Closed 25-26
Dec

Gleesons Townhouse & Restaurant
RESTAURANT WITH ROOMS

☎ 090 6626954 🖹 090 6627425
Market Square
e-mail: info@gleesonstownhouse.com
dir: in town centre next to tourist office

This 19th-century cut-limestone town house has been
very tastefully restored. The bedrooms and suites are
decorated and furnished to a high standard. Dinner is
served nightly in the Manse Restaurant and there is an
extensive lunch and afternoon tea menu in the café or in

the beautifully landscaped front courtyard. Conference
facilities and secure car parking are available.

Rooms 19 (2 pri facs) (1 fmly)

CO SLIGO

COLLOONEY
Map 1 B5

Markree Castle
★★★ 75% HOTEL

☎ 071 9167800 🖹 071 9167840
e-mail: markree@iol.ie
dir: off N4 at Collooney rdbt, take R290 towards
Dromahaire. Just N of junct with N17, 11km S of Sligo,
hotel gates on right after 1km

The castle, which has been in the Cooper family for over
370 years, is a gem of Irish Victorian architecture. The
bedrooms vary in size and style, and all in keeping with
the character of the building. Dinner is served in the
spectacular Louis XIV-styled dining room. Horse riding,
archery and clay-pigeon shooting can be arranged on the
estate.

Rooms 30 (1 fmly) (3 GF) (15 smoking) **S** €100-€165;
D €150-€260 (incl. bkfst)* **Facilities** STV FTV Fishing
Hiking Archery Clay pigeon shooting Wi-fi **Conf** Class 50
Board 40 Thtr 75 Del from €120 to €160* **Services** Lift
Parking 120 **Notes** LB Civ Wed 120

SLIGO
Map 1 B5

Radisson SAS Hotel & Spa Sligo
★★★★ 75% HOTEL

☎ 071 9140008 🖹 071 9140005
Rosses Point Rd, Ballincar
e-mail: info.sligo@radissonsas.com
dir: from N4 into Sligo to main bridge. Take R291 on left.
Hotel 1.5m on right

Located two miles north of the town overlooking Sligo
Bay, this new hotel offers a range of bedroom suites and
a very well-equipped leisure centre. The spacious lounges
and restaurant make the most of the bay views as do
some of the extensive meeting and banqueting facilities.

Rooms 132 (13 fmly) (32 GF) (19 smoking) **S** €90-€180;
D €180-€400 (incl. bkfst) **Facilities** Spa STV 🕾 Gym
Steam room Outdoor Canadian hot tub Treatment rooms
Thermal suite Xmas New Year Wi-fi **Conf** Class 420
Board 40 Thtr 750 Del from €169 to €260 **Services** Lift
Air con **Parking** 395 **Notes** LB ⊗ Civ Wed 750

SLIGO continued

Glasshouse

★★★★ 74% ⊛ HOTEL

☎ 071 9194300 📠 071 9194301
Swan Point
e-mail: info@theglasshouse.ie
dir: N4 Relief Road. Right at 2nd junct. Left at Post Office on Wine St. Hotel on right

This landmark building in the centre of town makes a bold statement with its cutting edge design and contemporary decor. Cheerful colours are used throughout the hotel; the bedrooms have excellent facilities including LCD TVs, workspace and internet access. There is a first floor café bar, a ground floor bar and a Mediterranean-style restaurant with great river views. Secure underground parking is complimentary to residents.

Rooms 116 **S** €85-€140; **D** €120-€200 (incl. bkfst)
Facilities STV FTV New Year Wi-fi **Conf** Class 100 Board 60 Thtr 120 **Services** Lift **Parking** 250 **Notes** LB ⊗ Closed 24-25 Dec Civ Wed 120

The Clarion Hotel Sligo

★★★★ 74% HOTEL

☎ 071 9119000 & 9119006 📠 071 9119001
Ballinode
e-mail: info@clarionhotelssligo.com
dir: On N side of Sligo off Enniskillen road (N16). Hotel opposite Sligo Institute of Technology

This imposing stone built hotel is located on an elevated site close to town, the regional college and hospital. It offers particularly spacious bedrooms and suites. The public areas comprise lounge areas, Sinergie Restaurant, Kudos bar and a well equipped Sano Vitae leisure centre. The original church building houses some of the extensive, modern conference facilities.

Rooms 165 (90 fmly) (46 GF) **Facilities** Spa ⊙ supervised Gym Gym classes ♫ New Year Wi-fi **Conf** Class 300 Board 80 Thtr 500 **Services** Lift **Parking** 250 **Notes** ⊗ Closed 24-26 Dec

Sligo Park

★★★ 78% HOTEL

☎ 071 9190400 📠 071 9169556
Pearse Rd
e-mail: sligo@leehotels.com
dir: On N4 to Sligo take Carrowroe/R287 exit. Follow signs for Sligo R287. Hotel 1m on right

Set in seven acres on the southern side of town, this hotel is well positioned for visiting the many attractions of the North West and Yeats' Country. Bedrooms are spacious and appointed to a high standard. There are two dining options, plus good leisure and banqueting facilities.

Rooms 137 (10 fmly) (45 GF) (35 smoking) **S** €89-€172; **D** €105-€185 (incl. bkfst)* **Facilities** ⊙ supervised ⊇ Gym Holistic treatment suite Plunge pool Steam room ♫

Xmas New Year Wi-fi **Conf** Class 290 Board 80 Thtr 550 **Services** Lift **Parking** 200 **Notes** LB ⊗ RS 24-26 Dec

CASHEL — Map 1 C3

Cashel Palace Hotel

★★★★ 80% ⊛ HOTEL

☎ 062 62707 📠 062 61521
e-mail: reception@cashel-palace.ie
dir: On N8 through town centre, hotel on main street near lights

The Rock of Cashel, floodlit at night, forms the dramatic backdrop to this fine 18th-century house. Once an archbishop's palace, it is elegantly furnished with antiques and fine art. The drawing room has garden access, and luxurious bedrooms in the main house are very comfortable; those in the adjacent mews are ideal for families.

Rooms 23 (10 annexe) (8 fmly) **S** €175-€185; **D** €225-€430 (incl. bkfst)* **Facilities** Fishing Private path to Rock of Cashel ♫ Wi-fi **Conf** Class 45 Board 40 Thtr 80 **Services** Lift **Parking** 35 **Notes** LB ⊗ Closed 24-26 Dec Civ Wed 130

CLONMEL — Map 1 C2

Hotel Minella

IRISH
COUNTRY
HOTELS

★★★ 80% HOTEL

☎ 052 22388 📠 052 24381
e-mail: frontdesk@hotelminella.ie
web: www.hotelminella.ie
dir: S of River Suir

This family-run hotel is set in nine acres of well-tended gardens on the banks of the Suir River. Originating from the 1860s, the public areas include a cocktail bar and a range of lounges; some of the bedrooms are particularly spacious. The leisure centre in the grounds is noteworthy. Two-bedroom holiday homes are also available.

Rooms 70 (8 fmly) (14 GF) **Facilities** ⊙ ⊇ Fishing ⤵ Gym Aerobics room **Conf** Class 300 Board 20 Thtr 500 **Services** Lift **Parking** 100 **Notes** ⊗ Closed 24-28 Dec

DUNDRUM — Map 1 C3

Dundrum House Hotel, Golf & Leisure Resort

★★★ 75% HOTEL

☎ 062 71116 📠 062 71366
e-mail: info@dundrumh@iol.ie
dir: R505 follow for 7m. Far side of Knockaville, hotel approx 0.5m on left

This Georgian mansion dates from 1730 and was tastefully restored by the Crowe family. Bedrooms vary in style and are comfortably furnished rooms in the original house with antique pieces and the new rooms feature a modern theme. There are relaxing lounges with open fires and a fine dining room, with more informal food available in the golf club. The extensive facilities include a leisure centre and an 18-hole championship golf course.

Rooms 68 (12 fmly) **S** €65-€150; **D** €100-€250 (incl. bkfst)* **Facilities** STV FTV ↧ 18 Putt green Fishing Gym Wellness suites ♫ New Year **Conf** Class 100 Board 70 Thtr 400 **Services** Lift **Parking** 300 **Notes** LB ⊗ Closed 21-26 Dec

ROSCREA — Map 1 C3

Racket Hall Country Golf & Conference Hotel

★★★ 70% HOTEL

☎ 0505 21748 📠 0505 23701
Dublin Rd
e-mail: reservations@rackethall.ie
dir: N7/N62

Ideally situated on the N7 just outside the heritage town of Roscrea, this long established house has been a popular stopping point for travellers for many years. It has well-equipped bedrooms. Lilly Bridges' bar offers food from early morning till late in the evening, with more formal fare in the restaurant.

Rooms 40 (19 fmly) (14 GF) **S** €69-€119; **D** €129-€199 (incl. bkfst)* **Facilities** FTV Xmas New Year **Conf** Class 250 Board 150 Thtr 550 **Services** Lift Air con **Parking** 150 **Notes** LB ⊗ Civ Wed

CO WATERFORD

ARDMORE — Map 1 C2

Cliff House

[U]

☎ 024 87800 📄 024 87820
e-mail: info@thecliffhousehotel.com
dir: N25 to Ardmore. Hotel at end of village via The Middle Road

Currently the rating for this establishment is not confirmed. This may be due to a change of ownership or because it has only recently joined the AA rating scheme. For further details please see the AA website: www.theAA.com

Rooms 39 (8 fmly) (7 GF) **S** €180-€450; **D** €180-€450 (incl. bkfst) **Facilities** Spa STV FTV ☾ supervised Fishing Gym Sauna Steam room Relaxation room Wi-fi Child facilities **Conf** Class 30 Board 20 Thtr 50 **Services** Lift Air con **Parking** 20 **Notes** LB ⊗ Closed Jan-14 Feb

DUNGARVAN — Map 1 C2

Lawlors

★★★ 68% HOTEL

☎ 058 41122 & 41056 📄 058 41000
e-mail: info@lawlorshotel.com
dir: off N25

This town centre hotel enjoys a busy local trade especially in the bar where food is served throughout the day. The Davitts Restaurant offers a wide choice of Italian, Mexican and seafood dishes. The bedrooms are of varying sizes; some are particularly spacious. Conference and meeting rooms are available. Public parking is nearby.

Rooms 89 (8 fmly) **Facilities** ♬ New Year Wi-fi **Conf** Class 215 Board 420 Thtr 420 **Services** Lift **Notes** Closed 25 Dec

TRAMORE — Map 1 C2

Majestic

★★★ 69% HOTEL

☎ 051 381761 📄 051 381766
e-mail: info@majestic-hotel.ie
dir: Exit N25 through Waterford onto R675 to Tramore. Hotel on right, opposite lake

A warm welcome awaits visitors to this long established, family friendly hotel in the holiday resort of Tramore. Many of the comfortable and well-equipped bedrooms have sea views. Public areas offer a selection of lounges, a traditional bar and spacious restaurant. The facilities at 'Splashworld' across from the hotel are available to residents.

Rooms 60 (4 fmly) **Facilities** Free access to Splashworld swimming pool & leisure club ♬ Xmas Child facilities **Services** Lift **Parking** 10 **Notes** LB ⊗ Civ Wed 250

WATERFORD — Map 1 C2

INSPECTORS' CHOICE

Waterford Castle

★★★★ ⊛⊛ HOTEL

☎ 051 878203 📄 051 879316
The Island
e-mail: info@waterfordcastle.com
dir: From city centre turn onto Dunmore East Rd, 1.5m, pass hospital, 0.5m left after lights, ferry at bottom of road

This enchanting and picturesque castle dates back to Norman times and is located on a 320-acre island just a five minute journey from the mainland by chain-link ferry. Bedrooms vary in style and size, but all are individually decorated and offer high standards of comfort. Dinner is served in the oak-panelled Munster Room, with breakfast taken in the conservatory. The 18-hole golf course is set in beautiful parkland where deer can be seen.

Rooms 19 (2 fmly) (4 GF) **S** €160-€245; **D** €195-€640* **Facilities** ♪ 18 ⛳ Putt green Boules Archery Clay pigeon shooting ♬ New Year Wi-fi **Conf** Board 15 Thtr 30 **Services** Lift **Parking** 50 **Notes** LB ⊗ RS 1st wk Jan-Feb Civ Wed 110

Faithlegg House

★★★★ 76% ⊛ HOTEL

☎ 051 382000 📄 051 382010
Faithlegg
e-mail: reservations@fhh.ie
web: www.faithlegg.com
dir: From Waterford follow Dunmore East Rd then Cheerpoint Rd

This hotel is surrounded by a championship golf course and overlooks the estuary of the River Suir. The house has 14 original bedrooms, and the rest are in an adjacent modern block. There is a range of comfortable lounges together with comprehensive meeting facilities. The leisure and treatment rooms are the perfect way to work off the excesses of the food offered in the Roseville Restaurant.

Rooms 82 (6 fmly) (30 GF) (16 smoking) **Facilities** STV ☾ supervised ♪ 18 ⛳ Putt green Gym ♬ New Year Wi-fi **Conf** Class 90 Board 44 Thtr 180 **Services** Lift **Parking** 100 **Notes** LB ⊗ Closed 20-27 Dec

Athenaeum House

★★★ 79% ⊛ HOTEL

☎ 051 833999 📄 051 833977
Christendon, Ferrybank
e-mail: info@athenaeumhousehotel.com
web: www.athenaeumhousehotel.com
dir: N25 to Wexford, through 1st lights, right, right again into Abbey Rd. 1st right after bridge, hotel on right

Set in parkland overlooking the banks of the River Suir and Waterford city, this hotel was originally built in the 18th century. The public rooms have been sympathetically restored in keeping with the age of the building, yet with a contemporary twist. Bedrooms are spacious and comfortably furnished. Zak's is the bright airy restaurant where innovative food is served.

Rooms 29 (5 GF) **S** €88-€150; **D** €120-€180 (incl. bkfst)* **Facilities** FTV ♬ New Year Wi-fi **Conf** Class 35 Board 45 Thtr 40 **Services** Lift **Parking** 35 **Notes** LB ⊗ Closed 24-26 Dec Civ Wed 50

Granville

★★★ 79% HOTEL

☎ 051 305555 📄 051 305566
The Quay
e-mail: stay@granville-hotel.ie
web: www.granville-hotel.ie
dir: take N25 to waterfront, city centre, opposite Clock Tower

Centrally located on the quayside, this long established hotel is appointed to a very high standard, while still keeping its true character. The bedrooms come in a choice of standard or executive, and are all well equipped and very comfortable. Friendliness and hospitality are hallmarks of a stay here.

Rooms 100 (5 fmly) (10 smoking) **S** €80-€140; **D** €110-€250 (incl. bkfst) **Facilities** STV ♬ New Year **Conf** Class 150 Board 30 Thtr 200 Del from €110 to €150* **Services** Lift **Parking** 300 (charged) **Notes** LB ⊗ Closed 25-26 Dec

See advert on page 750

WATERFORD continued

Dooley's

★★★ 75% HOTEL

☎ 051 873531 📄 051 870262
30 The Quay
e-mail: hotel@dooleys-hotel.ie
dir: on N25, close to Discover Ireland Centre

Situated on the quay in Waterford overlooking the River Suir at the harbour mouth, this hotel has been run by the same family for three generations and offers friendly and relaxed atmosphere. The contemporary public areas include the New Ship Restaurant, and also the Dry Dock Bar for more casual dining. Bedrooms are attractively decorated and offer a good standard of comfort. There is a car park opposite the hotel.

Rooms 113 (3 fmly) (40 smoking) **S** €70–€130; **D** €120–€198 (incl. bkfst)* **Facilities** STV ♫ New Year Wi-fi **Conf** Class 150 Board 100 Thtr 240 **Services** Lift **Notes** ⊗ Closed 25-27 Dec

Tower

★★★ 75%

☎ 051 875801 & 862300 📄 051 870129
The Mall
e-mail: info@thw.ie
web: www.towerhotelgroup.ie
dir: opp Reginald's Tower in town centre. Hotel at end of quay

This long established hotel includes two smart restaurants, a riverside bar and smart bedrooms together with three river view suites. Parking is provided at the rear.

Rooms 139 (6 fmly) **Facilities** ◎ supervised Gym ♫ Xmas Child facilities **Conf** Class 250 Board 80 Thtr 500 **Services** Lift **Parking** 100 **Notes** LB ⊗ Closed 24-28 Dec

Waterford Manor

★★★ 70% HOTEL

☎ 051 377814 📄 051 354545
Killotteran, Butlerstown
e-mail: sales@waterfordmanorhotel.ie
dir: N25 from Waterford to Cork, right 2m after Waterford Crystal, left at end of road, hotel on right

Dating back to 1730 this manor house is set in delightful landscaped and wooded grounds. It provides high quality accommodation as well as extensive conference and banqueting facilities. Public areas include a charming drawing room and restaurant for intimate dining, plus a brasserie with its own bar that serves a carvery lunch daily.

Rooms 21 (3 fmly) **Facilities** ♨ **Conf** Class 300 Board 40 Thtr 600 **Parking** 400 **Notes** LB ⊗ RS 25 Dec

Travelodge Waterford

BUDGET HOTEL

☎ 051 358885 📄 051 358890
Cork Rd
web: www.travelodge.co.uk
dir: on N25, 1km from Waterford Glass Visitors' Centre

Travelodge offers good quality, good value, modern accommodation. Ideal for families, the spacious en suite bedrooms include remote-control TV, tea and coffee-making facilities and comfortable beds. Meals can be taken at the nearby family restaurant. See also the Hotel Groups pages.

Rooms 32 **S** fr €40; **D** fr €40

Hodson Bay

★★★★ 75% ® HOTEL

☎ 090 6442000 📄 090 6442020
Hodson Bay
e-mail: info@hodsonbayhotel.com
dir: from N6 take N61 to Roscommon. Turn right. Hotel 1km on Lough Ree

On the shores of Lough Ree, four kilometres from Athlone, this hotel has its own marina and is surrounded by the

Granville Hotel

The Quay, Waterford, Co Waterford, Republic of Ireland
Tel: 051 305555
Fax: 051 305566
Email: stay@granville-hotel.ie
www.granville-hotel.ie

golf course. Spacious public areas are comfortable, with a carvery bar, an attractive restaurant and excellent conference and banqueting facilities. The spacious bedrooms have been designed to take in the magnificent lake views. The hotel has a leisure centre and treatment rooms.

Rooms 182 (32 fmly) (11 GF) **Facilities** ⓢ supervised ♨ 18 Fishing Gym Steam room Sauna Thermal suite ♫ Xmas New Year Wi-fi Child facilities **Conf** Class 250 Board 200 Thtr 700 **Services** Lift **Parking** 300 **Notes** LB ⊗

Glasson Golf Hotel & Country Club

Ⓤ HOTEL

☎ 090 6485120 ▣ 090 6485444
Glasson
e-mail: info@glassongolf.ie
dir: 6m N of Athlone on N55

Currently the rating for this establishment is not confirmed. This may be due to a change of ownership or because it has only recently joined the AA rating scheme. For further details please see the AA website: www.theAA.com

Rooms 65 (13 fmly) (27 GF) **Facilities** ♨ 21 Putt green New Year Wi-fi **Conf** Class 50 Board 30 Thtr 120 **Services** Lift **Parking** 150 **Notes** LB ⊗

Wineport Lodge

◉ RESTAURANT WITH ROOMS

☎ 090 6439010 ▣ 090 6485471
Glasson
e-mail: lodge@wineport.ie
dir: From N6 (Dublin/Galway road) take N55 north (Longford/Cavan exit) at Athlone. Left at Dog & Duck pub. Lodge 1m on left

Set in a wonderful location right on the shores of the inner lakes of Lough Rea on the Shannon and three miles north of Athlone. Guests can arrive by road or water, dine on the deck or in the attractive dining room. Cuisine is modern with innovative use of the best of local produce. Most of the luxurious bedrooms and suites have balconies - the perfect setting for breakfast. There is a Canadian hot tub on the roof terrace.

Rooms 29 (27 en suite) (3 fmly) (15 GF)

MULLINGAR Map 1 C4

Mullingar Park

★★★★ 77% HOTEL

☎ 044 9344446 & 9337500 ▣ 044 9335937
Dublin Rd
e-mail: info@mullingarparkhotel.com
web: www.mullingarparkhotel.com
dir: N4 junct 9, take exit for Mullingar

Just two kilometres from Mullingar towards Dublin, this hotel has much to offer. Spacious public areas, flexible banqueting suites and a well-equipped leisure centre are complemented by comfortably appointed bedrooms. The friendly staff are very guest focused. The Terrace Restaurant is particularly popular for its lunch buffet.

Rooms 95 (12 fmly) (39 smoking) **S** €150-€180; **D** €160-€230 (incl. bkfst) **Facilities** Spa STV ⓢ supervised Gym Aerobic studio Childrens' pool Hydrotherapy pool New Year Wi-fi **Conf** Class 750 Board 40 Thtr 1200 Del from €220 to €260 **Services** Lift **Parking** 500 **Notes** LB ⊗ Closed 24-26 Dec Civ Wed 500

CO WEXFORD

BUNCLODY Map 1 D3

Carlton Millrace

★★★★ 76% HOTEL

☎ 053 9375100 ▣ 053 9375124
e-mail: info@millrace.ie
dir: In town on Carlow/Wexford road (N80)

Located on the edge of the picturesque town of Bunclody, this hotel offers well-appointed bedrooms and smartly presented public areas, not least of which is the rooftop Lady Lucy restaurant. Separate leisure centres are also a feature. Some self-catering family suites are available.

Rooms 72 (12 fmly) **S** €84-€150; **D** €118-€250 (incl. bkfst) **Facilities** Spa STV ⓢ supervised Fishing Gym ♫ Wi-fi **Conf** Class 100 Board 50 Thtr 250 **Services** Lift Air con **Parking** 100 **Notes** LB ⊗ Closed 23-26 Dec Civ Wed 180

COURTOWN HARBOUR Map 1 D3

Courtown

★★★ 63% HOTEL

☎ 055 25210 & 25108 ▣ 055 25304
e-mail: info@courtownhotel.com
dir: Turn left on approach to Gorey, 5km on left

Situated in the town centre, near to the beach and an 18-hole golf course, this family run hotel offers relaxing public areas. There is a comfortable lounge, spacious bar and an attractive restaurant, and the leisure centre includes a swimming pool, gym and solarium.

Rooms 21 (4 fmly) **Facilities** ⓢ supervised ♨ Gym Squash Steam room Massage Crazy golf ♫ **Parking** 10 **Notes** ⊗ Closed mid Nov-early Mar

---

ENNISCORTHY Map 1 D3

Riverside Park

★★★ 72% HOTEL

☎ 053 9237800 ▣ 053 9237900
The Promenade
e-mail: info@riversideparkhotel.com
dir: 0.5km from New Bridge, centre of Enniscorthy town, N11 Dublin/Rosslare Rd

This modern hotel is situated on the banks of the River Slaney, and has a dramatically designed foyer; the public areas all take full advantage of the riverside views, including the Promenade Bar. There are two dining options, casual dining is available every night in the Alamo, with more formal dining in The Moorings at peak periods. Bedrooms have every modern comfort, some with balconies. Guests have full use of the leisure centre.

Rooms 60 (15 fmly) (10 smoking) **S** €120-€140; **D** €189-€220 (incl. bkfst) **Facilities** STV ⓢ supervised Gym ♫ New Year Wi-fi **Conf** Class 250 Board 100 Thtr 750 Del from €135 to €150 **Services** Lift **Parking** 150 **Notes** LB ⊗ Closed 24-25 Dec RS Good Fri

Treacy's

★★★ 68% HOTEL

☎ 054 37798 ▣ 054 37733
Templeshannon
e-mail: info@treacyshotel.com
dir: N11 into Enniscorthy, over bridge in left lane. Hotel on right

This modern hotel is family run and conveniently located near the town centre. There is a choice of dining options in the Chang Thai and Begenal Harvey restaurants, with Benedict's super-pub open at weekends. Guests have complimentary use of the nearby car park and a discount at the Waterfront Leisure Centre.

Rooms 59 (3 fmly) **Facilities** ⓢ supervised Gym Steam room Discount at adjacent leisure complex ♫ Child facilities **Services** Lift **Parking** 70 **Notes** LB ⊗ Closed 23-25 Dec

GOREY Map 1 D3

Amber Springs
★★★★ 77% HOTEL

☎ 053 9484000 ▤ 053 9484494
Wexford Rd
e-mail: info@ambersprings.ie
dir: 500mtrs from Gorey by-pass at junct 23

This new hotel on the Wexford road is within walking distance of the town. Bedrooms are spacious and very comfortable, and guests have full use of the leisure facilities. Dining in Kelby's Bistro is a highlight of a visit, with a combination of interesting food and really friendly service.

Rooms 80 (18 fmly) **Facilities** Spa ☺ supervised Gym Supervised children's play area 6-11pm ♫ Xmas New Year Wi-fi Child facilities **Conf** Class 450 Board 30 Thtr 700 **Services** Lift Air con **Parking** 178 **Notes** ⊗ Civ Wed 700

Ashdown Park Hotel
★★★★ 75% ⊛ HOTEL

☎ 053 9480500 ▤ 053 94777
The Coach Rd
e-mail: info@ashdownparkhotel.com
web: www.ashdownparkhotel.com
dir: N11 exit 22, on approaching Gorey, 1st left before railway bridge, hotel on left

Situated on an elevated position overlooking the town, this modern hotel has excellent health, leisure and banqueting facilities. There are comfortable lounges and two dining options - the popular carvery bar and first-floor, fine dining restaurant. Bedrooms are spacious and well equipped. Close to golf, beaches and hill walking.

Rooms 79 (12 fmly) (20 GF) **S** €90-€115; **D** €180-€230 (incl. bkfst) **Facilities** ☺ supervised Gym Leisure centre Gym Beauty salon Spa treatments ♫ New Year Wi-fi **Conf** Class 315 Board 100 Thtr 800 **Services** Lift **Parking** 150 **Notes** LB ⊗ Closed 25 Dec Civ Wed 200

INSPECTORS' CHOICE

Marlfield House Hotel
★★★ ⊛⊛ COUNTRY HOUSE HOTEL

☎ 053 9421124 ▤ 053 9421572
e-mail: info@marlfieldhouse.ie
dir: 1.5 hrs S of Dublin off N11, 1m outside Gorey on Courtown Road

This Regency-style building has been sympathetically extended and developed into an excellent hotel. An atmosphere of elegance and luxury permeates every corner of the house, underpinned by truly friendly and professional service led by the Bowe family who are always in evidence. The bedrooms are decorated in keeping with the style of the house, with some really spacious rooms and suites on the ground floor. Dinner in the restaurant is always a highlight of a stay at Marlfield.

Rooms 20 (3 fmly) (6 GF) **Facilities** ☺ ⚘ **Conf** Board 20 Thtr 60 **Parking** 50 **Notes** LB Closed 15 Dec-30 Jan

NEW ROSS Map 1 C3

Cedar Lodge
★★★ 74% HOTEL

IRISH COUNTRY HOTELS

☎ 051 428386 & 428436 ▤ 051 428222
Carrigbyrne, Newbawn
e-mail: cedarlodge@eircom.net
web: www.prideofeirehotels.com
dir: On N25 between Wexford & New Ross

Cedar Lodge sits in a tranquil setting beneath the slopes of Carrigbyrne Forest, just a 30-minute drive from Rosslare Port. The Martin family extend warm hospitality and provide good food in the charming conservatory restaurant with its central log fire. Many of the spacious, thoughtfully appointed bedrooms overlook the attractively landscaped gardens.

Rooms 28 (2 fmly) (10 GF) **S** €115-€165; **D** €150-€200 (incl. bkfst) **Conf** Class 60 Board 60 Thtr 100 Del from €175 to €200 **Parking** 60 **Notes** LB ⊗ Closed 21 Dec-Jan

Brandon House Hotel & Solas Croi Eco Spa
★★★ 72% HOTEL

☎ 051 421703 ▤ 051 421567
e-mail: reception@brandonhousehotel.ie
dir: In New Ross over O' Honrahan bridge, turn right along quay, hotel on left, on N25

Located on the eastern approach to New Ross, this well established property offers a range of comfortable bedroom styles together with good conference rooms, public areas and a choice of dining options. Excellent leisure facilities are available to guests, and a spectacular spa is under construction.

Rooms 79 (18 fmly) (39 GF) **Facilities** Spa ☺ supervised Gym Hydrotherapy Grotto ♫ New Year Wi-fi **Conf** Class 306 Board 96 Thtr 416 **Parking** 160 **Notes** LB ⊗ Closed 24-26 Dec

ROSSLARE
Map 1 D2

INSPECTORS' CHOICE

Kelly's Resort Hotel & Spa
★★★★ ⊛ HOTEL

☎ 053 9132114 📠 053 9132222
e-mail: info@kellys.ie
dir: 20km from Wexford town, turn off N25 onto Rosslare/Wexford road, signed Rosslare Strand

The Kelly Family have been offering hospitality here since 1895, where together with a dedicated team, they provide very professional and friendly service. The resort overlooks the sandy beach and is within minutes of the Ferry Port at Rosslare. Bedrooms are thoughtfully equipped and comfortably furnished. The extensive leisure facilities include a smart spa, swimming pools, a crèche, young adults' programme and spacious well-tended gardens. The bistro, La Marine, serves food to AA rosette standard.

Rooms 118 (15 fmly) (20 GF) **Facilities** Spa ⊛ supervised ⌘ ⌘ Gym Bowls Plunge pool Badminton Crazy golf Canadian hot tub 🎵 Wi-fi Child facilities **Conf** Class 30 Board 20 Thtr 30 **Services** Lift **Parking** 120 **Notes** ⊗ Closed mid Dec-late Feb

WEXFORD
Map 1 D3

Whites of Wexford
★★★★ 77% HOTEL

☎ 053 9122311 📠 053 9145000
Abbey St
e-mail: info@whitesofwexford.ie
dir: on Abbey St, Wexford Town

This long established hotel in the centre of the town has undergone major development in recent years. It now offers a fine range of bedroom styles all in smart contemporary schemes. Public areas are bright and airy and include a number of dining options. Excellent conference and leisure facilities are available, as is an underground car park.

Rooms 157 (50 annexe) (74 fmly) **S** €95-€120; **D** €130-€190 (incl. bkfst) **Facilities** Spa STV ⊛ supervised Gym Cryotherapy clinic High performance centre 🎵 Xmas New Year Wi-fi **Conf** Class 532 Board 126 Thtr 1110 **Services** Lift Air con **Parking** 250 **Notes** LB ⊗ Closed 24-26 Dec Civ Wed 200

Talbot Hotel Conference & Leisure Centre
★★★★ 72% HOTEL

☎ 053 9122566 & 9155559 📠 053 9123377
The Quay
e-mail: sales@talbothotel.ie
dir: N11 from Dublin, follow Wexford signs, hotel at end of quay on right

Centrally situated on the quayside, this hotel offers well-equipped bedrooms with custom-made oak furniture and attractive decor; naturally many enjoy splendid sea views. Public areas include a spacious foyer, comfortable lounges and the Ballast Quay bar, serving food all day. The attractive Oyster Lane Restaurant also serves some interesting dishes. Good leisure facilities are complimentary to residents.

Rooms 109 (8 fmly) **S** €85-€115; **D** fr €110 (incl. bkfst)* **Facilities** Spa ⊛ supervised Gym Talbot Tigers Club 🎵 Xmas New Year Wi-fi Child facilities **Conf** Class 250 Board 110 Thtr 450 **Services** Lift Air con **Parking** 160 **Notes** ⊗ Closed 24-25 Dec Civ Wed 300

Whitford House Hotel Health & Leisure Club
★★★ 75% ⊛ HOTEL

☎ 053 9143444 📠 053 9146399
New Line Rd
e-mail: info@whitford.ie
web: www.whitford.ie
dir: Just off N25 (Duncannon rdbt) take exit for R733 (Wexford), hotel immediately left

This is a friendly family-run hotel just two kilometres from the town centre and within easy reach of the Rosslare Ferry. Comfortable bedrooms range from standard to the spacious and luxuriously decorated deluxe. Public areas include a choice of lounges and the popular Forthside Bar Bistro where a carvery is served. More formal meals are on offer in the award-winning Seasons Restaurant.

Rooms 36 (28 fmly) (18 GF) **S** €68-€124; **D** €110-€198 (incl. bkfst)* **Facilities** Spa FTV ⊛ supervised Gym Children's playground 🎵 Xmas New Year Wi-fi **Conf** Class 45 Board 25 Thtr 50 **Parking** 200 **Notes** LB ⊗ RS 24-27 Dec Civ Wed 180

Maldon Hotel Wexford
★★★ 72% HOTEL

☎ 053 9172000 📠 053 9172001
Barntown
e-mail: res.wexford@maldonhotels.com

Five minutes from the town on the New Ross exit on the N25, this hotel is ideal for both the corporate and leisure user. All the bedrooms are comfortable and well equipped, and are matched by a number of dining options. The Club Vitae fitness centre is complimentary to guests.

Rooms 107 (20 fmly) (22 GF) **Facilities** Spa ⊛ supervised Gym 🎵 New Year Wi-fi **Conf** Class 40 Board 30 Thtr 60 **Services** Lift **Parking** 250 **Notes** LB ⊗ Closed 23-27 Dec Civ Wed 300

Riverbank House Hotel
★★★ 68% HOTEL

☎ 053 9123611 📠 053 9123342
e-mail: river@indigo.ie
dir: beside Wexford Bridge on R741

Overlooking the estuary of the Slaney River, this hotel is at the foot of the Wexford Bridge, a short distance from the town centre. Both the bar and restaurant have views of the harbour. The bedrooms are well equipped and comfortable. Impressive banqueting facilities are available.

Rooms 23 (6 fmly) (7 GF) **Facilities** 🎵 Child facilities **Conf** Class 180 Board 48 Thtr 350 **Services** Lift **Parking** 25 **Notes** LB ⊗ Closed 24-25 Dec

Newbay Country House & Restaurant
⊛ RESTAURANT WITH ROOMS

☎ 053 42779 📠 053 46318
Newbay, Carrick
e-mail: newbay@newbayhouse.com
dir: A11 from Wexford Bridge and turn right towards N25. Turn left before Quality Hotel and next right

Built in the 1820s, but only offering accommodation for some ten years, Newbay offers a choice of two dining areas, the casual Cellar Bistro on the lower floor, or the more formal restaurant in the original house. Unsurprisingly, seafood is a passion here. The freshest catch only has to travel a few hundred yards. The very comfortable bedrooms are situated in both the house and a wing. Some have four-posters and all have lovely views.

Rooms 11 (11 en suite) (1 fmly) (6 smoking)

CO WICKLOW

ARKLOW — Map 1 D3

Arklow Bay

★★★ 75% HOTEL

☎ 0402 32309 ▤ 0402 32300
Ferrybank
e-mail: sales@arklowbay.com
dir: off N11 at by-pass for Arklow. 1m turn left, hotel 200yds on left

This hotel enjoys panoramic views of Arklow Bay, and many of the well-appointed bedrooms take full advantage of this. The public areas are decorated in a contemporary style, including the Ferrybank Lounge that offers a bar food menu. For more formal dining, Howard's Restaurant opens for dinner, and there's a carvery each Sunday. Extensive leisure and spa treatment facilities are available.

Rooms 92 (3 fmly) (27 GF) **Facilities** Spa ⊛ supervised Gym ♫ Xmas New Year Child facilities **Conf** Class 200 Board 60 Thtr 500 **Services** Lift **Parking** 100 **Notes** ⊗ Civ Wed 350

AUGHRIM — Map 1 D3

Lawless

★★★ 64% HOTEL

IRISH
COUNTRY
HOTELS

☎ 0402 36146 ▤ 0402 36384
e-mail: reservations@lawlesshotel.ie
dir: N11 to Rathnew, R752 to Rathdrum, R753 to Aughrim. Hotel between bridges on outskirts of village

Established in 1787, this family-run hotel is located in the pretty village of Aughrim. Bedrooms are individually decorated and some enjoy river views. The inviting public areas include a comfortable lounge, smart restaurant and a very popular Thirsty Trout Bar and conservatory where food is served all day. Close to many golf courses and there is a trout-angling park nearby.

Rooms 14 (2 fmly) **Facilities** ⌇ **Conf** Class 60 Board 40 Thtr 100 **Parking** 40 **Notes** LB ⊗ Closed 23-26 Dec Civ Wed 330

BRAY — Map 1 D4

Royal Hotel & Leisure Centre

★★★ 71% HOTEL

☎ 01 2862935 & 2724900 ▤ 01 2867373
Main St
e-mail: royal@regencyhotels.com
dir: from N11, 1st exit for Bray, 2nd exit from rdbt, through 2 sets of lights, across bridge, hotel on left

Located in the town centre and walking distance from the seafront at Bray and close to Dun Laoighaire ferry port. Public areas offer comfortable lounges, traditional bar and The Heritage Restaurant. Bedrooms vary in size and are well appointed. There is a well-equipped leisure centre and a supervised car park is available.

Rooms 130 (10 fmly) **Facilities** ⊛ supervised Gym Massage & beauty clinic Therapy room Whirlpool spa Creche ♫ Xmas Wi-fi **Conf** Class 300 Board 200 Thtr 500 **Services** Lift **Parking** 60 (charged) **Notes** LB ⊗ Civ Wed 300

DELGANY — Map 1 D3

Glenview

★★★★ 74% HOTEL

☎ 01 2873399 ▤ 01 2877511
Glen O' the Downs
e-mail: sales@glenviewhotel.com
dir: from Dublin city centre follow signs for N11, past Bray on N11 southbound

Set in a lovely hillside location, overlooking terraced gardens, this hotel boasts an excellent range of leisure and conference facilities. Impressive public areas include a conservatory bar, lounge and choice of dining options. The bedrooms are spacious and many enjoy great views over the valley. A championship golf course, horse riding and many tourist amenities are available nearby.

Rooms 70 (11 fmly) (16 GF) **Facilities** ⊛ supervised ⌇ Gym Aerobics studio Massage Beauty treatment room ♫ Xmas Child facilities **Conf** Class 120 Board 50 Thtr 220 **Services** Lift **Parking** 200 **Notes** ⊗

GLENDALOUGH — Map 1 D3

The Glendalough

★★★ 69% HOTEL

☎ 0404 45135 ▤ 0404 45142
e-mail: info@glendaloughhotel.ie
dir: N11 to Kilmacongue, right onto R755, straight on at Caragh then right onto R756

Mountains and forest provide the setting for this long-established hotel at the edge of the famed monastic site. Many of the well-appointed bedrooms have superb views. Food is served daily in the very popular bar while relaxing dinners are served in the charming restaurant that overlooks the river and forest.

Rooms 44 (3 fmly) **Facilities** STV Fishing ♫ Wi-fi **Conf** Class 150 Board 50 Thtr 200 **Services** Lift **Parking** 100 **Notes** ⊗ Closed Dec-Jan

MACREDDIN — Map 1 D3

HOTEL OF THE YEAR

The Brooklodge Hotel & Wells Spa

★★★★ 86% ⊛⊛ HOTEL

☎ 0402 36444 ▤ 0402 36580
e-mail: brooklodge@macreddin.ie
web: www.brooklodge.com
dir: N11 to Rathnew, R752 to Rathdrum, R753 to Aughrim follow signs to Macreddin Village

A luxury country-house hotel complex, in a village setting, which includes Acton's pub, Orchard Café and retail outlets. Bedrooms in the original house are very comfortable, and mezzanine suites are situated in the landscaped grounds. Newly added is Brook Hall with ground-floor and first floor bedrooms overlooking the 18th green of the golf course. The award-winning Strawberry Tree Restaurant is a truly romantic setting, specialising in organic and wild foods. The Wells Spa Centre offers extensive treatments and leisure facilities. AA Hotel of the Year for the Republic of Ireland 2008-9

Rooms 90 (32 annexe) (27 fmly) (4 GF) **Facilities** Spa STV FTV ⊛ ⌇ ♨ 18 Putt green Gym Archery Clay pigeon shooting Falconry Shiatsu Massage Off road driving Xmas New Year Wi-fi **Conf** Class 120 Board 40 Thtr 300 **Services** Lift **Parking** 200

Marriott Druids Glen Hotel & Country Club

Marriott HOTELS & RESORTS

★★★★★ 84% HOTEL

☎ 01 2870800   🖹 01 2870801
e-mail: mhrs.dubgs.reservations@marriotthotels.com.
web: www.marriottdruidsglen.com.uk
dir: N11 S'bound, off at Newtownmountkennedy. Follow signs for hotel

This hotel, situated between the Wicklow Mountains and the coast, has two fabulous golf courses and a range of smart indoor leisure facilities and treatment rooms. Bedrooms have been equipped to the highest standard and service is delivered in a most professional manner, and always with a smile. Guests may choose to dine in Druid's Brasserie or the more formal Flynn's Restaurant.

Rooms 145 **Facilities** Spa ⚒ ♨ 18 Putt green Gym Plunge pool Xmas New Year Wi-fi **Conf** Class 180 Board 30 Thtr 400 **Services** Lift Air con **Parking** 350 **Notes** ⊗

Hunter's

★★★ 74% ⚫ HOTEL

IRELAND'S BLUE BOOK

☎ 0404 40106   🖹 0404 40338
e-mail: reception@hunters.ie
dir: 1.5km from village off N11

One of Ireland's oldest coaching inns, this charming country house was built in 1720 and is full of character and atmosphere. The comfortable bedrooms have wonderful views over prize-winning gardens that border the River Vartry. The restaurant has a good reputation for carefully prepared dishes which make the best use of high quality local produce, including fruit and vegetables from the hotel's own garden.

Rooms 16 (2 fmly) (2 GF) **Conf** Class 40 Board 16 Thtr 40 **Parking** 50 **Notes** LB ⊗ Closed 24-26 Dec

Woodenbridge

★★★ 70% ⚫ HOTEL

☎ 0402 35146   🖹 0402 35573
e-mail: reservations@woodenbridgehotel.com
dir: between Avoca & Arklow, off N11.

Situated in the beautiful Vale of Avoca and owner-managed by the hospitable O'Brien family this smart hotel is beside the Woodenbridge Golf Club. Public areas are comfortable with open fires and good food is assured in the Italian restaurant. The lodge bedrooms are well equipped, spacious and enjoy a peaceful riverside setting.

Rooms 23 (13 fmly) **S** €60-€85; **D** €90-€150 (incl. bkfst)* **Facilities** Pool table ♫ Xmas **Conf** Class 200 Board 200 Thtr 200 **Parking** 100 **Notes** LB ⊗

Rock

★★★★ 78% ⚫⚫ HOTEL

☎ 00 350 200 73000   🖹 00 350 200 73513
Europa Rd
e-mail: rockhotel@gibtelecom.net
web: www.rockhotelgibraltar.com
dir: From airport follow tourist board signs. Hotel on left half way up Europa Rd

Enjoying a prime elevated location directly below the Rock, this long established art deco styled hotel has been the destination of celebrities and royalty since it was built in 1932. Bedrooms are spacious and well equipped and many boast stunning coastal views that stretch across the Mediterranean to Morocco. Staff are friendly and service is delivered with flair and enthusiasm. Creative dinners and hearty breakfasts can be enjoyed in the stylish restaurant.

Rooms 104 (25 smoking) **S** £90-£135; **D** £90-£135 (incl. bkfst) **Facilities** STV ⚡ supervised ♫ Xmas New Year Wi-fi **Conf** Class 24 Board 30 Thtr 70 **Services** Lift Air con **Parking** 40 **Notes** LB RS 5 Oct-1 Apr Civ Wed 40

See advert on page 756

Caleta

★★★★ 75% ⚫⚫ HOTEL

☎ 00 350 200 76501   🖹 00 350 200 42143
Sir Herbert Miles Rd, PO Box 73
e-mail: sales@caletahotel.gi
web: www.caletahotel.com
dir: Enter Gibraltar via Spanish border & cross runway. At 1st rdbt turn left, hotel in 2kms

For travellers arriving to Gibraltar by air the Caleta is an eye catching coastal landmark that can be spotted by planes arriving from the east. This imposing and stylish hotel sits on a cliff top and all sea-facing rooms enjoy panoramic views across the straights to Morocco. Bedrooms vary in size and style with some boasting spacious balconies, flat screen TVs and mini bars. Several dining venues are available but Nunos provides the award winning fine dining Italian experience. Staff are friendly, service is professional.

Rooms 161 (89 annexe) (13 fmly) **Facilities** ⚡ supervised Gym Health & beauty club Xmas **Conf** Class 172 Board 85 Thtr 200 **Services** Lift **Parking** 32 **Notes** LB ⊗ Civ Wed 300

O'Callaghan Eliott

★★★★ 75% HOTEL

☎ 00 350 200 70500 & 200 75905
🖹 00 350 200 70243
2 Governor's Pde
e-mail: eliott@ocallaghanhotels.com
web: www.ocallaghanhotels.com

Located in the heart of the old town, this hotel provides a convenient central base for exploring the duty free shopping district and other key attractions on foot. The bedrooms are stylish, spacious and well equipped. The roof top restaurant provides stunning bay views whilst guests can also take a swim in the roof top pool.

Rooms 120 **S** £145-£270; **D** £145-£270* **Facilities** STV ⚡ Gym ♫ Xmas New Year Wi-fi **Conf** Class 80 Board 70 Thtr 180 **Services** Lift Air con **Parking** 17 **Notes** LB ⊗ Civ Wed 120

An oasis...

...in a busy world!

Bedrooms
104 bedrooms and suites in a colonial style all with a sea view

Conference facilities
Full upgraded conference facilities available for board meetings, training courses and presentations

Internet Facilities
Wireless broadband available throughout the hotel

Weddings
The Rock is an ideal wedding venue whether it be a small intimate wedding or large family gathering. We are also a recognised venue for civil marriages and ceremonies can now be conducted in various parts of the hotel

Banqueting
Weddings, banqueting, private dining or office parties catered for

Swimming pool
Outdoor swimming pool with pool side bar and pool side menu. We welcome private pool membership, our Lido Club, with private pool hire for parties and barbecues and children's parties

Restaurant
The restaurant has stunning views over the bay. Our "house" menu is excellent value for three courses including an aperitif Manzanilla, olives and coffee. A full à la carte menu along with a superb eclectic wine list is also available

Wisteria Terrace
The Wisteria Terrace for lunches, dinner, barbecues, afternoon teas, evening drinks and informal dining

Barbary Bar
Barbary Bar and terrace for a relaxing drink and, for the wine buff, a choice of nine wines by the glass

Lounges
Take a good old fashioned English tea in one of the spacious lounges

 Europa Road, Gibraltar
Tel: (+350) 200 73000 Fax: (+350) 200 73513
E-mail: info@rockhotel.gi
Web site: www.rockhotelgibraltar.com
78%

Index of Hotels

The Automobile Association would like to thank the following photographers and companies for their assistance in the preparation of this book.

Abbreviations for the picture credits are as follows: (t) top; (b) bottom; (l) left; (r) right; (c) centre (AA) AA World Travel Library.

7 Rhubarb-the Restaurant at Prestonfield; 8tl Jesmond Dene House Hotel & Restaurant; 8br Handpicked Hotels, Norton House Hotel & Restaurant; 9tl Lake Country House Hotel & Spa; 9br The Brooklodge Hotel & Wells Spa; 10tr, 10bl, 10br Q Hotels; 11bl, 11tr, 11br Hotel du Vin; 12, 13bl, 13bc, 13br, 14, 15 AA World Travel Library; 16, 17t Hotel du Vin; 17b Malmaison; 18t, 18b Malmaison; 19 Hotel du Vin; 20tl, 20bl, 20r One Aldwych, London; 21bl Hotel du Vin; 21tr Queensbury Hotel, Bath; 21br Malmaison; 22, 23cr Stockbyte; 23br Photodisc; 24 AA/J Smith; 25 & 26 The Pool House Hotel; 27 Photodisc; 28/9 Luton Hoo Hotel; 30 The Randolph Hotel, Oxford; 31 Bovey Castle; 44 AA/A Mockford & N Bonetti; 315 AA/C Sawyer; 589 AA/S Anderson; 668 AA/S Lewis; 706 AA/S McBride; 785 AA/J Smith; 786l AA/C Sawyer; 787bc TongRo Image Stock/Alamy.

Every effort has been made to trace the copyright holders, and we apologise in advance for any accidental errors. We would be happy to apply the corrections in the following edition of this publication.

Additional information

Hints on booking your stay

It's always worth booking as early as possible, particularly for the peak holiday period from the beginning of June to the end of September. Bear in mind that Easter and other public holidays may be busy too and in some parts of Scotland, the ski season is a peak holiday period. Some hotels will ask for a deposit or full payment in advance, especially for one-night bookings. And some hotels charge half-board (bed, breakfast and dinner) whether you require the meals or not, while others may only accept full-board bookings. Not all hotels will accept advance bookings for bed and breakfast, overnight or short stays. Some will not take reservations from mid week.

Once a booking is confirmed, let the hotel know at once if you are unable to keep your reservation. If the hotel cannot re-let your room you may be liable to pay about two-thirds of the room price (a deposit will count towards this payment). In Britain a legally binding contract is made when you accept an offer of accommodation, either in writing or by telephone, and illness is not accepted as a release from this contract. You are advised to take out insurance against possible cancellation, for example AA Single Trip Insurance (telephone 0845 092 0606).

Booking online

Locating and booking somewhere to stay can be a time-consuming process, but you can search quickly and easily online for a place that best suits your needs. Simply visit www.theAA.com/hotels to search for full details from around 8,000 quality rated hotels and B&Bs in Great Britain and Ireland. Then either check availability and book online by clicking on the 'Booking' button, or contact the establishment direct for any further information.

Prices

The AA encourages the use of the Hotel Industry Voluntary Code of Booking Practice, which aims to ensure that guests know how much they will have to pay and what services and facilities are included, before entering a financially binding agreement. If the price has not previously been confirmed in writing, guests should be given a card stipulating the total obligatory charge when they register at reception.

The Tourism (Sleeping Accommodation Price Display) Order of 1977 compels hotels, travel accommodation, guest houses, farmhouses, inns and self-catering accommodation with four or more letting bedrooms, to display

in entrance halls the minimum and maximum price for one or two persons but they may vary without warning.

Facilities for disabled guests

The final stage (Part III) of the Disability Discrimination Act (access to Goods and Services) came into force in October 2004. This means that service providers may have to make permanent adjustments to their premises. For further information, see the government website www.direct.gov.uk/en/DisabledPeople/RightsAndObligations/DisabilityRights/DG_4001068

Please note: AA inspectors are not accredited to make inspections under the National Accessibility Scheme. We indicate in entries if an establishment has ground floor rooms; and if a hotel tells us that they have disabled facilities this is included in the description.

The establishments in this guide should all be aware of their responsibilities under the Act. We recommend that you always telephone in advance to ensure that the establishment you have chosen has appropriate facilities.

Useful Websites

www.holidaycare.org.uk
www.dptac.gov.uk/door-to-door

Licensing Laws

Licensing laws differ in England, Wales, Scotland, the Republic of Ireland, the Isle of Man, the Isles of Scilly and the Channel Islands. Public houses are generally open from mid morning to early afternoon, and from about 6 or 7pm until 11pm, although closing times may be earlier or later and some pubs are open all afternoon. Unless otherwise stated, establishments listed are licensed to serve alcohol. Hotel residents can obtain alcoholic drinks at all times, if the licensee is prepared to serve them. Non-residents eating at the hotel restaurant can have drinks with meals. Children under 14 may be excluded from bars where no food is served. Those under 18 may not purchase or consume alcoholic drinks.

Club licence means that drinks are served to club members only, 48 hours must lapse between joining and ordering. The Fire Precautions Act does not apply to the Channel Islands, Republic of Ireland, or the Isle of Man, which have their own rules. As far as we are aware, all hotels listed in Great Britain have applied for and not been refused a fire certificate. For information on Ireland see page 708

Website Addresses

Where website addresses are included they have been supplied and specified by the respective establishment. Such Websites are not under the control of The Automobile Association Developments Limited and as such the AA has no control over them and will not accept any responsibility or liability in respect of any and all matters whatsoever relating to such Websites including access, content, material and functionality. By including the addresses of third party Websites the AA does not intend to solicit business or offer any security to any person in any country, directly or indirectly.

Bank and Public Holidays 2009

New Year's Day	1st January
New Year's Holiday	2nd January (Scotland)
Good Friday	10th April
Easter Monday	13th April
May Day Bank Holiday	4th May
Spring Bank Holiday	25th May
August Holiday	3rd August (Scotland)
Late Summer Holiday	31st August
Christmas Day	25th December
Boxing Day	26th December

AA star classification

AA Assessment

In collaboration with VisitBritain, VisitScotland and VisitWales, the AA developed Common Quality Standards for inspecting and rating accommodation. These standards and rating categories are now applied throughout the British Isles.

Any hotel applying for AA recognition receives an unannounced visit from an AA inspector to check standards. The hotels with full entries in this guide have all paid an annual fee for AA inspection, recognition and rating.

AA inspectors pay as a guest for their inspection visit, they do not accept free hospitality of any kind. Although AA inspectors do not stay overnight at Budget Hotels they do carry out regular visits to verify standards and procedures.

A guide to some of the general expectations for each star classification is as follows:

★ One Star

Polite, courteous staff providing a relatively informal yet competent style of service, available during the day and evening to receive guests

- At least one designated eating area open to residents for breakfast
- If dinner is offered it should be on at least five days a week, with last orders no later than 6.30pm
- Television in bedroom
- Majority of rooms en suite, bath or shower room available at all times

★★ Two Star

As for one star, plus

- At least one restaurant or dining room open to residents for breakfast (and for dinner at least five days a week)
- Last orders for dinner no earlier than 7pm
- Television in bedroom
- En suite or private bath or shower and WC

★★★ Three Star

- Management and staff smartly and professionally presented and usually uniformed
- A dedicated receptionist on duty at peak times
- At least one restaurant or dining room open to residents and non-residents for breakfast and dinner whenever the hotel is open
- Last orders for dinner no earlier than 8pm
- Remote-control television, direct-dial telephone
- En suite bath or shower and WC.

★★★★ Four Star

- A formal, professional staffing structure with smartly presented, uniformed staff anticipating and responding to your needs or requests. Usually spacious, well-appointed public areas
- Reception staffed 24 hours by well-trained staff
- Express checkout facilities where appropriate
- Porterage available on request
- Night porter available
- At least one restaurant open to residents and non-residents for breakfast and dinner seven days per week, and lunch to be available in a designated eating area
- Last orders for dinner no earlier than 9pm
- En suite bath with fixed overhead shower and WC

★★★★★ Five Star

- Luxurious accommodation and public areas with a range of extra facilities. First time guests shown to their bedroom
- Multilingual service
- Guest accounts well explained and presented
- Porterage offered
- Guests greeted at hotel entrance, full concierge service provided
- At least one restaurant open to residents and non-residents for all meals seven days per week
- Last orders for dinner no earlier than 10pm
- High-quality menu and wine list
- Evening service to turn down the beds. Remote-control television, direct-dial telephone at bedside and desk, a range of luxury toiletries, bath sheets and robes. En suite bathroom incorporating fixed overhead shower and WC

★ Inspectors' Choice

Each year we select the best hotels in each rating. These hotels stand out as the very best in the British Isles, regardless of style. Red Star hotels appear in highlighted panels throughout the guide. Inspectors' Choice Restaurant with Rooms are establishments that have been awarded the highest accommodation rating under the AA Bed & Breakfast scheme.

AA Rosette Awards

Out of the many thousands of restaurants in the UK, the AA identifies over 1,900 as the best. The following is an outline of what to expect from restaurants with AA Rosette Awards.

◉ Excellent local restaurants serving food prepared with care, understanding and skill, using good quality ingredients.

◉◉ The best local restaurants, which aim for and achieve higher standards, better consistency and where a greater precision is apparent in the cooking. There will be obvious attention to the selection of quality ingredients.

◉◉◉ Outstanding restaurants that demand recognition well beyond their local area.

◉◉◉◉ Amongst the very best restaurants in the British Isles, where the cooking demands national recognition.

◉◉◉◉◉ The finest restaurants in the British Isles, where the cooking stands comparison with the best in the world.

County Maps

England

1 Bedfordshire
2 Berkshire
3 Bristol
4 Buckinghamshire
5 Cambridgeshire
6 Greater Manchester
7 Herefordshire
8 Hertfordshire
9 Leicestershire
10 Northamptonshire
11 Nottinghamshire
12 Rutland
13 Staffordshire
14 Warwickshire
15 West Midlands
16 Worcestershire

Scotland

17 City of Glasgow
18 Clackmannanshire
19 East Ayrshire
20 East Dunbartonshire
21 East Renfrewshire
22 Perth & Kinross
23 Renfrewshire
24 South Lanarkshire
25 West Dunbartonshire

Wales

26 Blaenau Gwent
27 Bridgend
28 Caerphilly
29 Denbighshire
30 Flintshire
31 Merthyr Tydfil
32 Monmouthshire
33 Neath Port Talbot
34 Newport
35 Rhondda Cynon Taff
36 Torfaen
37 Vale of Glamorgan
38 Wrexham

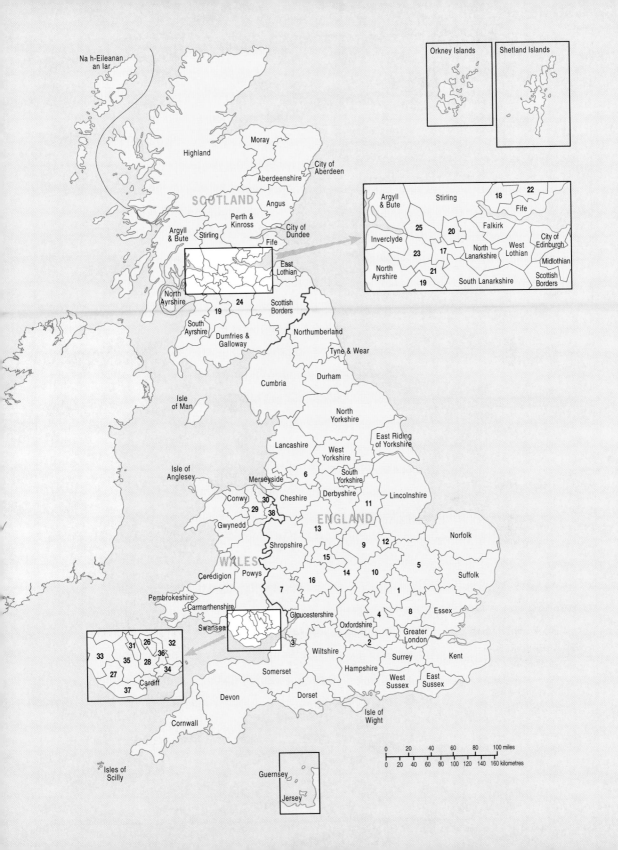

Na h-Eileanan
an Iar

Highland

Moray

City of
Aberdeen

Aberdeenshire

SCOTLAND

Angus

Perth &
Kinross

City of
Dundee

Argyll
& Bute

Stirling

Fife

East
Lothian

North
Ayrshire

19   24

South
Ayrshire

Scottish
Borders

Dumfries &
Galloway

Northumberland

Tyne & Wear

Durham

Cumbria

Isle
of Man

North
Yorkshire

East Riding
of Yorkshire

Lancashire

West
Yorkshire

Isle of
Anglesey

6

Merseyside

South
Yorkshire

Lincolnshire

Conwy

30

Cheshire

Derbyshire

29

11

Gwynedd

38

ENGLAND

13

Norfolk

Shropshire

9   12

WALES

15

14   10   5

Ceredigion

Powys

16   1

Suffolk

Pembrokeshire

7

Carmarthenshire

4   8

Essex

Swansea

Gloucestershire

Oxfordshire

Greater
London

3

2

Wiltshire

Surrey

Kent

Somerset

Hampshire

West
Sussex

East
Sussex

Devon

Dorset

Isle of
Wight

Cornwall

Isles of
Scilly

Guernsey

Jersey

Orkney Islands

Shetland Islands

Argyll
& Bute

Stirling

18   22

Fife

25   20

Falkirk

Inverclyde

17   North
Lanarkshire

West
Lothian

City of
Edinburgh

23

North
Ayrshire

21

Midlothian

19   South Lanarkshire

Scottish
Borders

31 26 32

33   36

35 28   34

27

Cardiff

37

0   20   40   60   80   100 miles

0 20 40 60 80 100 120 140 160 kilometres

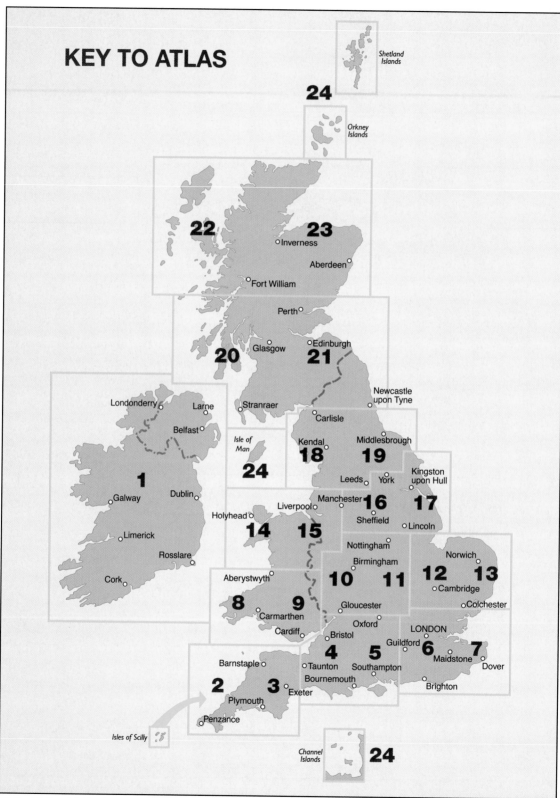

KEY TO ATLAS

Shetland Islands
24

Orkney Islands

22   **23**
Inverness
Aberdeen
Fort William

Perth
20   Glasgow   Edinburgh   **21**

Newcastle upon Tyne

Stranraer
Carlisle

Londonderry   Larne
Belfast
Isle of Man   Kendal   Middlesbrough
24   **18**   **19**

1   Leeds   York   Kingston upon Hull
Galway   Dublin   Liverpool   Manchester   **16**   **17**
Holyhead   Sheffield   Lincoln
Limerick   **14**   **15**
Rosslare   Nottingham
Cork   Birmingham   Norwich
Aberystwyth   **10**   **11**   **12**   **13**
8   **9**   Cambridge
Carmarthen   Gloucester   Colchester
Cardiff   Oxford   LONDON
Bristol   Guildford   **6**   **7**
Barnstaple   **4**   **5**   Maidstone
Taunton   Southampton   Brighton   Dover
2   **3**   Exeter   Bournemouth
Plymouth
Penzance

Isles of Scilly

Channel Islands   **24**

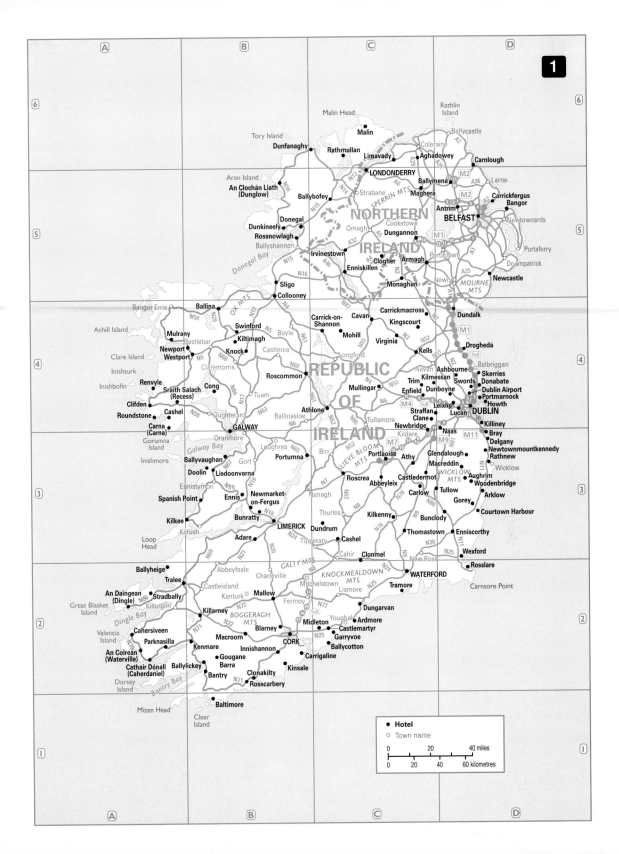

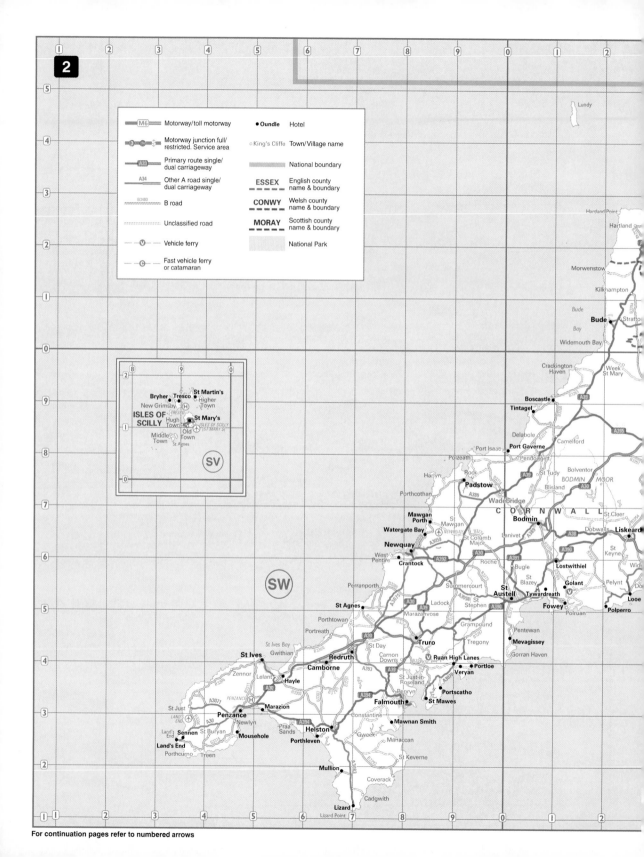

2

M6	Motorway/toll motorway
	Motorway junction full/restricted. Service area
A33	Primary route single/dual carriageway
A34	Other A road single/dual carriageway
B3480	B road
	Unclassified road
V	Vehicle ferry
C	Fast vehicle ferry or catamaran
● Oundle	Hotel
○ King's Cliffe	Town/Village name
	National boundary
ESSEX	English county name & boundary
CONWY	Welsh county name & boundary
MORAY	Scottish county name & boundary
	National Park

ISLES OF SCILLY

Bryher · Tresco · **St Martin's** · Higher Town · New Grimsby · Hugh Town · **St Mary's** · Old Town · Middle Town · St Agnes

SV

SW

Lundy

Hartland Point · Hartland · Morwenstow · Kilkhampton · Bude · Bude · Stratton · Bay · Widemouth Bay · Crackington Haven · Week St Mary

Boscastle · Tintagel · Delabole · Camelford · Bolventor · **BODMIN MOOR** · Blisland · St Tudy · Port Isaac · Port Gaverne · Pendoggett · Polzeath · Rock · Harlyn · **Padstow** · Wadebridge · **Bodmin** · Dobwalls · **Liskeard** · St Cleer · St Keyne · Porthcothan · St Mawgan · **C O R N W A L L** · Mawgan Porth · St Mawgan · St Columb Major · **NEWQUAY** · Lanivet · Bugle · St Blazey · **Lostwithiel** · **Golant** · Pelynt · Watergate Bay · **Newquay** · West Pentire · **Crantock** · Roche · Summercourt · **St Austell** · **Tywardreath** · **Fowey** · **Looe** · Perranporth · Ladock · St Stephen · Polruan · **Polperro** · **St Agnes** · Marazanvose · Grampound · Pentewan · **Mevagissey** · Porthtowan · Portreath · St Day · Carnon Downs · **Truro** · Tregony · Gorran Haven · St Ives Bay · Gwithian · **St Ives** · **Redruth** · **Ruan High Lanes** · **Portloe** · Lelant · **Camborne** · Carnon Downs · **Veryan** · Zennor · **Hayle** · St Just-in-Roseland · **Portscatho** · St Just · PENZANCE · Penryn · **St Mawes** · Marazion · **Falmouth** · **Penzance** · Newlyn · Praa Sands · Constantine · **Mawnan Smith** · Sennen · St Buryan · **Mousehole** · **Helston** · Gweek · Manaccan · **Land's End** · Porthleven · Porthcurno · Treen · **Porthleven** · St Keverne · **Mullion** · Coverack · Cadgwith · **Lizard** · Lizard Point

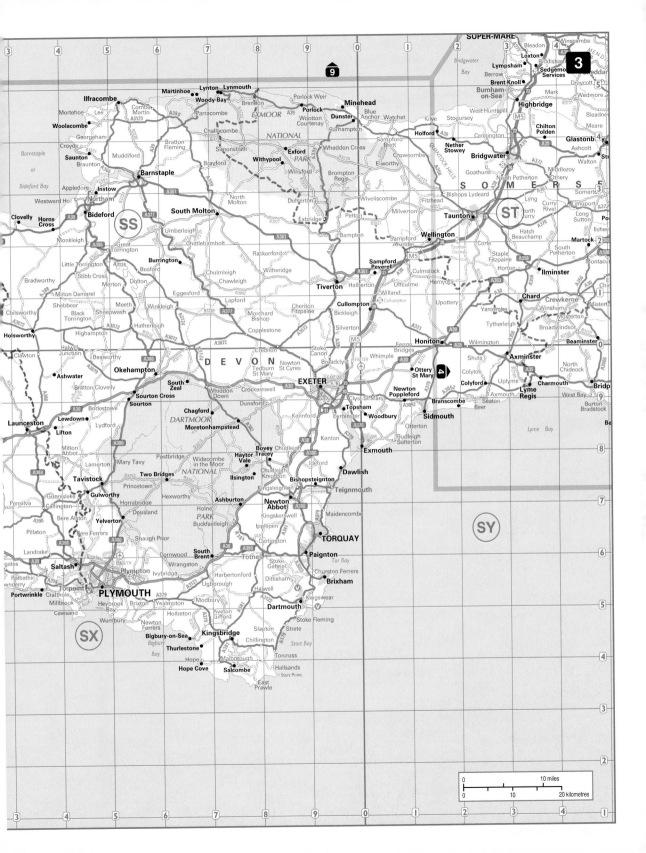

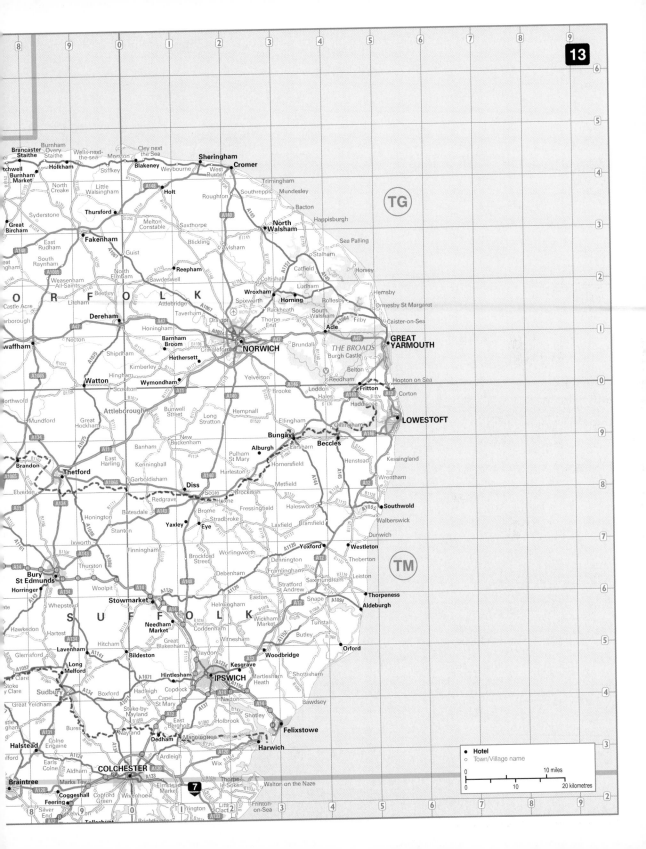

14

ISLE OF
ANGLESEY

Cemaes
Amlwch
Llanerchymedd
Holyhead
Llanfachraeth
Benllech
Red
Wharf Bay
Llangoed
Llandudno
Rhôs-
on-Sea
Rhy
Deganwy
Colwyn Bay
Trearddur Bay
Pentraeth
Penmaenmawr
Conwy
Abergel
Holy
Island
Rhosneigr
Llangefni
Menai
Bridge
Beaumaris
Bangor
Llanfairfechan
Llansantffraid
Glan Conwy
Betws-yn-Rhos
Llandulas
Aberffraw
Llanfair
P.G.
Y Felinheli
Llanllechid
Bethesda
Tal-y-Cafn
Llangernyw
Llanfair
Talhaiarn
Her
Llansannan
Newborough
Caernarfon
Llanrug
Trefriw
Llanrwst
CONWY
Bylchau
Bontnewydd
Llanberis
Capel Curig
Caernarfon
Bay
Llandwrog
Llanwnda
Betws-y-Coed
Dolwyddelan
Penmachno
Pentrefoelas
Cerrigydrudion
Penygroes
Rhyd Ddu
Clynnog-fawr
Y Maerd
SH
Beddgelert
S N O W D O N I A
Blaenau Ffestiniog
Llanaelhaearn
Prenteg
Ffestiniog
Morfa Nefyn
PENINSULA
Tremadog
Maentwrog
Nefyn
Llanystumdwy
Penrhyndeudraeth
NATIONAL
Bodfuan
Porthmadog
Bala
LLÊN
Criccieth
Borth-y-Gest
Portmeirion
Talsarnau
Sarn
Pwllheli
Trawsfynydd
G W Y N E D D
Llanbedrog
Harlech
PARK
Llanuwchllyn
Aberdaron
Y Rhiw
Abersoch
Llanbedr
Ganllwyd
Bardsey
Island
Dyffryn Ardudwy
Tal-y-bont
Dolgellau
Dinas-Mawddwy
Barmouth
Fairbourne
Mallwyd
Langadfan
Llwyngwril
Corris
Cemmaes
Road
Llanbrynmair
Y Bryncrug
Pennal
Tywyn
Machynlleth
Carno
SN
Aberdyfi
Eglwysfach
Borth
Tal-y-bont
9
CARDIGAN BAY
Llandre
Llanidloes
Aberystwyth
Capel
Bangor
Ponterwyd

Hotel
○ Town/Village name

0		10 miles
0	10	20 kilometres

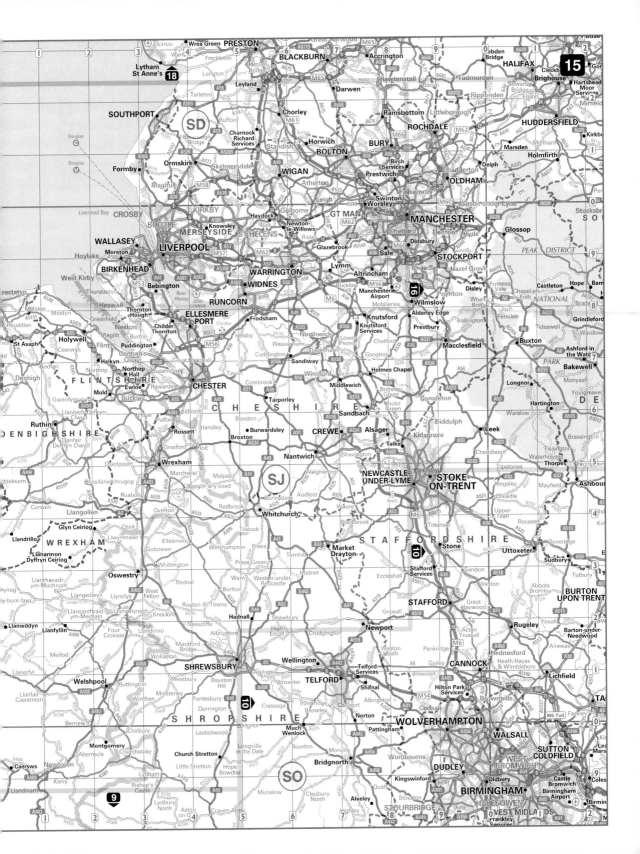

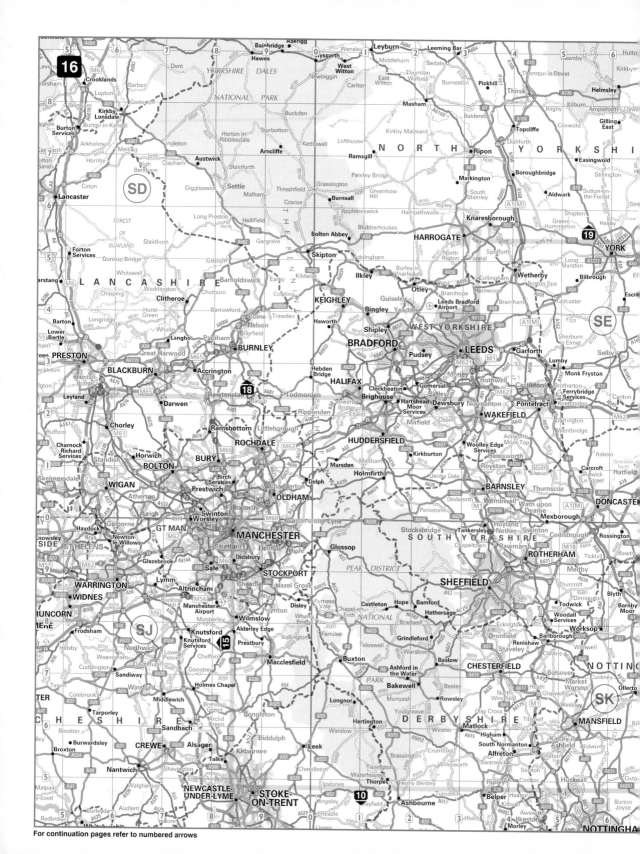

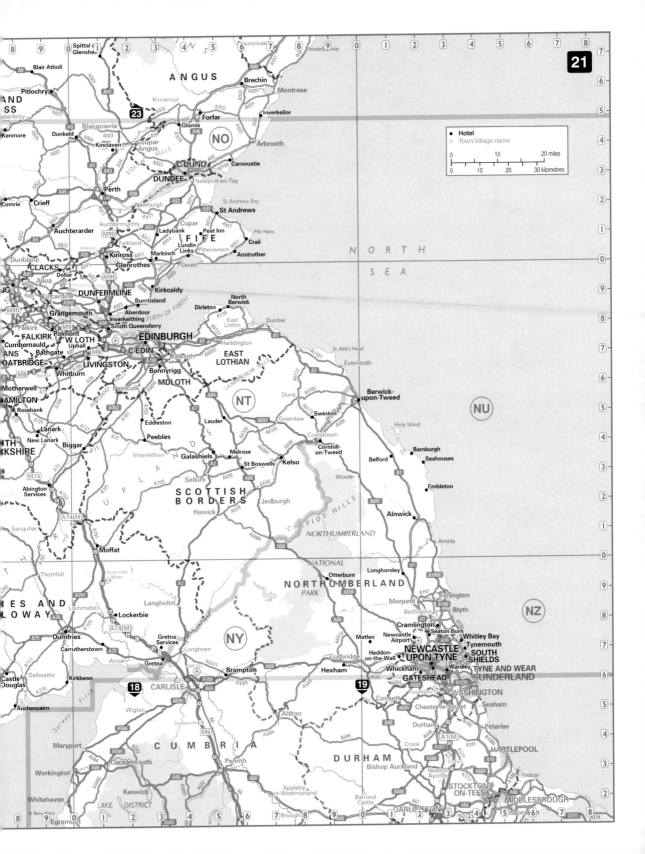

NA

NB

Cape Wrath

Rudha Rhobhanais
(Butt of Lewis)
Port Nis
(Port of Ness)

Cellar
Head

Handa Island

Scourie

A894

A837

Inchnadamph

Great
Bernera

ISLE

OF

LEWIS

Carlabhagh
(Carloway)

Tiumpan
Head

A858

A857

A858

A859

Steornabhagh
(Stornoway)

A859

A858

Lochinver

A835

**NA H–EILEANAN
AN IAR**

Scarp

THE MINCH

Ullapool

A837

Taransay

Tairbeart
(Tarbert)

Scalpay

Gruinard
Bay

A832

**Sgarasta Bheag
(Scarista)**

HARRIS

A859

Poolewe

Gairloch

THE LITTLE MINCH

Pabbay

Boreray

Bernaray

Uig

A855

Kinlochewe

A832

Torridon

A832

Shieldaig

Achnasheen

OUTER HEBRIDES

NORTH UIST

A865

Loch nam Madadh
(Lochmaddy)

A867

Ronay

NG

A896

HIGHLANDS

A890

NF

A865

Wiay

Colbost

Dunvegan

**Skeabost
Bridge**

A850

ISLE

Portree

Raasay

A863

Inner Sound

Plockton

Cannich

SOUTH
UIST

A865

Drynoch

Struan

OF

A87

Scalpay

**Kyle of
Lochalsh**

NORTH WEST

Loch Baghasdail
(Lochboisdale)

SKYE

Broadford

A87

Eriskay

Soay

Isleornsay

A807

BARRA

A888

Canna

Rùm

Ardvasar

Sound of Sleat

A851

A87

Invergarry

Bàgh a Chaisteil
(Castlebay)

Sandray

Mallaig

A830

A87

Mingulay

Eigg

INNER HEBRIDES

Muck

Glenfinnan

A830

Spean Bridge

A82

**Roy
Bridge**

NL

Point of
Ardnamurchan

NM

Acharacle

A861

Fort William

Coll

Arinagour

Tobermory

A884

Strontian

Onich

Kinlochleven

A82

Tiree

Scarinish

A861

**South
Ballachulish**

A828

Port Appin

ISLE

A849

Lochaline

Eriska

A828

Lismore

Connel

A85

20

Ulva

OF

Craignure

Kerrera

Oban

A85

Dalmally

Iona
Fionnphort

A849

MULL

Lorne

Kilchrenan

Cranlarich

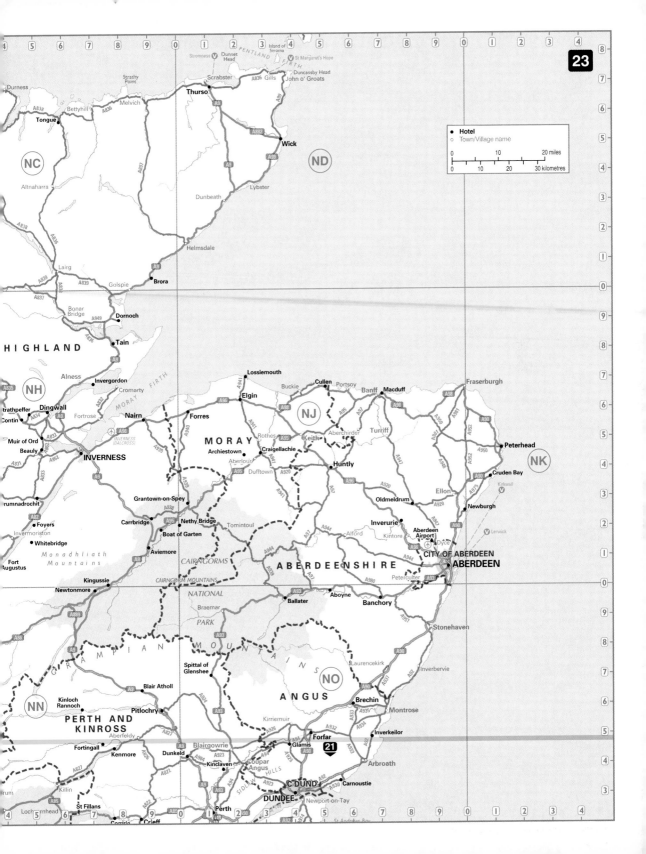

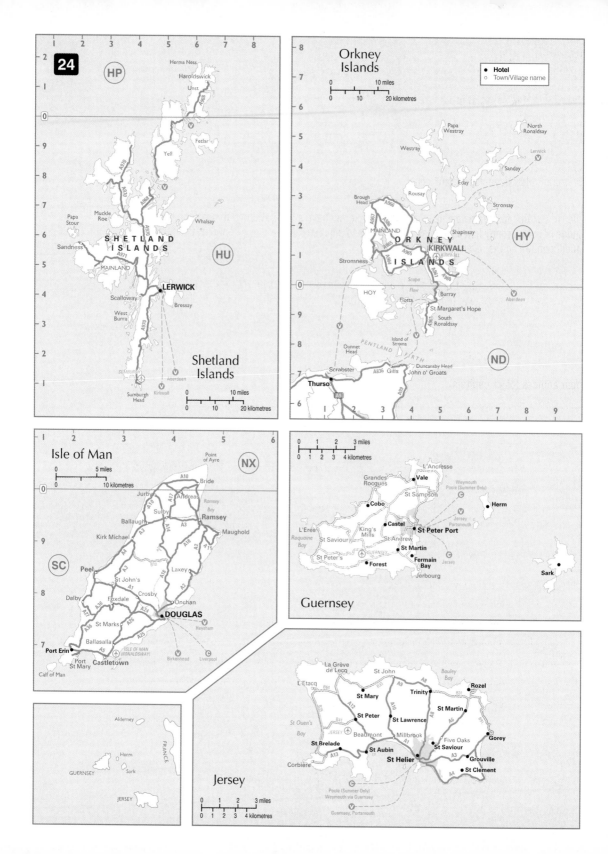

Readers' Report Form

Please use this form to recommend any hotel where you have stayed, whether it is included in the guide or not currently listed. You can also help us to improve the guide by completing the short questionnaire on the reverse.

The AA does not undertake to arbitrate between guide readers and hotels, or to obtain compensation or engage in protracted correspondence.

Date:

Your name (block capitals)

Your address (block capitals)

....

....

....

....

....

....

e-mail address:

Name of hotel:

Comments ....

....

....

....

....

....

....

....

(please attach a separate sheet if necessary)

Please tick here if you DO NOT wish to receive details of AA offers or products

PTO

Have you bought this guide before?   Yes   No

Have you bought any other accommodation, restaurant, pub or food guides recently?
If yes, which ones?

....

....

....

Why did you buy this guide? (circle all that apply)

holiday   short break   business travel   special occasion
overnight stop   find a venue for an event e.g. conference
other ....

How often do you stay in hotels? (circle one choice)

more than once a month once a month   once in 2-3 months
once in six months   once a year   less than once a year

Please answer these questions to help us make improvements to the guide:
Which of these factors are most important when choosing a hotel?

price   location   awards/ratings   service
decor/surroundings   previous experience   recommendation
other (please state) ....

Do you read the editorial features in the guide?   Yes   No

Do you use the location atlas?   Yes   No

What elements of the guide do you find the most useful when choosing somewhere to stay?

description   photo   advertisement   star rating

Can you suggest any improvements to the guide?

....

....

....

....